O9-CFU-541

THE WRITER'S HANDBOOK

The Writer's Handbook

2000 Edition

Edited by

SYLVIA K. BURACK
Editor, The Writer

Publishers   THE WRITER, INC.   Boston

Copyright © 1999
by
The Writer, Inc.

"Adult and Young Readers: What Do They Have in Common?," by Joan Aiken. Copyright © 1998 Joan Aiken Enterprises Ltd.

"Writing Matters," by Julia Alvarez. Copyright © 1998 by Julia Alvarez. This essay appears in an unabridged form in *Something to Declare,* Algonquin Books of Chapel Hill, 1998. By permission of Susan Bergholz Literary Services, New York. All rights reserved.

"Creative Nonfiction Writing," by Rita Berman. Copyright © 1997 by Rita Berman.

"The Supporting Cast in Your Novel," by Barbara Delinsky. Copyright © 1998 by Barbara Delinsky.

"Tricks of the Wizard's Trade," by Susan Dexter. Copyright © 1997 by Susan Dexter.

"Killing Off Characters. . .and Other Editorial Whims," by Louise Munro Foley. Copyright © 1997 by Louise Munro Foley.

"The Creative Power of Doing Nothing," by Colleen Mariah Rae, adapted from a chapter in *Movies in the Mind,* by Colleen Mariah Rae, published by Sherman Asher Publishing. Copyright © 1996 by Colleen Mariah Rae.

All rights reserved, including the right to
reproduce this book or parts thereof in any form.

Library of Congress Catalog Card Number: 36-28596
ISBN: 0-87116-187-7

Printed in the United States of America

CONTENTS

WITHDRAWN

JAN - - 2000

SPECIALIZED FICTION

NONFICTION: ARTICLES AND BOOKS

POETRY

PLAYWRITING

JUVENILE AND YOUNG ADULT

Background
for Writers

❑ 1

WRITING AND INSPIRATION

BY JAY PARINI

FOR THIRTY YEARS OR SO, I'VE BEEN SITTING DOWN AT MY DESK EVERY morning to write. I stay there, usually for three or four hours, whether or not anything comes. It's much like being a grocer: You have to open the shop and wait for customers; if any come, all is well and good. But even if nobody turns up, the obligation to keep business hours remains.

Despite this discipline, and the consolations of literary shopkeeping, I do—like all writers—fret over inspiration. The eternal question that faces everyone in this profession is where do stories, poems, and novels come from? Then comes the further, more vexing, question: Once you've got the idea for a poem or piece of fiction, how do you actually embody that idea in a fully realized work of art? That is, how do you "give to airy nothings," as Shakespeare wrote in *A Midsummer Night's Dream*, "a local habitation and a name"?

It should be obvious that the chief source of inspiration for any writer is experience. William Faulkner was once asked how much of his fiction came from his personal life, and he responded:

> "I can't say. I never counted up. Because 'how much' is not important. A writer needs three things, experience, observation, and imagination, any two of which, at times any one of which, can supply the lack of the others. With me, a story usually begins with a single idea or memory or mental picture. The writing of the story is simply a matter of working up to that moment, to explain why it happened or what it caused to follow. A writer is trying to create believable people in credible moving situations in the most moving way he can. Obviously he must use as one of his tools the environment he knows."*

I write poetry and fiction, with no sense of preferring one to the other. Poetry, at least for me, is a way of paying attention to the daily

---

Writers at Work: The Paris Review Interviews, ed. Malcolm Cowley. (New York: Viking, 1958), 133

3

fluctuations of experience. It is a seeking after grace. Poetic language is not, like the language of fiction, necessarily a vehicle for communication in the strictest sense. Poetry embodies, and often extends, the experience of the writer. Wallace Stevens once spoke of "The poem of the mind in the act of finding / What will suffice," and I think any poet can understand what he meant by those suggestive lines. In an age of disbelief, when there is so little solace or consolation in the culture at large, poetry is about finding a language adequate to our experience. Poets write to make sense of their own experience, to give it body and shape; ideally, others will read their poems and find them "useful" in some way, but the main use is always for the poets themselves. (Perhaps this explains why so much poetry is obscure?)

Fiction, on the other hand, seems to derive from a very different impulse: the wish to tell a story, to communicate experience within the generic boundaries of narrative. The desire to tell a story is ancient, and most writers do not have to look for ideas so much as wonder how to isolate and contain those springing forth naturally. (Writers block, I submit, is not so much the lack of a story to tell as a lack of confidence to tell it.)

When Robert Penn Warren, the great poet and novelist, was in his early eighties, he told me that he still had five or six novels in his head. They were, he said, "like airplanes circling an airport, waiting for permission to land." I find myself in much the same predicament.

With poems, I have always found that receptivity is everything. You have to be on the lookout for poems; in a way, they are there already, but you can't snag them unless you have your pen in hand, your notebook open. My ritual over many years has been to go to a local diner for breakfast and sit with a notebook open. I wait patiently, sometimes making lists of favorite words, thinking up titles for unwritten poems, or trying out phrases. The poems spring from those phrases, one phrase building upon another.

Thomas Campion (1567–1620) once usefully defined poetry as "a system of linked sounds." I like to build poems on that notion, linking sounds by various means, including the most obvious, such as rhyme (I love slant rhymes best) or alliteration. But there are other ways to link sounds: You might create interlocking metaphors, or—if you have a bent for philology—think of the roots of words, linking them by a principle of association.

Let me give an example of linking from a recent poem of my own, "Rain Before Nightfall."

Late August, and the long soft hills
are wet with light;
a silken dusk, with shifting thunder
in the middle distance. Chills
of fall have not yet quite
brought everything to ruin.

And I stop to look, to listen
under eaves. The yellow rain
slides down the lawn,
it feathers through the pine,
makes lilacs glisten,
all the waxy leaves. The air
is almost fit for drinking,
and my heart is drenched,
my thirst for something
more than I can see
is briefly quenched.

The circumstances under which I wrote this poem come vividly to mind. I was visiting the summer home of Robert Frost, in Ripton, Vermont. It was early evening, and I was alone. A sudden rain had recently swept the fields and forest, and the house was dripping as I sat on the little screened-in porch. As often happens in New England, the weather changed dramatically, and now a bright yellow sun flooded the landscape; I could hardly believe the yellowness of everything, even the grass and trees. I was overcome with a fierce sense of longing and joy, one of those exquisite and painfully mixed emotions that occasionally overwhelm us. My urge to get this experience down on paper was almost uncontainable.

I remember writing "a silken dusk," then waiting for a long time. Then I wrote, "the long soft hills are wet with light." With these phrases in hand, I was able to push forward, adding the "shifting thunder"—a gift from the skies. I kept telling myself to describe whatever was before me, remembering Wallace Stevens' great line: "Description is revelation." More than anything else, I wanted not to lose focus, to keep my eye on the object: the landscape, which through meditation would yield a spiritual essence. I wanted to find what Seamus Heaney has called "the music of what happens."

Soon I began linking the sounds of this poem, letting the l-sounds and s-sounds recur, almost like a pulse. I decided, instinctively, not to follow any rigid rhyme scheme but to rhyme as needed, so in the fourth line "hills" married "Chills." "Light" hitched up with "quite." These were traditional end-rhymes, but I hooked up "thunder," which concludes the third line, with "under," the first word in the eighth line. Internal rhyming is essential, I think, in stitching together poems. One should always think of rhyming as a form of echo, just as rhythm should be considered a pulse, not a metronomic tick-tock. I especially enjoyed rhyming "rain" with "ruin," a slant rhyme.

One hears a lot about the "New Formalism" these days, but there is nothing behind this phrase. Good poets have always used form as needed. Likewise, they have broken forms when the demand, which issues from the internal requirements of the poem, insisted that the form be abandoned. As anyone who has tried writing poetry knows (or ought to), no verse is really free if the poet hopes to construct a memorable poem. Those who choose to write in free verse should be aware that every line has a meter, and that words invariably create a music as their vowels and consonants collide. The poet has to manage these collisions with skill and tact.

Rhythms beget rhythms. In "Rain Before Nightfall," I recall starting with that line of "sprung" blank verse: "Late August, and the long soft hills," then quickly deciding to vary the pace with "are wet with light." As usual with me, I counted the stresses in each line, letting the unstressed syllables fall or gather as they would. This technique has its roots in Anglo-Saxon and Middle English poetry, and it allows for a more natural mesh of speaking voice with rhythmical unit.

The frightening thing about writing is that rules often get you nowhere. Poets and writers of fiction must, finally, achieve that mysterious thing called "a voice" on their own. But how do they do that? In truth, it's hard *not* to do it. All human beings have a distinct and original voice, as unique as their own thumbprints. When you hear someone you know speaking over the phone, even with your hand over the receiver so that the words themselves are indistinct, you can still tell who is talking. People have a particular way of hanging words together, of generating syntax; the rhythms in every speaking voice are almost invariably unique. The point of good writing is to utilize these individual aspects of a writer's voice, and that is where technique comes in. In poetry, it is where the discipline of language enters: knowing how to control the flow, the pulse of the line; keeping the imagery fresh and concrete; following the metaphors as far as they will go, but breaking them off when they have gone too far. Again, there are no rules here: You learn by trial and error. You must write badly at first, then revise, drawing closer and closer to the unique voice that is already latent but somehow obscured.

For writers of fiction, many of the same issues obtain, although the demands of storytelling are different from those of lyric poetry. Faulkner is on the mark when he says a writer must draw on "experience, observation, and imagination." But experience is foremost. The texture of daily life must find its way into all good fiction. Some writers—John Updike is a perfect example—have created a vast shelf of books devoted to this principle. He evokes the world with such astonishing particularity, as when (in a story called "Leaf Season") he describes driving through Vermont in the fall to experience "the leaves, whole valleys and mountains of them—the strident pinks and scarlets of the maples, the clangorous gold of the hickories, the accompanying brasses of birch and beech—on both sides of the road, rise after rise, a heavenly tumult tied to our dull earth only by broad bands of evergreen and outcropping of granite." The translation of experience into language must be, for Updike, almost instinctual by this point in his career.

For most writers—myself included—mere description of the world's glittering surface is not enough. I find myself eager to tell a story, to feel that surge through plot as characters entangle themselves in situations and need rescuing. Like Warren, I usually have five or six novels in my head, and I feel perpetually pressed for time to get them down on paper. This isn't to say there are not many days when, as I suggested earlier, I don't sit in the grocery store without customers. After thirty years, I still find myself puzzled by this thing called "inspiration." Why does the energy flow from unseen, bountiful sources one day, then dry up the next? I doubt that anyone can answer this, but there are ways of dealing with a seeming lack of inspiration.

Let me stay with the grocery store metaphor. The grocer can always do other things when nobody comes into the shop: He can study his accounts or wash the vegetables; he can sweep the floor and check his inventory. I find the parallel duties in writing extremely calming and useful. That is, I like to make lists of future characters or draw diagrams of plots. I can always go back and groom old passages, improving the rhythms of awkward sentences, finding glitches, substituting fresh metaphors and adjectives for clichés, which inevitably occur. If worse comes to worse, I can always read. For inspiration, I turn to Updike, Vidal, Marquez, Borges, Heaney, Frost. I have a private shelf of favorite writers, and I have spent blissful days rereading passages that I have virtually committed to memory. This reading often sparks my own writing.

When I'm working on a novel or story, I like to keep that "slight forward tilt" in the plot that Updike once mentioned. But how to keep the narrative moving, generate narrative momentum, that *sine qua non* without which any work of fiction is dead on the page?

I once spent a year on the Amalfi coast of Italy, and by lucky chance my neighbor was Gore Vidal. We became friends, and I learned a good deal about the writing life from him. One day I was working on a piece of fiction in which two characters were discussing the philosophy of Heidegger. I asked Gore if it were possible for two characters in a novel to discuss Heidegger for about twenty pages without losing the reader's interest. He looked at me with a droll smile and said, "Only if the characters are sitting in a railway car, and the reader knows there is a bomb under their seat."

I often recall that comment. In fact, I make a point to ask myself at regular intervals as I'm working: Is there a bomb under the seat? Without it, I know I may lose the narrative compulsion essential to good fiction.

More so than in poetry, fiction demands a vast commitment to the desk. I don't think it's possible to succeed in writing fiction without a huge capacity to sit in a desk chair and keep your attention focused on the task at hand for long periods. But this is also the reward of the art: that sense of being swept into a wholly separate world that is nevertheless contingent upon the one outside. You come to appreciate the intense pleasure of giving "a local habitation and a name" to vague intimations, those "airy nothings" that accost us daily in the shower, as we fall asleep or stumble awake, as we drive the children to school or sip a mug of coffee in the neighborhood diner.

You also come to realize that inspiration is only the beginning. As Alfred North Whitehead once said, "The art of literature, vocal or written, is to adjust the language so that it embodies what it indicates." That is, the poem or story, the novel or play, must somehow enact what it seeks to evoke. And here, the writer's craft comes into play, a discipline learned by trial and error, reading, writing, and revising, and long empty hours when the clock ticks slowly on the wall, and the cash register seems woefully, terrifyingly empty.

❏ 2

WRITING WITH JOY

BY JANE YOLEN

THERE ARE WRITERS WHO BELIEVE THAT WRITING *IS* AGONY, AND that's the best anyone can say of it. Gene Fowler's famous words are quoted all the time: "Writing is easy: All you do is sit staring at a blank sheet of paper until the drops of blood form on your forehead." Or Red Smith's infamous creed: "There's nothing to writing. All you do is sit down at a typewriter and open a vein."

But that's a messy way of working! And blood is extremely hard to get off of white paper.

Now, I am one of those people who makes a distinction between being a writer and being an author. A writer puts words on a page. An author lives in story. A writer is conversant with the keyboard, the author with character.

Roland Barthes has said: "The author performs a function; the writer an activity." We are talking here about the difference between desire and obsession; between hobby and life. But in either case, I suggest you learn to write not with blood and fear, but with joy.

Why joy?

It's a personal choice.

First of all, I am not a masochist willing to submit myself day after day to something that brings me pain. And I do mean day after day. Like an athlete or a dancer, I am uncomfortable—and even damaged—by a day away from my work.

Second, one need not have an unhappy life to write tragedy. Or conversely, one need not be deliriously happy all the time to write comedy. (In fact, many stand-up comics admit to being miserable much of the time.) Shakespeare was neither a king nor a fool, not a Moor or a Jew. He never saw a real fairy, and he was never asea in a tempest. His life was somewhere between happy and sad, as are most authors' lives. Yet he could write tragedy, comedy, and all between.

Authors are like actors; we get under the skins of our characters, inhabiting their lives for a while. We just don't have to live on and on with them forever. I have written about dragons, mermaids, angels, and kings. Never met any up close. I have even written a murder mystery, but I did not have to murder someone in order to write it. Still—don't mess with me. After doing my research, I *do* know how!

Third, writing for a living is much easier than spending a lot of time in a therapist's chair. Cheaper, too. Authors get to parade their neuroses in public disguised as story. If we are lucky, we get paid for doing it. And we get applause as well. As Kurt Vonnegut said: "Writers get to treat their mental illnesses every day."

Writing fiction—and poetry—is a bit like dreaming. You can find out what is troubling you on a deeper level. That one's writing goes out and touches someone else on that same level—though differently—is one of the pieces of magic that attends to art.

But I speak of *choosing* joy as if it were truly a matter of choice. For some people it is not. For some, agony oils the writing machine.

So—if you find that writing with pain is part of your process, I will not try and talk you out of it. After all, who am I to argue when Susan Sontag proclaims: "You have to sink down to a level of hopelessness and desperation to find the book that you can write." Or when Fran Lebowitz complains: "I just write when fear overtakes me." Or when Georges Simenon confesses: "Writing is not a profession but a vocation of unhappiness."

I may consider them whiners more than writers, but it is simply their way. Just don't ask me to stand by and give them a literary Heimlich maneuver when they get a bit of plot stuck in their throats.

❑ 3

An End to Writer's Block!

By Sandra Scofield

I'M IMPATIENT WITH THE VERY IDEA OF WRITER'S BLOCK, BUT IT doesn't mean I don't know it when I see it—or feel it. Panic, lassitude, depression: any or all may be symptoms, but whatever the version, the sure thing is the writing stops and heartache starts. The late poet William Stafford used to say, "Lower your standards, and write." He wasn't one to wait around for the perfect moment. Dig for ore, and maybe you'll find a gem. He wasn't encouraging inferior writing, and neither am I, but he was right in saying that you can't just sit it out. The way to end writer's block is to replace it with habits that keep you confident and productive.

After years of experience and observation, I've identified these factors as primary contributors to writer's block: *(1) Lack of research; (2) Lack of imagination; (3) Lack of focus; (4) Lack of confidence.*

Before I talk about the problems separately, I have to say that they all have a common thread: Too often, the writer starts writing too soon, with unreasonable expectations. I've heard many writers say they just "start writing and see where it goes," and if that works for you, well, you're one of the lucky ones. But many writers—especially beginners—tell me that just jumping in at the start of a particular story (or, heaven help them, a novel) is a sure route to a dead end. I'm all for free writing, *as long as you have no expectations or standards.* There are dozens of books to give you ideas for writing practice, but practice, by definition, isn't the actual game. The harder it is for you to write a "real story," the more you probably need to do the kind of writing that has no pressure, no criteria for success. Find a stimulus, and "warm up" this way, every day if you like. The writer Carol Bly tells her students to write an autobiography, a fine way to write past your hang-ups, to explore the fertile ground of memory, and to put words on a page without the burden of invention. I tell writers to write a "credo," a statement

12

of beliefs: What values mean the most to you? What scares you? What "news" would you like to spread? *What are you trying to figure out about the world?* You'll learn things about yourself, and you'll have concepts to help you evaluate the *content* of your work. I do it once a year; my credo is always evolving.

Research

Writing historical fiction carries the obvious dictum to learn as much as you can about your subject. What you may not realize, however, is that "research" includes all the information and observations that will help you develop characters and structure in any story. When I knew I wanted to set my novel in a Mexican village near an expatriate colony, I read about retirement in Mexico. I talked to several people who had spent time in Chapala, near Guadalajara, and others who knew San Miguel de Allende. Finally, I flew down and spent ten days exploring the region around Lake Chapala. I took the cheap buses; I hired taxi drivers to take me to remote villages. I sat in squares and talked my observations into a microcassette recorder. I took photographs of buildings and panoramas, market stalls, and the like. (I prefer to jot down notes about people unobtrusively.) I tried foods I hadn't eaten before. When I wanted to show my character Mr. Riley growing braver—he's too timid to go to Egypt!—I put him in those buses, and set a plate of tripe in front of him.

Of course, we can't always travel. When I was researching *Plain Seeing*, in order to write the 39 pages that take place in 1942 Hollywood, I read biographies of film stars and looked at books of photographs. I viewed a dozen movies from that period. I didn't know what I was looking for, yet I found it: a movie for my character to act in; the ambiance of a screen test; the details of a starlet's contract. It took a pleasurable month, and at the end, I had the confidence to write the chapter. If you feel "dry," you may just need to feed yourself from the springs of research.

Imagination

You must cultivate an agile mind. Learn that the elements of a story are all malleable. Stretch your creativity. Form a story group, in which writers share oral stories. Use family stories, memories of "embarrassing moments" or "something you lost." Fill in the unknown in a news-paper clipping. Read a published story and have everyone make up a different ending. Many books suggest story starters. Play with them *orally* so that you push yourself to work nimbly without worrying about style. Before I wrote *A Chance to See Egypt*, which I thought of as a kind of folk tale, I participated in a workshop in which we made up our own fairy tales and myths.

Apply these same playful principles to work in progress. When I feel stuck, I get out a big sheet of paper and write my characters' names and everything I know about them. Then I set about changing one feature about each to see what effect it has on their interactions. Try brain-storming questions and answering them in as many ways as you can. The most creative question is *What if . . . ?* Don't get attached to an idea too quickly; the next idea might be better. When something clicks, get right back to writing.

Focus

Here's my prejudice: When I set out, I want to have some idea of where I'm going. I may amend my story ten times over before I've finished it. Tell the story simply, in a few pages, knowing it's only a sketch. Go back to your credo, and ask yourself if you're pursuing something that really matters to you. (A false goal will kill your story.) Try to "see" a strong image in the story, and describe it. Where does it fit? Are you moving *from* it or *toward* it? In *A Chance to See Egypt*, I imagined a young woman in a moving Jeep on a dusty road, her long black hair blowing. That became an important moment of transition in the novel. In *Plain Seeing*, the picture of a young pregnant girl stepping down from a train reverberates throughout the novel, which is about the ways the loss of a parent haunts a child's life ever after.

Confidence

You can see by now that I believe "writing-aerobics" build muscles, i.e., skills; those skills build confidence. Nevertheless, writers are much affected by emotions. Publishing is tough. You've been rejected more times than you can count. You see writers whose work you don't like reaping rewards, or you see so many writers you admire you can't imag-ine there's any room for you. Your day is crammed, and you aren't giving writing enough time. You don't want to write, and you don't want to quit.

Give yourself a break. Remind yourself of what you have accomplished. Look through your notebooks (you *do* keep a notebook!); you'll be amazed at the ideas you've had. Make a fresh copy of a successful story (or a successful scene), and ask a friend to read it and tell you it's good. That's right; ask for praise. You can look at your weaknesses some other time. Read about the craft. Go to a writers' conference, and hang out with people who love what you love.

Also, kid yourself into offhandedness. I keep index cards by my bed and by the couch, and any time of day or night I jot down ideas. I'm not committed to them, so it's easy, and later, when I have a pile, I transcribe them and see what I've got. I write little playlets of dialogue instead of a scene, so I can hear the characters; of course it's not going into my novel that way, so I don't feel self-conscious. Before I write a scene, I daydream it over and over. I write jacket copy for the book this is going to be someday, even a review or two! Write one line you hope will be said about your work, and tack it above your desk.

Do your drafting on the back of used pages, or on cheap colored paper, so you are fully aware that it doesn't really count; it's just a first try. Team up with a friend and check in every week (every day?) and tell one another one idea you've had. No time? No ideas? Write one sentence. That's right, one sentence. Maybe it'll grow to one paragraph, or you'll discover a fresh idea. Set a timer for ten minutes and get up guiltlessly when it rings. I've written seven novels in ten years, and I've hardly ever worked longer than two hours at a sitting. The thing is, I sit down often!

You're the only one who knows how important writing is to you. You don't have to hurry; you *shouldn't* hurry. Seek the pleasure of discovery, and breathe through the tough times. Writer's block isn't a wall of bricks; it's as ephemeral as dust motes. Walk right through.

❏ 4

Tools of the
Writer's Trade

By Christopher Scanlan

In Shakespeare's time, itinerant actors who took their plays from village to town carried bags bulging with the tools of their art— scraps of costume, props, jars of paint. A writer's tools can be every bit as colorful and creative, and they won't take up as much room. Rummage through your memory and imagination to see if you find long-forgotten tools you can dust off.

Here are the tools I found and use: a tightrope, a net, a pair of shoes, a loom, six words, an accelerator pedal, and a time clock.

A tightrope

Take a risk with your writing every day. Submit to the magazine of your dreams. Conceive the next Great American Novel. The risks I've taken as a writer—pitching an ambitious project, calling for an interview with a reputed mobster, sending a short story back out in the mail the day it returned in my self-addressed envelope—have opened new doors and, more important, encouraged me to take other risks. Stretch an imaginary tightrope above your desk and walk across it every day.

A net

The best writers I know cast trawler's nets on stories. And they cast them wide and deep. They'll interview ten people, listening and waiting, to get the one quote that sums up the theme. They'll spend hours trolling for the anecdote that reveals the story. They'll sift through records and reports, looking for the one specific that explains the universal or the detail that captures the person or conveys the setting. I once wrote a story about a family in Utah whose daughter was a suspected victim of serial murderer Ted Bundy. During my visit, I noticed that a light switch next to the front door had a piece of tape over it so no one could turn it off. When I asked about it, the mother said she always left the light on until her daughter came home. The light had been burning for twelve years, a symbol of one family's unending grief.

A pair of shoes

Empathy, an ability to feel what another person feels, may be the writer's most important tool. Empathy is different from sympathy: It's one thing to feel sorry for a rape victim; it's another to imagine and write persuasively to recreate the constant terrors and distrust sown in the victim's mind. To write about a young widow in my story "School Uniform," I had to imagine the problems of a woman coping with her own grief and that of her children:

> After the funeral, Maddy had made sure that each child had something of Jim's. It was torture to handle his things, but she spread them out on their bed one night after the children were asleep and made choices. Anna draped his rosary from the mirror on her makeup table; Martin kept his paper route money secured in his father's silver money clip. Brian filled the brass candy dish that Jim used as an ashtray with his POGS and Sega Genesis cartridges. Daniel kept his baseball cards in Jim's billfold. There were days she wished she could have thrown everything out, and had she been alone, she might have moved away, started somewhere fresh with nothing to remind her of what had been, all she had lost when he died, leaving her at 38 with four children. And on nights like this, when there was trouble with Daniel, again, she wanted to give up.

When you write about a character, try to walk in that person's shoes.

A loom

Writers, like all artists, help society understand the connections that bind us. They identify patterns. Raymond Carver said, "writing is just a process of connections. Things begin to connect. A line here, a word here." Are you weaving connections in your stories? In your reading? In your life? Are you asking yourself what line goes to what line, and what makes a whole? "Only connect!" urged E.M. Forster. Turn your computer into a loom that weaves stories.

Six words

Thinking is the hardest part about writing and the one writers are likeliest to bypass. When I'm writing nonfiction, I try not to start writing until I've answered two questions: "What's the news?" and "What's the story?" Whatever the genre—essay, article or short story—effective writing conveys a single dominant message. To discover that theme or focus, try to sum up your story in six words, a phrase that captures the tension of the story. For a story about a teenage runaway hit by a train and rescued by another teen, my six words are "Lost, Then Found, On the Tracks." Why six words? No reason, except that in discipline, there is freedom.

An accelerator pedal

Free writing is the writer's equivalent of putting the pedal to the metal. I often start writing workshops by asking participants to write about "My Favorite Soup." It loosens the fingers, memory, and imagination. I surprised myself recently by describing post-Thanksgiving turkey soup:

> Most holidays have a "Do Not Resuscitate" sign on them. At the end of Christmas everybody vows that next year will be different, we'll pick names, not buy for everybody. It's too expensive, too time-consuming. But turkey soup puts a holiday on a respirator for a few more days of life, enough time to remember and savor the memories of the family around the table.

Speeding on a highway is a sure-fire route to an accident, but doing it on the page or computer screen creates an opportunity for fortunate accidents—those flashes of unconscious irony or insight that can trigger a story or take you and your readers deeper into one.

A time clock

Writers write. It's that simple—and that hard. If you're not writing regularly and for *at least* 15 minutes before your day job, then you're not a writer. Many times I resist; the writing is terrible, I'm too tired, I have no ideas, and then I remember that words beget other words. I stifle my whining and set to work, just for a little while, I tell myself. Almost always, I discover writing I had never imagined before I began, and those are the times I feel most like a writer. Put an imaginary time clock on your desk, right next to your computer. Punch in.

❑ 5

TAKING THE STING OUT
OF REJECTION

BY EILEEN GOUDGE

IN MY MIND'S EYE, I CAN STILL SEE IT—A SKINNY WHITE ENVELOPE floating just out of reach. Tantalizing as a fabled city of yore shimmering on some distant horizon. I'm referring, of course, to the ultimate prize of every free-lance writer: the acceptance letter. My dream version reads as follows:

> Dear Jane (John),
>   Your manuscript arrived on my desk yesterday. I read it at once, and was immediately hooked. Bravo! Yours is the most original voice I've come across in years. Needless to say, my esteemed colleagues and I are very excited about the prospect of introducing you to our readers, and would consider it an honor to publish your article/ short story/ novel. If the enclosed contract meets with your approval, please sign and return it, and a check for the sum of $10,000 will be on its way to you shortly.
>
>   Sincerely,
>
>   Joe Editor

Needless to say, I never received such a letter. The closest I got to Cibola, back in those early years as a struggling free-lance writer, was that every so often, tucked in with the slew of self-addressed stamped envelopes cramming my mailbox, there would be a slim white envelope to make my pulse race and my hopes soar. More often than not, it was a note from some kindly editor apologizing for the several-months delay in getting back to me, and informing me that my manuscript had been passed on to another (presumably more senior) editor, and was "currently under consideration." Occasionally, however, the envelope would contain an acceptance letter, or even a small check from some small publication no one had ever heard of. Just enough to keep that flickering flame going . . . as well as ending any possibility that this feverish obsession of mine—yes, *obsession*, as anyone with a mother-in-law who constantly asks, "when are you going to give up and get a *real* job?" knows—would be lifting anytime in this millennium.

Mostly, though, what I remember were the rejection slips. Piles and piles of them, spilling out of my mailbox, overflowing my wastebasket, jammed (those with even a word or two of scribbled encouragement) into a box by my desk. In those days I lived in a small seaside town where the mailman knew everyone on his route and would honk his horn whenever he spotted anything in the mail that looked even remotely like glad tidings. I would stop in the middle of what I was doing—washing dishes, hanging out wet laundry, or banging away at my ancient Underwood typewriter—to dash outside, only to find an overdue notice for some bill, a must-see-to-believe-offer-of-a-lifetime, or an invitation to the opening of a new shopping mall. A letter from a friend was a welcome distraction. It alleviated, if only for a few minutes, the onslaught of rejection that seemed to be coming at me from all directions—a constant drumbeat telling me I was a failure, I was never going to make a go of this, I'd been foolish to think I had the talent to be a published writer.

Could I have done anything differently to hasten my journey on the road to success? Not really. Looking back, I see all those rejections as a rite of passage, something nearly every writer has to go through, a literary boot camp so to speak, in order to earn his or her stripes. Now, with twenty-six years of experience under my belt, I also know that there *are* ways to soften the blow of rejection, and arrive at a more positive perspective—one that can increase your odds of getting one of those skinny white envelopes in place of a dog-eared SASE.

First and foremost: You're not alone. The best way to take the sting out of rejection is to join, or form, a writers group. Misery loves company, and no company but that of other struggling writers understands *this* brand of misery quite so well. I'm not recommending a steady diet of moaning and whining, though a little bit can go a long way in helping you let go of some of that pent-up frustration. What I *am* saying is there's strength in numbers. In sharing your experiences you're bound to receive, along with ideas and suggestions for improving your manuscript, some valuable tips from others who've forged the trail ahead of you. Someone may know of an editor or agent who's particularly open to receiving unsolicited submissions, or a publication looking for articles on a specific subject.

That's exactly how I got my first big break. I'd gotten together with several of my pals to form just such a group. A short while later, I learned from my friend Susan of a book packager who'd recently started a line of teen romances called "Sweet Dreams." I immediately fired off a query, and soon was rewarded with a contract. That led to another, even bigger break: the opportunity to help launch "Sweet Valley High," which went on to become the most popular teen series of all time. (In typical when-it-rains-it-pours fashion, I wrote five of the first twelve titles, a 150-page manuscript every six weeks.) After a move to New York, and a limited run with a teen series of my own, I started work on my first hardcover novel for adults, *Garden of Lies*. Two years later, I was looking at a two-book contract for close to a million dollars.

Sound too good to be true? That's what *I* thought at the time. In hindsight, though, I see it more as a triumph of perseverance than a lucky strike. All those rejections had honed me in some way—as does the chisel with which a sculptor chips away the excess from a block of stone that will become a beautiful and enduring statue. I emerged from that painful period not only a *better* writer, but a *triumphant* one. I had proven to myself, if to no one else, that I had the guts, as well as the talent, to make a go of this.

I can't stress this enough: *To stand even a slim chance of getting published you must be willing to walk through fire.* By that I mean you have to swallow your pride and listen to the truth, even when it hurts. Bear the slings and arrows of well-meaning friends and family who smile in fond bemusement at what they view to be a fairly useless pursuit. And let's not forget those close-but-no-cigar letters from editors and agents who see merit in your manuscript—but not enough to publish it.

If I had a dollar for every would-be author, usually a friend of a friend, whose proposal or manuscript I've offered to take a look at, but who never got up the courage to send it, I'd be rich enough to retire. Yes, that's one way of avoiding the pain of criticism or possible rejection, but it gets you nowhere, and in the end all it shows is that you aren't really cut out to be a writer. Talent isn't everything! You could be a diamond in the rough, a Steinbeck in the making, but if you're not prepared to get kicked around a bit, forget it.

I remember the exhilaration of my first check—twenty whole dollars for a short article titled, "An Egg in Your Car Can Save You Money." I was so excited, I wanted to frame it, but I needed the money to buy groceries. I framed a Xerox instead—my diploma from the School of Hard Knocks.

So you've collected your share of rejection slips, braved the harsh storm of criticism, bared your soul to your peers, and you *still* come up empty-handed. What are you doing wrong? Are there any shortcuts you should know about?

Sometimes all you need is a bit more patience. But if you're anything like *me*, chances are you're not seeing the whole picture, and could use a little boost. Here are some tips I've learned along the way for minimizing the wait, while maximizing your chances of getting positive feedback.

Some years back, when I first moved to New York, I had the good fortune to hook up with a top literary agent, whom shortly thereafter I ended up marrying. The marriage didn't stand the test of time, but I walked away with a wealth of experience. Have you ever wondered what it would be like to be a fly on the wall of a literary agent's office? Well, I lived that fantasy. Literally. I saw firsthand what it was like: the tide of manuscripts that poured in each day, the harried agents with overflowing desks and bookshelves, the mail room piled with return envelopes on the way back to their senders, the phones flashing with calls from desperate authors. Not a cheerful sight, but certainly a humbling one.

What I learned was this: *First*, the competition, while not always keen, can be overwhelming in terms of sheer number. In order for *your* precious pearl to emerge shining from the tide of flotsam and jetsam that washes in each day, you have to stand out in some way. *Not* by doodling daisies in the margins, enclosing nude photos of yourself, or a diamond pinkie ring (You think I'm making this up? I actually witnessed it!), but by a strict and unwavering adherence to excellence.

Start with a one-page, well-thought-out query letter. The agent had two piles on his desk. Everything typed on a single sheet of paper went into one pile. Usually, it got read within a day or two. The other pile, for letters and queries of two pages or more, would often sit unread for weeks until he got around to it. *Everything you need to say can be said in a single page.* If it means taking the time to slice, dice, and shave your query until you've excised every shred of excess flab, so be it. Nine times out of ten, you'll end up with a better letter, and a quicker response that's more likely to net a positive result.

To start with, succinctly but persuasively state why this extremely busy agent (or editor) should take the time to read the manuscript you wish to send. This can be summed up in a brief but intriguing one-or-two paragraph synopsis, coupled with any background or area of expertise you bring to the subject. If you grew up in the slums you're writing about, be sure to include a vivid thumbnail sketch of your own inspiring triumph over adversity. If you teach literature at a university, by all means mention it. Not only will this help convince the agent/editor that you know what you're talking about, it will help him or her visualize, and hopefully remember, you, the author.

Last but not least, your presentation must be letter perfect: not a single typo, a misspelled word, typeface that's hard to read—any of which can be the kiss of death. To a busy agent, any sign, however small or insignificant in your eyes, of someone who didn't take the time to comb through the letter for mistakes, will suggest the manuscript isn't worth considering. If you've come this far, it's worth the extra effort to go the distance.

I'm reminded of a true story from those days. One Saturday when the front door of the agency had been left open and unattended, a thief made off with an oriental rug and antique mirror. The police were clueless, and the trail cold. A few months later, the agent received a call from an inmate at Rykers Island—the thief who'd made off with our valuables and had been jailed for another, similar crime. He said he'd be happy to return our stolen goods, on one condition: that the agent read his manuscript. Clearly this aspiring writer would stop at nothing to get published!

I'm not suggesting you plan a heist. What's important to keep in mind is that rejection isn't always personal. Sometimes, it's simply the wrong idea, or just bad timing. There might have been a rash of articles or books on that subject recently. Or the editor you've approached with a book on cats is allergic to felines. Or that you've caught the person on a day when *everything* he's reading seems hopeless. To sum it all up: Put your best foot forward, and don't stress out if you don't get the desired result. In the long run, you'll win.

Recently, a women's magazine editor suggested I come up with a few ideas for an article. We discussed a few possibilities, and I followed up with a one-page proposal. Weeks went by. The editor phoned to apologize for the delay; she was awaiting word from her Editor-in-Chief. The end result? I received a nice letter saying that my idea wasn't quite right for them, and I should try again with something else. It didn't count that millions of copies of my novels have been sold around the world—this particular idea just wasn't up their alley! Nothing personal, and, *not an indictment of my writing ability.*

What did I take away from this experience? Well, it hurt a little, I confess—a pinch to the old ego. Then I sat back and took stock of all I *had* accomplished, and felt a lot better. I understood that nothing that's worth anything is achieved by less than an unstinting effort . . . not to mention buckets of blood, sweat, and tears. I felt lucky to have persevered. To be counted among the few who have made it, if not to the peak, then far enough up to admire the view.

❏ 6

BREAKING THE RULES

BY ALISON SINCLAIR

HANDS UP, EVERYONE WHO HAS EVER BEEN TOLD, "WRITE WHAT YOU Know."

Hands up, everyone who has heard, "Show, Don't Tell."

If there's a writer who hasn't heard either at some point early in his or her career, I'd consider that person fortunate indeed.

(They've surely heard the third—Stand up, please, anyone who hasn't—"You'll Never Make a Living at It!")

Though intolerant of abusers of the common apostrophe, I am a tender-hearted soul. I will not advocate the slaughtering of sacred cows, even in metaphor, but I would advocate firmly turning them out to pasture. Here's why.

1) Writers should *not* be urged to write what they know. They should be urged to write what they care about, care about passionately, argumentatively, gracelessly, if need be. Knowledge can be acquired, whether through books, the world wide web, or stoking or stroking an expert. (People love to talk about their own personal passions.) Knowledge can be acquired in the absence of caring. Ask any diligent student working just for a grade, or a responsible adult making a living in a job he or she dislikes. But caring, unlike knowledge, cannot be acquired at second hand. Knowledge gives writing authority—I cannot dispute that—but caring gives writing life.

A few years ago, in Canada, where I now live, and in particular amongst the community of women writers, there came a call that women of the majority culture (i.e., white) should not impersonate, in writing, minority characters. It was an act of appropriation. In one respect, I could see the justice of it, that the way would be cleared for writers from minorities to speak in their own voice. In another, I could see that it struck at the fundamental nature of writing. By raising "write what you know (and *only* what you know)" to a formal imperative, the imaginative projection of experience unlike one's own—experience not known but imagined—was denied. The controversy has settled, but I remember it, the questions it raised about balancing social justice and imaginative liberties, and the threat I felt it posed to the life of the imagination.

2) Every writing book somewhere says, "Show, don't tell." That phrase should come with a health warning: "Keep out of reach of novices." Like cellophane wrapping, it can suffocate. As many beginning writers do, I believed it. In my first novel, a character went out to meet a woman about whom he'd heard a great deal. So he got out bed, got dressed, went downstairs, had a conversation with other people in the house, and he was given an errand, which he did, which led to another conversation, and he walked downhill. I described everything he saw on the way, and ten pages on he finally met her. It was a good meeting, if I say so myself, but when the book was accepted (not, I suspect, for what I had done, but for what the editor thought I might yet do), the editor decreed CUT. And cut I did. I discovered, under her rigorous tutelage, that you show only what you absolutely have to, tell what you can't avoid, and leave the rest out. The final version of that chapter had my couple face to face in two-and-a-half pages. They went on to have a turbulent though happy life together (most of it long after the final line of the book because that had nothing to do with the problem set up in the first chapter). Paragraphs and paragraphs of "showing" were dispensed with in a few sentences or even words. And the book was by far the better for it.

Even in a 150,000-word novel, there is no space for "show," no scenes that can be given over to "I just wanted to show that this society was egalitarian." If these things are part of the story, they will be revealed through the action. If they are not, they are irrelevant; they can be narrated, briefly, or left out. "Tell" is a powerful tool for keeping minor matters in their place.

3) There are any number of Rules propounded for writers (which in itself is probably a reflection of Maugham's Three Rules, noted below. Nothing generates regulation like uncertainty): ONE MUST WRITE ONE THOUSAND WORDS EVERY DAY (honored more in the breach than in the

observance; writers have lives, too). NEVER START A NOVEL WITH DIA-
LOGUE (did anybody tell Tolstoy?). DO NOT TALK ABOUT YOUR WRIT-
ING; YOU'LL TALK IT OUT; or alternatively, IF YOU CAN'T TELL
SOMEONE ELSE YOUR PLOT, IT'S NO GOOD. NOVELS ABOUT (fill in the
blank) DO NOT SELL, etc.

For every writer who swears by a Rule, there is one as good, as successful, as sagacious and temperate, who breaks it. For myself, I believe
in Somerset Maugham's Three Rules, Le Guin's Advice, and Granny
Weatherwax's Principle. Maugham observed that there were Three
Rules of Writing; unfortunately, no one knows what they are. Le Guin's
Advice (from *The Language of the Night*): "No matter how any story
begins, it ends typed in good, clear, black text on one side of white
paper, with name and address on each page."*

Granny Weatherwax's Principle is: "When you break the rules, break
'em good and hard."†

---

*This predates the electronic age. Things have become more complicated since, so this
rule should be amended to: Read submission instructions in the latest issue.

†Granny Weatherwax is a witch (Terry Pratchett's *Wyrd Sisters*).

❏ 7

ARE YOU READING ENOUGH?

BY MAGGIE MURPHY

WE TAKE IT AS A GIVEN THAT THOSE OF US WHO LONG TO SEE OUR words in print love to read, but are you reading *enough?* We'd be surprised if an art student rarely visited art museums, or a would-be actor repeatedly turned down free theatre tickets. Yet it's a common lament among editors that many aspiring writers desperate to sell their manuscripts have scant acquaintance with the wonderful literary works already in libraries and bookstores.

Reading inspires us, sparks new ideas, and teaches us by example how to write effectively. The best writers I know, published and unpublished, are voracious readers. When you read interviews with accomplished writers, take special note of how frequently they describe themselves as *readers* in love with books.

If you aren't nurturing yourself as a reader, you're short-changing yourself as a writer. Here are ten tips to invigorate your reading program:

1) Read widely

The best literary menu provides plenty of variety. Most writers do have special loves: One of mine is children's literature. Still, you don't want to limit your reading to only your favorite literary field.

Read widely, and you'll discover galaxies of exciting worlds to explore.

In addition, reading plays, poems, fairy tales, and myths is invaluable to writers crafting in quite different fields. As just two examples, take plays and poetry.

Whether you're writing a mystery, a science fiction novella, or the Great American Novel, you can learn a great deal about dynamic writing from reading William Shakespeare's *Macbeth* or any other powerful play. In plays, you'll find excellent examples of dialogue that develops character and speeds the plot along. You'll also get a feel for presenting your story in scenes and, by examining the way a playwright handles entrances and exits, get your characters in and out of those scenes smoothly.

Then there's the oft-neglected world of poetry, a magical realm of vivid imagery and fanciful leaps. Reading poetry, everything from the delicate word-web of a Matsuo Bashō haiku to Samuel Taylor Coleridge's enchanting *Christabel*, will encourage you to weave more artful and inimitable tapestries with your prose.

2) Keep a "books finished" list

I started such a list in college nearly 20 years ago, and it's been a good way to monitor my reading life. If you suddenly stop adding to a "books read" list, you're more likely to head for the library or bookstore instead of letting several bookless weeks slide by.

It's rewarding to see your list grow. Remember that reading is an accomplishment as well as an enjoyable activity. There is no round of applause when you finish the last page of a marathon read like Victor Hugo's *Les Misérables*, but adding it to your "books finished" list is a small way to celebrate your reading success.

3) Always bring a book along

How often have you found yourself in a crowded waiting room wishing you had a book with you?

To make book-carrying more convenient, look for some "light reading" that is literally just that. If the hardback you're reading is too heavy, buy the same book secondhand in paperback, if available, and slip it into your bag. Choose slim books to read on your daily travels, such as Robert Louis Stevenson's classic novella *Dr. Jekyll and Mr. Hyde*.

4) Listen to books on tape

Audio books can transform a boring car trip into a literary adventure. Books on tape are also excellent for people who feel too tired to read in bed at night.

You'll find a tempting selection of audio books available in bookstores and public libraries. You can listen to the poems of Emily Dickinson, or a full-cast performance of Shakespeare's *A Midsummer Night's Dream.*

The sound of a well-trained voice reading to you is entrancing. Just slip in a cassette, and it's like having Scheherazade entertain you. It's especially meaningful to put yourself under the spell of the spoken word. With your own writing, you're striving to create polished work that stands the "read it out loud" test.

5) Read to a friend

Enjoy the experience of reading out loud to a friend, relative, child, or other book lover. This is a rewarding way to share a book.

6) Create your own reading theme

Focus on time travel, sea or ghost stories. Save the theme reading lists you find in magazines, and on library flyers and bookmarks. Read Charlotte Brontë's *Jane Eyre,* and then Jean Rhys's *Wide Sargasso Sea,* a haunting novel with an inventive tie-in to the Brontë classic. Read writers associated with places you're visiting, such as Dickens when you're in London.

One of my reading themes centered on Newbery Medal-winning children's books. Without this self-assignment, I doubt I'd have bought a used copy of Dhan Gopal Mukerji's *Gay-Neck: The Story of a Pigeon,* the Newbery award winner in 1928, now a little-known book, but rich with achingly beautiful descriptions of India.

7) Find book buddies

When a friend recommends a book she's just finished, I try to read it soon after so it will still be fresh in her mind for discussion.

One of my friends and I have had interesting conversations about works as different as Banana Yoshimoto's lyrical novel *Kitchen* and Jon Krakauer's gripping *Into Thin Air: A Personal Account of the Mt. Everest Disaster.*

And there's nothing like visiting with a book friend who shares your literary tastes. My mother is my children's book buddy because she understands that good children's books can be literature. We've talked about children's stories set on islands, brave storybook mice, and the verse of Mother Goose.

8) Join a book group

As a member of a book group, you have the opportunity to share the joy of books with others, while stretching yourself as a reader. Check listings in bookstore, library, and community center newsletters.

9) Go online

The Internet is an amazing resource for bibliophiles. For example, the online bookseller Amazon.com features just about every literary offering you can imagine, including book lists, author interviews, and even free e-mailed book recommendations.

Just one caution here: Exploring the Internet is like flipping through an enchanted magazine that will never have a last page. Don't be lured into doing so much reading *about* reading that you wind up staring at your computer screen for hours instead of opening a good book.

10) When you can't read a lot, at least read a little

People with frantic daily schedules often make little headway reading demanding tomes, become discouraged, and stop reading much at all. If you're facing a particularly hectic time, avoid this trap by reading plays, poems, or the fine short stories in good literary journals or collections. Try reading children's books such as C.S. Lewis's *The Lion, the Witch and the Wardrobe*. This book is packed with adventure and wisdom, yet it is written for shorter attention spans. In just six pages, you've left England and entered the magical land of Narnia.

When I'm very busy, I also like to set out certain books that don't need to be read cover to cover but are ideal for dipping into again and again, titles like *Grimms' Fairy Tales*, Ingri and Edgar Parin d'Aulaire's *Norse Gods and Giants*, and *The Arabian Nights*. (Even Sindbad the sailor's narrative is conveniently broken up into seven voyages.) For writers, such myths and tales are the bedrock of storytelling.

□ 8

IMPROVING YOUR WRITING LIFE

BY BILL VOSSLER

WRITING IS FUNDAMENTALLY ABOUT SOLVING PROBLEMS. SO IF YOU want to write, and write better, you must learn to confront the myriad problems that arise, large (what is my character like?) and small (does the comma go here or here?), and then overcome these impediments that slow your writing, or derail it entirely.

Here are nine problems you must learn to solve if you want to further your writing career:

1. Not expecting problems. As a professional writer, I expect to encounter problems every time I write; you must, too. But it is not enough to learn to *expect* problems; you must *believe* you will be able to solve them. Many can be solved immediately and easily; but a stubborn few will require prolonged thought or reworking until they are solved. (In those cases, the first time through I often do what I can, then insert "BLANK" or "???" into the text, and continue with the flow of my writing, returning to solve the thorny problem later.)

2. Easy writing. How is easy writing an impediment? In three ways:
First, if your first draft comes easily, you can mistakenly believe that all writing is easy, which it most certainly is not. (It's not impossibly difficult either, as some writers would have you believe.)
Second, when you encounter difficult or protracted writing, as in rewriting or editing, you might be tempted to skip these most important steps, or to toss the piece of writing aside, because you think it will take too much effort.
Third, your editor might say, "This piece is a no-go."

3. Stick-to-it-ive-ness. To finish a piece of writing—indeed to be a writer—requires great perseverance, but it can become a problem when you don't know when to let go, and you spend all your time researching, for instance, instead of writing.

Or perhaps, you *do* know you should let go, but then you'd have to take on another, different, and perhaps more formidable writing project, and it's easier to stay with a known one. So it is important to learn when you're finished with a piece (for a while, or permanently)—when more rewriting won't help it, and the piece is as good as you can make it—and then move on to another piece.

4. Flitting from project to project. To succeed at writing, a writer needs optimism and idealism; those same traits will help you come up with new ideas.

Finding ideas can be so much fun, however, that some writers don't do much else; or they may discover that developing an idea might be harder work than they thought: Either they don't know how to go about it, or the idea becomes more and more unpalatable. Their solution? Find a brighter flower; switch to another idea.

There's nothing wrong with working on several ideas/pieces at one time, of course, or even moving from one idea to the next during a single work period (I do it all the time), *unless* you make a habit of abandoning an idea without developing it, and jumping to another idea that seems more fun. Serial idea-ism, so to speak.

Writing success stems from taking one worthy idea, developing it to its fullest, and finishing it.

5. Outlines. An outline is a wonderful tool; it helps you organize, shows you quickly what you know (or don't know), delineates the project, points out duplication or missing areas, and much more.

But the process of writing is fluid and malleable, and a piece that begins at point A and is headed toward point D may at any time veer off to point G or Z. If that new direction is legitimate, it is imperative that you alter—even abandon—your outline. An outline is best used as a dim road instead of a solid, well-lighted highway.

6. Rabbit ears. Many new writers short-circuit their careers because when they finish one piece and send it off, they sit with their ears held high, waiting to hear, hoping to hear, wanting to hear, instead of moving on to their next project.

Think of it this way: No matter what you do, the editorial process will grind on, slowly and deliberately. You can do little to change it.

So it is important that, once you've finished with a writing project, you sit down at the keyboard and start the next one.

7. Falling in love—with your words, that is. The standard advice is to draw a line through your favorite parts of your writing. There is some truth in this. If you especially love a turn of phrase or an idea or concept in your writing, it's very possible that you are too close to those words and cannot make hard judgments about them, the hard judgments needed to improve your piece.

So put the piece away for a few days (weeks would be better). When you return to it, you'll see it with new eyes. What might at first have seemed wonderful and fitting, may not fit—may even turn ghastly and pale by the light of the new day.

8. Believing the advice of other writers. This is slippery ground. It is important to use experienced writers as mentors, as information sources, as strangers to guide you through the thorny pathways to that far land of good and smooth writing.

But it is also important to learn your own way, to begin to pick and choose only the information and advice from other writers that will work for *you* and be most useful to *you*, even if it means ignoring some of the professional writer's advice; after all, this is your writing life.

That said, it's important to know yourself well enough to understand whether you ignore a writer's advice because it won't work for you, or simply because it means hard work. If you aren't sure, then take the advice. No one can ever take your writing experience away from you.

9. Fun. How can fun possibly be an impediment? As you write more and more and have more and more fun, all you'll want to do for your life's work is write, because writing ends up being more fun than any person should ever be allowed to have!

❑ 9

WRITING MATTERS

BY JULIA ALVAREZ

ONE OF THE QUESTIONS THAT ALWAYS COMES UP DURING QUESTION-and-answer periods is about the writing life. The more sophisticated, practiced questioners usually ask me, "Can you tell us something about your process as a writer?"

In part, this is the curiosity we all have about each other's "processes," to use the terminology of my experienced questioner. We need to tell, and we also want to know (don't we?) the secret heart of each other's life. Perhaps that is why we love good novels and poems—because we can enter, without shame or without encountering defensiveness or embarrassment, the intimate lives of other people.

But the other part of my questioner's curiosity about the writing life has to do with a sense we all have that if we can only get a hold of the secret ingredients of the writing process, we will become better writers. We will have an easier time of it if we only find that magic pencil or know at which hour to start and at which hour to quit and what to sip that might help us come up with the next word in a sentence.

I always tell my questioners the truth: Listen, there are no magic solutions to the hard work of writing. There is no place to put the writing desk that will draw more words out of you. I had a friend who claimed that an east-west alignment was the best one for writing. The writing would then flow and be more in tune with the positive energies. The north-south alignment would cause blocks as well as bad dreams if your bed was also thus aligned.

See, I tell my questioners, isn't this silly?

But even as I say so, I know I am talking out of both sides of my mouth. I admit that after getting my friend's tip, I lined up my writing desk (and my bed) in the east-west configuration. It wasn't that I thought my writing or my dream life would improve, but I am so impressionable that I was afraid that I'd be thinking and worrying about my alignment instead of my line breaks. And such fretting would affect my writing adversely. Even as recently as this very day, I walk into my study first thing in the morning, and I fill up my bowl of clear water and place it on my desk. And though no one told me to do this, I somehow feel this is the right way to start a writing day.

Of course, that fresh bowl of water sits on my desk on good *and* bad writing days. I know these little ceremonies will not change the kind of day before me. My daily writing rituals are small ways in which I contain my dread and affirm my joy and celebrate the mystery and excitement of the calling to be a writer.

I use the word *calling* in the old religious sense: a commitment to a life connected to deeper, more profound forces (or so I hope) than the marketplace, or the academy, or the hectic blur of activity that my daily life is often all about. But precisely because it is a way of life, not just a job, the writing life can be difficult to combine with other lives that require that same kind of passion and commitment—the teaching life, the family life, the parenting life, and so on. And since we writers tend to be intense people, whatever other lives we com-bine with our writing life, we will want to live them intensely, too. Some of us are better at this kind of juggling than others.

After twenty-five years of clumsy juggling—marriages, friendships, teaching, writing, community work, political work, child caring—I think I've finally figured out what the proper balance is for me. Let me emphasize that this is not a prescription for anyone else. But alas, I'm of the Gerald Ford school of writers who can't chew gum and write iambic pentameter at the same time. I can do two, maybe three intense lives at once: writing and being in a family; writing and teaching and being in a family; writing and teaching and doing political work; but if I try to add a fourth or fifth, I fall apart, that is, the writing stops, which for me is the same thing as saying I fall apart.

But still, I keep juggling, picking up one life and another and another, putting aside the writing from time to time. We have only one life, after all, and we have to live so many lives with it. (Another reason the writing life appeals so much is that you can be, at least on paper, all those selves whose lives you can't possibly live out in the one life you've got.)

Living other lives enriches our writing life. The tension between them can sometimes exhaust us, this is true—but the struggle also makes the hard-won hours at the writing desk all the more precious. And if we are committed to our writing, the way we lead our other lives can make them lives-in-waiting to be writing lives.

For me, the writing life doesn't just happen when I sit at the writing desk. It is a life lived with a centering principle, and mine is this: that I will pay close attention to this world I find myself in. "My heart keeps open house," was the way the poet Theodore Roethke put it in a poem. And rendering in language what one sees through the opened windows and doors of that house is a way of bearing witness to the mystery of what it is to be alive in this world.

This is all very high-minded and inspirational, my questioner puts in, but what about when we are alone at our writing desks, feeling wretchedly anxious, wondering if there is anything in us worth putting down?

Let me take you through the trials and tribulations of a typical writing day. It might help as you also set out onto that blank page, encounter one adventure or mishap after another, and wonder—do other writers go through this?

The answer is probably yes.

Not much has happened at six-twenty or so in the morning when I enter my writing room above the garage. I like it this way. The mind is free of household details, worries, commitments, voices, problems to solve.

My mood entering the room depends on what happened with my writing the day before. If the previous day was a good one, I look forward to the new writing day. If I was stuck or uninspired, I feel apprehensive. In short, I can't agree more with Hemingway's advice that a writer should always end his writing day knowing where he is headed next. It makes it easier to come back to work.

The first thing I do in my study every morning is read poetry (Jane Kenyon, George Herbert, Rita Dove, Robert Frost, Elizabeth Bishop, Rhina Espaillat, Jane Shore, Emily Dickinson . . .). This is the first music I hear, the most essential. Interestingly, I like to follow the reading of poetry with some prose, as if, having been to the heights I need to come back down to earth.

I consider this early-morning reading a combination of pleasure-reading time when I read the works and authors I most love and finger-exercise reading time, when I am tuning my own voice to the music of the English language as played by its best writers. There's an old Yiddish story about a rabbi who walks out in a rich neighborhood and meets a watchman walking up and down. "For whom are you working?" the rabbi asks. The watchman tells him, and then in his turn, he asks the rabbi, "And whom are you working for, rabbi?" The words strike the rabbi like a shaft. "I am not working for anybody just yet," he barely manages to reply. Then he walks up and down beside the man for a long time and finally asks him, "Will you be my servant?" The watchman says, "I should like to, but what would be my duties?"

"To remind me," the rabbi says.

I read my favorite writers to remind me of the quality of writing I am aiming for.

Now, it's time to set out: Pencil poised, I read through the hard copy that I ran off at the end of yesterday's writing day. I used to write everything out by longhand, and when I was reasonably sure I had a final draft, I'd type it up on my old Selectric. But now, I usually write all my prose drafts right out on the computer, though I need to write out my poems in longhand, to make each word by hand.

This is also true of certain passages of prose and certainly true for times when I am stuck in a novel or story. Writing by hand relieves some of the pressure of seeing something tentative flashed before me on the screen with that authority that print gives to writing. "This is just for me," I tell myself, as I scratch out a draft in pencil. Often, these scribblings turn into little bridges, tendrils that take me safely to the other side of silence. When I'm finally on my way, I head back to the computer.

But even my hard copies look as if they've been written by hand. As I revise, I begin to hear the way I want a passage to sound. About the third or fourth draft, if I'm lucky, I start to see the shape of what I am writing, the way an essay will go, a character will react, a poem unfold.

Sometimes if Bill and I go on a long car trip, I'll read him what I am working on. This is a wonderful opportunity to "hear" what I've written. The process of reading my work to someone else does tear apart that beauteous coating of self-love in which my own creation comes enveloped. I start to hear what I've written as it would sound to somebody else.

When I'm done with proofing the hard copy of the story or chapter or poem, I take a little break. This is one of the pleasures of working at home. I can take these refreshing breathers from the intensity of the writing: go iron a shirt or clean out a drawer or wrap up my sister's birthday present.

After my break, I take a deep breath. What I now do is transcribe all my handwritten revisions on to my computer, before I launch out into the empty space of the next section of the story or essay or the chapter in a novel. This is probably the most intense time of the writing day. I am on my way, but I don't know exactly where it is I am going. But that's why I'm writing: to find out.

On the good days, an excitement builds up as I push off into the language, and sentence seems to follow sentence. I catch myself smiling or laughing out loud or sometimes even weeping as I move through a scene or a stanza. Certainly writing seems to integrate parts of me that are usually at odds. As I write, I feel unaccountably whole; I disappear! That is the irony of this self-absorbed profession: The goal finally is to vanish. On bad days, on the other hand, I don't disappear. Instead, I'm stuck with the blank screen before me. I take more and more breaks. I wander out on the deck and look longingly south toward the little spire of the Congregational church and wish another life for myself. Oh, dear, what have I done with my life?

I have chosen it, that's what I've done. So I take several deep breaths and go back upstairs and sit myself down and work over the passage that will not come. As Flannery O'Connor attested: "Every morning between 9 and 12, I go to my room and sit before a piece of paper. Many times, I just sit for three hours with no ideas coming to me. But I know one thing: If an idea does come between 9 and 12, I am there ready for it." The amazing thing for me is that years later, reading the story or novel or poem, I can't tell the passages that were easy to write, the ones that came forth like "greased lightning" from those other passages that made me want to give up writing and take up another life.

On occasion, when all else fails, I take the rest of the day "off." I finish reading the poet or novelist with whom I began the day or I complain to my journal or I look through a picture book of shoes one of my characters might wear. But all the while I am feeling profound self doubt—as if I were one of those cartoon characters who runs off a cliff, and suddenly looks down only to discover, there's no ground beneath her feet!

At the end of the writing day (about two-thirty or three in the afternoon), I leave the room over the garage. I put on my running clothes, and I go for a run. In part, this exercise does make me feel better. But one of the best perks of running has been that it allows me to follow Hemingway's advice. I don't always know where I am headed in my writing at the end of the work day, but after I run, I usually have one or two good ideas. Running helps me work out glitches in my writing and gives me all kinds of unexpected insights. While I run down past the Fields's house, through Tucker Development, down to the route that goes into town, and then back, I've understood what a character is feeling or how I'm going to organize an essay or what I will title my novel. I've also had a zillion conversations with dozens of worrisome people, which is much better than trying to have these conversations with them while I am trying to write. Also, since I am not near a phone, I am not tempted to call them up and actually have it out with them. I've saved a lot of friendships and relationships and spared myself plenty of heartaches this way.

After the run, the rest of the workday is taken up by what I call the writing biz part of being a writer. What this involves, in large part, is responding to the publicity machine that now seems to be a necessary component of being a published writer. Answering mail, returning phone calls, responding to unsolicited manuscripts from strangers or to galleys from editors who would so appreciate my putting in a good word for this young writer or translation or series. Ironically, all this attention can sometimes amount to distraction that keeps me from doing the work that brought these requests to my door in the first place.

I could just ignore these requests. But all along the way, I found helpers who did read my manuscript, did give me a little of their busy day. These are favors I can never pay back, I can only pass on. And so I do try to answer my own mail and read as many galleys by new writers as I possibly can and return phone calls to those who need advice I might be able to give.

When I'm finally finished with my writing biz or I've put it aside in the growing pile for tomorrow, I head to town to run errands or see a friend or attend a talk at the college. As the fields and farms give way to houses and lawns, I feel as if I'm reentering the world. After having been so intensely a part of a fictional world, I love this daily chance to connect with the small town I live in, to find out how everybody else is doing.

How's it going? everyone asks me, as if they really want to know all about my writing day.

At the end of a good reading, the audience lingers. It's late in Salt Lake City or Portland or Iowa City. Outside the bookstore windows, the sky is dark and star-studded. Then, that last hand goes up, and someone in the back row wants to know, "So, does writing really matter?"

This once really happened to me on a book tour. I felt as if I'd just been hit "upside the head," an expression I like so much because it sounds like the blow was so hard, the preposition got jerked around, too. Does writing matter? I sure hope so, I wanted to say. I've published six books. I've spent most of my thinking life, which is now over thirty years, writing. *Does writing really matter?* It was the hardest, and the best, question I've been asked anywhere.

Let's take out the *really*, I said. It makes me nervous. I don't *really* know much of anything, which is why I write, to find things out. Does writing matter?

It matters, of course, it matters. But it matters in such a small, almost invisible way that it doesn't seem very important. In fact, that's why I trust it, the tiny rearrangements and insights in our hearts that art accomplishes. It's how I, anyhow, learned to see with vision and perplexity and honesty and continue to learn to see. How I keep the windows and doors open instead of shutting myself up inside the things I "believe" and have personally experienced. How I move out beyond the safe, small version of my life to live other lives. "Not only to be one self," the poet Robert Desnos wrote about the power of the imagination, "but to become each one."

And this happens not because I'm a writer or, as some questioners put it, "a creative person." I'll bet that even those who aren't writers, those who are concerned with making some sense of this ongoing journey would admit this: that it's by what people have written and continue to write, our stories and creations, that we understand who we are. In a world without any books, we would not be the same kind of critter. "Art is not the world," Muriel Rukeyser reminds us, "but a knowing of the world. It prepares us."

Prepares us for what? I have to admit that I don't really know what it prepares us for. For our work in the world, I suppose. Prepares us to live our lives more intentionally, ethically, richly. A hand shoots up.

"You mean to say that if Hitler had read Tolstoy he would have been a better person?"

Let's say that it would have been worth a try. Let's say that if little Hitler had been caught up in reading Shakespeare or Tolstoy and was moved to the extent that the best books move us, he might not have become who he became. But maybe, Tolstoy or no Tolstoy, Hitler would still have been Hitler. We live, after all, in a flawed world of flawed beings. In fact, some very fine writers who have written some lovely things are not very nice people.

But I still insist that while writing or entering into the writing of another, they were better people. If for no other reason than they were not out there, causing trouble. Writing is a form of vision, and I agree with that proverb that says, "Where there is no vision, the people perish." The artist keeps that vision alive, cleared of the muck and refuse and junk and little dishonesties that always collect and begin to cloud our view of the world around us.

It is the end of the reading. My readers, who for this brief evening have become real people with questions about my writing life, come forward to have their books signed and offer some new insight or ask a further question. That they care matters. That they are living fuller versions of themselves and of each one because they have read books matters. This is why writing matters. It clarifies and intensifies; it reduces our sense of isolation and connects us to each other.

❑ 10

BEGINNING

BY EDITH KONECKY

THE MOST ENIGMATIC, AWESOME, AND COURAGEOUS ASPECT OF WRITing fiction is, to me, the mystery of beginning, to begin writing in the first place, that first time. What is the urge, where does it spring from? And, having begun, how do you go on to begin each new story, and, even more incredibly, each new novel?

Storytelling undoubtedly goes back to whatever time it was when human beings found their tongues and began to shape sounds into language. There in the cave, at the center of a circle, sits the storyteller, probably a woman, because she wanted, needed, words to speak to her child. She likes to *use* words and delights in inventing new ones to fill the gaps, or to name whatever new has happened. So there she sits, telling a story. Most likely it's a true story, something remembered or heard from another person. Because there's little else to do at night, she tells her stories over and over, and when she notices that her listeners, bored to death, are falling asleep, she begins to change the stories, to embroider them, to enliven them—to lie. "Well, here's something new," someone says, waking up.

Encouraged, she lies a little more. And a little more. She begins to make up people who never really were, and to invent things that happened to them. She finds she can even invent places she's never seen— and that may not even exist—and describe their landscape and their weather. By now it's no longer lying; it's storytelling. Our cavewoman has discovered fiction. And once launched on this dangerous pursuit, there is no stopping her.

But why did *she* choose to be the storyteller? Her counterpart smashed roots and berries and smeared stories on the walls of caves, but for her, it was words. She was never one who took words, new as they were, for granted. Very early, she learned to love words and to respect them for their grace and power, not merely for their utility. She saw that words, when carefully chosen, had the power to teach, to convey meaning, to explain, to express feeling, to ignite the imagination, to bring the hairy beasts in the cave closer into the ring of human experience.

So because of her special affinity for language, our cavewoman has learned to use words effectively to enlighten and to entertain. In the making of fiction, she isn't telling the story only to others, she's telling it to herself. It's possible that she herself doesn't know what is going to happen next and can't wait to find out. She has discovered that words help thought to evolve, to be refined, just as thought helps words to evolve. The process is marvelously reciprocal.

Then, too, there is a feeling of power, of being in control in a world where so little is known. She can redesign her world, her experience of life, make order and sense out of chaos. And most important, as in all creativity, she is making something that wasn't there before.

But there are dangers. As our cavewoman sits at the center of her circle, the center of attention, she can make her listeners laugh and sometimes even cry. If she is very good, they will stay awake. If she is very, *very* good, they will be rapt, their eyes will shine, and at the end they may even make a little fuss over her, which sometimes can be mistaken for love. There is something about all this that is seductive. She is being warmed by more than the fire in the cave.

But this is a by-product, or it had better be; she is no longer there merely to entertain and to be warmed by her audience. She has something else in mind: her own vision. She is creating something that matters. If the emphasis is more on her than on the work, she will become glib and showoffy, and the work will be false, dishonest. For, above all, what she has discovered is that her lies, her fiction, must tell a truth that is truer than truth.

Now let eons pass. Print evolves and so does our storyteller. She now has another reason for beginning. She is a reader, has loved books from an early age, loved the idea of people writing them and of the worlds to which they took her. Often, during puberty or adolescence, when there is that desperate need to express those terrible, almost unbearable, unformed and nameless yearnings, she begins with poetry.

But there are other differences. Our storyteller has become a silent recluse, scribbling away in the solitude of, with luck, a room of her own. Months, more often years, may go by with no one knowing what she is doing, thinking, writing, and no one to care whether she does it or not. Others are out in the world earning their keep at more practical pursuits, and their rewards are more immediate and tangible. More often than not, our—let's call her, now, a novelist—will finish her book and no one will want to publish it. After a couple of years, she puts it away in a drawer, or if it is published, it will have as little effect as if she *had* put it away in a drawer. But by now she is scarcely aware of it because she has long since made another beginning and is busily at work on another book. Oh, she may feel a little sorry for herself, but self-pity isn't useful, and so she gets on with it.

Why *do* writers get on with it? What makes them get up every day and begin again, for every day is a new and frightening beginning? No doubt there are as many reasons as there are writers. I think I write for all the unmystical reasons, and also because I wouldn't know what else to do with myself.

But how *does* one begin every day, since every new day is fraught with peril? I have never approached my typewriter, now my computer, without fear—fear that there will be nothing there, that the muse has fled in the night, deserted me forever, as though inspiration is quantifiable, that if something does come, it will be wrong, or stupid, or old hat. There are periods when I'll do anything to avoid my desk. There are suddenly urgent errands to the bank, the dry cleaner, the supermarket. I'll fix the vacuum cleaner plug, hang bookshelves, stare off into space for an hour or more, eat lunch, write letters—anything—but never with pleasure, always with a tightness in my stomach, a cramp of guilt, because I've reached an age when time has shrunk, when days have so few hours in them, when I'm aware that there is no longer time for everything. Sooner or later I must face my neurotic self. Do I really not want to do it and, if not, why don't I, like most people, just not do it? But it's not that simple. I do and I don't want to do it. What I don't want is to *begin* to do it. I *do* want to be in the middle of doing it.

For there *are* days when nothing comes, when my mind is blank or moves like a slug dying in a dish of beer, or what comes is all wrong. And that *is* death. And there are days when, given a chance, the words leap and frolic, and my characters speak and think and act, have minds of their own, and do and say exactly what's right. And that is the opposite of death. There is nothing to compare to it. It's what writing is all about.

So it is, after all, a matter of life and death, and I tell myself that I must have the courage—and the patience—to face the beginnings. And the confidence that ought to be born of past experience but somehow never is.

More specifically, there isn't just the beginning of a new writing day, but the beginning of a new piece of work, a new story, a new book. Because I'm not a disciplined, orderly, or really a conscious writer/ thinker, because I'm more instinctual than intellectual and rarely start a story or book knowing clearly what I want to say, I must put myself into a sort of trance, turn my attention inward, become absolutely unaware of those distractions that I can so easily succumb to, fooling myself into the belief that I've put in another kind of day's work. I must go to this other dark and quiet place and wait to see what's there. And what's there for me has almost always begun with a name, if not in the first sentence, then in the next. I have no idea where the name comes from, or to whom it belongs, but it's in finding out whose it is that the story begins to happen. There she is, this creature, but who is she? Is she going to speak? Oh, she's speaking already, that's *her* voice. Where is she and what is she doing? She's indignant, she's fussed, she's angry. Why?

Well, she's going to tell me why. And her telling is my novel.

❏ 11

MYTHS OF THE WRITING LIFE

BY JAMES A. RITCHIE

RECENTLY I'VE FOUND THAT MANY OF THE OLD TRIED AND TRUE rules of fiction writing, and the writing life in general, have come under attack. So I think it's time to set the record straight.

Myth: You don't have to write everyday.

Fact: Well, no, you don't. You don't have to write at all. There probably isn't a soul in the world who will care if you never write another word.

And, yes it is possible to sell a few short stories, a few articles, a little of this and a pinch of that, if you write only on Saturday, or during the full moon, or whenever the mood hits. You may even legitimately call yourself a writer—small "w"—by working in this manner.

But unless you work at least five or six days a week, no excuses, you will never be able to call yourself a Professional Writer, meaning a writer who earns a living from writing fiction. And because writing, like playing the violin, requires hundreds and thousands of hours of practice to get right, you will never develop your talent to the fullest unless you write nearly everyday.

Even if you succeed financially, the first million or so words you write will screech and jangle the nerves as will a violin played by a rank beginner.

And anyone who tells you otherwise is a dilettante, a dabbler.

Myth: Procrastination is no more than your subconscious telling you the story isn't ready to be written.

Fact: No, procrastination is your way of telling the world you're too lazy and too soft to stick it out when the writing gets tough. Good writing is always difficult, always hard work. Anytime the words are flowing too easily you'd better look at your hole card.

Unless, when you're old and gray, you're certain you'll be content looking back and realizing you published only a tiny fraction of what you might have, and that most of it was mediocre at best, get over the notion that procrastination is ever a good thing.

Myth: It isn't the writing that matters, it's the act of creating, and since a writer works all the time, you're creating even when you're fishing, crocheting, or watching a football game, as long as you're *thinking* about writing.

Fact: Horse hockey. There may be some truth to the statement that a writer works all the time, but it's only at the keyboard that a writer creates anything.

At best, the work a writer does in his or her mind between stints at the keyboard is only planning to create. It's easy to justify anything, but justified or not, I can guarantee Joe Blow, that writer down the street with half your talent but twice your drive, is going to succeed much sooner that you do if you buy into this one.

Myth: It's the editor's job to fix my bad grammar (style, paragraph, plot line, etc.).

Fact: Why should he? I was once—briefly and small time—an editor. I quickly learned two things. One: many, many would-be writers expect editors to do everything, from correcting horrific spelling to transcribing handwritten manuscripts, to teaching them how to write basic English.

An editor's job is actually pretty simple when it comes to manuscripts: Keep the ones good enough to publish and reject the others. That's all there is to it.

Yes, once an editor finds a good story, one that really could see publication as is, he or she will say, "Now, let's see what we can do to make this story even better."

But, that's it. Editors should not be expected to rewrite, correct grammar or spelling (except for an occasional typo), or give writing lessons. And they do not ever read handwritten manuscripts.

I also learned that editors do not enjoy rejecting stories. Editors, in fact, love finding stories good enough to publish. So don't blame the editor if you receive a rejection slip instead of an acceptance letter.

Myth: You can't get an agent until you've been published, and you can't get published until you have an agent.

Fact: This one is nonsense. Agents are in the business of finding new, publishable writers. It's how agents, at least reputable agents, earn their money. But the key word is *publishable.* Almost all agents read queries, and so do many publishers.

Myth: Big name writers get such large advances there's no money left over for the rest of us.

Fact: There's a grain of truth in this, but there is a reason for it. Simply, big name writers get big bucks because they write big novels that sell in big numbers.

But remember that just about every big name writer out there was once an obscure, unpublished writer who earned very little or nothing. They may even have believed the same myth.

Instead of wasting energy griping about how much money somebody else makes, study what she does and how she does it. Then, one of these days, you may pull down huge advances while others gripe about you.

Myth: You must have a college education to be a professional writer.

Fact: I hope not. I dropped out of school in the eighth grade. I did take a G.E.D. test years later, but that's it. I tried college for a few months, quickly realized my time would be much better spent writing, and dropped out without taking a single writing course.

And I'm now working on my sixth novel.

Myth: A would-be fiction writer shouldn't read other people's fiction because it will unduly influence his own writing.

Fact: If you don't read other people's fiction, and lots of it, you will never, ever succeed as a writer. Period.

You *want* to be influenced. In the early stages of your career, and even when you're established, studying other writers, and imitating their style, is exactly how you learn to write well yourself. There is no other way. So read everything, and read often.

Myth: Writing fiction is an art, and rewriting only obscures the artist's spontaneous vision.

Fact: Yes, writing fiction is an art. But it's also a craft. Failure to rewrite will guarantee that the artist's vision will never be seen by anyone except those unfortunate friends and family members forced to read it.

How much rewriting is enough? Beats me. Dean Koontz claims to rewrite each page an average of 26 times. Ernest Hemingway is said to have rewritten *A Farewell to Arms* 39 times.

My own rule is to rewrite until it's either as good as I can get it, or until I'm so sick of the process I can't take it any more. As Hemingway explained in an interview, you rewrite until you get the words right, then you stop.

The competition is fierce. Getting the words "almost right" isn't going to get you anything except rejection slips to paper your office walls.

Myth: You must be certifiably insane to be a fiction writer.

Fact: All right, so this one is true.

❑ 12

BUILDING A LASTING WRITERS' GROUP

BY D.M. ROSNER

OFTEN, A WRITER IS HIS OWN WORST CRITIC. AS A MEMBER OF A WRITers' group since its inception in 1989, I've found that participation in a good critique group is not only helpful in keeping my perspective and polishing my work, but is also inspirational during those inevitable dry spells. Experience has also taught me, however, that there are a number of pitfalls any new writers' group should be careful to avoid. If you're thinking about starting a writers' group, here are some ideas that may help.

Forming your group

All you really need to start your writers' group are other writers and a place to meet with them. Here are some ideas:

- If you know any writers, ask them if they would like to form a writers' group. If you don't know any other writers, try visiting a local college campus (evening writing classes draw writers of all ages and abilities). Another good place to meet writers is at writers' conferences, listings of which can be found in most writers' magazines.
- Try to keep the group small. More than five or six members may limit the ability of the group to critique one another's work. (Some groups are much larger; but if you choose to have a larger group, you may need to limit critiques to only a few members' work per meeting.)

Once you've gathered some writers, hold an initial meeting. You'll need to make the following decisions:

- How often to meet; what time; where; and for how long. (For instance, our group meets at 7:00 every other Monday night at members' homes or at coffee bars, for approximately two hours.)

51

- What kind of writing you wish as the focus of your group. (My group, for example, is for fiction writers. Some groups are for poetry only, while others cover a wide range of forms.)
- How much material each author can submit for critique at each meeting. (Ten pages per person per meeting is generally a good place to start.)
- Whether members prefer to read the work to be critiqued at home and bring comments to the meeting, or have authors read their work aloud at the meeting and invite comment. (We bring our work to the meetings and read it aloud—this can be helpful to the authors in catching errors, getting the rhythm of a sentence, or feeling out dialogue.)
- What ground rules to use, including choosing a leader or mediator.
- Whether or not you wish to write bylaws, to establish clearly the group's expectations of new members. These can come in handy as your group grows.
- Whether or not you wish to have each member report in on what he or she has accomplished since the previous meeting, and if so, who will keep a record of this information.

A word about critiques

The purpose of a critique group is to provide honest comments on members' work. Don't forget that many writers—new writers in particular—have fragile egos, but there is such a thing as being too nice. If something about a member's piece isn't working for you, it's important to share that with the writer, in a direct but gentle way.

Here are some things to remember when critiquing:

- Be honest when critiquing one another's work, but be diplomatic in your approach when offering suggestions.
- Give a balanced critique, taking care to point out the parts that work well, as well as those that don't.
- Explain the reasons for your comments or suggestions.
- Don't argue with another member's opinion of your work. If you don't agree with the changes suggested, just don't use them. (If you don't understand why the suggestion was made, you may politely ask the person giving the critique to clarify the comment.)

If your members are new to the art of tactful critiquing, you may want to create a checklist, or guidelines, for critiquing. This could be helpful in reminding members to share positive opinions, point out areas that need work, and provide reasons for each.

Common pitfalls

It's been rare that we've had to ask a member to leave our group, but it has happened. We've learned from our mistakes over the years, and have established bylaws and a screening process for new members, to avoid potential problems. Here are some tips that might help you avoid such problems:

- Be very clear about *exactly* what you expect from your members. Something as simple as expecting them to come to every meeting can cause misunderstanding and resentment.
- Be sure your members all share the same level of dedication. Your group can be serious or informal, but it's best not to try to mix the two.
- Every member should be expected to put an equal level of effort into critiquing one another's work.
- If you have a problem with a member's level of participation in the group (or method of critique, or anything else), the leader or mediator should talk to him or her about it, as diplomatically as possible. This may not always work (and the member may choose to drop out of the group), but sometimes what seems to be a major problem is nothing more than a minor misunderstanding blown out of proportion.

Keeping your group alive

My writers' group has stayed together so long because luckily, our members are serious writers who are dedicated to one another. Sure, we've had some members who have come and gone, but many have left only because they've moved out of state, and we all still keep in touch.

If you want your group to last, it's important to find others who share your level of dedication. Whenever new members join, explain to them how you feel about your group, to avoid potential problems later.

Don't feel that your group has to be limited to its scheduled meetings, either. In addition to regular meetings, our group also holds a variety of special events, such as:

- *Novel's Day*, during which we meet for a full day of work on our own individual projects. Writing in a room full of other working writers is very inspiring. (We hold three or more such days each year.)
- *Annual Halloween party*, for which we write a story to be read at the party (and come dressed as one of our characters).
- *Annual retreat,* held over long a weekend, usually at a bed & breakfast, and which is rather like an extended Novel's Day.

Writer's groups can be helpful, inspiring, and a lot of fun. For more ideas, stop by our website at: http://pages.cthome.net/6ft_ferrets/

❏ 13

THE STATUE IN THE SLAB

BY EDITH PEARLMAN

I AM NOT ONE OF THOSE LUCKY WRITERS INTO WHOSE EARS A THRILLing tale is confided on a train, in front of whose eyes an anguished romance is enacted at a seaside hotel. My fictions begin as fragments, more irritating than inspiring. For instance: I find myself thinking of elderly Manhattan widows in apartments, resentfully growing frail. Or: In a dream a lost child and her mysteriously damaged younger sister, reunited, exchange a few surreal words. Also: I notice a patient waiting outside an X-ray office, shivering in his johnny. He is ignored by the surly attendant, who resembles a South American general.

No story yet—only pebbles in my shoe.

Standing at a distance from my desk, I glower. Then the ghost of Michelangelo taps me on the shoulder. Michelangelo claimed that he didn't create his statues but rather, released them. Find a slab of marble, he told younger artists; then take away everything that *isn't* the statue.

I need a slab of marble. And I can't order it from Carrara. I have to build it, myself, around one of those damned pebbles.

This slab, which will later be ruthlessly hacked at, must be first made pretty big. It must contain a believable city or village—I've set my tales all over the world. It must contain buildings with doors, roofs, back stairs—my stories have played themselves out in a tobacco shop, a soup kitchen, a museum, a pharmacy; in houses and lonely flats. The slab must hold history, and perhaps a vision of the future. Inside the slab lurk characters and their children and their handkerchiefs and their Uzis.

So I read. I read about the streets my characters walk in and the wars they endure; about the work they do; about the diseases hiding in their bodies; about the pills they crave and the drink they can't leave alone.

And I play. For the sake of one story, I lost innumerable games of chess. For the sake of another, I spent a week using my left hand only.

And I write. Sentences, paragraphs, pages; reminders on three-by-five cards; a string of adjectives on the back of a charge receipt. I arrange and rearrange my characters' biographies, and also their rooms. I imagine their fantasies and I dream their dreams. I turn them toward each other and then transcribe their stunned declarations of love, their helpless lies. I design their wardrobes, and I equip them with hobbies (more reading!) and enemies and possessions. This material will continue to pile up. Not a comma will be discarded until the story is finished, revised, ripped into pieces, begun again, finished again, revised again, submitted again *and* again, finally published. My manual typewriter does not know how to delete. My wastebasket holds pussy willows, not crumpled papers. My folders stretch and eventually split open; still, the dossier expands. Nothing leaves this room! That diamond pin which in an early draft seems too flashy for the heroine may, in the final draft, illuminate the entire story. That excessive metaphor, mercilessly pared, may become not only apt but irreplaceable.

What a mound of pages! At last it resembles a slab of marble. I walk around it, riffle silently through it—and, when I'm lucky, my tale's contour and its hinted truth reveal themselves in the depths of the slab. An elderly widow, visited wearily by her children one by one, will decide to leave her home: Independence can be cruelty. The lost child, before she finds her way back to her family, will foresee that her future is inseparable from her afflicted sister's: in chance begins responsibility. The X-ray technician, rattling on to a stranger about his bedeviled country, will learn from his own words and his own omissions the nature of loyalty: flexible as a snake.

The story cannot be as dense as the slab of details I've constructed. No reader wants to know the name of the coffee shop the widow visits daily; or the etiology of the condition of the younger sister; or the succession of rulers in the country the X-ray technician has fled. These chunks of information would only encumber a short story.

But *I* know the chunks of information. I designed the coffee shop and installed its tolerant proprietor; my widow loves what she must leave. I read a shelf of books about the younger sister's affliction; her sweet face is properly vacant, her gestures properly vague. I invented the corrupt regimes that the X-ray technician refers to only by their soubriquets—The Coffee Revolution, The Month of the Colonels.

Now I chip away at whatever is not necessary, and polish and repolish what's left—leaving, I hope, characters who are affecting and a situation that is tense and a resolution that is satisfying.

What a mess, this way of writing. It is lengthy and indirect; it ignores the notion that art is a free expression of self; it slams the door on autobiography; it leaves shards all over the floor.

On the other hand, efficiency is a third-rate virtue. Self-expression is often self-indulgence, best kept in firm check. Autobiography knows all too well how to creep in through the keyhole. And those shards— sometimes they lodge like pebbles in my shoe, and become the centers of new slabs to be doggedly built up and then doggedly reduced, until all that is left is the story.

□ 14

THE JOURNEY INWARD

BY KATHERINE PATERSON

"DO YOU KEEP A JOURNAL?" NO, I ANSWER A BIT RED-FACED, BECAUSE I know that *real* writers keep voluminous journals so fascinating that the world can hardly wait until they die to read the published versions. But it's not quite true. I do make journal-like entries in used schoolgirl spiral notebooks, on odd scraps of paper, in fairly anonymous computer files. These notations are all so embarrassing that I am hoping for at least a week's notice to hunt them down and destroy all the bits and pieces before my demise.

I write these entries, you see, only when I can't write what I want to write. If they were collected and published, the reader could logically conclude that I was not only totally inept as a writer but that I lacked integration of personality at best, and at worst, was dangerously depressed.

If I had kept a proper journal, these neurotic passages would be seen in context, but such is not the case. If my writing is going well, why would I waste time talking about it? I'd be doing it. So if these notes survive me, they will give whatever segment of posterity might happen upon them a very skewed view of my mental state.

The reason I am nattering on about this is that I have come to realize that I am not alone. As soon as my books (after years of struggle) began to be published, I started to get questions from people that I had trouble answering in any helpful way: "Do you use a pen and pad or do you write on a typewriter?" (Nowadays, "computer" is always included in this question, but I'm talking about twenty years ago.)

"Whatever works," I'd say. Which was true. Sometimes I wrote first drafts by hand, sometimes on the typewriter; often I'd switch back and forth in an attempt to keep the flow going. The questioner would thank me politely, but, looking back, I know now that I had failed her.

"Do you have a regular schedule everyday or do you just write when you feel inspired?" the person would ask earnestly. I am ashamed to say, I would often laugh at this. "If I wrote only when I was inspired," I'd say, "I'd write about three days a year. Books don't get written in three days a year."

Occasionally, the question (and now, I know, all these were the same question) would be framed more baldly. "How do you begin?" "Well," I would say, "you sit down in front of the typewriter, roll in a sheet of paper and . . ."

If I ever gave any of you one of those answers, or if any other writer has ever given you similar tripe, I would like to apologize publicly. I was asked, in whatever disguise, a truly important question, and I finessed the answer into a one-liner.

How *do* you begin? It is not an idle or trick question. It is a cry from the heart.

I know. That's what all those aborted journal notes are about. They are the cry when I simply cannot begin. When no inspiration ever comes, when neither pen, nor pencil, nor typewriter, nor state-of-the-art computer can unloose what's raging about inside me.

So what happens? Well, something must. I've begun and ended over and over again through the years. There are several novels out there with my name on the cover. Somehow I figured out how to begin. Once the book is finished, the memory of the effort dims—until you're trying to begin the next one.

Well, I'm there now. I have to begin again. What have I done those other times? How have I gotten from that feeling of stony hopelessness? How do I break through that barrier as hard as sunbaked earth to the springs of creativity?

Sometimes, I know, I have a conversation with myself on paper:

What's the matter?

What do you mean "what's the matter?" You know perfectly well. I want to write, but I can't think of a thing to say.

Not a single thing?

Not a single thing worth saying.

You're scared what you might say won't be up to snuff? Scared people might laugh at you? Scared you might despise yourself?

Well, it is scary. How do I know there's still anything in here?

You don't. You just have to let it flow. If you start judging, you'll cut off the flow—you've already cut off the flow from all appearances—before it starts.

Grump.

Ah yes, we never learn, do we? Whatever happened to that wonderful idea of getting up so early in the morning that the critic in you was still asleep?

How do I know it will work this time?

You won't know if you don't try. But then, trying is risky, and you do seem a bit timid to me.

You don't know what it's like pouring out your guts to the world.

I don't?

Well, you don't care as much as I do.

Of course I do. I just happen to know that it is so important to my psychic health to do this that I'm willing to take the risk. You, my friend, seem to want all the creative juices inside you to curdle and poison the whole system.

You're nothing but a two-bit psychologist.

Well, I've been right before.

But how do I begin?

I don't know. Why don't we just get up at five tomorrow, come to the machine and type like fury for an hour and see what happens? Could be fun. Critic won't be up, and we won't ever have to show anybody what we've done.

Now you understand why I have to burn this stuff before I die. My posthumous reputation as a sane person of more than moderate intelligence hangs in the balance. But living writers, in order to keep writing, have to forget about posthumous reputations. We have to become, quite literally, like little children. We have to remember our early griefs and embarrassments. Talk aloud to ourselves. Make up imaginary companions. We have to play.

Have you ever watched children fooling with play dough or finger-paint? They mess around to see what will emerge, and they fiddle with what comes out. Occasionally, you will see a sad child, one that has decided beforehand what he wants to do. He stamps his foot because the picture on the page or the green blob on the table falls short of the vision in his head. But he is, thankfully, a rarity, already too concerned with adult approval.

The unspoiled child allows herself to be surprised with what comes out of herself. She takes joy in the material, patting it and rolling it and shaping it. She is not too quick to name it. And, unless some grownup interferes, she is not a judge but a lover of whatever comes from her heart through her hands. This child knows that what she has created is marvelous simply because she has made it. No one else could make this wonderful thing because it has come out of her.

What treasures we have inside ourselves—not just joy and delight but also pain and darkness. Only I can share the treasures of the human spirit that are within me. No one else has *these* thoughts, *these* feelings, *these* relationships, *these* experiences, *these* truths.

How do I begin? You could start, as I often do, by talking to yourself. The dialogue may help you understand what is holding you back. Are you afraid that deep down inside you are really shallow? That when you take that dark voyage deep within yourself, you will find there is no treasure to share? Trust me. There is. Don't let your fear stop you. Begin early in the morning before that critical adult within wakes up. Like a child, pour out what is inside you, not listening to anything but the stream of life within you. Read Dorothea Brande's classic *On Becoming a Writer,* in which she suggests that you put off for several days reading what you have written in the wee hours. Then when you do read it you may discern a repeated theme pointing you to what you want to begin writing about.

Begin, Anne Lamott suggests in her wonderful book *Bird by Bird,* in the form of a letter. Tell your child or a trusted friend stories from your past. Exploring childhood is almost always an effective wedge into what's inside you. And didn't you mean to share those stories with your children someday anyhow?

While I was in the midst of revising this article, my husband happened to bring home Julia Cameron's book, *The Artist's Way.* Cameron suggests three pages of longhand every morning as soon as you get up. I decided to give the "morning pages" a try and heartily recommend the practice, though these pages, too, will need to be destroyed before I die.

When I was trying to begin the book which finally became *Flip-Flop Girl* (and you should see the anguished notes along the way!), I just began writing down the name of every child I could remember from the fourth grade at Calvin H. Wiley School. Sometimes I appended a note that explained why that child's name was still in my head. Early-morning exercises explored ways the story might go, and I rejected most of them, but out of those fourth-grade names and painful betrayals a story began to grow. Judging from the notes, it was over a year in developing and many more months in the actual writing. But I did begin, and I did finish. There's a bit of courage for the next journey inward.

Now it's your turn. Bon voyage.

❑ 15

THE CREATIVE POWER OF DOING NOTHING

BY COLLEEN MARIAH RAE

LET'S SAY YOU'VE BEEN WORKING ON A STORY. IT'S COMING, BUT IT'S not coming fast enough. What will speed things up? Surprisingly: *Doing nothing.* Now's the time to turn to your unconscious and to let it do the work for you.

This is often the hardest part of the writing process but an essential part of the creative process. For a week, allow the unconscious to do its work. And, paradoxically, without any conscious effort on your part, your creative product will grow.

The trick is to do nothing long enough for the work to come to fruition in your unconscious. But because this is hard, what follow are some tips for *what to do when you're doing nothing; and how to do nothing so effectively that your story will pop from you full-blown.*

So, for the first tip: *What to do when you're doing nothing.*

It's always important to know where you're going, if you have any hope of reaching your goal. Here, the goal's a finished story that pops like Athena from the head of Zeus, and the only way to achieve this is through doing things that unclutter the unconscious sufficiently to allow it to devote full-time to the job.

This is the time to cook, build a model, swim, play chess, hike, paint, play music, or repair a toaster—whatever it is that puts you into that "time out of time state," where you lose all track of time. What you're looking for are activities that allow you to *immerse* yourself in an experience without thought. Whatever takes you away from the ceaseless round of chatter unclutters the unconscious. What works for you? Include it in your day, every day, because each day takes you through the same cycle of creativity in an abbreviated way.

For me, painting is the best "immersion" activity. I can so lose myself in the process that when I stop, I discover surprisingly that hours have passed. While I'm painting, I'm not thinking. But I'm not floating in a sea of no-thought: I'm doing what Aldous Huxley thought so important he had birds in his fictional country in *Island* crying "Attention, attention, attention." I am focused in on what I'm doing with a highly concentrated attention.

So that's what to do when you're doing nothing: anything that allows you to immerse yourself fully in the activity and at the same time challenges you enough, but not too much. Do anything, that is, but write. During this stage of the process, do anything but write—even one word. And, don't tell your story to anyone. Telling it will dissipate the energy. Keeping your story inside creates a pressure-cooker sensation— eventually you will feel as though you're going to explode if you can't let your story out. And that's the sensation you're aiming for.

Now for the second tip: *How to do nothing so effectively that your story will pop from you full-blown.* This is often the most fun, because it isn't so "hands-off" as immersion. You can really feel you're doing something to work with your unconscious—even though you *are* letting go and trusting the unconscious to do the work for you. I call this *active incubation,* because you're building bridges between the conscious and the unconscious mind.

One of these bridges you probably know well: How often have you said, "Let me sleep on it"? It's one of the best problem-solving tools we have. And it works for writing so well that I've come to believe that I couldn't write a darn thing worth publishing if I couldn't sleep on it. I'll go to sleep unclear of how to proceed in a story and wake in the morning with the answer.

You can also build bridges during your waking hours. Either way, it's still the same process: You have to silence your analytical mind long enough to let the unconscious speak. You have probably had a few such experiences: Names you couldn't remember an hour before come to you as soon as you get into the mind-numbing rhythm of vacuuming, or as you're washing the car, you recall what it is you forgot to buy at the store.

I make use of active incubation every day I write. I don't take a shower until I get stuck in my writing stint for the day, because invariably it's in the shower that ideas pop up. My writing journals are filled with "shower thought" notations.

Other things that shift me from that "stuck" analytical place also include water: I love to sit by a waterfall or any running water—even the fountains in shopping malls will do. Find your own. Some writers get unstuck sitting by a fire; some with candlelight; some while they meditate. Others can't write if they aren't driving. One of my students puts Grieg on the car stereo and drives across the desert, preferably during lightning storms. Any activity that stops analytical thought lets inspiration surface. And just a suggestion: Always keep a small notebook with you, so you won't forget your breakthroughs—write them down!

But there's more to active incubation than just getting out of your own way. This is the time to work actively with your unconscious. One way to do that is through what I call a "nightly recap." Lie in bed in the dark and try to visualize your story as clearly as possible; let all the details come alive for you. Summon the smells, tastes, textures, emotions, sounds. Make them as vivid as you can. You may find yourself in a state similar to Robert Louis Stevenson's, who was thrashing about in his bed one night, greatly alarming his wife. She woke him up, infuriating Stevenson, who yelled, "I was dreaming a fine bogey tale!" The nightmare from which he had been unwillingly awakened was the premise for *Dr. Jekyll and Mr. Hyde.*

When you wake in the morning after such a night, don't get out of bed. Stay there, moving only to pick up your already open notebook and uncapped pen. Write without thinking—anything about your story that comes to mind. Write for at least five minutes before you get up. Then close your notebook without reading what you've written. You'll read it later—when this period of doing nothing comes to an end. To read it too soon flips you into analytical thought.

"Silent movies" is another technique that helps build the pressure. Set a timer for ten minutes, and then sit without thinking until the timer rings. If thoughts do come, just let them move through your mind; don't hold onto them. Stay still. For the next ten minutes, see your story as a movie in your mind. Make it as vivid as you can; flesh out the details. Go back and forth, back and forth. Stop the projector, reverse the film, run it forward again. See it more and more clearly each time it reels by. Watch, but do not let yourself write—no matter how strong the urge.

Finally, for the last ten minutes, sit quietly without consciously thinking, until your urge to write is so strong that you just can't resist it. Then, and only then, pick up your pen and write.

Make these silent movies as often as you can during the days of this period of doing nothing. If you can't spend a full 30 minutes on it, cut back to five-minute segments. Remember: Don't read anything you write.

There's another aspect to this part of the creative process that's often given short shrift: solitude. Give yourself time alone each day, even if it's only to take a walk. A quiet walk alone can help your writing more than you'll ever know.

What if you do all this, and no story seems ready to pop into your head? In his autobiography, *Education of a Wandering Man*, Louis L'Amour said,

> There are so many wonderful stories to be written, and so much material to be used. When I hear people talking of writer's block, I am amazed. Start writing, no matter about what. The water does not flow until the faucet is turned on. You can sit and look at a page for a long time and nothing will happen. Start writing, and it will.

That's every writer's secret: not waiting for the muse. Give yourself a week at most to do nothing, then sit down to write.

Set yourself a schedule, and give yourself a goal. When I was writing fiction full-time, my writing hours were 7:00 a.m. till noon. My goal was to write five pages per day. Sometimes I finished the five pages *before* noon, and then I was free to stop. Sometimes I finished the five pages by noon, but even if I hadn't, I still stopped. It's a goal, not a stick.

When your writing is coming easily, it feels too good to stop. I rarely would stop if I had finished my five pages before noon, for instance. But I always remembered advice that came from a *Paris Review* interview with Ernest Hemingway. Although he wrote only in the morning, he said he would make a point of stopping before he'd written everything that was in him that day to write. It's great advice. If you know what's going to happen in the next scene, it'll prime your pump the following day.

Become aware of your own pattern. You may work best doing 16-hour-a-day stints for three weeks straight. Or you may find you can write only one hour a day without exhausting yourself. So schedule an hour and set a goal of a page a day. Even if you write only five pages a week, you'll still have produced 260 pages in one year. That's a whole book! The important thing is to find your own pattern—and then make it a habit. Good habits are just as hard to break as bad ones.

Rollo May's message in *The Courage to Create* is that for the creative person, fear never goes away. How can it? When we're working with the unconscious, as we must do in writing fiction, we walk up to the abyss every day and jump in. A very scary process! Allow yourself time to sharpen pencils or stare out the window for ten minutes or so before you start. After that, stay in your chair until your allotted hours are up, whether you've written anything or not. You'll find that the sheer boredom of doing nothing is often a catalyst to a remarkable gush of words.

❏ 16

THE WORD POLICE

BY BETH LEVINE

IT'S SUNDAY NIGHT AND THE SMELL OF CHINESE FOOD HANGS LOW over the city. Two figures are poised outside of a neon-lit overpriced specialty food store.

"Look, Joe, here's another one: 'Gormet Pastries,'" Lisa observes.

"Don't these people have any respect for the law? Let's take him in," Joe sighs, exasperated.

Joe pulls down on his snap brim hat. He and Lisa (and that's *Lisa;* not Leesa, Lysa, or Lise), a woman with determinedly clicking high heels, enter the aforementioned "Gormet Pastries."

The owner, a member of the I-Dress-Only-In-Black-And-Not-Because-It's-Slimming tribe, eyes them disdainfully. "Can I help you?" he asks faintly.

"Are you the proprietor of . . . *Gourmet* Pastries?" Lisa inquires, annoyed. This jerk can't spell and he's looking down on *her?*

"Yes. Is there a problem?"

The couple looks at each other meaningfully before whipping out their pocket-sized New Webster's Dictionaries.

"Word Police," Joe says with a penetrating stare. The owner turns pale, and his eyes start to dart around the store. Joe points to the back of the sign in the window and sure enough, there is *GORMET* in all its purple shame. The owner pales. "I . . . uh . . . guess I never noticed," he stammers.

"No, you people never do!" Joe exclaims. "Don't you ever *proof* things before shelling out your money? Day after day, you come in here and you never *noticed* a sign three feet high?"

Lisa puts her hand on his arm. "Easy, Joe," she says quietly. Turning to the owner, she asks, "What's your name, buddy?"

"Lonnee. L O N N . . ." He stops when he sees Joe and Lisa's faces turn pale. They are looking at a sign behind the counter that reads *Baking Done on Premise.*

68

"What is that?" Joe asks curtly. "You bake with the hope that it might come out right?" Lonnee looks confused, as Joe begins to tie two copies of *The Chicago Manual of Style* to Lonnee's wrists. The three begin to shuffle to the door, while Lisa reads him his rights.

"You have the right to remain silent—something we prefer, actually. You have the right to remain literate. In the absence of this ability, you have the right to an English professor, which the court will provide."

Lonnee raises his head in defiance. "Ha! I just catered an affair for Edwin Newman; he'll defend me! He owes me!"

"I don't think so. The man has principles—and that's *ples* not *pals*," snaps Joe. He sadly shakes his head and looks at Lisa. "Pathetic, isn't it?"

As they pass, the customers of the soon-to-be renamed Gourmet Pastries watch in open-mouthed horror. "He seemed to pay such attention to details. Who knew?" says one.

A mother looks down at her ashen-faced 10-year-old son. "See, sonny? He probably cheated his way through spelling class, too. Thought he could get away with it. See? It always catches up to you." The boy bursts into tears. (When he grows up, he will produce an Academy Award-winning documentary on his experiences, "Scared Grammatical.")

Later, Joe and Lisa emerge from the New York Public Library as the former owner of Gormet Pastries is bundled off into a library bus.

"What a dope," says Joe. "I'm glad they threw the book at him, not that he could read it. Imagine—dragging Edwin Newman's name into it!"

"Let's go get a cup of coffee," says Lisa. She takes Joe's arm, and they proceed to Bagels 'N Stuff. Joe balks when he sees the sign.

Lisa reassures him, "Well, it's a little cutesy, but I think colloquially it's correct." Joe stares at her intently as they enter the restaurant.

Ten minutes later, the two are relaxing in a booth.

"How'd you get into this crazy business, Joe?" Lisa asks meditatively.

"I started as a copy editor at a book publisher. I loved the job, but then to save money, the publisher . . ." Lisa leans over and pats his hand. Joe bravely continues, "The publisher started allowing books to go to press with *Britishisms* intact so they wouldn't have to spend money to reset type. *Colour* instead of *color,* that sort of thing. I said no. This far I will bend and no further.

"Turns out my boss used to work for McDonald's and was the one responsible for 'Over 5 billion sold,' not even knowing it should be 'More than 5 billion.' He was that sloppy. So he fired me! That's when I realized my true vocation: Cleaning up this ungrammatical city of ours."

Lisa sighs. "Sometimes I wonder if it really does matter."

Joe spills his coffee. "What? How can you possibly say that?"

"Oh, *more than, over. Gourmet* with or without a u, does it really amount to," she pauses before uttering the cliche, "a hill of beans?"

Now it's Joe's turn to reach for her hand. "Don't burn out on me now, baby. It happens to others, but not to us. It's in our blood."

Lisa's eyes well up. "I can't take it anymore. Everywhere I go—the bank, the sandwich shops, dry cleaners—there are typos everywhere. I went to buy a co-op, but when I saw the awning said 'Two Fourty,' I couldn't do it. I have no friends, because I'm always correcting them. Countermen hate me, because I'm forever pointing out that it's ice*d* tea, not *ice* tea. And don't even talk to me about apostrophes; they show up everywhere but where they are supposed to. Joe," Lisa's tears spill out, "I want to be like other people. I want to be sloppy."

Joe takes his hand away. "But we can't be like other people. We're a breed. We're . . . The Word Police. If we slip, it's the end of the civilized world, the demise of the society of Safire and Newman and Webster. It means the Lonnees and McDonald's of the world win."

Restlessly, Joe taps the end of his pencil on the tabletop. "Language defines what we can think," he continues. "I believe undisciplined, careless writing makes for undisciplined, careless thinking. How can you formulate ideas without appropriate tools—clarity, attention to detail? Without them, the world's thinking becomes muddled and uninformed. The mind is a muscle. Use it or lose it."

"We could go away, Joe," Lisa says plaintively through her sobs. "We could go to France. We don't speak French, so we'd never know when something was incorrect."

"Sorry, Lisa, I can't turn my back on murderers of the mother tongue. I need the facts, ma'am." Joe gives Lisa a despairing look, and then throws a dollar on the table. Coat collar up, hat brim pulled down, he sadly leaves Lisa and Bagels 'N Stuff behind, but not before pointing out to the amazed proprietor that *decaffeinated* has two Fs in it.

"I'll let you off with a warning this time," he says, exiting to chase a passing exterminator's truck with *MICES, TERMITES AND ROACHES* written on the side.

Back at the table, Lisa watches him go and says softly to herself, "I'll miss ya, Joe. Paris would of been swell." She shudders after mouthing the foul words of her new world. Picking up her decafeinated coffee, she drinks the bitter cup.

How To Write—
Techniques

❏ GENERAL FICTION

❏ 17

ADULT AND YOUNG READERS:
WHAT DO THEY HAVE IN COMMON?

BY JOAN AIKEN

PEOPLE WHO KNOW THAT I WRITE BOOKS FOR BOTH ADULTS AND CHILdren sometimes ask me: What is the difference between those kinds of writing? Do you have a different attitude toward what you write? Is the vocabulary different? What about the plots? The characters? Why do you *want* to write for both sets of readers?

As I grow older, I find these questions harder to answer, perhaps because the gap between the two sets of readers grows narrower—either in reality or in my mind. Looking about at other writers who also produce books read by both sets of readers—Russell Hoban, Peter Dickinson, Nina Bawden, Judy Blume—I suspect that the same thing is happening to them: They are beginning to write for a non-age reader who falls somewhere between the two groups—or, and this is just as likely, the readers themselves are changing. (For instance, there is now a vast readership who grew up forty years ago on the works of C.S. Lewis and Tolkien, and now have that built-in addiction.) Younger readers are turning to older books, and older readers go back to the pleasures found in fantasy and adventure stories.

It is like Kipling's wonderful change-over in *The Story of the Armadillos:*

> Can't curl but can swim
> Slow-Solid, that's him
> Curls up but can't swim
> Stickly-prickly, that's him

Perhaps I have it the wrong way 'round, but it doesn't matter, that is really the point of the story. It is no use learning a formula to help you with your work because, inevitably if you do so, a whole set of circumstances will change and the formula will fail you.

One thing we can be sure of: Older readers grow lazier, while younger readers are more adventurous and prepared to work harder. My grandchildren tackle books that I would not have the stamina to attempt, but our tastes still overlap. When they visit me, I read them my favorite passages from classic fiction—the shipwreck from Masefield's marvelous *Bird of Dawning*, or the gripping episode in Hugo's *Les Misérables* when Jean Valjean rescues poor little Cosette from the rapacious Thénardier family—and we have that unmatchable feeling of silent rapport when everybody's imagination is equally engaged.

But, although the area of common enjoyment is, I think, growing larger, there are still no-go areas on both sides. Few adults, for instance, would read Louisa Alcott these days; she is too sanctimonious, too quick to point a moral, though her plots and characters are still full of life, and young readers, girls especially, are still held by them. Few readers under twenty undertake Marcel Proust or Henry James with much enjoyment, because the action is too slow, the emphasis lies in character analysis.

There is one rule that still holds firm: In a story for young readers, the action *must* be swift, continuous, and immediately gripping. I was proud to find myself recently included in the new *Oxford Dictionary of Quotations* for my remark that Sir Walter Scott's leisurely opening of *Ivanhoe* ("In that pleasant district of merry England . . . etc.") would, these days, be accompanied by the sound of books slapping shut all over the library.*

And there are plenty of universal themes that still and always will engage the emotions and sympathies of both young and adult readers.

Injustice, for example. Injustice is the unbearable pain throughout the story that made *Jane Eyre* an instant bestseller and has kept it in print from 1847 to 1999. Why should poor little Jane, who has done nothing wrong, be treated so harshly by the odious Reed family? Once the reader's sympathies are engaged on Jane's behalf, the trick is done, there is no chance of closing the book until her wrongs have been righted. Arthur Ransome is an English writer whose children's adventure stories have somewhat gone out of fashion now, perhaps because several of them are written to formula. The children set themselves, or are set, a project, to make a map of the locality, or whatever, and by hard work,

---

The Way to Write for Children, St. Martin's Press

it is just completed as the story ends. But one, *The Big Six*, is very different from the others because in it the group of children who are the main characters are unjustly accused of theft and vandalism and the whole neighborhood turns against them. They become pariahs and have to clear themselves and nail their accusers by a series of heroic efforts. The fact that there are actual villains to contend with, instead of just the forces of nature, makes this book outstanding among the others.

Shakespeare has an elegant and skillful touch in mingling an injustice theme with a comedy motif, as in *The Merchant of Venice*, where the very grim Shylock-Antonio legal case focused on the horrifying pound-of-flesh penalty is contrasted with the light-hearted nonsense over rings and caskets. The injustice is done, first to Antonio, then to Shylock, giving a deeper resonance to the whole. Similarly in *Much Ado About Nothing*, the absurd Beatrice-Benedick story would hardly hold water on its own, if it were not counterpointed by Claudio's totally unjust accusations against poor Hero and the (highly improbable) unmasking of his scheme by Dogberry & Co. (It really takes Shakespeare to get away with this plot.)

Injustice is of course the theme of many classic folktales, starting from Cinderella. My favorite is a Croation story, "Stribor's Forest," in which a poor old mother is abominably treated by her daughter-in-law, who is really a snake turned into a girl, and has a snake's nature. She sets her mother-in-law impossible tasks, such as going to the forest for strawberries on a snowy winter's day. The good old mother is helped with her tasks by a tribe of benevolent forest elves, who finally offer to rescue her from her plight by restoring her to her girlhood in a magically created village in the enchanted forest. But realizing that, if this happens, her son would no longer exist, she chooses to go back to her life of hardship. This unprecedented choice undoes all the magic, and the son's wife becomes a snake again. This story, as well as having the classic folktale ingredients, is genuinely touching. Injustice has also formed the basis of many thriller and mystery stories, and can make the difference between a flat whodunit and an engrossing page-turner. Dorothy Sayers's *Strong Poison*, for instance, has terrific tension because Harriet Vane, the central character, is standing trial for her lover's murder. The jury can't agree, and there is only one month before the retrial in which to find proof that Harriet didn't commit the murder. The time element, and the fact that the reader is sure from the start that

Harriet is innocent, make this one of Sayers's best. Dick Francis, in his thriller *Enquiry*, uses a similar situation: His hero/narrator and the trainer he works for are barred from racing after being falsely accused of cheating in a race; owners are taking their horses away from the trainer (time element again), so there is only a limited period in which to prove that the accusation is false. Having the narrator as hero is an advantage here because he is able to tell the reader from the start that the charge is an unjust one.

I used the injustice theme myself in my Felix Brooke trilogy. Crossed wires seem to happen more in historical fiction than in contemporary work; perhaps because it is so much easier now to pick up the telephone and sort matters out. (As Stephen Leacock said, if only, when Othello had demanded, "Where is that handkerchief?," Desdemona had the presence of mind to answer, "I sent it to the laundry, darling," much trouble would have been saved.)

In my Felix Brooke stories I have the goodhearted but wild and impetuous hero run away from his uptight, strait-laced Spanish family because they are harsh with him, believing him to be illegitimate. When that situation is straightened out, he goes off to rescue the children of a man who is accused of being mad, and a traitor to his country. Felix very soon begins to realize that these are false accusations being circulated by the man's malevolent wife. In fact, the situation is the exact reverse of what he has been told, but by the time Felix is aware of this, he is on top of a cliff in the Pyrenees with three children, one seriously ill and one killed by poison.

Reconciliation is another universal theme that operates equally well in juvenile and adult fiction—the slow (or it may be sudden) coming together of two characters who have been opposed, if not actual enemies, throughout the story.

Dumas uses it in *The Three Musketeers*. All through the story, a character called Rochefort has been opposing and hindering D'Artagnan at every turn. They are mostly prevented by circumstances from actually fighting; but on the very last page, the epilogue, when all has been tidied up and a great many people have died, Dumas nonchalantly mentions to the reader: "D'Artagnan fought three duels with Rochefort and wounded him three times." D'Artagnan tells Rochefort, "If we have another fight, I shall probably kill you." Rochefort replies, "In that case it would be better for us both to forgive and forget. . .upon which they shook hands, this time in friendship."

In *Our Mutual Friend*, Dickens has a terrific cat-and-dog relationship between one of the heroines, spoiled little Bella Wilfer, and the hero, Rokesmith, whose real name is Harmon. He has been left a fortune on condition that he marry Bella, at that time unkown to him. Objecting to this arbitrary arrangement, Harmon contrives the pretense that he has been drowned, and presents himself to Bella merely as her family's lodger, somebody's unimportant secretary. Dickens has a lot of fun over this situation, as Bella first slights, teases, and spurns the humble Rokesmith, and then can't help falling in love with him (as he has with her already) and finally agrees to marry him, still without knowing that he is the real heir. The final revelation is enough to make the modern reader squirm with embarrassment, but Victorian readers lapped it up.

Georgette Heyer used the theme in half a dozen of her novels: A hates B adapts well to a Regency setting. And so did Jane Austen in *Pride & Prejudice*. Of course the fact that the antipathy is based on sexual attraction pushes the story up toward the adult market. Similarly, in E.M. Forster's *A Room with a View*, until the last chapter Lucy thinks she can't stand George; and the very same situation turns up in *Anne of Green Gables*, with Anne detesting the uppish, teasing Gilbert Blythe who puts her down at school. Hostilities crackle on briskly throughout the plot until Gilbert self-sacrificingly gives up a job so that Anne can have it, and the scene is set for romance to spring up between them.

It is much more entertaining for the writer—and the reader—to set the two main characters at loggerheads so they can display all their worst characteristics. In my school library, we used to have a wonderful weepie, *The Flight of the Heron* by D.K. Broster, about the Scottish clans rising against the English. The Scots hero mistakenly thinks that his English counterpart has betrayed him, and the misunderstanding is cleared up only at the very end when the dying Englishman, before he breathes his last, has just enough time to gasp out, "I always liked you!"

Must adult and juvenile characters differ? Obviously, characters in adult fiction can be more complex, can be depicted at greater depth and length, while young readers want to get on with the plot; they are not in the market for deep motivation and analysis, but the *type* of character may be basically the same for both age groups. King Arthur and Sir

Gawaine and Robin Hood, after all, began as heroes of adult fiction before they were adopted into the juvenile library. And an untidy, impatient problem-solver such as Sara Paretsky's V.I. Warshawski is equally welcome in both.

Reviewing the theme of overlap from children's to adult novels and vice versa, it struck me that I have a character who seems to have established himself with a foot in both camps. He is a somewhat inept, but intelligent and well-meaning British peer of the realm who wandered out of my last Jane Austen sequel, *The Youngest Miss Ward*, where, as Lord Camber, he goes off to found a Utopian community on the banks of the Susquehanna river. In *Dangerous Games*, my latest Dido Twite novel, as Lord Herondale, he is on a Pacific island searching for games to amuse the ailing King James III; and now he has turned up as the brother of Lady Catherine de Bourgh in yet another Austen spin-off. Vague, chatty, floundering, his heart in the right place and liable to cause his friends untold trouble, he is a kind of Sorceror's Apprentice. I have no idea where he came from, he is like no one I know, but I think it highly probable that he will turn up again, no doubt where least expected, whether in a juvenile or an adult story, who can say? Writing is like that. It continually takes the writer by surprise.

❏ 18

Rooting For Your Characters

By Barnaby Conrad

In *The Writer* magazine, Mary Higgins Clark is quoted as saying: "I like to create people the reader can root for."

Every would-be writer should tattoo that statement on his or her forehead! It is the very essence of the writing of fiction.

For example: Do you root for Romeo to overcome the Montague-Capulet feud and get his Juliet? Do you pull for the good Dr. Jekyll to conquer his alter ego, Mr. Hyde? For the wronged Count of Monte Cristo to get revenge on the men who sent him to prison? For the gutsy Scarlett O'Hara to get Tara back? For the gentle, retarded Lenny to find a safe haven in *Of Mice and Men*? For a young F.B.I. agent to outmaneuver the omnivorous Hannibal Lecter in *The Silence of the Lambs*? For the novice John Grisham lawyer to win his case in court? For clever Kay Scarpetta to use forensics to find the solution of the murders?

Of course you do: We all do, or these books would not have grabbed readers as they do and earned the popularity they enjoy.

In every story, readers must pull for something—or more specifically, *somebody*, a character with whom they can empathize. Every protagonist must want something and want it badly, whether it be an impoverished young girl who yearns for a nice dress for a dance, or a framed prisoner, frantic to find the real killer of his wife, or a general in battle who must take a defended hill or lose the battle, or an aged actor who desperately needs to get the small part in a film.

The reader needs to know what the character wants and understand why it is so important to him or her, whether it be wanting a requited love, the vice presidency of a bank, or simple revenge and justice.

Now for the major question: How do you as the writer make the reader identify with a character?

First: Your character must be in some sort of trouble, difficulty, peril, dangerous situation, or dilemma. One writer has said, "I only write about characters who are at the end of their rope."

Tolstoy once said: "My most successful stories are the ones where the reader hasn't known whose side I was on."

Ah, but Tolstoy himself knew whose side he was on! He was always on the side of the person in the most trouble, the character the readers would most want to achieve his goal. The same is true for Elmore Leonard: His characters are often reprehensible ex-jail birds, but because they are trying to go straight, the reader wants them to stay out of trouble. Caring about a person who has done something bad or even criminal but seeks redemption has a long and honorable history in classical fiction. For instance, Michael Henchard in Thomas Hardy's *The Mayor of Casterbridge*, when drunk, sells his wife and daughter to a sailor but is terribly remorseful ever after. (Parenthetically, James Michener stated that the first chapter of this Hardy novel is the most riveting of any novel in English.) Raskolnikov, in Dostoevsky's *Crime and Punishment*, commits a heinous murder, but he tries desperately to atone for it, and so we care about him.

In a like manner, in the beginning of Tom Wolfe's recent blockbuster, *A Man in Full*, we thoroughly dislike the egotistical tycoon, Charles Croker, but we root for him when he changes his ways, just as we do for Ebenezer Scrooge in Dickens's *A Christmas Carol*.

Having mentioned Wolfe's novel, it is worth studying how the author skillfully makes you sympathetic to the young protagonist, Conrad Hensley, almost instantly. How? He has Hensley save a fellow factory worker from an accident that would have been fatal. As Thackeray said, "Bravery never goes out of fashion," and readers instantly like the young man. As if that weren't enough, Hensley is subsequently jailed for a minor infraction he didn't commit, which escalates into a full prison sentence. Now the reader is really rooting for him, and when he escapes from prison readers are with him one hundred percent.

Escape is a powerful and seductive literary aphrodisiac; we want Huck Finn to escape from his abusive father, for Yossarian to escape from the madness of war in *Catch 22*, for Rabbitt Engstrom to leave behind the drab world John Updike has created for him, and for the prisoner in Stephen King's *Shawshank Redemption* to escape from the penitentiary.

In short, what makes us root for a character in fiction is usually what makes us root for a person in real life. Take the case of Christopher Reeve, the actor made famous by his role as Superman and then by the terrible riding accident that left him a quadriplegic. Do we pull for him in his efforts to rehabilitate himself? Of course we do, but why?

1) Because he has a terrible problem that might have happened to any of us.
2) He is struggling mightily to overcome his misfortune.
3) We empathize with his goal, i.e. to walk again.
4) He shows no self-pity.
5) He exhibits humor, courage, intelligence, and determination.

All of these qualities and conditions, if applied to a fictional character, would instantly make the reader empathize, and hence root for him or her to attain the desired goal.

(Actually, Jeffery Deaver, in his best-selling mysteries, features a totally paralyzed forensic expert, Lincoln Rhyme, whom readers like because he has many of the same qualities as Christopher Reeve.)

So: Think of the story or novel you are working on and ask yourself these questions:

1) Does my protagonist have an immediate and important problem?
2) Is he trying to solve it by his own efforts?
3) Is the goal something the reader wants the protagonist to attain?
4) And most important—for whom am I rooting?

❑ 19

FRAMING THE STRUCTURE OF A NOVEL

BY CAROL SHIELDS

A NOVEL IS A WILD AND OVERFLOWING THING. ITS NARRATIVE, EVEN when it is short and straightforward, includes a sort of encyclopedia of fact and notation and the gray spots in between, jumping from idea to idea, leaping continents and centuries and changes of mood. Novels—at least the novels I love to read—are stuffed with people, events, emotional upheavals and plateaus of despair. Its scenes dramatize arrivals, departures, births, marriages and murder, success and failure—the unsorted debris of existence, in fact, and yet its chaotic offerings are, when I look closely, attached to a finely stretched wire of authorly intention that reaches from the first page to the last.

How do novelists keep all this disorderly material on track? For years I fretted about the impossibility of the task, and kept putting off actually writing a novel. A novel, it seemed to me, was too big for someone who had scarcely been able to bring logic to a short story. Novels sprawled, or at least pretended to sprawl. Surely, characters or threads of thought got lost in the spreading chess game of prose, and no one could control it, least of all the inexperienced and fettered person sitting at the typewriter.

But I was getting close to forty, and, like many writers before me, I arrived at the now-or-never moment. Luckily for me, writing a master's thesis in my mid-thirties gave me a chip of courage; for the first time I had completed a *long* piece of writing and had discovered what should have been spectacularly self-evident: that long pieces of writing are made up of short pieces somehow sewn together.

Happily, my master's dissertation, about a pioneer writer of the 19th century, also contributed material for the novel. There were so many interesting footnotes I hadn't been able to incorporate, so much conjectural material that had been inadmissible in a scholarly document. And so, like my mother, who never threw out two tablespoons of leftover peas if she could help it, I decided to use up my research notes, to hand them over to a character I named Judith Gill, who, if the truth were known, was not at all that different from me—a woman nearing forty, a wife, a mother, a suburbanite—and someone who, like me, had an interest in history and in the idea of biography.

Because Judith Gill was part of an academic community, I arrived at the idea of using the academic year as a framework. My nine chapters were titled September, October, November, and so on, right through May. I didn't know where the novel was going, what its *substance* would be, but I found myself with a *structure* I could handle.

This structure felt to me like a series of similar-sized boxcars lined up on a track, nine of them. All I had to do was fill them up with "stuff," and I would have my novel. Every day when I sat down to write I called up in my head the image of boxcars, much as we call up images on our computers. It kept me sane, the knowledge that my un-ruly, unsorted thoughts could be distributed along the timeline, each in its own container.

I've heard of writers who do complex outlines of their novels, but, in fact, I've never met one of these eager outliners. Writing for me is generated out of writing. I honestly don't know where I'm going. The ideas come as I push forward—some days there are too many swarming possibilities and other days not enough. But at least with that first novel, later published as *Small Ceremonies*, I had found a vehicle—my slowly loaded train—that allowed me to keep track of my novelistic bits and pieces.

My second novel, *The Box Garden*, was also built on the practical contrivance of a timeline, seven long chapters that more or less approxi-mated the events of one week—approximate because I wanted to avoid being *too* schematic. I thought of these chapters as seven wire hangers on a coat rack. I didn't know what would be suspended from these hangers, but I knew their position and order. This novel was more com-pact in its events than the first, the temperature was correspondingly higher, and more intense. The image of *my fictional week* was less im-portant for the novel—which could have spilled into months or years—than it was for me, the writer; it gave me a disciplined structure that I could call on, depend on, and lean on. It made the maddening work of the novel writing easier.

I don't know how other writers organize their material, but I suspect that each of us finds a way to keep control. I had a very clear image for my novel *Swann*, a book that broke free of many of the traditional narrative patterns I was accustomed to. Because of the point of view of the novel—four characters in search of a subject—I wanted the book to be built on four independent novellas with a concluding dramatization, each leaning just slightly on the others for coherence. This matrix swam into my mind very early in the writing. I was not absolutely wedded to it, but worked toward it, relying on it and returning to it when I felt myself going off on wasteful tangents.

The original structure for my novel, *The Republic of Love*, failed. My plan was to write a love story (a tricky business in these cynical times) by using a short notation from each day of a year, giving my book 365 related segments. This proved impossible, for I soon saw my novel swelling toward what looked like a thousand pages. I abandoned the plan and chose daily segments stretching from Easter to Christmas, a more manageable framework. The chapters of the novel alternate between the two lovers, Fay and Tom, and each chapter covers the events of one week, moving always forward on the timeline.

When I came to write *The Stone Diaries*, I again felt I needed a working image. I decided on a series of Chinese nesting boxes. I, the novelist, was constructing the big outside box; my heroine, Daisy Goodwill, struggling to understand her life, was making the next box, and the inside box was empty, a reminder to me of my original premise: that I was writing an account of a woman who was absent from her own existence. This organizing principle with its solid and easily retrievable image was not sketched out on paper and it certainly wasn't projected onto the reader. Instead, it served as my scaffold, my silent working orders and *aide-mémoire*.

These concrete structures—concrete in my mind, that is—have been tactically useful, but they have also forced me to open my mind to new ways of organizing fiction. We've all heard the rumor: The novel is dead. I don't believe this for a moment, but I do think certain traditional structures have lost their relevance. The old conflict/solution set-up feels too easy for me, too manipulative, and too often leading to what seems no more than a photo opportunity for people in crisis.

The structure of these kinds of novels could be diagrammed on a blackboard, a gently inclined line representing the rising action, then a sudden escalatory peak, followed by a steep plunge which demonstrated the dénouement and then the resolution. I remember feeling quite worshipful in the presence of that ascending line. The novel as boxed kit, as scientific demonstration, and furthermore it was teachable.

It wasn't until I had been teaching literature for several years and passing on these inscribed truths to others that I started to lose faith. The diagram, which I had by then drawn on the blackboard perhaps fifty or sixty times, began one day to look like nothing so much as a bent spatula, and yet my students, hunched over the seminar table, were dutifully copying this absurd image into their notes.

Suddenly, I wasn't interested in the problem-solution story I had grown up with. The form seemed crafted out of the old quest myth in which obstacles were overcome and victories realized. None of this seemed applicable to the lives of women, nor to most of the men I knew, whose stories had more to do with the texture of daily life and the spirit of community than with personal battles, goals, mountaintops, and prizes.

About that time, I had started to pay attention to the way women, sitting around a table, for instance, tell each other stories. I noticed that women tended to deal in the episodic, to suppress what was smoothly linear, to set up digressions, little side stories which were not really digressions at all but integral parts of the story. These parts might contain gathered insights, or they might exist for their expressiveness alone, but they were, I felt, what a life was made of.

After my second novel, I had abandoned the kind of people-in-crisis set-up that was the engine of so much realistic fiction. This meddling with form, though, was so gradual and tentative that I had scarcely been aware of it. Now I was. I felt emboldened enough to allow the fictions I was writing to fill up on the natural gas of the quotidian, and, without venturing into the inaccessible, to find new and possibly subversive structures.

More and more I trusted daily detail, wondering why domesticity, the shaggy beast that eats up fifty percent of our lives, had been shoved aside by fiction writers. Was it too dull, too insignificant, too flattened out, too obvious? I wanted wallpaper in my novels, cereal bowls, cupboards, cousins, buses, local elections, head colds, cramps, newspapers, and I abandoned Chekhov's dictum that if there is a rifle hanging over the fireplace, it must go off before the story ends. A rifle could hang over a fireplace for countless other reasons. For atmosphere, to give texture, to comment on the owner of the house, to ignite a scene with its presence, not its ammunition.

The inclusion of domestic detail seemed much more to me than just an extra suitcase taken on board to use up my weight allowance. Diurnal surfaces could be observed by a fiction writer with a kind of deliberate squint that distorts but also sharpens beyond ordinary vision, bringing forward what might be called the subjunctive mode of one's self or others, a world of dreams, possibilities, and parallel realities.

In short, I want to write novels that were both tighter and looser. I wanted to create new structures that would give stability to the less stable material of my books and help me stay on course. And I wanted, then, to fill those structures with randomness, with side stories, surface details, potted histories, drifting thoughts—the whole raw material, in fact, of our lives. It meant taking a chance, looking around, tapping out words, shifting my sentences and paragraphs, getting the noises in my head onto paper, making something new.

In a sense, I use my structure as narrative bones, and partially to replace plot—which I more and more distrust. (I'm comforted by something that Patrick White, the Australian novelist, once said: that he never worried about plot. What he wrote was life going on toward death.) This is what interests me: the arc of a human life.

These are interesting times for a writer. The strands of reality that enter the newest of our novels are looser, more random and discursive. More altogether seems possible. The visual media, television and film, have appropriated the old linear set-ups, leaving fiction, by default, the more interesting—to me—territory of the reflective consciousness, the inside of the head where most of our lives are lived.

In the books I read—and I find hard to separate my life as a reader from that as a writer—I look first to language that possesses an accuracy that cannot really exist without leaving its trace of deliberation. I want, too, the risky articulation of what I recognize but haven't yet articulated myself. And finally, I hope for some fresh news from another country which satisfies, by its modesty, a microscopic enlargement of my vision of the world. I wouldn't dream of asking for more.

❏ 20

SEVEN KEYS TO EFFECTIVE DIALOGUE

BY MARTIN NAPARSTECK

GOOD DIALOGUE MAKES CHARACTERS IN A STORY SOUND LIKE REAL people talking, yet no one I know talks like a character, even in the best novels. This seeming contradiction can be explained by examining the seven attributes of good dialogue.

1. **Every voice is unique.**

In my novel *A Hero's Welcome,* Culver and Mabel talk:

> "Hi," she said softly.
> "Hi."
> "You feeling better?"
> "Yeah."
> "You had too much to drink."
> "I know."
> "Maybe you should go back to your room and sleep it off."
> "I would miss the party."
> "It's not much fun anyway."
> "Maybe I should have some coffee?"

Although both characters are products of middle-class, Eastern America, they are individuals, and I tried to keep that in mind. I tried to reflect Mabel's caring for Culver's condition and to capture Culver's condition—near-drunkenness—and a desire to continue the conversation. She speaks in longer sentences and controls the subject; he often speaks in incomplete sentences and only in response to her verbal initiatives. The differences may be subtle, but readers are unlikely to confuse who is speaking, despite the lack of attribution. Any time you have two or more characters speaking, make their rhythms differ. Some can speak staccato, some can speak with flow, some can use profanity, others can use big and fancy words. Assign a different voice to each character.

2. **Don't make speeches.**

Unless your character is running for president or teaching a literature class or is pompous, don't let him rant on for more than three or four sentences without being interrupted by another character. In my novel *War Song,* Fernandez says,

> "In case you never heard, war is hell. War is hell. Some people got to get killed so others can live in freedom. I know that might sound corny to you, but if enough people believed it this world would be a lot better off."

Then he's cut off by a character who finds his little speech pompous.

In real life we don't usually tolerate being lectured at. Sitting in a classroom or in a church, we might have to, but not always even then. We prefer a chance to respond. In a bar or a living room, we're likely to respond with our own opinion before the speaker gets too carried away. Your characters should display the same intolerance.

3. **Authors are not tape recorders.**

In "Deep in the Hole," a short story published in *Aethlon,* I have Mickey, a member of his college's baseball team, say to his literature professor, "I have a game on Wednesday and I wonder if it would be all right if I skipped the class. I can read all the. . . ." Because it's a highly autobiographical story, and because I was tremendously awkward in speech in the late 60's, I feel certain the real-life dialogue this bit of fiction is based upon went something like this: "Eh, I have, eh, you know, a game on Wednesday and I, eh, wonder, would it be, eh, all right. . . ." All those "ehs" and that "you know" may be O.K. for a sentence or two, but for a whole story it would not only annoy most readers, but would distract them to the point of losing them. A fiction writer is not a journalist, and he has no obligation to act like a stenographer or a tape recorder. The idea is to capture both the essence and the underlying emotion of what's said, not to reproduce a transcript.

4. **People tell more little lies than big ones.**

Probably most people who commit a murder will tell the police they didn't do it. Big lies are part of life and should be part of stories. But most of us don't get that much opportunity to tell big lies (most of us will never be asked by the police if we committed a murder). But smaller lies are part of our everyday conversations. In my *Ellery Queen* short story, "The 9:13," two men are alone in a train station, and one tells the other his name is Thunder, but two pages later he says:

> "My name ain't Thunder."
> "What?"
> "My name ain't Thunder."
> "No?"
> "No, it ain't."
> "Oh."
> "Ain't you curious what it is?"
> Joe stammered a bit.
> "It's Eddie."
> "I—I see."
> "Ain't you curious why I told ya it was Thunder?"
> "Yes, I suppose so. Why?"
> "Why what?"
> "Why did you tell me your name was Thunder?"
> "I ain't gonna tell ya."

Eddie's lie has no real purpose, but the fact that he chose to tell this particular lie in this particular manner reveals something about his character. Not everyone's playfulness is malevolent. Have your characters lie about small things in a manner that reveals who they are.

5. Dialogue is made up of monologues.

When someone is speaking to you, consider how you typically devote part of your attention to what she's saying, but you are also focused on what you're going to say when it's your turn to speak. In "Getting Shot," a short story of mine published in *Mississippi Review,* a soldier who has been wounded in Vietnam is told by his lieutenant:

> "You're gonna get a Purple Heart out of this. What do you think about that?"
> "Not much." I'm smiling like a teenage kid just got his first lay, and the Louey, he knows it.
> He pats my right shoulder. "Sure, sure." He adds, "Sure."

Although the narrator responds to what the lieutenant has said, he clearly has something else on his mind, part of which reflects the false bravado he assumes the situation requires. The lieutenant, while detecting that and playing along, uses a bit of staccato speech to end that portion of the conversation so he can move on to other things.

6. **Every word in dialogue represents a choice.**

Every word you ever spoke in your life represented a choice. You could have chosen to be silent. You could have used another word. Consider this bit of dialogue (from *War Song*): "Don't you wanna go home?" It could have been, "Do you not desire to return to your home?" Or, "Have you no desire to go home again?" The choice is based on who the character is. One test that works for me is to write the same bit of dialogue a dozen or more times, at least in my mind, sometimes on my computer screen, and then, only then, to decide which is most appropriate for a particular character under this particular circumstance. Chances are the first words you choose are not the ones that best reflect the character. As with all other writing, nothing improves dialogue like rewriting.

7. **All dialogue should reveal character and/or advance plot.**

I have never included a piece of dialogue like this in any story I've ever written (thank the great muse):

> He told me how to get to Salt Lake City from Logan.
> "Take Valley West Highway until you come to the Interstate 15 interchange and proceed on to the interstate, going south, for about 90 miles, and when you come to the exit marked 600 north, get off and follow the signs to downtown." Thanks to his accurate and detailed directions I found my way to Salt Lake City safely.

Any dialogue that simply exchanges information between characters (who was the 26th president of the U.S., what does antidisestablishment mean) is static. Stories need to move forward. Just as you never need to say the character walked to the other side of the room (unless it's the first time this guy has walked in 10 years), you never need to reveal how someone learned the directions from here to there. Just assume, as your readers will, that there are some bits of conversation we know take place in real life but which are far too boring to include in a story.

But do let a character say, "You're fired," even though it reveals a bit of information the listener didn't know, because it changes the life of the poor guy. If the dialogue doesn't change the listener's life, no matter how slightly, or help us better understand who the speaker is, leave it out.

Each of the first six examples I've given help make the speakers sound like real people. But only the seventh one is likely to reflect accurately a real bit of conversation. And that's the one you should never use.

❑ 21

HOW TO BRING YOUR SETTINGS TO LIFE

BY MOIRA ALLEN

GOD, IT'S BEEN SAID, IS IN THE DETAILS. SO, TOO, IS MUCH OF THE work of a writer. Too little detail leaves your characters wandering through the narrative equivalent of an empty stage. Too much, and you risk the tombstone effect: gray blocks of description that tempt the reader to skip and skim, looking for action.

To set your stage properly, it's important to choose the most appropriate, vivid details possible. It's equally important, however, to present those details in a way that will engage your reader. The following techniques can help you keep your reader focused both on your descriptions and on your story.

Reveal setting through motion

Few people walk into a room and instantly absorb every detail of their surroundings. Often, however, we expect the reader to do just that by introducing a scene with a block of text that completely halts the action.

As an alternative, let your description unfold as the character moves through the scene. Ask yourself which details your character would notice immediately and which might register more slowly.

Suppose, for example, that your heroine, a secretary of humble origins, has just entered the mansion of a millionaire. What would she notice first? How would she react to her surroundings?

Let her observe how soft the rich Persian carpet feels underfoot, how it muffles her footfalls, how she's almost tempted to remove her shoes. Does she recognize any of the masterpieces on the walls, or do they make her feel even more out of place because she doesn't know a Cezanne from a Monet? Don't tell readers the sofa is soft until she actually sinks into it. Let her smell the leather cushions, mingling with the fragrance of hothouse flowers filling a cut-crystal vase on a nearby table.

Use active verbs to set the scene—but use them wisely. Don't inform the reader that "a heavy marble table dominated the room"; force your character to detour around it. Instead of explaining that "light glittered and danced from the crystal chandelier," let your character blink, dazzled by the prismatic display.

"Walking through" a description breaks the details into small nuggets and scatters them throughout the scene, so the reader never feels overwhelmed or bored. However, doing this raises another important question: Which character should do the walking?

Reveal setting through a character's level of experience

What your character knows will directly influence what she sees. Suppose, for example, that your humble secretary really doesn't know a Cezanne from a Monet, or whether the carpet is Persian or Moroccan. Perhaps she doesn't even know whether it's wool or polyester. If these details are important, how can you convey them?

You could, of course, introduce the haughty owner of the mansion and allow him to reveal your heroine's ignorance. Or, you could write the scene entirely from the owner's perspective. Keep in mind, however, that different characters will perceive the same surroundings in very different ways, depending on the character's familiarity (or lack of familiarity) with the setting.

Imagine, for example, that you're describing a stretch of windswept coastline from the perspective of a fisherman who has spent his entire life in the region. What would he notice? From the color of the sky or changes in the wind, he might make deductions about the next day's weather and sailing conditions. When he observes seabirds wheeling against the clouds, they are not "gulls" to him, but terns and gannets and petrels—easily identified by his experienced eye by the shape of their wings or pattern of their flight.

Equally important, however, are the things he might not notice. Being so familiar with the area, he might pay little attention to the fantastic shapes of the rocks, or the gnarled driftwood littering the beach. He hardly notices the bite of the wind through his cable-knit sweater or the tang of salt in the air, and he's oblivious to the stench of rotting kelp-mats that have washed ashore.

Now suppose an accountant from the big city is trudging along that same beach. Bundled up in the latest Northwest Outfitters down jacket, he's still shivering—and can't imagine why the fisherman beside him, who isn't even wearing a sweater, isn't freezing to death. He keeps stumbling over half-buried pieces of driftwood and knows that the sand is ruining his Italian loafers. From the way the waves pound against the beach, it's obvious a major storm is brewing. The very thought of bad weather makes him nauseous, as does the stench of rotting seaweed (he doesn't think of it as "kelp") and dead fish.

Each of these characters' perceptions of the beach will be profoundly influenced by his background and experience. Bear in mind, however, that "familiar" doesn't imply a positive outlook, nor is the "unfamiliar" necessarily synonymous with "negative." Your accountant may, in fact, regard the beach as an idyllic vacation spot—rugged, romantic, isolated, just the place to make him feel as if he's really getting in touch with nature and leaving the rat race of the city behind. The fisherman, on the other hand, may loathe the ocean, feeling trapped by the whims of the wind and weather that he must battle each day for his livelihood. This bring us to the next point.

Reveal setting through the mood of your character

What we see is profoundly influenced by what we feel. The same should be true for our characters. Filtering a scene through a character's feelings can profoundly influence what the reader "sees." Two characters, for example, could "see" exactly the same setting, yet perceive it in opposite ways.

Suppose, for example, that a motorist has strolled a short distance into an archtypical stretch of British moorland. Across a stretch of blossoming gorse, she sees ruins of some ancient watch tower, now little more than a jumble of stones crowning the next hill (or "tor," as her guidebook puts it).

The temptation is irresistible. Flicking at dandelion heads with her walking stick, our intrepid motorist hikes up the slope, breathing in the scents of grass and clover, admiring the lichen patterns on the gray granite boulders. At last, warmed by the sun and her exertions, she leans back against a rock and watches clouds drift overhead like fuzzy sheep herded by a gentle wind. A falcon shrills from a nearby hollow, its cry a pleasant reminder of how far she has come from the roar and rumble of the city.

A pleasant picture? By now, your reader might be considering travel arrangements to Dartmoor. But what if your motorist is in a different mood? What if her car has broken down, and she has been unable to find help? Perhaps she started across the moor because she thought she saw a house or hut, but was dismayed to find that it was only a ruin, and a creepy one at that. The tower's scattered stones, half-buried in weeds and tangled grasses, remind her of grave markers worn faceless with time. Its silent emptiness speaks of secrets, of desolation that welcomes no trespassers. Though the sun is high, scudding clouds cast a pall over the landscape, and the eerie, lonesome cry of some unseen bird reminds her just how far she has strayed from civilization.

When this traveler looks at the gorse, she sees thorns, not blossoms. When she looks at clouds, she sees no faithful shapes, only the threat of rain to add to her troubles. She wants to get out of this situation, while your reader is on the edge of his seat, expecting something far worse than a creepy ruin to appear on this character's horizon!

Reveal setting through the senses

A character's familiarity with a setting and his or her emotional perception of that setting will influence and be influenced by the senses. Our stranded motorist, for example, may not notice the fragrance of the grass, but she will be keenly aware of the cold wind. Our accountant notices odors the fisherman ignores, while the fisherman detects subtle variations in the color of the sky that are meaningless to the accountant.

Different sensory details evoke different reactions. For example, people process visual information primarily at the cognitive level: We make decisions and take action based on what we see. When writers describe a scene in terms of visual observations, they are appealing to the reader's intellect.

Emotions, however, are often affected by what we hear. Think of the effects of a favorite piece of music, the sound of a person's voice, the whistle of a train. In conversation, tone of voice is a more reliable indicator of mood and meaning than words alone. Sounds can make us shudder, shiver, jump—or relax and smile. Scenes that include sounds—fingers scraping a blackboard, the distant baying of a hound— are more likely to evoke an emotional response.

Smell has the remarkable ability to evoke memories. While not everyone is taken back to childhood by "the smell of bread baking," we all have olfactory memories that can trigger a scene, a recollection of an event or person. Think of someone's perfume, the smell of new-car leather, the odor of wet dog. Then describe that smell so that your reader is *there*.

Touch evokes a sensory response. Romance writers know they'll get more mileage out of writing "he trailed his fingertips along her spine" than "he whispered sweet nothings in her ear." The first can evoke a shiver of shared sensory pleasure; the second is just words. Let your reader feel the silkiness of a cat's fur, the roughness of castle stones, the prickly warmth of your hero's flannel shirt beneath his lover's fingertips. Let your heroine's feet ache, let the wind raise goosebumps on her flesh, let the gorse thorns draw blood.

Finally, there is taste, which is closely related to smell in its ability to evoke memories. Taste, however, is perhaps the most difficult to incorporate into a setting; often, it simply doesn't belong there. Your heroine isn't going to start licking the castle stones, and it isn't time for lunch. "Taste" images should be used sparingly and appropriately, or you may end up with a character who seems more preoccupied with food than with the issues of the story.

The goal of description is to create a well-designed set that provides the perfect background for your characters—a setting that *stays* in the background, without overwhelming the scene or interrupting the story. In real life, we explore our surroundings through our actions, experience them through our senses, understand (or fail to understand) them through our knowledge and experience, and respond to them through our emotions. When your characters do the same, readers will keep turning pages—and not just because they're waiting for something interesting to happen!

❏ 22

Pacing Your Novel

By Margaret Chittenden

WHEN I BEGIN TO PLOT A NOVEL, I TEND TO THINK OF MY BRAIN AS A stockpot: I just throw ideas into it and let them simmer. It's no coincidence that one of my favorite quotes from the I Ching is, "Before the beginning of great brilliance, there must be chaos."

At first, I don't believe in being too organized. Eventually however, I get ready to write my synopsis—my plan—my plot, try to combine all the elements and make order out of the chaos.

The writer of popular fiction usually sets up a situation that creates suspense and anticipation, then shows what the fallout from that is, using cause and effect: If this happens, what would be the result, and what would that cause to happen, and what would be the consequence, until the situation is resolved and the loose ends are tied up. That's a very basic outline for a novel, but it gets the plot off to a good start.

One of the flaws I've seen most often when reading other writers' manuscripts is a beginning that's too slow. I don't think your characters have to show up on page one in the middle of a gunfight, but there should be a sense that something is happening or is about to happen. No reader is going to read patiently on while waiting for the suspense to begin.

Here are a few things to look at that have to do with pacing; I'll leave it up to you to decide if you should consider them before plotting, before writing, during writing, after you have finished the first draft . . . never. No one who writes for a living has gone up a mountain and been given a set of stone tablets with the rules of writing etched into them. If anything I suggest doesn't work for you, discard it and work it out your own way.

Try to have an opening that will engage your reader's attention right away. It is often the first page that sells a book to an editor or to a reader. It has to be interesting. What works best for me is to have more than one person on the scene and people *doing* things, rather than sitting around talking or thinking. Don't have anyone musing in a bathtub. Flying around waiting to land in an airplane is another dangerous situation—dangerous for boredom, that is.

People often talk about starting with a narrative hook, which is O.K. if it works. Unfortunately, some writers interpret that to mean starting with an enormously dramatic action scene, whether it belongs in the story or not. I'm happy if a book starts with something intriguing.

Earl Emerson, author of the Thomas Black mystery series and the Mac Fontana mystery series, always comes up with intriguing beginnings. For example:

> On Saturday, some ghoul murdered my dog. It surprises you when they do something like that. I expect to be flattened by snarling eighteen wheelers on the freeway. I expect to be lunged at by booze hounds with broken beer bottles in taverns. I expect to be slapped by loose women who aren't quite as loose as I thought. But it surprises you when some spook caves in your dog's skull on a rainy Saturday evening. (*The Rainy City*, Avon Books)

> It was raining when they rolled me out of the big Lincoln and into the ditch. (*Yellow Dog Party*, Ballantine Books)

I always check my first sentences to make sure they will generate questions in the reader's mind. This sets my plot in motion, because I have to answer those questions.

If your pace seems too slow at any point in the book, think action. Your characters don't have to be battling savage hordes—unless that's an integral part of the story—but it helps if they are doing *something*. This doesn't necessarily have to be vital for the story. Sometimes you need a scene in which two people are simply swapping information, or getting to know each other, or perhaps having an argument. And it doesn't have to be while they are eating lunch. Most books have too many meals in them. (Mine do. I have to cut out several meals when I'm revising.) The reader will understand that your characters eat. You can even say, "They ate dinner, then. . . ."

Your story also gets much more interesting and thus speeds up the pace if you put your characters in a variety of scenes. The first time I remember noticing this was in Sue Grafton's novel, *A is for Alibi*, in which the main character, Kinsey Millhone, has lunch with one person, then goes to visit the office of another. My interest really perked up when Kinsey goes to question a dog groomer. The constant references to what the woman is doing and what the dogs are doing brought this scene alive, and taught me about the importance of using a variety of settings. In my mystery, *Dead Beat and Deadly* (Kensington), there are a couple of meals, but there's also an interview with a former homeless person after he's found a place to stay—and the "furniture" is a little unusual. There's a scene at a hair stylist's salon; one at a veterinarian's clinic; one in a women's rest room; one in an alley; and then, because my series is set in a country-western tavern, there are scenes on the dance floor and at the bar.

In *Dying to Sing* (Kensington), I had my sleuth, Charlie Plato, and her sidekick Zack Hunter hike over the Golden Gate Bridge with a doctor from whom they're trying to get some information about the murder victim. The Golden Gate Bridge had nothing to do with the story, nor did the freighter that passed under the bridge, or the waves people were riding below them, but those activities added interest to what might otherwise have been a rather dry question-and-answer scene, thus increasing the pace of the story.

Pacing does not always mean going fast; sometimes it's actually necessary to slow it down. Check your story (preferably after you have written it) to see if the pace of each section seems right. If the scene is an important one with all kinds of ramifications, you might want to slow the pace a bit. If the scene follows one of lickety-split action, you might want to slow that down, too, to give the reader a bit of a rest. Non-stop action can get just as boring as no action at all.

I discussed the subject of pacing with Dale Furutani, author of the Samurai Trilogy and the Ken Tanaka Mystery Series, and he wrote, "I think the biggest mistake writers make is in thinking they have to move at a frenetic pace throughout a book. In classical music, there are beautiful, quiet interludes to set a level from which the more vigorous passages can ascend. Without setting this base, you just have forty minutes of loud noise. In writing, we talk about the tricks to increase pace (shorter sentences, ever ascending action, more action verbs, shorter chapters, etc.), but we don't usually talk about the techniques to create the interludes (poetic language, appeal to emotions like solitude and love, interesting diversions from the main plotline, etc.)."

I agree with this, though I'd add a caveat. You shouldn't play too much beautiful music without having something going on. One place you must think about timing is at the end of your story. It must not be too abrupt, or the reader might not believe it could happen that way. It must not drag on too long, either. You have to study the pacing of your endings carefully to make sure they will satisfy the reader.

If, however, people have been sitting around talking for a while, you'll want to speed things up. And if you have an action scene, you don't want to insert extraneous details that will slow it down. Or make it unbelievable.

Every once in a while I'll read a book in which the action is hot and heavy, with the villain breathing down the hero and heroine's neck— this is no time for the hero to notice what beautiful eyes the heroine has. Or for the heroine to wonder how old the hero is and if he's married. Nor is it the time to describe the snow melting off the pine branches.

If you want to create atmosphere and stretch out suspense by having the heroine hide behind a tree in the forest while the villain creeps slowly toward her, then by all means have the snow melting off the pines. It's a question of balancing the atmosphere with the action.

You'll slow down a story if you stop the action to show what a character looks like. However, if you want to show the person in a way that brings him or her to life, don't give a complete description all at once, but rather note the things you would note when you first meet someone—height, approximate age, general physique, coloring. You may notice the color of the eyes the next time you meet, along with a mouth set in a grim expression, a weak chin, or hairstyle.

The way a person dresses tells a lot about him or her, so take the time to describe the clothing. In *Dead Beat and Deadly*, here is how I presented Zack Hunter, who stars in a weekly TV series. We're in Charlie Plato's viewpoint:

> He looked great. He always does. Unfortunately. His long legs and lean hips were packed into his jeans just right. As Sheriff Lazarro, Zack had dressed in all black clothing—jeans, cowboy hat, Western shirt, Tony Lama Boots. This outfit had worked as well for Lazarro as it had for Johnny Cash, and it proved so successful in snaring the ladies that Zack had made it his signature suit, as much a part of him as his green eyes and wry smile and the straight black eyebrows that slanted whimsically upward above his nose.

Now, that's quite a lot of words, but I think you get a lot of information about Zack and a little about Charlie, too, and it's not necessary for me to talk much about Zack's appearance after that. If I have him put on or take off his cowboy hat, or raise those slanted eyebrows, you'll see him the way I want you to see him. So I'm really saving words in the long run.

Although I've noted that pacing also refers to slowing the story down from time to time, the flaw in many stories is that they move with the pace of a snail; most need speeding up. When I've finished a book, I go over each scene and ask myself, "What is happening?" And if nothing is, I look carefully to see if action is necessary.

Using transitions is the best way to pick up the pace. Transitions get you from place to place or person to person without your having to give all the details. "Later," "The following day," "Meanwhile back at the ranch." Quite often there is no need to tell how the character or characters got from here to there; you can just start another chapter or scene without worrying about what happened in between. You can even hop over a whole week, if the adjoining scenes lend themselves to that.

But here again, there will be times when you should make a slower transition. In some cases, there has to be a complete change of mood, and you have to prepare the reader for it. Or in a particular case, you might not want to hop over several days with a single word. You just have to examine the scene before and the scene after, listening to the internal rhythm of each, and then decide how long the transition should be. Think of a transition as the stepping stone that gets you from one place or one time period to another.

I began by talking about the sort of primordial soup I start with when I'm plotting a novel. Getting out of that soup is sometimes a problem, but if you keep the setup, anticipation, action, and resolution in mind, you'll bring order out of the chaos, and pick up—or slow down—your pace as necessary.

❑ 23

How to Write a Novel: Questions and Answers

By Sidney Sheldon

Q. *What is the hardest part of being a writer and the most rewarding?*

A. I love writing, so I don't find it hard. For me, the act of creation is the most exciting thing in the world. The most rewarding part is knowing you will bring pleasure to millions of people.

Q. *What type of people most often succeed as writers?*

A. You have to have basic talent. You have to love what you are doing. You have to work very hard and persevere against all of the rejections you get in the beginning. You have to keep pounding on all the gates until they open up.

Q. *Have any particular novelists been mentors?*

A. I was influenced by George Bernard Shaw, W. Somerset Maugham, Christopher Fry, and Ernest Hemingway.

Q. *When was your work first published?*

A. I sold my first poem when I was 10 years old and my first screenplay when I was 22.

Q. *Self-discipline is a problem for writers in all genres, but especially for novelists, who must spend months and even years on one project. How does a writer stay focused on a project over a long period of time?*

A. I work from 9:30 in the morning until 6:00 in the afternoon every day during the week. Sometimes I'll continue the same schedule over the weekend, or use that time to edit and make additional notes for future chapters. It's really not a matter of discipline for me; I write every day because I enjoy it.

Q. *Is there any other type of writing that you have done or would like to do?*

A. Before I wrote my first novel, I wrote Broadway plays, motion pictures, and television scripts. I love every form of writing.

Q. *How do you keep your novels and characters "contemporary"?*

A. My novels and characters remain contemporary because I prefer to write about the most exciting and dynamic period in our history—the present. I also feel that my readers can more easily identify with the characters and their story if it takes place in a contemporary setting.

Q. *How do you choose locale for your stories?*

A. I start with a single character, and the story evolves from that character. I try to write about glamorous places, because I think readers like to live vicariously through the characters. In *Rage of Angels* I thought Manhattan would be an exciting place for Jennifer Parker to live. In *Master of the Game*, Jamie MacGregor was involved in the diamond business, so South Africa, London, and New York were logical locales.

Q. *Your plots are always very involved and complicated. What do you think keeps them believable? What keeps them from becoming far-fetched?*

A. I think my books are believable because the characters are real to me. I feel my readers sense that, and therefore come to share my compassion for the characters and their plights and care about what happens to them.

Q. *Do you consciously try to balance your characters in one story— good versus evil, for instance? How do you determine the number of characters you include?*

A. I do not consciously try to balance my characters with regard to good versus evil. I do not believe in black or white characterizations. I think there is some good in the most evil person, as well as a bit of evil in the best of people. I try to make my characters as real as possible, so that readers can identify with them. As for the number of characters, it does not matter, as long as they are all interesting.

Q. *Are there ever characters that you have trouble with, i.e., that you think are important to the story, but that just don't seem to come across as real people?*

A. My characters are all real to me. I do run into trouble sometimes when I allow minor characters to run away with the story and take up too many pages. I have to go back and throw out the majority of those pages. The character of Old Samuel in *Bloodline* is an example of my failure to keep a minor player in check. I had to throw out 150 pages on Old Samuel.

Q. *What do you think is the most important characteristic of a protagonist? Or an antagonist?*

A. The most important characteristic of any character—protagonist or antagonist—is reality, making them absolutely believable.

Q. *How do you determine the length of a story?*

A. The characters determine the length.

Q. *Once you've developed an idea and then a plot for a story, how do you work it into a novel? Do you write episode by episode, so that each chapter ends with a "page-turner"?*

A. While I consciously make sure that all the chapters in my novels end on a "page-turner," I do not break down the plot by episode. The characters determine where one chapter ends and another one begins.

Q. *Do you think beginning fiction writers should write short stories before they try their hand at a novel?*

A. I think the decision to start out by writing short stories before tackling novels is a personal one. It is up to the writer to determine what makes him or her comfortable.

Q. *Do you think the adaptations of your novels for television have been successful? Have you worked on the adaptations or have others developed them on their own?*

A. I serve as Executive Producer on adaptations of my novels for television. Some of the mini-series have been more successful than others, due in large part to the problems involved in transferring printed material to the screen. My participation in the project is usually confined to overall script approval. I prefer to spend my time working on novels.

Q. *You have been enormously successful as a playwright, screenwriter, and novelist. Is there one type of writing you prefer? Why? Do the techniques of one, like playwriting, overlap with fiction? How? And can a writer improve his dialogue writing by learning to write plays?*

A. My first love is writing novels. No other media offers me such a vast canvas on which to spin sweeping panoramic tales. I cherish this freedom of expression. However, it was my experience as a screenwriter and playwright that prepared me for writing novels. A playwright deals with dialogue. If the dialogue is not good, the play will not be good, so the playwright's bread and butter depends on sharp dialogue-writing skills.

Q. *What do you think are the most important roles writers play in this country?*

A. I think writers in any country can make an enormous contribution by giving their readers an insight into themselves.

Q. *Why did you choose the type of writing that you do?*

A. I did not choose the type of writing I do. It chose me.

❑ 24

CAPTURE THE READER'S IMAGINATION

BY KARIN MCQUILLAN

READING IS A COLLABORATION BETWEEN THE IMAGINATION OF THE writer and the imagination of the reader. It is the writer's challenge to enable readers to create in their own minds the characters and the events the author has imagined. Given the necessary cues, the reader will be transported to an imaginary world, moved to tears or laughter, and be caught up in the story till the last word. If the author breaks the illusion by faulty writing, the reader will lose conviction.

The common advice "show, don't tell" is the key to success, but it can take years for beginning writers to work out what this actually means. The urge to explain instead of to fictionalize is natural, because it is the way we communicate in conversation. When we tell people about our experiences, they are learning it secondhand: We tell what happened; we don't recreate it in words. We add our thoughts, our analysis, describe our reaction.

The fictional illusion

In fiction, the writer's task is to create the illusion of a firsthand experience. This is the rendering of a scene that unfolds before readers' eyes as if they were there. It is a bit of magic, a tour de force that transforms black marks on a page into vivid settings, peopled by living characters caught up in a web of relationships and action. In fiction, "getting the idea across" is the enemy of that experiential illusion. Readers don't want an abstract idea; they want reality. That is the writer's challenge.

Writers often report that they watch the scene taking place in their mind's eye like a movie, and write it down. If only this were so! All too often, by the time this "movie" gets on the page, it is visually static; having scene after scene with characters talking about something exciting that happened offstage, or interminable close-ups of the main character's face with a voice-over narrating her thoughts about the off-stage event, would never hold an audience's attention.

The challenge is to write as if you're watching a movie unfold before you, *with the sound turned off.* Write as if you cannot use exposition or interior monologue; these have their place, but your writing will be stronger if you do not rely on them to create the story. Explanations cannot create the living dream that will capture your reader's imagination. From the action, setting, and body language, the reader should be able to grasp what's happening and feel the emotional impact of the scene. If you can't "turn the sound off" in your fictional narrative and have the visualized elements carry the scene, then those elements are not strong enough.

Readers want to be there

A key rule for writing a successful novel flows immediately from this discipline. You have to show events happening in front of the reader. This means putting the major scenes, the exciting scenes, the revealing scenes, the love scenes, the violent scenes—the difficult-to-write scenes—in your novel. To enlist the reader's imagination, you must have the courage to imagine scenes far outside your own experience. That is the challenge and reward of being a fiction writer.

I have read many unpublished manuscripts of murder mysteries by beginning writers in which the discovery of the body occurs offstage, the arrival of the police occurs offstage, the quarrels between characters take place offstage. The detective is kept busy hearing about all this in snappy dialogue from colorful characters. But it isn't enough. Readers want to hear, see, smell, taste and touch it themselves. They want to see more than just people talking, no matter how witty or belligerent they are.

Dramatize your ideas

The writer must show the reader many things, some concrete, some conceptual. Use your imagination to dramatize the concepts, giving them outward form in behavior, gesture, and setting so that the character's inner feelings can be rendered as graphically as the shape of his nose. Not only do you show where the characters are, and how they

look, but you show who they are, what they are feeling, how they relate
to other people, using all the tools available: setting, dialogue, viewpoint, voice, stage action, plot, sentence structure, and even word
choice.

"Show, don't tell" means that you never put your ideas about the
character on the page; those belong in your note file. You put down
exactly the right information to give your readers the experience, so
they come to the idea themselves. For example, you don't write, "She
was a beautiful woman." That is an idea. It could apply to a million
women, all different. The reader doesn't know what to imagine.

You don't write, "She was a tall, gorgeous blond." That is a generic
description, lacking the uniqueness of life. Clichés are by definition
ideas worn thin from overuse, a shorthand that replaces imagination.
No matter how vivid a cliché may seem, it will not evoke anything fresh
or personal in the readers' mind.

Show your blond with spare, powerful details of action, setting, and
body language. If your details are well chosen, the reader will fill in the
entire picture and visualize her as a specific, living woman, and see her
beauty and feel its impact.

Here is the readers' first look at the model, Candy Svenson, in my
African mystery, *Deadly Safari*:

> The staff were craning their necks to peer past the dining tent. I turned to
> see what they were staring at.
> Candy Svenson emerged from her afternoon nap. She stood framed by the
> tent awning. A mane of tawny hair stood out wildly from her head. A yellow
> robe with enormous padded shoulders and bird tracks all over it hung open
> and revealed a skintight green satin nightgown underneath. She stepped for-
> ward and stretched languorously.

There are only two sentences actually describing Candy's mane of
hair and tight satin nightgown. The rest shows her in action, and the
effect she has on the male staff, thus creating a strong impression in the
reader's mind of a striking, unrestrained, sensual woman who likes to
attract attention.

Notice I left almost everything to the reader's own imagination: the
shape of Candy's features, the color of her eyes, the shape of her figure,
whether voluptuous or willowy. Is her skin soft and yielding, or smooth
and muscular? I don't say, but my reader knows. The reader will fill in

all those details with her own imagination's lexicon of a sexy, beautiful woman, more vivid and convincing than any tracing of Candy's nose and breasts and skin that I could do. Each reader will have created her own Candy, but they will all have the essential elements necessary for the story.

The five rules of effective rendering

How do you know what details to select? Here are five basic rules: *Do not describe the obvious*; *visualize the scene through your viewpoint character*; *choose details that are unique in time and place*; *appeal to the five senses*; and *select details that evoke emotion*.

Extended description calls attention to the writing, thus blurring the reader's illusion of simply being there. Control the urge to write long blocks of description. Readers may enjoy that in Jane Austen, but they will skip over such paragraphs in a contemporary book. The solution: Work description into sentences involving stage action, plot or characterization. Make every word work triple time.

Effective details don't state the obvious. You can't create the illusion of a specific beach, or the feeling of being at the beach, by saying the sky was blue with puffy white clouds, and there were seagulls. When you don't demand anything of your own imagination, you won't enlist the reader's capacity for fantasy, either. Such a commonplace description doesn't set off personal associations or sense impressions to give life to this particular imaginary beach. It is an abstraction of a beach, in no place and no time, and it will never seem real.

The second rule is to see the scene through your narrator's eyes and attitude. Not all summer days are alike, and they are not the same to all people, or even to the same person at different moments. What would your point of view character notice, given his or her personality and what is happening in the story? The actual words you choose will have to be in your character's voice, that is, using the vocabulary, sentence structure, and pacing that suit your character's identity. What your character will notice on a particular sunny day will depend on her frame of mind, and will communicate her feelings to the reader. It must be congruent with both plot and character.

Here is my heroine Jazz as she radios in the discovery of the murdered body of her friend. I don't say Jazz is terribly upset. I describe

sunlight and two birds. Those concrete details enable the reader to visualize Jazz as a physical being at a particular time and place, feeling a
burden of pain and horror:

> I called in and gave detailed instructions on how to find Emmet's camp.
> The sun came in through the open roof hatch and fell in a burning patch on
> my back. I could feel sweat trickling between my shoulder blades. . . .A
> shadow passed over me, then another, bird-swift. Two vultures fell from the
> sky. They tipped their wings from side to side to hasten their descent, greedy
> to share in the possible spoils.

Notice I did not explain that a Land Rover has a roof hatch. Respect
readers' ability to construct the image of something they are familiar
with, like car sun roofs. I focus on the sense impression of the sun
burning her back and sweat trickling down her skin. This is not a
friendly, happy sun, because Jazz is feeling the oppression and hostility
of the world at that moment. Appealing to the five senses makes the
idea of a hot African sun take on an oppressive physical reality.

I don't state the idea that vultures began to gather. I help the reader
see them from Jazz's perspective, and with her careful observation of
animals: She feels the shadow, sees how vultures tip their wings to fall
to earth as quickly as possible, because as a safari guide, she is a person
who notices such things. Readers visualize and recoil from the greedy
vultures, and I leave the rest to their imagination.

Anytime you anchor your reader in a unique moment in time, you are
recreating the experience of real life. Here's a sunny morning later in
the book, when Jazz is in a very different mood. I don't need to mention
the sun for the reader to imagine it and feel in a sunny frame of mind.
The sun is indicated by the detail of the golden grass, anchored in the
specificity of Kenya's dry season. Again, there is a bird, not generic,
but a particular one, standing too close to the road:

> Once I set off, my spirits rose. I love driving by myself. We were nearing
> the end of the dry season, and the grass was sere, straw white and pale gold.
> A yellow-billed stork stood stiff and unmoving inches from the car as I
> whisked by. His gaudy yellow bill was topped with a band of bright red
> across his face, and I couldn't help but smile at such a cheerful sight.

Through describing Jazz driving past grass and a bird, I have given
the reader a setting so vivid they feel the wind of the car, feel the

vastness of Africa, feel themselves smile inwardly. I have also shown the reader Jazz's mood, her intimate observation of wildlife and the seasons, a sense of her natural vitality and her independence. Concepts (It was a sunny day. Jazz cheered up because she likes to drive. The grass was yellow. She saw a stork.) tend to be unidimensional, while living details mimic the rich, multi-layered experience of reality.

The importance of accuracy

Accuracy is absolutely essential for illusion. You probably have never found a corpse, but if you describe the discovery of a murder victim with the authority of accurate sights, sounds, smells, and plausible behavior, the reader will readily follow along. If you count on your readers not knowing anything relevant to a crime scene themselves and make it all up, you will lose readers who *do* know something about the topic—doctors, lawyers, cops. Multiply this effect through all the scenes in your book, all the areas of in-depth knowledge you touch on, and that "accuracy doesn't matter" will lose you a lot of readers.

For example, like millions of other Americans, I am an avid gardener. If your hero is walking up the steps to his beloved's house in Boston, humming a tune and stopping to sniff April's roses, I will not be smelling roses with him. Nor will I be enjoying his romantic mood, as I was a moment before. That "April's rose" has popped me right out of the story. Instead of being caught up in the fictional illusion, I am aware of the ignorant author, who doesn't know that April in Boston gives us daffodils, or maybe a doorstep container of pansies. I know that roses don't arrive till June, and are the promise of summer, not heralds of spring. In other words, a single word of careless, inaccurate writing has broken the illusion for countless readers.

Do I have to do research on every single statement? the beginner wails. Obviously that's both impractical and death to the imagination. What is called for is respecting what you know and what you don't. If you don't know about the progression of bloom through the seasons, then don't use flowers to convey the ardor of spring.

It is better to choose a detail you personally know: It will not only be accurate, it will have the lifelike quality of uniqueness and specificity. Perhaps the roses you're thinking of actually are a sign of spring, in the person of a flower vendor who appears in April at the top of the subway stairs: Put the vendor in the book, and it will come to life, instead of the phony garden roses that killed the scene.

If you need to be specific about something outside your experience—as in the make of a gun at the scene of the crime—then some research is called for. Looking up guns in a book will do, but if you make the effort to go to a shop and handle actual handguns, or even better, go to a range and do some shooting, your imaginary gun will become far more convincing. You will not only learn the proper make, size, and so on, you will have the heft of it in your hand, the smell in your nostrils, your inner sensations of holding or shooting a gun.

In some mystery novels, the kind of gun used is not terribly important, and you can get away with vagueness, respecting the cardinal rule of not stating anything that's actually false. But if you're writing a tough private eye tale in which your main character would know and care about firearms, then you must educate yourself so you can ground your fantasies in reality.

Fiction allows us to transcend our lonely individuality and glimpse the world through another's eyes. The author gives the gift of an imagined world. Readers can receive the gift only if they join in with their imagination to realize that world. The tools of this magic are prosaic elements of the writing craft: point of view, dialogue, action, description, well-written prose, research. Readers want to discover your imagined world. Do your job, and they will do the rest.

❑ 25

STORYTELLING, OLD AND NEW

BY ELIZABETH SPENCER

BEING A SOUTHERNER, A MISSISSIPPIAN, HAD A GOOD DEAL TO DO, I now believe, with my ever having started to write at all, though I did not have any notion about this at the time it all began. Having had stories read to me and having listened to them being told aloud since I could understand speech, I began quite naturally as soon as I could write to fashion stories of my own. I now can see that my kind of part-country, part-small-town Southerners *believed* in stories and still remain, in my experience, unique in this regard. They believed, that is, in events and the people concerned in them, both from the near and distant past, and paid attention to getting things straight, a habit which alone can give true dignity to character, for it defeats the snap judgment, the easy answer, the label and the smear. Bible stories, thus, which were heard at home and in church, were taken literally, and though the Greek and Roman myths that were read aloud to me, along with Arthurian legend and many others, were described as "just" stories, the distinction was one I found easy to escape; maybe I did not want to make it. And we heard oral stories, too: Civil War accounts and tragic things, some relating to people we could actually see uptown almost any day. All ran together in my head at that magic time—I trace any good books I have written, or stories, right back to them.

Starting at the other end of things, however, is what the writer who daily faces the blank sheet must do: that is to say, O.K. about childhood, what about now?

From motion to repose

The work of fiction begins for the writer and reader alike, I feel, when the confusing outer show of things can be swept aside, when something happens that gives access to the dangerous secret pulse of life. What is really going on? This is the question that continually tantalizes and

117

excites. For the fiction writer, the way of getting the answer is by telling the story.

Right back to stories. You see how quick it was.

A story is a thing in itself. It has a right to be without making any apology about what it means, or how its politics and religion and pedigree and nationality may be labeled. The name of the writer can be guessed at by the stories he puts down, but the writer is not the story any more than an architect is a building. The events in a true—that is to say, real—story are a complex of many things, inexhaustibly rich, able to be circled around like a statue or made at a touch to create new patterns like a kaleidoscope. Such a story may be absorbed sensually or pondered about reasonably; it may be talked about by friends or strangers in the presence or the absence of the writer. The story should be allowed to take in all its basic wants. It may want discipline, but it may not get it, depending upon how greedy it is or how obsessed the writer is about it. A story has the curious, twofold quality of seeming all in motion and at times even in upheaval while it is being told, but when finished, of having reached its natural confines and attained repose. Many times characters seem to have life outside the story in which they engage. So much the better; the story will not question this.

A silent magnetism

Each story I have written commenced in a moment, usually unforeseen, when out of some puzzlement, bewilderment, or wonder, some response to actual happening, my total imagination was drawn up out of itself; a silent magnetism, without my willing it, had taken charge. What was it all about? It is just as well for the writer to pause here and consider. Not that the writer will take the imprint, literally, of people and event—though for some writers the main worry falls here. To me, it is rather the power of the story that one should be warned about: Don't enter that lion's cage without knowing about lions. For the writer enters alone. He may be eaten up, or mauled, or decide to get the hell out of there, but even if all goes splendidly and ends in fine form, the person who comes out is not the same one who went in.

Anyone who takes stories as an essential part of life is only recognizing the obvious. Religion, love, psychiatry, families, nations, wars and history have all become deeply mixed up with stories and so find no way to shed them without violating or even destroying their own natures. Every human being is deeply involved with at least one story—his own. (The Southern tendency to get involved with family stories has accounted for the larger part of Southern fiction—if we add to this hunting stories and war stories, then we have just about accounted for all of it.) The present faint-hearted tone that some critics now adopt when discussing the future of fiction is surprising, for stories, being part of the primal nature of human expression, are in one way or another going to continue to be told. What disturbs us all, I believe, is the debasement of the story into something mass-made, machine-tooled, slick and false. (The lion was stuffed or drugged or doctored some way.) At its highest level, a story is a free art form, daring to explore and risk, to claim that it recognizes truth . . . and that even when inventive, what it imagines is, in terms it can splendidly determine, true.

A common note

At a level short of this highest fiction, but shared by it, many group stories exist, the bulk of which never get written down. They are told every day, repeated, embellished, continued, or allowed to die, and some are better than others; inventive and factual at once, both commonplace and myth-like, they grow among humanity like mistletoe in oaks. They are much better than average TV fare, and anyone who wants to write should start collecting everyday accounts that are passed about offices, campuses, neighborhoods, or within family situations, noticing whatever there is to be found of humor and terror, character, achievement, failure, triumph, tragedy, irony and delight. The modern theme of self-exploration with heavy emphasis on the private sexual nature and fantasy has been done to the point of weariness. Can we think of ourselves again in communion with others, in communities either small, medium or large, which may be torn apart disastrously or find a common note, an accord? One word for it maybe, is love.

□ 26

MATTERS OF FACT:
FICTION WRITERS AS RESEARCHERS

BY SHARON OARD WARNER

A FEW INTERESTING FACTS ON HONEY BEES:

1. Worker bees irritate the queen to prepare her to fly. She has to lose a little weight before she can take to the air.
2. The queen flies only once, going a distance of seven or eight miles so as not to mate with her brothers.
3. Mating occurs in the air, and after the act is completed, the drone dies and falls to the ground. (I could make all sorts of wise cracks here, but I'll refrain.)

This is the first use I've had for a whole legal pad full of notes I took in a beekeeping class a few summers ago. I registered for the class because I intended to write about a beekeeper, and to that end, I took faithful notes. More than two years have passed, and my beekeeper has yet to show himself. I do have firm possession of a radiologist who reads tarot cards, and I'm hoping to give her the beekeeper for a husband. As of this morning, she has yet to embrace him, but I'm optimistic about working it out. I intend to use some of this material on bees, but it's obvious that I'm not going to do all of it justice. If you need a stray bee fact or two, you're welcome to the above. Interesting though these facts are, I doubt that I'll find a place for them.

A few additional facts:

1. Bees don't like carbon dioxide, so when you work with them, be sure to breathe out the side of your mouth. (Try doing that, just to see how it feels.)
2. When a bee stings, she will die, but in the process she'll leave a "mad bee" smell on your skin, a smell that makes other bees want to sting you as well.
3. The mad bee smell is easy to identify: It smells for all the world like bananas with a little solvent mixed in.

Keep your hands off these facts. I can almost guarantee I'll use them sooner or later, and probably sooner. These are the kinds of facts that authenticate character and offer opportunities to advance a plot. They're active facts that carry a sensory charge. Let me show you what I mean: Once the radiologist acquiesces and agrees to be married to the beekeeper, one of the first things he'll do is lumber out to the hives and check on his bees. Maybe he has someone else with him, his daughter Sophie say, and he'll tell her a little about how to handle the combs. Already, I can predict that Sophie will insist on getting stung. She's that sort of girl. And there we have it: the "mad bee" smell all over Sophie, enticing the other bees to sink their stingers into the soft skin of her upper arm and to swarm menacingly about her face. "Get away, Sophie!" her father will yell, wresting the comb from her hands. But Sophie will refuse because she's sixteen and more hormones than good sense.

This one little scene requires more facts than might be readily apparent. The three I've listed will launch the scene, but they won't complete it. Almost immediately, others will be necessary. Without them, the scene will lose steam, and the plot will stall. As it turns out, fiction and fictional characters take their vitality from facts, from real-life detail, which means that writers of fiction are in the business of research. We're fact hoarders—accumulating, sorting, and storing details that give our stories life.

Some of the fact-finding is rather mundane, but research need not be dull. The beekeeping class and my trip to the beekeeper's house to "handle" the bees were recent highlights. (No, I did not get stung while I held the combs, nor did I wear gloves or a veil. Are you impressed? Well, you shouldn't be. These were gentle bees.) I think of this early research as a sort of "grounding" because I use these facts to situate my main characters in their milieu. Where do these people I'm writing about live? In which city, on what street, in this house or that? What do they do for a living? What are their hobbies, besides beekeeping, of course? Their fears? Their joys? To answer these questions, it's necessary to leave the computer and enter the world.

Sometimes, these forays take me only as far as the local library or bookstore. Books, newspapers, and magazines often provide sufficient information. For instance, I recently bought a book called *Beekeeping,* which advertises itself as a "Complete Owner's Manual," all you need to be a beekeeper or to create one. Like everything else, it's not what it claims to be, but it will answer some of my questions. What sort of questions? Well, here's one: To write the scene where stubborn Sophie invites a bee sting, I need to know the season, and the decision can't be arbitrary. From my bee class, I learned that bees winter, a state akin to hibernation, and that wintering lasts longer in certain areas of the country than in others. The farther north you live, the trickier this wintering process can be, but I digress.

And digress again: It's important to know facts, yes, but it's just as important to recognize when enough is enough. Lengthy and in-depth research carries its own liabilities. Think about it. Having spent time, energy and *el dinero* on acquiring precious facts, how likely are you to squander them? Not bloody likely. Which leads perfectly good writers to stuff their narratives with tangential information, just to justify that expensive tome on medieval bedroom practices or the weekend trip to Amarillo for local color. Don't overdo it; that's my advice. I almost quit reading that wonderful novel *Snow Falling on Cedars* for exactly this reason. There's only so much I want to know about fishing boats, and David Guterson tested my patience more than once. (I realize he won the PEN Faulkner and all, but no one is perfect.)

But don't let's go to Puget Sound, beautiful though it is. Let's stay in arid Albuquerque with the beekeeper. He lives right in town with me, in the North Valley, on the other side of the Rio Grande. So we've established place. What about the season? Checking my handy-dandy beekeeping book, I note that by mid-April the hive will be quite active. The desert is blooming, and nectar is plentiful. (Before I write this scene, I'll need to know exactly which plants bloom in April in Albuquerque, because the beekeeper is not only concerned with his insects; he's also concerned with their food sources. Lumbering out to check the hive, he'll be thinking about goldenrod, prickly pear, and Palmer lupine.) By April, the old bees that wintered over are dying off, and the young bees are taking their place. The brood nest will have swelled to six to eight combs, providing the beekeeper with something to check. And I'm guessing that the young bees are more likely to sting. I'll have to check to make sure, but if they're anything like teenage Sophie, they're hotheaded and impulsive.

To tell the truth, Sophie is the real subject of my book, and I'll let you in on a secret not even her parents know. Sophie's pregnant. Now

I've been pregnant, twice actually, so I don't need to research the various stages of pregnancy. I remember them all too well. But I've never been pregnant as a teenager, and certainly not as a teenager in 1998, and this does require some investigation. Before I began to work on this project—so far, I've written two short stories on these characters, and the stories themselves are a kind of research, a way of developing characters and familiarizing myself with the material—I read *Reviving Ophelia: Saving the Selves of Adolescent Girls.* The author, Mary Pipher, is a clinical psychologist in private practice in Lincoln, Nebraska. I also went to a reading and talk Ms. Pipher gave at a local bookstore, which proved helpful in a larger sense. It provided context and some sense of urgency. Ms. Pipher is very concerned about plight of teenage girls in the 1990s.

> Girls know they are losing themselves. One girl said, "Everything good in me died in junior high." Wholeness is shattered by the chaos of adolescence. Girls become fragments, their selves split into mysterious contradictions. They are sensitive and tenderhearted, mean and competitive, superficial and idealistic. They are confident in the morning, and overwhelmed with anxiety by nightfall. They rush through their days with wild energy and then collapse into lethargy. They try on new roles every week—this week the good student, next week the delinquent, and the next, the artist. . . . Much of their behavior is unreadable. Their problems are complicated and metaphorical—eating disorders, school phobias, and self-inflicted injuries. I need to ask again and again in a dozen different ways, "What are you trying to tell me?"

This is precisely the question I'm asking of Sophie, again and again, and the answers she provides will do much to shape the material for the novel. Thus, *Reviving Ophelia* provides me with a necessary cultural perspective, one I will certainly find useful, but this "grounding" I'm talking about is something more elemental. It's a matter of territory, of the actual earth on which a character walks.

So where does Sophie walk? Well, she walks around high school for one thing. Sophie goes to Valley High School in Albuquerque, which is, not so coincidentally, where my son goes to school as well. My son Corey is a sophomore, and Sophie is a senior, so it's not likely they'll run into one another, which is just as well because Sophie is not, as mothers say, a "good influence." She's got troubles, that girl. Still, my son's attendance at Valley is as useful to me as Ms. Pipher's book. Maybe more useful. I go to the high school frequently, and whenever I do, I take note of the place itself and of the kids who spend their days there.

Valley is one of the oldest high schools in Albuquerque. From all appearances, the main buildings date from the fifties. The campus has been maintained over the years, but in piecemeal fashion: In "senior circle," new picnic tables hunker up to crumbling cement benches. The library is now labeled the Media Center, but it houses a modest collection of moldy-looking books, not a computer in plain sight. The carpet in the Media Center is a horrible shade of puke green, and appears to have been laid down in the late sixties or early seventies when all the adults went temporarily color blind. I was around then, but still coming of age, and so I don't have to take responsibility for that carpet. At the last meeting of the Parent's Advisory Council—yes, I'm a member— the principal, a gracious and energetic man named Toby Herrera, voiced his hope that the carpet would soon be replaced. We all nodded vigorously and tried not to look down.

At an earlier meeting this year, Mr. Herrera happened to mention that Albuquerque has a high school specifically designed for pregnant teens. (Is this a step forward or backward? I can't decide.) The school is called New Futures, and the facility includes counseling for new and expectant mothers as well as on-site day care. When Mr. Herrera mentioned this school, I thought of Sophie, for whom New Futures will be an option, and I also thought of my own high-school career, when the girls who got pregnant had no options whatsoever. By and large, they did not have abortions, unless they crossed the border into Mexico—we're talking pre-Roe vs. Wade here—and they did not stay in school. What they did do, I suppose, was to get married, if the boy in question had the presence of mind or the generosity to propose, or else they slipped away to a home for unwed mothers in Fort Worth. I used to hear girls whisper about that place. It might have been, might still be, a humane and cheerful alternative to living at home or jumping off a cliff; I don't know. But at the time, it seemed a sort of prison where everything was stripped away, first your identity, your family and your friends, and finally, your baby, as well.

But Sophie lives in a different world, and it's one I need to know about. As Mr. Herrera was quick to point out, pregnant girls can choose to go to school at New Futures or they can stay at their home school. In other words, Sophie can continue to attend Valley, and knowing Sophie,

I imagine that's what she'll do. Of course, that decision will simplify my research tasks a bit because it means I won't have to scout out New Futures. One of the most important aspects of this "grounding" is to gain a firm sense of place, and here we're talking about everything from the time period to the city to the weather.

Naturally, Sophie blames her several bee stings on Daddy, then runs sobbing into the house. Ahh, yes, the house. What color is the back door Sophie slams behind her? And is her room at the front of the house or the back? For me, identifying home is one of the most important early research tasks. Before I can accomplish much in the way of characterization and plot, I must know where my characters live, and by this, I mean a particular house with particular windows that look out on particular plants and alleys and streets. Imagining the house does not work for me. It's too ephemeral—made-up people in a made-up house. The walls begin to waver and shift before my eyes, the kitchen to slide from one end of the house to the other, the garage to attach then unattach. Just where did I put that third bedroom, I wonder, and what was on the walls? Sooner or later, the occupants feel a tremor beneath their feet; they're threatened with imaginary collapse. Everything has its limits, you see, my imagination included.

So where to find a real house? My own doesn't work. I live there, my husband and children live there. We don't have room for a fictional family, and besides, they're bound to have entirely different tastes from mine. They're better housekeepers; they find time to dust thoroughly and not just swipe at the surfaces of things. Or maybe they're worse: Maybe pet hair gathers in the corners of the rooms, and dirty plates and coffee cups collect beside the bed and on top of the toilet tank. What I need, you see, is somebody else's home, full of furniture and magazines and knick knacks, but without occupants. A ready-made set.

For my first novel, I had a piece of luck. My family was in Austin, Texas, for the holidays, which is where the novel takes place, and my husband and I spent New Year's Eve with a friend who just happened to be house-sitting for an entire year. So there we were, drinking a little wine and listening to The Gypsy Kings, my husband and his friend Mark discussing, yawn, the University of Texas basketball team. An hour passed, and they moved on to the Dallas Cowboys. To keep from nodding off, I got up and had a look around. I took note of the flamingoes in the study, a whole motley crew of flamingoes—plastic ones, metal ones, and a wooden flamingo that swung from the ceiling. I puzzled over a small black and white TV on the counter in the bathroom, and the red tile floor in the kitchen. I peered out the bedroom windows and weighed myself on the scales. Nosy, you say. Yes, you're absolutely right, but I didn't open the medicine chest or any of the drawers. I didn't try on clothes, like the main character in Raymond Carver's story, "Neighbors." I just made a leisurely stroll around the premises. Later, when the characters in my first novel took up residence in this house, I had only to turn on The Gypsy Kings to bring it all back. Perfect.

For the second novel, I had to take action. No gift houses this time around. So I "feigned" and pretended to be a potential home buyer. Dragging my husband along to make it look good, I scouted several houses. I had ideas about where the beekeeper and his family would live. For one thing, I wanted them to reside in the North Valley, because I like it there, and because Sophie is already enrolled at Valley High School. She has friends there. We wouldn't want to move her at this late date. And the beekeeper requires land with flowering plants around his house, as well as a nearby water source. Bees have to drink.

Beforehand, I studied newspaper ads, choosing houses for description, location, price, and size. All these houses were occupied and previously owned. In each case, a real estate person was hosting an open house, so no one would be inconvenienced. The first houses we saw were all wrong. In a strange turn of events, we happened to go to a house which was the scene of a terrible murder, a story that had been on the news and in the papers for weeks, a death befitting a Dostoevsky novel. I won't go into details, as they will plunge you into despair. The real estate agent, who was clearly ill at ease, referred to the crime obliquely, mentioning it to us in order to be "up front." He'd been ordered by the court to sell the house, he said. What could he do? Indeed, I thought. His situation deserved its own novel. Before, the house had seemed dreary, broken up in odd ways, old and neglected. But afterwards, it seemed more than gloomy; it seemed downright haunted. Naturally, my husband and I hightailed it out of there, retreating to the car where we sat in shock for a few minutes before pulling slowly away, leaving the real estate agent to pace back and forth in the family room, an honest man who would surely be trapped in this tragic house for countless Sundays to come.

Quite naturally, we were tempted to abandon house hunting, for that day anyway, but we decided to forge on, and now I'm glad we did. The third house was perfect, or close to perfect, more expensive than the house I imagined for Sophie and her parents, but otherwise ideal. I took away a real estate brochure that I covered with notes. Here's the realtor's description: "This wonderful custom adobe home offers a quiet private retreat with views, Northern New Mexico decor, and room for horses." Or bees, lots of bees. The house is situated on 1.3 acres. It's a territorial style home with a pitched metal roof, a long front porch, brick floors and window ledges, vigas, latillas, and tile accents. (Live in Albuquerque for a few years, and you'll be able to sling these terms, too.) The house is shaped in an L; one wing is eighteen years old, the other only seven, but it was constructed to look old. The upstairs windows offer a view of the bosque, which is Spanish for woods. Whenever you see the bosque, you know the river is close by. Beyond the bosque, two inactive volcanoes rise like the humps of a camel's back. You want to move there, right? So did I, but I didn't have an extra $332,500. Yep, that was the asking price.

Though I can't have the house in reality, I've taken possession of it in my imagination. Sophie and her parents live there, and in order to give the family the financial wherewithal to afford this little hacienda in the midst of the city, I gave the mother, Peggy, a career that would bring in the big bucks, or at least the medium-sized bucks. Hence, her job as a radiologist. Actually, my reasons for making her a radiologist are a bit more complicated. I imagine Peggy to be a woman of extraordinary insight, someone who can see into people, very nearly a psychic.

Not surprisingly, Peggy's profession and her interest in tarot cards were suggested to me by some of the paraphernalia I noted in the house. The back upstairs bedroom was occupied by a young woman named Zoe (test papers in evidence), whose interests in Buddhism and acupuncture were also on display. An altar stood at one end of the room, and among the books on Zoe's desk was *The Book of Shiatsu* as well as a plastic body model for both the meridianal and extraordinary points. I made notes quickly because my husband insisted we not linger. He had compunctions about my nosiness, but I maintain that I did no one any harm, and again, I only looked at the things that were out in the open. Already, I've altered the particulars. Peggy is not a Buddhist, nor does she do acupuncture. But she does concern herself with what can't be seen on the surface, and it was Zoe's room that put this idea in my head. Thank you, Zoe.

But nothing comes free. I know about tarot cards because I took a class when I was seventeen and intent on the future. I still have the cards and the books. But here's a piece of research I have yet to do. I have to learn about the daily life of a radiologist: hours, tasks, and so forth. Having been to one fairly recently, I have a general sense of what radiologists do, but I need to know a great deal more. Already, I've lined up a lunch date with an acquaintance who used to work for a group of radiologists. And I have library sources. That won't be enough, of course, but it will get me started. The task is to find out how radiologists *think,* how they integrate their work in their day to day lives. Because radiologists aren't just radiologists at work. Like the rest of us, they carry their work away with them, and use it to understand the world.

The same is true for writers, of course, and for visual artists, photographers, assistant principals, day care workers, police officers, and doctors. A few years back, I asked my gynecologist so many questions about abortion that he quipped I could write off the visit as research, which, not so coincidentally, is exactly what it was.

Fiction writers are researchers. We can't help it. It's part and parcel of who we are. In restaurants, we crane our heads to listen to conversations taking place around us; we note accents and idiosyncratic speech patterns. At the mall, we stare at the strangers milling about, all of them people with homes to go to, children to care for, lives to lead. They have secrets these strangers, and we imagine what they are. It turns out that research isn't a distinct process, something with a beginning and end. It's ongoing, part and parcel of our lives. It is, in some sense, *our* secret.

One more interesting bee fact:

> When working with bees, wear white or light-colored clothing. Bees are attracted to red and black.

They're bees, you see. They can't help it.

❑ 27

WRITING ABOUT YOUR OWN BACKYARD

BY SHELBY HEARON

WE'RE TOLD TO WRITE ABOUT WHAT WE KNOW. BUT OFTEN IT IS DIFFI-cult to write about a place you know too well, a place that was home to you. I lived in this house, we say, on this street, and my parents were, well, my parents. My conclusion, after a recent trip back to Austin, Texas, attempting to write about a house and town I lived in for so many years, is that we have to distinguish what we know from what our characters know.

For example, suppose you go back to the hillside where you used to sit with your high scool love (long since gone), and you find it now the site of one of a cluster of overpriced, oversized homes with a view. In this case, you don't want to write about How Things Have Changed or Aren't Developers Awful.

You want your early memory to be *something your character doesn't know and learns about.* Say she's living in that fine home, trying to adjust to being on the rich side of town looking down on where she used to live, and she finds out that years ago someone in the story used to sit on that very slope in her garden, when there wasn't a home in sight, and dream about the future. Who was the dreamer? Her mother? The girl in high school who took her beau? Her husband, with someone that he can't forget? In any case, you are letting your character learn something you already know. You are sharing with the reader the fresh-ness of her discovery, her glimpse at the hope, the scent in the air, the longing, that you once experienced. So, *even though you know it al-ready, your character doesn't.*

Here's a real example from my past, which I used in my novel *Ella in Bloom.* Years ago, after a divorce, I rented an apartment in Austin that backed onto a springed stream called Barton Creek. Right outside the sliding glass doors of my otherwise ordinary, tiny efficiency, was a deck high in the treetops, with the sound of the rushing stream down below. I loved the place, and it was there I experienced the joy of living alone for the first time in my life. So, in the book, my narrator does not know there are apartments now built on what was once just a grassy bluff. She ends up there quite by accident; she learns about the place I knew so well.

Conversely, the other way you can bring to life a place almost too familiar to begin to write about, is by discovering *something you don't know but your character does*. Because she has to know everything about this topic/activity/locale, and you don't know anything, you have to research it in order to give your character authentic details and feelings concerning it.

The Austin I lived in and reared my children in was a country-music-loving community centered around the University of Texas and the state Capitol. Now, however, Austin is primarily a high-tech city, a silicon valley. There are nine hundred computer companies in the city and abutting townships. All this part of the larger Austin area is unknown to me, and, therefore, has to be a part of the lives of some of my characters; and as they live and work in that part of the county, the reader (and I!) learn about it, too.

I'll give an example. Poring over the newest *Texas Almanac* (a most marvelous fact-filled source), I noticed that Pflugerville, which I recall as a tiny German wide-spot-in-the-road with a good bakery and about 150 people, had become a town of 15,000, many of whom worked for Dell. Since this looked like a good, concrete, manageable place to start learning (you can't start with something large and vague like "the computer industry"), I subscribed to the local newspaper—who could resist receiving the weekly *Pflugerville Pflag?*—to learn about the news and schools and real estate in the language of the people who lived there. I also hung around a realty office, ate a few wonderful plates of barbeque, took a roll of film, and, finally, placed my narrator's boyfriend *in a neighborhood new to me, but not to him*.

Sometimes what helps you bring a familiar place to life is finding out what new things people do to make a living; changes in economics are as much a part of conveying a sense of place as changes in population or rainfall. Again, perusing the *Texas Almanac*—in this case to refresh my memory about the towns and waterways and precipitation levels of some of the counties where my people's people were from—I happened upon an item under agribusiness: raises *ratites*. A word I'd never even heard before. The term refers to birds that can't fly (resist that metaphor!), in other words, ostriches and emus. Emus! A new world.

I called the Texas Fish, Game and Wildlife Commission and found out that emus were considered livestock, not game. When I called the Extension Division of Texas A & M, they referred me to a branch office in Ector County (home of the University of Texas, Permian Basin). But it wasn't the reams of material that these agreeable people sent that went into the story, but their language, their responses. I found there was a "Save the Emus" group that considered emus an endangered species; that the people who raised them for food thought them "nothing but overgrown chickens"; that the ranchers who bred them to tan for leather raged with frustration because they needed the tanned leather to make the chaps and gauntlets to protect them against the emus' slashing claws. As is usually the case with "place setting" details, not a lot of this information got into the text, but, then, when the inevitable Texas drought hit, the effect of the baking dry skies was made more concrete, more specific. The emus all had to be slaughtered along with the cattle.

There is a third case you should consider in writing about your own backyard: When you know the place and people and your character needs to know also, you make this distinction: *You knew them as they were; your character knows them as they might have been.* My parents' home, once mine, sprawling, in disrepair—with its secret stairway from the attic, its oversized closets that let you slip into other rooms from the back, its sixty-foot-long screened porch and squirrels in the crawlspace—now has new owners. It has a new address, fronting on a side street, a new glassed-in porch, a smart structural face-lift, upscale interiors. I wanted to use that house in my novel, to fix it on the page much as you might fix a photo in an album, a bee in amber. But I did not put the remembered house or my real remembered parents in the story, rather, I put the couple they might have been, the home they might have furnished. The old father, an historian, always at his desk writing his own past, is not my daddy, a geologist with a non-human view of time; the mother, always in her garden watching her winged and four-legged visitors, living only in the present, is not my mama, whose mind was focused on her and the world's troubled past.

Sometimes you write about your own home place to recover it, sometimes to redress it, sometimes merely to recall it. But in any case, such

a remembrance of things past is a dialogue between you and your storyteller. Either you introduce her to your homesickness for that hillside
where you used to sit with your love under the stars, or she takes you
to a country café, where, over a plate of green-mesquite smoked ribs,
she tells you what's new in your own backyard.

❏ 28

THE MANY HATS OF A
FICTION WRITER

BY MADELEINE COSTIGAN

AS A FICTION WRITER TODAY, YOU WEAR MANY HATS. YOU'RE YOUR own boss, your own editor, and probably your own agent. When you play so many roles how do you keep them all in balance? It isn't easy, but it can be done.

1. Be a realistic boss.

You have to take yourself seriously as a writer before you can expect anyone else to take you seriously. Establish professional work habits early on, and believe in yourself enough to stick to them. Even if your office is a corner of the basement or an alcove under the eaves, do everything you can to make it as user-friendly as possible. Something wonderful is happening here.

Write every day. The more you write, the more fluent your writing will become. In the beginning you may be writing around what you want to say instead of getting to the core. Keep writing. The route may be circuitous but after you zero in on what you truly want to say, you'll see that during all those false starts and detoured storylines, you weren't wasting time, as you feared. You were developing as a writer, developing a discerning eye and ear, finding your own voice, learning to respect self-imposed deadlines.

You may be the only person who knows you're working when you're doing what your grandmother would call woolgathering, but who else needs to know? Alice Munro says that when her family sees her staring at the wall, she tells them she's thinking, even though she knows she's somewhere between thinking and a trancelike state. Toni Morrison refers to entering a space she can only call nonsecular. Every writer has such moments of reaching deeper and deeper levels of concentration, and whatever label you use to describe what you're doing, you soon learn that during such moments answers frequently come to nagging problems that days of writing won't solve. That's part of the mystery of writing fiction.

Some days you may become so immersed in your work that you lose all sense of time; there are those who might say all sense. For some writers the best course is to work until the vein is exhausted. Ernest Hemingway liked to stop when he knew what was going to happen next. Choose the method that suits you.

Other days nothing you write seems to work. Here's where keeping a notebook can be useful. Not only does it get you into the habit of writing every day, but while browsing through it you may come across a scene written at random, or a snatch of conversation that regenerates your enthusiasm for the work-in-progress, and changes your perspective. For me, it has always been fascinating to see how unrelated bits and pieces can meld to form a symmetrical whole.

In the beginning, you really need professional reaction to your work, but that's when it's most difficult to get. A plain rejection slip tells you nothing. If possible, join a local writers' group or go to a writers' conference. It can be most illuminating to listen to other writers discuss your work, and, if you've done your homework, probably not nearly so painful as you fear. The company of other writers can be wonderfully sustaining and exhilarating throughout your writing life.

2. Be a tough editor.

The first time you submit a story to a magazine you're competing with professionals. Most new writers send work out too soon. The hope is that it will quickly find a home at a top magazine. When instead, it meets with rejection, the writer may easily become discouraged. It may be that what you had hoped was a well-turned short story is actually a first draft. While a first draft is not finished work, it is tangible, concrete, and best of all, something to revise. Sidney Sheldon says he writes as many as a dozen drafts.

Take your story scene by scene and put it to the test: Does each scene unfold naturally, move the story forward? If a scene is static, work on it until it crystallizes. One way to do this may be to get your characters talking.

Or it may be that a scene is unnecessary. What you really need is a smooth transition. Sometimes beginning writers include a scene because they don't know how to get a character from here to there without explaining. When you find yourself having difficulty getting a character from the telephone to the agreed-upon meeting, you might well consider skipping the interim scene.

Is your opening compelling? If you were reading a story while standing at the airport magazine rack, waiting for your plane to be called, would you be unable to put the magazine back after reading only the first few lines? Toni Morrison has said that her favorite opening line is from *Tar Baby: He thought he was safe.* He isn't safe. Why isn't he? With five short words Toni Morrison has involved the reader in her character's dilemma.

Is your language fresh? Or cliché bound?

Reading fine writing is a good way to develop your ear for the precise word. What a difference if instead of writing, *They persevered in their conversation,* Jane Austen had chosen a different verb.

Is your setting an integral part of the story? Is it reader oriented? Offer a few telling details and the reader will extrapolate. In a story that takes place in a school building, mentioning the scarred, pitted lockers or the smell of linseed oil may be enough to suggest authenticity. In a different school, the sight of students hunched at computer terminals or passing through metal detectors might do it.

Are your characters real? Does your reader know and care about them? Many writers work with the contrast between a character's thoughts and words to reveal a character. When I was writing "A Small But Perfect Crime," I used this technique. Harold Burgoyne, principal of Howell Middle School has discovered that Charlie Patch, son of Burgoyne's cardiologist, has been vandalizing the school. The following conversation takes place between Burgoyne and Karl Webb, a teacher at the school:

> "Fraley is steamed over the vandalism," Burgoyne said. "It's ruining our image."
> Image was the stuff of life to Burgoyne. "Vandalism can't be tolerated," Karl said, waiting for Burgoyne to show his hand.
> "I've never considered Charlie to be Howell Middle School material," Burgoyne continued. "We've got to finesse this one, Webb. Sending Charlie to the youth center would be a grave mistake. Keeping him here is not in the best interest of Howell." Burgoyne's watery blue eyes gave Karl a searching look. "You know how dedicated I am to this school's best interest?"
> "Indeed." To himself, Karl called the language he spoke to Burgoyne, 'pedageese.'

Burgoyne leaned forward, his hands taut. "Charlie Patch is a year older than his classmates. It would be helpful to all concerned if two of his teachers recommended that Charlie be skipped into Jefferson High, where it won't be quite so easy for him to dominate the other students. I'm counting on your recommendation, Webb, and Ira Carpenter's as well."

"Brilliant," Karl said.

Does your dialogue ring true? It may be that your character says what a real person would say in a given situation, but that isn't a sufficient test for good dialogue. True, your dialogue should create the illusion of real speech, but it should also advance the plot, economically characterize, or evoke an emotional response from the reader. It must also be much shorter than real conversation.

Try listening with even more concentration than you give to talking. You want more than the gist of what you're hearing. Listen for cadence, word order, flavor, figures of speech, all the revelations each of us makes on a daily basis. And then write in your notebook whatever strikes you as useful.

Do you have a good title?

Many editors consider a title to be an editorial decision. They know their readers and what will attract those readers. Sometimes a title has to fit with an illustration, and must be changed because of space limitations. Even though it may be discarded, you still need an intriguing title for your work. It's the first thing the editor sees.

3. Be a tireless agent.

Many major magazines have stopped publishing fiction. Very few literary agents today handle short stories. It's up to you to place your own work.

First, do some research at the library. Read several issues of any magazine you think might find your story suitable. Skimming only one issue can be misleading and cause you to waste time and postage.

List the magazines according to your order of preference, making sure you've chosen the appropriate editor's name from the masthead. What's in a name? Maybe the difference between acceptance and rejection. You don't want to address your manuscript in the generic, or risk mailing it off to the magazine trusting that someone there will route it to the proper person. It's too easy for that someone to whip out a rejection slip and send your story winging back.

Not all magazines, particularly literary journals, are available at the local library or bookstore. Study writers' magazines for information about these and send for sample copies. While literary magazines offer little financial compensation for your work, they are valuable showcases, read by publishers, editors, and agents.

How long should you wait to hear from an editor concerning the fate of your story? I used to advise six weeks, but I now think three months is more realistic. Before a manuscript is accepted it is usually read by several editors. Very few editors can afford to read in the course of the business day; they do most of their manuscript reading after hours.

And yes, there are gradations of rejections. The most disappointing is the plain rejection slip. Even a handwritten note is encouraging.

A signed letter from an editor indicates more interest. And a detailed letter referring to your story's strengths and weaknesses demonstrates thoughtful consideration.

Close, but no cigar, you may think. Think again. You are now being taken seriously as a writer. Several people on the editorial staff have probably read your story, seen its merit, and passed it on to the editor who wrote to you. Editors do not have time to write letters to writers unless they see promise and real talent in the manuscript.

Now it's your turn to accept and reject. If you find more than one editor making the same criticism, take the editors' words to heart and rework the story accordingly. Incorporate the suggestions you find worthwhile. Those that seem irrelevant, file for later review. You can always throw them away after you sell the story. Like a good stew, criticism is best evaluated after it simmers a while.

When an editor expresses an interest in seeing more of your work, respond with a new story in a timely manner. This story may meet with acceptance—which is why it's so very important to work on something new while you're waiting. Which brings us back to being a realistic boss.

❏ 29

THE PLOT THICKENS

BY BARBARA SHAPIRO

SOME WRITERS CAN SIT DOWN AND BEGIN A NOVEL WITHOUT KNOWING where it will end, trusting in the process to bring their story to a successful conclusion. I'm not that trusting. And I'm not that brave. I don't have the guts to begin a book until I know there *is* an end—and a middle, too. I need to have a rough outline that allows me to believe my idea might someday be transformed into a successful novel. Some writers need a working title; I need a working plot.

A substantial segment of the writing community turns its collective nose up at the mere mention of the word "plot"—particularly if that plot is devised before writing has begun. "Plot is not what novels are about," they claim. "Novels are about feelings and characters and ideas. Plot is for TV movies." Novels *are* about feelings and characters and ideas, but novels are, above all else, stories, and it is through the story that the characters' feelings and the author's ideas are revealed. A handy equation is: Story equals plot equals novel. But what exactly *is* a story?

A story is a tale with a beginning, a middle, and an end. It's a quest. Your protagonist goes after something she wants very badly— something she gets, or doesn't get, by the end. Whether it's returning to Kansas (Dorothy in *The Wizard of Oz*) or killing the witch ("Hansel and Gretel"), this journey is the story, the plot, the means by which your characters' strengths and weaknesses are unveiled, his or her lessons learned. It is the trip you and your protagonist and your reader all make together.

All human beings have the same features, yet the magic of the human race is that we all look different. The same holds true for plot. While the specifics of your plot are unique, there is an underlying structure that it shares with other stories—and it is this structure that you can use to develop your working plot.

Human beings have been telling stories and listening to stories as long as there have been human beings, and there is a structure to these stories. Tell the story without the right structure and risk losing your listeners. Find this structure, and your job as a novelist will be easier; you will understand your readers' expectations and be able to meet them. Follow this plot structure and add your own voice, your own words, your own creativity, and you will have a unique novel that works.

Discovering and understanding the underlying structure of the novel will help you develop your working plot even before you begin writing. It will get you moving by assuring you that you are on the right path. In my career, I have used this concept to come up with a number of tricks to help me discover where my novel is going—and to get myself going. These tricks can be translated into four exercises: (1) classical structure; (2) plot statement; (3) the disturbance; and (4) the crisis.

Step 1: Classical structure

There is a long-running argument among writers as to exactly how many different stories there are. Some say there are an infinite number, some say there are 47 or 36 or 103, and others say there is only one. I am a member of the "only one story" school. I believe this one story is the skeleton upon which almost all successful novels are hung—this story *is* the underlying structure. If I can figure out how *my* story hangs on this skeleton, I can begin to move forward. This is how the story goes:

> There once was a woman who had a terrible problem enter her life (*the disturbance*). She decided that she was going to solve/get rid of her problem so she devised a plan (*goal*). But whenever she put this plan into action, everything around her worked against her (*conflicts*) until the problem had grown even worse and she seemed even further then ever from reaching her goal. At this darkest moment (*crisis*), the woman made a decision based on who she was and what she had learned in the story. Through this decision and the resulting action (*climax*), her problem was resolved (*resolution*) in either a positive (*happy ending*) or negative way (*unhappy ending*).

The first step to understanding and using story structure is to break the classic story into its component parts. The key elements are: the disturbance; the goal; the conflicts; the crisis; the climax—the sacrifice and the unconscious need filled from the backstory; and the resolution. Once this is clear to you, then you can transpose these components into your particular story. To accomplish this, ask yourself the following five questions:

What is the disturbance? Some terrible or wonderful or serendipitous event that comes into your protagonist's life, upsets her equilibrium and causes her to develop a goal that propels her through your story. A tornado, for instance.

What is the protagonist's goal? To get out of Oz and return to Kansas.

What are some of the conflicts that stand in her way? The key to creating a successful story is putting obstacles in your protagonist's path—external, internal, and interpersonal. Create opposition and frustration to force her to fall back on who she is, and what she knows, to overcome the hurdles you have created. No hurdles, no conflict, no story. Conflict is what moves your story forward and what develops your protagonist's character.

What specific crisis will she face in the end?
How will she resolve this crisis?

Once you have answered these questions, you will have the skeletal outline for a story that is the basis for almost every successful novel written, and you may find you are ready to begin. If this is the case, dive right in. Unfortunately, for me, this is not enough. I need to do a bit more.

Step 2: Plot statement

A plot statement is a one-sentence, high-concept summary of the set-up of your story. It is what you might pitch to a producer to whom you were trying to sell a movie—or to an agent to whom you are trying to sell a book. To write this statement all you need to know is your protagonist, the disturbance, his goal, and what is at stake.

"Dorothy Gale (protagonist) must find her way home (goal/stakes) after a tornado blows her into the strange land (disturbance) full of evil witches and magical wizards," is the plot statement for Frank Baum's *The Wizard of Oz*.

"Jay Gatsby (protagonist) must win back the love of Daisy Buchanan (goal) to give meaning to his meaningless life (stakes) after he buys a mansion across the water from the one in which Daisy lives (disturbance)," is the plot statement for F. Scott Fitzgerald's *The Great Gatsby.*

"Delia Grinstead (protagonist) must create a new life for herself (goal/stakes) after she impulsively walks away from her three children and long-term marriage," is the plot statement for Anne Tyler's *Ladder of Years.*

"Suki Jacobs (protagonist) must discover what really happened on the night Jonah Ward was killed (goal) before her teenage daughter is arrested for a murder she didn't commit (stakes), but that she did predict (disturbance)," is the plot statement for my latest book, *Blind Spot.*

What's the plot statement for yours?

Step 3: The disturbance

Although you already have a rough idea of what the disturbance of your story is, it is useful to make it more specific. This isn't just any disturbance: It is a particular event that begins the action of your particular story, throws your protagonist into turmoil, and forces her to devise a specific goal that will place her on the path that will lead her to *her* crisis. It is the "particular" aspect of these events that makes your story unique. To discover your disturbance—and, in many ways, your character—ask yourself the following question: "What is the worst thing that can happen to my protagonist, but will ultimately be the best thing that could happen to her?"

What does your protagonist need to learn? Her lesson is your readers' lesson: It is the theme of your book. What life lesson do you want to teach? Once you have answered these questions, you will be able to develop a character whose story resonates to your theme—a character whose backstory reflects what she needs to learn and whose journey within your story teaches it to her.

The disturbance in my second book, *Blameless,* occurs when Dr. Diana Marcus' patient, James Hutchins, commits suicide. It is the worst thing for Diana because it tears her life apart:

She begins to question herself as a psychologist.

A wrongful death and malpractice suit is filed by the Hutchins family, jeopardizing Diana's teaching position and practice as a psychologist.

She is publicly humiliated when the media disclose her unprofessional behavior.

Her husband Craig becomes suspicious, and their marriage is jeopardized.

Diana's inability to save James mirrors her childhood tragedy when she was unable to save her younger sister, and taps into all of her deepest insecurities.

This all sounds pretty terrible, but, like life, it's not all bad. James' death is also a good thing for Diana, because it forces her to face her tragic flaws and try to correct them:

She acknowledges her professional mistakes, making her a better therapist.

She and her husband rediscover their relationship.

She learns that she cannot cure everyone.

She forgives herself for her sister's death.

In order to come up with this disturbance, I had to delve deeply into Diana's present life and develop a past for her that would create a character who needed to learn this lesson. This process deepened both Diana and my plot.

How is your disturbance the best and worst thing that could happen to your protagonist?

Step 4: The crisis

The crisis of your novel is the major decision point for your protagonist. It reveals who she really is and what the experience has taught her. Its seeds are in the disturbance, and all the conflicts lead inexorably to this specific crisis, this specific decision and its specific resolution. But the decision can't be a simple one. If the choice is too easy, your reader will be unsatisfied. Therefore, you must create a decision that has both good and bad consequences, that has both gains and sacrifices, so that your reader will not know which choice your protagonist will make. To determine the crisis in your story, ask yourself the following questions:

What is the event that precipitates the crisis?

What is the decision the protagonist must make?

What does she learn in the decision-making process?
How does the decision reveal who she is (the backstory)?
How does her decision reflect on what happened to her in this story?
What does she lose in the decision (the sacrifice)?
What does she gain from her decision?
How is the decision turned into action?
How does the decision resolve the plot?

When I was developing the plot for *Blameless,* I asked myself the above questions and came up with these answers:

> James shows up at Diana's apartment and holds a gun to his head; he tells her that if she tells him not to shoot himself, he won't.
>
> Diana must decide whether to stop James from killing himself.
>
> Diana learns that everyone cannot be saved, that she cannot save everyone, and she is not responsible for James.
>
> Diana overcomes her belief that it is her mission to save everyone, realizes that she is not responsible for her sister's death, and ultimately forgives herself for it.
>
> Diana struggles with her need to control her career, her marriage, her patients, and herself.
>
> James will be dead, and she will be responsible for not stopping him.
>
> A dangerous murderer will be dead, and Diana will remove the threat to herself and her unborn baby.
>
> Diana doesn't say anything, and James blows his brains out.
>
> James really is dead, and Diana is cleared of his murder.

So if you aren't as brave a writer as you'd like to be—or if that mythical muse just won't appear—try these four exercises. You just might discover that you aren't that cowardly after all. And that novel might just get finished.

□ 30

POINT OF VIEW

BY ROBIN WHITE

IN FICTION, THE HIDDEN PERSUADER BEHIND ANY STORY IS A POINT OF view that focuses your narrative, involves your reader, and temporarily suspends all other realities, save the one on the page. Your prose may be artful, and your story clever, but if your point of view is ineffective, the work can seem like so many rows of flat black letters on a dull white page. On the other hand, there may be nothing special about your prose or story, but if your point of view is arresting, your words will spring to life.

Since point of view is so important, how do we go about choosing the right one—apart from just stumbling upon it? First, you must recognize that for any given story there are many different points of view, not merely the shift from third person to first, first to omniscient. And it can be creatively stimulating to try different ones until you find the one that will not let you (or your reader) go. Because every individual is unique, no two people ever see things in quite the same way, and shifting the viewpoint from one to another can enhance how readers see what writers want them to see.

For example, let's take the story of "Little Red Riding Hood." As the story goes, a little girl named after her riding cape sets out one day to take a basket of treats to her grandmother, who lives alone in a gloomy forest patroled by an English-speaking wolf. We don't know why Grandma doesn't stay with Riding Hood's parents (one of whom has to be her child); and we have no idea why our young heroine has been sent off by herself through wild-animal territory. We are told only that she is confronted by the wolf, who stupidly fails to eat her at once and instead sneaks around to Grandma's house, strips and devours the old lady, dons her clothes, gets into her bed, and soon manages to snack on the grandchild. Then a huntsman comes to the rescue, kills the wolf, and saves Grandma and Red Riding Hood, removing them alive, we're told, from the wolf's belly.

So, how do you handle this story? One way is to see things from the little girl's point of view: Her father is a deadbeat, her mother is having an affair, and Grandma is desperately in need of food and company. So off goes Little Red on a good will mission and discovers that the world away from home can be hazardous. This point of view rests on the premise that smart girls who venture into wolf territory need to befriend the local huntsman.

But how do things look from the wolf's point of view? There is Mrs. Wolf—yes, *Mrs.*—just trying to get food for her cubs, maybe change the way people tend to look on all wolves as male, when along comes a chance to engage in intergenerational dialogue, persuade young and old to save the forest, and be kind to wild animals. Unfortunately, before the dialogue can begin, Huntsman knocks on the door, hoping to sell Grandma some venison. Mrs. Wolf runs for her life, and Riding Hood makes the news by telling everyone that she and Grandma had been eaten alive. This point of view might advance the argument that everyone's little darling was nothing but a liar, responsible for starting a lot of bad PR for timber wolves, who are really shy creatures who avoid people.

Events can also be seen from Grandma's point of view, the huntsman's, the parents', the neighbor's, even a wolf cub's, as well as that of a psychologist, social worker, reporter, and so on. To turn things around—not assume that life has only one reality—is the surest way to discover your internal reality and create an illusion of reality that will grip the reader.

In addition to inspiring new insights, the effort to explore various points of view can also help you avoid offending someone unintentionally. For example, if you have seen things from the huntsman's point of view, you may be less likely to tackle the side issues of animal rights and the NRA, infuriating the proponents and opponents of both. Or if you have seen things from Grandma's point of view, you won't tend to say something that annoys the AARP. But an even more important reason to explore differing viewpoints is that writing itself is an act of faith—faith in the unseen, faith that an evolving truth does exist, and that fragmented sensory evidence is the external symptom of it. We seek the truth, believe in the truth as if it were singular, yet is there ever a whole, single, unchanging truth?

When giving testimony in a court of law, for instance, those who testify are asked to swear to tell "the truth, the whole truth, and nothing but the truth," and everyone usually so swears. But whose truth? What makes the difference between individual truths? What might be true for one, might not be true for another? Two people can witness the same event and give conflicting accounts of it. Even family members can experience something together and later on disagree about what happened.

The more writers grapple with viewpoint, the better they understand that what they see is conditioned by what they believe. Personal beliefs in turn are conditioned by time and by group beliefs. The truth thus tends to be encompassed rather than known, and a writer's ability to encompass it is a process that involves point of view.

One ironclad rule about point of view states that in a short story the writer should never switch from first- to third-person, or vice versa. J. D. Salinger is the only writer I know of who broke this rule, and did so successfully in his famous short story, "For Esmé—with Love and Squalor," when he changed his first-person narrator into a third-person protagonist. He did this by disarming the reader with humor: "I'm still around, but from here on in, for reasons I'm not at liberty to disclose, I've disguised myself so cunningly that even the cleverest reader will fail to recognize me." Thereafter, Staff Sergeant X takes over, and readers are moved, not put off. But what would happen if Salinger had chosen to see things not from the viewpoint of an adult male but through the eyes of Esmé, or her little brother, or perhaps a relative or close friend? Could the shift from first- to third-person have worked? And how would the impact have changed if the story had been told entirely in first person or entirely in third person?

Another interesting choice of viewpoint is Hemingway's, in "The Short Happy Life of Francis Macomber." The story opens: "It was now lunch time and they were all sitting under the double green fly of the dining tent pretending that nothing had happened." "They" includes Macomber, his wife, and Wilson the safari leader. The action could be viewed through the eyes of any one of them, or of one of the servants. Instead, Hemingway elects the omniscient point of view, which allows him to shift from one person to another, for the most part favoring Wilson, and thus avoiding literary disaster when Mrs. Macomber sleeps with him and later on "accidentally" shoots her husband. This detached, often dry way of seeing things is what conveys a profound sense of irony.

Now let's consider Fitzgerald's curious use of third-person adult male to tell a clearly autobiographical story, "Babylon Revisited," in which Charlie, a recovering alcoholic, fails to regain custody of his daughter, Honoria, from the Peters, relatives with whom the child is living. Some writers might be tempted to tell the story from Honoria's point of view to show how it feels to live with relatives who blame your father for your mother's death. Others might choose Mrs. Peters' point of view to dramatize her seething rage against Charlie. And I would have chosen Charlie's point of view in first- instead of third-person to help him vent his grief: wife dead, only child in her sister's custody. But Fitzgerald chose third person in order to convey a sense of total sadness—glitter gone, old friendships fled—making it one of his most memorable short stories.

I can also cite one of my own stories, "First Voice," as an example, because it involved a struggle with point of view. The story was about what happens when Aaron, the eldest son of American missionaries in South India, decides to become a sannyasi, or Hindu holyman (tantamount to what might happen if the first son of a prominent American surgeon decided to become a witch doctor). While the story eventually aroused the interest of American youth in Hindu culture, I had to shift point of view until I found the one that came alive for me. Since I am the eldest son of American missionaries, the logical viewpoint might have been Aaron's, in first- or third-person.

That did not work; it left me feeling uninvolved. So did the viewpoints of Aaron's parents, his sister, and one of his Indian friends. Then I created Samuel, a younger brother close enough to be a caring go-between, who looked at things from his point of view, so the story took off, in first person. Although the events narrated never occurred, readers continue to think that I must have gone through some revolutionary experiences in India. I did, but trying to become a Hindu holyman was not one of them.

When your point of view is working, it will draw into its vortex a host of sensory details—the evidence of touch, smell, taste, sight, and sound—that will breathe life into your words and validate what you are trying to say. And once this happens, your characters—not you—take charge, controlling the story. That is a great moment, well worth working for.

□ 31

WRITERS AND THEIR READERS

BY NORMA FOX MAZER

A NOVEL I WROTE OVER A NUMBER OF YEARS, *WHEN SHE WAS GOOD*, is the story of Em Thurkill and her struggle to live with and then come out from under the shadow of her abusive older sister, Pamela. Since the novel was published (fall, 1997) to the kind of reviews writers dream about, a shadow seems to have fallen over Em's story, one characterized mainly by the word "bleak." Questions were raised: Why do writers write these bleak books? Do young readers want to read bleak books? Or will they be repelled by them?

I don't choose to write bleak books. Writing a novel is, for me, like a kind of marriage that I enter in a somewhat dazed state of love, believing that this will be (at last!) a perfect union, blessed by all—relatives and readers. This is the honeymoon phase.

Then reality intervenes: I got married to this idea; now I have to live with it. Frustration enters the relationship. I dream of divorce, but being of a faithful nature, I stick with what I've chosen. And often, I'm rewarded: I find myself back once more in a state of bliss: ideas come; language, images.

But long before all this, there's something else: I'll call it the courtship. How we got to know each other. How I decided to take to this idea, to stay true to it. My courtship with *When She Was Good* had its first stirrings years ago. We had four kids and a two-family house shared with my parents, in the old working-class section of Syracuse, with its crowded, flat-roofed houses, churches on every corner, and tiny brilliant gardens.

After 10 years in the apartment below my parents, we were itchy from being constantly under the parental eye. No one said any of this in so many words. We were an almost Puritanically restrained and inhibited bunch. We all adored books and from grandparents to youngest child read voraciously. But when it came to feelings, too often we went mute or glowered at each other.

My husband and I realized we had to break free. Driven by equal amounts of guilt, love, and irritation, we found them a good apartment in a good building in a pleasant neighborhood.

My mother had a gift for friendship, and quite soon made friends in the new building. One of these was a woman who lived with her sister. The sister did some kind of knitting—dolls, perhaps. Once, I met the friend, a tall, gawky woman who seemed younger than her years, and a little frightened beneath her sudden, on-and-off smile.

Sometime later, my mother showed me a note the woman had written her. Something about this note, its tone of clenched intensity, made me think that she was in love with my mother. I didn't say this. My mother would have been shocked and embarrassed.

A few years later, I read an article on loneliness in America. The evidence pointed to the existence of two single older women for every single older man. A sad picture for women, if they believed happiness lay in pairing up. But why did people always have to be in pairs? I began to plan a novel about three older people who would fall in love with each other in various combinations. Like the statistics, two women, one man. Each one alone, each lonely. There was overweight Warren, a shoe salesman, who'd grown up in the shadow of his two older brothers. And Louise, feisty and energetic, with two disappointed and disappointing daughters. And Em, who lived with her domineering older sister, who busily knit doll-like figures.

For years I worked on this novel whenever I could. As time went on, I stayed with it even in the most extreme moments of despair at how long I'd been dallying and getting nowhere, or at least not where I wanted to go—which was to The End. As happens, over a long period of intimacy with anyone, I came to know my characters well. I knew, for instance, Em's childhood in detail.

I introduced my three characters to each other. They had a dinner party. They went to the beach. They took a trip. One of them had a heart attack. Things happened, which is good. Things must happen in a novel. But I could never get to the end of their story. Every time I approached it, a leaden feeling overtook me. It wasn't a structural problem, but more that something was emotionally lacking. I wasn't convinced.

I wrote other books. I wrote articles and short stories. But this story and those three people were always with me. At any moment, walking home from a movie, driving to the dentist, standing in line in the super-market, I would be mentally writing and revising. This went on for years. I became disgusted. Why couldn't I finish this story? I wanted to hate it. I did hate it. I announced to my husband that I was through with it. It was unwritable. I was going to delete it from my computer. Kill it. No mercy. Dead.

"Don't do that," he said. "There's too much good stuff there." He was telling me to get back in the harness. I bared my teeth and made sulking, resentful noises, but back I went, writing and rewriting, invent-ing new scenes, finding out more things about my character. But, really, what else did I have to know? I was already better acquainted with these people than with any of my friends. I could write a book about each one of them, I said. But stubbornly, I kept trying to cram them all into the same story.

Then I went to a Christmas party in New York City. A few hundred literary types were jammed into a small space, everyone shouting to be heard over the din, everyone smiling and waving—exactly the kind of scene that makes me want to creep into a corner. Someone I knew stopped me. "It's barbaric, isn't it?" I shouted.

"What?" he shouted back. "A barbershop? I've been looking for a good one."

"Bar-bar-ic!" I mouthed.

"Barbara? I haven't seen her. She looks great, though."

"I thought so, too," I said.

He looked pleased that I agreed with him. At that moment, I would have agreed with anything. Because, behind me, I had just heard—or thought I heard—someone say "real tough young adult stuff." Maybe I heard the words "real tough." Maybe I didn't. Maybe I just needed to hear those words. Whatever. In that instant, I knew that I should write the novel around Em alone. And I felt—absurdly, and wrongly, but thrillingly—that her story had sprung full blown into my mind.

I went to work the next morning around 3:30. It was impossible for me to sleep. From the pages I'd written over the years, I pulled every scene and incident in which Em figured. A lot of pages. In these pages were Em's childhood, her life with her sister, scenes alone, scenes with her and Louise, with her and Warren, with the three of them together. I had more than I needed and much less than I needed. I had written in third person, but now I wanted a closer, more intimate voice. Months later, I heard or found the line, "I never thought Pamela would die," and from that moment the form my book would take—which was not a straightforward linear narrative—became entirely clear to me.

As I wrote on, I worried. I worried about getting the book published. Everyone—whoever Everyone is—was saying no one wanted young adult books anymore. What was wanted were stories for younger kids, scary stories, funny stories, lighthearted stories. What I was writing might be scary, but not goosebump-scary, and it sure wasn't cute or adorable or lovable. It was a domestic story, like almost everything I've written, but more intense, starker, honed down to the bone.

Is this the definition of bleak? And if so, who did I think the audience was? I envisioned older readers, both adults and those people caught between *what is, what was, and what will be*—in other words, teens. No longer children, not yet adults, bright, imaginative, bewildered, and buffeted by emotions, hormones, adults, and everyone else's ideas—by everything, in fact, which we, as adults, presumably have put in place, dealt with, and understand.

Being a writer for this audience means entering a teenage mind, maybe the mind I once had, and yet never leaving the one I have now. While I write, I'm adult, teenager, and writer, and a struggle goes on among these selves.

As a teenager, my view is restricted. As a writer, I can hope for my characters, but promise nothing. While I know that the world is not as grim as it sometimes looks, at times it is even grimmer. I can't get in there and prop up my character. I have to stay with her, with who *she* is and what *she* perceives. I have to follow the scent, keep my nose to the trail, even if it begins in sorrow and fear and ends without much hope; even if it's bleak, because bleak is part of the world, too. The real world.

As things turned out, I didn't have a hard time finding a publisher. One editor told me he cried when he read the manuscript. Although another editor was interested, the first won my heart with his tears. He was a careful, and I might even say, loving editor for my book. I was so lucky. I lived with Em for a long time, and I was happy to let her go into the world.

My analogy of novel writing to marriage is faulty. Marriages often end with sadness—the death of the marriage or the death of a partner. But writing a book and finding a publisher brings about the opposite—a kind of birth. No, wrong again. Newborns are not pitched into the world and bid goodbye, Godspeed, and good luck. But that's more or less the way it goes with books. It's no longer up to the writer, but to the readers to embrace our books, to nourish them, to keep them alive. Though I love readers—how could I exist without them?—rather than my going where they are, I want them to come along with me.

Writing and publishing books that have been labeled "bleak" implies our faith in our readers, faith that they are hungry for and ready for more than a TV gloss on life. And a belief that it's important to give it to them. Faith, too, that they are ready to see a larger world or a different world, maybe not an ideal world, but a world that I believe is true and real.

□ 32

PUTTING EMOTION INTO YOUR FICTION

BY BHARTI KIRCHNER

LAUGH, SCREAM AND WEEP BEFORE YOUR KEYBOARD; MAKE YOUR reader feel. I kept this in mind when I started writing my first novel, *Shiva Dancing*. In developing characters, plot, and setting, I looked for every opportunity to make an emotional impact on the reader. Often, as I composed a sentence or paragraph, I felt the emotion myself.

Why are emotions important? Because they're more compelling than ideas, facts, and reasoning, which are the stuff of nonfiction. In fiction, the character must act from emotion, rather than from reason. And emotional truth is the reward readers hope to get from a novel. They will not turn to the next chapter or even the next page unless the material engages their emotions.

What emotions? Love and hate, joy and despair, fear and hope. Those are the significant ones to develop over a novel or chapter. But there are others—pride, timidity, shame, and humiliation—that move people and characters minute to minute, word to word.

Whether simple and understated or complex and dramatic, emotions need to be conveyed in a story, first by developing sympathetic characters. The more readers identify or sympathize with your protagonist, the more they'll feel her emotions and be curious enough to turn the page.

In the first chapter of *Shiva Dancing,* for example, seven-year-old Meena is kidnapped by bandits from her village in Rajasthan on the night of her wedding. The girl cries as she's snatched away from her mother's loving embrace by two big men on camels. Her old grandfather, who shuffled after them, looks on helplessly. This incident is meant to draw an emotional response from the reader. At the end of the chapter Meena's found by an American couple in a train far away from her village. They're about to take her to their home in New Delhi, where they're temporarily posted, when the chapter ends. The reader is likely to ask at this point: What's going to happen to Meena? Will she ever find her village? Where will she end up?

Turn to the next chapter.

If emotion is important, the question is: How do you, the writer, actually depict it on paper? And how does the reader know what that emotion is? The cardinal rule is: *Show, don't tell.* In other words, stating a mental condition directly may not convince the reader. For example:

> She was anxious.

In real life, you observe someone's behavior and draw appropriate conclusions. The example below from *The Power of the Sword* by Wilbur Smith *shows* that the character is agitated:

> Centaine was too keyed up to sit down. She stood in the center of the floor and looked at the pictures on the fireplace wall without actually seeing them.

You can also *show* an emotion through a character's thought. This is often effective, since a person may not reveal his true feeling in his speech. Use a simile, as Alice Hoffman does in *Second Nature:*

> He just couldn't shake the feeling of dread; he was like an old woman, waiting for disaster to strike.

Notice how much more effective the above is than saying:

> He was afraid.

Use physical symptoms. Readers are convinced of an emotion only when they recognize a physical reaction similar to one they've experienced themselves: a racing heart, stiff legs, or cold palms. Here's one of Meena's reactions in *Shiva Dancing,* but first a bit about the story and the scene where she finds herself.

Meena is adopted by the American couple, who raise her in San Francisco. When we meet her again, she's 35, a software techie, working for a Bay Area company. In one scene, Meena goes to a bookstore to attend a reading by Antoine Peterson, a celebrity novelist she has met briefly on one previous occasion. After the reading, he invites her for tea. Just when the chai is tasting "creamy smooth," and the tabla music has reached a crescendo, Antoine mentions his upcoming marriage to Liv and their honeymoon. Meena's reaction?

> Her tea tasted cold and weak. She set her cup down, trying to keep her hand steady.

An emotion, however, is not an end in itself. Describing it in a vacuum is never enough. You have to combine facts and action with emotion to create an illusion of reality. Here's an example from *The Rest of Life* by Mary Gordon.

> She gets into the train, one of the first to board. [action and fact] Everything is still and quiet. [fact] Then the train starts up with an insulting lurch. [emotion]

Though I try to bring out a character's feelings even during the first draft, I find I never catch them one hundred per cent. Revision is the perfect time to check for the following: What are the various emotional situations in which the protagonist has found herself? How does she react to the stimulus? Look for a sentence, some piece of dialogue, or a flashback where emotions can be injected. Nostalgia, a milestone in life, a return to some place previously visited, are potential sources.

In *Shiva Dancing*, Meena returns to her village after an absence of three decades. As she arrives with her driver, she notices that the thatched-roof houses have been replaced by newer buildings. She can't recognize any of the sights. She's eager to find her mother. The reader knows—but Meena doesn't—that her mother is long dead. Meena meets a schoolboy on the street and asks, in one poignant moment, about her mother:

> "My mother made clothes for the kids. She embroidered their names on their baby sari. Everyone in the village came to her."
> The shocking reply that comes to Meena through her driver is:
> His mother buys ready-made clothes for him.

Use sizzle in your dialogue: Inane comments, yes-and-no answers might do in real life, but speech in fiction must have the effect of potential shockers. In *Shiva Dancing*, Antoine returns from a book tour and immediately goes to visit Meena at her apartment. There, he finds Carlos, a close friend of Meena's, who tells him Meena has left for India.

Antoine doesn't like Carlos in the first place, and now he has the task of finding out where she is actually staying. Carlos, protective of Meena, has been unwilling up to this point to share any information about her. Finally, the outwardly polite Carlos explodes:

> "She had strong feelings for you. I've never seen Meena get so excited about a man. And what do you do? You build up her hopes, then dump her the day Liv comes back. Pardon me if I'm getting a little emotional. Meena's my friend. It hurts me to see her cut up like that."
> "I didn't mean to hurt her," Antoine said. "My situation is different now."
> "It better be."

The words used in a dialogue can be simple, but just repeating a phrase can intensify the emotion. Here's Alice Hoffman in *Second Nature:*

> "Help me up," Richard Aaron shouted over the sound of the hooves hitting against the earth. "Just help me up."

A person's words may be a smoke screen, but her voice, facial expression, and gestures can be a dead giveaway. Notice how Gail Godwin does this in *The Finishing School:*

> Her chin shot up so fast that it set in motion the crest of her feathery haircut. "Where did you hear about them?"

Another place where an emotional quality can be imparted is in the setting. *Create an atmosphere:* A dark house on a stormy night has a sinister connotation, whereas a sunny day on a beach is quite the opposite. You can make effective use of the environment to set a mood. This is equivalent to using background music in a movie to highlight the action on the screen. In this example from *Shiva Dancing,* Meena is about to attend a staff meeting at Software International Company. There's tension among her coworkers. The scene opens with a short description of the conference room:

> Sunlight streamed in through the room's only window, casting shadows of the saucerlike leaves of the potted plants on the wall *without warming the room.*

The italics is mine. When selecting from a number of details in a surrounding, pick only those elements relevant for the character, those that bring an emotional surge. Here's novelist Antoine in *Shiva Dancing* arriving in Calcutta in pursuit of Meena. He feels lonely and uncertain. Everything he sees through his taxi window on the way to the hotel is colored by his present mental condition:

> Antoine's eyes watered as acrid charcoal smoke from a clay oven on the sidewalk drifted in through the open car window. Along with the smoke came the smell of freshly baked flat bread. A young woman in a yellow-orange sari browned the puffy *roti* rounds over the fire. Her deep eyes and rhythmic gestures reminded him of Meena. He yearned for fresh bread made just for him.

Use symbolism. A symbol is a habit, an object, an event, almost anything charged with a hidden meaning that stems from association. In *Shiva Dancing,* a symbol used for Meena is her thirst, which, in effect, is her longing for her desert homeland. In her San Francisco office, she always keeps a glass of water on her desk and sips from it often. The true meaning of this ritualistic habit is revealed to her only after she finally returns to her village.

> "Tubewell," the boy said, pointing. He rushed to it and levered the handle until water gushed out. Meena made a cup of her hands, drank deeply and splashed the remainder on her face. As she did so, she went back in time when she was tiny. Mataji would hold a glass of well water to her mouth. This clear earth water tasted the same. She had missed it. Without knowing it, she had been thirsty all these years.

Collect "feeling" words: Avoid overusing common words, such as "loving," "calm," or "blissful." Consider cataloguing your own feelings in a notebook and using them for your characters. Here are some examples:

Animated	Exasperated
Diffident	Sated
Bubbly	Petrified
Refreshed	Crushed

Regardless of what techniques are used, ultimately it's the writer's own emotions that set the tone of a scene or piece of fiction. As a preparation for writing, it might be necessary for you to revisit an incident in the past and try to identify and relive an emotion. Or, like an actor, you might assume a new role and experience a new set of emotions. The choice of words, the length of a sentence, the pacing of paragraphs all broadcast to readers how they should feel. In general, short sentences and paragraphs heighten the drama, whereas longer, more leisurely writing gives the reader more breathing space.

Avoid sentimentality. As important as emotions are, don't overemphasize powerful ones such as loss and grief. Readers feel manipulated when presented with one misery after another. You may summarize such happenings or provide relief by using humor and insight. In general, the stronger the emotion, the more you need to restrain your passion in describing it.

To sum up, don't be afraid to transfer one or more emotional experiences of laughter, pain, or agony to your readers. They may curse you because they burned the rice, dropped their aerobics routine, and were late for work, but they won't put your book down.

❏ 33

GET YOUR NOVEL BACK ON TRACK: A SOLUTION TO WRITER'S BLOCK

BY MAYNARD ALLINGTON

I ONCE ASKED A SUCCESSFUL NOVELIST IN THE HORROR GENRE HOW HE handled writer's block. His reply was, "I've never had it." He went on to say his enthusiasm, while writing, was always so high and his creative excitement so keen, that writer's block never hit him.

It seemed to me a simplistic answer, though it's true that enthusiasm confers temporary immunity to writer's block. The malady isn't likely to strike when you are writing, let's say, a first chapter and that creative fire is burning in your brain. But for most of us, this fervor diminishes early on in a novel, and we have to subsist on the short rations of technique and discipline. For novelists new at the craft this can be a starvation diet, and the hunger pangs invariably take the form of writer's block.

Just as pain serves a vital purpose in sending to the brain a signal that something is wrong, so does writer's block. Most of the time, it's telling us there's a flaw in the architecture of the novel. The worst mistake you can make is trying to write through it. That's like exercising when you have an injury, which can only make it worse.

When writer's block hits, use it to your advantage. Try to diagnose the problem. Check the major components of your novel—premise, plot, and characters—to see if they are *functional*. I generally use three steps in this process, and can usually locate the trouble.

Step 1

Examine the *premise* of your story. Is it *big* enough to carry a novel through three or four hundred pages of manuscript? Premise grows out of theme. The theme of Robert Penn Warren's *All the King's Men*, for example, is *power corrupts*. The premise builds from this into a microcosm of a plot: *A backwoods country boy, idealistic at first, rises from obscurity to political prominence through deceit, intimidation, and venality. He betrays those closest to him; and in his ascent to a near dictatorship he corrupts the system and is corrupted by it.* Consider the panoramic sweep of this premise. Clearly, it will require a *large* cast of characters to tell the story, and the material lends itself to the development of conflict.

Here's an opposite example—William Styron's novella, *A Tidewater Morning. A boy recalls the day his mother died, and how her dying affected the routine events of that day, altering the course of his life.* A powerful premise, but a *small* one. A literary scenario such as this can support only a few characters. While there is much interior movement, the plot is choreographed around just a few events. The premise could never sustain a long narrative. Styron added two other (long) short stories to make a trilogy out of this small masterpiece. The three pieces are connected only by having the same narrator and a common theme (confronting death). Each has a different premise.

Back to your novel-in-progress: For five or six chapters, the story has moved well, but suddenly you find yourself in a literary blind alley. You can't expand your material. The paralyzing inertia of writer's block settles on your imagination like a drop of deadly curare. What do you do?

Always check your premise, first. Match it against the two models I've described. If it's not a *big* premise, you can't construct a novel from it. Perhaps the material can be used in a novella, or a long short story, or you may be able to develop a new premise on the same theme.

Step 2

Examine your cast of characters. How well do they interact with each other? In *Gone with the Wind*, the first time Scarlett sees Rhett Butler staring at her in a crowd, there is a psychosexual voltage between them that lasts throughout the novel. Imagine this story without Rhett. It would sink into a stereotypic love triangle between Scarlett, Ashley, and Melanie. Still a *big* premise because of the Civil War canvas, but it would lose its literary thrust, and forfeit its stature as a great novel.

The chemistry between Scarlett and Rhett that drives *Gone with the Wind* is vital to every novel. As a novelist, you can cast anyone you choose to fill the leading roles, but unless there is that special chemistry between them, you're inviting writer's block. Heroes and heroines—and, yes, supporting characters—who have no psychological depth or intelligence are a poor ensemble for a novel. Simple people say simple things to each other. After a few exchanges, dialogue collapses. Characters with intrinsic psychological conflicts or opposing goals will create their own dialogue when you bring them together on a page.

Unskilled novelists tend to focus on physical descriptions of their players, ignoring the psychological dimension. Dostoyevsky's understanding of this more than a century ago set his novels apart. The best characters in fiction have always been driven by complex psychological issues in their lives. These issues shape the way they think, talk, and react to events and to other characters. Dramatic tension is best achieved when characters, especially of opposite sexes, have some degree of conflict in their psychological make-up. This gives literary force to their dialogue. (Jimmy Porter and Helena Charles in British playwright John Osborne's play *Look Back in Anger* are prime examples.)

Of course, you should focus a great deal of thought on this element of your novel before you even begin to write. Mentally audition different characters for a role and select the one whose presence in a scene will consistently spark conflict. If your dialogue doesn't seem to go anywhere, or sounds flat, chances are, you failed to do this. But it's never too late to fix the problem. Sometimes the solution can be as simple as changing a character's background.

Step 3

If you still haven't isolated the source of your writer's block, make a detailed search of your plot. A story line, which forms an unbroken arc through a beginning, middle, and end of your novel, is an extension of a premise. A plot fits in pieces (chapters) into a story line. Given the same story line, no two writers will choreograph the same plot. Conflict is the literary oxygen a plot needs in order to breathe. Deprive it of that for even a short period, and anoxia sets in.

I use the "Fish rule" to detect breaks in conflict. First told to me by the editor of a professional journal, this rule has proved the most useful advice I've ever received about writing, and now I am entrusting it to you.

The "Fish rule" comes from the following story: The owner of a fish market decided to put a sign in his window. He wrote the following on butcher paper:

FRESH
FISH
FOR SALE
AT THIS STORE
TODAY

The sign didn't look right, and he drew a line through At This Store. Then he asked himself, "Why say Today? If I put the sign in the window, people will know it's today." So he crossed out Today. Next, he decided that For Sale wasn't needed, since any idiot would know that he didn't give fish away. And why say Fresh? Obviously he wouldn't sell fish that had gone bad.

In the end, only one word survived: Fish.

This little story embodies the whole mystique of writing. To begin with, you must apply it to sentences. Next, use it to eliminate paragraphs and snatches of dialogue that don't move the story forward. And when the process has become second nature to you, test it against whole chapters.

It sounds simple, but once you internalize the "Fish rule" and make it part of your creative persona, the effect can be amazing.

Let's assume you've eliminated premise and characters as the source of your writer's block. The flaw lies in the plot, where the oxygen line to conflict was cut, and the writing was left brain dead. How do you repair the damage? First look at the scene (or even the whole chapter). Is it critical to the story line? If so, could the material be presented in a different form?

I ran into this problem in writing my third novel, *The Court of Blue Shadows,* set in Nazi Germany. The lead, Paul Krenek, is a half-Jew who has survived the death camps. I'd written a chapter in which Paul's mildly retarded, five-year-old sister, Liesl, is killed by lethal injection in a children's psychiatric ward as part of the euthanasia program carried out by German doctors. The scene was graphically described, and the chapter certainly did not lack conflict, but I felt troubling symptoms of writer's block as I worked on it. Somehow it didn't fit into that part of the novel. The emotion seemed to me dangerously close to bathos; at best, it was heavy-handed. Finally, I cut out the whole thing. The material, still vital to the plot, went into a later chapter in which Paul, after the war, is tracking down the men responsible for the little girl's murder. He learns what happened to Liesl from a nurse who assisted the doctor in the psychiatric ward when the injection of iodine was given. I found that the scene, in this form, had far more dramatic power, if only because it was underplayed.

You can often reshape a plot in this fashion without losing any of the power of the story line. Usually, the writer's block disappears with the discarded material. A novel is the material of human experience expressed as an original vision. Writer's block is a natural part of the creative process. Be skeptical of those who insist that it's all in the mind, and who peddle quack remedies. Enthusiasm, sadly, does not come in cans. But you don't need a miracle agent to beat writer's block at its true source.

□ 34

USING *REAL* PEOPLE IN YOUR STORIES

BY EILEEN HERBERT JORDAN

WHEN HENRY JAMES DESCRIBED HIS WRITING METHODS, HE WROTE OF how fitting he had found it to place a willful heroine in the gardens of an estate he had long admired, and thus capture her, thereby introducing his readers to Isabel Archer in *Portrait of a Lady*. That may have been fine for Henry James, but it's not going to help you much. Your story is about your willful mother-in-law, who doesn't want to be captured in print, and no matter where you place her, when she reads your story, she's not going to like it, and God knows what it will do to your family relationships!

There isn't a writer, dead or alive, who has not had this problem. In fact, through the years there has been so much conflict between writers and those they write about (or those who *think* they are written about) that I don't presume to come up with a solution. But a few things *have* worked for me when I have had an idea for a story and been stopped by the thought, *Oh, I can't say that about her—she'll never speak to me again.* . . . a thought that has stopped me a lot. And it's no wonder—the dilemma is very real.

If all good writing comes from life—and I believe it does—and we fail to tap the source, we end with cardboard figures whose every move is unreal, and whose story is usually unpublishable. Still, in the world we live in, most of us are not misogynists (or man haters, either); in fact, we court approval and dislike living in alienation. Yet writing is what we do, the thing that defines us, and we have to do it the best we can.

Writing instructors are fond of suggesting that the psyches of two or three people we know can be mingled to produce one in a story. Like many similar suggestions, this one *doesn't* work more often that it *does,* and at best, it takes considerable skill. We are, after all, engaged in the

164

business of mixing the characteristics of different people—not in making soup. But before you despair, try these approaches:

Change genders. This doesn't always work, of course, but it does more often than you would think. Recall the family situations you have observed in which daughters behaved exactly as their fathers had, sons mirrored the reactions of mothers, etc. When a character's emotions and actions are not solely motivated by his gender, it is perfectly viable to make the switch and get away with it.

Do a makeover. It's often been said that inside every short, fat person there lies a tall and willowy one, yearning to be free. Well, you can do it. I have done it often and have not been found out yet, although once it did boomerang and work in reverse. I wrote a story about the romance of a friend of mine. Aware that magazines crave youth and beauty, I made my heroine younger, slimmer, taller, and quite a bit more lissome than my friend.

I also set the romance in Manhattan (it actually took place in the suburbs) because I knew the area, and I knew the sneaky magic of liaisons that begin there. The story was published, but not right away, having been rejected the first time around by an editor I knew slightly. She admitted later that the problem was she couldn't bear the thought of seeing it in print because she felt that I had invaded her privacy and written *her* story. Her reaction was a total surprise to me, and ironic, too—after all my duplicity in fashioning the characters! The second editor, without the same baggage, bought it.

Despite the above example, however, a makeover does not consist merely of a few cosmetic touches. It is a process of imbuing your protagonist with a star quality she did not have before. Most of us don't believe we are stars and never recognize ourselves as such.

Change the label. We are captives of our identity, defined by labels we have acquired, sometimes by choice, often not. We are mothers, daughters, sisters, neighbors. This can be changed. After you have explored the gender possibilities, making your mother your father, try making your neighbor your sister, your daughter your roommate, your mother your best friend. Simply take the person you know, foibles intact, and give her a new identity.

Recently, I wrote a story that I felt might not be popular with the person who inspired it. I solved the problem by identifying her at the beginning as a grandmother. Except for the age requirement, grandmotherhood had nothing whatsoever to do with my story, so it didn't matter. What I did know was that the person in question was *not* a grandmother and had no urge to become one; her eyes would glaze over as she read the word, and she never would connect any part of what followed with herself. I was right.

Change the skill. To many people a skill or talent is as much a part of them as a thumbprint. So, in fact, is a lack of ability—we are all very aware of what we *can't* do. Let me give you an example. I have two sons, and I write about them often. But in a short story, you should not have too many characters, or you will lose your reader in the crowd. I write about my sons, therefore, as one person. They try to guess who's who and sometimes succeed, but sometimes I fool them. The main character in one of my recent stories was a dead ringer for my younger boy, until the climax, which involved his swimming across a lake.

"Well, Mom," he said, "this one's not me—I know that. You know I don't swim."

Obviously, if what you are writing is totally involved with a cross-country skier, a ballroom dancer, or the soul of a poet, you can't do much about it. But if the skill doesn't matter to the plot, taking it away, changing it, or, perhaps, conferring it on another character can blur recognition with no harm done.

Don't think "Know Thyself" works for everyone. You may be surprised at the number of people who believe they could never be fooled; they're sure they would recognize themselves—but they don't. If you write a story that you know may expose someone, remember that—then cross your fingers.

I know a successful writer who was determined never to exploit friends, family, or acquaintances, and she never did until she completed a novel, reread it, and found, to her horror, that one of the main characters was a clone of somebody she knew, a character who had somehow slipped from the writer's unconscious onto the printed page. Not only that, the character was not a flattering clone, either; she was Matilda, the evil force who drove the story. And it was too late to do anything about it—except wait and see.

That did not take long. Shortly after the book was published, at a party, the writer gazed across the room and her eyes locked with those of her nemesis. She stopped still and just stood there silently, racking her brains for an approach as the other woman began walking toward her. What to do?

Should she start the conversation with a burst of pleasantries, ignoring the issue?

Should she apologize right away, call writers like herself insensitive clods—and see what happens?

Should she just lie?

The woman reached her side, and grabbing her arm, she said, "I've read your novel. I couldn't put it down. It's just wonderful. . . ." There was a pause. "Just one thing . . ."

My friend swallowed hard.

"How do you ever dream up those characters? I could never do that. Or maybe I just never meet people like that. That Matilda is a monster—and so real! Congratulations!"

So she got away with it—by a stroke of sheer luck. And you may, too. For a writer it is the ideal solution to the problem, and it is not one he forgets, either. It has been almost forty years since Neil Simon's first play, *Come Blow Your Horn,* opened and he can still remember how worried he was that the character of the household head would be offensive to his father, upon whom the play was entirely based. Worried, that is, until his father came to him afterwards, shook his head and said, "I know so many men just like him."

On the other hand, Truman Capote lost all his friends when he made their identities obvious in a short story. So if you would rather take precautions, try some I have suggested. It gets easier with practice—in fact, the characters you create grow so real, you feel as if you've made new friends!

❏ 35

TURNING YOUR EXPERIENCE INTO FICTION

BY EDWARD HOWER

"THAT WOULD MAKE A GOOD STORY—YOU OUGHT TO WRITE IT!" How many times have you heard people say this, after you've told them about some interesting experience?

But if you're like me, you may not *want* to write directly about yourself, except perhaps in your private journal. This doesn't mean, however, that your own life can't be used as material for fiction. Using your own experiences as starting places for stories or novels gives your work an authenticity that made-up adventures may lack. A great many fiction writers have mined their own pasts—some of them over and over throughout their careers.

Advantages of starting with yourself

Writing stories that are similar to real-life occurrences allows you to relive and to re-examine your life. In fiction, you can explore all the might-have-beens of your past. You can experience the loves that didn't quite happen but that might have proved blissful or (more interestingly) disastrous in tragic or amusing ways. You can delve into your worst fears, describing what might have happened if you hadn't been so careful about trusting strangers or about avoiding life's dark alleys.

And by creating characters similar to yourself and to people you've known, you can get a perspective on your past that couldn't come from direct, analytic examination. One of the most gratifying experiences I had in writing my last novel was getting to know my family all over again in ways I'd never previously considered. Some anger resurfaced, but so did a lot of compassion. And I finally got a kind of closure on my sometimes painful childhood that had eluded me before.

I've emphasized writing about the past here rather than about the present. This is because I think it's a lot more productive to deal with material from which you have psychic distance.

Selective memory can produce interesting, emotionally charged material for fiction. Recent events, however, are hard to deal with creatively. Immediate reality intrudes, and issues unresolved in life resist resolution in fiction.

Searching your life

Here's an exercise I used while I was writing my semi-autobiographical novel, *Night Train Blues*. I've frequently given the exercise to students in my creative writing workshops, too. It's designed to help retrieve buried memories and then transform them into usable images, characters, and episodes for stories or longer fiction.

First, decide on a period in your life you'd like to write about. A year in your past in which emotionally intense experiences happened is often the best one. This doesn't mean that the events need to be melodramatic. Small traumas and triumphs often make the best material for fiction, especially if they involve people you've had strong feelings about. Events that caused you to change your attitude toward yourself and other people are especially good. For this reason, many writers choose a period from childhood or adolescence—the times of many emotional changes.

Start the exercise in a quiet place, alone. Get comfortable, close your eyes, and take slow deep breaths. Now imagine yourself going home during the time period you've chosen. Picture yourself approaching the place where you lived. Imagine entering it. What do you see . . . hear . . . smell? Go into the next room. What's there? Now go into the room in which you kept your personal possessions. Stand in the middle of the floor and look around. What do you see . . . hear . . . smell? Now go to some object that was especially precious to you. Hold it. Feel it. Turn it around. Get to know it again with as many senses as possible. Then ask yourself: Why did I choose this object?

As soon as you're ready, open your eyes and start writing as fast as you can. First describe the object in great detail. If you want to discuss people and events associated with it, that's fine, too. Finally, write about the object's importance to you. You might give yourself ten to fifteen minutes for the entire exercise. Don't edit what you write. Don't even pause to look back over it—fill as much paper as you can. If you write fast, you'll fill at least a page, probably more.

When I did this exercise, the object I found was an old wooden radio with a cloth dial and an orange light that glowed behind it. I mentally ran my fingers over its smooth, rounded surfaces. I put my nose up to it and smelled the dusty cloth warmed by the pale bulb behind it. I twisted the dial, and listened to my favorite childhood stations.

Thinking about the radio's meaning for me, I remembered the warm relationship I'd had with the person who gave it to me. The radio also reacquainted me with country songs I later came to associate with an important character in my novel, my young hero's wandering older brother. So I gave my fictional narrator a radio similar to the one I'd had, and I let him find solace in its music, too.

My students have also come up with radios given to them by important people in their lives. Dolls and stuffed animals, sports equipment, pictures, china figurines, tools, articles of clothing—all have been highly evocative objects that eventually radiated emotions not only for the writers but for their fictional characters as well. Cars, records, and clothes were important items for people returning to adolescence. Each freshly-recalled object resonated with feelings about rebellion, first love, and newfound freedoms.

Transforming truth into fiction

Now it's time to turn this object into the central image of a story or novel chapter. Write "If this were fiction . . ." at the top of a page. Give yourself a different name. You are now a fictional character, one who resembles you but who will gradually develop his or her own personality as you continue working.

Then jot down some answers to these questions:

Character development
1. What does the choice of this object tell about the character (A—"you") who chose it?
   • Who is A? Describe this person quickly.

2. Imagine that another character (B) gave A the object.
   • Who is B? Describe B quickly.
   • What is B's relationship to A?

3. Imagine that yet another character (C) wants the object.
   • Who is C? Describe C quickly.
   • What is C's relationship to B and A?

When trying to imagine B and C, you might choose people from your own life or people like them who might have given you the object or might have coveted it. Characters often come from composites of several people you knew—the physical attributes of one person, the voice of another, the sense of humor or the mannerisms of another.

One way to get to know characters not modeled after yourself is to start the visualization exercise again, this time treating someone you knew as you did the object in the previous exercise. Follow the person around in your visualization, observing and listening closely. Then write a fast page or two about what you discovered.

Another good way to understand a character is to make lists of his or her attributes and preferences. Jot down his or her favorite clothes, food, TV show, brand of car, breed of dog, film hero, period in history, childhood memory, and so forth. Say what religious, political, and ethical beliefs the character has. Expand the list until you feel you know as much about this fictional person as you do about your best friend. You may not use much of this material in the actual story, but it gives you the background of the character that you need in order to write with authority.

Plot development

The treasured object can give you some ideas about what storyline to follow. Try answering these questions:

1. **A and the object**
   • Why does A treasure it? What will A do with it?
   • What problems might result from his having it?

2. **B and the object**
   • Where did B get the object? Why did B give it to A?
   • What problems might result from B giving it to A?

3. **C and the object**
   • Why does C want the object?
   • What problems might result from C trying to get it?

All plots involve conflicts—thus the emphasis on problems. Once you've listed some conflicts, choose one that interests you and try answering some more questions:

1. What events might foreshadow this conflict?
2. What dramatic action might result from this conflict?
3. How might the conflict be resolved?

By this time, you've probably discovered that although the story has ostensibly been about an object, it's really about people. One is a central character who probably resembles you in some ways, and one or more other characters are based—closely or loosely, it doesn't matter—on people you've known.

Deciding on a setting

To become familiar with your fictional locale, try closing your eyes and visualizing the place where you found the object in the original exercise. Observe the details of the room, the sounds you hear from the other rooms, and the view from the windows. Then, as if you were a bird, fly out a window to observe the neighborhood, the town or city, the county or region. Pay attention to details—the clothes people are wearing, the kinds of cars in the streets, the signs in shop windows. Smell the smells. Listen to the sounds of life. Feel the energy given off by ball parks, bars, beaches, playgrounds, political rallies. After you've flown around for a while, return to your region . . . neighborhood . . . dwelling . . . and room—for a last look-around.

Then start writing as fast as you can about things you've discovered on your journey. You might want to draw a quick map with concentric circles radiating out from your own small world. You don't need to include everything you found—this isn't a memory test. But do go into detail about discoveries that stand out sharply. Be aware that the best details of a setting give off strong emotions, providing atmosphere for your characters to move around in. The way they respond to their environment will help define who they are and what they do.

Development of a theme

To get a grip on the story's meaning, it will be helpful to go back to the treasured object at least one more time and answer these questions:

1. How does the object resemble
   - You
   - character A
   - character B and/or C

2. What effect does the object have on the relationship
   - between A and B
   - between B and C
   - between A and C

Again, you'll probably discover that whatever your story means, it has to do with people developing relationships with each other, entering into conflicts, and trying to find resolutions to them. The treasured object may fade in importance by the time you've finished the story's last draft. But it will have served its purpose.

Truth and invention

What if the characters and plot of your fiction closely resemble real people and/or events that have actually occurred? Does it matter?

I don't think it does. If you use the *techniques* of fiction-writing—characterization, plot, conflict, dialogue, description, and so on—then what you'll have at the end will be fiction, regardless of its source.

But you may still find that similarities between your life and your fiction inhibit your creative writing. You might also worry that readers who know you could be disturbed by what you write. In this case, you can do what a great many authors have done throughout history (sometimes on the advice of their attorneys)—make alterations in their fiction to avoid resemblances to actual people, places, and events.

- With characters, change one or more of these attributes: size, shape, hair color, accent, nationality, clothes
- Change the story's setting to a different region
- Move the story backward or forward in time

Having made these changes, you'll probably have to change other details of the fictional work in order to fit in the new material. This in itself can become part of the creative process, helping you to imagine more and remember less. At the end, even those who know you best may not be clear about what you've recalled and what you've made up. And you may not be sure, yourself.

If this happens, you may be certain you've moved from autobiography to fiction—one of the most interesting and satisfying ways in which your writing can develop.

❑ Specialized Fiction

❑ 36

FACT AND FICTION: THE STUFF THAT DREAMS ARE MADE OF

BY REX BURNS

IT IS FAIRLY USUAL FOR NOVELISTS TO USE REAL SITUATIONS, EVENTS, and stories as the basis for creating their fiction. Daniel Defoe based *Robinson Crusoe* on Thomas Selkirk's biography, and Edgar Allan Poe "solved" a New York homicide by extrapolating from details reported in the newspapers. I'm sure readers can think of many other tales not marketed as "faction" that are still "based on fact."

Several of my books, too, have been "based on fact." *The Avenging Angel*, for one, grew out of newspaper articles dealing with renegade Mormon polygamists at war with each other in Colorado, Utah, and Mexico. Many of the central events in *The Alvarez Journal* were drawn from court documents of a case tried in Denver in the early 1970's.

The importance of this nice-to-know information is not that writers seek and find ideas in real life—where else do they find them?—but that real life by itself, undigested, seldom makes a complete story. Generally, the factual information from newspaper articles, court documents, personal memoirs, etc. serves as a source for the events of a fictional story, but plot, and especially character, tend to come from an author's imagination.

For me, imagination is the tool by which factual happenings are converted into a story with structure and purpose. This function of imagination can occur in several ways: inventing fictional characters who perform the actual deeds; discovering motivations that were obscure or not present in the actual events; finding metaphors for other aspects of life in the actions; structuring the given events into the shape of a meaningful conclusion. Although this may sound cut and dried, of course it isn't. In fact, it can generate the excitement and fun of creativity that helps make up for the long hours at the keyboard.

A glimpse at *The Alvarez Journal* may offer some insight into how the givens of an actual story might be transmuted into fiction.

The principal document on which I based this novel is an affidavit sworn by the investigating officer and filed in Denver district court. Like most other open court documents, it was available to the public for a search and copy fee. Like most of those legal documents, the affidavit is in formulaic phrase and structure: "I, _____, being first duly sworn, upon oath depose and state as follows: . . ." What follows is a fill-in-the-blanks format which first lists the detective's credentials, establishes probable cause for his investigation, and enumerates the methods by which information was obtained: "1. Information from three (3) previously reliable, confidential informants, hereinafter referred to as informant A, informant B and informant C"; "2. Surveillance conducted by the affiant in conjunction with other members of . . ." ; "3. Routine investigative procedures such as an enchange of information with. . . ." Then follows the conclusion the detective came to: ". . . that ____ and ____ and other persons as yet unknown are committing, have committed, or are about to commit violations of 1963, C.R.S. 48-5-20(1), as amended, to wit: illegal transportation of narcotic drugs, conspiracy to illegally transport narcotic drugs, possession of narcotic drugs for sale, and conspiracy to possess narcotic drugs for sale." The language here is copied from the Colorado Revised Statutes in the usually justified belief that a defense lawyer will not challenge the established definition of the suspected crimes. This technique is vital in court; but it makes pretty boring reading in fiction, and even a plodding writer feels the itch to make the prose style a bit more lively.

The body of the affidavit details the information gathered through the three methods mentioned in the document's introduction. This is where the writer's imagination begins to work full time, and it starts with a barrage of questions that stimulate the imagination and flesh out the facts of the affidavit.

To illustrate, here is a quotation from the affidavit and some of the questions raised in my mind as I considered the material from the writer's perspective of generating character and plot.

Affidavit: "A. I have received information from a previously reliable, confidential informant (hereinafter referred to as informant A), whose information has resulted in the arrests of dangerous and (sic) narcotic drug violators, and the confiscation of large quantities of heroin, mari-

juana, and dangerous drugs on numerous previous occasions, that ____
and ____ are presently engaged in the dealing and trafficking of narcot-
ics, namely heroin. Informant A, who has been for the past three years,
and is currently, an associate of ____ and ____, related to this affiant
on or about October 15, 1971, the following information . . ."

One of the first questions I—like the accused—would ask, is, who is
Informant A? Other questions that I—*unlike* the accused—might ask
are, What caused Informant A to get in touch with the detective or vice
versa? How did Informant A get close enough to the accused to be able
to quote the accused's citing of names and addresses, his method of
cutting and distribution of heroin, his profits? What is the relationship
between Informant A and the detective? In short, the facts alone are
essential and central in the actual court testimony, and they are also
important to the action of the novel. But from the novelist's point of
view, even more important are the scenes in which "Informant A" gathers and delivers those facts to the detective.

The fictional stimulus to my detective, Gabe Wager, to pursue the
crime based on this particular affidavit came via a brief and pro forma
notice from another police agency: "Time for one more item before
quitting for the day—an envelope opened, retaped, his name scrawled
over the original address in Sergeant Johnston's handwriting: 'Gabe,
check it out.' . . . The letter was from the Seattle office of the Drug
Enforcement Agency, stating that one Eddie Hart—busted in Seattle by
DEA agents—named the Rare Things Import Shop, 1543 West Thirty-
eighty Street, Denver, Colorado, as a front for smuggling marijuana
into the United States at the rate of five hundred to a thousand pounds
a week."

The alert reader will have noted that the actual affidavit states heroin
as the controlled substance, while the fictional passage above states
"marijuana." I—admittedly on rewrite—changed the substance as an
element of plot. The tip Wager gets from the DEA is not entirely accurate in every detail; like other forms of gossip, tips seldom are. However, this imaginative change enabled me to pace the discovery to the
novel's length and to add another element of mystery to the plot. The
point, of course, is that in fiction, the facts of a real event are subject to
change in the interests of structuring a good story. After all, the art of
fiction writing is the art of lying gracefully.

This routine tip will eventually lead to the central story of this novel, but Wager does not know that yet. He begins the process of "checking it out" through searching the department's contact files, cruising by the establishment to observe, and especially, by asking his informants about the Rare Things Import Shop and its manager, Rafael Alvarez.

As the affidavit implies, informants are key to the discovery and prosecution of much criminal activity, and—for the story teller—this places them on or near center stage. In the passage below is the fictional representation of Wager's meeting with "Informant A" of the affidavit:

> Wager carried his beer over. "Hello, Leonardo."
> "What the hell do you want, Wager?"
> "Rafael Alvarez. What do you hear of him?"
> Leonard tapped a cigarette on the plank table. "I'm goddamn tired of you leaning on me when you feel like it."
> "My friend," said Wager in his gentlest accent, "I own you."

Through this scene, as Wager puts pressure on the reluctant and resentful Leonard to gather information on Alvarez, the use of an imagined conflict defines the characters of both men and establishes their relationship. In addition, the scene ends with implications for the plot:

> ". . . Wager, I can't even make contact that soon!"
> "You hustle a little, my friend. Or you'll have a vacation in colorful Canyon City."
> Even in the dimness he saw Leonard's face pale so that the drooping mustache looked black against his lips. "They'd kill me."
> "I know. Eleven. Tomorrow night."

None of this, of course, is in the affidavit; but all of it derived from the facts worked on by my imagination. Informant A became a principal character in the fictional narrative because story and scene demanded it; he shows through his actions the deeds summed up in the affidavit. As the novel progresses, Wager brings increased pressure on Leonard to produce more information by threatening him with exposure as a snitch. Two or three chapters later, Wager and Leonard meet again:

> Wager leaned down and murmured toward the ear nestled in bushy sideburns. "I hear he's heavy into heroin."
> Leonard's soft face jerked back, dark eyes wide. "You didn't hear that from me!"
> "I should have, *amigicito*."
> The eyes blinked twice, three times. "You son of a bitch."

"Think about it—you say people know you've been asking questions. I can put out the word I heard it from you."

"You son of a bitch."

"Or I can give you some cover."

"You set me up!"

"You're goddamn right I did. And if you don't produce, you are dead. Cold dead. You check in with me in three days with some solid information or the word goes out about our meeting tonight." He left Leonard staring at the cloudy ice cubes in his drink, a sour expression on his face, from his stomach or from Wager or from both.

About halfway through the novel, Wager eventually gets his information from Informant A. Leonard, now too terrified to leave his hotel room, knows he is marked to be killed by Alvarez. Wager pays him the snitch fee and forces him onto a bus to New York.

Leonard seemed to lose air, shriveling up inside the grimy suit that was too big to start with, until he looked half the size he was. "Wager, I don't want to go. I don't even know anybody there. I'm gonna die there, I know it."

"You're dead if you stay here, and I don't want your carcass in my territory."

Leonard stared at Wager and started to speak. Then he stopped. Then blurted, "I used to think maybe it was almost a game between you and me. You know, we bad mouth each other and then you say you're not going to give me any bread and I say I'm not going to give you any information, and we both know we'll deal in the end. It was a kind of game." He paused and picked with dirty fingernails at a thread on his cuff. "Christ, Wager, I don't know nobody in New York. Please don't send me there."

"There's the bus. It's loading now."

"It never was a game with you, was it? I mean the way it was for me?"

Wager said nothing; he pulled the man after him toward the open door of the bus where a gray-uniformed driver stood checking tickets and helping an old lady reach the first step.

"Wager, of all the people I know, and I know some bad dudes, you're the worst. You are a real bastard."

"You want a kiss goodbye?"

The last image of Informant A in this fictional representation is of him boarding the bus as Wager turns to walk away.

As author, I may feel sorry for someone whose life is as lost and wasted as Leonard's, but Wager, as fictional cop, does not. His character is shown to be in determined and single-minded pursuit of his case, working in a world where life is hard and "games" are delusions, and where trust, affection, and human respect have been replaced by power.

While none of these thematic elements exists in the original affidavit, the facts of that affidavit and my questions arising from those facts provided the impetus for creating this storyline and its scenes. The result was that Informant A and the facts he offered became Leonard, his life, and his relationship with Wager, and also defined Wager's world. In short, the writer's imagination by working on the facts of real life produced a story.

❏ 37

SECRETS OF ROMANTIC CONFLICT

BY VANESSA GRANT

ROMANCE IS A MASSIVE MARKET, WITH THOUSANDS OF DEVELOPING writers struggling to crack it. Those who succeed know how to create and resolve romantic conflict to sustain suspense.

Romance literature tells us that love is the most powerful force in our lives. A story that does not convey this message is not a romance, although it may contain a romantic subplot.

Even romances that end unhappily, like *Casablanca* and *Bridges of Madison County,* show readers how love can help one achieve personal growth. In the best romances, this powerful love-message is inseparable from story conflict and suspense.

What is romantic conflict?

In a romance, falling in love creates problems for both hero and heroine, but ultimately love's power provides the solution. During their romantic journey, characters must experience both internal and external conflict as they struggle to achieve their goals.

Internal conflict is the result of a character's wanting two incompatible things. A hero wants love, yet fears being vulnerable. A heroine must keep a secret, although her moral code demands honesty.

In my novel, *Hidden Memories*, my heroine Abby has a secret. Her daughter Trish was conceived with Ryan, a stranger she met when she was in shock after her husband's death. Abby knows she should be honest about her daughter's real father, but fears the consequences of telling the truth. She wants to be an honest person, but she wants to hide the truth. Because she can't have both, she struggles inwardly.

If your characters don't experience internal conflict, you're telling the reader that the issues in this story aren't important enough to worry about. Internal conflict is essential, but external conflict generates excitement. If your hero and heroine don't experience *external* threats to their goals, they'll spend the book agonizing about the internal struggle and your reader will become impatient. External conflict occurs when characters struggle with each other over opposing goals. When characters with opposing goals have transactions with each other, conflict moves out in the open, becoming visible to readers and other characters.

Whenever a character experiencing internal conflict acts in response to that struggle, it becomes externalized and may create conflict with other characters. Abby's internal conflict, when she acts on it, has the potential to affect Ryan, her daughter, her daughter's grandfather, and her parents.

In Chapter One, Abby tries to hide when she recognizes Ryan across a crowded room. He could expose her secret and throw her life into turmoil. Even before Abby makes the first move in her struggle with this hero, she's fighting with her conscience, Ryan's right to know his child, and her desire to avoid exposure. When Ryan recognizes Abby, his attempt to learn all he can about her threatens to expose her secret even more. She fears he'll learn she has a daughter and realize he's the father. Abby's frightened response to the external conflict generates intensifying internal conflict.

In your novel, external conflict should always intensify the internal conflict.

Ryan wants to know why Abby disappeared after their brief affair. Once he learns she's had his child, he wants to form a strong relationship with his daughter. Because Abby wants to maintain the fiction that Trish is her dead husband's daughter, she can't let him have what he wants. Their opposing goals create both internal and external conflict.

Every step in the external struggle between Ryan and Abby makes Abby's internal conflict worse. Because of her internal conflict, when the external conflict begins, her reactions are instinctive, not logical. Characters experiencing heightened internal conflict often behave irrationally.

Abby is under stress, attacked from outside by Ryan, from inside by her own conscience. She tries to hide, to pretend, to evade. Ryan becomes suspicious. Abby's mother, who likes Ryan, makes things worse when she tries some matchmaking. As Abby and Ryan fall in love, both internal and external conflict skyrocket.

With strong internal conflict and strong interlinking external conflict, the stakes rise. The reader fears it won't work out for these characters. Will Abby drive Ryan away with her inability to live openly with the truth? Will Ryan become angry and leave? The more uncertainty readers feel over the outcome, the more satisfied they will be when hero and heroine come together in the end.

As your story progresses, the conflict must change and develop. Your hero and heroine must have trouble getting what they want, they must worry about it, doubting whether their relationship can work. For good reasons, they must offend one another. We all commit offenses against people we love because we're tired, worried, or afraid we're not loved as much as we love. Those are valid emotional reasons arising from our internal conflicts. They generate transactions that are part of external conflict.

In a love story, the conflict eventually develops to make the reader ask: "Do hero and heroine care enough about each other to make the necessary compromises? Can they trust each other enough to reveal their inner selves and commit to a believable, lasting relationship?

How to create conflict

Conflict is created when goals meet obstacles. To create conflict, first give your character an important goal, then have someone oppose that goal.

Every strong desire has its corresponding fear. If you combine your character's goal to a fear, you'll achieve a high level of internal conflict when things begin to go wrong. Abby's goal of keeping her secret is attached to her fear of what will happen if the truth becomes known. Her late husband was a famous artist, and although he destroyed Abby's sense of self, the world believed their marriage was idyllic. Now, however, if the truth is exposed, both Abby and her daughter will suffer.

Strong goals conceal strong fears.

By the time Ryan discovers Abby's lie, they are struggling with their own new relationship. The external conflict issues have grown. They are in conflict over Ryan's desire to be acknowledged as Trish's father, Abby's fear of committing to another disastrous relationship, and his insistence that they marry and become a family.

To create conflict in your story, give your character a goal, then ask yourself what fear hides behind that goal. The more powerful the fear, the higher the level of conflict. If your hero's goal is financial power, why is money so important to him? What does he fear? Did he live in severe poverty as a child? Perhaps he vowed never to be poor again. If he fears poverty, intensify the fear by making it personal. Perhaps his baby brother had a disease requiring expensive medical care. The hero worked a paper route, mowed lawns, and dug ditches for extra money, but it wasn't enough. The brother died.

This hero has a deep emotional fear that someone he loves will suffer again, and he won't be able to provide enough. With this fear behind his drive to achieve wealth, any threat to his financial security will create strong internal conflict. If this hero must choose between money and the woman he loves, all his fears about poverty will be aroused, and he'll be thrown into severe conflict. If he chooses money, he'll lose his love and the joy in life. If he chooses love, he'll lose the money and may be unable to keep his love safe. Unless your story is a tragedy, the hero will have to win the battle against his demons and choose love. His struggle will involve pain, suffering, and sacrifice.

From conflict to resolution

A good story begins by putting forth a *story question* in the reader's mind. In a romance novel, the story question is usually, "Will heroine and hero overcome the obstacles to love—*their conflict issues*—and find happiness?"

In *Hidden Memories,* Abby's opening conflict arises from her internal struggle between honesty and fear. As the story progresses, the conflict changes and develops. When Ryan discovers Trish is his daughter, he wants Abby to marry him so that they can be a family, but she believes their marriage would be a disaster. Abby and Ryan still struggle over their daughter's identity, but a new element has been added: Abby's fear of the pain she risks if she surrenders to her growing love for Ryan and agrees to marry him.

As your story progresses, new problems should continue to emerge as the romantic conflict moves through several stages: beginning, middle, black moment, and ending. Ideally, the beginning of your story will create suspense and curiosity in your reader by showing or hinting at internal or external conflict. If you didn't put conflict in the first page of your manuscript, try beginning the story at a different point.

Here are a few examples from the opening paragraphs of my own stories:

> It couldn't be him!
> Abby had dreamed him in nightmares, dreams suppressed and almost forgotten. A man's head and shoulders glimpsed across a room . . .
>
> from *Hidden Memories*
>
> Eight hours was too long. She should have walked right up to Connar and faced him this morning at the exhibition. "Let's talk," she should have said.
>
> from *Yesterday's Vows*
>
> "We may have to turn back!" the pilot shouted over the engine noise.
> "Can't you give it a try?" Sarah squinted to see through the windscreen and wished herself back in her Vancouver office.
>
> from *Nothing Less Than Love*

If you begin your story by tossing your characters into strong conflict—with themselves, each other, or circumstances—you'll be off to a good start. As your story progresses, your characters should face a series of problems that create increasing conflict, thus forcing them to wrestle with the real issue. A satisfying novel pits characters against overwhelming odds, then leaves them to struggle through disaster after disaster until victory is won.

Heroine and hero may have a wonderful time on a date. They may laugh, make love, even get married, but despite their ultimate victories, the problems keep coming until happiness seems impossible. The harder you make life for your characters, the better your readers will like the book. Until you reach the final scene, every transaction must present new problems, or new developments to old problems. Forget everything you ever learned about being nice to people. To be a good storyteller, you must treat your characters terribly, throwing their worst fears in their faces

In a satisfying romance, the suspense between hero and heroine culminates in a black moment when all seems lost. To be powerful, the black moment must emerge from the personality and fears of your characters, and it must be deeply related to the conflict issue. The more powerful your moment, the more satisfying the resolution.

It is only after the black moment, when hero and heroine realize that they've lost each other, that they can experience the full strength of their love. In the aftermath of the black moment, hero and heroine each realize that their relationship matters more than the convictions they held so rigidly. After this realization, they are willing to make the necessary sacrifice to achieve their happy ending.

Panicked by Ryan's demands for marriage and her own fears, Abby finally succeeds in driving Ryan away, only to realize how bleak life will be without the man she loves. If the conflict is based on your characters' fears and personal history, the sacrifice must be related. The hero who fears poverty must sacrifice the illusion that money can prevent personal loss. Abby, who fears exposure, must embrace truth and risk herself.

To achieve a happy ending, lovers must always sacrifice their need to protect themselves against abandonment. They must allow themselves to become vulnerable, to risk broken hearts and grief, before they can win the prize of true intimacy.

It is only at the end of the romance novel, when hero and heroine make their sacrifices and emerge victorious over the conflicts that threaten their future, that the reader's suspense is ended with the satisfying answer to the story question.

Can this couple overcome the obstacles to love and find a happy ending?

Yes, they can, but it isn't easy.

❏ 38

WRITING MYSTERY NOVELS: SOME MODEST HINTS AND WARNINGS

BY GWENDOLINE BUTLER

THE MYSTERY NOVEL, MUCH MORE THAN THE MAINSTREAM NOVEL, must appear spontaneous, but it cannot be so. No one was better at this than its begetter, Wilkie Collins, Agatha Christie in her prime, and my favorite writer, Elizabeth Daly. At the moment I would award the palm to the English writer Reginald Hill, and I wish Raymond Chandler was not dead, but Ross Macdonald took his place marvelously (in a slightly different mystery style), and so did his wife Margaret Millar. Her books read as if they were just happening to someone she knew.

Contrivance is necessary, because the mystery novel must contain a puzzle, a problem to be solved. A question must be raised for the reader to brood over, and then it must be resolved, logically, so the reader believes. There is an unspoken contract with the readers that they will be treated fairly by the author and given an honest answer somewhere in the book. There is trust between the writer and the reader: You do not cheat. At the same time, you cannot be totally straightforward. After all, this is a mystery novel, so you have to sustain reader interest. I've found that it is often wise to make several mysteries hang upon one big one, say, a death in unusual circumstances. Or you know there is a body, but it has completely disappeared. How? Why? Or a body may be found, hidden in another grave. Either a modern one or a stone age tumulus that is being excavated. Again, how and why? Perhaps the body has red socks on—and nothing else.

All these "clues" help because as one after another of the minor puzzles is solved, they are steps to the main solution. No fudging is allowed; there must be a good, practical reason for the killer to dispose of the body in this way. Not just a mad murderer with a taste for a stone age burial mound and red socks!

You can see from all this that the mystery cannot just resolve itself;

189

it must have a solver or a detective, a person who is believable and who uses techniques that are real. You cannot pretend or invent techniques, especially as readers grow ever more sophisticated. What sort of a detective? Well, the days of amateur detectives, like Lord Peter Wimsey, are over—much enjoyed but finished—so as the writer, you have a choice: You can keep the action brisk and compressed so that your non-professional detective can clear up everything before the police get there, or you can have a pro, either a policeman or scientist of some sort, or a lawyer. If you have a police officer, it is advisable to read up on police procedure or get to know a police detective, because readers today are very knowledgeable. I like to have a police officer, myself, but if you do so, you must remember to make your detective story entertaining as well as accurate. The mystery novel is very elastic: It is not just a puzzle; it should also reflect society, its manners, and its problems. The spy story or the thriller can, to a certain extent, be a fairy story; the crime story never can.

The detective stories of the 30's and 40's tended to be puzzles, such as those solved by the New York detective Inspector Queen and his son Ellery. The Queen novels posed a problem and then demanded the reader solve it. To a certain extent, this was even the case with Hercule Poirot, as depicted by Agatha Christie, but she had an engaging way of winding the reader into her stories. To my mind, the modern detective story reads better if the plot does not depend on a cunning alibi.

All the same, it is still a puzzle story with which you want to tantalize readers before letting them see the truth. It's good if they can gradually work the problem out, bit by bit; but technically, I think it is much better, more satisfying, if readers come up with the answers by degrees, rather than in one great denouement—although a final thunderbolt, if you can manage it, is splendid.

Because a mystery story raises questions, you have to be careful of your technique. To my mind it is vital to know the end before you write the beginning, although within that framework, I like the plot to grow toward its ending. I would feel it dishonest to begin with one murderer in mind, but then to change it halfway through; that would mean that any killer would do, provided there was a surprise. Not everyone would agree with me there. Some writers might consider this too strict a rule.

In my crime novels, the detective is the questioner, so I give him (or her) the focus, and tell the story mainly through his or her eyes. You may prefer to have the narrator an innocent before whose eyes the story unfolds, but make sure that such a story is told in the first person. There are drawbacks here: Since the narrator cannot be everywhere, he or she will have to rely on reported evidence. The first-person narrator has been suspect ever since Agatha Christie, in *The Murder of Roger Ackroyd*, used the device in a devastating way. No writer has dared to do it quite like that again.

It is probably wiser to avoid too crowded a Dickensian scene, but you do need some interesting secondary characters among whom to hide the victim and the killer. A surprise victim is always a welcome touch, so the reader can say: "I didn't expect *that* one to get killed!" But secondary and minor characters have other uses besides providing handy victims. They can help explain plot points and push the action forward. And I feel that they must have real reason for being a part of the plot, indeed for being in the novel at all. I even like a walk-on character to have a real reason for being in the story. You can't always do this, of course, and part of being a writer is inventing a likable, amusing character, so don't deny yourself this pleasure. I have to admit that I have several times invented a cat or a dog as a character for my amusement. Of course, I try to give them some plot point: They can find a body or bite the killer. Others could do that, of course, but the animals are my present to myself.

Minor characters can present a problem: You as the writer can get too interested in them and upset the balance of the plot. Take, for example, this imaginary plot: A woman newspaper editor is stabbed in her office. The murderer is, in fact, her estranged husband, but the false clues suggest it is a political killing, since she is famous for her right-wing views and has quarreled with an MP with whom she has had an affair. He is suspect number one. But the dead woman's daughter is a fashion editor for another paper and might interest the writer who enjoys using models, photographers, and eccentric couturiers as characters. Great fun, but they are not the main plot. You may be tempted to develop this aspect of the plot, but you should control it. Though it may be amusing, plotwise it is a dead end. Go back to the mainstream—the daughter and her relationship with her father and mother. It is a family murder, not a political one.

Very important, too, is the setting of the crime. Make it as real as possible and know your way around it. There was a period when maps were popular, and they do make the scene concrete, but the mystery novel has widened its territory and no longer is confined to, say, a country house or a college. Even the books about the Oxford colleges where Inspector Morse works do not provide a map, as did the Oxford book introducing Inspector Appleby of long ago. Today the emphasis is more psychological and scientific, rather than on alibis and maps.

Finally, there are a few very practical points that you should remember as you write your mystery:

If you find it hard to remember names, you should write them down as soon as you have the characters on the scene; keep a handwritten list at your elbow. Also, be sure to avoid names that are too much alike or begin with the same letter.

If you have a character who is part of a series—for example, the detective with his or her friends, secretaries, and assistants—it is wise to keep a list with a short biography for each one!

All this is a gospel of perfection, but I must confess that I have just written the first chapter of a novel in which a character meant to be secondary has walked onto the page with such energy that I know he means to stay there.

❑ 39

IDEAS IN SCIENCE FICTION

BY POUL ANDERSON

"WHERE DO YOU GET YOUR IDEAS?"

Probably every sort of writer hears this question once in a while, but science fiction writers surely more than most. In the past it often took the form, "Where do you get those crazy ideas?" but since then the field has become quite widely accepted, even respectable. Discoveries in science and advances in technology have given dazzling proof that science fiction's visions are not absurd. Meanwhile, such popular shows as "Star Trek" and *StarWars* have made many of those concepts—space travel, time travel, alien intelligences, artificial intelligences, genetic engineering, and much more—common currency.

Now, nobody claims that science fiction predicts the future or explores the universe. No "future history" has matched the actual course of events. We writers failed to anticipate a heap of developments, all the way from the Internet and its revolutionary impact, to the use of galaxies as gravitational lenses. We seized on them only as they came to pass. The few times a story has come near the mark, it's been on the shotgun principle: Put out enough different notions, and you have a chance of making an occasional hit. Moreover, a number of our standard motifs—most obviously time travel and travel faster than light—may well prove to be forever impossible.

But then, we aren't in the business of prophecy; we're storytellers. We look at the cosmos around us, wonder what this or that *might* imply, and express our thoughts in fictional, human terms.

The question "Where do you get your ideas?" is legitimate. Science fiction is preeminently a literature of ideas. The answer is: the world. Anything whatsoever may spark a story—a personal experience, something that happened to someone else, something read or seen or heard or watched on a screen, a news item, a mathematical calculation, a dream, a chance remark—anything. What counts is what you do with it. This tie to reality, however remote and unlikely it may become, is perhaps what distinguishes science fiction from fantasy. (Not that fantasy doesn't include many fine works, but it isn't what I shall be discussing.)

Admittedly, there's a lot of bad science fiction around, most conspicuously in the movies and on television, but also abundant on the newsstands and in bookstores. Characters are cardboard; plots are cookie-cutter; the underlying ideas, if any, are either ridiculous or old and worn-out, with no attempt made at the touch of originality that would freshen them a bit. We won't say more about this. If you want to write science fiction, you want it to be good, don't you?

You'll find yourself in excellent company. A significant amount of what appears in print meets high literary as well as intellectual standards while being a pleasure to read. The sheer volume of published science fiction nowadays is such that some of the good science fiction gets overlooked, lost in the pile of trash. However, some does deservedly well. Editors remain eager to discover strong new voices. In addition, although novels dominate, the science fiction (and mystery) magazines and anthologies are almost the only surviving homes for short stories. A budding writer would do well to start with them, gaining experience and reputation before making the investment of time and effort that a book requires.

First, though, you had better be reasonably familiar with the field and enjoy it. Life's too short to struggle with stuff that bores you. Also, if you don't know what's been done, you're too apt to waste your energy reinventing the wheel. Thus, "attack from outer space" is an ancient theme. Set forth baldly, it will only draw yawns. Yet it can still succeed, if the author presents unique, thought-provoking aspects. What are the aliens like? You can design interesting, hitherto unknown beings. Why are they here? After all, a technology capable of crossing interstellar space should be able to produce everything its people want at home. How do humans react? It won't be uniformly. For instance, throughout history on Earth, again and again a local faction has allied itself with foreign invaders, hoping they will crush its hated neighbors.

In my opinion, two streams run through science fiction. The first traces back to Jules Verne. It is "the idea as hero." His tales are mainly concerned with the concept—a submarine, a journey to the center of the planet, and so on. The second derives from H.G. Wells. His own ideas were brilliant, but he didn't care how implausible they might be, an invisible man or a time machine or whatever. He concentrated on the characters, their emotions and interactions.

Today, we usually speak of these two streams as "hard" and "soft" science fiction. Needless to say, they were never completely separate. Verne's characters are lively, sometimes memorable. When he chose to, Wells could write a story focused on a future development: for example, "The Land Ironclads," which foresaw the military tank. Ideally, the streams unify in a tale that meets both scientific and conventional literary standards. Though this is not exactly common, our best writers have achieved it oftener than one might think.

Indeed, not just the quantity but the diversity of current science fiction is amazing. You can find everything from the wonderfully conceived and carefully executed planets of Hal Clement to the far-flung romances of Jack Vance, from the gritty sociology of Frederick Pohl through the headlong adventure of S.M. Stirling, to the humor and sensitivity of Gordon R. Dickson—all of them, and many more, first-class reading. This is another reason for writers to know what their colleagues have been doing. It inspires.

In this short piece I can't take up the purely literary side. I'm not sure that any "how to" about it can be taught, except for advising that you experience widely, meditate on that experience, learn something about everything, and read the great works of world literature. But perhaps I can offer a few suggestions about sources of ideas and what can be accomplished by taking thought.

We begin with science and technology. You want to keep up with these fields anyway. In this day and age, I don't see how any person can be called educated who doesn't. Besides, they're boundlessly rich fountainheads of exciting story possibilities. You don't need a professional degree. Yes, Gregory Benford is a physicist who as a sideline writes novels of high literary quality; but Greg Bear is a layman whose work, equally well-written, also goes believably to the frontiers of our knowledge and beyond. We have no dearth of fascinating, authoritative books and periodicals that report from these frontiers. Prowl the bookstores and libraries; consider joining the Library of Science book club. Among magazines, I'll list *Science News, Discover, Scientific American,* and the British *New Scientist.* I subscribe to several others, too, but these four, especially the first, have the most general coverage that I know of.

All fiction deals with people. Even the rare story that has no humans in it is necessarily told from a human viewpoint. I've mentioned personal experience and the masterworks of the world as means of gaining a deeper understanding. We acquire knowledge of a more structured kind from history, anthropology, psychology, and other studies of our species. Among the benefits, we find that our twentieth-century Western civilization is not the only expression of human variousness, and probably won't be the final one. What we learn we can transmute into exotic story situations.

We can't do this mechanically. At least, attempts to generate a setting by simply changing names have had pretty dismal results. The writer's imagination must come into play, along with hard thought.

As an example of how different sources flow together, doubtless not the best but closely known to me, let me bring in my novel *The People of the Wind*. For a long time I'd wanted to write a story about a planet colonized jointly by humans and a nonhuman race. Traveling in France, I happened on the Alsatian city of Belfort. Although ethnically German, the Alsatians are fiercely patriotic French citizens. The heroic resistance of Belfort during the Franco-Prussian War caused it to be spared the annexation to Germany that the rest of the province suffered from 1871 to 1918. Ah-ha! Subjecting my planet to this kind of stress should dramatically highlight its mixed society.

In my last conversation with the late John Campbell, editor of *Analog* magazine, he tossed off the idea that post-mammalian evolution may produce a kind of biological supercharger, powered by the animal's motion and conferring tremendous cursive ability. I saw at once that this would also enable a man-sized creature with a man-sized brain to fly on a planet similar to Earth. Such a species would be satisfyingly alien to ours, but communication and cooperation were not ruled out.

These elements were a bare beginning. The planet, while habitable, would not be a copy of Earth. It would have its own characteristics and its own native life. In addition, human and nonhuman colonists would introduce plants and animals from their home worlds. Thus we'd get a mixed ecology, too. All of this needed working out in detail. Likewise did the aliens. Their anatomy had to be functional. The power of flight would basically influence their psyches. So would its energy demands;

they'd be obligate carnivores, highly territorial. What social arrangements could they make? What would their languages sound like? What religions might they have? How would they and the humans influence each other? And the humans themselves wouldn't be the same as us today, when the story was set centuries in the future.

A great deal of effort went into such questions before any actual writing started, but I've seldom had more fun, and I hope the end product was interesting and vivid.

Be prepared for arguments. Science fiction readers are bright, well-informed, and good-naturedly scrappy. Thus, Larry Niven's *Ringworld* is a marvelously complete visualization of a splendid concept, a world in the form of a gigantic ring around its sun and the myriad cultures that could arise on so vast an area. It deserved the sales and awards it won. Nevertheless, several persons pointed out that he'd gotten the rotation of the Earth backward, others that the structure would be gravitationally unstable. He corrected the first mistake in a second edition. To explain how Ringworld was kept in orbit, he wrote a sequel, which naturally became more of a tour and which also was a publishing success. I too have received valuable critiques, information, and suggestions from readers—almost as much as from the conversations with my wife. Contacts like these are a major reward of writing science fiction.

Note well, Niven didn't wish tedious lectures on us. He never does. People and places come to life in the course of story events. Often a hint is enough. Robert Heinlein was an absolute master of this technique. Such casual-looking phrases as "The door dilated" or "A police car was balanced on the rooftop" throw us straight into the future. He could do this because he had very fully developed his background. He could pick and choose what items to show.

In a way, we science fiction writers are professional daydreamers. We give our readers what we have imagined. But that imagining should spring from reality, which is infinitely varied and surprising; and beneath the color, suspense, stylistic experimentation, and all else, it should make sense.

❏ 40

You Don't Need a History Degree to Write Historical Fiction

By Cynthia Bass

READERS WHO LOVE HISTORICAL NOVELS DEMAND MORE FROM THEIR fiction than good stories with compelling characters. They hope to relive the past. They expect accuracy; they value atmosphere; they search for interesting bits of information. They want to look up from a book and say, "I didn't know they had pretzels during the Civil War!"

For writers of historical fiction, this means that we need to know some real history. But even if your primary memory of high school history is a lot of naps, don't panic! It isn't necessary to know everything. There are several easy ways to get all the information you need to help you write a detailed, informative, high-quality historical novel—without a history degree. Here's how you do it:

Master the basic facts

The first (and most difficult) step is to learn the major facts about your time period. For this you need some trustworthy *secondary sources*.

A "secondary source" is a history or biography written by an expert in the field. *Battle Cry of Freedom*, by James MacPherson, and *A Distant Mirror*, by Barbara Tuchman, are examples of excellent secondary sources. Libraries and bookstores are full of choices for every conceivable time and place.

A good secondary source uses information that is cited, either in footnotes or annotations in the back of the book. There also should be a bibliography, with references to other sources. Footnotes and a bibliography are of crucial importance: They show that the author is not just presenting a partisan viewpoint without any serious research. Also, they're useful in helping you locate further research materials.

I use three simple tests to judge the "trustworthiness" of a secondary source. First, is it cited by *other* secondary sources? This practice is known as cross-citing. If a book is not cross-cited, it's unlikely that its interpretation can be used with confidence.

My second test for trustworthiness is the publisher. Reputable publishers may seem to publish a lot of bad fiction, but they don't, as a rule, bring out bad history.

Example: Recently, when researching my new novel about German physicists and the atomic bomb, I found a book at my library that argued that England, not Nazi Germany, started World War II. In view of the fact that WW II began when the Nazis invaded Poland, this assertion sounded suspicious. So I checked the publisher and found no listing for them. Later, I found out they're known for publishing pro-Nazi books—definitely the kind of sources to avoid.

My third test is the writing. Trustworthy secondary sources are seldom exciting, and they're often even a little boring, because what's important to the writers is the information, not the style.

How do you tell when you've read enough secondary sources? When you feel that you know what happened during the time period you've chosen. This may take one book or a dozen, but the day will come that your period holds no more surprises. Now for the fun: the details.

Making the jump from overview to close-up

A historical novel is successful if it makes you feel you're living in the period. As a writer, you can achieve that success by using *primary sources*. A "primary source" is a source created in the past for the use of the people living at that time. Primary sources have the immediacy and freshness of something intended for daily consumption, and using them extensively gives your novel the specificity of real life. Three primary sources are invaluable for historical novelists:

1. *Newspapers and magazines*
Newspapers and magazines tell a lot about a society. Don't read *only* the news, though; read advertisements, letters to the editor, "human interest" stories and help-wanted ads. You're not so much seeking information as immersion. You want to know what everyday life was like.

Consider advertisements. When researching my second novel,

Maiden Voyage, which took place on the *Titanic*, I checked out a copy of *Collier's*—a once-popular, now defunct magazine—in which I saw an ad for catsup. This ad opened up my main character's world for me. It showed me that 1912 was an era of mass production and that people splurged on non-essential items. On the label I saw a "pure food" stamp and a "wholesomeness rating." This meant people were worried about food purity and contamination of manufactured goods. Then I read the copy. Catsup is being touted as "good for the female figure—high in nutrients, promotes slimness." Oh, my—they were already pushing weight loss. All this from one ad!

Besides regular advertisements, check the help-wanted ads, to learn not only what jobs were available and how much they paid, but as a microcosm of a society. For example, in 1912, help-wanted ads in Boston routinely excluded Irish applicants; in New York, Italians; in Seattle, Chinese. They also describe 60-hour work weeks, mandatory church attendance, and minimum height and weight requirements (these positions often required some heavy lifting). References to any of this will do wonders for the authenticity of your fiction.

Letters to the editor and special-interest articles are also gold mines. They tell you what people of the time thought important. For example, most letters to the editor in Great Britain on the eve of the First World War concern Ireland, not Germany, while in France, special-interest articles all center on a murder trial. Only in Germany and Austria do the letters and articles mention a possible war.

2. *Fiction*

Reading fiction published in your time period will help you discover how people of the time spoke. One of the worst mood-breakers in fiction is the anachronism. It's also one of the most obvious; even the most non-historically-minded reader will catch these goofs (the word "goof," by the way, is from World War I; don't have a lady-in-waiting for Catherine the Great say it!).

Another benefit of reading fiction of your time period is that you sometimes discover expressions you think of as "modern" have been around for a long time. I never realized that use of the verb "make" to mean "seduce" was a time-honored practice till I saw it in Balzac's *Cousin Bette*.

Read both "good" and "popular" fiction from the period—good because it shows standards of the day, popular because it shows how people actually spoke in everyday life.

3. *Letters and diaries*

Letters and diaries are incredibly rich sources for the details of daily existence—food, fashion, health, family, love. Because letters and diaries were written for private consumption, they often brought up topics not seen as fit to print. Thus, they can provide you with an intimate knowledge of your period never found in the more self-conscious primary sources mentioned above.

Example: One of the narrators of my first novel, *Sherman's March*, is General Sherman ("War is hell") himself. At the outset, I knew quite a bit about his Civil War exploits: the burning of Atlanta, the March to the Sea. What I didn't know (and never would have dreamed) is how many female "acquaintances" he had in the South. I learned about these women from his letters, and I used the information to write a chapter in which he meets an old lover.

How far back should you go?

Your research should go further back than the main time period of your novel, because characters often remember events from their pasts, and you need to know what those memories are. For a main character, I would go back to when he or she is approximately three years old. For instance, all the action in *Sherman's March* takes place during the three weeks of Sherman's March to the Sea (1864); still, I had to go back to 1823 (when Sherman was three years old) to know what sort of memories he had, so that his reveries would sound like those of a real person.

And don't think you can avoid this research by creating only young characters! If *any* character is older, you need insight into his memories, too. One of the most boring clichés in fiction is the generic geezer, spouting off about the good old days, without giving a concrete example of those good old days, because the author stopped her research too soon. If a character reminisces about her teen-age years during the Great Depression, don't have her remember a romantic dance with a long-lost beau; have her remember dancing to "Tangerine."

When can you stop the research and start writing?

This one's easy. You stop when the period you've been researching feels real to you. And as soon as you reach this point, make sure you *do* stop: Don't use endless research as an excuse not to write your novel. Find some reliable secondary material and a variety of primary sources; learn what you can; gain confidence; and then start writing.

One final word about research: Research can make history come alive, but it can't by itself do the same for your characters. That's because the essence of character isn't the facts of the past but your characters' passions as they respond to that past. So make sure to fill your head with facts before you start, but make doubly sure that your heart goes into your fiction.

❑ 41

Partners in Crime

By Marcia Muller

LIKE MANY CRIME WRITERS, I CAME TO THE GENRE THROUGH MY LOVE of reading, and the novels that most appealed to me were those featuring private investigators. Possibly because I don't respond well to any type of authority, I was fascinated by detectives who, unhampered by regulations and procedure, would set off down the mean streets to right wrongs, strong and unafraid. As one who had always wanted to write, I'd then dream of creating my own character who would walk those streets, strong and unafraid.

Unfortunately, almost all the fictional models at that time were male, and while I could empathize with men and understand them on an individual basis, of course I didn't know the slightest thing about actually *being* male. Thus, the character I'd dream of creating was always a woman.

By the time I'd seriously begun to consider writing a novel featuring a private investigator of my own, I'd discovered several authors who were doing excellent characterization within the framework of the crime novel. Bill Pronzini (whom I did not know at the time, but to whom I'm now married) wrote about a detective who had no name, yet I knew intimate details about him that made him more real to me than many characters *with* names. Lillian O'Donnell had created New York City policewoman Norah Mulcahaney who, in addition to a lively professional life, found time to marry; her family life provided a rich backdrop to the cases she solved.

When I sat down to write my first (never published, and quite horrible) Sharon McCone novel, I was well aware that I could create a woman who would conform to the stereotype of the hard-bitten loner with the whiskey bottle in the desk drawer. Or I could make her a camera who observed the world around her without fully reacting or interacting. Or, at the far end of the spectrum, I could create a woman who would be a fully developed individual.

Sharon McCone, I decided, was to be as close to a real person as possible. Like real people she would age, grow, change; experience joy and sorrow, love and hatred—in short, the full range of human emotions. In addition, McCone was to live within the same framework most of us do, complete with family, friends, coworkers, and lovers; each of her cases would constitute one more major event in an ongoing biography. This choice also had a practical basis. In writing crime fiction, the author frequently asks the reader to suspend disbelief in situations that are not likely to occur in real life. Private investigators do not, as a rule, solve dozens of murder cases over the course of their careers. And what few criminals they do encounter do not tend to be as clever and intelligent as their fictional counterparts. To make the story convincing to the reader, the character and day-to-day details of her life had to be firmly grounded in reality.

The choice made, I realized I hadn't a clue as to how to go about creating such an individual. I had a name: Sharon, for my college roommate; McCone, for the late John McCone, former head of the CIA (a joke, since politically Sharon is as far from any CIA employee as one can get). I also had a location, San Francisco, my adopted home city. But as for the rest . . . ?

Should I make my character like me in background, lifestyle, appearance, and spirit? Certainly not! At the time I had no job, no recognizable skills, no prospects, a failing marriage, and was afraid of my own shadow. I longed to be three or four inches taller, to be fifteen to twenty pounds lighter, to be able to eat all the ice cream I wanted and never gain an ounce. And I was vehemently opposed to making Sharon's background similar to mine, lest I fall into the trap of undisciplined autobiographical writing.

I therefore began building McCone's character by giving her a background as different from mine as I could make it. She is a native Californian; I am not. She comes from a large blue-collar family; I do not. She put herself through the University of California at Berkeley by working as a security guard; I was supported by my parents during my six years at the University of Michigan. And Sharon has exotic Native American features and long black hair, is enviably tall and slender, and can eat whatever she likes without gaining weight. Since I don't possess such qualities, I wanted to spend time with a character who did.

At the time I was developing McCone, I was participating in an informal writers' workshop that met every week; fear of having nothing to read aloud at the sessions drove me daily to the typewriter. I chose to take the suggestion of the group leader (a published author) to work up a biographical sheet on McCone, in which I fine-tuned the other details of her life: names of parents and siblings; likes and dislikes; religious and political attitudes; talents and weaknesses; even the circumstances of her first sexual experience.

By the time I'd completed the biographical sheet, McCone finally emerged as real to me. Still, it was in a form that was more like a questionnaire than a work of fiction. At this point I was forced to face the fact that the only way to develop a character fully is to write her. And write her, and write her. . . .

Anyone who claims that first manuscripts aren't simply learning exercises is either exceptionally gifted or completely deluded. My early efforts were stiff and wooden and—with the exception of McCone's narrative voice, which was the same from the very first—totally different from what eventually saw publication.

I was insecure as to how to go about constructing a mystery, and in spite of my resolve to let the events flow from character, I found the stories becoming very plot-driven. I manipulated secondary characters and their actions to fit the plot; kept elaborate charts showing what every person was doing at every moment during the story; wrote long accounts of the back story (the events that set the crime in motion). I wasted paper, time, and energy concocting cryptic clues, red herrings, and unnecessary complications. Even after my third novel manuscript was accepted for publication, I continued to fall back on stock scenes and situations: ongoing antagonism between private investigator and police; the standard body-finding scene; the obligatory talk about the case in the office of Sharon's boss.

Fortunately, through all of this, McCone came into her own as a person and also became my full partner in fictional crime. I take little credit for this; it simply happened. Writers constantly talk about how their characters "just take over," and when I hear myself doing the same, I feel vaguely embarrassed, but it *does* happen, and is vitally important to any long-running series.

My theory about this phenomenon is that knowing one's character intimately allows the writer to tap into her subconscious, which usually works far ahead of the conscious mind. The fictional character's actions and reactions often have little to do with the writer's original intention. In this area, McCone has served me well.

I first experienced her determination to be her own person while writing the second book in the series, *Ask the Cards a Question* (1982). In my previous efforts, Sharon had many analytical conversations about her cases with her boss, Hank Zahn, and they inevitably took place in his office at All Souls Legal Cooperative, the poverty law firm where she worked. A third of the way through *Cards,* it seemed time for one of these talks, so I had Sharon leave her office for Hank's. But contrary to my intentions, she detoured down the hall to the desk of the co-op's secretary, Ted, to ask him where Hank was, and in doing so, she—and I—took a look around the big Victorian that housed All Souls. What I saw was a goldmine in terms of places to set scenes and characters to play in them: There were rooms, lots of them; there were attorneys and paralegal workers and other support staff, some of whom lived there communally, and often had potlucks and parties and poker games. As in any situation where people live and work at close quarters, there was the opportunity for conflict and resolution.

Where Hank Zahn had once been the only partner who had an identity, I now began to flesh out others. A number of them became important in McCone's life. They began to demand more important roles, and soon I realized that they—as well as McCone—would determine the direction that the series as a whole would take.

The development of fully realized characters is essential to creating a strong series. Without them, the author is simply manipulating cardboard people aimed at a specific—and usually contrived—end. Eventually the writer will become bored with the artificiality of the story and lose all sense of identification with the characters. And if the writer is bored, imagine the poor reader!

Over the twenty years I've been writing the McCone series, I've made a number of choices and changes, and each of these came from within Sharon's character and her reactions and interactions with others. This involves a firm commitment on my part to remain flexible, willing to switch directions mid-stream. Initially, this was a rather frightening process, but the rewards have proved considerable.

Different facets of McCone's character have been revealed to me by her interactions with other characters. A violent confrontation with a man she considered the most evil person she'd ever encountered, and the choice she made in dealing with him, affirmed that she was unable to step over the line into pointless violence. Another confrontation, this time when the lives of people she cared about were at stake, demonstrated that she could take violent action when the circumstances justified it.

During the past four years, McCone has revealed feelings and attitudes that have dictated radical changes in the overall direction of the series—long before I considered making any. When the All Souls partners threatened to confine Sharon to a desk job (*Wolf in the Shadows,* 1993), I'd originally intended for them to work out some sort of compromise, coupled with expanding the scope of her responsibilities. At the end of the novel, I was still undecided as to the nature of that compromise. But at the beginning of the next novel in the series, *Till the Butchers Cut Him Down* (1994), McCone made the decision for me: She decided to leave the co-op and establish her own agency, while retaining offices in the house—thus permitting her to continue her association with people for whom she cared.

But only months after her new office furniture was delivered, McCone began to doubt the wisdom of her decision. As I was writing a scene in *A Wild and Lonely Place* (1995), I found her saying, "No wonder I avoided having clients come to the office. . . . Actually, a lot of things about All Souls were beginning to pale for me." Her doubts mirrored my own, which I'd scarcely confronted until that point. She decided for me that the time had come to leave All Souls; time, in fact, for All Souls to become defunct. With roots in the 1970s, it was an outmoded institution; my attempts to bring it into the 1990s with its virtues intact had failed.

But in what direction to go? And where? Certainly not a stereotypical seedy office where McCone would keep a bottle in her desk drawer. And certainly not a suite in a high-rent building; she is too frugal for that.

The answer came to me while I was walking on the Embarcadero, San Francisco's waterfront boulevard, with a friend who was talking about some people she knew who had offices in a renovated pier. I looked around, spotted the San Francisco fireboat station, and noted a space between it and Pier 24 that was almost large enough for a fictional Pier 24½. The surrounding area was an exciting one, undergoing a renaissance; artists' lofts, lively clubs, trendy restaurants, and unusual sorts of enterprises abounded. And there was also San Francisco's rich maritime history, which offered many possibilities. Immediately, Sharon McCone made the decision to move her offices to Pier 24½.

But would I be forced to abandon Hank Zahn, his wife Anne-Marie Altman, Rae Kelleher, and Ted Smalley? Of course not. The co-op had paled for Anne-Marie several books before; it would now do the same for Hank, and they would decide to form their own law firm, then ask McCone to share a suite of offices with them. As for Rae and Ted, they would need jobs when All Souls went under, so Ted would come along as office manager, Rae as the first of what McCone hoped would be many operatives. Without delay, Sharon, Hank, and Anne-Marie signed a lease for space at Pier 24½.

A long and intimate association with well-rounded characters can not only enrich a series, but also an author's life. Over the years, I've found myself moving closer to McCone in spirit. Where she was once the independent, strong, brave half of the partnership, I've now become more independent, strong, and brave myself.

It's strange but gratifying to know that my own creation has empowered me. That's what the series is all about: to entertain and inspire the reader; perhaps to make some readers think more seriously about an issue that's important to McCone and me; and to give escape and pleasure to those who buy our books.

❏ 42

SELLING SPECULATIVE FICTION

BY LESLIE WHAT

THE GENRE KNOWN AS SCIENCE FICTION AND FANTASY IS MUCH MORE than rocket ships, dystopias, and elves. This might explain why some critics and writers prefer to call it "the literature of the fantastic" or "speculative fiction"—SF for short. SF magazines and anthologies publish a mix of unclassifiable fiction, magical realism, urban fantasy, alternative history, high fantasy, and hard science fiction. No matter what you call it, speculative fiction is a great field for the new writer.

Editors actively seek out talent: They attend conventions; make virtual appearances on-line; teach at workshops or conferences; and read unsolicited submissions from unknowns—unceremoniously known as "slush." Leading SF magazines publish only ten to twelve of every thousand manuscripts submitted; fortunately for new writers, every editor is a reader hoping to find precious words in that mountain of paper. And there are ways to make your work stand out, at least long enough for the editor to notice your name.

My first professionally published story, "King for a Day" (*Asimov's Science Fiction*), postulated that there were so many Elvis impersonators in Hell, the *real* Elvis had a hard time finding work. In my satiric vision of the afterlife, John Lennon waited in line to see himself. The acceptance was a bit of a surprise, because I hadn't been sure if "King for a Day" was *really* science fiction. But I was sure about the important things: The story was fast-paced, original, and lively; the manuscript proofread to the best of my ability. The rest was up to the editor.

Though the creative side may be in the writing, selling fiction is business, and in business, deals can be broken by a clumsy introduction. Take time to come up with a title that creates interest and excitement in the story. A knockout line from the text might do, or a portion of a quote that has always intrigued you. Titles can mirror the concept of the story. "Designated Hater" (*Magazine of Fantasy and Science Fic-*

tion) took its cue from the American League, but twisted the rules for the sake of the plot. "The Goddess is Alive, and Well, Living in New York City" (*Asimov's Science Fiction*) reworked a bumper sticker I saw on pre-1980 VW vans. Titles work best when they reflect both the tone and language of the story. "A Dark Fire, Burning from Within" (*Realms of Fantasy*) tells the reader not to expect one of my lighthearted pieces, while "How to Feed Your Inner Troll" (*Asimov's Science Fiction*) suggests not only an encounter with a magical being, but a satire of pop psychology.

Think of the opening paragraphs of your story as an introduction to a prospective employer. Picture yourself standing face to face with the employer while you mumble on for pages before getting down to what you both mean and want to say. Not the most effective use of time. Rambling openings can keep an editor from reading to the end and giving your work the attention it deserves.

Analyze your beginning carefully. It should:

1) Evoke a sense of time and place. A reader expects a story to take place in the here and now, unless you say otherwise. If your story is set in the Italy of 2507, mention this at the start, or offer enough clues to prevent the revelation from coming as a surprise on page six. Clues can take the form of metaphor, dialogue, or straight narrative description.

2) Establish tone and authority through voice, word choice, theme, imagery, and detail. Prove that you are in control of your story by a correct use of grammar and a healthy respect for the conventions of language.

3) Introduce major character(s), hint at ages, gender, socioeconomic background. This can be the barest introduction, to be elaborated upon throughout the story.

4) Foreshadow major story problems and introduce minor ones.

A beginning that accomplishes as much of the above as possible will increase its chances for publication. Here's an example from "Smelling of Earth, Dreaming of Sky" (*Asimov's Science Fiction*):

Sunday at church:
In his sermon, the minister preaches that the first man was made from earth.

"Adamah," he begins, "common clay begat Adam, common man." Adam of earth, who thought he knew better than God and was forced to leave Paradise.

"We all—every one of us—came from that very clay," says the minister. "With this humble beginning, the Bible teaches that not one of us is better than the rest."

I groan, disagreeing. The minister must be referring to the commoners.

This opening makes clear who the story is about, and also hints at possible conflicts. Each new piece of information builds on what has previously been established. The next few paragraphs reveal that the narrator is an angel, sent back to perform one good deed. The somber tone of the writing, the deliberate use of present tense to magnify the feelings of a character who is trapped, the angry voice coupled with the spare choice of details, suggest that she will be unlikely to fulfill her mission. (Note: The title came from an earlier work that another editor had rejected with a note, "Title great, story stinks." The truth hurt, but he was right. I kept the title, tossed the story, then wrote a better one in its place.)

Selling wonders

Gardner Dozois, the editor of *Asimov's Science Fiction,* compares himself to P. T. Barnum, who sold wonders and marvels for money. "If there's no wonder or marvel in the content of your story," says Dozois, "then it's going to be a hard sell."

Editors want stories that are interesting and entertaining, unique, and logically consistent in their own way. Read what is being published now for clues of where to send your work. Magazines like *Analog* and *Science Fiction Age* are unlikely to publish a "Gnomes on Vacation" story, while *Realms of Fantasy* might not be the first place to send a story featuring "Physicists Who Save Themselves Before the Sun Goes Nova." Of course, there are always exceptions.

Instead of trying to clone what you read, view ideas through a prism to see them in a different light. For "Mothers' Day," (*Realms of Fantasy*), I took the legend of the Pied Piper one step further. What would it *really* be like, I wondered, for a man stuck inside a cave with all those children? The resulting story was a sympathetic yet satiric look at a man living with what he *never* bargained for.

It's fine to reuse a premise if you do something different. You must take the premise where no writer has gone before. A story cannot have time travel or virtual reality as the only focus; it must use the idea as background setting, what editor Dozois calls "The furniture of plot." In "Compatibility Clause" (*Fantasy and Science Fiction*), I borrowed heavily from William Gibson, my experiences and observations at video arcades, and themes of married life. The story is about a wife (Mrs. Claus on the night before Christmas), desperate to communicate with her husband, a busy man with an addictive personality. I combined real-life tensions with a fantasy world and a science fiction gimmick to create a story.

Hard sells

You might have trouble selling what is known as a *Translation Story:* the Western set on Alpha IV, with blasters instead of shotguns, and spaceships instead of horses. As a general rule, the fantastic or scientific idea must be an integral part of the story and not put there just to set up your theme or add interest to the plot.

Other hard sells include the surprise ending: the *deus ex machina,* where the resolution occurs as if by the hand of God; the story set in virtual reality (unbeknownst to the characters, who are revealed as imaginary only at story's end); stories that take place in dreams; Adam and Eve at the end of the world; stories with joke endings. If you've written one of the above, send it out anyway, but if you get back form letter rejections, you might try changing tactics. You will not be able to sell stories based on Star Trek or any licensed characters, or stories that are spin-offs from trademarked games.

Stories about ghosts are said to be a hard sell, though I've sold several. The key to selling a ghost story might be figuring out what the ghost represents on a symbolic level, as well as knowing why the ghost is needed in the story. Little-known legends reinterpreted through your unique vision can be a source of ideas for new and inventive ghost stories. "Beside the Well" (*Bending the Landscape: Fantasy,* White Wolf Publishing 1997) was based on a Korean folk tale, but with a few unexpected twists that fit the theme of the anthology. "Clinging to a Thread" (*Fantasy and Science Fiction*) presented ghosts through their physical connection to the objects they once touched. Vampires have been done to death (sorry), but an inventive writer might come up with a way to make them fresh.

Your story must be about the day, the person, and the event—not just any day or any person who happens to be trapped in some fascinating scenario. If another person could just as easily replace the central character, if the angel is merely symbolic and could be replaced by a Western Union man, if the effect of time travel is the same as if your character just got out of jail, you'd better rethink what you've written.

Why this person? Why today? Why is THIS fantastic element necessary? In general, these questions must be answered for the story to sell. Otherwise, let yourself go wild. In the field of speculative fiction, stories are limited only by imagination.

DEFINITIONS

Cyberpunk: Combines street-smart punks with the hi-tech world of computers and neural networks.

Hard Science Fiction: SF where the scientific idea is central to the plot, conflict, and resolution in the story.

Urban Fantasy/Contemporary Fantasy: Magic in modern-day settings, also called "North American magical realism."

High Fantasy: Often set in feudal or medieval societies where magical beings reside.

Alternative History: Looking at how an alternative past would change the present.

WEB SITES OF INTEREST

1) <http://critique.org/users/critters> On-line workshop, support, critiques, advice.

2) <http://www.sff.net> Author newsgroups, marketing information, and a private on-line critique group.

3) <http://www.speculations.com> News of open anthologies, magazine guidelines.

4) <http://users.aol.com/marketlist> Marketing information.

□ 43

DETECTIVE NOVELS: THE PACT BETWEEN AUTHORS AND READERS

BY IAN RANKIN

I HAD LITTLE INTEREST IN DETECTIVE STORIES UNTIL I FOUND THAT I'D accidentally written one.

My first Inspector John Rebus novel was not meant to be a whodunit. It was not meant to be the first book in a series that has now reached double figures. At the time I wrote it, I was a postgraduate student in Edinburgh, studying literary theory and the Scottish novel. I thought I was updating *Dr. Jekyll and Mr. Hyde,* delivering a "Scots Gothic" for the 1980s, while also perhaps telling readers something about hidden aspects of the city of Edinburgh, aspects the tourists and day-trippers would never see.

That was my intention. The fact that I made my central character a policeman was (to me at the time) of little or no importance. I knew almost nothing about policing or the mechanics of the law; in retrospect, probably no bad thing: It's easy for the would-be author to be put off by procedure and detail, easy to be sidetracked into esoteric research. Maybe that's why so many fictional detectives have been amateurs (in the UK) or private eyes (in the US): These are people who either ignore or wilfully sidestep the proper procedures for investigating a murder. By using them, their authors can proceed in blissful ignorance of the mechanics of a criminal investigation.

In the early days, my writing really did seem to descend from a Muse, in that I depended upon a fertile imagination—and how fertile it was! With no family life, wife or mortgage worries to get in the way, I wrote *Knots & Crosses* in about five weeks. Because I'd already had one novel published (*The Flood),* an agent had approached me to ask if further novels were forthcoming. I handed her *Knots & Crosses,* and she offered valuable suggestions for changes I should make (such as pruning an overtangled flashback from fifty pages to a neater fifteen, or so). She then found me a London publisher, and the book crept into the world without making too much fuss. (I was on book five or six before I was earning enough to even contemplate becoming a full-time writer.)

So it was back to the day job and dreams of new stories. I'd gone on to publish two spy novels before someone asked the innocent question: "Whatever happened to that Edinburgh cop of yours?" By this time, I'd discovered that *Knots & Crosses* had been classified a crime novel, and that the *genre* had not ended (as I'd assumed) with Christie and Chandler. I was now reading and enjoying crime novels, and catching up on the history of the detective story. I discovered its long and noble tradition, and that while noted for rattling good yarns, it was also capable of dealing with serious questions and the moral and psychological depth usually associated with the "literary" or "serious" novel.

I also discovered that a pact exists between mystery authors and their readers, forcing certain constraints on the author. For example, there should be no *deus ex machina,* no sudden appearance of a new character at the end of a book who would turn out to be the miscreant, no twist which the reader couldn't have been expected to be able to work out. I found that because the whodunit constantly poses questions, there have to be ways of expressing them and answering them. Thus the usefulness of the sidekick ("But gracious me, Holmes, how did you come to that astonishing conclusion?!"), or the penultimate chapter's gathering of suspects ("So you see, Madame Bouvier, you could not possibly have been in the archdeacon's antechamber at ten minutes to midnight"). In the Holmes example, the sidekick (Watson) stands for the reader and allows the detective to answer the very questions readers have been asking themselves. In the second example, the book's plot is about to be summarized and explained, and the real villain unmasked, all for the readers' edification.

The problem with such tricks, even when the reader is a willing enough accomplice, is that, to my mind, they *are* tricky, and reduce the seriousness of the crime novel, and turn it into a game, a puzzle. This is fine if the author's intention is to provide fun, entertainment, some little mental challenge to while away the hours.

But my own intentions extended further, and in my Rebus books, the detective is a loner along the lines of the American private eye. He works on the margins of the police force, eschewing sidekicks and back-up, and though written in the third person, the style of the narrative has evolved so that readers are inside the detective's head most of the time, allowing them insights into his thinking. Further, the detective is never physically described, his face and physique a blank, allowing readers to impose their own interpretation on him. In effect, he becomes *their* character.

Some critics have shrewdly commented that Rebus is not the main character in the series, that my main character is Edinburgh itself, and the country of which it is capital. But Edinburgh can "boast" only six murders a year, while Glasgow, only forty miles to the west, notches up between sixty and seventy. I've been asked why I don't write about Glasgow; wouldn't it be a more fruitful setting for a crime novel? Perhaps, but I don't *know* Glasgow. I choose to live and work in Edinburgh. It's a city that fascinates me and puzzles me, and these feelings become part of the fabric of my stories. Because *I* am fascinated by my chosen city, perhaps part of that fascination will extend to the reader which was the whole point of the series all along, even before it *became* a series. It is a cliché perhaps, but in a very real sense we are all detectives, trying to make sense of the world around us. I set up problems for Rebus, and the pleasure for the reader is in joining him on an expedition toward the various solutions. This requires a measure of holding back. *I* may know whodunit, but readers will probably be disappointed if they work it out too quickly. Premature revelation is a constant worry. One way to solve it is to be unsure yourself who your villain is. Sometimes I'm on the third or fourth draft of a book before I decide which of my cast is to be the "baddie." The first draft for me is in itself an investigation: it's only when I start to write about my characters that I begin to sense what they are capable of, and what motives they might have for committing a crime.

Just as we are all detectives, so *all* fiction is mystery fiction, setting up questions that will be answered only if we read on. Ask yourself: What makes you turn the next page? Answer: the need to find out what happens next. A story must generate tension and leave things unsaid or unexplained (until near its climax), otherwise the reader will lose interest. If there are only so many plots in fiction, there are even fewer in the detective novel, and the problems with keeping a series going are many and varied. I doubt I'd have had the guts to begin a series using the alphabet, as Sue Grafton did, in the knowledge that twenty-five books on I'd still have to be writing about the same protagonist. How do you keep your character and your plots fresh? I've found that it pays to have a hero with a past—and not to unlock the door to this secret past too quickly. In *Knots & Crosses,* the plot is all down to events that happened to Rebus during his time in the British Army's crack SAS batallion. In future novels in the series, we learn a little more about his army service in Northern Ireland, about his early police cases, and about past family secrets and even boyhood mysteries.

These help add layer upon layer to the psychological make-up of the detective, as well as providing new material for plots. But in fact plots have never been that hard for me to find; most of them actually throw themselves at me: Some newspaper story or overheard anecdote in a bar will have me asking questions or railing at a miscarriage of justice. The crime novel is the perfect vehicle for dissecting society, since in fiction you can get away with saying things (between the lines) which, as newspaper reporting, could get you sued. And the detective is the perfect tool for the job, having, as he does, access to both the Establishment and society's dispossessed. In moving easily between these two worlds (and all stops in between), the detective can uncover all sorts of skeletons, from the personal (a character's hidden past, for example) to the public (conspiracies in high office).

In this sense, there are no limitations to where the crime novel can go. It may also explain why serious novels such as Don DeLillo's *Underworld* (and note that title) contain their fair share of mysteries, subterfuges, hidden identities, and murderers.

Here, then, are a few rules about the detective story, with the caveat that rules are there to be broken by writers with a strong enough disposition:

1) No cheating. Your murderer can't turn out to be a character you've suddenly introduced five pages from the end of the story. The reader must be given a fair chance of solving any puzzle in your book.

2) Having said this, I must admit that some sorts of cheating are actually expected, in that you're going to provide red herrings and false trails galore. These can be as outlandish as you like, as long as the reader is convinced they work within the context of the story. Note James Ellroy's tactic of peppering his novels with real historical characters. In this way, he dupes the reader into suspending disbelief, thinking: "That really did happen, and those people really did exist . . . so how

much of the rest of this story is true?" Once you've got readers reacting that way, you've got them hooked.

3) You can keep research as minimal as you like, but your book must read as *authentic*. In other words, the reader must be hoodwinked into thinking you know what you're talking about, which isn't the same as your actually knowing what you're talking about. A little knowledge will go a long way. Conversely, writers who know too much about a subject can end up putting too much of it into their novels, slowing the story and confusing the reader. The task for the author is to know how much to put in and how much to leave out. I believe in the "less is more" principle. *Showing* is always better than *telling*. Give an example rather than a long explanation. If you have 200 pages of notes on autopsy procedure, fine, but use all of it in a novel and you'll bore the pants off everyone. An autopsy scene of a couple of paragraphs can be every bit as convicing as one of twenty pages, and you stand less risk of descending into tedium or jargon.

4) Don't strain for novelty in your central character. We all know this problem: Since all detectives are much of a muchness, how can I get mine to stand out from the herd? Well, in fact the very familiarity of a typical detective can be satisfying to readers. They're happy to work with a hero who is little more than a cipher, as long as the plot is blistering. To put meat on your hero's bones, introduce flaws and foibles, and an interesting home life. You don't need to strain after this. Don't feel the need to make your protagonist a six-foot-five Icelandic woman with poor eyesight and a box-file of homemade recipe-cards to be dispensed one per chapter. Characterization can be more subtle, and every bit as effective at delineating your detective.

5) Go read Raymond Chandler's rules. Better still, make up your own.

□ 44

How To Generate
Suspense in Fiction

By John Lutz

SUSPENSE IN FICTION HAS BEEN DEFINED AS THE READER WONDERING what happens next. But for the writer, it has to be something much more than that, something better understood, and something the writer knows how to generate.

One way to help understand suspense is to realize that it is not simply curiosity. Curiosity keeps the readers turning pages by holding out the promise that they will eventually get answers to questions. In a classic puzzle mystery novel, this might happen in the last chapter, where the detective gathers all the characters in the drawing room and explains how the victim was found shot to death in his locked study without a gun being present and with no sound being heard, and who the murderer is and why. All loose ends will be tightly knotted, and the reader will be satisfied. But a good mystery, like any good novel or short story, requires something more—suspense.

Suspense is emotional. It is the reader experiencing vicariously what the story's main character is experiencing. Of course, this requires the reader to identify with the character. When the character feels emotional tumult, so on a certain level will the reader, and when the character suffers physical pain, maybe mild, sympathetic, and unconscious pain will cause the reader's grip to tighten on the book cover.

The first challenge for the suspense writer is to get the reader to identify with your character. You do this by giving the reader more than merely a description of the character and his surroundings. You want the reader—as soon as possible—to think, *Yes, I understand, I've been there, I know exactly how that feels.* The writer has to find common denominators in order to engage reader emotion.

Here's an example from my short story "High Stakes" (originally published in *The Saint Mystery Magazine*):

Ernie followed the bellhop into the crummy room at the Hayes Hotel, was shown the decrepit bathroom with its cracked porcelain, the black-and-white TV with its rolling picture. The bellhop, who was a teenager with a pimply complexion, smiled and waited. Ernie tipped him a dollar, which, considering that Ernie had no luggage other than the overnight bag he carried himself, seemed adequate. The bellhop sneered at him and left.

While all of us haven't checked into that kind of a hotel under those circumstances, most of us have traveled less than first-class and encountered a disdainful bellhop. The important points here are that the reader learns something about Ernie and his situation, and on a certain level, identifies with him and is beginning to feel what Ernie feels.

A story that relies mainly on clues and curiosity sends a different sort of initial signal to the reader. Compare the above with the opening paragraph of my puzzle mystery "Shock," that portends curiosity rather than suspense (from the 1996 anthology *Unusual Suspects*):

It was odd the way people in shock had a protective, calming armor against emotion, almost like a powerful deadening drug. And this was a shocking scene. Every lamp in the beach cottage blazed, illuminating detail and making it all the more vivid, the deeper to be etched into memory.

No emotion here—not even the introduction of the main character— but mostly an objective observation leading to the second paragraph in which the details referred to above are described for the reader to ponder. Curiosity, not suspense, which will come later. In this story, the reader primarily wants to learn more facts and what they mean; in "High Stakes," the reader mainly wants to learn more about Ernie and his predicament. The writer, of course, knows what the reader doesn't, and decides how the reader should feel about Ernie. In "Shock," I wanted the reader to feel sympathy for Ernie, to see him as one of life's underdogs:

He had spent most of his forty years in the starkly poor neighborhood of his birth; and if he wasn't the smartest guy around, he did possess a kind of gritty cunning that had enabled him to make his own erratic way in the world. And he had instinct, hunches, that led to backing the right horse sometimes, or playing the right card sometimes. Sometimes. He got by, anyway. Getting by was Ernie's game, and he just about broke even. He was not so much a winner as a survivor. There were people who resented even that.

No suspense here yet, but the groundwork is being laid. I wanted the reader's sympathy for Ernie because he's going to be forced out onto a high ledge by thugs, the window closed and locked behind him, his way to the left and right blocked, his only available direction down, and Ernie without wings. If the reader already feels sorry for Ernie, the reader is out on that ledge with him, vicariously feeling his terror. Paragraphs of detailed description aren't the slightest substitute for that kind of empathy:

> Vertigo hit him with hammer force. Twelve stories seemed like twelve miles. He could see the tops of foreshortened street lights, a few toylike cars turning at the intersection. His mind whirled, his head swam with terror. The ledge he was on seemed only a few inches wide and was barely visible, almost behind him, from his precarious point of view. His legs quivered weakly; his boots seemed to become detached from them, seemed to be stiff, awkward creatures with their own will that might betray him and send him plunging to his death. He could see so far—as if he were flying. Ernie clenched his eyes shut. He didn't let himself imagine what happened to flesh and bone when it met the pavement after a twelve-story drop.

Of course curiosity plays a role in this. Readers wonder how Ernie's going to get out of his predicament. But that isn't the primary hook here. Readers want Ernie to get safely off that ledge because they felt sorry for him even before he found himself in danger—and that's what places readers on the ledge, trembling in Ernie's boots.

Once you've established the essential character-reader identification, there are several techniques for generating and heightening suspense. One of them is the ticking clock: Your character has a time limit and must accomplish something difficult and dangerous, maybe something that means life or death, and time is fast ticking away. That's the situation in my *Alfred Hitchcock's Mystery Magazine* story, "Dead Man," when the main character realizes that the heavy door of an airtight vault has just swung shut behind him, sealing him inside with little hope of rescue:

> Masters had never in his life panicked, but never in his life had he had a harder time fighting panic than now. No one was due in the house until tomorrow morning, when Margaret would arrive to prepare breakfast, and the vault was completely airtight and escape-proof. Add to that the fact that someone had obviously set out to imprison him in the vault until he suffocated, and his chances of breathing fresh air again were negligible. Always one to face things squarely and calculate instantly, accurately, and realistically where he stood, Masters arrived at the conclusion that he was a dead man.

The goal here is to put the reader in the vault with Masters while time and oxygen dwindle. Here suspense must transcend mere curiosity. *How* Masters escapes shouldn't be more important to the reader than *if* he will somehow find a way to defy time and the odds against him.

Another way to create suspense is to let the reader know something your character doesn't suspect. Perhaps a time bomb can be ticking away in a minivan full of children, while the car-pooling mother drives, happy and unaware, toward a school. In this situation, we've combined the character's unawareness of impending danger along with the (this time literally) ticking clock. At this point, the reader should already care about your character and in addition will be concerned for the lives of the children and be drawn deeper into the story. Somewhere in the back of the reader's mind should be silent screaming: *Stop the van! Take the children and run!* In the best of circumstances for the writer, that's what comes of letting the reader know more than your character.

In my short story "Hector Gomez Provides," published in *Mike Shayne's Mystery Magazine*, a poor man, who earns his money diving from a high cliff into a tiny, rocky cove for the amusement of rich tourists, has been drugged but doesn't know it (though the reader does). His survival depends on his precise timing of an oncoming wave so the water in the cove is momentarily deep enough for him to knife into it safely and not be bashed to death on the rocks:

> At last, Hector saw an oncoming swell that would provide enough water when it entered the cove. He watched it approach, a rolling, glittering vast hill of water, shot with sunlight as if it contained thousands of diamonds.
> It seemed to take forever to reach the point Hector had chosen, where he knew it would begin to curl into a green, sloping wall for its assault on the cove. The point from where it would enter the cove only a moment before the plummeting Hector sliced into its cool depths.

The reader should of course be standing on the high, rocky ledge with Hector, not lounging safely below as a spectator.

And the reader must dive along with Hector:

> Hector didn't want to dive . . . But his right arm was already raised, signaling the turistas, all watching through admiring, apprehensive eyes. Many were peering through camera lenses, hastily setting F-stops and shutter speeds, not admitting to the secret desire to record on film a brave man's death. It was too late for Hector to turn away with self respect.
> As soon as he launched himself into the air . . .

If the writer's done a good job, maybe the reader will unconsciously catch his or her breath here.

Now let's combine the ticking clock with another way of creating suspense—atmosphere.

In this instance the reader knows that a killer lurks in the apartment of an unsuspecting woman arriving home. This isn't just any woman; the reader has gotten to know and like her. And it isn't just any apartment building, but an ornate, converted 19th-century bordello where long ago a grisly murder occurred and a similar murder might be committed tonight. Its floors and doors creak, and its walls are in need of paint and marked with ominous graffiti. The reader wants to know, needs to know, whether the woman will enter her apartment and be killed. Her key is already in her hand.

Then she's stopped in the dim hall by a neighbor who has a crush on her and wants her to go back outside with him and walk around the corner for a cup of coffee. The woman has always been a little leery of this guy and is undecided. We know he's nothing more than a love-struck, amiable pest, but she doesn't know that. Will she go back outside with the neighbor instead of inside to her apartment and almost certain death? Everything rides on what is to her a trivial decision. And if the reader cares enough about the woman to be standing in her shoes, we have suspense, generated not only by atmosphere, but by the fact that we're aware of something terrible and momentous that she doesn't suspect.

There are plenty of variations and combinations of these techniques used to create suspense in mystery stories, from Poe's "Pit and the Pendulum," in which with each repetitive swing a blade drops closer to a bound man's exposed throat, to a single woman living an outwardly normal life day after day with a new roommate she doesn't suspect (but the reader knows) is a psychotic killer.

The secret is to reach beyond curiosity and engage the reader's emotions. That's not always an easy thing for a writer to do, but armed with some easily obtained knowledge, it's certainly possible. The question everyone serious about writing good fiction has to ask him or herself is whether the effect is worth the effort.

There should be no suspense involved in waiting for the answer.

❑ 45

THE SUPPORTING CAST
IN YOUR NOVEL

BY BARBARA DELINSKY

WHEN I BEGAN FICTION WRITING, I DIDN'T HAVE TO THINK ABOUT minor characters and their role in a novel. In those days, I wrote 200-page novellas that were too short to allow for minor characters. That changed with my shift into full-length fiction. Suddenly my books were twice as long and twice as deep. They definitely called for a cast of characters that went beyond two or three stars.

So I began adding secondary characters. I had no formal training in creative writing, but common sense told me that the purpose of a supporting cast was to flesh out my hero and heroine by giving them lives independent of one another. To that end, I created parents who had raised those main characters, and siblings with whom they had grown up and competed. I created friends who shaped their early adulthood and former spouses who left them burned. I created children who affected not only their present, but their future.

In doing this, I instinctively applied the same rule that trial-and-error had taught me about fiction writing in general: Just as every scene has to have a purpose, so every character, no matter how minor, has to have a purpose. Tossing in a character solely for the sake of making a book longer is pure filler and unacceptable. Readers see through this ploy in no time flat—and feel cheated.

Looking back, now that I have over sixty full-length books to my credit, I can see method to my madness in creating a supporting cast. Minor characters add richness to a novel, no doubt about that, but there are dozens of ways in which they do so. For simplification's sake, I offer three general categories that describe what the supporting cast contributes: depth, breadth, and movement.

Let's start with movement, since it is the most obvious of the three. Minor characters are often introduced to propel a plot forward, and in

224

this role, they serve a specific purpose: to provide information or create a complication; as a sounding board, to help a major character work through an emotional dilemma; as an all-out villain whose evil deeds must be answered.

Plots in which minor characters have a role are most often action-driven. Mysteries fall into this category, as do legal thrillers, westerns, science fiction. Of my own recent books, *A Woman's Place* does so, too.

In this first-person novel, the main character, Claire Rafael, is a successful businesswoman whose husband, Dennis, sues her for divorce, demanding sole custody of the children, possession of their house, and huge alimony. Much of the story centers on Claire's fight to regain custody of the children.

Most of the minor characters in *A Woman's Place* are tools for moving the plot forward. Carmen Niko, Claire's lawyer, sets the legal wheels in motion. Judge E. Warren Selwey hears the case and makes decisions that have a direct impact on the plot. Dean Jenovitz is the psychologist whose role it is to interview Claire and Dennis, gain insight into them, and make a custody recommendation to the court. Phoebe Lowe, as Dennis's lawyer and potential significant other, is responsible for many of Dennis's actions, to which Claire must then respond.

A Woman's Place is more action-driven than some of my other novels. In *Three Wishes*, which I wrote immediately after it, minor characters serve a very different purpose: They bring breadth to the novel.

By breadth, I mean color—color, atmosphere, backdrop. *Three Wishes* is set in a small town in northern Vermont that itself is a vital part of the story. How to bring out the flavor of this oh-so-crucial-to-the-plot small town? Minor characters. They create the environment in which the major characters operate. Flash O'Neill, who owns the diner where the heroine works, adds the twist of modern chic that sets the tone of the town. Various regulars at the diner describe the businesses that keep the town solvent. Emma McGreevy, Eliot Bonner, and Earl Yarum represent the traditional, old-time triumvirate of power. Dotty Hale is the obligatory gossip; Julia Dean is the newcomer who illustrates the town's capacity for warmth; Verity Greene is the bohemian who pushes the town's limits of trust.

These minor characters add breadth to *Three Wishes* in the form of a physical environment, but minor characters can also add emotional breadth. This often takes the form of a sub-plot or two that echo—and hence reinforce—the major theme of the book.

My novel *Coast Road* is the best example I can give of the emotional element. It is the story of Rachel and Jack, artist and architect respectively, who have been divorced for six years, after ten years of marriage. When Rachel is in a near fatal accident, Jack receives a middle-of-the-night call that brings him to her bedside and puts him in charge of their two teenage daughters. During sixteen days of trying to coax Rachel out of her coma, he becomes immersed in an in-depth analysis of not only of his marriage, but of parenthood.

Loyalty—as in fighting for what matters most—emerges as a major theme in this examination. Loyalty is also the theme of several subplots driven by the supporting characters. Just as Jack comes to realize that he wasn't there emotionally for his wife during the later years of their marriage, he finds himself talking about loyalty with his fifteen-year-old daughter as she straddles a social crossroad; with his thirteen-year-old daughter, as she cares for her sick cat; and with his ex-wife's best friend as she tries to explain the deepest meaning of friendship. This echoing of the theme among the supporting cast helps Jack understand and resolve his own larger issue of loyalty.

Coast Road is also a good example of the third type of contribution minor characters can make—depth. Depth is crucial to novels like this that are heavily emotional and largely character-driven. The starring players in such novels must be three-dimensional. The supporting cast is instrumental in making them so.

Each supporting cast member is chosen to illuminate some aspect of the life or personality of a major character. In the case of family members, the illumination has to do with the passage of time. Family members share a history with the major character. Their thoughts and personalities help explain the "why" of the main character's behavior. They offer glimpses of the main character in childhood, adolescence, adulthood, and serve as a mechanism that allows the writer to reach into the past or imagine the future.

But depth has another dimension as well. Here, minor characters help round out a picture of the major characters in the present tense. These would be friends, neighbors, colleagues—all of whom, through words, action, or mere presence, say something about who and what the main character is as the story unfolds.

Again, *Coast Road* is an apt illustration. The female lead lies comatose for nine-tenths of the book. How, then, is her voice heard? This was the challenge I set for myself in writing the book. The answer? Through the supporting cast. Rachel may lie in a coma, but she remains the main character through a depth offered by her daughters, her best friend, her book group, her mother, and, yes, the husband she divorced six years before.

One of the questions I'm most frequently asked is whether I create the plot before the characters, or vice versa. A natural follow-up to that question is whether star players are created before the supporting cast. My answer to both questions is the same: It depends on the novel. The general assumption would be that major characters are created first, and minor characters are added as needed, rather like salt and pepper, for flavor; yes, this is what happens most often. But there are exceptions. I recently finished writing a book with another small-town setting, and I actually had half a dozen members of the supporting cast already chosen, while I was still grappling with the major theme of the book and, hence, the identity of the stars.

Neither way is right or wrong. What *is* wrong is if a writer gets so hung up on which should come first that he or she is stalled and can't write at all!

A note here on point of view. Some very successful writers brainhop, relating the innermost thoughts of even the most peripheral minor character. I am uncomfortable doing that. For one thing, I like to write an entire scene from one point of view, that of the character with the most at stake emotionally. For another, I think that introducing so many diverse—and often irrelevant—elements dilutes the effectiveness of the emotions. Since my novels have become known for their emotional impact, this method is working for me. The bottom line is that you must think about what the strength of your book will be, and make point-of-view decisions accordingly.

Making the wrong point-of-view decision is but one of several dangers I would caution you against, where the supporting cast is concerned.

Another is introducing the supporting cast at the outset of the book, before you introduce a main character or two. Readers can be like ducklings. They will imprint on the first character they meet. If that character is a peripheral one, there will be confusion and a delay in their relating to the main character. Too long a delay, and the reader becomes detached emotionally, closes the book, and is lost.

Similarly, if the supporting cast is so much more likable than the leading players that readers don't care about the leading players, they won't read on, you've lost them. If part of your plot makes the good guys look bad for a while, that's fine, but keep in mind that you walk a tightrope. The reader has to care what happens. If your supporting cast can make the reader care enough to keep reading until the major characters pick up the ball, your problem is solved.

Conversely, a minor character who is overly loud, bad, quirky or glaring may divert the reader's attention from the flow of the plot. I call this the "cauliflower breast" issue, named after a love scene I once read, a beautifully lyrical piece in which the author suddenly likened the heroine's breast to cauliflower. That stopped me short, ice water on any passion I might have imagined. Jarring minor characters can have the same effect. Keep in mind that every minor character must have a role in supporting the major characters. If the jarring has a definite purpose, it may work. If, however, you have simply created a wonderfully weird minor player on the spur of the moment, think twice about it. Such a player may drag the reader too far afield, and might best be saved for its own starring role.

Those caveats aside, I can't stress strongly enough the positive role that the supporting cast can play. Alone, a major character is like the right hand picking out single notes on a piano. The notes may have rhythm and a tune; in the hands of a maestro, they may even have feeling and heart. But the tune remains largely one-dimensional until a second player, the left hand, joins in. When that left hand picks out single notes of a complementary theme, you have a pleasant duet. Add chords by either or both hands, and you have a full-bodied song. The supporting cast in a novel supply the notes in those chords. They shouldn't overpower, jar, or bore. Used to their fullest, they turn a song into a song that is beautiful, meaningful, and memorable.

❑ 46

WRITING THE SUPERNATURAL NOVEL

BY ELIZABETH HAND

I'VE ALWAYS THOUGHT THAT THE OLDEST PROFESSION WAS THAT OF storyteller—in particular, the teller of supernatural tales. A look at the cave paintings in France or Spain will show you how far back our hunger for the fantastic goes: men with the heads of beasts, figures crouching in the darkness, skulls and shadows and unblinking eyes. Take a glance at the current bestseller list, and you'll see that we haven't moved that far in the last twenty thousand years. Books by Anne Rice, Stephen King, Joyce Carol Oates, and Clive Barker, among many others, continue to feed our taste for dark wine and the perils of walking after midnight. But how to join the ranks of those whose novels explore the sinister side of town?

First, let me distinguish between supernatural fiction and its tough (and very successful) younger cousin, the horror novel. Horror novels depend heavily upon the mechanics of plot, less-than-subtle characterizations, and shock value—what Stephen King calls "going for the gross-out." In spirit and execution, they aren't that different from the "penny dreadfuls" of a century ago, crude but effective entertainments that tend to have a short shelf life. Unlike more stylized works such as *Dracula, The Turn of the Screw* or *The Shining,* most horror novels lose their ability to chill the second time around—they just don't stand up to rereading. As Edmund Wilson put it, "The only horror in these fictions is the horror of bad taste and bad art."

In the wake of Stephen King's success, the 1980's was a boom decade for horror fiction. But the market was flooded with so many books—and so many second-rate Stephen King imitators—that publishers and readers alike grew wary. With the dwindling reading public, it's far more difficult today to get a supernatural novel into print.

But the readers *are* there. And they're quite a sophisticated audience, which makes it both more challenging, and more fun, to write the sort of novel that will appeal to someone who prefers *The Vampire Lestat* to the *The Creeping Bore.*

More than other genres, supernatural fiction is defined by *atmosphere* and *characterization.* By atmosphere, I mean the author's ability to evoke a mood or place viscerally by the use of original and elegant, almost *seductive* language. Science fiction and fantasy also rely heavily upon unusual settings and wordplay, often against a backdrop of other, imagined, worlds. But the most successful supernatural novels are set in *our* world. Their narrative tension, their very ability to frighten and transport us, derives from a conflict between the macabre and the mundane, between everyday reality and the threatening *other*—whether revenant, werewolf, or demonic godling—that seeks to destroy it.

The roots of supernatural fiction lie in the gothic romances of the eighteenth and nineteenth centuries with their gloomy settings, imperiled narrators and ghostly visitations. Even today these remain potent elements. Witness Anne Rice's vampire Lestat during a perambulation about prerevolutionary Paris:

> The cold seemed worse in Paris. It wasn't as clean as it had been in the mountains. The poor hovered in doorways, shivering and hungry, the crooked unpaved streets were thick with filthy slush. I saw barefoot children suffering before my very eyes, and more neglected corpses lying about than ever before. I was never so glad of the fur-lined cape as I was then. . . .

Much of the pleasure in Rice's work comes from her detailed evocations of real, yet highly romanticized, places: New Orleans, Paris, San Francisco. It pays to have firsthand knowledge of some desirable piece of occult real estate: Readers love the thrill of an offbeat setting, but they also like recognizing familiar landmarks. So, Stephen King has staked out rural Maine as his fictional backyard. The incomparable Shirley Jackson (whose classic "The Lottery" has chilled generations of readers) also turns to New England for the horrific doings in *The Haunting of Hill House, The Bird's Nest* and *We Have Always Lived in the Castle.* Daphne du Maurier's novella "Don't Look Now" gives us a tourist couple lost amidst the winding alleys of Venice, a notion creepy enough to have inspired Ian McEwan's nightmarish *The Comfort of Strangers.* Just about any setting will do, if you can imbue it with an aura of beauty and menace. My neo-gothic novel *Waking the Moon* takes place in that most pedestrian and bureaucratic of cities, Washington, D.C. But by counterpointing the city's workaday drabness with exotic descriptions of its lesser-known corners, I was able to suggest that an ancient evil might lurk near Capitol Hill:

> From the Shrine's bell tower came the first deep tones of the carillon calling the hour. I turned, and saw in the distance the domes and columns of the Capitol glimmering in the twilight, bone-colored, ghostly; and behind it still more ghostly buildings, their columned porticoes and marble arches all seeming to melt into the haze of green and violet darkness that descended upon them like sleep.

Style, of course, is a matter of taste and technique, and as with all writing, your most important tools should be a good thesaurus and dictionary. (Good taste in reading helps, but is probably not necessary.) A thesaurus can transform even the oldest and most unpalatable of chestnuts. "It was a dark and stormy night" becomes "Somber and tenebrous, the vespertine hour approached."

The danger, of course, is that such elevated diction easily falls into self-parody. But when well-done, it can quickly seduce the reader into believing in—well, in any number of marvelous things:

> Last night I dreamt that I woke to hear some strange, barely audible sound from downstairs—a kind of thin tintinnabulation, like those coloured-glass bird scarers which in my childhood were still sold for hanging up to glitter and tinkle in the garden breeze. I thought I went downstairs to the drawing room. The doors of the china cabinets were standing open, but all the figures were in their places—the Bow Liberty and Matrimony, the Four Seasons of Neale earthenware, the Reinecke girl on her cow; yes, and she herself—the Girl in a Swing. It was from these that the sound came, for they were weeping.

This is from Richard Adams's superb *The Girl in a Swing,* to my mind the best supernatural novel I've ever read. One of the problems in writing supernatural fiction stems from the fact that "ghost stories" are nearly always better when they are really *stories,* rather than full-length novels. Indeed, many of the classic works of dark fantasy—*The Turn of the Screw,* Charlotte Gilman's "The Yellow Wallpaper," Oliver Onions's "The Beckoning Fair One"—are novellas, a form that particularly suits the supernatural, but which is a hard sell: too short for publishers looking for meaty bestsellers, too long for a magazine market that thrives on the 5,000- to 7,000-word story. It is very difficult to sustain a high level of suspense for several hundred pages. Chapter after chapter of awful doings too often just become awful, with the "cliff-hanger" effect ultimately boring the reader.

Characterization is one way of avoiding this pitfall. If your central characters are intriguing, you don't need a constant stream of ghoulish doings to hold a reader's attention. Think of Anne Rice's Lestat, whose melancholy persona has seen him through several sequels. Or the callow student narrator of Donna Tartt's *The Secret History,* a novel which has only a hint of the supernatural about it, but which is more terrifying than any number of haunted houses:

> Does such a thing as "the fatal flaw," that showy dark crack running down the middle of a life, exist outside literature? I used to think it didn't. Now I think it does. And I think that mine is this: a morbid longing for the picturesque at all costs.

The Secret History is told in the first person, as are *The Girl in a Swing,* Rice's *Vampire Chronicles,* and *Waking the Moon.* In supernatural fiction, it is not enough that the protagonist compel our interest. Readers must also be able to truly *identify* with him, to experience his growing sense of unease as his familiar world gradually crumbles in the face of some dark intruder, be it spirit or succubus. That is why the first-person narrator is so prevalent in supernatural tales. It is also why most uncanny novels feature individuals whose very *normalcy* is what sets them apart from others. Like us, they do not believe in ghosts, which makes it all the worse when a ghost actually does appear.

But "normal" does not necessarily mean "dull." Richard Papen, the narrator of *The Secret History,* is drawn into a murderous conspiracy when his college friends seek to evoke Dionysos one drunken winter night. In *The Girl in a Swing,* Alan Desland is a middle-aged bachelor whose most distinguishing characteristic is his extraordinary *niceness*—until he becomes obsessed with the beautiful Kathe, who may be the incarnation of a goddess—or of a woman who murdered her own children. And in C. S. Lewis's classic *That Hideous Strength,* an entire peaceful English village is besieged by the forces of darkness.

As with all good fiction, it is important that the central characters are *changed* by their experiences, whether for good or ill. Lazy writers often use mere physical transformations to effect this change: The heroine becomes a vampire. Or the heroine is prevented from becoming a vampire. Or the heroine is killed. Far more eerie is the plight of the eponymous hero of Peter Ackroyd's terrifying *Hawksmoor,* a police detective who finds himself drawn into a series of cult murders that took place in London churches two hundred years before:

> Hawksmoor looked for relief from the darkness of wood, stone and metal but he could find none; and the silence of the church had once again descended as he sat down upon a small chair and covered his face. And he allowed it to grow dark.

While he is very much a twentieth-century man, Nicholas Hawksmoor's unwanted clairvoyance gives him a glimpse of horrors he is unable to forget, and forever alters his perception of the power of good and evil in the world and in his work.

In many ways, the intricacies of *plot* are less central to supernatural fiction than is *pacing* (another reason why short stories usually work better than novels). A careful balance must be achieved between scenes of the ordinary and the otherworldly. Usually, a writer alternates the two, with the balance gradually tipping in favor of the unreal: Think of Dracula moving from Transylvania to London, and bringing with him a miasma of palpable evil that slowly infects all around him. In *Waking the Moon,* my heroine's involvement with the supernatural parallels her love affair in the real world. However you choose to do it, don't let the magical elements overwhelm your story completely.

Especially, don't let the Big Supernatural Payoff come too *soon.* (The only thing worse that killing off all your werewolves fifty pages before the end is penning these dreadful words: IT WAS ALL A DREAM.) Think of your novel in musical terms: You wouldn't really want to listen to one Wagnerian aria after another, would you? Well, neither would you want to read page after page of mysterious knockings, stakes through the heart, and screams at midnight.

Finally, dare to be different. Does the world really need another vampire novel? How about a lamia instead? Or an evil tree? As always, it's a good idea to be well-read in your chosen genre, so that you don't waste time and ink reinventing Frankenstein's monster. In addition to the works mentioned above, there is a wealth of terrific short supernatural fiction that can teach as well as chill you. *Great Tales of Terror and the Supernatural* (edited by Herbert A. Wise and Phyllis Fraser) is perhaps the indispensable anthology. There are also collections by great writers such as Poe, Robert Aickman, John Collier, Edith Wharton, Isak Dinesen, Sheridan Le Fanu, M. R. James, and many, many others. Jack Sullivan has written two books that I refer to constantly: *Elegant Nightmares* and *Lost Souls,* classic studies of English ghost stories that can serve as a crash course on how to write elegant horror. These, along with Stephen King's nonfiction *Danse Macabre,* should put you well on your way to creating your own eldritch novel. Happy haunting!

❏ 47

How Real History Fits Into the Historical Novel

By Thomas Fleming

TOO MANY WRITERS—AND NOT A FEW READERS—TEND TO THINK OF nonfiction and fiction as opposites—a twain that should never meet. Throughout my career, I have taken a very different approach. While I am writing a nonfiction book or article, I am constantly looking for situations, events, characters, that present an opening to the imagination.

For example, I received an assignment to write an article about the 1942 Battle of Savo Island, the disastrous naval engagement off Guadalcanal in which the Japanese inflicted a stunning defeat on the Americans. As I assembled the research, I discovered that the *USS Chicago,* the acting flagship of the American cruiser squadron, had unaccountably sailed *away* from the attacking Japanese soon after the midnight assault began. The other American cruisers were sunk. The *Chicago's* captain was relieved of duty and later shot himself rather than face a court of inquiry.

I asked myself: What if the captain of that disgraced ship was replaced by his Annapolis roommate, his closest friend? How would the new captain handle the job? Would he investigate what had happened aboard the ship on that terrible night, and perhaps destroy his friend's career? In a flash, the plot of my novel, *Time and Tide,* leaped into my mind. I created an imaginary cruiser, the *USS Jefferson City,* which became the guilt-haunted ship. I peopled it with a crew tormented by the memory of Savo Island. As they struggled to redeem themselves and the Captain tried to redefine his relationship with his friend, who had always been the superior voice, the naval war in the Pacific unfolded around them, seen from a dramatic new perspective.

Sometimes it is a special insight into a historical character that triggers an imaginative explosion. While working on a profile of General

John J. Pershing, the American commander in World War I, I discovered that shortly before he went to France, his wife and three children were killed in a fire at the Presidio, the San Francisco army base. What did that tragedy do to the general's soul? I wondered. Did it have an impact on his conduct in France? How could that be dramatized?

What if Pershing had a close army friend who had sustained a similar loss? Enter Colonel Malvern Hill Bliss, the central character of my novel, *Over There.* He is speeding down a highway outside San Antonio, drunk and demoralized by the death of his wife and son from a terrorist machete in the Philippines. Before this opening chapter ends, Pershing has dragged Bliss out of a brothel and ordered him to prepare to depart for France with him in 24 hours. The Pershing that Bliss reveals to the reader is a very different man from the Iron General in the history books—and so is the World War that both of them fight.

My novel *Dreams of Glory* is another novel whose genesis was derived from a nonfiction book. I was writing *The Forgotten Victory,* an account of the 1780 battle of Springfield, when I came across the story of a black American soldier found in a snowdrift outside George Washington's headquarters in Morristown, with a bayonet in his chest. Washington's army was about 15% black by this time. Who had killed this man? Apparently no one ever found out.

Again, this fact exploded into a whole novel in my imagination. What if the black soldier was a spy who was killed in the intelligence war that raged between the two armies? The result was a book that reveals a dark underside of the Revolutionary struggle.

By now it should be apparent that a historical novel is not "made up." Its vitality can and should come from history itself, and the deeper its roots in reality, the better.

Another trigger to the imagination may be the discovery of a little-known set of historical facts or a situation that has relevance to our own time. I believe a prime function of the historical novel is to surprise as well as intrigue the reader.

A few years ago, I was fascinated to discover that before the American Revolution, New York City was 25% black—mostly slaves. In the 1740s the blacks concocted a plot to sack the city and hand it over to the French in exchange for their freedom.

How would this startling set of facts fit into a novel? I wanted to tell the story from the inside, retaining sympathy for the slaves, yet seeing the episode in all its complexity. What if there were someone in the conspiracy who saw it differently? I created Clara Flowers, a beautiful black woman who was captured and raised by Seneca Indians, then repatriated to the white world at seventeen. She became the main character of my recently published novel, *Remember The Morning*.

Growing up in the so-called middle ground around the Great Lakes, where whites and Indians mingled, Clara has a different view of race relations. As her role grew in my mind, I saw she could also illuminate women's experience in pre-revolutionary America. I created a Dutch woman, Catalyntie Van Vorst, with whom Clara shared her Indian captivity. Catalyntie becomes a successful merchant, not unusual among the American Dutch. Although the slave revolt strains their relationship, their early bonding as Senecas and their common identity as women enable them to continue their friendship.

To make this work, I had to learn the mores and customs of the "middle ground," the intricacies of the fur trade, the local politics of colonial New York, and the global politics of the struggle for world supremacy between Catholic France and Protestant England. It all began with the seed of my original discovery about the startling role of the blacks in New York, two hundred years before Harlem and Bedford-Stuyvesant. As good historical novels should, this book resonates in our own time, making us think about our present dilemmas in a new way.

Similarly, one of the primary insights of my twenty-five years of research into the American Revolution was the little-known fact that in some states, such as New Jersey, the struggle was a civil war. Brothers fought brothers and sisters fell in love with their brothers' or their fathers' enemies.

Swiftly, my imagination created a character who could convey this startling ambiguity. What if an ex-British officer named Jonathan Gifford married an American widow, adopted her two children, and opened a tavern on the Kings Highway in New Jersey? Into the tavern—and the story—would swirl loyalists and neutrals and ferocious rebels, eager to hang every waverer in sight. It would be especially poignant if Gifford's stepson, Kemble Stapleton, was the local Robespierre. Thus was born my novel *Liberty Tavern,* which told the story of Gifford's gradual conversion to the American cause—and Kemble's education in the complexities of Revolutionary politics.

Crucial to the success of every work of historical fiction is a thorough

knowledge of the period, so that the imaginary events fit plausibly into
the known history of the time. This "veracious imagination" (a term
coined by English novelist George Eliot and revived by Cornell critic
Cushing Stout) is a vital ingredient in meshing real history and the
imaginative, symbolic events that the novelist is adding to the story.
Without this background knowledge, the writer may create "improbable truths," something the father of the American historical novel,
James Fenimore Cooper, felt was a primary danger in interweaving the
imaginative and the real.

Achieving this fit is not as daunting as it seems at first. Rich as the
historical record is, it is not so crowded with information that the creation of an imaginary character like Malvern Hill Bliss or Clara Flowers
strains plausibility. On the contrary, by giving the reader a closeup of
the historical experience, it may make the story even more plausible.

Real characters, such as Pershing, George Washington, Adolf Hitler,
Franklin D. Roosevelt have appeared in my novels, alongside the imaginary ones. It is extremely important to present such historical figures
accurately. To portray Washington as a drunk or Pershing as a coward,
for instance, would be a serious violation of the novelist's historical
responsibilities.

But dialogue *can* be invented for these historical figures. In my novel
Loyalties, for instance, I have a scene in which F.D.R. reveals his patho-
logical hatred of the German people—a little-known fact that plays a
large part in the novel's plot (and was a major factor in prolonging
World War II). I put words in F.D.R.'s mouth that are based on extensive
research, making them not only plausible but probable.

There is another reason for grasping the great issues and inner spiritual and psychological struggles of a whole period. *Remember the
Morning,* for instance, is more than the story of Clara Flowers' and
Catalyntie Van Vorst's search for security and love. As the story unfolds, they both get emotionally involved with a raw young would-be
soldier named Malcolm Stapleton. The growing American dissatisfac-
tion with England's corrupt imperial control of America becomes the
book's leitmotif. Out of the racial and personal turmoil in the forefront
of the novel, an awakening sense of a separate American destiny
emerges. The drums of the American Revolution are thudding in the
distance as the story ends, adding substance and a deeper meaning to
the book.

The historical novelist has to be even more selective than the historian in constructing his narrative. His goal is emotional truth—a considerable leap beyond factual truth. Historians seldom deal with personal emotions in history. In the novel, such emotions are the primary focus of the story. This means that you cannot describe every battle of World War I while writing about Bliss and Pershing in France. You have to choose one or two battles in which their inner anguish becomes visible. It means you can shift the timing of a historical event a few years in either direction in order to increase the emotional intensity—as I did with the black revolt in *Dreams of Glory.*

Perhaps the least understood role of reality in the historical novel is the way research can supply you with details that deepen and otherwise improve the story you are telling. In *Loyalties,* the main character, Berthe Von Hoffmann, an agent for the German Resistance to Hitler, is kidnapped from Madrid by her former lover, who is working for the Nazis. The American protagonist Jonathan Talbot follows them to Grenada. The imperatives of the plot require Talbot to kill the Nazi.

I found myself recoiling from a scene which was routine spy novel huggermugger. Something else was needed. In another day's research on Grenada, I discovered that inside the famed Moslem palace, the Alhambra, was a crude Spanish palace built by King Charles V. On one of its walls was an enormous painting of a column of refugees plodding into the distance. "The Expulsion of the Jews" by Emilio Sala depicted the decision of King Ferdinand and Queen Isabella to banish the Jews from Spain in 1492.

I had the ingredient I needed to create an original scene that fit perfectly into the story. While the Nazi gazes up at the painting and remarks that he hoped to persuade the Spanish government to let him bring it to Berlin, Talbot slips a silken cord around the Nazi's throat and strangles him. It was not my imagination that transformed this scene from cliche to meaningful drama; it was research—reality—fact.

More and more, I have come to think of these two sides of a historical novel as competing themes in a piece of music. Ultimately, fact can and should be woven into fiction so seamlessly, readers never stop to ask what is true in the literal sense and what is imaginative. All that should matter is the conviction that they are being taken inside events in a new revelatory, personal way. It takes hard work—but it is tremendously satisfying to write a book that engages readers' heads and hearts.

❑ 48

STRESS-FREE TURKEYS
AND MURDER

BY ANNE GEORGE

A COUPLE OF THANKSGIVINGS AGO, WHEN I TOOK MY TURKEY FROM the freezer, I discovered a card attached to the yellow plastic netting. It proclaimed that this was a "stress-free turkey raised in the shade of pecan trees." Since I was about to do all sorts of terrible things to this bird, including stuffing and eating it, the fact that it had had a happy youth was hardly comforting. The card, instead of assuring me that the meat would be tender, turned the frozen lump in my kitchen sink into a turkey with a past.

I'm not crazy. I stuffed it, cooked it until the thermometer popped out, and served it on the turkey platter I bring out twice a year. We all enjoyed it.

But, oh, the power of words. As soon as I read the card, I rushed for my notebook and copied it down. And the "stress-free turkey" shows up several times in my novel *Murder Gets a Life*. It even gave me the name of one of the families, Turkett.

In the notebook I keep in my purse at all times, I jot down things that strike me as funny or unusual. Recently, three men, two from Bangladesh and one from Cincinnati, were trapped in the elevator in the huge iron statue of Vulcan that overlooks Birmingham, Alabama. I used the incident in my last book, but I put Mary Alice Tate Sullivan Nachman Crane, one of the sisters in my Southern Sisters Mystery series, in with them. Mary Alice is six feet tall, admits to weighing two hundred fifty pounds and, as her brother-in-law says, has the nerve of a bad tooth. She has also been widowed by three wealthy men, all of whom were twenty-eight years older than she. The other sister, Patricia Anne Tate Hollowell, is a retired school teacher, petite, long-married to a husband she adores. They live in Birmingham, are in their sixties, and keep stumbling over bodies.

240

I know these women. I know their families, their friends, the communities in which they live. I know what they order at Morrison's Cafeteria. I wouldn't dare write about them otherwise. This is the old "write what you know about" advice. Well, it's true. I received a letter from a woman in Arizona telling me that you couldn't drive down Lakeshore from a shopping center and turn left into Samford University. You can. They've built a new shopping center since the lady left Birmingham. But it reminded me of how important it is not to be careless when you're writing about a specific location.

I began writing humorous mystery novels after twenty years of writing serious poetry. From that background, I learned the importance of each word; that concrete words are the foundation of all good writing, and that a sense of place is a necessity. Poems, short stories, novels—all must be grounded in a place.

From my poetry background, I also picked up what I consider the necessary habit of reading aloud what I've written. When you're reading a poem aloud and you stumble, you know the rhythm isn't right. Now I do the same thing with my novels. Each day when I sit down to write, I read aloud what I wrote the day before. If I stumble badly over the dialogue or some part of a paragraph, I usually find that it's too wordy. Rhythm is an essential element of writing not emphasized enough. Not that you want to be sing-songy. Not at all. But smooth. Then a sharp, deliberate change in rhythm can be used to signify something important to your reader. Reading aloud is especially important for dialogue. We don't talk the way we write. We talk in half-sentences, with exclamations and contractions.

My characters talk with southern accents. They say, "I'm fixing to go to the store," or "Do you reckon he's coming?" My copy editor appreciates the colloquialisms and has stopped me only a few times, once for "He stuck his head in the door" (she added "way"), and "Let's pick up the house" (changed to "straighten"). My dialogue has been described as being right on the money. Do they think I could do a British accent? I'll stick to what I know. Believe me, it's safer. And I'll keep reading it out loud.

Each of the two sisters in this mystery series has her own way of speaking. I'm working on my seventh novel in the series now, and I know them so well, that it's no problem. Mary Alice, the older, larger, bossier sister tends to make pronouncements. Patricia Anne, who has been known to correct her sister's grammar, is slightly more hesitant. She'll say, "I think." Mary Alice just says, "It is." In *Murder on a Bad Hair Day*, Patricia Anne and Mary Alice are in a barbecue restaurant and Patricia Anne is worried about the dirty windows. Mary Alice announces it's not dirt, it's just grease, and eats happily.

On the other hand, when faced with a real emergency, it's Patricia Anne who is the stronger one. Mary Alice tends to fall apart. Sometimes, though, she surprises me, which is the joy of writing a series. There is room for the characters to grow, for their families to change, for me to get to know them better.

My novels are character driven. I know that if you can get the murder on the first page, it's great. P.D. James can do this; I can't get a body in until the third or fourth chapter. First I have to introduce the sisters, let my readers get to know them as I do. I usually keep them as the only two characters in the first chapter. I don't want to confuse the reader by throwing too many people in too soon. I do try to establish the basis of the story early on, and I usually do this by having the sisters talk about it. In *Murder on a Girls' Night Out*, the first in the series, Mary Alice announces that she has bought a country-western bar. This is what sets everything in motion. In the book I am working on now, their cousin Pukey Lukey, so called because of his childhood carsickness, shows up with the news that his wife of forty years has run off with another man. It will take them several chapters to find a body. If you can go the P.D. James route, though, get that body in there quickly.

In writing, we don't have the luxury of using body language to help us communicate. But we do have simple words, which are the paint with which we create our word pictures. Years ago, I had a great teacher who made me cut every word of four or more syllables, and every three-syllable word (ing's and ed's weren't counted).

"Now," he said, "what's left is the gold. Use it."

It's a lesson I've never forgotten. What I had to work with were words of Anglo-Saxon derivation. Of course we can't limit ourselves to nothing but these words, but I still think of them as the "gold," especially the strong verbs, the most important words in every sentence. The men and women in my novels walk at the edge of a cliff. They don't perambulate beside the precipice.

People often ask me how I came to write mysteries. Actually, the sisters made their first appearance in a short story entitled "Where Have

You Gone, Shirley Temple," based on a true incident. They were in an antique mall looking for a Shirley Temple doll to replace the one Mary Alice swore Patricia Anne had lost over fifty years before. A tornado hit (Patricia Anne hadn't been watching the Weather Channel; it was all her fault), and they ended up under a drop-leaf Duncan Phyfe table, fussing. The sisters were so well received, and I was so fond of them, that I knew I wanted to do more with them. I'm not good at plotting, so I challenged myself to see if I could write a mystery. And I did. I actually fit all of the pieces together and sold it.

"It was the voice," my editor said. "And I laughed at the sisters by page two."

Voice. Your voice. The distinctive quality that announces, "Hey, it's ME writing this. This is what I believe. This is what I am." You owe it to your readers to show them who you are. And that takes courage. It takes baring a little of your soul.

In *Murder Makes Waves*, the sisters witness a turtle laying her eggs. This is the way Patricia Anne describes it:

> On the horizon, lightning streaked across a cloud, and moments later we heard distant, muffled thunder. I looked at the dark water of the Gulf, at the turtle laying her eggs, at my daughter, her face filled with awe as she knelt in the sand, at all of us caught in a small pool of light on this beach on this primal night. It was something I'll always remember.

This is my voice. I hope my readers recognize it as true.

But when you're writing a murder mystery, even a cozy, you've got to kill somebody off. And what did I, the real-life Patricia Anne, know about that? I knew I'd better not try to have someone killed with a gun. I'd make a fool of myself. My husband has an old B.B. gun, the only weapon in our house. So I realized that the people in my novels would have to die some other way.

My veterinarian came through for the second book in the series. I took my cat in for her shots and asked him how I could kill a woman with hair products. He knew exactly how and was delighted to tell me.

The Okaloosa County Sheriff's department kept me from making a bad mistake in *Murder Makes Waves*. The sisters find a body on the beach, and I assumed the county sheriff would investigate, but something told me I'd better check it out. I got my chance at a mall in Fort Walton Beach, Florida, where I happened to notice that there was a sheriff's substation. I asked the employees there who would investigate a body on the beach.

"Is it wet?" they wanted to know.

I said yes, it was on the beach.

"The Florida Marine Patrol investigates the wet ones."

They seemed so disappointed, I put two bodies in that book; one was snug and dry in a condo so the Okaloosa County sheriff could be involved, too.

Big lesson learned. I now call about anything that's questionable. My local fire department helped me with an arson question. I'm on a first-name basis with my neighborhood policemen, who are an invaluable resource. Fortunately my daughter is a lawyer, so I get a lot of answers from her about criminal procedures.

I don't outline. I know I should, and I recommend it. But when I do, the person who is the designated murderer invariably gets killed about halfway through the book. So around chapter thirteen, I begin to get panicky. I have to decide who did it. I have several good friends who have been kind enough to read what I've written and say who they think did it. Though they usually choose different people, it's still helpful to get their comments. If there is a writing group available close to you, join it. It doesn't have to be a mystery writing group. We all need support and advice. For instance, my group advised me while I was writing the third book that I should let the sisters find the body, that their different reactions would tell so much about their characters. They were absolutely right, and I've done that in every book since.

I wish I could say I write every day, but I don't. That doesn't mean I'm not working. A lot of a writer's work is done while she's cooking supper or exercising. Plots must be thought out, characters developed. But get to the notebook or the computer as soon as you can to put those thoughts down.

One final piece of advice that seems so simple: Send your work to publishers. Don't be hesitant. But know your market. A friend and I owned Druid Press for ten years, and for listings in the literary market directories, we were very specific about what we published: We wanted short fiction and unrhymed poems under forty lines in length. Period. We received nonfiction manuscripts, epic novels, autobiographies. Sometimes the postage on these tomes ran three or four dollars. A total waste. We also received many query letters with no SASE included, and we simply couldn't afford to respond. We sold the company seven years ago, and we're still getting manuscripts. Don't waste your money and time. Make sure your mystery goes to a publisher who publishes mysteries. And if that manuscript is returned, send it out again. A clean copy. When I was in publishing, I actually received manuscripts with other editors' comments on them. Be professional. Follow the rules.

And keep that notebook handy. The world is full of stress-free turkeys waiting for you to write about. Just do it!

❏ 49

TRICKS OF THE WIZARD'S TRADE

BY SUSAN DEXTER

FANTASY IS THE OLDEST FORM OF LITERATURE—THE GREAT UMBRELLA that arches over *all* fiction. Fantasy is also a marketing category, shelved and intermingled with science fiction, wearing scaly dragons on its covers in place of shiny spaceships. Fantasy's themes spring from the collective unconscious. Fantasy is populated by archetypes and demons common to us all. Our dreams and our nightmares. Fairy tales.

It's *hard* to be original in this genre. But limits are illusions. Consider: We have but 26 letters in our alphabet. And they'd best be used in combinations readers will recognize as *words*. Now, *there's* a limit. Music? Even worse, but composers don't seem to mind that there are only so many notes to go around.

"Never been done before" may truly be impossible. But "Never been done like *that* before"? That sounds like a goal to me. *Star Wars* didn't wow the world because it was a *new* idea; it resonates with audiences because it's a very *old* story: a fairy tale, right down to the princess. Retell an old tale—do it in a fresh way, and your readers will gasp in wonder. Do it well, and you'll have editors drooling.

The first trick in a wizard's bag is this: Look at your sources of inspiration. Be a *reader,* before you begin to write. Read new fantasies. Keep up with the field. Read the classics. Comic books aren't forbidden fruit—just don't make them an exclusive diet. Read fairy tales. Read folklore. Study the magic and mythologies of many cultures. If you feed your subconscious properly, it will supply your storytelling needs.

Go to your public library. Breathe in the fresh air and book dust. Surf the Net later. No need to memorize the Dewey System to graze the shelves productively. The 200's are philosophy and religion—*all* religions. Folklore lives in the 398.2's—right next to the prettified fairy tales "retold for children." You'll find original folk tales that will make your hair stand on end and get your juices flowing. Arrowsmith's *Field Guide to the Little People* will convince you that elves are neither Disney critters nor the fantasy analogue of Vulcans, but beings far more ancient and interesting. *The Golden Bough,* Frazer's study of myth and religion, supplied the magical system my wizard Tristan used in *The Ring of Allaire* and its two sequels. I doubt that a thousand authors mining day and night could exhaust that book's possibilities.

Remember the hero has a *thousand* faces. If you confine your reading to role-playing manuals, the stirring high fantasy you hope to craft will be a pale, weak thing, a fifth-generation videotape. Recycled characters stuck in a plot that's a copy of an imitation of Tolkien won't excite an editor these days. Read to understand what the classic themes are. Tolkien based *The Lord of the Rings* solidly on the northern European mythic tradition. It's not a copy of anything, but we respond to it as something familiar.

Fantastic elements work only if you make *reality* real. If I carelessly give my horses "paws," will you believe what I tell you about dragons? So think about the nuts and bolts, and don't trust Hollywood to do it for you. Castles—where did people *live* in them? Surely everyone wasn't born a princess. Who grows the food, does the laundry, cleans up after the knights' horses? When you research actual medieval cultures, you'll turn up truths far stranger than anything you could *invent.* Your characters should have real lives, with routines, habits, responsibilities. Most of us have to work for a living, and while being a princess may be a full-time job, being an elf is not. My title character in *The Wind-Witch* stands out from the pack of fantasy heroines: Not only is she *not* a princess, but she has a job—two jobs: She's a farmer and a weaver. Getting her sheep through lambing season matters just as much to Druyan as warding off a barbarian invasion or discovering her magical talents. That makes her *real,* for all that she can literally whistle up a storm. Readers can identify with her.

Magic was the science of its day. Science is of fairly recent origin. Both science and magic seek to explain and control the natural world, usually for a man's benefit. Study belief systems. Decide what suits your story, and stick to that. Don't throw in random demons just because they sound cool. Plan your world, if you want it to work for you.

Maps are more than endpaper decorations, and you should start drawing one before you ever start writing your fantasy. Never mind your quest-bound characters: A map will keep *you,* the author, from getting lost. If the desperate ride from Castle A to Castle B takes three days, then the trip back from B to A can take *longer* once the pressure's off; but if the journey takes *less* time, you have major explaining to do. Maps can spare you such *faux pas.*

Maps can suggest plot solutions. In the real world, things are where they are for good reasons. Castles protect and are not built where there's nothing worth contesting. Towns are tied to trade; they grow where roads cross, beside safe harbors. As I began to write *The Wind-Witch,* I had established in an earlier book that my Esdragon had a cliffy coast and treacherous seas. Now I needed it to suffer an invasion—by sea. Where could the invaders strike? Well, the Eral are after plunder, so they want towns. And Esdragon's towns—as in the real-world town of Cornwall, on which I based my fictional duchy—are mostly at the mouths of the rivers that drain the upland moors and reach the sea as broad estuaries. I put rivers on my map, decided which were navigable for any distance—and *presto!* I had many places for my raiders to plunder, distant from one another, spots for Druyan to try to protect from the back of her magic-bred horse.

A primitive map has charm—perhaps one of your characters drew it—but there are tricks to convincing cartography. You can't draw a straight line without a ruler? Relax! Nobody can, and there are rather few straight lines in nature anyway. Now get yourself a real map. Any continent or bit of one will do. Put tracing paper over your selection. Pencil some outlines, imagining how the coast changes as the sea level rises—or falls. Hills become islands, islands change into peninsulas. Valleys become arms of the sea. The combination of wind and wave nibbles cliffs, isolating outcrops. It's your pick.

Change the scale. Use an island to make a continent, or vice versa. Turn your map upside down. When I designed Esdragon and Calandra, I basically used Europe—but I stood it on end, balanced on the tip of Portugal. Copy the shape of the water spot on your ceiling or the last patch of snow lingering on your sidewalk.

Study actual maps. Where do rivers flow? How do they look? Mountain ranges trap rain and alter climate. So where will your forest be? Your dry grasslands? Your band of unicorn hunters needs to cross the Dragonspike Mountains. Where are the passes? Are they open year-round or only seasonally? The threat of being trapped by an early winter can add drama. A map will remind you of that.

God, as Mies van der Rohe said, is in the details. As the creator of your paper world, you have responsibilities. *You* must concern yourself with the details, for there is no *Fodor's Guide to Middle Earth,* or Esdragon, or your elfin kingdom. Which brings us to the Rule of Names.

Basic rules for name use apply to all fiction. Just as you vary your sentence lengths, so you should choose names with differing lengths and sounds. Your names must not all begin with the same letter of the alphabet. Characters and countries must not be easily confused with one another. A name that brings to mind an over-the-counter remedy will not work for your hero.

World-makers need to name *everything.* Adam got off easy doing just the animals! I need to name kingdoms, heroes, continents, castles, islands, mountains, rivers, lakes, gods, horses, magic swords and cats. Unlike the author of the police procedural, I can't get my names by stabbing a random finger into the phone book.

Names in fantasy present special pleasures and certain problems. Names must always be apt, but you can toss off grand heroic names without the twinge of conscience you'd feel about giving such names to real children who'd be attending real-world schools. Remember, though, that names are tools. They make your invented world convincing and solid, but they must evoke the feel of *your* world. You can't just put the *Encyclopedia of Mythology* into a blender. In folkloric tradition, names have serious power: To know a creature's true name is to control it. That power carries over into fiction. Poorly chosen names can strain your reader's willing suspension of disbelief until it snaps. And then where are you?

You will be wise not to leave your naming to chance, or to the last minute. Under the pressure of mid-paragraph, you will either heave up a melange of x's, q's, and z's, or you'll clutch and settle for names as bland as tapioca. Planning ahead avoids both extremes. Compile a list of useful names.

You can keep that list in your PC or on the backs of old envelopes, but a small notebook is the handiest. I use an address book—durably hardbound, alphabetized pages, large enough not to be easily mislaid. I list names down the left margins, circling those I use and noting where.

I may reuse a name from time to time, certain names being as common in Esdragon as John is in this world.

I glean and gather from sources readily available to all. Start with baby-name books. The older thebetter; you aren't after the trendy and popular. Copy whatever catches your eye. Histories of popular names offer archaic forms and less common variants. Rhisiart, in *The Wizard's Shadow,* is a name that is simply a Welsh version of Richard. The Welsh struggle to represent with their alphabet the sounds of a name they got from Norman French gives the name an exotic look.

Invent your own names. Dickens did it. Lord Dunsany was a master at it. Tolkien invented whole *languages* and took his names from them. You may enjoy playing with sounds. When I wrote *The Ring of Allaire,* I struggled for a week for a proper name for Valadan, my immortal warhorse. Wanting a proud, noble, brave name, I began with *val,* from valiant, and went on from there. Whereas Kessallia in *The Prince of Ill Luck* just popped out of my subconscious one day. Learn to spot a "keeper" like that.

Use the phone book. Use the newspaper—all those lists of engagements, weddings, obituaries. Chop off the front half of a name, or use just the ending. Stick a syllable of one name onto part of another. Minor changes yield fresh names. Switching just one letter made Robert into *Robart,* and gave Druyan's brother a familiar yet not ordinary name.

Watch movie credits. Watch the Olympics—you'll hear scads of less usual names, like Oksana, and they're *spelled* for you, right on the screen. What could be easier?

Once you have your names, use them wisely. Pick those that fit your story and its cultures. Save the rest for your next project.

The true test of imagination may be to name a cat, as Samuel Butler said. I doubt that correctly naming a dragon is far down the difficulty scale, though. World-making and myth-making are not for the faint-hearted, nor the short attention span. The good news: No license is required! Only the will to do the job right—which is the *real* power behind *any* wizard's spell.

❑ 50

TWILIGHT FOR HIGH NOON: TODAY'S WESTERN

BY LOREN D. ESTLEMAN

PARDON ME WHILE I INDULGE IN SOME SELF-CONGRATULATION: I WAS right. In 1981, when TV sitcoms and big-screen space operas had all but crowded out the traditional western, and Louis L'Amour's career was drawing to a close with Tom Clancy's ascendant, I went out on a limb in an article for *The Writer* Magazine and predicted the triumphant return of frontier fiction.

Only four years later, Larry McMurtry's monumental tale of a cattle drive, *Lonesome Dove,* swept to the top of *The New York Times* bestseller list and captured the Pulitzer Prize. The subsequent TV adaptation gunned down the ratings competition, saved the endangered television miniseries from extinction, and spawned three successful sequels and a regular series. In the meantime, *Dances with Wolves,* Kevin Costner's epic motion picture based on Michael Blake's acclaimed novel about a white man living with Indians, recovered its investment ten times over and took seven Academy Awards. Next in the chute was Clint Eastwood's *Unforgiven,* a grittily realistic movie about an Old West assassin, and the big winner at the Academy Awards in 1993.

The effect on Hollywood was as sudden and startling as the Gunfight at the O.K. Corral. Immediately, every major studio gave the green light to western productions that had been languishing in its story department for years. By the middle of the 1990s, more westerns were opening in the nation's theaters than at any time since the 1950s.

The pundits who had smugly announced the permanent closing of the frontier were stumped for an explanation. Writers of westerns were not.

What *Lonesome Dove, Dances with Wolves,* and *Unforgiven* have in common that set them apart from the long stream of *High Noon* imitations of decades past was a regard for authentic history. The flawed, emotionally repressed cattlemen of *Lonesome Dove* had as little in com-

251

mon with the heroic cowboys of 1946's *Red River* as Kevin Costner's flesh-and-blood Sioux had with the cardboard savages of the old B western; and there was certainly little of John Wayne's swagger or Gary Cooper's stoic self-sacrifice in Clint Eastwood's gunfighter, a drunken, whoring killer. They presented raw, unflinching portraits of imperfect humanity that audiences the world over recognized as genuine.

Not every entry in this spate of big-screen westerns was successful. Those that failed were dismal attempts to revive the old mythology of fast-draw contests and heroic loners with no visible means of support, dedicating their lives to the eradication of evil. Time was when these stereotypes were fresh and popular. But an increasingly sophisticated public, made cynical by real-life assassinations and corruption in high places, demands realistic characters in plausible situations.

TV documentaries such as Ken Burns's *The West,* and exhaustive revisionist histories such as Dee Brown's *Bury My Heart at Wounded Knee,* Paula Mitchell Marks's *And Die in the West,* and Evan S. Connell's *Son of the Morning Star,* have all reached wide audiences who can no longer be expected to embrace tall tales directed at readers who never ventured west of Chicago. Responding to a growing appetite for historical accuracy, a new breed of western writer is mining primary resources for people and facts that require no dramatization to attract reader interest.

Fortunately, there is no shortage of such raw material. The historical James Butler Hickok and Martha Jane Cannary were far more complex and interesting than the Wild Bill and Calamity Jane of fiction, and the thousands of less noted participants in the Westward Expansion all loom larger than life in our pampered time. Consider the haunted, burned-out expressions on the faces of those long-dead prairie wives photographed in front of their mean soddies. Yes, there were women out West; and theirs is but one of the many hundreds of tales that have yet to be told.

The traditional western is dying out, along with the readership that made it popular. Today's publishers have jettisoned the very word "western," substituting the labels "frontier fiction" and "American historical." Books herded into these categories are immediately distinguishable from their predecessors, first, by their length—100,000 words plus, as opposed to the 60,000-word horse operas of old—second, by their covers, which feature great sweeps of land and ethnically diverse casts instead of WASPish gunslingers facing off on a dusty street—third, by their reviews. *Publishers Weekly, The New York Times,* and the *Bloomsbury Review* take serious notice of these books as often now as they ignored the work of Luke Short and Ernest Haycox in the past. Today's western writers demonstrate a deeper understanding of the role of the American West in the shaping of a nation, and consequently of that nation's place in the history of the world.

As a writer, I welcome the larger canvas. In the past, I often felt constrained by the need to tell a grand story in a narrow space, and once ran afoul of an editor at Doubleday when an early entry in my Page Murdock series ran more than 300 pages in manuscript. Compare that with the freedom I felt to include this passage in Murdock's adventure, *City of Widows* (Forge, 1994):

> Desert heat doesn't follow any of the standard rules. You'd expect it to be worst when the sun is straight up, but a hat will protect you from it then. When the only shade for miles is on the wrong side of the shrubbery you're using for cover, there is no hiding from that afternoon slant. I turned up my collar and unfastened my cuffs and pulled them down over the backs of my hands, but I could feel my skin turning red and shrinking under the fabric. Pinheads of sweat marched along the edge of my leather hatband and tracked down into my eyes, stinging like fire ants. The water in the canteen tasted like hot metal. I wanted the Montana snow, blue as the veins in Colleen Bower's throat with the mountain runoff coursing through it carrying shards of white ice . . .

That editor would probably have insisted I make do with the bare statement "It was hot," and get to the shooting. The end of space restrictions allows me to enlist the climate and topography of the West as characters in the plot.

One of the most significant—and progressive—developments of the new western has been the increase in women writers. Their ability to empathize with the courageous women who left behind the security of civilization to build a new life in the wilderness is largely responsible for the western's acceptance in the literary mainstream. In the past, the few women who ventured into the genre, including Dorothy M. Johnson ("The Man Who Shot Liberty Valance," "A Man Called Horse") and Willa Cather (*My Antonia, Death Comes for the Archbishop*) were obliged to write from the male point of view. Successors such as Lucia St. Clair Robson, author of *Ride the Wind,* told from the perspective of Comanche captive Cynthia Ann Parker, have changed all that—to everyone's benefit.

Consider this frontier fiction staple—the showing of a notorious outlaw's corpse for profit—as transformed by Deborah Morgan in her short story "Mrs. Crawford's Odyssey" (*How the West Was Read,* Durkin Hayes, 1996), simply by adopting the point of view of the dead man's mother:

> This could not be her twenty-two-year-old son. Matthew had golden features, sunlit hair, a strong, square-set jaw. Laid out before her was an old man, bald, with flesh of a blue-white translucency, like watered-down milk. The heavily rouged cheekbones emphasized vast, dark hollows that should have been a jawline.
>
> Someone had made a terrible mistake, she was sure of it. She grabbed at that thread of hope, caught it, held it taut. This eased her, and she approached the deceased like any slight acquaintance might—respectfully, but thankful it's not one of your own. Only when she was leaning over the body did she discover death's ruse and see, unmistakably, her child.
>
> She clasped her hand over her mouth, a futile attempt to contain her emotions. Tears flowed until she believed that she would never be able to cry again.
>
> "My dear, precious boy," she said at last, "what have they done to you?"

Few male writers could write so poignantly and convincingly about a woman regarding the lifeless body of the boy to whom she gave birth.

Publishers are actively seeking women interested in tapping the rich vein of material concerning women out West. The market has rarely been so open to newcomers.

The West was settled by many different kinds of people: whites, blacks, Indians, immigrants, consumptives, heroes, and scoundrels. Bill Hotchkiss's *The Medicine Calf* and *Ammahabas* absorbingly follow the life of Jim Beckwourth, the black trapper and fur trader who became a Crow chief, and Cherokee writer Robert J. Conley (*The Dark Island, Crazy Snake*) stands at the summit of an impressive career built upon the Native American experience. In the heyday of the traditional western, such characters were regulated to secondary roles, either as villains or as comic foils.

When in my *Writer* article I first echoed Horace Greeley's advice "Go West," the necessary reference material resided only in libraries, bookstores, and county courthouses. Today, the writer with access to a computer can tap into a wealth of information on the geography, living conditions, and history of the West through the Internet. Rounding up the facts has never been so easy, but be warned: There is no longer an excuse for getting them wrong. Today's readers have the same access, and if you err, you will hear from them.

The timespan embraced by the new western is limitless. Once restricted to the bare quarter-century between the end of the Civil War in 1865 and the closing of the frontier in 1890, it now encompasses prehistoric Indian life as exemplified by the "People" series written by anthropologists W. Michael and Kathleen O'Neal Gear (*People of the Fire, People of the Silence,* and many more), and the struggles of modern westerners to come to terms with their heritage, as recounted by John L. Moore in *The Breaking of Ezra Riley.*

Freed from the tyranny of "acceptable" timeframes, I took advantage of all I had learned about the West in twenty years of researching and writing westerns to tell a fictional story based on the mysterious life of the musician who wrote the famous ballad "Jesse James." History knows nothing of this individual beyond the name he signed to his composition, so I co-opted him as representative of the itinerant modern minstrels whose music brought romance to the frontier and preserved its legend. My novel *Billy Gashade* (Forge, 1997) follows its narrator from his fateful role in the New York draft riots of 1863 to his final stint as a ghostwriter of songs for Gene Autry musicals in 1935 Hollywood:

> . . . I don't regret much. I've known some of the best and worst men of my time, survived events that sent better men than I to their graves more than half a century ago and as I was told by one of the strong, intelligent women who have charted the course of my life, I have my gift. Unlike its composer, the song I wrote fifty-three years ago grows stronger each year. A month hardly passes that I don't hear it on the radio or in a supper place with a live performer, usually at the request of one of the patrons, even if whoever sings it usually leaves out the last verse:

> > *This song was made by Billy Gashade*
> > *Just as soon as the news did arrive.*
> > *He said there was no man with the law in his hand*
> > *That could take Jesse James alive.*

The "best and worst men"—and women—of Billy's time include Jesse James, Boss Tweed, Edith Wharton, Allan Pinkerton, Oscar Wilde, George Armstrong Custer, and Greta Garbo. The liberty offered by the new western permitted me to include people and places not commonly associated with the "western," and thus to help stretch the limits; for the history of what was once dismissed as the Great American Desert is the history of America.

The mystique of the frontier has always been freedom: from restrictions, from convention, from one's past. Today, at long last, the western itself offers that same freedom, as well as the opportunity for the writer—any writer—to slap his or her brand on an exciting, expanding market. So saddle up.

❑ NONFICTION: ARTICLES AND BOOKS

❑ 51

THE MAKER'S EYE

BY DONALD M. MURRAY

WHEN BEGINNING WRITERS COMPLETE THEIR FIRST DRAFT, THEY USUally read it through to correct typographical errors and consider the job of writing done. When professional writers complete their first draft, they usually feel they are at the start of the writing process. Now that they have a draft, they can begin writing.

That difference in attitude is the difference between amateur and professional, inexperience and experience, journeyman and craftsman. Most productive writers share the feeling that the first draft (and most of those that follow) is an opportunity to discover what they have to say and how they can best say it.

To produce a progression of drafts, each of which says more and says it better, writers have to develop a special reading skill. In school we are taught to read what is on the page. We try to comprehend what authors have said, what they meant, and what are the implications of their words.

The writers of such drafts must be their own best enemy. They must accept the criticism of others and be suspicious of it; they must accept the praise of others and be even more suspicious of it. They cannot depend on others. They must detach themselves from their own page so they can apply both their caring and their craft to their own work.

Detachment is not easy. It takes ego to write. I need to say, "I am here. Listen. I have something important to say." Then, after our egos have produced a draft, we must read when our judgment may be at its worst, when we are close to the euphoric moment of creation. Writers must learn to protect themselves from their own egos.

Just as dangerous as protective writers are despairing ones, those who think everything they do is terrible, dreadful, awful. If they are to publish, they must save what is effective on the page while cutting away what doesn't work. Writers must hear and respect their own voice.

Remember how each craftsperson you have seen—the carpenter eyeing the level of a shelf, the mechanic listening to the motor—takes the instinctive step back. This is what writers have to do when they read their own work.

It is far easier for most beginning writers to understand the need for rereading and rewriting than it is to understand how to go about it. Published writers don't necessarily break down the various stages of rewriting and editing, they just go ahead and do it.

There is nothing virtuous in the rewriting process. It is simply an essential condition of life for most writers. There are writers who do very little rewriting, mostly because they have the capacity and experience to create and review a large number of invisible drafts in their minds before they get to the page. And many writers perform all of the tasks of revision simultaneously, page by page, rather than draft by draft. But it is still possible to break down the process of rereading one's own work into the sequence most published writers follow and which beginning writers should follow as they study their own pages.

Seven elements

Many writers just scan their manuscript at first, reading as quickly as possible for problems of subject and form. They stand back from the more technical details of language so they can spot any weaknesses in content or in organization. Each writer works in an individual way, but I know from my studies of the writing process that most writers read their manuscripts as I do, paying close attention to seven key elements of effective writing.

The first is *subject*. Do I have anything to say? If I am lucky, I will find that I do have something to say, often more than I expected. If the subject is not clear, or if it is not yet limited or defined enough for me to proceed, I step back and try to catch the focus of what I *may* say in a line that may become a title or the first sentence of the piece. If not, I write my way toward meaning with discovery drafts that usually make the subject come clear.

The next point I check is *audience*. Like most writers, I write first for myself, to explore and then share my world. But the aim of writing is communication, not just self-expression. I ask myself if there is an audience for what I am writing, if anyone will need or enjoy what I have to say.

Form is usually considered after audience. Form, or genre, is the vehicle that will carry what I have to say to my readers, and it should grow out of my subject. If I have a character, my subject may grow into a short story, a magazine profile, a novel, a biography, or a play. It depends on what I have to say and to whom I wish to say it. When I reread my manuscript, I ask if the form is suitable, if it works, if it will carry my meaning to my reader.

Once I have the appropriate form, I survey the *structure*, the order of what I have to say. Every good piece of writing is built on a solid framework of logic or argument or narrative or motivation; it is a line that runs through the entire piece of writing and holds it together. If I read my manuscript and cannot spot this essential thread, I stop writing until I find something to weave my writing together.

The manuscript that has order must also have *development*. Each part of it must be built in a way that will prepare the reader for the next part. Description, documentation, action, dialogue, metaphor—these and many other devices flesh out the skeleton so that the reader will be able to understand what is written. How much development? That's like asking how much garlic. It depends on the cook, the casserole, and to whom it is going to be served. This is the question that the writer will be answering as he reads his piece of writing through from beginning to end, and answering it will lead him to the sixth element.

The writer must be sure of his *dimensions*. This means that there should be something more than structure and development, that there should be a pleasing proportion among all of the parts. I cannot decide on a dimension without seeing all of the parts of writing together. I examine each section of the writing in its relationship to all of the other sections.

Finally, I listen for *tone*. Any piece of writing is held together by that invisible force, the writer's voice. Tone is my style, tone is all that is on the page and off the page, tone is grace, wit, anger—the spirit that drives a piece of writing forward.

Potentialities and alternatives

When I have a draft that has subject, audience, form, structure, development, dimension, and tone, then I am ready to begin the careful process of line-by-line editing. Each line, each word has to be right.

Now I read my copy with infinite care. I often read aloud, calling on my ear's experience with language. Does this sound right—or this? I read and listen and revise, back and forth from eye to page to ear to page. I find I must do this careful editing at short runs, fifteen or twenty minutes, or I become too kind to myself.

Slowly, I move from word to word, looking through the word to see the subject. Good writing is, in a sense, invisible. It should enable the reader to see the subject, not the writer. Every word should be true— true to what the writer has to say. And each word must be precise in its relation to the words that have gone before and the words that will follow.

This sounds tedious, but it isn't. Making something right is immensely satisfying, and the writer who once was lost in a swamp of potentialities now has the chance to work with the most technical skills of language. And even in the process of the most careful editing, there is the joy of language. Words have double meanings, even triple and quadruple meanings. Each word has its own tone, its opportunity for connotation and denotation and nuance. And when I connect words, there is always the chance of the sudden insight, the unexpected clarification.

The maker's eye moves back and forth from word to phrase to sentence to paragraph to sentence to phrase to word. I look at my sentences for variety and balance in form and structure, and at the interior of the paragraph for coherence, unity and emphasis. I play with figurative language, decide to repeat or not, to create a parallelism for emphasis. I work over my copy until I achieve a manuscript that appears effortless to the reader.

I learned something about this process when I first wore bifocals. I thought that when I was editing I was working line by line. But I discovered that I had to order special editing glasses, even though the bottom section of my bifocals have a greater expanse of glass than ordinary glasses. While I am editing, my eyes are unconsciously flicking back and forth across the whole page, or back to another page, or forward to another page. The limited bifocal view through the lower half of my glasses is not enough. Each line must be seen in its relationship to every other line.

When does this process end? The maker's eye is never satisfied, for he knows that each word in his copy is tentative. Writing, to the writer, is alive, something that is full of potential and alternative, something that can grow beyond its own dream. The writer reads to discover what he has said—and then to say it better.

A piece of writing is never finished. It is delivered to a deadline, torn out of the typewriter on demand, sent off with a sense of frustration and incompleteness. Just as writers know they must stop avoiding writing and write, they also know they must send their copy off to be published, although it is not quite right yet—if only they had another couple of days, just another run at it, perhaps. . . .

□ 52

WRITING THE
PERSONAL ESSAY

BY EILEEN HERBERT JORDAN

IF YOU ARE ACTIVELY WRITING THESE DAYS, CHANCES ARE YOU ARE either exploring or attempting to do a personal essay. Call it a form whose time has come, though in reality it has been on the rise now for longer than you think. It played a part in chasing the short story off the pages of magazines. Since then, its big brother, the Memoir, has been busy doing the same thing to the novel on book lists.

Editors seem to be clamoring for the truth. When I noticed this trend, I began to write essays, trying to learn as I went along. I have now published enough, it seems, to make people ask me if I have a secret formula—or are there any guidelines? I don't know of any, and I have no rules. Maybe there are none. It is a business of opinion, and what I do have is an accumulation of opinions that may lead you in the right direction; more often than not they try to explain what *not* to do. Let's take them one at a time.

Don't think it is easy. This will be your first stumbling block, and, in fact, it is the hardest one to get beyond. After all, in a personal essay there is no plot, no characterization. There is no dialogue to invent, no motivations to contrive, no strange backgrounds to explore. There is no research—what you don't know, you omit. How much simpler could it be? Just wait. Before you know it you will be longing for your nemesis, the plot (real life so seldom has any). If you have done investigative writing, you will wish for the experts you need only to quote to make your point. You will be driving on a strange road—and getting nowhere. *In order to work, a personal essay must have the bones of a story under its skin.* It doesn't emerge from your head full blown. It comes out slowly, and when it does, it better have a beginning, a middle, and an end.

Don't try to do it alone. This may strike you as strange advice, espe-

264

cially to give writers, those paragons of isolation, but I have a point. You write alone, but the ideas and the emotions in an essay often arise from an exchange of viewpoints with others. Some will have experiences similar to yours, and by listening to them, you will get an insight you didn't have before. The personal essay is the most highly subjective kind of writing, with the possible exception of poetry, so, especially when you're starting, you may choose highly personal themes—fine, if you make a point. Better to ask around and discover the nerve hit most often by the situation you have chosen.

I once wrote about the death of my dog. This single piece brought more mail than anything the magazine had ever published. Naturally, most of the letters were from readers who had lost dogs they loved, too. Why tell me? Because before reading my essay they could not believe that anyone had ever loved a dog the way they loved theirs—and now they were bonded with me in love and loss. I didn't know what I was doing beforehand—I just let it all hang out.

Though sometimes that works well, as it did here, you can't always depend on it. Why in the world would an editor want to publish your particular version of a high or a low moment in your life unless you write with the kind of insight that makes readers see themselves again as they were then—or see themselves perhaps for the first time? Comparing notes often helps.

Don't make things up. Gilding the lily doesn't work here. If your imagination runs riot as soon as you sit down to write, count your blessings and write fiction. This applies to names, too. If the person I'm writing about doesn't want to be identified (some love it, some hate it), I say "my son" and not, "my son, Joseph." I do not say "my son, whom I will call Boris"—if I do, some reader will mutter, "Hey, what's she hiding?"

But don't tell everything. Anyone who has studied the short story knows that each sentence is leading to something; the same is true with the personal essay. Just because you don't have a dramatic tale to wrap up, there's no excuse for you to rattle on about every move you made, every stitch you wore, every flower in the garden, every breeze that blew—most likely, none of this matters. Keep your eye on the point you're making from the first sentence on.

Get mad, but don't get cranky. It is good for the soul and good for the reader to sound off in print about something that makes you *mad.*

Take a stand, fight for what you believe, a small issue or a giant one—it doesn't matter. You *must* mean it, and if you do and your fire is bright, you will be amazed at the response you receive from those who feel the same way—and from those who don't! What you *don't* want to do is simply to bemoan the dreary state of the world these days and your particular angst. We all have our little miseries—we don't have to read about yours. Now, if you can do it with wit, that is something else entirely. I can't judge it. One is funny or one is not, and, if you are, it is your most precious commodity.

Don't be coy. If you are pretty, talented, rich, bright or whatever, and any of these attributes is relevant to what you are writing, admit it. It only muddles the point if you don't. If it is no part of what you are writing, don't bring it up. If you were 40 when the episode you are recounting happened, don't say you were 20, or even 30. The gears shift differently with time. And, above all, never attempt to convince the reader of your honesty by saying, *I am not a writer.* That's something he may find out fast enough himself!

There is one thing I have not mentioned, although it is often a key factor—timing. Timing in writing an essay is not, under certain circumstances, unlike timing in life: absolutely vital and rarely predictable. Of course, it can work for you. You have in your head a treasure trove of holidays, anniversaries, and special moments. As your writing progresses, you will know precisely when the markets you favor need material for every one of them. But then there are times when you are caught short, when something happens that you never expected would, that you never wanted to face. Do you write about it? When—and how?

When I first heard that Frank Sinatra was very ill, I thought, well, now I should write my own Sinatra memory. I resisted. For one thing, news of his condition was coming only from the tabloid press, and I didn't trust them. But there was another reason: I couldn't face it, because I knew what the ending had to be. And, without closure, who cared? Who cared that I was once 16 and in the throes of a romance as doomed as it can only be at that age? And who cares that, to muffle the pain, I went out and bought my first Sinatra record? I carried it home, set the package on the floor, tripped, and because records broke as easily as hearts did in those days, shattered it. I cried off and on all day, not for the lost love (whatever *his* name was), but for the lost notes of

"I'll Never Smile Again," which I knew were meant just for me—if only I could hear them.

Later in the year Sinatra died, and I could have written it then, but the lead time was against me, as it so often is, so I never did.

I don't suggest that you do that. I think you should write what you want to write—keep it tender, keep it funny, keep it yours—and hope for the best. That's what a personal essay is all about. For while it has the rules of journalism as its base, the who, when, where, why, and how, I like to think that, at its best, the personal essay has something else as well—something I call the journalism of heart.

□ 53

SLEUTH, HUNTER, BIOGRAPHER

BY LINDA SIMON

ONE OF MY FAVORITE BIOGRAPHIES IS RICHARD HOLMES'S *FOOTSTEPS: Adventures of a Romantic Biographer*. In it, Holmes does not give us what we might expect—a chronological study of one subject—but instead, he records his own travels in search of some great British Romantic writers, including Robert Louis Stevenson, Percy Bysshe Shelley, William Wordsworth, and Mary Wollstonecraft. One admiring critic summed up the book's merits: "This exhilarating book, part biography, part autobiography, shows the biographer as sleuth and huntsman, tracking his subjects through space and time."

Not all biographies are quite as exhilarating, but the critic's words could be applied to any biographer's task: We are all part sleuth, part hunter as we travel into the past and through unfamiliar landscapes in search of our subject. For writers with boundless curiosity and a genuine respect for other people's lives, writing biography is a satisfying and illuminating project.

Your subject

Biographical subjects may be found anywhere. Your mother's uncle, the one who emigrated from Norway at the turn of the century, may be as interesting a subject as a renowned artist or statesman. A biographical subject need not be famous to the world; it is up to you, as biographer, to make that subject interesting to others. If your subject is a family member or friend, he or she may have lived a private, unheralded life—but a life no less worthy of a biography. Other subjects may have touched fame, but never achieved it for themselves. Jean Strouse, the biographer of Alice James, sister of the novelist Henry and philosopher William, coined the term "semi-private lives" to describe men and women who lived in the shadows of more famous people, but whose own lives were fairly ordinary. One of my own subjects, Alice B.

Toklas, lived a "semi-private" life in comparison with her more famous companion, Gertrude Stein. And another of my subjects, Margaret Beaufort, also lived a "semi-private" life, in comparison with her more famous son, King Henry VII, and her notorious grandson, Henry VIII.

Writing about Margaret Beaufort gave me a chance to explore the lives of women in fifteenth-century England. Although Beaufort surely was a member of the aristocracy, still she shared some experiences— childbirth, for example, and widowhood—with other women of the time. Initially, I decided to write about her because she was the matriarch of the House of Tudor; but as I explored various sources, I became increasingly interested in the ways that she helped me understand the daily life of medieval women.

Margaret Beaufort, not yet sixteen, was living in Wales at the end of her first pregnancy. Her husband was in England at the time, and when labor began, she was alone, without family, in a cold, stone castle, unable to speak the language of her servants. I found a fifteenth-century gynecological manual to help me understand how young Margaret would have been cared for during childbirth. She delivered her son in a bare room, with walls a foot thick, tended by midwives who brought her strange oils and potions and who sat beside her on an oddly shaped birthing stool. Surely Margaret knew that her life—like that of all women at the time—was at risk from childbirth; and just as surely she knew that infant mortality was frighteningly high. But the birth went well: She lived and so did her son. And the thin, frail young woman quickly rallied to a newly-discovered strength when it came time to name the boy: She refused to name him after his Welsh father or grandfather, but instead insisted on a regal English name. He would be Henry, and he would be king.

Even though Margaret Beaufort was a noble woman, there were few sources available to me that gave evidence of her life and experiences, especially as a child and young wife and mother. But there were enough sources, scarce as they were, to enable me to feel confident that I could reveal the significant events and context for her life.

Make sure there are sources

As much as you may care about your subject, you cannot write a biography without sufficient historical and biographical sources. Those sources include letters, diaries, journals, interviews, memoirs, creative writing, and works of art such as paintings or films. Such sources are available in many collections—some private (in your parents' attic), some public (in libraries or museums).

The reference room of a good local or college library has many reference sources that may help you find out what material, published and unpublished, is available about your subject. Among these is the *Biography Index,* which lists references to books and more than two thousand periodicals for a wide range of subjects, including major figures in the arts, sports, science, and politics. You may also want to consult one of the many standard biographical dictionaries, such as *Dictionary of National Biography* (for British figures) or the *Dictionary of American Biography.* The *Biographical Dictionaries Master Index* can direct you to an entry about your subject in one hundred biographical dictionaries. For contemporary subjects, you may want to consult *Current Biography,* a monthly journal that began publication in 1940, offering biographical information on men and women in the news. Many public libraries subscribe to this journal and keep bound issues on their reference shelves. In addition to these general dictionaries, there are many specialized biographical dictionaries focused on gender, race, profession, or time period.

To find unpublished material about your subject (manuscripts or letters your subject may have written), you may consult directories of libraries that contain archives or manuscript collections. These directories include *American Literary Manuscripts,* the *Directory of Archives and Manuscript Repositories in the United States,* and *The National Union Catalog of Manuscript Collections.* Tracking down your subject in these reference books is often slow and tedious work, but it is a necessary first step in the research process.

Once you locate sources for your subject, you may be able to order photocopies of the material you need. Sometimes, however, you may need to travel to collections to do research. Before you leave on a research trip, however, it is helpful to know as precisely as possible what the library holds, what you are looking for, and how much material is available. If you plan a two-day trip and discover two weeks of reading, you will leave the library frustrated.

If your subject has been written about before, a previous biography can be invaluable in giving you a start for research. Consult the book's bibliography and notes for references to library archives. But don't stop there. Libraries are always in the process of adding to their collections. New material about your subject may have become available since the publication of books or articles. It's your job to find that new material.

Stay organized

Any researcher needs to be well-organized. For my own work, I keep notes in three places: file folders, which contain photocopies of sources; 5"7" index cards, on which I write notes taken from books or articles; and computer files, where I also keep notes from readings, interviews, and other sources. At the end of a project, I may have several drawers of file folders, hundreds and hundreds of index cards, and many computer files—far more material than will ever make its way into the finished book. But this excess is necessary so I can select what I need for a coherent and energetic narrative.

Biographers find their own way of organizing notes: Mine is to keep index cards devoted to the names of people that figure in my subject's life. Whenever someone is mentioned in a letter or book, I make an index card. When I see a reference to that person in another source, I pull out the card and take notes. In that way, I find it easy to compose small biographical sketches of the person when he or she first appears in the biography.

Other biographers may organize material chronologically or they may organize notes related to events in their subject's life. There is no right way to organize, but you need to be consistent and meticulous in both note-taking and documentation. Write down the author, title, and publication information for every published book that you use, and make sure you note the name of the library for every unpublished letter or manuscript you use. Your readers will expect careful documentation in whatever you publish. For writers who need to brush up on documentation, such reference sources as the *MLA Handbook* or the *Chicago Manual of Style* are helpful.

Keep asking questions

As a biographer, you do not serve as a conduit through which your subject tells his or her own life. Instead, you are an active questioner about that life. You are always in search of understanding why and how your subject acted, rather than merely chronicling those actions. You are interested in relationships, in motivation, in the dimensions of your subject's personality that may have been hidden from public view.

The questions that you ask about a subject's life reflect ways of understanding human behavior that come largely from your own experiences. If, for example, you discover that your subject was a person who tried to control or manipulate the behavior of others, your own experiences with such a person will color the way you portray and understand such behavior. Some biographers also rely on psychological theory to explain behavior, bringing to their sources ideas from such famous thinkers as Freud, Jung, Karen Horney, or a host of other theorists. If you decide to take such an approach, you need to remember that your sources, however rich they are, do not provide as complete a "case history" as a psychoanalyst might glean from years of therapy sessions. Usually, it is safer to *suggest* a theorist's explanation for your subject's behavior, rather than to claim that the explanation is airtight.

Similarly, some biographers bring to their work assumptions about gender or class that reflect the work of feminist or cultural critics. You need to be careful, though, about ascribing your subject's dreams and desires to social forces or personal expectations that may or may not have been applicable at the time in which your subject lived.

Create contexts

Biographers are interested in more than the events of one person's life. They must look at the contexts—historical, cultural, and physical—in which that person lived. Every public event, of course, does not affect each person in the same way; still, the biographer needs to be aware of the history swirling around his or her subject: How did a war, an economic depression, or attitudes of racism or sexism affect the subject's life? How was the subject shaped by growing up on a farm in central Kansas, in a castle in Wales, on the city streets of nineteenth-century Manhattan? "You pick up things spending time on the native ground, taking your time, listening, poking through the old local papers," said David McCullough, biographer of Harry Truman and Theodore Roosevelt. Sometimes, though, it is not possible for a biographer to travel to that "native ground." Richard Holmes came to France in 1964 hoping to discover the landscape that Robert Louis Stevenson had traversed in 1878. In some places, the hills, the woods, and the villages seemed unchanged from the late nineteenth century; in other places, Holmes wandered "dazed and disappointed" because sites had so greatly altered. In the end, however, armed with Stevenson's travel diary and letters, Holmes used his talents as "Baskerville Hound," as he put it, to reinvent the reality of Stevenson's life. *Footsteps* testifies to the achievement of his—and of any biographer's—goal: to enter the inner landscape of another human being's mind and feelings, and to share the adventure of that discovery with readers.

❏ 54

Turn Your Vacation Into Article Sales

By Roberta Sandler

You want to take a vacation and get paid for it. But how?

During your last vacation, did you visit a museum, a tropical beach, a historic or popular attraction, or a strip of antique shops? Why not turn such experiences into travel articles? Why not get paid for honestly evaluating and relating your vacation impressions?

As a freelance travel writer, I've stood among ancient Greek ruins, faced the Barbary apes of Gibraltar, browsed the pricey boutiques of Monaco, watched Island women slice coconuts at a Martinique marketplace, and gasped at the raw beauty of Alaskan glaciers. That's the fun part. The hard part is that to be effective in showing readers what to expect from a site, I must do exhaustive research, preparation, exploration, and fact-checking before I write my article. But what pleasure in seeing my travel articles in print, and in helping readers discover our world.

Here's how you can turn your vacations into articles.

Prepare

Before you take your trip, get in touch with the Convention and Visitors Bureau and the Chamber of Commerce of the town you'll be visiting. Request a calendar of events, and information about the area's history, size, exact location, dining and accommodations, landmarks and attractions. This will be useful for the article and the sidebar. Find out whether the town is known for something special, or has a nickname. For example, St. Marys, Georgia, is known as America's "Rock Shrimp Capital." Petersburg, Virginia, is the site of the longest siege of the Civil War. This information may become a hook opening for your article.

Call the town's Historical Society or Preservation Society (the Chamber or Visitors Bureau is likely to have the phone number). Ask whether a volunteer will set up a day and time to guide you around the city. These volunteers can contrast the town's past with its present.

In Hannibal, Missouri, lifelong resident Susan Stark drove me past her childhood home, originally the home of her grandfather, who knew Samuel Clemens (Mark Twain).

When Sandy Craig, operator of "Tour St. Augustine," guided me around the Old City, she told me that she could trace her geneology in St. Augustine to the 1600s, when her ancestor, a Spanish soldier, first arrived. That gave her wonderful historical anecdotes to pass along to me.

When you arrive at your destination, peruse the local newspaper for fairs, festivals, or other events scheduled during your visit. Thumb through the local Yellow Pages. Under "Museums" and "Attractions," can you find an art museum or sculpture garden with an unusual collection, or a historic building that hosts an unusual museum? For instance, the Karpeles Manuscript Library Museum, with its massive collection of rare documents, has branches in only seven American cities (Jacksonville, Duluth, Buffalo, Charleston, Tacoma, Santa Barbara, and Montecito). The Knott House Museum, built in 1843 in Tallahassee, Florida, is known as "the house that rhymes." Former resident Luella Knott wrote poems to her furniture. The poems are tied to the furniture with ribbons.

Write about where you live. Hoffman's Chocolate Factory and Garden is only 20 minutes from my home in West Palm Beach, but I have written about it as an unusual tourist attraction. The garden has whimsical topiary, a waterfall, a gazebo, and toy trains tracking through a miniature village.

Explore

Readers often like the offbeat, the unexpected, so be sure to visit the town's popular sights and landmarks, but look for the unusual. Along Monument Avenue in Richmond, Virginia, the bronze statues of Civil War heroes are expected, but the statue of tennis ace Arthur Ashe is a surprise.

Speaking of statues, you can make them the sole subject of a travel article. And that one article can lead you down a path paved with money. Here's my proudest illustration: Several years ago, I took a cruise to Alaska. I sold my article about the cruise ship and the ports, but I also wrote a separate article about the statue at Juneau's harborfront of Patsy Ann, a deaf dog with a remarkable ability to "hear" when a ship was nearing the harbor. In the 1930s, Juneau's mayor proclaimed Patsy Ann as the city's official canine greeter. More than 50 years later, Juneau locals erected the statue.

There are two essential lessons to be learned from my Patsy Ann piece. First, when you visit a destination, look at the big picture, but also zero in on the details (Juneau as a topic, and Patsy Ann as a topic within a topic).

Second, retain the copyright and create reprint opportunities for your article, which will produce additional income. My Patsy Ann article first appeared in *Hearing Health* Magazine, along with my two photos ($180). I then sold it to a publisher of cruise travel magazines ($300 plus $50 for the photo), to a newspaper for seniors ($100), and to *Good Dog* Magazine ($50). It was reprinted as a chapter in *Chicken Soup For The Dog Lover's Soul* ($1,000). As a filler, it appeared in a bank newsletter ($55) and *Pet Life* Magazine ($100). About $1,800! Thanks, Patsy Ann. Although *Pet Life* and *Good Dog* magazines are aimed at the same readership, one Patsy Ann piece was a full article, and the other was a filler. When you sell reprints of a previously published article, it shouldn't be to a competing publication unless you let the editor know. It is then up to him or her whether to reprint the article.

Travel editors like roundup articles, so think in terms of multiples that the town offers: Tampa's Five Best Antique Shops; St. Augustine's Most Romantic Bed and Breakfasts. My travel roundups have included "America's Celebrity Museums"; "What's On Cruise Lines' Private Islands?"; "On-site Pet Kennels: Another Feature of Florida's Theme Parks."

Better still if the roundup ties in with a timely event. My article, "Tracing George Washington's Footsteps Through Virginia," covers sites, from birth to death, where George left his imprint as a man, rather than as a military figure. Since 1999 was the Bicentennial of Washington's death, and Virginia celebrated with numerous exhibitions and celebrations, my article appeared in several newspapers during the year.

Observe

Use your senses. Don't glance—observe. Do locals speak with a twang, or use colloquialisms? What gives pace and character to the town? A horse and buggy clip-clopping on cobblestone? Taxis weaving a serpentine path through traffic? A market ripe with the smell of fresh produce? Convey a sense of place; for example, this excerpt is from my article about serene Santa Rosa Beach, Florida, which appeared in the *Miami Herald*:

> Walter Huettel thought someone was playing a joke on him. Beneath the palmetto, bay leaf, and pine trees that canopy his property, two wooden crosses suddenly appeared to serve as markers for the graves of two deceased animals.
> "Then, the kids in the neighborhood asked me if I'd let them bury wildlife that gets killed while crossing the road," Huettel says. That's how the tiny wildlife cemetery began, a short path away from Bayou Arts and Antiques, the pottery and art studio Huettel shares with his wife Cathy in the peaceful Florida Panhandle town of Santa Rosa Beach.

In sharp contrast, the energetic feel of historic Ybor City in Tampa is reflected in the lead-in to my article which appeared in the *Sun Sentinel*'s Sunday magazine, *Sunshine*:

> Ybor City stimulates the senses with the sounds of jazz and blues, the savory taste of Cuban and Creole foods, the strong aroma of Cuban coffee and cigars, and the visual pleasure of globed lampposts, wrought-iron balconies, and red-brick buildings that echo the city's heyday as the Cigar Capital of the World.

Write to market

Don't merely state, ". . . is a friendly city." Give examples. Be positive, but be objective. Editors don't want puff pieces. If a B&B isn't well maintained despite its historical significance, say so. If a museum is disappointing, explain why. Read many travel articles to analyze how the informative and entertaining components, woven together, enlighten and guide the reader.

Editors like sidebars that list directions, where to dine, where to stay, whom to contact for information, etc. All names, addresses, spellings, must be correct. Verify.

Newspaper travel sections and travel magazines aren't the only markets for your articles and fillers. Travel features appear in inflight, retirement, lifestyle, general interest, pet, parenting, trade, and regional publications. Some editors prefer travel features written in first person; others prefer third person. To find out, read previous issues of a publication, or call to ask about its style preference. As for queries, most magazine editors usually prefer a written query, but newspaper travel editors haven't objected to my pitching a three-sentence e-mail or phone query.

If you write travel articles, life will become an enchanting journey for you and your readers.

❏ 55

PROFILES TAKE COURAGE

BY BOB SCHULTZ

THE NERVOUS MAN IN THE RUMPLED SPORTS COAT PICKED UP THE handgun from its place near the microphone, lifted one slat of the mini-blind, and watched as the slow-moving car disappeared around the corner. "Can't be too careful after all those death threats," he said. "Now, what else does your magazine want to know about me?"

All articles on interviewing stress how to put the person you're interviewing at ease, but none of them told me how to put myself at ease as I jumped every time I heard the slightest noise outside for the rest of that interview. Some profiles take courage.

Interviewing locally famous, or notorious, characters like this conservative talk-show host has been one of my more regular sources of by-lines and income. The skills I have acquired interviewing a small-town mayor or the local handwriting analyst are the same skills I've used to interview celebrities. What skills do you need to start seeing your by-line on profiles? Here are the steps I follow:

Find an interesting subject. Where can you find people interesting enough to profile in local newspapers and regional magazines? Everywhere! Look in the phone book for unusual businesses, and you may find people like the owner of the Used Car Factory, who turns out "new" roadsters or brings that old Chevy back to life so it looks as good, or better, than it did when it rolled off the assembly line. If Halloween or New Year's is coming up, that store with all the old costumes might make an interesting story, with some great photo possibilities.

Follow local news articles and watch for those little human interest pieces. A handwriting analyst in a local fraud trial turned out to be an expert on Elvis Presley's handwriting. An arresting officer in another case turned out to be a singer in a rock and roll band comprised of uniformed officers.

Do your research. Before you ask your first question, you need to know something about the person you're interviewing, or about the career or activity that makes the person noteworthy. If he's a radio talk show host, tape a few shows and listen to them to become familiar with his favorite themes and strongest opinions. If she's a handwriting expert, pick up a book on handwriting analysis or on crime investigation to get enough background to ask relevant questions. If he's a famous author, read a book or two along with book reviews of his work to see what the critics think of his work.

Respect your subject. You don't have to fall in love with or agree with everything the person you're profiling says, but you do have to respect him or her enough to write an article that is accurate and fair. If you look down on your subject, your arrogance will show through, diminishing the reader's respect and interest in the person.

You don't have to believe in psychics to write good articles on a local psychic. Your job is to get to know the person well enough to illuminate the qualities that will make this person interesting to readers.

Hook your reader. Once you have the background you need, start writing. You need a lead paragraph that will hook readers and keep them reading till the end. They may never have heard of the person you're profiling and never thought about doing whatever it is that the person does, so you have to work to draw them into the article. Here is an opening paragraph to an article I wrote on a local boudoir photographer:

> Considering what she isn't wearing, perhaps she just stepped out of a shower. Reclining in peace and apparent solitude, she takes a bite from a juicy red apple. Slowly, a huge serpent slithers up from behind her.

Wonder what happens next? I hope so. If you don't entice readers with your opening paragraph, they're probably already skipping on to the next article, so the hook is critical.

Use anecdotes and interesting quotes. If you think the person you're interviewing should be in the hall of fame, just telling readers your opinion probably won't carry much weight. You are much more likely to be convincing by describing an activity or a comment that illustrates your opinion.

As I interviewed a woman with multiple sclerosis confined to a wheelchair, I noticed that she didn't have any "handicap" plates on her van. "Oh, I don't ever use those parking places," she said. "Those are for people who'd have breathing trouble or other problems if they couldn't park close. Remember, I'm not disabled." And, of course, she isn't disabled, because she refuses to see herself that way. But, she said it better than I could.

Letting a person you disagree with speak his or her mind will give readers information that will help them form their own opinions. In an article about a basketball coach, I acknowledged that the coach felt that his being labeled a blatant sexist was due to some out-of-context quotes. I found his original statement and quoted it in its entirety. When readers had a chance to read his complete statement, the coach came across as "blatantly sexist," but he did it in his own words!

Surprise the reader. Anecdotes and quotes that surprise readers usually keep them reading for more, as do anecdotes that reveal the humanity in larger-than-life people.

During an interview with Ray Bradbury, he showed me the autographs of people like Jean Harlow and W.C. Fields that he collected when he was a youngster in Los Angeles. But the note he seemed to treasure most was from someone much less famous—his daughter: "Mom, I don't know what time I'll be home, but I will be safe. P.S. One of the cats threw up on the stairs." That simple quote brought home the fact that my profile was about Ray Bradbury, father and husband, not just Ray Bradbury, author.

Be positive, but don't "puff." Those too-good-to-be-true articles about celebrities are often called "puff" pieces. The magazine or newspaper generally looks for a positive article about someone from an industry that advertises in the publication, or a famous person. The trick is to show the person's good qualities without making your profile sound like a nomination for sainthood.

To make it clear that a local TV news anchorman had not let his fame go to his head, he closed his interview with these words: "Don't tell my mother I'm a newsman. She thinks I'm a piano player in a whore-house." I used that quote as the ending of my profile.

Wrap it up. Second in importance only to the hook that draws read-ers in, is an ending that will keep them thinking about your article after they finish it. An illustration of giving your profile a big finish comes from an article I wrote on Robin Cook. I had ended a review of one of Mr. Cook's medical thrillers by mentioning that I was going in to have two wisdom teeth taken out the next day and I was grateful that Cook hadn't written any books to scare me out of that surgery. After reading my review, Mr. Cook wrote to me, saying, "I wanted you to know that my next book will be called *Tooth* . . . a thriller about wisdom teeth!"

Fictionalize it. Take the real-life characters you've interviewed and profiled and mix and match them to create characters for your fiction. Change that conservative talk show host into a liberal talk show hostess. Create a series sleuth out of that handwriting analyst. Keep track of the comments, the habits, the eccentricities of the fascinating people you profile, and then recycle revised versions of those people into your short stories and novels.

There are many good reasons to write profiles. They get you away from your solitary word processor and out interacting with interesting people; they give you experience conducting interviews, connect you with local experts you can call on later, and provide you with bits and pieces for creating memorable fictional characters that are deeply rooted in reality.

There are plenty of interesting people out there just waiting to tell their stories. They might as well tell them to you. Just ask them to check their guns at the door.

❏ 56

CREATIVE NONFICTION WRITING

BY RITA BERMAN

WHAT IS CREATIVE NONFICTION? IS IT A NEW GENRE OF WRITING? AN oxymoron? Fictionalized facts? While it sounds like a contradiction in terms, creative nonfiction is a new description for an old skill: that of writing well-crafted salable articles. For today's market, however, nonfiction writers are allowed, even encouraged, to incorporate certain fiction techniques and to use the first-person "I."

Formerly, the formal style, using a neutral voice, is now recognized as distancing the writer from the reader, whereas writing from the first-person viewpoint can help with reader identification that is further magnified if the writer's experiences or comments resonate or connect with the reader's life. That is why seemingly ordinary concerns of everyday life, such as health, diet, sex, money, and travel can provide good potential topics for creative nonfiction. The range of creative nonfiction includes feature articles, memoirs, essays, personality profiles, travel pieces, how-to's and even contemporary, political, or other social issues pieces.

Because editors have switched from asking "just give me the facts," to "tell me a story," *how* you tell the story is where creative nonfiction comes in. In other words, the article remains nonfiction because the content is based on fact and is not created or made up, but you have more freedom in the actual writing of it. That calls for embellishing and enhancing, narrating instead of reporting, dressing up the bare facts by using fiction techniques such as setting of mood, providing description of place, expressing emotion, and often incorporating dialogue or flashbacks.

Before describing some of the fiction elements you could use, it might be helpful to review the basic structure of an article. You must catch the reader's interest in the introduction; in the next section identify your topic; in the body of the piece present your material; and close by drawing a conclusion or repeating a key point.

Your task is to write your article like a storyteller, not as a gatherer of facts. Take those facts and filter them through your eyes. Provide details so that you add to, but don't change the information you have gathered. And as you write, keep your potential readers in mind, so that you angle the story to their needs.

My article on graphology, "Unlocking Secrets in Handwriting Can Help Hiring" (*Triangle Business*), began with an opening quote from my source, Mary Gallagher, a handwriting expert:

> "Looking at how applicants cross their t's or dot their i's is one way to decide whether to hire an individual." So said Mary Gallagher, a certified graphoanalyst. More than 5,000 companies use handwriting analysis as a hiring aid. . . . Employers need the edge to know not only what the applicant projects but also what he or she is capable of doing.

Having aroused the readers' interest, a brief summary about the history of graphology came next, and then I continued with examples of what handwriting might reveal. Quotes from other people who had used Gallagher's services, including a manager who had ignored her findings, gave balance to the piece.

Framing the story

For this particular piece, I used the technique of framing the story to make a satisfactory ending: I circled around to the beginning by referring to the opening paragraph. For creative nonfiction, this is an excellent way of tying the article together, satisfying the curiosity you have aroused and leaving the reader with a resonant image of all that has gone before. You might draw a conclusion, make an evaluation, or point out a question that still needs an answer.

In this instance I ended by informing readers of how companies obtain a sample of handwriting from applicants in order to study it; they have prospective employees state in their own handwriting why they believe they are qualified for the job.

Atmosphere and mood

Specific details are highly significant in nonfiction to help the reader visualize the place or the event you are describing. They add interest and color and convey atmosphere and mood to the setting, locale, time of year, and even the weather in your article. General statements, such as, "We went to a museum, which we found interesting," fall flat without supporting detail. Use fiction techniques to describe what you saw in the museum.

Make note of your impressions and reactions as you conduct your research. Whether you are taking a tour, arriving at a new destination, or interviewing someone for a personal profile, these impressions and observations may turn out to be the lead or heart of your piece when you come to write it.

Example: In a piece about redevelopment and housing in Jamaica for *Town and Country Planning Journal,* I opened with a description of what I had seen in the drive from the airport:

> The coast road from the airport is a narrow lane overlooked by small and large estates. Plantations, old great houses, and tiny country towns dot the hillside. Snaking by resort hotels and sugar-cane fields, some of which are now being developed into housing estates, the life of the country appeared before us as we turned each bend on the main north-coast road.

Writing in first person

Your nonfiction pieces will come alive creatively when you incorporate your personal observations. Use all of your senses. Tell your readers what you tasted, saw, touched, heard. . . . By personalizing the piece, it becomes your own. No other article will have that voice—your voice.

Instead of saying that there were vendors at the site and leaving it at that, I described my encounter with them in "Spain, New and Old Faces," published in *Leader Magazine:*

> . . . As we stepped down from the bus, we were accosted by a group of women darting in front of us, each waving a lace tablecloth. Having caught our attention, they shouted prices at us in Spanish, jabbing their fingers in the air to indicate how many thousands of pesetas they wanted.
>
> To indicate that I wanted a smaller cloth, and round, I made a circle with my hands. They understood. An older woman held up a tablecloth while a young girl held up five fingers, 50,000 pesetas. I countered with two fingers. She shook her head and held up four fingers. I then showed cash—25,000 pesetas (approximately $25). She took two bills, but wanted "another finger," total of $30. No deal. I pointed to an embroidered rectangular cloth and the finger shaking started all over again. . . . I got both tablecloths for $53.

By revealing the interaction that took place, I enhanced the story and by adding color and humor, made the piece more interesting than if I had baldly stated that I spoke no Spanish, but we came to a deal.

Reveal your characters

Creative nonfiction is frequently about people. We're all curious about how other people live, what they do, and how they think. For personality profiles, draw on the external cues that you observed while doing the interview. Describe the subject's quirks, mannerisms, or appearance, what he wore, how he moved his body as he spoke. Movement can reveal and imply at the same time. "Shifting in his chair" conveys an image quite different from "settling in his chair."

Dialogue

The fiction writer makes up dialogue, but in creative nonfiction you take the dialogue from your interview notes or tapes, using direct quotes from your sources, instead of paraphrasing. This adds verbal color to your piece and encourages your readers to draw their own conclusions—an excellent way to present a controversial topic or viewpoint.

I used provocative statements about women and their reactions to conflict as my lead for a piece for *Women Executive's Bulletin:*

> Most women fear conflict—perhaps more than men fear it. . . . Many women give contradictory signals. For example, when they are under stress and trying to communicate, they often smile, unconsciously suggesting to the other person that this isn't such a serious situation, according to Dr. Ruth D. Anderson, Associate Professor of Speech Communication.

Next, I offered some significant details on how we learn to communicate:

> The communication skills we learn early in life are those that we use when we reach managerial and executive positions: to accept conflict as a normal, everyday occurrence, then to understand how to handle conflict. Think back to how your mother, or any other female authority figure in the household you grew up in, dealt with conflict. If she screamed, do you scream?

Here's another "tell me more" quote that I used for a general-interest article on buying or selling a house, a concern of many Americans:

"The consumer has the right to bargain," said Andrew M. Barr, a real estate broker. "It isn't a rigid situation. Some houses are easier to sell than others. Why charge 6% when you can do it for 3% and sell it in a week? That's fair to the consumer and fair to us."

Published in the *Virginia Cardinal,* my article explored the sensitive topic of brokers' commission and informed the reader about available alternatives in the Washington D.C. area, the flexible fee system, or using a consumer-oriented advisory service.

Flashbacks

Flashbacks are another fiction device you might consider using to provide a change of pace. By means of the flashback you can expand your story and take the reader in a direction different from where you began. Example: "As the train drew into the station, I remembered the last time I visited London. . . ." Or, "As he spoke of his father I was remembering our first meeting, more than 20 years ago. . . ."

With this technique, you can introduce something significant from the past that has bearing on the present. To help the reader make the transition back to the present, insert a transitional phrase or word, such as "now" or "today," and continue with the present-day account.

Writing about my own experience as a temporary worker some years ago, I used a flashback to go back to when the Kelly Girl organization began in 1946, transitioning to a change of name of Kelly Temporary Services in the 1980's, then continued with more of my work experiences and ended with a forecast about the future direction of temporary work.

Know your readership

As you write, keep in mind the readers you want to reach; you need to know for whom you are writing. This calls for studying your possible markets before you commence writing, research that will be helpful when you shape the story. For example, some magazines publish only descriptive essays, while others prefer nuts-and-bolts information. After you have studied the market listings as well as writers' guidelines and read several issues of the magazine, you will know what the readers like and how to aim your articles to their preferred style.

Knowing my readership helped me slant my piece, "Pick up on the

Shell Game," for *The Army, Navy, Air Force Times Magazine*. I opened with:

> When Navy man Jim Wadsworth was stationed in New Guinea 30 years ago, he stooped over and picked up a shell on the beach. By that simple act, he found himself hooked on a hobby—shell collecting.
>
> Shelling has given many military families special pleasures. Any number can play; there are no sex or age barriers. You don't have to be an expert or spend a cent, unless you want to become a professional shell collector. Shells can be traded with other collectors or bought like stamps from a dealer.

That paragraph linked the hobby of shell collecting to military families, who were the readers of this particular magazine. By focusing the angle of the story to those readers, I achieved publication.

Creative nonfiction is not a new genre, but a new description for articles based on fact but written in fictional form. Creative nonfiction uses mood, setting, descriptions of place, action, people, senses, thoughts, and feelings. It may use dialogue and flashbacks. The first-person viewpoint adds to reader identification, catches their attention. Your personal impressions and comments can help make your nonfiction unique.

□ 57

THE KEY TO INTERVIEWING SUCCESS

BY JOY PARISE

IF YOU WANT TO ADVANCE IN YOUR ARTICLE WRITING, INCORPORATE the opinions of outside professionals to enliven and enrich your work. If done properly, a good interview provides not only plenty of material that will add depth to an article, but also valuable ideas and sources for future projects.

The actual interview is no place for on-site training. Much of the success of an interview will depend on your behind-the-scenes preparation to make sure that your subject is enough at ease to talk freely and openly to you. With experience, you'll learn techniques that work best for you. The following are some methods that can help you on your way to interviewing success.

1. If at all possible, arrange for a face-to-face interview. While a telephone call can give you the information you need, an in-person interview will more than pay off. Eye contact with your subject will help relax him or her, and being able to describe his or her gestures, appearance, and surroundings can make your writing come alive.

Once you have phoned and arranged the interview, follow up with a note thanking the person and confirming the time and place, and enclose a simple business card, if you have one. If you'll need any specific information, photos, statistics, or phone numbers, alert your subject in your note so that he or she can have them handy. Don't send specific questions that you'll be asking. Nothing is worse than sitting down in front of the subject who reads stilted and scripted answers to you.

2. Make the most of your interviewing time, and give your subject the maximum amount of time to talk. Prepare your questions in advance so that you don't flounder. To create an atmosphere of easy conversation, don't keep the list of questions in front of you. Tuck them inside the cover of your notepad or place them discreetly to the side to peek at now and then. Be familiar enough with your questions in advance to be flexible if new material from your subject's comments and responses pops up, if your interview takes an interesting new slant, or if your prepared order doesn't work. Although your prepared questions will help keep you on course, don't be close-minded. Keep alert. You may find a whole line of discussion to pursue spontaneously.

3. Structure your questions around a preliminary outline. Try to keep the outline of your article in your mind before you go into the interview so that you ask your questions in sequence. This will make it easier later to work from your notes rather than facing a hodgepodge of information you have to organize.

When I interview someone for a feature, I structure my articles in a specific way. Drawing a picture in words of the gestures, appearance, or surroundings tells why this person is interesting enough to be written about. That's how I try to capture the readers' attention so that they will become interested enough to want to know more about this person—and keep reading.

I then go into the subject's area of expertise and give enough objective and colorful information so that readers say, "I didn't know that." (Editors often tell me that they found my articles very informative; they learned a lot.) Then I swing back to the person I'm interviewing and ask about his or her goals for the future.

Whatever your style, make a plan in advance so that you have a good idea where you want to steer your interview.

4. Dress for success. Making a good appearance begins with being on time. If you're interviewing someone important enough to be interviewed, then his or her time is important, too. Respect it.

Dress in a way to put your subject at ease. Don't underestimate this step. If you're going to a corporation, wear a suit. If you're going to a small business, try a sports jacket. If you're going to a cowboy barn, try jeans. For a sports club, neat slacks. The idea is to make your subject comfortable enough to relate to you and want to help you write a good article.

5. Let your instincts take over. If for some reason you're having a really hard time with the interview, let your subject know it. Some years ago, I was sent to cover a riding clinic at an out-of-state stable. The owner was very rude and cold. After trying to get quotes from him—to make him look good—and getting nowhere, I looked at him and lightly said, "Come on, give me a break. Help me out here." Since he knew he was being obnoxious (but was probably never called on it), he immediately tuned in and started talking.

Another time, I was asked to do an article on a whole family. The editor had tried to write a piece about them but had found them almost impossible to interview. Though they were willing to sit down with me, they found it hard to make anything other than the "name, rank, and serial number" types of comments.

When I walked into their house, to my horror I found the whole family sitting around the table. Self-conscious in front of each other, no one spoke. From the corner of the table, one person would meekly add a bit of information. I went home and waited for a few days, then phoned that person. I told him that he sounded as if he had so much background to tell me about (which he did), and I asked if I could meet with him alone so that I could write a "good" article. We met again at his house, sat under a lovely tree, and talked for an hour about the family history and their achievements in the horse world. The tree became the central symbol for the stability of the family, and the article turned out much better than I'd ever imagined it would.

Don't be afraid to ask for more if you are not getting what you need, but do so tactfully and honestly.

6. Bring a tape recorder. Be prepared to take notes to back up what's on the tape. The recorder is good for capturing the exact ways that people speak, as well as names and figures and other information that takes too much time to write. This is important in drawing a picture of your subject. Furthermore, the flow of your subject's speech as opposed to yours in your writing will help keep the rhythm of your article interesting.

A third and more subtle use of the tape recorder comes in when it is shut off. I've gotten some of my best quotes when the interview appears to be formally over and the people you're interviewing tend to relax and open up.

Once, when I was interviewing a successful professional horseman, he walked me to the door of his stable, and looking out over his forty-acre farm, he waved his arm and said, "I'm so lucky. I'm so lucky. I'm forty years old and doing what I love!"

I began the article with that gesture and those words. Since the article showed that he had attained what he had through hard work and dedication, not luck, his humility endeared him to the readers. In fact, he said he never got so much positive feedback from any other article written about him. The fact was that he was a nice guy, and it showed—particularly when the interview was "officially" over.

7. Let your subject really talk. Ask your subject what he or she thinks is important, and what he or she would like you to write. You'll be amazed!

Once when I was interviewing a man who had won at a horse show, I asked him what he would like me to say. He talked about his stable's successful breeding program—something few people knew about, although it was highly successful.

Not only did it add more information to the article, but it provided me with material for a second article on that stable—an eight-page piece I wrote the next year for a national magazine.

8. Show your appreciation. Get to your interview on time, leave on time, and be polite. Remember, you're not the important person here; the person you're interviewing is. Send a copy of your published article with a thank-you note.

9. Look inside yourself. If you're not getting a successful interview after careful preparation, then look inside. Were you sincerely interested in the person you interviewed? Dogs, horses, and kids know when someone dislikes them, but they warm up with people they know they can trust. People being interviewed do, too. Put your best foot forward, and you can't fail.

❑ 58

How to Write and Sell Humorous Greeting Cards

By Donna Gephart

WRITING GREETING CARDS FOLLOWS THE FOUR SIMPLE BASICS OF OTHER types of writing:

1. Read published greeting cards.
2. Write intensely and creatively.
3. Edit mercilessly.
4. Submit professionally.

First things first

Read greeting cards. Before I sit to write a batch of greeting cards, I'll spend an hour and a half in a card shop or any other store that sells greeting cards reading every funny card I can find. After all, if you write romances, you read romances. If you write horror, you read horror.

Also, read anything that might give you an idea for a card; copy on a cereal box, ads, slogans, billboards, or poems might inspire a card idea.

You should also send for submission guidelines. Simply send a self-addressed, stamped envelope to the editorial department of a greeting card company with a note saying, "Please send guidelines." You can obtain addresses from various sources. Look on the back of the cards on the racks. Consult market lists of greeting card companies. Visit the web site of the National Greeting Card Association which offers its members an online list of companies at http://www.greetingcard.org.

Before putting pen to paper, keep a few things in mind:

- Though women purchase between 80–90% of all greeting cards, many men are successful in the field because they are able to think like women.
- When writing, keep a real person in mind, whether it's a best

friend, sister, ex-boyfriend, etc., and write as though you're going to give the card to this person. It's a sure-fire trick to guarantee your card is salable.

- Finally, write what editors need. Birthday is the most popular occasion.

Editors are starving for fresh, innovative ways to wish someone a happy birthday. Christmas and Valentine's Day are the most popular seasonal occasions. (Remember, though, that even smaller companies buy seasonal ideas up to a year ahead of time.)

I usually write surrounded by things to inspire me. If I'm writing birthday cards, I browse lists I've created that have to do with birthdays, for instance, one which details the physical aspects of aging: false teeth, age spots, the need to wear glasses, etc. I'll pair items on the list and try to find connections or think of multiple meanings for an item. For example, glasses can mean reading glasses or drinking glasses. That thought inspired this card. (O = outside or front of card; I = inside of card.)

> O: Here' s a birthday present you can really sink your teeth into . . .
> I: (Drinking glass containing false teeth)
> (Kalan, Inc.)

Besides the lists I've created about particular topics, I love to read through humorous quotations. Clichés can always be twisted into a new way to say something. A rhyming dictionary and thesaurus should be close at hand. And I collect fascinating facts. Did you know a cat has thirty-two muscles in each ear? And a goldfish has a memory span of three seconds? I even knew a writer who kept old love letters and various kinds of cologne in her desk to inspire her when she wrote cards for Valentine's Day.

It's all in the format

As you read greeting cards, you'll notice that certain formats or set-ups are used again and again. There are several formats into which you can try to fit your ideas with examples from cards I've published. Use these as a guide, but don't let them restrict your creativity.

1. *Lists.* "Top ten" lists were quite popular for awhile and some still are, such as the Top Ten Reasons to be Glad You're Having Another Birthday or Top Ten Reasons I Love You. Shorter lists also work well. Example:

> O: You' re 21—an adult now. It' s time to make some very serious decisions about your future . . .
> I: bottles or cans
> domestic or imported
> by itself or with a shot
> top shelf or the cheap stuff
> shaken or stirred
> dry or on the rocks
> with a twist or without
> straight or with a mixer (Gibson Greetings)

2. *A pun or play on words.*

> O: Congratulations on your pregnancy.
> I: You deserve a standing ovulation. (InnoVisions)

3. *Using the physical properties of the card itself, such as color, weight, measurements, etc.*

> O: (Hunk photo) Your Christmas present is exactly seven inches long . . .
> I: by five inches wide. And when you're done staring at it, you can put it back in the envelope. (Gibson Greetings)

4. *Riddles with a personal twist. A question ending with an unexpected answer.*

> O: Valentine's Day Riddle: What would it mean if you were hot, sweaty and panting heavily?
> I: It would mean the batteries in the remote control died and you had to get up and change the channel yourself. (Gibson Greetings)

5. *Statement of "fact" that can begin with "Did you know . . ." or "Statistics prove . . ."*

> O: Hey Bachelorette! Studies prove there are many devices to increase a man's sexual desire. Leave it to you to find one that reduces it.
> I: A wedding ring. Congratulations! (Smart Alex)

6. *Short poem, often with a twist ending.*

> O: Happy birthday to you.
> You live in the zoo.
> You look like a monkey.
> I: But you're really my sister. (Gibson Greetings)

7. *Exaggeration*

> O: Is it possible for you to read this birthday card without wearing glasses?
> I: Sure, if you can stretch your arm to Cleveland. Happy Birthday. (Oatmeal Studios)

8. *Comparison. Finding the similarities or dissimilarities between two separate items.*

> O: What's the difference between men and birthdays?
> I: We can live without men. (Gibson Greetings)

9. *Parody a well-known document or expression.*
The following is a parody of the Miranda Rights that an officer must read to a person being arrested:

> O: HALT! Valentine's Day Police. Your complete cooperation will be appreciated.
> I: You will be confined overnight in the bedroom. A thorough strip search and frisking will be provided. You have the right to remain naked. Anything I have can and will be held against you. Any questions? (Gibson Greetings)

Editing

After you've written your hot new greeting cards, let them cool completely. Take the dog for a walk. Throw in a load of laundry. Discover the joys of in-line skating. Go on a cruise. Just get away from your ideas. Far away. Pull them out again after several days or even weeks. Now edit your card as you would any other type of writing. Eliminate words that don't work. If your punch line seems flat, stretch to find something more original or cut it. Make sure the card is one you would send to someone or would enjoy receiving. Do you think you heard this joke somewhere before? If so, strike it. On the other hand, if your card idea still makes you laugh out loud after time away from it, you've got a winner, and you're ready to organize your ideas into a professional presentation.

Submitting like a pro

Editors at greeting card companies are swamped with misspelled submissions, flat ideas and poor grammar. These are returned immediately. On the other hand, every editor has several writers with whom she works closely and often; writers who submit original ideas, presented professionally. They are your competition. Here's how to compete:

After editing your card ideas, type each one on a 3″ x 5″ index card. On the top corner of each index card, put a code number. For example, a simple one like B-37 would be the 37th Birthday card I've written. Or V-98 is the 98th Valentine's Day card. An editor will refer to your ideas using these code numbers.

Type two identical index cards for each idea. One card stays in your files. (On the back of the one you keep, list the companies to whom you send it.) The other index card goes to the greeting card company. (On the back of this one, type your name, address and phone number so the editor can contact you when she wants to buy your card.)

Gather a batch of card ideas, and put them in an envelope along with a SASE. For your records, keep a copy of every card you're sending out with a cover sheet listing date, name of company, and which ideas you sent.

The waiting period

Having spent nearly seven years as the editor at a greeting card company, I can tell you what happens to your submission after it reaches an editor's desk.

First, your envelope is dropped into a drawer with dozens of other envelopes.

Second, after your friendly editor is back from attending meetings, analyzing sales data, working on the latest new product line, and proofreading finished cards, she'll pull out the envelopes from her drawer, and read the contents of each one.

You can expect one of three responses:

1) A form rejection letter. Editors can't accept all the good cards they receive because of space and budget constraints, so if your ideas are returned to you, make a note of it on your records and get them out to another company . . . the same day.

2) A hold letter. An editor may hold one or two ideas from your batch and return the rest. It will take several weeks to make the rounds at meetings to seek approval to purchase them. Not all "holds" are purchased, but your odds are often very good.

Make a note of the holds on your records, and send the others to the next company on your list.

3) A contract will be sent to you for one or more of your card ideas. Sign it. Wait a couple of weeks for the check. (You can expect to earn anywhere from fifty to a hundred and fifty dollars for each one accepted, depending on the rates of a particular company. No royalties are paid, and the company buys all rights.) Be happy! You're a published greeting card writer. In several months, you may receive samples of the card(s) you sold.

General do's and don'ts

1. Don't submit artwork. If an illustration is integral to understanding the joke, describe it briefly.

2. Do wait six to eight weeks before mailing a polite reminder note. And another four to six weeks to withdraw your ideas if you haven't heard a word.

3. Don't submit simultaneously to several companies. You're in a bad position if two editors want the same idea.

4. Do remove a card idea from circulation once it's sold. Remember: The greeting card company buys all rights.

5. Don't call, question or harangue an editor about her decision.

6. Do have as much fun writing and submitting greeting cards as thousands of people will have reading and sending your published cards.

7. Don't give up after a few rejections. Even top-selling greeting card writers get rejections. Keep reading, writing, revising, and submitting.

Finally, if you enjoy writing greeting card copy, you might also enjoy creating novelty products—key rings, T-shirts, etc. Although the markets for these products have shrunk over the past few years, there are still a few companies seeking Post-It notepads and novelty buttons (witty one-liners).

Writing greeting cards is a profitable field, highly receptive to innovative, professional writing, even if you've never sold a greeting card before.

□ 59

BECOMING A BIOGRAPHER

BY WILLIAM SCHOELL

TO BECOME A BIOGRAPHER, YOU MUST FIRST BE INTRIGUED BY OTHER people's lives. You must have a good understanding of human nature and a willingness to ask the tough questions, both of yourself, your subject, and the people who knew him or her. You must understand the difference between biography and memoir, and know the right approach to take to your biography depending on the subject and related factors.

Of course, first, you must choose your subject. An important basic factor is your enthusiasm level; there's nothing worse than spending months or years writing about somebody you have no deep interest in. Is there a particular historical figure or a contemporary celebrity whose life or work you admire, whose background you'd like to explore? If you find yourself wondering what kind of childhood this person had, what kind of relationship he or she had with his spouses and children and coworkers, what went on behind the scenes, then it's a good bet other people have the same curiosity. Then finding the answers to your questions will not be a chore to you, but rather a welcome revelation.

Next, you must decide if you are truly the right person to write this biography. A genuine interest in the subject and writing talent are, of course, prerequisites and the ones that matter the most. But today's publishers also like their authors to have some background related to the subject's, or even a vague connection. (Keep in mind that if by any chance you knew your subject personally or had some kind of relationship with him or her, you'll be writing what might more appropriately be called a *memoir,* that is, your personal recollections of the subject. This is the difference between a straight biography, of, say, Tennessee Williams by an author who may or may not ever have met him, and a book on the playwright written by his brother or a close friend who knew him well.)

You do not need to know or have known your subject personally to write a good biography about him. However, if you want to write about a filmmaker, an actor, or a director, it would be helpful to have written a few film reviews or filmmaker profiles, even if only for a local paper. If your subject is a composer, singer, or conductor, then some background in music will indicate you will have a better understanding than the rest of us as to what drives this person. If you've written an interview or an article about one of today's celebrities, it will certainly help sell a biography of him.

When you've decided on your subject, the next step is to think seriously about the subject's marketability. If the person is very obscure, it might be better to try first to sell a magazine article rather than a book. Then again, perhaps this person's obscurity is entirely undeserved. Perhaps there is something "special" about this person that gives him or her historical validity and therefore contemporary interest. For instance, the bestseller lists in recent years have featured biographies of women who were feminists long before the word was in fashion, and African-Americans whose contribution to society had never before been fully explored. There have also been successful biographies published about people whose sole claim to fame is the people they knew and worked with.

If you're uncertain how publishers might react to your subject, test the waters by querying a magazine or two. A published piece enclosed with your book proposal will show the editor that others thought your subject would be interesting to a mass audience. Your proposal should make clear that there's much more to say about the person, that there's plenty of room to develop things you only mentioned in the article.

Suppose you have a strong interest in chronicling someone's life, but there really is no special "hook" on which to hang your proposal. The person was not ahead of his time in any particular way; she does not fit neatly into any modern trends. Query a smaller firm or publisher, one less concerned with the bottom line. Trade publishers—that is, publishers whose books are sold in bookstores—are understandably concerned with sales potential, and frankly, a biography of an obscure person who did not do anything *very* significant, will not get past the sales representative who sits in at all editorial board meetings.

Even a small press, however, will want subjects who have done *something* significant: Your Uncle Joe may have been a marvelous character, but if he's never painted, written, composed, made a film, or left some kind of unique achievement behind, there probably isn't a book in him.

Also remember that most small firms pay tiny advances if they pay any at all, so if you need to take a leave of absence from your job to do research for your biography, you might, regrettably, have to move on to a more commercial subject.

As for historical subjects, publishers want a fresh approach to major figures, books that reveal, rather than rehash. If your subject is not internationally famous, you must explain why he is important and what his contribution was, and especially, *why* people might be interested in reading about him. When it comes to modern-day celebrities, there is one basic rule of thumb. Are people talking about him or her? There's little point in trying to market to a major trade publisher a biography of a film or rock star who hasn't worked or been in the public eye (or gossip columns) in years—unless he or she has reached cult status like Elvis or Marilyn.

After choosing your subject, you have to decide on the tone and style of your book. Largely, these will be set by the subject's achievement: A book on major figures like Beethoven, or Winston Churchill, whose life played out across an international arena in a fascinating, frenetic time period, will require a very serious, profound approach. On the other hand, books on Brad Pitt, Leonardo DiCaprio, or the Spice Girls, whose accomplishments and fame are recent and don't have a large body of work, and whose fans are primarily teenagers, should be comparatively light and breezy. An artist like Laurence Olivier would require an in-depth approach; a movie star like Marilyn Monroe with her much narrower range should get a much lighter treatment. However, because Monroe was involved with world-famous men (and because recent biographers have created such a "mystery" about her death), some biographers feel an intense approach to her life is the only way to go. Look at your subject with an objective eye and then decide on the appropriate tone and style. Sometimes it's not the subject but the events she was embroiled in and the people she knew that determine what kind of book you should write.

Your proposal should consist of an introduction mentioning the highlights of your subject's life, the things that make him memorable, and any fresh theories you have regarding his life and work. The rest should be a chapter-by-chapter outline showing that you have knowledge of his life and times and can effectively organize the material. If you've never published a book before, the publisher or agent will probably want to see a sample chapter or two. These do not necessarily have to be the first two chapters but could be a part of your subject's life or career that particularly intrigues you and information that you have special access to and develop in later chapters.

By this time, you should have read everything you could find on your subject. As you read, make a note of published "facts" that bother you or seem inconsistent. Biographers often make conjectures about their subjects that may or may not be supported by facts. Make a list of questions about your subject that you'll want to answer in your book. Is this person's public reputation (good or bad) deserved? What areas of her life and work have never been adequately explored? In addition to books and magazines available in the public library, remember that there may be collections in special libraries or museums—personal letters, private papers, notes and diaries—that relate to your subject.

When you've exhausted the books and files in the library, make a list of every living person (or their offspring) who might have known or worked with your subject. Famous people can often be contacted through professional organizations like Actors Equity, the Screen Actors Guild, the Authors Guild, and Mystery Writers of America; others may be in the phone book or can be reached via their employers or universities. Sometimes the best anecdotes and information come not from other big names, who may have reasons for putting a "spin" on their memories, but from ordinary people who have crossed paths with your subject in interesting ways. Each person you speak to may be able to provide the names and phone numbers of others who knew or have some information about your subject.

If the person you're writing about has already been the subject of several biographies, or one good recent one, you might want to consider a different, non-chronological approach. When I did my book on Al Pacino, I found that a pretty comprehensive biography about him had already been published. I decided to have a biographical section up front in my book and then to concentrate on the actor's career—one chapter for each film—with a final section on his stage work. In this way, I was able to analyze his films and acting style more intensely than would have been possible in a regular biography. When several Steven Spielberg adult biographies were published just as I was putting together a proposal for one, I decided to target mine for the young adult market. Sometimes it's a good idea to expand upon or refocus your original plan, as my coauthor and I did when we found that several Frank Sinatra books were coming out at once. We decided, therefore, to do a book on the entire Rat Pack—Sinatra, Dean Martin, Sammy Davis, Jr., Peter Lawford, Joey Bishop—instead.

To organize your material better, use file folders, one for each chapter, that will include. photocopies, tear sheets, phone numbers, transcripts, and a list of other material too large to fit in the folder—books, videos, audio cassettes—that you will need to refer to when you do the writing. Give yourself at least several months to complete your research (although you can work on certain chapters as you gather the material). Keep in mind that busy people—whether it's the director of a Rat Pack movie or a college professor who wrote a thesis on a classical composer—can take months to answer your letters or return your phone calls.

Whether your book winds up in the bookstore or on the library shelf, you'll have the satisfaction of knowing that as a biographer you've helped illuminate the lives and careers of people that the world should know more about.

❑ 60

HOW TO BREAK INTO
NEWSPAPER WRITING

BY LISA COFFEY

HAVE YOU EVER READ A NEWSPAPER ARTICLE, OPINION PIECE, OR FEA-
ture story and said to yourself, "I could write something like that, only
about 100 times better"? If so, you've clearly got the confidence; now
save the hyperbole for the supermarket tabloids and let's get started.

The first step is to study the newspaper for which you wish to write.
Note content, flavor, style, and approximate word count for different
types of pieces. Ask yourself: Would my article/column fit well in this
newspaper? Because of ad layouts and page designs, editors must adhere to certain word count constraints. So, if opinion columns on the
editorial page generally run 750 words, don't submit something twice
that length.

No writing method is set in stone, but one sound approach is to tackle
a topic in stages. Follow the 4 R's: *Reflection, Reporting, Reconstruction*, and *Revision.*

Reflection involves pondering an issue and determining whether there
is in fact a conflict or problem requiring focus, investigation, and resolution. For example, a former Section 8 (housing program designed to
create affordable housing) program manager phoned our newspaper
about a disturbing trend he had seen: Tenants who trashed their rental
units were rightly evicted, only to be recertified to obtain housing at
other Section 8 units. Was that a problem? Yes. Landlords, unable to
recoup damages from impoverished tenants, were pulling out of the
Section 8 program. Fewer landlords meant a growing shortage of such
housing for those who truly needed it. Further, destructive tenants were
never punished for their behavior—no penalty, no deterrent. This is
where you define the issue, establishing the premise of your piece. Now
you're ready for your next step.

Reporting involves getting the who, what, when, where, why, and how of the story, in addition to establishing for readers why they should care. For the Section 8 editorial series, I contacted numerous Section 8 landlords, tenants, the Indiana Department of Human Services, and the Legal Services Organization, and I acquired photos and a wealth of other information from the former program manager who initially called the newspaper. I also enumerated solutions—one of which was adopted by the then Housing and Urban Development Secretary Jack Kemp after he read the series—and the ramifications to U.S. taxpayers if they didn't demand accountability from the government's entitlement program administrators. Sources of information for your article or column are available from experts and laymen on both sides of an issue, from your local library, on-line databases such as NEXIS and Data Times (often available through your local library), and public records (with most documents available through the federal Freedom of Information Act and state companion "sunshine" laws). Try to get as much information as possible during your reflection stage. You probably won't use everything, but the more you gather and review, the more likely you are to write a balanced, well-rounded story.

Reconstruction involves arranging your material into a logical, coherent, and attention-grabbing form readers can understand. Break down the reconstruction phase into four S's: the Stopper, the Synopsis, the Supporting Material, and the Summary.

• *The Stopper* is that eye-catching lead, the opening statement or paragraph that makes the reader want to read more. For my Section 8 series, I began with a quote from a Section 8 landlord: "It's like a swarm of locusts going through an area. . . . There are places here in the city where Section 8 tenants have literally destroyed the community." It was an ugly comment, but it was the heart of the series' raison d'être: to tell an ugly story and to try to do something about it. Or how about this lead to a story about the U.S. Department of Agriculture sending subsidies to deceased farmers: "The dead don't tell tales; they're too busy collecting USDA benefits." Sometimes light humor may be appropriate to draw attention to a serious story. Make the lead the most arresting part—not necessarily the meat, but the attention-grabber that will make readers want to continue.

• *The Synopsis* is a focus statement, a clarification of the issue at hand. "Legal Services Organization's summer victory, which prevents termination of destructive tenants from the Section 8 housing program, could turn into a winter defeat for the very group whom Legal Services and the courts sought to protect—low-income tenants." It is from the synopsis—the statement of the problem or conflict, the issue you wish to address in your writing—that the rest of your article will flow. The synopsis isn't meant to be exciting or cute: It explains, defines, and steers your readers toward what is to come.

- *Supporting material* is just that—the quotes, statistics, hard facts, examples and other documentation that build your piece and help the reader form a truly informed opinion on the issues under discussion. Don't forget to cite all sources and always get permission before quoting someone directly.

- *The Summary* is a simple restatement of the issues, with proposed action.

Revision involves eliminating the extraneous or repetitious material, checking your facts, and double-checking your sources. This is where you may discover that you should shift your story in a totally new direction. Don't be afraid to do that. Be flexible. Let what will help readers the most be your guide.

What to write

Write a news feature or column describing a personal event that gave you new insight or a greater degree of compassion for others. Write a travel piece about an unusual place you or your family recently visited. Do a local celebrity profile from an unusual angle—the state legislator whose toughest "race" was against cancer. Offer to cover school board meetings or other news in your neighborhood; most newspapers have sections featuring "zoned" news from specific parts of town or a region and often are in the market for "correspondents" from those areas. Write a how-to column on a topic the paper doesn't regularly feature: tax strategies, dog grooming, housecleaning tips, ethnic cooking, summer/winter automotive maintenance, gardening, child-rearing, single parenthood. If your article is good, you may be asked to write a column on the subject on a regular basis. But be sure to do your homework.

When to write it

If the President just signed a welfare bill, and you've been following the welfare debate in Congress and can offer cogent analysis of the pros and cons of the legislation that now is law, opinion editors want to hear from you—right away. Speed is of essence. Many issues will be around for a long time—crime, education, the national debt, foreign policy—but when a news event occurs, the media must respond and do so quickly, explaining, analyzing, predicting, and offering articles that tie into the event. Fresh voices are often welcome, especially if a national event can be reported from a local angle.

Where to submit

Call a newspaper in which you'd like to see your work published. Have a finished piece or well-defined proposal ready. Ask to speak to the city, state, sports, fashion or opinion page (op-ed) editor, depending on whether your submission is city news, state news, sports news, etc. The editor may ask you to send your material by e-mail, regular mail or fax; conversely, they may not be interested. You'll never know until you try. In fact, that's how I—with no journalism credentials—ended up working at *The Indianapolis News*; I made a cold call to the editor, proposing a weekly column idea. He liked it, I started writing it, and several months later, when a position opened up on the paper's editorial staff, he offered it to me, and I've been working there for almost ten years. Take a chance; the worst thing that can happen is for an editor to say no.

In what format to submit

Help the editor! For many newspapers, the faster you can get your story or column in, and the sooner it can be put into their typesetting/pagination system, the more inclined the editor will be to buy it. Some publications, however, may not use the Internet for copy transmission; be sure to ask. Also, submit your material in the format (single-spaced vs. double-spaced, etc.) requested by the newspaper, which will have its own preferences.

Some words to the wise

* Write the way you talk. Be concise and precise. Don't try to impress with big words and long sentences. Communicate clearly and authoritatively.

* Bone up on grammar, spelling, and punctuation. Get a copy of *The Elements of Style* by Strunk and White and *The Associated Press' Stylebook*, which nearly all newspapers follow. Some writers with the most to say have the least chance of saying it in print because their grammar, spelling and punctuation are so poor that an editor is turned off immediately.

* Get a good thesaurus or book of synonyms. You'll learn about precise writing as you study synonyms and their subtle semantic differences. Your ability to convey various shades of meaning through your words is akin to an artist's ability to create meaning through his or her brush strokes, shading techniques, and color palette. Write what you want to convey, nothing more, nothing less.

* Do not depend on your spellchecker! It cannot differentiate words that are correctly spelled but have completely different meanings.

The key

Newspapers strive for truth, fairness and accuracy, not only because libel laws demand it, but because the philosophical and constitutional justification for a free press crumbles without it. Always remember, "If in doubt, cut it out," until you can verify the information.

* If you were a mother, would you want to read that your son, in custody, but not yet convicted, is: 1) a "murderer"; or 2) an "alleged murderer"? Neither one, but if you had a choice, you'd probably prefer the latter. Watch your wording, not just to avoid libel, but to be sure it's true and accurate.

* If a reporter quoted you in the newspaper, how would you feel if your words were twisted, even if unintentionally? Do the best, most accurate job you can, but also know that mistakes may be made— printed corrections and a personal apology are the proper responses in those cases. Newspapers, especially dailies, have a great impact on the community; their circulation alone gives them the power to create consensus on the issues of the day. They can uncover truth or fuel gossip; they capture the spirit of the age, and they also help shape it. It should be every newspaper journalist's solemn goal to disseminate truth in a way that elevates, not degrades, that spirit.

□ 61

MILITARY MONEY:
CASHING IN ON OLD WAR STORIES

BY LANCE Q. ZEDRIC

IF YOU'VE ALWAYS WANTED TO WRITE FOR MILITARY MAGAZINES, BUT never considered yourself an expert, relax—you don't have to be an expert or even a veteran to break into this well-paying free-lance market. It's easier than you think, and often the best material can be found in an old history book or even right next door.

There are plenty of topics bivouacked out there. All you have to do is ask. Everyone knows a family member, friend or neighbor who served in the military. And they all have an old war story to tell. The kind old man next door might have been a celebrated war hero or a Medal of Honor winner! Your grandfather, father, aunt or uncle might have served aboard a ship with Admiral Nimitz, eaten Christmas dinner with General Patton, or participated in a historic event. Millions of stories are waiting to be told.

After you've blown the dust off *U.S. History 101,* turn to the sections on World War I, World War II, Korea, the Vietnam War, and even the more recent military ventures, and you will find accounts of important battles, commanders, or military events that, with a little research and a fresh angle, will provide ideal material for an interesting article.

Recon the market. Research military publications, and become familiar with their readership. A sound battle plan will prevent having your article become a rejection slip casualty.

The military market ranges from general to specific. For example, *VFW Magazine* (Veterans of Foreign Wars) and *American Legion Magazine* have readerships of more than two million veterans from every branch of the military. They publish various articles on training, weaponry, tactics, veterans legislation, active and former units, military personalities and nostalgia. Publications with such large readerships prefer articles that appeal to as many of their readers as possible. They focus on events involving large military units, such as Army and Marine divisions, Navy fleets, and Air Force Squadrons. Smaller publications, on the other hand, cater to more defined audiences. *Behind The Lines: The Journal of U.S. Special Operations,* specializes in articles on elite U.S. units, such as the Green Berets and Navy SEALs; others focus on respective branches of the military. *Army Magazine* appeals to Army veterans; *All Hands* and *Navy Times* to the Navy; and *Air Force Times* to the Air Force. Magazines like *Civil War Illustrated, World War II* and *Vietnam,* among others, appeal to enthusiasts of a particular war.

Editors are always on the lookout for articles offering new insights on prominent military leaders and for anniversary articles commemorating notable battles and events. But most publications prefer articles on major anniversaries, such as the fifth, tenth, twenty-fifth, fiftieth, and one-hundredth.

But military publications aren't limited to anniversary themes. Anything to do with the home front is also desirable. Whether it's an article on industrial war production, sending care packages to a family member overseas, or collecting "sweetheart pins," the possibilities are endless. Read past issues and look for a theme.

It will save time and effort to consult a calendar. Since most magazines require at least four months' lead time, allow ample time to query, research, and write an article. If you're writing a 50th-anniversary article on the armistice during the Korean War, which occurred in June 1953, send your query or article to the editor by February 2003.

But be careful. War recollections can be a professional minefield. Here are a couple of tips to remember when interviewing a war veteran for an article:

Never write a military article based solely on a personal recollection. As years pass, war stories tend to be exaggerated and important details omitted. Whether intentional or not, veterans often "embellish" their experiences and recollections. What might have been a five-minute skirmish with a squad of enemy troops armed with pistols in 1944, may, more than fifty years later, become a bloody, year-long siege against two divisions of crack troops armed with automatic rifles! So, beware. Ask the veteran you're interviewing for specific times, dates, locations, books, articles, documents, and for the name of anyone who could "help verify" the account.

Use tact when interviewing a veteran. War is often the most traumatic event in a person's life, and it can be an ongoing source of great pain. Don't begin an interview with "how many people did you kill?" or "tell me what it's like to kill somebody." Insensitivity will guarantee failure. Ease into the interview, and allow the person time to relax and learn more about you. For example, ask an open question, such as "tell me what you were doing before you left for military service." As your subjects relax, ask specific questions. But steer clear of potentially sensitive questions until a solid rapport is established. Always put the veteran's feelings first.

If you want to research a specific military unit, but can't find anyone who served in it, don't give up. Most units have a veterans' association and are listed with the Office of the Chief of Military History in Washington, D.C. Another approach is to consult reunion announcements listed in military magazines; these usually provide a phone number to call for information. Explain that you are researching an article on their unit, and chances are a membership roster will be in the mail.

When you need detailed accounts of a particular unit, government institutions are the best source. The National Archives at Suitland, Maryland, contains enough information for the most ambitious military article. The United States Military History Institute at Carlisle Barracks, Pennsylvania, is an outstanding repository for unit histories and contains the personal papers of some of the country's most outstanding military figures. Service academy libraries at West Point, Annapolis, and Colorado Springs, along with military post libraries across the nation, also have extensive unit histories and rare documents. But call first and obtain clearance. Admittance is not guaranteed.

Good photographs can sell an article. In many cases, military photographs are easy to obtain. Most veterans have a few snapshots and will eagerly show them or lend them to you to be copied. With luck, a rare one-of-a-kind photo might turn a reluctant would-be editor into an eager, all-too-happy-to-write-you-a-check editor!

Photographs can also be purchased from several government sources. The Still Photo Branch of the National Archives in College Park, Maryland, is one. It will research its photo files and provide a partial listing on three topics. You then select a commercial contractor from a list to produce the photographs.

Other government sources in the Washington, D.C., area maintain extensive photo files and offer similar services. The Department of Defense Still Media Records Center provides Army, Navy, Air Force, and Marine Corps photographs from 1954 to the present. The Smithsonian's National Air and Space Museum has Air Force photographs prior to 1954. Coast Guard photographs are available through the Commandant at Coast Guard Headquarters.

If time is short, consult the ad sections of military magazines. Military photo catalogues are available from a number of private suppliers. The photos might cost more, but they will arrive much faster than if they were ordered from Uncle Sam. And an 8 x 10 B&W photo may sell a $500 article.

After concluding your research and obtaining photographs, it's time to write. Here are a few more helpful tips:

1. Write tight and factually. The military audience is knowledgeable and will not be won over with flowery prose or fluffy writing. They appreciate facts and hate filler. Most readers are veterans and know how to cut through fat to get to the point.

2. Use quotes from participants when possible. Put the reader in a muddy foxhole alongside a bedraggled infantryman. Put him or her in the cockpit of a bullet-ridden F-14 screaming toward a Soviet MIG at mach 1 with guns blazing! Let the reader take part in the action.

3. Extol duty, honor and country. Patriotism sells, especially with readers of military magazines. Don't be afraid to wave the flag responsibly.

Whether you write about an elite unit fighting its way out from behind enemy lines against insurmountable odds, recount the monumental invasion of Normandy, or retell the sad story of a soldier's loneliness far from home, if you do your homework and follow a few simple rules, you should be well on your way to breaking into this lucrative market. Salute!

❑ 62

THE KEY TO SUCCESSFUL PERSONAL ESSAYS

BY JOHN LENGER

WHEN WRITING PERSONAL ESSAYS, MANY WRITERS DON'T REALIZE THE essential distinction between something they want to write and something that's worthy of publication. That distinction can be summed up as: It is not "something important happened to me and everyone should know about it," it is "something happened to me and it might be important to you, the reader."

As essential as that distinction is, many writers blunder blindly past the subtle difference, barraging editors with personal essays that wind up in the round file. Overwhelmed with "me, me, me!" missives, many publications have curtailed the columns in which such material used to flourish. And no wonder; "me, me, me!" is fine if you're practicing music; otherwise, no one else wants to hear you sing so much about yourself.

But it's not too late to reinvigorate the personal essay—especially since there are indications that editors might now be more receptive to well-written personal essays than they have been. Memoirs—which in essence are book-length personal essays—seem to be more popular than ever; books such as Frank McCourt's *Angela's Ashes* win major awards and top the best-seller lists. As life becomes more and more complicated, readers are searching for friendly and personal connections provided in personal essays. They want to know how someone—perhaps you—dealt with a dramatic situation, overcame an obstacle, or solved a problem. At the same time, newspapers and magazines are trying to be less formal, less distant from their readers, and are publishing more personal perspectives with reader appeal in their pages.

And many of the misguided "me" writers have something interesting to say, if only they can figure out how to say it. The secret is telling a story, rather than just imparting information. The successful personal essay follows ten guidelines and provides answers to questions all writers should ask themselves: What do readers want?

1) Tell readers about *their* problems—*not yours*. Your readers' sympathy for you as a writer extends only so far as they can identify with you and your problems. If, for example, you begin your essay by telling them about how rich, beautiful and successful you are, what is there for them to relate to? They are only interested in knowing that you were once like them—poor and without hope of changing—until something you did helped you overcome the obstacles. Your readers are interested in what positive thing you did so that they can do something similar to bring about similar results for them. (Or, as in the case of many personal essays, how can they prevent having something terrible happen to them?) Whatever story you're trying to tell—how you lost 50 pounds, were attacked by a swarm of bees, married someone you met on the Internet—the unwritten opening is always, "I was once like you, then something marvelous (dreadful) happened and changed my life."

2) Don't hit readers with a hammer; lull them with a lullaby. Unlike a news story, in which a writer wants to state the crucial fact in the opening paragraph, in the personal essay an oblique approach works best. That's because the crucial fact you're relating is not really crucial to anyone but you. Readers will go along for the ride because they expect to be entertained, outraged, frightened or informed by your essay. They don't want an update from a stockmarket ticker—a piece of information like "Beverly broke her arm"—they want to be told a story. "Beverly broke her arm . . . and you won't believe what happened next!"

3) Engage readers emotionally. Especially if you're writing about serious things. Readers want to be your friends, to share your secrets, to laugh at your jokes, to take your side. That's why people become readers; they're looking for that emotional connection. There are two things that readers won't abide: Being preached at and being bored.

4) Don't overstate your case. Frank McCourt won a Pulitzer Prize for his memoir *Angela's Ashes*, about growing up poor in Ireland. Reviewer after reviewer has praised McCourt for his straight-ahead writing style. As Patti Hartigan put it in *The Boston Globe*, the story is "told through the clear, unanalytical gaze of a child's eyes. In the hands of any other writer, *Angela's Ashes* might have been another green parade of stereotypes: the alcoholic father, the long-suffering mother, Father O'Malley, Glocca Morra, leprechauns, and all. McCourt knows he's flirting with clichés, but he tells a tale so honest and specific, it makes your eyes sting." When you're writing your personal essay, follow the lead of a master: Be honest and specific. Make the readers' eyes sting.

5) Leave out unnecessary details. Many beginning writers get hung up on telling things just exactly as they happened, in detail after excruciating detail. But that's not what good writing is. Good writing requires you to separate the important from the unimportant. If you crave second-by-second detail, buy a video camera, but don't invite anybody else to watch.

6) Be aware of the metaphoric implications of what you write. James Carroll's memoir about how the Vietnam War affected his family is called *An American Requiem: God, My Father and the War that Came Between Us.* This book, which won the National Book Award for 1996, tells a very personal story about how the war divided his family, but it also presents the Carroll family as a metaphor for the United States; it's as much about how America was divided by the war as it is about the war's effect on one particular family. In the same way, Caroline Knapp, in *Drinking, A Love Story,* and Elizabeth Wurtzel, in *Prozac Nation,* recount their respective personal struggles with alcoholism and depression as a way of saying something about the larger cultural problems of addiction and mental illness.

7) Write with authority. It's amazing how many people write essays that are apologetic —"I know you don't want to read about me, but . . . "—or are so lacking in detail that readers wonder if the writer was actually present for these important events in her life. If you're writing about your struggles with a broken arm, don't write about it as your doctor would. Instead, write as you would if you were talking to a friend. *It hurt. I cried. I thought, how am I going to drive the kids to* *school? Why did this happen to me?* This is your story, after all. Tell it; don't apologize for it.

8) Tie your essay to an idea or event to which many people can relate. Are you a mother? A veteran? A person of Irish ancestry? Then there are special days in which everyone else celebrates you, and during those times, they would especially like to read your story. The impact—and the salability—of your essay on your wartime experiences increases a hundred-fold in the period just before Veterans' Day. The same thing happens with the essay recalling your father's or mother's wartime experiences and how they affected you. Cokie Roberts' collection of personal essays, *We Are Our Mothers' Daughters*, appeared in bookstores right before Mother's Day. This sort of thing is entirely predictable. *The Boston Globe* for Mother's Day 1998 printed three essays about motherhood in its Focus section: two personal essays, one each by a staff writer and a free-lancer, and another essay by two academics who had conducted research on how difficult it is to be a mother. For Mother's Day next year, why not write an essay about *your* mother? Or *your* children?

9) Let your readers be participants. Don't tell readers what they should think about what happened to you. Let them bring something to the reading of your piece, so that it's a conversation instead of a sermon. Can you imagine, for instance, actors on stage saying at the end of a performance, "O.K. You're all supposed to feel happy now because that was a comedy"? Of course not. Respect your readers. If you've done your job, they will get the point.

10) Complete the transaction. Now that you've invited them into your essay, readers want questions answered. They want to know how things ended. They want a sense of closure.

Why do so many writers not follow through on their good beginnings? They seem to extend a friendly hand to their readers, then become shy, retreating into generalities or dribbling off into nothingness.

To write is a bold action. So be bold! Put yourself on the line emotionally. Readers want to read about you—as long as you're also writing about them.

❑ 63

SNOOPING IN THE PAST: WRITING HISTORICAL BIOGRAPHIES

BY LAURIE WINN CARLSON

THE PAST FEW YEARS HAVE SEEN BIOGRAPHIES OF PEOPLE FROM THE past propelled onto bestseller lists across the country: *Undaunted Courage,* Stephen Ambrose's biography of Meriwether Lewis; *Unredeemed Captive,* by John Demos, the story of Eunice Williams and the French and Indian War; *No Ordinary Time,* the story of Franklin and Eleanor Roosevelt by Doris Kearns Goodwin, and several biographies of Jane Austen, to name only a few.

The spectacular sales of historical biographies prove that the public wants stories about heroes and heroines, whether their lives involved statesmanship, exploration, or writing literature. People read biographies for many of the same reasons they read novels: to be entertained, to be informed, to be comforted or inspired, to identify with successful people, to live somebody else's life for a while. There's every reason to write historical biographies if you like historical research, enjoy learning about people, and can master the elements of good storytelling.

How does a writer go about retelling the life of a historical person in a way that grabs first an editor, then the reader? Even the most intriguing person's life can be incredibly boring unless presented with creativity and skill. Writing historical biographies requires a combination of techniques from nonfiction and fiction writing, and like the novelist, the first decision the biographer makes is, "Whose story can I tell?" Just like creating a main character in a novel, choosing the subjects for biographies is all-important. Who they are, the times they lived in, and the choices they made are what keeps the narrative going.

The main character

The person you choose to write about must be someone with whom readers will want to identify. That doesn't mean they have to be saints—

readers like to read about "bad guys," too, and biographies of history's villains can make compelling reading. Just be careful to select someone whose life and character pique your interest. I decided to write about women missionaries in the West because they were different from our commonly held perceptions—they were feminists rather than conventional nineteenth-century wives and mothers—and that makes their story intriguing and interesting to today's readers.

Avoid stereotypes: They are too boring. Challenge your preconceptions, search for people who tried to break the mold society had created for them, who strived to do something different and worthwhile, even if they made poor decisions or met with failure. Similar to a protagonist in a novel, good biographies follow the "hero's journey." Writers need to examine a person's life, the hurdles and obstructions he or she met, and how that person overcame them. If he or she failed miserably, perhaps that failure can be understood better or differently from today's perspective.

Like the novelist, as a biographer you want to reveal a person's character bit by bit, showing rather than telling. Using the subject's own writings (diaries, letters) as well as what others wrote or said about the person can be very revealing, but, of course, other people's opinions can be biased, based on personal resentments or jealousies. How you interpret the facts determines whether or not your biography will have true depth and dimension. You'll want to reveal details about your subject's life throughout your book, looking for ways to stir readers' emotions by creating drama and tension, even some suspense, to propel them forward.

Setting

For historical biographies, time and place are extremely important to the picture of the subject's life. What best-selling biographies have in common is that they examine lives of people who lived in periods of turmoil and action, and are carefully researched and scrupulously accurate. In addition, they are written in a lively narrative style that engages and holds readers' interest.

As you choose the person to write about, look at the geographic setting and the time period and social class in which they lived. Time and place achieve a symbolic importance in a biography, as they do in a novel. In biographies, the setting is another character of sorts; it provides hurdles the protagonist must overcome. An impoverished childhood, geographic isolation, ramifications of social class—these all become part of the setting in a biography. When writing about a woman of the early nineteenth century, it makes a great deal of difference whether she lived in a settled New England village or on the Ohio frontier. Where and when she lived is part of her life's story.

When you're casting about for a particular subject for your biography, look for people who lived in exciting times. That will make the entire story much more interesting and provide conflicts outside the person's inner character.

Other characters

Biographies, like novels, have antagonists or villains. Your subject may be young, idealistic, duty-bound; the "bad guys" can be treacherous weather, distance, rugged terrain, armed and dangerous dissidents, time running out, lack of funds, or simply the dark side of human nature. You will also need to identify and include people who helped the protagonist: lovers, mentors, siblings, rescuers, friends, or confidants. Adding these elements will enrich the biography—you will not simply be retelling chronological events in a dead person's life—and will eventually give the biography a sort of climactic resolution.

When you choose a suitable subject to write about, be careful not to choose someone you're in love with—and be sure not to fall in love with the subject as you write. Be alert for evidence of character failings in even the most righteous subject's life: Those natural flaws, mistakes, and weaknesses make the character more well-rounded and real.

Theme

Once you've selected the subject for your biography, ask yourself: Why do I want to write about this person? It's an important question because it gives you the theme for the book. What topics, besides the facts of the person's life, will you include? What broader issues will you address as you tell about this particular person and the times he or she lived in? The theme is really the story you are telling, whether it's about an ordinary person trying to save the farm, a business, society, or whether the theme is one of family devotion, escape from intolerable conditions, or how to overcome adversity and become a leader. These are the overall themes you should really be exploring when you write a person's life from the past.

Study psychological motivation, and place the person's life within the times in which he or she lived. Don't judge his or her efforts (or lack of them) by today's social standards, but determine the expectations of the period in which your subject lived and how he or she did or did not live up to them.

Structure

Most biographies are pretty much chronological, because that's how lives are lived. But you can jump around or diverge somewhat to keep the narrative dramatic as well as realistic. What you're trying to do is to write in scenes, like a playwright. Plan your story around the incidents or events with the most dramatic potential. Select scenes that are visual, full of conflict, danger, failure, suffering, turning points, beginnings, discoveries, and successes. You can't recount all the events in the person's life, but only the most important, dramatic ones; perhaps limit the scope of the book to a span of only a few years or a decade, rather than an entire lifetime. Omit details of childhood, education, old age, or other times when your subject's life held little conflict or excitement. Focus your narrative on the times and events that shaped the subject's life.

Research

Research strongly affects your selection of a subject. You certainly can't select someone about whom there's practically nothing known, because then you have to invent the facts, in which case you should switch from writing a biography to writing a historical novel.

If you want to write about someone with an extensive written record—diaries, court records, letters, and military records—you'll have no problem with research. If, however, you choose a female subject who wasn't famous enough to have left behind lots of written records (and most women in history would fall into this category), you'll need to search harder for information, and can perhaps write a group biography, as I did. This will enable you to use what several women wrote about each other, and by comparing and contrasting their lives, you'll be able to produce a strong narrative.

Researching the biography is all-important in giving your writing authenticity; the use of specialized jargon of the day, and specific details gleaned from your research will help make your book credible. The foods people ate, the fabric used in the clothing they wore, the specific illnesses and medicines they were subject to—these all help the reader become more involved in the story you are telling and make your words ring true. This research takes time, but these tiny details makes the subject's life become more real to you, too. The words I found in missionary hymns of the 1830s made me see how women connected becoming a missionary with going to far-off lands for adventure. I would have never discovered that fact if I'd simply accepted that they sang "generic" church hymns. The exact words in the hymns provided a rich resource for understanding the people who sang them. As you do your research, you should at times be surprised, or else you simply aren't digging enough.

A last question to ask as you set about writing a biography: Why would anyone else want to read about this person? Your answer will help you identify your theme and focus, and maintain the energy and effort it takes to complete a project as time-consuming and difficult as writing a historical biography. A satisfying mix of personality, historical setting, and human nature, moving along a chronological continuum, gives you (and your readers) a story to enjoy and remember.

If there's one other thing a historical biographer needs, it's a passion for digging into the lives of people, finding out all you can about them and the times in which they lived—along with the drive to tell others about it. An unquenchable desire for gossip (backed up by research, mind you) goes a long way, too!

□ 64

WRITING WITH A GREEN THUMB

BY MARY E. MAURER

Help Wanted: Enthusiastic writer with hands-on gardening experience or professional gardener with hands-on writing experience. Please send articles, fillers, tips, essays, interviews, profiles, photo features, or craft ideas to any of the dozen of home and garden magazines now featured at your local newsstand.

You probably won't find an ad for a "garden writer" in your local paper, but if you have a green thumb, or know someone who does, there is a flourishing field waiting to be harvested. It took me five years till I finally had the sense to combine my two passions, writing and gardening.

To meet the demand for gardening and landscaping advice, the number of "home and garden" magazines and columns has blossomed into a significant market for writers, photographers, and gardeners with practical ideas. Whether you enjoy gardening or you just appreciate your neighbor's garden, there are many opportunities in this field if you follow a few guidelines.

First, be honest about your gardening experience, interests, and abilities. Are you interested in plants, creative landscaping, breeding techniques, garden pests, medicinal herbs, or historical gardens? Do you know any interesting gardeners? Do you live near a major botanical garden or arboretum? Are there flower clubs or shows in your city? This is a vital step, because some editors respect free-lance writers who are interested in gardening and willing to do research; others absolutely insist that writers be experienced gardeners.

Next, decide what area of green-thumb writing you want to try first. Most articles published by the major gardening magazines fit one of the following categories:

Basic plant identification and care. A couple of years ago I wrote an article about cleomes, one of my favorite flowers, for *Flower and*

Garden. Articles for this category might also include "Dividing Perennials," "Growing Antique Roses," "Six Sizzling Chile Peppers," or "Your Guide to Spring Pruning." These are often feature articles and should include photos and sources from which readers can obtain plants and/or seeds. Many magazines also like photocopies of your resources. This category also includes advice and tips, which can be written as short fillers or grouped into a feature article. *Woman's Day* ran an interesting "round-up" piece called "41 Secrets of Great Gardeners."

Home landscape and design. Many gardening magazines focus specifically on designing landscapes for a particular home, location, "look," color scheme, etc. *Fine Gardening* focuses on landscape and ornamental gardening. *Garden Design* is "devoted to the fine art of garden design." Others may be primarily interested in vegetable gardening, but also use annual features on "designing an herb garden" or "creating a cottage garden." Also, many general, regional, home and garden, and trade magazines use articles about landscaping. You may also find markets in newspaper "lifestyle" sections.

Environmental concerns. If you are a gardening buff, you know that gardeners are sharply divided over the use of pesticides and herbicides. *Organic Gardening* makes its views against chemicals in gardening very clear. Others, like *Flower and Garden*, take a more moderate stance and often give readers natural and chemical options. Read at least six back issues of a magazine and pay particular attention to the advertisements to help you understand the magazine's viewpoint on environmental issues. These publications also use articles about soil amendment, composting, native plants, and conservation of wild areas.

Garden showcase/profile. This is one of the best categories for free lancers with limited gardening knowledge. Avid gardeners love to talk about their gardens and give advice. They love to give tours and usually welcome photographers. According to the editor of *Garden Design*, "Our greatest need is for extraordinary private gardens." You can locate them by contacting nurseries, garden clubs, friends, or your local newspaper. A profile of a gardener is much like an interview/profile of anyone else. However, remember that gardening magazines are looking for unique ideas, new techniques, time-saving advice, stunning landscapes,

or extraordinary plant collections. And don't forget that this category
also includes outstanding community and public gardens.

Indoor and container gardening. Houseplants and greenhouse gardening are of interest to many city dwellers. This is also another category that can land you in "non-gardening" publications, since many
frequently use articles about houseplants. *Family Circle*, for example,
ran an article on "Potted Pleasures," which included several container
gardens and groupings.

Equipment and technology. The burgeoning interest in gardening
has led to an even greater interest in time- and labor-saving devices.
Articles about everything from tillers and tractors to garden design software and the latest "how-to" books and videos would be of interest to
magazines in this category. *Family Circle's Easy Gardening* published
an article on hand tools titled, "Weed It and Reap," and also ran a
review of garden tractors.

Vegetable/fruit production and harvesting. This is the mainstay of
many gardening magazines. In addition to the basics of planting and
harvesting edibles, you could also write about cooking and preserving
them. Don't forget articles about gardening in different zones, or trying
new varieties of vegetables and fruit.

Garden history and folklore. There is a feeling of nostalgia that
unites most gardeners. We recall the gardens of our parents and grandparents and swear that the harvests were bigger, the fragrances sweeter.
Burpee's heirloom seed catalogue begins with this introduction: "One
of the most exciting trends in gardening today is the growing interest in
heirloom or antique varieties of vegetables and flowers." You can tap
into this market with articles like "Grandma's Favorite Vines," "Heirloom Vegetables for Your Garden," or "Posies from the Past." Or you
may want to write about famous gardens like those of Monet or Thomas
Jefferson, or gardens visited by tourists in England, Holland, and other
countries. This is a more limited market, but still an option.

Flower shows and sources. Many of these articles are staff-written,
but you may have a foot in the door if you live close to or in your travels

have visited a major show or an interesting nursery. Most early spring editions of traditional gardening magazines include articles about new varieties and discoveries.

Gardening "lifestyles." This is the potpourri category that includes all the topics tied to gardening in various ways. You can explore the psychology of gardening, medicinal uses of wildflowers, or tell humorous anecdotes about gardeners. You can describe how to build a birdhouse, create a paved path, or put in a sprinkler system. *Birds & Blooms* published an article about making scented soaps. An article in *Country Home/Country Gardens* showed how to make a plant tower out of willow posts. You might write about crafts using flowers or how best to photograph flowers. Some magazines even carry recipes and cartoons. I've read gardening articles about birdwatching, raising koi, attracting butterflies, hosting a garden party, making pressed-flower greeting cards, raising chickens, and making a peach pie. Last year *Flower and Garden* published an article on how to transport your plants when you move!

As you can see, the opportunities are endless, but study the markets to find your niche. Read at least six gardening magazines. Check your usual writing markets for gardening departments, annual gardening issues, or features. Decide which magazine seems the most compatible with your writing style and gardening interests and experience. Write for guidelines of any magazine that interests you as a possible market.

There is one more piece of advice that you'll need before writing with a green thumb. Gardening is a seasonal avocation. Be sure that you understand the concept of planting/harvesting cycles, and note the lead time for your target magazines. Many plan their main articles 10 to 18 months in advance, so it's important to query about major features.

If you're looking for a way to expand your writing opportunities, garden writing may be the perfect field for you. It certainly works for me. Now, when I'm outside digging in the dirt instead of sitting in front of my computer, I just tell myself I'm "researching a new article"!

□ 65

THE HOW-TOS OF
HOW-TOS

BY LINDA SLATER

I HAVE BEEN WRITING AND SELLING HOW-TO ARTICLES FOR ABOUT twenty years. Most editors are willing to consider a well-crafted article that helps other people learn how to do something well. I have sold many articles and have not been immune to rejection either, so I feel I have been through the School of Hard Knocks several times! Here are my best tips for selling that how-to article:

1. **Never give up.** If an article is rejected by *Mother Earth News,* try *Back Home* or *Countryside.* I once sent an article to eight different magazines before it sold. Your article won't be published gathering dust on the shelf.

2. **Revise.** If an article is rejected, reread it and see what might make it sparkle. Does it need better, more detailed photographs? Do you need a few more quotes from other, more varied experts? Is the article dated?

3. **Read at least ten issues** of the magazine you are aiming to sell to. What style do they favor? Are the articles formal or informal and conversational? Carefully study the photographs. Are the articles fifty percent text and fifty percent photos? Does humor fit this magazine's style? Now you know how to slant your article.

4. **Try new markets** that had been unknown to you. I once sent a garden article to a small magazine I found in my doctor's office. I am now the garden editor of that magazine! Risk-taking is healthy for all writers. You might be surprised where you might sell your article on flyfishing for women. I took a risk once and sent an article on self-esteem to a magazine for large women, *Big Beautiful Woman*, and sold it. Spend ten minutes every day studying market lists on books on writing at your library or at home. You may be amazed at which magazine or newspaper will buy your how-to article.

5. **Keep an "idea file"** for those days when inspiration won't come. Several kinds of articles from various publications get me going. For example, I keep a garden idea file, a self-help idea file, and a general human-interest idea file. If I read about a local artist or unusual character, I cut out the article so that I'll remember to try an article similar to that or in more depth about that subject. A news story about a flood or fire might turn into a human-interest piece or an article on flood or fire insurance, with examples of people who have lost everything because they weren't insured.

6. **Ask for feedback.** Ask friends or family to read your article and give you good or bad feedback. Is the piece clear and easy to read? Do the photographs help tell the reader how to do something? You will learn from each feedback you receive. Take a deep breath and try it.

7. **Stay in touch with local events.** Keep a calendar of local and state fairs, festivals, competitions, and events. Visit some of these events and see whom you can meet and talk to. Take photos of local artists, musicians, crafts-people, and writers. Could you turn any of these interviews into a how-to piece on drawing or painting? Sewing or fishing? Quilting or boating? One woman in my area compiled and self-published a booklet on "How to Compete in Art Fairs and Festivals and Sell Your Work," and sold several thousand copies at art fairs and through the mail. I once took photos of four weavers at a show and sold an article about them to a regional publication, and another time, I did a profile of a woman who paints on gourds and sells them for hundreds of dollars.

8. **Write about your passionate interests.** I am wild about gardening, so I love interviewing area gardeners, talking to people who run nurseries, and telling others how to garden. I make my own herbal teas, so I sent an article on this topic to *Mother Earth News*. They bought it, used it in the magazine, then paid me again when they reprinted it in an anthology. I sold an article to an environmental magazine on gardening with my children, and one on how to quit smoking to a health food publication. If you love angels or miracles, you have the germ of an article idea. (Hint: Anything with the word "soul" in it seems to sell these days!)

9. **Solve a problem.** This type of article tells readers how to overcome a problem or solve a dilemma in their everyday lives. It could be about how to take out coffee stains or cleaning the house with non-

toxic chemicals, how to catch bass or grow spinach. This kind of article may require some research or interviews with local or national experts. I find that if I have at least five quotes in an article from experts who live all over the country, it has more credibility. I check the library for names of experts in the field and write or call them. Once Joyce Brothers called me back while I was baking cookies and surprised me with her promptness. For ideas, ask your friends or relatives what kinds of problems they are trying to solve. (Hint: Many of my friends are struggling with how to communicate with their teenager and how to pay for their children's college education. Remember, there are 40 million baby boomers now thinking about these problems.)

10. **Tailor your article to a specific market.** Check and recheck your article for spelling, grammar, and punctuation. Ask people to proof it, read it, give you feedback. Enclose an SASE, and send your article out! If it is rejected, revise and send it out the next day to another market. Your article will not sell sitting on your desk or waiting for you to make it perfect.

❏ 66

THE BUSINESS OF WRITING ABOUT BUSINESS

BY CHRISTINE M. GOLDBECK

WALL STREET REPORTERS AREN'T THE ONLY WRITERS MAKING MONEY from the business community. Most business journals and regional weekly or monthly publications dealing with issues and information important to business people depend on free-lance writers, and pay well for the articles they receive or assign.

Step one to breaking into this market is to tell yourself that business is not intimidating or boring. That you aren't an M. B. A., that you flunked high school economics, that you don't know the difference between a mutual fund and a certificate of deposit—none of this really matters. The business community is not an ogre, and all business people are not stuffed shirts who are too busy with the bottom line to talk about their industry or their enterprise. Nor is business writing non-creative and rigidly routine.

In fact, many business owners and operators like to share their expertise and experiences. So, not only will you get bylines and make money writing about business, you will learn a lot.

Call the local Chamber of Commerce or any other business support agency to inquire whether there is a business journal published in your area, and check your newspaper to see whether it has a business page. Bigger daily papers usually run such a page in each issue. Smaller dailies often publish a business page on a weekly basis.

Business story subjects run the gamut: new businesses, profiles of business people, the grand opening of a business, a store reopening a year after it was destroyed by fire, trends in an industry, affirmative action contracts, a bankrupt bagel shop, a new product sold in the area, college bookstores selling quarts of milk for continuing education students . . . as long as it relates to doing business and you can write it for business people, you're in.

A newspaper editor will want samples of your published works in order to assess your ability to write interesting business copy. Business journals usually have writer's guidelines and on request, will mail them to you, along with a sample issue. Therefore, that byline might be but a telephone call to an editor away.

Let's say you've received a go-ahead from a business editor on an article about a business in your community. Now what?

You will of course want to set up an appointment to interview the owner, and to be prepared for that interview by learning something about him or her, the company, and the industry. Your local community library, as well as area university libraries, are great places to obtain information on the businesses and types of industries in the area. Take time to familiarize yourself with all the information that is available.

These are some of the references you should consult for background information on a company or a business executive:

- **Annual reports.** A public company's annual report contains helpful information (in addition to the stuff they write for stockholders). Look for statistics that reveal financial information about the company.
- **Trade journals** (magazines and newspapers devoted to a specific industry).
- **Local chambers of commerce and business associations.** Staffs at such agencies are usually good about giving you some information about their member companies, many of which are small- to medium-size private enterprises. So, if you need to know the identity of the president of Aunt Mabel's Meatballs, call the Chamber of Commerce nearest to the location of the business.
- **Commercial on-line services, the Internet, and the World Wide Web.** Here you'll find a wealth of information about industry trends and specific companies and business leaders. (For a recent piece on how high paper prices are affecting profit in a number of industries, I went to an on-line newsstand, searched under the key words "paper," "costs," and "paper prices," and got more information than I was able to use. But, it certainly gave me a lot of background, which I used to formulate questions for my interviews.) Dun & Bradstreet and other business references can also be contacted via the Internet.

Like a typical newspaper or magazine article, a business feature is built on the five Ws (*who, what, where, when,* and *why*—and don't forget *how*), answering such questions as:

What is the business: What does it make or what services does it provide for sale? Where is it located? How long has the company been in business? How does it market its product or service?

Once you have that vital information, you will need to focus on the people who run the business, asking every interviewee from whom you need information the following kinds of questions:

- What is your business strategy?
- How are you marketing your product?
- How much did you invest to start the business? Did you get loans, and if so, what kind?
- Who is your competition and how do you try to stay ahead of them?
- How much do you charge for your product?
- Is this a sole proprietorship, a privately held company, or a public operation?
- What are your annual sales?
- How many employees do you have?

Let's say you're going to write about your neighbor who makes meatballs and sells them to local supermarkets. If your piece is for a mainstream newspaper, the editor will probably instruct you to take what is called a "general assignment approach," which simply means you will have to use a style the average newspaper reader will understand and find satisfying. You won't use business lingo, and you will find something interesting, even homey, about your subject or topic and center your story on that specific point.

You will ask your subject how, when, and where she got started, why she wanted to sell her meatballs, and what made her think this business could be profitable. What did she do before making meatballs?

Your lead might read:

Up to her elbows in ground beef, Susan Tucker fondly recalls the times she and her Aunt Mabel made meatballs for the Saint Mary's Church socials. A year ago, Tucker gave up her 7-to-3 job sewing collars on coats to sell "Aunt

Mabel's Meatballs." "Too bad Mabel isn't here to see how good business has been," she says.

This type of human interest piece, extolling personal success, the local church, and good old Aunt Mabel, sells mainstream newspapers.

If your piece is for a business journal, you'll need to handle it a little differently, since you are writing for a different audience—business people.

Something like this might work:

> An Olive County businesswoman last year used a recipe for homemade meatballs to launch a business that currently employs ten people. Susan Tucker, the owner of Aunt Mabel's Meatballs, started the business in the kitchen of her Brownsville home. Within six months, she had made enough money to purchase and renovate an old restaurant located in Brownsville's commercial district, where she and her employees now make meatballs for wholesale and retail sales. They package and ship their product to a number of supermarkets and restaurants in the region and sell hot meatball hoagies to downtown shoppers, as well.
>
> "I started out making and selling meatballs wholesale to places like Acme Market and Joe's Spaghetti House," Tucker says. "After we moved into this building, I thought it would be a good idea to sell the product retail, so I started selling sandwiches and fresh meatballs from here. That proved to be a good decision, too."
>
> Tucker invested no capital when she launched the business. She says there was little overhead cost, and she quickly recouped what she paid for beef, eggs, and the other ingredients by selling the meatballs for $2.99 per pound.

See the difference? It's the same story, but tailored for a different readership.

This method of getting the information and writing a business journal piece can be used for any type of business or industry. Here's another example, using a service industry executive as the source:

> The president of Bridgetown Health Services Inc. says his company now sells medical insurance to small businesses that have fewer than five employees. Owen Johnson says that the small business health plan was created in order to stay competitive in the ever-evolving health industry. The new policy was put on the market October 1, and within two months, the company had signed up 500 small businesses.
>
> "There are major competitors trying to break into this marketplace. We wanted to get a jump on them. By selling our 'Small Business Health Plan,' we believe we have entrenched ourselves in the Northeast Pennsylvania medical insurance field," Johnson said. "It proved to be a good business decision."

Reporting on business is not difficult when you know your subject, get the vital information, then ask those extra questions specific to doing business in a particular field. If you were writing a piece about a fire, a murder, a local church yard sale, a visit from the Pope, you would ask questions specific to that event or person. This is really all you will do in business writing: You will write the story so that your readers— business people—will be informed and entertained. Also, you'll build up your publication credits, make new contacts, and learn interesting things about the people in your area.

Reference materials I recommend and which you may want to have on hand include *The Associated Press Stylebook and Libel Manual,* which contains a section on business writing, and *BusinessSpeak,* compiled by Dick Schaaf and Margaret Kaeter (Warner Books). Both should be available through a local bookstore or in a good public or business library.

Trade groups with information about business journals include the Association of Area Business Publications, 5820 Wilshire Blvd., Suite 500, Los Angeles, CA 90036, (213) 937-5514, and The Network of City Business Journals, 120 W. Morehead St., Suite 420, Charlotte, NC 28202, (800) 433-4565.

There are also professional societies for business writers. Write the Society of American Business Editors and Writers, University of Missouri, 76 Gannett Hall, Columbia, MO 65211, or the American Business Press, 675 Third Ave., Suite 415, New York, NY 10017.

❑ 67

TRUE CRIME WRITING:
A DYNAMIC FIELD

BY PETER A. DEPREE

FEW GENRES IN JOURNALISM TODAY ARE AS EXCITING AND PROFITABLE as true crime, whether article or book. Although this piece focuses on the true crime article, many of the techniques and methods discussed in the following six steps are readily applicable to the true crime book.

STEP ONE: *Researching the field.* Buy several true crime magazines and spend a rainy afternoon getting a feel for the slant and depth of the articles. Jot down what you liked and didn't like about them. Then, dash off a request to the editorial office of one or two of the magazines for the writers guidelines (include the requisite SASE).

STEP TWO: *Finding a crime.* Visit your local library and look in the index of the biggest newspaper in your area under the heading Murder/ Manslaughter, going back about four years, and photocopy those index pages. (Most crimes more than four or five years old are too stale to fit the slant of true detective magazines.) Highlight the crimes that seem most likely to make interesting true crime pieces. The few sentences describing each article will give you a good feel for the highlights of the case. Select about half a dozen cases that look promising. As you peruse them, you will whittle down the group for one reason or another until you're left with one or two that have all the elements you need for an effective true crime piece. Most detective magazine guidelines will help you narrow them down: The crime is always murder; the "perp" (police parlance for perpetrator) has been convicted; there was a substantial investigation leading to the arrest; the crime took place reasonably near your area (important, since you'll have to go to the court to gather research); and photos are available for illustration.

STEP THREE: *Doing the research.* First, with the index as a guide, collect all available newspaper articles on the crime you've selected so you can make an outline before reading the trial transcript. Your library should have either back issues or microfilm (provided you followed Step One and picked a case no more than four years old). If there are two or more newspapers in your area that covered the crime, get copies of all of them. Often, pertinent details were printed by one paper but not the other.

STEP FOUR: *Reading the trial transcript.* Call the clerk's office of the court where the trial took place and ask for the case number on the crime and whether the transcript is available to the public (it usually is). By now you should have a three- or four-page outline based on all the articles you've read. Take your outline and a lot of paper and pens to the courthouse, and be prepared to spend a whole day reading the trial record; even a trial that lasted only three or four days can fill several bound volumes. (When I was doing research for a book on the Nights-talker serial killer case in Los Angeles, the court record was 100,000 pages long and filled three shopping carts!) Skim and make notes of the quotes and material you'll need; this will be a lot easier if you've prepared your outline carefully, since you'll already know the key names to watch for—the lead detective, prosecutor, defense attorney, victim, witnesses, responding officer, and so forth. You'll need to look for material on several different levels simultaneously: details for accuracy, dramatic quotes, colorful background, etc. There will usually be far more of these elements than you could possibly pack into an article, so you have the luxury of choosing only the very best. You may discover a brand-new form of writing frustration when you have to slash all those dramatic prosecutorial summations and subplots down to the required word count.

Use whatever form of research you're comfortable with. I find a combination of scribbling notes in my own pseudo-shorthand and dictating into a hand-held recorder suits me. (Pack enough spare batteries and tapes!) I can mumble into my recorder faster than I can write. Having photocopies made at the court is usually prohibitively expensive, so copy very selectively. As a rule of thumb, the parts of a transcript that yield the most important factual information are the opening remarks of both attorneys; the questioning of the lead detective; the testimony of expert witnesses such as forensic technicians; and the summing up of both attorneys. A couple of tips: Dates are especially important, and so are names.

Almost as important as the transcript is the court file. Specify to the court clerk that you would like that as well as the transcript.

STEP FIVE: *Writing the article.* Reread the writers guidelines for the magazine to which you're submitting your piece, then write the kind of article *you* would find exciting and surprising (or shocking) to read. Chances are that if a particular detail, scene, or quote piques your interest, it belongs in your piece. Don't get lost in boring minutiae, but do remember that sprinkling in telling details seasons the piece and sharpens the focus.

If your detective used a K9 dog to search for evidence, you might mention that it was a Rottweiler named Butch, with a mangled ear. If the ballistics expert test-fired the gun, you could throw in that detail, noting that he fired it into a slab of gel, then retrieved the bullet and viewed it under a comparison microscope for tell-tale striations, and so on. The trial transcript is packed with details like these that make your article stand out from a "made-up" detective story.

As you're writing, watch your length. Editors are not impressed with articles that run a few thousand words over their suggested length.

STEP SIX: *Secondary wrap-up research.* True crime editors are picky about certain details, especially names (check those writers guidelines again!). If you mention "Mr. Gordon," you should specify that he is Commissioner John Gordon of the Gotham City Police Department. Change the names of witnesses or family members, for obvious reasons. Go back to the library to check the details that will give your writing authority. For instance, if the crime was committed with a shotgun and you don't know a pump-action from an over-&-under, you need to do some minor research to find out. If your crime involves DNA fingerprinting, you'll need to spend no more than an hour in the library to find enough useful facts to give your article a little snap. I recently wrote an article on a killer who was suffering from paranoid schizophrenia. In just four pages in two college psych textbooks—twenty minutes' investment of my time—I came up with more than enough facts for my piece.

What to watch out for

There are at least four articles in my computer that are almost completely written, but went nowhere. Why? Because I made stupid, unnecessary mistakes—mistakes that *you* would never make if you follow a few simple rules. The following three are non-negotiable:

1) *Never start on an article without querying the magazine first.* Nothing is quite as frustrating as writing twenty detailed pages on the Longbow rapist, only to discover that Joe Bland already sold that piece to your target magazine a year ago. You now have a pile of perfectly good kindling.

2) *Always make doubly sure the trial transcript is available.* You should never have to invest more than one or two full days in researching the transcript and court file, but that doesn't help when on the day you need it you learn that the whole file was shipped five hundred miles away so the appeals judges could study it at their leisure. (We're talking *months* here.)

3) *Never start an article without making sure photos are available.* Etch this in stone. No true crime magazine will run an article without *at least* three photos. The minimum basics are a photo of the perp; one of the victim; one of the crime scene. These can be what I call "documentary-grade"; sometimes, even a particularly sharp photo clipped from a newspaper will suffice. But query your target magazine first, and always make sure the picture is in the public domain (i.e., a high school yearbook photo of the killer, a photo of the victim distributed to all the papers, a snapshot of the bank building where an armed robbery took place).

True crime writing might be called entry-level journalism. If you can write a tightly researched and entertaining piece following these suggestions, you'll have a better chance of success.

❏ 68

WRITING NEWSPAPER OPINION ARTICLES

BY WENDY DAGER

IF YOU HAVE STRONG OPINIONS ON ISSUES THAT AFFECT OUR DAILY lives, as well as good basic writing skills, you should try your hand at writing newspaper opinion articles. Here are some tips to start you off:

1. Identify your markets.

The best way to get into newspaper opinion writing is by invitation. Look closely and you'll find these invitations in many local papers. Every Saturday, for example, the *Ventura County Star* in Southern California runs the "Pulse Page," a section of the newspaper that has short pieces—about 400 words—on timely issues. A recent invitation for "Pulse Page" submissions read, "TELL US—Higher education is often touted as a way to prepare people to participate in the emerging global economy. Some, however, decry any materialistic aim for higher education. What do you think is the purpose of education?" This is not a request for letters to the editor, but for columns written by educators, politicians, housewives, and free-lance writers—for which they are paid.

Other papers, such as *The Los Angeles Daily News*, occasionally ask readers for opinions on issues affecting the community. There are also calls for articles in other parts of some newspapers. *The Star* has a weekly column in its "Fast Forward" business section called the "Best of Everything," featuring humorous takes on the necessity of household items, from record players to typewriters to cotton balls—all by different writers.

You should not submit your opinion piece simultaneously to newspapers, unless you are in the business of self-syndication. If the editor of one newspaper can't use it, then you may send it to another paper.

Out-of-state newspapers will consider opinion pieces from writers in other parts of the country, but many editors are interested only in local viewpoints from unknown authors.

The newspaper market is entirely different from the magazine market, which publishes less frequently and has more specific needs. Timeliness is of utmost importance in newspaper writing, and though editors look for good writing, they will often take a piece somewhat less polished than one aimed for a magazine. If a newspaper editor receives an opinion piece based on a personal experience that is particularly heartwarming or gut-wrenching—like a Holocaust victim's memoir— even though it doesn't quite fit his format, he may still accept it just because the topic strikes a nerve.

2. Go light on the "I."

The best kind of opinion articles—and the easiest to read and follow—are those that express intelligent viewpoints without whining, ranting, or preaching. Sometimes, the pieces that are the most fun to write are those that whine, rant, and preach—but they make you sound as if you are on the attack, rather than expressing an objective, informed, intelligent opinion. If you think it's difficult to give an opinion without editorializing or writing emotionally, do your best *to avoid using the pronoun "I."* Look at this excerpt from a published article about 76-year-old astronaut John Glenn:

> So, NASA took it upon their genius selves to come up with something new. A gimmick for the next millennium. Let's get the oldest guy we can find, they said, someone who used to be an astronaut—someone who is still a hero to many of us—and stick him into space.

This is obviously not a verbatim account. It is just how I imagined a NASA employee might come up with the idea of putting John Glenn into space. But nowhere in those few sentences did I say, "*my* opinion is," or "here's what *I* think"; I avoided the use of "I" and focused attention directly on the issue. In addition, the use of "we" in editorials invites camaraderie with the reader. It also can inspire strong letters to the editor—the comments of those who do not agree with your opinion. Not necessarily a bad thing, as controversy sells papers.

3. Use humor whenever possible.

If you read the works of writers like Andy Rooney, who often addresses serious subjects with humor, you'll find there's a rhythm to it. Funny line, funny line—and then, boom! Right to the heart of the matter—suddenly serious to grab the reader's attention.

Ask yourself, why is this subject interesting? What is funny about it? How is it ironic? Irony—a sophisticated form of humor—is very important when it comes to offering opinions. If you read the op-ed page in any newspaper, you will find at least one article in which the author has used examples of irony—which often highlight the hypocrisy of politicians, actors, and other public figures.

4. Add verifiable statistical information and direct quotes.

Doing this will back up your opinion. In writing a longer, assigned article about the growing crime rate among young people, I added some quotes from politicians, as well as statistical information about the rate of growth of that particular area of crime. All this factual information was used to back up what was strictly an opinion piece. Not that my opinion on the causes of youthful crime wasn't rooted in fact—but it sounded more authoritative once I had the experts to back me up. Make sure your sources for statistical information and quotes are reliable. Any editor will appreciate your ability to do your own research.

5. Quote the experts.

What are you going to write about? I have a friend who has limitless material for her opinion pieces. As a woman, she writes about the unending supply of women's issues, and as a career counselor, she is also an expert in a field related to a large number of social issues. Do you have expert knowledge about something? Isn't one of the first rules of writing to write what you know?

6. Anticipate anniversaries.

Take note of anniversary dates for events that are of significant cultural importance: Roe *v.* Wade, the first moon landing, the 1994 Northridge earthquake, Woodstock. Where were you when John F. Kennedy was shot? What does the civil rights movement mean to you—how were you affected? How does it affect you today? For newspapers, submit this type of article two to three weeks in advance of the anniversary dates. And if your piece is very personal, it's O.K. to use the "I" word. Many magazines also want a personal focus. Study issues of magazines like *Woman's Day* and *Newsweek*, both of which accept free-lance op-ed submissions.

7. Don't cover "tired" topics.

Avoid writing about what has been overdone—unless you have a *fresh* viewpoint. Be realistic. Nobody wants to hear what you have to say about the Princess Di tragedy *unless you were in the car next to hers at the time of the crash.* Take timely issues, as I did with the diet drug Phen-Fen, and put a different spin on them. The medical problems with the drug itself were big news, but I wrote an article about those who got rich from it. It was a subject people were talking about, but I had not seen that aspect addressed in the papers.

8. Scour the papers for obscure news items.

Use small news items as a way to focus on the bigger picture. I recently read an article about a Good Samaritan who offered to help a stranded motorist. The motorist actually commanded his dog to attack the Good Samaritan. A salable opinion piece for this news story might be that it sometimes doesn't pay to help someone in need.

I once wrote about a public figure who made an insulting remark to a radio news reporter he thought was pregnant. Based on a tiny article buried in the middle pages of the paper, one I felt was deserving of further attention, my piece commented on people's lack of tact when it comes to many personal issues.

9. Don't say too much.

The approximate length of a newspaper op-ed is 600 to 750 words. Certainly, if you are assigned an article with a specific word count, or if you are writing a piece for a section of a magazine that typically runs a certain length, don't exceed the required number of words. If you go on too long, you run the risk of rambling. Avoid tackling too many aspects of one issue. If the article is too short, however, perhaps it is not a worthwhile subject for a complete piece, and you may include more than one aspect of the topic.

Submit your newspaper articles via mail, fax, or e-mail, if editors accept submissions in that form. Follow up with a phone call. Sometimes editors get busy, so you have to call or write them to inquire about the status of your submission; if an editor doesn't let you know soon that he can't use your article, it may be dated by the time you're able to submit it elsewhere. If your piece is accepted, call or e-mail to thank the editor.

Payment for newspaper shorts ranges from $25 to $100 for a 600-word piece, with $50 being average.

10. Write fast.

Timeliness is crucial for most newspaper opinion pieces. It takes me about two hours to write a 600-word article—maybe a little longer for extra editing—then I immediately fax it to the newspaper for consideration. If you are writing about a current news story as an unknown writer, you must try to get your piece on the editor's desk *first*—before syndicated writers send their stories over the wires. The advantage you have is that syndicated writers are generally not aware of what is going on in your community.

The rewards for writing a newspaper opinion piece far outweigh those few critical letters to the editor your words may incite. The positive feedback you'll receive, along with the occasional check, make it worthwhile to share your views with newspaper readers.

❑ Poetry

❏ 69

THE INSTANT OF KNOWING

BY JOSEPHINE JACOBSEN

I AM NEITHER SO IMPERTINENT NOR SO NAÏVE AS TO WORK TOWARD A definition of poetry, but I want to tell a story, a true story that implies as much of a definition as I have come by.

The center of everything is the poem. Nothing is important in comparison to that. Anything that in some valid way is not directly connected with that current of energy which is the poem is dispensable.

The naming of things, which is the poet's function, is not, like a science, progressive. It is circular, and each passage of the circle is unique.

Often the poet brings back very little from the instant of knowing. Sometimes—rarely—he brings back something that combines two worlds: something germane to what Yeats called "the artifice of eternity"—the made and the eternal. Such poetry may wear any mode: the august, the raucous, the witty, the tragic. Nothing could matter less. Poetry is energy, and it is poetic energy that is the source of that instant of knowing that the poet tries to name. The test for the true poetic energy is, it seems to me, the only universal test that can be applied to poetry.

In the process of naming things, the poet is caught at once in the problem of naming his own time, the problem of what was called "relevancy" until that word's exhaustion gave everyone empathetic fatigue. In naming his own time, the poet may be one of those rare writers who reach community in a working solitude, though seldom in a personal one. Ionesco writes: "For solitude is not *separation* but *meditation*, and we know that social groups . . . are most often a collection of solitary human beings. . . ."

For solitary writers, the group experience in the pursuit of their own work is a negative experience. They work alone; the poem's inception and execution is as secret as a film's development in a darkroom. They learn, ravenously, from their fellows, their betters, the great dead, their own guts; from talk, from print, by osmosis; but they are not, and can never be, group members. Most poets, on the other hand, as John Ciardi pointed out, have at some phase of their working life as poets been part of a group, and these have the stimulation and reinforcement that fly like sparks from the contact with congenial minds with the same general approach, objectives, and dislikes. But groups can also generate group-think—that curious amalgam that bounces back and forth, carrying always some measure of other-directed debris.

The brief story I want to tell is completely concerned with that energy and how it travels and the mysterious fact that certain words, in a certain arrangement, and with a certain cadence, start up a chain reaction explained by nothing in the words themselves or in their content.

Once, after a speech I gave, a hot controversy arose as to what degree of analysis of a poem is possible without destroying the life of the poem. A number of teachers in the audience felt that poems could be, and were, dismembered to the point of death. Others held out, very stoutly indeed, for the belief that the more you studied the poem, the more it meant to you. I understand very well the first point of view, having some years ago had a class for teachers of poetry who had been so disheartened by the poetry analysis to which they themselves as students had been subjected, that they cordially disliked poetry and were now trying to learn to reapproach it. On the other hand, it is impossible to denigrate the joy and comprehension that come from a close textual reading. It seems to me that the solution of the basic problem—as Robert Frost has pointed out—lies in acknowledging as the most important element that point of mystery which is the core of the poem, that untranslatable quasar that can never fully be put into the prose of exposition. Certain words, in a certain cadence.

"Ah sunflower! weary of time, who countest the steps of the Sun." It would be impossible to find simpler or more daily words. Or, "I have been one acquainted with the night." It is something that is not music and is not talk and is both; but what it does, every single time, is touch the nerve that knows. It is, literally, an instant of knowing—of something simultaneously strange and familiar; something already known but now discovered.

More than fifty years ago, on a cold autumn afternoon, my husband and I were exploring some of the small side roads in the northern mountains of New Hampshire. One such road went over the crest of a hill and past a small and thoroughly overgrown cemetery, which obviously hadn't been used in the past decade. We stopped the car, and got out, and started wandering around in the tall grass, reading some of the tombstones. Some of them were tilted at angles, and some had lost letters to the weather. They said all the usual things—"Beloved wife of . . ." "He giveth his beloved rest . . ." A few said "Infant Son" or "Infant Daughter," and there were quite a lot of children. It was cold in the wind, and we started back to our car. Just before we got to the gate, which was rusted and rather lopsided, I saw a carving of a pair of clasped hands, on a leaning stone, and stooped down to look at the inscription. There was a woman's name but no relationship, and under the name and the date were carved two lines of poetry. They said:

> It is a fearful thing to love
> What Death can touch.

Eleven words, ten of them monosyllables. Immediately I thought, I know those lines; but I didn't, in the sense of placing them, and neither did my husband, though he had had exactly the same sense of recognition. They hung in my mind as though every hour they were going to place themselves. I quoted them a few times to people I thought might recognize them; always there was the same reaction: "Yes, I know that . . ." But no one did.

A few months later, I wrote a longish and unsatisfactory poem about a wartime cemetery, and in it, I quoted the epitaph from the tombstone. Later, I forgot about the poem, but I didn't forget the two lines I did not write; they were there.

About four or five years later, after an illness, I came home from the hospital and found some piled-up issues of *Commonweal*. Leafing through them, I noticed a review of a play that had just opened in New York, by a poet whose work had interested me when I saw his Pulitzer Prize-winning play, *Hogan's Goat*. The poet was William Alfred and the verse-play under review was his *Agamemnon*. The review, a very favorable one, after praising the poetry and the stature of the play, went on to say that the play reached its climax in Cassandra's cry, "It is a fearful thing to love what death can touch."

I don't think I have ever had such an eerie sensation. I kept reading the words over, waiting for them to change in some particular. Then I sat down, in a sort of superstitious panic, and wrote a letter to William Alfred, and asked him where he had gotten those two lines, as I had a special reason for wanting to know. He wrote back at once to say that evidently the copy of the published play, which he had sent me, hadn't arrived. It came in the next day, and there was a note in the front which said that Cassandra's cry, "It is a fearful thing to love what death can touch," was from a poem by Josephine Jacobsen and had been quoted to him by C. Page Smith, the historian.

When I was preparing this piece, I did what I had waited many years to do—I wrote to William Alfred and asked him what, exactly, he remembered. This is what he wrote me, as new to me then as it is to you now:

> It was Columbus Day, 1950. C. Page Smith had arranged a trip under the aegis of Samuel Eliot Morison, to Plymouth, to look at where the Mayflower had first landed. Professor Morison had recently lost his wife. Part of the tour, on that gray cold day, was the graveyard . . . of the pilgrims, on a small hill above the harbor. As we looked out over the sea from the rise, Page told Professor Morison of that poem of yours and of the New Hampshire tombstone . . . it haunted me as it haunts me still.

Those eleven words, put together by an unknown human being, carved by someone's hand on a grassed-over tombstone, in a deserted New Hampshire graveyard, had struck—in a chain of energy, unbelievable but natural—into my mind, then into my poem; had extricated themselves from that inferior substance, and struck through the mind of another writer so forcefully that he had been compelled to speak them to a poet-dramatist, who put them at the core of the poem that was his play; and the reviewer found them rising from that play to arrest him and put them, as the play's climax, onto the page of a magazine, later held by the person who had received their impact from the stone in the grass in the graveyard.

I think that the whole meaning of the instant of knowing lies in that circuit. A knowledge of what we already knew becomes for an instant so devastatingly fresh that it could be contained no more than a flash of lightning. The arrangement of the oldest human fact into certain special sounds, in a certain sequence. It is the thing that cannot be argued with. And I have always felt almost superstitious about the story, because it is such a complete one; it is, to me, of the essence of poetry. Whenever I hear someone trying to define poetry or hear myself working toward a definition, I think of that carved stone sending out its terrible energy to that nerve of knowledge in the hearer, the reader, which transmits it.

This is the live energy that keeps the mass from corruption: the venal poet who writes, the editor who publishes, the critic who analyzes, the reader who reads. What that energy speaks to is our knowledge, but a dormant, denied-by-habit knowledge that is kindled to response in the rare instant.

That energy is the common quality that brings poets together.

❑ 70

THE SHOCK OF GOOD POETRY

BY JANE HIRSHFIELD

WHAT IS THE MEANING OF A "LITTLE" MAGAZINE IN THE LIFE OF poetry in American culture today? Is it a forum for the inquisitive reader to see what is being written, what kinds of thoughts and forms of thought are occupying the minds and hearts of writers both established and unknown? Is it a place for those writers to put their work forward first to the doorkeeping editors, then to readers—a kind of gladiatorial testing ground, perhaps? Is it, as the deconstructionists might pro-pose, a locus for the prevailing cultural tendencies of mind and style to im-pose themselves further, or, as the experimentalist avant-garde might propose, a place where the marginal can find a small space in which to be heard, to wedge a clearing amid established patterns of speech and of being?

These are real questions, even interesting ones, but they are also tired ones. I will confess that when opening the envelopes of poems sent on to me by the unfailingly gracious staff of *Ploughshares*, I did not con-sider my activity as guest editor a chance to impose or explore any theory of art and culture. I did not consider the role of the words I read in regard to the culture at large. I did not consider the role of "poetry," or whether or not it "matters." I did not consider—though I did no-tice—the way certain themes and types of poems recurred from submis-sion to submission. What I considered was the poems: the words on the page, and the effect they had on my heart and mind and body as I let them enter my being. And what I hoped for, each time I turned to a fresh page, was nothing less than to find myself moved and transformed.

Make no mistake: I consider such a moment of transformation a radi-cal event. Radical in both senses of the word—an extraordinary poem requires of its reader a fundamental revolution in being, and also returns the reader to some deep root of being which has been present in us from the start. It may be that both senses are necessary for our survival: We live so much of the time in a state of estrangement from ourselves. Estranged from the possibility of a real knowledge of our own experience, estranged from our own hearts, we wander the hours and years in a kind of day-blindness, lost in the alleyways of an expected life. It is easier, certainly, to navigate a life we believe is predictable, is knowable, is known. And the costs? Bearable—until some event forces us to realize it has all been a dream, a falseness, and we must recover the ability to see not what we wish to see, but what is: a wholly surprising world.

A good poem offers always some entrance into and reminder of the fact that genuine experience is unexpected. A good poem shocks us awake, one way or another—through its beauty, its insight, its music, it shakes or seduces the reader out of the common gaze and into a genuine looking. It breaks the sleepwalking habit in our eyes, in our ears, in our mouths, and sets us adrift in a small raft under a vast night-sky of stars. We feel ourselves moving, too, above a vast, cold-streaming current carrying inner-lit sea creatures, tangles of kelp strands, fishes. Thus we learn the deep clefts of the mid-ocean land-rifts; thus the wave-blanketed mountains rise up before us as islands, a new habitation for heart and mind.

We depart the known ease in order to arrive somewhere other than where we were. We travel by poem, as by any other means, in order to see for ourselves more than was seen.

The record of those travels matters—one person's word-wakened knowledge becomes another's. We seed poems into magazines, into books, onto the Internet, over the radio, whether to be met by two million people or two hundred, because we are beings who learn from one another how to become our full selves. The pages of *Ploughshares*, filled year by year with new poems and new stories chosen by new selectors, matter to me immensely because on any of them I may meet the few words that will suddenly cast me into a widened humanness, a widened knowledge and range of being.

This encounter of words and reader occurs in privacy, in silence; if any of these pages becomes such a moment of liberation for any of its readers, it is unlikely that I or the words' author will ever hear of it. Yet I have utter confidence that the sum of such moments is one of the essential ways that both individuals and cultures move forward—into awakening; into first the recognition of and then responsibility for our kinship with others; into agreement that this life in all its harshness and beauty is one we want not merely to get through blindly, but make our own. And so we say of a good poem, of a good story, "powerful."

Recently, Czeslaw Milosz mentioned to me his theory that Walt Whitman was responsible for the First World War. "You see," he said, "by the end of the nineteenth century, Whitman began to be widely translated, and all the young revolutionaries of Europe read eagerly and took to heart this new cry for democratic being . . ." Then there is the letter I once received from a woman who had read *The Ink Dark Moon*:* "I heard in those ancient poems what was missing from my life, and ended my marriage." I remember, too, my own return from a period of prolonged depression, a dark hibernation of being; after months of not reading anything, I found one voice I could tolerate—Rilke's. Slowly, surely, his intimate, inward murmuring guided me back to the terrifying shoals of aliveness.

I offer this powerful and dangerous thing into your hands, a "little" magazine. It has been a pleasure to be part of its coming into existence.

---

* *The Ink Dark Moon* is a collection of translations by Jane Hirshfield of two women poets of the 9th- and 10th-century Japanese Court, who were among the creators of the Japanese lyric.

❏ 71

STARTING A POEM

BY PETER MEINKE

MOST BEGINNING POETS DON'T HAVE TROUBLE STARTING A POEM; YOU probably have started hundreds. It's *finishing* a poem that's difficult, and more challenging. But sometimes everyone gets stuck: the dread writer's block.

I no longer worry about this, knowing from experience that a little fallow time is sometimes needed, to let the soil rejuvenate. The Romantic poets had a favorite metaphor for creativity, the Aeolian harp—a harp with stretched strings often placed in windows so that when the wind blew, it would make music. Many of these poets looked upon themselves as writers who waited passively for inspiration to blow through them:

> And what if all of animated nature
> Be but organic Harps diversely framed,
> That tremble into thought, as o'er them sweeps
> Plastic and vast, one intellectual breeze,
> At once the Soul of each, and God of all?
> (from "The Eolian Harp," by Samuel Taylor Coleridge)

Well, we *are* harps, and inspiration is real, but we can fan the breeze a little ourselves. The first way is to relax and be patient. Something will come, the breeze will pick up again. To help this along, however, it's good to have a regular time and place for writing poems. Just as you can train yourself to remember dreams, you can train yourself to be receptive to the poetic ideas circulating around and inside you.

A notebook can be a great help; just pick a phrase out of it, transfer it to your computer, or typewriter, or legal pad, and see what comes. The simple act of carrying a notebook around and writing in it can make you a more observant person, and more likely to write poetry.

Poets are natural spies and eavesdroppers; they should be seers (*see-ers*), as well.

Figure out whether silence or music sparks your creative energy. I need silence before I can concentrate, but many writers prefer working while listening to music, usually classical. Hart Crane was famous for writing his poems to the strains of Ravel's "Bolero"; Frank O'Hara turned on Rachmaninoff concertos. I've known several city poets who couldn't write in the country: too quiet, or the birds and crickets bothered them.

Poetry can and does get written anywhere, and under any conditions. Some poets write standing up, some write in bed, many have written in prison, but it makes sense to help your writing along however you can. If you have a place where you regularly go to write—spending hours and hours in a room of your own—you should make it comfortable: a good chair at the right height to avoid back problems or carpal tunnel syndrome; a desk with enough room to spread out; a good light; a window (unless you're like Marcel Proust and prefer a cork-lined room); the usual supplies: pencils, pens, paper, envelopes, stapler, Scotch tape, scissors, calendar.

I have a file cabinet, which every poet needs after writing for several years: drafts, letters from editors, letters from writers, correspondence, articles to save, deadlines. The business of poetry churns out a lot of paperwork!

You may like some pictures or photos on your desk and walls. On my wall there's a blown-up photograph my wife took of Yeats's tombstone in Drumcliff churchyard: "Cast a cold eye / On life, on death. / Horseman, pass by!" Also on my wall is a James Thurber sketch of himself and a poster/photograph of my favorite artist, Camille Pissarro. A couple of beer coasters from Neuchâtel protect the much-scarred desk from new coffee stains. It's far from plush, but it's comfortable; it's the place I go to write.

The need, as always, is to be able to clear your mind and concentrate, and try to sink deep within yourself to find the poem, which can appear from anywhere. Robert Frost said, "A poem begins as a lump in the throat, a sense of wrong, a homesickness, a lovesickness. . . . It finds the thought and the thought finds the word." Sometimes you can't control your surroundings, and you just have to give writing your best shot, from wherever you are.

Recipe

Let's say you want to write a poem
yes?
a good poem maybe not The Second Coming but
your hair is getting thin already and
where's your Dover Beach?

Everything seems somehow out of reach
no?
all of a sudden everyone's walking faster than you and
you catch yourself sometimes staring not at girls

You live in at least two worlds
yes?
one fuzzy one where you always push
the doors that say pull and
one clear cold one where you live alone

This is the one where your poem is
yes?
no
It's in the other one
tear your anthologies into small pieces
use them as mulch for your begonias and
begin with your hands

(first published in *Poetry*)

This poem speaks for itself, but I can perhaps get it to talk faster by saying a little about it. The image of the poet isolated in his or her own world is pervasive in our society: the "clear cold one where you live alone." And it's true that for the most part, you're alone when writing. But Yeats was right when he wrote, in "The Circus Animals' Desertion," "I must lie down where all the ladders start, / In the foul rag-and-bone shop of the heart." That is to say, poems should come from the crowded real world, not the rarefied romantic one. And although you should read as much as you can of the great poets who have gone before you, if you hope to write poetry over any length of time, you must also grow *out* of the anthologies and find your own voice. Your poems must emerge from your own experience, even—or perhaps particularly—from your most painful experience. So "begin with your hands" means you should 1) sit down and begin to write, and 2) dig into the roots of your own life (the anthologies will make excellent mulch).

"Recipe" also has a subliminal message: *Poetry is that special language with which much care is taken.* Although the lines may seem to be written in light chatty free verse, closer inspection will show it's not all that "free." Rhymes or near-rhymes link the stanzas (beach/reach, girls/worlds, alone/poem). The next-to-last line of each stanza ends with the conjunction "and." A five-line structure is repeated up to the last stanza when the two-line reversal ("no/It's in the other one") extends that stanza to seven. Also notice the alliteration (cold/clear, begonias/begin), the odd hyphenation (walk-/ing), the disjointed sentence structure ("staring not at girls").

All of these details represent decisions I had to make, ideas I had, effects—successful or not—that I was consciously striving for while writing "Recipe." The reader shouldn't even be aware of them, at least not at first. But they're important. They make the poem a poem.

Your story is interesting to you because of what happened. What will make your story interesting to others is the way you tell it. What you should always be looking for when starting a poem is finding and using fresh language. In "Recipe," the perky "yes/no" structure with its reversal was enough to get me going. Almost all poets have their "Writing a Poem" poem—there must be thousands of them!—so why add another? My job as a writer was to make it verbally lively, funny, sad, helpful—*worth reading.* Some poems aren't worth reading, just as, in a sense, some people aren't worth meeting, although these judgments and reactions vary widely with the individual. To make your poem readable, attack it, as you begin, with the same physical intensity and pleasure that a child uses working with Play-Doh, or building blocks, putting it together a handful at a time. The energy that goes into writing your poem will be the energy that shines out of it.

Many writers, finding themselves stuck, are able to get going again by concentrating on some ordinary object around them. I might look out my window and describe the live oak there. Two kinds of Spanish moss, hanging and balled, cling to it. A limb looks dead. A bald patch is spreading on the main trunk. One limb is much longer than the others, reaching toward the sun; a bluejay on it is eyeing a mockingbird with suspicion. I can say so much about this tree! You can do the same with a waste basket or a bottle of Liquid Paper or the wires leading to your electric outlets. Poems begin with close observation, so the act of describing something within view is a good exercise, and with luck and care, you can find yourself writing a real poem.

One other suggestion I should add about starting. Write as fast as you can think and feel, uncritically, for as long as you can. Just let it all flow out. See where the poem's going, and try to get there. Afterwards, you can take all the time you want to rewrite.

I mentioned before that I often write past the point that I need to; when I reread what I've written, I see I've repeated myself, or spelled out the obvious. Usually in rewriting, my poems shrink. Of course, many poets don't work that way. Apparently Dylan Thomas would labor all morning on a single line, perfect it, and then head to the pub. The next day, another line, and so on until a poem was done. But most poets do it the other way around: Write the first draft fast, then spend however much time it takes on making a poem out of it.

Beginning a poem may be like diving into a strange lake. You can look all you want, you can prepare all morning, you can study the water, you can stick your toe in, but sooner or later you have to jump. This takes courage, as does any important act that has no guarantee of a successful conclusion. Still, when you hit that water and look around, there's nothing else quite so exciting.

□ 72

Becoming a Poet

By Diana O'Hehir

Talking becomes poetry as walking becomes dancing," wrote poet Josephine Miles in her introduction to *The Poem, A Critical Anthology* (Prentice-Hall). "It takes on form to give shape to a mood or an idea."

Yes. We've all felt that. During those moments of pure felicity when poetry welled up and became our natural medium, when writing seemed loving and straightforward, a natural activity. But what about those other times when writing was difficult? How do you not only become a poet, but how do you keep on being one?

It's the first day of a fall course I'm teaching called "Creative Writing. Poetry." "How many of you," I ask, "are poets?"

My naïve question produces only three raised hands. I don't ask how many of the others here would *like* to be poets; instead, I start inquiring about what difficulties are imagined. And in no time I have a long list, most of its items familiar:

"How do I get started?"

"I used to write. Now I can't."

"How do I know I'm any good?"

Yes, almost everyone in this varied group (the ages range from seventeen to fifty-five) would like to be a poet. But fear of poetry—"because it's so difficult . . . so important . . . so different . . ." is a major complaint of this class.

"I don't have any ideas. When my life's not dramatic, I don't know what to write about."

"Somebody said, write your dreams. But I don't remember my dreams." At this point I ask everyone to grab a sheet of paper and list seven objects she really hates. "Objects, artifacts from ordinary life that irritate you, gizmos that won't do their job or get in your way. Things you really feel strongly about. Stuff that springs to mind when I say

360

hate. You can see them clearly. Remember, you're listing objects, not human beings, not events. Things you can touch and see—clock-radio, television set, purple scarf, leaky ballpoint pen."

The class settles in with enthusiasm to list stuff they hate. "No," I answer a question, "your list isn't a poem, though it looks something like it on the page. But if you choose one of those hated items—the one you see most vividly, whose physical details you know best—you'll probably be able to write about it. And maybe that's the beginning of a poem."

A hand goes up. "Somebody said that if I wrote a poem that rhymed you wouldn't let me stay in the class."

This question produces such enormous issues of craft, discipline, originality, and control, calls for such a long lecture on form, its use and abuse, that I move on completely. "Now," I announce enthusiastically, "we're going to look at some poems by professional poets, poems that will give you a lift; you'll notice that one of the most beautiful and moving of these is rhymed throughout."

I've been writing poetry all my life and some of the students are just about to begin, but our problems are much the same. We face issues of self-worth and of dogged application, questions of how to keep going. (Remember that Emily Dickinson had only five poems published in her lifetime; William Blake printed his own poems by hand and died a pauper.) At home now, after my class, I'm drawing up a mental list, a list for myself. It's short and stupid and obvious; it includes a series of instructions to myself and a list of recipes to overcome block.

The recipes at least are specific and direct. They sound simple-minded; they don't always work, but they're a place to begin.

First, here's an anti-block measure that we all know: Find a friend, at least one friend to whom you can show your work. This person should ideally be another writer with whom you trade reactions. And it helps if the friend (a) likes your work; (b) is not too competitive; and (c) writes a lot, so that he or she is eager for you to show up with your poems.

And second (related and also simple-minded), get yourself into a group of writers. Choose this group with enormous care. Not too large a group, one with some people your own age, people whose work you respect, and at least one of whom is a better poet than you. Writers who offer genuine criticism but aren't destructive. Not at all. Not the least little bit!

There are lots of small anti-block devices. Sometimes these work; often they don't.

Vary your routine. If you use a computer, try a yellow pad. Pen instead of pencil. Different chair, different table, back to light instead of facing the view, etc.

Vary your routine *dramatically.* Leave home, go to San Francisco or Hoboken and sit in a park. Claim a table in a coffeehouse. Public libraries are great for composition; if you're like me, you feel enclosed and comforted by public libraries.

Imitate. Read voraciously and then shamelessly imitate a poet whom you really respect. After a while, you may get the surprise of finding you sound like that poet, but different, good in your own way.

Imitate *other* **art (not writing).** Music, painting, sculpture, architecture? I don't mean to write *about* these arts, but to try to reinterpret them. What would a poetic version of the *Nabucco* Hebrew Chorus be like? Of the Vietnam Memorial?

Use a newspaper headline as a first line of a poem. (Or a quote. Or someone else's first line. Or a line of instruction for your computer/shampoo/pancake mix.)

And so on, and on. Look out your window and react, in poetry, to the first thing you see. Write about your dreams. If you don't remember dreams, get a reproduction of a surrealist painting—Dali, di Chirico, Chagall, or whoever—and try to describe it. Write a letter in poetry to someone you hate, to somebody you used to love, or to someone you loved too late. *From* someone you've wronged. Obviously, all these devices are tricks to get you started. Maybe some of them will produce meaningful work, maybe none will, but you *will* be writing, if only briefly.

So, what good are tricks? Well, anything that works, works. But beyond such questions as "How do I get some words on the page *today?*"

are fundamental issues of commitment and address: Why are we doing this? How do I make myself feel like a poet?

Back home in my room, I translate my class's questions into a more simple catch-all question for myself: How do I keep going?

Read, I tell myself. Read poetry, lots of it, poems that are strange and thorny, that make my scalp prickle. (That's how Alice B. Toklas knew she was in the presence of genius.) Read many other works, too, the more difficult and challenging, the better. I'm lazy; I like to ignore this straightforward instruction. But on the few occasions when I follow it I'm really happiest, glowing with a sense of Calvinist rightness, fighting with ideas that stretch my mind. Not knowledge I can copy or imitate, but astronomy, geology, physics (I don't understand that one at all), philosophy. Beside me is a stack of books that I need to review each time I pick them up.

Difficult reading can lead to poetry; exotic flotsam can surface unexpectedly. "Almost always my poems begin with a small scrap of language," William Matthews says, "—a few words or an image."* And he goes on to make a comparison between deep-sea diving and poetic process.

A second instruction to myself involves honesty. It sounds feeble-minded to say *try to be completely honest with yourself; don't tell lies to yourself.* Of course we're honest; who fakes inside the safe haven of her own writing? Well, I do. I'm not talking about creative invention and imagination, which are absolutely necessary. I'm talking about dis-honesty in recognizing my own true attitudes. I pretend I can write in a fashionable style that's not mine. Or I pretend to a point a view, not mine, which might get me published. Oddly enough, these efforts never work; poems written that way are bad and weak, imitations of imita-tions; I know this and so does the editor of the magazine I'm hoping to fool.

Editors of magazines? Publication? How do you get published? There are, of course, simple rules about the way a manuscript should look, about knowing the magazine you're submitting your poems to. But, if you want to keep going, to think of yourself as a poet, do that sending out automatically and then forget it. Ridiculous? Impossible? Yes, al-

---

*From *50 Contemporary Poets: The Creative Process.* Alberta T. Turner, Editor. (David McKay and Co.)

most. But watching the mailbox is highly destructive. Maybe you can trade duties with a friend: "I'll send yours, you send mine." This friend who reads your work *is* publication; remind yourself of that. And that thrill from getting published lasts only about ten minutes.

My final instruction to myself is one some poets don't agree with, but I find it essential. Edit. Everyone has an editorial personality as well as a creative, intuitive one. Don't let that editorial personality interfere with your original creative process. At the time of inspiration, the editorial self can be an anti-muse that stops you before you start. But go back later, after a month, a year, and review rigorously, with all the honesty and judgment you have. Be thorough and incisive. Forgive nothing. There's a liberating sense of rightness that comes when a poem finally meets your own exact standards. Marvin Bell says, "I remember carrying a draft of the poem, at first on yellow sheets, later, ironically, a Xerox of a draft—on trips, finally, all the way to Europe. I let it lie, awaiting a clear perspective. . . . I wanted the poem to speak as the objects and occasions had spoken to me: haltingly, correctingly, without a posed moment to make famous."

We're back to Josephine Miles's statement about poetry, that it gives shape or mood to an idea. What a simple, unassuming concept, and what a fantastically ambitious and disturbing one. No wonder we poets are excited and disturbed by our job.

□ 73

THE POET AS HYBRID MEMOIRIST

BY MOLLY PEACOCK

FOR SOME PEOPLE KEEPING THEIR GIRLHOOD PROMISES MAKES A DEFINI-tion of hell on earth, but abiding by my promises became a definition of heaven. By the age of eight I had already decided: a) not to have children, b) to marry Humankind's Best Friend (I had my eye on the collie down the street), c) to become a painter with an easel and a real beret, and d) to use at least gigantic, at best colossal words. Now it is a deep pleasure to glance up at my husband (whom I can easily call my best friend), then look across the desk to see the four books of poetry I've written, and know that I've become a word-painter—sans easel and beret. But when I wrote my fifth book, a memoir called *Paradise, Piece by Piece* all about the choices I've made in my life, I had to learn a new skill—writing prose. Like a painter attempting to make a sculpture, I didn't know at first how to construct a prose book.

Should I, like a sociologist, conduct interviews about how *other* people made crucial choices? Or, like a journalist, make a cultural essay? Or was I really on a poet's search, a quest for understanding? I quickly realized that I couldn't do interviews and cull statistics. I would have to use a poet's skills.

One way poets understand what they discover is by tenderly examining that discovery with words. This examination must have the lightest touch—the poet as physician, with deft hands. The process of describing, even though it is exterior, draws on the deeply unconscious interior of the describer. My challenge was to examine aspects of my life unmentioned and buried; I would have to feel my way toward them, relying on my senses and intuitions to provide language for my descriptions. So much in the culture would have you fight or ignore your own instincts that it is a relief and an adventure to have only them to trust.

Even though I was planning to write about how I came to construct my life as an adult, I knew I had to go to the place where the senses are sharpest: childhood. When I entered scenes of my growing up in working-class Buffalo in the 1950s and in rural upstate New York, my senses rang with truths, and I began hearing again what I had forgotten for decades, the voices of my family imprinted from long ago. I was their duckling.

As soon as I made myself small, crouched under the kitchen table on the green linoleum floor where I often played with my coloring books and crayons, I could picture the feet on the floor, taste the wax of the crayon I wasn't supposed to put in my mouth, and most importantly, hear their voices. Critics have wondered how people can put dialogue in their memoirs—surely they don't remember the actual words and their sequence. But as a poet learns to listen to deeply internal rhythms, I listened to the deeply internalized voices of my family. I could "hear" them speak. I could mimic them the way only a child mimics a parent or a teacher, with—as any teacher knows—appalling accuracy. Thus, as I remembered each situation and reinserted myself into it, remaking myself small, reattuning myself to the feelings of being in that place and at that time, I reheard their voices, now coming out of my own heart, that is, my own mouth. (Sometimes my heart *was* in my mouth as I felt my way into my past.) I discovered that what I heard was crucial to the assembling of the reasons for my most unusual choice to be childfree—especially when I remembered the voices of the grownups as they reiterated, "Don't ever have children, Molly," and all the contradictory feelings I felt when that statement was repeated.

Thus, the dialogue I made up for the memoir isn't "invented" like the dialogue of a novel; it is reconjured from an attunement with the past. I do know the difference, because later on in the writing of my book, I created characters and did indeed invent dialogue. I found myself writing a hybrid memoir, one that incorporated fictional characters. I wanted to be careful of other people's privacy, even though, as a poet who has used my life freely in my work, I understood I would be interrupting my own.

But how would my apprehensions become a book? Would the discoveries be discrete and individual, like poems? Surely not, I worried, afraid of putting a big, huge prose book together. Surely so, another voice inside me said, why not use the same principle? So I did what anyone does to get a big job done: made the book step by step. I would go to a place and time in my life and just start writing; because I'd picked a certain moment, the writing had a natural border. Then, like beads, I began stringing the sections together. Of course, I made many of these "necklaces" over time. After all, the book took me six years to write—just about as long as a book of my poems takes. But each time I reassembled the pieces of the book, I was reacknowledging, and coming first to understand, and then to love, all the people and circumstances of my life, even the really terrible ones.

As a matter of fact, it was the terrible times I started off with. The first scene I wrote was where my Dad, in a rage, tears off the legs of the maple kitchen table after throwing a hot pan of corn at the wall, just missing my head. These times were dark beads, blue-black like lapis lazuli. I did not have the gold beads, the humor, the love and friendship, the art that I also joyfully experienced and embodied. The early "necklaces" had grouped all the things that prevented me from developing normally in a relentless line before me. Seeing them made me understand a crucial aspect of my choice not to have children: I had not made only a reactive, negative decision; this was the dark side of a galaxy that was also lit by positive choices, ambitions, and desires.

When I began to supply the light to the book, I wrote about the funny, happy, spiritual, and sloppily artistic side of my personality and my life. Suddenly I was laughing out loud. This humor swathed cold situations with the love that became apparent to me only after I realized how only partially true the coldness was.

And there had been aspects of my life that were obscure to me because I had a full palette. All the pieces were coming into place, especially that essential aspect of being that my first tries had ignored: spirituality. Now religion, with all my goofy interpretations, and art, the activity that had saved my life by enabling me to focus, were vitally present as choices toward a healthy whole. I was getting a complete picture—and I had really become a complete woman: a poet, a wife, a friend, a daughter, a sister, a teacher, a public person with opinions and goals she understood with zest and without apology.

As my roles became clear to me, so did aspects of certain characters. And this is where the novelistic side to this nonfiction book comes in. My goal of concentrating on the many facets of a single issue made me up the level of craft from beading to the techniques of the jeweler. Not only did I have to give emeralds their complex faces, I had to provide settings for them. Because my parents and sister were dead, I felt I could set them in a context that would tell the truth because I was free to explore the ambiguities of love and hatred that made our family what it was. My husband Mike, a literature professor, understood very well what my work was all about, and he both trusted and permitted me to say anything I wanted about him. My cousin, likewise, trusted me to represent him as he was. My friends also trusted me, but who was I to tell their stories baldly and from the outside? Now the book was becoming more of an artful enterprise, full of themes, motifs, and balancing. I have many and varied friends. Could they all be given appropriate character portraits and numbers of pages? Could I remain loyal and also air their stories? In response, I melded composites of all my dearest friends into two characters, Maggie and Lily. Opposing them is another fictional character, the novelist Mariah Moore. She is a product of all the negative voices that were inside me, the noisy jury of criticism in my head. My poet's training in narrowing, and structuring, was at work, creating a hybrid memoir that took the excitement of scenes from my life and set them against the decisions—sometimes wacky, sometimes wise—that resulted.

Yet I hated the idea of precious "poetic" prose. I wanted to write straight to the heart of an ordinary reader, because I myself am an ordinary human who found herself under extraordinary pressure. This demanded metaphor.

Single metaphors, infrequently placed so that they pop up in the landscape like errant flowers, let each character bloom. When my sister—in an antique beaded flapper dress and bare dirty feet—accosts me in an Upper East Side supermarket, she winks one conspiratorial eye, "just like a macaw." With that comparison, she becomes the complex person she was: bred in a kind of jungle, but willing, within her own wildness, to become a tame pet. Very often in poetry, when an animal is evoked, the "natural" self of the speaker is about to appear.

I had to turn the light of metaphor on myself, too. Food and sex, the signs of life, flourish everywhere in *Paradise, Piece by Piece*. Was I conscious of these metaphors? Oh, yes—and no. Once I found myself using them, I tried to continue. Our intuition operates in spite of us, but when we become aware of it, and let it guide us through the rest of our conscious life—our freedom shapes our destiny.

The rhythm of language is part of the *hap* of the book. ("Hap" is the

Old English root of "happen" and "happiness" and means "fate" or "fortune.") I began *Paradise, Piece by Piece* just after I reunited with my lost lover from high school, the man who, a year later, would become my husband. To rest in the grasp of a love that went its own secret way through a wilderness of years and suddenly revealed itself, gave intimate meaning to my experience of fate and hap. And so I was able to write through the panoply of feelings in all the stages of my life so far—smelling, touching, and tasting them.

❑ 74

A Serious Look at Light Verse

By Rosemarie Williamson

I HAVE BEEN WRITING AND SELLING LIGHT VERSE FOR NEARLY THIRTY years. As an art school graduate (who had always enjoyed humorous writing), I had been undecided about my career choice until I enrolled in a creative writing course at a then-nearby New Jersey university. When my professor, who was both knowledgeable and enthusiastic, happened to spot a few of my verses lying around on the table beside my assignment pad, she got very excited. "These are great," she said. "Send them out—flood the market!"

I will never forget her words. I did indeed send my light verse out, to two of the markets she had suggested. To my utter amazement, within a week I received an acceptance from both *Good Housekeeping* magazine and *The Saturday Evening Post*. Hallelujah—I was hooked!

An early acceptance by *The Saturday Evening Post* was "Cost Plus":

> She sells
> Sea shells
> By the sea shore.
> Sam sells
> Clam shells
> For a bit more.

A sale to *Good Housekeeping* from the same period was "Mob Psychology":

> You join the bargain-hunting group,
> Grabbing and unfolding—
> Then find the only thing you want
> Is what some stranger's holding.

This is all well and good, you may be thinking, but how does the verse itself come about? Surely it doesn't evolve full-blown? Not at all. There are a few simple rules to remember, and within these confines, your creativity can run wild. First, you must have a funny idea. (If you find something amusing, chances are others will, too.) Everyday events provide one of the richest sources for humor; the office, supermarket, church, sporting events, shopping mall—all can produce laughable situations.

Possibly the easiest and most common poetic form for humor is the four-line verse, called the quatrain. The quatrain is a neat little package whose length makes it ideal for use as a magazine filler, or for other spots where space is limited. Its brevity is particularly suited to telling a "joke in rhyme," which essentially defines light verse. Making each word count, the first three lines build up to the fourth line, the all-important punch line.

Second in importance is the title, which can serve one or more functions. Titles can provide background material, act as lead-ins, or simply be relevant wordplay. Remember that a clever title is your first chance to catch an editor's eye.

Following are two favorite titles of mine—which may have been instrumental in selling the verses:

Of All the Gauls!

Caesar's legions, so we're told,
Were famous for their marches.
Which may account for Rome today
Being full of fallen arches.

(*The Wall Street Journal*)

Handwriting on the Cave

A caveman's life was fraught with fear,
His world was full of predators,
And it's much the same for modern man,
Except we call them creditors.

(*The American Legion Magazine*)

A word about meter

In a humorous poem the meter (or rhythm or beat) should be regular and simple, to make sure that readers' (or listeners') attention will focus on the words and not be distracted by unexpected changes in rhythm.

Otherwise, double entendres and other forms of wordplay could easily be missed. Irregular and even innovative meter certainly has a place in the poetic scheme of things. Long, rambling epics, elegiac stanzas, and free verse are all perfectly acceptable forms, but they're *not* light verse—whose format is quite different.

Two examples of uncomplicated metric lines come to mind. Familiar to most of us, the first line is from a nursery rhyme, and the second from a Christmas carol:

MAry, MAry, QUITE conTRAry

and its inverse

it CAME upON a MIDnight CLEAR

You will notice that I have capitalized the accented or "stressed" syllables; the unaccented or "unstressed" syllables are in lower case. The first line starts with a stressed syllable, the second with an unstressed one. Either would be a splendid vehicle for light verse. (No need, here, to go into the intricacies of "iambic tetrameter," etc. Life is complicated enough! I just remembered that years ago I wrote a short verse called "They Trod on My Trochee"—which remains unsold!)

So far we have a boffo title and a knee-slapping punch line, but what about the other lines? Not to mention the rhyme scheme—what is appropriate for light verse? The first three lines of a humorous quatrain should provide fodder for the grand finale in the fourth line. If the last line concerns a dog, the build-up lines could be full of canine humor— "Dry Bones," old sayings, puppy puns, etc. When my children were growing up, we had a family dog. Kids-plus-dog inspired the following poem, which ran in *The Saturday Evening Post*:

Dog Days

School is out, the weather's nippy—
They forecast snow; the kids yell "Yippee!"
And greet the flakes with eager glance,
But Fido views the scene askance—
"Although for kids it has its assets,
It's enough to BURY us poor bassets!"

I had more to say about the subject than usual, so I extended it into a set of three couplets.

The most common rhyme scheme for a quatrain is to have the second and fourth lines rhyme. Frequently, the first and third lines also rhyme (but with a different end-rhyme sound from lines #2 and #4). The following verse (which I sold to *The Wall Street Journal*) demonstrates the most common rhyme scheme:

Gag Rule

While dental work for some is painful,
And frequently induces squawking,
My complaint is somewhat different—
It means I have to give up talking!

While you'll be aware of the second/fourth line rhyme in this poem (a copy of which hangs in my dentist's office!), there are other things going on as well. You'll note the dentist-related wordplay of the title. The word "squawking" is funny-sounding—even more so when associated with supposedly mature adults. The last line, however, is the real clincher, with its surprise ending.

Endowed with a good sense of humor, you're already halfway there, and the rest of the trip is fun.

Markets

An investment that's sure to pay long-term dividends is the purchase of a few books: an introduction to poetry that explains basic terms and concepts, as well as that perennial poet's pal, a rhyming dictionary. Public libraries are virtual wellsprings of information about and examples of light verse by well-known humor writers—from the amiable Robert Benchley to the tart-tongued Dorothy Parker.

Several of the so-called slick magazines are good markets for light verse. This can be an off again-on again situation, however, so it's best to check recent issues to determine their current editorial policy.

Literary and college magazines can be good markets for beginning as well as established verse writers. *Cimarron Review,* a publication of Oklahoma State University, bought two of my verses, one of which follows:

From "A" to Zebra

Our kids described their zoo trip to us,
Excitedly, at home that night:
"We saw most animals in color—
But the striped one was in black and white."

A real plus in writing light verse is the fact that the entire process can be just plain FUN! Not many professions can offer such an enticing "perk." With practice, you can learn to view life's little annoyances as raw material for humor—it becomes positively addictive. After writing—and selling—light verse for nearly thirty years, I find the challenge just as exciting today as when I started out, and that's saying quite a bit.

□ 75

WRITING A POEM:
TECHNIQUE AND INTUITION

BY GREG GLAZNER

ANY SUCCESSFUL WRITER NEEDS, AMONG OTHER THINGS, TWO RADI-
cally different abilities: technique and intuition. Technique is learned
consciously; it gives us the ability to make conscious decisions about
craft and criticism. Intuition must be enhanced unconsciously; it makes
use of our attitudes, chance happenings that nevertheless "work" in a
poem, and that baffling experience no one understands and which we
sometimes call "inspiration."

The following exercises focus on technique, but they also encourage
intuitive writing. Exercises are one way of making it possible for poems
to happen *through* us, of getting us in condition for those unpredictable
times when intuition pushes us toward lines we didn't think we were
capable of.

One exercise that helps writers incorporate surprise and spontaneity
in their work was developed by my co-editor at *Countermeasures* magazine, Jon Davis. I sometimes use it in my classes, but it works just as
well for the solitary writer as it does for a group of students.

First, write twenty or so unrelated words and phrases on individual
slips of paper—"In Her Room," "Jungle Plants," and "Cable Television," for example—again, phrases that seem completely unrelated. Select several phrases at random. Now, incorporate the random phrases in
successive lines of a poem. The object is to make the unrelated phrases
relate somehow—through image, tone, style, narrative, or some combination of these. The exercise often produces lines that are surprising
and intuitive, yet oddly coherent as well. These qualities give power to
Jon Davis's own poetry. In this section of his "The Ochre World," I've
italicized connecting words and associations in lines that seem, at first
glance, to leap from one unconnected image to the next: "The *star*-
nosed mole popped out of the earth like a *log*, flopped on its belly. / Its

progress across the hardpan was like the progress of a *canoe* paddled by children. / In Vermont, in summer, my brother and I commandeered our host's *canoe* and paddled into the *starry* night. / If meaning is a stew, these nouns, these verbs, this handful of adjectives must *float* in a broth before they can be digested. / Were we, that night, the *lake's* intelligence?" (This last line is, as well, an allusion to a famous passage in Wordsworth's *Prelude* in which he "borrows" a canoe.)

While this exercise encourages the poet to incorporate unpredictable connections in a poem, I sometimes use a quite different one that sharpens the writer's ear for rhythms. In a class in graduate school that focused on Walt Whitman and Philip Levine, our professor, poet Patricia Goedicke, asked us to take a famous short poem as a model and mimic in a poem of our own every aspect of its rhythms—using the model's syllable count, its placement of accented and unaccented syllables, and the pauses indicated by commas and periods.

The most common difficulty with this exercise is trying to *hear* the play of stressed and unstressed syllables in a poem. If this is the case for you, take this first step: Mark the accented and unaccented syllables of multi-syllabic *words*—not of entire poems. Then check yourself against the dictionary's markings. When you can mark single words successfully, you'll have much less trouble marking lines of poetry. Hearing stressed syllables in a poem is exactly like hearing them in individual words.

I chose section 9 of Whitman's "Song of Myself" as a model because I'd been feeling imprisoned by iambs (˘ ´) and wanted to explore freer rhythmic possibilities. Whitman's last two lines seemed, in particular, both free in their rhythms and extremely well-written. How so? Listen to the play of iambs (˘ ´) and anapests (˘ ˘ ´). "Ĭ júmp frŏm thĕ cróss-beăms ănd seíze thĕ clóveř ănd tímŏthў , / Ănd řoll heád ŏveř heéls ănd tángle mў háir fŭll ŏf wísps." The last two lines of my imitation (opposite in tone, but almost identical in rhythm) went "Ĭ walk tŏ thĕ creék-bĕd ănd tośs iň grável ănd wórrў thiňgs, / Ănd tĕll nó ŏne bŭt crows ănd gráckles hŏw dárklў ĭt góes." Not "finished lines" by a longshot, but the feel of that exercise must have resurfaced to help me later, when I wrote, in iambs, the opening lines of "The Metaphysician's Weekend"—"Tŏ soóthe mўsélf, I've stepped oŭtside, / bŭt éveň heře, it's chemĭstřy: /" and then immediately broke that rhythm with something quite different: "boóze iň thĕ blóodstřeam, thĕ blínd lawn / rísing undĕrnéath m̆e ăs t̆he stréetliğht / ĭs dĕlivéred̆ dŏẃnwărd." Look at all those anapests playing off of the line's other rhythms. The exercise had compelled me to take Whitman's rhythms into my head and send them back out, later, in my poem.

I don't want to overstate the case. Writing several drafts of original poems (I wrote more than fifty drafts of the first section of "The Metaphysician's Weekend") is probably the most important way, overall, to learn to write poetry. But exercises *are* an efficient means for addressing specific aspects of poetry.

One I've invented may help you get past the hurdle that almost all beginning poets struggle with: writing in a stiff, stilted voice.

To begin with, make a tape recording of yourself telling some sort of colorful anecdote. Now play it back and take note of the kinds of words, rhythms, and phrases you used most naturally. That is, take note of the kind of *voice* you've used. For example, you may have used a chummy voice full of farfetched comparisons: "You couldn't have beat sense into his head any more than you could have beat rocket science into a pit bull." You may have leaned on trendy phrases: "He was a totally rad head-banging type of guy with black tattoos and rings hanging out of him everywhere." Maybe you spoke in an earnest voice using emphatic repetitions: "I couldn't say that to her, not with so many people watching us. I just couldn't. There was no way to say anything about it until the next day." (This stage of analysis is even more enjoyable if you can find a writing partner. In this case, you'll analyze each other's voice.) Once you've arrived at a preliminary understanding of the kind of voice you chose naturally, try writing a poem making use of it.

Clearly, the oral voice is not any sort of end-all. Many other kinds of voice might serve you as well. And no one would claim an exercise as an accomplished work of poetry. But I'd count "a rad head-banging type of guy with black tattoos and rings hanging out of him" as a dramatic improvement over "His dark rage, despair, and empty longing were more infinite than the eternal black sky"—the sort of lines beginning writers often come up with before working through the exercise.

Sometimes writers are encouraged to think of technical exercises as a way to generate finished pieces and to publish them or read them in public, if possible. I'd like to suggest a different approach. So much of the focus in the poetry world these days is on quick self-gratification. When you pour your energy into writing a merely competent poem, one that is more or less "publishable" or one that seems to express how you were feeling at a given moment, or a poem flashy enough to conjure up applause at an open mike or a poetry slam—then an atmosphere alien to real poetry takes hold. Narrow self-interest starts to choke everything else out.

But if the growing interest in poetry were to move somehow in a different direction, toward, say, the love of all accomplished writing—no matter who writes it—then the development of technique and intuition through exercises would become steps on a long, rich journey one never completes. If by some extremely unlikely combination of will and inspiration and talent and good luck, you write a poem brilliant enough to last, then obviously, the devotion has been worth the effort. Less obviously, however, even if one's own work falls short, the effort has still been worthwhile. There's still that irreplaceable, strenuous pleasure, that rare kind of understanding we encounter when we take art seriously.

What's wrong with this as a kind of incantation for poets of all stripes?: *We paid attention in great detail to the work we loved, through close reading and sometimes, through imitations. We knew the marvelous singing qualities of our language intimately, knew them in our minds and in our hands. We understood the best poetry to be such a fine thing that poets—beginning poets working on technical exercises, mid-career poets working on a third or fourth book, even great poets like Walt Whitman—had, at their best, worked not primarily for short-lived attention, but to serve a vibrant, powerful art.*

With some attention to a broader purpose, writing exercises are far from being a quick fix. They become part of a slow, deepening intensification of experience that's only possible through language.

❑ 76

CREATE YOUR OWN POET'S LIBRARY

BY DAVID KIRBY

MOST WRITERS I KNOW HAVE A COLLECTION OF TOTEMS ON OR NEAR their desks: a photo of Whitman, a strand of heather from the Brontës' parsonage, a fortune-cookie slip promising great success. These are our power objects, the ritual devices we gaze at, touch, even talk to as we prepare to shoulder the mantle of authorship. Where would we be without them?

Well, we'd probably be right there at our desks anyway, doing the best we can. But good writing comes more easily when it takes place within a rich, familiar environment that not only locates us in a sympathetic time and space but also reminds us of a larger context, that realm where the immortals dwell. A friendly physical setting is a point of departure for a writer as well as a source of continuous encouragement during that long journey we make every day through an often-strange landscape of fresh feelings and new ideas.

I've got my gadgets and gizmos—postcards, mementoes, strange things I've put on my desk unthinkingly but for some reason never removed—yet books are the things that help me the most with my own writing. I always use the same coffee cup, a chipped, badly stained object that my sons gave me years ago, though in a pinch I suppose I could drink my morning jolt of "rocket fuel" from some other vessel. But there are certain books I find indispensable. One person's lifesaver is another's dust trap, of course, so I trust you'll edit this list to meet your own requirements as you compile or revise your poet's bookshelf. Some of these items are available on CD-ROM or come already included in a computer's hard drive. However, even the most computer-centric writers I know still surround themselves with their favorite books.

Personally, I couldn't get along without:

(1) A dictionary, probably two. Almost any dictionary will do for daily use as long as it is comprehensive enough to be useful and small

379

enough so that you can handle it comfortably. After that, it's nice to have *Webster's Third New International Dictionary* (Merriam-Webster), or, even better, the *Oxford English Dictionary* (Oxford University Press), which comes in a compact (i.e., small-print version). Mark Twain said that the difference between the right word and the one that is almost right is the difference between "lightning" and "lightning bug," and certainly the dictionary's principal purpose is to steer the writer toward the most precise expression. But it can also be used as a aid to inspiration. The poet Carolyn Knox writes a poetry that is so lush and word-drunk that I once asked her, "Do you just look through the dictionary sometimes for interesting words?" Her answer was, "Of course. Don't you?" I didn't then, but I do now.

(2) The Bible. The Judeo-Christian tradition permeates the whole of Western culture. But our ordinary lives are shaped by religious language as well; just listen to what a self-described atheist says when he pounds his thumb with a hammer and you'll see what I mean. The Garden of Eden, the Flood, the Marriage of Cana: these are timeless stories of innocence, righteousness, and love, chapters in a rich anthology that addresses our deepest sorrows and our highest hopes. From Dante to Dickinson, writers have always borrowed from the Bible and always will.

As with the dictionary, any standard version will do, though an index is essential. The Bible is a big book in more ways than one, and if you're looking for the story of Abraham and Isaac, you won't want to spend hours wandering in the desert with Moses and the Chosen People.

(3) A real thesaurus. I say "real" because these days, every computer comes equipped with a thesaurus of sorts, but to date there is no substitute for *Roget's International Thesaurus* (HarperCollins). For instance, if I want to consider synonyms for "totem," which occurs in the first sentence of this article, I can hit the Alt-F1 keys on my keyboard, but then the screen tells me "Word Not Found" in my computer thesaurus. On the other hand, if I look up "totem" in *Roget's,* I can choose from "earmark," "emblem," "token," and "badge" as well as "genius," "demon," "good angel," and a dozen other choices. This is one more case of the computer being faster but not better than the book.

Besides, computer tools don't really encourage serendipity. Again, imagine you're looking up "totem." Your computer may tell you there's no such word, but on the way to looking it up in *Roget's,* you may (as I just did) stumble across "stiacciato," which can be used in place of "mask," "plague," "medallion," "cameo," etc. A real thesaurus reminds us of the richness of our language in a way that the more efficient if single-minded computer cannot.

(4) A one-volume encyclopedia. Of course a multi–volume set would be ideal, but something along the lines of *The Columbia Encyclopedia* (Columbia University Press) is ideal for most purposes, especially when you take shelf space into account as well as cost.

(5) *Bartlett's Familiar Quotations* (Little, Brown). Did Samuel Johnson say "A little knowledge is a dangerous thing" or "A little learning is a dangerous thing"? You often hear the former, but the latter is correct. And by the way, Alexander Pope said it, not Johnson.

(6) A current edition of an almanac, such as the *World Almanac* (World Almanac). Recently I was writing a poem about rhythm and blues and I needed to find out when Fats Domino was born, and that's not the kind of thing you're going to find in the encyclopedia. (Answer: February 26, 1928.)

(7) Langford Reed's *The Writer's Rhyming Dictionary,* with an introduction by John Holmes (The Writer, Inc.). Even a free-verse poet will from time to time want to find a word with a very particular sound, and this or a similar book will lead you to the right one. It will also surprise you: how else would you learn that the rhymes for "Christmas" include "anabasse," "contrabass," "octobass," "Boreas," "isinglass," and "galloglass," as well as a bunch of words you already know?

Yes, the version of Windows on my computer has a rhymer, but I value it more for its speed than for its usefulness. For as with the dictionary and the thesaurus, the rhyming dictionary permits the kind of happy accident of which wonderful poems are made. Speaking of which . . .

(8) Jack Elster's *There's a Word for It!* (Pocket Books) is an engrossing guide to all those words you know exist even if you don't know

what they are. Thanks to Elster, I found out that I am a "cruciverbalist." No, not someone who nails grammar books to boards—a cruciverbalist is a devotee of crossword puzzles.

More seriously, suppose you want to describe someone who hates men. Everyone knows that a woman hater is a "misogynist." "Misanthrope" isn't the word you want, because a misanthrope hates everyone. But a "misandrist" is someone who hates men only.

(9) *The Oxford Companion to American Literature* and *The Oxford Companion to English Literature* (Oxford University Press). These two books, like the next item on this list, keep me out of trouble because through them I stay connected with the great tradition out of which all writing flows. After all, you can't do something new unless you have an idea of what has already been done.

Right now I'm working on a poem about my recent trip to Venice, so before I began to write I reminded myself of what Shakespeare said about that city in *The Merchant of Venice* and *Othello*. I don't plan to outdo Shakespeare, of course, but I do want to say something different from what he said.

(10) At least one anthology of classic poetry. This can range from such manageable volumes as Oscar Williams' *Immortal Poems* (Pocket Books) or William Harmon's *The Concise Columbia Book of Poetry* (Columbia University Press), which contains the 100 poems included most often in more than 400 anthologies, to the thousand-plus-page textbook you kept from your college days. Again, the point is to be able to connect with the best of the past and use it in the best way.

(11) Half a dozen current poetry collections. Obviously a poet's connection with the past is essential, but it is equally clear that poets need to learn from their contemporaries. Right now I'm looking at the spines of recent books by Primo Levi, Marilyn Hacker, Reginald Shepherd, and Dorothy Barresi; I also see two anthologies, the *Coffeehouse Poetry Anthology* edited by June King and Larry Smith (Bottom Dog Press), which emphasizes the oral tradition, and *The Party Train: A Collection of North American Prose Poetry,* edited by Robert Alexander, Mark Vinz, and C. W. Truesdale (New Rivers Press). A sumptuous feast is served 24 hours a day within the modest space these books occupy, and

whenever I pick up one of these collections, I am certain of getting my Recommended Daily Allowance of Vitamin P.

As with the older poetry, this new writing is not something I want either to duplicate or deny. What I seek in these pages is inspiration, an inkling of what has been done and what remains for me to do. This is the part of my poet's bookshelf that changes most frequently, and it is the part least likely to be cloned by any other poet. Vitamin P takes many different forms, and you know which poets are best for you.

(12) A book from The Wild Card Category. You have a further chance to personalize your poet's bookshelf by including something so outlandish that only you would find it useful. One of my favorite books in this category is *The Romance Writers' Phrase Book* by Jean Kent and Candace Shelton (Berkley Publishing Group). This is a book of over 3,000 "tags" or one-line descriptions used to convey emotion—or passion, actually, since romance heroes and heroines seem never to do anything halfway.

In the "Eyes" chapter, for example, you will find such headings as "Expression," "Color," "Movement," and so on, with dozens of tags under each, such as (from "Expression") "her wide-eyed innocence was merely a smoke screen," "his eyes were cold and proud," and "his eyes glowed with a savage inner fire." I love to dip into this book whenever I think I'm being too stiff or pedantic. Then my own eyes begin to glow with a savage inner fire as I return—no, swagger—to my task.

Are these the books you need to make your own poetry the best it can be? Many of them are, no doubt, whereas others may strike you as unimportant. The idea is to create your own poet's bookshelf and stock it with works that will, like old friends, gaze down upon you and murmur silent encouragement as you pursue your craft.

□ 77

WHAT MAKES A GOOD POETRY WORKSHOP?

BY ELIZABETH BILLER CHAPMAN AND EVE SUTTON

IT IS EARLY EVENING ON A QUIET STREET IN A CALIFORNIA SUBURB. If you were standing outside the front door of one home, you'd hear a mixture of voices from the living room—giddy, firm, accusing, tender—punctuated by silence, and laughter raucous as a freshman dorm.

Peering through the front window, you'd see a cozy circle of couches and chairs, a small table of refreshments, stacks of paper, and ten or twelve adults who banter with the easy familiarity of old friends. Welcome to the Thursday Night Poets.

Much has been written about the vicious world of workshops, wolf packs that leave their victim's entrails on the floor. At the other extreme are gatherings so "supportive" that one's ego is coddled at the expense of one's writing.

We are fortunate to belong to a group that is both gentle and constructive. Here are our hints for starting a critique group, and for making it successful.

When and where

Choose a consistent time, day, and location: We meet on Thursday evenings, September to June, a holdover from the years when most of us were enrolled in a poetry class offered by a local community college.

What's available: reference books, especially dictionaries; assorted poetry—Shakespeare, Norton anthologies, lots of contemporary writers; food and drink.

Who's in, and why

Size: The group should be large enough for productive discussion, small enough so it doesn't feel impersonal or overwhelming. Not everyone can attend every week. We've found that if our group includes

384

12–15 people, we're likely to have a good number—eight or more—at each meeting.

Level: We've made a decision not to include poets who were still learning the elementary skills of the craft, because we wished to work at a more advanced level. However, we do have some members who started writing poetry just a few years ago, along with some who have decades of experience.

Diversity: Our group includes both genders, and a range of ages, backgrounds, occupations, income levels, and living situations. When a poem makes a reference to a particular place, religion, or experience, it's likely that at least one member of the group will recognize it from an insider's perspective, and at least one member will not. We can discuss how to present that reference in a way that is clear, but not condescending.

Guidelines

This is our customary format—it is not unique. As members arrive, they place their poems, enough copies to go around, face down on the table. This is the Stack, which is passed around 15 minutes after the official Start Time—not as simple as it sounds, since people want to stop and read the poems!

The poet reads his or her poem aloud. A silence follows. If they wish, members write comments on their copies to hand back to to the poet later. Then we discuss, beginning with a "holistic" comment on the overall poem or effect, positive attributes, what works well. Other comments, suggestions, changes. A basic axiom: Every criticism implies its opposite.

Workshop atmosphere: energy

The most important thing: generosity of tone and spirit. This is not the same as sappy: "You're a nice person, and this is a nice poem." It means everyone must be willing to make an effort to find something positive to say about each poem. It is more important than laser-like wit or "being right."

Examples

1. A helpful suggestion for change, from "Shedding a Layer" by S. Gaines:

> Torn from an old magazine
> this richly colored advertisement:
> "The Timelessness of Diamonds."

Comment: It would be stronger without the second line (which "tells" more than it "shows").

Revised version:

> Torn from an old magazine
> "The Timelessness of Diamonds."

2. A revision, based on a workshop comment, from "Parting" by E. B. Chapman, written for a mentor, about to move away:

> Last night I heard an owl, clearly, five hoots.
> Difficult thatched bird, was that you?
> announcing your departure all along the creekbed . . .

Comment: The second adjective modifying "bird" was originally "wise"; triter and more "mental" than the other imagery.

3. A poem we all agreed on: It works as is; leave it alone:

Saving Time
by E. Sutton

> I hoard each fragment
> against winter dark: gilt-edged
> notch of mountain at dawn, glint
> of blue-lake afternoon, evening's book
> for dessert outdoors. I'll never return
> the daylight I've saved.

In conclusion

We'd like to end with some advice from our former poetry teacher, who, though comfortably retired, still follows our progress. Here, then, are two of Richard Maxwell's Maxims:

1. Dive in; if you pussyfoot around, testing the water, you'll never get wet.
2. Remember, you don't have to be doing this, but you really like to.

P. S. Have fun!

❑ 78

The Poet's Choice: Lyric or Narrative

By Gregory Orr

Poets are haunted by the dream of perfection in a way that writers in no other literary art form are. And unity is one of those mysterious elements interwoven with poetry's fatal dream of its own perfection.

Unity is something almost all poets and those writing about poetry have insisted upon as an essential element. But things become complicated when we decide to define unity, because there are many definitions leading to many different kinds of poems.

Suppose we begin with two kinds of poems and the distinct kind of unity each might aspire to: *lyric poems* and *narrative poems.* They aren't different kinds of poems; they actually exist on a spectrum with (pure) lyric on one end and (pure) narrative on the other. I've put the adjective "pure" in parentheses because there is no such beast; every lyric has some element of narrative in it, even if it is only an implied dramatic context for its words. Similarly, every narrative has some lyric element, if only a metaphor placed at a crucial point or the heightening of its rhythmic texture, as it approaches its narrative climax. Lyric and narrative are part of a continuum, and it is extremely interesting to take a number of your poems and try to locate them along this spectrum. Ask yourself: Is this sonnet more lyric than narrative? And how does it compare with any of my other poems in terms of lyric and narrative elements? Which is dominant?

Lyrics and narratives are the products of different sensibilities or of the same sensibility operating in two distinct ways. These differences can be understood by comparing them with the making of a sculpture. There are two basic ways of making a piece of sculpture: carving and modeling.

The carving method involves taking a piece of stone or wood and cutting away toward some desired or intuited shape *within* the original block. The finished piece emerges as the extra material is stripped away.

The modeling method requires the sculptor to construct a skeletal structure out of wood or metal that essentially defines the shape of the piece, much as our skeleton defines the shape of our bodies. This structure is called an armature. Once the armature is constructed, the sculptor proceeds by slapping lumps of clay or plaster on it to flesh out the shape. This modeling technique is one of accretion: The sculptor has added material to make his piece, and the finished piece is larger than what he or she began with. Also, the carving technique results in a piece that is smaller than the original stone the sculptor began with.

What do these two techniques have to do with poetry? They correspond to the lyric and narrative modes. The lyric poem is created like the carved sculpture—the poet intuits a hidden, compelling shape within the language of the first draft. The secret is to carve away, to eliminate the excess as you work your way toward the lyric's secret center. The motto of the lyric is somewhat mystical: "Less is more."

The author of narrative, on the other hand, has a different purpose: If the lyric poet seeks a hidden center, then the narrative poet wants to tell a story—this happened, and then that happened. He or she wants to add material, to keep moving, to find out what is over the next hill. The narrative poem is a kind of journey, and it needs to add action to action, event to event, line to line. Narrative poems get longer as they are rewritten, because the narrative poet discovers his or her meanings by asking, "What next?" and pushing a poem's protagonist further by adding one line to the next. One of the cleverest definitions of narrative thinking comes from contemporary poet Frank O'Hara, who spoke of his work as his "I-did-this-and-then-I-did-that" poems. O'Hara's remark sounds almost glib, but he's articulating the secret of how a narrative gets made. The narrative poet's motto is the sensible: "More is more."

The narrative poem wanders across a landscape, propelled by verbs and unified by the need to have a beginning, middle, and end that relate to each other. The narrative poem is searching for something and won't be happy (complete, unified) until it has found it. The lyric poem has a different shape—it *constellates* around a single center, usually an emotional center: a dominant feeling. If the shape of a narrative is a line meandering down the page, then the shape of a lyric is that of a snowflake or crystal. The lyric is not searching, because it already knows what it knows, what it feels. Browning caught this already-knowing when he said "the lyric poet digs where he stands." The lyric poet digs into his or her emotion, a single, centered thing.

Needless to say, neither the narrative nor the lyric is "right"; each can be merely a direction a poet might take a poem. But they also reflect inclinations a poet has, and as such, they can be more deeply rooted in the dominant psychology of a poet.

Robert Frost is a prime modern example of a narrative temperament—not that his poems contain no lyric moments, but that the lyric was seldom his aim, and lyric unity was not what he usually sought. William Carlos Williams would be my candidate for a poet whose primary temperament is lyric.

What do I mean by lyric and narrative unity? Aristotle, who in the fifth century B.C. became the first poet-friendly critic with his *Poetics,* knew that unity was essential to the dramatic effectiveness of poetry. His idea of poetry was essentially narrative, and he proposed that what could unify narrative poetry was this: that it describe a single action. He further insisted that there had to be a beginning, a middle, and an end to this action, and that these three parts should be in a harmonious relationship.

When Robert Frost writes his poem "Directive," he is giving us a quintessential narrative poem, which will take the form of a journey, the poet-speaker offering himself to us as a guide. We travel over a landscape toward the ruins of a vanished village (we are also, in a sense, traveling backward in time). It is the narrative as journey, the narrative as a series of actions where *verbs,* those action words, move us forward from one sentence to the next. How will Frost's "Directive" achieve narrative unity? By arriving at a significant location (the village, the spring behind the deserted house) and making a significant discovery (the cup hidden in the hollow tree). We have journeyed a long way, we have journeyed from being "lost" and disoriented to being "found" and located.

Here is Edmund Waller's 17th-century lyric "On a Girdle." The girdle he celebrates is an embroidered sash or belt women then wore around their waists, not the "foundation garment" in modern use:

On a Girdle

That which her slender waist confined
Shall now my joyful temples bind;
No monarch but would give his crown
His arms might do what this had done.

It was my heaven's extremest sphere,
The pale which held that lovely deer;
My joy, my grief, my hope, my love
Did all within this circle move.

A narrow compass! and yet there
Dwelt all that's good, and all that's fair.
Give me but what this ribband bound,
Take all the rest the sun goes round.

(1664)

Waller's poem achieves lyric unity through two methods. One is through the single emotion that motivates and animates the poem: praise of the beloved. The poet is at pains to tell us how enraptured he is at the thought of his beloved: He'd rather have her in his arms than the whole world in his possession. Notice that Waller sticks with the single emotion and takes it all the way through the poem. Lyrics tend to do that—locate their single, central emotion and take it to the limit.

The second unifying element in Waller's poem is "technical," i.e., the recurring use of circle images and metaphors. Almost everything is a circle starting (and ending) with the sash that encircles his beloved's waist. He puts the sash around his head, and that reminds him of the circle of a king's crown and arms around a woman's waist. In stanza two he thinks of heavenly spheres and the circle of fence (pale) that might confine a deer; in stanza three, he thinks of her waist again, and (the final line) the giant orbit of the sun around the earth (here he's using the old earth-centered cosmic scheme).

The reason I chose Waller's poem rather than, say, a William Carlos William lyric is this: The very technique that unifies Waller's lyric—a series of metaphors—would work *against* narrative unity.

Why? How? Simply this: Metaphors slow a poem down. The more metaphors, the slower the going. The reader has to stop and think about (and savor) the comparisons. But narrative poems thrive on momentum; they need to keep moving. A good narrative poet knows to beware of metaphors and use them sparingly. Metaphors are a lyric poet's friend, but they can disrupt narrative unity, which is based on unfolding action.

A lyric poem can go wrong in many ways: Most commonly, the first draft has not sufficiently surrounded its emotional or imagistic character. (In this situation, when the sculptor revises by carving the block of wood, he ends up with no more than a toothpick, or even less.)

Similarly, when a narrative poem goes wrong, it can get completely lost and wander aimlessly. Remember that in Frost's poem, the speaker/poet/guide knows exactly where his poem is taking readers, even if they don't.

If a poem you're working on is giving you trouble, try to locate it on the spectrum that goes from lyric to narrative. If your poem aspires to narrative, then keep it moving with verbs and action, and ask yourself where this story best begins, how it develops, how it is resolved. If your poem aspires to lyric, ask where its emotional or imagistic center is, and see if you can strengthen it by stripping away extra material.

❑ 79

FINDING THE RIGHT FORM
FOR YOUR POEM

BY N. I. CLAUSSON

AS A POET AND TEACHER, WHAT I NOTICE MOST ABOUT THE POEMS OF beginning poets (in addition to the lack of concreteness and specificity) is that their form seems arbitrary, that there is no reason for a poem to have the number of lines it does, for the line breaks to come where they do, or for the poem to be long and narrow, short and wide, or divided into four-line stanzas (quatrains) with one extra line at the end. I often get the impression that I could rearrange the lines and stanzas without affecting the poem's meaning. In short, the poet has not mastered form.

Form is not a convenient container into which you can pour your meaning. Trying to define form so it is instantly intelligible to beginning poets (or even to experienced ones) is very difficult. It is much easier to say what form is *not*.

When you jot down a note to a friend asking her to take out the garbage and phone Mary to invite her to the barbecue, it really doesn't matter how many sentences you use or where you end one line and start another. But poems are not notes (as anyone who has read William Carlos Williams' "This Is Just to Say" will know). Poetry is a field of writing in which how you say it is just as important as what you say. But even that definition doesn't nail down what I'm trying to get across. Poetry is an area of writing in which meaning is determined by form. In the successful poem, form creates meaning.

The best way to explain this concept is with an example. I've chosen Linda Pastan's "love poem." (If you haven't read any of Pastan's poetry, you have a real treat in store for you.) Here's the poem:

love poem

I want to write you
a love poem as headlong
as our creek
after thaw
when we stand
on its dangerous
banks and watch it carry
with it every twig
every dry leaf and branch
in its path
every scruple
when we see it
so swollen
with runoff
that even as we watch
we must grab each
other or
get our shoes
soaked we must
grab each other

If the meaning of this poem were simply *in the words* Pastan has brilliantly chosen, then we could rearrange them into a different configuration and the meaning should not change, or change so little as to be insignificant. Let's do that. Here is my "rearrangement" (of course, it is one of many possible versions):

I want to write you a love poem
as headlong as our creek after thaw

when we stand on its dangerous banks
and watch it carry with it every twig,
every dry leaf and branch in its path,
    every scruple;

when we see it so swollen with runoff
that even as we watch
we must grab each other and step back.

We must grab each other,
or get our shoes soaked.
We must grab each other.

Linda Pastan's "love poem" is reprinted here from *The Imperfect Paradise,* © 1988 by Linda Pastan, and published by permission of the publishers, W. W. Norton & Company.

In one sense, the two versions say the same thing. I have not added or deleted a single word, or changed the order of any words, although I have added punctuation. But the difference between the two poems is enormous. It is the difference between a successful poem and a stillborn one. And that difference is a difference of form.

What is most noticeable about the form of Pastan's poem is that it enacts or duplicates in language both the movement of the creek during spring thaw and the emotional release of the speaker. Like many love poems, this one is organized around a controlling metaphor, which here compares being in love to being swept down a creek during spring thaw; being in love is like being in the power of an uncontrollable natural force. The lover can no more control her or his feelings than the objects in the stream (twig, leaf, and branch) can control their movement. That feeling of being in the power of an uncontrollable force somehow has to get into the poem; and the only way for this to happen in poetry is for the form of the poem in some way to embody that feeling. The meaning of the words alone cannot convey that experience; it's the form the words take on the page that convey the speaker's state of mind.

But the poem is not just saying that love is like a powerful force of nature. It is also saying that *the poem itself* is "as headlong / as our creek / after thaw." The poem has to be like the creek. The problem is how, in language, to create the experience of being carried headlong along a creek like a branch or a leaf. The only way to do this is through the movement of the words on the page—that is, through *form.* In reading Pastan's poem, the reader experiences—through the form of the poem—the headlong feeling of the speaker. The reader moves headlong through the poem, unable to pause at any point to catch his or her breath. The reason for this is that there are no periods or capital letters separating the three sentences of the poem; there are no pauses at the end of any of the lines (they are all enjambed); and the poem is printed on the page as one long, narrow stanza without breaks or subdivisions. The words rush past the reader just as the turbulent creek rushes past the speaker.

But what about my version? What's wrong with it? There is a contradiction at the heart of the poem: The words are saying one thing (that love is an irresistible natural force and that a love poem must carry the reader along like the victim of this force), but the form of the poem is saying just the opposite: that one can talk about the headlong, uncontrolled force of love in language as controlled and logical as the language of a chemistry textbook. Notice how my line and stanza breaks neatly coincide with grammatical and syntactic units. It isn't that my poem lacks form; it's that the form is inappropriate for *this* poem. In short, I have not solved the problem of how to make the form of the poem consistent with the propositions that the words are making about love and about love poems. My poem is stillborn.

Is there any other form that Pastan could have chosen to gain the effect she wants? Perhaps, but I doubt it. True, she could have written the poem in long lines that go almost from margin to margin. The first line of such a version might be: "I want to write you a love poem as headlong as our creek after thaw . . ." Such a poem would of course create a strong sense of irresistible forward movement, but something would be missing. In Pastan's poem the short enjambed lines create a sense of jerky disorientation that is perfect to covey the sense of the jerky, unpredictable movements of the objects in the stream. Long lines would create a sense of steady, predictable forward movement. But that is not the feeling Pastan wants to create. It still would not have been the best form for her poem.

To a large extent the problem of writing poetry is the problem of how to solve similar problems of form. Once you realize this fact, you will find that you are writing much better poems because what you say and how you say it will be inseparable. The proof will be in the noticeable decline in rejection letters in your mailbox.

Of course, writing a good poem is much more than a matter of form. For a poem to be good, the poet has to have something worthwhile to say: If you find the perfect form in which to say something that should have been left unsaid, you will not have written a successful poem. Nor will having something worthwhile to say in itself make you a poet. Only saying something significant in the most significant form will make you a significant poet.

❏ 80

POETS SPEAK IN MANY VOICES

BY GEORGE KEITHLEY

WRITERS OF THE PERSONA POEM—A DRAMATIC MONOLOGUE SPOKEN IN the voice of a character created by its author—often find it one of the most rewarding of poetic forms. And often for the same reasons that delight readers: At its best, the poem may be surprising, insightful, and dramatic, all at the same time.

While *persona* may refer to the speaker of any poem, the term *persona poem,* in current usage, refers to a poem spoken by a central character other than the author. Immediately you see one of its attractions: It invites us to enter the consciousness of a creature other than oneself. Who hasn't, at some time, wondered what it would be like to be someone else? Or tried to understand how the world might look when viewed from a perspective other than our own? Well, for the duration of each persona poem, the poet thinks and feels and speaks as someone else; perhaps a person of a different sex, age, nationality, or culture.

Because of this different perspective, in which the poet assumes the role of someone else, the persona poem differs essentially from a lyric poem (in which the speaker is the author) or a narrative poem (written in the third person about other people and their experiences).

Among the best-known examples of the persona poem are some of the most admired poems in the English language: Robert Browning's "My Last Duchess," T.S. Eliot's "Journey of the Magi," W.B. Yeats's "Crazy Jane Talks with the Bishop," and Hart Crane's "Repose of Rivers" (a monologue in the mind of the Mississippi River).

As that last example suggests, the *persona,* or speaking-consciousness of the poem, needn't be a person. Poems in this form have also been written from the imagined intelligence of rain, snow, fog, fire, sheep, frogs, bears, horses, whales, characters from fairy tales, and the constellations in the night sky.

Whether they are historical figures or fictional ones, human or nonhuman, the speakers of these poems bring to both the poet and the reader many voices that might otherwise have remained silent, not only in the world around us, but also within ourselves.

A few of the many successful persona poems written by modern poets are Linda Pastan's "Old Woman," Galway Kinnell's "The Bear," Louise Bogan's "Cassandra," James Wright's "Saint Judas," and Gwendolyn Brooks's "We Real Cool" and "Big Bessie Throws her Son into the Street." The telling nature of these titles is no accident. The reader of a persona poem should learn from the title or the first lines of the poem exactly who is speaking, and perhaps—something of the situation that has moved the speaker to address us.

Keep the identity of the speaker clear and direct. Since you're asking the reader to embark on a journey into the consciousness of another being, often one in inner turmoil, let the identity of that figure be clear from the start. The poem's essential mystery lies in what the speaker reveals to readers, and in the language in which the revelation is expressed. In one of the most famous persona poems, Browning offers the title "My Last Duchess," and the speaker, the Duke, begins:

> That's my last Duchess painted on the wall,
> Looking as if she were alive. I call
> That piece a wonder now . . .

Immediately the reader knows that the Duchess has died, and her widowed husband cares more about her portrait than he cared for her.

In my book, *Earth's Eye,* I included a poem, "Waiting for Winter," which begins:

> I think of my name, Julia Grahm,
> and hold my hands so in a circle,
> making my mind obey my mind.

In the first line the speaker gives readers her name and invites them to see that introspection and self-restraint are her significant features. (She'll go on to reveal that, in her forties, living alone, she's keenly attuned to the promptings of her body and soul.)

Similarly, in the same book, my poem, "In Early Spring," begins with a young woman saying:

> In early spring I felt the weight
> of his legs
> upon my own. I undid my dress,
> we watched the wind row
> across the water . . .

At this point, I hope the poem has established the voice of its central character and has suggested her situation.

About the speaker's situation—remember that the persona poem is a *dramatic* monologue. Ask yourself: What is it about this situation that causes my character to experience an intensity of insight and emotion? What is the urgency that compels this person to speak? What makes us eager to reveal ourselves to others? When you can answer these questions, you're ready to write the poem and hope to see it published.

Once the nature of your central character is apparent to you, and the figure has begun to reveal itself, you then have the speaking-consciousness that is vital to the persona poem, and you're ready to move on, within the life of that character. I often visit a diner where a waitress, as she places food before her customers, smiles, and says: "There you go!" As if she's recognizing our hunger, our anticipation, and our readiness to begin. That feeling of release, of freedom to explore, is typical of the poet and the reader, meeting each other in the persona poem. For the poem offers a wide range of physical and psychological experience not often accessible to us. Writing it, or reading it, we inhabit another life—or perhaps a part of our own consciousness of which we're usually unaware.

I tend to write the persona poem for two different purposes. One is to allow myself to enter a state of feeling, a state of being, and to speak from within that context, which previously had been unknown to me. It might mean empathizing with a character of a far different nature, but by assuming the thoughts and feelings of that speaker, to the extent that I give voice to them, I might come to a better understanding of the "character" of that figure. On the other hand, the persona might be very compatible, but I find it difficult to write about myself in the first person, so the dramatic figure, the persona, is a mask that allows me to speak, free of an otherwise stifling inhibition.

A word of caution. Much has been said about the ethics of appropriating someone else's culture or history: a poet pretending to be someone he or she is not, in order to capitalize on a history of suffering that the writer hasn't endured. The rule is simple: Don't do it. You write with your head and your heart. Your conscience will tell you if your empathy is authentic. Or not. A virtue of the persona poem is that it affords both poet and reader an opportunity for understanding and compassion.

A second reason for writing the persona poem is that often the central figure is involved in a dramatic situation or story. Taking on the character of the figure is a way of entering the story. The speaking figure is itself our invitation to enter the poem.

So the persona poem will be most compelling if the main figure, the speaking-consciousness, is at the center of a dramatic situation, for the moral and psychological pressures of a conflict will bring thought and feeling into focus. Why is that persona compelling to us? Why at this particular moment? If the poem's central character, its speaking voice, is encountered at a moment of dramatic tension, or moral consequence, or significant insight, the answer will be evident to the poet and the reader alike.

The drama that compels our interest may or may not be apparent from the character's actions. What's vitally important is the poet's understanding of the character's inner nature at the moment when it's revealed to the reader. In "The Pleading Child," another poem in *Earth's Eye,* I tried to evoke the troubled joy a young boy experiences one winter night with his parents and his sister, in what might otherwise seem a very peaceful environment:

> After Christmas Mass the strains
> of carols call us to the flesh
> and blood figures in the stable crèche:
> "Joy to the world! the Savior reigns . . ."
>
> Joseph, Mary, and the Child in white.
> Kneeling, the Kings set down their pomp
> and gifts. We troop into the night—
> Moon, lift up your little lamp.
>
> The stone bridge straddles the stiff creek.
> Skate blades slung back, two sharp boys slip
> off the ice. Beyond the bridge we grip
> each other's hands to climb the bleak
> hill. My sister whispers, "Look!"

Fresh tracks pock the snow, dogs romp
down the road in a ragged pack—
Moon, lift up your little lamp.

Something more than the snow or chill
makes my mother stop and weep.
Something her heart had hidden deep
within the winter pulses still:
Silent in the sparkling dark,
lovers bundle past the pump
house and pause. Only their eyes speak—
Moon, lift up your little lamp.

Father shoulders Julia over
a steep drift. Why do I cry?
Mother's singing, ". . . the sounding joy,
Repeat the sounding joy." I shiver
in my short coat and she stoops to fold
her arms around me. Gladly we tramp
home across the glittering cold—
Moon, hold up your happy lamp!

Whether the resulting persona poem is a character study or the evolving of a story, there is, at the heart of the poem, a figure who compels our attention. The writer's interest in this figure might be an impulse toward compassion, or humor, or the desire to come to understand different aspects of human nature or the natural world. Or it might be a desire to explore the drama of the character's situation.

Each of these is a fundamental motive for writing, and the persona poem results from the combination of introspection, examination, and drama. It is a dramatic form, and a poetic medium, but it is also, and essentially, a poem. So it must live and prosper according to those qualities of language, rhythm, tension, and imagery that we give it.

The possibilities for subjects in the persona poem are limited only by our imagination and our willingness to take risks—which is another way of saying that it's time to get to work. Now, for however long it takes to write the poem, you find yourself becoming (and giving voice to):

- A teacher facing her third-grade class on the first morning of the school year.
- A man watching a baseball game with his father who is recovering from a stroke.

- The almost silent snowfall that settles upon a pine forest.
- A parent attending the military funeral of an only son, killed in combat.
- A woman riding the subway home to her apartment while she considers a recent marriage proposal that she's not quite willing to accept. Or reject.
- A river flowing swiftly under a fine spring rain.
- A child walking thoughtfully through the dappled shade of a fruit orchard on a summer morning.
- A man who stands in a public parking lot looking at his red pickup truck, while two police officers pull his arms behind his back and handcuff his wrists.
- An owl gliding over a frozen field at twilight.
- A stand-up comic waiting to go on stage in a small theater.
- An elderly woman picking her way through a city park, a bag of groceries in her arms, while her granddaughter skips ahead of her into the deepening dusk.
- A colt running through a field of grass glossy with sunlight.

"There you go!"

❏ Playwriting

❑ 81

TRANSFORMING STORY INTO PLOT

BY DAVID COPELIN

WHAT *IS* A PLOT, ANYWAY? WHAT'S THE DIFFERENCE BETWEEN A PLOT and a story? And how do you create one from another?

Here's a classic distinction: "The queen died, and then the king died" is a story. "The queen died, and then the king died *of grief*" is a plot. *Story*, then, is the events of a play, in whatever order you choose to tell them. *Plot* concerns the relationship among these events and the characters who enact them.

We can infer that our king and queen had more than a political marriage, that their public relationship contained (and probably concealed) a powerful emotional bond. In such a case, our hypothetical king's death may be explained to his subjects as an emotional response to the loss of his queen. How sad! How moving! But what if, behind the scenes, a darker political struggle is taking place? What if the king's death means the end of one dynasty and the establishment of another, with a civil war to decide which dynasty will rule? Yes, the king's grief was deep, but did it *really* cause his death? Or was it a convenient coincidence? As Shakespeare put it (cynically): "Men have died from time to time, and worms have eaten them; but not for love." Then how *did* the king die? For that matter, how did the *queen* die? What if . . . ? Or could the king's grief and a political struggle be *simultaneous truths?* Of course they could.

As you see, the dramatic possibilities inherent in this situation are limitless.

In such a case, plot and character influence each other in many ways, and as the playwright, you determine which influences are most important.

As a practical matter, the story of your play is likely to develop well before its plot does, because all the linkages among events and characters—both obvious and subtle—that make up an effective plot are usually a result of several drafts. Getting the story elements right, and presenting them in the most effective order, is hard enough; but making a plot out of the story, a plot in which every moment gives just enough information and no more, in which the play's forward movement is both unmistakable and compelling, is even harder.

Fortunately, the complicated and lengthy process of creating a play from an idea, or an image, or a character, or whatever you start from, is ultimately more fascinating than frustrating. Don't worry if your plot isn't completely clear to you at the outset. Don't worry if you don't know all there is to know about each character before you start writing your script. Some playwrights create random lists of character traits, then sculpt each list into a person. Try this, and see if it works for you. Or you may be more comfortable imagining a character as a whole, and discovering additional traits as they reveal themselves in the course of your writing the play.

Alternatively, you may start with an event, then say, "What kind of character would most likely be involved in such an event?" Or (and better) "What kind of character would be highly *un*likely to be involved in such an event, and what would happen if he or she *were* so involved?"

In your first draft, feel free to begin with bits and pieces of your story. Don't worry, at this point, about unity, coherence, or emphasis. Step by step, make each event or transaction into a scene; each scene into a series of scenes that fit together according to your dramatic vision; each series of scenes into an act; each act into a play. Take your time, building the overall structure out of smaller units. You need not write the play in chronological order. In later drafts, you can cut, add, rearrange, expand, contract—do whatever is necessary to make those bits and pieces fit together seamlessly.

Traditionally, a play is supposed to have a beginning, a middle, and an end; plays that do so are highly satisfying to most audiences. But you can make an arbitrary choice of where in a story to start and where to end. Those choices will define the middle. Remember, you can always use a *flashback* or *flash-forward,* as the structure of your play may require.

One common test for the effectiveness of a play is whether or not it has *forward motion*, but while *most* plays need to move forward through time with some urgency, there are some really great plays that do not.

Their motion is circular or spiral, their force centripetal. Their action meanders, and their characters seem stuck in time and place.

Consider Anton Chekhov's plays, in which the leisure of the landed Russian gentry conceals a dim, anguished perception that nothing they do will keep their world from coming to an end. A lot happens in Chekhov, but it tends to happen *offstage*. Chekhov dramatizes a world that seems to have no drama, except for the occasional intense moment; deftly, he turns the typical plot-rich 19th-century play into examinations of character so subtle, yet so powerful, that generations of actors have found exploring roles in his plays to be indispensable for their training. Chekhov's plays don't have much forward motion in the traditional sense, because they reveal a world that is autumnal, burnt out, yet they manage to proceed to their dramatically logical end with seemingly effortless grace.

Nevertheless, many dramatic authors today, and many audiences, expect a play to move forward clearly and quickly, partly because they have been conditioned by thousands of hours of film and television to mistake *action* for *drama*. In our daily lives, we learn to experience time primarily as linear. In our dreams, however, we experience time in many other ways, so plays with dream-like, imaginative structures tend to be less linear than plays that attempt to replicate the recognizable external world. Hamlet says that the purpose of theatre is "to hold, as 'twere, the mirror up to nature." You, the playwright, get to decide what sort of mirror, and what aspect of nature. For example, Harold Pinter's play *Betrayal* begins after its events have taken place, and tells its story backwards. The audience experiences how memory revises our lives, and how actions that destroy human relationships may begin in a chance word here, a careless gesture there. In a different mode, Tennessee Williams created *The Glass Menagerie* consciously as a dream-play. Time swirls, history repeats itself, "real" objects become symbols, and so on. On stage, private dreams may become public magic.

Most playwrights follow a "forward motion" model, in which story elements are kept or discarded to the degree that they move the plot toward its climax and conclusion. Forward motion gathers momentum, so that a play seems to move faster and faster as it nears its most revealing moment. This is the technique Sophocles used in as early a play as *Oedipus Rex*: He created the sensation of increasing speed by making each successive scene shorter (and therefore more intense) than the preceding one, until the play's ultimate, inexorable revelation.

Sophocles' invention is thoroughly adaptable to our time. *Glengarry Glen Ross*, David Mamet's feisty, funny play about sleazy Chicago real-estate salesmen, is an excellent contemporary example of the Sophoclean model of forward motion—and yet Sophocles is probably the last influence you'll think of if you read or see Mamet's play. *Glengarry*'s combination of verbal jazz, lean structure, and ruthless analysis of petty capitalism seems utterly American and up-to-date.

This is an important reason for you to acquaint yourself with as many plays as possible. Imagine using a 2,500-year-old technique for thoroughly modern purposes! There's no need to reinvent the wheel, but rediscovering what makes it turn can be very helpful to any playwright.

Sometimes a plot is described in terms of "rising action," "climax," and "falling action," generally to show how dramatic stories move from A to B to C. Plays structured this way often have impressive power and clarity, but not all viable dramatic paths are linear. These days, more and more dramatic material that is fragmented, or repetitive in subtle ways, or is simply a series of blackout sketches, finds its way to successful performance. Nevertheless, because "forward motion" has such power over us, many playwrights' work is criticized for what it *doesn't do* rather than appreciated for what it *does*—especially if the play's motion is seemingly static. Any play, no matter how much it seems to hold an objective mirror up to everyday reality, is in fact an imaginative creation in which the playwright has the option of reaffirming the commonly accepted rules of time, space, and behavior, or inventing new ones. Whatever the playwright's choice, the more consistently and tellingly these rules are applied, the more persuasive the play will be.

Plays that appear to be about the world we all share are easier to appreciate than plays about worlds that exist only in the writer's mind, but of course this depends on the writer. August Strindberg worked quite effectively in both modes. *The Father* is ruthlessly objective, while *The Ghost Sonata* is much more obviously a dream play. The same dark comic sensibility informs both dramas, but in the first, forward motion is relentless. In the second, motion comes in many diverse forms. If you compare these texts to Canadian playwright George F. Walker's *Suburban Motel* cycle, you'll see how forward motion and circular repetition can be combined. I wouldn't have thought of mixing together the sensibilities of Sam Shepard and the Marx Brothers, but Walker did, and the result is wacky, preposterous theatre with a great core of human truth.

If your talent is for writing non-linear and/or non-realistic plays, it's up to you to provide alternate sources of dramatic energy. Here are a few such sources: progressive revelation of character (e.g., Emily Mann's *Still Life*), increasing emotional intensity (e.g., Sam Shepard's *Buried Child*), more powerful imagery of states of inertia (e.g. Samuel Beckett's *Happy Days*), vivid theatrical poetry (e.g. Federico Garcia-Lorca's *Blood Wedding*). *Something* has to take the place of forward motion, or your play will be wan and tepid.

You can, of course, combine linear and non-linear elements in your play, or realistic scenes and non-realistic scenes. This sort of dramatic counterpoint has exciting theatrical possibilities.

There are many techniques that will help you turn your story into a plot:

1. *Follow your instincts about which elements of your story deserve the most stage time.*

2. *As you draft and redraft, you will notice patterns emerging in your story. Make linkages among these patterns through the repetition and development of language, symbols, and sounds, as appropriate to the characters and situation—so that you are working on verbal, visual, and aural dimensions of your play simultaneously.* How does Shakespeare use the witches in *Macbeth* to create atmosphere, provide information, and dramatize the interplay between the ordinary and the occult? How does David Mamet's *American Buffalo* make verbal repetition and the focus on small rituals coexist in a wholly appropriate and resonant context? Read Mamet's description of the play's setting, and notice how the setting and the dialogue complement each other.

3. *If your plot is starting to feel too convoluted, try "storyboarding" it.* Borrow a technique from film writing: Put units of action on index cards, then put each index card on your wall. Does the first way you arranged each card make sense to you? Do you need all the cards? Are there gaps in the pattern? If so, do you need to fill these gaps? How can you rearrange the cards so that a different, perhaps more provocative, pattern begins to emerge? Follow that trail!

4. *As the playwright, only you know which events in the early part*

of a play will in retrospect be seen as significant. Theatre people refer
to such an event as a *setup.* To complete the structural (and emotional)
circle, a setup must be followed, usually at some distance, by a *payoff.*
This is usually some sort of surprise, some event or revelation that in
retrospect is inevitable, without having been predictable in advance.
Oscar Wilde's preposterous coincidences, late in *The Importance of
Being Earnest,* are wonderful examples of payoffs, absurd and delight-
ful at the same time.

Make sure, therefore, that your setups stay concealed, but don't forget
that there must be a payoff—unless you choose, for some good reason,
not to pay off a setup, to leave the structural-emotional circle unclosed.
To look at it from another angle: In writing a payoff, make sure that
you go back and locate the setup. If there isn't one, invent one. Then
hide it.

Hidden setups that are paid off openly and tellingly occur in Edward
Albee's *Who's Afraid of Virginia Woolf?*, when the offstage child is
revealed as a fantasy with the emotional impact of reality; in Shakespeare's *Macbeth,* when Birnam Wood *does* come to Dunsinane, though
not in the form we expect; and in Bertolt Brecht's *Mother Courage,*
when the significance of Swiss Cheese's nickname becomes chillingly
clear.

5. *What can you cut without weakening your play's structure?* If
your first answer is "Nothing!"—look again.

6. *Be careful about #5.* August Wilson's plays, such as *Fences, The
Piano Lesson,* and *Seven Guitars,* are characterized by a loose, open
architecture and a lot of rambling discourse that can seem repetitive and
verbose. But since Wilson is dramatizing a culture with a complicated
attitude about time and how best to pass it, it makes some sense for his
plays to unfold slowly, with a lot of fits and starts and blind alleys. The
rough edges of Wilson's writing, the meandering and curlicues, become
attributes of an identifiable individual *style* of playwriting. This style
may not be suitable for every playwright, but it is an artistic choice.

In other words, don't be too quick to homogenize your work. You
have a right to your idiosyncrasies; in the end, they may be more valuable than you expected.

7. *There is a certain satisfaction to tying up all the loose ends of a
play neatly, as in the much-abused, little-appreciated "well-made"
play; but this sort of tightly contrived and controlled playwriting has*

few advocates today. It survives most obviously in TV sitcoms and movies. A looser structure seems to suit many contemporary playwrights. There may be a greater satisfaction in leaving some elements unresolved, so that the audience is left wanting to know what happens to the characters even after the play is over. This is more like life itself, in which few questions are answered totally and unambiguously.

For example, in Arthur Miller's *Death of a Salesman*, the author focuses most of our attention on Willy Loman, his (anti)hero. But this major focus is buttressed by a strong secondary focus on Willy's family. What happens to Linda, Biff, and Happy after Willy's suicide? We never really learn, so part of the significance of Willy's choice is lost to us. But, you can't write about everything at once. Choosing *which* elements to leave unresolved is the mark of a master, and this mastery is the result of practice.

After reading *Death of a Salesman*, read Donald Margulies' *The Loman Family Picnic*. There's a lesson here about the constructive use of an older play to inspire a new one, and the illumination of the older play by the newer one. Tom Stoppard's plays *Rosencrantz and Guildenstern are Dead*, *The Real Inspector Hound*, and *Travesties* are both tributes to and parodies of, respectively, Shakespeare's *Hamlet*, any Agatha Christie murder mystery, and Oscar Wilde's *The Importance of Being Earnest*. The most significant fact to keep in mind, though, is that each of Stoppard's plays stands perfectly well on its own. You don't need to have read or seen the plays that inspired them, but if you have, you get an extra measure of enjoyment from the echoes, and can learn from the ways this approach has been used.

8. *Make your exposition serve multiple purposes. Exposition* is information about characters and events from the past or present that an audience needs to know to appreciate onstage action fully.

Although audiences *want* to know what's going on at every moment, they don't *need* to know. Suspense is an important attribute in a play, because it reinforces an audience's curiosity and helps provide some of the forward motion. So when should you provide vital information? For many purposes, at the latest possible moment. This does *not* mean that you save all crucial information until the play's last five minutes, then tell the audience everything you've withheld; but make sure you've explored indirect ways of giving information before you do so directly.

One of the most effective ways to do this is to have your characters discuss what actions they are *going to* take, rather than what they have done in the past. You'll find that any necessary background or character information will emerge organically, so that you don't have to slow your play down by giving the audience chunks of the past.

In contemporary plays, exposition is almost never *just* exposition; it often contains action as well as other kinds of information. Emily Mann's *Execution of Justice* dramatizes the famous and controversial murder trial of Dan White, the San Francisco politician who shot Mayor George Moscone and gay activist Harvey Milk in 1975. The play's strategy is to give us a kaleidoscopic view of the community in which it takes place. The profusion and sprawl of actual events, the candid reminiscences of people involved in the trial, and volumes of court testimony are all challenges to the playwright's need for dramatic economy. They were also her raw material.

Given this complexity, every moment in *Execution of Justice* had to serve several purposes simultaneously. The drama opens with two characters speaking. They are both onstage, close to each other, yet they seldom acknowledge each other's presence. They represent two opposing factions in the community and in the play. One of the characters is an unnamed San Francisco policeman who wears a "Free Dan White" T-shirt under his uniform; the other is Sister Boom-Boom, a gay transvestite in a nun's habit. From the first moment of the play, we are confronted with a kind of civic schizophrenia. The scene sets the tone for the play, and introduces us to its larger subject: the conflict of different value systems within the same community. It is exposition disguised as action.

You may never confront the challenge of effective exposition to such a degree in your own work, but *Execution of Justice* is a good example of how to rise to such a challenge.

9. *"Show, don't tell" means don't say directly in words what you can convey indirectly through behavior, and never, ever sermonize.* This is generally gospel for contemporary playwrights. But, as Sportin' Life says of that *other* gospel, "It ain't necessarily so." There are exceptions. Look at Tony Kushner's play *Slavs! (Thinking About the Problems of Virtue and Happiness)* for a recent example of "breaking the rules" and getting away with it. This play begins with a character reading to the audience out of a book! There are few clearer ways of saying outright, "Let's save time. This is what you need to know." I admire the

playwright's nerve, his willingness to do whatever he felt the situation required, and "show, don't tell" be damned. You may never start a play with a lecture, and I hope that doing so never becomes fashionable; but it *is* part of the available stock of playwriting strategies.

There are many ways of turning a story—whether totally fictional or taken from headlines like *Execution of Justice*—into a plot, then into a play. Whether character, structure, theatricality, or mood predominates depends very much on choices you make and the sort of effect you are trying to achieve: Even the most rigid dramatic structure is really quite malleable.

Consider, for example, what Ibsen did with the "well-made" play of his time, and what Shakespeare did with the Elizabethan dramatic forms he inherited. Look at the idiosyncratic contemporary comedies of the late Charles Ludlam, plays such as *Camille (A Tearjerker)*, *Der Ring Gott Farblonjet*, *The Bourgeois Avant-Garde*, *The Mystery of Irma Vep*—unique, yet clearly inspired by such older dramatic forms as Restoration comedy and Victorian melodrama. Bertolt Brecht was famous for updating older dramatic structures into contemporary forms. His *Mother Courage* and *The Caucasian Chalk Circle,* for example, revised an open, Shakespearean, "epic" way of writing plays. Don't be afraid to mine the past for intriguing ways to turn your stories into play plots. Don't be afraid to invent new ways to do so, either.

❏ 82

THE DEVIL'S IN THE REWRITE

BY JULIE JENSEN

REWRITING IS LIKE MILK OR EXERCISE—EITHER YOU LIKE IT OR YOU don't. Also like milk and exercise, it's necessary. So it's best if we all learn to like it. Better yet, if we all learn to love it.

Because theater is a collaborative art form, writing for the stage is full of rewriting: Directors, actors, designers all play a part. They all have opinions, and they all affect the play, either overtly or covertly. Some of them will actually tell you how to rewrite; others will just make choices that make the text changes necessary.

It's wise to be open-minded about rewrites. The best playwrights listen, cull the suggestions, and make the changes they find genuinely helpful. Unwise playwrights take all suggestions and try to incorporate them. Foolish playwrights listen to no one and make no changes at all.

Here are a few suggestions, things to keep in mind during the rewriting process.

The first concerns **plot.** Ask yourself this question: What's the difference between the character at the beginning of the play and at the end? In other words, did something happen? Think back on your favorite plays. Compare the leading character at the beginning with the one at the end. Look at Romeo and Juliet when we first meet them. By the end, of course, they are dead. But they have done more than just die. They've been through a lot. And that's good. One sign of a good plot.

The second test concerns **structure.** Are the events in an arc? Arc implies an arch. But arc is also more elastic than that. Arc is a bubble in the wind, stretching. It's a good shape for a play.

Next, make sure you've written **beats.** Beats are the small units of a play. Beats in a play correspond to paragraphs in prose. They should have beginnings, middles, and ends. It's easiest to define a beat as the time between a character's starting to pursue a goal and the point at which he achieves it, changes it, or stops. That section or segment is a beat.

Can a beat be short? Of course. Sometimes a piece of stage business is a whole beat. The character reads the note, thinks a second, wads it up, and tosses it into the fire. That's a beat. A beat might also be a page or two long. A woman wants her husband to wrap a present for their child. Her pursuit of that goal is a beat. Her reasons compose the element of the beat. She's running late, she's got to change her clothes, and the child will be home at any moment. When she grabs the box, tosses it on the couch, and decides to wrap it herself, that's the end of the beat.

The reason you write in beats is simple: You want your play to be made up of sections rather than isolated lines. It's also easy for actors to play beats. They understand them instinctively and will endeavor to supply them if you don't. The structure of the action is also easier to apprehend if it's divided into beats. Could you have a good piece of prose in which there were no paragraphs? Well, perhaps, but I doubt it. We think in sections. We feel in sections. Sections help us divide up an experience.

Now then, a radical suggestion: Don't think about *expanding* your play. Think about *cutting* it. If expansion is really a goal, think about adding events, not expanding dialogue. In general, playwrights worry entirely too much about their work being too short. Most people in the audience worry about a play being too long. Try packing a lot of events into a small section of time rather than scattering a few events over a long period of time.

Recently, I was standing in a theater lobby, waiting to see a new play. Someone came out with news that the play was only 95 minutes long, with one intermission. We were buoyant. And yet, I'll bet anything that the playwright had tormented herself about whether the play was long enough.

I had a similar experience at the opening of a college production of a musical. "It's three hours and twenty minutes long," someone said. We were all disappointed. I myself was inconsolable. One couple frowned and left.

Theater experiences need to be intense and, in general, shorter than they were in the past. Audiences just won't put up with a lot of talk. They certainly can't put up with the boredom. And overlong plays threaten both.

My best advice is to rewrite the play to please the audience and yourself. Examine your own responses to experiences in the theater. Then go ahead and be ruthless. Cut any scene not necessary to the story, even if it contains some of your favorite bits, lines, or ideas. *Especially* if it contains your favorite bits, lines, or ideas, cut it. If it doesn't further the story, it sticks out as "writerly," calls attention to itself, to the writing. And that is a no-no, the writer equivalent to a show-off child. Embarrassing rather than impressive.

Cut also any repeated beats. That means any beats in which the character repeats the same tactics in pursuit of a goal. Say, for example, that a character wants his sister to leave the room. His first tactic is to lure her out, his second is to threaten her, his third is to insult her. If he threatens her twice, it is less effective than if he threatens her only once.

Now we are at the micro-editing stage. Pare down the individual lines. Make sure they're economical. What if a character says something like, "Oh, hell, Bill, how many times do I have to tell you? You just don't understand anything." All right. But check to see if the line would be better if it read, "Hell, Bill, you just don't understand anything." Then take a look at that version. Maybe it would be better yet if it read, "You understand nothing." Make sure you've tested every line every possible way. Almost always, the most economical version is the best.

A writer with a particularly good ear will often imitate speech, and that can be wonderful. But it can also lead to extra beats in a line, especially at the beginning. For example, a character will say something like, "Well, yes, I know, but I also like horses." Far better if the character says, "I also like horses." It's cleaner, sharper, in some way more surprising. But most of all, it moves the scene along. It steps forward rather than marching in place, and then stepping forward.

You can also sharpen the individual lines by letting a character go on the offensive. What if the line reads, "I don't know. I don't think you understand." We know already that the lead-in sentence is unnecessary. But the second sentence is inert. What if, instead, it reads, "You. What do you understand?" You've said the same thing, you've shortened the speech, and you've also issued a challenge. The line is sharper, cleaner, better. And probably the scene is, too.

On the other hand, the character might surprise you, and say, "It smells like Campbell's Vegetable Soup in here." Good for him. Surprises are wonderful. Most plays have too few of them.

That leads me to another suggestion. Note the images you're using. (Images are figures of speech that appeal to one of the five senses.) Quite consciously, make sure that your images are interesting, subtle, fun. And while you're at it, check to see if they appeal to at least four of the five senses. Of the senses—sight, touch, smell, taste, and hearing—we tend to overdo images of sight and neglect all the others.

This next suggestion is quite radical: If you're having trouble with a section you've rewritten several times, try using iambics (a two-syllable foot, the first unaccented, the second accented). They are very easy rhythm structures, quite natural to English. They make the language rock, give it a sense of momentum. (By the way, you need not worry about the pentameter part or any other number of feet to the line. The important thing is the iambic.)

Practice some lines. Don't worry about meaning. Pay attention only to the rhythm: Ta-DUM, ta-DUM, ta-DUM. Here's an example: "In fact, the words are in my mind. But God himself could hardly give them voice." Good old iambic. Write more lines, just for practice. "You can't believe I'm dead tonight. I've gone and said too much." Language is pure sound and rhythm. Just practice the rocking motion.

Now take a look at some of your awkward lines. See if letting them rock back and forth will help you move the scene along.

One final suggestion (I like to apply this one after I've been playing with the details, the mechanics, because it is a marked contrast): Test your play for truth. Is what you're saying true? Is what this character says and does true? You can learn to finesse anything, but make sure you don't lose your soul in the process. All the technical expertise in the world can't compensate for a play that lies.

□ 83

WHEN THE WELL RUNS DRY

BY KENT R. BROWN

YOU'VE FINISHED THAT SCATHING DIATRIBE AGAINST SOMETHING OR other, and that hysterical comedy about the time you and three longtime women friends from Cape May, New Jersey, were stranded in a country 'n western bar in Amarillo, Texas. Now what? Your audience is hungry for something new, original, daring, funny but not silly, silly but not stupid, serious but not a complete downer, and your blank computer screen is daring you to knock its socks off. And nothing's coming. You've run dry!

It's a fact. As storytellers, you sometimes get stuck, run out of steam. Or perhaps you find yourself writing the same play over and over again, using similar themes, situations, and characters. You need to expand your skills by varying your plots and characterizations. Where then do you go for artistic stimulation? The answer? Everywhere. History, myth, biographies, diaries, letters, newspapers, obituaries, and the yellow pages—all are possible sources of inspiration.

Reading history, whether ancient or current, places us at the center of the social, political, scientific, and military revolutions that left their mark on human development. We can explore the public and private lives of Jefferson, Lincoln, Madame Curie, or Louis XIV. We can research the Ming Dynasty, Alexander's conquest of the western world, the Great Depression, the role of women in science or the influence of immigration on the social fabric of America. The possibilities are endless. We can continue our fascination with whatever our favorite themes might be, but we must draw our characters, accurately or with artistic embellishments, from the fabric of history.

History is full of fascinating people, but perhaps you don't have the time or, truthfully, the interest to wade through scholarly analyses. You're willing to be enriched and all that, but you really want to write the five- to six-character play with no more than one or two settings. If so, start reading the newspaper. You do read the newspaper, you say, but nothing leaps out at you. Why would it? *You* have to improvise, speculate.

Over several mornings, with *The New York Times* and two local newspapers before me, I decided to see what plots and characters might be hiding within the articles I read. I tried to keep an eye out for conflict, that situation in which two energies go up against one another. Without conflict, without making choices, there is little drama. Here goes.

• **Article:** The opening of a new art gallery. The drama: A photographer/artist who "sees" life as a set of flat planes and surfaces has difficulty communicating his/her own heart. Maybe a parent is dying and the artist tries to convey emotion through drawings or photographs. But the parent is blind. The play takes place in the gallery, perhaps, or in the summer cottage where the artist, estranged over the years, has come to say goodbye. What might happen? The possibilities are endless.

• **Article:** A biographer has elected to focus on embarrassing/sexual behavior engaged in by the subject of the biography. The drama: The biographer is approached by the subject's last surviving family member and is asked to expunge this unflattering period/episode/event in the subject's background. But the biographer needs the publication to break into an august circle of celebrity biographers. The issues are fascinating. Does any singular action actually reflect the essence of an individual? Are reputations built upon truths or fiction? Is honesty really the best policy?

• **Article:** The need to establish an investment strategy at an early age to insure that a child's college tuition will be fully funded. The drama: A single father/mother, having made disastrous financial decisions, resolves to take money from a teen-age child's education fund to cover loans or bad debts. Where is the play set? In the living room, fine, but how about a playground? On a teeter-totter? It might be dynamic to see an adult and fully-grown child coming to terms with the parent's flaws, surrounded by toys of symbolic innocence and hope. Maybe this is really a play for young people focusing on two children who set out to help their father/mother who is ill at home and has lost his/her job. How might they help out? What difficulties might they encounter?

- **Article:** Legal vs. emotional claim to items in an estate. The drama: A niece or long-distant relative appears after a funeral claiming title to an object that has been willed to her sister with whom she has had a stormy relationship. What rights do the sisters really have? What evidence will they each produce? What do they know about the family, the deceased, each other? What are the *real* stakes here?

- **Article:** A longtime social club has been meeting in an old house that is up for sale. The members face displacement. The drama: One of the club members is the buyer but does not want the others to continue meeting there. Why? I don't know yet, but if I started to explore the energy inherent in the situation, something would emerge.

- **Article:** A mother and two sick children are stranded by the side of the road in bad weather. The drama: A grown daughter, her ailing mother, and her two teen-age children are stranded at a roadside picnic rest stop. Two men approach and offer their assistance, which requires one of the stranded family members to go with one of the men while the second man stays with the family. I'm intrigued.

- **Article:** A retrospective piece looking at the Mars Rover and efforts of the engineers and scientists. The drama: What must it be like to devote one's life effort to a machine? Is it to benefit the human race, or is it motivated by a desire for celebrity? What about the scientists' families and the time the scientists spent away from loved ones? Perhaps a scientist tries to excite his children to share his enthusiasm for the work, but the children rebel because of his absence. Maybe this play is set in the backyard in a tent or a lean-to the father helped build. And the children refuse to come inside the house.

For a little comedy, try the absurd:

- **Article:** Older children in greater numbers seek money and financial assistance from their parents. The comedy: A scruffy, slightly degenerate father seeks financial aid from his grown child. But the grown child is such a poor manager of money that the father moves in with him or her and tries to manage not only the child's financial life but the child's love life as well.

- **Article:** A feature on an unfamous writer of famous jingles. The comedy: A quiet, unassuming writer of greeting cards and jingles is approached by a mobster/unsavory character to write a tribute for the mob/gang's boss on the eve of . . . something or other. I haven't figured it out quite yet, but maybe the writer falls in love with the gangster's daughter or wife or mistress!

At the core of these speculations must always be the search for an energy opposite to that generated by the protagonist. And don't require all the questions you may have about the material to be fully known before you begin to write. Many writers launch into their work letting the impulse and energy guide their inquiry. Often, too, the ending is not what they originally thought it was going to be. That's not necessarily bad. The exploration most likely will unearth future plot or character possibilities.

I used several issues of *USA Today* in writing my play, *The Phoenix Dimension*. The inciting event was actually supplied by a friend who answered his phone one morning and heard a woman's voice plead, "Help me." My friend didn't recognize the voice, thought it was a prank, and hung up. But he couldn't get back to sleep. What if the plea was genuine, what if he had stayed on the phone longer? Concurrently, I had become increasingly fed up with America's obsession with violence. Indulgent and confessional talk shows, depressing nightly news, and hundreds of articles about how we damage ourselves in so many ways in this country—all this had been fueling my frustration. *The Phoenix Dimension* fused together these two separate but thematically related states.

A ringing telephone is heard in the dark. A man in his 50s answers it. A woman's voice is heard. He hangs up. She calls back. He is hooked. She has a seductive voice and seems to know a great deal about his life, even warning him that his job is in jeopardy. A man of simple means, his full identity has been invested in his work. He becomes wary. She calls him at his office, but he never gave out his work number. His world begins to come apart. Younger employees want his job, and the boss seems eager to see the man leave the company. By the end of the play, and without ever having met her directly, the woman has persuaded him to kill his boss, who happens to be the woman's husband.

To create the impression of being off-center and no longer in control of a stable environment, I wrote a series of sound bites influenced by jingles, discount and grocery store announcements, radio and television talk shows, and predominantly, from those thumbnail news items *USA Today* lists under the heading of each state. These were interspersed throughout the play, between scenes, as my central character dressed, went to work, stared out the window, sat in a bar, and so on. Also, I never allowed him to leave the stage, thus intensifying his sense of being assaulted by the frantic and often absurd dimensions of life. For several months, I read these news snippets to learn about murders, bizarre marital difficulties, gang killings, killer bee attacks, and a host of other actual events. Each was tailored to underscore specific moments in the play, or to serve as ironic counterpoints to the action. I don't believe I could have made up all the items I used. In this instance, truth was stranger than fiction but served my fictional needs perfectly.

Besides history, biography, personal observations, and journalism, what's left? Obituaries. Here's what you'll find:

• A rural farmer who fought in W.W. II, fathered seven children, lost his farm in a major Midwest flood, played Santa Claus at annual Rotary Christmas festivities, sang with a barbershop quartet, survived three wives, and lived to be ninety-seven years of age. And that's just what was printed in the obituary! What influence might his W.W. II experiences have had on his attitude toward life? What made him want to play Santa Claus?

• A single mother in the south, with three adopted children of mixed heritage, who earned her living as a professional mourner, a tutor in Italian, a nurse, and a choir singer who often sang at ten church services per week. She served on the state's Welfare Commission and generated funding initiatives for the Special Olympics. What conflicts did she have with her children, her employers? How did she spend whatever quiet time came her way, or was she driven to prove something to herself or to someone else?

• A Ph.D. university scholar of hard sciences who was a sports photographer and National Science Foundation Fellowship recipient, a Formula 1 race car driver, and loved ballet and classical music. Was this a man who valued control and precision but enjoyed dealing with risky variables as he raced around the track?

Finally, if you are really pressed for time, and are fed up with the alcoholic fathers, insensitive psychiatrists, and arrogant teachers that always seem to turn up in your cast lists, try this: Open a telephone book and turn to the yellow pages. You'll be amazed at the countless occupations, associations, and businesses that keep this country moving but seldom walk the stage: air conditioning contractors, termite controllers, animal welfare directors, antique dealers, architects, auto supply owners/workers/secretaries, bank examiners, birth center directors, private bodyguards, billiard parlor owners, bookbinders, burial vault salespersons, caterers, chiropractors, ministers, crane operators, kitchen designers, elevator inspectors—I'll stop here.

Imagine the options! You can mix and match your characters as you do your wardrobe. How about a crane operator father who is an opera buff? Why not? Or a chiropractor who studied film in college and knows the dialogue to all the films by John Ford and plays out a different scene each time he's working on a client. Or maybe there's a play about a burial vault salesperson who meets an antique dealer/mortician/ bookbinder who wants to be buried in a specially designed vault that plays Dixie whenever the doors are opened. Well, this last idea may or may not fly, but give it a try. The point here is that what we do and how we elect to spend our time and our energy tells volumes about our values—and our characters' values, as well.

To develop a rich appreciation for how fascinating people's lives can be, read the oral histories compiled by Studs Terkel: *The Good War, Hard Times, Working,* and *American Dreams.* The personal tales of fear, joy, aspiration, and regret are riveting, superior tributes to human tenacity. Also, for a personal perspective on history, take a look at *Eyewitness to History,* edited by John Carey, for examples of life as it was lived from the siege of Jerusalem in 70 A.D. to the fall of Ferdinand Marcos in 1986.

To see how history and nonfiction can inform the theatrical imagination, take a good look at Robert Bolt's *A Man for All Seasons;* Robert Schenkkan's *The Kentucky Cycle;* James Goldman's *The Lion in Winter; Clarence Darrow,* by David Rintels; *Becket,* by Jean Anouilh; the musical *Quilters,* by Molly Newman (book) and Barbara Damashek (book, music and lyrics); and *Across the Plains,* by Sandra Fenichel Asher.

Root your work in reality, but remember, fact alone is not drama. You have to push it, shape it, tease it into a dramatic work that can be more truthful to the spirit of human condition than the facts that created it.

❑ 84

FINDING A THEME
FOR YOUR PLAY

BY PETER SAGAL

USUALLY WHEN PEOPLE ASK ME WHAT MY PLAYS ARE ABOUT, I HEM
and haw and squint off into the sky and then come up with something
like, "Well, there's this guy, and he has this dog. . . . and then this army
invades. . . . well, it's really kind of a love story, in the end." I feel
silly, and my questioner hasn't learned anything, which may be right,
because if he wants to know what the play is about, he should see
the thing. I mean, we write immortal works of dramatic literature, not
slogans.

But I recently wrote a play that could be summarized in a single
sentence.* This was a first for me, and because of this, and because the
sentence in question invoked some political and moral questions, I became instantly known as a Dramatist of Serious Theme. This makes me
bristle, because like every other normal writer, I resent any praise that
is not universal. What are my comedies, chopped liver?

Nonetheless, I'm now known as a guy with something to say, and
I've been asked here to give some tips on how to say it, that is, how to
approach the problem of Theme in playwriting. (That raises the ancil-
lary question of how you write a play when you have *nothing* to say,
which is a problem I face daily.) Somebody—I think it was Woody
Allen quoting Samuel Goldwyn—said that people go to the theater for
entertainment; if you want to send a message, call Western Union. But
the theater has changed a lot and seems to be surviving only because of
its toehold in Meaning; i.e., movies and TV may give you cleavage and
explosions, etc., but if you want to learn something, come to the theater.
Somebody else said—and this time I know, it was the actor Simon

---

*"A Jewish lawyer defends the First Amendment rights of a man who says the Holo-
caust did not happen." (*Denial,* Long Wharf Theater, Dec. 1995)

Callow—that in this day and age, going to the theater for "entertain-ment" is like going to a restaurant for indigestion.

So how to approach the theme play, the political or "problem" play? First of all, it seems to me that the playwright should always begin not from a statement, but a question. It is boring to be told an opinion, but it is interesting to be asked for your own. Thus, a writer who sets off to tell us, "Racism is bad!," for example, will probably ultimately irritate the audience, because they know that racism is bad and they're sorry, but frankly they don't feel that they had to pay $20 or whatever to be told again. But a writer who asks the audience, "Why is racism bad?" or even "Is racism ever justified?" will hold the playgoers' attention, because they may never have thought about it before, and their answers may surprise or please or horrify the playwright.

Once you have framed your question in an interesting and provoca-tive way, how do you dramatize it? Here we fall into the great Un-known, because the answer depends on your particular vision of drama and the theater, and my answer may not suit you and your purposes. For example, if you're Brecht, you'll pose your question by writing it on a banner and hanging it upstage center. What I do is try to make the Thematic Problem into a personal one.

Sometimes it's obvious how to do this, sometimes it's not. If you're writing about True Love, then clearly your play will need some lovers. If it's about racism, then a racist or two will be in order. More compli-cated questions require more complicated solutions, but part of your job as a dramatist (some would say your *whole* job) is to find that telling situation, that moment of crisis and decision plucked from the entire span of an infinite number of imaginary lifetimes, that perfectly distills the essence of the question you're addressing. For example, let's say you want to write about the tension between duty to self and duty to country. You want to write about a solider. But which solider, in which war? An Englishman fighting in World War I? A Jew fighting in World War II? An Asian American fighting in Vietnam? Any situation will give different emphases to different sides of your question. How do you choose?

In considering this choice, remember that the worst sin the dramatist can commit is to lie to an audience. In this context, it means putting a question out there and then making the answer easy or simple when it's not. There's a great temptation when asking an important question—

"Will True Love Always Triumph?"—to go immediately for the best and most comforting answer—"Yes!"—and ignore all the evidence to the contrary that's in the world, in your heart, in your own play. Consider *King Lear*. Its answer to that particular question would be a resounding *No,* so during the 17th century, the play was rewritten by Nahum Tate to answer *Yes:* Cordelia, quite alive at the end, united with Edmund and her loving father. That rewritten version was rejected by history for, among other things, being a lie.

So if you are going to ask a tough question, and you should, you must be merciless in your search for the answer. Let the situation of the play be rife with ambiguity and doubt. Let your characters be contradictory, holding both bad and good within them. Let the most horrible opinions be held by the most pleasant and attractive people. Let good people do terrible things to one another; let them react to kindness with anger and to attacks with fear. Because that's what happens in the real world, and if by chance you do want to say, ultimately, something good—that Love will triumph, that freedom is precious and worth fighting for—it won't help your case to set your play in a fantasy world where these things come easier than they actually are.

What I've often done is to take a character I admire and like, and then either put that character in a very difficult position, or cause him or her to do something rather unpleasant and then have to deal with the results. In my play *Denial* I took a character who was very confident in her support of free speech and confronted her with another character—very charming, by the way—who made her want to scream and strike out every time he opened his mouth. In *Angels in America,* by Tony Kushner, a lead character, who is charming and sympathetic and funny, abandons his lover in time of crisis, so we are left to ask ourselves—we, who think of ourselves as charming and sympathetic and funny—if when the time came, we might do the same thing.

The second worst sin in the theater, after lying, is to be boring. In fact, it's often in the pursuit of not being boring that we end up telling our worst lies. There's a strong temptation—driven by the market and our own inclination to be cheerful—to preach to the choir. The theater of today desperately wants to say something Useful and Good about the world; it wants to condemn what needs condemning and praise what needs praising, according to the mores of the day. But the problem is that unless you do that from a deeply informed, dramatically charged, almost universally comprehending place, you're going to bore the heck out of your audience.

How do you achieve that kind of aesthetic Buddha-nature, where you comprehend everything, where all forces balance, where the true strengths and faultlines of the universe reveal themselves?

Work hard, write every day, and tell the truth. It may not work, but nothing else will.

❏ JUVENILE AND YOUNG ADULT

❑ 85

THE OUCH FACTOR

BY SID FLEISCHMAN

WHEN I FIRST BEGAN TO WRITE FICTION, I MADE EVERY MISTAKE known to the world of moveable type. I even pioneered mistakes as yet undiscovered. In my haste to keep a story moving, I was apt to leap from action to action, unwilling to pause for reactions. If one of my characters hit his thumb with a hammer, I didn't give him time to say ouch.

I hadn't a clue to the story muscle that reactions provide. They are, of course, dramatic punctuation, focusing and intensifying passing moments. But they may be more. Somewhere along the way, I discovered the power of reaction to reveal character, to jump start a dying scene—and even, as I will explain, to give an unexpected direction to a story-in-progress. I regard reaction as one of a writer's loyal company of friends.

Take this situation: A nine-year-old boy is sent to a foreign city, to be met at the airport by a grumpy uncle. When Uncle Grump fails to turn up, the boy hops a bus and walks in on the relative. Grump dismisses the matter with not even an apology. All this dramatic fodder is told, not shown, at the speed of light in a couple of narrative paragraphs.

What's wrong here? The "ouches" are missing. Discovering no one there to meet him at the airport—a strong dramatic situation—the abandoned boy *must* react. Is he scared? Does he wonder if his uncle is sick? Dead? Didn't the old man receive the letter to say he would be arriving? Maybe Uncle Grump really doesn't want him to visit. What should he do? Reaction would jump start the scene.

And how about that cardboard uncle? The way he responds will peg his character. *Arrogant*: "You're a day early, boy!" *Addled*: "Dear me, dear me, who'd you say you were?" *Guilt-stricken*: "You poor lad, you must be starved! Mollie, set a plate for the boy and bring a dunce cap for me."

I'm not certain what wised me up to the full range and impact of reaction. My education may have started with the famous World War II news picture of the Frenchman on a Paris boulevard trying to hold back his tears as he watches the invading Germans come goose-stepping by.

That face, caught in a moment of profound tragedy, was a reaction shot. One could read a life story into it.

Reaction! How had I managed to treat it so cavalierly?

Motion pictures have been described as the art of *action and reaction.* There is even the well-defined "reaction shot." The next time you watch a movie on TV, turn off the sound and watch the reaction shots flicker by like exclamation points. To punch up the moment, savvy comedians invented a trunkload of reactions: "takes," "double takes," mouth-spraying "spit takes." Who could forget Edgar Kennedy's slow burn?

And then I saw an amazing newspaper item (one that seems to recur about every twenty years) about a convict, about to be let out of prison, *who doesn't want to leave.* There blossomed in my head that marvel of them all—what I have come to call the "contrary reaction."

When a character's response is contrary to the normal and the ex-pected, but somehow made logical—that's pure story oxygen.

Isn't that what makes O. Henry's story, "The Ransom of Red Chief," such a charmer and so memorable? An insufferable nine-year-old kid, you'll recall, is kidnapped and forced to hide out in a cave—to his utter delight! There he plays Indian chief. Finally:

> "Red Chief," says I to the kid, "would you like to go home?"
> "Aw, what for?" says he. "I don't have any fun at home. I hate to go to school. I like to camp out. You won't take me back home again, Snake-eye, will you?"

In due time, the family demands a "ransom" from the kidnappers to take the tyke *back.* How's that for contrary reaction?

I use these reversals whenever I see a good opportunity. In my Gold Rush novel, *Bandit's Moon* (Greenwillow Books), my eleven-year-old heroine, Annyrose, should flee for her life at the sight of the notoriously bloodthirsty bandit, Joaquín Murieta and his gang. She does the reverse. Standing her ground, she pleads, "Sir . . . take me with you!"

Naturally, I had to set up a situation and a rationale so that the reader would not regard the girl as certifiable. That was easy. I made Joaquín her immediate opportunity to escape from a greater villain, that horror in petticoats, O.O. Mary. At the same time the reverse "take" enabled me to establish Annyrose's feisty, unflappable and resourceful character. It all worked beautifully, and the novel was designated a Notable Book by the American Library Association.

In an earlier novel, *By the Great Horn Spoon!* (Little, Brown), I opened the story with two stowaways, Jack and the family butler, Praiseworthy, on a ship bound for California. They rise from two potato barrels where they have been hiding. Watch the reverse reaction:

> "I suggest that we see what can be done about improving our accommodations," said Praiseworthy, tapping his bowler hat firmly in place. "Shall we go?"
>
> "Go?" Jack replied. "Go where?" He fully expected to pass the voyage below decks with the cargo. He had read dire accounts of the treatment handed out to stowaways on ships of the sea.
>
> "Why, to pay our respects to the captain," said Praiseworthy.
>
> "*The captain!*" The words very nearly caught in his throat. "But he'll put us in chains—*or worse!*"
>
> "Leave that to me," said Praiseworthy, with an airy lift of the eyebrow. "Come along. . . ."

The direction of another one of my novels was profoundly changed when I tried out a bit of contrary reaction in a boy and dog story, *Jim Ugly* (Greenwillow Books). Here I was dealing with the reaction of a one-man dog, Jim Ugly, to the death of his master. The dog, half wolf, might normally mourn the death at the nearby gravesite. Then I wondered how it would play if I reversed the reaction, with the dog showing no interest in the spot. Here it reaches a climax:

> I hauled up on the rope and pointed to the burying ground. "This way, Jim Ugly. Dad's in there."
>
> Jim Ugly gave me a twitchy look, as if to say I didn't have enough brains to know my way outdoors without printed instructions. . . .
>
> My eyes tightened on the tombstones leaning up against the sunset. I knew for a sudden fact what Jim Ugly had known all along. My dad wasn't buried there. His scent wasn't on that rough, hammered-together coffin. The hair on my neck shot up.

If the boy's father wasn't in the pine box, where was he? That became the novel, thanks to Jim Ugly's contrary reaction.

And you'll remember what happened to the fellow who bit into a savory French pastry. The remembered taste of that *petite madeleine* in childhood, as Proust described his reaction, set the narrator off on a six-volume memory trip.

Shake hands with the ouch factor. It's an author's friend.

❏ 86

SAILING THE CRAFT OF
CHILDREN'S POETRY

BY J. PATRICK LEWIS

NOT LONG AGO, A YOUNG WOMAN WHO WANTED DESPERATELY TO write children's poetry asked me for some advice. "Which poets do you enjoy reading?" I asked her encouragingly. "Good heavens," she said, "I never *read* poetry. After all, I wouldn't want to be affected by what others have written."

That little encounter brought to mind my own benighted, late-in-life experience when I first discovered "Lady Poetry." I was just on the sunlight side of forty, laboring in other fields (professing Economics!) for most of my adult life. Don't ask what or who turned my head. I honestly don't remember, though to that source or gentle soul I now extend a swashbuckling bow.

Enthusiasm and commitment, hard work and long hours at the writer's trade I offered in spades, as the making of poems, especially children's verse, took hold of me—obsessively. My first efforts so startled me with their brilliance that I couldn't wait to show the world what I had wrought: "Going down and down/For the good turf. Digging," as Seamus Heaney memorably put it. Needless to add, it wasn't long before I escaped that rarefied air and realized that what I'd penned was abominable doggerel. Forgive the redundancy, but I am at pains to emphasize the true awfulness of my mid-life "juvenilia," now, mercifully, mulch in a landfill.

What was absent was a sense of craft, because I had read almost no poetry. I didn't know that poems are, as Mary Oliver says, "fires for the cold, ropes let down to the lost, something as necessary as bread in the pockets of the hungry." What to do? What I did was to stop writing. For three years. I immersed myself in the bone and the marrow of poetry—adult's and children's, classics and new—before I dared to take up a pen again.

435

I'm not sure if any of that experience justifies pontificating on "what children's poets should do." So these few tips I offer humbly to those who would plow these fields:

Never fear failure, that cold, hardhearted friend, but friend nonetheless. The novelist Allan Gurganus has said, in another context, that, "In America, the true 'F-word' is Failure." When I make school visits I emphasize how important it is to fail—regularly. What comes easy is cheesy. Schools should award prizes to kids who say, "Hey, I failed three times today—and that was before lunch!" A lesson for grown-up poets, too. Every writer's toolkit should come with a regulation, extra-large wastebasket.

Learn the rules of prosody—metrics, verse forms, rhythm, rhyme. Most people learn to play the guitar by first understanding chords. Or they become plumbers by learning the trade's techniques. Poets are no exception.

Once you know the rules, go ahead and break them. Especially for children who are cutting their teeth on language, sound is vital to sense *and* nonsense. Most of my children's verses do indeed rhyme. But I encourage teachers to *dis*courage the very young from rhyming. As T. S. Eliot says of the naming of cats, rhyming "is not one of your holiday games." It takes time and skill, two essentials that children have precious little of. They invariably opt for the cheap nonsense neologism that they mistakenly believe to be poetry. If, as an adult cobbler of children's verse, you choose to write in rhyme, beware: The bar of excellence rises a notch or two because contrived rhymes are so easy to write—yet painful to read.

Let me elaborate. A well-intentioned children's magazine once gave a different word—one word each—to three other children's poets and me. Our charge was to rhyme that word four times in a quatrain within one minute over the telephone! "We will then publish the results," the editor said, "as a challenge and an inspiration to our young readers." Foolishly, all four of us rose to the bait, and all four "poems" appeared in the next issue of the magazine. I don't know if there were any subsequent howls to the editor, but there should have been. Each poem was, how should I say this? Horrid. And a poor lesson for aspiring poets. Writing poetry is not a race against time. It is composition, not competition. Like painting, poetry requires a slow hand.

Keep children's poems fairly short. For better or (in my opinion) worse, the increasing speed of the world no longer provides shelter or comfort to epics, ballads, long narrative poems. Publishers find little to like about them. And after a trying day at home or office, parents are unlikely to relish a bedtime reading of, say, even the masterful eighteen (*18!*) stanzas of Lewis Carroll's "The Walrus and the Carpenter."

When I am asked where ideas come from, I state the obvious: everywhere. Generally, the sources are three: reading; observing; and remembering your own childhood or experiences with your children. Look for inspiration around the corner, in a food court, at a soccer game, in the grocery line, at the aquarium. Muses hang out everywhere, but most notably in the pages of books. What I told the young lady I mentioned at the outset is that, quite apart from the sheer thrill of reading, another poet's words or lines might be the catalyst for her own magnum opus.

To increase your chances of publication, look to themes that have general appeal: holidays; seasons; birthdays; food; colors; sports. There are far too few poems on math and science. If you can write a love poem that isn't "sincere," more power to you. An anthologist recently asked me for a poem about school. Does this qualify?

> Knives can harm you, heaven forbid!
> Axes may disarm you, kid.
> Guillotines are harmful, but . . .
> There's nothing like a paper cut.

Apparently not. The poem didn't make it into the school anthology, but, happily, it found worthy homes elsewhere.

This little ditty of mine appeared in the Food Section of several regional newspapers:

> God made the rooster,
> God made the hen,
> But Ma made the chicken
> Pot pie! Amen.

Even the sky—and pie—is not the limit. Unanchor your imagination. No subject is out of bounds for poetry.

Or choose a theme of your own. Last year, thumbing through *The Guinness Book of World Records*, I was inspired to write a collection

of "extreme poems." *A Toast of Mosts & A Feast of Leasts* (Harcourt/
Creative) should appear in time for Y2K.

Write a bookmark poem (long and skinny), a dream poem, or an
acrostic poem:

> Libraries
> Are
> Necessary
> Gardens,
> Unsurpassed
> At
> Growing
> Excitement.

Write a list poem by starting with a color:

Violet is . . .

> my cat's tongue
> lavender out on a holiday
> blush pears
> bruised peaches
> pain gone away
> Earth from six miles high
> the color of dreams after midnight
> the afternoon glancing off a grackle's back
> the flower that bears her name

To write for children, be the child that still lives in you. How often
do children find themselves talking to someone or something that can't
talk back? An uncooperative soccer ball, spilled orange juice, a cozy
doll? If you write a poem in a voice that addresses the voiceless, this is
an apostrophe poem. Left alone, children often speak in an apostrophe
voice, addressing the moon, a mouse, a blade of grass, even an absent
person. For instance:

Sea, Who Are You?

> A quilt of blue on blue?
> An ocean in disguise?
> An endless mirror to
> The self-important skies?
> The city of the strange?

The country of the deep?
The wind's first practice range?
The secrets seagulls keep?
The home to buried hills . . .
Oh what's a mystery for?
The empire that builds
Gold borders on a shore.

Don't be afraid to imitate! Pianists learn by practicing other people's works; so can poets. You may discover that what you have written is actually better than the original, or a scintillating parody of it, duly acknowledged, of course.

Do you like riddles? I can tell you from my school visit experiences, riddles are a natural vein to mine. Kids love them, perhaps because they are tickled to be an interactive part of guessing the answer:

To folks in Maine,
They're red and round,
And you can find 'em
Underground.
In Idaho,
They're brown and big.
They still grow under-
Ground. You dig?

Immediately obvious to you, but not necessarily to second-graders. Like all forms of poetry, riddle poems are more difficult to write than they seem.

Children are extremely visual, which is why concrete poetry is another exciting avenue for them—and for you—to explore. It's impossible to make great claims for shape poems, apart from their cleverness on the page. But again, it's the aspect of the word play that students find, well, playful, and that sets them to thinking.

Haiku, cinquains, limericks, double dactyls—try them all on for size. And don't forget the first rule you learned, probably at a much younger age than I did: Find your own voice. Better yet, find your own voices.

The great Dr. Seuss certainly had a distinctive, recognizable style. You always know a Seuss poem when you meet one. But he was a most notable and very successful exception, which is why, I suppose, too many people writing for children try in vain to substitute his voice for their own. It has always seemed to me more virtuous, or more fun at least, to write in so many styles that no single poem can be traced back to you. There is a challenge so daunting that you are bound to fail over and over again.

And that's the best part. Nothing succeeds like failure.

❏ 87

GET YOUR READER INVOLVED

BY ANNE WARREN SMITH

CERTAIN STORIES INVITE READERS IN AND HOLD THEM TIGHT; THEY feel magnetized or glued, unable to put the book down. They connive to outwit the villains, guffaw at the protagonist's antics, and long after they've finished reading, they catch themselves still living in that other world, still caring for the characters. If you can write that kind of book for young adults, your story will win out over all the other enticements today's young adults face.

The best writing for young adults is interactive; it forges a partnership with the reader. How do writers achieve this? The answer lies in the language—specifically in the nouns and verbs and sensory details they use. Small stuff, you may think, but I'm talking here about *final* revisions. Once you are satisfied that your characters and plot are as good as you can make them, take time to look at individual words. Every word has the power to magnetize.

Make your nouns specific

At first, you're lazy and may write, "Eat all your vegetables," or "Don't tease that dog." How much more effective if you say, "Eat all your beet greens," or "Don't tease that pit bull." Name every vegetable and dog—every generic noun—in your prose. In his award-winning book, *Blue Skin of the Sea,* although Graham Salisbury speaks of "rubble" as his characters enter a disaster area, he gets specific right away:

> The rubble crammed up into the back end of the river was incredible—splintered buildings, boulders, cars, bent and twisted steel beams, dead fish, telephone poles, and cane trash. And a sampan as long as Dad's, red hull to the sky. . . . Steel parking meters were bent flat to the sidewalks. Where buildings had once been, there were only vacant cement pads. The houses, shops, and boats lay farther back, in shattered heaps, with men digging through them. Fish trapped in puddled gutters flopped hopelessly in brown, foot-deep ponds.

441

Another kind of specificity—proper nouns—will also engage your young adult readers. Here are the enticing first lines of Salisbury's novel:

> A noon-high Hawaiian sun poured over the jungled flanks of the Big Island, spreading down into the village of Kailua-Kona and the blistering metal bed of Uncle Harley's fish truck. Keo and I sat across from each other on the black rubber inner tubes that Uncle Harley, Keo's father, had gotten for us at the Chevron Station in Holualoa.

Actual places that exist on a map and an uncle with a real name lend verisimilitude and flavor to the story. And a Chevron station isn't just a generic gas station; the name instantly evokes a red and white picture in the minds of most readers.

Choose strong verbs

In my own early drafts, I use the first verb that occurs to me. For example, I may have written that Tom, my young adult hero, *walked* through the forest. I need then to consider whether he *staggered, marched, moseyed, crept, sauntered,* or *strode* through the forest. Or did he *skip, trudge, amble,* or *tiptoe*? Each of these verbs evokes a different picture of what Tom was really doing and, most important, how he felt about it. This is where the writer turns the reader into a partner. If I choose *amble*, my reader thinks, "Tom's relaxed, not a bit worried." Furthermore, the reader is more apt to *believe* Tom is relaxed than if I had simply told him so.

In a second reading of my story, I find I've written that Tom's friend Linda ate a hamburger, but it's more likely that, depending on her frame of mind (and the condition of her braces), she *munched, gummed, pigged out, picked at, wolfed, gulped, chomped,* or *chewed*. Choose any one of these verbs and you can *see* her. Paul Zindel's creepy fantasy, *Doom Stone*, teems with evocative verbs. Notice how *sprang, shrieked, fled*, and *burst* work for him:

> Like a tick on a burning match cover, the monster sprang whole from the cage, landing against the far wall. It shrieked, its flesh on fire as it fled for the cellar door. With a single motion it burst the doors from their hinges.

Reading Salisbury's *Blue Skin of the Sea* again, you see how he uses powerful verbs to show his character's fear of deep water and at the same time his fascination with it:

The mask pushed in on my face and small streams of water dripped in at my temples. The ocean filled my ears and pressed in painfully. We floated in an air of watery space with a crackling, snapping, buzzing sound all around us. A small puddle began to gather in the mask, below my nose, nearly panicking me.

But for a moment I looked beyond the puddle, amazed at the islands of coral that broke the sandy ocean floor. Silent fish circled and hung in small schools far beneath my feet, their backs dark and bullet shaped. A huge parrot fish nibbled at the edge of a mass of coral, then suddenly darted away and sailed to a stop farther out.

As if the verbs *pushed, filled, pressed, floated, circled, hung, nibbled, darted,* and *sailed* aren't enough, Salisbury adds *crackling, snapping, buzzing, and panicking.*

Add power with sensory details

Never underestimate the power of sensory details. I always need to add and refine the sensory details in my own final drafts, and the work is well worth the effort. Sensory details are the warhorses that crank up tension, create mood and atmosphere, and breathe life into our characters.Here are some examples:

In my hypothetical story, Tom's younger brother Jerry, normally a happy-go-lucky kid, is walking down a dark alley. I already know enough to use *creeping* instead of *walking* since I want the reader to know that Jerry's afraid. Now, suppose I increase Jerry's (and therefore the reader's) fear by adding carefully selected sensory details: I choose the smell of urine, the rasp of a garbage can on the pavement, the flash of a cat's eyes from the top of the fence, and the prickly chill of bricks against Jerry's back as he presses against the wall. Smells, sounds, sights, textures. Did I forget taste? Here is a possible one: "He tasted sour apple fear—acid, rancid—worse than anything he'd ever tasted before." As you incorporate more sensory details into a scene you are writing, watch the tension thermometer rise.

Sensory details also increase tension by forcing your narrative into slow motion, like nightmares in which you can barely move your leaden feet to avoid being run over by the speeding locomotive. In *Probably Nick Swansen,* Virginia Euwer Wolff stops time by heightening background sounds that otherwise might not be noticed:

There was a fierce quiet in the living room. You could hear the lawn sprinkler ticking and a fly angry on the windowsill looking for a way out. Nick looked at his mother and dad. If he got killed, they wouldn't have any children left at all.

In *Alias,* by M.E. Ryan, the protagonist knows he's not supposed to look in a box that belongs to his mother. Here's how his sense of hearing is heightened:

> The box was old and worn from years of travel. The stars and crescents were faded, the cardboard lid frayed at the edges.
> My hands were shaking so badly, I almost dropped it.
> I paused a moment and listened. Was something ticking inside the box?
> Nope—just the alarm clock in the corner. I swallowed a few times, took a deep breath, and opened the box.

In *The True Confessions of Charlotte Doyle,* the author, Avi, could have told the reader that Charlotte, the fourteen-year-old protagonist, was excited. Instead he lets the reader participate. Notice the details:

> Everywhere I looked great canvas sails of gray, from mainsail to main royal, from flying jib to trysail, were bellied out. Beyond the sails stretched the sky itself, as blue as a baby's bluest eyes, while the greenish sea, crowned with lacy caps of foaming white rushed by with unrelenting speed. The *Seahawk* had gone to sea.

Readers share Charlotte's excitement as her adventure begins. A few pages later, however, Avi describes the same scene, this time, with details and verbs that foretell disaster:

> Though the *Seahawk* heaved and rolled, creaked and groaned, her sails hung limply. The sky was different too; low, with a heavy dampness that instantly wet my face, though I felt nothing so distinct as rain. As for the sea, it was almost the same color as the sky, a menacing claylike gray. And yet, it was in constant motion, its surface heaving rhythmically like the chest of some vast, discomforted sleeper.

Gary Paulsen in *Sisters/Hermanas* uses sensory details to characterize fourteen-year-old Rosa, an illegal immigrant who is a prostitute on the streets of Houston. He doesn't tell his readers that Rosa is a sympathetic character; they *know* she is when they read the following:

> In the middle [of her room] was a bed made of wood with burned edges and covered with burned brands that she sometimes ran her fingers over in the late mornings when she awakened. . . . The bed was a kind of nest for

her. Sometimes when she was hurt, when the men hurt her, she would come back to the room and curl into the center of the bed with the blanket that had the soft, silky edge wrapped around her and take comfort there, rubbing the silk between her fingers until she slept.

Be selective with your details. Discard those that readers will automatically understand. In *Probably Nick Swansen*, Virginia Euwer Wolff carefully chooses the sensory details that are most likely to take us into the mind of a young man who is learning disabled. Here's her very successful first paragraph:

> Room 19 was dressed up. It crackled with sounds, and party smells came from everywhere. Green streamers hung from the ceiling, two tables were covered with junk food, and more things were arriving every time you turned around—hot dogs, homemade brownies, three kinds of potato chips. A giant homemade poster was trying to come unhinged from its masking tape over the blackboard, and it said in huge red letters, "Yay, Shana."

Consider the details Wolff does *not* put in. Any teenager can fill in the ordinary blanks of chalk dust or desktop graffiti. Wolff uses the space to introduce a character in whose mind a room might be "dressed up," or where a poster might seem to be alive—in short, the kind of person many teenage readers might avoid in real life.

Practice

Beyond being aware of the amazing power of specific nouns and verbs and sensory details when writing for young adults, here are some ideas that may help you improve your young adult stories:

- Read the prize-winning books I've quoted here and ask your librarian about other outstanding books for young adult readers. Read them once for enjoyment and then again, paying particular attention to nouns, verbs, and sensory details.
- Write pairs of sentences using weak verbs and strong verbs.
- Write a paragraph that uses general nouns, then rewrite it using specific ones.
- Write a scene in which you incorporate every one of the five senses. Write it over and over using different sensory details each time to evoke a different emotion: joy, sadness, fear, or horror.
- Scrutinize your current writing. Evaluate each noun and verb. See

what sensory details you can add. Remember that just any verb or any detail won't do. Use artistic judgment to select ones that increase tension, evoke pictures, conjure atmosphere, and give characters their identity and sympathetic qualities.

Think of the young adult reader as your partner. Give your readers the best raw material, and they will leap into your story and stay with you to The End.

❑ 88

WRITING NONFICTION FOR YOUNG READERS

BY NANCY WARREN FERRELL

AS A PUBLISHED AUTHOR OF NONFICTION FOR YOUNG READERS, I'VE often been approached by people who say they have a great idea and want to write a book, but they are not sure where to start.

First, go to your public library and study the type of books you want to write. See how other authors handle their material, and get a sense of the different grade and age levels of the books in print. Check *Books in Print* to see how many books have already been written on your topic. Obviously, if several have been published for the same age group in recent years, it might be best to turn to another topic, unless your slant is fresh.

Note the names of the publishers who bring out certain kinds of books. It's a waste of time and postage to submit nonfiction to a company that publishes only fiction. You can also locate marketing information in the Book Publishers section of this book. In addition, consult current publishers' catalogues found in the children's department of the library. Or you can write for catalogues and guidelines from the publishers themselves.

While at the library, locate books on creative writing and check references in them. Take a few home to study writing techniques. If you find one or two books you really like, order them from the publishers or buy them from the bookstore to start your home library.

After completing some preliminary research on your topic, write a one-page query letter to an appropriate publisher to see if their house is interested in your subject. In the letter, describe what you have in mind and how you plan to approach the material. Be sure to indicate if you have special knowledge of your topic, such as work experience. You might also write a brief outline of your proposed book to include with your query.

447

If you have photographs or know they are available, mention that in your query. Ordinarily, an author is not responsible for illustrations or photographs in books. Nevertheless, some writers who take good pictures should indicate their credentials. Arrangements for publication and payment are made in the final contract.

Send your proposal to about five publishers, including an SASE (self-addressed, stamped envelope) with each one. Note this information on a file card so you know to whom and when you submitted the queries.

Usually, you receive responses to your queries—yes or no. Let's say a publisher likes your idea, and after some talk and negotiation, you sign a contract. You will often receive comments and suggestions from your editor to help you shape your book to fit the publisher's needs. Now the serious work begins.

Check out a number of books on your topic from the library—both adult and juvenile. Read and make copies of specific magazine articles you can locate. Surf the Internet for additional material.

On 4″ × 6″ file cards, note such information as the title, author, where located, etc., for each book, article, or contact you may consult. Keeping a record of this data will help you build a bibliography if you should need one; it also gives a specific reference point if you wish to add information to your manuscript or check facts during the revision process. Otherwise, you could be frantically looking through piles of books and papers trying to find a quote or a fact that your editor has questioned. Taking time for these reference cards at the start of your research proves its worth over and over.

If it's important as part of your research to interview people in an agency or business, go to the top. Make appointments beforehand. As an example, when I researched my book on the U.S. Coast Guard, I arranged an appointment with the Alaskan commander, a rear admiral. I described my project, and he in turn sent a memo to the local offices explaining who I was, and requesting their cooperation. This clearance proved invaluable. Everyone I met took me seriously, and was willing to help.

As you read and digest your subject material, you might find that distant locations have valuable information or photographs you need. Write letters so that data can be coming back to you as you get farther into your project. Be sure to write a quick "thank you" when you receive the material.

Arrange for any on-scene experiences you know would be interesting. This can be the most fun, because you are actively doing, feeling, and understanding the excitement you want to convey to young readers. If, for example, you are writing a book about fishing, go fish; if writing about a historical site, visit that location to get a true-life experience, and then pass as much as you can on to your readers.

My most exciting hands-on experience was going up in a Coast Guard search-and-rescue helicopter to take photographs. Again, this experience was cleared through the rear admiral first. At Sitka Air Station, the flight mechanic fitted me out in an orange mustang suit. I was briefed beforehand, and up we went. When the chopper flew high above Sitka harbor, a crew member wrapped a gunner's belt around my waist, hooked me onto a strap, and opened the cabin doors. There I was, breathless, the toes of my shoes clamped to the door sill, with nothing but air in front and beneath me! "There you are," a crew member said, "take all the pictures you want."

At this point, you should be aware of the one universal warning that flashes like a red light: Do not talk down to young readers; this is not a writing mistake, but a way of thinking—you cannot correct it with a comma or a paragraph break. Respect your readers, show them you have something fascinating to tell them, and give them credit for absorbing the information.

What I've found helpful in writing for elementary-grade readers is to conjure up, say, some eight-year-olds and figuratively plunk them down in front of me. Then I begin writing with them in mind. If I sense they are getting restless or do not seem to understand, I'm not doing my job.

While you are absorbing information on your subject, keep an eye out for unusual facts and anecdotes to include in your final version. For instance, while doing research for *U.S. Air Force,* I learned that when the first U.S. air force was formed in 1907, the division had no aircraft, and only three men—none of whom could fly a plane! To me that was a startling, amazing fact that had to be shared with young readers.

During this research-gathering stage, you have only a general idea of how to handle your material. Normally, it does not come in a rush, but in bits and pieces until a smooth, balanced manuscript emerges. There are changes, reorganization, insertions, deletions. It takes time and work.

Then when you actually begin writing, keep certain techniques in mind:

Make your verbs active, appeal to the five senses, and use dialogue to give life to your words. If possible, use actual dialogue from journals and letters, keeping in mind that youngsters can be experts in certain fields, too. Experts give authority to your writing. When I needed an expert role-model for my *Alaska: A Land in Motion* geography book, I located a 12-year-old boy who was the first young person to climb the highest mountain in North America—Mt. McKinley.

Make your chapter headings and openings as interesting as possible. One chapter heading in my book, *Battle of the Little Bighorn,* for example, was the Sioux Indian battle cry, "It is a good day to die!" In my book, *The New World of Amateur Radio,* I told of the strange behavior of cattle several hours before an Alaska earthquake. Grab your readers from the start, and pull them in.

Use newspaper headlines, actual cassette tape dialogues, bumper stickers, etc. in your narrative. In my *Fishing Industry* book, for instance, I duplicated actual boat radio talk. For my diplomacy book, *Passports to Peace,* I used authentic secret code phrases, and added excitement to *U.S. Air Force* by including video dialogue of a real intercept of a Russian fighter plane entering U.S. air space. Besides adding drama, these short units help break up text, catch the reader's eye and hold his or her interest.

Make adult role-models real; show your young readers that even successful adults, with all their accomplishments, have weaknesses, too. I found that a cadet in the first U.S. Coast Guard Academy class, who later became national commander, had trouble with seasickness. Mentioning this human frailty gave this role model another dimension.

When possible, relate your writing to the interest of young readers. For instance, when I focused on the devastation of an earthquake, I described it and found a photograph of an elementary school affected by the disaster. When I related the public's reaction to George Custer's death in *Battle of the Little Bighorn,* I mentioned school students in Custer's hometown. Such material personalizes the text for your readers.

Take care with your paragraphs. If you want real punch, use one-word or one-sentence paragraphs. But use this technique sparingly, or the "punch" will lose its power from overuse. And in the reverse, do not make your paragraphs too long. Lengthy paragraphs suggest detailed description, which often turns off the young reader. Breaking up paragraphs makes the material more inviting.

During this whole process of writing and working with an editor, remember that writing is a business. Meet your deadlines. Do not promise something you cannot deliver. Be sensitive to suggested changes. Proving that you are reliable and reasonable shows you can handle another project.

Once your book is published, good things may happen: You may receive letters from young readers and may be asked to speak to school or community groups, and publishers may prove to be more receptive to your new book ideas. So, if you are inspired to write, write. Remember, if your ideas remain in your head, or your written drafts remain in a drawer, nothing will happen at all. Send your manuscripts out. To quote my 12-year-old McKinley mountain climber, "Go for it!"

Practical Advice

You might locate a local writer's organization. Members of such groups give encouragement, critique creative work, and help with marketing information. They are, so to speak, your personal cheering section.

For a broader view, join a national organization such as the Society of Children's Book Writers and Illustrators; you do not have to be a published author to join. Their monthly bulletins not only present practical information to members, but the Society also prints materials that deal with marketing, manuscript format, how-to books on writing, copyright and tax data, and much more—mostly for the price of postage. Becoming a member gives newcomers a sense of purpose. (Society of Children's Book Writers and Illustrators, 8271 Beverly Blvd., Los Angeles, CA 90048. Yearly membership is $50.00.)

❏ 89

TEN TIPS ON WRITING
PICTURE BOOKS

BY DIANE MAYR

AS A CHILDREN'S LIBRARIAN, I DO STORY HOURS FOR PRESCHOOLERS ages 3 to 5. Children this age have developed language skills, but aren't yet able to read on their own. After more than 1,500 story hours, I know what these children like. By sharing this knowledge I hope to improve the chances of my wowing young patrons with some great picture book—yours.

Tip #1: READ. When wannabe writers tell me they have written a book for children, I ask them to compare their book to something already in print. I'm usually met with a blank stare, or "I haven't read many children's books." If you haven't read what's out there, how do you know if your book is better than—or as good as—the rest? How do you know your version of "The Three Little Pigs" is different enough from the traditional one to attract a child's (or publisher's) attention? [Suggestions of titles to "study" will be shown in brackets.]

Tip #2: BE BRIEF. Good books for preschoolers run 800 words or less—sometimes considerably less. Look at the word counts of some of the "classics": *The Very Hungry Caterpillar* (Eric Carle)—225; *If You Give A Mouse A Cookie* (Laura Joffe Numeroff)—291; *The Snowy Day* (Ezra Jack Keats)—319; and *Corduroy* (Don Freeman)—708.

Don't use a lot of description, the illustrator will fill in the details. (You may, though, wish to provide notes, separate from the text, about illustrative elements crucial to your story.) A balance of dialogue and narration works best.

Tip #3: TELL A GOOD STORY. If your forte is "mood" pieces, then you're not aiming for the preschool audience. For them, something has to happen, and the story must have a beginning, a middle, and an end. The ending must not be ambiguous; predictability is expected.

Have you heard of the "rule of three"? The main character must complete three tasks, or face three foes, before winning the day. The rule has worked for generations of talespinners; try letting your heroine face the monster under the bed three times before she develops the courage to banish it. [Read: *The Wolf's Chicken Stew*, by Keiko Kasza]

Tip #4: KNOW THE PRESCHOOL PSYCHE. Preschoolers are strongly tied to their homes and family. They enjoy hearing about situations they're familiar with such as the arrival of a new baby. It's your task to develop a twist on a familiar theme, but make the twist believable. [Read: *Julius, The Baby Of The World*, by Kevin Henkes]

As adults, we have a tendency to dismiss a preschooler's fears and "problems" as inconsequential, but they're very real. They need to be addressed and dealt with reassuringly. [Read: *Rosie's Baby Tooth*, by Maryann Macdonald]

The problems adults see as significant—death, divorce, abuse, etc.— are topics for bibliotherapy; such books have a place, but are not for the general audience. Nor are 3-to 5-year-olds the audience for a picture book that tries to explain the Holocaust. Childhood is short but critical in the development of character. Preschoolers deserve to feel secure.

Animals often appear as the characters in picture books, but don't allow the talking animals in your stories to do things a child wouldn't do. For example, don't have Baby Monkey cross a busy street by herself. If you do, preschoolers will invariably ask, "Where's the Mommy?" If Baby Monkey needs to cross the street without Mom in order to advance your plot, leave it in, but don't arbitrarily dismiss a young monkey's (child's) need to depend on responsible adults. [Read: *Baby Duck And the Bad Eyeglasses*, by Amy Hest]

Tip #5: SUREFIRE PLEASERS. Preschoolers love humor! But, they're not looking for subtlety. Think pratfalls without pain. Sophisticated punning is out, but nonsense words draw a laugh. [Read: *Froggie Gets Dressed*, by Jonathan London; *Contrary Mary*, by Anita Jeram; *Tacky The Penguin*, by Helen Lester; *Mother Makes A Mistake*, by Ann Dorer]

Noises are always a hit. Preschoolers will "moo" and "quack" along with the reader—and love doing it! [Read: *Is This A House For Hermit*

Crab?, by Amy McDonald; *Peace At Last,* by Jill Murphy; *Small Green Snake,* by Libba Moore Gray]

Allow the audience to discover a "secret" before the main character does. Little kids, so frequently put down by older siblings, more advanced peers, and even by adults, appreciate the opportunity to feel "smarter" than someone else. This device is often used by puppeteers who have the audience see the villain before the lead puppet does. If you've ever heard the gleeful screams, "Look behind you! He's behind you!", then you know how successful this can be with preschoolers. [Read: any of Frank Asch's books about Bear. Two good examples: *Mooncake* and *Bread And Honey*]

Questions scattered throughout the story—for example, "Should he look under the bed?"—allow interaction between the child and the story. Kids love to interact! [Read: *The Noisy Book,* by Margaret Wise Brown]

Tip #6: PICTURES ARE ESSENTIAL. If your story makes sense without visual clues, then it is not a picture book. Text and pictures must contribute equally to telling the story. (One note of caution: Unless you are an accomplished artist/illustrator, do not attempt to illustrate your own work if you plan to submit it to a trade publisher. You need not seek out an illustrator, the illustrator will be selected by your publisher.) [Read: *King Bidgood's In The Bathtub,* by Audrey Wood, illustrated by Don Wood]

Tip #7: WATCH YOUR LANGUAGE! Preschoolers tend to take what you say literally. If I read aloud—"'Look, it's snowing!' he cried."—without a doubt, a child will interrupt me to ask, "Why is he crying?" Use "he said" or "he shouted."

Nothing destroys the flow of a story like having to stop to explain an unfamiliar term. Use language with which today's children are comfortable. Don't use "frock" for dress or "dungarees" for jeans.

Tip #8: LEARN THE 3 "R's." Repetition, rhythm, and rhyme work well with the younger set. Traditional folktales like "The Little Red Hen" still appeal to them because of the repetition. Rhyme, unfortunately, can kill a story if it's not done well. Rather than write a story entirely in rhyme, try a few repetitive rhyming sentences. [Read: *Millions Of Cats,* by Wanda Gag; *A Cake For Barney,* by Joyce Dunbar]

Tip #9: READ ALOUD. Read your story out loud and listen. If you stumble, nine times out of ten, there's something wrong with the writing. When it finally sounds right to you, try reading it to someone else for continuity and clarity.

Tip #10: MAKE A DUMMY. Fold eight pieces of paper in half and staple at the fold. You now have a 32-page dummy. Cut and paste your words onto the pages, leaving the first three pages blank for front matter. You'll need to make decisions on length. Is the story too short? Too long? Does it flow smoothly? You may want to make notes about the pictures you envision for each page or spread. The suspense in a story could be jeopardized by raising a problem in the text on a left-hand page and having a picture on the right-hand page provide the solution. Remember, preschoolers are "reading" the illustrations as you're reading the words. It's preferable to have a page turn before providing resolutions or answers.

Bonus Tip: Make Friends with Your Children's Librarian. She can introduce you to the classic picture books, as well as to the best of what's currently being published. She'll have review journals and publishers' catalogues for you to look at, and she can double as a critical reader.

I've been waiting more than ten years for the perfect picture book to share with my story hour kids; I can wait a little longer for you to write it!

❑ 90

BRINGING HISTORY TO LIFE
FOR CHILDREN

BY DEBORAH M. PRUM

DID YOU KNOW PETER THE GREAT PRACTICED DENTISTRY ON HIS SUBjects? That Botticelli means "little barrel"? Or that Ivan III's new wife was so heavy, she broke her bed the first night she stayed at the Czar's palace?

With marvelous facts like these at our disposal, there is no excuse for subjecting children to boringly written history. Of course, the primary purpose of writing history for kids is to instruct, not to entertain. However, once you lose a child's interest, you risk losing your audience. A good writer achieves a balance, presenting facts and concepts in a way that will entice a young reader to read on cheerfully and willingly.

Keep them awake with verbs

Nothing puts someone to sleep faster than the use of boring verbs. Granted, when you are writing about past events, you naturally tend to use verbs like "was, were, had been," but entangling your prose in passive constructions will slow down forward movement in your piece.

Whenever you can, use active image verbs. Consider these two sentences:

> By the mid-sixteenth century, the unhappy serfs were hungry and became violent.
> Starving serfs stormed the palace, destroying furnishings and attacking the royal guards.

Make them laugh

Use humor liberally in your writing. Catchy subtitles help, especially when you have to discuss subjects that ordinarily may not appeal to children. The subtitle "The Burning of the Papal Bull—*Not* a Barbecue!" will attract more interest than "Martin Luther Rebels."

When appropriate, include a cartoon. A cartoon will draw a child's eyes to a page. You can use a cartoon to poke fun with your material (i.e. a picture of Botticelli dressed in a barrel, apropos of his nickname). Or, you can use a cartoon to make a point. A cartoon depicting the disputing political parties prior to the Civil War may serve to inform your reader as effectively as a paragraph on the subject.

Highlighting an amusing fact makes children more likely to plow through less interesting information. For example, in a discussion of the Gutenberg press, you can start by mentioning that Johann Gutenberg started out life as "John Gooseflesh" (Gensfleisch). Once you have grabbed their attention, then you can go on to talk about the somewhat drier details of your topic.

Be careful when using humor. Avoid the temptation to distort fact in order to be funny.

Using sidebars

Not all factual information or lists may fit smoothly into your text, and may slow the pacing of your piece. For material that is tangential to your primary point, sidebars are a useful way to handle these problems.

A sidebar enables you to include greater detail on a topic without disrupting your narrative flow. Sidebars can give your reader an in-depth view of the period you are discussing. For a piece on the Civil War, you might include a few recipes of the dishes popular at the time. Or, if you are discussing Leonardo Da Vinci, you might include a list of all his inventions. Every once in a while, it doesn't hurt to include a nonsensical sidebar, like this one:

Places Marco Polo did *not* explore:
1. Lizard Lick, North Carolina
2. Walla Walla, Washington
3. Newark, New Jersey

When writing about history for children, you can easily get bogged down in confusing details. Good organization of your material is essential. A young child reading about the first few centuries of Russian history will be tempted to think that every last Russian of importance was named Ivan or Fedor. Of course, that's not true. But, you have to provide a way to sort through potentially confusing material. There are several ways to help your readers:

One is to show a detailed family tree at the beginning of your chapter, including dates, actions for which the person is famous, and nicknames (i.e. Ivan the Great, Ivan the Terrible, Fedor the Feebleminded).

If you must discuss many events occurring over several years, consider using a time line to show the "who, what, and when" of any era in a clear and simple way.

Another way to help a child understand some of the forces contributing to an event is to tell a story. How did a lightning storm change Martin Luther's life? Talk about the time Borgia betrayed the Duke of Urbino: Borgia borrowed, then used the Duke's own weapons to attack his city. Mention that Peter III played with lead soldiers and dolls, and ultimately lost the Russian Empire to his wife, Catherine the Great. By telling these stories, you will make your material far more interesting and you will give children a better sense of history.

Controversy

Don't shy away from controversy. Make it your ally. Use the tension controversial issues create to add excitement to your text. When possible, tell both sides of the story. Readers know that historians disagree. Help your readers form their own opinions by including direct quotes from the controversial figures, quotes of correspondence, or transcripts of debates. Give the children a chance to hear both sides and an opportunity to develop their critical thinking skills.

Not all historians agree, but you can make controversy work for you. That statement will not come as a shock to most adults, yet it does pose a problem for writers. Which side of the story do you present to young readers? Maybe the "facts" are clear (although, not always), but one historian may slant a discussion in a completely different way from another.

For example, what about Machiavelli? Was he an ogre, an opportunist with dangerous political ideas? Was he a practical political scientist who merely described reality? Does the answer lie somewhere in between? Those are good questions, debated by one and all. How should you present the topic to children?

Fascinating beginnings

You must capture your young reader's attention at the beginning of a chapter and end it in a way that will make that child want to go on to the next chapter.

Begin with an interesting fact or a question: "What does the word 'Medici' mean to you? 1) an interesting pasta dish, 2) a new foreign convertible, 3) a deadly tropical disease, or 4) none of the above."

Capture your reader's attention by opening a chapter with a scene from everyday life at the time your book takes place. (Make it clear that this event "might" have happened but don't veer from accepted fact.) For example, you could start a chapter on Thomas Jefferson by describing him playing his violin for some guests in his drawing room at Monticello.

Ending your chapter well is just as important as beginning well. You want your reader to finish your book. Make a statement that will pique the child's curiosity.

Insofar as possible, make your book a visual pleasure. If you are writing about Ben Franklin, see if you can find museum photographs of his pot-bellied stove. Look for pictures of Catherine the Great's crown or Galileo's telescope. If you are discussing a war or an explorer, include colorful maps.

When writing history for children, be certain that you know your audience. Spend some time around the age group for whom you are writing. Listen to the words they use. Pay attention to how they form their sentences. Figure out what they think is funny. Then, in your own writing, use syntax slightly more complex than what they used. Include a few unfamiliar terms, but be certain to highlight and define any new word. When you are presenting a concept that is foreign to your readers, compare it with one they already understand.

Once your material is written, test it on a child you know. Find a curmudgeonly person who is a reluctant reader. You will be sure to get some valuable comments. A grumpy child will provide a good first test for your material. Then, if you have the opportunity, read your manuscript in front of a classroom of kids. Are your words greeted with excitement and interest, or just yawns and glassy-eyed stares? If you see tired looks and drooping eyelids, enliven your prose accordingly. However, if the children want to know more, you've got a winner.

□ 91

WRITING BIOGRAPHIES FOR YOUNG PEOPLE

BY JAMES CROSS GIBLIN

THERE WAS A TIME WHEN IT WAS ACCEPTED PRACTICE FOR YOUNG PEOPLE's biographies to whitewash their subjects to a certain extent. For example, juvenile biographies either ignored or gave a once-over-lightly treatment to personal failings like a drinking problem, and they scrupulously avoided any mention of complications in their subjects' sex lives.

Such whitewashing was intended to serve several different purposes. It protected the subject's reputation and made him or her a more suitable role model, one of the main goals of juvenile biographies in earlier periods. At the same time it shielded young readers from some of life's harsher realities.

All this has changed in the last twenty-five or thirty years as an increased openness in the arts and the media has spread to the field of children's literature. Young people who watch TV talk shows after school and dip into celebrity tell-all books expect more realism in the biographies that are written expressly for them. As a consequence, juvenile biographies of Franklin D. Roosevelt now acknowledge that he had a mistress, and young adult studies of John F. Kennedy frankly discuss his health problems and womanizing.

Today, the chief goal of a young people's biography is not to establish a role model but rather to provide solid, honest information about a man or woman worth knowing for one reason or another. However, a children's writer still has to make judgments about what facts to include in the biography and how much emphasis to give them. These judgments aren't always easy to arrive at, as I've discovered with the biographies I've written for young people. Each book presents its own unique problems, for which unique solutions must be found.

Much depends on the age of the intended audience. For example, when I was writing a picture book biography of George Washington for

ages six to nine, I felt it was important to describe Washington's changing attitude toward slavery, from easy acceptance in youth to rejection
as he grew older. With that background in place, I was confident even
quite young readers could grasp the significance of Washington's will,
which specified that his slaves would be freed after the death of his
wife, Martha.

A picture book biography of Thomas Jefferson presented a much
more complex set of problems. Although Jefferson had written in the
Declaration of Independence that "all men are created equal," he never
rejected the concept of slavery as Washington did. How could he? The
very existence of his beloved Monticello depended on slave labor. After
much thought, I decided there was no way I could avoid discussing
Jefferson's conflicted position. But I tried to present it as clearly and
simply as possible and was careful not to let the discussion overshadow
Jefferson's many accomplishments.

The role of the slave Sally Hemings proved harder to deal with.
Whenever I mentioned in talks with writers that I was doing a biography
of Jefferson, African-Americans in the audience invariably asked how
I was going to treat Sally. I told them I intended to incorporate items
from the historical record in the main text—that Sally had come into
Jefferson's household as part of his wife's inheritance from her father;
had accompanied Jefferson's younger daughter to Paris when Jefferson
was the American ambassador to France; and had become one of the
most trusted house slaves at Monticello in her later years.

In the back matter, along with other additional information, I said I'd
include the story that one of Sally's sons, Madison Hemings, told an
Ohio journalist in the mid-19th century. According to Madison, Jefferson had made Sally his mistress after his wife's death and had fathered
her seven children, five of whom lived to adulthood and three of whom
"passed" as white.

My editor felt that the latter story, aside from being controversial,
would be too complicated for six-to-nine-year-olds to absorb. She urged
me to leave it out, and in the end I decided she was right. If the book had
been directed toward an upper elementary or young adult readership, I
would have insisted on the story's retention. But I decided it was probably too involved for a younger audience.

However, the references to Sally Hemings remain in the body of the
book, letting readers know that a slave by that name figured in Thomas

Jefferson's life. When those same readers grow older, they can read about Sally in greater detail in other books about Jefferson. Meanwhile, my book—while not going deeply into the matter—will at least have introduced Sally to them instead of pretending she didn't exist.

Biographies for older children confront the writer with a different set of difficulties. What sort of balance do you aim for between the subject's achievements and his failings? This question was brought home to me in a particularly vivid way when I was working on a biography of Charles A. Lindbergh for ages ten to fourteen. Rarely in American history has there been such a sharp dichotomy between a subject's accomplishments—in Lindbergh's case his almost incredible solo flight to Paris in 1927, along with his other contributions to aviation—and his errors, namely his flirtation with fascism in the 1930s and his open admiration of Nazi Germany.

If I'd been writing a biography for adults, I might well have focused more intently on the part Lindbergh played in bringing about the appeasement of Adolf Hitler at Munich and his subsequent speeches urging the United States to take an isolationist stand with regard to the war in Europe. But while I went into this phase of Lindbergh's life in some detail, I decided it was my duty as a biographer for young people to "accentuate the positive," as the old song lyric goes.

An adult biographer may choose to expose or debunk his subject, assuming that readers will be able to compare his version of the person's life with other, more favorable accounts. I don't believe that option is open to the juvenile biographer, whose readers will most likely have little or no prior knowledge of the subject and thus will be unable to make comparisons. Such readers deserve a more even-handed introduction to the person.

Of course, that wouldn't be possible if one were writing about a destructive personality like Adolf Hitler, Joseph Stalin, or Senator Joseph McCarthy. But even in the portrayal of someone as reviled as these men, the juvenile biographer would have the responsibility of trying to help young readers understand how a human being could be capable of such inhuman acts. In other words, the writer wouldn't simply wallow in the person's excesses, as some adult biographers might be tempted to do, but instead would try to offer a full-scale portrait and locate the sources of the person's evil actions.

If you're thinking about writing a biography for young people, here are a few questions you would do well to ask yourself. Having the answers in hand should save you time when you're researching and writing the project.

Depending on the age group of the readers, how best can you convey an accurate, three-dimensional picture of the subject in ways that the intended audience can comprehend?

If the book is for younger children, should you discuss the seamier aspects of the subject's life, or merely hint at them and leave a fuller treatment to biographers for older children?

If you're writing for an older audience, how much space should you devote to the darker side of the subject's life and experience? In a biography of sports star Magic Johnson, for example, should you go into detail about the promiscuous behavior that, by Johnson's own account, was responsible for his becoming infected with the AIDS virus, or should you merely mention it in passing?

As you seek answers to these questions, you'll have to rely ultimately on your own good taste and judgment, combined with your knowledge of the prevailing standards in the children's book field. Perhaps the most decisive factor of all, though, will be your feeling for the subject.

Jean Fritz, the author of many award-winning biographies for young people, once said that she had to like a subject tremendously before she could write about the person. I'd amend that to say I must be *fascinated* by a subject in order to invest the time and energy needed to discover what makes the person tick.

The intensity of your fascination with your subject should be of great help as you decide how much weight to give the person's positive and negative aspects. It should also communicate itself to young people, making them want to keep on reading about the intriguing man or woman at the center of your biography.

❏ 92

When You Write Humor for Children

By Julie Anne Peters

Children are born to laugh. In fact, humor is thought to be the first expressive form of communication. Good writers understand the value of humor when they write for children. Not only does humor entertain and amuse them, but it lures the most reluctant reader.

When my first book, *The Stinky Sneakers Contest,* was selected by third-grade children in Greater Kansas City as their favorite book of 1995, I was delighted—and shocked. Humorous books rarely win awards. In the kingdom of exalted literature, humor is relegated to serfdom. But the award confirmed my belief that even though funny books infrequently win prestigious literary prizes, they do become children's favorites.

Writers often tell me, "I'm not a funny person. I can't write humor." Piffle! Betsy Byars, grandmistress of humorous children's books, reveals the secret. "The funniest word in the vocabulary of a second grader," she says, "is 'underwear.'" Use it liberally. "Poo poo" works for preschoolers. Or you can rise above so-called potty humor and choose one of the standard humor devices that follow.

Surprise

Writers and illustrators of picture books are guaranteed laughter or smiles by springing the unexpected on their young readers. Books are the perfect vehicle for creating humor through surprise. James Stevenson demonstrates this very effectively in his book, *Quick! Turn the Page.*

To bring about surprise, take an expected event or consequence and create the unexpected. A boy bounces a ball. He expects it to go up and come down. Page one: Ball goes up. Page two: A wild monkey in a banyan tree snatches the ball and steals off to . . . ? Next page. Surprise can delight page after page, intermittently, or just once, with a surprise ending. Read Judith Viorst's poem, "Mother Doesn't Want a Dog," for a classic example of a surprise ending.

Exaggeration

The earliest American humor used exaggeration in its purest form: larger-than-life heroes performing superhuman feats. Remember Pecos Bill, Paul Bunyan, and John Henry? The American tall tale is still a favored form of humor for children. Anne Isaac's *Swamp Angel* moves this classic genre into the 1990s with her female superheroine. Not only does Swamp Angel fend off Thundering Tarnation, the marauding bear, she has to prove herself to taunting backwoodsmen who'd have her stay at home, quilting.

Transcendental toasters, madcap Martians, and articulate animals are all examples of truth stretching. My favorite mouthy mammal is the mutt, Martha, in Susan Meddaugh's *Martha Speaks.* After Martha dog eats a bowl of alphabet soup, she becomes quite the loquacious pooch. "You people are so bossy. COME! SIT! STAY! You never say please."

Journey beyond the bounds of possibility to create exaggerated humor. How about a plucky petunia? A daring doormat? Even preschool children can differentiate between the real and unreal as they gleefully embrace the fun in make-believe.

Word and language play

With wordplay, language is key to the rhythm, sound, and rhyme that carries your story forward. Readers become reciters. Jack Prelutsky, Shel Silverstein, and Joyce Armor are wizards of wordplay in their witty poetry. Nancy Shaw's "Sheep" books are shear joy (yes, pun intended).

If you're not a poet and you know it, try your hand at literal translation. *Amelia Bedelia* books by Peggy Parish teach you how. Amelia Bedelia, the indomitable maid, takes every order, every conversation, every suggestion literally, and sets herself up for catastrophe. Children love trying to predict the consequences of Amelia's misunderstandings.

Role reversal

Eugene Trivizas chose role reversal to retell a classic fairy tale in his *The Three Little Wolves and the Big Bad Pig.* To make the most effective use of role reversal, choose familiar characters acting out of character. Turn everyday events topsy-turvy. Harry Allard uses children's perceptions about substitute teachers (whether true or not) when he changes meek, mild Miss Nelson into bleak, vile Viola Swamp. You may choose to switch family members, as Mary Rodgers did with her mother/daughter exchange in *Freaky Friday,* or people and their pets, aliens with automobiles, princes and paupers. Stay away from twins, though. It's been done and done and done.

Nonsense

Nonsense includes incongruity and absurdity, ridiculous premises, and illogical series of events. What makes a nonsense book funny is its weirdness. *Imogene's Antlers,* by David Small, is the story of a young girl who wakes up one day to find she's grown antlers. This is a problem. Imogene has trouble getting dressed; she can't fit through narrow doorways; her antlers get caught in the chandelier. Even worse, her mother keeps fainting at the sight of her. Though children recognize the absurdity of Imogene's situation, they also see how well she copes with her sudden disability. This book speaks to children's physical differences, which is a fundamental value of humor.

Literary humor helps children grow. It offers distancing from pain, from change and insecurity, from cruelty, disaster and loss. Children are not always sophisticated or mature enough emotionally to laugh at themselves. Humorous books with subtle serious themes offer children ways to deal positively with life's inequities. They offer a magic mirror, through which children's problems—and their solutions—can be reflected back.

Slapstick

Farce and horseplay have been part of the American humor scene since vaudeville—maybe before. Who knows what Neanderthals did for fun? Physical humor appeals to the child in all of us. Hectic, frenetic chases and bumbling, stumbling characters cause chaos in the pages of children's books. Your plot will immediately pick up pace if you include a frantic fiasco or two. Check out Betsy Byars' *Golly Sisters.* May-May and Rose's calamitous capers are rip-roaring fun. Avi used slapstick masterfully in his book *Romeo and Juliet Together (And Alive)*

At Last! His high schoolers' rendition of Shakespeare's masterpiece would make The Bard weep (with tears of laughter).

Satire

You can achieve humor by poking fun at human vices, human foibles or the general social order, which rarely makes sense to children, so they love to see it pulverized on paper. My favorite satirical series is "The Stupids," by Harry Allard. I swear these people lived next door to me when I was growing up. James Marshall's illustrations add hilarity to the humor.

To write effective satire for children, you must recognize the ridiculous in youngsters' lives. Make fun of uppity people's pretensions, lampoon restrictions, and spoof the silly societal mores children are expected to embrace. Create characters who teeter on the edge, who challenge the status quo—and thrive. Read Sid Fleischman's *The Whipping Boy* for a lesson in writing satire.

Adolescent angst

Family and school stories, growing up and coming-of-age novels make up the bulk of children's humorous fiction. Adolescence just seems to lend itself to humor. Laughter helps older children deal with life's larger dilemmas: death, divorce, disability, senility, loss, and unwelcome change. Reading about characters who successfully and humorously overcome obstacles provides children with painless lessons on how to handle their own problems.

For my book *B.J.'s Billion-Dollar Bet,* I started with a troublesome topic—betting. Frequently, I overhear conversations between kids who are placing bets: "Oh, sure. I bet you," or "Wanna bet? Come on, let's bet on it." And they bet away valuable items—clothing, sports card collections, lunch money. To show the consequences of betting, I created B.J. Byner, a compulsive gambler who bets and loses all of his possessions, then begins to bet away his family's belongings. When B.J. loses his mother's lottery ticket in a wager, then finds out the ticket is a fifty-million-dollar winner, he has to get that ticket back!

I hope young readers will see that the risks of gambling are considerable; the losses more than they may be willing or able to pay. Betting can result in loss of friendship, family conflict, and, as with any addiction, loss of control and self-respect. If I hadn't chosen a humorous premise for this book, it would have been too preachy.

Middle-grade and young adult novels include more urbane, cerebral humor. These young people are developing their own individual views of the world, and social relationships take on a major role.

For my middle-grade novel, *How Do You Spell Geek?*, I began with a funny, offbeat character, Lurlene Brueggemeyer, the geek, and built the story around her. The issues are serious ones—judging people by their appearance, shifting alliances between friends, peer pressure, and self-examination, but I gave my main character, Ann, a sarcastic sense of humor and a wry way of watching her world get weird, which seems to lighten the load.

Read the masters of middle-grade humor: Ellen Conford, Barbara Park, Beverly Cleary, Betsy Byars, Daniel Pinkwater, and Jerry Spinelli, among many, many others.

There are humor writers who defy classification; they relate to their audiences through rebellion, radicalism, and general outrageousness. Three young adult authors who fall into this special category are M.E. Kerr, Richard Peck, and Paul Zindel. Their books validate an emerging adult's individuality, passion, and self-expression.

If you plan to try your hand at humor, steer clear of targeting a specific age group. I've received letters from eight-year-olds who are reading my junior high novel, *Risky Friends.* And I'm sure you know high schoolers who still get a hoot out of Dr. Seuss. Even though sense of humor evolves as we grow older, we never lose appreciation for the books that made us laugh when we were younger.

Humor writing is a spontaneous act. It comes from deep within, from your own wacky way of looking at the world. One word of caution: Humor has power. What we laugh at, we make light of. What we laugh at, we legitimize and condone. Cruelty is never funny. Violence isn't funny. Torture, torment, neglect, war, hatred, and preying on others' misfortunes are not subjects for children's humor. There's a fine line between sarcasm and cynicism; between light-spirited and mean-spirited. So be aware. If you do write humor for children, observe the limits.

There's more than one way to connect with children through humor (beyond using "underwear"). In fact, with all the techniques available, and given the fact that children laugh easily, your chances of eliciting gleeful responses are excellent.

❑ 93

WRITE FOR CHILDREN'S MAGAZINES

BY BEVERLY J. LETCHWORTH

CHILDREN'S MAGAZINES OFFER AN EXCITING VEHICLE FOR THE WRITER. It's a Starship ride of challenge and fun, stimulating and rewarding throughout the journey. Where else can a writer find the variety, short length, and better chance of publication than in children's magazines?

The variety alone tantalizes the imagination. Children's magazines want fiction, nonfiction, poetry, puzzles, games, jokes, crafts, recipes, party ideas—welcome spice for any writer's life.

The relatively short wordage of magazine material is also appealing. Most middle-grade magazines want stories and articles of no more than 1,000 words, maybe 1,200 at the most. Material for the younger set is restricted to perhaps 500 to 700 words. So your time in writing such pieces is much less than if you wrote a middle-grade or young adult novel.

Magazines are usually published monthly, so they need a steady supply of material, making your chances of publication greater. You may have only a one percent chance of selling a book, but your odds go up to about fifteen percent in selling to magazines.

Of course, it helps if you know children and can still remember what it feels like to be a child. Do you know what interests today's children? How they occupy their time? What pressures and stresses they face in today's world? What they worry about, what they fear, what they crave? Society today is different from what it was like twenty years ago. You need to know those differences and how they're shaping our young people.

Also keep attuned to children's conversations. How do they speak? How do they act and react?

When you're writing stories and articles for children's magazines, keep your material lively and captivating. Create exciting word images.

Use plenty of dialogue and strong verbs. Throw in humor and vivid figures of speech. Ask questions and inject touches of mystery here and there.

Keep your stories focused and write "tight." You simply don't have room for excess wordage. No unimportant dialogue or unnecessary characters. No multiple subplots or long stretches of description. In nonfiction, no inconsequential data or unrelated facts.

Pay attention to slant, tone, and purpose. Notice what kinds of stories and articles, poetry and fillers the magazine uses and how many of each it prints each month. Is fantasy included? Mysteries? Adventure? Multicultural material? Biography? History? Nature pieces? Does poetry rhyme, or is free verse used?

Notice vocabulary, sentence length and structure, word length. Do stories include many characters or few? Do they encompass long time spans, or do plots run their course in a day or an afternoon? Answering all of these questions adds to your knowledge of the magazine and thus increases your chance of selling your material.

Don't add obvious morals or messages to your stories; most magazines don't want them. Above all, don't write down to children. This disregard of their ability will turn them off immediately. Any interaction with children today will quickly convince you that they are more sophisticated than they were in previous generations.

Not only do you have to know how to write for children, but you have to know how to market the work you've written. Magazine markets for children's writers abound, but to acquire marketing skills, you must study as many magazines as you can. Check them out from your library; send away for sample copies. The market listings in this handbook and in *The Writer* magazine inform you about the magazines that will send sample copies for a fee. Naturally, you can't send away for all of them, but choose six or eight that you think will fit your writing style, and study them well.

Market listings describe the kinds of materials magazines want, but unless you have the magazines in hand, you will not know the flavor and style they prefer. Every magazine has a special tone and slant, some purpose in the material they present to their young readers. The slogan of *Highlights for Children*, "fun with a purpose," indicates that *Highlights* wants material that is entertaining for children, but also instructive.

Follow directions in market listings. Don't send a 1,000-word article to a magazine that wants pieces of only 500 words. Don't submit free verse to a magazine that uses only rhymed poetry. Don't send fiction to a nonfiction magazine. This advice sounds so basic and obvious it hardly needs to be said, but editors constantly complain about the inappropriate material they receive.

Studying magazines may seem tedious, but in the end it will pay off because you'll have a better idea of what magazine fits your style. For example: You'd have a better chance of selling a myth or folk tale to *Cricket Magazine* than to *Highlights for Children*, which doesn't publish such tales as routinely as *Cricket*.

Continue doing your homework as you study the magazines. Though marketing your work is often tedious, time-consuming, and frustrating, you must constantly read, read, read writer's magazines and newsletters to learn about new markets, merging markets, closed markets, marketing trends, and policy changes. The magazine market is generally not as changeable as the children's book market, but you need to be knowledgeable about it to be successful.

Attend writers' conferences, seminars, workshops. Be on the lookout for marketing tips, new publications, receptive editors. You'll reap not only writing techniques, but marketing how-tos as well.

Join an established writers' group with experienced writers. You'll profit from a bonanza of tested information about all aspects of the writing profession, and receive support for your efforts.

Above all, don't quit too soon. When the going gets rough, keep writing and submitting anyway. The three P's—persistence, practice, and patience—are your best tools.

Writing for children demands a specialized knowledge and spirit, but because it's a "calling" for writers, it remains a joyful, stimulating experience. Writing for children's magazines gives you the opportunity to go along on that exciting, continuous adventure.

□ 94

FORGET THE ALAMO: WRITING HISTORY FOR CHILDREN

BY SYLVIA WHITMAN

GROWING UP, I FELT THE SAME WAY ABOUT HISTORY AS I DID ABOUT spinach: Everybody said it was good for me, and I detested it. Elections, treaties, dates, and more dates—what a bore! Luckily, I loved to read. Just as I managed to meet my minimum RDA of vitamins with frozen peas and grape juice, I got a rough sense of the past through biographies and novels like *Johnny Tremaine* (1943), Esther Forbes's award-winning story of an apprentice silversmith on the eve of the American Revolution. The last thing I ever expected, though, was that I would end up writing history books that teachers could inflict upon kids.

I first started to enjoy history in college in the early 1980s. By then "social history" had moved into the academic mainstream. Although it would seem that social historians should be poring over the guest list of the Boston Tea Party, they are more likely to be studying the propaganda of rebellion or 18th-century perceptions of Native Americans. Social historians are the "big picture" people: They tend to highlight change instead of chronology; to focus on processes rather than events; to think in terms of decades instead of weeks or months; to follow the transmutations of ideas as they trickle down from the intelligentsia and trickle up from popular culture. Also, in the 1980s, stirrings of multiculturalism were beginning to influence scholarship, and women's studies was gaining respectability. I had long taken an interest in the activities of my mother and grandmothers, my personal links to the past. At last, academia was encouraging me to place family history in a broader context.

Developments at the university level have influenced elementary and secondary school curricula. Time lines are now merely a springboard in many history classes. Teachers searching for books and periodicals to enrich textbook fare and stimulate research projects have helped feed a boom in nonfiction of all kinds for children. If you're interested in writing about the past you have a captive audience.

Fact vs. fiction

Most of the biographies I devoured as a child read like novels. I remember in particular one about Clara Barton, founder of the American Red Cross. In the opening chapter, Clara is celebrating her sixth birthday. As she divides up her cake, she forgets to leave herself a piece. Although the scene skillfully makes a point about Clara's selflessness, the author would never get away with all that embellishment today. It's historical fiction, not history.

Teachers and publishers expect authors to adhere to certain scholarly conventions. You can conjecture from the evidence; you can contrast opposing viewpoints; you can report conversations documented in journals or letters or tape recordings. But you can never invent characters or recreate dialogue. Writing "pure" history requires a sort of collage mentality. You have to search out the juiciest facts, then juxtapose them to support your points.

Going to the sources

Some authors avoid putting any of their own words into the collage by compiling anthologies of first-person quotes. This cut-and-paste approach asks young readers to extrapolate a lot. I prefer to blend primary and secondary sources—combining accounts by people who lived through or witnessed events with analysis and reports by academics or journalists. By paraphrasing, quoting, and interpreting, you can give more structure to the collage. You can also scale history down to an elementary reading level.

Before I begin a first draft, I survey the topic in the library to find out what's on the shelf, what's in print, and what might be available through interlibrary loan. My proposals always include an outline and a bibliography. Neither is considered binding, but they force me to think early about structure, about themes, and especially about the variety of my sources.

Cast your net widely. Researching *Hernando de Soto and the Explorers of the American South,* I relied on four published accounts. Luis Hernandez de Biedma described the group's wanderings. Although both de Soto's secretary and a Portuguese nobleman documented the ruthlessness of the Spaniards, the latter also admired his leader's panache. Garcilaso de la Vega, a 16th-century mestizo historian who nicknamed himself "the Inca," didn't travel with the expedition, but his romantic version based on interviews with survivors stands out for its sympathetic portrayal of Native Americans. Instead of designating one chronicle as the "true" version, I juggled all four. I let my readers see the seams of history—the biases of the winesses, and the "facts" on which they disagreed.

With secondary sources, try to draw on recent work by young historians as well as classics by old masters. Essential to my book *This Land Is Your Land: The American Conservation Movement* was William Cronon's *Changes in the Land: Indians, Colonists, and the Ecology of New England* (1983). Each generation rewrites history. It's not coincidence that Cronon published his groundbreaking study about the colonial deforestation and economic exploitation of the Atlantic coast after Earth Day 1970. Even if you're writing about Pilgrims, make sure you've skimmed titles from the past three decades.

And don't overlook related works in other disciplines—art history, literature, anthropology, sociology, even science. To find out about Native American trail building for *Get Up and Go! The History of American Road Travel,* for instance, I consulted several anthropological studies of the Iroquois. A balanced bibliography always results in a better book.

Don't limit your search for lively details to books, either. I love leafing through old magazines to get a feel for an era through ads, advice columns, radio shows, and lyrics. I often use song titles as section headings, such as "You'd Be So Nice To Come Home To" (a WWII era hit) or "Fifteen Kisses on a Gallon of Gas" (an early car tune).

As Studs Terkel has demonstrated in his many collections of interviews, oral history brings the past to life. I've used personal reminiscences in all of my "People's History" books. In addition to quoting from Terkel's *The Good War* and other first-person accounts, I always try to do some original research. Posting notes on the bulletin board at a local senior center produced a lode of informants on WWII, including a charming saxophone player who had joined the Marines in order to play in the band and had ended up a Japanese POW. Most newspapers list community meetings, and I added some color to *This Land Is Your*

Land by attending a local reunion of the Civilian Conservation Corps. To track down a talkative trucker, I started with a phone call to a garage listed in the Yellow Pages. If you have access to the Internet, you can easily contact people beyond your neighborhood. From a small town in New York, I arranged interviews with transportation engineers on the West Coast by posting a note in a cyberspace discussion group. Eloquent or unpolished, these voices add texture to the collage. Their conversational tone makes history more accessible to young readers.

Nothing beats photographs for pulling the past out of the mist. Much admired authors like Russell Freedman (*Franklin Delano Roosevelt,* 1990) and Jerry Stanley (*Children of the Dust Bowl,* 1992) write books that are almost photo essays. Although most publishers, like mine, handle all the layout and illustration, editors always appreciate ideas. If you come across an exciting photo, make a photocopy—with credit information—to submit with your manuscript. Because color is expensive to print and stock photo agencies often charge hefty fees, black-and-white "public domain" snapshots from libraries, historical societies, and government agencies are usually more attractive. A small publisher might expect you to round up illustrations yourself. If you don't find appropriate pictures in published material and don't have time to comb through archives, you could hire a photo researcher.

These are a few major archives:

*Library of Congress, Prints and Photographs Division, Washington, DC 20540
*National Archives and Records Administration, Still Picture Branch, 8601 Adelphi Road, College Park, MD 20740
*International Museum of Photography, George Eastman House, 900 East Avenue, Rochester, NY 14618

The three C's

Although most authors present history as a narrative, it may take other forms, too. In *Ticket to the Twenties: A Time Traveler's Guide* (1993), Mary Blocksma breaks down the decade into flashy chapters on everything from jive talk to breakfast. Did you know the first electric pop-up toaster hit the market in 1926? Instead of merely listing the presidents, consult *How the White House Really Works* (1989), George Sullivan's "upstairs, downstairs" tour of 1600 Pennsylvania Avenue.

While most titles fall into the categories of biography, survey, or "issue" book, your imagination is the only limit.

Once I begin writing, I stick to the three C's—*clarity, context,* and *cohesion.* Although the vocabulary you use may be simple, writing for children is often harder than writing for adults. Just try summarizing the causes of World War II in a paragraph or two for someone with no knowledge of European history. To the degree possible, keep background brief, points clear; write straightforward topic sentences, and leave the nuance to the details.

To aid the reader in evaluating an event or a person, try to include context about the period. This is the sort of low-key background that often appears in popular histories for adults, from Frederick Allen's *Only Yesterday: An Informal History of the 1920s* (1931) to David Brinkley's *Washington Goes To War* (1988). Whether you write about Earth Day or Ralph Nader or highway planning in the '60s and '70s, remind your readers that in those decades, Americans were beginning to "question authority." Since many children today have working moms, they may not appreciate the change in women's roles that "Rosie the Riveter" represented during the 1940s. Therefore, in *"V" Is for Victory: The American Home Front During World War II,* I discuss the public relations efforts of the government Office of War Information and the ads that defense plants ran to encourage people to apply for wartime work. Make it real. Describe the smell of Main Street in the heyday of horse-drawn wagons or the pastimes of Sunday afternoons before the advent of television and the NFL.

Finally, focus on themes. In a biography, you might want to trace the influence of a particular trait or skill over a lifetime—for instance, Rachel Carson's keen observation. Describing the World War II home front, I emphasized Americans' shared sense of purpose, despite racial and ethnic tensions. Since authors for young people face strict limits (in some cases, several centuries compressed into 60 pages of manuscript), they have to cull their research ruthlessly. The key-concept method gives you criteria for deciding what to keep and what to discard. Writing history, after all, is the art of pulling facts out of a grab bag and turning them into a story worth remembering.

❑ 95

WRITING MYSTERIES FOR YOUNG PEOPLE

BY PEG KEHRET

PART OF THE JOY OF WRITING FOR CHILDREN IS THE LETTERS THEY send me. One of my favorite letters said, "It took my teacher two weeks to read *Nightmare Mountain* to our class. You wrote it in three days. Wasn't that hard to do?"

I have never written a book in three days! *Nightmare Mountain* took me nine months, and then my editor asked for revisions. Writing mysteries for children is not easy or fast, but it is fun and enormously satisfying. Here are some hints to help you write a mystery that will satisfy young readers.

*Begin the novel in an exciting place. Sometimes this means rearranging your material after the book is written. I wrote *Nightmare Mountain* in chronological order, but when it was finished, I realized there was too much background information at the beginning of the book. Although it was necessary information, it gave the story a slow start.

I took a letter from the middle of the novel and made it my opening. Now the book begins: "Dear Mom, Someone's trying to kill me." The letter is less than a page long; it became my whole first chapter. Chapter two starts at the true beginning, with the necessary background information. At the end of chapter six, Molly finally picks up her pen and writes to her mother, but meanwhile that letter has generated suspense throughout the first five chapters.

When you finish your first draft, read through it to see if there is a more exciting scene with which to open your novel. If so, try moving that scene to the beginning of the story.

Another good way to open a mystery is with intriguing dialogue. A fourth-grade teacher told me that she once read the first paragraph of six novels to her class and then let them vote on which book she would read aloud to them. My book, *Horror at the Haunted House,* was the students' choice. Here is my beginning: "Hey, Ellen! I'm going to get my head chopped off."

Such an opening makes the readers curious. They will want to read on, to see where the opening leads.

*Be sure all of the dialogue is appropriate to the character. A young child does not speak the same way his parents do; a belligerent teenager will sound different from one who is trying to please. The funny kid should get the laugh lines.

I try not to use current slang, even in dialogue. It dates a book too quickly. These days, kids say *awesome.* Several years ago, it was *rad* and before that, *groovy* was in. A book for children will often stay in print a long time; don't make it seem old-fashioned by using language that doesn't last.

*Give your protagonist a personal problem in addition to the main story problem. This will add depth to your story and will help you create a more believable and sympathetic character. For example: In *Night of Fear,* the main story problem is that T.J. is abducted. The personal problem is his unhappiness over the changes in his grandmother, who has Alzheimer's disease. Grandma Ruth, through T.J.'s memories, becomes a major character and her disease creates reader sympathy. Tension is also increased as readers wait to find out if Grandma Ruth got home safely after T.J. was forced to leave her alone. Because T.J. cares deeply about his grandma, the readers care, too.

*The title of any book for children must grab young readers and create curiosity; for a mystery, the title should also hint at danger. My working title for *Terror at the Zoo* was *Zoo Night,* but that title did not suggest any danger or conflict. (The editor said it sounded like a nonfiction title.) *Terror at the Zoo* makes it clear that the book is a suspense novel, and it arouses the curiosity of potential readers who wonder what scary event happens at the zoo.

Another editor once suggested that I try to use an action verb in every title. I have done so several times, with good results.

*Provide new information. Kids like to learn interesting facts, and if you weave the information in as a natural part of the plot, your readers learn easily and naturally. In *Horror at the Haunted House,* a collection of antique Wedgwood is important to the plot, as are historical scenes about Joan of Arc.

The characters in *Backstage Fright* find a stolen Van Gogh painting. I could have used a fictitious artist, but by using Van Gogh I introduced young readers to a great artist, thus broadening the learning experience of the students and the classroom usefulness of the book.

In *Race To Disaster,* the children take their dog, Bone Breath, to do pet therapy at a nursing home where they realize that an elderly patient has witnessed a murder. A subplot involves a patient who is drawn out of a shock-induced silence by continued exposure to the dog. Children who read that book get a mystery about a pair of diamond thieves, and also information about pet therapy and how it works.

When I am writing the first draft of a book, I ask myself, "What will children learn from this book? What new topic can I introduce?" Often, unusual information adds a plot twist that I would not have thought of otherwise.

*Put some humor in every book. If your mystery involves a serious problem, humor will give a much-needed lightening of mood. It does the same in a suspense book in which the tension is high page after page. A character who makes kids laugh will quickly become a favorite, and readers will beg for more books about him. But make it genuine humor, not bathroom jokes or put-down jokes that make fun of someone.

*End every chapter with a cliffhanger. I've had children complain, "Why do you always quit at the good parts?" These are the same kids who then say they loved the book and couldn't put it down. The chapter ending makes the reader want to continue.

Sometimes while I'm writing I'll come up with a sentence that I realize would make a good chapter ending. When that happens, I space down a couple of lines to remind myself that this would be a good spot for a break. Other times, I need to rewrite until I have a good cliffhanger sentence for the end of each chapter. Here is an example of a chapter ending from *Danger at the Fair:*

> Corey couldn't let the man get away. Forgetting his promise to stay with Ellen, he took off across the fairgrounds after the thief.

*Make the first paragraph of each chapter short and compelling. At the end of a chapter, readers will usually peek ahead, to see what happens next. If they see a long narrative, they may decide to put the book aside and go play soccer. But if the next chapter begins, "Hey, Ellen!" Corey waved from the sidewalk. "We got a video of you on fire!," chances are they'll keep reading.

*Let your book reflect who you are and what you stand for. This will help with that all-important quality, voice.

Certain themes surface over and over in my mysteries: kindness to all creatures; violence is not a solution; each of us is responsible for our own actions. My main characters are outraged by people who dump unwanted pets (*Desert Danger*).

The antiviolence message is strong in *Night of Fear* when Grandma Ruth tells T.J. to "win with your wits, not with your fists," and in *Race to Disaster* when Rosie and Kayo organize Goodbye Guns Day at their school.

You can't write from a soapbox; you need to write stories, not sermons. But if your characters deal with social and ethical problems, your mystery has a definite plus.

*Don't mimic what's already popular. For several years, the juvenile mystery market has been flooded with Goosebumps wannabes, but editors look for fresh ideas and new voices.

It's far better to risk writing a mystery that reflects your unique vision, than to attempt to imitate what some other writer did. Be true to yourself. Write what you love to write, and your writing will attract like-minded readers.

*Ask authorities to check your book for accuracy. There's nothing worse than having a reader point out that you have made an error. (Unfortunately, I know this from personal experience.) If you are dealing with factual information, double-check everything. *Terror at the Zoo* was read by two people from the education department of Seattle's Woodland Park Zoo, where the story is set. Whatever flaws the book may have, I know the information about the zoo and its animals is correct. My latest novel, *The Volcano Disaster,* deals with the eruption of Mount St. Helens. I did extensive research, but I also had the manuscript read by the Lead Interpreter at the Mount St. Helens Visitors' Center.

I have never had anyone turn down my request to check a manuscript. Actually, they seem delighted to share their knowledge. I do include their names on my acknowledgments page, and, of course, I see that each person who has helped me receives a signed copy of the book on publication.

*Make your mystery an appropriate length. If it's too long (more than 200 pages) it may be intimidating to all but the most enthusiastic young reader. A good length for juvenile mysteries is 125 to 150 double-spaced manuscript pages.

*Read current award-winning juvenile mysteries to become familiar with the best style and content. The Mystery Writers of America presents an Edgar each year to a juvenile mystery novel.

Many states have annual children's book award programs, in which students are encouraged to read selected titles and then vote for their favorite. A glance at the master list from any of these programs shows a large number of mysteries, which are often the books that win the prize.

School Library Journal and *The Horn Book* are magazines that review children's books and announce awards. Look for mysteries that have won a state children's book award, such as the Iowa Children's Choice Award, the Indiana Young Hoosier Award, or the Pacific Northwest Young Readers Choice Award. These books are recommended by librarians and are popular with young readers. Study them to see how the authors did it.

*Last, but most important of all, put the words on paper. Write until you have a first draft of at least 125 pages. Then go back and, using these hints, revise and polish your manuscript. You may end up with an award-winning mystery and wonderful letters such as this: "Dear Peg Kehret, Can I start helping you write your storys? I aldredy have an idea. It is called Atack of the Killer Strawberries. Your $nul fan, Melissa."

❑ Editing and Marketing

❑ 96

WHAT DO AGENTS WANT?

BY NANCY LOVE

AGENTS SAY THEY WANT NEW WRITERS, BUT WHEN YOU SEND A QUERY or a proposal, they fire back, "No thanks!" What are you to make of this mixed message? Aside from those agents who really do not welcome new clients, the rest of us need a continuous supply of fresh offerings to submit to publishers, but since we are in the publishing business to sell books, we are constantly trying to select those we think publishers want. The question we ask is: *What do publishers want?*

Death by mid-list

The conventional wisdom these days is, *Publishers do not want mid-list books.* The term "mid-list" refers to the place a book has in a publishing house catalogue. It is a book that is not "front-list" (books listed in the first few pages of the catalogue and declared thereby best-seller material), and it is not "back-list" (perennials listed in the back of the catalogue and kept in print season after season). Translation: Only best sellers need apply. That leaves high and dry the nice, little literary or commercial novel with no break-out potential. And what about first novels?

The reality is, mid-list and first novels *do* get published, often by smaller publishing houses, many of which have fine reputations for discriminating taste, and then the authors are poached by the mainstream houses that didn't have the guts to take a chance themselves. Or they are championed by stubborn editors at the larger houses who want to nurture a talented writer or who have enough clout to bulldoze through the disapproval of sales and marketing departments.

Another reality is that it is often easier to get a first novel accepted than a second if the first one bombed. Enter the Dread Sales Record. Once you have a sales history documented in bookstore computers everywhere, it will follow you around for the rest of your publishing

485

life, and can be amended only by subsequent successes that balance out the failures, or by changing your name.

One of the dirty little secrets of agentry is that many agents will avoid novels with either of the above potential problems (i.e., a mid-list book or a second book that follows a wipe-out first book), but might be less than candid about sharing these reasons for rejection.

Appetite for nonfiction

Sure, publishers want front-list nonfiction titles, too, but are more welcoming to a mid-list book that has a potential of being back-listed. Most fiction is here today, gone tomorrow, but a nonfiction title that yields even modest, but steady, revenue may be kept around for a number of years. Many publishers will take on a "small" book they believe will not only earn out, but will generate income in the long run.

But before you rejoice prematurely, remember that today publishers have an insatiable appetite for credentials attached to nonfiction books. Backing by an authority or institution is important, and for some books, essential. A health book needs a genuine medical (doctor, hospital, or health organization) imprimatur, foreword, or co-authorship. A cookbook needs a food establishment tie-in (restaurateur, chef, or TV or print food personality. For large publishers, credentials are a must for an offer of even a minimal advance on a nonfiction book. To really hit pay dirt, you might need more than credentials; it will also help if you have a "platform"—a following or a guaranteed promise of advance sales. In this scenario, the author is not just a gardening authority, but she can also attach the name of the Garden Clubs of America to her book and a promise that the organization will offer it as a premium to their members.

The agent connection: Do you even want one?

If you write short fiction or articles, academic or textbooks, or poetry, you don't need or want an agent. Often, writers of literary fiction also do better on their own when approaching smaller publishers or college presses that agents may not deal with because of slow response time and low or non-existent advances.

I know writers of both fiction and nonfiction who—initially, anyhow—like to represent themselves and do well at it. But be prepared to spend a lot of downtime with the nitty-gritty of that process. You might also come out ahead if you have connections and are more comfortable being in control.

Getting in the agent's door

What makes the difference?

Agents often specialize. First, research your target. Find out if you are in the right place before you waste your stamp and everyone's time. Use listings in authors' source books. Scan books that are similar to yours for an acknowledgment of an agent. Use the name of the workshop leader or fellow writer who referred you. Go to writers' conferences where you might meet appropriate agents. Collect their cards and use the connection when you are querying.

Winning queries and proposals

There are whole books devoted to this subject, so I will stress just a few points:

- Queries need to be positive, succinct, yet contain the facts about who you are and what the book is about. A query is like a short story in which every word has to count. A novel can ramble a bit, but short stories and queries don't have that luxury.
- There is no excuse for bad spelling or grammar. If you and your computer can't be counted on to proofread, ask a friend to read your work.
- Proposals and summaries of novels can be more expansive, but they also should be professionally crafted. Your writing ability and skills are being judged in everything you submit.
- There is nothing in a nonfiction proposal more important than a marketing plan. Make suggestions for how the publisher can promote the book, and even more essential, tell the publisher how you can help. Do you have media contacts? Are you an experienced speaker? Do you have lists of newsletters in your field that might review or write about the book? Do you lecture at meetings where the book can be sold or flyers can be distributed? Do you have a web site or belong to an organization that does and will promote your book? You get the idea.

Authors frequently respond to a request for this information by saying, "I write the book. That's my job. Selling the book is the job of the
publisher." Unfortunately, while that might have been true at one time,
it is no longer. Even when large advances are involved, I have discovered that publishers need and expect input from authors, and their cooperation and willingness to pitch in with ideas and commitment.

As an agent, I have to be sensitive to that point of view, so I find
myself making decisions on whether or not to take on an author based
not only on what she has to say and how well she says it, but on her
credentials, her visibility, and on her ability to promote and become
involved in publicity. Also, if you are able to put aside some of your
advance to pay for publicity and perhaps a publicist, be sure to let the
agent know this.

A marketing plan is not usually expected from a novelist, but it is a
pleasant and welcome surprise if one is forthcoming. Fiction is promoted, too, by in-store placement, author appearances, book jacket
blurbs. Sales of mysteries are helped by authors who are active in such
organizations as the Mystery Writers of America (regional branches),
Sisters in Crime, and other mystery writer organzations that support
their members and boost their visibility. All novelists can start a minor
groundswell by making themselves known at local bookstores, by placing items in neighborhood newspapers, and by using other local media.
Some writers have reached out to store buyers with mailings of postcards, bookmarks or reading copies. Signal your readiness to participate, and make known what contacts you have, when you are
approaching an agent.

Start out by writing the big, the bold, the grabber novel every agent
is going to want. This works only if an author feels that option is viable.
I strongly believe a writer has to have a passion for the book she is
writing, whether it is fiction or nonfiction, or it probably isn't going to
work.

Till death do us part

You've succeeded in attracting an agent; now what? I would advise
waiting until an agent indicates an interest before plunging in with such
nuts-and-bolts questions as, What is your commission? Which other
writers do you represent? Do you use a contract?

I'm in favor of author-agent contracts, because they spell out the understanding and obligations of the two parties, not the least of which is how either one can end the relationship. Basically, unless an agent commits a serious breach, she is on the contract with the publisher for the life of the contract. There should be, however, an agreed-upon procedure for dissolving the author-agent contract.

After all, the author-agent relationship is the business equivalent of a marriage. Attracting the partner is just the beginning.

❑ 97

How to Get the Most From the Internet

By Moira Allen

THE INTERNET IS CHANGING THE WAY WRITERS DO BUSINESS—FROM the way we conduct research to the way we submit material to editors. Using the Web can save time and money, give you a break from the isolation of writing, and provide access to resources from around the world—no matter where you live.

Despite what some doomsayers say, the Web isn't likely to replace books and magazines any time soon. It isn't going to destroy our livelihood (even if print publications disappeared tomorrow, writers would still be needed to supply the words that appear on-line). It's simply another technology—one that offers significant advantages to writers, if you know how to make it work for you. The following tips can help you improve your writing skills, your writing sales, and your writing life.

1. Conduct research more effectively

The first reason most writers turn to the Internet is for information: facts and figures for articles, background information for novels and stories.

Internet search engines (such as **Infoseek** [www.infoseek.com], **Lycos** [www.Lycos.com], or **Alta Vista** [www.AltaVista.com]) let you conduct research on a grand scale—or to search out minute details. For example, if you're looking for "everything there is to know" about Roman Britain, a well-designed search engine can take you to archaeological sites that post up-to-the-minute excavation reports; to museums that offer detailed information on their collections; to translations of original documents; and to "living history" sites that "recreate" the period on-line. You'll also find links to scholarly articles, and articles

490

published in magazines like **British Archaeology** [britac3.britac.ac.uk/
cba/ba/] or **British Heritage** [www.thehistorynet.com/BritishHeritage/
articles/].

On the other hand, if you want only a single detail about Roman
Britain—e.g., details about the lesser-known Antonine Wall—the Internet will simplify that search as well. Just look for "Antonine Wall"
(put it in quotes so that the search engine will treat it as a single term),
and within minutes, you'll get a detailed, illustrated description of the
second-century bathhouse at Bearsden Fort.

On-line bookstores can also aid your research. You may not be able
to find the latest English Heritage volume on Roman Britain at your
local bookstore, but you can find it at **Amazon.com** [www.amazon.-
com] or **Barnes and Noble** [www.BarnesandNoble.com]. As traditional bookstores lean increasingly toward popular titles and subjects,
on-line bookstores are the place to look for hard-to-find references—
and in many cases the book will be in your mailbox within two days.

2. Locate experts to interview

Quite often, your on-line research will turn up just the person you
need for an in-depth interview. Many experts host their own web sites;
others are often associated with universities, government organizations,
and commercial and private agencies. Associations often list directories
on-line, enabling you to locate experts both locally and globally.

If you know the name of the author of a book on the topic you're
researching, try searching for that author directly. If no web site pops
up, visit Amazon.com to see if the author's book listing offers a link to
a home page, or an e-mail address. Another option is to search a directory of author web-pages.

Once you've located an expert, it's often easiest to make your preliminary request for an interview via e-mail. Some experts prefer to be
"interviewed" by e-mail as well; you may also have the option of conducting an interview through an on-line chat session or via free "chat"
software such as **ICQ** [www.icq.com].

3. Find new markets

Today, more and more magazines have web sites as well as print
editions. Many post archives of previously published articles, giving

you an excellent way to determine what type of material the magazine prefers—and what subjects have recently been covered.

To locate a magazine, type its name as a URL (e.g., "www.mymagazine.com") into your browser's "Go To" section. If this doesn't take you directly to the magazine's web site, you can try to locate it through a search engine, or through an "electronic newsstand" such as **The Ecola Newsstand** [www.ecola.com], which lists thousands of magazines, newspapers, and other media by name, category, and even by country of publication. Electronic newsstands are also an excellent way to locate English-language markets in other countries, to which you can try to sell reprints. Two good sources of British publications, for example, include **Magazines in the United Kingdom** [travelconnections.com/Magazines/Unitedkingdom.htm] and **Media UK** [www.mediauk.com/directory/].

Several guideline databases are also available on-line, among them **The Writers' Guidelines Database** [mav.net/guidelines/]. You can also find databases of specific genre guidelines, such as **The Market List** [www.marketlist.com], a guide to speculative fiction publications.

Finally, if you're looking for electronic publications, check a directory of e-zines, such as **John Labovitz's E-Zine List** [www.meer.net/johnl/e-zine-list/index.html] or **NewJour's Electronic Journals and Newsletters Archive** [gort.ucsd.edu/newjour].

4. Contact editors by e-mail

Many magazine editors find it faster and easier to respond to queries submitted via e-mail than those sent by traditional "snail mail"—no envelopes or postage required! Others prefer writers to make "first contact" by letter, but use e-mail to correspond with regular contributors.

To find out whether an editor accepts "e-queries," check the magazine's guidelines on-line. If a preference is not specified, send a brief note to the editorial e-mail address asking whether e-mail queries are acceptable. (If you receive no response, assume the answer is no!)

An e-mail query should be just as formal and detailed as a traditional query. The only real difference is that your name, electronic address, and date are automatically included in the header. (Be sure to add a subject.) Some writers include their postal address, telephone, and/or fax number, as well.

Many publications are also willing to accept *solicited* material by e-mail, enabling them to transfer it directly into their computer system. However, never e-mail unsolicited material until you know the editor is willing to accept it in this format.

When writing material that you plan to e-mail, do not use any special formatting characters, and turn off "smart quotes" in your word-processing system. Otherwise, they will be transmitted in bizarre symbols that make your e-mail difficult to read. Whether e-mailing a query or an article, always include the entire text within the body of the e-mail; don't rely on attachments.

5. Promote yourself

Most ISPs (Internet Service Providers) offer free web space as part of your monthly connection package. If yours does not, other sites, such as **Geocities** [www.geocities.com/main/info/], offer free space for noncommercial sites.

Through your own web site, you can attract new readers, impress editors with "clips," and interact with your audience. If you have a book in print, the Internet offers a host of free promotional opportunities (see **Promoting Your Book on the Internet** [www.inkspot.com/feature/promotion.html]). You can also use a site to offer biographical information, announce booksignings and conference appearances, or market your writing services.

The cost of developing a web site ranges from "free" if you do it yourself (HTML code is not difficult to learn), to several hundred dollars if you pay a professional designer. (For information on creating your own web site, try Kevin Werbach's **Bare Bones Guide to HTML** [werbach.com/ barebones/].) Keep in mind that content is the key to a successful site: Snazzy design won't hook readers, but good copy will.

6. Join a writers group

If you'd like to "meet" with writers who share your interests or who work in the same field, an on-line discussion group is a good place to start. Dozens of e-mail lists are available; members simply post messages to a central address, and those messages are forwarded automatically to the entire list. Other "groups" meet through "electronic bulletin boards" that are hosted on the Usenet and are accessed through a news-reader (which usually comes with your browser).

Nor are your options limited to writers groups. You'll find literally thousands of special interest discussion groups on-line, addressing every imaginable topic. Do you have a passion for Arthurian legend? A fascination with archaeology? A yen for oriental cooking? No matter what your interest, you'll find a group that shares it (and may also be an excellent source of information and anecdotes for your research).

Several sites allow you to search for discussion groups by topic, and also to search for specific topics of discussion within those groups. Some of the most popular include **CataList** [www.lsoft.com/ lists/ listref.html], **DejaNews** [www.dejanews.com] and **Liszt** [www. liszt.com].

7. Join a critique group

Like writers groups, critique groups bring together writers who share an interest in a particular genre or subject, and who review and comment upon one another's work. Some groups are open to writers of any level of experience; others prefer to bring together writers of comparable expertise.

Most critique groups operate by e-mail, but offer a web site that provides information on membership rules and criteria. Members are usually expected to provide a certain number of critiques per month to remain on the active list (and to be eligible to post their own submissions). You'll find a list of critique groups and sources of critiquing information at **Tips for Writers: Critiques** [www.olywa.net/peregrine/ critique.html].

8. Take a class

Dozens of universities and independent organizations host on-line writing classes, offering flexibility, the chance to work with established authors, and privacy. Many are less expensive than "real-time" courses, and allow you to "meet" with your professor and do homework on your own schedule.

Guidelines differ, but the general approach to on-line course work is simple: The instructor posts "lectures" and reading and homework assignments on a web site. Students turn in writing assignments via e-mail and receive comments in the same way. They may also participate in e-mail "discussion sessions" or (in some cases) in real-time "chat" sessions. One good source of information on "virtual universities" is the **EdSurf Adult Distance Education Internet Surf Shack** [www.edsurf. net/edshack/).

For less formal instruction, you might want to visit an "OWL" (On-line Writing Laboratory). Dozens of university English departments host OWLs, offering handouts on various writing topics, grammar help, exercises, and even one-on-one instruction. An extensive directory of OWLs, with a link to a directory of OWL handouts and on-line tutoring sources, can be found at Colgate University's **National Writing Centers Association** [departments.colgate.edu/diw/NWCAOWLS.html].

9. Join a club

Many writing associations, including local clubs and national writing groups, have gone on-line. For a list, see **Inkspot's** directory of Writers' Associations [www.inkspot.com/network/assoc.html].

You'll also find a home page for each of the major genre associations, including:

Horror Writers Association [www.horror.org]
Mystery Writers of America [www.bookwire.com/mwa/]
Romance Writers of America [www.rwanational.com/]
Science Fiction/Fantasy Writers' Association [www.sfwa.org/]
Western Writers of America [www.imt.net/~gedison/wwahome.html]

These associations offer articles on how to write effectively within the genre, market information, links to author pages and interviews with well-known authors, agent information, and much more.

10. Subscribe to an on-line writing magazine (or two)

There are several on-line writers publications available—free! A publication is considered a "newsletter" if it is delivered via e-mail, an "e-zine" if you must visit the web site to read it.

One of the best-known newsletters is **Inklings** [www.inkspot.com/inklings], which is e-mailed biweekly and contains a mix of articles, market listings, and announcements of web sites of interest to writers. **Writers On Line** [www.novalearn.com/wol/] is a good example of an e-zine, featuring articles and columns by several well-known authors. Another good e-zine is **NovelAdvice** [www.noveladvice.com], a semi-monthly publication on "the craft of writing."

Finally, a word of warning. As you chat with writers, critique submissions, take classes, read articles, and just generally browse the Net, don't forget to leave time for the most important task of all: writing! The Internet is a useful tool, but it can also become addictive. It's also a far more enjoyable means of procrastination than, say, cleaning your desk. So set yourself a time limit when you start to surf, and once you've reached it, shut down your browser, disconnect your modem, and get back to work!

❑ 98

THE THREE-STEP QUERY LETTER

BY B. J. BASSETT

A QUERY LETTER IS A LETTER ASKING AN EDITOR IF HE OR SHE IS INTER-ested in an article you want to write. It is a "sales pitch." Your letter in an editor's hand is like getting your foot in the publisher's door.

Never be afraid to write to an editor. Editors are people just like you and me. They have good days and bad days. I have found some nice editors to work with, and you can, too.

With a query letter you try to sell your idea, and you sell yourself as the best person to write it. It takes less time to write a letter than an article, and you find out if there is a market for your article idea. The query letter is a tool. You are trying to sell your writing with this tool, so do your best writing.

Before you write a query letter, think your idea through and ask yourself, "What is the focus of the piece?" Then address your letter to a specific editor by name. You can find the name of the individual on the masthead in a current copy of the magazine you want to write for. For magazines that are not readily available, check the current edition of a writer's magazine or directory in the reference section of your library.

Write a straightforward, interesting letter about one page in length, and single-spaced.

There are three parts (or steps) to a query letter: step one, the introduction; step two, the middle; and step three, where you sell yourself as the best person to write the piece.

Step 1: The Introduction

Make your first sentence a powerful one that will grab the editor's attention; this first sentence can come from your article. The introduction can also include examples, anecdotes, statistics (cite sources), and quotes from experts (use names). The editor wants to care about your piece, and your job is to make the editor care.

497

Step 2: The Middle

Now that you have the editor's attention, you need to provide some information. Tell what you plan to do with a brief description of your article. State your idea in a nutshell. Be specific about your focus and viewpoint. Is your piece personal experience, factual, how-to, or an interview? Include any quotes, statistics, anecdotes, and facts available, and provide a plan of how you will organize your article. Also, indicate the word count of your piece and the availability of photos.

Most beginning writers write on speculation (meaning that you write the piece and the editor has the option to buy or reject it). When you agree to work "on speculation" you, not the editor, are taking the risk. Let the editor know that you are willing to write on speculation.

Step 3: Sell Yourself

In the last paragraph, you need to sell yourself. Tell why you are qualified to write this piece. Include any relevant personal experience, special background, or education that qualifies you to write it.

Be honest and positive. If you do not have any professional writing experience, never say, "I'm only a beginner" or "I've never been published." If you have publication credits, include a couple of your best writing samples (tearsheets) that reveal your thinking process and writing style.

Don't be overly concerned if you haven't published in well-known periodicals; even a good piece from a campus or local paper, or an unpublished sample, can reveal your writing style or subject expertise.

The last sentence of your query letter should leave the editor in the driver's seat. Write something like: "I look forward to your reply." Enclose a SASE (a self addressed stamped envelope), and put your query letter in the mail.

That's all there is to it!

You can expect a reply from the magazine, even if it's only a form letter. If you do not receive a reply after a month has passed, you can write a follow-up letter, indicating that you would like a reply within two weeks so that you can offer the idea elsewhere. If the idea is rejected, make a list of possible markets, and send the query to another editor.

You may send the same query letter to several editors at the same time. This is called simultaneous or multiple querying.

Writing query letters takes practice, so don't get discouraged, or give up after only writing one or two. Your query letters will improve.

SAMPLE LETTERS

The following query letters did what I wanted them to do: They resulted in sales. You, too, can write letters that bring you sales.

Dear (editor's name):

In September we celebrate Grandparents' Day. I'd like to submit an 850-word nostalgia piece, on speculation, about my grandparents.

Grandpa died when I was five, and cancer took Grandma eight years later. Soon after Grandma died, I was given a piece of paper on which Grandma had written each grandchild's name, and beside each was listed one of her possessions. Beside my name was "silver salt and pepper shakers." I was delighted to have something that had belonged to my grandparents.

Some people wouldn't think I was left much, but my grandparents gave me so much more than material things. They gave me themselves, their love, and I inherited their characteristics. Those characteristics have helped me through life.

Your readers will remember their own experiences on the special day set aside for grandparents. I have black-and-white photos.

Some of my published credits include *Woman's World, True Experience*, David C. Cook Publishing, and Standard Publishing.

I look forward to your reply.

Dear (editor's name):

After folding what seemed hundreds of rebellious yards of satin and lace, Melanie and I placed her wedding dress in the box and carefully put the lid over it. But the lid kept popping off. While on my knees, I positioned the top of my body on the box with my derriere stuck up in the air. (I never do things the easy way.) Giggling, Melanie struggled to wrap the thick string around the huge box.

I joked, "I know you wanted candid photos of the wedding, but I hope you don't plan to take a picture of this!" Melanie and I have always shared a close relationship, and this was a happy time for us, but there was a time about six years ago when I didn't know if Melanie would have a wedding day or even a future. At that time she was the victim of the dreaded disease anorexia nervosa, or self starvation.

The above paragraphs are taken from "Starved." It's a personal experience piece about our family's struggle with anorexia nervosa. Written by my daughter, Melanie, and me, it shows how she overcame a disease that affects one million young women and the people who love them.

The manuscript is 2,000 words long with two sidebars of about 100 words each. (Some Characteristics of an Anorexic and Information About Anorexia Nervosa). Photos are available. I look forward to your reply.

Dear (editor's name):

"We made it!" Carl Schneider shouted into the cellular phone as he arrived in Paris. With his co-driver/navigator, Don Jones, Schneider completed the grueling 45-day Peking to Paris Motor Challenge in a 1954 Packard. They were one of ten American teams that competed.

The world's first international motor rally went from Peking to Paris in 1907. Ninety years later, the longest competitive drive ever organized for vintage and classic motor cars was held September 6 through October 18, 1997. For 45 days, 100 cars from 23 nations raced 16,000 kilometres across 13 countries. This was the first time Westerners drove their own cars through China, Tibet, Nepal, Pakistan, and Iran, and it will be recorded in the Guinness World Book of Records.

Carl, Don, and the '54 Packard appeared on the *Today Show*, and celebrated send-offs in New York and San Francisco. Family and friends kept in touch and received daily progress reports from Carl and Don through a cellular phone and a web site.

I find this race fascinating, and I think your readers will, too. I will write the piece in accordance with your word-length requirements and will feature the adventure and endurance of the drivers and of the '54 Packard. Like the Energizer Bunny, the drivers and the '54 Packard kept going, and going, and going. Photos are available.

My published credits and a sample of my writing are enclosed. Thank you for your time and consideration. I look forward to your reply.

You, too, can get your foot in the publisher's door. Follow the three steps, and watch those acceptances roll in.

❑ 99

How to Get a Literary Agent

By Lewis Burke Frumkes

EACH YEAR AT THE WRITERS' CONFERENCE I RUN AT MARYMOUNT Manhattan College in New York City, the most popular panel is always the one on literary agents.

The reason for this popularity is that writers think they may be able to secure a good agent by attending the panel, or at the very least, that they will learn just what agents are looking for. Maybe, if a writer is lucky, he will be able to strike up a relationship with one of the agents on the panel and convince him or her to take him on as a new client. Maybe the agent will sense the writer's talent and potential and ask to see his or her work. By this time the writer is already fantasizing about being the next Saul Bellow or Barbara Taylor Bradford or Patricia Cornwell or John Grisham, because the agents on the panel all represent clients of this caliber. The writer imagines the millions he will receive from the auction of his manuscript: *Simon & Schuster offers 3 million for Sanguine Rudebaker's first novel . . . No, wait! HarperCollins offers 5 million . . . Simon & Schuster ups the bid to 7 million.* Instant fame and fortune are there for the taking: All the writer has to do is get an agent.

Is this realistic? "Of course not," says Eugene Winnick, the president of McIntosh and Otis, a leading literary agency that represents, for example, Mary Higgins Clark, one of the world's most successful mystery writers. "The odds against the beginning writer's becoming a best-selling author are astronomical. Nor should the writer be concerned with just fame and glory. Those who have the Hollywood starlet mentality and pursue only glitz and glamour as an end seldom produce anything of consequence. Writers who do become successful authors usually do so because they feel compelled to write, to follow their muse. They are passionate about their work and *must* write because it's what they love to do. The writer who is serious about writing must surrender his image of being rich and famous and be true to his craft."

501

Nevertheless, agents are important. While they cannot guarantee you sales, they certainly have a better shot at making a sale than you do. Agents know just which publishing houses would be interested in your book; they don't send out your manuscript randomly. And when they do send it out under their imprimatur, they usually send it to an editor who is senior at the publishing house. If you send your manuscript to the publisher, over the transom, it will probably be read by a low-level reader who may return it to you, never having shown it to anyone higher up.

Consider too that in the event a sale is made, your agent is the perfect person to negotiate the contract for you. Your agent regards you as a professional and will fight for the highest possible payment for your work. Your agent believes in you or he wouldn't be representing you. After all, he doesn't make any money unless he can sell your book. Think about that: The agent may charge you fifteen percent, but he won't receive his percentage unless he sells your book. Any way you look at it, fifteen percent of nothing is still nothing. However, if your agent manages to sell your book for a million dollars, you will most likely feel comfortable paying him fifteen percent for his hard work. (Curious how generous we become when we are counting millions!)

According to literary agent Tom Wallace of the Wallace Agency, "In negotiating with the publisher, your agent will retain certain rights you never dreamed of, never even knew existed." On the off chance that your book becomes a fabulous bestseller and sells umpteen-gazillion copies, you will appreciate that your agent did not sell Internet rights or the rights for Togoland, and Mauritius, and the intergalactic airwaves. "Your agent understands the importance of these rights," says Wallace, "and will exploit your manuscript to its maximum potential either by retaining certain subsidiary rights, or making sure the publisher pays top dollar to get them."

Also, in addition to being your agent/lawyer, he may also act as your financial consultant. Writers, by and large, are notoriously inept when it comes to finances, and often need advice in this area. Also, working together in close collaboration over a period of years, writers and agents often become close friends. It is a wonderful but underappreciated aspect of the agent/writer relationship.

Naturally, friendship is not the most important thing you are seeking from an agent, at least not initially; it is a byproduct. You are seeking an advocate who believes in you and will represent you in the best possible manner to publishers—and that is what you generally get. An agent who takes you on as a client believes in your work; he believes he can sell your work; he truly thinks you are talented, or he wouldn't agree to represent you. This already says something terrific about your agent . . . he has good taste.

At this point I assume we agree that having an agent is worthwhile. So when do you begin looking for an agent? Well, not when you are trying to sell your first essay or short story to a magazine; no agent will try to sell one short story, or an essay, or article for you. There is not enough money in it, and besides, it is something you can do yourself. In fact, it's very good experience for you to get to know the magazine markets, and to learn how to deal with editors. Book projects are different. Many publishers today won't even look seriously at an unagented book, so this is the time you need an agent. For their part, agents generally want to handle a book, because it will potentially involve a larger amount of money, perhaps an auction, and also because it really reflects your work in a more serious way.

O.K., so how do you find the agent? One of the most common ways is to ask writer-friends to recommend a good one. If you don't know any professional writers with agents, you should probably get in touch with The Association of Authors' Representatives (10 Astor Pl., 3rd Floor, New York, NY 10003), which will send you a list of their members for a $7 check or money order and a 55¢ SASE (self-addressed, stamped envelope). And there are many other organizations, some quite specific, such as The Screen Actors Guild, or The Romance Writers of America, which will also send you lists. Finally, you can consult this book's list of first-rate agents who don't charge reading fees, or any of the books on agenting that can be found in the reference section of the library, or possibly, in a good bookstore.

Tom Wallace suggests another way. "One overlooked method of obtaining an agent or an editor," he says, "is to pick up a book by an author you admire and whose work is similar in type to your own, then comb the author's acknowledgments. This may yield the names of his agent and his editor."

Now that you've narrowed the field and zeroed in on the agent or agents you want to represent you . . . how do you make your approach?

"Send a query letter first, with an SASE," says Robin Rue of the

Writers House. "If the agent is interested, he or she will get back to you, asking to see more of your work."

Jonathan Dolger, of the Jonathan Dolger Literary Agency, says, "Usually I can tell quickly from a query—whether the author writes fiction or nonfiction—if it is worth following up. If fiction, I prefer a synopsis and a couple of chapters, and if nonfiction, I want to know why the book is different from all the other books on that subject now on the market. This also helps me in my presentation to the publishers."

Good agents are highly sought after for all the reasons I have outlined earlier and because everyone wants to be represented by a top agent— someone who represents successful writers and brings in the big-dollar contracts. This is only natural. People have heard that Amanda Urban, Andrew Wylie, Molly Friedrich, Ginger Barber, Lynn Nesbit, and Mort Janklow are "super-agents" who represent celebrity clients, big-time writers. It's as if the provenance of the agent accrues to you. Thus it is not uncommon to hear a writer subtly drop into a conversation that his agent represents Norman Mailer or John Updike or Tom Wolfe or Cynthia Ozick, or whoever the fashionable writer at the time is. However, beginning writers must keep in mind that what is more important than who the agent represents is that he love your work, and believe in you, and be willing to get out there and be an advocate for you. It won't do you any good if your agent represents only the most distinguished writers but leaves you at the gate, and pushes only the work of his star clients. You are better served by an agent who will give you and your work the attention it deserves, not put you on a back burner and leave you to deal with his secretary when she has the time.

"Put another way," says Carol Mann, a literary agent who has a mix of high-profile clients as well as unknowns, "it's only common sense that an agent with a lot of high-profile clients will not have as much time for you and your work. You are clearly better off with an agent who has an intuitive feeling for your work and will personally pick up the phone for you when you need her."

Suppose after approaching several agents, more than one is interested in your work. What do you do? Clearly, you are in a good position. You must realize that while personality is important, you are not marrying the agent. You obviously will want to go with the agent who convinces you she can do the best for you in terms of selling your work and managing your career. But it won't hurt for you and the agent to be compatible. If you live in New York, take the agent to lunch. You can meet face to face and ask any questions you may have. After you have lunched with your various prospects . . . go with your gut feeling. It is that simple. There probably will not even be a formal contract between you. Your contract is a handshake. Clearly, no agent can compel you to give her your work, and conversely, you cannot force an agent to represent you well if she doesn't wish to.

Never question the agent who thinks you have talent. Probably you have, and probably the agent who recognizes it is someone you should think seriously about having represent you; you don't want to pursue an agent who doesn't want you.

❏ 100

THE AUTHOR/EDITOR CONNECTION

BY EVE BUNTING

AT A WRITERS' CONFERENCE ONCE, I HEARD AN AUTHOR STATE: "Make no mistake. The writer and the editor are enemies. He's always on the side of the publisher and not on yours." I was astonished and appalled. This has never been my experience. Never.

As a children's book writer who "publishes around," I have several editors, male and female, young and older. Since I don't work through an agent, my contacts are directly author to editor. I have always been treated fairly and have always had the assurance that we are a team, striving for the best possible book.

This is not to say there have not been disagreements. Of course there have. But with compromise on both sides we have always been able to work a problem out.

To establish and keep a good relationship, there are some things the author should bear in mind.

1) Be prepared to listen when your editor suggests changes. Yes, the book is yours. Yes, every word is as perfect as you have been able to make it. But the editor has had a lot of experience, knows what works and what doesn't, and is as anxious as you are for a quality book. **But**, be prepared to take a stand if you feel you are right. Present your case. Be factual. Be reasonable. Chances are she (I'm using the generic "she" because I have more female editors than male) will come around to your thinking. Be gracious if you are proven wrong. The best editors during discussion will be careful to ask: "Do you agree?" and will often say: "Of course, you have the last word." That may not be exactly true, but it leaves room for further discussion.

2) Try to realize that your editor is a person who works hard. Do not burden her with unnecessary questions and complaints. Yes, you want to know how your book is coming along. It's O.K. to ask. But not every

week. When it's finally published, you want to know how it is selling. Call the royalty department. Yes, you are upset that you can't find a copy in your local bookstore. Call the sales department and ask if they know why.

You don't think your work has been promoted with enough enthusiasm? (A lot of us feel that way. I was going to say *most* of us, but perhaps many authors are totally satisfied. I don't know any of them!) Talk to the Promotions Department to suggest what they might do, as well as what you are willing to do: bookstore signings, school visits, visits to your local library. Perhaps it can be a joint project between you and the publisher.

3) If you submit a new manuscript to your editor, try not to be irate if she doesn't get back to you right away. Understand that she has a workload that allows only a small percentage of her time to be spent reading manuscripts—even yours. She has meetings coming out of her ears!

4) If your editor tells you that your book will not be published this year, and possibly not until the following fall, or the spring after that, bite the bullet. Publishers' lists fill up, and you have to realize that you are going to have your book scheduled where (a), there is a slot for it, or (b), where the publisher feels it will sell best. There's no point in ranting and raving in your very understandable impatience. Your editor will bless you for not being difficult.

5) When you are asked to make corrections on a manuscript or galleys, do them promptly. The editor is making deadlines herself. Being on time can determine whether or not your book makes that list where it's slotted. If your manuscript is not ready, another book may replace yours.

6) Be absolutely certain of your facts. An error in a nonfiction book is unforgivable, and it is equally unforgivable in fiction. A reader or reviewer is going to pick up on it. Children's books are particularly open to scrutiny. The embarrassment of an error falls on the editor and copy editor, but yours is the primary accountability. A mistake will not endear you to anyone. In my very first middle-grade novel, I made an

incredible blunder: I put the Statue of Liberty in New York Harbor a year before it was actually there! Horrors! No one caught it, except an astute librarian who challenged me on it while I stood at a podium, talking about the book. Double horrors! I will never forget that moment nor the lesson I learned. Since I was a fairly recent immigrant from Ireland, I managed to exclaim, "Oh! Forgive me! I thought that wonderful statue was always there, welcoming the tired and the poor as she welcomed me." That got applause instead of boos! It was corrected in the next printing.

7) For picture book writers who are not fortunate enough to be able to illustrate their books, the key words are "be reasonable." Of course, we want the very best artists in the country—in the world—to illustrate our books. Surely, this is not too much to ask! You pine for Trina Schart Hyman. You know she'd do an exquisite job. You lust after Barbara Cooney. Her style would be just perfect for your book. And how about Chris Van Allsburg? But if you are reasonable, you will know that every picture book author wants those illustrators and others equally wonderful, equally famous. The reality is that we are probably not going to get any one of them. It is all right to ask, but don't be aggrieved or petulant if it doesn't happen. Usually the artist is chosen by the editor in consultation with the art department and after much perusal of sample art and already published picture books. They are usually very good at choosing just the right artist. Perhaps they come up with a "first time" artist, and your first reaction is likely to be, "Oh, no! Not for *my* book!" But all wonderful illustrators start somewhere. I personally have discovered the thrill of having newish, relatively unknown artists turn out to be smash hits and lift my books beyond the ordinary to the extraordinary. I thank them. And I thank my editors. They know I trust them.

8) Try to accept the fact that you are not your editor's only author. She is juggling four, six, eight other writers and illustrators, too. She can't give you her undivided attention. You may think another author is getting more than her fair share of attention. That may be true. But that author may have paid her dues in many years of good books. One of her books may have made a million dollars for the company. It may have earned a lot of money and prestige-making awards. It's been said that 20% of a publisher's list supports the other 80%. Another author's

book and the attention it gets may be making it possible for your book to get published.

9) If, by unfortunate chance, your editor has to turn down your next manuscript, take a deep breath and swallow your disappointment. When she says she's sorry, she probably is. An editor does not easily reject a book, especially if she has worked with the author before. It is easier to be the bearer of pleasant news. Your editor may have fought for your book with a publishing committee and lost. Say, "I'm sorry, too. Can you give me any idea why you decided against it?" Listen to what she says. You may want to make changes before you submit it elsewhere. And remember, you may want to try her with another manuscript in the future, so keep that relationship cordial.

10) Remember that your editor is human. Show appreciation for her efforts in making your book the thing of beauty that it is. Flowers, candy, or other gifts are unnecessary. A simple thank-you note is sufficient.

Ten points about how to keep that author/editor relationship warm and cordial. A word or two about the editor/author relationship. What should an author expect to get from her editor?

- As quick a reading of a new manuscript as possible.
- As quick a response as possible.
- Enthusiasm.
- Open-mindedness.
- Support of the book with the sales and publicity departments.
- Attentiveness to your misgivings, if any.
- A commitment to keep in touch. Not to hear what is happening to your book is horrible, and since you would be out of line to bug her, she should be courteous and keep you informed.
- Praise. Insecure as we are, we need a certain amount of TLC.
- The assurance that author and editor are in this together. It's *your* book.
- To be a person of her word. If she says she'll call, write, see you, then you have the right to assume she is dependable, as you are.

So . . . we have a good author/editor relationship, and a good book. Working together, with consideration for one another, we've done it!

□ 101

KILLING OFF CHARACTERS . . . AND OTHER EDITORIAL WHIMS

BY LOUISE MUNRO FOLEY

EDITORIAL COMMENTS ARE SELDOM GREETED WITH ENTHUSIASM BY writers, but most writers drag themselves—however ungraciously—back to the keyboard to make the changes requested by the editors. Over the years I have often gnashed my teeth as I capitulated to editors' suggestions, but found that in most cases the points they made were valid. Furthermore, the editors' advice aided me on future books as well, helping me to identify recurring pitfalls of my own making—sort of a signal to keep me from repeating errors over and over again.

Did I learn from my mistakes? Yes, indeed.

My first mistake was selling the first book I ever wrote. After dropping over half a dozen transoms and being promptly being shipped back to me, it finally sold to Random House. That was the good news. The bad news was my attitude. This is a snap, right? Knock out a book, persevere in sending it out, and you'll eventually get a check in the mail. Not quite. My next three book manuscripts and their numerous form rejection slips still reside in my filing cabinet, silent reminders against getting too cocky.

Lesson 1: Respect the craft and the competition.

I learned something else from that first book: The letter I received from Random House expressing their interest led off with a mysterious line. "Several of us have enjoyed reading this chapter. When may we see the rest of the book?"

Well! Obviously there was a difference of opinion here about what age group I was writing for. I was thinking in terms of a picture book, but the vocabulary I had used prompted the editor to see it as a book for older readers. I did what any anxious writer would do: Using the same characters, I sat down and wrote more "books" (to me), "chapters" (to them), and sent them off.

Lesson 2: Know the age level you're writing for.

O.K. I was learning to follow the rules, and one piece of advice we've all heard repeatedly is *write what you know.* I could do that. With two sports-playing sons, I set out to cash in on those hot-dusty—cold-rainy (take your seasonal pick) hours I had spent on bleachers in local parks. I wrote a picture book about baseball. This time, I had the language level right, but the opening was all wrong. Delacorte expressed an interest. An editor called me, saying, "Your story starts out on page eleven." The first ten pages were cut before *Somebody Stole Second* was published, with my page eleven as page one.

I still tend to go through a narrative "warming-up" process when I start a new book, but a sign on my office wall—"Your story starts on page 11"—reminds me to do some heavy editing before sending out a manuscript.

Lesson 3: Introduce the protagonist and the problem quickly.

If you think that losing ten pages is bad, listen up. Figuring that I was on a sports roll, I turned my attention to football. (*Tackle 22,* Delacorte) This time the editor didn't stop at cutting pages. "You don't need this many kids," he groused. "Young readers will get confused." He killed off characters. Three of them. And had the survivors deliver the dialogue of my three excised players. In retrospect, I felt he was right.

Lesson 4: Don't overpopulate your book.

My next editorial lesson came when an editor I had previously worked with invited me to write a story about sibling rivalry. Would I give it a try? Would I?! Piece of cake! As the middle daughter in a family of three girls, I knew everything there was to know about sibling rivalry.

I wrote the book. Five-year-old Sammy finds restrictions are imposed on his lifestyle after the arrival of his baby sister: He doesn't go to the park as often; he has to curtail noisy activities during her naps; he gets less attention from neighbors and family.

But even with a relatively satisfying ending—after he came to grips with the changes—the book was a hard sell. Although the idea had been suggested by the editor, the folks at Western Publishing sensed there was something wrong with my manuscript. Several editors had a go at it, and the rewrites were drudgery. Finally, the correct diagnosis was made: The problem was with the flashbacks. In making comparisons, Sammy would think back to what it was like before baby sister's arrival. And picture-book kids don't handle flashbacks very well.

I solved the problem by introducing Grandma and a friend who could talk (in the present) with Sammy, about how it used to be, thus eliminating the flashbacks.

Lesson 5: Avoid flashbacks in books for readers eight years old or younger.

Then there was was my "now you see it, now you don't" picture book—the vanishing act of my repertoire. By the time the editor got through writing her "suggestions," my locale was changed from rural to suburban; neighbors became family friends; a brother was now a neighbor; and a number of plot elements were dumped and replaced. The editor's letter ran over half as long as the book; I shelved my manuscript and wrote *her* book.

A cop-out? No, for this compelling reason. The editor had a slot in a series for the book she outlined, and I wanted to make the sale.

She hadn't asked me to write something to which I was philosophically or ethically opposed; "her" book wasn't better or worse than mine, it was just different.

Lesson 6: If you get an assignment, write it to spec.

Should we, as writers, always be compliant? Should we just roll over and play dead when editorial fingers snap? No, of course not. But be aware that putting up a fight doesn't always assure a win. Here's my horror story.

After teaching a class for six years on "Writing and Selling Non-Sexist Books for Children" at the university and community college level, I considered that I knew the language and nuances of sexism that creep into books for kids, sending subtle but lasting skewed messages. And I conscientiously kept them out of my work . . . unless I deliberately wanted them there for a good reason.

Such was the case with *Ghost Train* (Bantam), in which one of my male characters uttered a sentence that upset the editor (the third one to work on the book, thanks to the transient nature of publishing people).

The storyline goes like this: In a desperate attempt to salvage some of the peach crop when a trucker's strike halts shipping in the Okanagan Valley, my character suggests they have a Peach Festival to lure tourists.

Harry, the orchard owner, excited about the idea, says: "I'll get some of my lady friends to bake pies. . . ."

"No," says the editor. "Delete 'lady.' It's sexist."

"Wait a minute," I argued. "Harry's fifty years old. A bachelor. A farmer. He doesn't know any *men* who bake pies. It's perfectly logical for him to say 'lady friends.' This is the way he would normally talk. It has to do with the integrity of his character."

I lost. In the published book, the editor has Harry saying that his housekeeper can get some of her friends together to bake pies . . . a statement that has its own sexist connotation.

Lesson 7: Fight to keep your character's dialogue in sync with his or her personality, and don't willingly sacrifice a persona in order to suit the editor.

The most puzzling piece of advice I've ever had from an editor came when I was working on book four in *The Vampire Cat Series* (TOR) for middle-aged readers.

In my outline, I had the villainous vampire come down with chicken pox, transmitted by the little brother of the girl protagonist.

"I don't think so," said the editor.

"Why not?" I asked.

"It's not realistic," she replied.

"Oh. Realistic," I repeated.

I hung up the phone, promising to give it some thought.

In a series that featured a talking cat, a host of vampires, and a feline underground spy network, her response called for some intense deliberation on my part. I'm still working on it.

Lesson 8: Don't ever lose your sense of humor.

❏ 102

NEGOTIATING THE BOOK CONTRACT

BY SHERRI L. BURR

YOUR DREAM IS ABOUT TO BE REALIZED. YOUR FIRST BOOK CONTRACT arrives in the mail. You go directly to the advance clause. It is exactly as you agreed. You look no further, sign the contract, and return it, confident of your great deal.

You are deliriously happy, until one day you run into an experienced writing friend. She's unhappy because she has not received a single royalty from her publisher since her advance.

"How could that happen?" you ask.

"I never read the fine print that said royalties were paid on net proceeds. I thought I'd be paid on the gross sales price. Instead, the publisher is paying me a percentage based on the amount that is received from booksellers, minus a few deductions for shipping costs and other overhead charges. My current statement says I owe the publisher money."

"That's terrible," you reply, secretly wondering if the same thing could happen to you. You rush home, take out your contract, and begin to read it. You are appalled by what you find and wonder what to do.

While this may never have happened to you, it serves as a reminder to review your contract carefully before signing. It is easy to understand why writers do not read their book contracts carefully. Contracts are usually written in "legal garbage-ese" and printed in the smallest type that the best computer scientists can design. The saying, "The big print giveth and the small print taketh away," is particularly appropriate to book contracts.

But don't despair; all contracts are negotiable. You just need to invest some time in determining what rights you should keep, and what rights the publisher will want. Here are some important issues to consider when reviewing your contract:

Manuscript clause

Many book contracts begin with a standard clause dealing with the specifics of the manuscript: the title, the name of the author, the length, the due date, how many copies you must deliver in hard copy and on disk. Sometimes, in this clause the publisher reserves the right to reject the final manuscript as unacceptable or unpublishable.

A savvy negotiator may be able to get the publisher to waive this clause, but don't count on it. Instead, try to insert that the publisher's right of rejection must be "reasonably exercised," which is often implied in the contract. Publishers rarely reject a manuscript at the final stages, unless they think that it is unpublishable.

What makes a manuscript unpublishable? The final draft may not be as well written as the initial proposal. Or the subject of the book has become dated: A psychological profile of Bob Dole that might have sold in 1992 would not be acceptable today. Or the manuscript may contain damaging information about a prominent family, and the publisher becomes worried about potential libel suits. For these and other reasons, the publisher will insist on keeping an "out" clause in the contract, permitting the return of all rights to the author.

If a publisher does exercise its "out" clause, what happens to your advance? Often, the advance is tied to the production of an acceptable manuscript. Under most contracts, if the publisher deems your manuscript unacceptable, you must refund the advance.

In Joan Collins' well-publicized dispute with Random House, however, a jury ruled that she did not have to return her advance—even though Random House found her manuscript unacceptable—and that the company had to pay her part of the additional monies due on her contract. Instead of the usual clause that the author must produce an "acceptable" manuscript, Ms. Collins' contract merely required her to produce a "completed" manuscript. Although this case has been unusual for the publicity it generated, there have been other instances where the publisher, as an act of good will, has permitted the author to keep the advance.

Copyright issues

Ideally, the contract should provide that the publisher will register the copyright *in the name of the author.* Some contracts, particularly those from university and small presses, state that the publisher will register the copyright *in the name of the publisher,* but this clause is negotiable.

The "Rights and Royalties" clauses are critical for you to understand. If your publisher has only the capacity to publish your book in English and distribute it in Canada and the United States, why grant the publisher all the rights to your book, including the right to publish it in any translation throughout the world? Instead, tell the publisher that you want to sell the rights only to the English-language edition in specific countries. Also, consider selling the publisher audio and electronic rights only if the company has these divisions. If not, retain the rights for sales at a later date.

If your publisher is a major conglomerate with movie divisions and your book has movie potential, consider granting the publisher the movie rights, but only if you are sure that you or your agent could not sell the movie rights yourselves for more profit. Ask your agent about his contacts with Hollywood and whether he has sub-agency relations with Hollywood agents.

You should also be aware that the publisher may ask to split the movie rights 50–50. Try to negotiate to a more profitable (60–40, 75–25, 85–15) split, because the publisher will be acting as your agent.

Royalty provisions

Traditional publishers typically offer a royalty fee of 10% to 15% on the retail price for hardcover books, but less for paperback. On mass market paperback books, publishers may print 500,000 copies or more, offer authors a 5% royalty, and sell the books in discount markets such as K-Mart and Wal-Mart. Writers or their agents can propose a royalty schedule. For example, after the first 10,000 or 50,000 or 100,000 or so in sales, the royalty fee increases according to an agreed-upon scale.

Some smaller presses offer payment on net proceeds because they sell fewer copies and therefore receive less money. Make sure the term "net proceeds" is concretely defined in your contract; it is important to specify that net proceeds include the money that the publisher receives from its sales. In a net profit deal, you should be able to negotiate a higher royalty percentage payment, at least 10% to 15% or more.

Accounting provisions

Accounting provisions indicate when you can expect to receive royalty checks. Most trade publishers have semiannual accountings; most academic and small presses have annual accountings. Payments are made within 30 to 90 days following the close of the accounting period.

These provisions may be difficult to negotiate because they often depend on the publisher's overall accounting practices. However, trade publishers have been known to provide shorter accounting periods for their best-selling authors who are generating a great deal of revenue. You can ask for a similar arrangement, but if you do not yet fall into this category, do not be surprised if your publisher resists setting up a different system for you.

Warranties

Almost impossible to negotiate, these clauses require the author to guarantee to the publisher that:

- the author is the sole creator and owner of the work.
- the work has not been previously published.
- the work does not violate another work's copyright.
- the work does not violate anyone's right of privacy.
- the work does not libel or defame anyone.
- the work does not violate any government regulation.

If you or your work violates the above warranties, the publisher has a right to cancel the contract.

Warranty clauses are often accompanied by an indemnity provision, requiring the author to indemnify, or repay, the publisher, should the work violate a warranty provision. If the publisher is sued because of the author's work, the author must defend the lawsuit and reimburse the publisher for any related expenses.

Expenses, permissions, and fair use

Publishers may grant authors budgets to cover certain expenses, such as those connected with travel or interviews. This is obviously a negotiable point, though it may be difficult for a first-time book author to negotiate reimbursement for such expenses.

If you plan to quote from copyrighted works, you should get the permission of the copyright holder (usually either the author or the publisher) to do so. Sometimes the publisher will grant a budget for permission fees; other times, you must cover the cost of such permissions.

In some cases, authors claim a fair-use privilege to use other people's work, such as when critiquing it, in which case permission is not needed. Determining whether the fair-use privilege applies requires authors to use their best judgment. However, you should be aware that if the copyright owner sues, you have to pay to defend both yourself and the publisher.

New editions, author's copies, out of print

The contract may also specify that the publisher has the first right to publish further editions of the work. This should be a negotiable item. Authors of a continuing series (such as mysteries) and textbook publications should beware of such clauses, because they may give the publisher the right to name other writers to produce additional editions. Obviously, the original author would want to retain this right.

The author's copies clause specifies how many free copies of your book you will receive, and the cost of any additional copies you may want to purchase. Sometimes these clauses specify that you cannot re-sell reduced-price copies. Try to strike this portion of the clause or spell out circumstances where resale would be permitted, such as when you sell copies at a lecture, conference, or book signing.

Also, make sure that the contract provides that when the book goes out of print, all rights revert to the author.

Assignment

A clause that has become standard in the era of mergers and acquisitions is the assignment clause, granting the publisher the right to assign the contract to another publisher. You could easily sell your book to Publisher A only to have Publisher Q purchase or merge with Publisher A soon thereafter. With an assignment clause, Publisher Q would assume the responsibility for publishing your book. You would be protected because the book would still be published.

Your contract may contain fewer clauses than those mentioned here, or it may be more extensive. Whether it's long or short, in large or small print, you should read your contract carefully! You will not only avoid royalty payment shock, but also prevent your book contract dreams from becoming nightmares should some unforeseen disaster strike. Having read your contract, you will know that the price of a magnifying glass could prove a good investment!

❑ INTERVIEWS

❏ 103

A CONVERSATION WITH
SUE MILLER

BY LEWIS BURKE FRUMKES

Lewis Burke Frumkes: Sue Miller's new novel, *While I Was Gone*, is out just now from Knopf. You remember Sue, of course, from *The Good Mother*, and she's also written several other novels including *Inventing the Abbotts*, *Family Pictures*, *For Love,* and *The Distinguished Guest.* Let me begin by asking you to talk about the themes of fidelity and infidelity a little bit in relationship to *While I Was Gone.*

Sue Miller: It actually is an odd book in the sense that it's talking about fidelity and infidelity and yet an infidelity does not quite occur. It's more the potential, the interest in it on the part of the main character, whose name is Jo Becker. She's very drawn to someone other than her husband, while also loving her husband. I think I was interested in that question, actually, of intent and guilt. At what point are we guilty of something? Is it when we are thinking of it, or when we are acting on it? There is a lot of questioning in this book about who we really are; the good things we've done, the bad things we've done or just whatever we present to the world. So I wanted to have this be an unacted-on desire on Jo's part, but, nonetheless, one that she would have acted on had conditions been right.

LBF: Well, you have very eloquently probed the philosophical underpinnings of this phenomenon. Now, Jo Becker is a veterinarian who spent some formative and happy years in a commune in Cambridge, a wonderful place. I don't want to give the whole novel away, but set us up with the commune and what transpires.

SM: It is in 1968 that she lives in this commune for a while. She's actually in flight from an earlier marriage, a marriage that fails, and she goes so far as to assume a false name, just sort of on impulse. She gives a name that comes to her head as she is being interviewed for this group house, and moves in. She is a person who has been a "good girl" in many ways all her life. Even her marriage was the result of being a good girl. She married very sensibly and well and everyone, except Jo, was very pleased with what she did. The group house is sort of wild and free and for her represents all possibility, all potentiality. Everyone there sees himself or herself as secretly a great artist of one kind or another. And they are. One is an artist. One is a musician. There is a scientist. Someone struggling to write a novel. There is a young poverty lawyer. Yet the lives they lead are what I think would have been very typical for a Cambridge group house at that time. There was a lot of smoking dope. One character, named Dana, the other woman in the house, is like the other members in the sense of "oh, this is what one does." There is no sense of ownership.

LBF: And she is this beautiful blond with striking features.

SM: Yes, and Jo is very drawn to her because she is a very lovely and energetically loving sort of unselfconscious person. Jo lives there for about seven or eight months and then something terrible happens that makes the whole thing sort of explode. Everyone is grief-stricken and horrified, and the members of the house go their separate ways. Jo carries around with her both the sense of potential and possibility and this joyous moment when she was young as well as the horrifying ending of it as two different signals about life that are very much a part of who she becomes later on. She goes back home, just by chance takes a job in a veterinarian's office. This makes her realize that she is very drawn to this, in a way, as a healing: The animals are very trusting and simple, and this seems a wonderful relief to her from the pain and complexity of the life she led up until that point.

LBF: Around 1990 a young mother was murdered on Sparks Street in Cambridge—you may remember—and the murder was never solved. It was speculated that a husband or son might have been involved. Did this in any way spark the murder in your book?

SM: Actually no. A similar sort of Harvard-based murder took place back in the time that I was writing about. I went to talk to the homicide department in Cambridge because I wasn't sure how things worked technically: Who arrives first at the scene? Who arrives second? When does an ambulance get called? When does the body get moved? That sort of thing. But, there was a detective there who remembered that murder very well and talked about it with me. It was a graduate student in Anthropology at Harvard that was murdered in an apartment near Harvard Square. Her body was wrapped a certain way and there were some kinds of powder put on her that made the police think it was a kind of tribal rite and that someone from the anthropology department must have done it. But they never solved that murder. I was living in Cambridge at the time as a young married woman with a child, and was terrified. It was very scary to imagine some person moving around Cambridge who had done this. And that was what was on my mind when I wrote the novel.

LBF: Let's leave something for the readers to enjoy in this wonderful book. Let us turn now to Sue Miller. You exploded with your first book, *The Good Mother*. It was a bestseller. You secured a major reputation at that time. What was that like? Tell us when you started writing, and how it led up to *The Good Mother*.

SM: I've been writing all my life, actually. As a kid, in college.

LBF: Where did you go to college?

SM: I went to Harvard. I wrote a terrible novel right after college. I didn't write very much after that, because I was married, then I had a child, and then I got divorced and started working. During that period I had been reading contemporary novels, which most college students haven't read a lot of. You were supposed to be reading non-contemporary novels. But around the time I was 35 or so I began to write very seriously, with a greater sense of confidence.

LBF: Whose novels were you reading?

SM: At that time, anyone that I could get my hands on: Updike and Bellow. Those were the "big names." Joyce Carol Oates, Joan Didion, anyone. And I began to submit short stories here and there. I also applied for a fellowship. I remember talking to another writer who suggested I go to a writing program. I told her I couldn't afford it, but she said, "No, no, they pay you." And they did, they paid me almost as much as I had been making working in daycare. That one-year program really turned things around for me because after that I got another one-year fellowship. That allowed me to write another unpublished novel.

But I began to write notes then, and I learned from writing that novel that didn't get published what I needed to do as a corrective in my own writing. And, in a way, *The Good Mother* was me teaching myself to write a novel that had a plot, which is something. . .

LBF: Something you'd left out?

SM: Yeah. Everything else was there but the plot. And so, for people who found it overplotted, that was the answer. What I was trying to do and what I was learning to do was to write a novel that told a story and carried the meaning I was trying to get at, instead of just writing the meaning down on the page.

LBF: Were you surprised at the success of *The Good Mother*?

SM: Oh, terribly. I had thought I was writing sort of a literary novel that—if I was lucky—would sell 5000 copies, and 10,000 copies if I was *really* lucky. And then I would go on and the next book might sell a little bit more. Maybe eventually I would be a mid-list writer.

LBF: Who is your literary agent?

SM: Maxine Groffsky, who had taken me on when I was just doing short stories. But, I think she realized the potential when she saw the manuscript of *The Good Mother*. But she never said it overtly to me, which I think was very wise. She didn't make me nervous or scared of anything I was writing. I just went on doing what I was doing. When I finished it, Maxine said, "Well, let me tell you what I am going to do with this." And I said, "Don't tell me anything. Just sell it the way you think it should be sold; I don't want to be thinking about it." She submitted it to many places that I did not imagine she would. She said this is going to be a great success. It was at that point that it occurred to me that my life was going to be different from the life I'd thought I was going to have because it was clear that people saw this as a book that was going to have commercial success. I was very lucky I had Ted Solotaroff for my first editor; he is someone who took my book seriously.

LBF: Good person to have in your corner.

SM: Yes, absolutely. And he really focused on the writing.

LBF: How do you write? Do you write longhand? Do you write on a computer?

SM: I do longhand for the first draft. And I try to write in the morning because there is less going on in my head. I'm mostly pretty focused on the imaginary people. Then I put everything into the computer because it is so easy to revise.

LBF: Do you think of the plot first or is it character-driven?

SM: It's usually more idea-driven. Some themes I am wanting to get at or I am thinking about. The plot and the characters usually come at the same time as I am working out how I'll play with the ideas that I have. It's hard to think about what comes first because it seems to get mixed up.

LBF: How long does it take you to write a novel?

SM: This one took about two years and that has been fairly typical for me. It had been four years between novels, because I made a false start on a nonfiction book.

LBF: Of all your characters, from Jo Becker to going back to any of your other novels, which character has the most Sue Miller in her?

SM: I feel I am pretty evenly distributed in them all. There is a side of me that if I emphasized to the nth degree would equal this character and I am talking about the male characters, too.

LBF: Was there an Eli (a character in *While I Was Gone*) in your life?

SM: No. But, I feel that I can be the mother in *Family Pictures*, let's say, as well as the daughter or the father. In *While I Was Gone*, I feel that I am Daniel, Jo's husband. I understood him and I was with him when I was writing this novel. But also her daughters. Each one of them, particularly Cass, was this rock-and-roll type and I can imagine myself doing that, too.

LBF: Would you like to see *While I Was Gone* made into a film?

SM: It's early. It might well be. They are very interested in books in Hollywood for reasons which elude me because translating them to the screen is so difficult.

LBF: Well, this has a lot of elements which, deftly done, could make a wonderful film.

SM: It's a very dramatic book, very cinematic in some ways. And it's very propulsive. It moves forward after a certain point with a lot of energy.

LBF: What advice would you give to writers starting out?

SM: Read. There are formal demands of the novel or short story, and you learn them by reading. I really felt that my apprenticeship was in the amount of reading I did. I read three or four books a week, as fast as I could. I learned a great deal about how a novel was put together, how a story was put together—things that could not have been explained, that I couldn't have learned from a lecture, but just by feeling my way through. To me that seems the first step. I was startled at how many students hadn't read enough to really know that they needed to be shaping something. They couldn't just write their heart out as some of the more fantastic writers do. There needed to be some response to a form.

LBF: Can you give us a hint as to where your next book is heading?

SM: It's again domestic realism, which is my specialty, I am told. But, yes, I am interested in—and this is very general—two people of quite different ages who grew up in very different worlds and having those worlds collide.

LBF: Very interesting.
SM: I think it will be.

❑ 104

A CONVERSATION WITH
WALLY LAMB

BY LEWIS BURKE FRUMKES

Lewis Burke Frumkes: Wally Lamb is a wonderful writer who made a big reputation with a first novel, called *She's Come Undone,* and his second book, *I Know This Much Is True*, a large, sprawling story. Wally, tell us how *I Know This Much Is True* came about. It's a fascinating tale. Can you introduce it?

Wally Lamb: *I Know Much Is True* is a novel about identical twins, Thomas and Dominick Birdsey, one of whom develops paranoid schizophrenia when the twins are in their first year of college. The book starts in 1990, just as the Persian Gulf crisis is gearing up, and Thomas, the schizophrenic twin, commits an act of self-mutilation that triggers the progress of the novel. But the novel also goes backward in time to the twins' past, their childhood, and even further back into their grandfather's life.

LBF: How did you come up with the idea?

WL: In the wake of my first novel, *She's Come Undone*, I sat down to do a second one and spun my wheels for several weeks. Finally, a picture came into my head, a sort of moving picture of a guy driving down the middle of a rural road in Connecticut in a pickup truck because he couldn't sleep. I began to toy with that voice, and I became aware very early on that it was the voice of anger and despair, but I didn't know anything about this guy. So day after day I sat down at my computer, put in my x-number of hours, and little by little I figured out this guy's life. Eventually, he became Dominick, and after about four or five weeks I realized that part of his problem, part of his despair and anger, had to do with his brother. At that point, I didn't know the brother was an identical twin. For me, writing fiction is sort of a gradual process of discovery. I had Thomas Birdsey's eccentric behavior long before I had a diagnosis for him. After writing several scenes, I consulted a psychiatrist and said, "If a guy is acting this way, that way, and the other way, what would be a probable diagnosis?" He answered, "It sounds like paranoid schizophrenia." I then felt it was incumbent on me to learn what I could about that illness, because I had a lot of the stereotypical assumptions about that disease. I had written myself into a place where I had to learn, so that I could write about it as truly as possible.

LBF: Somewhere in this novel Dominick pays a visit to a grandfather. There's a lot of interesting stuff that goes on, and you go into a magical voice, a mythical voice. Would you describe that? Why does he go to visit the grandfather?

WL: The grandfather's story was probably the easiest ride I've ever had as a fiction writer. It came fairly early into what was to be a five-and-a-half year process. Although I've never visited Sicily, the grandfather's voice was very real to me, and in some ways I can't explain, the story was almost writing itself in a voice with a lot of magical elements to it. The grandfather is a pompous character who belittles other people in his family. What it turned into was sort of the beating heart of the entire novel. When I start working with material, I have no idea what the meaning of the book is going to be or how that's going to surface, but the grandfather's story became a sort of cautionary tale. Simultaneously, as I was writing this, I was also reading *Tales of My Native Town,* by a wonderful turn-of-the-century Sicilian writer named Gabriele D'Annunzio, and picked up some of the terrific local color from it; that had a really strong influence on me.

LBF: *I Know This Much Is True* is a wonderful novel, and I'm not going to deconstruct it. I'd like to turn for a moment to your first book, *She's Come Undone,* a coming-of-age story that was a major hit. Tell us about Wally Lamb, the writer.

WL: I was born and raised in a blue-collar town, Norwich, Connecticut, and grew up with older sisters and older girl cousins who lived just down the street, in a primarily "girl gang" sort of neighborhood. I didn't have a particularly *lonely* childhood, but it was a *solitary* childhood. Early on, I was in the role of the observer of all this wild and exotic behavior going on around me in the neighborhood. I graduated from the University of Connecticut and bounced right back to the high school that I had attended, where I taught English for the next 25 years. When I began to write fiction, I realized that up to that point I had been teaching writing in a way that was not particularly useful for writers. My teaching was very traditional, assigning a number of topics, and then reacting after the fact with marginal notes and grades. But when I started to write myself, I threw out everything I knew about how to teach writing, and turned more into being a facilitator that encouraged students to find their own subject matter. I left the traditional classroom but stayed at the school, and designed a Writing Center that went across the curriculum. One period I would be working with art classes, the next period, with creative writing students, and then I'd work with a history group.

LBF: Were you surprised by the success of *She's Come Undone?*
WL: Yes, I was. It went beyond my wildest expectations. The novel took me a long time to write. I did it piecemeal on weekends and vacations.

LBF: How long?
WL: Almost nine years. I was completely ignorant of the whole business side of writing: agents, editors, and publishing companies. I just kept writing. The only fantasy that I would allow myself during that eight- to nine-year period was that maybe there was some slim chance that it might be published somewhere. I've been baffled by the response.

LBF: Were the publishers, Pocket Books, surprised by the reaction to the book?
WL: My editor at Pocket, Judith Regan, championed the book right from the beginning. She tells the story of how she was just going to read ten "polite" pages and send it back. Instead, she stayed up all night to read it and she never stopped being the book's champion and promoter.

LBF: Your writing style is not only engaging, but it's very accessible. It feels easy, comfortable, and it apparently appeals to the literary world as well as to the ordinary readers. Who were your literary models and heroes growing up?

WL: I didn't particularly love to read when I was a kid. The first book that mattered to me mattered to a lot of teenagers—J.D. Salinger's *The Catcher in the Rye*. Another early book that I just loved and was amazed and dazzled by was *To Kill a Mockingbird,* by Harper Lee. When I went off to college, I intended to be an art major, but early on, in an introduction to a literature class, I had occasion to read Scott Fitzgerald's *The Great Gatsby*. What fascinated me about it was realizing that writing could exist on several different levels at once and the writing that was between the lines. So I swerved in a direction I hadn't intended: I became an English major and was off and running.

LBF : Obviously you love language. Do you have favorite words—words that either surprise you because they crop up more often than they should, or words that you're drawn to or that you think are particularly beautiful?

WL: Gosh, yes. Since I was a kid, for some reason, I've always loved the word *chandelier*. I love the way it flows. I love the flow of language, and very often there's a connection between that and, for me, the sound of running water. I know when I'm having a bad writing day, one of the ways I can dislodge things is to go where I can hear the sound of water: to a stream or a waterfall near where we live. My most creative place is the shower. That's where the characters start telling me a story. Usually it's some combination of early morning physical exercise and shower water that will do it for me. Just the other day, I had the beginning of a character come to mind, and my impulse was to say, "Look, I'm on this book tour now. Can you stick around for another couple of months until I get through the process of selling this one, and then we'll talk?"

Another word that means a lot to me, both as a writer and as a person, is the word *renovation*. I think that ultimately that's the message of *I Know This Much Is True*. If you do the hard work of "renovating" your life and understanding who you *are* outside of or beyond the context of who you *were* and were born, and back to who your ancestors were, that renovation will point the way in which to go.

LBF: When you are not writing, what writers do you read?

WL: I'm a great admirer of Margaret Atwood. Her work goes here and there and everywhere, and each new book takes you to unpredictable places. John Updike is certainly one of my heroes and Toni Morrison as well.

LBF: Has either of your novels been optioned for film?

WL: Yes. *She's Come Undone* was optioned and purchased by Warner Brothers. I'm excited about that. And right now, there is some film interest in *I Know This Much Is True*.

LBF: Do you write longhand, do you write on a word processor? Do you write at night, during the day?

WL: I've always been a morning person, and my creativity evaporates as the day goes on. I find I can't do any kind of creative writing past maybe one, two, or three o'clock in the afternoon. And the earlier I get started, the better. *She's Come Undone* was largely written in longhand with the cheapest of the Bic pens, on looseleaf paper.

LBF: What advice would you give to young writers starting out?

WL: Probably the first thing that writers should do is detach themselves from the fantasy of bestsellerdom. Engage in the process of writing, bring patience to the job, and know that writing is more about grunt work than inspiration, and that revision is the real writing.

LBF: Has the immense success you've had changed your life?

WL: In the wake of the Oprah Book Club phenomenon of 1997, the telephone didn't stop ringing. Up to that point I had written at home. I have a character flaw in that I have trouble saying no to people. I found that I was giving away all of my writing time to being "author." Writing and being an author began to compete, so the way that I solved it and was able to finish the second book was to rent a little apartment that was dedicated only to writing fiction. It's about seven or eight miles from where I live, and I purposely didn't furnish it or put anything on the walls, not even bookcases. The only thing that it has is a table and computer and lots of paper, and its chief selling point is that there's no telephone. My wife and kids know how to get hold of me in case of an emergency, but it's sort of like entering the Biosphere.

LBF: In a material way, have you indulged yourself?

WL: When Oprah called, and we knew that the book was going to take off, I remember saying to my wife that night, "You know, the only thing that I want to do is to give back some of these good blessings, and buy a really cool stereo."

❑ 105

A Conversation with John Berendt

By Kristine F. Anderson

Kristine F. Anderson: Did you think *Midnight in the Garden of Good and Evil* would become a bestseller?

John Berendt: No! I spent seven years working on it without a publisher's advance. People thought I was crazy, but I didn't want to have to meet a deadline or owe anyone money. When I sent the finished manuscript to my agent, she sent it back and said it was too local. But, fortunately, she turned out to be wrong.

KFA: Why do you think it turned out to be such a success?

JB: The story is entertaining and compelling because it's true. The people are real, but I changed some names. And Savannah is a beautiful place that has been completely overlooked by the rest of the country and writers. The story would not have worked as well in a different setting.

Midnight has no genre. It's not really a novel, but there are fictional techniques in it; it's not really a travel book, but there's travel in it; and it's not really a true crime story, but there's a murder in it. The bookstores don't know where to put it. When it comes off the bestseller list, it will probably be impossible to find.

KFA: You were born in upstate New York and worked as an *Esquire* columnist in New York City. Why did you decide to write a novel about a Southern city?

JB: As a columnist, I was skimming the surface of everything—I did something different every month and could never go into depth on anything. I yearned to wallow in something. When I went to Savannah for a weekend on a whim in 1982, I fell in love with the people and the place. It's a seductive city, and I immediately got caught up in its spell. But I didn't decide to write a book about it until three years later.

KFA: Did your experience as a columnist help you in writing this book?

JB: Yes—a lot of writers use too many words and go off on tangents. I used the skills I'd learned as an editor and magazine writer. I'd been writing short pieces, and, even if the writing was serious, I tried to entertain the reader's imagination. And I mean "entertain" in the broadest sense—in other words, hold his attention.

I wrote the book chapters as if they were articles or profiles for *Esquire*. I would ask myself if the picture in the reader's head was moving along properly as the story progressed. And I was always concerned that the reader not be lost or bored.

KFA: Did you write every day?

JB: Yes. I started as soon as I got up and often worked late at night. I didn't have any routine, but I wrote, read, edited, did research, or talked with people about ideas every day.

KFA: What was writing the book like?

JB: Writing the book was a learning experience for me. The years I spent working on it were more instructive than all my years in college.

When I arrived in Savannah, I had a northern point of view and certain things immediately jumped out at me. I knew I had to get them down quickly, or they would soon seem routine. I spent the first year doing intense research, recording impressions and interviewing people. I didn't write a word of the book that first year.

I started out writing in third-person, but I didn't like the way it sounded, so I shifted to first-person. I found myself writing without expressing my point of view. There was no need for me to comment on the characters or events because they were so colorful, they spoke for themselves. I didn't want to force a point of view on the reader—which is probably why the book appeals to a variety of people and has been translated into 19 languages, including Croatian.

KFA: Did you work from an outline?

JB: I didn't make an outline because it would have kept changing, but I did make a laundry list of things I wanted to include, and I kept shifting those items into an order that made sense. And I had some idea of the ending.

KFA: What was the most difficult part of writing the book?

JB: The biggest challenge for any writer, especially those writing nonfiction, is finding characters worth writing about. I found a mother lode in Savannah. The storytelling tradition is alive and well in the South. When people heard I was writing a book, they were eager to talk with me. And many were larger-than-life, ready-for-prime-time exhibitionists.

Then I had to figure out some structure and how to tie individual stories into a running narrative. The subtitle of the book is "A Savannah Story," but that's actually a ruse: The book is really one hundred Savannah stories. I used a lot of little literary devices to tie the stories together. In writing about real stories, I used fictional techniques, which made it seem more like a novel.

For instance, the character of Joe Odom keeps popping up throughout the book, commenting on my progress in Savannah. He's really the glue that holds the stories together. So is the setting—everything happens in Savannah. My being the narrator is another unifying device, and so is the murder story.

KFA: You're considered to be a skilled stylist. Did you spend a lot of time revising your material?

JB: I was constantly revising and polishing—that's why the book took seven years to finish. One of the most important things a writer does is find a voice. When I found my voice, I discovered my rhythm. I write in a style that can be read aloud, and I want the sound and rhythm to be right. I'd read sections of the book to friends. Sometimes I'd call my home in New York and read sections into the answering machine, and then call back and listen. Getting some distance between me and my writing helped me to be more objective.

KFA: Did you want to write the screenplay?

JB: No, I let the experts do it. If I'd written the screenplay, the movie would have been 25 hours long.

KFA: Will there be a sequel to *Midnight*?

JB: Definitely not. I'm not sure what my next project will be.

KFA: What advice would you give writers?

JB: Writing is never easy—even for professionals. "Write and keep on writing" is the best advice I can give.

❏ 106

A CONVERSATION WITH DORIS LESSING

BY LEWIS BURKE FRUMKES

Lewis Burke Frumkes: Doris Lessing, one of our most distinguished writers living today, has published over 30 books, probably the most well-known of them *The Golden Notebook.* Her newest books are *Mara and Dan: An Adventure,* and *Walking in the Shade, 1949–1962,* the second volume of her astonishing autobiography, both published by HarperCollins. Doris, you once submitted a book to your publisher under a pseudonym, Jane Somers. What prompted you to do that little prank?

Doris Lessing: One reason is that writers often feel they're stereotyped and have a set of images stuck to them that they can't get out from under. I thought it might be quite amusing to challenge that a bit.

Two main publishers turned the book down. I know that neither of them read it, and I saw the readers' reports, which were extremely patronizing, and it made me remember how patronized young writers often are. Then a very bright young woman at my very first British publisher, Michael Joseph, took it, not knowing it was mine. She said it reminded her of a young Doris Lessing, and my agent said, "Please, just keep quiet!" Now what impressed me about that was, two big publishing houses, one in England and one in the United States, could keep the secret, absolutely, whereas I'd only mentioned this in confidence to just one person in the literary world.

LBF: It really shook up the publishing world.

DL: I think they were quite cross with me. It was hilarious. I got the kind of reviews that promising young writers get: "We must keep an eye on this young writer."

LBF: Tell us about yourself, Doris. You had a very unusual childhood.

DL: I was born in Persia in a town that was destroyed in the Iran-Iraq war. My father was working for the Imperial Bank of Persia. Then, being a romantic, wanting to be free, he became a farmer in southern Rhodesia. He found himself with a wife, two small children, and a governess, in the middle of unstumped bush in a district that was just being opened up. So I was brought up in the bush, which was the luckiest thing that ever happened to me. I went to a Roman Catholic convent, where I was always ill, and I was a dropout.

LBF: What drew you to language and letters?

DL: The bookcases on the farm were full of the best and greatest literature—all the English classics, all the great children's writers from England and America, which my mother ordered, and then I started ordering books on my own. I read all the great Russians and Proust, of course.

LBF: When did you turn your own hand at writing?

DL: I wrote a book in southern Rhodesia when I was 24 or 25.

LBF: And you've been writing ever since with increasing success. What happened to *The Golden Notebook*, which received such big attention?

DL: At that particular time, my whole life was in total chaos: It was the end of the Communist party, everybody I knew was in disarray, and all that energy went into the book. I made a very tight frame for the book, which meant I had to concentrate within the framework. Why do some books take off and others don't? I don't know.

LBF: Is it your favorite book?

DL: No, it isn't. I do understand why people find it interesting. If you've lived through something, you don't find it interesting; in fact, you might even get bored with it because you've done that.

LBF: Is it fun or is it annoying to hear from readers, "Oh I love you," or, "You're not like what I expected." Is it tiresome after a while or do you enjoy it?

DL: I really don't think it's got much to do with me. It's not what

I'm about. What I'm about is writing my books in my room when I'm alone and getting on with it.

LBF: Talk about that. Do you write on a computer, longhand, on a typewriter?

DL: Longhand, no. I still use an old-fashioned typewriter. I can't bring myself to upset my brain by writing on a word processor, but I have to because there are no typists left anymore. What I used to do is hand over a scrappy old manuscript to a typist, but now no one can type, and they can't be bothered to look to see how many mistakes they've made. So I have to learn to use a word processor.

LBF: Do you write at night, or during the day, or once in a while, or all the time?

DL: Ideally, I like to write from 8:00 in the morning to 12 or 1. That's my best time. But the trouble is, there's a plumber and a roofer, and a washing machine, so it's very hard to get a straight run.

LBF: If you could have written a book, other than one of your own, that you would have been very proud to have written, what book would it be?

DL: Leaving aside *War and Peace* and all of Dostoevsky, how about Gogol's *The Overcoat,* which is probably the most perfect little book ever written. Have you read it?

LBF: I haven't.
DL: It's the saddest, most beautiful little book.

LBF: I will read it. Doris, what advice would you give to writers starting out?

DL: I always give the same advice, and it's very boring, which is that they have to work hard. There's a great temptation because it's so easy to word-process or whatever to think that they just have to do it and then there it is and it's fine. But in actual fact, you learn to write by writing, and tearing it up, and tearing it up, and doing it again, and by reading a lot of good books. You learn to acquire a style of your own and a sense of discrimination because you've read the best. But a lot of the young writers can't be bothered to do that.

LBF: Do you socialize with other writers?

DL: I don't go in for the literary life. I have good friends, like Margaret Drabble, but I don't go to literary parties very much. I don't have time, you know. I'm an obsessive writer. When one book is finished the wolf is slapping at my heels.

LBF: Is it more fun for you to do fiction than nonfiction?

DL: Though I have sweated blood over accuracy for my autobiography, I already know it's got three mistakes, and I had a researcher. If you write fiction, it doesn't matter.

❑ 107

A CONVERSATION WITH
MARTIN AMIS

BY LEWIS BURKE FRUMKES

Lewis Burke Frumkes: Martin Amis, one of the finest writers on our side of the Atlantic, has a new book out called *Heavy Water,* published by Harmony Books. Martin, this book is extraordinary, interesting in so many ways. In one of the stories, you have a screenwriter who is writing about three gorgons who have an idea for coming back and opening one of these escort agencies. It was just so hilarious. The stories in *Heavy Water* were written over how many years?

Martin Amis: Actually, twenty-two. The first story is dated 1975, when I was 26. They span that length of time because I write short stories at a reasonably steady rate. So, three stories were stranded back in time, and the rest are actually recent. But there is no design in the book. It's just the old principle of when you've got enough short stories, you just sling them into a book.

LBF: Each one is more fun than the other. But, there is one extraordinary story at the end, "What Happened to Me on My Holiday." How did that story originate in your mind?

MA: Perhaps only once or twice in a writer's life will a short story happen to you, and that story happened to me. It happened to my children, and I wrote the story in a morning because it was all there in front of me. But then I decided that it would be too transparent if written in normal English. And so it's written in an eleven-year-old's sarcastic, facetious notion of what an American accent sounds like. But, he's using that device as a way to delay his apprehension of death, which is what the story is really about. He's fending off death until the last few lines, when the story reverts to the clarity of English and you feel that the experience is being absorbed.

LBF: Michiko Kakutani of *The New York Times,* who's not an easy critic, fell in love with that story. She felt you reached out on so many levels that she was extraordinarily moved by it. . . .Let's turn to Martin Amis the man, the writer, the personality, and talk a little about you. You are the son of a very successful man. Sometimes having a celebrated forebear must be very difficult, but sometimes it opens all kinds of doors. I don't for a minute mean to suggest that your gifts are not your own; and certainly noted writers from Updike to Bellow have sung your praises. What was it like having Kingsley Amis for a father?

MA: That's a topic that has been much in my mind, because I am writing a memoir about him and about me and others. It was always a very close relationship, based on humor and good nature and generosity and support. We did have a few spats in the press, but we disagreed more in print than we did around the sitting room. On literary questions, really. What it comes down to is that he felt that the novel should be entertainment, and my novels, I suppose, are more "worked at," more literary than his. He was also a poet, and he had poetry as an avenue on which he could slow things down and be linguistically very precise. I didn't have that outlet, so it all went into my novels. But although he thought my work was pretentious, he did concede that I was the best of a bad lot. You're always likely to scorn the upcoming generation, and it's equally natural to revere your forebears.

LBF: When did you start writing?

MA: Not until I began my first novel. When I went to the university I wrote a few scenes but I wasn't one of those kids who writes an epic poem at the age of eleven and then a series of dramas. I wasn't precocious. But I do think all writers begin to be writers in adolescence. That's the natural time when you write poems and keep a diary and a notebook and begin to explore your own consciousness and yourself. Writers are just the regressives who never grew out of that. I believe a writer needs an element of innocence despite all the supposedly flashy sophistication and gaudiness of "worked-at" prose. There's still a route back to your childhood and adolescence, and a literary man is a) a literary man; b) an angry man; and c) an innocent. It's a necessary component.

LBF: You live quite a colorful life. You have been much admired and much criticized and much just the subject of conversation because not only are you at the top of your field as a writer, but you live a sort of international social life. What is the real Martin Amis all about? What is the essence of Martin Amis? How do you respond to the people looking in who paint you in various ways?

MA: The basic unit is the writer, and that means someone who is most alive when he is alone. I see myself as sitting in my study all day. That is the basic unit in my life—the day in my study in which everything comes. Nurturing a preoccupation. Protecting your solitude. In my case, with four children and one more on the way, there seems to be the permanent battle for solitude.

LBF: So you are, to some extent, a family man as well?

MA: Yes. I'll give you an example: When I was growing up, it was only in the direst emergency that you knocked on the study door of the father who'd whip around in his chair and say, "What?"—although he was very soft and friendly when he wasn't in his study. It was with trepidation that you approached his door. I'm astonished when *my* boys wander up into my study without so much as a "May I come in?"

LBF: They don't fear you?

MA: They don't fear me at all. They sort of respect what I do, but there is no aura of un-interruptibility that my father managed to evoke.

LBF: How long ago did your father die?
MA: He died in '95.

LBF: So he had an opportunity to see much of your success.
MA: Oh, yes.

LBF: Was he very proud of you?

MA: I think he was, but he was slightly resentful of being outflanked. A woman came up to him once at a party and asked, "How does it feel to have a son who is more famous than you are?" and he said, "He isn't more famous than I am." And she said, "He is *much* more famous than you are." My father told that story, but I think with some irritation.

LBF: As someone who loves language, uses words well, do you have favorite words? Words that crop up more often than other words, or that you are particularly fond of because of euphony or any other reason?

MA: I have crushes on words. *Quiddity* was showing up more often than it should in my stuff, and my father used to say that I used the word *sweaty* too often. But you have these crushes and then the infatuation passes. But all writers have key words. In Conrad it's *ineffable*, *terrible*, words of that kind. In Henry James it's words with eight syllables that mean delicate. When you deal in words, you have your preoccupations.

LBF: Do you write in long hand? On a computer? On a typewriter? At night? During the day?

MA: I can work all through the day and it is a wrench sometimes to stop around seven. I don't work at night. I might make notes at night, but when the day is over I need to recuperate for the next day. I always work in long hand and when I get the whole thing written—perhaps not in the right order, and perhaps not sufficiently polished—I type it up and then retype it. But this memoir I am writing is the first book I've written on a computer, and I'm hoping that will eliminate the middle stage. I use my computer only as a sort of advanced typewriter. I don't use any of its functions besides the word count and I seem to have a very provincial computer that underlines, in a squiggly red line, almost every other word I use.

LBF: Because they are neologisms?

MA: Words not recognized by my computer. All foreign cities and all names. I don't want to fall into the trap that I think is there for people who use computers for creative writing that nothing is ever really finished, because it is so easy to go back and rewrite a phrase. My father had a rule: Don't put it down unless it's right, and stay with it until it is right. There's that danger and also the more elusive one, that the cursor is there and the whole thing is humming. It gives you the impression that you're thinking even though you're not.

LBF: Whose work inspired you to write? Whose work did you read? Whose work did you love?

MA: I was very slow to come to literature. I spent my teens reading comics, and then my later teens rereading those comics. But when I did come to it, I came to it whole. It was actually the poets I read hungrily— the romantics, the Victorians, Milton, Shakespeare. I had a good appetite for anthologies. I came to the novel a little later, and then it was in the English tradition.

LBF: What do you read now when you're not writing?

MA: I read Don DeLillo, Saul Bellow, John Updike, Norman Mailer—all the obvious senior Americans.

LBF: What about the well-regarded British novelists?

MA: I read those contemporaries of mine with dread, because you can't get out of it. My two closest novelist friends, Salman Rushdie and Ian McEwan, I read with great pleasure and admiration.

LBF: What is the title of the memoir you're working on?

MA: I'm not sure yet. The one I am toying with is *The Experience.*

LBF: Martin, if you were giving advice to young writers starting out, what would you tell them?

MA: Two things. I think these are the only useful bits of advice: Write about what you know; don't write tremendously elaborate fantasies. Be specific, be concrete, write about details of life you see, and not necessarily about yourself, but the world. That's more fun. Point two, just get going and keep going. Dismiss anxiety. Just proceed to the end.

❑ 108

A Conversation with
Elinor Lipman

By Susan Kelly

Susan Kelly: Elinor Lipman began writing fiction in 1979. Her first short story, "Catering," was published in *Yankee* Magazine, and was followed by stories and reviews in *Ascent, Cosmopolitan, Playgirl, The Ladies' Home Journal, Wigwag, The New York Times, Self,* and *New England Living,* among others. Her first novel, *Then She Found Me,* published in 1990, won wide critical acclaim, and was followed by *The Way Men Act, Isabel's Bed,* and her most recent novel, *The Inn at Lake Devine.* Elinor, was there any special reason that you started as a short story writer and abandoned that form for the novel?

Elinor Lipman: For me, short stories were developmental. I had to start somewhere, and the idea of writing a novel was just too daunting. My next step was my book of seven connected short stories—*Into Love and Out Again.* Then I said to my agent, "I really want to write a novel. Do you think I can?" She replied, "Anyone who can write seven connected stories can certainly write a novel." I never looked back. I found it easier to write a novel, despite the time involved. It takes me thirteen to eighteen months to do a novel. I feel very comfortable getting up in the morning and continuing with what I did the day before and not having to think up a brand-new idea and brand-new characters.

SK: So you always know what you have to do on a given day?

EL: Yes. Each new chapter presents a bit of an obstacle, but nothing like having to come up with a new short story. There was also a pragmatic side to my decision to become a novelist. It was a year between the time I finished the short story collection and its publication. That year I wrote eight stories and sold only three of them. I thought, "What kind of odds are these?"

SK: Was *Then She Found Me* inspired by a real-life incident?

EL: When I did readings from that book, there was always someone at the end of the line waiting to talk to me, either an adoptee looking for her birth mother, or a birth mother looking for her daughter, or an adoptive mother. My answer to whether I was impelled to write about the adoption theme by something in my own background is, "Yes and no." My original intent was to have the novel that was to become *Then She Found Me* involve the protagonist's discovery that the woman she thought was her aunt was in fact her mother.

SK: How did you resolve this in your novel?

EL: I heard that a friend of mine had married a man who'd been born in this country in 1948. When he was about twenty-five, he did some research and found that his biological mother had been a Holocaust survivor who had come to this country, become pregnant, and had given her baby away. I was so stunned by this story that I had to create my own characters. I could *not,* however, make [my Holocaust survivors] Trude and Julius Epner give up a baby, so I switched things and made *them* the adoptive parents.

I didn't come to the theme because of anything in my own life, but it had always seemed to me an exceedingly dramatic and emotional topic. I had no agenda. I wasn't setting out to be the spokesperson either for or against adoption.

SK: When you write, are you theme-driven, character-driven, or plot-driven?

EL: My fiction definitely starts as character-driven, and then I become very aware of story pacing. I want to *tell* a story. Character can take you only so far. I want my stories to be *real* stories. I want to *deliver.*

Asked how he managed to keep his novels fast-paced, Elmore Leonard answered, "I try to leave out the parts that the reader would skip." I always try to cut the fat, with the result that I often have to go back and add fat when it comes to description. When writing dialogue, I have to go back and put in the "stage directions." I'm constantly aware of the story: I want it to go someplace. I want to reward the reader.

SK: You really seem fascinated by male-female relationships, which can be so convoluted that it seems like an inexhaustible topic.

EL: Yes, but it lends itself more to comedy than do scenes of domestic life.

SK: In *Isabel's Bed,* you have a triangular relationship. There's the mistress, the wife, and the husband, who is shot to death by the wife before we ever meet him. And then there's the third woman, Harriet Mahoney, who is the lopped-off corner of the triangle. What was the inspiration behind that?

EL: After I finished *The Way Men Act,* I was trying to think of a topic for a new novel. I read in the newspaper that Ivana Trump was looking for someone to ghostwrite *her* novel. Pocket Books (then my publisher) was going to pay the ghostwriter a million dollars. I called them and said, "What about me?" The people at Pocket Books were very nice but told me that I had "too distinctive a literary voice," and it wasn't Ivana's.

SK: Your latest novel, *The Inn at Lake Devine,* is about anti-Semitism. It strikes me as absolutely breathtaking that you could write a comic novel about such a subject. Was it inspired by an incident in your own childhood?

EL: Well, that is certainly the case. In 1961, my mother wrote to a hotel in Vermont requesting information about room rates and the availability of rooms. She received a prompt reply: "Our guests who feel most comfortable here and return year after year are Gentiles." I've never forgotten that letter. Restricting Jews from hotels was not illegal then, but I remember the look on my mother's face; I even remember the stationery the letter was written on.

When I sent the idea for *The Inn at Lake Devine* to my editor, she responded enthusiastically. "This is it. This is your new novel." When I said I wasn't sure whether I could sustain the idea and turn it into a novel, she replied, "You have to." When I asked why, she said, "Because no one has ever written a novel about anti-Semitism in a comedic fashion." I took that as my charge.

SK: *The Inn at Lake Devine is* funny, but there are elements of great sadness in it.

EL: Yes, in Part Two, serious, if not tragic, things happen. I remember consulting my editor again, saying, "I don't know if I can do this," and she said, "You'll do it the way you do other things, and you'll make it obliquely funny."

SK: You're Jewish. Was it painful for you to write this book, living every day with anti-Semitism, in your head and on the page?

EL: I hate to sound shallow, but it wasn't painful. It's not the same as facing it every day of your real life—which doesn't happen. You hear the occasional comment from a person who doesn't know you're Jewish—most Jews have experienced that kind of thing—but for the most part, people are too polite to say anything like that to your face.

SK: Are there any writers who have particularly influenced you?

EL: It's never a conscious thing. I think my style has always been my own. My father loved funny writers like Ring Lardner and was always pressing me to read him. "Read this, read that. Read 'Alibi Ike,' the best short story ever written." I definitely came away with the feeling that good fiction is funny fiction.

A writing teacher at the Radcliffe Institute suggested that I read Grace Paley and Fay Weldon because "They are funny, but they do so much more." I think that planted the idea in my head that comedy was not a goal. I've always wanted the comedy in my books to be situational. The goal was not to make jokes. Reading Grace Paley and Fay Weldon opened my eyes to the kind of writing that had a layer of poignancy underneath it.

SK: Would you ever like to experiment with any other form, say plays? I know you love to write dialogue.

EL: Before I wrote novels, if someone came to me and said, "Write a play; we'll produce it," I'd probably do one. But I've become pragmatic; I know what it takes to write a novel and what you have to do to get it published. With plays, I don't know the steps to take, and I don't really have the time to educate myself.

SK: What advice do you give to students about writing?

EL: I talk about dialogue. I call that lecture, "When Dialogue Isn't Working." Everyone thinks he can write dialogue. That's just the starting point. But then it doesn't sound right, it doesn't sound real.

SK: How do you make it sound real?

EL: When dialogue isn't working, ask what's missing: facial expressions, physical details of pauses, gestures, glances that give conversation its timing. Part of the dialogue question is attribution. You need to make those attributions disappear. Readers involved in a story don't read the "saids" and "says." On the third or fourth revision of a novel, I start to take out some of the attributions.

Then there's description, which I feel should never be mannered or authorial. It shouldn't be there just to show off how well one can do it. I learned this when I judged a contest and read about seventy-five book-length collections of stories. I was astonished to find how many stories began with descriptions of the sky. It was always foreboding and purple. I thought, "There's a lesson for me here," and that is, it's a cliché. Weather is essential to a story only *sometimes, maybe.* A lot of description is self-conscious and showing off. It should help the reader see the place or the character. Beyond that, it should disappear.

SK: Have you ever considered writing a really bleak tragedy?

EL: *Never!* And I'll tell you why: They're a dime a dozen. Slush piles are made up of bleak tragedies.

SK: What would you do if an editor asked you to write a really lurid, graphic sex scene?

EL: It wouldn't happen. Editors know my work.

SK: To shift our focus. . .How do you like being compared to Jane Austen?

EL: Every writer, sooner or later, gets compared to Jane Austen. The first time it happened to me was for *The Way Men Act.* I was thrilled. I wanted that blurb on my book jackets forever. If your fiction is seen as part comedy of manners, part having to do with people of marriageable age, in a wry tone, you will get compared to Jane Austen.

SK: If you were interviewing yourself, what question would you ask and how would you answer it?

EL: I don't know how to turn this into a question, but I would like readers to focus on what is generally overshadowed by character and turns of the plot. Reviewers don't talk about writing style. I take great pains with every word; I polish my prose as brightly as it can be polished.

❏ 109

A CONVERSATION WITH
T. CORAGHESSAN BOYLE

BY LEWIS BURKE FRUMKES

Lewis Burke Frumkes: T. Coraghessan Boyle, you are considered one of the country's outstanding, and sometimes controversial novelists. Your work includes *The Tortilla Curtain, Without a Hero, The Road to Wellville, East is East, If the River Was Whisky, World's End*—which won the PEN Faulkner Award for Fiction—*Greasy Lake, Budding Prospects, Water Music, Descent of Man*, and your most recent novel, *Riven Rock. Riven Rock* is a departure in some ways, from your earlier novels, isn't it?

T. Coraghessan Boyle: I work to achieve that. I think the curse of the writer is to repeat himself. *Riven Rock* is a departure in that it is based on a true story, and I stick very close to an actual story that kind of fell into my lap.

LBF: How did that come about?

TCB: Well, here I am, an honest, hardworking, decent human being who used to live in Peekskill, New York, and now lives in the paradise of the world, Santa Barbara, California. I moved there about four years ago, and at the time, my wife discovered a story in a book by a local historian of Santa Barbara, about the days of the great estates. This area, Montecito in particular, was founded by a millionaire industrialist from the East and the Midwest.

Riven Rock is about Stanley McCormick, the son of the guy who invented the reaper. The McCormicks, along with the Armors, the Pullmans, and the Swifts, built monumental mansions in Montecito. The McCormick mansion was called "Riven Rock." The property is still there, but the main house is gone. The theater house remains, where Stanley McCormick was entertained. It's about a mile from where I live now and is still called "Riven Rock," because on the estate there was a piece of rock that had been split in two by a tree that grew up through it. It seemed to me a perfect metaphor for Stanley McCormick, who suffered from schizophrenia. The front cover of the novel shows a picture of the actual people the novel is about—Stanley McCormick and his wife, Katherine Dexter McCormick—on their wedding day in front of her chateau in Switzerland.

LBF: Stanley is, or is presented as, a bit of a sex maniac.

TCB: That's one thing that attracted me to the story, I have to admit. In the popular press, he was called a "sexual maniac" because they didn't know about schizophrenia in those days. They didn't know that it was a primarily inherited disease. Stanley was a fine artist and athlete who graduated cum laude from Princeton in 1896. He was six-feet-four, a vigorous man, very handsome. Katherine was every bit his equal. She is the first female to graduate in sciences from MIT. She became very powerful in the suffrage movement and finally in Planned Parenthood. A socialite, she was a very brilliant, beautiful, wealthy woman. Some of the press accounts of the day called their marriage "the match of the year." But Stanley came from a very repressive household. He had a lot of sexual problems that didn't manifest themselves until after the marriage, which was never consummated. The frustration of that, plus schizophrenia, put him over the line: He had a complete breakdown and became catatonic, a condition that can manifest itself in manic, violent actions. And in these manic periods, he began to assault any woman he saw—his mother, his sisters, his wife—anybody walking down the street. So he had to be confined for the rest of his life at Riven Rock. But the fascinating thing is that for the first 20 years of that confinement—from 1908 to 1928—he wasn't allowed to see a woman. He lived entirely with men.

LBF: That's an incredible setup for a novel. Aristotle said that the tragic hero must be high-born, because no one cares much if a plumber loses his job. But these are incredibly wealthy, attractive people. It's almost classic in the sense that they stumble into that horrible situation.

TCB: It *is* like a classic tragedy. In fact, that's one of the things that attracted me to the story. But the tumble is greater. I suppose they have what everybody wants—love, good looks, and money. I like to oppose the haves and the have nots. In this novel, I've invented a character based closely on the four male nurses who came to Montecito from Boston, where Stanley had his breakdown, and they remained as his nurses for the rest of their lives. The character I invented is Eddie O'Kane. At the turn of the century, he was in his twenties, working at a Boston asylum with patients who had the same problem as Stanley, but didn't have Stanley's wealth and connections; it was a step up for Eddie to work for the McCormicks. He spent his entire life in Montecito. That gave me the opportunity to examine Stanley from a working-class perspective.

LBF: We haven't talked about Katherine yet.

TCB: Katherine becomes the heroine of the book about halfway through. As the structure is evolving, we start with Stanley's breakdown, and Eddie O'Kane. Then we go all the way back in time and retrace how Katherine and Stanley met, fell in love, got married, and so on.

LBF: It's a love story.

TCB: It's a big love story. I like the way the structure evolved, because Katherine then becomes the central figure as the book goes on, and it ends with her. She was really an extraordinary woman. No one knew much about her because, in her time and class, it was considered very gauche to be before the press or give a speech at a rally. She worked very closely with Margaret Sanger, and before that with many women in the women's movement. She was the organizer, and helped finance a lot of it. No one knows much about her except Armond Fields, her biographer. He's a very kind man who shared a lot of his material about Katherine with me. So I was able to give a pretty accurate portrait of her. But of course, *Riven Rock* is a novel, and I invent conversations.

LBF: I want to turn away from the novel for a moment and talk about you. You are often referred to as iconoclastic: You're a very intelligent, nice, funny guy. Do you consider yourself iconoclastic?

TCB: Well, I'm a baby boomer, spoiled by my parents, and I'm a monster of ego unleashed upon the world today. I've never had to obey anybody or do anything in the real world. I've always done exactly as I pleased, for better or worse.

LBF: How'd you get into writing?

TCB: I was a student at SUNY-Potsdam. I went there to be a music major but found I really couldn't hack that at the age of 17. I just started to read outside my classes—literature and history. I wound up being a history and English major; when I wandered into a creative writing class as a junior, I realized that writing was what I could do. I'm dedicated to teaching, and I've been very fortunate to have a large, ever-growing reading audience, and that becomes very remunerative. I don't need to teach any more, but I do two days a week at the University of Southern California, because I really do believe in it. I want to encourage my students and create the next generation of writers and readers, and I want to write books.

LBF: Are you already playing with ideas for another book?

TCB: Sure. I have another book coming out.

LBF: Another novel?

TCB: No, it's the collected stories. The first 25 years of my stories—everything I've done—some new stories, some uncollected ones that have been in anthologies. I'm reading material for my next novel, which will have something to do with environmental concerns, particularly what our species has done to damage the environment. It's going to be a joyfully pessimistic, hilarious, black, nasty book.

LBF: When you write these "joyfully pessimistic, nasty books," do you use a computer or do you do it longhand?

TCB: I've worked all these years on a portable typewriter my mother gave me when I went away to college at the age of 17. I still compose on the typewriter, but my two sons, 11 and 15, have recently integrated me into doing a final draft on the word processor. I enter my typewritten draft into the word processor, which then allows me easily to expand things, and change things a little bit here and there.

LBF: When do you write? All day, at night, when you're inspired?

TCB: Seven days a week, I get up in the morning, do my work, and when I look up it's 1 or 2 in the afternoon. Then I have a sandwich and go out and get some physical exercise.

LBF: What writers did you read as a youngster? Who may have inspired you to be a writer?

TCB: In my undergraduate days—we're talking about the late sixties and early seventies—the only writers I knew were current. I didn't have a good grounding in what came before. That's why I got a Ph.D. at Iowa. I decided I ought to know something about literature—writers like Flannery O'Connor, Thomas Pynchon, Gunter Grass, Donald Barthelme, people who had a wicked comic sensibility, a black humor. Also novelists who had a great historical perspective appealed to me, and that's what I read and loved.

LBF: I can see a lot of these influences in your work. What writers do you read for pleasure today?

TCB: Anybody who's good. My favorites among the current crop of writers my age are Martin Amis, Louise Erdrich, Richard Ford, and Denis Johnson.

LBF: What would you say to young writers starting out?

TCB: Read constantly. And read what's happening right now. A lot of young writers have tremendous talent, and they could probably tell you every night the lineup of the TV shows, the new CDs coming out. But they don't know much about current writers. They know plenty about what came before, because they're studying that in class. I think they come to this art of writing with a kind of naïveté. But writing is a synthesis—something you do over a period of time, a period of history. So you have to read, and read voluminously.

LBF: If you were reviewing your own style and novels, do you feel that you are closer to Conrad than to E.B. White? How would you characterize your work?

TCB: My style is unique, which is not to say I can't alternate it with a short, punchy line. I have a larger vocabulary and a larger view than many writers that are my contemporaries. I edit myself and deliver something that is pretty well formed and shaped. Every writer has gifts and weaknesses, and I think I have a gift for structure. I always have an idea of how long it will take to work out a given idea, whether it's a short story or a novel. I think my style is very baroque, elaborate, and rich. That is something that is unique to me.

LBF: Most reviewers say you're a great storyteller—which you are.

TCB: I think a lot of novelists, particularly academic novelists, lose track of the fact that literature is not something that is on the shelf in the academy, with the public out here being ignorant, and the writer is over here being equally ignorant, and you need some genius critic to mediate. Good literature is a living, brilliant, great thing that speaks to you on an individual and personal level. You're the reader. I think the essence of it is telling a story. It's entertainment. It's not something to be taught in a classroom, necessarily. To be alive and be good, it has to be a good story that grabs you by the nose and doesn't let you go till The End.

❏ 110

A CONVERSATION WITH ROBERT PINSKY

BY SUSAN KELLY

Susan Kelly: Originally appointed Poet Laureate of the United States in March, 1997, Robert Pinsky was recently reappointed to serve a third year. A prolific poet, Mr. Pinsky has received a number of prestigious awards for his work and is a professor at Boston University. His major project as Poet Laureate is the Favorite Poem Project, for which he has recorded 1,000 Americans from across the country reading or reciting their favorite poems. When completed, this will be an audio and video archive of poems Americans love best.

Now, to Mr. Pinsky. . . . When did you begin writing?

Robert Pinsky: That's a hard question for me to answer because so much of my poetry I write in my head. And in a way, most of my work I *don't* write: I'm thinking sounds in my head. I've been doing that all my life.

SK: So poetry is something that interested you as a child.

RP: It interested me, but I didn't know there was an art to it. I would always be thinking the sounds of words, and making up little chants in my mind. I can't remember *not* doing this, although it's not that I sat down at a typewriter or had a pad and pencil in my hand all the time. I was always thinking things up that I would chant or say aloud.

SK: What were your early influences?

RP: One of the first writers I loved was Mark Twain. I must have read *Huckleberry Finn* first, but I loved a lot of the minor Twain. I read the Tom Sawyer books, *Pudd'nhead Wilson, Life on the Mississippi.* I thought *Roughing It* was one of the funniest things I'd ever read.

I also read Dickens . . . and the *Alice in Wonderland* books were incredibly important to me. As a child, I read them over and over again.

SK: What was there about them that impressed you?

RP: It might have to do with the fact that they're *writers'* books, that there's so much about language in them. There's definitely a sinister quality to them, and Carroll had a great, great imagination.

SK: All children love to have poetry read and recited to them, but that love seems to be replaced by what is almost fear in adulthood. Very few adults read poetry.

RP: I don't agree with you there. I've received tens of thousands of letters to the contrary. I agree that many people are afraid of poetry and lose their love of it, but for the Favorite Poem Project I've heard from all kinds of corporation executives and parole officers, and . . . I get hundreds of letters every day from Americans who have poems they love.

SK: In doing this project, have there been any surprises in terms of a certain type of person liking a certain poem?

RP: Absolutely. A lot of people don't cleave to professional expectations. As in art generally, that connection is very mysterious.

SK: You disputed my feeling that adults don't love poetry. I'm thinking of the teaching setting, and how terrorized a lot of college students are at the thought of reading a poem.

RP: One thing that I hope the Project will accomplish is to have some effect on the teaching of poetry. Too much of our teaching of poetry has proceeded as though the reason for a poem to exist is to have smart things said about it. Well, I *like* smart things, I approve of smart things, but a poem is not an occasion for saying smart things. A poem is something that sounds terrific when it is read aloud. That's the nature of the art. I think that school, alas, has inculcated the idea that a poem is something that makes you nervous, because it's a test to see if you're clever.

SK: Yes, I can see that.

RP: How discouraging it is for those of us who write poetry to have people say, "Did I get it? Is this right?" As though you're creating these difficult puzzles, while, on the contrary, you're trying to pour your heart out.

SK: How do *you* go about teaching poetry?

RP: I ask every student in the class to compile and type up an anthology of thirty or forty pages that provides a definition by example of what the student means when he or she uses the word "poetry," so that it is the student's responsibility to provide the sources. When I give the anthology assignment, I have the students make copies of the contents page and give it to everyone else in the class. Then everyone in the class has a kind of recommended reading list.

SK: You are influenced by the English medieval and Renaissance poets, aren't you?

RP: Renaissance, yes. The 16th and 17th centuries, very much.

SK: Which poets do you feel close to?

RP: The poets who seem very close to my own language are people like Ben Jonson, George Herbert, George Gascoigne, and Thomas Campion.

SK: Let me move on to some general literary questions. Are there any themes you find yourself returning to?

RP: Sometimes I think that everything I've ever written has to do with the human tendency to create things, on a very humble level as well as an exalted one. Every morning most of us make a little work of art that consists of how we dress and what we do with our hair. And there's the way people landscape their houses and how they paint them and add shutters and storm windows. What people do to the interior of their cars or to make their offices look a certain way. . .all the way up to great works of art. "Culture-making," if you want to call it that. . .there's an awful lot of that in my work.

SK: How has your poetry changed over the years, since your first book? Have you changed form in any way?

RP: I think that's for the critics to say.

SK: Have you made a conscious effort to change?

RP: Well, you always try not to repeat yourself, to do something new. I'm not sure that when I'm trying to make a poem I'm thinking about the form and subject as two things. I'm just saying things to myself and trying to shape them into art.

SK: A couple of poets I've spoken to have said that sometimes the more formal the prosody of the poem, the more free they feel to express ideas. The constraints of craft are somehow liberating.

RP: I think whatever you do, you're trying to have that quality. In some ways, the free verse poem has to be just as formal as the poem in iambic lines and rhymes. Your ideal is the same.

SK: Are there any current trends in literature that you particularly like or dislike?

RP: I never think about trends. I always feel it's the artist's job, almost by definition, to ignore trends.

SK: Is there any particular lesson you try to impart to your students?

RP: Perhaps that knowledge has to be acquired in a very individual, personal, and possibly even bodily way. If you want to be a writer, you have to study great works. There's more to learn by that than by pursuing rules or finding out what everyone else around you is doing, or imitating the currently fashionable modes.

SK: That's interesting, because I used to tell my students, "If you want to learn how to write well, read good books. Read a lot!"

RP: Exactly.

SK: What are you writing now?

RP: I'm writing a book of poems. The first poem in the book is called "Ode to Meaning." The alphabet comes into the book a lot.

SK: It's always interesting to me to hear how people engage in the process of writing. Sometimes it comes in great bursts, and sometimes in little drips and drops. Sometimes it leaks out and sometimes it pours out.

RP: I guess most of us experience it that way.

SK: People often ask me, "What is your routine when you write?" It's almost as if they think there's a charm. Do you get that question, too?

RP: In my book *The Sounds of Poetry,* there's a chapter called "Theory." It's a page and a half long, and the first sentence of it is: "There are no rules."

SK: Have you been asked if you use a word processor?
RP: Oh, sure.

SK: I asked a friend what was behind that question, and he said, "I think it makes writing *seem* less like magic."
RP: I think there's a lot to that. It makes sense.

Where to Sell

Where to Sell

All information in these lists concerning the needs and requirements of magazines, book publishing companies, and theaters comes directly from the editors, publishers, and directors, but personnel and addresses change, as do requirements. No published listing can give as clear a picture of editorial needs and tastes as a careful study of several issues of a magazine or a book catalogue, and writers should never submit material without first thoroughly researching the prospective market. If a magazine is not available in the local library or on the newsstand, write directly to the editor for the price of a sample copy; contact the publicity department of a book publisher for an up-to-date catalogue, or a theater for a current schedule. Many companies also offer a formal set of writers guidelines, available for an SASE (self-addressed, stamped envelope) upon request.

While some of the more established markets may seem difficult to break into, especially for the beginner, there are thousands of lesser-known publications where editors will consider submissions from first-time free lancers.

All manuscripts must be typed double-space and submitted with self-addressed envelopes bearing postage sufficient for the return of the material. If a manuscript need not be returned, note this with the submission, and enclose an SASE or a self-addressed, stamped postcard for editorial reply. Use good white paper; onion skin and erasable bond are not acceptable. *Always* keep a copy of the manuscript, since occasionally material is lost in the mail. Magazines may take several weeks, or longer, to read and report on submissions. If an editor has not reported on a manuscript after a reasonable length of time, write a brief, courteous letter of inquiry.

Some publishers will accept, and may in fact prefer, work submitted on computer disk, usually noting the procedure and type of disk in their writers guidelines.

ARTICLE MARKETS

The magazines in the following list are in the market for free-lance articles in many categories. Unless listings state otherwise, a writer should submit a query first, including a brief description of the proposed article and any relevant qualifications or credits. A few editors want to see samples of published work, if available.

Submit photos or slides *only* if the editor has specifically requested them. A self-addressed envelope with postage sufficient to cover the return of the manuscript or the answer to a query should accompany all submissions.

GENERAL-INTEREST PUBLICATIONS

AIR & SPACE/SMITHSONIAN—901 D St. S.W., 10th Fl., Washington, DC 20024-2518. George Larson, Ed. General-interest articles, 1,000 to 3,500 words, on aerospace experience, past, present, and future. Pays varying rates, on acceptance. Query.

AIR FORCE TIMES—See *Times News Service.*

AMERICAN JOURNALISM REVIEW—1117 Journalism Bldg., University of Maryland, College Park, MD 20742-7111. Rem Rieder, Ed. Articles, 500 to 5,000 words, on print, broadcast, and electronic journalism. Query.

THE AMERICAN LEGION—Box 1055, Indianapolis, IN 46206. John B. Raughter, Ed. Articles, 750 to 2,000 words, on current world affairs, public policy, and subjects of contemporary interest. Payment is negotiable, on acceptance. Query.

AMERICAS—OAS, 19th and Constitution Ave. N.W., Washington, DC 20006. James Patrick Kiernan, Dir. & Ed. Rebecca Read Medrano, Man. Ed. Features, 2,500 to 4,000 words, on Latin America and the Caribbean. Wide focus: anthropology, the arts, travel, science, and development. "We prefer stories that can be well-illustrated." No political material. Pays from $400, on publication. Query.

ARMY TIMES—See *Times News Service.*

ASIAN PAGES—P.O. Box 11932, St. Paul, MN 55111-0932. Cheryl Weiberg, Ed.-in-Chief. Biweekly newspaper tabloid. Profiles and news events, 500 words; short stories, 500 to 750 words; poetry, 100 words; and Asian-related fillers. "All material must have a strong, non-offensive Asian slant." SASE required for response. Pays $40 for articles, $25 for photos/cartoons, on publication.

THE ATLANTIC MONTHLY—77 N. Washington St., Boston, MA 02114. William Whitworth, Ed. Not currently accepting any material.

BON APPETIT—6300 Wilshire Blvd., Los Angeles, CA 90048. Barbara Fairchild, Exec. Ed. Articles on fine cooking (menu format or single focus), entertaining at home, kitchen design, new tableware, food-focused humor, personal essays, cooking classes, and gastronomically focused travel. Pays varying rates, on acceptance; buys all rights. Query with samples of published work.

BRAZZIL—P.O. Box 50536, Los Angeles, CA 90050-0536. Rodney Mello, Ed. Monthly. Articles, written in English, 800 to 5,000 words, on Brazil and its culture. Features include politics, economy, ecology, tourism, literature, and the arts. Some short stories in Portuguese. Pays $20 to $50 and copies, on publication. Web site: www.brazzil.com.

BUTTON—Box 26, Lunenburg, MA 01462. Attn: Terry Ryder. Biannual. Sheet music, recipes, how-to's, celebrity gossip, book and album reviews, poetry, short stories, and essays. Query for guidelines. Pays honorarium and subscriptions.

CAPPER'S—1503 S.W. 42nd St., Topeka, KS 66609-1265. Ann Crahan, Ed. Articles, 500 to 700 words: human-interest, personal experience for family section, historical. Payment varies, on publication.

CHANGE: THE MAGAZINE OF HIGHER LEARNING—1319 18th St. N.W., Washington, DC 20036. Attn: Ed. Dept. Well-researched features, 2,500 to 3,500 words, on programs, people, and institutions of higher education; and columns, 700 to 2,000 words. "We can't usually pay for unsolicited articles."

THE CHRISTIAN SCIENCE MONITOR—One Norway St., Boston, MA 02115. Articles, 800 words, for "Arts and Leisure," Jennifer Wolcott, Ed.; "Learning," Amelia Newcomb, Ed.; "Ideas," Jim Bencivengia, Ed.; "Home and Family," David Scott, Ed. Essays and poetry on the "Home Forum Page"; guest columns for "Opinion Page." Pay varies, on acceptance. Original material only, exclusive rights for 90 days.

CHRONICLES—The Rockford Institute, 928 N. Main St., Rockford, IL 61103. Thomas Fleming, Ed. "A Magazine of American Culture." Articles and poetry that displays craftsmanship and a sense of form. "Read the magazine first to get a feel for what we do." No fiction, fillers or jokes. Payment varies.

CIVILIZATION—Library of Congress, 575 Lexington Ave., 33rd Fl., New York, NY 10022. Regan Solmo, Man. Ed. Thought-provoking nonfiction articles and essays; some book reviews and puzzles. "Writers should read the magazine to get a sense of our editorial needs." Guidelines are not available. Query. Payment varies.

COLUMBIA—1 Columbus Plaza, New Haven, CT 06507-3326. Tim S. Hickey, Ed. Journal of the Knights of Columbus. Articles, 500 to 1,200 words, on a wide variety of topics of interest to K. of C. members, their families, and the Catholic layman: current events, religion, education, art, etc. Pays $250 to $600, on acceptance.

THE COMPASS—365 Washington Ave., Brooklyn, NY 11238. J.A. Randall, Ed. True stories, to 1,500 words, on the sea and sea trades. Pays $1,000, on acceptance. Query with SASE.

CONSUMERS DIGEST—8001 N. Lincoln Ave., 6th Fl., Skokie, IL

60077. John Manos, Ed. Articles, 500 to 3,000 words, on subjects of interest to consumers: products and services, automobiles, health, fitness, consumer legal affairs, and personal money management. Photos. Pays from 35¢ to 50¢ a word, extra for photos, on publication. Buys all rights. Query with resumé and published clips.

COSMOPOLITAN—224 W. 57th St., New York, NY 10019. Kate White, Ed. Steve Perrine, Exec. Ed. Articles, to 3,000 words, and features, 500 to 2,000 words, on issues affecting young career women. Query.

COUNTRY JOURNAL—4 High Ridge Park, Stamford, CT 06905. Josh Garskof, Man. Ed. Articles, 500 to 1,500 words, for country and small-town residents. Helpful, authoritative pieces; how-to projects, small-scale farming, and gardening. Pays $75 to $500, on acceptance. Send SASE for guidelines. Query with SASE.

CULTUREFRONT—150 Broadway, Suite 1700, New York, NY 10038. Attn: Ed. "A Magazine of the Humanities." Nonfiction and occasional fiction articles, to 2,500 words, related to theme. "News and a variety of views on the production, interpretation, and politics of culture." No payment. Query for current themes.

DIVERSION MAGAZINE—1790 Broadway, New York, NY 10019. Tom Passavant, Ed.-in-Chief. Articles, 600 to 2,000 words, on travel, sports, hobbies, entertainment, food, etc., of interest to physicians at leisure. Photos. Pays from $500, on acceptance. Query.

DOSSIER—277B E. Paces Ferry Rd., Atlanta, GA 30305. Published 8 times per year. Fiction, nonfiction, poetry, and fillers, all varying lengths, on business, home, health, fitness, and travel. Payment varies, on publication. Query or send complete manuscript.

EBONY—820 S. Michigan, Chicago, IL 60605. Lerone Bennett, Jr., Exec. Ed. "We do not solicit free-lance material."

THE ELKS MAGAZINE—425 W. Diversey Parkway, Chicago, IL 60614. Anna L. Idol, Man. Ed. Articles, 1,500 to 2,500 words, on technology, business, sports, and topics of current interest, for non-urban audience with above-average income. Pays 20¢ a word, on acceptance. Send manuscript with SASE; no queries please.

EMERGE—BET Plaza, 1900 W. Place N.E., Washington, DC 20018. Florestine Purnell, Man. Ed. "Black America's Newsmagazine." Articles, 1,200 to 2,000 words, on current issues, ideas, or news personalities of interest to successful, well-informed African-Americans. Department pieces, 650 to 700 words, on a number of subjects. Pays 50¢ a word, on publication. Query.

ESQUIRE—250 W. 55th St., New York, NY 10019. David Granger, Ed.-in-Chief. Helene F. Rubinstein, Ed. Dir. Peter Griffin, Deputy Ed. Articles, 2,500 to 6,500 words, for intelligent adult audience. Pay varies, on acceptance. Query with published clips; complete manuscripts from unpublished writers. SASE required.

ESSENCE—1500 Broadway, New York, NY 10036. Susan L. Taylor, Ed.-in-Chief. Monique Greenwood, Exec. Ed. Provocative articles, 800 to 2,500 words, about black women in America today: self-help, how-to pieces, business and finance, work, parenting, health, celebrity profiles, and political issues. Pays varying rates, on acceptance. Query required.

FAMILY CIRCLE—375 Lexington Ave., New York, NY 10017. Nancy Clark, Deputy Ed. Articles, to 2,000 words, on "women who make a difference," "profiles in courage/love" (dramatic narratives), opinion pieces on topics of general interest, humor essays. Pays top rates, on acceptance. Query required.

FRIENDLY EXCHANGE—P.O. Box 2120, Warren, MI 48090-2120. Dan Grantham, Ed. Articles, 700 to 1,500 words, offering readers "news you can use," on lifestyle issues, such as home, health, personal finance, and travel. Photos. Pays $400 to $1,000, extra for photos. Query required. Guidelines.

THE FUTURIST—World Future Society, 7910 Woodmont Ave., Suite 450, Bethesda, MD 20814. Cynthia Wagner, Man. Ed. Features, 1,000 to 5,000 words, on subjects pertaining to the future: environment, education, business, science, technology, etc. Submit complete manuscript with brief bio and SASE. Pays in copies.

GEIST—1014 Homer St., #103, Vancouver, BC, Canada V6B 2W9. Attn: Editorial Board. Quarterly. "The Canadian Magazine of Ideas and Culture." Creative nonfiction, 200 to 1,000 words; excerpts, 300 to 1,500 words, from works in progress; long essays and short stories, 2,000 to 5,000 words. Payment varies, on publication. Query for longer pieces.

GLAMOUR—350 Madison Ave., New York, NY 10017. Bonnie Fuller, Ed.-in-Chief. Editorial approach is "how-to" for women, 18 to 35. Articles on careers, health, psychology, interpersonal relationships, etc. Fashion, health, and beauty material staff-written. Pays from $1,000 for 1,500- to 2,000-word articles, from $1,500 for longer pieces, on acceptance.

GOOD HOUSEKEEPING—959 Eighth Ave., New York, NY 10019. Lisa Benenson, Articles Ed. Articles, 2,500 words, on a unique or trend-setting event; family relationships; personal medical pieces dealing with an unusual illness, treatment, and result; personal problems and how they were solved. Short essays, 750 to 1,000 words, on family life or relationships. Pays first-time writers $500 to $750 for short, essay-type articles; $1,500 to $2,000 for full-length articles, on acceptance. "Payment scale rises for writers with whom we work frequently." Buys all rights, though the writer retains the right to use material from the article as part of a book project. Queries preferred. Guidelines.

GRIT—1503 S.W. 42nd St., Topeka, KS 66609. Donna Doyle, Ed.-in-Chief. Articles, 1,200 to 1,500 words, on people, home and garden, lifestyles, friends and family, reminiscences, grandparenting, Americana. Send complete manuscript with photos (submissions with photos are reviewed and considered first). SASE required; guidelines available. Pays 15¢ to 22¢ a word for features, flat rate for departments, extra for photos, on publication. Allow at least six months for review. Submissions will not be acknowledged, nor will status updates be given.

HARPER'S BAZAAR—1700 Broadway, 37th Fl., New York, NY 10019. Katherine Betts, Ed.-in-Chief. Articles for sophisticated women on current issues, books, art, film, travel, fashion and beauty. Send queries with one- to three-paragraph proposal; include clips and SASE. Rarely accepts fiction. Payment varies.

HISPANIC MAGAZINE—999 Ponce de Leon Blvd., Suite 600, Coral Gables, FL 33134. Managing Ed. General-interest English-language monthly covering career, business, politics, and culture. "We confront issues affecting the Hispanic community, but we prefer to emphasize solutions rather than problems." Features run 1,400 to 2,500 words; shorter pieces for "Hispanic Journal" and "Portfolio" sections. Features pay $450; shorter pieces, $75 to $150. Query.

HOUSE BEAUTIFUL—1700 Broadway, New York, NY 10019. Elaine Greene, Features Ed. One personal memoir each month, "Thoughts of Home," with high literary standards. Pays $1 per word, on acceptance. Query with detailed outline and SASE. Guidelines.

IDEALS—P.O. Box 305300, Nashville, TN 37230. Lisa Ragan, Ed. Articles, 800 to 1,000 words; poetry, 12 to 50 lines. Light, nostalgic pieces. Payment varies. SASE for guidelines.

ITALIAN AMERICA—219 E St. N.E., Washington, DC 20002-4922. Brenda K. Dalessandro, Ed. "The Official Publication of the Order Sons of Italy in America." Quarterly. Articles, 1,000 to 2,500 words, and fillers, 500 to 750 words, on people, institutions, and events of interest to the Italian-American community. Also book reviews. Payment varies, on publication. Queries preferred.

KIWANIS—3636 Woodview Trace, Indianapolis, IN 46268. Chuck Jonak, Man. Ed. Articles, 1,200 to 2,500 words, on home; family; international issues; the social, health, and emotional needs of youth (especially under age 6); career and community concerns of business and professional people. No travel pieces, interviews, profiles. Pays $400 to $1,000, on acceptance. Query. Send SASE for guidelines.

LADIES' HOME JOURNAL—125 Park Ave., New York, NY 10017. Pam O'Brien, Articles. Ed. Articles on contemporary subjects of interest to women. "See masthead for specific-topic editors and address appropriate editor." Query with SASE required.

LISTEN MAGAZINE—55 W. Oak Ridge Dr., Hagerstown, MD 21740. Lincoln Steed, Ed. Articles, 1,000 to 1,200 words, on problems of alcohol and drug abuse, for teenagers; personality profiles; self-improvement articles, and drug-free activities. Photos. Pays 5¢ to 7¢ a word, extra for photos, on acceptance. Guidelines. Sample issues available. Query.

MCCALL'S—375 Lexington Ave., New York, NY 10017. Attn: Articles Ed. Articles, 1,000 to 1,800 words, on current issues, human interest, family relationships. Payment varies, on acceptance. SASE.

MADEMOISELLE—350 Madison Ave., New York, NY 10017. Faye Haun, Man. Ed. Articles, 750 to 2,500 words, on subjects of interest to single, working women in their twenties. Reporting pieces, essays, first-person accounts, and humor; how-tos on personal relationships, work, and fitness. No fiction. Pays excellent rates, on acceptance. SASE required. Query with clips.

METROPOLITAN HOME—1633 Broadway, New York, NY 10019. Attn: Michael Lassell, Articles Dept. Service and informational articles for residents of houses, co-ops, lofts, and condominiums, on real estate, equity, wine and spirits, collecting, etc. Interior design and home furnishing articles with emphasis on lifestyle. Pay varies. Query with clips.

MOTHER EARTH NEWS—49 E. 21st St., 11th Fl., New York, NY 10010. Matthew Scanlon, Ed. Articles for rural and urban readers: home improvements, how-tos, indoor and outdoor gardening, health, food, ecology, energy, and consumerism. Pays varying rates, on acceptance.

MOTHER JONES—731 Market St., Suite 600, San Francisco, CA 94103. Roger Cohn, Ed. Investigative articles, political essays, cultural analyses, multicultural issues. "OutFront" pieces, 250 to 500 words. Query with SASE.

MS.—20 Exchange Pl., 22nd Fl., New York, NY 10005. Attn: Manuscript Ed. Articles relating to feminism, women's roles, and social change; reporting, essays, theory, and analysis. No poetry or fiction. Pays market rates. Query with resumé, clips, and SASE.

NATIONAL ENQUIRER—Lantana, FL 33464. Attn: C. Montgomery. Mass audience: topical news, celebrities, how-to, scientific discoveries, human drama, adventure, medical news, personalities. Photos. Query (2 to 3 sentences, with source) with SASE.

NAVY TIMES—See *Times News Service.*

THE NEW YORK TIMES MAGAZINE—229 W. 43rd St., New York, NY 10036. Attn: Articles Ed. Timely articles, approximately 3,000 words, on news items, forthcoming events, trends, culture, entertainment, etc. Pays to $2,500 for major articles, on acceptance. Query with clips.

THE NEW YORKER—20 W. 43rd St., New York, NY 10036. Send submissions to appropriate Editor (Fact, Fiction, or Poetry). Factual and biographical articles for "Profiles," "Reporter at Large," etc. Pays good rates, on acceptance. Query.

NEWSWEEK—251 W. 57th St., New York, NY 10019-1894. Attn: My Turn. Original personal (first person) opinion essays, 850 to 900 words, for "My Turn" column; must contain verifiable facts. Submit manuscript with SASE. Pays $1,000, on publication.

PARADE—711 Third Ave., New York, NY 10017. Articles Ed. National Sunday newspaper magazine. Factual and authoritative articles, 1,200 to 1,500 words, on subjects of national interest: social issues, common health concerns, sports, community problem-solving, and extraordinary achievements of ordinary people. "We seek unique angles on all topics." No fiction, poetry, cartoons, games, nostalgia, quotes, or puzzles. Pays from $1,000. Query with two writing samples and SASE.

PENTHOUSE—277 Park Ave., 4th Fl., New York, NY 10172-0003. Peter Bloch, Ed. Lavada B. Nahon, Sr. Ed. General-interest or controversial articles, to 5,000 words. Pays to $1 a word, on acceptance.

PEOPLE WEEKLY—Time-Life Bldg., Rockefeller Ctr., New York, NY 10020. John Saar, Asst. Man. Ed. "Vast majority of material is staff-written." Will consider article proposals, 3 to 4 paragraphs, on timely, entertaining, and topical personalities. Pays good rates, on acceptance.

PLAYBOY—9242 Beverly Blvd., Beverly Hills, CA 90210. Stephen Randall, Exec. Ed. Sophisticated articles, 4,000 to 6,000 words, of interest to urban men. Humor, satire. Pays on acceptance. Query.

PLAYGIRL—801 Second Ave., 9th Fl., New York, NY 10017. Sandra Mardenfeld, Man. Ed. Articles, 750 to 3,000 words, on sexuality, relationships, and celebrities for women ages 18 and up. Erotic fiction, 1,500 to 2,500 words. Query with clips. Pays negotiable rates, after acceptance.

PRESERVATION—1785 Massachusetts Ave. N.W., Washington, DC 20036. Robert Wilson, Ed. Feature articles from published writers, 1,500 to 4,000 words, on the built environment, place, preservation issues, and people involved in preserving America's heritage. Mostly free-lance. Query.

QUEEN'S QUARTERLY—Queens Univ., Kingston, Ont., Canada K7L 3N6. Boris Castel, Ed. Articles, to 5,000 words, on a wide range of topics, and fiction, to 5,000 words. Poetry; send no more than 6 poems. B&W art. Pays to $400, on publication.

READER'S DIGEST—Readers Digest Road, Pleasantville, NY 10570-7000. Kenneth Tomlinson, Ed.-in-Chief. Unsolicited manuscripts will not be read or returned. General-interest articles already in print and well-developed story proposals will be considered. Send reprint or query to any editor on the masthead.

REAL PEOPLE—450 7th Ave., Suite 1701, New York, NY 10123-0073. Alex Polner, Ed. True stories, to 500 words, on interesting people, strange occupations and hobbies, eye opening stories about people, places and odd happenings. Pays $25 to $50, on publication; send submissions to "Real Shorts," Brad Hamilton, Ed. Query for interviews, 1,000 to 1,800 words, with movie or TV actors, musicians, and other entertainment celebrities. Pays $150 to $350, on publication. SASE.

REDBOOK—224 W. 57th St., New York, NY 10019. Andrea Bauman, Ed. Articles, 1,000 to 2,500 words, on subjects related to relationships, marriage, sex, current social issues, crime, human interest, health, psychology, and parenting. Payment varies, on acceptance. Query with clips.

ROLLING STONE—1290 Ave. of the Americas, 2nd Fl., New York, NY 10104. Attn: Ed. Magazine of American music, culture, and politics. No fiction. "We rarely accept free-lance material." Query.

THE ROTARIAN—1560 Sherman Ave., Evanston, IL 60201-3698. Charles W. Pratt, Ed. Cary Silver, Managing Ed. Articles, 1,200 to 2,000 words, on international social and economic issues, business and management, human relationships, travel, sports, environment, science and technology; humor. Pays good rates, on acceptance. Query.

RUSSIAN LIFE—89 Main St., #2, Montpelier, VT 05602-2948. Mikhail Ivanov, Ed. Articles, 1,000 to 3,000 words, on Russian culture, travel, history, politics, art, business and society. "We do not want stories about personal trips to Russia, editorials on developments in Russia, or articles that promote the services of a specific company, organization, or government agency." Query. Pays 7¢ to 10¢ a word; $20 to $30 per photo, on publication.

THE SATURDAY EVENING POST—1100 Waterway Blvd., Indianapolis, IN 46202. Ted Kreiter, Exec. Ed. Family-oriented articles, 1,500 to 3,000 words: humor, preventive medicine, health and fitness, destination-oriented travel pieces (not personal experience), celebrity profiles, the arts, and sciences. Pays varying rates, on publication. Queries preferred.

SMITHSONIAN MAGAZINE—900 Jefferson Dr., Washington, DC 20560. Marlane A. Liddell, Articles Ed. Articles on history, art, natural history, physical science, profiles, etc. Query with clips.

SPORTS ILLUSTRATED—1271 Ave. of the Americas, New York, NY 10020. Chris Hunt, Articles Ed. Query. Rarely uses free-lance material.

STAR—660 White Plains Rd., Tarrytown, NY 10591. Attn: Ed. Dept. Topical articles, 50 to 800 words, on show business and celebrities, health, fitness, parenting, and diet and food. Pays varying rates.

SUCCESS—733 Third Ave., 10th Fl., New York, NY 10017. Joanna Smith Bers, Ed. Profiles of successful entrepreneurs; how-to articles on raising money and building a successful small business; science, psychology, behavior, and motivation articles, 500 to 3,500 words. Query with resumé and two clips.

TIMES NEWS SERVICE—Army Times Publishing Co., Springfield, VA 22159. Attn: R&R Ed. Articles, 500 to 750 words, that are informative, helpful, entertaining, and stimulating to a military audience for "R&R" newspaper section. Pays $75 to $100, on acceptance. Also, 1,000- to 1,200-word articles on careers after military service, travel, finance, and education for *Army Times, Navy Times,* and *Air Force Times.* Address Supplements Ed. Pays $125 to $275, on acceptance. Guidelines.

TOWN & COUNTRY—1700 Broadway, New York, NY 10019. Pamela Fiori, Ed.-in-Chief. Considers one-page proposals for articles. Include clips and resumé. Rarely buys unsolicited manuscripts.

TRAVEL & LEISURE—1120 Ave. of the Americas, New York, NY 10036. Nancy Novogrod, Ed.-in-Chief. Articles, 800 to 3,000 words, on destinations and travel-related activities. Regional pieces for regional editions. Pays varying rates, on acceptance. Query.

TV GUIDE—Radnor, PA 19088. Barry Golson, Exec. Ed. Short, light, brightly written pieces about humorous or offbeat angles of television and industry trends. (Majority of personality pieces are staff-written.) Pays on acceptance. Query.

URB—1680 N. Vine St., Suite 1012, Los Angeles, CA 90028-8836. Stacy Osbaum, Ed. Bimonthly. Features, varying lengths on dance and underground hip-hop music, featuring profiles of emerging musicians, singers, and groups. Pays about 10¢ a word, on publication. Query.

VANITY FAIR—350 Madison Ave., New York, NY 10017. Attn: Submissions (Specify News, Arts, or Culture). Pays on acceptance. Query.

VILLAGE VOICE—36 Cooper Sq., New York, NY 10003. Doug Simmons, Man. Ed. Articles, 500 to 2,000 words, on current or controversial topics. Pays $100 to $1,500, on acceptance. Query or send manuscript with SASE.

WASHINGTON POST MAGAZINE—*The Washington Post,* 1150 15th St. N.W., Washington, DC 20071. John Cotter, Sr. Ed. Essays, profiles, and Washington-oriented general-interest pieces, to 5,000 words, on business, arts and culture, politics, science, sports, education, children, relationships, behavior, etc. Pays from $1,000, after acceptance.

WOMAN'S DAY—1633 Broadway, New York, NY 10019. Stephanie Abarbanel, Sr. Articles Ed. Articles, 500 to 1,800 words, on subjects of interest to women: marriage, family health, money management, interpersonal relationships, changing lifestyles, etc. Dramatic first-person narratives about women who have experienced medical miracles or other triumphs, or have overcome common problems, such as being overweight. SASE required. Pays top rates, on acceptance. Query; unsolicited manuscripts not accepted.

YANKEE—Yankee Publishing Co., P.O. Box 520, Dublin, NH 03444.

Judson D. Hale, Ed. Articles, to 2,500 words, with New England angle. Photos. Pays $150 to $2,000 (average $800), on acceptance. Query required.

CURRENT EVENTS, POLITICS

AMERICAN CITY & COUNTY—6151 Powers Ferry Rd. N.W., Atlanta, GA 30339-2959. Janet Ward, Ed. 600 to 2,500 words, on local government issues (wastewater, water, solid waste, financial management, information technology, etc.). "Our readers are elected and appointed local government leaders. Guidelines.

THE AMERICAN LEGION—Box 1055, Indianapolis, IN 46206. John B. Raughter, Ed. Articles, 750 to 2,000 words, on current world affairs, public policy, and subjects of contemporary interest. Pays $500 to $3,000, on acceptance. Query.

THE AMERICAN SCHOLAR—1811 Q St. N.W., Washington, DC 20009-9974. Anne Fadiman, Ed. Non-technical articles and essays, 3,500 to 4,000 words, on current affairs, the American cultural scene, politics, arts, religion, and science. Pays to $500, on acceptance.

THE AMICUS JOURNAL—Natural Resources Defense Council, 40 W. 20th St., New York, NY 10011. Kathrin Day Lassila, Ed. Investigative articles, profiles, book reviews, and essays, related to the environment, especially national and international environmental policy. Also poetry "rooted in nature." Pays varying rates, on publication. Queries with clips required.

THE ATLANTIC MONTHLY—77 N. Washington St., Boston, MA 02114. William Whitworth, Ed. Not currently accepting material.

BRIARPATCH—2138 McIntyre St., Regina, Saskatchewan, Canada S4P 2R7. George Manz, Man. Ed. "Saskatchewan's Independent Newsmagazine." Left-wing articles, 600 to 1,200 words, on politics, women's issues, environment, labor, international affairs for Canadian activists involved in social change issues. Pays in copies. Queries preferred.

BUILD MAGAZINE—423 W. 55th St., 8th Fl., New York, NY 10019. Dara Mayers, Ed-in-Chief. Quarterly. Articles and photos geared toward helping "16- to 30-year olds in the political, creative, and organizing realms" change the world. Query; no unsolicited manuscripts. Pays $100 per printed page, 30 days after publication.

CALIFORNIA JOURNAL—2101 K St., Sacramento, CA 95816. A.G. Block, Ed. "Independent analysis of politics and government." Balanced articles, 1,500 words, related to California government and politics. Advocacy pieces, 800 words. Pays to $1000 for articles, on publication. (No payment for advocacy pieces.) Query.

CAMPAIGNS & ELECTIONS—1414 22nd St., Washington, DC 20037. Ron Faucheux, Ed. Feature articles, 700 to 4,000 words, related to the strategies, techniques, trends, and personalities of political campaigning. Campaign case studies, 1,500 to 3,000 words; how-to articles, 700 to 2,000 words, on specific aspects of campaigning; items, 100 to 800 words, for "Inside Politics"; and in-depth studies, 700 to 3,000 words, of public opinion, election results, and political trends that help form campaign strategy. Pays in subscriptions and free admission to certain public seminars.

CHURCH & STATE—1816 Jefferson Pl. N.W., Washington, DC 20036.

Joseph L. Conn, Ed. Articles, 600 to 2,600 words, on issues of religious liberty and church-state relations, promoting the concept of church-state separation. Pays varying rates, on acceptance. Query.

COMMENTARY—165 E. 56th St., New York, NY 10022. Neal Kozodoy, Ed. Articles, 5,000 to 7,000 words, on contemporary issues, Jewish affairs, social sciences, religious thought, culture. Serious fiction; book reviews. Pays on publication.

COMMONWEAL—475 Riverside Dr., New York, NY 10115. Margaret O'Brien Steinfels, Ed. Catholic. Articles, to 3,000 words, on political, social, religious, and literary subjects. Pays 3¢ a word, on acceptance.

CULTUREFRONT—150 Broadway, Suite 1700, New York, NY 10038. Attn: Ed. "A Magazine of the Humanities." Nonfiction and occasional fiction articles, 2,500 words, related to theme. "News and a variety of views on the production, interpretation, and politics of culture." No payment. Query for current themes.

CURRENT HISTORY—4225 Main St., Philadelphia, PA 19127. William W. Finan, Jr., Ed. Country-specific political science and current affairs articles, to 20 pages. Hard analysis written in a lively manner. "We devote each issue to a specific region or country. Writers should be experts with up-to-date knowledge of the region." Queries preferred. Pays $300, on publication.

EMERGE—BET Plaza, 1900 W. Place N.E., Washington, DC 20018. Florestine Purnell, Man. Ed. "Black America's Newsmagazine." Articles, 1,200 to 2,000 words, on current issues, ideas, or news personalities of interest to successful, well-informed African-Americans. Department pieces, 650 to 700 words, on a number of subjects. Pays 50¢ a word, on publication. Query.

FIRST THINGS—156 Fifth Ave., #400, New York, NY 10010-7002. James Nuechterlein, Ed. Published 10 times a year. Essays and general social commentary, 1,500 words or 4,000 to 6,000 words, for academics, clergy, and general educated readership, on the role of religion in public life. Also, poetry, 4 to 40 lines. Pays $300 to $800, on publication.

FOREIGN SERVICE JOURNAL—2101 E St. N.W., Washington, DC 20037. Articles of interest to the Foreign Service and the US diplomatic community. Pays to 35¢ a word, on publication. Query. E-mail: journal@afsa.org

THE FREEMAN—Foundation for Economic Education, 30 S. Broadway, Irvington-on-Hudson, NY 10533. Sheldon Richman, Ed.; Beth Hoffman, Man. Ed. Articles, to 3,500 words, on economic, political, and moral implications of private property, voluntary exchange, and individual choice. Pays 10¢ a word, on publication.

IN THESE TIMES—2040 N. Milwaukee Ave., Chicago, IL 60647. Joel Bleifuss, Ed. Biweekly. Articles, 1,500 to 2,500 words, on politics, the environment, labor, women's issues, etc. "A magazine with a progressive political perspective. Please read before querying us." Payment varies, on publication. Query.

INQUIRER MAGAZINE—*Philadelphia Inquirer*, P.O. Box 8263, 400 N. Broad St., Philadelphia, PA 19101. Ms. Avery Rome, Ed. Local-interest features, 500 to 7,000 words. Profiles of national figures in politics, entertainment, etc. Pays varying rates, on publication. Query.

IRISH AMERICA—432 Park Ave. S., Suite 1503, New York, NY 10016.

Patricia Harty, Ed. Articles, 1,500 to 2,000 words, of interest to Irish-American audience; preferred topics include history, sports, the arts, and politics. Pays 10¢ a word, after publication. Query.

MIDSTREAM— 633 Third Ave., 21st Fl., New York, NY 10017. Joel Carmichael, Ed. Articles of international and Jewish/Zionist concern. Pays 5¢ a word, after publication. Allow 3 months for response.

MOMENT MAGAZINE— 4710 41st St. N.W., Washington, DC 20016. Hershel Shanks, Ed. Sophisticated articles, 2,500 to 5,000 words, on Jewish culture, politics, religion, and personalities. Columns, to 1,500 words, with uncommon perspectives on contemporary issues, humor, strong anecdotes. Book reviews, 400 words. Pays $40 to $600.

MOTHER JONES— 731 Market St., Suite 600, San Francisco, CA 94103. Roger Cohn, Ed. Investigative articles and political essays. Pays $1,000 to $3,000 for feature articles, after acceptance. Query with clips and SASE.

THE NATION— 33 Irving Place, 8th fl., New York, NY 10003. Katrina vanden Heuvel, Ed. Articles, 1,500 to 2,500 words, on politics and culture from a liberal/left perspective. Editorials, 750 to 1,000 words. Pays $75 per published page, to $300, on publication. Query.

THE NEW YORK TIMES MAGAZINE— 229 W. 43rd St., New York, NY 10036. Attn: Articles Ed. Timely articles, approximately 4,000 words, on news items, trends, culture, etc. Pays $1,000 for short pieces, from $2,500 for major articles, on acceptance. Query with clips.

THE NEW YORKER— 20 W. 43rd St., New York, NY 10036. Attn: Ed., "Comment." Political/social essays, 1,000 words. Pays on acceptance. Query.

ON THE ISSUES—Merle Hoffman Enterprises, Inc., 97-77 Queens Blvd., Suite 1120, Forest Hills, NY 11374-3317. Jan Goodwin, Ed. "The Progressive Woman's Quarterly." Articles, up to 2,000 words, on political or social issues. Movie, music, and book reviews, 500 to 750 words. Query. Payment varies, on publication.

POLICY REVIEW— 214 Massachusetts Ave. N.E., Washington, DC 20002. Attn: Articles Ed. Bimonthly. Essays and articles of general intellectual interest, 800 to 5,000 words, on politics, social criticism, and public policy. "We are the flagship journal of The Heritage Foundation, a conservative public policy research institute. We use articles that highlight private sector and local government alternatives to welfare state politics." Pays about $500, on publication.

THE PROGRESSIVE— 409 E. Main St., Madison, WI 53703. Matthew Rothschild, Ed. Articles, 500 to 4,000 words, on political and social problems. Pays $100 to $500, on publication.

PUBLIC CITIZEN MAGAZINE— 1600 20th St. N.W., Washington, DC 20009. Bob Mentzinger, Ed. Investigative reports and articles of timely political interest, for members of Public Citizen: consumer rights, health and safety, environmental protection, safe energy, tax reform, international trade, and government and corporate accountability. Photos, illustrations. Honorarium.

SATURDAY NIGHT— 184 Front St. E., Suite 400, Toronto, Ont., Canada M5A 4N3. Paul Tough, Ed. Canada's oldest magazine of politics, social issues, culture, and business. Features, 1,000 to 5,000 words, and columns, 800 to

3,000 words; fiction, to 3,000 words. Must have Canadian tie-in. Payment varies, on acceptance.

TIKKUN— 26 Fell St., San Francisco, CA 94102. Michael Lerner, Ed. "A Bimonthly Jewish Critique of Politics, Culture & Society." Articles and fiction, 2,400 to 3,000 words. Poetry. "Read a copy to get a sense of what we publish. We are always interested in work pertaining to contemporary culture." Pays in copies. E-mail: magazine@tikkun.org.

VFW MAGAZINE— 406 W. 34th St., Kansas City, MO 64111. Richard K. Kolb, Ed. Articles, 1,000 words, related to current foreign policy and defense, American armed forces abroad, and international events affecting U.S. national security. Also, up-to-date articles on veteran concerns and issues affecting veterans. Pays to $500, on acceptance. Query. Guidelines.

REGIONAL AND CITY PUBLICATIONS

ADIRONDACK LIFE— P.O. Box 410, Jay, NY 12941. Elizabeth Folwell, Ed. Features, to 5,000 words, on outdoor and environmental activities and issues, arts, wilderness, wildlife, profiles, history, and fiction; focus is entirely on the Adirondack Park region of New York State. Pays to 25¢ a word, 30 days after acceptance. Query.

ALABAMA HERITAGE— The Univ. of Alabama, Box 870342, Tuscaloosa, AL 35487-0342. Suzanne Wolfe, Ed. Quarterly. Articles, to 5,000 words, on local, state, and regional history: art, literature, language, archaeology, music, religion, architecture, and natural history. Query, mentioning availability of photos and illustrations. Pays an honorarium, on publication, plus 10 copies. Guidelines.

ALASKA— 4220 B St., Suite 210, Anchorage, AK 99503. Bruce Woods, Ed. Articles, 1,500 words, on life in Alaska. Pays varying rates, on publication. Guidelines.

ALBERTA SWEETGRASS— Aboriginal Multi-Media Society of Alberta, 15001 112th Ave., Edmonton, Alberta, Canada T5M 2V6. Tabloid. Articles, 100 to 1,000 words (most often 500 to 800 words; briefs, 100 to 150 words): features, profiles, and community-based articles all with an Alberta angle.

APPRISE— See *Central PA.*

ARIZONA HIGHWAYS— 2039 W. Lewis Ave., Phoenix, AZ 85009. Robert J. Early, Ed. Third-person experience articles, 1,200 to 1,800 words, on travel in Arizona; pieces on adventure, humor, lifestyles, nostalgia, history, archaeology, nature, etc. Departments also using personal experience pieces include "Mileposts," "Focus on Nature," "Along the Way," "Back Road Adventures," "Hiking," "Great Weekends," and "Arizona Humor." Pays 35¢ to 55¢ a word, on acceptance. Query required. Guidelines.

ASPEN MAGAZINE— P.O. Box G-3, Aspen, CO 81612-7452. Ms. Jamie Miller, Man. Ed. Bimonthly. Articles, 500 to 1,000 words, of interest to readers in Aspen, Colorado. Payment varies, on publication. Query.

ATLANTA HOMES AND LIFESTYLES— 1100 Johnson Ferry Rd., #595, Atlanta, GA 30342-1746. Attn: Eds. Articles with a local angle. Department pieces for "Around Atlanta," "Design Takes," "Great Escapes," and "Quick Fix." Pays $50 to $300 for departments; $300 to $400 for features, on acceptance.

ATLANTA MAGAZINE— 1360 Peachtree St. N.E., Atlanta, GA 30309-3214. Lee Walburn, Ed. Articles from 2,000 to 5,000 words, and fillers from 100 to 200 words. Departments include "On My Mind" and "Night Out." Payment is negotiable and made on acceptance. Query for guidelines.

BACK HOME IN KENTUCKY—P.O. Box 681629, Franklin, TN 37068-1629. Nanci P. Gregg, Man. Ed. Articles on Kentucky history, travel, craftsmen and artisans, Kentucky cooks, and "colorful" characters; limited personal nostalgia specifically related to Kentucky. Pays $25 to $100 for articles with B&W or color photos. Queries preferred.

BALTIMORE MAGAZINE— 1000 Lancaster St., Suite 400, Baltimore, MD 21202. Margaret Guroff, Man. Ed. Articles, 500 to 3,000 words, on people, places, and things in the Baltimore metropolitan area. Consumer advice, investigative pieces, profiles, humor, and personal experience pieces. Payment varies, on publication. Query required.

BIG APPLE PARENT—(formerly *The Big Apple Parents' Paper*) 9 E. 38th St., New York, NY 10016. Helen Rosengren Freedman, Man. Ed. Articles, 500 to 750 words, for New York City parents. Pays $35 to $50, on publication. Buys first New York City rights.

BIG SKY JOURNAL—P.O. Box 1069, Bozeman, MT 59771. Michelle A. Orton, Man. Ed. Published 5 times a year. Articles, to 2,500 words, and fiction to 4,000 words, on Montana art and architecture, hunting and fishing, ranching and recreation. Payment varies, on publication. Query.

BLUE RIDGE COUNTRY—P.O. Box 21535, Roanoke, VA 24018. Kurt Rheinheimer, Ed. Bimonthly. Regional articles, 1,200 to 2,000 words, that "explore and extol the beauty, history, and travel opportunities in the mountain regions of VA, NC, WV, TN, KY, MD, SC, and GA." Color slides or B&W prints considered. Pays $200 for photo-features, on publication. Queries preferred.

THE BOSTON GLOBE MAGAZINE—*The Boston Globe,* P.O. Box 2378, Boston, MA 02107-2378. Nick King, Ed. General-interest articles on regional topics and profiles, 2,500 to 5,000 words. Query and SASE required.

BOSTON MAGAZINE— 300 Massachusetts Ave., Boston, MA 02115. Lisa Gerson, Ed. Asst. Informative, entertaining features, 1,000 to 3,000 words, on Boston-area personalities, institutions, and phenomena. Query. Pays to $2,000, on publication.

BUFFALO SPREE MAGAZINE— 5678 Main St., Williamsville, NY 14221. Larry Levite and David McDuff, Pubs. Articles of local interest, to 1,800 words, for readers in the western New York region. Fiction, to 2,000 words; poetry. Pays $125 to $200, $25 for poetry, on publication.

BUSINESS IN BROWARD—P.O. Box 460669, Ft. Lauderdale, FL 33346-0669. Sherry Friedlander, Ed. Published 8 times a year. Articles, 1,000 words, on small business in eastern Florida county. Pay varies, on acceptance.

CANADIAN GEOGRAPHIC— 39 McArthur Ave., Vanier, Ont., Canada K1L 8L7. Rick Boychuk, Ed. "Making Canada Better Known to Canadians and to the World." Articles on interesting places, nature and wildlife in Canada. Payment varies, on acceptance. Query.

CAPE COD LIFE—P.O. Box 1385, Pocasset, MA 02559-1385. Nancy E. Berry, Man. Ed. Articles, to 2,000 words, on current events, business, art, history, gardening, and nautical lifestyle on Cape Cod, Martha's Vineyard, and Nantucket. Pays 15¢ a word, 30 days after publication. Query.

CARIBBEAN TRAVEL AND LIFE— 330 W. Canton Ave., Winter Park, FL 32789. Steve Blount, Ed. Articles, 500 to 3,000 words, on all aspects of travel, recreation, leisure, and culture in the Caribbean, the Bahamas, and Bermuda. Pays $75 to $750, on publication. Query with published clips.

CAROLOGUE—South Carolina Historical Society, 100 Meeting St., Charleston, SC 29401-2299. Peter A. Rerig, Ed. General-interest articles, to 10 pages, on South Carolina history. Queries preferred. Pays in copies.

CENTRAL PA—(formerly *Apprise*) P.O. Box 2954, 1982 Locust Ln., Harrisburg, PA 17105. Steve Kennedy, Exec. Ed. Articles, 1,500 to 3,500 words, of regional (central Pennsylvania) interest, including profiles of notable central Pennsylvanians, and broadly based articles of social interest that "enlighten and inform." Pays 10¢ a word, on publication.

CHARLESTON MAGAZINE—P.O. Box 1794, Mt. Pleasant, SC 29465. Louise Chase Dettman, Ed. Quarterly. Seeks nonfiction pertaining to Charleston, South Carolina. Past features have discussed topics such as secret winter getaways, holiday gift ideas, and local homeless shelters. Departments include "In Good Taste," "Top of the Shelf," "Midday Recipes," and "Cityscape." Payment varies, on publication. Query for guidelines.

CHICAGO— 500 N. Dearborn, Suite 1200, Chicago, IL 60610. Shane Tritsch, Man. Ed. Articles, 1,000 to 5,000 words, related to Chicago. Pays varying rates, on acceptance. Query.

CHICAGO HISTORY—Clark St. at North Ave., Chicago, IL 60614. Rosemary Adams, Ed. Articles, to 4,500 words, on Chicago's urban, political, social, and cultural history. Pays to $250, on publication. Query.

CINCINNATI MAGAZINE—One Centennial Plaza, 705 Central Ave., Suite 370, Cincinnati, OH 45202. Kitty Morgan, Ed. Articles, 500 to 3,500 words, on Cincinnati people and issues. Pays $50 to $500. Query with writing sample.

COLORADO BUSINESS—7009 S. Potomac, Englewood, CO 80112. David Lewis, Ed. Articles, varying lengths, on business, business personalities, and economic trends in Colorado. Preference given to Colorado residents. Pays on acceptance. Query.

COLORADO HOMES AND LIFESTYLES—7009 S. Potomac St., Englewood, CO 80112. Evalyn K. McGraw, Ed. Bimonthly. Articles, 1,300 to 1,500 words, with a focus on Colorado homes and interiors. Features cover upscale homes and unusual lifestyles. Department pieces, 1,100 to 1,300 words, cover architecture, artists, food and wine, design trends, profiles, gardening, and travel. Pays $150 to $300, on acceptance. Guidelines. Query.

COMMON GROUND MAGAZINE—P.O. Box 99, McVeytown, PA 17051-0099. Ruth Dunmire, Pam Brumbaugh, Eds. Quarterly. General-interest articles, 500 to 5,000 words, related to central Pennsylvania's Juniata River Valley and its rural lifestyle. Related fiction, 1,000 to 2,000 words. Poetry, to 12 lines. Fillers, photos, and cartoons. Pays $25 to $200 for articles, $5 to $15 for fillers, and $5 to $25 for photos, on publication. Guidelines.

COMMONWEALTH—177 Tremont St., 5th Fl., Boston, MA 02111. Dave Denison, Ed. Articles, 2,000 to 4,500 words, on politics, government, and public policy issues affecting Massachusetts citizens. Payment varies, on acceptance. Query.

CONNECTICUT — 35 Nutmeg Dr., Trumbull, CT 06611. Charles Monagan, Ed. Articles, 1,500 to 3,500 words, on Connecticut topics, issues, people, and lifestyles. Pays $500 to $1,200, within 30 days of acceptance.

CONNECTICUT FAMILY — See *New York Family.*

CRAIN'S DETROIT BUSINESS — 1400 Woodbridge, Detroit, MI 48207. Cindy Goodaker, Exec. Ed. Business articles, 500 to 1,000 words, about Detroit, for Detroit business readers. Pays $10 per inch, on publication. Query required.

DELAWARE TODAY — P.O. Box 2800, Wilmington, DE 19805. Ted Spiker, Ed. Service articles, profiles, news, etc., on topics of local interest. Pays $150 for department pieces, $200 to $500 for features, on publication. Queries with clips required.

DOSSIER — 277 B E. Paces Ferry Rd., Atlanta, GA 30305. Ed. Published 8 times per year. Fiction, nonfiction, poetry, and fillers, all varying lengths, on business, home, health, fitness, and travel; all geared toward people living in or around Atlanta. Payment varies, and is made on publication. Query or send complete manuscript.

DOWN EAST — Camden, ME 04843. Attn: Manuscript Ed. Articles, 1,500 to 2,500 words, on all aspects of life in Maine. Photos. Pays on acceptance. Query.

EASTSIDE PARENT — Northwest Parent Publishing, 1530 Westlake Ave. N., Suite 600, Seattle, WA 98109. Virginia Smyth, Ed. Articles, 300 to 2,500 words, for parents of children ages 14 and under. Pays $50 to $500, on publication. Queries preferred. Also publishes *Pierce County Parent, Portland Parent, Puget Sound Parent* and *Snohomish County Parent.*

ERIE & CHAUTAUQUA MAGAZINE — 317 W. Sixth St., Erie, PA 16507. K. L. Kalvelage, Ed./Pub. Margaret Fisher Cutler, Assoc. Ed. Feature articles, to 2,500 words, on issues of interest to upscale readers in the Erie, Warren, and Crawford counties (PA), and Chautauqua (NY) county. Pieces with regional relevance. Pays after publication. Query preferred, with writing samples. Guidelines.

FAMILY TIMES — P.O. Box 932, Eau Claire, WI 54702. Nancy Walter, Ed. Articles, from 800 words, for parents in the Chippewa Valley, WI. Pays $35 to $50, on publication. Queries preferred. Guidelines.

FLORIDA WILDLIFE — 620 S. Meridian St., Tallahassee, FL 32399-1600. Attn: Ed. Bimonthly of the Florida Game and Fresh Water Fish Commission. Articles, 800 to 1,500 words, that promote native flora and fauna, hunting, fishing in Florida's fresh waters, outdoor ethics, and conservation of Florida's natural resources. Pays $50 per published page. SASE for guidelines and how-to-submit memo.

GARDEN SHOWCASE — P.O. Box 23669, Portland, OR 97281-3669. Lynn Lustberg, Ed. Montly. Articles, to 1,000 words, on gardening. Features cover a wide range of gardening ideas, but all must have a connection to the Willamette Valley. Also accepts slides or transparencies of trees, shrubs, perennials, and gardens in that area. Payment is $125, on publication. Query.

GET UP & GO! — (formerly *Northwest Prime Time Journal*) 10827 NE

68th St., Kirkland, WA 98033. Neil Strother, Pub./Ed. News and features on the Northwest for readers 50 and older. Pays whatever the market can bear, on publication. Limited market.

GO MAGAZINE—6600 Executive Circle Dr., Charlotte, NC 28212-8250. Tom Crosby, Ed. Focuses on travel and auto safety in North and South Carolina, as well as their neighboring states. Pays 15¢ a word, on publication.

GOLDENSEAL—The Cultural Ctr., 1900 Kanawha Blvd. E., Charleston, WV 25305-0300. John Lilly, Ed. Quarterly. Articles, 1,000 and 3,000 words, on West Virginia history, folklife, folk art and crafts, and music of a traditional nature. Pays 10¢ a word, on publication. Guidelines.

GRAND RAPIDS—549 Ottawa N.W., Grand Rapids, MI 49503. Carole R. Valade, Ed. Service articles (dining guide, travel, personal finance, humor) and issue-oriented pieces related to Grand Rapids, Michigan. Pays $35 to $200, on publication. Query.

GULF COAST GOLFER—See *North Texas Golfer.*

HAWAII—1210 Auahi St., Suite 231, Honolulu, HI 96814. John Hollon, Ed. Bimonthly. Articles, 1,000 to 2,500 words, related to Hawaii. Pays 10¢ and up a word, on publication. Query.

HIGH COUNTRY NEWS—Box 1090, Paonia, CO 81428. Betsy Marston, Ed. Biweekly. Articles, 2,000 words, and roundups, 750 words, on western environmental issues, public lands management, rural community, and natural resource issues; profiles of western innovators; pieces on western politics. "Writers must take regional approach." B&W photos. Pays 20¢ a word, on publication. Query with clips.

ILLINOIS ENTERTAINER—124 W. Polk, Suite 103, Chicago, IL 60605. Michael C. Harris, Ed. Articles, 500 to 1,500 words, on local and national entertainment (emphasis on alternative music) in the greater Chicago area. Personality profiles; interviews; reviews. Photos. Pays varying rates, on publication. Query preferred.

INDIANAPOLIS MONTHLY—40 Monument Circle, Suite 100, Indianapolis, IN 46204. Sam Stall, Ed. Articles: IndyScene (trendy "quick hits"), to 200 words, $50; departments, 1,500 to 2,500 words, $250 to $350; features, 2,500 to 4,000 words, $400 to $500. Topics: profiles, sports, business, travel, crime, controversy, service, first-person essays, book excerpts, etc. All material must have an Indianapolis/Indiana focus. Pays on publication.

INQUIRER MAGAZINE—*Philadelphia Inquirer,* P.O. Box 8263, 400 N. Broad St., Philadelphia, PA 19101. Ms. Avery Rome, Ed. Articles, 1,500 to 2,000 words, and 3,000 to 4,500 words, on politics, science, arts and culture, business, lifestyles and entertainment, sports, health, psychology, education, religion, and humor. Pays varying rates. Query.

THE IOWAN MAGAZINE—504 E. Locust, Des Moines, IA 50309. Jay P. Wagner, Ed. Articles, 1,000 to 3,000 words, on business, arts, people, and history of Iowa. Essays and poetry on life in Iowa. Photos a plus. Payment varies, on acceptance. Query required.

ISLAND LIFE—P.O. Box 929, Sanibel Island, FL 33957. Joan Hooper, Ed. Articles, 500 to 1,200 words, with photos, on wildlife, flora and fauna, design and decor, the arts, shelling, local sports, historical sites, etc., directly related to the islands of Sanibel, Captiva, Marco, Estero, or Gasparilla. No first-person articles. Pays on publication.

JACKSONVILLE—White Publishing Co., 1032 Hendricks Ave., Jacksonville, FL 32207. Joseph White, Ed. Service pieces and articles, 1,500 to 2,500 words, on issues and personalities of interest to readers in the greater Jacksonville area. Department pieces, 1,200 to 1,500 words, on business, health, travel, personal finance, real estate, arts and entertainment, sports, dining out, food. Home and garden articles on local homeowners, interior designers, remodelers, gardeners, craftsmen, etc., 1,000 to 2,000 words. Pays $200 to $500, on publication. Query required. Guidelines.

JOURNAL OF THE WEST—1531 Yuma, Box 1009, Manhattan, KS 66505-1009. Robin Higham, Ed. Articles, to 20 pages, on the history and culture of the West, then and now. Pays in copies.

KANSAS!—Kansas Dept. of Commerce, 700 S.W. Harrison, Suite 1300, Topeka, KS 66603-3957. Andrea Glenn, Ed. Quarterly. Articles, 1,000 to 1,250 words, on attractions and events of Kansas. Color slides. Pays to $300, on acceptance. Query.

KANSAS CITY MAGAZINE—118 Southwest Blvd., Kansas City, MO 64108. Zim Loy, Ed. Articles, 250 to 3,500 words, of interest to readers in Kansas City. Pays to 30¢ a word, on acceptance. Query.

LAKE SUPERIOR MAGAZINE—P.O. Box 16417, Duluth, MN 55816-0417. Paul Hayden, Ed. Articles with emphasis on Lake Superior regional subjects: historical and topical pieces that highlight the people, places, and events that affect the Lake Superior region. Pictorial essays; humor and occasional fiction. Quality photos enhance submissions. "Writers must have a thorough knowledge of the subject and how it relates to our region." Pays to $600, extra for photos, on publication. Query.

THE LOOK—P.O. Box 272, Cranford, NJ 07016-0272. John R. Hawks, Pub. Articles, 1,500 to 3,000 words, on fashion, student life, employment, relationships, and profiles of interest to local (NJ) readers ages 16 to 26. Also, beach stories and articles about the New Jersey shore. Pays $30 to $200, on publication.

LOS ANGELES MAGAZINE—11100 Santa Monica Blvd., 7th Fl., Los Angeles, CA 90025. Spencer Beck, Ed. Articles, to 3,000 words, of interest to sophisticated, affluent southern Californians, preferably with local focus on a lifestyle topic. Payment varies. Query.

LOUISVILLE—137 W. Muhammad Ali Blvd., Suite 101, Louisville, KY 40202. Dan Crutcher, Ed. Articles, 1,000 to 2,000 words, on community issues, personalities, and entertainment in the Louisville area. Photos. Pays from $50, on acceptance. Query; articles on assignment only. Limited market.

MEMPHIS—Contemporary Media, Box 256, Memphis, TN 38101. Richard Banks, Ed. Articles, 1,500 to 4,000 words, on a wide variety of topics related to Memphis and the Mid-South region: politics, education, sports, business, history, etc. Profiles; investigative pieces. Pays $50 to $500, on publication. Query. SASE for guidelines.

METROKIDS—1080 N. Delaware Ave., Suite 702, Philadelphia, PA 19125. Nancy Lisagor, Ed. Tabloid. Features and department pieces, 500 to 1,000 words, on regional family entertainment and children's issues in the Philadelphia metropolitan region. Pays $25 to $75, on publication.

MIAMI METRO MAGAZINE—(formerly *South Florida Magazine*) 800 Douglas Rd., Suite 500, Coral Gables, FL 33134. Nancy Moore, Ed. Features, 1,100 to 2,000 words, and department pieces, 200 to 1,300 words, on news, profiles, and hot topics related to south Florida. Short, bright items, 200 to 400 words. Pays $75 to $700, within 30 days of acceptance. Query.

MICHIGAN LIVING—Auto Club of Michigan, 1 Auto Club Dr., Dearborn, MI 48126-9982. Ron Garbinski, Ed. Informative travel articles, 300 to 1,500 words, on U.S. and Canadian tourist attractions and recreational opportunities; special interest in Michigan. Pays $55 to $500 (rates vary for photos), on publication. Send queries only.

MID-WEST OUTDOORS—111 Shore Dr., Hinsdale, IL 60521-5885. Gene Laulunen, Ed. Articles, to 1,500 words, with photos, on where, when, and how to fish and hunt, within 600 miles of Chicago. Pays $25, on publication.

MILWAUKEE MAGAZINE—312 E. Buffalo, Milwaukee, WI 53202. John Fennell, Ed. Profiles, investigative articles, and service pieces, 2,000 to 4,000 words; local tie-in a must. No fiction. Pays $400 to $1,000, on publication. Query preferred.

MINNESOTA MONTHLY—Lumber Exchange Bldg., 10 S. Fifth St., Suite 1000, Minneapolis, MN 55402. David Mahoney, Ed. Articles, to 4,000 words, on people, places, events, and issues in Minnesota. Pays $50 to $1,000, on acceptance. Query.

MONTANA MAGAZINE—P.O. Box 5630, Helena, MT 59604. Beverly R. Magley, Ed. Recreation, travel, general interest, regional profiles, photoessays. Montana-oriented only. B&W prints, color slides. Pays 15¢ a word, on publication.

MPLS. ST. PAUL—220 S. 6th St., Suite 500, Minneapolis, MN 55402-4507. Brian E. Anderson, Ed. In-depth articles, features, profiles, and service pieces about the Minneapolis-St. Paul area, 300 to 4,000 words. Pays to $2,500.

NEBRASKA HISTORY—P.O. Box 82554, Lincoln, NE 68501. James E. Potter, Ed. Articles, 3,000 to 7,000 words, on the history of Nebraska and the Great Plains. B&W line drawings. Pays in copies. Cash prize awarded to one article each year.

NEVADA MAGAZINE—401 N. Carson St., Carson City, NV 89701. David Moore, Ed. Carolyn Graham, Assoc. Ed. Articles, 500 to 700 or 1,500 to 1,800 words, on topics related to Nevada: travel, history, recreation, profiles, humor, and attractions. Special section on Nevada events and shows. Photos. Pay varies, on publication.

NEW FRONTIERS OF NEW MEXICO—P.O. Box 1299, Tijeras, NM 87059. Wally Gordon, Ed./Pub. Fiction and in-depth nonfiction, to 3,000 words, related to New Mexico and the Southwest. Humor, to 1,000 words. Poetry, to 100 lines. Pays $25 to $200, on publication.

NEW JERSEY REPORTER—The Ctr. for Analysis of Public Issues, 164 Nassau St., Princeton, NJ 08542. Mark Magyar, Ed. In-depth articles, 1,000 to 4,000 words, on New Jersey politics and public affairs. Pays $175 to $800, on publication. Query required.

NEW MEXICO JOURNEY—10501 Montgomery Blvd. N.E., Albuquerque, NM 87111-3848. Bimonthly. Travel magazine for AAA New Mexico members. Departments include: "Inside Story," "Journey Through New Mexico," "The Way I See It," and "Recalls." Send for guidelines.

NEW MEXICO MAGAZINE—Lew Wallace Bldg., 495 Old Santa Fe Trail, Santa Fe, NM 87501. Attn: Ed. Articles, 250 to 2,000 words, on New Mexico subjects. No poetry or fiction. Pays about 30¢ a word, on acceptance. Query.

NEW YORK FAMILY—141 Halstead Ave., Suite 3D, Mamaroneck, NY 10543. David Parker, Publishing Dir. Betsy F. Woolf, Ed. Articles related to family life in New York City. Pays $50 to $200, on publication. Same requirements for *Westchester Family* and *Connecticut Family.*

NEWPORT LIFE—55 Memorial Blvd., Newport, RI 02840. Lynne Tungett, Publisher. John Pantalone, Ed. Quarterly. Annual City Guide. Articles, 500 to 2,500 words, on people, places, attractions of Newport County: general-interest, historical, profiles, international celebrities, and social and political issues. Departments, 200 to 750 words: sailing, dining, food & wind, home & garden, and the arts in Newport County. Photos must be available for all articles. Query. SASE.

NORTH DAKOTA HORIZONS—P.O. Box 2639, Bismarck, ND 58502. Lyle Halvorson, Ed. Quarterly. Articles, about 2,500 words, on people, places, and events in North Dakota. Photos. Pays $75 to $300, on publication.

NORTH GEORGIA JOURNAL—P.O. Box 127, Roswell, GA 30077. Olin Jackson, Pub./Ed. History, travel, and lifestyle features, 2,000 to 3,000 words, on north Georgia; need human-interest approach and must be written in first person. Include interviews. Photos a plus. Pays $75 to $300, on acceptance. Query.

NORTH TEXAS GOLFER—9182 Old Katy Rd., Suite 212, Houston, TX 77055. David Widener, Man. Ed. Articles, 800 to 1,500 words, involving local golfers or related directly to north Texas. Pays from $50 to $350, on publication. Query. Same requirements for *Gulf Coast Golfer* (related to south Texas).

NORTHEAST MAGAZINE—*The Hartford Courant,* 285 Broad St., Hartford, CT 06115. Jane Bronfman, Ed. Asst. Articles spun off the news and compelling personal stories, 750 to 3,000 words, that reflect the concerns of Connecticut residents. Pays $250 to $1,000, on acceptance. Send appropriate SASE. Responds in 2 to 3 months.

NORTHERN LIGHTS—Box 8084, Missoula, MT 59807-8084. Attn: Deborah Clow. Articles, 500 to 3,000 words, about the contemporary West. "We look for finely crafted personal essays that illuminate what it means to live in the contemporary West. We're looking to bust the New York and Hollywood stereotypes." Pays 10¢ a word, on publication.

NORTHWEST PRIME TIME JOURNAL—See *Get Up & Go!*

NORTHWEST REGIONAL MAGAZINES—P.O. Box 18000, Florence, OR 97439-0130. Attn: Jim Forst or Judy Fleagle. All submissions considered for use in *Oregon Coast, Oregon Outside* and *Northwest Travel.* Articles, 800 to 2,000 words, pertaining to travel, history, town/city profiles, events, outside activities, and nature. News releases, 200 to 500 words. Articles with photos (slides) preferred. Pays $50 to $300, after publication. Guidelines with SASE.

NORTHWEST TRAVEL—See *Northwest Regional Magazines.*

NOW & THEN—CASS/ETSU, P.O. Box 70556, Johnson City, TN 37614-0556. Jane Harris Woodside, Ed. Fiction and nonfiction, 1,500 to 3,000 words: short stories, articles, interviews, essays, memoirs, book reviews. Pieces must be related to theme of issue and have some connection to the Appalachian region. Also photos and drawings. SASE for guidelines and current themes. Pays $15 to $75, on publication.

OHIO MAGAZINE—62 E. Broad St., Columbus, OH 43215. Shannon Jackson, Ed. Focuses on travel around the state, with profiles of people, cities, and towns of Ohio; pieces on historic sites, tourist attractions, little-known spots. Lengths and payment vary. Query with clips.

OKLAHOMA TODAY—15 N. Robinson, Suite 100, Oklahoma City, OK 73102. Louisa McCune, Ed. Articles, 250 to 4,000 words: travel; profiles; history; nature and outdoor recreation; and arts. All material must have regional tie-in. Pays $25 to $750, on publication. Queries preferred. Guidelines available with SASE. Website: www.oklahomatoday.com

ORANGE COAST—3701 Birch St., Suite 100, Newport Beach, CA 92660. Patrick Mott, Ed. Articles, 2,000 to 3,000 words, of interest to educated Orange County residents. "Escape" (weekend travel) and "Close-Up" (personality profile), approx. 650 words, and 200-word pieces for "Short Cuts" (local phenomena). Query with clips. Pays $400 to $800 for features; $100 to $200 for departments; $50 for "Short Cuts," after acceptance. Guidelines.

ORANGE COUNTY WOMAN—3701 Birch St., #100, Newport Beach, CA 92660-2618. Janine Robinson, Ed. Articles, 500 to 1,500 words, for and about women living in Orange County, CA. "Our readers are highly educated, upscale women who are looking for information that will make their busy lives more efficient and gratifying. We cover everything from family issues to health and beauty." Must have strong local angle. SASE for guidelines. Payment is $50 to $3000, on acceptance.

OREGON COAST—See *Northwest Regional Magazines.*

OREGON OUTSIDE—Northwest Regional Magazines, Box 18000, Florence, OR 97439-0130. Judy Fleagle, Co-Ed. Quarterly. Articles, 1,000 to 1,500 words, on Oregon and the outdoors, "all kinds of adventure, from walks for families to extreme skiing." Prefers to receive manuscript/photo packages. Pays $100 to $350, on publication. Query.

ORLANDO MAGAZINE—260 Maitland Ave., Suite 2000, Altamonte Springs, FL 32701. Brooke Lange, Ed. Locally based articles and department pieces, lengths vary, for residents of Central Florida. Query with clips.

OUR STATE: DOWN HOME IN NORTH CAROLINA—P.O. Box 4552, Greensboro, NC 27404. Mary Ellis, Ed. Articles, 1,200 to 1,500 words, on people, history, and travel in North Carolina. Photos. Pays on publication.

PALM SPRINGS LIFE—Desert Publications, 303 N. Indian Canyon Dr., P.O. Box 2724, Palm Springs, CA 92263. Stewart Weiner, Ed. Articles, 1,000 to 3,000 words, of interest to "wealthy, upscale people who live and/or play in the desert." Pays $150 to $500 for features, $25 to $75 for short profiles, on publication. Query required.

PENNSYLVANIA MAGAZINE—Box 576, Camp Hill, PA 17001-0576. Matthew K. Holliday, Ed. General-interest features with a Pennsylvania focus.

All articles must be accompanied by photocopies of possible illustrations. Query. Guidelines.

PERSIMMON HILL—1700 N.E. 63rd St., Oklahoma City, OK 73111. M.J. Van Deventer, Ed. Published by the National Cowboy Hall of Fame. Articles, 1,500 to 2,000 words, on Western history and art, cowboys, ranching, and nature. Top-quality illustrations a must. Pays from $100 to $250, on publication. Query.

PHOENIX MAGAZINE—5555 N. 7th Ave., Suite B200, Phoenix, AZ 85013. Beth Deveny, Ed. Articles, 1,000 to 3,000 words, on topics of interest to Phoenix-area residents. Pays $300 to $1,500, on publication. Query.

PIERCE COUNTY PARENT—See *Eastside Parent.*

PITTSBURGH—4802 Fifth Ave., Pittsburgh, PA 15213. Attn: Man. Ed. Profiles, from 300 to 3,000 words, feature stories and service pieces, from 1,200 to 3,000 words, and in-depth news features, to 5,000 words, geared to western Pennsylvania, eastern Ohio, northern West Virginia, and western Maryland readers. Pays from $300, on publication. Query with outline. Local travel stories, to 300 words, pay $150. Must query first.

PITTSBURGH POST GAZETTE—34 Blvd. of the Allies, Pittsburgh, PA 15230. Sharon Eberson, Ed. Sunday magazine. Well-written, well-organized, in-depth articles of regional interest, 1,000 to 3,500 words, on issues, personalities, human interest, historical moments. No fiction, hobbies, how-tos or "timely events" pieces. Pays from $350, on publication. Query.

PORTLAND MAGAZINE—578 Congress St., Portland, ME 04101. Colin Sargent, Ed. "Maine's City Magazine." Articles on local people, legends, culture, and trends. Fiction, to 750 words. Pays on publication. Query preferred.

PORTLAND PARENT—See *Eastside Parent.*

PROVINCETOWN ARTS—650 Commercial St., Provincetown, MA 02657. Christopher Busa, Ed. Annual. Interviews, profiles, essays, 1,500 to 4,000 words. Mainstream fiction and novel excerpts, 500 to 5,000 words. Poems, submit up to 3 at a time. "We have a broad focus on the artists and writers who inhabit or visit Cape Cod." Pays from $125 for articles; $75 to $300 for fiction; $25 to $150 for poems, on publication.

PUGET SOUND PARENT—See *Eastside Parent.*

RANGE MAGAZINE—106 E. Adams, Suite 201, Carson City, NV 89706. C.J. Hadley, Ed. Quarterly. "The Cowboy Spirit on America's Outback." Articles, 500 to 2,000 words, on issues that threaten the West, its people, lifestyles, lands, and wildlife. "Our main purpose is to present public awareness of the positive presence of ranching operations on America's rangelands." Payment varies, on publication. Query preferred.

RECREATION NEWS—P.O. Box 32335, Washington, DC 20007-0635. Henry T. Dunbar, Ed. Articles, 900 to 2,200 words, on recreation and travel around the mid-Atlantic region for government and private sector workers in the Washington, DC area. "Articles should have a conversational tone that's lean and brisk." Pays $50 for reprints, to $300 for cover articles, on publication. Queries preferred. Guidelines.

RHODE ISLAND MONTHLY—280 Kinsley Ave., Providence, RI 02903. Sarah Francis, Man. Ed. Features, 1,000 to 4,000 words, ranging from investigative reporting and in-depth profiles to service pieces and visual stories, on Rhode Island and southeastern Massachusetts. Seasonal material, 1,000 to 2,000 words. Fillers, 150 to 500 words, on Rhode Island places, customs, people, events, products and services, restaurants and food. Pays $250 to $1,000 for features; $25 to $50 for shorts, on publication. Query.

ROCKY MOUNTAIN GARDENER—P.O. Box 18537, Boulder, CO 80308. Susan Martineau, Pub./Ed.-in-Chief. Quarterly. How-to articles, 1,000 to 1,200 words, on regional techniques and varieties; profiles of regional gardeners and gardens, 1,000 to 1,500 words; book reviews and production reviews, 800 to 1,000 words. "Articles must be focused on Rocky Mountain area from New Mexico to Montana. We prefer new, novel, or specific information, not just general gardening topics." Pays 10¢ a word, on publication.

RURAL LIVING—4201 Dominion Blvd., Suite 101, Glen Allen, VA 23060. Richard G. Johnstone, Jr., Ed. Features, 1,000 to 1,500 words, on people, places, historic sites in Virginia and Maryland's Eastern Shore. Queries required. Pays $150 to $200 for articles, on publication.

RURALITE—P.O. Box 558, Forest Grove, OR 97116. Attn: Ed. or Feature Ed. Articles, 800 to 2,000 words, of interest to a primarily rural and small-town audience in OR, WA, ID, WY, NV, northern CA, and AK. "Think pieces" affecting rural/urban interests, regional history and celebrations, self-help, profiles, etc. No fiction or poetry. Pays $30 to $400, on acceptance. Queries required. Guidelines.

SACRAMENTO MAGAZINE—4471 D St., Sacramento, CA 95819. Krista Hendricks Minard, Ed. Features, 2,500 words, on a broad range of topics related to the region. Department pieces, 1,200 to 1,500 words, and short pieces, 400 words, for "City Lights" column. Pays $50 to $300, on publication. Query.

SAN DIEGO MAGAZINE—4206 W. Point Loma Blvd., P.O. Box 85409, San Diego, CA 92138. Tom Blair, Ed. Virginia Butterfield, Exec. Ed. Ron Donoho, Man. Ed. Articles, 1,500 to 3,000 words, on local personalities, politics, lifestyles, business, history, etc., relating to San Diego area. Photos. Pays $250 to $750, on publication. Query with clips.

SAN DIEGO READER—P.O. Box 85803, San Diego, CA 92186. Jim Holman, Ed. Literate articles, 2,500 to 10,000 words, on the San Diego region. Pays $500 to $2,000, on publication.

SAN FRANCISCO—243 Vallejo, San Francisco, CA 94111. Dale Eastman, Ed. Service features, profiles of local newsmakers, and investigative pieces of local issues, 2,500 to 3,000 words. News items, 250 to 800 words, on subjects ranging from business to arts to politics. Payment varies, on acceptance. Query required.

SAN FRANCISCO BUSINESS TIMES—275 Battery St., Suite 940, San Francisco, CA 94111. Steve Symanovich, Ed. Business-oriented articles, about 20 column inches. Limited free-lance market. Pays $250 to $350, on publication. Query.

SAN FRANCISCO EXAMINER MAGAZINE—*San Francisco Examiner*, 110 Fifth St., San Francisco, CA 94103. Attn: Ed. Articles, 1,200 to 3,000 words, on lifestyles, issues, business, history, events, and people in northern California. Query. Pays varying rates.

SAN JOSE—11 W. St. John St., Suite 702, San Jose, CA 95113. Attn: Editor. Monthly magazine for Silicon Valley, featuring departments such as

"The Marriage of Wine and Food" and "Chefs D'oeuvre." Also, events such as the AT&T National Pro-Am Golf Tournament, the San Jose film festival, and stories on the lives of famous persons. Query.

SASKATCHEWAN SAGE—Aboriginal Multi-Media Society of Alberta, 15001 112th Ave., Edmonton, Alberta, Canada T5M 2V6. Debora Lockyer, Man. Ed. Tabloid. Articles, 100 to 1,000 words, most often 500 to 800 words; briefs 100 to 150 words, features, profiles, and community-based articles with a Saskatchewan angle.

SAVANNAH MAGAZINE—P.O. Box 1088, Savannah, GA 31402. Linda Wittish, Ed. Articles, 2,500 to 3,500 words, on people and events in and around Savannah and the region. Historical articles, 1,500 to 2,500 words, of local interest. Reviews, 500 to 750 words, of Savannah-based books and authors. Short pieces, 500 to 750 words, on weekend getaways near Savannah. Pays $75 to $350, after acceptance. Submit complete manuscript. Guidelines.

SEATTLE—701 Dexter Ave. N., Suite 101, Seattle, WA 98109. Giselle Smith, Ed. City, local issues, home, and lifestyle articles, 500 to 2,000 words, relating directly to the greater Seattle area. Personality profiles. Pays $100 to $700, on publication. Guidelines.

SEATTLE WEEKLY—1008 Western, Suite 300, Seattle, WA 98104. Knute Berger, Ed. Articles, 250 to 4,000 words, from a Northwest perspective. Pays $25 to $800, on publication. Query. Guidelines.

SEATTLE'S CHILD—Northwest Parent Publishing, 1530 Westlake Ave. N, Suite 600, Seattle, WA 98109. Ann Bergman, Ed. Articles, 400 to 2,500 words, of interest to parents, educators, and childcare providers of children 14 and under, and investigative reports and consumer tips on issues affecting families in the Puget Sound region. Pays $75 to $500, on publication. Query required.

SENIOR MAGAZINE—3565 S. Higuera St., San Luis Obispo, CA 93401. Attn: Ed. Articles, 600 to 900 words: personality profiles, travel pieces, articles about new things, places, business, sports, movies, television, and health; book reviews (of new or outstanding older books) of interest to seniors. Pays $1.50 per inch; $10 to $25 for B&W photos, on publication.

SILENT SPORTS—717 10th St., P.O. Box 152, Waupaca, WI 54981. Attn: Ed. Articles, 1,000 to 2,000 words, on canoeing, bicycling, cross-country skiing, running, hiking, backpacking, snowshoeing, inline skating, and other "silent" sports, in the upper Midwest region. "Articles must focus on the upper Midwest. No articles about places, people, or events outside the region." Pays $40 to $100 for features; $20 to $50 for fillers, on publication. Query.

SNOHOMISH COUNTY PARENT—See *Eastside Parent.*

SOUTH CAROLINA HISTORICAL MAGAZINE—South Carolina Historical Society, 100 Meeting St., Charleston, SC 29401-2299. W. Eric Emerson, Ed. Scholarly articles, to 25 pages with footnotes, on all areas of South Carolina history. Pays in copies.

SOUTH CAROLINA WILDLIFE—P.O. Box 167, Columbia, SC 29202-0167. Attn: Man. Ed. Articles, 1,000 to 2,000 words, with regional outdoors focus: conservation, natural history and wildlife, recreation. Profiles. Pays from 15¢ a word. Query.

SOUTH FLORIDA MAGAZINE—See *Miami Metro Magazine.*

SOUTHERN CULTURES—Ctr. for the Study of the American South, CB #3355, Manning Hall, UNC-CH, Chapel Hill, NC 27599-3355. Dave Shaw, Man. Ed. Articles, 15 to 25 typed pages, on folk, popular, and high culture of the South. "We're interested in submissions from a wide variety of intellectual traditions that deal with ways of life, thought, belief, and expression in the United States South." Pays in copies.

SOUTHWEST ART—5444 Westheimer, Suite 1440, Houston, TX 77056. Margaret L. Brown, Ed.-in-Chief. Articles, 1,200 to 1,800 words, on the artists, art collectors, museum exhibitions, gallery events and dealers, art history, and art trends west of the Mississippi River. Particularly interested in representational or figurative arts. Pays from $500, on acceptance. Query with at least 20 slides of artwork.

SUNSET MAGAZINE—80 Willow Rd., Menlo Park, CA 94025. Rosalie Muller Wright, Ed. Western regional. Limited free-lance market, but some need for western travel. Query; include clips.

SUNSHINE: THE SUNDAY MAGAZINE OF THE SUN-SENTINAL—*The Sun-Sentinel,* 200 E. Las Olas Blvd., Ft. Lauderdale, FL 33301-2293. Mark Gauert, Ed. Articles, 1,000 to 3,000 words, on topics of interest to south Floridians. Pays $300 to $1,200, on acceptance. Query. Guidelines.

SWEAT—736 E. Loyola Dr., Tempe, AZ 85282. Joan Westlake, Ed. "South West Exercise And Training." Articles, 500 to 1,200 words, on sports, wellness, and fitness with an Arizona angle. "No personal columns or tales. We want journalism. Articles must relate specifically to Arizona or Arizonans." Pays $25 to $60 for articles; $15 to $70 for photos, on publication. Queries required; no unsolicited manuscripts. E-mail preferred: westwoman@aol.com

TALLAHASSEE MAGAZINE—P.O. Box 1837, Tallahassee, FL 32302-1837. Kathy Grobe, Man. Ed. Articles, 800 to 1,500 words, on the life, people, and history of the north Florida-south Georgia area. Pays on acceptance. Query.

TEXAS HIGHWAYS MAGAZINE—P.O. Box 141009, Austin, TX 78714-1009. Jack Lowry, Ed. Texas travel, history, and scenic features, 200 to 1,800 words. Pays about 40¢ to 50¢ a word, $80 to $550 per photo. Query. Guidelines.

TEXAS MONTHLY—P.O. Box 1569, Austin, TX 78767-1569. Gregory Curtis, Ed. Features, 2,500 to 5,000 words, and departments, to 2,500 words, on art, architecture, food, education, business, politics, etc. "We like solidly researched pieces that uncover issues of public concern, reveal offbeat and previously unreported topics, or use a novel approach to familiar topics." Pays varying rates, on acceptance. Queries required.

TEXAS PARKS & WILDLIFE—3000 S. Interstate Hwy. 35, Suite 120, Austin, TX 78704. Articles, 400 to 1,500 words, promoting the conservation and enjoyment of Texas wildlife, parks, waters, and all outdoors. Features on hunting, fishing, birding, camping, and the environment. Photos a plus. Pays 30¢ to 50¢ per word, on acceptance; extra for photos.

TIMELINE—1982 Velma Ave., Columbus, OH 43211-2497. Christopher S. Duckworth, Ed. Articles, 1,000 to 6,000 words, on history of Ohio (politics, economics, social, and natural history) for lay readers in the Midwest. Pays $100 to $900, on acceptance. Queries preferred. SASE for guidelines.

TORONTO LIFE—59 Front St. E., Toronto, Ont., Canada M5E 1B3.

John Macfarlane, Ed. Articles, 1,500 to 4,500 words, on Toronto. Pays $1,500 to $3,500, on acceptance. Query.

TUCSON LIFESTYLE—Old Pueblo Press, 7000 E. Tanque Verde, Tucson, AZ 85715. Sue Giles, Ed.-in-Chief. Local slant to all articles on businesses, lifestyles, the arts, homes, fashion, and travel in the Southwest. Payment varies, on acceptance. Query preferred.

VALLEY MAGAZINE—11151 Laurel Canyon Blvd., San Fernando, CA 91340. Bonnie Steele, Ed. Articles, 1,000 to 1,500 words, on celebrities, issues, education, health, business, dining, and entertaining, etc., in the San Fernando Valley. Pays $100 to $350, within 8 weeks of acceptance.

VERMONT LIFE— 6 Baldwin St., Montpelier, VT 05602. Tom Slayton, Ed.-in-Chief. Articles, 500 to 3,000 words, on Vermont subjects only. Pays 25¢ a word, extra for photos. Query preferred.

VIRGINIA BUSINESS—411 E. Franklin St., Suite 105, Richmond, VA 23219. James Bacon, Publisher. Articles, 1,000 to 2,500 words, related to the business scene in Virginia. Pays varying rates, on acceptance. Query required.

VIRGINIA WILDLIFE—P.O. Box 11104, Richmond, VA 23230-1104. Attn: Ed. Articles, 800 to 1,200 words, with Virginia tie-in, on fishing, hunting, wildlife management, outdoor safety and ethics, etc. Articles may be accompanied by color photos. Pays from 18¢ a word, extra for photos, on publication. Query.

WASHINGTON FLYER—Suite 700, 1707 L St., NW, Washington, DC 20036. Stefanie Berry, Assoc. Ed. Bimonthly. Local and travel publication for upscale Washingtonians and visitors. Nonfiction briefs and features, from 350 to 1,500 words. Color photographs. Pays $150 to $800, on publication. Query. Rarely uses freelance material. Send SASE for guidelines.

WASHINGTON POST MAGAZINE—*The Washington Post*, 1150 15th St. N.W., Washington, DC 20071. T. A. Frail, Man. Ed. Personal-experience essays, profiles, and general-interest pieces, to 6,000 words, on business, arts and culture, politics, science, sports, education, children, relationships, behavior, etc. Articles should be of interest to people living in Washington, DC, area. Pays from $750, on acceptance. Limited market.

THE WASHINGTONIAN—1828 L St. N.W., Suite 200, Washington, DC 20036. John Limpert, Ed. Helpful, informative articles, 1,000 to 4,000 words, on DC-related topics. Pays 50¢ a word, on publication.

WESTCHESTER FAMILY—See *New York Family.*

WESTERN SPORTSMAN—2002 Quebec Avenue, Suite 201, Saskatoon, Saskatchewan, Canada S7K 1W4. George Gruenefeld, Ed. Informative articles, to 2,500 words, on hunting, fishing, and outdoor experiences in British Columbia, Alberta, Saskatchewan, and Manitoba. How-tos, where-tos, cartoons. Photos. Pays $75 to $300.

WESTWAYS—P.O. Box 25001, Santa Ana, CA 92799-5001. Attn: Ed. Articles, 1,000 to 2,500 words, on travel in California, western U.S., greater U.S., and overseas. Pays from 50¢ a word, on acceptance. Query.

WINDSPEAKER—Aboriginal Multi-Media Society of Alberta, 15001 112th Ave., Edmonton, Alberta, Canada T5M 2V6. Debora Lockyer, Ed. Tabloid. Features, news items, sports, op-ed pieces, columns, etc., 200 to 1,000 words, concerning Canada's Aboriginal peoples. Pays from $3 per published inch, after publication. Query. Guidelines.

WINDY CITY SPORTS—1450 W. Randolph, Chicago, IL 60607. Jeff Banowetz, Ed. Articles, to 1,000 words, on amateur sports in the Chicago area. Queries required. Pays $100, on publication.

WISCONSIN TRAILS—P.O. Box 5650, Madison, WI 53705. Scott Klug, Ed./Pub., Kate Bast, Man. Ed. Articles, 1,500 to 2,000 words, on regional topics: outdoors, lifestyle, events, history, arts, adventure, travel; profiles of artists, craftspeople, and regional personalities. Pays 25¢ per word, on publication. Query in writing.

THE WREN MAGAZINE—(formerly *Wyoming Rural Electric News*) 340 W. B St., Suite 101, Casper, WY 82601. Kris Wendtland, Ed. Articles, 500 to 900 words, on issues relevant to rural Wyoming. Wyoming writers given preference. Pays to $140, on publication.

WYOMING RURAL ELECTRIC NEWS—See *The Wren Magazine.*

YANKEE—Yankee Publishing Co., P.O. Box 520, Dublin, NH 03444. Judson D. Hale, Ed. Articles and fiction, 500 to 2,500 words, on New England and New England people. Pays $500 to $2,500 for features, on acceptance. Query required.

TRAVEL ARTICLES

AAA TODAY—378 Whooping Loop, Suite 1272, Altamonte Springs, FL 32701. Margaret Cavanaugh, Ed. Bimonthly. Articles, 1,000 to 1,200 words, on travel in Pennsylvania, West Virginia, New York, Massachusetts, and Ohio. International destinations as well. Color photos. Pays $300 to $400, on publication.

ADVENTURE JOURNAL—650 S. Orcas St., Suite 103, Seattle, WA 98108. Kristina Schreck, Man Ed. Bimonthly. Travel articles, 2,500 to 3,000 words, on risky wild adventures; 700 to 2,000 words, on shorter trips with information on where to stay and what to do. Profiles and essays also used. Emphasis on both domestic and international travel. Pays 15¢ a word, for unsolicited submissions, within 30 days of publication.

AIR FAIR: THE MAGAZINE FOR AIRLINE EMPLOYEES—See *Interline Adventures: The Magazine for Airline Employees.*

AIR FORCE TIMES—See *Times News Service.*

ARIZONA HIGHWAYS—2039 W. Lewis Ave., Phoenix, AZ 85009. Richard G. Stahl, Sr. Ed. Informal, well-researched personal-experience and travel articles, 1,600 to 1,800 words, focusing on a specific city or region in Arizona. Also articles dealing with nature, environment, flora and fauna, history, anthropology, archaeology, hiking. Departments for personal-experience pieces include "Focus on Nature," "Along the Way," "Back Road Adventures," "Hiking," and "Arizona Humor." Pays 35¢ to 55¢ a word, on acceptance. Query with published clips only. Guidelines.

ARMY TIMES—See *Times News Service.*

BIG WORLD—P.O. Box 8743-A, Lancaster, PA 17604. Jim Fortney, Ed. Quarterly. Articles, 500 to 4,000 words, that offer advice on working and studying abroad, humorous anecdotes, first-person experiences, or other "down-to-earth" travel information. "For people who prefer to spend their traveling time responsibly discovering, exploring, and learning, in touch with locals and their traditions, and in harmony with their environment." Pays $10 to $20 for articles, $5 to $20 for photos, on publication. Web page: www.bigworld.com

BLUE RIDGE COUNTRY—P.O. Box 21535, Roanoke, VA 24018. Kurt Rheinheimer, Ed. Regional travel articles, 750 to 1,200 words, on destinations and backroad drives in the mountain regions of VA, NC, WV, TN, KY, MD, SC, and GA. Color slides and B&W prints considered. Pays to $200 for photo-features, on publication. Queries preferred.

CANADIAN DIVER & WATERSPORT—See *Diver Magazine.*

COAST TO COAST—2575 Vista del Mar Dr., Ventura, CA 93001. Valerie Law, Ed. Membership publication for Coast to Coast Resorts, private camping and resort clubs across North America. Focuses on "travel, recreation, and good times." Destination features focus on a North American city or region, going beyond typical tourist stops to interview locals. Activity or recreation features introduce readers to a sport, hobby, or other diversion. Also features on RV lifestyle. Send queries or manuscripts. Payment is $350 to $600, on acceptance, for 1,500- to 2,500-word articles.

CONDE NAST TRAVELER—360 Madison Ave., New York, NY 10017. Alison Humes, Features Ed. Uses very little free-lance material.

CRUISE TRAVEL—990 Grove St., Evanston, IL 60201. Robert Meyers, Ed. Charles Doherty, Man. Ed. Ship-, port-, and cruise-of-the-month features, 800 to 2,000 words; cruise guides; cruise roundups; cruise company profiles; travel suggestions for one-day port stops. "Photo-features strongly recommended." Payment varies, on acceptance. Query (by mail only) with sample color photos.

DIVER MAGAZINE—230-11780 Hammersmith Way, Richmond, B.C., Canada V7A 5E3. Stephanie Bold, Ed. Illustrated articles, 500 to 1,000 words, on dive destinations. Shorter pieces are also welcome. "Travel features should be brief and accompanied by excellent slides and/or prints and a map. Unsolicited articles will be reviewed only from August to October and will be considered for *Diver Magazine* and *Canadian Diver & Watersport.*" Guidelines. Limited market.

ENDLESS VACATION—Box 80260, Indianapolis, IN 46280. Laurie D. Borman, Ed. Travel features, to 1,500 words; primarily on North American destinations, some international destinations. Pays on acceptance. Query preferred. Send SASE for guidelines. Limited market.

FAMILY CIRCLE—110 Fifth Ave., New York, NY 10011. Sylvia Barsotti, Sr. Ed. Travel articles, to 1,500 words. Concept travel pieces should appeal to a national audience and focus on affordable activities for families; prefer service-filled, theme-oriented travel pieces or first-person family vacation stories. Payment varies, on acceptance. Query.

GO MAGAZINE—6600 Executive Circle Dr., Charlotte, NC 28212-8250. Tom Crosby, Ed. Focuses on travel and auto safety in North and South Carolina, as well as their neighboring states. Pays 15¢ per word, on publication.

HAWAII—1210 Auahi St., Suite 231, Honolulu, HI 96814. John Hollon, Ed. Bimonthly. Articles, 1,000 to 2,500 words, related to Hawaii. Pays 10¢ and up a word, on publication. Query.

INDIA CURRENTS—P.O. Box 21285, San Jose, CA 95151. Arvind Kumar, Submissions Ed. First-person accounts, 1,500 words, of trips to India or the subcontinent. Helpful tips for first-time travelers. Prefer descriptions of people-to-people interactions. Pays in subscriptions.

INTERLINE ADVENTURES: THE MAGAZINE FOR AIRLINE EMPLOYEES—(formerly *Air Fair: The Magazine for Airline Employees*) 211 E. 7th St., #1100, Austin, TX 78701. Christina Kosta, Ed. Travel articles, 800 to 2,500 words, with photos, on shopping, sightseeing, dining, and nightlife for airline employees. Prices, discount information, and addresses must be included. Pays $250 to $500, upon publication.

ISLANDS—P.O. Box 4728, Santa Barbara, CA 93140-4728. Joan Tapper, Ed.-in-Chief. Destination features, 2,500 to 4,000 words, on islands around the world as well as department pieces and front-of-the-book items on island-related topics. Pays from 50¢ a word, on acceptance. Query with clips required. Guidelines.

JOURNEYS—5301 S. Federal Circle, Littleton, CO 80123. Kara Skruck, Ed. Annual. Departments, 800 words, and features, 1,800 words, on destinations and travel experiences. "Our readers are mature and well-traveled." Query with clips and list of potential cities/countries or other story topics. Pays 75¢ per word, on acceptance.

MAIDEN VOYAGES—109 Minna St., Suite 240, San Francisco, CA 94105. Nanette C-Lee, Ed. Quarterly. "The Indispensable Guide to Women's Travel." Articles, to 1,500 words, and departments, to 750 words. "Heartfelt and transformative articles in a strong 'female' voice, and sweaty adventure tales." Pays $50 for articles with photos, $35 for departments with photos, on acceptance. Manuscripts only.

MICHIGAN LIVING—Automobile Club of Michigan, 1 Auto Club Dr., Dearborn, MI 48126. Ron Garbinski, Ed. Informative travel articles, 200 to 2,000 words, on U.S. and Canadian tourist attractions and recreational opportunities; special interest in Michigan. Pays $55 to $500 (rates vary for photos), on publication.

THE MIDWEST MOTORIST—See *The Midwest Traveler.*

THE MIDWEST TRAVELER—(formerly *The Midwest Motorist*) 12901 N. Forty Dr., St. Louis, MO 63141. Michael Right, Ed. Articles, 1,000 to 1,500 words, with color slides, on domestic and foreign travel. Pays from $150, on acceptance.

MOUNTAIN LIVING MAGAZINE—7009 S. Potomac, Englewood, CO 80112. Attn: Ed. Travel articles, 1,200 to 1,500 words, on cities, regions, establishments in the mountainous regions of the world. Pays $200 to $300, on acceptance.

NATIONAL GEOGRAPHIC—1145 17th St. N.W., Washington, DC 20036. William Allen, Ed. First-person articles on geography, exploration, natural history, archaeology, and science: 40% staff-written; 60% written by published authors. Does not consider unsolicited manuscripts.

NATIONAL GEOGRAPHIC ADVENTURE—104 W. 40th St., 17th Fl., New York, NY 10018. John Rasmus, Ed.-in-Chief. Bimonthly. Articles on adventure, travel, and outdoor pursuits; profiles of famous adventurers. Departments, 2,000 to 3,000 words, focus on adventurous lifestyles and personalities. Features, 4,000 to 8,000 words, are "in-depth, descriptive pieces on celebrities of adventure, gripping accounts of ground-breaking expeditions and scientific exploration, and intriguing, unknown historical tales." Compass section includes a variety of topics, varying lengths, and shows readers how to "bring adventure into their own lives." Query with at least 3 published clips. Send for guidelines. Payment varies.

NATIONAL MOTORIST—National Automobile Club, 1151 E. Hillsdale Blvd., Foster City, CA 94404. Jane Offers, Ed. Quarterly. Illustrated articles, 500 to 1,100 words, for California motorists, on motoring in the West, domestic and international travel, car care, roads, news, transportation, personalities, places, etc. Color slides. Pays from 10¢ a word, on acceptance. Pays for photos on publication. SASE required.

NAVY TIMES—See *Times News Service.*

NEW MEXICO JOURNEY—10501 Montgomery Blvd. N.E., Albuquerque, NM 87111-3848. Bimonthly. Magazine for AAA members in New Mexico. Departments include: "Inside Story," "Journey Through New Mexico," "The Way I See It," and "Recalls." Query for guidelines.

NEW YORK DAILY NEWS—450 W. 33rd St., New York, NY 10001. Linda Perney, Travel Ed. Articles, 700 to 900 words, on all manner of travel. Price information must be included. B&W or color photos or slides. Pays $100 to $200 (extra for photos), on publication.

THE NEW YORK TIMES—229 W. 43rd St., New York, NY 10036. Nancy Newhouse, Travel Ed. Query with SASE required; include writer's background, description of proposed article. Pays on acceptance.

NORTHWEST REGIONAL MAGAZINES—P.O. Box 18000, Florence, OR 97439. Attn: Judy Fleagle or Jim Forst. All submissions considered for use in *Oregon Coast* and *Northwest Travel.* Articles, 800 to 2,000 words, on travel, history, town/city profiles, outdoor activities, events, and nature. News releases, 200 to 500 words. Articles with slides preferred. Pays $50 to $300, after publication. Guidelines with SASE.

NORTHWEST TRAVEL—See *Northwest Regional Magazines.*

OREGON COAST—See *Northwest Regional Magazines.*

OREGON OUTSIDE—Northwest Regional Magazines, Box 18000, 1525 12th St., Florence, OR 97439-0130. Judy Fleagle, Jim Forst, Eds. Quarterly. Articles, 1,000 to 1,500 words, on Oregon and the outdoors, "all kinds of adventure, from walks for families to extreme skiing." Prefers to receive manuscript/photo packages. Pays $100 to $350, on publication. Query.

ROUTE 66 MAGAZINE—326 W. Route 66, Williams, AZ 86046-2427. Paul Taylor, Ed. Articles, 1,500 to 2,000 words, on travel and life along Route 66 between Chicago and Los Angeles. Also, fillers, jokes, and puzzles, for the Children's Page. B&W photographs. Pays $20 per column, 45 days after publication. Query.

SACRAMENTO MAGAZINE—4471 D St., Sacramento, CA 95819. Krista Hendricks Minard, Ed. Articles, 1,000 to 1,500 words, on destinations within a 6-hour drive of Sacramento. Pay varies, on publication. Query.

SPECIALTY TRAVEL INDEX—305 San Anselmo Ave., #313, San Anselmo, CA 94960. C. Steen Hansen, Co-Pub./Ed. Semiannual directory of adventure vacation tour companies, destinations, and vacation packages. Articles, 1,250 words, with special-interest, adventure type travel accounts and information. Pays 20¢ per word, on receipt of complete materials. Slides and photos considered. Queries preferred.

STUDENT WORLD TRAVELER—638 Camino de los Mares, C-240, San Clemente, CA 92673. Attn: Ed. Focus is on helping college students planning to work, study, or travel abroad. Articles written by college students and recent college graduates who have explored the places about which they write.

TEXAS HIGHWAYS MAGAZINE—P.O. Box 141009, Austin, TX 78714-1009. Jack Lowry, Ed. Travel, historical, cultural, scenic features on Texas, 200 to 1,800 words. Pays about 40¢ to 50¢ a word; photos $80 to $400. Guidelines.

TIMES NEWS SERVICE—Army Times Publishing Co., Springfield, VA 22159. Attn: R&R Ed. Travel articles, 700 words, on places of special interest to military people for use in "R&R" newspaper section. "We like travel articles to focus on a single destination but with short sidebar covering other things to see in the area." Pays $100, on acceptance. Pays $35 for original color slides or prints. Also, travel pieces, 1,000 words, for supplements to *Army Times*, *Navy Times*, and *Air Force Times*. Address Supplements Ed. Pays $125 to $200, on acceptance. Guidelines.

TRANSITIONS ABROAD—18 Hulst Rd., Box 1300, Amherst, MA 01004-1300. David Cline, Man. Ed. Articles for overseas travelers of all ages who seek an enriching, in-depth experience of the culture: work, study, travel, budget tips. Include practical, first-hand information. Emphasis on travel for personal enrichment. "Eager to work with inexperienced writers who want to share information not usually found in guidebooks. High percentage of material is from free lancers. Also seeking articles from writers with special expertise on cultural travel opportunities for specific types of travelers: seniors, students, families, etc." B&W photos a plus. Pays $2 per column inch, after publication. SASE required for guidelines and editorial calendar.

TRAVEL AMERICA—World Publishing Co., 990 Grove St., Evanston, IL 60201-4370. Randy Mink, Man. Ed. Robert Meyers, Ed. Features, 800 to 1,200 words, on U.S. vacation destinations. Pays up to $300, on acceptance. Top-quality color slides a must. Query.

TRAVEL & LEISURE—1120 Ave. of the Americas, New York, NY 10036. Nancy Novogrod, Ed.-in-Chief. Articles, 800 to 3,000 words, on destinations and travel-related activities. Short pieces for "Strategies" and "T&L Reports." Pays on acceptance: $2,500 to $5,000 for features; $750 to $1,500 for departments; $50 to $300 for short pieces. Query; articles on assignment.

TRAVEL SMART—40 Beechdale Rd., Dobbs Ferry, NY 10522-3098. Attn: Ed. Short pieces, 250 to 1,000 words, about interesting, unusual and/or economical places. Give specific details on hotels, restaurants, transportation, and costs. Pays on publication. "Send manila envelope with 2 first-class stamps for copy and guidelines." Query on longer pieces.

TRAVELERS' TALES, INC.—P.O. Box 610160, Redwood City, CA 94061. Attn: Ed. Personal travel stories and anecdotes, to 2,500 words, for book anthologies focused on a specific country or theme. Payment varies, on publication. Guidelines.

TRIPS: A TRAVEL JOURNAL—Suite 245, 155 Filbert St., Oakland, CA 94607. Tony Stucker, Ed.-in-Chief. For the active, adventurous traveler. Seeks irreverent articles about unique, interesting travel destinations. Nonfiction, from 500 to 5,000 words; and fillers, from 150 to 500 words. Also accepts photographs and slides. Payment is 20¢ to 25¢ per word, on publication. Query.

WASHINGTON FLYER—Suite 700, 1707 L. St. NW, Washington, DC 20036. Stefanie Berry, Assoc. Ed. Bimonthly. Travel publication for the upscale Washington residents and visitors. Nonfiction briefs and features, from 350 to 1,500 words. Color photographs. Pays $150 to $800, on publication. Query.

WESTWAYS—P.O. Box 25001, Santa Ana, CA 92799-5001. Attn: Ed. Travel articles, 1,300 to 2,500 words, on southern California, the West, domestic and foreign destinations. Pays $1 a word, on acceptance.

INFLIGHT MAGAZINES

ABOARD—100 Almeria Ave., Suite 220, Coral Gables, FL 33134. Attn: Ed. Dept. Inflight magazine of 15 Latin American international airlines in Chile, Dominican Republic, Ecuador, Venezuela, Costa Rica, Guatemala, El Salvador, Bolivia, Nicaragua, Honduras, Uruguay, and Paraguay. Articles, 1,200 to 1,500 words, with photos, on these countries and on science, sports, technology, adventure, wildlife, fashion, business, ecology, and gastronomy. No political stories. Pays $100 for articles; $100 for photos; $150 for articles with photos, on acceptance and on publication. Query.

ALASKA AIRLINES MAGAZINE—2701 First Ave., Suite 250, Seattle, WA 98121. Paul Frichtl, Ed. Articles, 250 to 2,500 words, on business, travel, and profiles of regional personalities for West Coast business travelers. Payment varies, on publication. Query.

AMERICA WEST AIRLINES MAGAZINE—Skyword Marketing Inc., 4636 E. Elwood St., Suite 5, Phoenix, AZ 85040-1963. Michael Derr, Ed. Business trends, first-person profiles, destination pieces, fiction, arts and culture, 500 to 2,000 words; thoughtful essays. Pays from $250, on publication. Clips and SASE required. Guidelines. Very limited market.

AMERICAN WAY—P.O. Box 619640, DFW Airport, Fort Worth, TX 75261-9640. Tiffany Franke, Assoc. Ed. Travel, business, food and wine, health, and technology. Departments, 400 to 1,000 words. Sojourns travel stories to 200 words. Features, 1,500 to 2,000 words. Query with SASE.

HEMISPHERES—1301 Carolina St., Greensboro, NC 27401. Randy Johnson, Ed. United Airlines inflight magazine. Articles, 1,200 to 1,500 words, on business, investing, travel, sports, family, food and wine, etc., that inform and entertain sophisticated, well-traveled readers. "The magazine strives for a unique global perspective presented in a fresh, strong, and artful graphic environment." Pays good rates, on acceptance. Query. Guidelines with SASE.

HORIZON AIR MAGAZINE—2701 First Ave., #250, Seattle, WA 98121-1123. Michele Dill, Man. Ed. Business and travel articles on the companies, people, issues, and trends that define the Northwest. News items, 200 to 500 words, and profiles for "The Region" section. Other department pieces, 1,800 words, cover corporate and industry profiles, regional issue analysis, travel, and community profiles; main features, 2,500 words. Pays $100 to $600, on publication.

US AIRWAYS ATTACHÉ—(formerly *USAIR Magazine*) 1301 Carolina St., Greensboro, NC 27401. Articles, 400 to 2,500 words, on "the finer things in life." Paragons department offers short pieces touting the best of the best;

Informed Sources department contains experts' opinions and knowledge on a variety of topics. No politics or Hollywood issues. Pays $1 a word, on acceptance.

WOMEN'S PUBLICATIONS

BBW: BIG BEAUTIFUL WOMAN—8484 Wilshire Blvd., Suite 900, Beverly Hills, CA 90211. Theresa Flynt-Gaerke, Pub. Dir. Articles, 1,500 words, of interest to women ages 25 to 50, especially large-size women, including interviews with successful large-size women and personal accounts of how to cope with difficult situations. Tips on restaurants, airlines, stores, etc., that treat large women with respect. Payment varies, on publication. Query.

BRIDAL GUIDE—Globe Communications Corp., 3 E. 54th St., New York, NY 10022. Diane Forden, Ed.-in-Chief. Denise Schipani, Man. Ed. Laurie Bain Wilson, Travel Ed. Bimonthly. Articles, 1,500 to 3,000 words, on wedding planning, relationships, sexuality, health and nutrition, psychology, travel, and finance. No beauty, fashion articles; no fiction, essays, poetry. Pays on acceptance. Query with SASE.

BRIDE'S—140 E. 45th St., New York, NY 10017. Sally Kilbridge, Man. Ed. Articles, 800 to 3,000 words, for engaged couples or newlyweds, on wedding planning, relationships, communication, sex, decorating, finances, careers, remarriage, health, birth control, religion, in-laws. Major editorial subjects: home, wedding, and honeymoon (send honeymoon queries to Travel Dept.). No fiction or poetry. Pays from 50¢ a word, on acceptance.

COMPLETE WOMAN—875 N. Michigan Ave., Suite 3434, Chicago, IL 60611. Bonnie L. Krueger, Ed. Lora Wintz, Sr. Ed. Articles, 1,000 to 2,000 words, with how-to sidebars, giving practical advice to women on love, sex, careers, health, personal relationships, etc. Also interested in reprints. Pays varying rates, on publication. Query with clips.

COSMOPOLITAN—224 W. 57th St., New York, NY 10019. Kate White, Ed. John Searles, Fiction and Books Ed. Articles, to 3,000 words, and features, 500 to 2,000 words, on issues affecting young career women, with emphasis on jobs and personal life. Fiction on male-female relationships: short shorts, 1,500 to 3,000 words; short stories, 3,000 to 4,000 words; condensed published novels, 25,000 words. "We generally only print fiction that is excerpted from a novel being published." SASE required. Payment varies.

COUNTRY WOMAN—P.O. Box 989, Greendale, WI 53129. Kathy Pohl, Exec. Ed. Profiles of country women (photo-feature packages), inspirational, reflective pieces. Personal-experience, nostalgia, humor, service-oriented articles, original crafts, and how-to features, to 1,000 words, of interest to country women. Pays $25 to $75 for crafts, humor, nostalgia; pays $150 for photo-features, on acceptance.

ELLE—1633 Broadway, New York, NY 10019. Amy Gross, Ed. Dir. Articles, varying lengths, for fashion-conscious women, ages 20 to 50. Subjects include beauty, health, fitness, travel, entertainment, and lifestyles. Pays top rates, on publication. Query required.

ESSENCE—1500 Broadway, New York, NY 10036. Susan L. Taylor, Ed.-in-Chief. Monique Greenwood, Exec. Ed. Provocative articles, 800 to 2,500 words, about black women in America today: self-help, how-to pieces, business and finance, work, parenting, health, celebrity profiles, art, travel, and political issues. Fiction, 800 to 2,500 words. Pays varying rates, on acceptance. Query for articles.

EXECUTIVE FEMALE—135 W. 50th St., New York, NY 10020. Kim Calero, Pres. Articles, 750 to 2,500 words, on managing people, time, money, companies, and careers for women in business. Pays varying rates, on acceptance. Query.

FAMILY CIRCLE—375 Lexington Ave., New York, NY 10017. Nancy Clark, Deputy Ed. Articles, to 2,000 words, on "women who have made a difference," marriage, family, and child-care and elder-care issues; consumer affairs, psychology, humor, health, nutrition, and fitness. Pays top rates, on acceptance. Query required.

FIT PREGNANCY—21100 Erwin St., Woodland Hills, CA 91367-3712. Peg Moline, Ed. Articles, 500 to 2,000 words, on pregnant women's and post-partum health, nutrition, and physical fitness. No fiction or poetry. Payment varies, on publication. Query.

GLAMOUR—350 Madison Ave., New York, NY 10017. Bonnie Fuller, Ed.-in-Chief. Laurie Sprague, Man. Ed. Articles, from 1,000 words, on careers, health, psychology, politics, current events, interpersonal relationships, etc., for women ages 18 to 35. Fashion, entertainment, travel, food, and beauty pieces staff-written. Pays from $500, on acceptance. Query Articles Ed.

GOLF DIGEST WOMAN—P.O. Box 395, Trumbull, CT 06611-0395. Liz Comte Reisman, Ed. "We want to help our readers play better, have fun, and play with the best stuff available." Interested in previously published authors (in national magazines) who have in-depth knowledge of golf and golf-related subjects.

GOOD HOUSEKEEPING—959 Eighth Ave., New York, NY 10019. Lisa Benenson, Articles Ed. Lee Quarfoot, Fiction Ed. Articles, about 2,500 words, for married working women with children 18 and younger. Social issues, dramatic personal narratives, medical news, marriage, friendship, psychology, crime, finances, work, parenting, and consumer issues. Best places to break in: "Better Way" (short, advice-driven takes on health, money, safety, and consumer issues) and profiles (short takes on interesting or heroic women or families). No submissions on food, beauty, needlework, or crafts. Short stories, 2,000 to 5,000 words, with strong identification for women. Unsolicited fiction not returned; if no response in 6 weeks, assume work was unsuitable. Pays top rates, on acceptance. Guidelines. Query with SASE for nonfiction.

HARPER'S BAZAAR—1700 Broadway, 37th Fl., New York, NY 10019. Katherine Betts, Ed.-in-Chief. Articles, 1,500 to 2,500 words, for active, sophisticated women: the arts, world affairs, travel, families, education, careers, health, and sexuality. Payment varies, on acceptance. No unsolicited manuscripts; query with SASE.

IRIS: A JOURNAL ABOUT WOMEN—The Women's Ctr., Box 323, HSC, Univ. of Virginia, Charlottesville, VA 22908. Eileen Boris, Ed. Semiannual. Fiction, 2,500 to 4,000 words; book reviews, 900 words for a single book, 1,500 words for combined review; articles, 2,500 to 4,000 words; poetry, any length; personal essays to 2,500 words; photos and art essays; short humor. All material must focus on women's issues. Pays in subscription. E-mail: iris@virginia.edu.

THE JOYFUL WOMAN—P.O. Box 90028, Chattanooga, TN 37412. Joy Rice Martin, Ed. Joanna Rice, Ed. Asst. Fiction, 500 to 1,000 words, for women with a "Christian commitment." Also first-person inspirational true stories, profiles of Christian women, practical and Bible-oriented how-to articles. Pays 3¢ to 4¢ a word, on publication. Queries required.

LADIES' HOME JOURNAL—125 Park Ave., New York, NY 10017. Myrna Blyth, Pub. Dir./Ed.-in-Chief. Articles of interest to women. Send queries to: Deborah Pike, Sr. Ed. (relationships/sex and psychology); Elena Rover, Ed. (health/medical); Melina Gerosa, Sr. Ed. (celebrity/entertainment); Pamela Guthrie O'Brien, Articles Ed. (news/general interest); Shana Aborn, Features Ed. (personal experience). Fiction accepted through literary agents only. Guidelines.

MCCALL'S—375 Lexington Ave., New York, NY 10017. Attn: Articles Ed. Human-interest, self-help, social issues, and popular psychology articles, 1,200 to 2,000 words. Also publishes "Couples," first person essays, 1,400 words; "Families," how-to articles, 1,400 words; "Health Sense," short, newsy items; and "Medical Report," health-related items, 1,200 words. Query with SASE. Payment varies, on acceptance.

MADEMOISELLE—350 Madison Ave., New York, NY 10017. Faye Haun, Man. Ed. Articles, 1,000 to 3,000 words, on work, relationships, health, and trends of interest to single, working women in their early to mid-twenties. Reporting pieces, essays, first-person accounts, and humor. No fiction. Submit query with clips and SASE. Pays excellent rates, on acceptance.

MAMM—349 W. 12th St., New York, NY 10014-1796. Submissions. Monthly. Articles on women's health, mainly, cancer prevention, treatment, and survival. Survivor profiles, conventional and alternative treatment information, investigative features, essays, and cutting-edge news. Query with clips or send complete manuscript. SASE. Payment varies, and is made within 45 days of acceptance.

MODERN BRIDE—249 W. 17th St., New York, NY 10011. Mary Ann Cavlin, Exec. Ed. Articles, 1,500 to 2,000 words, for bride and groom, on wedding planning, financial planning, juggling career and home, etc. Pays $600 to $1,200, on acceptance.

MS.—20 Exchange Pl., 22nd Fl., New York, NY 10005. Attn: Manuscript Ed. Articles relating to feminism, women's roles, and social change; national and international news reporting, profiles, essays, theory, and analysis. No fiction or poetry accepted, acknowledged, or returned. Query with resume and published clips.

NA'AMAT WOMAN—200 Madison Ave., Suite 2120, New York, NY 10016. Judith A. Sokoloff, Ed. Articles on Jewish culture, women's issues, social and political topics, and Israel, 1,500 to 3,000 words. Short stories with a Jewish theme. Pays 10¢ a word, on publication.

NATURAL LIVING TODAY—175 Varick St., 9th Fl., New York, NY 10014. Attn: Ed. Dept. Bimonthly. Articles, 1,000 to 2,000 words, on all aspects of a natural lifestyle for women. Pays $75 to $200, on publication. Query.

NEW WOMAN—733 3rd Ave., 12th Fl., New York, NY 10017. Attn: Manuscripts and Proposals. Articles for women ages 25 to 49, on self-discovery, self-development, and self-esteem. Features: relationships, careers, health and fitness, money, fashion, beauty, food and nutrition, travel features with self-growth angle, and essays by and about women pacesetters. Pays about $1 a word, on acceptance. Query with SASE.

ON THE ISSUES—Merle Hoffman Enterprises Ltd., 97-77 Queens Blvd., Suite 1120, Forest Hills, NY 11374-3317. Jan Goodwin, Ed. "The Progressive Woman's Quarterly." Articles, to 2,500 words, on political or social issues. Movie, music, and book reviews, 500 to 750 words. Payment varies, on publication. Query.

PLAYGIRL—801 Second Ave., New York, NY 10017. Claire Harth, Ed.-in-Chief. Send queries to: Sandra Mardenfeld, Man. Ed. Erotic entertainment for women. Insightful articles on sexuality and romance; sizzling fiction, humor, and in-depth celebrity interviews of interest to contemporary women. Pays varying rates, after acceptance. Query with clips. Guidelines.

REDBOOK—224 W. 57th St., New York, NY 10019. Christina Boyle, Stephanie Young, Sr. Eds., Health. Dawn Raffel, Fiction Ed. Andrea Bauman, Articles Ed. For mothers, ages 25 to 45. Short stories, 10 to 15 typed pages; dramatic inspirational narratives, 1,000 to 2,000 words. SASE required. Pays on acceptance. Query with writing samples for articles. Guidelines.

SELF—350 Madison Ave., New York, NY 10017. Attn: Ed. "We no longer accept unsolicited manuscripts or queries."

TODAY'S CHRISTIAN WOMAN—465 Gundersen Dr., Carol Stream, IL 60188. Ramona Cramer Tucker, Ed. Articles, 1,500 to 1,800 words, that are "warm and personal in tone, full of real-life anecdotes that deal with marriage, parenting, friendship, spiritual life, single life, health, work, and self." Humorous anecdotes, 150 words, that have a Christian slant. Payment varies, on acceptance. Queries required. Guidelines.

WOMAN'S DAY—1633 Broadway, New York, NY 10019. Stephanie Abarbanel, Sr. Articles Ed. Human-interest or service-oriented articles, 750 to 1,200 words, on marriage, child-rearing, health, careers, relationships, money management. Dramatic first-person narratives of medical miracles, rescues, women's experiences, etc. "We respond to queries promptly; unsolicited manuscripts are returned unread." SASE. Pays standard rates, on acceptance.

WOMAN'S TOUCH—1445 Boonville Ave., Springfield, MO 65802-1894. Lillian Sparks, Ed. Aleda Swartzendruber, Man. Ed. Inspirational articles, 500 to 1,500 words, for Christian women. Pays on publication. Allow 3 months for response. Submit complete manuscript. Guidelines and editorial calendar.

WOMEN IN BUSINESS—American Business Women's Assn., 9100 Ward Pkwy., Box 8728, Kansas City, MO 64114-0728. Susan Fitch Swanson, Communications Dir. Currently overstocked; not accepting material for 1999. How-to business features, 1,000 to 1,500 words, for working women ages 35 to 55, business trends, small-business ownership, self-improvement, and retirement issues. Profiles of ABWA members only. Pays on acceptance. Query required.

WOMEN'S SPORTS & FITNESS—342 Madison Ave., New York, NY 10017. Lucy S. Danziger, Ed.-in-Chief. Articles on fitness, nutrition, outdoor sports; how-tos; profiles; adventure travel pieces; and controversial issues or reported stories in women's sports, 500 to 2,000 words. Pays on acceptance.

WORKING MOTHER—MacDonald Communications, 135 W. 50th St., 16th Fl., New York, NY 10020. Attn: Ed. Dept. Articles, to 2,000 words, that help women in their task of juggling job, home, and family. "We like pieces that solve or illuminate a problem unique to our readers." Payment varies, on acceptance.

WORKING WOMAN—135 W. 50th St., Suite 16, New York, NY 10020-1201. Articles, 200 to 1,500 words, on business and finance. "Our readers are high level executives and entrepreneurs who are looking for newsworthy information about the changing marketplace and its effects on their businesses and careers." Query. Pays from $250, on acceptance.

MEN'S PUBLICATIONS

ESQUIRE—250 W. 55th St., New York, NY 10019. David Granger, Ed.-in-Chief. Peter Griffin, Deputy Ed. Articles, 2,500 to 4,000 words, for intelligent audience. Pays varying rates, on acceptance. Query with clips and SASE.

GALLERY—401 Park Ave. S., New York, NY 10016-8802. Will Romano, Ed. Dir. Megan Green, Copy Ed. Articles, investigative pieces, interviews, profiles, to 2,500 words, for sophisticated men. Short humor, satire, service pieces, fiction, and erotic fiction. Photos. Erotic fiction is the only fiction currently accepted. Query. Guidelines.

GQ—350 Madison Ave., New York, NY 10017. No free-lance queries or manuscripts.

ICON—595 Broadway, 4th Fl., New York, NY 10012. Philip Zabriskie, Sr. Ed. "Very balanced and critical" in-depth profiles, 4,000 to 6,000 words, of interest to men. "We are interested in accomplishment, all forms and all industries. Pays $1 a word, on publication. Query required.

MEN'S HEALTH—Rodale Press, 33 E. Minor St., Emmaus, PA 18098. Tom McGrath, Sr. Ed. Articles, 1,000 to 2,500 words, on fitness, diet, health, relationships, and careers for men ages 25 to 55. Pays from 50¢ a word, on acceptance. Query.

MEN'S JOURNAL—1290 Ave. of the Americas, New York, NY 10104-0298. Attn: Editorial. Articles and profiles, 2,000 to 7,000 words, of interest to active men age 25 to 49. Travel, fitness, health, adventure, participatory sports. Service articles for equipment and fitness sections, 400 to 1,800 words. Pays "good rates," on acceptance. Query.

NEW MAN—600 Rinehart Rd., Lake Mary, FL 32746. Brian Peterson, Ed. No longer accepting unsolicited manuscripts.

PENTHOUSE—277 Park Ave., 4th Fl., New York, NY 10172-0003. Peter Bloch, Ed. Lavada B. Nahon, Sr. Ed. General-interest profiles, interviews, or investigative articles, to 5,000 words. No unsolicited fiction. Pays on acceptance.

PLAYBOY—9242 Beverly Blvd., Beverly Hills, CA 90210. Stephen Randall, Exec. Ed. Articles, 3,500 to 6,000 words, and sophisticated fiction, 1,000 to 10,000 words (5,000 preferred), for urban men. (Address fiction to Attn: Fiction Ed.) Humor; satire. Science fiction. Pays to $5,000 for articles and fiction, $2,000 for short-shorts, on acceptance. SASE required.

SENIORS MAGAZINES

AARP BULLETIN— 601 E St. N.W., Washington, DC 20049. Elliot Carlson, Ed. Publication of the American Association of Retired Persons. Payment varies, on acceptance. Query required.

GET UP & GO!—(formerly *Senior Highlights*) 500 Fesler St., Suite 101, El Cajon, CA 92020. Laura Impastato, Ed. Articles, 400 to 700 words, for mature adults, 50 and older; focus is on Southern California. Articles on profiles, programs, hobbies, and travel of local interest only. Good photos or graphics required. Reports in 60 days. Fees negotiated.

GET UP & GO! NEWSMAGAZINE—(formerly *Mature Lifestyles.*) 4575 Via Royale, #110, Ft. Myers, FL 33919. Linda Heffley, Ed. Articles, 500 to 700 words, for readers over 50 in Florida. No fiction or poetry. Florida angle a must. Pays $75, on publication.

GOOD TIMES—Robert Morris Bldg., 100 N. 17th St., 9th Fl., Philadelphia, PA 19103. Karen Detwiler, Ed.-in-Chief. Mature lifestyle magazine for readers 50 years and older in Pennsylvania. Articles, to 1,500 words, on medical issues, health, travel, finance, fashion, gardening, fitness, legal issues, celebrities, lifestyles, and relationships. Payment varies, on publication. Query with samples and resumé.

LIFE LINES MAGAZINE—129 N. 10th St., Rm. 418, Lincoln, NE 68508-3627. Dena Rust Zimmer, Ed. Short stories, "Sports and Hobbies," "Remember When . . . ," "Travels With . . . ," and "Perspectives on Aging," to 450 words. Poetry, to 50 lines. Fillers and short humor, "the shorter the better." No payment.

MATURE LIFESTYLES—P.O. Box 44327, Madison, WI 53744. Sue Sveum, Ed. "South Central Wisconsin's Newspaper for the Active 50-Plus Population." Syndicated national coverage and local free lance.

MATURE LIFESTYLES—See *Get Up & Go! Newsmagazine.*

MATURE LIVING—127 Ninth Ave. N., Nashville, TN 37234-0140. Al Shackleford, Ed. Fiction and human-interest articles, to 1,200 words, for senior adults. Must be consistent with Christian principles. Payment varies, on acceptance.

MATURE OUTLOOK—Meredith Corp., 1716 Locust St., Des Moines, IA 50309. Peggy Person, Ed. Bimonthly. Upbeat, contemporary articles, 75 to 2,000 words, for readers 50 and older. Regular topics include health, money, food, travel, leisure, and stories of real people. Pays $50 to $1,500, on acceptance. Query required. Guidelines.

MATURE YEARS—201 Eighth Ave. S., P.O. Box 801, Nashville, TN 37202. Marvin W. Cropsey, Ed. Articles of interest to older adults: health and fitness, personal finance, hobbies and inspiration. Anecdotes, to 300 words, poems, cartoons, jokes, and puzzles for older adults. "A Christian magazine that seeks to build faith. We always show older adults in a favorable light." Include name, address, and social security number with all submissions. Allow 2 months for response.

MILESTONES—246 S. 22nd St., Philadelphia, PA 19103. Robert Epp, Dir. Cathy Green, Ed. Tabloid published 10 times a year. News articles and features, 750 to 1,000 words, on humor, personalities, political issues, etc., for readers 50 and older. Articles are written by staff and local writers only.

MODERN MATURITY—601 E. St. N.W., Washington, DC 20049. Hugh Delehanty, Ed. Articles, 400 to 2,000 words, on careers, workplace, human interest, living, finance, relationships, and consumerism for readers over 50. Query. Pays $500 to $2,500, on acceptance.

NEW CHOICES: LIVING EVEN BETTER AFTER 50—Reader's Digest Publications, Reader's Digest Rd., Pleasantville, NY 10570. Greg Daugherty, Ed.-in-Chief. Service magazine for people ages 50 and older. Articles on health, personal finance, and travel. Payment varies, on acceptance. Query.

NEW JERSEY 50+ PLUS—1830 US Rt. 9, Toms River, NJ 08755-1210. Pat Jasin, Ed. Articles on finance, health, travel, and social issues for older readers. Pays in copies. Query required.

THE RETIRED OFFICER MAGAZINE—201 N. Washington St., Alexandria, VA 22314. Attn: Manuscripts Ed. Articles, 800 to 2,000 words, of interest to military members and their families. Current military/political affairs, recent military history (especially Vietnam and Korea), military family lifestyles, health, money, second careers. Photos a plus. Pays to $1,300, on acceptance. Queries required. Send for guidelines. E-mail: editor@troa.org. Web: www.troa.org/serv/pubs/mag/guidelines.asp.

SENIOR HIGHLIGHTS—See *Get Up & Go!*

SENIOR MAGAZINE—3565 S. Higuera St., San Luis Obispo, CA 93401. Attn: Ed. Articles, 900 to 1,200 words, of interest to men and women 40+; personality profiles, travel pieces, articles about new things, places, business, sports, movies, television, and health. Reviews of new or outstanding older books. Pays $1.50 per inch; $10 to $25 for B&W photos, on publication.

SENIOR TIMES—Suite 814, 1102 Pleasant St., Worcester, MA 01602-1232. Edwin H. Gledhill, Ed. Short stories, historical or people oriented, 500 to 1,200 words. Articles, 500 to 1,200 words, on arts, travel, local interest, entertainment, and positive role models for aging. Poetry, 10 to 200 words. No payment.

HOME & GARDEN/FOOD & WINE

AFRICAN VIOLET MAGAZINE—2375 North St., Beaumont, TX 77702. Ruth Rumsey, Ed. Articles, 700 to 1,400 words, on growing methods for African violets; history and personal experience with African violets. Violet-related poetry. No payment.

THE AMERICAN GARDENER—7931 E. Boulevard Dr., Alexandria, VA 22308-1300. David J. Ellis, Ed. Bimonthly. Articles, to 2,500 words, for American ornamental gardeners: profiles of prominent horticulturists, plant research and plant hunting, events and personalities in horticultural history, plant lore and literature, the politics of horticulture, etc. Humorous pieces for "Offshoots." "We run very few how-to articles." Pays $100 to $500, on publication. Query with SASE preferred.

AMERICAN ROSE—P.O. Box 30,000, Shreveport, LA 71130. Beth Smiley, Man. Ed. Articles on home rose gardens: varieties, products, helpful advice, rose care, etc.

ATLANTA HOMES AND LIFESTYLES—1100 Johnson Ferry Rd., #595, Atlanta, GA 30342-1746. Attn: Eds. Articles with a local angle. Department pieces for "Around Atlanta," "Design Takes," "Great Escapes," and

"Quick Fix." Pays $50 to $300 for departments; $300 to $400 for features, on acceptance.

BETTER HOMES AND GARDENS—1716 Locust St., Des Moines, IA 50309-3023. Jean LemMon, Ed. Articles, to 2,000 words, on health, travel, parenting, and education. Pays top rates, on acceptance. Query.

BON APPETIT—6300 Wilshire Blvd., Los Angeles, CA 90048. Barbara Fairchild, Exec. Ed. Articles on fine cooking (menu format or single focus), cooking classes, and gastronomically focused travel. Query with clips. Pays varying rates, on acceptance.

BRIDE'S—140 E. 45th St., New York, NY 10017. Sally Kilbridge, Man. Ed. Articles, 800 to 2,000 words, for engaged couples or newlyweds on wedding planning, home and decorating, and honeymoon. No fiction or poetry. Send travel queries to Travel Dept. Pay starts at 50¢ per word, on acceptance.

CANADIAN GARDENING—340 Ferrier St., Suite 210, Markham, Ont., Canada L3R 2Z5. Rebecca Hanes-Fox, Ed. Features, 1,200 to 2,500 words, that help avid home gardeners in Canada solve problems or inspire them with garden ideas; Canadian angle imperative. How-to pieces, to 1,000 words, on garden projects; include introduction and step-by-step instructions. Profiles of gardens, to 2,000 words. Department pieces, 200 to 400 words. Pays $75 to $700, on acceptance. Queries preferred.

CAROLINA GARDENER—P.O. Box 4504, Greensboro, NC 27404. L.A. Jackson, Ed. Bimonthly. Articles, 750 to 1,000 words, specific to southeast gardening: profiles of gardens in the southeast and of new cultivars or "good ol' southern heirlooms." Slides and illustrations should be available to accompany articles. Pays $150, on publication. Query required.

CHEF—Talcott Communications Corp., 20 N. Wacker Dr., Suite 1865, Chicago, IL 60606. Brent T. Frei, Ed.-in-Chief. "The Food Magazine for Professionals." Articles, 800 to 1,200 words, that offer professionals in the food-service business ideas for food marketing, preparation, and presentation. Pays $200 to $300, on publication.

CHILE PEPPER—1227 W. Magnolia Ave., Fort Worth, TX 76104. Joel Gregory, Pub. Eddie Lee Rider, Jr., Exec. Ed. Food and travel articles, 1,000 to 1,500 words. "No general and obvious articles, such as 'My Favorite Chile Con Carne.' We want first-person articles about spicy world cuisine." No fillers. Payment varies, on publication. Queries required.

COLORADO HOMES AND LIFESTYLES—7009 S. Potomac St., Englewood, CO 80112. Evalyn K. McGraw, Ed. Bimonthly. Articles, 1,300 to 1,500 words, with a focus on primarily upscale Colorado homes and interiors. Department pieces, 1,100 to 1,300 words, cover architecture, artists, design trends, profiles, gardening, food and wine, and travel. Pays $150 to $300, on acceptance. Guidelines. Written query.

COOKING LIGHT—P.O. Box 1748, Birmingham, AL 35201. Doug Crichton, Ed. Articles on fitness, exercise, health and healthful cooking, nutrition, and healthful recipes. Query with clips and SASE.

COOK'S ILLUSTRATED—17 Station St., Brookline, MA 02445. Barbara Bourassa, Man. Ed. Bimonthly. Articles that emphasize techniques of home cooking with master recipes, careful testing, trial and error. Payment varies, within 60 days of acceptance. Query. Guidelines.

COUNTRY GARDENS—1716 Locust St., Des Moines, IA 50309-3023. LuAnn Brandsen, Ed. Bimonthly. Garden-related how-tos and profiles of gardeners, 750 to 1,500 words. Department pieces, 500 to 700 words, on garden-related travel, food, projects, decorating, entertaining. "The gardens we feature are informal, lush, and old-fashioned. Stories emphasize both inspiration and information." Pays $450 to $1,500 for columns; $350 to $800 for features, on acceptance. Query required.

COUNTRY LIVING—224 W. 57th St., New York, NY 10019. Marjorie E. Gage, Sr. Ed. Articles, 800 to 1,200 words, on decorating, antiques, cooking, travel, home building, crafts, and gardens. "Most material is written in-house; limited free-lance needs." Payment varies, on acceptance. Query preferred.

DESIGN CONCEPT—820 W. Jackson Blvd., #450, Chicago, IL 60607-3026. Rebecca Rolfes, Ed. Biannual. "An Interior Design Magazine from Pier 1 Imports." Features for and interviews with professional interior designers, 800 to 1,200 words. Pays about 50¢ a word, on publication. Query.

FANCY FOOD—Talcott Communications Corp., 20 N. Wacker Dr., Suite 1865, Chicago, IL 60606. Paddy Buratto, Ed. Dir. "The Business Magazine for Specialty Foods, Coffee and Tea, Natural Foods, Confections, and Upscale Housewares." Articles, 2,000 words, related to gourmet food. Pays $250–$500, on publication.

FINE GARDENING—The Taunton Press, P.O. Box 5506, Newtown, CT 06470-5506. LeeAnne White, Ed. Bimonthly. Articles, 800 to 2,000 words, for readers with a serious interest in gardening: how-tos, garden design, as well as pieces on specific plants or garden tools. "Our primary focus is on ornamental gardening and landscaping." Picture possibilities are very important. Pays $300 to $1,200 per story story on a project basis, part on acceptance, part on completed galley. Photos, $75 to $500. Query. Guidelines.

FLOWER & GARDEN MAGAZINE—4645 Belleview, Kansas City, MO 64112. Attn: Ed. Practical how-to articles, 500 to 1,000 words, on home gardening and landscaping. Photos a plus. Pays varying rates, on acceptance (on publication for photos). Query.

FOOD & WINE—1120 Ave. of the Americas, New York, NY 10036. Dana Cowin, Ed.-in-Chief. Mary Ellen Ward, Man. Ed. No unsolicited material.

GARDEN DESIGN—100 Ave. of the Americas, 7th Fl., New York, NY 10013. Douglas Brenner, Ed. Garden-related features, 500 to 1,000 words, on private, public, and community gardens; articles on art and history as they relate to gardens.

GARDEN SHOWCASE—P.O. Box 23669, Portland, OR 97281-3669. Lynn Lustberg, Ed. Monthly. Articles, to 1,000 words, on gardening. Features cover a wide range of gardening ideas, but all must have a connection to the Willamette Valley. Also accepts slides or transparencies of trees, shrubs, perennials, and gardens in that area. Payment is $125, on publication. Query.

GOURMET: THE MAGAZINE OF GOOD LIVING—Conde Nast, 360 Madison Ave., New York, NY 10017. Attn: Ed. No unsolicited manuscripts; query.

GROWERTALKS—P.O. Box 9, 335 N. River St., Batavia, IL 60510-0009. Chris Beytes, Ed. Articles, 800 to 2,600 words, that help commercial greenhouse growers (not florist/retailers or home gardeners) do their jobs better: trends, successes in new types of production, marketing, business management, new crops, and issues facing the industry. Payment varies, on publication. Queries preferred.

THE HERB COMPANION—Herb Companion Press, 201 E. Fourth St., Loveland, CO 80537. Robyn Griggs Lawrence, Ed. Bimonthly. Articles, 1,500 to 3,000 words; fillers, 75 to 150 words. Practical horticultural information, original recipes illustrating the use of herbs, thoroughly researched historical insights, step-by-step instructions for herbal craft projects, book reviews. Pays 33¢ per word, on publication.

THE HERB QUARTERLY—P. O. Box 689, San Anselmo, CA 94960. Linda Sparrowe, Ed. Articles, 2,000 to 4,000 words, on herbs: practical uses, cultivation, gourmet cooking, landscaping, herb tradition, medicinal herbs, crafts ideas, unique garden designs, profiles of herb garden experts, and practical how-tos for the herb businessperson. Include garden design when possible. Pays on publication. Guidelines; send SASE.

HOME MAGAZINE—1633 Broadway, 44th Fl., New York, NY 10019. Gale Steves, Ed.-in-Chief. Linda Lentz, Articles Ed. Articles of interest to homeowners: architecture, remodeling, decorating, products, project ideas, landscaping and gardening, financial aspects of home ownership, home offices, home-related environmental and ecological topics. Pays varying rates, on acceptance. Query, with summary of 50 to 200 words.

HOME MECHANIX—See *Today's Homeowner.*

HOME POOL & BAR-B-QUE—P.O. Box 272, Cranford, NJ 07016-0272. John R. Hawks, Pub. Articles about pool maintenance, design, safety, products, bar-b-que recipes. Pays $30 to $100, on publication.

HORTICULTURE—98 N. Washington St., Boston, MA 02114. Thomas C. Cooper, Ed. Published 10 times a year. Authoritative, well-written articles, 500 to 2,500 words, on all aspects of gardening. Pays competitive rates, on publication. Query.

HOUSE BEAUTIFUL—1700 Broadway, New York, NY 10019. Jane Margoues, Features Ed. & Travel Ed. Service articles related to the home. Pieces on design, travel, and gardening. Query with detailed outline and photos if relevant. Guidelines.

KITCHEN GARDEN—P.O. Box 5506, Newtown, CT 06470-5506. Editorial. Bimonthly. Nonfiction articles, varying lengths, for home gardeners who "love to grow their own vegetables, fruits, and herbs and use them in cooking." Features include "Plant Profiles," Garden Profiles," Techniques," "Design," "Projects," and "Cooking." Pays $150 per page, half on acceptance, half on publication. Query.

LOG HOME LIVING—P.O. Box 220039, Chantilly, VA 20153. Janice Brewster, Exec. Ed. Articles, 1,000 to 1,500 words, on modern manufactured and handcrafted kit log homes: homeowner profiles, design and decor features. Pays $350 to $550, on acceptance.

THE MAINE ORGANIC FARMER & GARDENER—RR 2, Box 594, Lincolnville, ME 04849. Jean English, Ed. Quarterly. How-to articles and profiles, 100 to 2,500 words, for organic farmers and gardeners, consumers who care about healthful foods, and activists. Tips, 100 to 250 words. "Our readers want good solid information about farming and gardening, nothing soft." Pays about 6¢ a word, on publication. Queries preferred.

METROPOLITAN HOME—1633 Broadway, New York, NY 10019. Michael Lassell, Articles Dir. Service and informational articles for residents of houses, co-ops, lofts, and condominiums, on real estate, equity, wine and spirits, collecting, trends, etc. Interior design and home furnishing articles with emphasis on lifestyle. Payment varies. Query.

MOTHER EARTH NEWS—Sussex Publishers, 49 E. 21st St., 11th Fl., New York, NY 10010. Ed. Bimonthly featuring articles on organic gardening, building projects, holistic health, alternative energy projects, wild foods, and environment and conservation. "We are dedicated to helping our readers become more self-sufficient, financially independent, and environmentally aware." Photos and diagrams a plus. No fiction. Payment varies, on publication.

NATIONAL GARDENING MAGAZINE—180 Flynn Ave., Burlington, VT 05401. Michael MacCaskey, Ed.-in-Chief. News, department, and feature articles, 300 to 2,000 words. The magazine of the National Gardening Association, the largest association of home gardeners in the U.S. Written and edited for all home gardeners, beginning or advanced. Informative, how-to articles on all aspects of home gardening. Most articles are assigned.

OLD-HOUSE INTERIORS—2 Main St., Gloucester, MA 01930. Regina Cole, Sr. Ed. Articles of 300 to 1,500 words, on architecture, decorative arts, and history; should be illustrated in some way as this is an art-driven magazine. Query required. Clips acceptable. Payment is $1 a word, or $200 page minimum, on acceptance.

ROCKY MOUNTAIN GARDENER—P.O. Box 18537, Boulder, CO 80308. Susan Martineau, Pub./Ed.-in-Chief. Quarterly. How-to articles, 500 to 1,000 words, on regional techniques and varieties; profiles of regional gardeners and gardens, 500 to 1,000 words; book reviews and production reviews, 300 to 500 words; regional columns (esp. from Utah, Wyoming, and Montana), 200 to 300 words. "Articles must be focused on Rocky Mountain area from New Mexico to Montana. We prefer new, novel, or specific information, not just general gardening topics." Pays 10¢ a word, on publication.

TODAY'S HOMEOWNER —(formerly *Home Mechanix*) 2 Park Ave., New York, NY 10016. Paul Spring, Ed. Articles on home improvement and home-related topics including money management, home care, home environment, home security, yard care, design and remodeling, tools, repair and maintenance, electronics, new products and appliances, building materials, lighting and electrical, home decor.

WINE SPECTATOR—387 Park Ave. S., New York, NY 10016. Jim Gordon, Man. Ed. Features, 600 to 2,000 words, preferably with photos, on news and people in the wine world, travel, food, and other lifestyle topics. Pays from $400, extra for photos, on publication. Query required.

WINES & VINES—1800 Lincoln Ave., San Rafael, CA 94901. Philip E. Hiaring, Ed. Articles, 2,000 words, on grape and wine industry, emphasizing marketing, management, and production. Pays 15¢ a word, on acceptance.

FAMILY & PARENTING MAGAZINES

ADOPTIVE FAMILIES MAGAZINE—2309 Como Ave., St. Paul, MN 55108. Linda Lynch, Ed. Bimonthly. Articles, 1,500 to 2,500 words, on living in an adoptive family and other adoption issues. Photos of families, adults, or children. Payment is negotiable. Query. Web: www.adoptivefam.org.

AMERICAN BABY—Primedia Consumer Magazines, 249 W. 17th St., New York, NY 10011. Judith Nolte, Ed. Articles, 1,000 to 2,000 words, for new or expectant parents on prenatal and infant care. Personal experience, 900 to 1,200 words, (do not submit in diary format). Department pieces, 50 to 350 words, for "Crib Notes" (news and feature topics). No fiction, fantasy pieces, dreamy musings, or poetry. Pays $800 to $2,000 for articles, $500 for departments, on acceptance. Guidelines.

ATLANTA PARENT—2346 Perimeter Park Dr., Ste. 101, Atlanta, GA 30341. Peggy Middendorf, Ed. Articles, 800 to 2,000 words, on parenting and baby topics. Related humor, 800 to 1,500 words. Photos of parents and/or children. Pays $15 to $30 an article; $15 for photos, on publication.

BABY MAGAZINE—124 E. 40th St., Suite 1101, New York, NY 10016. Jeanne Muchnick, Ed. Bimonthly. Parenting articles, 750 to 1,500 words, geared toward women in the last trimester of pregnancy and the first year of baby's life. "We want how-to and personal articles designed to smooth the transitions from pregnancy to parenthood." Payment varies, on acceptance. Query.

BABY TALK—1325 Avenue of the Americas, New York, NY 10019. Susan Kane, Ed. Articles, 1,000 to 3,000 words, by professionals, on pregnancy, babies, baby care, women's health, child development, work and family, etc. No poetry. Query by mail. Pays varying rates, on acceptance. SASE required.

BAY AREA BABY—See *Bay Area Parent.*

BAY AREA PARENT—401 Alberto Way, Suite A, Los Gatos, CA 95032-5404. Mary Brence Martin, Ed. Articles, 1,200 to 1,400 words, on local parenting issues for readers in California's Santa Clara County and the South Bay area. Query. Mention availability of B&W photos. Pays 6¢ a word, $10 to $15 for photos, on publication. Also publishes *Valley Parent* for central Contra Costa County and the tri-valley area of Alameda County, *Parenting Bay Area Teens, Bay Area Baby, Preschool & Childcare Finder,* and *Education and Enrichment Guide.*

BIG APPLE PARENT—9 E. 38th St., New York, NY 10016. Helen Rosengren Freedman, Man. Ed. Articles, 500 to 750 words, for NYC parents. Pays $35 to $50, on publication. Buys first NYC rights. E-mail: parentspaper@mindspring.com.

CATHOLIC PARENT—Our Sunday Visitor, Inc., 200 Noll Plaza, Huntington, IN 46750. Woodeene Koenig-Bricker, Ed. Features, how-tos, and general-interest articles, 800 to 1,000 words, dealing with the issues of raising children "with solid values in today's changing world. Keep it anecdotal and practical with an emphasis on values and family life." Payment varies, on acceptance. Guidelines.

CENTRAL CALIFORNIA PARENT—2037 W. Bullard, #131, Fresno, CA 93711. Sally Cook, Pub. Articles, 500 to 1,500 words, of interest to parents. Payment varies, on publication.

CHILDSPLAY—280 N. Main St., E. Longmeadow, MA 01028. Editor. "The Parenting Publication for Western Massachusetts." Articles, 1,000 to

1,500 words, for "upwardly mobile, educated parents of children under 12." Payment varies, on publication.

CHRISTIAN HOME & SCHOOL—3350 E. Paris Ave. S.E., Grand Rapids, MI 49512. Gordon L. Bordewyk, Ed. Articles for parents in Canada and the U.S. who send their children to Christian schools and are concerned about the challenges facing Christian families today. Pays $125 to $200, on publication. Send SASE for guidelines or 9"x12" SASE with 4 first-class stamps for guidelines and sample issue.

CHRISTIAN PARENTING TODAY—4050 Lee Vance View, Colorado Springs, CO 80918. Erin Healy, Ed. Articles, 900 to 2,000 words, dealing with raising children with Christian principles. Departments: "Parent Exchange," 25 to 100 words, on problem-solving ideas that have worked for parents; "Life in our House," insightful anecdotes, 25 to 100 words, about humorous things said at home. Queries preferred for articles. Pays 15¢ to 25¢ a word, on publication. Pays $40 for "Parent Exchange," $25 for "Life in our House." Guidelines.

CONNECTICUT FAMILY—See *New York Family.*

DOVETAIL INSTITUTE FOR INTERFAITH FAMILY RE-SOURCES—(formerly *Dovetail Publishing*) 775 Simon Greenwell Lane, Boston, KY 40107. Mary Heléne Rosenbaum, Ed. Articles and essays, 800 to 1,000 words, on topics of interest to interfaith (Jewish/Christian) families. Related cartoons, humor, and photos also used. Payment varies.

EASTSIDE PARENT—Northwest Parent Publishing, 1530 Westlake Ave. N, Suite 600, Seattle, WA 98109. Virginia Smyth, Ed. Articles, 300 to 2,500 words, for parents of children under 14. Readers tend to be professional, two-career families. Queries preferred. Pays $50 to $600, on publication. Also publishes *Pierce County Parent, Portland Parent, Puget Sound Parent* and *Snohomish County Parent.*

EDUCATION AND ENRICHMENT GUIDE—See *Bay Area Parent.*

EXCEPTIONAL PARENT—555 Kinderkamack Rd., Oradell, NJ 07649-1517. Maxwell J. Schleifer, Ed.-in-Chief. Articles, to 1,500 words, for parents and professionals caring for children and young adults with disabilities. Practical ideas and techniques on parenting, technology, research, legislation, and rehabilitation. Query. Pays $50, 60 days after publication.

EXPECTING—See *Parents Expecting.*

FAMILYFUN—Walt Disney Publishing Group, 244 Main St., Northampton, MA 01060. Send queries on articles, to 1,500 words, on family activities to Activities Ed. Payment varies, on acceptance.

FAMILY LIFE—1633 Broadway, 41st Fl., New York, NY 10019. Peter Herbst, Ed.-in-Chief. Published 10 times a year. Articles for parents of children ages 3 to 12. Payment varies (generally $1 a word), on acceptance. Limited market. Query required.

FAMILY TIMES—P.O. Box 932, Eau Claire, WI 54702. Ann Gorton, Ed. Articles, from 800 words, on children and parenting issues: health, education, raising children, how-tos, new studies and programs for educating parents. Pays $35 to $50, on publication. Query preferred. Guidelines.

GROWING CHILD/GROWING PARENT—22 N. Second St., P.O. Box 620, Lafayette, IN 47902-0620. Nancy Kleckner, Ed. Articles, to 1,500 words, on subjects of interest to parents of children under 6. No personal experience pieces or poetry. Guidelines.

JOYFUL TIMES— 60 Vultee Rd., Sedona, AZ 86351. Peggy Jenkins, Ed. Bimonthly internet publication "dedicated to activating and nurturing our inner joy, the energy of love." Articles, 500 to 800 words, that "explore how society and education can more effectively nurture both children and adults to express their fullest potential, thus releasing their inner joy." Web: www. JOY4U.org.

L.A. BABY—See *Wingate Enterprises, Ltd.*

L.A. PARENT—See *Wingate Enterprises, Ltd.*

LANDMARK COMMUNICATIONS, INC.—(formerly *Windmill Publishing, Inc.*) 5700 Thurston Ave., Ste. 133, Virginia Beach, VA 23455. Jennifer O'Donnell, Ed. Parenting Publications of America. Informational articles, 800 to 1,100 words, for regional parenting tabloids, including *Tidewater Parent* and *Peninsula Parent.* Pays $40 to $60, within two weeks of publication.

METROKIDS— 1080 N. Delaware Ave., Suite 702, Philadelphia, PA 19125. Amanda Hathaway, Exec. Ed. Tabloid for Delaware Valley families. Features and department pieces, 500 to 1,000 words, on parenting, regional travel, local kids' programs, nutrition, and product reviews. Pays $25 to $50, on publication.

MOSAICA DIGEST—P.O. Box 340272, Brooklyn, NY 11234-0272. Attn: Submission Dept. Joseph Ginberg, Pres. Fiction, 1,500 to 4,000 words; articles, 1,500 to 3,000 words; fillers, 100 to 300 words, of interest to Jewish families. First-person pieces, humor, travel, and history. Articles of Jewish interest are preferred (not articles about religion or religious issues). "We are a family-oriented magazine, and everything must be squeaky clean! No profanity, etc." Reprints are preferred. Pays to $50, on publication.

MOTHERING—P.O. Box 1690, Santa Fe, NM 87504. Ashisha, Sr. Ed. Bimonthly. Articles, to 2,000 words, on natural family living, covering topics such as pregnancy, birthing, parenting, etc. "We're looking for articles that have a strong point of view and come from the heart." Also poetry, 3 to 20 lines. Pays $200 to $500 and higher, on publication. Query.

NEW YORK FAMILY— 141 Halstead Ave., Suite 3D, Mamaroneck, NY 10543. David Parker, Pub. Betsy F. Woolf, Ed. Articles related to family life in New York City and general parenting topics. Pays $50 to $200. Same requirements for *Westchester Family* and *Connecticut Family.*

PARENTGUIDE NEWS— 419 Park Ave. S., 13th Fl., New York, NY 10016. Jenine M. DeLuca, Ed.-in-Chief. Articles, 1,000 to 1,500 words, related to families and parenting issues: trends, profiles, health, education, travel, fashion, calendar of events, seasonal topics, reader's opinions, special programs, products, etc. Humor and women's section.

PARENTING—See *Wingate Enterprises, Ltd.*

PARENTING— 1325 Avenue of the Americas, New York, NY 10019. Attn: Articles Ed. Articles, 500 to 3,000 words, on education, health, fitness, nutrition, child development, psychology, and social issues for parents of young children. Query.

PARENTING BAY AREA TEENS—See *Bay Area Parent.*

PARENTS— 685 Third Ave., New York, NY 10017. Ann Pleshette Murphy, Ed. Articles, 1,500 to 2,500 words, on parenting, family, women's and community issues, etc. Informal style with quotes from experts. Pays from $1,000, on acceptance. Query.

PARENTS EXPECTING—(formerly *Expecting*) 375 Lexington Ave., New York, NY 10017. Maija Johnson, Ed. Not buying any new material in the foreseeable future.

PARENTS EXPRESS—921 South St., Philadelphia, PA 19147. Sharon Sexton, Ed. Articles on children and family topics for Philadelphia-area parents. Pays $120 to $250 for first rights, $25 to $35 for reprints, on publication.

PARENTS RAISING TEENS AND PRE-TEENS—14682 N. 74th St., Scottsdale, AZ 85260. Sue Kauffman, Pub. Bimonthly. Geared towards parents of teens, especially articles on communicating with teens, choosing battles, and enforcing limits with respect. Prefers articles written by parents, teachers, doctors, and psychologists. Send for guidelines.

PENINSULA PARENT—See *Landmark Communications.*

PIERCE COUNTY PARENT—See *Eastside Parent.*

PORTLAND PARENT—See *Eastside Parent.*

PRESCHOOL & CHILDCARE FINDER—See *Bay Area Parent.*

PUGET SOUND PARENT—See *Eastside Parent.*

REUNIONS MAGAZINE—P.O. Box 11727, Milwaukee, WI 53211-0727. Edith Wagner, Ed. Positive and instructive articles related to reunions (family, class, military reunions, searching, and some genealogy). "The magazine is reunion organizers speaking to reunion organizers. No class reunion catharsis stories." Pays honoraria and copies. www.reunionsmag.com. E-mail: reunions@etecpc.com

SAN DIEGO PARENT—See *Wingate Enterprises, Ltd.*

SCHOLASTIC PARENT & CHILD—555 Broadway, New York, NY 10012-3919. Susan Schneider, Ed. Bimonthly. Articles, 600 to 900 words, on childhood education and development. "We are the learning link between home and school." Payment varies, on acceptance. Query; no unsolicited manuscripts. SASE.

SEATTLE'S CHILD—Northwest Parent Publishing, 1530 Westlake Ave. N., Suite 600, Seattle, WA 98109. Ann Bergman, Ed. Articles, 400 to 2,500 words, of interest to parents, educators, and childcare providers of children under 12, plus investigative reports and consumer tips on issues affecting families in the Puget Sound region. Pays $75 to $600, on publication. Query.

SESAME STREET PARENTS—One Lincoln Plaza, New York, NY 10023. Articles, 800 to 2,500 words. Articles on health to Sandra Lee, Sr. Ed.; articles on family finance to Arleen Love, Assoc. Ed.; articles on education, computer material to Karin DeStefano, Lifestyle Ed. Personal essays and other articles of interest to any editor. "Covers parenting issues for families with young children (to 8 years old)." Pays $1 per word, up to 6 weeks after acceptance. SASE for guidelines.

SNOHOMISH COUNTY PARENT—See *Eastside Parent.*

TIDEWATER PARENT—See *Landmark Communications.*

TOLEDO AREA PARENT NEWS—1120 Adams St., Toledo, OH 43624. Reid Ahlbeck, Ed. Articles on parenting, child and family health, and other family topics, 750 to 1,200 words. Writers must be from Northwest Ohio and Southern Michigan. Pays $75 to $100 per article, on acceptance. Query required.

TWINS—The Magazine for Parent of Multiples, 5350 S. Roslyn St., Suite 400, Englewood, CO 80111. Susan J. Alt, Ed.-in-Chief. Send submissions to Betsy McLinda, Asst. Ed. Features, 1,100 to 1,300 words, third person. Departments, 750 words, first person. "Articles must be multiples specific and focus on every day issues parents of twins, triplets, and more face. Features should have 2 to 3 professional and/or parental experience sources. Payment is $75 to $250, on publication. Query or send complete manuscript.

VALLEY PARENT—See *Bay Area Parent.*

WESTCHESTER FAMILY—See *New York Family.*

WINDMILL PUBLISHING, INC.—See *Landmark Communications, Inc.*

WINGATE ENTERPRISES, LTD.—443 E. Irving Dr., Burbank, CA 91504. Attn: Eds. Publishes city-based parenting magazines with strong "service-to-parent" slant. Articles, 1,000 words, on child development, health, nutrition, and education. *San Diego Parent* covers San Diego area; *Parenting* covers the Orange County, CA, area; *L.A. Parent* is geared toward parents of children to age 10. Pays $100 to $350, on acceptance. Query.

WORKING MOTHER—MacDonald Communications, 135 W. 50th St., New York, NY 10020. Attn: Ed. Dept. Articles, to 2,000 words, that help women juggle job, home, and family. Payment varies, on acceptance.

LIFESTYLE MAGAZINES

ABLE—P.O. Box 395, Old Bethpage, NY 11804-0395. Angela Miele Melledy, Ed. Monthly. "Positively for, by, and about the disabled." Nonfiction to 500 words. Pays $25 on publication. Color and B&W photos.

ACCENT ON LIVING—P.O. Box 700, Bloomington, IL 61702-0700. Betty Garee, Ed. Quarterly. Articles, 800 to 1,000 words, for physically disabled consumers, mostly mobility impaired. Topics include travel, problem solving, and accessibility. "We like articles on devices or how-to information that make tasks easier." Pays 10¢ a word, on publication. Query.

AMERICAN HEALTH—(formerly *American Health for Women.*) Reader's Digest Road, Pleasantville, NY 10570. Attn: Ed. Dept. Lively, authoritative articles, 1,000 to 2,000 words, on women's health, nutrition, mental health, fitness, and a healthy lifestyle. Payment varies, but is made on acceptance. Query with clips.

AQUARIUS: A SIGN OF THE TIMES—1035 Green St., Roswell, GA 30075. Dan Liss, Ed. Articles, 800 words (with photos or illustrations), on New Age lifestyles and positive thought, holistic health, metaphysics, spirituality, environment. No payment. E-mail: aquariusnews@mindspring.com.

AVATAR JOURNAL—237 N. Westmonte Dr., Altamonte Springs, FL 32714. Miken Chappell, Ed. Bimonthly. Articles, 500 words, on self-development, awakening consciousness, and spiritual enlightenment. "Spiritual in nature. Pieces that teach a lesson, paradigm shifts, epiphany experiences, anecdotes with theme of obtaining enlightenment, healing, inspiration, metaphysics." Pays $100 for articles; $50 for poems, on publication.

BACKHOME—P.O. Box 70, Hendersonville, NC 28793. Lorna K. Loveless, Ed. Articles, 800 to 2,500 words, on alternative building methods, renewable energy, organic gardening, livestock, home schooling, home business, healthful cooking. "We hope to provide readers with ways to gain more control over their lives by becoming more self-sufficient: raising their own food, making their own repairs, using alternative energy, etc. We do not promote 'dropping out' of society, but ways to become better citizens and caretakers of the planet." Pays $25 per page; $20 for photos, on publication. Queries preferred.

BUILD MAGAZINE—423 W. 55th St., 8th Fl., New York, NY 10019. Dara Mayers, Ed-in-Chief. Quarterly. Articles and photos geared towards helping "16- to 30-year olds in the political, creative, and organizing realms" change the world. Query; no unsolicited manuscripts. Pays $100 per printed page, 30 days after publication.

CAPPER'S—Editorial Dept., 1503 S.W. 42nd St., Topeka, KS 66609-1265. Ann Crahan, Ed. Human-interest, personal-experience, historical articles, 300 to 700 words. Poetry, to 16 lines, on nature, home, family. Novel-length fiction for serialization. Letters on women's interests, recipes, and hints for "Heart of the Home." Jokes. Children's writing and art section. Pays for poetry, on acceptance; manuscripts, on publication.

THE CHRISTIAN SCIENCE MONITOR—One Norway St., Boston, MA 02115. David Clark Scott, Homefront Ed. Newspaper. Articles on lifestyle trends, women's rights, family, and parenting. Pays varying rates, on acceptance.

COMMON BOUNDARY—7005 Florida St., Chevy Chase, MD 20815. Attn: Manuscript Ed. Bimonthly. Feature articles, 3,000 to 4,000 words, exploring the connections between psychology, spirituality, and creativity. Essays, book reviews, department pieces (1,500 to 1,800 words), and 500-word news items. Readers are mental health professionals, pastoral counselors, spiritual directors, and lay readers.

CURIO—P.O. Box 522, Bronxville, NY 10708-0522. Mickey Z., Ed. Quarterly. Articles, to 3,000 words; essays, to 2,000 words; reviews, to 300 words; interviews, in Q & A format. Features "lively coverage and analysis of arts, politics, health, entertainment, and lifestyle issues. No fiction. Payment varies, on publication.

DIALOGUE: A WORLD OF IDEAS FOR VISUALLY IMPAIRED PEOPLE OF ALL AGES—P.O. Box 5181, Salem, OR 97304-0181. Carol McCarl, Ed. Quarterly. Articles, 800 to 1,200 words, and poetry, to 20 lines, for visually impaired youth and adults. Career opportunities, educational skills, and recreational activities. "We want to give readers an opportunity to learn about interesting and successful people who are visually impaired." Payment varies, on publication. Queries preferred. SASE.

FATE—P.O. Box 64383, St. Paul, MN 55164-0383. Attn: Ed. Factual fillers; journalistic reports on ghosts, UFOs, psychic phenomena, other paranormal topics, to 3,000 words; personal mystical experiences to 500 words. Pays 10¢ a word.

FELLOWSHIP—Box 271, Nyack, NY 10960-0271. Richard Deats, Ed. Bimonthly. Published by the Fellowship of Reconciliation, an interfaith, pacifist organization. Features, 1,500 to 2,000 words, and articles, 750 words, "dealing with nonviolence, opposition to war, and a just and peaceful world community." Photo-essays (B&W photos, include caption information). SASE required. Pays in copies and subscription. Queries preferred.

FILIPINAS MAGAZINE—363 El Camino Real, S. San Francisco, CA 94080. Mona Lisa Yuchengco, Pub. Monthly. "Aims to provide Filipino-Americans with a sense of identity, community, and pride." Cover stories, 1,500 to 2,000 words; profiles, 900 to 2,000 words; reviews and other features, 600 to 1,200 words. Photos welcome. Query with resumé and three writing samples. Pays $50 to $100, on publication.

FRIENDLY EXCHANGE—P.O. Box 2120, Warren, MI 48090-2120. Dan Grantham, Ed. Articles, 700 to 1,500 words, offering readers "news you can use," on lifestyle issues such as home, health, personal finance, and travel. Pays $400 to $1,000. Query required. Guidelines.

GERMAN LIFE—Zeitgeist Publishing, 1068 National Hwy., La Vale, MD 21502. Heidi Whitesell, Ed. Bimonthly. Articles, 500 to 2,500 words, on German culture, its past and present, and how America has been influenced by its German immigrants: history, travel, people, the arts, and social and political issues. Fillers, 50 to 200 words. Pays $300 to $500 for full-length articles, to $80 for short pieces and fillers, on publication. Queries preferred.

GNOSIS—P.O. Box 14217, San Francisco, CA 94114. Richard Smoley, Ed. Articles, to 4,000 words, on esoteric and mystical traditions of the West; 1,000-word news items related to current events in esoteric spirituality; book reviews, 250 to 1,000 words; interviews with spiritual leaders, authors, and scholars. Pays $100 to $250 per article, on publication. Query for current themes.

GOOD TIMES—Robert Morris Bldg., 100 N. 17th St., 9th Fl., Philadelphia, PA 19103. Karen Detwiler, Ed.-in-Chief. Mature lifestyle magazine for people 50 years and older. Articles, 1,200 to 1,500 words, on medical issues, health, travel, finance, gardening, fitness, legal issues, celebrities, lifestyles, and relationships. Guidelines. Payment varies, on publication. Query.

THE GREEN MAN—See *Pan Gaia.*

HEART & SOUL—BET Publications, One BET Plaza, 1900 W. Place N.E., Washington, D.C. 20018. Yanick Rice Lamb, Ed. Dir. Articles, 800 to 1,500 words, on health, beauty, fitness, nutrition, and relationships for African-American women. "We aim to be the African-American woman's ultimate guide to total well-being—body, mind, and spirit." Payment varies, on acceptance. Queries preferred.

HOPE MAGAZINE—Box 160, Brooklin, ME 04616. Kimberly Ridley, Ed. Quarterly. Articles, 150 to 5,000 words, about people making a difference. No nostalgia, sentimental, political, opinion, or religious pieces. Pays 30¢ a word, on publication. Query with clips.

INSIDE MAGAZINE—226 S. 16th St., Philadelphia, PA 19102-3392. Jane Biberman, Ed. Jewish lifestyle magazine. Articles, 1,500 to 3,000 words, on Jewish issues, health, finance, and the arts. Pays $75 to $600 for departments; $600 to $1,200 for features, after publication. Queries required; send clips if available.

INSIDER MAGAZINE—4124 W. Oakton, Skokie, IL 60076. Rita Cook, Ed. Dir. Articles, 750 to 1,500 words, on issues, career, politics, sports, and entertainment. "We are mainly a college publication, but to appeal to college readers you must write above them." Pays 1¢ to 5¢ a word, on publication.

Queries preferred. Western Office: 11168 Acama St., #3, N. Hollywood, CA 91602-3039.

INTERRACE—P.O. Box 17479, Beverly Hills, CA 90209. Candy Mills, Ed. Articles, 800 to 2,500 words, with an interracial, intercultural, or interethnic theme: news, commentary, personal accounts, exposés, historical, interviews, transracial adoption, biracial/multiracial topics, etc. No fiction. "Not limited to black/white issues. Interaction between blacks, whites, Asians, Latinos, Native Americans, etc., is also desired." Pays in subscription and copies.

INTUITION—P.O. Box 460773, San Francisco, CA 94146. Colleen Mauro, Ed. Bimonthy. Articles, 750 to 6,000 words, on intuition, creativity, and spiritual development. Departments, 750 to 2,000 words, include profiles; "Frontier Science," breakthroughs pertaining to parapsychology, creativity, etc.; "Intuitive Tools," history and application of a traditional approach to accessing information. Pays $25 for book reviews to $1,200 for cover articles.

JEWISH CURRENTS—22 E. 17th St., #601, New York, NY 10003. Morris U. Schappes, Ed. Articles and book reviews, 2,400 to 3,000 words, on progressive Jewish culture or history: Holocaust resistance commemoration, Black-Jewish relations, Yiddish literature and culture, Jewish labor struggles. "We are a secular Jewish magazine." No fiction. No payment.

THE JEWISH HOMEMAKER—391 Troy Ave., Brooklyn, NY 11213. Avi Goldstein, Ed. Published 4 times a year. Articles, 1,200 to 2,000 words, for a traditional/Orthodox Jewish audience. Parenting, marriage, humor. Payment varies, on publication. No reprints. Query.

JOURNAL AMERICA—P.O. Box 459, Hewitt, NJ 07421. Glen Malmgren, Ed. Tabloid. Fiction and nonfiction, 200 to 1,000 words, on science and nature or "true but strange stories." Pays in subscription.

LINK: THE COLLEGE MAGAZINE—32 E. 57th St., 12th Fl., New York, NY 10022. Torey Marcus, Ed.-in-Chief. News, lifestyle, and issues for college students. Short features, 300 to 500 words, on college culture. Well-researched, insightful, authoritative articles, 2,000 to 3,000 words, on academics, education news, breaking stories, lifestyle, and trends; also how-to and informational pieces. Pays $100 to $1,500, on publication. Query. Guidelines.

MAGICAL BLEND—133½ Broadway St., Chico, CA 95928-5317. Michael Peter Langevin, Ed. Nonfiction; positive, uplifting articles, to 3,000 words, on spiritual exploration, alternative health, social change, self improvement, stimulating creativity, lifestyles, and interviews.

MEN'S JOURNAL—1290 Ave. of the Americas, New York, NY 10104-0298. Attn: Editorial. Lifestyle magazine for active men ages 25 to 49. Articles and profiles, 2,000 to 7,000 words, on travel, fitness, health, adventure, and participatory sports. Service articles, 400 to 800 words, for equipment and fitness sections. Pays "good rates," on acceptance. Query.

MOMENT MAGAZINE—4710 41st St. N.W., Washington, DC 20016. Attn: Ed. Dept. A conversation on Jewish culture, politics, and religion. "Notes and News/5759": sharp, surprising 250-word pieces on Jewish events, people, and living. "Olam/The Jewish World": well-written, colorful 800 to 1,500 word first-person "letters from" and sophisticated reporting. Book reviews, to 400 words. Query for 1,500 to 3,500 word features. E-mail: editor@momentmag. com. Pays $50 to $1,000.

MOUNTAIN LIVING MAGAZINE—7009 S. Potomac, Englewood,

CO 80112. Irene Rawlings, Ed. Articles, 1,200 to 1,500 words, on topics related to mountains: travel, home design, architecture, gardening, art, cuisine, sports, and people. Pays $50 to $400, on acceptance. E-mail: rawlings@winc.usa.com

NATIVE PEOPLES MAGAZINE—The Arts and Lifeways, 5333 N. 7th St., Suite C-224, Phoenix, AZ 85014-2804. Gary Avey, Publisher. Ben Winton, Ed. Quarterly, full-color on Native Americans. Articles, 1,800 to 2,800 words. Authentic and positive portrayals of present traditional and cultural practices necessary. Pays 25¢ a word, on publication. Query, include availability of photos. Guidelines and sample copy. SASE.

NEW AGE, THE JOURNAL FOR HOLISTIC LIVING—42 Pleasant St., Watertown, MA 02472. Jenny Cook, Ed. Articles for readers who take an active interest in social change, personal growth, health, and contemporary issues. Features, 2,000 to 4,000 words; columns, 750 to 1,500 words; short news items, 150 words; and first-person narratives, 750 to 1,500 words. Pays varying rates, after acceptance.

NEW CHOICES: LIVING EVEN BETTER AFTER 50—Reader's Digest Publications, Reader's Digest Road, Pleasantville, NY 10570. Greg Daugherty, Ed.-in-Chief. Service magazine for people ages 50 to 65. Articles on health, personal finance, travel, etc. Payment varies, on acceptance.

THE NEW YORK TIMES MAGAZINE—229 W. 43rd St., New York, NY 10036. Topical, personal pieces, 900 words, for "Lives." Pays $1,000, on acceptance.

OUT—The Soho Bldg., 110 Greene St., Suite 600, New York, NY 10012. James Collard, Ed.-in-Chief. Articles, 50 to 8,000 words, on various subjects (current affairs, culture, fitness, finance, etc.) of interest to gay and lesbian readers. Payment varies, on publication. Query. Guidelines.

PALM SPRINGS LIFE—Desert Publications, 303 N. Indian Canyon Dr., Palm Springs, CA 92262. Stewart Weiner, Ed. Articles, 1,000 to 3,000 words, of interest to "wealthy, upscale people who live and/or play in the desert." Pays $150 to $500 for features, $25 to $75 for short profiles, on publication. Query required.

PAN GAIA—(formerly *The Green Man*) P.O. Box 641, Point Arena, CA 95468-0641. Diane Conn Darling, Ed. "Exploring the Pagan World." Articles, 1,500 to 3,000 words. Pays 1¢ per word. Query for guidelines.

PLUS: THE MAGAZINE OF POSITIVE THINKING—66 E. Main St., Pawling, NY 12564. Ric Cox, Ed. Published 10 times a year. Practical howto pieces, to 2,300 words, and fillers, varying lengths, with an "emphasis on faith or positive thinking." Payment is made on publication.

PRESENCESENSE—P.O. Box 547, Rancocas, NJ 08073. Attn: Editor. Bimonthly. Articles of varying lengths, on social customs, etiquette, and lifestyle issues. Past issues have included articles on flying the flag, selecting and serving cheese, and analyzing marriage myths. Currently seeking material from free-lance writers, artists, and photographers. SASE for guidelines.

ROBB REPORT—1 Acton Pl., Acton, MA 01720. Steven Castle, Ed. Consumer magazine for the high-end/luxury market. Features on lifestyles, home interiors, boats, travel, investment opportunities, exotic automobiles, business, technology, etc. Payment varies, on publication. Query with SASE and published clips.

SAGEWOMAN—P.O. Box 641, Point Arena, CA 95468-0641. Anne Newkirk Niven, Ed. Quarterly. Articles, 200 to 5,000 words, on issues of concern to pagan and spiritually minded women. Material which expresses an earth-centered spirituality: personal experience, Goddess lore, ritual material, interviews, humor, and reviews. Accepts material by women only. Pays 1¢ a word, from $10, on publication.

SAVEUR—100 Ave. of the Americas, 7th Fl., New York, NY 10013. Colman Andrews, Ed. Rarely assigns restaurant-based pieces, and sections such as "Classic" and "Source" are almost always staff-written. Queries should be detailed and specific, and personal ties to the subject mattter are important. Articles, to 2, 000 words. Pays on acceptance.

SCIENCE OF MIND—P.O. Box 75127, Los Angeles, CA 90075. Elaine Sonne, Ed. Articles, 1,500 to 2,000 words, that offer a thoughtful perspective on how to experience greater self-acceptance, empowerment, and a meaningful life. "Achieving wholeness through applying spiritual principles is the primary focus." Inspiring first-person pieces, 1,000 to 2,000 words. Interviews with notable spiritual leaders, 3,500 words. Poetry, to 28 lines. Pays $25 per page.

T'AI CHI—P.O. Box 26156, Los Angeles, CA 90026. Marvin Smalheiser, Ed. Articles, 1,200 to 4,000 words, on T'ai Chi Ch'uan, other internal martial arts and related topics such as qigong, Chinese medicine and healing practices, Chinese philosophy and culture, health, meditation, fitness, and self-improvement. Pays $75 to $500, on publication. Query required. Guidelines. SASE.

TROIKA—P.O. Box 1006, Weston, CT 06883. Celia Meadow, Ed. Quarterly. Articles, 2,000 to 2,500 words, and columns, 750 to 1,400 words, for arts, health, science, human interest, international interests, business, leisure, ethics, and personal finance. "For educated, affluent baby-boomers, who are seeking to balance their personal achievements, family commitments, and community involvement." Pays $250 to $1,000, on publication. Query.

US AIRWAYS ATTACHÉ—(formerly *USAIR Magazine*) 1301 Carolina St., Greensboro, NC 27401. Articles, 400 to 2,500 words, on "the finer things in life." Paragons department offers short pieces touting the best of the best; Informed Sources deparment contains experts' opinions and knowledge on a variety of topics. No politics or Hollywood issues. Pays $1 a word, on acceptance.

USAIR MAGAZINE—See *US Airways Attaché.*

VENTURE INWARD—215 67th Ave. , Virginia Beach, VA 23451. A. Robert Smith, Ed. Articles, to 4,000 words, on metaphysical and spiritual development subjects. Prefer personal experience. Opinion pieces, to 800 words, for "Guest Column." "Turning Point," to 800 words, on an inspiring personal turning point experience. "The Mystical Way," to 1,500 words, on a personal paranormal experience. "Holistic Health," brief accounts of success using Edgar Cayce remedies. Book reviews, to 500 words. Pays $30 to $300, on publication. Query.

WEIGHT WATCHERS MAGAZINE—2100 Lakeshore Dr., Birmingham, AL 35209. Exec. Ed. Articles on fashion, beauty, food, health, nutrition, fitness, and weight-loss motivation and success. Pays on acceptance. Query with clips required. Guidelines.

WHOLE LIFE TIMES—21225 Pacific Coast Hwy., Suite B, P.O. Box 1187, Malibu, CA 90265. Liz Finch, Assoc. Ed. Tabloid. Feature articles, 2,000 words, with a holistic perspective. Departments and columns, 800 words. Well-researched articles on the environment, current political issues, women's issues, and new developments in health, as well as how-to, humor, new product information, personal growth, and interviews. Pays 5¢ to 10¢ a word for features only, 30 days after publication.

WIRED—520 Third St., San Francisco, CA 94107-1427. Christina Gangei, Ed. Asst. Lifestyle magazine for the "digital generation." Articles, essays, profiles, fiction, and other material that discusses the "meaning and context" of digital technology in today's world. Guidelines. Payment varies, on acceptance.

YES! A JOURNAL OF POSITIVE FUTURES—Box 10818, Bainbridge Island, WA 98110. Tracy Rysavy, Assoc. Ed. Quarterly. Articles, 1,500 to 2,500 words; poetry, 200 to 500 words; photos and drawings. Focus is on "ways people are working to create a more just, sustainable, and compassionate world." Don't simply expose problems; highlight a practical solution. Query. Pays $20 to $50, on publication.

YOGA JOURNAL—2054 University Ave., Berkeley, CA 94704. Kathryn Arnold, Ed. Articles, 1,200 to 4,000 words, on holistic health, spirituality, and yoga. Pays $100 to $3,000, on acceptance.

SPORTS & RECREATION

ADVENTURE CYCLIST—Adventure Cycling Assn., P.O. Box 8308, Missoula, MT 59807. Daniel D'Ambrosio, Ed. Articles, 1,200 to 2,500 words: accounts of bicycle tours in the U.S. and overseas, interviews, personal-experience pieces, humor, and news shorts. Pay is negotiable.

ADVENTURE JOURNAL—(formerly *Adventure West*) 650 S. Orcas St., Suite 103, Seattle, WA 98108. Kristina Schreck, Man. Ed. Bimonthly. Recreational travel articles, 2,500 to 3,500 words, on risky wild adventures; 700 to 1,200 words, on shorter trips that offer a high degree of excitement; and service pieces, 700 to 1,200 words, on short excursions. Profiles and essays also used. Pays 15¢ a word, on publication. Include clips.

ADVENTURE WEST—See *Adventure Journal.*

AKC GAZETTE—51 Madison Ave., New York, NY 10010. Mark Roland, Features Ed. "The official journal for the sport of purebred dogs." Articles, 1,000 to 2,500 words, relating to purebred dogs, for serious fanciers. Pays $200 to $450, on acceptance. Queries preferred.

THE AMERICAN FIELD—542 S. Dearborn, Chicago, IL 60605. B.J. Matthys, Man. Ed. Yarns about hunting trips, bird-shooting; articles to 1,500 words, on dogs and field trials, emphasizing conservation of game resources. Pays varying rates, on acceptance.

AMERICAN HUNTER—NRA Publications, 11250 Waples Mill Rd., Fairfax, VA 22030. John Zent, Ed. Articles, 1,400 to 2,000 words, on hunting. Photos. Pays on acceptance. Guidelines.

AMERICAN MOTORCYCLIST—American Motorcyclist Assn., 33 Collegeview Rd., Westerville, OH 43081-1484. Greg Harrison, Ed. Articles and fiction, to 3,000 words, on motorcycling: news coverage, personalities, tours. Photos. Pays varying rates, on publication. Query with SASE.

THE AMERICAN RIFLEMAN—11250 Waples Mill Rd., Fairfax, VA 22030. Mark Keefe, Man. Ed. Factual articles on use and enjoyment of sporting firearms. Pays on acceptance.

AMERICAN SQUAREDANCE MAGAZINE—P.O. Box 777, North Scituate, RI 02857. Ed & Pat Juaire, Eds. Articles and fiction, 1,000 to 1,500 words, related to square dancing. Poetry. Fillers, to 100 words. Pays $1.50 per column inch.

AMY LOVE'S REAL SPORTS—P.O. Box 8204, San Jose, CA 95155-8204. Jill McManus Bimonthly. Articles, on girls' and women's sports (with a focus on team sports), and emphasizing the drama of competition. Queries preferred. Pay varies, on publication. Web site: www.loves-real-sports.com.

ATLANTIC SALMON JOURNAL—P.O. Box 429, St. Andrews, N.B., Canada E0G 2X0. Jim Gourlay, Ed. Articles, 1,500 to 3,000 words, related to Atlantic salmon: fishing, conservation, ecology, travel, politics, biology, how-tos, anecdotes. Pays $100 to $400, on publication.

BACKPACKER MAGAZINE—Rodale Press, 33 E. Minor St., Emmaus, PA 18098. Thom Hogan, Exec. Ed. Articles, 250 to 3,000 words, on self-propelled backcountry travel: backpacking, kayaking/canoeing, mountaineering; technique, nordic skiing, health, natural science. Photos. Pays varying rates. Query editor Tom Shealey. Website: www.bpbasecamp.com.

THE BACKSTRETCH—P.O. Box 7065, Louisville, KY 40257-0065. Sam Ramor, Manager. United Thoroughbred Trainers of America. Feature articles, with photos, on subjects related to thoroughbred horse racing. Pays after publication. Sample issue and guidelines on request.

BACKWOODSMAN—P.O. Box 627, Westcliffe, CO 81252. Charlie Richie, Ed. Articles for the twentieth-century frontiersman: muzzleloading, primitive weapons, black powder cartridge guns, woodslore, survival, homesteading, trapping, etc. Historical and how-to articles. No payment.

BASEBALL FORECAST, BASEBALL ILLUSTRATED—See *Hockey Illustrated.*

BASKETBALL FORECAST—See *Hockey Illustrated.*

BASSIN'—NatCom, Inc., 5300 CityPlex Tower, 2448 E. 81st St., Tulsa, OK 74137-4207. Mark Chesnut, Exec. Ed. Articles, 1,200 to 1,400 words, on how and where to bass fish, for the amateur fisherman. Pays $350 to $500, on acceptance. Query.

BASSMASTER MAGAZINE—B.A.S.S. Publications, P.O. Box 17900, Montgomery, AL 36141. Dave Precht, Ed. Articles, 1,500 to 2,000 words, with photos, on freshwater black bass and striped bass. "Short Casts" pieces, 400 to 800 words, on news, views, and items of interest. Pays $200 to $500, on acceptance. Query.

BAY & DELTA YACHTSMAN—155 Glendale Ave., #11, Sparks, NV 89431-5751. Don Abbott, Publisher Cruising stories and features, how-tos. Must have northern California tie-in. Photos and illustrations. Pays varying rates.

BC OUTDOORS—300-780 Beatty St., Vancouver, B.C., Canada V6B 2M1. Karl Bruhn, Ed. Articles, to 1,500 words, on fishing, hunting, conservation, and all forms of non-competitive outdoor recreation in British Columbia. Photos. Pays from 20¢ to 27¢ a word, on publication.

BICYCLE GUIDE—See *Bicyclist.*

BICYCLING—135 N. 6th St., Emmaus, PA 18098. Stan Zukowski, Man. Ed. Articles, 500 to 2,500 words, for cyclists, on recreational riding, fitness training, nutrition, bike maintenance, equipment, racing and touring, covering all aspects of the sport: road, mountain biking, leisure, etc. Photos, illustrations. Pays $50 to $2,000, on acceptance. Guidelines.

BICYCLIST—(formerly *Bicycle Guide*) 6420 Wilshire Blvd., Los Angeles, CA 90048-5515. Editor Articles on cycling history, personality profiles, and photos for all-road cycling enthusiasts. Pays varying rates, on publication. Buys all rights. Query with clips.

BIKE RACING NATION—(formerly *Cycling U.S.A.*) One Olympic Plaza, Colorado Springs, CO 80909. B.J. Hoeptner, Man. Ed. Articles, 500 to 1,000 words, on bicycle racing. Payment depends on nature of article and information included. E-mail: media@usacycling.org.

BIRD WATCHER'S DIGEST—P.O. Box 110, Marietta, OH 45750. William H. Thompson, III, Ed. Articles, 600 to 2,500 words, for bird watchers: first-person accounts; how-tos; pieces on backyard-related topics; profiles of bird species. Pays from $100, on publication. Submit complete manuscript. SASE for guidelines.

BLACK BELT—P.O. Box 918, Santa Clarita, CA 91380-9018. Attn: Ed. Articles related to self-defense: how-tos on fitness and technique; historical, travel, philosophical subjects. Pays $100 to $300, on publication. Guidelines.

BOW & ARROW HUNTING—265 S. Anita, Suite 120, Orange, CA 92868. Bob Torres, Ed. Articles, 1,200 to 2,500 words, with color slides, B&W or color photos, on bowhunting; profiles and technical pieces, primarily on deer hunting. Pays $250 to $500, on acceptance. Same address and mechanical requirements for *Gun World.*

BOWHUNTER MAGAZINE—6405 Flank Dr., Harrisburg, PA 17112. M.R. James, Ed.-in-Chief. Dwight Schuh, Ed. Informative, entertaining features, 500 to 2,000 words, on bow-and-arrow hunting. Fillers. Photos. "Study magazine first." Pays $100 to $400, on acceptance.

BOWLING—5301 S. 76th St., Greendale, WI 53129. David Yeghiaian, Ed. Articles, to 1,500 words, on all aspects of bowling, especially human interest. Profiles. "We're looking for unique, unusual stories about bowling people and places, and occasionally publish business articles." Pays varying rates, on publication. Query required.

BUCKMASTERS WHITETAIL MAGAZINE—P.O. Box 244022, Montgomery, AL 36124-4022. Russell Thornberry, Exec. Ed. Semiannual. Articles and fiction, 2,500 words, for serious sportsmen. "Big Buck Adventures" articles capture the details and the adventure of the hunt of a newly discovered trophy. Fresh, new whitetail hunting how-tos; new biological information about whitetail deer that might help hunters; entertaining deer stories; and other department pieces. Photos a plus. Pays $250 to $400 for articles, on acceptance. Guidelines.

BUGLE—Rocky Mountain Elk Foundation, P.O. Box 8249, Missoula, MT 59807-8249. Lee Cromrich, Ed. Asst. Bi-monthly. Fiction and nonfiction, 1,500 to 4,000 words, on elk and elk hunting. Department pieces, 1,000 to 3,000 words, for: "Thoughts and Theories"; "Situation Ethics"; and "Women in the Outdoors." Pays 20¢ a word, on acceptance.

CANOE AND KAYAK MAGAZINE—P.O. Box 3146, Kirkland, WA 98083. Jan Nesset, Ed.-in-Chief. Features, 1,600 to 2,500 words; department pieces, 500 to 1,000 words. Topics include canoeing or kayaking adventures, destinations, boat and equipment reviews, techniques and how-tos, short essays, camping, environment, safety, humor, health, history, etc. Pays 12.5¢ a word, on publication. Query preferred. Guidelines.

CAR AND DRIVER—2002 Hogback Rd., Ann Arbor, MI 48105. Csaba Csere, Ed.-in-Chief. Articles, to 2,500 words, for enthusiasts, on new cars, classic cars, industry topics. "Ninety percent staff-written. Query with clips. No unsolicited manuscripts." Pays to $2,500, on acceptance.

CAR CRAFT—6420 Wilshire Blvd., Los Angeles, CA 90048. David Freiburger, Ed. Articles and photo-features on high performance street machines, drag cars, racing events; technical pieces; action photos. Pays from $150 per page, on publication.

CASCADES EAST—716 N.E. Fourth St., P.O. Box 5784, Bend, OR 97708. Geoff Hill, Ed./Pub. Articles, 1,000 to 2,000 words, on outdoor activities (fishing, hunting, golfing, backpacking, rafting, skiing, snowmobiling, etc.), history, special events, and scenic tours in central Oregon Cascades. Photos. Pays 5¢ to 15¢ a word, extra for photos, on publication.

CHESAPEAKE BAY MAGAZINE—1819 Bay Ridge Ave., Annapolis, MD 21403. Tim Sayles, Ed. Articles, to 2,500 words, on boating, fishing, destinations, people, history, and traditions on the Chesapeake Bay. Photos. Pays $100 to $700, on acceptance. Query.

COAST TO COAST—2575 Vista del Mar Dr., Ventura, CA 93001. Valerie Law, Ed. Membership publication for Coast to Coast Resorts, private camping and resort clubs across North America. Focuses on "travel, recreation, and good times." Destination features focus on a North American city or region, going beyond typical tourist stops to interview locals. Activity or recreation features introduce readers to a sport, hobby, or other diversion. Also features on RV lifestyle. Send queries or manuscripts. Pays $350 to $600, on acceptance, for 1,500- to 2,500-word pieces.

CROSS COUNTRY SKIER—P.O. Box 50120, Minneapolis, MN 55405. Jim Chase, Ed. Published October through February. Articles, to 2,000 words, on all aspects of cross-country skiing. Departments, 1,000 to 1,500 words, on ski maintenance, skiing techniques, health and fitness. Pays $300 to $700 for features, $100 to $350 for departments, on publication. Query.

CYCLE WORLD—1499 Monrovia Ave., Newport Beach, CA 92663. David Edwards, Ed.-in-Chief. Technical and feature articles, 1,500 to 2,500 words, for motorcycle enthusiasts. Photos. Pays on publication. Query.

CYCLING USA—See *Bike Racing Nation.*

DANCE DRILL—1212 Ynez Ave., Redondo Beach, CA 90277. Dr. Kay Crawford, Ed. Quarterly. Articles, fiction, poetry, fillers, and humor related to the pep arts (dance drill, flags, cheerleading, majorettes, or pom pon girls). Payment varies, on publication.

DANCE SPIRIT—250 W. 57th St., Ste. 1701, New York, NY 10107. Julie Davis, Ed. Monthly. Articles on training, instruction and technique, choreography, dance styles, and profiles of dancers, geared toward dancers of all disciplines. Photos accepted. Payment varies, on publication.

THE DIVER—P.O. Box 28, St. Petersburg, FL 33731-0028. Bob Taylor, Ed. Articles on divers, coaches, officials, springboard and platform techniques, training tips, etc. Pays $15 to $50, extra for photos ($5 to $10 for cartoons), on publication.

DIVER MAGAZINE—230-11780 Hammersmith Way, Richmond, B.C., Canada V7A 5E3. Stephanie Bold, Ed. Illustrated articles, 500 to 1,000 words, on dive destinations. Shorter pieces are also welcome. "Travel features should be brief and accompanied by excellent slides and/or prints and a map. Unsolicited articles will be reviewed only from August to October. Pays $2.50 per column inch, on publication. Guidelines. Limited market.

ELYSIAN FIELDS QUARTERLY—2034 Marshall Ave., St. Paul, MN 55104. Tom Goldstein, Ed. Articles, to 4,000 words, and poetry, fiction, essays, interviews, humor, and opinion pieces, all related to baseball. Pays in copies. SASE for guidelines.

EQUUS—Fleet Street Corp., 656 Quince Orchard Rd., Gaithersburg, MD 20878. Laurie Prinz, Ed. Articles, 1,000 to 3,000 words, on all breeds of horses, covering their health, care, the latest advances in equine medicine and research. "Attempt to speak as one horseperson to another." Pays $100 to $400, on publication.

FAMILY MOTOR COACHING—8291 Clough Pike, Cincinnati, OH 45244-2796. Robbin Gould, Ed. Articles, 1,500 to 2,000 words, on technical topics and travel routes and destinations accessible by motorhome. Payment varies, on acceptance. Query preferred.

FIELD & STREAM—2 Park Ave., New York, NY 10016. Duncan Barnes, Ed. Articles, 1,000 to 2,000 words, on hunting, fishing. Short articles, to 1,000 words. Fillers, 75 to 500 words. Cartoons. Pays from $800 for feature articles with photos, $75 to $500 for fillers, $100 for cartoons, on acceptance. Query for articles.

THE FLORIDA HORSE—P.O. Box 2106, Ocala, FL 34478. Dan L. Mearns, Ed. Articles, 1,500 words, on Florida thoroughbred breeding and racing. Also veterinary articles, financial articles, and articles of general interest. Pays $100 to $200, on publication. Query.

FLY FISHERMAN—6405 Flank Dr., Harrisburg, PA 17112. Philip Hanyok, Man. Ed. Query.

FLY ROD & REEL—P.O. Box 370, Camden, ME 04843. James E. Butler, Ed. Fly-fishing pieces, 2,000 to 2,500 words, and occasional fiction; articles on the culture and history of the areas being fished. Pays on acceptance. Query.

FOOTBALL DIGEST—Century Publishing Co., 990 Grove St., Evanston, IL 60201. Jim O'Connor, Ed.-in-Chief. William Wagner, Senior Assoc. Ed. Nonfiction articles, 1,500 to 2,500 words, for the hard-core football fan: profiles of pro and college stars, nostalgia, trends in the sport. Pays on publication. Query.

FOOTBALL FORECAST—See *Hockey Illustrated.*

FUR-FISH-GAME—2878 E. Main St., Columbus, OH 43209. Mitch Cox, Ed. Illustrated articles, 800 to 2,500 words, preferably with how-to angle, on hunting, fishing, trapping, dogs, camping, or other outdoor topics. Some humorous or where-to articles. Pays to $150, on acceptance.

GAME AND FISH PUBLICATIONS—P.O. Box 741, Marietta, GA 30061. Attn: Ed. Dept. Publishes 30 monthly outdoor magazines for 48 states. Articles, 1,500 to 2,500 words, on hunting and fishing. How-tos, where-tos, and adventure pieces. Profiles of successful hunters and fishermen. No hiking, canoeing, camping, or backpacking pieces. Pays $125 to $175 for state-specific articles, $200 to $250 for multi-state articles, before publication. Pays $25 to $75 for interior photos. $250 for covers.

GOLF DIGEST—5520 Park Ave., Trumbull, CT 06611. Jerry Tarde, Ed. Currently not accepting material.

GOLF DIGEST WOMAN—P.O. Box 395, Trumbull, CT 06611-0395. Liz Comte Reisman, Ed. "We want to help our readers play better, have fun, and play with the best stuff available." Interested in previously published authors (in national magazines) who have in-depth knowledge of golf and golf-related subjects. Pays varying rates, on publication.

GOLF FOR WOMEN—125 Park Ave., 15th Fl., New York, NY 10017. Leslie Day, Ed.-in-Chief. Golf lifestyle magazine for avid women golfers. Includes travel, instruction, fashion, equipment, news. Query with clips.

GOLF JOURNAL—Golf House, P.O. Box 708, Far Hills, NJ 07931-0708. Brett Avery, Ed. Official publication of the United States Golf Association. A general-interest magazine on the game with articles on a variety of contemporary and historic topics. Pays varying rates, on publication.

GOLF MAGAZINE—2 Park Ave., New York, NY 10016. Jim Frank, Ed. Articles, 1,000 words with photos, on golf history and travel (places to play around the world); profiles of professional tour players. Shorts, to 500 words. Pays 75¢ a word, on acceptance. Queries preferred.

THE GREYHOUND REVIEW—National Greyhound Assn., Box 543, Abilene, KS 67410. Tim Horan, Man. Ed. Articles, 1,000 to 10,000 words, pertaining to the greyhound racing industry: how-to, historical nostalgia, interviews. Pays $85 to $150, on publication.

GULF COAST GOLFER—See *North Texas Golfer.*

GUN DIGEST—Krause Publications, Inc., 700 E. State St., Iola, WI 54990. Ken Warner, Ed. Well-researched articles, to 5,000 words, on guns and shooting, equipment, etc. Photos. Pays from 10¢ a word, on acceptance. Query.

GUN DOG—P.O. Box 35098, Des Moines, IA 50315. Rick Van Etten, Man. Ed. Features, 1,000 to 2,500 words, with photos, on bird hunting: how-tos, where-tos, dog training, canine medicine, breeding strategy. Fiction. Humor. Pays $150 to $300 for fillers and short articles, $150 to $450 for features, on acceptance.

GUN WORLD—See *Bow & Arrow Hunting.*

GUNGAMES—Box 516, Moreno Valley, CA 92556. Roni Toldanes, Ed. Monthly. Articles and fiction, 1,200 to 1,500 words, about "the fun side of guns and shooting. No self-defense articles." Related poetry, to 300 words. Pays $250 to $350, on publication.

HANG GLIDING—U.S. Hang Gliding Assn., P.O. Box 1330, Colorado Springs, CO 80901-1330. Gilbert Dodgen, Ed. Articles, 2 to 3 pages, on hang gliding. Pays to $50, on publication. Query.

HOCKEY ILLUSTRATED—Lexington Library, Inc., 233 Park Ave. S., New York, NY 10003. Stephen Ciacciarelli, Ed. Articles, 2,500 words, on hockey players and teams. Pays $125, on publication. Query. Same address and requirements for *Baseball Illustrated, Wrestling World, Pro Basketball Illustrated, Pro Football Illustrated, Baseball Forecast, Pro Football Preview, Football Forecast,* and *Basketball Forecast.*

HORSE & RIDER—1597 Cole Blvd., Suite 350, Golden, CO 80401. Kathy Kadash-Swan, Ed. Articles, 500 to 2,000 words, with photos, on western riding and training, and general horse care geared to the performance horse. Pays varying rates, on acceptance. Buys first N.A. serial rights. Guidelines.

HOT BOAT—Sport Publications, 8484 Wilshire Blvd., #900, Beverly Hills, CA 90211. Brett Bayne, Ed. Family-oriented articles, 600 to 1,000 words, on motorized water sport events and personalities: general-interest, how-to, and technical features. Pays $85 to $300, on publication. Query.

INSIDE SPORTS—990 Grove St., Evanston, IL 60201. Kenneth Leiker, Ed. In-depth, insightful nonfiction sports articles, player profiles relating to baseball, football, basketball, hockey, auto racing, and boxing. Payment varies, on publication. Query.

INSIDE TEXAS RUNNING—9514 Bristlebrook Dr., Houston, TX 77083-6193. Joanne Schmidt, Ed. Articles and fillers on running in Texas. Pays $35 to $100 for articles; $10 for short fillers; $10 to $25 for photos, on acceptance.

KITPLANES—8745 Aero Dr., Suite 105, San Diego, CA 92123. Dave Martin, Ed. Articles, 1,000 to 4,000 words, on all aspects of design, construction, and performance of aircraft built from kits and plans by home craftsmen. Pays $70 per page, on publication.

LAKELAND BOATING—500 Davis St., Suite 1000, Evanston, IL 60201-5047. Randall W. Hess, Ed. Articles for powerboat owners on the Great Lakes and other area waterways, on long-distance cruising, short trips, maintenance, equipment, history, regional personalities and events, fishing, and environment. Photos. Pays on publication. Query. Guidelines. Website: www.lakelandboating.com.

MEN'S HEALTH—Rodale Press, 33 E. Minor St., Emmaus, PA 18098. David Zinczenko, Sr. Ed. Articles, 1,000 to 2,500 words, on sports, fitness, diet, health, nutrition, relationships, and travel, for men ages 25 to 55. Pays from 50¢ a word, on acceptance. Query.

MICHIGAN OUT-OF-DOORS—P.O. Box 30235, Lansing, MI 48909. Dennis Knickerbocker, Ed. Features, 1,000 to 1,500 words, on hunting, fishing, camping, hiking, sailing, wildlife, and conservation in Michigan. Pays $90 to $180, on acceptance.

MID-WEST OUTDOORS—111 Shore Dr., Hinsdale, IL 60521-5885. Gene Laulunen, Ed. Articles, 1,000 to 1,500 words, with photos, on where, when, and how to fish and hunt in the Midwest. No Canadian material. Pays $15 to $35, on publication.

MOTOR TREND—6420 Wilshire Blvd., Los Angeles, CA 90048-5515. C. Van Tune, Ed. Articles, 250 to 2,000 words, on autos, racing, events, histories, and profiles. Color photos. Pay varies, on acceptance. Query.

MOTORHOME MAGAZINE—2575 Vista Del Mar, Ventura, CA

93001. Sherry McBride, Man. Ed. Articles, to 1,800 words, with color slides, on motorhome travel, activities, and how-to pieces. Pays to $600, on acceptance.

MOUNTAIN SPORTS & LIVING—(formerly *Snow Country*) 810 Seventh Ave., 4th fl., New York, NY 10019. Attn: Ed. Dept. Published 8 times a year. Features, 2,500 to 3,000 words, and articles, 1,000 words on skiing, mountain biking, camping, rafting and other year-round mountain sports, as well as lifestyle issues. First-person adventure articles, travel pieces, service-oriented articles, profiles of ski-town residents. "Mountain Views," 100- to 400-word pieces on people and points of view, anecdotes, trends, issues. Query with clips and resume. Pays 80¢ a word, on acceptance.

MUSHING—P.O. Box 149, Ester, AK 99725-0149. Todd Hoener, Ed. Dog-driving how-tos, profiles, and features, 1,500 to 2,000 words; and department pieces, 500 to 1,000 words, for competitive and recreational dogsled drivers, weight pullers, dog packers, and skijorers. International audience. Photos. Pays $20 to $175, on publication. Queries preferred. Guidelines and sample issue on request. Web site: www.mushing.com.

MUZZLE BLASTS—P.O. Box 67, Friendship, IN 47021-0067. Terri Trowbridge, Dir. of Pub. Articles, 500 to 1,500 words, on hunting with muzzle-loading rifles, technical aspects of the rifles, historical pieces. Pays $50 to $400, on publication. Send for guidelines.

NATIONAL GEOGRAPHIC ADVENTURE—104 W. 40th St., 17th Fl., New York, NY 10018. John Rasmus, Ed.-in-Chief. Bimonthly. Articles on adventure, travel, and outdoor pursuits; profiles of famous adventurers. Departments, 2,000 to 3,000 words, on adventurous lifestyles and personalities. Features, 4,000 to 8,000 words, are "in-depth, descriptive pieces on celebrities of adventure, gripping accounts of ground-breaking expeditions and scientific exploration, and intriguing, unknown historical tales." Compass section includes a variety of topics, varying lengths, and shows readers how to "bring adventure into their own lives." Query with at least 3 published clips. Send for guidelines. Payment varies.

NEW YORK OUTDOORS—Allsport Publishing Corp., 51 Atlantic Ave., Floral Park, NY 11001. Scott Shane, Ed.-in-Chief. Features, to 1,500 words, with B&W prints or color transparencies, on any aspect of outdoor sports travel or adventure in northeast U.S. Pays to $250 for major features. Queries preferred.

NORTH TEXAS GOLFER—9182 Old Katy Rd., Suite 212, Houston, TX 77055. Bob Gray, Pub. Articles, 800 to 1,500 words, of interest to golfers in north Texas. Fees and guidelines upon request. Queries required. Same requirements for *Gulf Coast Golfer* (for golfers in south Texas).

OFFSHORE—220 Reservoir St., Suite 9, Needham , MA 02494-3133. Betsy Frawley Haggerty, Ed. Articles, 500 to 2,500 words, on boats, people, places, maritime history, and events along the New England, New York, and New Jersey coasts. Writers should be knowledgeable boaters. Photos a plus. Pays $125 to $500.

OPEN WHEEL—65 Parker St., #2, Newburyport, MA 01950. Rus S., Ed. Articles, to 6,000 words, on open wheel drivers, races, and vehicles. Photos. Pays to $400 on publication.

OREGON CYCLING—455 W. 1st Ave., Eugene, OR 97401. Kurt

Kamin, Ed. Ten times yearly. Informative and entertaining articles related to bicycling in the Pacific Northwest. Photos and drawings welcome. No payment for first three articles; pays $20 to $50 for subsequent articles.

OUTDOOR AMERICA—707 Conservation Ln., Gaithersburg, MD 20878-2983. Attn: Ed. Quarterly publication of the Izaak Walton League of America. Articles, 1,500 to 3,000 words, on natural resource conservation issues and outdoor recreation, with emphasis on IWLA member/chapter tie-in; especially fishing, hunting, and camping. Also, short items, 500 to 750 words. Pays 30¢ a word. Query with clips. No unsolicited manuscripts.

OUTDOOR CANADA—340 Ferrier St., Suite 210, Markham, Ont., Canada L3R 2Z5. James Little, Ed. Published 8 times yearly. Articles, 1,500 to 3,000 words, on fishing, camping, hiking, canoeing, and wildlife. Pays $500 and upwards, on acceptance.

OUTSIDE—Outside Plaza, 400 Market St., Santa Fe, NM 87501. No unsolicited material.

PADDLER MAGAZINE—P.O. Box 775450, Steamboat Springs, CO 80477. Eugene Buchanan, Ed. Dir. Articles on canoeing, kayaking, rafting, sea kayaking. "Best way to break in is to target a specific department, i.e. 'Hotlines,' 'Paddle People,' etc." Pays 15¢ to 25¢ a word, on publication. Query preferred. Guidelines.

PENNSYLVANIA ANGLER AND BOATER—Pennsylvania Fish and Boat Commission, P.O. Box 67000, Harrisburg, PA 17106-7000. Attn: Art Michaels, Ed. Articles, 500 to 3,000 words, with photos, on freshwater fishing and boating in Pennsylvania. Pays $50 to $300, on acceptance. Must send SASE with all material. Query. Guidelines.

PENNSYLVANIA GAME NEWS—Game Commission, 2001 Elmerton Ave., Harrisburg, PA 17110-9797. Bob Mitchell, Ed. Articles, to 2,500 words, on hunting, wildlife, and other outdoor subjects, except fishing and boating. Photos. Pays from 6¢ a word, extra for photos, on acceptance.

PETERSEN'S BOWHUNTING—6420 Wilshire Blvd., Los Angeles, CA 90048-5515. Jay Michael Strangis, Ed. How-to articles, 2,000 to 2,500 words, on bowhunting. Also pieces on where to bowhunt, unusual techniques and equipment, and profiles of successful bowhunters will also be considered. Photos must accompany all manuscripts. Pays $300 to $400, on acceptance. Query with SASE.

POWER AND MOTORYACHT—249 W. 17th St., New York, NY 10011. Diane M. Byrne, Sr. Ed. Articles, 1,000 to 2,000 words, for owners of powerboats, 24 feet and larger. Seamanship, ship's systems, maintenance, sportfishing news, travel destinations, profiles of individuals working to improve the marine environment. "For our readers, powerboating is truly a lifestyle, not just a hobby." Pays $500 to $1,000, on acceptance. Query required.

POWERBOAT—1691 Spinnaker Dr., Suite 206, Ventura, CA 93001. Eric Colby, Ed. Articles, to 2,000 words, with photos, for high performance powerboat owners, on outstanding achievements, water-skiing, competitions; technical articles on hull and engine developments; how-to pieces. Pays $300 to $1,000, on publication. Query and writing samples required. No unsolicited manuscripts.

PRACTICAL HORSEMAN—Box 589, Unionville, PA 19375. Mandy

Lorraine, Ed. How-to articles conveying leading experts' advice on English riding, training, and horse care. Pays on acceptance. Query with clips.

PRIVATE PILOT MAGAZINE—265 S. Anita Dr., Suite 120, Orange, CA 92868-3310. Bill Fedorko, Exec. Ed. Fly-in destinations, hands-on, how-to, informative articles, 1,500 to 3,000 words, for general aviation pilots, aircraft owners, and aviation enthusiasts. Quality photos. Pays $400 to $700, on publication. Query.

PRO BASKETBALL ILLUSTRATED, PRO FOOTBALL ILLUSTRATED, PRO FOOTBALL REVIEW—See *Hockey Illustrated*.

RESTORATION—P.O. Box 50046, Dept. TW, Tucson, AZ 85703-1046. W.R. Haessner, Ed. Articles, 1,200 to 1,800 words, on restoration projects in general, as well as restoration of autos, trucks, planes, trains, etc., and related building (bridges and structures). Photos. Pays from $25 per page, on publication. Queries required.

RUNNER TRIATHLETE NEWS—P.O. Box 19909, Houston, TX 77224. Lance Phegley, Ed. Articles on running for road racing and multi-sport enthusiasts (triathlons) in TX, OK, NM, LA, and AR. Payment varies, on publication.

SAFARI—4800 W. Gates Pass Rd., Tucson, AZ 85745. William Quimby, Publications Dir. Merrik Bush-Pirkle, Manuscripts Ed. Articles, 2,000 words, on worldwide big game hunting and/or conservation projects of Safari Club International's local chapters. Pays $200, extra for photos, on publication. E-mail: editorsci@earthlink.net.

SAILING—125 E. Main St., Port Washington, WI 53074. M. L. Hutchins, Ed. Features, 700 to 1,500 words, with photos, on cruising and racing; first-person accounts; profiles of boats and regattas. Query for technical or how-to pieces. Pays varying rates, 30 days after publication. Guidelines.

SALT WATER SPORTSMAN—263 Summer St., Boston, MA 02210. Barry Gibson, Ed. Articles, 1,200 to 1,500 words, on how anglers can improve their skills, and on new places to fish off the coast of the U.S. and Canada, Central America, the Caribbean, and Bermuda. Photos a plus. Pays $350 to $700, on acceptance. Query.

SEA KAYAKER—P.O. Box 17170, Seattle, WA 98107-0870. Christopher Cunningham, Ed. Articles, 1,500 to 4,000 words, on ocean kayaking. Related fiction. Pays 12¢ a word, on publication. Query with clips and SASE.

SILENT SPORTS—717 10th St., P.O. Box 152, Waupaca, WI 54981-9990. Attn: Ed. Articles, 1,000 to 2,000 words, on bicycling, cross country skiing, running, canoeing, hiking, backpacking, and other "silent" sports. Must have regional (upper Midwest) focus. Pays $50 to $100 for features; $20 to $50 for fillers, on publication. Query.

SKI RACING INTERNATIONAL—Box 1125, Rt. 100, Waitsfield, VT 05673. John Hilferty, Consulting Ed. Articles by experts on race techniques and conditioning secrets. Coverage of World Cup, pro, collegiate, and junior ski and snowboard competition. Comprehensive results. Photos. Rates vary.

SKIN DIVER MAGAZINE—6420 Wilshire Blvd., Los Angeles, CA 90048-5515. Bonnie J. Cardone, Ed. Illustrated articles, 500 to 1,000 words, on scuba diving activities, equipment, and dive sites. Pays $50 per published page, on publication.

SKYDIVING MAGAZINE—1725 N. Lexington Ave., DeLand, FL 32724. Sue Clifton, Ed. Timely news articles, 300 to 800 words, relating to sport and military parachuting. Fillers. Photos. Pays $25 to $200, extra for photos, on publication.

SNOW COUNTRY—See *Mountain Sports & Living.*

SNOWEST—520 Park Ave., Idaho Falls, ID 83402. Lane Lindstrom, Ed. Articles, 1,200 words, on snowmobiling in the western states. Pays to $100, on publication.

THE SNOWSHOER—Box 458, Washburn, WI 54891. Jim Radtke, Ed. Fiction and articles on snowshoeing, 1,000 to 1,500 words. Pays 5¢ a word, on publication. Queries preferred.

SOCCER JR.—27 Unquowa Rd., Fairfield, CT 06430. Joe Provey, Ed. Articles, fiction, and fillers related to soccer for readers in 5th and 6th grade. Pays $450 for features; $250 for department pieces, on acceptance. Query.

SOUTH CAROLINA WILDLIFE—P. O. Box 167, Columbia, SC 29202-0167. John E. Davis, Ed. Articles, 1,000 to 2,000 words, with state and regional outdoor focus: conservation, natural history, wildlife, and recreation. Profiles, how-tos. Pays on acceptance. ˙

SPORTS ILLUSTRATED—1271 Ave. of the Americas, New York, NY 10020. Chris Hunt, Articles Ed. Query.

SPORTS ILLUSTRATED FOR KIDS—1271 Ave. of the Americas, New York, NY 10020. Steve Malley, Dept. Man. Ed. Articles, 800 words, (submit to Bob Der) and short features, 500 to 600 words, (submit to Erin Egan) for 8- to 13-year-olds. "Most articles are staff-written. Department pieces are the best bet for free lancers." (Read magazine and guidelines to learn about specific departments.) Puzzles and games (submit to Nick Friedman). No fiction or poetry. Pays $500 for departments, $1,000 to $1,250 for articles, on acceptance. Query required.

STOCK CAR RACING—65 Parker St., #2, Newburyport, MA 01950. Dick Berggren, Feature Ed. Articles, to 6,000 words, on stock car drivers, races, and vehicles. Photos. Pays to $500, on publication.

SURFING—P.O. Box 3010, San Clemente, CA 92674. Jamie Brisick, Exec. Ed. Skip Snead, Ed. Skip Snead, Asst. Ed. Short newsy and humorous articles, 200 to 500 words. No first-person travel articles. "Knowledge of the sport is essential." Pays varying rates, on publication.

SWEAT—736 E. Loyola Dr., Tempe, AZ 85282. Joan Westlake, Ed. Articles, 500 to 1,200 words, on sports or fitness with an Arizona angle. "No personal articles or tales. We want journalism. Articles must relate specifically to Arizona or Arizonans." Pays $25 to $60 for articles; $12 to $70 for photos, on publication. Queries required; no unsolicited manuscripts. E-mail preferred: westwoman@aol.com.

T'AI CHI—P.O. Box 26156, Los Angeles, CA 90026. Marvin Smalheiser, Ed. Articles, 800 to 4,000 words, on T'ai Chi Ch'uan, other internal martial arts and related topics such as qigong, Chinese medicine and healing practices, Chinese philosophy and culture, health, meditation, fitness, and self-improvement. Pays $75 to $500, on publication. Query required. Guidelines.

TENNIS—810 Seventh Ave., 4th fl., Trumbull, CT 10019. Mark Woodruff, Ed. Instructional articles, features, profiles of tennis stars, grassroots articles, humor, 800 to 2,500 words. Photos. Payment varies, on publication. No phone queries

TENNIS WEEK—341 Madison Ave., #600, New York, NY 10017-3705. Eugene L. Scott, Pub. Kim Kodl, Heather Holland, Randy Master, Man. Eds. In-depth, researched articles, from 1,000 words, on current issues and personalities in the game. Pays $125, on publication.

TRAILER BOATS—20700 Belshaw Ave., Carson, CA 90746-3510. Jim Hendricks, Ed.; Ron Eldridge, Man. Ed. Lifestyle, technical and how-to articles, 500 to 2,000 words, on boat, trailer, or tow vehicle maintenance and operation; skiing, fishing, and cruising. Fillers, humor. Pays $100 to $700, on acceptance.

TRIATHLETE—2037 San Elijo, Cardiff, CA 92007. Christina Gandolfo, Man. Ed. Published 12 times yearly. Articles, varying lengths, pertaining to the sport of triathlon. Color slides. Pays 20¢ a word, on publication. Query.

VELONEWS—1830 N. 55th St., Boulder, CO 80301. John Wilcockson, Ed. John Rezell, Sr. Ed. Articles, 500 to 1,500 words, on competitive cycling, training, nutrition; profiles, interviews. No how-to or touring articles. "We focus on the elite of the sport." Pay varies, on publication. E-mail: jrezzell@ 7dogs.com.

THE WATER SKIER—799 Overlook Dr., Winter Haven, FL 33884. Scott Atkinson, Man. Ed. Feature articles on water skiing. Pays varying rates, on publication.

THE WESTERN HORSEMAN—P.O. Box 7980, Colorado Springs, CO 80933-7980. Pat Close, Ed. Articles, about 1,500 words, with photos, on care and training of horses; farm, ranch, and stable management; health care and veterinary medicine. Pays to $800, on acceptance.

WESTERN SPORTSMAN—2002 Quebec Ave., Suite 201, Saskatoon, Sask., Canada S7K 1W4. George Gruenefeld, Ed. Articles, to 2,500 words, on hunting and fishing in British Columbia, Alberta, Saskatchewan, and Manitoba; how-to pieces. Photos. Pays $75 to $300, on publication.

WINDY CITY SPORTS—1450 W. Randolph, Chicago, IL 60607. Jeff Banowetz, Ed. Articles, 1,000 words, on amateur sports in Chicago. Pays $100, on publication. Query required.

WRESTLING WORLD—See *Hockey Illustrated*.

YACHTING—20 E. Elm St., Greenwich, CT 06830. Charles Barthold, Ed. Articles, 1,500 words, on upscale recreational power and sail boating. How-to and personal-experience pieces. Photos. Pays $350 to $1,000, on acceptance. Queries preferred.

AUTOMOTIVE MAGAZINES

CAR AND DRIVER—2002 Hogback Rd., Ann Arbor, MI 48105. Steve Spence, Man. Ed. Articles and profiles, to 2,500 words, on unusual people or manufacturers involved in cars, racing, etc. "Ninety-five percent staff-written. Query with clips. No unsolicited manuscripts." Pays to $2,500, on acceptance.

CAR CRAFT—6420 Wilshire Blvd., Los Angeles, CA 90048. David Freiburger, Ed. Articles and photo-features on high performance street machines, drag cars, racing events; technical pieces; action photos. Pays from $150 per page, on publication.

CYCLE WORLD—1499 Monrovia Ave., Newport Beach, CA 92663. David Edwards, Ed.-in-Chief. Technical and feature articles, 1,500 to 2,500 words, for motorcycle enthusiasts. Photos. Pays $100 to $200 per page, on publication. Query.

MOTOR TREND—6420 Wilshire Blvd., Los Angeles, CA 90048-5515. C. Van Tune, Ed. Articles, 250 to 2,000 words, on autos, auto history, racing, events, and profiles. Photos required. Pay varies, on acceptance. Query.

OPEN WHEEL—See *Stock Car Racing*.

RESTORATION—P.O. Box 50046, Dept. TW, Tucson, AZ 85703-1046. W.R. Haessner, Ed. Articles, 1,200 to 1,800 words, on restoration of autos, trucks, planes, trains, etc., and buildings (bridges, structures, etc.). Photos. Pays from $25 per page, on publication. Queries required.

RIDER—2575 Vista Del Mar Dr., Ventura, CA 93001. Mark Tuttle Jr., Ed. Articles, to 2,000 words, with color slides, on travel, touring, commuting, and camping motorcyclists. Pays $100 to $750, on publication. Query.

ROAD & TRACK—1499 Monrovia Ave., Newport Beach, CA 92663. Ellida Maki, Man. Ed. Short automotive articles, to 450 words, of a "timeless nature" for knowledgeable car enthusiasts. Pays on publication. Query.

ROAD KING—Hammock Publishing, 3322 W. End Ave., Suite 700, Nashville, TN 37203. Tom Berg, Ed. Bill Hudgins, Ed. Dir. Bimonthly. Articles, 300 to 1,500 words, on business of trucking from a driver's point of view; profiles of drivers and their rigs; technical aspects of trucking equipment; trucking history; travel destinations near major interstates; humor; fillers. No fiction. Include clips with submission. Pays negotiable rates, on acceptance.

STOCK CAR RACING—65 Parker St., #2, Newburyport, MA 01950. Dick Berggren, Ed. Features, technical automotive pieces, and profiles of interesting racing personalities, to 6,000 words, for oval track racing enthusiasts. Fillers. Pays $75 to $350, on publication. Same requirements for *Open Wheel*.

FITNESS MAGAZINES

AMERICAN FITNESS—15250 Ventura Blvd., Suite 200, Sherman Oaks, CA 91403. Peg Jordan, R.N., Ed. Articles, 500 to 1,500 words, on exercise, health, research, trends, research, nutrition, alternative paths, etc. Illustrations, photos.

FIT MAGAZINE—1700 Broadway, New York, NY 10019. Lisa Klugman, Ed. Lively, readable service-oriented articles, 800 to 1,200 words, on exercise, nutrition, lifestyle, and health for women ages 18 to 35. Writers should have some background in or knowledge of sports, fitness, and/or health. Also considers 500-word essays for "Finally Fit" column by readers who have lost weight and kept it off. Pays $300 to $500, on publication. Query.

FITNESS—Gruner & Jahr USA Publishing, 375 Lexington Ave., New York, NY 10017-5514. Sarah Mahoney, Ed.-in-Chief. Articles, 500 to 2,000 words, on health, exercise, sports, nutrition, diet, psychological well-being, alternative therapies, sex, and beauty for readers around 30 years old. Queries required. Pays approximately $1 per word, on acceptance.

IDEA HEALTH & FITNESS SOURCE—(formerly *Idea Today*) 6190 Cornerstone Ct. E., Suite 204, San Diego, CA 92121-3773. Ed. Practical articles, 1,000 to 3,000 words, on new exercise programs, business management, nutrition, sports medicine, dance-exercise, and one-to-one training techniques.

Articles must be geared toward the group fitness instructor, exercise studio owner or manager, or personal trainer. No consumer or general health articles. Payment is negotiable, on acceptance. Query preferred.

IDEA PERSONAL TRAINER—6190 Cornerstone Ct. E., Suite 204, San Diego, CA 92121-3773. Ed. Association publication for personal fitness trainers. Articles on exercise science; program design; profiles of successful trainers; business, legal, and marketing topics; tips for networking with other trainers and with allied medical professionals; client counseling; and training tips. "What's New" column includes industry news, products, and research. Query. Payment varies, on acceptance.

IDEA TODAY—See *Idea Health & Fitness Source.*

INSIDE TEXAS RUNNING—9514 Bristlebrook Dr., Houston, TX 77083-6193. Joanne Schmidt, Ed. Articles and fillers on running in Texas. Pays $35 to $100 for articles; $10 to $25 for photos and short fillers, on acceptance.

MEN'S FITNESS—21100 Erwin St., Woodland Hills, CA 91367. Jerry Kindela, Ed.-in-Chief. Features, 1,500 to 1,800 words, and department pieces, 1,200 to 1,500 words, dealing with fitness. Pay varies, 6 weeks after acceptance. Limited market.

MEN'S HEALTH—Rodale Press, 33 E. Minor St., Emmaus, PA 18098. Lou Schuler, Fitness Ed. Articles, 1,000 to 2,500 words, on fitness, diet, health, relationships, sports, and travel, for men ages 25 to 55. Pays from 50¢ a word, on acceptance. Query.

THE PHYSICIAN AND SPORTSMEDICINE—4530 W. 77th St., Minneapolis, MN 55435. Susan Hawthorne, Exec. Ed. News articles. Sports medicine angle necessary. Pays $300 to $500, on acceptance. Query. Guidelines.

SHAPE—21100 Erwin St., Woodland Hills, CA 91367-3772. Peg Moline, Ed. Dir. Articles, 1,200 to 1,500 words, with new and interesting ideas on the physical and mental side of getting and staying in shape; reports, 300 to 400 words, on journal research. Payment varies, on publication. Guidelines. Limited market.

SWEAT—736 E. Loyola Dr., Tempe, AZ 85282. Joan Westlake, Ed. Articles, 500 to 1,200 words, on amateur sports, outdoor activities, wellness, or fitness with an Arizona angle. "No self-indulgent or personal tales. We want investigative pieces. Articles must relate specifically to Arizona or Arizonans." Pays $25 to $60 for articles; $15 to $70 for photos, on publication. Queries required; no unsolicited manuscripts. Web site: Westwoman@aol.com

VEGETARIAN TIMES—4 High Ridge Park, Stamford, CT 06905. Donna Sapolin, Ed. Dir. Articles, 1,200 to 2,500 words, on vegetarian cooking, nutrition, health and fitness, and profiles of prominent vegetarians. "News Items" and "In Print" (book reviews), to 500 words. "Herbalist" pieces, to 1,800 words, on medicinal uses of herbs. Queries required. Pays $75 to $1,000, on acceptance. Guidelines.

VIM & VIGOR—1010 E. Missouri Ave., Phoenix, AZ 85014. Jenn Woolson, Ed. Positive articles, with accurate medical facts, on health and fitness, 1,200 to 2,000 words, by assignment only. Writers may submit qualifications for assignment. Pays $500, on acceptance. Guidelines with SASE.

THE WALKING MAGAZINE—45 Bromfield St., 8th Fl., Boston, MA

02108. Seth Bauer, Ed. Articles, 1,500 to 2,500 words, on fitness, health, equipment, nutrition, travel and adventure, and other walking-related topics. Shorter pieces, 150 to 800 words, and essays for "Ramblings" page. Photos welcome. Pays $750 to $1,800 for features, $100 to $500 for department pieces, within a week of acceptance. Guidelines.

WEIGHT WATCHERS MAGAZINE—2100 Lakeshore Dr., Birmingham, AL 35209. Articles on health, nutrition, fitness, and weight-loss motivation and success. Pays from $1 per word, on acceptance. Query with clips required. Guidelines available.

WOMEN'S SPORTS & FITNESS—342 Madison Ave., New York, NY 10017. Mary Gail Pezzimenti, Man. Ed. Bimonthly. Articles on fitness, nutrition, outdoor sports, and equipment; how-tos; profiles; emerging sports; adventure travel pieces; and controversial issues or reported stories in women's sports, 500 to 2,000 words. Pays on publication.

YOGA JOURNAL—2054 University Ave., Berkeley, CA 94704. Kathryn Arnold, Ed. Articles, 300 to 6,000 words, on holistic health, meditation, conscious living, spirituality, and yoga. Pays $75 to $3,000, on acceptance.

CONSUMER/PERSONAL FINANCE

BLACK ENTERPRISE—130 Fifth Ave., New York, NY 10011. Earl G. Graves, Ed. Articles on money management, careers, political issues, entrepreneurship, high technology, and lifestyles for black professionals. Profiles. Pays on acceptance. Query.

COMPLETE WOMAN—875 N. Michigan Ave., Suite 3434, Chicago, IL 60611. Bonnie Krueger, Ed. Lora Wintz, Sr. Ed. Articles, 1,000 to 2,000 words, with how-to sidebars, giving advice to women. Also interested in reprints. Pays varying rates, on publication. Query with clips.

CONSUMERS DIGEST—8001 N. Lincoln Ave., 6th Fl., Skokie, IL 60077. John Manos, Ed. Articles, 500 to 3,000 words, on subjects of interest to consumers: products and services, automobiles, travel, health, fitness, consumer legal affairs, and personal money management. Photos. Pays 50¢ a word, extra for photos, on acceptance. Query with resumé and clips.

ESSENCE—1500 Broadway, New York, NY 10036. Susan L. Taylor, Ed.-in-Chief. Monique Greenwood, Ed. Articles, 800 to 2,500 words, for black women in America today, on business and finance, as well as health, art, travel, politics, and celebrity profiles, self-help pieces, how-tos. Payment varies, on acceptance. Query.

FAMILY CIRCLE—375 Lexington Ave., New York, NY 10017. Ann Matturo, Jennifer Pirtle, Editor-Writers. Enterprising, creative, and practical articles, 1,000 to 1,500 words, on investing, smart ways to save money, and consumer news on smart shopping. Pays $1 a word, on acceptance. Query with clips.

HOME MECHANIX—See *Today's Homeowner.*

KIPLINGER'S PERSONAL FINANCE MAGAZINE—1729 H St. N.W., Washington, DC 20006. Attn: Ed. Dept. Articles on personal finance (i.e., buying insurance, mutual funds). Pays varying rates, on acceptance. Query required.

KIWANIS—3636 Woodview Trace, Indianapolis, IN 46468. Chuck Jonak, Man. Ed. Articles, 1,200 to 2,500 words, on financial planning for younger families and retirement planning for older people. Pays $400 to $1,000, on acceptance. Query required.

THE MONEYPAPER—1010 Mamaroneck Ave., Mamaroneck, NY 10543. Vita Nelson, Ed. Financial news and money-saving ideas; particularly interested in information about companies with dividend reinvestment plans. Brief, well-researched articles on personal finance, money management, saving, earning, investing, taxes, insurance, and related subjects. Pays $75 for articles, on publication. Query with resumé and writing sample.

NEW CHOICES: LIVING EVEN BETTER AFTER 50—Reader's Digest Publications, Reader's Digest Rd., Pleasantville, NY 10570. Greg Daugherty, Ed.-in-Chief. News and service magazine for people ages 50 and older. Articles on retirement planning, financial strategies, housing options, as well as health and fitness, travel, leisure pursuits, etc. Payment varies, on acceptance.

OUT—The Soho Bldg., 110 Greene St., Suite 600, New York, NY 10012. James Collard, Ed.-in-Chief. Articles, 50 to 8,000 words, on arts, politics, fashion, finance and other subjects for gay and lesbian readers. No fiction or poetry. Guidelines. Query.

ROBB REPORT—1 Acton Pl., Acton, MA 01720. Steven Castle, Ed. Features on investment opportunities for high-end/luxury market. Lifestyle articles, home interiors, boats, travel, exotic automobiles, business, technology, etc. Payment varies, on publication. Query with SASE and clips.

TODAY'S HOMEOWNER—(formerly *Home Mechanix*) 2 Park Ave., New York, NY 10016. Paul Spring, Ed.-in-Chief. Home improvement articles, remodeling, maintenance, home finances. Time- or money-saving tips for the home and yard. Pays from $900 for features. Up to 15% free-lance material.

WOMAN'S DAY—1633 Broadway, New York, NY 10019. Stephanie Abarbanel, Sr. Articles Ed. Articles, 750 to 1,500 words, on financial matters of interest to a broad range of women. Pays to $1 per word, on acceptance. Query with SASE. No unsolicited manuscripts.

YOUR MONEY—8001 N. Lincoln Ave., Skokie, IL 60077. Dennis Fertig, Ed. Informative, jargon-free personal finance articles, to 2,500 words, for the general reader, on investment opportunities and personal finance. Pays 50¢ a word, on acceptance. Query Brook Hessel, Asst. Ed. with clips for assignment. (Do not send manuscripts on disks.)

BUSINESS & TRADE PUBLICATIONS

ACROSS THE BOARD—845 Third Ave., New York, NY 10022. Christy Eidson, Asst. to the Ed. Articles, 1,000 to 4,000 words, on a variety of topics of interest to business executives; straight business angle not required. Payment varies, on publication.

ALTERNATIVE ENERGY RETAILER—P.O. Box 2180, Waterbury, CT 06722. David Johnston, Ed. Feature articles, 1,000 words, for retailers of hearth products, including appliances that burn wood, coal, pellets, and gas, and hearth accessories and services. Interviews with successful retailers, stressing the how-to. B&W photos. Pays $200, extra for photos, on publication. Query.

AMERICAN BANKER—One State Street Plaza, New York, NY 10004. Phil Roosevelt, Ed. Articles, 1,000 to 3,000 words, on banking and financial services, technology in banking, consumer financial services, investment products. Pays varying rates, on publication. Query preferred.

AMERICAN COIN-OP—500 N. Dearborn St., Chicago, IL 60610-9988. Paul Partika, Ed. Articles, to 2,500 words, with photos, on successful coin-operated laundries: management, promotion, decor, maintenance, etc. Pays from 8¢ a word, $8 per B&W photo, 2 weeks prior to publication. Query. Send SASE for guidelines.

AMERICAN DEMOGRAPHICS—P.O. Box 68, Ithaca, NY 14851-9989. Shannon Dortch, Sr. Ed. Articles, 500 to 2,000 words, on the four key elements of a consumer market (its size, its needs and wants, its ability to pay, and how it can be reached), with specific examples of how companies market to consumers. Readers include marketers, advertisers, and strategic planners. Pays $100 to $500, on acceptance. Query.

AMERICAN MEDICAL NEWS—515 N. State St., Chicago, IL 60610. Greg Borzo, Topic Ed. Articles, 900 to 1,500 words, on socioeconomic developments in health care of interest to physicians across the country. Seeks well-researched, innovative pieces about health and science from physician's perspective. Pays $500 to $1,500, on acceptance. Query required. Guidelines.

AMERICAN SCHOOL & UNIVERSITY—P.O. Box 12901, 9800 Metcalf, Overland Park, KS 66212-2216. Joe Agron, Ed. Articles and case studies, 1,200 to 1,500 words, on design, construction, operation, and management of school and university facilities. Queries preferred.

ARCHITECTURE—1515 Broadway, New York, NY 10036. Reed Kroloff, Ed. Articles, to 2,000 words, on architecture, building technology, professional practice. Pays 50¢ a word.

AREA DEVELOPMENT MAGAZINE—400 Post Ave., Westbury, NY 11590. Geraldine Gambale, Ed. Articles for top executives of industrial companies on sites and facility planning. Pays 25¢ a word. Query.

ART BUSINESS NEWS—270 Madison Ave., 6th Fl., New York, NY 10016. Julie Macdonald, Ed. Articles, 1,000 words, for art dealers and framers, on trends and events of national importance to the art and framing industry, and relevant business subjects. Payment varies, on publication. Query preferred.

AUTOMATED BUILDER—1445 Donlon St., Suite 16, Ventura, CA 93003. Don Carlson, Ed. Articles, 500 to 750 words, on various types of home manufacturers and dealers with slides or color prints. Pays $300, on acceptance, for articles with photos. Query required.

BARRON'S—200 Liberty St., New York, NY 10281. Edwin A. Finn, Jr., Ed./Pres. Investment-interest articles. Query Richard Rescigno, Man. Ed.

BARTENDER—P.O. Box 158, Liberty Corner, NJ 07938. Jaclyn W. Foley, Pub./Ed. Quarterly. Articles, 100 to 1,000 words, emphasizing liquor and bartending for bartenders, tavern owners, and owners of restaurants with full-service liquor licenses. Department pieces, 200 to 1,000 words, and related fillers, 25 to 100 words. Pays $50 to $200 for articles, $5 to $25 for fillers, on publication.

BEAUTY EDUCATION—3 Columbia Cir., Albany, NY 12212. Articles, 750 to 1,000 words, that provide beauty educators, trainers, and professionals in the cosmetology industry with information, skills, and techniques on such topics as hairstyling, makeup, aromatherapy, retailing, massage, and beauty careers. Send SASE for editorial calendar and themes. Articles on assignment only. Pays in copies. Query.

BICYCLE RETAILER AND INDUSTRY NEWS—502 W. Cordova Rd., Santa Fe, NM 87501. Michael Gamstetter, Ed. Articles, to 1,200 words, on employee management, employment strategies, and general business subjects for bicycle manufacturers, distributors, and retailers. Pays 20¢ a word (higher rates for more complex articles), plus expenses, within 30 days of publication. Query.

BOATING INDUSTRY—National Trade Publications, 13 Century Hill Dr., Latham, NY 12110-2197. Anne Dantz, Man. Ed. Articles, 1,000 to 2,500 words, on recreational marine products, management, merchandising and selling, for boat dealers and marina owners/operators. Photos. Pays varying rates, on publication. Query.

BOOKPAGE—ProMotion, Inc., 2501 21st Ave. S., Suite 5, Nashville, TN 37212. Katherine H. Wyrick, Ed. Book reviews, 500 words, for a consumer-oriented tabloid used by booksellers and libraries to promote new titles and authors. Query with writing samples and areas of interest; Editor will make assignments for reviews. Pays $20 per review. Guidelines.

BUILDER—Hanley-Wood, Inc., One Thomas Cir. N.W., Suite 600, Washington, DC 20005. Boyce Thompson, Ed. Articles, to 1,500 words, on trends and news in home building: design, marketing, new products, etc. Pays negotiable rates, on acceptance. Query.

BUSINESS AND COMMERCIAL AVIATION—4 International Dr., Rye Brook, NY 10573. Attn: Ed. Articles, 2,500 words, with photos, for pilots, on use of private aircraft for business transportation. Pays $100 to $500, on acceptance. Query.

BUSINESS MARKETING—740 N. Rush St., Chicago, IL 60611. Karen Egolf, Ed. Articles on marketing, advertising, and promoting products and services to business buyers. Pays competitive rates, on acceptance. Queries required.

BUSINESS START-UPS—2392 Morse Ave., Irvine, CA 92614-6234. Karen Axelton, Man. Ed. Monthly. Articles, 1,200 to 1,500 words, targeted at entrepreneurs ages 23 to 35; focus on starting a new business, motivational ideas, and growth strategies. Pays $400 and up, on acceptance. Guidelines. Query.

BUSINESS TIMES—P.O. Box 580, 315 Peck St., New Haven, CT 06513. Joel MacClaren, Ed. Articles on Connecticut-based businesses and corporations. Query.

CALIFORNIA LAWYER—1390 Market St., Suite 1210, San Francisco, CA 94102. Thomas Brom, Sr. Ed. Articles, 2,500 to 3,000 words, for attorneys in California, on legal subjects (or the legal aspects of a given political or social issue); how-tos on improving legal skills and law office technology. Pays $300 to $2,000, on acceptance. Query.

CAMPGROUND MANAGEMENT—P.O. Box 5000, Lake Forest, IL 60045-5000. Mike Byrnes, Ed. Detailed articles, 500 to 2,000 words, on managing recreational vehicle campgrounds. Photos. Pays $50 to $200, after publication.

CHEF—Talcott Communications Corp., 20 N. Wacker Dr., Suite 1865, Chicago, IL 60606. Brent T. Frei, Ed.-in-Chief. "The Food Magazine for Professionals." Articles, 600 to 1,200 words, that offer professionals in the food-service business ideas for food marketing, preparation, and presentation. Pays $100 to $300, on publication.

CHIEF EXECUTIVE—733 Third Ave., 21st Fl., New York, NY 10017. J.P. Donlon, Ed.-in-Chief. CEO bylines. Articles, 2,000 to 2,500 words, on management, financial, or global business issues of direct concern to CEOs only. Departments, 750 words, on investments, corporate finance, technology/ internet, and emerging markets. Pays varying rates, on acceptance. Query required.

CLEANING AND MAINTENANCE MANAGEMENT MAGA-ZINE—13 Century Hill Dr., Latham, NY 12110-2197. Dominic Tom, Man. Ed. Articles, 500 to 1,200 words, on managing efficient cleaning and custodial/ maintenance operations; also technical/mechanical how-tos. Photos encouraged. Pays to $300 for commissioned features, on publication. Query. Guidelines.

CLUB MANAGEMENT—8730 Big Bend Blvd., St. Louis, MO 63114. Tom Finan, Pub. Teri Finan, Ed. The official magazine of the Club Managers Assn. of America. Features, to 2,000 words, and news items, from 100 words, on management, budget, cuisine, personnel, government regulations, etc., for executives who run private clubs. "Writing should be tight and conversational, with liberal use of quotes." Color photos usually required with manuscript. Query preferred. Guidelines.

COLORADO BUSINESS—7009 S. Potomac, Englewood, CO 80112. David Lewis, Ed. Articles, varying lengths, on business, business personalities, and economic trends in Colorado. Preference given to Colorado residents. Pays on acceptance. Query.

COMMERCIAL CARRIER JOURNAL—201 King of Prussia Rd., Radnor, PA 19089. Paul Richards, Exec. Ed. Thoroughly researched articles on private fleets and for-hire trucking operations. Pays from $50, on acceptance. Queries required.

COMPUTER GRAPHICS WORLD—10 Tara Blvd., Suite 500, Nashua, NH 03062-2801. Phil LoPiccolo, Ed. Articles, 1,000 to 3,000 words, on computer graphics technology and its use in science, engineering, architecture, film and broadcast, and interactive entertainment. Computer-generated images. Pays $600 to $1,000 per article, on acceptance. Query.

THE CONSTRUCTION SPECIFIER—Construction Specifications Institute, 601 Madison St., Alexandria, VA 22314. Anne Scott, Ed. Technical articles, 1,000 to 3,000 words, on the "nuts and bolts" of nonresidential construction, for owners/facility managers, architects, engineers, specifiers, contractors, and manufacturers.

CONVENIENCE STORE NEWS—233 Park Ave. S., 6th Fl., New York, NY 10003. John Callanan, Ed.-in-Chief. Features and news items, 750 to 1,200 words, for convenience store owners and operators. Photos, with captions. Pays negotiated price for features; extra for photos, on publication. Query.

CONVERTING MAGAZINE—1350 E. Touhy Ave., P.O. Box 5080, Des Plaines, IL 60017-5080. Mark Spaulding, Ed.-in-Chief. Business articles, 750 to 1,500 words, serving the technical, trends, and productivity information needs of flexible-packaging converting companies, as well as manufacturers of labels, paperboard cartons, and other converted products. Payment varies, on publication. Query required.

COOKING FOR PROFIT—P.O. Box 267, Fond du Lac, WI 54936-0267. Colleen Phalen, Pub./Ed.-in-Chief. Articles, of varying lengths, for foodservice professionals: profiles of successful restaurants, chains, and franchises, schools, hospitals, nursing homes, or other "institutional feeders"; also case studies on successful energy management within the foodservice environment. Business to business articles of interest to foodservice professionals. Payment varies, on publication.

COSTUME! BUSINESS—Festivities Publications, Inc., 815 Haines St., Jacksonville, FL 32206-6025. Sara Summers, Ed. Quarterly. Costume-related articles, 1,200 to 1,500 words, for designers, manufacturers, retailers, and costumers. Queries preferred. Pays 15¢ per word, on publication. Web site: www.festivities-pub.com.

CRAIN'S CHICAGO BUSINESS—740 Rush St., Chicago, IL 60611. David Snyder, Ed. Business articles about the Chicago metropolitan area exclusively.

DAIRY FOODS MAGAZINE—Cahners Publishing Co., 1350 E. Touhy Ave., Des Plaines, IL 60018. Dave Fusaro, Ed. Articles, to 2,500 words, on innovative dairies, dairy processing operations, marketing successes, new products for milk handlers and makers of dairy products. Fillers, 25 to 150 words. Payment varies.

DEALERSCOPE CONSUMER ELECTRONICS MARKETPLACE—North American Publishing Co., 401 N. Broad St., Philadelphia, PA 19108. Janet Pinkerton, Ed. Articles, to 1,000 words, on new consumer electronics, computer and major electronics products, and any associated new technologies, coming to retail. Pays varying rates, on publication. Query with clips and resumé.

DIVIDENDS—Imagination Publishing, 820 W. Jackson, Suite 450, Chicago, IL 60607. Shannon Watts, Ed. Features, 1,500 to 1,800 words, of interest to small business owners and executives; departments, 500 to 600 words. Pays 75¢ a word, on publication. Query.

DRAPERIES & WINDOW COVERINGS—666 Dundee Rd., Suite 807, Northbrook, IL 60062-2769. Katie Sosnowchik, Ed. Articles, 1,000 to 2,000 words, for retailers, wholesalers, designers, and manufacturers of draperies and window, wall, and floor coverings. Profiles, with photos, of successful businesses in the industry; management and marketing related articles. Pays $150 to $250, after acceptance. Query.

EMPLOYEE SERVICES MANAGEMENT—NESRA, 2211 York Rd., Suite 207, Oak Brook, IL 60523. Cynthia M. Helson, Ed. Articles, 1,200 to 2,500 words, for human resource and employee service professionals on work/life issues, employee services, wellness, management and personal development. Pays in copies.

THE ENGRAVERS JOURNAL—26 Summit St., P.O. Box 318, Brighton, MI 48116. Rosemary Farrell, Man. Ed. Articles, of varying lengths, on topics related to the engraving industry or small business. Pays $150 to $300, on acceptance. Query.

ENTREPRENEUR—2392 Morse Ave., Irvine, CA 92614. Rieva Lesonsky, Ed. Dir. Articles for small business owners, on all aspects of running a business. Pay varies, on acceptance. Query required.

EXECUTIVE FEMALE—135 W. 50th St., New York, NY 10020. Kim Calero, President. Articles, 750 to 2,500 words, on managing people, time, money, companies, and careers, for women in business. Pays varying rates, on acceptance. Query.

FANCY FOOD—Talcott Communications Corp., 20 N. Wacker Dr., Suite 1865, Chicago, IL 60606. Carolyn Schwaar, Ed.-in-Chief. "The Business Magazine for Specialty Foods, Confections, and Upscale Housewares." Articles, 2,000 words, related to gourmet food. Pays $250 to $500, on publication.

FARM JOURNAL—1500 Market St., 28th Fl., Philadelphia, PA 19102-2181. Sonja Hillgren, Ed. Practical business articles, 500 to 1,500 words, with photos, on growing crops and raising livestock. Pays 20¢ to 50¢ a word, on acceptance. Query required.

FINANCIAL WORLD—1328 Broadway, New York, NY 10001. Seth E. Hoyt, Pres./Pub., Steven Taub, Ed.-in-Chief. Features and profiles of large companies and financial institutions and the people who run them. Pays varying rates, on publication. Query required.

FIRE CHIEF—35 E. Wacker Dr., Suite 700, Chicago, IL 60601-2198. Scott Baltic, Ed. Monthly. Articles, 1,000 to 5,000 words and department pieces, 1,200 to 1,800 words, for "Training Perspectives," "EMS Viewpoint," and "Sound Off," for fire officers. SASE for guidelines. Pays up to 30¢ per word, on publication.

FISHING TACKLE RETAILER MAGAZINE—P.O. Box 17151, Montgomery, AL 36141-0151. Dave Ellison, Ed. Deborah Johnson, Man. Ed. Articles, 300 to 1,250 words, for merchants who carry angling equipment. Business focus is required, and writers should provide practical information for improving management and merchandising. Pays varying rates, on acceptance.

FITNESS MANAGEMENT—P.O. Box 1198, Solana Beach, CA 92075. Ms. Ronale Tucker, Ed., Edward H. Pitts, Co-Publisher. Authoritative features, 750 to 2,500 words, and news shorts, 100 to 750 words, for owners, managers, and program directors of fitness centers. Content must be in keeping with current medical practice; no fads. Pays 8¢ a word, on publication. Query.

FLORIST—33031 Schoolcraft Rd., Livonia, MI 48105. Sallyann Moore, Man. Ed. Articles, to 1,500 words, on retail florist shop management.

FLOWERS &—11444 W. Olympic Blvd., Los Angeles, CA 90064. Joanne Jaffe, Ed.-in-Chief. Articles, 500 to 1,500 words, with how-to information for retail florists. Pays 50¢ a word, on acceptance. Query with clips.

FOOD MANAGEMENT—1100 Superior Ave., Cleveland, OH 44114. John Lawn, Ed. Articles on food service in hospitals, nursing homes, schools, colleges, prisons, businesses, and industrial sites. Trends, legislative issues, how-to pieces with management tie-in, and retail-oriented food service pieces. Query.

GENERAL AVIATION NEWS & FLYER—P.O. Box 39099, Tacoma, WA 98439-0099. Ben Sclair, Gen. Mgr. Articles, 500 to 2,500 words, of interest to "general aviation" pilots. Pays to $3 per column inch (approximately 40 words); within a month of publication, $10 for B&W photos; to $50 for color photos. Web site: www.flyer-online.com

GLASS DIGEST—18 E. 41st St., New York, NY 10017-6222. Julian Phillips, Ed. Articles, 1,200 to 1,500 words, on building projects and glass/metal dealers, distributors, storefront and glazing contractors. Pays varying rates, on publication.

GOLF COURSE NEWS—106 Lafayette St., Yarmouth, ME 04096. Mike Levans, Ed. Features and news analyses, 500 to 1,000 words, on all aspects of golf course maintenance, design, building, and management. Pays $200, on acceptance.

GOVERNMENT EXECUTIVE—1501 M St. N.W., Washington, DC 20005. Timothy Clark, Ed. Articles, 1,500 to 3,000 words, for civilian and military government workers at the management level.

GREENHOUSE MANAGEMENT & PRODUCTION—P.O. Box 1868, Fort Worth, TX 76101-1868. David Kuack, Ed. How-to articles, innovative production and/or marketing techniques, 500 to 1,800 words, accompanied by color slides, of interest to professional greenhouse growers. Pays $50 to $300, on acceptance. Query required.

GROWERTALKS—P.O. Box 9, 335 N. River St., Batavia, IL 60510-0009. Chris Beytes, Ed. Articles, 800 to 2,600 words, that help commercial greenhouse growers (not florist/retailers or home gardeners) do their jobs better: trends, successes in new types of production, marketing, business management, new crops, and issues facing the industry. Payment varies, on publication. Queries preferred.

HARDWARE TRADE—10617 France Ave. S., #225, Bloomington, MN 55431. Patt Patterson, Ed. Dir. Articles, 800 to 1,000 words, on unusual hardware and home center stores and promotions in the Northwest and Midwest. Photos. Query.

HARVARD BUSINESS REVIEW—Harvard Business School Publishing Corp., 60 Harvard Way, Boston, MA 02163. Request a copy of HBR's guidelines for authors, or query editors, in writing, on new ideas about management of interest to senior executives.

HEALTH FOODS BUSINESS—2 University Plaza, Suite 204, Hackensack, NJ 07601. Gina Geslewitz, Ed. Articles, 1,200 words, with photos, profiling health food stores. Pays on publication. Query. Guidelines.

HEALTH PRODUCTS BUSINESS—Cygnus Publishing, 445 Broad Hollow Rd., Suite 21, Melville, NY 11747. Jill Evans, Man. Ed. Articles, 500 to 1,500 words, on topics related to the health products industry. Photos welcome. Query with SASE preferred. Pays $50 to $200, on publication. E-mail: jill.evans@cygnuspub.com.

HEALTH PROGRESS—4455 Woodson Rd., St. Louis, MO 63134-3797. Judy Cassidy, Ed. Journal of the Catholic Health Assn. Features, 2,000 to 4,000 words, on hospital and nursing home management and administration, medical-moral questions, health care, public policy, technological developments in health care and their effects, nursing, financial and human resource management for health-care administrators, and innovative programs in hospitals and long-term care facilities. Payment negotiable. Query.

HEATING/PIPING/AIR CONDITIONING—1100 Superior Ave., Cleveland, OH 44114. Michael G. Ivanovich, Ed. Articles, to 3,500 words, on heating, piping, and air conditioning systems and related issues, such as indoor air quality and energy efficiency in Industrial plants and large buildings only;

engineering information. Pays $70 per printed page, on publication. Query. Web site: www.hpac.com.

HOSPITALS & HEALTH NETWORKS—One N. Franklin St., 29th Fl., Chicago, IL 60606. Kevin Lumsdon, Man. Ed. Articles, 300 to 2,200 words, for health care executives. Query.

HUMAN RESOURCE EXECUTIVE—LRP Publications Co., 747 Dresher Rd., Horsham, PA 19044-0980. David Shadovitz, Ed. Profiles and case stories, 1,800 to 2,200 words, of interest to people in the human resource profession. Pays varying rates, on acceptance. Queries required.

INCOME OPPORTUNITIES—1500 Broadway, Suite 600, New York, NY 10036-4015. Linda Molnar, Ed.-in-Chief. Articles on marketing, financing, and managing a small or home-based business, especially on a tight budget. Profiles of entrepreneurs who started their businesses on a shoestring. Pays varying rates, on acceptance. Query; no unsolicited manuscripts.

INDEPENDENT BUSINESS—125 Auburn Ct., Suite 100, Thousand Oaks, CA 91362. Maryann Hammers, Man. Ed. How-to articles, 1,200 to 2,000 words, of practical interest and value on all aspects of running a small business. Pays $550 to $1,500, on acceptance. Also, short fun profiles, about 400 words, on offbeat businesses; pays $50 to $100. Query. Guidelines available with SASE.

INDEPENDENT LIVING PROVIDER—See *Today's Home Healthcare Provider.*

INDUSTRY WEEK—1100 Superior Ave., Cleveland, OH 44114-2543. John R. Brandt, Ed.-in-Chief. Biweekly. Articles, varying lengths, on business and management. Departments include "Executive Briefing," "Emerging Technologies," "Finance," "Economic Trends," and "Executive Life." Payment varies, on acceptance. Query.

INSTANT & SMALL COMMERCIAL PRINTER—P.O. Box 7280, Libertyville, IL 60048. Anne Marie Mohan, Ed. Articles, 3 to 6 typed pages, for operators and employees of printing businesses specializing in retail printing and/or small commercial printing: case histories, how-tos, technical pieces, small-business management. Pays $150 to $250, extra for photos, on publication. Query.

INTERNATIONAL BUSINESS—9 E. 40th St., 10th Fl., New York, NY 10016. Linda Lynton, Ed.-in-Chief. Articles, 1,000 to 1,500 words, on global marketing strategies. Short pieces, 500 words, with tips on operating abroad. Profiles, 750 to 3,000 words, on individuals or companies. Pays 30¢ a word, on acceptance and on publication. Query with clips.

JEMS, JOURNAL OF EMERGENCY MEDICAL SERVICES—P.O. Box 2789, Carlsbad, CA 92018. A.J. Heightman, Ed.-in-Chief. Articles, 1,500 to 3,000 words, of interest to emergency medical providers (EMTs, paramedics, nurses, and physicians) who work in the EMS industry worldwide.

LLAMAS—P.O. Box 250, Jackson, CA 95642. Cheryl Dal Porto, Ed. "The International Camelid Journal," published 5 times yearly. Articles, 300 to 3,000 words, of interest to llama and alpaca owners. Pays $25 to $300, extra for photos, on publication. Query.

MACHINE DESIGN—Penton Publishing Co., 1100 Superior Ave., Cleveland, OH 44114. Ronald Khol, Ed. Articles, to 10 typed pages, on mechanical and electromechanical design topics for engineers. Pays varying rates, on publication. Submit outline or brief description.

MAINTENANCE TECHNOLOGY—1300 S. Grove Ave., Barrington, IL 60010. Robert C. Baldwin, Ed. Technical articles with how-to information on increasing the reliability and maintainability of electrical and mechanical systems and equipment. Readers are managers, supervisors, and engineers in all industries and facilities. Payment varies, on acceptance. Query.

MANAGE—2210 Arbor Blvd., Dayton, OH 45439. Doug Shaw, Ed. Articles, 800 to 1,000 words, on management and supervision for first-line and middle managers. "Please indicate word count on manuscript and enclose SASE." Pays 5¢ a word.

MARKETING NEWS—American Marketing Assn., 250 S. Wacker Dr., Chicago, IL 60606-5819. Lisa M. Keefe, Ed. Biweekly. Articles, 700 to 1,000 words, on every aspect of marketing, including advertising, sales promotion, direct marketing, telecommunications, consumer and business-to-business marketing, and market research. Pays $500 to $1,000, on publication. Query with appropriate clips.

MODERN HEALTHCARE—740 N. Rush St., Chicago, IL 60611. Clark Bell, Ed. News weekly covers management, finance, building design and construction, and new technology for hospitals, health maintenance organizations, nursing homes, and other health care institutions. Pays $200 to $400, on publication. Query; very limited free-lance market.

MODERN TIRE DEALER—P.O. Box 3599, Akron, OH 44309-3599. Lloyd Stoyer, Ed. Tire retailing and automotive service articles, 1,000 to 1,500 words, with photos, on independent tire dealers and retreaders. Pays $400 to $450, on publication. Query; articles by assignment only.

MUTUAL FUNDS—2200 S.W. 10th St., Deerfield Beach, FL 33442. Norman G. Fosback, Ed.-in-Chief. "Writers experienced in covering mutual funds for the print media should send resumé and clips." Pays to $1 a word, on acceptance.

NATIONAL FISHERMAN—121 Free St., P.O. Box 7438, Portland, ME 04112. Sam Smith, Ed. Articles, 200 to 2,000 words, aimed at commercial fishermen and boat builders. Pays $4 to $6 per inch, extra for photos, on publication. Query preferred.

NATION'S BUSINESS—1615 H St. N.W., Washington, DC 20062-2000. Articles on small-business topics, including management advice and success stories. Pays negotiable rates, on acceptance. Guidelines.

NEPHROLOGY NEWS & ISSUES—15150 N. Hayden Rd., Suite 101, Scottsdale, AZ 85260. Mark Neumann, Ed. News articles, human-interest features, and opinion essays on dialysis, kidney transplantation, and kidney disease.

THE NETWORK JOURNAL—139 Fulton St., Suite 407, New York, NY 10038. Jacqueline Mitchell, Man. Ed. Monthly newspaper. Articles, 800 to 1,500 words, on small business, personal finance, and career management of interest to African American small business owners and professionals. Profiles of entrepreneurs; how-to pieces; articles on sales and marketing, managing a small business and personal finance. Pays $50 to $100, on acceptance.

NEW CAREER WAYS NEWSLETTER—67 Melrose Ave., Haverhill,

MA 01830. William J. Bond, Ed. How-to articles, 1,500 to 2,000 words, on new skills used to move ahead at work in the 1990s, and new opporunities for today's home-based businesses. Pays varying rates, on publication. Query with outline and SASE. Same address and requirements for *Workskills Newsletter.*

THE NORTHERN LOGGER AND TIMBER PROCESSOR— Northeastern Logger's Assn., Inc., P.O. Box 69, Old Forge, NY 13420. Eric A. Johnson, Ed. Features, 1,000 to 2,000 words, of interest to the forest product industry. Photos. Pays 15¢ a word, on publication. Query preferred.

NSGA RETAIL FOCUS—National Sporting Goods Assoc., 1699 Wall St., Suite 700, Mt. Prospect, IL 60056. Larry Weindruch, Ed. Members magazine. Articles, 1,000 to 1,500 words, on sporting goods industry news and trends, the latest in new product information, and management and store operations. Payment varies, on publication. Query.

ONCE UPON A TIME—553 Winston Ct., St. Paul, MN 55118. Audrey B. Baird, Ed. "A 32-page magazine for Children's Writers and Illustrators." Quarterly. Articles, to 800 words: questions, insights, how-to articles, tips and experiences (no fiction) on the writing and illustrating life by published and unpublished writers. Also, short articles, 100 to 400 words. B&W artwork. No payment.

OPPORTUNITY MAGAZINE—18 E. 41st St., New York, NY 10017. Daniel Joelson, Ed. How-to articles for people who work at home, small business owners, and people interested in franchising and distributorships. Success stories. Payment varies, on publication. Query.

OPTOMETRIC ECONOMICS—See *Practice Strategies.*

PARTY & PAPER RETAILER—70 New Canaan Ave., Norwalk, CT 06850. Trisha McMahon Drain, Ed. Articles, 1,000 to 1,500 words, that offer employee, management, and retail marketing advice to the party or stationery store owner: display ideas, success stories; advertising, promotion, financial, and legal advice. "Articles grounded in facts and anecdotes are appreciated." Pay varies, on publication. Query with published clips.

PET BUSINESS—7-L Dundas Cir., Greensboro, NC 27407. Rita Davis, Ed. Brief, documented articles on animals and products found in pet stores; research findings; legislative/regulatory actions; business and marketing tips and trends. Pays 10¢ per word, on publication; pays $20 for photos.

PET PRODUCT NEWS—P.O. Box 6050, Mission Viejo, CA 92690. Mary K. McHale, Ed. Articles, 1,000 to 1,200 words, with photos, on pet shops, and pet and product merchandising. No fiction or news clippings. Pays $150 to $350, extra for photos. Query.

P.O.B.—Business News Publishing Co., 755 W. Big Beaver Rd., Suite 1000, Troy, MI 48084. Beth Wierzbinski, Ed. Technical and business articles, 1,000 to 4,000 words, for professionals and technicians in the surveying and mapping fields. Technical tips on field and office procedures and equipment maintenance. Pays $150 to $500, on acceptance.

POLICE MAGAZINE—6300 Yarrow Dr., Carlsbad, CA 92009-1597. Randall Resch, Ed. Articles and profiles, 1,000 to 3,000 words, on specialized groups, equipment, issues, and trends of interest to people in the law enforcement profession. Pays $100 to $400, on acceptance.

PRACTICE STRATEGIES—(formerly *Optometric Economics*) American Optometric Assn., 243 N. Lindbergh Blvd., St. Louis, MO 63141-7881. Gene Mitchell, Sr. Ed. Articles, 1,000 to 3,000 words, on private practice management for optometrists; direct, conversational style with how-to advice on how optometrists can build, improve, better manage, and enjoy their practices. Short humor and photos. Payment varies, on acceptance. Query.

PUBLIC RELATIONS QUARTERLY—P.O. Box 311, Rhinebeck, NY 12572. Paul Swift, Man. Ed. Articles, 1,500 to 3,500 words, on public relations, public affairs, communications, and writing. No payment. Queries preferred.

PUBLISH—Integrated Media, Inc., 501 Second St., San Francisco, CA 94107. Mard Naman, Man. Ed. Features, 1,500 to 2,000 words, and reviews, 400 to 800 words, on all aspects of computerized publishing. Pays $400 to $600 for reviews, $850 to $1,200 for full-length features, on acceptance.

PUBLISHERS WEEKLY—245 W. 17th St., New York, NY 10011. Daisy Maryles, Exec. Ed. Articles, 900 words, on a current issue or problem facing publishing and bookselling for "My Say" column. Articles for "Booksellers' Forum" may be somewhat longer. Payment varies.

QUICK PRINTING—Cygnus Publishing Inc., 445 Broad Hollow Rd., Melville, NY 11747. Gerald Walsh, Ed. Articles, 1,500 to 2,500 words, of interest to owners and operators of quick print shops, copy shops, and small commercial printers, on how to make their businesses more profitable; include photography/figures. Also, articles on using computers and peripherals in graphic arts applications. Pays from $150, on publication.

REMODELING—Hanley-Wood, Inc., One Thomas Cir. N.W., Suite 600, Washington, DC 20005. Paul Deffenbaugh, Ed. Articles, 250 to 1,700 words, on remodeling and industry news for residential and light commercial remodelers. Pays on acceptance. Query.

RESTAURANTS USA—1200 17th St. N.W., Washington, DC 20036-3097. Jennifer Batty, Ed. Publication of the National Restaurant Assn. Articles, 1,000 to 2,500 words, on the foodservice and restaurant business. Restaurant experience preferred. Pays $350 to $800, on acceptance. Query.

THE ROTARIAN—1560 Sherman Ave., Evanston, IL 60201-3698. Willmon L. White, Ed.-in-Chief. Charles W. Pratt, Ed. Cary Silver, Man. Ed. Articles, 1,200 to 2,000 words, on international social and economic issues, business and management, environment, science and technology, sports, and some humor, including cartoons. "No political or religious subjects." Pays good rates, on acceptance. Query.

THE RUSSIAN—8621 Wilshire Blvd., Suite 700, Beverly Hills, CA 90211. Martha Little, Ed. Articles, 1,000 to 2,000 words, on business ventures in Russia involving Western firms, Russian economic and political analysis, and business development in the U.S. pertaining to Russia. Also photographs, color slides, and drawings. Pays $150 to $500, up to 30 days after publication. Queries preferred.

RV BUSINESS—2575 Vista Del Mar Dr., Ventura, CA 93001. Sherman Goldenberg, Assoc. Pub. Articles, to 1,500 words, on RV industry news and product-related features. Articles on legislative matters affecting the industry. General business features rarely used. Pays varying rates.

SAFETY MANAGEMENT— 24 Rope Ferry Rd., Waterford, CT 06386. Jane Winkler, Ed. Interview-based articles, 1,500 words, for safety professionals, on improving workplace safety and health. Pays to 20¢ a word, on acceptance. Query.

SIGN BUILDER ILLUSTRATED— 4905 Pine Cone Dr., #2, Durham, NC 27707-5258. Bruce Amaro, Ed. Bimonthly. How-to articles and editorials, 1,500 to 2,500 words, on the sign industry. Pays $300 to $500, on acceptance.

SMALL PRESS REVIEW—Dustbooks, P.O. Box 100, Paradise, CA 95967. Len Fulton, Ed./Pub. Reviews, 200 words, of small literary books and magazines; tracks the publishing of small publishers and small-circulation magazines. Query.

SOFTWARE MAGAZINE—One Research Dr., Westborough, MA 01581. Patrick Porter, Ed. Technical features, to 1,800 words, for computer-literate MIS audience, on how various software products are used. Pays about $1,000 to $1,200, on publication. Query required. Calendar of scheduled editorial features available.

SOUTHERN LUMBERMAN—P.O. Box 681629, Franklin, TN 37068-1629. Nanci P. Gregg, Man. Ed. Articles on sawmill operations, interviews with industry leaders, how-to technical pieces with an emphasis on increasing sawmill production and efficiency and new installations. Pays $100 to $250 for articles with B&W photos. Queries preferred.

SOUVENIRS, GIFTS, AND NOVELTIES MAGAZINE—(formerly *Souvenirs and Novelties*) 7000 Terminal Sq., Suite 210, Upper Darby, PA 19082. Attn: Ed. Articles, 1,500 words, on retailing and merchandising collectible souvenir items for managers at zoos, museums, hotels, airports, and souvenir stores. Pays 12¢ a word, on publication.

STOCKBROKER MAGAZINE— 1655 E. Semoran Blvd., Suite 22, Apopka, FL 32703. Craig C. Rowe, Man. Ed. Quarterly. Informative, educational articles, 750 to 1,000 words, for stock brokers and investors. Pays in copies. Query.

STONE WORLD— 299 Market St., Suite 320, Saddle Brook, NJ 07663. Michael Reis, Ed. Articles, 750 to 1,500 words, on new trends in installing and designing with stone. For architects, interior designers, design professionals, and stone fabricators and dealers. Pays $6 per column inch, on publication. Query.

SUCCESSFUL FARMING— 1716 Locust St., Des Moines, IA 50309-3023. Gene Johnston, Man. Ed. Articles, to 2,000 words, for farming families, on all areas of business farming: money management, marketing, machinery, soils and crops, livestock, and buildings; profiles. Pays from $300, on acceptance. Query required.

TABLEWARE TODAY— 368 Essex Ave., Bloomfield, NJ 07003. Amy Stavis, Ed. Case histories and interviews, 1,500 to 2,500 words, with photos, on merchandising of tableware. Pays $100, per page, on publication. Query.

TANNING TRENDS— 3101 Page Ave., Jackson, MI 49203-2254. Joseph Levy, Ed. Articles on small businesses and skin care for tanning salon owners. Scientific pro-tanning articles and "smart tanning" pieces. Query for profiles. "Our aim is to boost salon owners to the 'next level' of small business ownership. Focus is on business principles with special emphasis on public relations and marketing." Payment varies, on publication.

TEA & COFFEE TRADE JOURNAL—130 W. 42nd St., Suite 1050, New York, NY 10036. Jane P. McCabe, Ed. Articles, 3 to 5 pages, on trade issues of importance to the tea and coffee industry. Pays 20¢ per word, on publication. Query.

TEXTILE WORLD—6151 Powers Ferry Rd., Atlanta, GA 30339. Mac Isaacs, Ed. Articles, 500 to 2,000 words, with photos, on manufacturing and finishing textiles. Pays varying rates, on acceptance.

TODAY'S $85,000 FREELANCE WRITER—P.O. Box 543, Oradell, NJ 07649. Brian Konradt, Ed. Bimonthly. Articles, to 1,000 words, on operating a profitable freelance commercial copywriting business and writing for down-sized corporations, large and small businesses, ad agencies, and other commercial markets. No fiction. Pays 10¢ a word, on acceptance. Guidelines. SASE.

TODAY'S HOME HEALTHCARE PROVIDER—(formerly *Independent Living Provider*) 26 Main St., Chatham, NJ 07928-2402. Nancy DelPizzo, Ed. Articles, from 1,200 words, on the home healthcare market. "We're looking for good writers." Payment varies, on publication. Send query or resumé.

TODAY'S SURGICAL NURSE—Slack, Inc., 6900 Grove Rd., Thorofare, NJ 08086. Frances R. DeStefano, Man. Ed. Clinical or general articles, from 2,000 words, of direct interest to operating room nurses.

TOURIST ATTRACTIONS AND PARKS—7000 Terminal Sq., Suite 210, Upper Darby, PA 19082. Articles, 1,500 words, on successful management of parks, entertainment centers, zoos, museums, arcades, fairs, arenas, and leisure attractions. Pays 12¢ a word, on publication. Query.

TRAILER/BODY BUILDERS—P.O. Box 66010, Houston, TX 77266. Paul Schenck, Ed. Articles on engineering, sales, and management ideas for truck body and truck trailer manufacturers. Pays from $100 per printed page, on acceptance.

TRAINING MAGAZINE—50 S. Ninth St., Minneapolis, MN 55402. Jack Gordon, Ed. Articles, 1,000 to 2,500 words, for managers of training and development activities in corporations, government, etc. Pays varying rates, on acceptance. Query.

TREASURY & RISK MANAGEMENT—111 W. 57th St., New York, NY 10019. Anthony Baldo, Ed. Nine issues per year. Articles, 200 to 3,000 words, on treasury management for corporate treasurers, CFOs, and vice presidents of finance. Pays 50¢ to $1 a word, on acceptance. Query. Seeks freelancers.

UNIQUE OPPORTUNITIES—455 S. 4th Ave., #1236, Louisville, KY 40202. Bett Coffman, Assoc. Ed. Articles, 2,000 to 3,000 words, that cover the economic, business, and career-related issues of interest to physicians who are interested in relocating or entering new practices. "Our goal is to educate physicians about how to evaluate career opportunities, negotiate the benefits offered, plan career moves, and provide information on the legal and economic aspects of accepting a position." Pays from 50¢ a word for features, on acceptance. Query.

WHO CARES: THE TOOL KIT FOR SOCIAL CHANGE—(formerly *Who Cares: The Magazine for People Who Do.*) 1436 U St., NW, Suite 201, Washington, DC 20009. Samantha Stainburn, Ed. Bimonthly. Business magazine for "people who do good works." Features, 1,500 to 3,500 words, on nonprofit management and innovative approaches to social change.

"Tool Box" pieces, 700 to 1,200 words, strategies for saving the world in a more efficient and effective way; "Civil Society" pieces, 700 to 1,200 words, on what's happening in government, corporations, communities, religious institutions, and schools. Send for guidelines and free sample. Payment varies, on publication.

WINES & VINES—1800 Lincoln Ave., San Rafael, CA 94901. Philip E. Hiaring, Ed. Articles, 2,000 words, on grape and wine industry, emphasizing marketing, management, vinyard techniques, and production. Pays 15¢ a word, on acceptance.

WOODSHOP NEWS—35 Pratt St., Essex, CT 06426-1185. Thomas Clark, Ed. Features, one to 3 typed pages, for and about people who work with wood: business stories, profiles, news. Pays from $40 to $250 minimum, on publication. Queries preferred.

WORKING WOMAN—230 Park Ave., New York, NY 10169. Articles, 350 to 2,500 words, on business and personal aspects of working women's lives. Pays from $300, on acceptance.

WORLD OIL—Gulf Publishing Co., P.O. Box 2608, Houston, TX 77252-2608. Robert E. Snyder, Ed. Engineering and operations articles, 3,000 to 4,000 words, on petroleum industry exploration, drilling, or production. Photos. Pays from $50 per printed page, on acceptance. Query.

WORLD WASTES—6151 Powers Ferry Rd. N.W., Atlanta, GA 30339. Bill Wolpin, Ed./Pub. Case studies, market analysis, and how-to articles, 1,000 to 2,000 words, with photos of refuse haulers, recyclers, landfill operators, resource recovery operations, and transfer stations, with solutions to problems in the field. Pays from $125 per printed page, on publication. Query preferred.

IN-HOUSE/ASSOCIATION MAGAZINES

Publications circulated to company employees (sometimes called house magazines or house organs) and to members of associations and organizations are excellent, well-paying markets for writers at all levels of experience. Large corporations publish these magazines to promote good will, familiarize readers with the company's services and products, and advise them about the issues and events concerning a particular cause or industry.

AARP BULLETIN—601 E St. N.W., Washington, DC 20049. Elliot Carlson, Ed. Publication of the American Assn. of Retired Persons. Payment varies, on acceptance. Query required.

THE AMERICAN GARDENER—7931 E. Boulevard Dr., Alexandria, VA 22308-1300. David J. Ellis, Ed. Bimonthly publication of the American Horticultural Society. Articles, to 2,500 words, for American ornamental gardeners: profiles of prominent horticulturists, plant research and plant hunting, events and personalities in horticulture history, plant lore and literature, the politics of horticulture, etc. Humorous pieces for "Offshoots." Pays $100 to $500, on publication. Query preferred.

CALIFORNIA HIGHWAY PATROLMAN—2030 V St., Sacramento, CA 95818-1730. Carol Perri, Ed. Articles on the CHP, its personnel, programs, history and mission, or any true-life police-related story that is exciting, action-packed, of great human interest or humorous. Photos a plus. Buys one-time rights; pays 2 1/2¢ a word, $5 for B&W photos, on publication. Guidelines and/or sample copy with 9x12 SASE.

CATHOLIC FORESTER—355 Shuman Blvd., P.O. Box 3012, Naperville, IL 60566-7012. Dorothy Deer, Ed. Official publication of the Catholic Order of Foresters, a fraternal life insurance organization for Catholics. General-interest articles and fiction, to 1,500 words, that deal with contemporary issues; no moralizing, explicit sex, or violence. Short, inspirational articles, to 500 words. "Need health and wellness, parenting, and financial articles." Pays 20¢ a word, on acceptance.

CATHOLIC LIBRARY WORLD—The Catholic Library Assn., 291 Springfield St., Chicopee, MA 01013-2839. Mary E. Gallagher, SSJ, Ed. Co-Chair. Articles for school librarians, academic librarians, and institutional archivists. No payment. Queries preferred.

COAST TO COAST—2575 Vista del Mar Dr., Ventura, CA 93001. Valerie Law, Ed. Membership publication for Coast to Coast Resorts, private camping and resort clubs across North America. Focus is on "travel, recreation, and good times." Destination features focus on a North American city or region, going beyond typical tourist stops to interview locals. Activity or recreation features introduce readers to a sport, hobby, or other diversion. Also features on RV lifestyle. Send queries or manuscripts. Payment is $350 to $600, on acceptance, for 1,500- to 2,500-word articles.

COLUMBIA—1 Columbus Plaza, New Haven, CT 06507-0901. Tim S. Hickey, Ed. Journal of the Knights of Columbus. Articles, 1,200 words, for Catholic families. No fiction. Pays up to $600 for articles, on acceptance.

THE COMPASS—365 Washington Ave., Brooklyn, NY 11238. J.A. Randall, Ed. True stories (no first-person accounts), to 2,000 words, on the sea, and sea trades. Pays $1,000, on acceptance. Query with SASE.

THE ELKS MAGAZINE—425 W. Diversey Pkwy., Chicago, IL 60614. Janell Neal, Ed. Asst. Articles, 1,500 to 2,500 words, on technology, sports, history, and topics of current interest; for non-urban audience. Pays 20¢ a word, on acceptance. No queries.

FIREHOUSE—Cygnus Publishing Co., 445 Broad Hollow Rd., Melville, NY 11747. Harvey Eisner, Ed.-in-Chief. Articles, 500 to 2,000 words: on-the-scene accounts of fires, trends in firefighting equipment, controversial fire-service issues, and lifestyles of firefighters. Query. SASE.

THE FURROW—John Deere-North American Agricultural Marketing Center, 11145 Thompson Ave., Lenexa, KS 66219. Karl Kessler, North American Ed. Specialized, illustrated articles on farming. Pays to $1,200, on acceptance.

FUTURIFIC INC.—Foundation for Optimism, 305 Madison Ave., #10B, New York, NY 10165. Charlotte Kellar, Ed. Forecasts of what will be. "Only optimistic material will get published. Solutions, not problems. We track all developments giving evidence to our increasing life expectancy, improving international coexistence, the global tendency toward peace, and improving economic trends. We also report on all new developments, economic, political, social, scientific, technical, medical or other that are making life easier, better and more enjoyable for the greatest number of people." Pays in copies. Queries preferred.

HARVARD MAGAZINE—7 Ware St., Cambridge, MA 02138-4037.

John Rosenberg, Ed. Articles, 500 to 5,000 words, with a connection to Harvard University. Pays from $100, on publication. Query required.

IDEA PERSONAL TRAINER—6190 Cornerstone Ct. E., Suite 204, San Diego, CA 92121-3773. Ed. For personal fitness trainers assn. Articles on exercise science; program design; profiles of successful trainers; business, legal, and marketing topics; tips for networking with other trainers and with allied medical professionals; client counseling; and training tips. "What's New" column includes industry news, products, and research. Payment varies, on acceptance. Query.

KIWANIS—3636 Woodview Trace, Indianapolis, IN 46268. Chuck Jonak, Man. Ed. Articles, 2,500 words (with 250- to 350-word sidebars), on lifestyle, relationships, world view, children's issues and concerns, education, trends, small business, religion, health, etc. No travel pieces, interviews, profiles. Pays $400 to $1,000, on acceptance. Query.

THE LION—300 22nd St., Oak Brook, IL 60523. Robert Kleinfelder, Sr. Ed. Official publication of Lions Clubs International. Articles, 800 to 2,000 words, and photo-essays, on club activities. Pays from $100 to $700, on acceptance. Query.

NEW HOLLAND NEWS—New Holland, N.A., Inc., P.O. Box 1895, New Holland, PA 17557. Attn: Ed. Articles, to 1,500 words, with strong color photo support, on agriculture and rural living. Pays on acceptance. Query.

THE NEW PHYSICIAN—American Medical Student Association, 1902 Association Dr., Reston, VA 20191. Amy Myers-Payne, Ed. Nine issues a year. Articles, 1,200 to 3,500 words, on social, ethical, and political issues for medical students. Query for departments. Pay is negotiable.

OPTIMIST MAGAZINE—4494 Lindell Blvd., St. Louis, MO 63108. Dena Hull, Man. Ed. Articles, to 1,000 words, on activities of local Optimist Clubs, and techniques for personal and club success. Pays from $100, on acceptance. Query.

RESTAURANTS USA—1200 17th St. N.W., Washington, DC 20036-3097. Jennifer Batty, Ed. Publication of the National Restaurant Assn. Articles, 1,000 to 2,500 words, on the foodservice and restaurant business. Restaurant experience preferred. Pays $350 to $800, on acceptance. No phone queries.

THE RETIRED OFFICER MAGAZINE—201 N. Washington St., Alexandria, VA 22314. Address the Manuscripts Ed. Articles, 1,800 to 2,000 words, of interest to military retirees and their families. Current military/national affairs, recent military history, health/medicine, and second-career opportunities. No fillers. Photos a plus. Pays to $1,300, on acceptance. Query. Guidelines.

THE ROTARIAN—1560 Sherman Ave., Evanston, IL 60201-3698. Willmon L. White, Ed.-in-Chief. Charles W. Pratt, Ed. Cary Silver, Man. Ed. Publication of Rotary International, world service organization of business and professional men and women. Articles, 1,200 to 2,000 words, on international social and economic issues, business and management, human relationships, travel, sports, environment, science and technology; humor. Pays good rates, on acceptance. Query.

THE SCHOOL ADMINISTRATOR—American Assn. of School Administrators, 1801 N. Moore St., Arlington, VA 22209-1813. Jay P. Goldman, Ed. Articles related to school administration (K through 12). "We seek articles about school system practices, policies, and programs that have widespread appeal." Pays in copies. Guidelines.

VFW MAGAZINE—406 W. 34th St., Kansas City, MO 64111. Richard K. Kolb, Ed. Articles, 1,000 words, related to current foreign policy and defense, American armed forces abroad, and international events affecting U.S. national security. Also, up-to-date articles on veteran concerns and issues affecting veterans. Pays to $500, on acceptance. Query. Guidelines.

RELIGIOUS MAGAZINES

AMERICA—106 W. 56th St., New York, NY 10019-3893. Thomas J. Reese, S.J., Ed. Articles, 1,000 to 2,500 words, on current affairs, family life, literary trends.

AMERICAN BIBLE SOCIETY RECORD—1865 Broadway, New York, NY 10023. David Singer, Man. Ed. Material related to work of American Bible Society: translating, publishing, distributing. All articles staff-written; accepts no free-lance material.

AMERICAN JEWISH HISTORY—American Jewish Historical Society, 2 Thornton Rd., Waltham, MA 02154. Dr. Marc Lee Raphael, Ed. Academic articles, 15 to 30 typed pages, on the settlement, history, and life of Jews in North and South America. Queries preferred. No payment.

AMIT MAGAZINE—817 Broadway, New York, NY 10003-4761. Rita Schwalb, Ed; Micheline Ratzersdorfer, Exec. Ed. Patricia Israel, Man. Ed. Articles, 1,000 to 2,000 words, of interest to Jewish women: Middle East, Israel, history, holidays, travel, culture, food.

ANGLICAN JOURNAL—600 Jarvis St., Toronto, Ont., Canada M4Y 2J6. Rev. David Harris, Ed. National newspaper of the Anglican Church of Canada. Articles, to 1,000 words, on news and features of the Anglican Church across the country and around the world, including social and ethical issues and human-interest subjects in a religious context. Pays 23¢ per published word, on publication. Query required.

THE BANNER—2850 Kalamazoo Ave. S.E., Grand Rapids, MI 49560. John D. Suk, Ed. Malcolm McBryde, Assoc. Ed. Fiction, to 2,500 words, nonfiction, to 1,800 words, and poetry, to 50 lines, for members of the Christian Reformed Church in North America. "The magazine's purpose is to inform, challenge, educate, comfort, and inspire members of the church." Also some church-related cartoons. Pays $125 to $200 for articles, $40 for poetry, on acceptance. Query preferred.

BAPTIST LEADER—American Baptist Churches-USA, P.O. Box 851, Valley Forge, PA 19482-0851. I. Dvirnak, Man.Ed. Practical how-to or thought-provoking articles, 1,200 to 2,000 words, for local church lay leaders, pastors, and Christian education staff.

BIBLE ADVOCATE—P.O. Box 33677, Denver, CO 80233. Calvin Burrell, Ed. Articles, 1,000 to 1,800 words, and fillers, 100 to 400 words, on Bible passages and Christian living; also teaching articles. Some poetry, 5 to 20 lines, on religious themes. Opinion pieces, to 650 words. "Be familiar with the doctrinal beliefs of the Church of God (Seventh Day). For example, they don't celebrate a traditional Easter or Christmas." Pays $15 to $35 for articles, $10 for poetry, on publication. Send for guidelines and theme list.

BREAD FOR GOD'S CHILDREN—P.O. Box 1017, Arcadia, FL 34265-1017. Judith M. Gibbs, Ed. Fiction (to 1,800 words for older children, to 800 words for younger) and articles (to 800 words) that apply the word of God to every situation. "We are an interdenominational teaching magazine for Christian families." Pays $20 for articles; to $50 for fiction, on publication. Guidelines.

BRIGADE LEADER—Box 150, Wheaton, IL 60189. Deborah Christensen, Man. Ed. Inspirational articles, 750 words, for Christian men who lead boys in Christian Service Brigade programs. "Most articles are written on assignment by experts; very few free lancers used. Query with clips and we'll contact you if we need you for an assignment. You must understand the Brigade program and be able to address issues Brigade leaders face." Pays $60 to $150.

CATECHIST—330 Progress Rd., Dayton, OH 45449. Patricia Fischer, Ed. Informational and how-to articles, 1,200 to 1,500 words, for Catholic teachers, coordinators, and administrators in religious education programs. Pays $25 to $100, on publication.

CATHOLIC DIGEST—2115 Summit Avenue, St. Paul, MN 55105-1081. Attn: Articles Ed. Articles, 1,000 to 3,500 words, on Catholic and general subjects. Fillers, to 300 words, on instances of kindness rewarded, for "Hearts Are Trumps"; accounts of good deeds, for "People Are Like That." Pays from $200 for original articles, $100 for reprints, on acceptance; $4 to $50 for fillers, on publication. Guidelines.

CATHOLIC FAITH & FAMILY—(formerly *Catholic Twin Circle*) 33 Rossotto Dr., Hamden, CT 06514. Loretta G. Seyer, Ed. Features, how-tos, and interviews, 1,000 to 2,000 words, of interest to Catholic families; include photos. Opinion or inspirational columns, 600 to 800 words. Strict attention to Catholic doctrine required. Enclose SASE. Pays $75 to $300 for articles, $75 for columns, on publication.

CATHOLIC NEAR EAST MAGAZINE—1011 First Ave., New York, NY 10022-4195. Michael La Civita, Exec. Ed. Bimonthly publication of CNEWA, a papal agency for humanitarian and pastoral support. Articles, 1,500 to 2,000 words, on people of the Middle East, northeast Africa, India, and eastern Europe: their faith, heritage, culture, and present state of affairs. Special interest in Eastern Christian churches. Color photos for all articles. Pays 20¢ per edited word. Query.

CATHOLIC PARENT—Our Sunday Visitor, Inc., 200 Noll Plaza, Huntington, IN 46750. Woodeene Koenig-Bricker, Ed. Features, how-tos, and general-interest articles, 800 to 1,000 words, for Catholic parents. "Keep it anecdotal and practical with an emphasis on values and family life. Don't preach." Payment varies, on acceptance.

CATHOLIC TWIN CIRCLE—See *Catholic Faith & Family.*

THE CHRISTIAN CENTURY—407 S. Dearborn St., Chicago, IL 60605. James M. Wall, Ed. Ecumenical. Articles, 1,500 to 3,000 words, with a religious angle, on political and social issues, international affairs, culture, the arts. Poetry, to 20 lines. Photos. Pays about $50 per printed page, extra for photos, on publication.

CHRISTIAN EDUCATION COUNSELOR—1445 Boonville Ave., Springfield, MO 65802-1894. Sylvia Lee, Ed. Articles, 600 to 800 words, on teaching and administrating Christian education in the local church, for local

Sunday school and Christian school personnel. Pays 5¢ to 10¢ a word, on acceptance.

CHRISTIAN EDUCATION JOURNAL—Trinity Evangelical Divinity School, 2065 Half Day Rd., Deerfield, IL 60015. Dr. Perry G. Downs, Ed. Articles, 10 to 25 typed pages, on Christian education topics.

CHRISTIAN HOME & SCHOOL—3350 E. Paris Ave. S.E., Grand Rapids, MI 49512. Gordon L. Bordewyk, Ed. Articles for parents in Canada and the U.S. who send their children to Christian schools and are concerned about the challenges facing Christian families today. Pays $125 to $200, on publication. Send SASE for guidelines.

CHRISTIAN PARENTING TODAY—4050 Lee Vance View, Colorado Springs, CO 80918. Erin Healy, Ed. Articles, 900 to 2,000 words, dealing with raising children with Christian principles. Departments: "Train Them Up," 600 to 700 words, on child development (spiritual, moral, character building); "Healthy & Safe," 300- to 400-word how-to pieces on keeping children emotional and physically safe, home and away; "The Lighter Side," humorous essays on family life, 600 to 700 words; "Parent Exchange," 25 to 100 words on problem-solving ideas that have worked for parents; "Life in Our House," insightful anecdotes, 25 to 100 words, about humorous things said at home. (Submissions for "Parent Exchange" and "Life in our House" are not acknowledged or returned.) Pays 15¢ to 25¢ a word, on publication. Pays $25 to $125 for department pieces. Guidelines; send SASE.

CHRISTIAN SOCIAL ACTION—100 Maryland Ave. N.E., Washington, DC 20002. Erik Alsgaard, Ed. Articles, 1,500 to 2,000 words, on social justice issues for people of faith. Pays $75 to $125, on publication.

CHRISTIANITY TODAY—465 Gundersen Dr., Carol Stream, IL 60188. Michael G. Maudlin, Man. Ed. Doctrinal social issues and interpretive essays, 1,500 to 3,000 words, from evangelical Protestant perspective. No fiction or poetry. Pays $200 to $500, on acceptance. Query.

CHURCH & STATE—1816 Jefferson Pl. N.W., Washington, DC 20036. Joseph L. Conn, Ed. Articles, 600 to 2,600 words, on issues of religious liberty and church-state relations, promoting the concept of church-state separation. Pays varying rates, on acceptance. Query.

CHURCH EDUCATOR—Educational Ministries, Inc., 165 Plaza Dr., Prescott, AZ 86303. Robert G. Davidson, Ed. How-to articles, to 1,750 words, on Christian education: activity projects, crafts, learning centers, games, bulletin boards, etc., for all church school, junior and high school programs, and adult study group ideas. Allow 3 months for response. Pays 3¢ a word, on publication.

THE CHURCH MUSICIAN—See *Church Musician Today.*

CHURCH MUSICIAN TODAY—(formerly *The Church Musician*) 127 Ninth Ave. N., Nashville, TN 37234. Jere Adams, Ed. Articles on choral techniques, instrumental groups, worship planning, music administration, directing choirs (all ages), rehearsal planning, music equipment, new technology, drama/ pageants and related subjects, hymn studies, book reviews, and music-related fillers. Pays 5½¢ a word, on acceptance.

CLUBHOUSE JR.—8605 Explorer Dr., Colorado Springs, CO 80920. Jesse Florea, Ed. Articles on Christian values aimed at children ages 4 to 8. Nonfiction, to 500 words, on real people, science, and nature; fiction, from 250 to 1,000 words; Bible stories, 250 to 800 words; rebus stories, to 200 words; poetry, to 250 words; and one-page puzzles. Pays $75 to $200 for all material except poetry, rebus stories, and puzzles. SASE for guidelines.

COLUMBIA—1 Columbus Plaza, New Haven, CT 06507-0901. Tim S. Hickey, Ed. Knights of Columbus. Articles, 1,500 words, for Catholic families. No fiction. Pays up to $600 for articles, on acceptance.

COMMENTARY—165 E. 56th St., New York, NY 10022. Neal Kozodoy, Ed. Articles, 5,000 to 7,000 words, on contemporary issues, Jewish affairs, social sciences, religious thought, culture. Serious fiction; book reviews. Pays on publication.

COMMONWEAL—475 Riverside Dr., New York, NY 10115. Margaret O'Brien Steinfels, Ed. Catholic. Articles, to 3,000 words, on political, religious, social, and literary subjects. Pays 3¢ a word, on acceptance.

THE COVENANT COMPANION—5101 N. Francisco Ave., Chicago, IL 60625. Jane K. Swanson-Nystrom, Ed. Articles, 800 to 1,800 words, with Christian implications published for members and attenders of Evangelical Covenant Church "seeking to inform, stimulate thought, and encourage dialogue on issues that impact the church and its members." Pays $35 to $75, on publication.

CRUSADER—P.O. Box 7259, Grand Rapids, MI 49510. G. Richard Broene, Ed. Fiction, 900 to 1,500 words, and articles, 400 to 1,000 words, for boys ages 9 to 14 that show how God is at work in their lives and in the world around them. Also, short fillers. Pays 4¢ to 6¢ a word, on acceptance.

DAILY MEDITATION—Box 2710, San Antonio, TX 78299. Emilia Devno, Ed. Inspirational, self-improvement, nonsectarian religious articles "showing the way to greater spiritual growth," 300 to 1,650 words. Fillers, to 350 words; verse, to 20 lines. Pays 1½¢ to 2¢ a word for prose; 14¢ a line for verse, on acceptance. SASE required.

DECISION—Billy Graham Evangelistic Assn., 1300 Harmon Pl., P.O. Box 779, Minneapolis, MN 55440-0779. Kersten Beckstrom, Interim Ed. Christian testimonies and teaching articles on evangelism and Christian nurturing, 800 to 1,200 words. Vignettes, 400 to 500 words. Pays varying rates, on publication.

DISCIPLESHIP JOURNAL—Box 35004, Colorado Springs, CO 80935. Susan Nikaido, Ed. Bimonthly. Nonfiction, from 1,500 to 2,500 words. Topics include: teaching on a Scripture passage, Teaching on a topic, and how-tos. Focus is on helping believers develop a deeper relationship with Jesus Christ. Book reviews, news articles, or articles about Christian organizations. Send SASE for themes. Pays 20¢ a word, on acceptance.

DREAMS & VISIONS—Skysong Press, 35 Peter St. S., Orillia, Ont., Canada L3V 5A8. Steve Stanton, Ed. New frontiers in Christian fiction. Eclectic fiction, 2,000 to 6,000 words, that "has literary value and is unique and relevant to Christian readers today." Pays ½¢ per word.

ENRICHMENT: A JOURNAL FOR PENTECOSTAL MINISTRY—1445 Boonville Ave., Springfield, MO 65802. Wayde I. Goodall, Ed. Articles, 1,200 to 1,500 words, slanted to ministers, on preaching, doctrine, practice; how-to features. Pays to 10¢ a word, on acceptance.

EVANGEL—Light and Life Communications, Box 535002, Indianapolis,

IN 46253-5002. Julie Innes, Ed. Free Methodist. Personal experience articles, 1,000 words; short devotional items, 300 to 500 words; fiction, 1,200 words, showing personal faith in Christ to be instrumental in solving problems. Send #10 SASE for sample copy and guidelines. Pays 4¢ a word for articles, $10 for poetry, on publication.

FAITH TODAY—M.I.P. Box 3745, Markham, Ontario, Canada L3R OY4. Larry Matthews, Interim Man. Ed. Articles, 1,500 words, on current issues and news relating to Evangelical Christians in Canada. Pays negotiable rates (usually 20¢ per word, Canadian), on publication. Queries required. E-mail: ft@efc-canada.com.

THE FAMILY DIGEST—P.O. Box 40137, Fort Wayne, IN 46804. Corine B. Erlandson, Ed. Articles, 700 to 1,200 words, on family life, Catholic subjects, seasonal, parish life, prayer, inspiration, how-to, spiritual life, for the Catholic reader. Also publishes short humorous anecdotes drawn from personal experience and light-hearted cartoons. Pays $40 to $60 per article; $20 for personal anecdotes; $30 for cartoons, 4 to 6 weeks after acceptance.

FELLOWSHIP—Box 271, Nyack, NY 10960-0271. Richard Deats, Ed. Bimonthly published by the Fellowship of Reconciliation, an interfaith, pacifist organization. Articles, 750 and 1,500 to 2,000 words; B&W photo-essays, on active nonviolence, peace and justice, opposition to war. "Articles for a just and peaceful world community." SASE required. Pays in copies and subscription. Queries preferred.

FELLOWSHIP IN PRAYER—See *Sacred Journey.*

FIRST THINGS—156 Fifth Ave., #400, New York, NY 10010-7002. James Nuechterlein, Ed. Published 10 times a year. Essays and social commentary, 1,500 words or 4,000 to 6,000 words, for academics, clergy, and general educated readership, on the role of religion in public life. Pays $300 to $800, on publication.

FOURSQUARE WORLD ADVANCE—1910 W. Sunset Blvd., Suite 200, P.O. Box 26902, Los Angeles, CA 90026. Ronald D. Williams, Ed. Official publication of the International Church of the Foursquare Gospel. Religious fiction and nonfiction, 1,000 to 1,200 words, and religious poetry. Pays $75, on publication. Guidelines.

FRIENDS JOURNAL—1206 Arch St., Philadelphia, PA 19107. Vinton Deming, Ed. Articles, to 2,000 words, reflecting Quaker life today: commentary on social issues, experiential articles, Quaker history, world affairs. Poetry, to 25 lines, and Quaker-related humor and crossword puzzles also considered. Pays in copies. Guidelines.

THE GEM—Box 926, Findlay, OH 45839-0926. Mac Cordell, Ed. Articles, 300 to 1,600 words, and fiction, 1,000 to 1,600 words: true-to-life experiences of God's help, of healed relationships, and of growing maturity in faith. For adolescents through senior citizens. Pays $15 for articles and fiction, $5 to $10 for fillers, after publication.

GLORY SONGS—127 Ninth Ave. N., Nashville, TN 37234. Jere V. Adams, Ed. For volunteer and part-time music directors and members of church choirs. Very easy music and accompaniments designed specifically for the small church (4 to 6 songs per issue). Includes 8-page pull-out with articles for choir members on leisure reading, music training, and choir projects. Pays 5½¢ per word, on acceptance.

GOSPEL HERALD—See *The Mennonite.*

GOSPEL TODAY—761 Old Hickory Blvd., Suite 205, Brentwood, TN 37027. Terea E. Harris, Pub. Published eight times a year. America's "leading gospel lifestyle magazine" and is aimed at African American Christians. Features, 1,000 to 3,500 words, on human interest stories on Christian personalities, events, and testimonials from Christian leaders. Book reviews also welcome. Features pay $150 to $250; columns pay $50 to $75. Query with ideas and for complete guidelines.

GROUP, THE YOUTH MINISTRY MAGAZINE—Box 481, Loveland, CO 80539. Rick Lawrence, Ed. Interdenominational magazine for leaders of junior and senior high school Christian youth groups. Articles, 500 to 1,700 words, about practical youth ministry principles, techniques, or activities. Short how-to pieces, to 300 words. Pays to $200 for articles, $35 for department pieces, on acceptance. Guidelines.

GUIDE—Review and Herald Publishing Assn., 55 W. Oak Ridge Dr., Hagerstown, MD 21740. Tim Lale, Ed. True stories, to 1,200 words, for Christian youth, ages 10 to 14. Pays 10¢ to 12¢ a word, on publication.

GUIDEPOSTS—16 E. 34th St., New York, NY 10016. Catherine Scott, Dept. Ed. True first-person stories, 250 to 1,500 words, stressing how people have used faith to overcome obstacles and live better lives. Anecdotal fillers, to 250 words. Pays $75 to $400 for full-length stories, $25 to $100 for fillers, on acceptance.

INSIDE MAGAZINE—226 S. 16th St., Philadelphia, PA 19102-3392. Jane Biberman, Ed. Jewish lifestyle magazine. Articles, 1,500 to 3,000 words, on Jewish issues, health, finance, and the arts. Pays $75 to $600, after publication. Queries required; send clips if available.

JEWISH CURRENTS—22 E. 17th St., #601, New York, NY 10003. Morris U. Schappes, Ed. Articles, 2,400 to 3,000 words, on Jewish history, Jewish secularism, progressivism, labor struggle, Holocaust and Holocaust-resistance, Black-Jewish relations, Israel, Yiddish culture. "We are pro-Israel though non-Zionist and a secular magazine; no religious articles." Overstocked with fiction and poetry. No payment.

THE JEWISH HOMEMAKER—391 Troy Ave., Brooklyn, NY 11213. Avraham M. Goldstein, Ed. Quarterly. Articles, 1,200 to 2,000 words, for a traditional/Orthodox Jewish audience. Payment varies, on publication. Query.

THE JEWISH MONTHLY—B'nai B'rith International, 1640 Rhode Island Ave. N.W., Washington, DC 20036. Eric Rozenman, Exec. Ed. Articles, 500 to 2,500 words, on politics, religion, history, culture, and social issues of Jewish concern with an emphasis on people. Pays $300 to $650 for features, on publication. Query with clips. E-mail: ijm@bnaibrith.org.

JOURNAL OF CHRISTIAN NURSING—P.O. Box 1650, Downers Grove, IL 60515-1650. Judy Shelly, Sr. Ed. Articles, 8 to 12 double-spaced pages, that help Christian nurses view nursing practice through the eyes of faith: spiritual care, ethics, values, healing and wholeness, psychology and religion, personal and professional ethics, etc. Priority given to nurse authors, though work by non-nurses will be considered. Pays $25 to $80. Guidelines and editorial calendar.

THE JOYFUL WOMAN—P.O. Box 90028, Chattanooga, TN 37412. Joy Rice Martin, Ed. Articles and fiction, 500 to 1,200 words, for Christian women: first-person inspirational true stories, profiles of Christian women, practical and biblically oriented how-to articles. Pays 3¢ to 4¢ a word, on publication. Queries required; no unsolicited manuscripts.

LEADERSHIP—465 Gundersen Dr., Carol Stream, IL 60188. Marshall Shelley, Ed. Articles, 500 to 3,000 words, on administration, finance, and/or programming of interest to ministers and church leaders. Personal stories of crisis in ministry. "We deal mainly with the how-to of running a church. We're not a theological journal but a practical one." Pays $50 to $350, on acceptance.

LIBERTY MAGAZINE—12501 Old Columbia Pike, Silver Spring, MD 20904-1608. Clifford R. Goldstein, Ed. Timely articles, to 2,500 words, and photo-essays, on religious freedom and church-state relations. Pays 6¢ to 8¢ a word, on acceptance. Query.

LIGHT AND LIFE—P.O. Box 535002, Indianapolis, IN 46253-5002. Doug Newton, Ed. Thoughtful articles about practical Christian living. Social and cultural analysis from an evangelical perspective. Pays 4¢ to 5¢ a word, on publication.

LIGUORIAN—Liguori, MO 63057-9999. Rev. Allan Weinert, Ed. Catholic. Articles and short stories, 1,500 to 1,700 words, on Christian values in modern life. Pays 10¢ to 12¢ a word, on acceptance.

THE LIVING LIGHT—U.S. Catholic Conference, Dept. of Education, Caldwell 345, The Catholic Univ. of America, Washington, DC 20064. Theoretical and practical articles, 1,500 to 4,000 words, on religious education, catechesis, and pastoral ministry.

THE LOOKOUT—8121 Hamilton Ave., Cincinnati, OH 45231. David Faust, Ed. Articles, 500 to 1,800 words, on spiritual growth, family issues, applying Christian faith to current issues, and people overcoming problems with Christian principles. Inspirational or humorous shorts, 500 to 800 words. Pays 5¢ to 15¢ a word, on acceptance.

THE LUTHERAN—8765 W. Higgins Rd., Chicago, IL 60631. Edgar R. Trexler, Ed. Articles, to 1,200 words, on Christian ideology, personal religious experiences, social and ethical issues, family life, church, and community of Evangelical Lutheran Church in America. Pays $100 to $500, on acceptance. Query required.

MARRIAGE PARTNERSHIP—Christianity Today, Inc., 465 Gundersen Dr., Carol Stream, IL 60188. Ron Lee, Ed. Articles, 500 to 2,000 words, related to marriage, for men and women who wish to fortify their relationship. Humor. Pays $40 to $300, on acceptance. Query required.

MARYKNOLL—Maryknoll, NY 10545. Joseph Veneroso, M. M., Ed. Frank Maurovich, Man. Ed. Magazine of the Catholic Foreign Mission Society of America. Articles, 800 to 1,000 words, and photos relating to missions or missioners overseas. Pays $150, on acceptance. Payment for photos made on publication.

MATURE LIVING—127 Ninth Ave. N., Nashville, TN 37234-0140. Al Shackleford, Ed. Fiction and human-interest articles, to 1,200 words, for senior adults. Must be consistent with Christian principles. Payment varies, on acceptance.

MATURE YEARS—201 Eighth Ave. S., P.O. Box 801, Nashville, TN 37202. Marvin W. Cropsey, Ed. Nondenominational quarterly. Articles, 1,500 to 2,000 words, on retirement or related subjects, inspiration. Humorous and serious fiction, 1,500 to 1,800 words. Travel pieces for seniors or with religious slant. Poetry, to 14 lines. Include social security number with manuscript. Guidelines.

THE MENNONITE—Merged with *Gospel Herald,* P.O. Box 347, Newton, KS 67114. J. Lorne Peachey, Ed.; Gordon Houser, Assoc. Ed. Articles, 1,200 words, that emphasize Christian themes. Pays 7¢ a word, on publication. Guidelines.

MESSENGER OF THE SACRED HEART—661 Greenwood Ave., Toronto, Ont., Canada M4J 4B3. Articles and short stories, about 1,500 words, for American and Canadian Catholics. Pays from 6¢ a word, on acceptance.

MIDSTREAM—633 Third Ave., 21st Fl., New York, NY 10017. Joel Carmichael, Ed. Jewish/Zionist-interest articles and book reviews. Fiction, to 3,000 words, and poetry. Pays 5¢ a word, after publication. Allow 3 months for response.

MINISTRY & LITURGY—(formerly *Modern Liturgy*) 160 E. Virginia St., #290, San Jose, CA 95112. Nick Wagner, Ed. Practical, imaginative how-to help for Roman Catholic liturgy planners. Pays in copies and subscription. Query required.

THE MIRACULOUS MEDAL—475 E. Chelten Ave., Philadelphia, PA 19144-5785. Rev. William J. O'Brien, C.M., Ed. Dir. Catholic. Fiction, to 2,400 words. Religious verse, to 20 lines. Pays from 2¢ a word for fiction, from 50¢ a line for poetry, on acceptance.

MODERN LITURGY—See *Ministry & Liturgy.*

MOMENT MAGAZINE—4710 41st St. N.W., Washington, DC 20016. Hershel Shanks, Ed. Sophisticated articles, 2,500 to 5,000 words, on Jewish culture, politics, religion, and personalities. Columns, to 1,500 words, with uncommon perspectives on contemporary issues, humor, strong anecdotes. Book reviews, 400 words. Pays $40 to $600.

MOMENTUM—National Catholic Educational Assn., 1077 30th St. N.W., Suite 100, Washington, DC 20007-3852. Margaret Bonilla, Ed. Articles, 500 to 1,500 words, on outstanding programs, issues, and research in education. Book reviews. Pays $25 to $75, on publication. Query.

MOODY MAGAZINE—820 N. La Salle Blvd., Chicago, IL 60610. Andrew Scheer, Man. Ed. Anecdotal articles, 1,200 to 2,000 words, on the evangelical Christian experience in the home, the community, and the workplace. Pays 15¢ to 20¢ a word, on acceptance. Query. No unsolicited manuscripts.

NATURE FRIEND—2727 TR 421, Sugarcreek, OH 44681. Stanley K. Brubaker, Ed. Monthly. Articles for children that "teach spiritual lessons; show them how to be kind to animals, plants, and nature; and increase their awareness of God." Also, some poetry, games, and fillers. Pays 5¢ per word for nonfiction; $15 for games and fillers. Send SASE for guidelines.

NEW ERA—50 E. North Temple, Salt Lake City, UT 84150. Larry A. Hiller, Man. Ed. Articles, 150 to 1,500 words, and fiction, to 2,000 words, for young Mormons. Poetry; photos. Pays 5¢ to 10¢ a word, 25¢ a line for poetry, on acceptance. Query.

NEW WORLD OUTLOOK—475 Riverside Dr., Rm. 1476, New York, NY 10115. Alma Graham, Ed. Articles, 500 to 2,000 words, illustrated with color photos, on United Methodist missions and Methodist-related programs and ministries. Focus on national, global, and women's and children's issues, and on men and youth in missions. Pays on publication. Query.

OBLATES—9480 N. De Mazenod Dr., Belleville, IL 62223-1160. Mary Mohrman, Manuscripts Ed. Christine Portell, Man. Ed. Articles, 500 to 600 words, that inspire, uplift, and motivate through positive Christian values in everyday life. Inspirational poetry, to 16 lines. Pays $80 for articles, $30 for poems, on acceptance. Send 2 first-class stamps and SASE for guidelines and sample copy.

THE OTHER SIDE—300 W. Apsley, Philadelphia, PA 19144. Doug Davidson, Nonfiction Ed. Bob Finegan, Fiction Ed. Jeanne Minahan, Poetry Ed. Independent, ecumenical Christian magazine devoted to issues of social justice, Christian spirituality, and the creative arts. Fiction, 500 to 5,000 words, that deepens readers' encounter with the mystery of God and the mystery of ourselves. Nonfiction, 500 to 4,000 words (most under 2,000 words), on contemporary social, political, economic, or racial issues in the U.S. or abroad. Poems, to 50 lines; submit up to 3 poems. Payment is 2 copies, a two-year subscription, plus $20 to $350 for articles; $75 to $250 for fiction; $15 for poems, on acceptance. Guidelines. Web site: www.theotherside.org.

OUR FAMILY—Box 249, Battleford, Sask., Canada S0M 0E0. Marie-Louise Ternier-Gommers, Ed. Articles, 1,000 to 3,000 words, for Catholic families, on modern society, family, marriage, current affairs, and spiritual topics. Humor; verse. Pays 7¢ to 10¢ (Canadian) a word for articles, 75¢ to $1 (Candian) a line for poetry, on acceptance. SAE with international reply coupons required with all submissions. Guidelines. E-mail: editor@ourfamilymagazine.com. See web site for guidelines and projected themes for 2000: www.ourfamilymagazine.com.

PASTORAL LIFE—Box 595, Canfield, OH 44406-0595. Anthony L. Chenevey, Ed. Articles, 2,000 to 2,500 words, addressing the problems of pastoral ministry. Pays 4¢ a word, on publication. Guidelines.

PENTECOSTAL EVANGEL—1445 Boonville Ave., Springfield, MO 65802. Hal Donaldson, Ed. Assemblies of God. Religious, personal experience, and devotional articles, 400 to 1,000 words. Pays 8¢ to 10¢ a word.

PERSPECTIVE—Pioneer Clubs, P.O. Box 788, Wheaton, IL 60189-0788. Rebecca Powell Parat, Ed. 3 times/year. Articles, 500 to 1,200 words, that provide growth for adult club leaders in leadership and relationship skills and offer encouragement and practical support. Readers are lay leaders of Pioneer Clubs for boys and girls (age 2 to 12th grade). "Most articles written on assignment; writers familiar with Pioneer Clubs who would be interested in working on assignment should contact us." Pays $30 to $120, on acceptance. Guidelines.

PIME WORLD—17330 Quincy St., Detroit, MI 48221. Ed. Articles, 600 to 1,200 words, on Catholic missionary work in South Asia, West Africa, and Latin America. Color photos. No fiction or poetry. Pays 10¢ a word, extra for photos, on publication.

POWER AND LIGHT—6401 The Paseo, Kansas City, MO 64131. Beula J. Postlewait, Preteen Ed. Fiction and nonfiction, 400 to 800 words, for grades 5 and 6, defining Christian experiences and demonstrating Christian values and beliefs. Pays 5¢ a word for multi-use rights, on publication.

THE PREACHER'S MAGAZINE—10814 E. Broadway, Spokane, WA

99206. Randal E. Denny, Ed. Scholarly and practical articles, 700 to 2,500 words, on areas of interest to Christian ministers: church administration, pastoral care, professional and personal growth, church music, finance, evangelism. Pays 3½¢ a word, on publication. Guidelines.

PRESBYTERIAN RECORD—50 Wynford Dr., Toronto, Ont., Canada M3C 1J7. John Congram, Ed. Fiction and nonfiction, 1,500 words, and poetry, any length. Short items, to 800 words, of a contemporary and often controversial nature for "Vox Populi." The purpose of the magazine is "to provide news, not only from our church but the church-at-large, and to fulfill both a pastoral and prophetic role among our people." Queries preferred. SAE with international reply coupons required. Pays about $50 (Canadian), on publication. Guidelines.

PRESBYTERIANS TODAY—100 Witherspoon, Louisville, KY 40202-1396. Eva Stimson, Ed. Articles, 1,200 to 1,500 words, of special interest to members of the Presbyterian Church (USA). Pays to $200, before publication.

THE PRIEST—200 Noll Plaza, Huntington, IN 46750-4304. Msgr. Owen F. Campion, Ed. Viewpoints, to 1,500 words, and articles, to 5,000 words, on life and ministry of priests, current theological developments, etc., for priests, permanent deacons, and seminarians. Pays $75 to $250, on acceptance.

PURPOSE—616 Walnut Ave., Scottdale, PA 15683-1999. James E. Horsch, Ed. Fiction, nonfiction, and fillers, to 750 words, on Christian discipleship and church-year related themes, with good photos; pieces of history, biography, science, hobbies, from a Christian perspective; Christian problem solving. First-person pieces preferred. Poetry, to 12 lines. "Send complete manuscript; no queries." Pays to 5¢ a word, to $2 a line for poetry, on acceptance.

QUEEN OF ALL HEARTS—26 S. Saxon Ave., Bay Shore, NY 11706-8993. J. Patrick Gaffney, S.M.M., Ed. Publication of Montfort Missionaries. Articles and fiction, 1,000 to 2,000 words, related to the Virgin Mary. Poetry. Pay varies, on acceptance.

THE QUIET HOUR—4050 Lee Vance View, Colorado Springs, CO 80919. Gary Wilde, Ed. Short devotionals. Pays $15, on acceptance. By assignment only; query.

RECONSTRUCTIONISM TODAY—30 Old Whitfield Rd., Accord, NY 12404. Lawrence Bush, Ed. Articles on contemporary Judaism and Jewish culture. No fiction or poetry. Pays in copies and subscription.

REVIEW FOR RELIGIOUS—3601 Lindell Blvd., St. Louis, MO 63108. David L. Fleming, S.J., Ed. Informative, practical, or inspirational articles, 1,500 to 5,000 words, from a Catholic spirituality tradition stemming from charisms of Catholic religious communities. Pays $6 per page, on publication. Guidelines.

SACRED JOURNEY: THE JOURNAL OF FELLOWSHIP IN PRAYER—(formerly *Fellowship in Prayer*) 291 Witherspoon St., Princeton, NJ 08542. Articles, to 1,500 words, relating to prayer, meditation, and the spiritual life as practiced by men and women of all faith traditions. Pays in copies. Guidelines.

ST. ANTHONY MESSENGER—1615 Republic St., Cincinnati, OH 45210-1298. Fr. Jack Wintz, O.F.M., Ed. Articles, 2,000 to 3,000 words, on personalities, major movements, education, family, religious and church issues, spiritual life, and social issues. Human-interest pieces. Humor; fiction, 2,000 to 3,000 words. Articles and stories should have religious implications, keeping a predominantly Roman Catholic readership in mind. Query for nonfiction. Pays 15¢ a word, on acceptance.

ST. JOSEPH'S MESSENGER—P.O. Box 288, Jersey City, NJ 07303-0288. Sister Mary Kuiken, Ed. Inspirational articles, 500 to 1,000 words, and fiction, 1,000 to 1,500 words. Verse, 4 to 40 lines. Payment varies, on publication.

SEEK—8121 Hamilton Ave., Cincinnati, OH 45231. Eileen H. Wilmoth, Ed. Articles and fiction, 400 to 1,200 words, on inspirational and controversial topics and timely religious issues. Christian testimonials. Pays 5¢ a word, on acceptance. 6" x 9" SASE for guidelines.

SHARING THE VICTORY—Fellowship of Christian Athletes, 8701 Leeds Rd., Kansas City, MO 64129. David Smale, Ed. Articles, interviews, and profiles, to 1,500 words, for co-ed Christian athletes and coaches in junior high, high school, college, and pros. Pays from $50, on publication. Query required.

SIGNS OF THE TIMES—P. O. Box 5353, Nampa, ID 83653-5353. Marvin Moore, Ed. Seventh-day Adventists. Articles, 500 to 2,000 words: features on Christians who have performed community services; first-person experiences, to 1,000 words; health, home, marriage, human-interest pieces; inspirational articles. Pays to 20¢ a word, on acceptance. Send 9x12 SASE with 3 first-class stamps for sample and guidelines.

SISTERS TODAY—The Liturgical Press, St. John's Abbey, Collegeville, MN 56321-7500. Articles, 500 to 3,500 words, on theology, social justice issues, and religious issues for women and the Church. Poetry, to 34 lines. Pays $5 per printed page, $10 per poem, on publication; $50 for color cover photos and $25 for B&W inside photos. Send articles to: Sister Mary Anthony Wagner, O.S.B., Ed., St. Benedict's Monastery, St. Joseph, MN 56374-2099. Send poetry to: Sister Virginia Micka, C.S.J.,1884 Randolph Ave., St. Paul, MN 55105.

SOCIAL JUSTICE REVIEW—3835 Westminster Pl., St. Louis, MO 63108-3409. Rev. John H. Miller, C.S.C., Ed. Articles, 2,000 to 3,000 words, on social problems in light of Catholic teaching and current scientific studies. Pays 2¢ a word, on publication.

SPIRITUAL LIFE—2131 Lincoln Rd. N.E., Washington, DC 20002-1199. Edward O'Donnell, O.C.D., Ed. Professional religious journal. Religious essays, 3,000 to 5,000 words, on spirituality in contemporary life. Pays from $50, on acceptance. Guidelines.

STANDARD—6401 The Paseo, Kansas City, MO 64131. Articles and fiction, 300 to 1,200 words; poetry, to 20 lines; fiction with Christian emphasis but not overtly preachy. Pays 3½¢ a word, on acceptance.

TEACHERS INTERACTION—3558 S. Jefferson Ave., St. Louis, MO 63118. Tom Nummela, Ed. Practical, educational, and inspirational articles, 600 to 1,200 words, for Christian teachers and how-to pieces, to 100 words, specifically for volunteer church school teachers. Pays $20 to $100, on publication. Freelance submissions accepted.

THEOLOGY TODAY—Box 29, Princeton, NJ 08542. Patrick D. Miller, Ed. Articles, 1,500 to 3,500 words, on theology, religion, and related social and philosophical issues. Literary criticism. Pays $50 to $200, on publication.

TIKKUN—26 Fell St., San Francisco, CA 94102. Michael Lerner, Ed. "A Bimonthly Jewish Critique of Politics, Culture, and Society." Articles and fiction, 2,400 to 3,000 words. Poetry. "Read a copy to get a sense of what we publish. We are always interested in work pertaining to contemporary culture." Pays in copies. E-mail: magazine@tikkun.org.

TODAY'S CHRISTIAN WOMAN—465 Gundersen Dr., Carol Stream, IL 60188. Ramona Cramer Tucker, Ed. Articles, 1,500 to 1,800 words, that are "warm and personal in tone, full of real-life anecdotes" that deal with marriage, parenting, friendship, spiritual life, self, single life, work, and hot issues from an evangelical Christian perspective. Payment varies, on acceptance. Queries required. Guidelines.

TURNING WHEEL—P.O. Box 4650, Berkeley, CA 94704. Susan Moon, Ed. Quarterly. Articles, poetry, reviews, and artwork. "Magazine is dedicated to Buddhist activism, bringing a Buddhist/spiritual perspective to matters of social and environmental justice." No payment.

UNITED SYNAGOGUE REVIEW—155 Fifth Ave., New York, NY 10010. Lois Goldrich, Ed. Articles, 1,000 to 1,200 words, on issues of interest to Conservative Jewish community. Query.

UNITY MAGAZINE—1901 N.W. Blue Pkwy., Unity School of Christianity, Unity Village, MO 64065. Philip White, Ed. Religious and inspirational articles, 1,000 to 1,800 words, on spiritual growth, health and healing, metaphysical, Bible interpretation, and prosperity. Poems. Pays 20¢ a word, on acceptance.

VISTA MAGAZINE—6060 Castleway Dr., Indianapolis, IN 46250-0434. Attn: Ed. Articles and adult fiction, on current Christian concerns and issues as well as fundamental issues of holiness and Christian living. Not accepting freelance material at this time.

THE WAR CRY—The Salvation Army, P.O. Box 269, Alexandria, VA 22313. Attn: Man Ed. Inspirational articles, 800 to 1,200 words, addressing modern life and issues. Short fiction, poetry, religious news and trends, Bible study, with emphasis on spiritual discernment and compassionate acts and ministries that correspond to the mission of the Salvation Army. Also short articles on evangelism and devotion, family life, parenting, coping with violence, revival, rehabilitation, and cross-cultural ministries, 350 to 450 words. Color photos. Pays 15¢ to 20¢ a word for articles, $35 to $200 for photos, on acceptance. E-mail: warcry@usa.salvation army.org. Web site: http://publications. salvationarmy.org.

WARNER PRESS—P.O. Box 2499, Anderson, IN 46018. Jennie Bishop, Senior Ed. Religious themes, sensitive prose, and inspirational verse for Sunday bulletins. Pays $20 to $35, on acceptance. Also accepts ideas for coloring and activity books. "Always looking for new products that will serve churches and their ministries." Writers must send SASE for guidelines.

WITH: THE MAGAZINE FOR RADICAL CHRISTIAN YOUTH—722 Main St., Box 347, Newton, KS 67114. Carol Duerksen, Ed. Fiction, 500 to 2,000 words; nonfiction, 500 to 1,600 words; and poetry, to 50 lines for Mennonite and Brethren teenagers. "Wholesome humor always gets a close read." B&W 8x10 photos accepted. Payment is 6¢ a word, on acceptance (4¢ a word for reprints).

WOMAN'S TOUCH—1445 Boonville, Springfield, MO 65802-1894.

Lillian Sparks, Ed. Aleda Swartzendruber, Man. Ed. Articles, 500 to 1,000 words, that provide help and inspiration to Christian women, strengthening family life, and reaching out in witness to others. Submit complete manuscript. Allow 3 months for response. Payment varies, on publication. Guidelines and editorial calendar.

YOUNG SALVATIONIST—The Salvation Army, 615 Slaters Ln., P.O. Box 269, Alexandria, VA 22313. Attn: Tim Clark, Man. Ed. Articles, 600 to 1,200 words, that teach the Christian view of everyday living, for teenagers. Short shorts, first-person testimonies, 600 to 800 words. Pays 15¢ a word (10¢ a word for reprints), on acceptance. SASE required. Send 8½×11 SASE (3 stamps) for theme list, guidelines, and sample copy.

‹ **YOUR CHURCH**—465 Gundersen Dr., Carol Stream, IL 60188. Phyllis Ten Elshof, Ed. Articles, to 1,000 words, about church business administration. Pays about 15¢ a word, on acceptance. Query required. Guidelines.

HEALTH

ACCENT ON LIVING—P. O. Box 700, Bloomington, IL 61702. Raymond C. Cheever, Pub. Betty Garee, Ed. Articles, 250 to 800 words, about physically disabled people, including their careers, recreation, sports, self-help devices, and ideas that can make daily routines easier. Good photos a plus. Pays 10¢ a word, on publication. Query.

AMERICAN BABY—Primedia Inc., 249 W. 17th St., New York, NY 10011. Judith Nolte, Ed. Articles, 1,000 to 2,000 words, for new or expectant parents on prenatal and infant care. Personal experience, 900 to 1,200 words (do not submit in diary format). Department pieces, 50 to 350 words, for "Crib Notes" (news and feature topics) and "Medical Update" (health and medicine). No fiction, fantasy pieces, dreamy musings, or poetry. Pays $500 to $1,000 for articles, $100 for departments, on acceptance. Guidelines.

AMERICAN FITNESS—15250 Ventura Blvd., Suite 200, Sherman Oaks, CA 91403. Peg Jordan, Ed. Ayn Nix, Man. Ed. Articles, 500 to 1,500 words, on exercise, health, trends, research, nutrition, alternative paths, etc. No first person stories. Illustrations, photos.

AMERICAN HEALTH —(formerly *American Health for Women*) Reader's Digest Road, Pleasantville, NY 10570. Attn: Editorial Dept. Lively, authoritative articles, 1,000 to 2,500 words, on women's health, alternative health, nutrition, mental health, and fitness. Query with clips. Pays on acceptance; fee is negotiated with assigning editor.

AMERICAN JOURNAL OF NURSING—345 Hudson St., New York, NY 10014. Santa J. Crisall, Ed. Dir. Articles, 1,500 to 2,000 words, with photos or illustrations, on nursing or disease processes. Query.

AQUARIUS: A SIGN OF THE TIMES—1035 Green St., Roswell, GA 30075. Dan Liss, Ed. Tabloid. Articles, 800 words (plus photo or illustration) on holistic health, metaphysics, spirituality, and the environment. "We are a great way for new writers to get clips." No payment. E-mail: aquariusnews@ mindspring.com.

ARTHRITIS TODAY—The Arthritis Foundation, 1330 W. Peachtree St., Atlanta, GA 30309. Cindy McDaniel, Ed. Research, self-help, how-to, general interest, general health, and lifestyle topics, and very few inspirational articles,

750 to 3,000 words, and briefs, 100 to 250 words. "The magazine is written to help people with arthritis live more productive, independent, and pain-free lives." Pays $500 to $2,000 for articles, $75 to $250 for briefs, on acceptance.

ASTHMA—3 Bridge St., Newton, MA 02158. Rachel Butler, Ed.-in-Chief. Bimonthly. Focus on how to manage asthma. Articles, to 1,200 words, on health and medical news, and human interest stories affecting children, adults, and the elderly. Photographs and drawings are also accepted. Pays on acceptance. Query.

BABY TALK—1325 Ave. of the Americas, New York, NY 10019. Susan Kane, Ed. Articles, 1,000 to 1,500 words, by parents or professionals, on women's health, babies and baby care, etc. No poetry. Pay varies, on acceptance. SASE required.

BETTER HEALTH—1450 Chapel St., New Haven, CT 06511. Cynthia Wolfe Boynton, Pub. Dir. Wellness and prevention magazine published by The Hospital of Saint Raphael in New Haven. Upbeat articles, 2,000 to 2,500 words, that encourage a healthier lifestyle. Articles must contain quotes and narrative from healthcare professionals at Saint Raphael's and other local services. No first-person or personal experience articles. Pays $500, on acceptance. Query with SASE.

COPING WITH ALLERGIES & ASTHMA—P.O. Box 682268, Franklin, TN 37068-2268. Attn: Ed. Published six times a year. Provides the "knowledge, hope, and inspiration necessary to help readers learn to live with their conditions in the best ways possible." Seeks original, unsolicited manuscripts and photography. No payment.

COPING WITH CANCER—(formerly *Coping: Living With Cancer*) P.O. Box 682268, Franklin, TN 37068. Kay Thomas, Ed. Uplifting and practical articles for people living with cancer: medical news, lifestyle issues, and inspiring personal essays. No payment.

CURRENT HEALTH—900 Skokie Blvd., Suite 200, Northbrook, IL 60062-4028. Carole Rubenstein, Ed. Published 8 times a year. Articles, varying lengths, on drug education, nutrition, fitness and exercise, first aid and safety, and environmental awareness. Two editions: *Current Health 1,* for grades 4 to 7, and *Current Health 2,* for grades 7 to 12. Payment varies, on publication. Query with clips and resumé; no unsolicited manuscripts.

DIABETES SELF-MANAGEMENT—150 W. 22nd St., New York, NY 10011. Ingrid Strauch, Managing Ed. Articles, 2,000 to 4,000 words, for people with diabetes who want to know more about controlling and managing it. Up-to-date and authoritative information on nutrition, pharmacology, exercise physiology, technological advances, self-help, and other how-to subjects. "Articles must be useful, instructive, and must have immediate application to the day-to-day life of our readers. We do not publish personal experience, profiles, exposés, or research breakthroughs." Query with one-page rationale, outline, writing samples, and SASE. Pays from $500, on publication. Buys all rights.

FIT PREGNANCY—21100 Erwin St., Woodland Hills, CA 91367-3712. Peg Moline, Ed. Articles, 500 to 2,000 words, on pregnant women's health, sports, and physical fitness. Payment varies, on publication. Query.

FITNESS—Gruner & Jahr USA Publishing, 375 Lexington Ave., New York, NY 10017. Sarah Mahoney, Ed.-in-Chief. Articles, 500 to 2,000 words, on health, exercise, sports, nutrition, diet, psychological well-being, alternative therapies, and beauty. Average reader is 30 years old. Query required. Pays $1 a word, on acceptance.

FITNESS PLUS—P.O. Box 672111, Bronx, NY 10467. Mathea Levine, Ed. Bimonthly. Articles, 1,000 to 3,000 words, on serious health and fitness training for men. Payment varies, on publication. Queries preferred.

HERBALGRAM—P.O. Box 144345, Austin, TX 78714-4345. Barbara Johnston, Man. Ed. Quarterly. Articles, 1,500 to 3,000 words, on herb and medicinal plant research, regulatory issues, market conditions, native plant conservation, and other aspects of herbal use. Pays in copies. Query.

HOSPITALS & HEALTH NETWORKS—One N. Franklin St., 29th Fl., Chicago, IL 60606. Kevin Lumsdon, Man. Ed. Articles, 800 to 900 words, for hospital administrators, on financing, staffing, coordinating, and providing facilities for health care services. Query.

IDEA HEALTH & FITNESS SOURCE—(formerly *Idea Today*) 6190 Cornerstone Ct. E., Suite 204, San Diego, CA 92121-3773. Ed. Practical articles, 1,000 to 3,000 words, on new exercise programs, business management, nutrition, health, motivation, sports medicine, group-exercise, and one-to-one training techniques. Articles must be geared toward the exercise studio owner or manager, personal trainer, and fitness instruction. No consumer or general health pieces. Payment negotiable, on acceptance. Query preferred. Guidelines.

IDEA PERSONAL TRAINER—6190 Cornerstone Ct. E., Suite 204, San Diego, CA 92121-3773. Michelle Zamora, Asst. Ed. Association publication for personal fitness trainers. Articles on exercise science; program design; profiles of successful trainers; business, legal, and marketing topics; tips for networking with other trainers and with allied medical professionals; client counseling; and training tips. "What's New" column includes industry news, products, and research. Payment varies, on acceptance. Query.

IDEA TODAY—See *Idea Health & Fitness Source.*

LET'S LIVE—P.O. Box 74908, Los Angeles, CA 90004. Laura Barnaby, Man. Ed., Articles, 1,500 to 1,800 words, on preventive medicine and nutrition, alternative medicine, diet, vitamins, herbs, exercise. Pays up to $800, depending on length, on publication. Query.

MAMM—349 W. 12th St., New York, NY 10014-1796. Submissions. Monthly. Articles on women's health, mainly cancer prevention, treatment, and survival. Survivor profiles, conventional and alternative treatment information, investigative features, essays, and cutting-edge news. Query with clips or send complete manuscript. SASE. Payment varies, and is made within 45 days of acceptance.

MEDIPHORS—P.O. Box 327, Bloomsburg, PA 17815. Dr. Eugene D. Radice, Ed. "A Literary Journal of the Health Professions." Short stories, essays, and commentary, 4,500 words, related to medicine and health. Poetry, to 30 lines. "We are not a technical journal of science. We do not publish research or review articles, except of a historical nature." Pays in copies. Guidelines.

THE NEW PHYSICIAN—American Medical Student Association, 1902 Association Dr., Reston, VA 20191. Amy Myers-Payne, Ed. Nine issues a year. Articles, 1,200 to 3,500 words, on social, ethical, and political issues of medical education. Pays $800 to $1,000 per feature-length article.

NURSING 99—1111 Bethlehem Pike, P.O. Box 908, Springhouse, PA

19477-0908. Patricia Nornhold, Exec. Dir. Most articles are clinically oriented, and written by nurses for direct caregivers. Also covers legal, ethical, and career aspects of nursing; narratives about personal nursing experiences. No poetry, cartoons, or puzzles. Pays $25 to $300, on publication. Query.

NUTRITION HEALTH REVIEW—P.O. Box 406, Haverford, PA 19041. Frank Ray Rifkin, Ed. Quarterly tabloid. Articles on medical progress, information relating to nutritional therapy, genetics, psychiatry, behavior therapy, surgery, pharmacology, animal health; vignettes relating to health and nutrition. "Vegetarian-oriented; we do not deal with subjects that favor animal testing, animal foods, cruelty to animals or recipes that contain animal products." Humor, cartoons. Pays on publication. Query.

THE PHOENIX—7152 Unity Ave. N., Brooklyn Ctr., MN 55429. Pat Samples, Ed. Tabloid. Articles, 800 to 1,500 words, on recovery, renewal, and growth. Department pieces for "Bodywise," "Family Skills," or "Personal Story." "Our readers are committed to physical, emotional, mental, and spiritual health and well-being. Read a sample copy to see what we publish." Pays 3¢ to 5¢ a word, on publication. Send SASE for guidelines and calendar.

THE PHYSICIAN AND SPORTSMEDICINE—4530 W. 77th St., Minneapolis, MN 55435. Susan Hawthorne, Exec. Ed. News articles; clinical articles coauthored with physician. Sports medicine angle necessary. Pays $300 to $1,400, on acceptance. Query. Guidelines.

PREVENTION—33 E. Minor St., Emmaus, PA 18098. Marty Munson, Man. Ed. Query required. No guidelines available. Limited market.

PSYCHOLOGY TODAY—Sussex Publishing, 49 E. 21st St., 11fl., New York, NY 10010. Aviva Patz, Exec. Ed. Bimonthly. Articles, 800 to 2,000 words, on timely subjects and news. Pays varying rates, on publication.

RX REMEDY—120 Post Rd. W., Westport, CT 06880. Val Weaver, Ed. Bimonthly. Articles, 600 to 2,500 words, on health and medication issues for readers 50 and over. Regular columns include "The Dispensary" and "The Nutrition Prescription." Query. Pays $1 to $1.25 a word, on acceptance.

TANNING TRENDS—3101 Page Ave., Jackson, MI 49203-2254. Joseph Levy, Ed. Articles on skin care and "smart tanning" for tanning salon owners. "We promote tanning clients responsibly and professionally." Payment varies, on publication.

TODAY'S SURGICAL NURSE—Slack, Inc., 6900 Grove Rd., Thorofare, NJ 08086. Frances R. DeStefano, Man. Ed. Clinical or general articles, from 2,000 words, of direct interest to surgical nurses.

VEGETARIAN TIMES—4 High Ridge Park, Stamford, CT 06905. Anne Russell, Ed. Dir. Articles, 1,200 to 2,500 words, on vegetarian cooking, nutrition, health and fitness, and profiles of prominent vegetarians. "News Items," to 500 words. "Herbalist" pieces, to 1,800 words, on medicinal uses of herbs. Queries required. Pays $75 to $1,000, on acceptance. Guidelines.

VEGETARIAN VOICE—P.O. Box 72, Dolgeville, NY 13329. Brian Graff, Exec. Ed. Quarterly. Informative, well-researched and/or inspiring articles, 600 to 1,800 words, on health, nutrition, animal rights, the environment, world hunger, etc. Pays in copies. Guidelines.

VIBRANT LIFE—55 W. Oak Ridge Dr., Hagerstown, MD 21740. Attn: Larry Becker, Ed. Features, 600 to 2,000 words, on total health: physical, mental, and spiritual. Upbeat articles on the family and how to live happier and healthier lives, emphasizing practical tips; Christian slant. Pays $80 to $250, on acceptance.

VIM & VIGOR—1010 E. Missouri Ave., Phoenix, AZ 85014. Jenn Woolson, Ed. Positive health and fitness articles, 1,200 to 2,000 words, with accurate medical facts. By assignment only; no queries or unsolicited manuscripts. Writers with feature- or news-writing ability may submit qualifications for assignment. Pays $500, on acceptance. Send SASE for guidelines.

THE WALKING MAGAZINE—45 Bromfield St., 8th Fl., Boston, MA 02108. Seth Bauer, Ed. Articles, 1,500 to 2,500 words, on fitness, health, equipment, nutrition, travel and adventure, famous walkers, and other walking-related topics. Shorter pieces, 150 to 800 words, and essays for "Ramblings" page. Color slides welcome. Pays $750 to $1,800 for features, $100 to $500 for department pieces, on acceptance. Guidelines.

YOGA JOURNAL—2054 University Ave., Berkeley, CA 94704. Kathryn Arnold, Ed. Articles, 300 to 6,000 words, on holistic health, meditation, conscious living, spirituality, and yoga. Pays $75 to $3,000, on acceptance.

YOUR HEALTH—5401 N.W. Broken Sound Blvd., Boca Raton, FL 33487. Susan Gregg, Ed.-in-Chief. Health and medical articles, 1,000 to 2,000 words, for a lay audience. Queries preferred. Pays 20¢ a word, on publication.

EDUCATION

THE ACORN MAGAZINE—8717 Mockingbird Road, Plateville, WI 53818. Attn: Ed. Quarterly. Read by librarians and elementary/preschool teachers. "We need stories with lots of action, sound, and excitement." Folktales from 200 to 300 words. Payment is copies and a free gift book.

AMERICAN SCHOOL & UNIVERSITY—P.O. Box 12901, 9800 Metcalf, Overland Park, KS 66212-2215. Joe Agron, Ed. Articles and case studies, 1,200 to 1,500 words, on design, construction, operation, and management of school and university facilities. Queries preferred.

BLACK ISSUES IN HIGHER EDUCATION—10520 Warwick Ave., Suite B-8, Fairfax, VA 22030-3136. Cheryl D. Fields, Exec. Ed. Biweekly. News and feature articles, 800 to 1,000 words, on blacks in post-secondary education. Also, fillers, to 250 words, on higher education and public policy. Pays about 25¢ per word, on publication. Query.

THE BOOK REPORT—Linworth Publishing, 480 E. Wilson Bridge Rd., Suite L, Worthington, OH 43085-2372. Carolyn Hamilton, Ed./Pub. "The Journal for Junior and Senior High Librarians." Articles, columns, and reviews by practicing educators about school libraries and librarians. Write for themes and guidelines. Also publishes *Library Talk,* "The Magazine for Elementary School Librarians" and *Technology Connection,* "The Magazine for Library and Media Specialists."

CABLE IN THE CLASSROOM—141 Portland St., #7100, Cambridge, MA 02139-1937. Al Race, Ed. Monthly. Articles, 200 to 1,200 words, for K through 12 teachers and media specialists, on upcoming educational cable television programs and creative ways to use those programs. Pays $100 to $500, on acceptance. Queries required.

CAREERS & THE DISABLED—See *Minority Engineer.*

CHANGE: THE MAGAZINE OF HIGHER LEARNING—1319 18th St. N.W., Washington, DC 20036. Attn: Man. Ed. Columns, 700 to 2,000 words, and in-depth features, 2,500 to 3,500 words, on programs, people, and institutions of higher education. "We can't usually pay for unsolicited articles."

CHRISTIAN EDUCATION JOURNAL—Trinity Evangelical Divinity School, 2065 Half Day Rd., Deerfield, IL 60015. Dr. Perry G. Downs, Ed. Articles, 10 to 25 typed pages, on Christian education topics.

CHRISTIAN EDUCATION LEADERSHIP—P.O. Box 2250, Cleveland, TN 37320-2250. Lance Colkmire, Ed. Quarterly. Articles, 500 to 1,200 words, that "encourage, inform, and inspire those who teach the Bible in the local church." No fiction, poetry, fillers, or artwork. Pays $25 to $55, on acceptance.

THE CLEARING HOUSE—Heldref Publications, 1319 18th St. N.W., Washington, DC 20036. Judy Cusick, Man. Ed. Bimonthly for middle level and high school teachers and administrators. Articles, 2,500 words, related to education: useful teaching practices, research findings, and experiments. Some opinion pieces and satirical articles related to education. Pays in copies.

COMMUNITY COLLEGE WEEK—10520 Warwick Ave., #B-8, Fairfax, VA 22030-3136. Scott Wright, Ed. Biweekly tabloid. Articles, to 1,000 words, related to education. Pays 25¢ a word, on publication. Queries preferred.

CREATIVE CLASSROOM—149 Fifth Ave., 12th Fl., New York, NY 10010. "Hands-on" magazine for elementary-school teachers. Articles on all curriculum areas, child developmental issues, technology and the Internet in the classroom, professional development, and issues facing K-6 teachers. SASE for guidelines and pay rates.

EARLY CHILDHOOD NEWS—330 Progress Rd., Dayton, OH 45449. Megan Shaw, Ed. Bimonthly. Fiction, 400 to 600 words; nonfiction, 600 to 2,200 words; and poetry, 400 to 600 words, for child care professionals. "Our purpose is to provide child care professionals with practical information, based upon educational theory, for use inside the classroom." Photographs. Pays $100 to $200, on publication. Query or send complete manuscript.

EQUAL OPPORTUNITY—See *Minority Engineer.*

GIFTED EDUCATION PRESS QUARTERLY—P.O. Box 1586, 10201 Yuma Ct., Manassas, VA 20108. Maurice Fisher, Pub. Articles, to 4,000 words, written by educators, laypersons, and parents of gifted children, on the problems of identifying and teaching gifted children and adolescents. "Interested in incisive analyses of current programs for the gifted and recommendations for improving the education of gifted students. Particularly interested in advocacy for gifted children, biographical sketches of highly gifted individuals, and the problems of teaching humanities, science, ethics, literature, and history to the gifted. Looking for highly imaginative and knowledgeable writers." Query required. Pays in subscription. Web site: www.cais.com/GEP.

THE HISPANIC OUTLOOK IN HIGHER EDUCATION—210 Rt. 4 East, Suite 310, Paramus, NJ 07652. Attn: Ed. Articles, 1,500 to 2,000 words, on the issues, concerns, and potential models for furthering the academic results of Hispanics in higher education. Queries are preferred. Payment varies, on publication. E-mail: pub@hispanicoutlook.com.

THE HORN BOOK MAGAZINE—56 Roland St., Suite 200, Boston, MA 02129. Roger Sutton, Ed.-in-Chief. Articles, 600 to 2,800 words, on books for young readers and related subjects for librarians, teachers, parents, etc. Payment varies, on publication. Send complete manuscript.

INDEPENDENT LIVING PROVIDER—See *Minority Engineer.*

INSTRUCTOR MAGAZINE—Scholastic, Inc., 555 Broadway, New York, NY 10012. Carol Mauro-Noon, Ed. Articles, 300 to 1,500 words, for teachers in grades K through 8. Payment varies, on acceptance.

JOURNAL OF SCHOOL LEADERSHIP—211 Hill Hall, College of Education, Univ. of Missouri-Columbia, Columbia, MO 65211. Dr. Paula M. Short, Ed. Bimonthly. Articulate, accurate, and authoritative articles on educational administration, particularly on translating research and theory into practice. No payment.

LEADERSHIP PUBLISHERS, INC.—P.O. Box 8358, Des Moines, IA 50301-8358. Attn: Dr. Lois F. Roets. Reference books for teachers of talented and gifted students, grades K to 12. Send SASE for catalogue and guidelines before submitting. Pays in royalty for books, and flat fee for booklets.

LIBRARY TALK—See *The Book Report.*

MINORITY ENGINEER—1160 E. Jericho Turnpike, Suite 200, Huntington, NY 11743. James Schneider, Ed. Articles, 1,000 to 1,500 words, for college students, on career opportunities; techniques of job hunting, and role-model profiles of professional minority engineers. Interviews. Pays 10¢ a word, on publication. Query. Also publishes: *Equal Opportunity*; *Careers & the Dis-ABLED*, query James Schneider; *Woman Engineer* and *Work Force Diversity*, query Editor Claudia Wheeler.

MOMENTUM—National Catholic Educational Assn., 1077 30th St. N.W., Suite 100, Washington, DC 20007-3852. Margaret Bonilla, Ed. Articles, 500 to 1,500 words, on outstanding programs, issues, and research in education. Book reviews. Query or send complete manuscript. No simultaneous submissions. Pays $25 to $75, on publication.

PHI DELTA KAPPAN—408 N. Union St., Box 789, Bloomington, IN 47402-0789. Pauline Gough, Ed. Articles, 1,000 to 4,000 words, on educational research, service, and leadership; issues, trends, and policy. Rarely pays for manuscripts.

REACHING TODAY'S YOUTH: THE COMMUNITY CIRCLE OF CARING JOURNAL—National Education Service, P.O. Box 8, Bloomington, IN 47402. Alan Blankstein, Sr. Ed. Articles, 1,500 to 2,500 words, that provide an interdisciplinary perspective on positive approaches to reaching and educating youth who are troubled, angry, or disconnected from school, peers, or family. Readers are educators, parents, youth care professionals, residential treatment staff, juvenile justice professionals, police, researchers, youth advocates, child and family psychologists, community members and students. Send SASE for guidelines and current themes.

SCHOLASTIC PARENT & CHILD—555 Broadway, New York, NY 10012-3919. Susan Schneider, Ed. Bimonthly. Articles, 600 to 900 words, on children's education and development. "We are the learning link between home and school." Payment varies, on acceptance. Query; no unsolicited manuscripts. SASE.

THE SCHOOL ADMINISTRATOR—American Assn. of School Administrators, 1801 N. Moore St., Arlington, VA 22209-1813. Jay P. Goldman,

Ed. Articles related to school administration (K through 12). "We seek articles about school system practices, policies, and programs that have widespread appeal." Pays in copies. Guidelines.

SCHOOL ARTS MAGAZINE— 50 Portland St., Worcester, MA 01608. Dr. Eldon Katter, Ed. Articles, 800 to 1,000 words, on art education with special application to the classroom: successful and meaningful approaches to teaching art, innovative art projects, uncommon applications of art techniques or equipment, etc. Photos. Pays varying rates, on publication. Guidelines.

SCHOOL SAFETY—National School Safety Ctr., 141 Duesenberg Dr., Suite 11, Westlake Village, CA 91362. Ronald D. Stephens, Exec. Ed. Published 8 times during the school year. Articles, 2,000 to 3,000 words, of use to educators, law enforcers, judges, and legislators on the prevention of drugs, gangs, weapons, bullying, discipline problems, and vandalism; also on-site security and character development as they relate to students and schools. No payment. Web site: www.nssc1.org.

TEACHING K-8— 40 Richards Ave., Norwalk, CT 06854. Patricia Broderick, Ed. Dir. Articles, 1,000 words on classroom-tested ideas and techniques for teaching students K-8th grade. Pays on publication. No queries.

TEACHING TOLERANCE—The Southern Poverty Law Center, 400 Washington Ave., Montgomery, AL 36104. Jim Carnes, Ed. Semiannual. Articles, teaching ideas, and reviews of other resources available to educators. Payment is $500 to $3,000, on acceptance, for features to 3,000 words; $300 to $800 for essays to 800 words; and $100 to $200, on publication, for "Idea Exchange" articles to 500 words. Query.

TECH DIRECTIONS— 3970 Varsity Drive, Ann Arbor, MI 48107-8623. Tom Bowden, Man. Ed. Articles, 6 to 10 double-spaced typed pages, for teachers and administrators in industrial, technology, and vocational educational fields, with particular interest in classroom projects, computer uses, and legislative issues. Pays $10 to $150, on publication. Guidelines.

TECHNOLOGY CONNECTION—See *The Book Report.*

TODAY'S CATHOLIC TEACHER— 330 Progress Rd., Dayton, OH 45449. Mary Noschang, Ed. Articles, 600 to 800 words, 1,000 to 1,200 words, and 1,200 to 1,500 words, on education, parent-teacher relationships, innovative teaching, teaching techniques, etc., of use to educators in Catholic schools. Pays $65 to $250, on publication. SASE required. Query. Guidelines.

WOMAN ENGINEER, WORK FORCE DIVERSITY—See *Minority Engineer.*

FARMING & AGRICULTURE

AMERICAN BEE JOURNAL— 51 N. Second St., Hamilton, IL 62341. Joe M. Graham, Ed. Articles on beekeeping, for professionals. Photos. Pays 75¢ a column inch, extra for photos, on publication.

BEE CULTURE— 623 W. Liberty St., Medina, OH 44256. Mr. Kim Flottum, Ed. Basic how-to articles, 500 to 2,000 words, on keeping bees and selling bee products. Slides or B&W prints. Payment varies, on acceptance and on publication. Queries preferred. E-mail address: kim@airoot.com.

THE BRAHMAN JOURNAL—P.O. Box 220, Eddy, TX 76524-0220.

Joe Brockett, Ed. Articles on Brahman cattle only. Photos. Pays $150 to $300, on publication. Queries preferred.

BUCKEYE FARM NEWS—Ohio Farm Bureau Federation, 2 Nationwide Plaza, Box 479, Columbus, OH 43216-0479. Lynn Snyder, Copy Ed. Articles, to 600 words, related to agriculture. Pays on publication. Query. Limited market.

DAIRY GOAT JOURNAL—P.O. Box 10, Lake Mills, WI 53551. Dave Thompson, Ed. Articles, to 1,500 words, on successful dairy goat owners, youths and interesting people associated with dairy goats. "Especially interested in practical husbandry ideas." Photos. Pays $50 to $150, on publication. Query.

FARM AND RANCH LIVING—5400 S. 60th St., Greendale, WI 53129. Nick Pabst, Ed. Articles, 1,000 words, on rural people and situations; nostalgia pieces; profiles of interesting farms and farmers, ranches and ranchers. Pays $15 to $300, on acceptance and on publication.

FARM INDUSTRY NEWS—7900 International Dr., Minneapolis, MN 55425. Kurt Lawton, Ed. Articles for farmers, on new products, machinery, equipment, chemicals, and seeds. Pays $350 to $500, on acceptance. Query required.

FARM JOURNAL—1500 Market St., 28th Fl., Philadelphia, PA 19102-2181. Sonja Hillgren, Ed. Articles, 500 to 1,500 words, with photos, on the business of farming. Pays 20¢ to 50¢ a word, on acceptance. Query.

FLORIDA GROWER —1555 Howell Branch Rd., Suite C-204, Winter Park, FL 32789. Frank Garner, Ed. Articles and case histories on Florida citrus and vegetable growers. Pays on publication. Query; buys little freelance material.

THE FURROW—John Deere-North American Agricultural Marketing Center, 11145 Thompson Ave., Lenexa, KS 66219-2302. Karl Kessler, N. American Ed. Specialized, illustrated articles on farming. Pays to $1,200, on acceptance.

THE LAND—P.O. Box 3169, Mankato, MN 56002-3169. Kevin Schulz, Ed. Articles on Minnesota agriculture and rural issues. Pays $30 to $60, on acceptance. Query required.

NATIONAL CATTLEMEN—5420 S. Quebec St., Englewood, CO 80111-1905. Curt Olson, Ed. Articles, 400 to 1,200 words, related to the cattle industry. Payment varies, on publication.

OHIO FARMER—117 W. Main St., Lancaster, OH 43130. Tim White, Ed. Technical articles on farming, rural living, etc., in Ohio. Pays $50 per column, on publication.

ONION WORLD—P.O. Box 9036, Yakima, WA 98909-9036. D. Brent Clement, Ed. Production and marketing articles, to 1,500 words (preferred length 1,200 words), for commercial onion growers and shippers. "Research oriented articles are of definite interest. No gardening articles." Pays about $5 per column inch, on publication. Query preferred.

PEANUT FARMER—3000 Highwoods Blvd., Suite 300, Raleigh, NC 27604-1029. Mary Evans, Ed. Articles, 500 to 2,000 words, on production and management practices in peanut farming. Pays $100 to $350, on publication.

PENNSYLVANIA FARMER—P.O. Box 4475, Gettysburg, PA 17325.

John R. Vogel, Ed. Articles on farmers in PA, DE, MD, and WV; timely business-of-farming concepts and successful farm management operations. Short pieces on humorous experiences in farming. Payment varies, on publication.

RURAL HERITAGE—281 Dean Ridge Ln., Gainesboro, TN 38562. Gail Damerow, Ed. How-to and feature articles, 800 to 1,200 words, related to present-day farming and logging with horses, mules, and oxen. Pays 5¢ a word, $10 for photos, on publication. Guidelines. E-mail: editor@ruralheritage.com. Web site: www.ruralheritage.com.

SHEEP! MAGAZINE—P.O. Box 10, Lake Mills, WI 53551. Dave Thompson, Ed. Articles, to 1,500 words, on successful shepherds, woolcrafts, sheep raising, and sheep dogs. "Especially interested in people who raise sheep successfully as a sideline enterprise." Photos. Pays $80 to $150, extra for photos, on publication. Query.

SMALL FARM TODAY—3903 W. Ridge Trail Rd., Clark, MO 65243-9525. Paul Berg, Man. Ed. Agriculture articles, 1,000 to 2,000 words, on preserving and promoting small farming, rural living, and "agripreneurship." How-to articles on alternative or traditional crops, livestock, and direct marketing. Pays 3½¢ a word, on publication. Query. E-mail: smallfarm@socket.net.

SMALL FARMER'S JOURNAL—P.O. Box 1627, Dept. 106, Sisters, OR 97759. Address the Eds. How-tos, humor, practical work horse information, livestock and produce marketing, gardening information, and articles appropriate to the independent family farm. Pays negotiable rates, on publication. Query.

SUCCESSFUL FARMING—1716 Locust St., Des Moines, IA 50309-3023. Gene Johnston, Man. Ed. Articles on farm production, business, and families; also farm personalities, health, leisure, and outdoor topics. Pays varying rates, on acceptance.

THE WESTERN PRODUCER—Box 2500, Saskatoon, Saskatchewan, Canada S7K 2C4. Address News Ed. Articles, to 800 words (prefer under 600 words), on agricultural and rural subjects, preferably with a Canadian slant. Photos. Pays from 23¢ a word; $50 to $100 for color photos, on publication.

THE WREN MAGAZINE—(formerly *Wyoming Rural Electric News*) 340 W. B St., Suite 101, Casper, WY 82601. Kris Wendtland, Ed. Articles, 500 to 900 words, on issues relevant to rural Wyoming. Articles should support personal and economic growth in Wyoming, social development, and education. Wyoming writers given preference. Pays $20 to $140, on publication. E-mail: wendtlnd@coffey.com.

WYOMING RURAL ELECTRIC NEWS—See *The Wren Magazine*.

ENVIRONMENT

ALTERNATIVES JOURNAL—Faculty of Environmental Studies, Univ. of Waterloo, Waterloo, Ontario, Canada N2L 3G1. Suzanne Galloway, Man. Ed. Quarterly. Feature articles, 4,000 words; notes, 200 to 500 words; and reports, 750 to 1,000 words, that focus on Canadian content in areas of environmental thought, policy, and action. No payment.

AMERICAN FORESTS—910 17th St., Suite 600, Washington, DC 20006. Michelle Robbins, Ed. Looking for skilled science writers for assignments documenting the use, enjoyment, and management of forests. Send clips.

AMERICAN SURVIVAL GUIDE—Y-Visionary, L.P., Suite 120, 2655 Anita Dr., Orange, CA 92868-3310. Jim Benson, Ed. Articles, 1,500 to 2,000 words, with photos, on human and natural forces that pose threats to everyday life, all forms of preparedness, food production and storage, self defense and weapons, etc. All text must be accompanied by photos (and vice versa). Pays $80 per published page, on publication. Query.

THE AMICUS JOURNAL—Natural Resources Defense Council, 40 W. 20th St., New York, NY 10011. Kathrin Day Lassila, Ed. Quarterly. Articles and book reviews on local, national and international environmental topics. (No fiction, speeches, or product reports accepted.) Pays varying rates, on publication. Query with clips required.

ANIMALS—350 S. Huntington Ave., Boston, MA 02130. Joni Praded, Dir./Ed. Informative, well-researched articles, to 2,500 words, on animal protection, national and international wildlife, pet care, conservation, and environmental issues that affect animals. No personal accounts or favorite pet stories. Pays from $350, on acceptance. Query.

ATLANTIC SALMON JOURNAL—P.O. Box 429, St. Andrews, N.B., Canada E0G 2X0. Jim Gourlay, Ed. Articles, 1,500 to 3,000 words, related to Atlantic salmon: fishing, conservation, ecology, travel, politics, biology, how-tos, anecdotes. Pays $100 to $400, on publication.

AUDUBON—700 Broadway, New York, NY 10003. Assistant.; Lisa Gosselin, Ed. Bimonthly. Articles, 150 to 4,000 words, on conservation and environmental issues, natural history, ecology, and related subjects. Payment varies, on acceptance. Send query with clips and SASE to Ed. Assistant.

THE BEAR DELUXE—(formerly *The Bear Essential*) P.O. Box 10342, Portland, OR 97296. Thomas L. Webb, Ed. Quarterly. Unique environmental articles, 750 to 3,500 words; essays, 250 to 2,500 words; artist profiles, 750 to 1,500 words; and reviews, 100 to 1,000 words. Fiction, 750 to 4,500 words (2,500 is ideal). Poetry. Pays 5¢ a word, after publication, and subscription. Query for nonfiction.

BIRD WATCHER'S DIGEST—P.O. Box 110, Marietta, OH 45750. William H. Thompson, III, Ed. Articles, 600 to 2,500 words, for bird watchers: first-person accounts; how-tos; pieces on backyard-related topics; profiles of bird species. Pays from $100, on publication. Write for guidelines. Submit complete manuscript with SASE.

BUGLE—Rocky Mountain Elk Foundation, P.O. Box 8249, Missoula, MT 59807-8249. Lee Cromrich, Ed. Asst. Bimonthly. Fiction and nonfiction, 1,500 to 4,000 words, on wildlife conservation, elk ecology and hunting. Department pieces, 1,000 to 3,000 words, for: "Thoughts and Theories"; "Situation Ethics"; and "Women in the Outdoors." Pays 20¢ a word, on acceptance.

CALIFORNIA WILD—(formerly *Pacific Discovery*) California Academy of Sciences, Golden Gate Park, San Francisco, CA 94118-4599. Gordy Slack, Assoc. Ed. Quarterly. Well-researched articles, 1,500 to 3,000 words, on natural history and preservation of the environment. Pays 25¢ a word, on publication. Query.

E: THE ENVIRONMENTAL MAGAZINE—Earth Action Network, Inc., P.O. Box 5098, Westport, CT 06881. Jim Motavalli, Ed. Environmental features, 4,000 words, and news for departments: 400 words for "In Brief"; and 1,000 words for "Currents." Pays 20¢ a word, on publication. Query.

EQUINOX—11450 Albert Hudon Blvd., Montreal North, Quebec, Canada H1G 3J9. Alan Morantz, Ed., Wayne Grady, Sci. Ed. Articles, 2,000 to 5,000 words, on popular geography, science, wildlife, natural history, the arts, travel, and adventure. Department pieces, 250 to 400 words, for "Nexus" (science and medicine). Pays $1,500 to $3,500 for features, $150 to $350 for short pieces, on acceptance.

FLORIDA WILDLIFE—620 S. Meridian St., Tallahassee, FL 32399-1600. Attn: Ed. Bimonthly of the Florida Game and Fresh Water Fish Commission. Articles, 800 to 1,200 words, that promote native flora and fauna, hunting, fishing in Florida's fresh waters, outdoor ethics, and conservation of Florida's natural resources. Pays $50 a page, on publication. SASE for "how to submit" memo.

HERBALGRAM—P.O. Box 201660, Austin, TX 78720. Barbara Johnston, Man. Ed. Quarterly. Articles, 1,500 to 3,000 words, on herb and medicinal plant research, regulatory issues, market conditions, native plant conservation, and other aspects of herbal use. Pays in copies. Query.

IN BUSINESS—419 State Ave., Emmaus, PA 18049-3097. Jerome Goldstein, Ed. Bimonthly. Articles, 1,500 words, for environmental entrepreneurs: reports on economically successful businesses that also demonstrate a commitment to the environment, advice on growing a "green" business, family-run businesses, home-based businesses, community ecological development, etc. Pays $100 to $250 for articles; $25 to $75 for department pieces, on publication. Query with clips.

INTERNATIONAL WILDLIFE—National Wildlife Federation, 8925 Leesburg Pike, Vienna, VA 22184. Jonathan Fisher, Ed. Articles, 2,000 words, that make nature, and human use and stewardship of it, understandable and interesting; covers wildlife and related issues outside the U.S. Pays $2,000 for full-length articles, on acceptance. Query with writing samples. SASE for guidelines.

MOTHER EARTH NEWS—Sussex Publishers, 49 E. 21st St., 11th Fl., New York, NY 10010. Ed. Bimonthly featuring articles on organic gardening, building projects, holistic health, alternative energy projects, wild foods, and environment and conservation. "We are dedicated to helping our readers become more self-sufficient, financially independent, and environmentally aware." Photos or diagrams a plus. No fiction. Payment varies, on publication.

NATIONAL WILDLIFE—8925 Leesburg Pike, Vienna, VA 22184. Mark Wexler, Ed. Articles, 1,000 to 2,500 words, on wildlife, conservation, environment; outdoor how-to pieces. Photos. Pays on acceptance. Query.

NATURE FRIEND—2727 TR 421, Sugarcreek, OH 44681. Stanley K. Brubaker, Ed. Monthly. Articles for children that "teach them to be kind to animals, plants, and nature." Also publishes some poetry, fillers, and games. Pays 5¢ per word for nonfiction; $15 for fillers and games. SASE for guidelines.

NEW HAMPSHIRE WILDLIFE—P.O. Box 239, Concord, NH 03302-0239. Marianne Conrad-Pres, Ed. Bimonthly tabloid. Fiction and nonfiction, 1,700 to 2,000 words. "Dedicated to preserving and protecting hunting, fishing, and trapping and for the conservation of fish and wildlife habitat." No payment.

THE NEW YORK STATE CONSERVATIONIST—50 Wolf Rd., Rm. 548, Albany, NY 12233-4502. R.W. Groneman, Ed. "The official magazine of the New York State Department of Environmental Conservation." Bimonthly.

Articles, varying lengths, on environmental/conservation programs and policies of New York. Pays $50 to $100 for articles; $15 for photos; and $50 for original artwork, on publication.

OUTDOOR AMERICA—707 Conservation Ln., Gaithersburg, MD 20878-2983. Attn: Articles Ed. Quarterly publication of the Izaak Walton League of America. Articles, 1,500 to 3,000 words, on natural resource conservation issues and outdoor recreation, with emphasis on IWLA member/chapter tie-in; especially fishing, hunting, and camping. Short items, 500 to 750 words. Pays 30¢ a word. Query with clips.

PACIFIC DISCOVERY—See *California Wild*.

SIERRA—85 2nd St., San Francisco, CA 94105. Joan Hamilton, Ed.-in-Chief. Articles, 750 to 2,500 words, on environmental and conservation topics, travel, hiking, backpacking, skiing, rafting, cycling. Photos. Pays from $500 to $2,000, extra for photos, on acceptance. Query with clips.

SPORTS AFIELD—250 W. 55th St., New York, NY 10019. John Atwood, Ed.-in-Chief. Articles, 500 to 2,000 words, on outdoor sports such as hiking, skiing, kayaking, mountain biking, hunting, fishing, survival, conservation, personal experiences. How-to pieces; humor, fiction. Payment varies, on acceptance.

TEXAS PARKS & WILDLIFE—Fountain Park Plaza, 3000 S. Interstate Hwy. 35, Suite 120, Austin, TX 78704. Susan Ebert, Ed. Articles, 800 to 2,500 words, promoting the conservation and enjoyment of Texas wildlife, parks, waters, and all outdoors. Features on hunting, fishing, birding, camping, and the environment. Photos a plus. Pays to $600, on acceptance; extra for photos.

VIRGINIA WILDLIFE—P.O. Box 11104, Richmond, VA 23230-1104. Attn: Ed. Articles, 500 to 1,200 words, on fishing, hunting, wildlife management, outdoor safety, ethics, etc. All material must have Virginia tie-in and may be accompanied by color photos. Pays from 18¢ a word, extra for photos, on publication. Query.

WHOLE EARTH—(formerly *Whole Earth Review*) 1408 Mission Ave., San Rafael, CA 94901. Attn: Ed. Quarterly. Articles and book reviews. "Good article material is often found in passionate personal statements or descriptions of the writer's activities." Pays $40 for reviews; payment varies for articles, on publication.

WILD OUTDOOR WORLD—Box 1249, Helena, MT 59624. Carolyn Cunningham, Ed. Dir. Articles, 600 to 800 words, on North American wildlife, for readers ages 8 to 12. Pays $100 to $500, on acceptance. Query. SASE.

WILDLIFE CONSERVATION—The Wildlife Conservation Society, Bronx, NY 10460. Nancy Simmons, Sr. Ed. First-person articles, 1,500 to 2,000 words, on "popular" natural history, "based on author's research and experience as opposed to textbook approach." Payment varies, on acceptance. Guidelines.

MEDIA & THE ARTS

THE AMERICAN ART JOURNAL—730 Fifth Ave., New York, NY 10019-4105. Jayne A. Kuchna, Ed. Scholarly articles, 2,000 to 10,000 words, on American art of the 17th through the mid-20th centuries. Photos. Pays $200 to $500, on acceptance.

AMERICAN INDIAN ART MAGAZINE—7314 E. Osborn Dr., Scottsdale, AZ 85251. Roanne P. Goldfein, Ed. Detailed articles, 10 to 20 double-spaced pages, on American Indian arts: painting, carving, beadwork, basketry, textiles, ceramics, jewelry, etc. Pays varying rates, on publication. Query.

AMERICAN JOURNALISM REVIEW—1117 Journalism Bldg., University of Maryland, College Park, MD 20742-7111. Rem Rieder, Ed. Articles, 500 to 5,000 words, on print or electronic journalism, ethics, and related issues. Query.

AMERICAN THEATRE—355 Lexington Ave., New York, NY 10017. Jim O'Quinn, Ed. Features, 250 to 2,500 words, on the theater and theater-related subjects. Departments include "Profiles," "Books," "Commentary," and "Media". Payment varies, on publication. Query.

AMERICAN VISIONS, THE MAGAZINE OF AFRO-AMERICAN CULTURE—1156 15th St. N.W., Suite 615, Washington, DC 20005. Joanne Harris, Ed. Articles, 1,500 to 2,500 words, and columns, 1,000 words, on African-American culture with a focus on the arts. Pays from $100 to $600, on publication. Query.

ART & ANTIQUES—2100 Powers Ferry Rd., Atlanta, GA 30339. Barbara S. Tapp, Ed. Research pieces, art and antiques in context (interiors), overviews, or personal narratives, 1,500 to 2,000 words, and news items, 250 to 350 words, on art or antiques. Pays 75¢ to $1 a word, on acceptance. Query with resumé and clips.

THE ARTIST'S MAGAZINE—1507 Dana Ave., Cincinnati, OH 45207. Sandra Carpenter, Ed. How-to features, 1,200 to 1,800 words, and department pieces for the working artist. Pays $150 to $350 for articles. Guidelines. Query.

BACK STAGE—1515 Broadway, 14th Fl., New York, NY 10036-8901. Sherry Eaker, Ed.-in-Chief "The Performing Arts Weekly." Service features about learning one's craft, dealing with succeeding in the business; interviews with actors, directors, and playwrights; industry tends. Payment varies, on publication. Queries required; articles on speculation.

BACK STAGE WEST—5055 Wilshire Blvd., 6th Fl., Los Angeles, CA 90036. Robert Kendt, Ed. Weekly. Articles and reviews for actor's trade paper for the West Coast. Query required. Pays 10¢ to 15¢ a word, on publication.

BLUEGRASS UNLIMITED—Box 111, Broad Run, VA 20137-0111. Peter V. Kuykendall, Ed. Articles, to 3,500 words, on bluegrass and traditional country music. Photos. Pays 8¢ to 10¢ a word, extra for photos.

BOMB—594 Broadway, Suite 905, New York, NY 10012. Editor Quarterly. Articles, varying lengths, on artists, musicians, writers, actors, and directors. Some fiction and poetry. Pays $100, on publication. Send complete manuscript.

CABLE IN THE CLASSROOM—141 Portland St., #8200, Cambridge, MA 02139-1937. Al Race, Ed. Monthly. Articles, 200 to 1,200 words, for K through 12 teachers and media specialists, on upcoming educational cable television programs and creative ways to use those programs. Pays $100 to $500, on acceptance. Queries required.

THE CHURCH MUSICIAN—See *Church Musician Today.*

CHURCH MUSICIAN TODAY—(formerly *The Church Musician*) 127 Ninth Ave. N., Nashville, TN 37234. Jere V. Adams, Ed. Articles on choral techniques, instrumental groups, worship planning, music administration, directing choirs (all ages), rehearsal planning, music equipment, new technology, drama/pageants and related subjects, hymn studies, book reviews, and music-related fillers. Pays 5½¢ a word for articles on hard copy; 6½¢ per word for articles on diskette, on acceptance.

CINEASTE—200 Park Ave. S., Suite 1601, New York, NY 10003-1503. Attn: Eds. Quarterly. Articles, 2,000 to 3,000 words, on the art and politics of the cinema. "Articles should discuss a film, film genre, a career, a theory, a movement, or related topic, in depth." Interviews with people in filmmaking. Department pieces, 1,000 to 1,500 words. Pays $75 to $100, on publication.

DANCE MAGAZINE—33 W. 60th St., New York, NY 10023. Richard Philp, Ed.-in-Chief. Articles on dancers, companies, history, professional concerns, young dancers, health, and current and upcoming news events. Photos: Query; limited free-lance market.

DANCE TEACHER—(formerly *Dance Teacher Now*) Lifestyle Ventures, 250 W. 57th St., Suite 420, New York, NY 10107. Susie Eley, Ed. Articles, 500 to 1,500 words, for professional dance educators, students, and other dance professionals on practical information for the teacher and/or business owner; economic and business issues related to the profession. Profiles of schools, methods, and people who are leaving their mark on dance. Must be thoroughly researched. Photos a plus. Query. Pays $100 to $300. E-mail: seley @lifestyleventures.com.

DECORATIVE ARTIST'S WORKBOOK—1507 Dana Ave., Cincinnati, OH 45207. Anne Hevener, Ed. How-to articles, 1,000 to 1,500 words, on decorative painting. "Painting projects only, not crafts." Profiles, 500 words, of up-and-coming painters for "The Artist of the Issue" column. Pays $150 to $300 for features; $100 to $150 for profiles, on acceptance. Query required.

DOUBLETAKE—1317 W. Pettigrew St., Durham, NC 27705. Attn: Manuscript Ed. Quarterly. Realistic fiction, narrative poetry, book excerpts, memoirs, essays, and cultural criticism. Color or B&W photo-essays, works in progress, and proposals "in the broadest definition of documentary work. We're looking for new and unexpected insights about the world around us." Payment varies, on acceptance. Guidelines. Query for nonfiction. SASE.

DRAMATICS—Educational Theatre Assoc., 2343 Auburn Ave., Cincinnati, OH 45219. Don Corathers, Ed. Articles, interviews, how-tos, 750 to 4,000 words, for high school students of the performing arts with an emphasis on theater practice: acting, directing, playwriting, technical subjects. Prefer articles that "could be used by a better-than-average high school teacher to teach students something about the performing arts." Also publishes plays. Pays $25 to $400 honorarium. Complete manuscripts preferred; graphics and photos accepted.

ELECTRONIC MUSICIAN MAGAZINE—6400 Hollis St., Suite 12, Emeryville, CA 94608. Mary Cosola, Managing Ed. Monthly. Articles, 1,500 to 3,500 words, on audio recording, live sound engineering, technical applications, and product reviews. Pays $350 to $750, on acceptance.

EMMY—5220 Lankershim Blvd., N. Hollywood, CA 91601-2800. Gail Polevoi, Man. Ed. Bimonthly. Articles, 2,000 words, related to the television industry: contemporary issues and trends in broadcast and cable; VIPs, especially those behind the scenes; and new technology. Pays from $900, on publication. "It is easier for newcomers to break in with shorter pieces rather than

full-length articles. These items can run 500 to 700 words; pay starts at $250."
Query.

THE ENGRAVERS JOURNAL—26 Summit St., P. O. Box 318, Brighton, MI 48116. Rosemary Farrell, Admin. Ed. Articles, varying lengths, on topics related to the engraving industry and small business operations. Pays $75 to $225, on acceptance. Query.

ENTERTAINMENT DESIGN—(formerly *Theatrecrafts International*) 32 W. 18th St., New York, NY 10011. Jacqueline Tien, Pub. David Johnson, Ed. Articles, 500 to 2,500 words, on design, technical, and management aspects of theater, opera, dance, television, and film for those in performing arts and the entertainment trade. Pays on acceptance. Query. Web site: www.eteenyc.net.

FILM COMMENT—70 Lincoln Ctr. Plaza, New York, NY 10023-6595. Richard T. Jameson, Ed. Bimonthly. Articles, 1,000 to 5,000 words, on films (new and old, foreign and domestic), as well as performers, writers, cinematographers, studios, national cinemas, genres. Opinion and historical pieces also used. Pays approximately 33¢ a word, on publication.

FILM QUARTERLY—Univ. of California Press Journals, 2120 Berkeley Way, Berkeley, CA 94720. Ann Martin, Ed. Historical, analytical, and critical articles, to 6,000 words; film reviews, book reviews. Guidelines.

GLORY SONGS—127 Ninth Ave. N., Nashville, TN 37234. Jere V. Adams, Ed. For volunteer and part-time music directors and members of church choirs. Very easy music and accompaniments designed specifically for the small church (4 to 6 songs per issue). The Glory Songs kit includes Director's Letter with articles for directors and choir members on leisure reading, music training, worship planning, and choir projects. Pays 5½ per word for hard copy; 6½ for diskette, on aceptance.

GUITAR PLAYER MAGAZINE—411 Borel Ave., Suite 100, San Mateo, CA 94402. Attn: Ed. Articles, from 200 words, on guitars and related subjects. Pays $100 to $600, on acceptance. Buys all rights.

INDEPENDENT FILM AND VIDEO MONTHLY—304 Hudson St., New York, NY 10013-1015. Patricia Thomson, Ed.-in-Chief. Articles on film, video, and new media. "Technical, practical, legal, and aesthetic coverage of the media arts fields." Pays 10¢ a word, on publication. Query.

INDIA CURRENTS—P.O. Box 21285, San Jose, CA 95151. Vandana Kumar, Managing Ed. Fiction, to 3,000 words, and articles, to 3,000 words, on Indian culture in the United States and Canada. Articles on Indian arts and entertainment. Also music reviews, 800 words; book reviews, 800 words; commentary on national or international events affecting the lives of Indians, 800 words; and travel articles, to 3,000 words. Pays in subscriptions.

INDIAN ARTIST—1807 Second St., #61, Santa Fe, NM 87505-3510. Michael Hice, Ed. Quarterly. Articles on contemporary Native American art and interviews with Native American artists, 200 to 2,300 words. Some fillers and photographs. Payment varies, on acceptance. Query.

INTERNATIONAL MUSICIAN—Paramount Bldg., 1501 Broadway, Suite 600, New York, NY 10036. Attn: Ed. Articles, 1,500 to 2,000 words, for professional musicians. Pays varying rates, on acceptance. Query.

IPI REPORT—132A Neff Annex, School of Journalism, University of Missouri, Columbia, MO 65211. Prof. Stuart Loory, Ed. Quarterly. Short articles on international journalism, press coverage, and free press issues around the world. Queries required. Send SASE for guidelines. (E-mail submissions preferred.) Pay varies, on publication. E-mail: stuartloory@jmail.jour. missouri.edu.

KEYBOARD MAGAZINE—Suite 100, 411 Borel Ave., San Mateo, CA 94402. Marvin Sanders, Ed. Articles, 300 to 5,000 words, on keyboard instruments, MIDI and computer technology, and players. Photos. Pays $200 to $600, on acceptance. Query.

MODERN DRUMMER—12 Old Bridge Rd., Cedar Grove, NJ 07009. Ronald L. Spagnardi, Ed. Articles, 500 to 2,000 words, on drumming: how-tos, interviews. Pays $50 to $500, on publication.

NEW ENGLAND ENTERTAINMENT DIGEST—P.O. Box 88, Burlington, MA 01803. Julie Ann Charest, Ed. News and features on the arts and entertainment industry in New England and New York. Pays $15 to $75, on publication, and 5$ per print of original photos.

OPERA NEWS—The Metropolitan Opera Guild, 70 Lincoln Ctr. Plaza, New York, NY 10023-6593. Rudolph S. Ranch, Ed. Articles, 600 to 2,500 words, on all aspects of opera. Payment varies, on publication. Query.

PEI (Photo Electronic Imaging) Magazine—229 Peachtree St. N.E., Suite 2200, International Tower, Atlanta, GA 30303. E. Sapwater, Exec. Ed. Articles, 1,000 to 3,000 words, on electronic imaging, computer graphics, desktop publishing, pre-press and commercial printing, multimedia, and web design. Material must be directly related to professional imaging trends and techniques. Query required; all articles on assignment only. Payment varies, on publication.

PERFORMANCE—1101 University Dr., Suite 108, Fort Worth, TX 76107. Jane Cohen, Ed.-in-Chief. The leading publication on the touring industry: concert promoters, booking agents, concert venues and clubs, as well as support services, such as lighting, sound, and staging companies.

PETERSEN'S PHOTOGRAPHIC—6420 Wilshire Blvd., Los Angeles, CA 90048-5515. Ron Leach, Ed. Articles and how-to pieces, with photos, on travel, portrait, action, and digital photography, for beginners, advanced amateurs, and professionals. Pays $125 per printed page, on publication.

PLAYBILL—52 Vanderbilt Ave., New York, NY 10017. Judy Samelson, Ed. No unsolicited manuscripts. PLAYBILL Magazine provides information necessary to the understanding and enjoyment of each Broadway production, certain Lincoln Center and Off-Broadway productions and regional attractions served. In addition to information about the attractions, it features articles by and about theatre personalities, fashion, entertainment, dining, etc.

POPULAR PHOTOGRAPHY—1633 Broadway, New York, NY 10019. Jason Schneider, Ed.-in-Chief. Illustrated how-to articles, 500 to 2,000 words, for serious amateur photographers. Query with outline and photos.

ROLLING STONE—1290 Ave. of the Americas, 2nd Fl., New York, NY 10104. Attn: Ed. Magazine of American music, culture, and politics. No fiction. Query; no unsolicited manuscripts. Rarely accepts free-lance material.

SCULPTURE FORUM—(formerly *Wildlife Art*) P.O. Box 390026, Edina, MN 55439. Robert J. Koenke, Ed. Informative, thought-provoking articles, 500 to 2,500 words, on wildlife and art topics. All media, including wood, bronze, stone, glass, and metal. Many features spotlight individual artists; query with photos or slides of artist's work. Guidelines. Payment varies, on acceptance. Query required.

THE SENIOR MUSICIAN—127 Ninth Ave. N., Nashville, TN 37234. Jere V. Adams, Ed. Quarterly music periodical. Easy choir music for senior adult choirs to use in worship, ministry, and recreation. Also includes leisure reading, music training, fellowship suggestions, and choir projects for personal growth. For music directors, pastors, organists, pianists, choir coordinators. Pays 5½¢ a word for hard copy; 6½ on diskette, on acceptance.

SOUTHWEST ART—5444 Westheimer, Suite 1440, Houston, TX 77056. Margaret L. Brown, Ed. Articles, 1,200 to 1,800 words, on the artists, art collectors, museum exhibitions, gallery events and dealers, art history, art trends, and Western American art. Particularly interested in representational or figurative arts. Pays from $400, on acceptance. Query with at least 20 slides of artwork to be featured.

STAGE DIRECTIONS—SMW Communications, Inc., 250 W. 57th St., Suite 420, New York, NY 10107. Stephen Peithman, Ed.-in-Chief. How-to articles, to 2,000 words, on acting, directing, costuming, makeup, lighting, set design and decoration, props, special effects, fundraising, and audience development for readers who are active in all aspects of community, regional, academic, or youth theater. Short pieces, 400 to 500 words, "are a good way to approach us first." Pays 10¢ a word, on publication. Guidelines.

STORYTELLING MAGAZINE—116½ W. Main St., Jonesborough, TN 37659. Attn: Eds. Features, 1,000 to 2,500 words, related to the oral tradition. News items, 200 to 400 words, and photos reflecting unusual storytelling events/applications. Query. "Limited free-lance opportunities." Pays in copies.

SURFACE—7 Isadora Duncan Ln., San Francisco, CA 94102. Jeremy Lin, Ed. Dir. Quarterly. Articles, 100 to 3,000 words, including celebrity interviews; reviews of art, music, and fashion. Payment varies, on publication.

TDR (THE DRAMA REVIEW): A JOURNAL OF PERFORMANCE STUDIES—721 Broadway, 6th Fl., New York, NY 10003. Richard Schechner, Ed. Eclectic articles on experimental performance and performance theory; cross-cultural, examining the social, political, historical, and theatrical contexts in which performance happens. Submit query or manuscript with SASE and IBM compatible disk. Pays $100 to $250, on publication.

THEATRECRAFTS INTERNATIONAL—See *Entertainment Design.*

U.S. ART—220 S. Sixth St., Suite 500, Minneapolis, MN 55402. Sara Gilbert, Ed. Features and artist profiles, 1,200 words, for collectors of limited-edition art prints. Query. Pays $300 to $450, within 30 days of acceptance.

VIDEOMAKER—P.O. Box 4591, Chico, CA 95927. Stephen Muratore, Ed. Authoritative, how-to articles geared to hobbyist and professional video camera/camcorder users: instructionals, editing, desktop video, audio and video production, innovative applications, tools and tips, industry developments, new products, etc. Pays varying rates, on publication. Queries preferred.

WEST ART—P.O. Box 6868, Auburn, CA 95604-6868. Martha Garcia, Ed. Features, 350 to 700 words, on fine arts and crafts. No hobbies. Photos. Pays 50¢ per column inch, on publication. SASE required.

WILDLIFE ART—See *Sculpture Forum.*

HOBBIES, CRAFTS, COLLECTING

AMERICAN HOW-TO—12301 Whitewater Dr., Suite 260, Minnetonka, MN 55343. Tom Sweeney, Ed. No unsolicited material.

AMERICAN WOODWORKER—Rodale Press, 33 E. Minor St., Emmaus, PA 18098. Tim Snyder, Exec. Ed. "A how-to bimonthly for the woodworking enthusiast." Technical or anecdotal articles, to 2,000 words, relating to woodworking or furniture design. Fillers, drawings, slides and photos considered. Pays from $150 per published page, on publication; regular contributors paid on acceptance. Queries preferred. Guidelines.

ANCESTRY—P.O. Box 990, Orem, UT 84057. Loretto Szucs, Exec. Ed. Jennifer Utley, Managing Ed. Bimonthly for professional Family Historians and hobbyists who are interested in getting the most out of their research. Articles, 1,500 to 4,000 words, that instruct (how-tos, research techniques, etc.) and inform (new research sources, new collections, etc.). No family histories, genealogies, or pedigree charts. Pays $50 to $1,500, on publication. Guidelines.

THE ANTIQUE TRADER WEEKLY—Box 1050, Dubuque, IA 52004. Kyle Husfloen, Ed. Articles, 1,000 to 2,000 words, on all types of antiques and collectors' items. Photos. Pays from $50 to $250, on publication. Query preferred. Buys all rights.

ANTIQUES & AUCTION NEWS—P.O. Box 500, Mount Joy, PA 17552. Denise Sater, Ed. Weekly newspaper. Factual articles, 600 to 1,500 words, on antiques, collectors, collections, and places of historic interest. Photos. Query required. Pays $10 to $35, after publication.

ANTIQUEWEEK—P.O. Box 90, Knightstown, IN 46148. Tom Hoepf, Ed., Central Edition; Connie Swaim, Ed., Eastern Edition. Weekly antique, auction, and collectors' newspaper. Articles, 500 to 2,000 words, on antiques, collectibles, genealogy, auction and antique show reports. Photos. Pays from $40 to $200 for in-depth articles, on publication. Query. Guidelines.

AOPA PILOT—421 Aviation Way, Frederick, MD 21701. Thomas B. Haines, Ed. Magazine of the Aircraft Owners and Pilots Assn. Articles, to 2,500 words, with photos, on general aviation for beginning and experienced pilots. Pays to $750.

THE AUCTION EXCHANGE—P.O. Box 57, Plainwell, MI 49080-0057. Attn: Ed. Weekly tabloid. Articles, 500 to 700 words, on auctions, antiques, collectibles, and Michigan history. "We have 9,000 subscribers who collect all sorts of things." Queries preferred.

AUTOGRAPH COLLECTOR MAGAZINE—510-A S. Corona Mall, Corona, CA 91719. Ev Phillips, Ed. Articles, 1,000 to 2,000 words, on all areas of autograph collecting: preservation, framing, and storage, specialty collections, documents and letters, collectors and dealers. Queries preferred. Guidelines. Payment varies.

BECKETT BASEBALL CARD MONTHLY—15850 Dallas Pkwy., Dallas, TX 75248. Mike McAllister, Ed. Articles, 500 to 2,000 words, geared to baseball card collecting, with an emphasis on the pleasures of the hobby. "We accept no stories with investment tips." Query. Pays $150 to $250, on acceptance. Guidelines.

BECKETT BASKETBALL CARD MONTHLY—15850 Dallas Pkwy., Dallas, TX 75248. Mike McAllister, Man. Ed. Articles, 400 to 1,000 words, on the sports-card hobby, especially basketball card collecting for readers 7 to 70. Query. Pays $100 to $250, on acceptance. Also publishes *Beckett Baseball Card Monthly, Beckett Sports Collectibles & Autographs, Beckett Football Card Monthly, Beckett Hockey Collector,* and *Beckett Racing and Motorsports Monthly.* SASE for guidelines.

BIRD TALK—Box 6050, Mission Viejo, CA 92690. Melissa Kauffman, Ed. Articles for pet bird owners: care and feeding, training, safety, outstanding personal adventures, exotic birds in their native countries, profiles of celebrities' pet birds, travel to bird parks or shows. Good transparencies a plus. Pays up to 10¢ a word, after publication. Query required.

BIRD WATCHER'S DIGEST—P.O. Box 110, Marietta, OH 45750. William H. Thompson III, Ed. Articles, 600 to 3,000 words, on bird-watching experiences and expeditions; interesting backyard topics and how-tos. Pays from $50, on publication. Allow 8 weeks for response.

BIRDER'S WORLD—P.O. Box 1612, Waukesha, WI 53187-1612. Greg Butcher, Ed. Bimonthly. Articles, 2,200 to 2,400 words, on all aspects of birding, especially on a particular species or the status of an endangered species. Tips on birding, attracting birds, or photographing them. Personal essays, 500 to 1,500 words. Book reviews, to 500 words. Pays $350 to $450 for features, on publication. Query preferred.

BREW YOUR OWN—Niche Publications, 216 F St., Suite 160, Davis, CA 95616. Craig Bystrynski, Ed. Practical how-to articles, 800 to 2,500 words, for homebrewers. Pays $50 to $150, on publication. Query.

THE CAROUSEL NEWS & TRADER—87 Park Ave. W., Suite 206, Mansfield, OH 44902. Attn: Ed. Features on carousel history and profiles of amusement park operators and carousel carvers of interest to band organ enthusiasts, carousel art collectors, preservationists, amusement park owners, artists, and restorationists. Pays $50 per published page, after publication. Guidelines.

CC MOTORCYCLE NEWSMAGAZINE—P.O. Box 808, Nyack, NY 10960. Ed. Monthly. Articles and fiction, 750 to 1,500 words, dealing with motorcycles. Also poetry, all lengths. Photos accepted. Submissions must be in electronic form. Send for guidelines. Pays $10 minimum, and $75 for stories with photos, 30 days after publication.

CHESS LIFE—3054 NYS Rte. 9W, New Windsor, NY 12553-7698. Glenn Petersen, Ed. Articles, 500 to 3,000 words, for members of the U.S. Chess Federation, on news, profiles, technical aspects of chess. Features on all aspects of chess: history, humor, puzzles, etc. Fiction, 500 to 2,000 words, related to chess. Photos. Pays varying rates, upon publication. Query; limited free-lance market.

CLASSIC TOY TRAINS—21027 Crossroads Cir., Waukesha, WI 53187. Attn: Ed. Articles, with photos, on toy train layouts and collections. Also toy train manufacturing history and repair/maintenance. Pays $75 per printed page, on acceptance. Query.

COLLECTOR EDITIONS—170 Fifth Ave., New York, NY 10010. Joan Muyskens Pursley, Ed. Articles, 750 to 1,500 words, on collectibles, mainly contemporary limited-edition figurines, plates, and prints. Pays $150 to $350, within 30 days of acceptance. Query with photos.

COLLECTORS JOURNAL—P.O. Box 601, Vinton, IA 52349. Connie

Gewecke, Ed. Weekly tabloid. Features, to 2,000 words, on antiques and collectibles. Pays $10 for articles, $15 for articles with photos, on publication.

COLLECTORS NEWS—P.O. Box 156, Grundy Ctr., IA 50638. Linda Kruger, Ed. Articles, to 1,000 words, on private collections, antiques, and collectibles, especially modern limited-edition collectibles, 20th-century nostalgia, Americana, glass and china, music, furniture, transportation, timepieces, jewelry, farm-related collectibles, and lamps; include quality color or B&W photos. Pays $1 per column inch; $25 for front-page color photos, on publication.

CRAFTING TRADITIONS—5400 S. 60th St., Greendale, WI 53129. Kathleen Anderson, Ed. All types of craft designs (needlepoint, quilting, woodworking, etc.) with complete instructions and full-size patterns. Pays from $25 to $250, on acceptance, for all rights.

CRAFTS 'N THINGS—2400 Devon, Suite 375, Des Plaines, IL 60018-4618. Nona Piorkowski, Ed. How-to articles on all kinds of crafts projects, with instructions. Send manuscript with instructions and photograph of the finished item. Pays $50 to $250, on acceptance.

DOLL WORLD—306 E. Parr Rd., Berne, IN 46711. Vicki Steensma, Ed. Explores the many aspects of dolls and doll collecting. Informative articles about doll history, both contemporary and antique, costume history, and tips on how to re-create the fashions of yesterday. Query for submission guidelines.

DOLLHOUSE MINIATURES—(formerly *Nutshell News*) 21027 Crossroads Cir., P.O. Box 1612, Waukesha, WI 53187. Kay Melchisedech Olson, Ed. Articles, 1,200 to 1,500 words, for dollhouse-scale miniatures enthusiasts, collectors, craftspeople, and hobbyists. Interested in artisan profiles and how-to projects. "Writers must be knowledgeable about scale miniatures." Color slides or B&W prints required. Payment varies, on acceptance. Query.

DOLLS, THE COLLECTOR'S MAGAZINE—170 Fifth Ave., New York, NY 10010. Stephanie Finnegan, Ed. Articles, 500 to 2,500 words, for knowledgeable doll collectors; sharply focused with a strong collecting angle, and concrete information (value, identification, restoration, etc.). Include high quality slides or transparencies. Pays $100 to $350, within 30 days of acceptance. Query.

DRUM! MAGAZINE—1275 Lincoln Ave., Suite 13, San Jose, CA 95125. Andy Doesschuk, Ed. Eight times a year. Technical magazine for drummers and percussionists. Nonfiction, such as interviews and product reviews, 350 to 3,000 words. Pays flat rate, on publication.

FIBERARTS—50 College St., Asheville, NC 28801. Ann Batchelder, Ed. Published 5 times yearly. Articles, 400 to 2,000 words, on contemporary trends in fiber sculpture, weaving, surface design, quilting, stitchery, papermaking, felting, basketry, and wearable art. Query with photos of subject, outline, and synopsis. Pays varying rates, on publication.

FIGURINES & COLLECTIBLES—Cowles Enthusiast Media, 6405 Flank Dr., Harrisburg, PA 17112. Mindy Kinsey, Man. Ed. Not currently accepting material.

FINE LINES—Box 101447, Pittsburgh, PA 15237. Deborah A. Novak, Ed. Publication of the Historic Needlework Guild. Articles, 500 to 1,500 words, about historic needlework, museums, famous historic needlework, or themes revolving around stitching (samplers, needlework tools, etc.). Pays varying rates, on acceptance. Queries required.

FINE WOODWORKING— 63 S. Main St., Newtown, CT 06470. Timothy Schreiner, Ed. Bimonthly. Articles on woodworking: basics of tool use, stock preparation and joinery, specialized techniques and finishing, shop-built tools, jigs and fixtures; or any stage of design, construction, finishing and installation of cabinetry and furniture. "We look for high-quality worksmanship, thoughtful designs, safe and proper procedures." Departments: "Methods of Work," "Q&A," "Master Class," "Finish Line," "Tools & Materials," and "Notes and Comment." Pays $150 per page, on publication; pays from $10 for short department pieces. Query.

FINESCALE MODELER—P.O. Box 1612, Waukesha, WI 53187. Terry Thompson, Ed. How-to articles for people who make nonoperating scale models of aircraft, automobiles, boats, and figures. Photos and drawings should accompany articles. One-page model-building hints and tips. Pays from $45 per published page, on acceptance. Query preferred.

FRESHWATER AND MARINE AQUARIUM—P.O. Box 487, Sierra Madre, CA 91025. Don Dewey, Ed. "The Magazine Dedicated To The Tropical Fish Enthusiast." How-to articles, varying lengths, on anything related to basic, semi-technical, and technical aspects of freshwater and marine aquariology. Payment is $50 to $350 for features, $50 to $250 for secondary articles, $100 to $200 for columns, and $25 to $75 for fillers. Send for guidelines.

GAMES—P.O. Box 184, Ft. Washington, PA 19034. R. Wayne Schmittberger, Ed.-in-Chief. "The magazine for creative minds at play." Features and short articles on games and playful, offbeat subjects. Visual and verbal puzzles, pop culture quizzes, brainteasers, contests, game reviews. Pays top rates, on publication. Send SASE for guidelines; specify writer's, crosswords, variety puzzles, or brainteasers.

GOLD AND TREASURE HUNTER—P.O. Box 47, Happy Camp, CA 96039. Gerry Westerkamp, Man. Ed. Bimonthly. Articles, 1,000 to 2,000 words, about people discovering gold and gems, metal detecting, and outdoor adventure. First-person experiences, adventure, profiles, and how-to. "We provide wholesome family recreation, exploration, and adventure." Pays 3¢ a word, after publication.

HERITAGE QUEST—American Genealogical Lending Library, P.O. Box 329, Bountiful, UT 84011. Leland Meitzler, Ed. Bimonthly. Genealogy how-to articles, 2 to 4 pages; national, international, or regional in scope. Pays $30 per published page, on publication.

THE HOME SHOP MACHINIST—2779 Aero Park Dr., Box 1810, Traverse City, MI 49685. Joe D. Rice, Ed. How-to articles on precision metalworking and foundry work. Accuracy and attention to detail a must. Pays $40 per published page, extra for photos and illustrations, on publication. Guidelines.

KITPLANES—8745 Aero Dr., Suite 105, San Diego, CA 92123. Dave Martin, Ed. Articles geared to the growing market of aircraft built from kits and plans by home craftsmen, on all aspects of design, construction, and performance, 1,000 to 2,500 words. Pays $70 per page, on publication.

LOST TREASURE—P.O. Box 451589, Grove, OK 74345. Patsy Beyerl, Man. Ed. How-to articles, legends, folklore, and stories of lost treasures. Also publishes *Treasure Cache* (annual): articles on documented treasure caches with sidebar telling how to search for cache highlighted in article. Pays 4¢ a word, $5 for photos, $100 for cover photos.

THE MIDATLANTIC ANTIQUES MAGAZINE—P.O. Box 908, Henderson, NC 27536. Lydia Stainback, Ed. Articles, 500 to 2,000 words, on antiques, collectibles, and related subjects. "We need show and auction reporters." Queries are preferred. Payment varies, on publication.

MILITARY HISTORY—Primedia History Group, 741 Miller Dr. S.E., #D2, Leesburg, VA 20175. Jon Guttman, Ed. Bimonthly. Features, 4,000 words with 500-word sidebars, on the strategy, tactics, and personalities of military history. Department pieces, 2,000 words, on intrigue, weaponry, and perspectives; book reviews. No fiction. Pays $200 to $400, on publication. Query. SASE for guidelines.

MINIATURE COLLECTOR—30595 Eight Mile Rd., Livonia, MI 48152-1761. Ruth Keessen, Pub. Articles, 800 to 1,200 words, with photos, on outstanding 1/12-scale (dollhouse) miniatures and the people who make and collect them. Original, illustrated how-to projects for making miniatures. Pays varying rates, within 30 days of acceptance. Query with photos.

MINIATURE QUILTS—See *Traditional Quiltworks.*

MODEL RAILROADER—21027 Crossroads Cir., P.O. Box 1612, Waukesha, WI 53187. Andy Sperandeo, Ed. Articles on model railroads, with photos of layout and equipment. Pays $90 per printed page, on acceptance. Query.

NEW ENGLAND ANTIQUES JOURNAL—4 Church St., Ware, MA 01082. Jody Young, Gen. Mgr. Jamie Mercier, Man. Ed. Well-researched articles, usually by recognized authorities in their field, 2,000 to 5,000 words, on antiques of interest to dealers or collectors; antiques market news, to 500 words; photos required. Pays from $100 to $250, on publication. Query or send manuscript. Reports in 2 to 4 weeks.

NUTSHELL NEWS—See *Dollhouse Miniatures.*

PETERSEN'S PHOTOGRAPHIC—6420 Wilshire Blvd., Los Angeles, CA 90048. Ron Leach, Ed. How-to articles on all phases of still photography of interest to the amateur and advanced photographer. Pays about $100 per printed page for article accompanied by photos, on publication.

POPULAR MECHANICS—224 W. 57th St., New York, NY 10019. Sarah Deem, Man. Ed. Articles, 300 to 1,500 words, on latest developments in mechanics, industry, science, telecommunications; features on hobbies with a mechanical slant; how-tos on home and shop projects; features on outdoor adventures, boating, and electronics. Photos and sketches a plus. Pays to $1,500; to $500 for short pieces, on acceptance. Buys all rights.

POPULAR WOODWORKING—1507 Dana Ave., Cincinnati, OH 45207. Steve Shanesy, Ed. Project articles, up to 3,000 words; techniques pieces, to 1,500 words, for the "modest production woodworker, small shop owner, wood craftsperson, intermediate hobbyist and woodcarver." Pays $500 to $1,000 for large, complicated projects; $100 to $500 for small projects and other features; pays on acceptance. Query with brief outline and photo of finished project.

QUILTING TODAY—See *Traditional Quiltworks.*

R/C MODELER MAGAZINE—P.O. Box 487, Sierra Madre, CA 91025. Patricia E. Crews, Ed. "The world's leading publication for the radio control model aircraft enthusiast." How-to articles, varying lengths, on anything related to radio control model aircraft, helicopters, boats, and cars. Payment is $50 to $350 for features; $50 to $250 for secondary articles; and $25 to $75 for fillers. Send for guidelines.

RAILROAD MODEL CRAFTSMAN—P.O. Box 700, Newton, NJ 07860-0700. William C. Schaumburg, Ed. How-to articles on scale model railroading; cars, operation, scenery, etc. Pays on publication.

RENAISSANCE MAGAZINE—Phantom Press Publications, 13 Appleton Rd., Nantucket, MA 02554. Kim Guarnaccia, Ed. Feature articles on history, costuming, heraldry, re-enactment, roleplaying, Renaissance faires, interviews, and reviews of medieval and Renaissance books, music, movies, and games. Pays 5¢ a word, on publication.

RESTORATION—P.O. Box 50046, Dept. TW, Tucson, AZ 85703-1046. W.R. Haessner, Ed. Articles, 1,200 to 1,800 words, on restoring and building machines, boats, autos, trucks, planes, trains, buildings, toys, tools, etc. Photos and art required. Pays from $25 per page, on publication. Query.

RUG HOOKING MAGAZINE—Stackpole Magazines, 500 Vaughn St., Harrisburg, PA 17110. Patrice Crowley, Ed. How-to and feature articles on rug hooking for beginners and advanced artists. Payment varies.

SCHOOL MATES—U.S. Chess Federation, 3054 NYS Rt. 9W, New Windsor, NY 12553-7698. Jay Hastings, Publications Dir. Articles and fiction, 250 to 800 words, and short fillers, related to chess for beginning chess players (primarily children, 8 to 15). "Primarily instructive material, but there's room for fun puzzles, cartoons, anecdotes, etc. All chess related. Articles on chess-playing celebrities are always of interest to us." Pays from $20, on publication. Query; limited free-lance market.

SEW NEWS—741 Corporate Circle, Suite A, Golden, CO 80401. Linda Turner Griepentrog, Ed. Articles, to 3,000 words, "that teach a specific technique, inspire a reader to try new sewing projects, or inform a reader about an interesting person, company, or project related to sewing, textiles, or fashion." Emphasis is on fashion (not craft) sewing. Pays $25 to $400, on acceptance. Queries required; no unsolicited manuscripts accepted.

SPORTS COLLECTORS DIGEST—Krause Publications, 700 E. State St., Iola, WI 54990. Tom Mortenson, Ed. Articles, 750 to 2,000 words, on old baseball card sets and other sports memorabilia and collectibles. Pays $50 to $100, on publication.

TEDDY BEAR REVIEW—Collector Communications Corp., 170 Fifth Ave., New York, NY 10010. Stephen L. Cronk, Ed. Articles on antique and contemporary teddy bears for makers, collectors, and enthusiasts. Pays $100 to $300, within 30 days of acceptance. Query with photos.

THREADS MAGAZINE—Taunton Press, 63 S. Main St., Box 5506, Newtown, CT 06470. Attn: Ed. Bimonthly. Technical pieces on garment construction by writers who are expert sewers, quilters, embellishers, and other needle workers. Pays $150 per published page, on publication.

TRADITIONAL QUILTWORKS—Chitra Publications, 2 Public Ave., Montrose, PA 18801. Attn: Ed. Team. Specific, quilt-related how-to articles, 700 to 1,500 words. Patterns, features, and department pieces. Completed manuscripts preferred. Pays $75 per published page, on publication. Also publishes *Quilting Today* and *Miniature Quilts*.

TRAINS—Kalmbach Publishing Co., 21027 Crossroads Cir., P.O. Box 1612, Waukesha, WI 53187. Attn: Ed. Assistant. Articles, first-person recalls, anecdotes, and poetry, all related to the field of railroading. Photos accepted. Pays on acceptance. Query.

TREASURE CACHE—See *Lost Treasure.*

WEST ART—Box 6868, Auburn, CA 95604-6868. Martha Garcia, Ed. Features, 350 to 700 words, on fine arts and crafts. No hobbies. Photos. Pays 50¢ per column inch, on publication. SASE required.

WESTERN & EASTERN TREASURES—P.O. Box 1598, Mercer Island, WA 98040-1598. Rosemary Anderson, Man. Ed. Illustrated articles, to 1,500 words, on treasure hunting and how-to metal-detecting tips. Pays 2¢ a word, extra for photos, on publication.

WILDFOWL CARVING AND COLLECTING—See *Wildfowl Carving Magazine.*

WILDFOWL CARVING MAGAZINE—(formerly *Wildfowl Carving and Collecting*) Stackpole Magazines, 500 Vaughn St., Harrisburg, PA 17110. Cathy Hart, Ed.-in-Chief. How-to and reference articles, of varying lengths, on bird carving; collecting antique and contemporary carvings. Query. Pays varying rates, on acceptance.

WOODENBOAT MAGAZINE—P.O. Box 78, Brooklin, ME 04616. Matthew Murphy, Ed. How-to and technical articles, 4,000 words, on construction, repair, and maintenance of wooden boats; design, history, and use of wooden boats; and profiles of outstanding wooden boat builders and designers. Pays $200 to $250 per 1,000 words. Query preferred.

WOODWORK—42 Digital Dr., Suite 5, Novato, CA 94949. John Lavine, Ed. Bimonthly. Articles for woodworkers on all aspects of woodworking (simple, complex, technical, or aesthetic). Pays $150 per published page; $35 to $75 for "Techniques," on publication. Queries or outlines (with slides) preferred.

YELLOWBACK LIBRARY—P.O. Box 36172, Des Moines, IA 50315. Gil O'Gara, Ed. Articles, 300 to 2,000 words, on boys'/girls' series literature (Hardy Boys, Nancy Drew, Tom Swift, etc.) for collectors, researchers, and dealers. "Especially welcome are interviews with, or articles by, past and present writers of juvenile series fiction." Pays in copies.

YESTERYEAR—P.O. Box 2, Princeton, WI 54968. Michael Jacobi, Ed. Articles on antiques and collectibles for readers in WI, IL, IA, MN, and surrounding states. Photos. Will consider regular columns on collecting or antiques. Pays from $20, on publication. Limited market.

ZYMURGY—Box 1679, Boulder, CO 80306-1679. Dena Nishek, Ed. Articles appealing to beer lovers and homebrewers. Pays after publication. Guidelines. Query.

SCIENCE & COMPUTERS

AD ASTRA—National Space Society, 600 Pennsylvania Ave. S.E., #201, Washington, DC 20003-4316. Frank Sietzen, Ed.-in-Chief. Lively, semi-technical features, to 2,000 words, on all aspects of international space exploration. Particularly interested in "Living in Space" articles; commercial space and human space flight technology. Pays $150 to $250, on publication. Query. Guidelines.

AMERICAN HERITAGE OF INVENTION & TECHNOLOGY—60 Fifth Ave., New York, NY 10011. Frederick Allen, Ed. Quarterly. Articles, 2,000 to 5,000 words, on history of technology in America, for the sophisticated general reader. Pays on acceptance. Query.

THE ANNALS OF IMPROBABLE RESEARCH—AIR, P.O. Box 380853, Cambridge, MA 02238. Marc Abrahams, Ed. Science humor, science reports and analysis, one to 4 pages. Brief science-related poetry. B&W photos. "This journal is the place to find the mischievous, funny, iconoclastic side of science." Guidelines. No payment.

ARCHAEOLOGY—135 William St., New York, NY 10038. Peter A. Young, Ed.-in-Chief. Articles on archaeology by professionals or lay people with a solid knowledge of the field. Pays $500 to $1,000, on acceptance. Query required.

ASTRONOMY—P.O. Box 1612, Waukesha, WI 53187. Bonnie Gordon, Ed. Dave Eicher, Man. Ed. Articles on astronomy, astrophysics, space programs, recent discoveries. Hobby pieces on equipment and celestial events; short news items. Query with short, detailed article proposal. Pays varying rates, on acceptance.

C/C++ USERS JOURNAL—1601 W. 23rd St., Suite 200, Lawrence, KS 66046-4153. Marc Briand, Editor-in-Chief. Practical, how-to articles, 2,500 words (including up to 250 lines of code) on C/C++ programming. Algorithms, class designs, book reviews, tutorials. No programming "religion." Pay varies, 10¢-12¢ a word, on publication. Query. Guidelines.

CLOSING THE GAP—526 Main St., P.O. Box 68, Henderson, MN 56044. Megan Turek, Man. Ed. Bimonthly tabloid. Articles, 700 to 1,500 words, that describe a particular microcomputer product that affects the education, vocation, recreation, mobility, communication, etc., of persons who are handicapped or disabled. Non-product related articles also used. Web site: www.closingthegap.com

COMPUTERSCENE MAGAZINE—5921 Jefferson St. N.E., #B, Albuquerque, NM 87109-3432. Greg Hansen, Man. Ed. Noel Hansen, Bus. Mgr. Computer-related articles and fiction, 800 to 1,500 words. "We provide New Mexico computer users with entertaining and informative articles on all aspects of computers: hardware, software, technology, productivity, advice, personal experience, even computer-related fiction." Fillers, 400 to 800 words. Pays $40 to $75, on publication. Send SASE for guidelines and editorial calendar.

ELECTRONICS NOW—500 Bi-County Blvd., Farmingdale, NY 11735. Carl Laron, Ed. Technical articles, 1,500 to 3,000 words, on all areas related to electronics. Pays $50 to $500 or more, on acceptance.

ENVIRONMENT—1319 18th St. N.W., Washington, DC 20036-1802. Barbara T. Richman, Man. Ed. Analytical articles, 2,500 to 5,000 words, on environmental science and policy issues, especially on a global scale. Detailed queries required. Pays $100 to $300.

FOCUS—Turnkey Publishing, Inc., P.O. Box 200549, Austin, TX 78720. Geri Farman, Ed. Articles, 700 to 4,000 words, on Data General computers. Photos a plus. Pays to $50, on publication. Query required.

NATURAL HISTORY—American Museum of Natural History, Central Park W. at 79th St., New York, NY 10024. Bruce Stutz, Ed.-in-Chief. Informative articles, to 3,000 words, on anthropology and natural sciences. "Strongly recommend that writers send SASE for guidelines and read our magazine." Pays from $1,000 for features, on acceptance. Query.

NETWORK WORLD—161 Worcester Rd., Framingham, MA 01701-9171. John Gallant, Ed. Articles, to 2,500 words, about applications of communications technology for management level users of data, voice, and video communications systems. Pays varying rates, on acceptance.

POPULAR ELECTRONICS—500 Bi-County Blvd., Farmingdale, NY 11735. Konstantinos Karagiannis, Ed. Features, 2,000 to 3,500 words, for electronics hobbyists and experimenters. "Our readers are science and electronics oriented, understand computer theory and operation, and like to build electronics projects." Fillers and cartoons. Pays $150 to $500, on acceptance.

POPULAR SCIENCE—2 Park Ave., New York, NY 10016. Fred Abatemarco, Ed.-in-Chief. Articles, with photos, on developments in science and technology. Short illustrated articles on new inventions and products; photoessays, book excerpts. Payment varies, on acceptance.

PUBLISH—Integrated Media, Inc., 501 Second St., San Francisco, CA 94107. Mard Naman, Man. Ed. Features, 1,500 to 2,000 words, and reviews, 400 to 800 words, on all aspects of computerized publishing. Pays $300 to $600 for reviews, $1000 to $1,400 for full-length features, on acceptance.

THE SCIENCES—655 Madison Ave., 16th Fl., New York, NY 10021. Peter G. Brown, Ed. Essays and features, 2,000 to 4,000 words, and book reviews, on all scientific disciplines. Pays honorarium, on publication. Query.

SCIENCEWORLD—Scholastic, Inc., 555 Broadway, New York, NY 10012-3999. Mark Bregman, Ed. Science articles, 750 words, and science news articles, 200 words, on life science, earth science, physical science, environmental science technology, and/or health for readers in grades 7 to 10 (ages 12 to 15). "Articles should include current, exciting science news. Writing should be lively and show an understanding of teens' perspectives and interests." Pays $100 to $125 for news items; $300 to $750 for features. Query with a well-researched proposal, suggested sources, 2 to 3 clips of your work, and SASE (or SASE for guidelines).

SKY & TELESCOPE—Sky Publishing Corp., P.O. Box 9111, Belmont, MA 02178-9111. Bud Sadler, Man. Ed. Articles for amateur and professional astronomers worldwide. Department pieces for "Amateur Astronomers," "Astronomical Computing," "Astro Imaging," "Telescope Plus," "Observer's Log," and "Gallery." Also, 800-word opinion pieces, for "Focal Point." Mention availability of diagrams and other illustrations. Pays 10¢ to 25¢ a word, on publication. Query required.

TECHNOLOGY & LEARNING—Miller Freeman, Inc., 600 Harrison St., San Francisco, CA 94107-1370. Judy Salpeter, Ed. Articles, to 3,000 words, for teachers of grades K through 12, about uses of computers and related technology in the classroom: human-interest and philosophical articles, how-to pieces, software reviews, and hands-on ideas. Payment varies, on acceptance.

TECHNOLOGY REVIEW—MIT, W59-200, Cambridge, MA 02139. John Benditt, Ed. General-interest articles on technology and innovation. Payment varies, on acceptance. Query.

YES MAG: CANADA'S SCIENCE MAGAZINE FOR KIDS—4175 Francisco Pl., Victoria, BC, Canada V8N 6H1. Shannon Hunt, Ed. Quarterly. Articles, 250 to 1,200 words, on science and technology topics for children 8 to 14. Topics include do-at-home projects, environmental updates, and profiles on Canadian students or scientists. Query preferred; send for guidelines. Pays 15¢ (Canadian) per word, on publication. Web site: www.yesmag.bc.ca.

ANIMALS

ANIMALS—350 S. Huntington Ave., Boston, MA 02130. Joni Praded, Dir./Ed. Informative, well-researched articles, to 2,500 words, on animal protection, national and international wildlife, pet care, conservation, and environmental issues that affect animals. No personal accounts or favorite pet stories. Pays from $350, on acceptance. Query.

THE ANIMALS' AGENDA—The Animal Rights Network, Inc., P.O. Box 25881, Baltimore, MD 21224. Jessica Duffy, Ed. Bimonthly. Features, to 2,500 words; news briefs, to 100 words; true stories, to 400 words; profiles, to 400 words; investigations, to 1,200 words; reviews, to 800 words; and commentaries, to 700 words. No unsolicited manuscripts. Query.

BIRD TALK—Box 6050, Mission Viejo, CA 92690. Melissa Kauffman, Ed. Articles for pet bird owners: care and feeding, training, safety, outstanding personal adventures, exotic birds in their native countries, profiles of celebrities' birds, travel to bird parks or bird shows. Pays 7¢ to 10¢ a word, after publication. Query required; good transparencies a plus.

CAT FANCY—P.O. Box 6050, Mission Viejo, CA 92690. Amanda Luke, Ed. Nonfiction, to 2,500 words, on cat care, health, grooming, etc. Pays 20¢ a word, on publication. Query with SASE required.

CATS—260 Madison Ave., 8th Fl., New York, NY 10016. Jane W. Reilly, Ed. Monthly. Articles, 1,200 to 3,200 words, on the health and welfare of cats. Photos. Pays $50 to $500, on acceptance. Query.

CATSUMER REPORT—P.O. Box 10069, Austin, TX 78766. Judith Becker, Ed. Articles, 800 to 1,100 words, for cat owners and cat lovers. "Do not 'speak' in the voice of a cat!" No fiction or poetry. Small payment, on publication.

DAIRY GOAT JOURNAL—P.O. Box 10, Lake Mills, WI 53551. Dave Thompson, Ed. Articles, to 1,500 words, on successful dairy goat owners, youths and interesting people associated with dairy goats. "Especially interested in practical husbandry ideas." Photos. Pays $50 to $150, on publication. Query.

EQUUS—Fleet Street Corp., 656 Quince Orchard Rd., Suite 600, Gaithersburg, MD 20878. Laurie Prinz, Ed. Articles, 1,000 to 3,000 words, on all breeds of horses, covering their health and care as well as the latest advances in equine medicine and research. "Attempt to speak as one horseperson to another." Pays $100 to $400, on publication.

THE FLORIDA HORSE—P.O. Box 2106, Ocala, FL 34478. Dan Mearns, Ed. Articles, 1,500 words, on Florida thoroughbred breeding and racing. Also veterinary articles, financial articles, and articles of general interest. Pays $100 to $200, on publication.

FRESHWATER AND MARINE AQUARIUM—P.O. Box 487, Sierra

Madre, CA 91024. Don Dewey, Ed. "The Magazine Dedicated To The Tropical Fish Enthusiast." "How-to" articles, varying lengths, on anything related to basic, semi-technical, and technical aspects of freshwater and marine aquariology. Payment is $50 to $350 for features, $50 to $250 for secondary articles, $50 to $150 for columns, and $25 to $75 for fillers. Send for guidelines.

GOOD DOG!—P.O. Box 10069, Austin, TX 78766-1069. Judi Becker, Ed. Bimonthly. "The Consumer Magazine for Dog Owners." Articles, one to two pages, that are informative and fun to read. No fiction. No material "written" by the dog. Small payment, on publication.

HORSE & RIDER—1597 Cole Blvd., Suite 350, Golden, CO 80401. Kathy Kadash-Swan, Ed. Articles, 500 to 3,000 words, with photos, on western training and general horse care: feeding, health, grooming, etc. Pays varying rates, on acceptance. Guidelines.

HORSE ILLUSTRATED—P.O. Box 6050, Mission Viejo, CA 92690. Moira C. Harris, Ed. Articles, 1,500 to 2,000 words, on all aspects of owning and caring for horses. Photos. Pays $300 to $400, on publication. Query.

HORSEMEN'S YANKEE PEDLAR—83 Leicester St., N. Oxford, MA 01537. Kelley R. Small, Pub. News and feature-length articles, about horses and horsemen in the Northeast. Photos. Pays $2 per published inch, on publication. Query.

I LOVE CATS—450 7th Ave., Suite 1701, New York, NY 10123. Lisa Allmendinger, Ed. Fiction, preferably 500 to 700 words, about cats. Articles, to 1,000 words. No poetry, puzzles, or humor. "Read the magazine, then request guidelines with SASE." Pays $40 to $250; $20 to $25 for fillers, on publication.

LLAMAS—P.O. Box 250, Jackson, CA 95642. Cheryl Dal Porto, Ed. "The International Camelid Journal," published 5 times yearly. Articles, 300 to 3,000 words, of interest to llama and alpaca owners. Pays $25 to $300, extra for photos, on publication. Query.

MUSHING—P.O. Box 149, Ester, AK 99725-0149. Todd Hoener, Pub. How-tos, innovations, history, profiles, interviews, and features related to sled dogs, 1,200 to 2,000 words, and department pieces, 500 to 1,000 words, for competitive and recreational dog drivers and skijorers. International audience. Photos. Pays $20 to $250, on publication. Send SASE for guidelines. E-mail: editor@mushing.com. Web site: www.mushing.com.

PETLIFE MAGAZINE—300 W. 3rd St., #1400, Ft. Worth, TX 76102. C. C. Risenhoover, Pub. Bimonthly. How-to pieces and human interest features, 500 to 1,500 words, for pet owners and pet lovers. No first-person pieces. Pays $150 to $300, on acceptance. Web site: www.petlife.com.

PRACTICAL HORSEMAN—Box 589, Unionville, PA 19375. Mandy Lorraine, Ed. How-to articles conveying leading experts' advice on English riding, training, and horse care. Payment varies, on acceptance. Query with clips.

SHEEP! MAGAZINE—P.O. Box 10, Lake Mills, WI 53551. Dave Thompson, Ed. Articles, to 1,500 words, on successful shepherds, woolcrafts, sheep raising, and sheep dogs. "Especially interested in people who raise sheep successfully as a sideline enterprise." Photos. Pays $15 to $150, extra for photos, on acceptance. Query.

THE WESTERN HORSEMAN—P.O. Box 7980, Colorado Springs, CO

80933-7980. Pat Close, Ed. Articles, 1,500 to 2,500 words, with photos, on care and training of horses; farm, ranch, and stable management; health care and veterinary medicine. Pays to $800, on acceptance.

WILDLIFE CONSERVATION—The Wildlife Conservation Society, Bronx, NY 10460. Nancy Simmons, Sr. Ed. Articles, 1,500 to 2,000 words, that "probe conservation controversies to search for answers and help save threatened species." Payment varies, on acceptance. Guidelines.

YOUNG RIDER—Box 8237, Lexington, KY 40533. Lesley Ward, Ed. Bimonthly. 1,200 word stories about horses and children. No overly sentimental stories, or stories with "goody two-shoes" characters. Photos. Query or send manuscript. Pays $120, on publication.

TRUE CRIME

DETECTIVE CASES—See *Globe Communications Corp.*

DETECTIVE DRAGNET—See *Globe Communications Corp.*

DETECTIVE FILES—See *Globe Communications Corp.*

GLOBE COMMUNICATIONS CORP.—1350 Sherbrooke St. W., Suite 600, Montreal, Quebec, Canada H3G 2T4. Dominick A. Merle, Ed. Factual accounts, 3,500 to 6,000 words, of "sensational crimes, preferably sex crimes, either pre-trial or after conviction." All articles will be considered for *Startling Detective, True Police Cases, Detective Files, Headquarters Detective, Detective Dragnet,* and *Detective Cases.* Query with pertinent information, including dates, site, names, etc. Pays $250 to $350, on acceptance; buys all rights.

HEADQUARTERS DETECTIVE—See *Globe Communications Corp.*

P.I. MAGAZINE: AMERICA'S PRIVATE INVESTIGATION JOURNAL—755 Bronx Ave., Toledo, OH 43609. Bob Mackowiak, Ed. Profiles of professional investigators containing true accounts of their most difficult cases. Pays $75 to $100, plus copies, on publication.

STARTLING DETECTIVE—See *Globe Communications Corp.*

TRUE POLICE CASES—See *Globe Communications Corp.*

MILITARY

AIR FORCE TIMES—See *Times News Service.*

AMERICA'S CIVIL WAR—Primedia History Group, 741 Miller Dr. S.E., Suite D-2, Leesburg, VA 20175. Roy Morris, Jr., Ed. Articles, 2,000 to 4,000 words, on the strategy, tactics, personalities, arms and equipment of the Civil War. Department pieces, 2,000 words. Query with illustration ideas. Pays from $150 to $300, on publication. Guidelines. SASE.

ARMY MAGAZINE—Box 1560, Arlington, VA 22210-0860. Mary B. French, Ed.-in-Chief. Features, 1,000 to 1,500 words, on military subjects. Essays, humor, history (especially World War II), news reports, first-person anecdotes. Pays 12¢ to 18¢ a word, $25 to $50 for anecdotes, on publication. Guidelines.

ARMY TIMES—See *Times News Service.*

COAST GUARD—Commandant (G-CP-1b),U.S. Coast Guard, 2100 2nd

St. S.W., Washington, DC 20593-0001. Veronica Cady, Ed. Articles on maritime topics, including search and rescue, law enforcement, maritime safety, protection of the marine environment, and related topics. Photos a plus. Pays in copies.

COMMAND—P.O. Box 4017, San Luis Obispo, CA 93403. Ty Bomba, Ed. Bimonthly. Articles, 800 to 10,000 words, on any facet of military history or current military affairs. "Popular, not scholarly, analytical military history." Pays 5¢ a word, on publication. Query.

MARINE CORPS GAZETTE—Box 1775, Quantico, VA 22134. Col. John E. Greenwood, Ed. Military articles, 500 to 2,000 words; features, 2,500 to 5,000 words; book reviews, 300 to 750 words. "Our magazine serves primarily as a forum for active duty officers to exchange views on professional, Marine Corps-related topics. Opportunity for 'outside' writers is limited." Queries preferred.

MILITARY—2122 28th St., Sacramento, CA 95818. Lt. Col. Michael Mark, Ed. Articles, 600 to 2,500 words, on firsthand experience in military service: World War II, Korea, Vietnam, and all current services. "Our magazine is about military history by the people who served. They are the best historians." No payment.

MILITARY HISTORY—Primedia History Group, 741 Miller Dr. S.E., #D2, Leesburg, VA 20175. Jon Guttman, Ed. Bimonthly. Features, 4,000 words with 500-word sidebars, on strategy and tactics of military history. Department pieces, 2,000 words, on intrigue, personality, weaponry, perspectives, and travel. Pays $200 to $400, on publication. Query with illustration ideas. Guidelines. SASE.

NATIONAL GUARD—One Massachusetts Ave. N.W., Washington, DC 20001-1431. John Goheen, Man. Ed. Articles on national defense. Payment varies, on publication.

NAVAL AVIATION NEWS—157-1 Washington Navy Yard, 901 M St. S.E., Washington, DC 20374-5059. Cdr. Jim Carlton, Ed. Bimonthly. Articles on Naval aviation history, technology, and news. No payment.

NAVY TIMES—See *Times News Service*.

OFF DUTY MAGAZINE—3505 Cadillac Ave., Suite 0-105, Costa Mesa, CA 92626. Tom Graves, Man. Ed. Travel articles, 1,800 to 2,000 words, for active-duty military Americans (age 20 to 40) and their families worldwide. Must have wide scope; no out-of-the-way places. Military angle essential. Photos. Pays from 20¢ a word, extra for photos, on acceptance. Query required. Guidelines. Limited market.

THE RETIRED OFFICER MAGAZINE—201 N. Washington St., Alexandria, VA 22314. Attn: Manuscripts Ed. Articles, to 2,000 words, of interest to uniformed services retirees and their families. Current military/political affairs, military history, health, money, military family lifestyles, travel, and general interest. Photos a plus. Pays to $1,350, on acceptance. Queries required; no unsolicited manuscripts. Guidelines available at web site: www.troa.org

TIMES NEWS SERVICE—Army Times Publishing Co., Springfield, VA 22159. Attn: R&R Ed. Free-lance material for "R&R" newspaper section. Articles about military life and its problems, as well as interesting things people are doing. Travel articles, 700 words, on places of interest to military people. Profiles, 600 to 700 words, on interesting members of the military community.

Personal-experience essays, 750 words. No fiction or poetry. Pays $75 to $100, on acceptance. Also articles, up to 1,200 words, for supplements to *Army Times*, *Navy Times*, and *Air Force Times*. Address Supplements Ed. Pays $125 to $350, on acceptance. Guidelines.

VFW MAGAZINE—406 W. 34th St., Kansas City, MO 64111. Richard K. Kolb, Ed. Articles, 1,000 words, related to current foreign policy and defense, American armed forces abroad, and international events affecting U.S. national security. Also, up-to-date articles on veteran concerns and issues affecting veterans. Pays to $500 on acceptance, unless specially commissioned. Query. Guidelines.

VIETNAM—Primedia History Group, 741 Miller Dr. S.E., Suite D-2, Leesburg, VA 20175. Col. Harry G. Summers, Jr., Ed. Articles, 2,000 to 4,000 words, on the strategy, tactics, personalities, arms, and equipment of the Vietnam War. Pays from $150 to $300, on publication. Query with illustration ideas. Guidelines. SASE.

WORLD WAR II—Primedia History Group, 741 Miller Dr. S.E., Leesburg, VA 20175. Michael Haskew, Ed. Articles, 4,000 words, on the strategy, tactics, personalities, arms, and equipment of World War II. Department pieces, 2,000 words. Pays from $100 to $200, on publication. Query with illustration ideas. Guidelines. SASE.

HISTORY

ALABAMA HERITAGE—The Univ. of Alabama, Box 870342, Tuscaloosa, AL 35487-0342. Suzanne Wolfe, Ed. Quarterly. Articles, to 5,000 words, on local, state, and regional history: art, literature, language, archaeology, music, religion, architecture, and natural history. Pays an honorarium, on publication, plus 10 copies. Query, mentioning availability of photos and illustrations. Guidelines.

AMERICAN HERITAGE OF INVENTION & TECHNOLOGY—60 Fifth Ave., New York, NY 10011. Frederick Allen, Ed. Quarterly. Articles, 2,000 to 5,000 words, on history of technology in America, for the sophisticated general reader. Query. Pays on acceptance.

AMERICAN HISTORY—6405 Flank Dr., Harrisburg, PA 17112. Attn: Tom Huntington. Articles, 3,000 to 5,000 words, soundly researched. Style should be popular, not scholarly, with a good focus and strong anecdotal material. No travelogues, fiction, or puzzles. Pays $300 to $650, on acceptance. Query. No unsolicited manuscripts.

AMERICAN JEWISH HISTORY—American Jewish Historical Society, 2 Thornton Rd., Waltham, MA 02154. Dr. Marc Lee Raphael, Ed. Articles, 25 to 35 typed pages, on American Jewish history. Queries preferred. No payment.

AMERICA'S CIVIL WAR—Primedia History Group, 741 Miller Dr. S.E., Suite D-2, Leesburg, VA 20175-8920. Roy Morris, Jr., Ed. Articles, 3,500 to 4,000 words, on the strategy, tactics, personalities, arms and equipment of the Civil War. Department pieces, 2,000 words. Query with illustration ideas. SASE for guidelines. Pays from $150 to $300, on publication. Web site: www.thehistorynet.com.

ANCESTRY—P.O. Box 990, Orem, UT 84057. Jennifer Utley, Man. Ed.

Bimonthly for professional Family Historians and hobbyists who are interested in getting the most out of their research. Articles, 1,500 to 3,000 words, that instruct (how-tos, research techniques, etc.) and inform (new research sources, new collections, etc.). No family histories, genealogies, or pedigree charts. Pays $150 to $500, on publication. Guidelines.

AVIATION HISTORY—Primedia History Group, 741 Miller Dr. S.E., Suite D-2, Leesburg, VA 20175-8920. Arthur Sanfelici, Ed. Bimonthly. Articles, 3,500 to 4,000 words with 500-word sidebars and excellent illustrations, on aeronautical history. Department pieces, 2,000 words. Pays $150 to $300, on publication. Query; SASE for guidelines. Web site: www.thehistorynet.com.

THE BEAVER—167 Lombard Ave., #478, Winnipeg, Manitoba, Canada R3B 0T6. A. Greenberg, Ed. Articles, 500 to 3,000 words, on Canadian history, "written to appeal to general readers." Payment varies, on publication. Queries preferred.

CAROLOGUE—South Carolina Historical Society, 100 Meeting St., Charleston, SC 29401-2299. Peter A. Rerig, Ed. General-interest articles, to 10 pages, on South Carolina history. Queries preferred. Pays in copies.

CHICAGO HISTORY—Clark St. at North Ave., Chicago, IL 60614. Rosemary Adams, Ed. Articles, to 4,500 words, on political, social, and cultural history of Chicago. Pays to $250, on publication. Query.

CIVIL WAR TIMES—6405 Flank Dr., Harrisburg, PA 17112. James Kushlan, Ed. Articles, 2,500 to 3,000 words, on the Civil War. "Accurate, annotated stories with strong narrative relying heavily on primary sources and the words of eyewitnesses. We prefer gripping, top-notch accounts of battles in the Eastern Theater of the war, eyewitness accounts (memoirs, diaries, letters), and common soldier photos." SASE for guidelines. Pays $400 to $650 for features, on acceptance.

COMMAND—P.O. Box 4017, San Luis Obispo, CA 93403. Ty Bomba, Ed. Bimonthly. Articles, 800 to 10,000 words, on any facet of military history or current military affairs. "Popular, not scholarly, analytical military history." Pays 5¢ a word, on publication. Query.

EARLY AMERICAN HOMES—6405 Flank Dr., Harrisburg, PA 17112. Mimi Handler, Ed. Articles, 1,000 to 3,000 words, on early American life: arts, crafts, furnishings, history, and architecture before 1850. Pays $50 to $500, on acceptance. Query.

EIGHTEENTH-CENTURY STUDIES—Dept. of French and Italian, Kresge Hall 152, Northwestern Univ., Evanston, IL 60208-2204. Bernadette Fort, Ed. Quarterly. Articles, to 7,500 words, on all aspects of the eighteenth century, especially those that are interdisciplinary or that are of general interest to scholars working in other disciplines. Blind submission policy: Submit 2 copies of manuscript; author's name and address should appear only on separate title page. No payment.

GOLDENSEAL—The Cultural Ctr., 1900 Kanawha Blvd. E., Charleston, WV 25305-0300. John Lilly, Ed. Features, 3,000 words, and shorter articles, 1,000 words, on traditional West Virginia culture and history. Oral histories, old and new B&W photos, research articles. Pays 10¢ a word, on publication. Guidelines.

THE GOLDFINCH—State Historical Society of Iowa, 402 Iowa Ave., Iowa City, IA 52240-1806. Millie Frese, Ed. Quarterly. Articles, 200 to 800 words, and short fiction on Iowa history for young people. "All articles must correspond to an upcoming theme." Pays in copies. Query for themes.

GOOD OLD DAYS—306 E. Parr Rd., Berne, IN 46711. Ken Tate, Ed. True stories (no fiction), 500 to 1,200 words, that took place between 1900 and 1955. Departments include: "Good Old Days on Wheels," about period autos, planes, trolleys, and other transportation; "Good Old Days in the Kitchen," favorite foods, appliances, recipes; "Home Remedies," hometown doctors, herbs and poultices, harrowing kitchen table operations, etc. Pays $15 to $75, on publication.

THE HIGHLANDER—560 Green Bay Rd., Suite 204, Winnetka, IL 60093. Sharon Kennedy Ray, Ed. Bimonthly. Articles, 1,300 to 2,200 words, related to Scottish history. "We do not use any articles on modern Scotland or current problems in Scotland." Pays $100 to $150, on acceptance. Photos must accompany manuscripts.

JOURNAL OF THE WEST—1531 Yuma, Box 1009, Manhattan, KS 66505-1009. Robin Higham, Ed. Articles, to 15 pages, devoted to the history and the culture of the West, then and now. B&W photos. Pays in copies or subscription.

LABOR'S HERITAGE—10000 New Hampshire Ave., Silver Spring, MD 20903. Quarterly. Illustrated journal of The George Meany Memorial Archives. Articles, 80 pages, for labor scholars, labor union members, and the general public. Pays in copies.

MILITARY HISTORY—Primedia History Group, 741 Miller Dr. S.E., Suite D-2, Leesburg, VA 20175-8920. Jon Guttman, Ed. Bimonthly. Features, 4,000 words with 500-word sidebars, on the strategy, tactics, and personalities of military history. Department pieces, 2,000 words, on intrigue, weaponry, personalities, and perspectives. Pays $200 to $400, on publication. Query. SASE for guidelines. Web site: www.thehistorynet.com.

MONTANA JOURNAL—P.O. Box 4087, Missoula, MT 59806. Mike Haser, Ed. Bimonthly tabloid. Human-interest articles, to 1,000 words, about the people, places, and events that helped build Montana. Pays 2¢ a word, on publication. Query preferred.

MONTANA, THE MAGAZINE OF WESTERN HISTORY—225 N. Roberts St., Box 201201, Helena, MT 59620-1201. Charles E. Rankin, Ed. Authentic articles, 3,500 to 5,500 words, on the history of the American and Canadian West; new interpretive approaches to major developments in western history. Footnotes or bibliography must accompany article. "Strict historical accuracy is essential." No fiction. Queries preferred. No payment. Web site: www.his.mt.gov.

NEBRASKA HISTORY—P.O. Box 82554, Lincoln, NE 68501. James E. Potter, Ed. Articles, 3,000 to 7,000 words, relating to the history of Nebraska and the Great Plains. B&W line drawings. Allow 60 days for response. Pays in copies. Cash prize awarded to one article each year.

NOW & THEN—CASS/ETSU, P.O. Box 70556, Johnson City, TN 37614-0556. Jane Harris Woodside, Ed. Fiction and nonfiction, 1,500 to 3,000 words: short stories, articles, interviews, essays, memoirs, book reviews. Pieces must be related to theme of issue and have some connection to the Appalachian region. Also photos and drawings. SASE for guidelines and current themes. Pays $15 to $75, on publication.

OLD WEST—P.O. Box 2107, Stillwater, OK 74076. Marcus Huff, Ed. Thoroughly researched and documented articles, 1,500 to 4,500 words, on the history of the American West. B&W 5x7 photos to illustrate articles. Queries are preferred. Pays 3¢ to 6¢ a word, on acceptance.

PENNSYLVANIA HERITAGE—P.O. Box 1026, Harrisburg, PA 17108-1026. Michael J. O'Malley III, Ed. Quarterly of the Pennsylvania Historical and Museum Commission and the Pennsylvania Heritage Society. Articles, 2,500 to 3,500 words, that "introduce readers to the state's rich culture and historic legacy. Seeks unusual and fresh angle to make history come to life, including pictorial or photo essays, interviews, travel/destination pieces." Prefers to see complete manuscript. Pays to $500, up to $100 for photos or drawings, on acceptance.

PERSIMMON HILL—1700 N.E. 63rd St., Oklahoma City, OK 73111. M.J. Van Deventer, Ed. Published by the National Cowboy Hall of Fame. Articles, 1,500 words, on western history and art, cowboys, ranching, and nature. Top-quality illustrations with captions a must. Pays from $150 to $250, on publication.

PROLOGUE—National Archives, NPOL, 8601 Adelphi Rd., College Park, MD 20740-6001. Quarterly. Articles, varying lengths, based on the holdings and programs of the National Archives, its regional archives, and the presidential libraries. Query. Pays in copies.

RENAISSANCE MAGAZINE—Phantom Press Publications, 13 Appleton Rd., Nantucket, MA 02554. Kim Guarnaccia, Ed. Feature articles on Renaissance and Medieval history, reenactments, roleplaying, and Renaissance faires. Interviews, reviews of Medieval and Renaissance books, music, movies, and games. Pays 5¢ a word, on publication.

RUSSIAN LIFE—89 Main St., #2, Montpelier, VT 05602-2948. Mikhail Ivanov, Ed. Articles, 1,000 to 3,000 words, on Russian culture, travel, history, politics, art, business, and society. "We do not want stories about personal trips to Russia, editorials on developments in Russia, or articles that promote the services of a specific company, organization, or government agency." Pays 7¢ to 10¢ a word; $20 to $30 per photo, on publication. Query.

SCOTTISH JOURNAL—P.O. Box 3165, Barrington, IL 60011. Angus J. Ray, Ed. Articles, 1,500 to 2,000 words, on Scottish history, famous Scots, clans, battles. Travel pieces on specific areas in Scotland. Queries preferred. Pays $150 to $200, on acceptance.

SOUTH CAROLINA HISTORICAL MAGAZINE—South Carolina Historical Society, 100 Meeting St., Charleston, SC 29401-2299. W. Eric Emerson, Ed. Scholarly articles, to 25 pages including footnotes, on South Carolina history. "Authors are encouraged to look at previous issues to be aware of previous scholarship." Pays in copies.

TRUE WEST—P.O. Box 2107, Stillwater, OK 74076-2107. Marcus Huff, Ed. True stories, 500 to 4,500 words, with photos, about the Old West to 1930. Some contemporary stories with historical slant. Source list required. Pays 3¢ to 6¢ a word, extra for B&W photos, on acceptance.

VIETNAM—Primedia History Group, 741 Miller Dr. S.E., Suite D-2, Leesburg, VA 20175-8920. Col. Harry G. Summers, Jr., Ed. Articles, 2,000 to 4,000 words, on the strategy, tactics, personalities, arms, and equipment of the

Vietnam War. Pays $150 to $300, on publication. Query with illustration ideas. SASE. Web site: www.thehistorynet.com.

THE WESTERN HISTORICAL QUARTERLY—Utah State Univ., Logan, UT 84322-0740. Anne M. Butler, Ed. Original articles about the American West, the Westward movement from the Atlantic to the Pacific, twentieth-century regional studies, Spanish borderlands, Canada, northern Mexico, Alaska, and Hawaii. No payment made.

WILD WEST—Primedia History Group, 741 Miller Dr. S.E., Suite D-2, Leesburg, VA 20175-8920. Gregory Lalire, Ed. Bimonthly. Features, to 4,000 words, with 500-word sidebars, and department pieces, 2,000 words, on Western history from the earliest North American settlements to the end of the 19th century. Pays $150 to $300, on publication. Query with SASE. Web site: www. thehistorynet.com.

WORLD WAR II—Primedia History Group, 741 Miller Dr. S.E., Suite D-2, Leesburg, VA 20175-8920. Michael Haskew, Ed. Articles, 3,500 to 4,000 words, on the strategy, tactics, personalities, arms, and equipment of World War II. Pays $100 to $200, on publication. Query with illustration ideas. SASE for editorial guidelines. Web site: www.thehistorynet.com.

COLLEGE, CAREERS

THE BLACK COLLEGIAN—140 Carondelet St., New Orleans, LA 70130. Robert G. Miller, Ed. Articles, to 2,000 words, on entry-level career opportunities, the job search process, how to prepare for entry-level positions, what to expect as an entry-level professional, and culture and experiences of African-American collegians. Audience: African-American juniors and seniors. Pays on publication. Query.

BYLINE—Box 130596, Edmond, OK 73013. Marcia Preston, Ed.-in-Chief. General fiction, 2,000 to 4,000 words. Nonfiction: 1,500- to 1,800-word features and 300- to 750-word special departments. Poetry, 10 to 30 lines preferred. Nonfiction and poetry must be about writing. Humor, 50 to 600 words, about writing. "We seek practical and motivational material that tells writers how they can succeed, not why they can't. Overdone topics: writers' block, the muse, rejection slips." Pays $5 to $10 for poetry; $15 to $35 for departments; $75 for features and $100 for short fiction, on acceptance.

CAMPUS LIFE—465 Gundersen Dr., Carol Stream, IL 60188. Chris Lutes, Ed. Articles reflecting Christian values and world view, for high school and college students. Humor, general fiction, and true, first-person experiences. "If we have a choice of fiction, how-to, and a strong first-person story, we'll go with the true story every time." Photo-essays, cartoons. Pays 15¢ to 20¢ a word, on acceptance. Query.

CAREER DIRECTIONS—21 N. Henry St., Edgerton, WI 53534. Diane Everson, Pres. and Pub. Tabloid. "Current News & Career Opportunities for Students." Career-related articles, 500 to 1,500 words, especially how-to. Pays $50 to $150, on acceptance. Also publishes the newsletter *Career Waves*, for career development professionals.

CAREER WAVES—See *Career Directions*.

CAREER WORLD—GLC. 900 Skokie Blvd., Suite 200, Northbrook, IL 60062-4028. Carole Rubenstein, Sr. Ed. Published 7 times a year, September through April/May. Gender-neutral articles about specific occupations and career awareness and development for junior and senior high school audience. Query with clips and resumé. Payment varies, on publication.

CAREERS & COLLEGES—989 Ave. of the Americas, New York, NY 10018. Don Rauf, Ed. Quarterly. Designed to give high school juniors and seniors advice on how to plan their future. Nonfiction, from 800 to 2,500 words. Topics include interesting, new takes on college admission, scholarships, financial aid, work skills, and careers. Payment is $300 to $800 per article, depending on length. Query.

CAREERS AND . . . —See *Careers and the College Grad.*

CAREERS AND THE COLLEGE GRAD—201 Broadway, Cambridge, MA 02139. Kathleen Grimes, Pub. Annual. Career-related articles, 1,500 to 2,000 words, for junior and senior liberal arts students. Career-related fillers, 500 words and line art or color prints. Queries preferred. No payment. Same address and requirements for *Careers and the MBA* (semiannual) for first- and second-year MBA students; *Careers and the Engineer* (semiannual) for junior and senior engineering students; *Careers and the Minority Lawyer* (semiannual) for law school students; *Careers and the International MBA*; *Careers and the Woman MBA; Careers and the Minority MBA*; and *Careers and the Minority Undergraduate.*

CAREERS & THE DISABLED—See *Minority Engineer.*

CIRCLE K—3636 Woodview Trace, Indianapolis, IN 46268-3196. Nicholas K. Drake, Exec. Ed. Serious and light articles, 1,500 to 1,700 words, on careers, college issues, trends, leadership development, self-help, community service and involvement. Pays $200 to $400, on acceptance. Queries preferred.

COLLEGE BOUND MAGAZINE—Ramholtz Publishing, Inc. 2071 Clove Rd., Suite 206, Staten Island, NY 10304. Gina LaGuardia, Ed. Six times during the academic year. (One national and various regional editions.) Articles, 200 to 1,000 words, to provide high school students a view of college life. High school and college related filler, 50 to 100 words. Send SASE for guidelines. Queries preferred. Pays $20 to $100, on publication. Web site: www.cbnet.com.

EQUAL OPPORTUNITY—See *Minority Engineer.*

INSIDER MAGAZINE—4124 W. Oakton, Skokie, IL 60201. Rita Cook, Ed. Dir. Articles, 700, 1,500, and 2,100 words, on issues, careers, politics, sports, and entertainment for readers ages 18 to 34. Pays 1¢ to 3¢ a word, on publication. Send SASE for themes. Web site: www.insidermag.com.

LINK: THE COLLEGE MAGAZINE—32 E. 57th St., 12th Fl., New York, NY 10022. Torey Marcus, Ed.-in-Chief. News, lifestyle, and issues for college students. Informational how-to and short features, 300 to 500 words, on education news, finances, academics, employment, lifestyles, trends, entertainment, sports, and culture. Well-researched, insightful, authoritative articles, 2,000 to 3,000 words. Pays 50¢ a word, on publication. Queries preferred. Guidelines. Web site: www.linkmag.com

MINORITY ENGINEER—1160 E. Jericho Turnpike, Suite 200, Huntington, NY 11743. James Schneider, Ed. Articles, 1,000 to 1,500 words, for college students, on career opportunities; techniques of job hunting; developments in and applications of new technologies. Interviews. Profiles. Pays 10¢ a word, on publication. Query. Same address and requirements for *Woman Engi-*

698   COLLEGE, CAREERS/OP-ED MARKETS

neer (address Anne Kelly), and *Equal Opportunity* and *Careers & the Dis-ABLED* (address James Schneider).

STUDY BREAKS MAGAZINE— 600 W. 28th St., #103, Austin, TX 78705. Gal Shweiki, Pub. Fillers, humor, jokes, etc., of interest to students at The Univ. of Texas at Austin, Texas Tech. Univ., Texas A & M Univ., Southwest Texas State Univ., and The Univ. of North Texas. Pays $15.

SUCCEED—Ramholtz Publishing Inc., 2071 Clove Rd., Suite 206, Staten Island, NY 10304. Gina LaGuardia, Ed.-in-Chief. Quarterly. Feature articles, 1,000 to 1,500 words, on topics of interest to professionals and current students interested in continuing education. Department pieces, 400 to 750 words, on financial advice; career-related profiles; news; book and software reviews, and information on other continuing education-related resources. Query with three writing clips. Guidelines and sample issues available. Pays $50 to $125, 30 days after publication. Responds in 4 to 6 weeks. E-mail: editorial@collegebound.net. Web site: www.cbnet.com.

UCLA MAGAZINE— 10920 Wilshire Blvd., Suite 1500, Los Angeles, CA 90024. David Greenwald, Ed. Quarterly. Articles, 2,000 words, must be related to UCLA through research, alumni, students, etc. Pays to $2,000, on acceptance. Queries required.

UNIQUE OPPORTUNITIES— 455 S. 4th Ave., #1236, Louisville, KY 40202. Bett Coffman, Assoc. Ed. Articles, 2,000 to 3,000 words, that cover economic, business, and career-related issues of interest to physicians who are looking for their first practice or looking to make a career move. "Our goal is to educate physicians about how to evaluate career opportunities, negotiate the benefits offered, plan career moves, and provide information on the legal and economic aspects of accepting a position." Pays 50¢ a word for features; $200 for profiles, on acceptance. Query.

WOMAN ENGINEER— See *Minority Engineer.*

OP-ED MARKETS

THE ATLANTA CONSTITUTION—P.O. Box 4689, Atlanta, GA 30302. Op-Ed Ed. Articles related to the Southeast, Georgia, or the Atlanta metropolitan area, 200 to 600 words, on a variety of topics: law, economics, politics, science, environment, performing and manipulative arts, humor, education; religious and seasonal topics. Pays $75 to $125, on publication. Submit complete manuscript.

THE BALTIMORE SUN—P.O. Box 1377, Baltimore, MD 21278-0001. Marilyn McCraven, Opinion-Commentary Page Ed. Articles, 600 to 1,500 words, on a wide range of topics: politics, education, foreign affairs, lifestyles, etc. Humor. Payment varies, on publication. Exclusive rights: MD and DC.

THE BOSTON GLOBE—P.O. Box 2378, Boston, MA 02107-2378. Marjorie Pritchard, Ed. Articles, to 700 words, on economics, education, environment, foreign affairs, and regional interest. Send complete manuscript. Exclusive rights: New England.

BOSTON HERALD—One Herald Sq., Boston, MA 02106. Attn: Editorial Page Ed. Pieces, 600 to 700 words, on economics, foreign affairs, politics, regional interest, and seasonal topics. Prefer submissions from regional writers. Payment varies, on publication. Exclusive rights: MA, RI, and NH.

THE CHARLOTTE OBSERVER—P.O. Box 30308, Charlotte, NC 28230-0308. Jane Pope, Deputy Ed., Editorial Pages. Well-written, thought-provoking articles, to 700 words. "We are only interested in articles on local (Carolinas) issues or that use local examples to illustrate other issues." Pays $50, on publication. No simultaneous submissions in NC or SC.

THE CHRISTIAN SCIENCE MONITOR—One Norway St., Boston, MA 02115. Clara Germani, Opinion Page Ed. Pieces, 400 to 900 words, on domestic and foreign affairs, economics, education, environment, law, media, politics, and cultural commentary. Pays up to $400, on acceptance. Retains all rights for 90 days after publication. E-mail: oped@csps.com

THE CLEVELAND PLAIN DEALER—1801 Superior Ave., Cleveland, OH 44114. Gloria Millner, Assoc. Ed. Pieces, 700 to 800 words, on a wide variety of subjects. Pays $75, on publication. E-mail: gmillner@plaind.com

DENVER POST—P.O. Box 1709, Denver, CO 80201. Bob Ewegen, Ed. Articles, 400 to 700 words, with local or regional angle. No payment for freelance submissions. Query.

DETROIT FREE PRESS—600 W. Fort St., Detroit, MI 48226. Attn: Op-Ed Ed. Opinion pieces, to 800 words, on domestic and foreign affairs, economics, education, environment, law, politics, and regional interest. Priority given to local writers or topics of local interest. Pays $50 to $100, on publication. Query. Exclusive rights: MI and northern OH.

THE DETROIT NEWS—615 W. Lafayette Blvd., Detroit, MI 48226. Attn: Richard Burr. Pieces, 500 to 750 words, on a wide variety of subjects. Pays $75, on publication. E-mail: oped@detnews.com. Fax: 313-222-6417.

INDIANAPOLIS STAR—P.O. Box 145, Indianapolis, IN 46206-0145. John H. Lyst, Ed. Articles, 700 to 800 words. Pays $40, on publication. Exclusive rights: IN.

LOS ANGELES TIMES—Times Mirror Sq., Los Angeles, CA 90053. Bob Berger, Op-Ed Ed. Commentary pieces, 650 to 700 words, on many subjects. "Not interested in nostalgia or first-person reaction to faraway events. Pieces must be exclusive." Payment varies, on publication. Limited market. SASE required. E-mail: op-ed@latimes.com.

THE NEW YORK TIMES—229 W. 43rd St., New York, NY 10036. Attn: Op-Ed Ed. Opinion pieces, 650 to 800 words, on any topic, including public policy, science, lifestyles, and ideas, etc. Include your address, daytime phone number, and social security number with submission. "If you haven't heard from us within 2 weeks, you can assume we are not using your piece. Include SASE if you want work returned." Pays on publication. Buys first North American rights.

NEWSDAY—"Viewpoints," 235 Pinelawn Rd., Melville, NY 11747. Noel Rubinton, "Viewpoints" Ed. Pieces, 700 to 800 words, on a variety of topics. Pays $150, on publication.

THE REGISTER GUARD—P.O. Box 10188, Eugene, OR 97440. Don Robinson, Editorial Page Ed. All subjects; regional angle preferred. Pays $25 to $50, on publication. Very limited use of non-local writers.

THE SACRAMENTO BEE—P.O. Box 15779, Sacramento, CA 95852-0779. Jewel A. Reilly, Op-Ed Ed. Op-ed pieces, to 750 words; state and regional topics preferred.

ST. LOUIS POST-DISPATCH—900 N. Tucker Blvd., St. Louis, MO 63101. Donna Korando, Commentary Ed. Articles, 700 words, on economics, education, science, politics, foreign and domestic affairs, and the environment. Pays $70, on publication. "Goal is to have at least half of the articles by local writers."

ST. PAUL PIONEER PRESS—345 Cedar St., St. Paul, MN 55101. Ronald D. Clark, Ed. Articles, to 750 words, on a variety of topics. Strongly prefer authors or topics with a connection to the area. Pays $75, on publication.

SEATTLE POST-INTELLIGENCER—P.O. Box 1909, Seattle, WA 98111. Sam R. Sperry, Op-ed Page Ed. Articles, 750 to 800 words, on foreign and domestic affairs, environment, education, politics, regional interest, religion, science, and seasonal material. Prefer writers who live in the Pacific Northwest. Pays $75 to $100, on publication. SASE required. Very limited market.

THE WALL STREET JOURNAL—Editorial Page, 200 Liberty St., New York, NY 10281. David B. Brooks, Op-Ed Ed. Articles, to 1,500 words, on politics, economics, law, education, environment, humor (occasionally), and foreign and domestic affairs. Articles must be timely, heavily reported, and of national interest by writers with expertise in their field. Pays $150 to $300, on publication.

WASHINGTON TIMES—3600 New York Ave. N.E., Washington, DC 20002. Frank Perley, Articles and Opinion Page Ed. Articles, 800 to 1,000 words, on a variety of subjects. No pieces written in the first-person. "Syndicated columnists cover the 'big' issues; find an area that is off the beaten path." Pays $150, on publication. Exclusive rights: Washington, DC, and Baltimore area.

ADULT MAGAZINES

CHIC—8484 Wilshire Blvd., Suite 900, Beverly Hills, CA 90211. Scott Schalin, Lisa Jenio, Exec. Eds. Sex-related articles, interviews, erotic fiction, 2,500 words. Query for articles. Pays $150 for brief interviews, $350 for fiction, on acceptance.

GENESIS—210 Route 4 E., Suite 401, Paramus, NJ 07652. Paul Gambino, Ed. Dir. Dan Davis, Man. Ed. Sexually explicit fiction and nonfiction features, 800 to 2,000 words. Celebrity interviews, photo-essays, product and film reviews. Pays on publication. Query with clips.

PENTHOUSE—277 Park Ave., 4th Fl., New York, NY 10172-0003. Peter Bloch, Ed. Lavada B. Nahon, Sr. Ed. Articles, to 5,000 words: general-interest profiles, interviews (with introduction), and investigative pieces. Pays on acceptance.

PLAYBOY—9242 Beverly Blvd., Beverly Hills, CA 90210. Stephen Randall, Exec. Ed. Articles, 3,500 to 6,000 words, and sophisticated fiction, 1,000 to 10,000 words (5,000 preferred), for urban men. Humor; satire. Science fiction. Pays to $5,000 for articles and fiction, $2,000 for short-shorts, on acceptance.

PLAYGIRL—801 Second Ave., New York, NY 10017. Sandra Mardenfeld, Man. Ed. Articles, 1,500 to 4,000 words, for women 18 and older. Pays varying rates, on acceptance.

VARIATIONS, FOR LIBERATED LOVERS—11 Penn Plaza, 12th Fl., New York, NY 10001. V. K. McCarty, Ed. Dir./Assoc. Pub. First-person true narrative descriptions of "a couple's enthusiasm, secrets, and exquisitely articulated sex scenes squarely focused within one of the magazine's pleasure categories." Pays $400, on acceptance.

FICTION MARKETS

This list gives the fiction requirements of general- and special-interest magazines, including those that publish detective and mystery, science fiction and fantasy, romance and confession stories. Other good markets for short fiction are the *College, Literary, and Little Magazines* where, though payment is modest (usually in copies only), publication can bring the work of a beginning writer to the attention of editors at the larger magazines. Juvenile fiction markets are listed under *Juvenile, Teenage, and Young Adult Magazines*. Publishers of book-length fiction manuscripts are listed under *Book Publishers*.

GENERAL FICTION

ABORIGINAL SF—P.O. Box 2449, Woburn, MA 01888-0849. Charles C. Ryan, Ed. Stories, 2,500 to 7,500 words, with a unique scientific idea, human or alien character, plot, and theme of lasting value; "must be science fiction; no fantasy, horror, or sword and sorcery." Pays $200. Send SASE for guidelines.

AFRICAN VOICES—270 W. 96th St., New York, NY 10025. Carolyn A. Butts, Exec. Ed. Quarterly. Humorous, erotic, and dramatic fiction, 500 to 2,500 words, by ethnic writers. Nonfiction, 500 to 1,500 words: investigative articles, artist profiles, essays, and first-person narratives. Poetry, to 50 lines. Include SASE; sample copies available for $5. Pays $25 for fiction, on publication, plus 5 copies of magazine. (Payment varies for nonfiction.)

AIM MAGAZINE—P.O. Box 1174, Maywood, IL 60153. Myron Apilado, Ed. Short stories, 800 to 3,000 words, geared to proving that people from different backgrounds are more alike than they are different. Story should not moralize. Pays from $15 to $25, on publication. Annual contest. $100 prize.

ALFRED HITCHCOCK MYSTERY MAGAZINE—475 Park Ave. S., New York, NY 10016. Cathleen Jordan, Ed. Well-plotted, plausible mystery, suspense, detection and crime stories, to 14,000 words; "ghost stories, humor, futuristic or atmospheric tales are all possible, as long as they include a crime or the suggestion of one." Pays 8¢ a word, on acceptance. Guidelines with SASE.

ANALOG SCIENCE FICTION AND FACT—475 Park Avenue S., New York, NY 10016. Stanley Schmidt, Ed. Science fiction, with strong characters in believable future or alien setting: short stories, 2,000 to 7,500 words; novelettes, 10,000 to 20,000 words; serials, to 70,000 words. Include SASE. Pays 5¢ to 8¢ a word, on acceptance. Query for novels.

ASIMOV'S SCIENCE FICTION MAGAZINE—475 Park Ave. S, 11th Fl., New York, NY 10016. Gardner Dozois, Ed. Short science fiction and fantasies, to 15,000 words. Pays 6¢ to 8¢ a word, on acceptance. Guidelines. Website: www.asimovs.com

THE ATLANTIC MONTHLY—77 N. Washington St., Boston, MA 02114. William Whitworth, Ed. No unsolicited material accepted.

THE BOSTON GLOBE MAGAZINE—*The Boston Globe,* P.O. Box 2378, Boston, MA 02107-2378. Nick King, Ed. Short stories, to 3,000 words. Include SASE. Pays on acceptance.

BOYS' LIFE—1325 W. Walnut Hill Ln., P.O. Box 152079, Irving, TX 75015-2079. Shannon Lowry, Fiction Ed. Publication of the Boy Scouts of America. Humor, mystery, science fiction, adventure, 1,200 words, for 8- to 18-year-old boys; study back issues. Pays from $750, on acceptance. Send SASE for guidelines. Send complete manuscript; no queries.

BUFFALO SPREE MAGAZINE—5698 Main St., Williamsville, NY 14221. David McDuff and Laurence Levite, Pubs. Fiction and humor, to 2,000 words, for thoughtful, intelligent readers in the western New York region. Pays $125 to $150, on publication.

BYLINE—Box 130596, Edmond, OK 73013. Marcia Preston, Ed.-in-Chief. Carolyn Wall, Assoc. Fiction Ed. General fiction, 2,000 to 4,000 words. Nonfiction: 1,500- to 1,800-word features and 300- to 750-word special departments. Poetry, 10 to 30 lines preferred. Nonfiction and poetry must be about writing. Humor, 100 to 600 words, about writing. "We seek practical and motivational material that tells writers how they can succeed, not why they can't. Overdone topics: writers' block, the muse, rejection slips." Pays $5 to $10 for poetry; $15 to $35 for departments; $50 for features; and $100 for short fiction, on acceptance. SASE for guidelines or see Web page: http://www. bylinemag.com.

CAPPER'S—1503 S.W. 42nd St., Topeka, KS 66609-1265. Ann Crahan, Ed. Fiction, 7,500 to 40,000 words (12,000 to 20,000 words preferred), for serialization. No profanity, violence, or explicit sex. Pays $75 to $300, on publication.

CATHOLIC FORESTER—355 Shuman Blvd., P.O. Box 3012, Naperville, IL 60566-7012. Dorothy Deer, Ed. Official publication of the Catholic Order of Foresters. Fiction, to 1,200 words (prefer shorter); "looking for more contemporary, meaningful stories dealing with life today." No sex, violence, romance, or "preachy" stories; religious angle not required. Pays 20¢ a word, on acceptance.

CHESS LIFE—3054 NYS Rte. 9W, New Windsor, NY 12553-7698. Glenn Petersen, Ed. Fiction, 500 to 2,000 words, related to chess for members of the U.S. Chess Federation. Also, articles, 500 to 3,000 words, on chess news, profiles, technical aspects of chess. Pays varying rates, on acceptance. Query; limited market.

COBBLESTONE: DISCOVER AMERICAN HISTORY —30 Grove St., Suite C, Peterborough, NH 03458-1454. Meg Chorlian, Ed. Historical fiction, 500 to 800 words, for children aged 8 to 14 years; must relate to theme. Pays 20¢ to 25¢ a word, on publication. Send SASE for guidelines.

COMMENTARY—165 E. 56th St., New York, NY 10022. Neal Kozodoy, Ed. Fiction, of high literary quality, on contemporary social or Jewish issues, from 5,000 to 7,000 words. Pays on publication.

COMMON GROUND MAGAZINE—P.O. Box 99, McVeytown, PA 17051-0099. Ruth Dunmire and Pam Brumbaugh, Eds. Quarterly. Fiction, 1,000 to 2,000 words, related to Central Pennsylvania's Juniata River Valley. Pays $25 to $200, on publication. Guidelines.

COSMOPOLITAN—224 W. 57th St., New York, NY 10019. Alison Broner, Sr. Books Ed. Novel excerpts; submissions must be sent by a publisher or agent. Payment rates are negotiable. SASE.

COUNTRY WOMAN—P.O. Box 989, Greendale, WI 53129. Kathy Pohl, Exec. Ed. Fiction, 750 to 1,000 words, of interest to rural women; protagonist must be a country woman. "Stories should focus on life in the country, its problems and joys, as experienced by country women; must be upbeat and positive." Pays $90 to $125, on acceptance.

CRICKET—P.O. Box 300, Peru, IL 61354-0300. Marianne Carus, Ed.-in-Chief. Fiction, 200 to 2,000 words, for 9- to 14-year-olds. Pays to 25¢ a word, on publication. SASE.

DISCOVERIES—WordAction Publishing Co., 6401 The Paseo, Kansas City, MO 64131. Attn: Asst. Ed. Weekly take-home paper designed to correlate with Evangelical Sunday school curriculum. Fiction, 500 words, for 8- to 10-year-olds. Stories should feature contemporary, true-to-life characters and should illustrate character building and scriptural application. No poetry. Pays 5¢ a word, on publication. Send SASE for guidelines and theme list.

ELLERY QUEEN'S MYSTERY MAGAZINE—475 Park Ave. S., New York, NY 10016. Janet Hutchings, Ed. High-quality detective, crime, and mystery stories, 1,500 to 10,000 words. Also "Minute Mysteries," 250 words, short verses, limericks, and novellas, to 17,000 words. "We like a mix of classic detection and suspenseful crime." "First Stories" by unpublished writers. Pays 3¢ to 8¢ a word, occasionally higher for established authors, on acceptance.

ESQUIRE—250 W. 55th St., New York, NY 10019. David Granger, Ed.-in-Chief. Send finished manuscript of short story; submit one at a time. No full-length novels. No pornography, science fiction, poetry, or "true romance" stories. Include SASE.

EVANGEL—Light and Life Communications, P.O. Box 535002, Indianapolis, IN 46253-5002. Julie Innes, Ed. Free Methodist. Fiction and nonfiction, to 1,200 words, with personal faith in Christ shown as instrumental in solving problems. Pays 4¢ a word, on publication. Send #10 SASE for sample copy and guidelines.

FICTION INTERNATIONAL—English Dept., San Diego State Univ., San Diego, CA 92182-8140. Harold Jaffe, Ed. Formally innovative and politically committed fiction and theory. Query for themes. Submit between September 1st and December 15th.

FLY ROD & REEL—P.O. Box 370, Camden, ME 04843. James E. Butler, Ed. Occasional fiction, 2,000 to 3,000 words, related to fly fishing. Payment varies, on acceptance.

GALLERY—401 Park Ave. S., New York, NY 10016-8802. Will Romano, Ed. Dir. Erotic fiction, to 2,500 words, for sophisticated men. We encourage quality work from unpublished writers." Pays $500, on publication. SASE for guidelines.

GLIMMER TRAIN PRESS—710 S.W. Madison St., #504, Portland, OR 97205. Susan Burmeister-Brown, Ed. Fiction, 1,200 to 7,500 words. "Eight stories in each quarterly magazine." Pays $500, on acceptance. Submit material in January, April, July, and October; allow 3 months for response. "Send SASE for guidelines before submitting."

GOOD HOUSEKEEPING—959 Eighth Ave., New York, NY 10019. Lee Quarfoot, Fiction Ed. Short stories, 1,000 to 3,000 words, with strong identification figures for women, by published writers and "beginners with demonstrable talent." Novel condensations or excerpts from about-to-be-published books only. Query; no longer accepts unsolicited manuscripts.

GRIT—1503 S.W. 42nd St., Topeka, KS 66609. Donna Doyle, Ed.-in-Chief. Short stories, 850 to 2,000 words; also historical, mystery, western, adventure, and romance serials (15,000 or more words in 1,000-word installments with cliff-hangers). Articles, 500 to 1,200 words. Serial fiction, 3,500 to 15,000 words. Should be upbeat, inspirational, wholesome and interesting to mature adults. No reference to drinking, smoking, drugs, sex, or violence. Also publishes true-story nostalgia. Pays up to 22¢ a word, on publication. All fiction submissions should be marked "Fiction Dept." Send $4 for sample copy. SASE for guidelines. Submissions will not be acknowledged, nor will status updates be given.

GUIDEPOSTS FOR KIDS—P.O. Box 638, Chesterton, IN 46304. Mary Lou Carney, Ed. Value-centered bimonthly for 7- to 12-year-olds. Problem fiction, mysteries, historicals, 1,000 to 1,400 words, with "realistic dialogue and sharp imagery. No preachy stories about Bible-toting children." Pays $300 to $500 for all rights, on acceptance. No reprints.

HARDBOILED—Gryphon Publications, P.O. Box 209, Brooklyn, NY 11228-0209. Gary Lovisi, Ed. Hard, cutting-edge crime fiction, to 3,000 words, "with impact." "It's a good idea to read an issue before submitting a story." Payment varies, on publication. Query for articles, book and film reviews.

HARPER'S MAGAZINE—666 Broadway, New York, NY 10012. Attn: Eds. Will consider unsolicited fiction manuscripts. Query for nonfiction (very limited market). No poetry. SASE required.

HIGHLIGHTS FOR CHILDREN—803 Church St., Honesdale, PA 18431-1824. Christine French Clark, Man. Ed. Fiction on sports, humor, adventure, mystery, folktales, etc., 900 words, for 8- to 12-year-olds. Easy rebus form, 100 to 120 words, and easy-to-read stories, to 500 words, for beginning readers. "We are partial to stories in which the protagonist solves a dilemma through his or her own resources." Pays from 14¢ a word, on acceptance. Buys all rights.

IRISH EDITION—903 E. Willow Grove Ave., Wyndmoor, PA 19038-7909. Jane M. Duffin, Ed. Short fiction, nonfiction, fillers, humor, and puzzles for Irish-American and Irish-born audience. Pay is negotiable and made on acceptance. Query.

THE JOYFUL WOMAN—P.O. Box 90028, Chattanooga, TN 37412. Joy Rice Martin, Ed. First-person inspirational true stories and sketches, 500 to

1,000 words; occasionally uses some fiction. Pays 3¢ to 4¢ a word, on publication.

LADIES' HOME JOURNAL—125 Park Ave., New York, NY 10017. Fiction; only accepted through agents.

THE MAGAZINE OF FANTASY AND SCIENCE FICTION—Box 1806, Madison Sq. Station, New York, NY 10159. Gordon Van Gelder, Ed. Fantasy and science fiction stories, to 25,000 words. Pays 5¢to 8¢ a word, on acceptance.

MATURE LIVING—127 Ninth Ave. N., Nashville, TN 37234. Al Shackleford, Ed. Fiction, 900 to 1,200 words, for senior adults. Must be consistent with Christian principles. Pays $75, on acceptance.

MIDSTREAM—633 Third Ave., 21st Fl., New York, NY 10017. Joel Carmichael, Ed. Fiction with a Jewish/Zionist reference, to 3,000 words. Pays 5¢a word, after publication. Allow one month for response.

NA'AMAT WOMAN—200 Madison Ave., 21st Fl., New York, NY 10016. Judith A. Sokoloff, Ed. Short stories, approximately 2,500 words, with Jewish theme. Pays 10¢ a word, on publication.

NEW MYSTERY MAGAZINE—The Flatiron Bldg., 101 W. 23rd St., PMB 7, New York, NY 10011. Charles Raisch, Ed. Quarterly. Mystery, crime, detection, and suspense short stories, 2,000 to 6,000 words, with "sympathetic characters in trouble and visual scenes." Book reviews, 250 to 2,000 words, of upcoming or recently published novels. Pays 3¢ to 10¢ a word, on publication. No guidelines; study back issues.

THE NEW YORKER—20 W. 43rd St., New York, NY 10036. Attn: Fiction Dept. Short stories, humor, and satire. Payment varies, on acceptance.

PLAYGIRL—801 Second Ave., New York, NY 10017. Sandra Mardenfeld, Man. Ed. Contemporary, erotic fiction, from a female perspective, 3,000 to 4,000 words. "Fantasy Forum," 1,000 to 2,000 words. Pays from $200; $25 to $100 for "Fantasy Forum", after acceptance.

POWER AND LIGHT—6401 The Paseo, Kansas City, MO 64131. Beula J. Postlewait, Preteen Ed. Fiction, 500 to 800 words, for grades 5 to 6, defining Christian experiences and values. Pays 5¢ a word for multiple-use rights, on publication.

PURPOSE—616 Walnut Ave., Scottdale, PA 15683-1999. James E. Horsch, Ed. Fiction, up to 750 words, on problem solving from a Christian point of view. Poetry, 3 to 12 lines. Pays to 5¢ a word for fiction; to $2 per line for poetry, on acceptance.

QUEEN'S QUARTERLY—Queens Univ., Kingston, Ont., Canada K7L 3N6. Attn: Fiction Ed. Fiction, to 5,000 words, in English and French. Pays to $300, on publication.

RANGER RICK—8925 Leesburg Pike, Vienna, VA 22184. Deborah Churchman, Fiction Ed. Photographers and artists wishing to send unsolicited portfolios should first write for photo and art guidelines. No unsolicited article queries or manuscripts.

ST. ANTHONY MESSENGER—1615 Republic St., Cincinnati, OH 45210-1298. Fr. Jack Wintz, O.F.M., Ed. Barbara Beckwith, Man. Ed. Fiction that makes readers think about issues, lifestyles, and values. Pays 15¢ a word, on acceptance. Queries or manuscripts accepted.

SEA KAYAKER—P.O. Box 17170, Seattle, WA 98107-0870. Christopher Cunningham, Ed. Short stories exclusively related to ocean kayaking, 1,000 to 3,000 words. Pays on publication.

SEVENTEEN—850 Third Ave., New York, NY 10022. Ben Schrank, Fiction Ed. High-quality, literary short fiction, to 4,000 words. Pays on acceptance.

STRAIGHT—8121 Hamilton Ave., Cincinnati, OH 45231. Heather E. Wallace, Ed. Well-constructed fiction, 1,000 to 1,500 words, showing Christian teens using Bible principles in everyday life. Contemporary, realistic teen characters a must. Most interested in school, church, dating, and family life stories. Pays 5¢ to 7¢ a word, on acceptance. Guidelines.

'TEEN—6420 Wilshire Blvd., Los Angeles, CA 90048-5515. Attn: Fiction Dept. Short stories, 2,500 to 4,000 words: mystery, teen situations, adventure, romance, humor for teens. Pays from $200, on acceptance.

TEEN LIFE—1445 Boonville Ave., Springfield, MO 65802-1894. Tammy Bicket, Ed. Fiction, to 1,200 words, for 13- to 19-year-olds. Articles, 500 to 1,000 words. Strong evangelical emphasis a must: believable characters working out their problems according to biblical principles. Buys first rights; pays on acceptance. Reprints considered.

TRUE CONFESSIONS—233 Park Ave. S., New York, NY 10003. Pat Byrdsong, Ed. Timely, emotional, first-person stories, 2,000 to 9,000 words, on romance, family life, and problems of today's young working-class women. Pays 5¢ a word, after publication.

WESTERN PEOPLE—Box 2500, Saskatoon, Sask., Canada S7K 2C4. Attn: Ed. Short stories, 1,200 to 2,500 words, on subjects or themes of interest to rural readers in western Canada. Pays $100 to $200, on acceptance. Enclose international reply coupons and SAE.

WOMAN'S WORLD—270 Sylvan Ave., Englewood Cliffs, NJ 07632. Attn: Fiction Dept. Fast-moving short stories, no more than 1,500 words, with realistic relationship theme. (Specify "romance" on outside of envelope.) Mini-mysteries, to 1,000 words, with "whodunit" or "howdunit" theme. (Specify "mini mystery" on envelope.) No science fiction, fantasy, or historical romance and no horror, ghost stories, or gratuitous violence. "Dialogue-driven romances help propel the story." Pays $1,000 for romances, $500 for mini-mysteries, on acceptance. SASE for guidelines and manuscript return.

YANKEE—Yankee Publishing Co., P.O. Box 520, Dublin, NH 03444. Judson Hale, Ed. Edie Clark, Fiction Ed. High-quality, literary short fiction, to 3,000 words (shorter preferred), with New England setting; no sap buckets or lobster pot stereotypes. Pays $1,000, on acceptance.

DETECTIVE & MYSTERY

ALFRED HITCHCOCK'S MYSTERY MAGAZINE—475 Park Avenue S., New York, NY 10016. Cathleen Jordan, Ed. Well-plotted, previously unpublished mystery, detective, suspense, and crime short stories, to 14,000 words. Submissions by new writers strongly encouraged. Pays 8¢ a word, on acceptance. No simultaneous submissions, please. (Submissions sent to *AHMM* are not considered for, or read by, *Ellery Queen's Mystery Magazine,* and vice versa.) Guidelines with SASE.

ARMCHAIR DETECTIVE—549 Park Ave., Suite 252, Scotch Plains, NJ 07076-1705. Elizabeth Foxwell, Ed.-in-Chief. Articles on mystery and detective fiction; biographical sketches, reviews, etc. No fiction. Pays $12 a printed page; reviews are unpaid. SASE for guidelines.

COZY DETECTIVE MYSTERY MAGAZINE—686 Jake Ct., McMinnville, OR 97128. David Rowell Workman, Sr. Ed. Charley Bradley, Story Ed. Mystery and suspense, fiction and nonfiction, to 5,000 words. Poems, to 20 lines. Pays in copies. Artwork and poems also needed.

ELLERY QUEEN'S MYSTERY MAGAZINE—475 Park Ave. S., New York, NY 10016. Janet Hutchings, Ed. Detective, crime, and mystery fiction, approximately 1,500 to 10,000 words. Occasionally publishes novelettes, to 20,000 words, by established authors and humorous mystery verse. No sex, sadism, or sensationalism. Particularly interested in new writers and "first stories." Pays 3¢ to 8¢ a word, occasionally higher for established authors, on acceptance.

HARDBOILED—Gryphon Publications, P.O. Box 209, Brooklyn, NY 11228-0209. Gary Lovisi, Ed. Hard, cutting-edge crime fiction (suspense, noir, private eye) to 3,000 words. Payment varies, on publication. Query for articles, book and film reviews, and longer fiction.

MURDEROUS INTENT—P.O. Box 5947, Vancouver, WA 98668-5947. Margo Power, Ed./Pub. Quarterly. Mystery and suspense stories and mystery-related articles, 2,000 to 4,000 words; fillers, to 750 words; poems, to 30 lines. "We love humor in mysteries. Surprise us!" Pays $10, on acceptance. No simultaneous submissions. Electronic submissions only. Send query letter with synopsis and length to: madison@teleport.com.

MYSTERY TIME—P.O. Box 2907, Decatur, IL 62524. Linda Hutton, Ed. Semiannual. Suspense, 1,500 words, and poems about mysteries, up to 16 lines. "We prefer female protagonists. No gore or violence." Pays $5, on acceptance.

NEW MYSTERY MAGAZINE—The Flatiron Bldg., 101 W. 23rd St., PMB 7, New York, NY 10011. Charles Raisch, Ed. Mystery, crime, detection, and suspense short stories, 2,000 to 6,000 words. No true crime. Book reviews, 250 to 2,000 words, of upcoming or recently published novels. Pays $15 to $500, on publication. No guidelines; study back issues.

SLEUTHHOUND MAGAZINE—P.O. Box 890294, Oklahoma City, OK 73189-0294. Peggy Farris, Ed. Quarterly. Articles, 500 to 2,000 words. How-to articles; book reviews; interviews with well-known writers. "No explicit sex, gore or extreme violence." Pays 3¢ to 6¢ a word, on publication.

SCIENCE FICTION & FANTASY

ABERRATIONS—P.O. Box 460430, San Francisco, CA 94146. Richard Blair, Man. Ed. Science fiction, horror, and fantasy, to 8,000 words. "Experimental, graphic, multi-genre is O.K. with science fiction/fantasy/horror tie-in." Pays ½¢ a word, on publication. Guidelines.

ABORIGINAL SF—P.O. Box 2449, Woburn, MA 01888-0849. Charles C. Ryan, Ed. Short stories, 2,500 to 7,500 words, and poetry, one to 2 typed pages, with strong science content, lively, unique characters, and well-designed plots. No sword and sorcery, horror, or fantasy. Pays $200 for fiction, $15 for poetry, $10 for science fiction jokes, and $20 for cartoons, on publication.

ABSOLUTE MAGNITUDE—P.O. Box 2988, Radford, VA 24143. Warren Lapine, Ed. Quarterly. Character-driven technical science fiction, 1,000 to 25,000 words. No fantasy, horror, satire, or funny science fiction. Pays 1¢ to 5¢ a word, on publication. Guidelines.

ADVENTURES OF SWORD & SORCERY—P.O. Box 807, Xenia, OH 45385. Randy Dannenfelser, Ed. Quarterly. High fantasy and heroic fantasy, 1,000 to 8,000 words. Pays 3¢ to 6¢ a word, on acceptance.

ANALOG SCIENCE FICTION AND FACT—475 Park Ave. S., New York, NY 10016. Stanley Schmidt, Ed. Science fiction with strong characters in believable future or alien setting: short stories, 2,000 to 7,500 words; novelettes, 10,000 to 20,000 words; serials, to 80,000 words. Also uses future-related articles. Pays to 7¢ a word, on acceptance. Query for serials and articles.

ASIMOV'S SCIENCE FICTION MAGAZINE—475 Park Ave. S., 11th Fl., New York, NY 10016. Gardner Dozois, Ed. Short, character-oriented science fiction and fantasy, to 15,000 words. Pays 5¢ to 8¢ a word, on acceptance. Guidelines.

DRAGON MAGAZINE—1801 Lind Ave. S.W., Renton, WA 98055. Dave Gross, Ed. Articles, 1,500 to 7,500 words, on fantasy and science fiction role-playing games. Fantasy, 1,500 to 8,000 words. Pays 5¢ to 8¢ a word for fiction, on acceptance. Pays 4¢ a word for articles, on publication. All submissions must include a disclosure form. Guidelines.

FANGORIA—475 Park Ave. S., 8th Fl., New York, NY 10016. Anthony Timpone, Ed. Published 10 times yearly. Movie, TV, and book previews, reviews, and interviews, 1,800 to 2,500 words, in connection with upcoming horror films. "A strong love of the genre and an appreciation and understanding of the magazine are essential." Pays $175 to $225, on publication. No fiction.

FANTASY MACABRE—P.O. Box 20610, Seattle, WA 98102. Jessica Salmonson, Ed. Fiction, to 3,000 words, including translations. "We look for a tale that is strong in atmosphere, with menace that is suggested and threatening rather than the result of dripping blood and gore." Pays 1¢ a word, to $30 per story, on publication. Also publishes *Fantasy & Terror* for poetry-in-prose pieces.

HADROSAUR TALES—Hadrosaur Productions, P.O. Box 8468, Las Cruces, NM 88006. David Summers, Ed. Semiannual. Literary science fiction and fantasy, 1,500 to 6,000 words. Science fiction- or fantasy-based poetry, one to 2 pages. No graphic horror or violence. Pays $6 for fiction; $2 per poem, on acceptance, plus copies.

HAUNTS—Nightshade Publications, Box 8068, Cranston, RI 02920-0068. Joseph K. Cherkes, Ed. Horror, fantasy, and science fiction with strong character development and solid plots, 1,500 to 8,000 words. No explicit sexual scenes, famous rewrites, or pure adventure. Pays $5 to $50 for fiction; $3 per poem (submit up to 3), on publication. Manuscripts read January 1st through June 1st. SASE.

IN DARKNESS ETERNAL—Stygian Vortex Publications, 113 Highland Park Dr., Athens, GA 30605-3577. Glenda Woodrum, Ed.-in-Chief. T'shai K., Fiction and Poetry Ed. Annual. Stories from 3,000 words, articles, and artwork by and for vampire enthusiasts. No stories about serial killers, prostitutes, or anything involving people becoming vampires from the bite of a vampire; no Dracula or other media related vampire tales. Payment is 50¢ per printed page; $1 to $3 for poetry. Query. Guidelines.

THE LEADING EDGE—3163 JKHB, Provo, UT 84602. David Burnett, Ed. Semiannual. Science fiction and fantasy, 3,000 to 12,000 words; poetry, to 600 lines; and articles, to 8,000 words, on science, scientific speculation, and literary criticism. No excessive profanity, overt violence, or excessive sexual situations. No simultaneous submissions. Pays 1¢ a word, on publication. Guidelines.

THE MAGAZINE OF FANTASY AND SCIENCE FICTION—Box 1806, Madison Sq. Station, New York, NY 10159-1806. Gordon Van Gelder, Ed. Fantasy and science fiction stories, to 15,000 words. Pays 5¢ to 7¢ a word, on acceptance.

MARION ZIMMER BRADLEY'S FANTASY MAGAZINE—P.O. Box 249, Berkeley, CA 94701. Marion Zimmer Bradley, Ed. Quarterly. Well-plotted stories, 3,500 to 4,000 words. Action and adventure fantasy "with no particular objection to modern settings." Send SASE for guidelines before submitting. Pays 3¢ to 10¢ a word, on acceptance.

NIGHT TERRORS—1202 W. Market St., Orrville, OH 44667-1710. Mr. D. E. Davidson, Ed. Stories of psychological horror, the supernatural or occult, from 2,000 to 5,000 words. Pays in copies and by arrangement with professional writers.

OF UNICORNS AND SPACE STATIONS—P.O. Box 97, Bountiful, UT 84011-0097. Gene Davis, Ed. Science fiction and fantasy, to 5,000 words. Poetry related to science fiction, science, or fantasy. "Do not staple or fold long manuscripts." Pays 1¢ per word for fiction; $5 for poems, on publication.

OMNI INTERNET—General Media International, 277 Park Ave., 4th Fl., New York, NY 10172-0003. Ellen Datlow, Fiction Ed. On-line magazine. Strong, realistic science fiction, 2,000 to 10,000 words, with good characterizations. "We want to intrigue our readers with mindbroadening, thought-provoking stories that will excite their sense of wonder." Some fantasy. No horror, ghost, or sword and sorcery tales. Pays $1,300 to $2,250, on acceptance. SASE. Web site: www.omnimag.com.

OUTER DARKNESS: WHERE NIGHTMARES ROAM UNLEASHED—1312 N. Delaware Pl., Tulsa, OK 74110. Dennis Kirk, Ed. Quarterly. Science fiction and horror, 1,500 to 5,000 words; nonfiction pertaining to legends, myths, folklore, etc., to 1,000 words; poetry, up to two digest-size pages; half-page fillers; and B&W photos and illustrations, to one digest-size page. Query for illustrations only. Pays in copies.

PIRATE WRITINGS: TALES OF FANTASY, MYSTERY & SCIENCE FICTION—P.O. Box 329, Brightwaters, NY 11718-0329. Edward J. McFadden, Pub./Ed. Tom Piccirilli, Assoc. Ed. Mystery, science fiction, fantasy, 250 to 6,000 words. Poetry, to 20 lines. Pays 1¢ to 5¢ a word.

SCAVENGER'S NEWSLETTER—519 Ellinwood, Osage City, KS 66523-1329. Janet Fox, Ed. Flash fiction, 1,200 words, in the genres of science fiction, fantasy, horror, and mystery. Articles, 1,000 words, pertaining to writing and art in those genres. Poems, to 10 lines, and humor, 500 to 700 words, for writers and artists. "Most of the magazine is market information." Pays $4 for fiction, articles, and cover art; $2 for humor, poems, and inside art, on acceptance. Website: www.cza.com/scav/index.html

SCIENCE FICTION CHRONICLE—P.O. Box 022730, Brooklyn, NY 11202-0056. Andrew Porter, Ed. News items, 300 to 800 words, for science fiction and fantasy readers, professionals, and booksellers. Interviews with authors, 3,000 to 5,000 words. No fiction. Pays 3.5¢ to 5¢ a word, on publication. Query. Sample issue, $1. E-mail: SFChronicle@Compuserve.com.

THE SFWA BULLETIN—522 Park Ave., Berkeley Heights, NJ 07922. John Betancourt, Ed. Quarterly. Science fiction or fantasy articles to 5,000 words. Pays 8¢ to 10 a word, on acceptance. No fiction. E-mail queries preferred: bulletin@sfwa.org.

TALEBONES—Fairwood Press, 10531 S.E. 250th Pl., #104, Kent, WA 98031. Patrick and Honna Swenson, Eds. Science fiction and dark fantasy, to 6,000 words. Articles, to 3,000 words, on the state of speculative fiction. Poetry. Cartoons with science fiction or fantasy themes. "We're looking for science fiction and dark fantasy with strong characters and entertaining story lines. Fiction should be more toward the darker side, without being pure horror." Pays 1¢ a word for fiction, 2¢ a word for the lead story, and $7 per poem, on acceptance.

THE ULTIMATE UNKNOWN—Combs Press, P.O. Box 219, Streamwood, IL 60107-0219. David D. Combs, Ed. Fiction and nonfiction on horror, science fiction, and the future, to 3,000 words. Related poetry, to 20 lines. Payment is one copy.

THE URBANITE: SURREAL & LIVELY & BIZARRE—Box 4737, Davenport, IA 52808. Mark McLaughlin, Ed. Published 3 times a year. Dark fantasy, horror (no gore), surrealism, reviews, and social commentary, to 3,000 words. Free verse poems, to 2 pages. Pays 2¢ to 3¢ a word; $10 for poetry, on acceptance. Query for themes. Web site: http://members.tripod.com/theurbanite.

WEIRD TALES—123 Crooked Ln., King of Prussia, PA 19406-2570. George Scithers, Pub. Darrell Schweitzer, Ed. Quarterly. Fantasy and horror (no science fiction), to 8,000 words. Pays about 3¢ per word, on acceptance. Guidelines.

CONFESSION & ROMANCE

BLACK CONFESSIONS—See *Black Romance.*

BLACK ROMANCE—233 Park Ave. S., New York, NY 10003. Marcia Y. Mahan, Ed. Romance fiction, 5,000 to 5,800 words, and relationship articles. Queries preferred. Pays $100 to $125, on publication. Also publishes *Black Secrets, Bronze Thrills, Black Confessions,* and *Jive.* Guidelines.

BLACK SECRETS—See *Black Romance.*

BRONZE THRILLS—See *Black Romance.*

INTIMACY—233 Park Ave. S., 7th Fl., New York, NY 10003. Marcia Y. Mahan, Ed. Fiction, 5,000 to 5,800 words, for black women ages 18 to 45; must have contemporary plot and contain 2 romantic and intimate love scenes. Pays $100 to $125, on publication. Guidelines.

JIVE—See *Black Romance.*

MODERN ROMANCES—See *True Life Stories.*

ROMANTIC HEARTS—P.O. Box 450669, Westlake, OH 44145. Debra Krauss, Ed./Pub. Short romantic fiction, 1,500 to 4,000 words; related how-to articles and essays with a romantic theme, 500 to 1,500 words; love poems, to 25 lines. "We are looking for heartwarming tales of love and romance that are rich with emotion and strong characterization." Pays in copies. Guidelines.

TRUE CONFESSIONS—233 Park Ave. S., New York, NY 10003. Pat Byrdsong, Ed. Timely, emotional, first-person stories, 1,000 to 9,000 words, on romance, family life, and problems of today's young blue-collar women. Pays 5¢ a word, after publication.

TRUE EXPERIENCE—233 Park Ave. S., New York, NY 10003. Rose Bernstein, Ed. Katherine Edwards, Assoc. Ed. Realistic first-person stories, 1,000 to 12,000 words, on family life, single life, love, romance, overcoming hardships, mysteries. Pays 3¢ a word, after publication.

TRUE LIFE STORIES—(formerly *Modern Romances*) 233 Park Ave. S., New York, NY 10003. Bridget Gayle, Ed. Romantic and topical confession stories, 4,000 to 10,000 words, written in first person, with reader-identification and strong emotional tone. Pays 5¢ a word, after publication. Buys all rights.

TRUE LOVE—233 Park Ave. S., New York, NY 10003. Alison Way, Ed. Fresh, young, true-to-life stories, on love and topics of current interest. Must be written in the past tense and first person. Pays 3¢ a word, after publication. Guidelines.

TRUE ROMANCE—233 Park Ave. S., New York, NY 10003. Pat Vitucci, Ed. True or true-to-life, dramatic and/or romantic first-person stories, 5,000 to 10,000 words. All genres: tragedy, mystery, peril, love, family struggles, etc. Topical themes. Love poems. "We enjoy working with new writers." Reports in 3 to 5 months. Pays 3¢ a word, a month after publication.

POETRY MARKETS

As the following list attests, the market for poetry in general magazines is rather limited: There aren't many general-interest magazines that use poetry, and in those that do, the competition to break into print is stiff, since editors use only a limited number of poems in each issue. In addition to the magazines listed here, writers may find their local newspapers receptive to poetry.

While poetry may be scant in general-interest magazines, it is the backbone of a majority of the college, little, and literary magazines (see page 713). Poets will also find a number of competitions offering cash awards for unpublished poems in the *Literary Prize Offers* list.

AMERICA—106 W. 56th St., New York, NY 10019. Patrick Samway, S.J., Literary Ed. Serious poetry, preferably in contemporary prose idiom, 10 to 25 lines. Occasional light verse. Submit 2 or 3 poems. Pays $1.40 per line, on publication. Guidelines.

THE AMERICAN SCHOLAR—Fourth Fl., 1785 Massachusetts Ave., NW, Washington, DC 20036. Anne Fadiman, Ed. Highly original poetry for college-educated, intellectual readers. Pays $50, on acceptance.

ASIAN PAGES—P.O. Box 11932, St. Paul, MN 55111-0932. Cheryl Weiberg, Ed.-in-Chief. Poetry, 100 words, with "a strong, non-offensive Asian slant." Pays on publication.

THE ATLANTIC MONTHLY—77 N. Washington St., Boston, MA 02114. Peter Davison, David Barber, Poetry Eds. Previously unpublished poetry of highest quality. Limited market; only 2 to 3 poems an issue. Interested in new poets. Occasionally uses light verse. "No simultaneous submissions; we make prompt decisions." Pays excellent rates, on acceptance.

CAPPER'S—1503 S.W. 42nd St., Topeka, KS 66609-1265. Ann Crahan, Ed. Free verse, light verse, traditional, nature, and inspirational poems, 4 to 16 lines, with simple everyday themes. Submit up to 6 poems at a time, with SASE. Pays $10 to $15, on acceptance.

CHILDREN'S PLAYMATE—P.O. Box 567, Indianapolis, IN 46206. Terry Harshman, Ed. Poetry for children, 6 to 8 years old, on good health, nutrition, exercise, safety, seasonal and humorous subjects. Pays from $30, on publication. Buys all rights.

THE CHRISTIAN SCIENCE MONITOR—One Norway St., Boston, MA 02115. Elizabeth Lund, Poetry Ed. Finely crafted poems that celebrate the extraordinary in the ordinary. Seasonal material always needed. No violence, sensuality, racism, death and disease, helplessness, hopelessness. Short poems preferred; submit no more than 5 poems at a time. SASE required. Pays varying rates, on publication.

COMMONWEAL—475 Riverside Dr., New York, NY 10115. Rosemary Deen, Poetry Ed. Catholic. Serious, witty poetry. Pays 50¢ a line, on publication. SASE required. No submissions accepted June to September.

COMPLETE WOMAN—Dept. P, 875 N. Michigan Ave., Suite 3434, Chicago, IL 60611. Attn: Poetry Ed. Send poetry with SASE.

COUNTRY WOMAN—P.O. Box 989, Greendale, WI 53129. Kathy Pohl, Exec. Ed. Traditional rural poetry and light verse, 4 to 30 lines, on rural experiences and country living; also seasonal poetry. Poems must rhyme. Pays $10 to $25, on acceptance.

EVANGEL—Light and Life Communications, Box 535002, Indianapolis, IN 46253-5002. Julie Innes, Ed. Free Methodist. Devotional or nature poetry, 8 to 16 lines. Pays $10, on publication. Guidelines available with SASE.

MATURE YEARS—201 Eighth Ave. S., P.O. Box 801, Nashville, TN 37202. Marvin W. Cropsey, Ed. United Methodist. Poetry, to 14 lines, on preretirement, retirement, Christianity, inspiration, seasonal subjects, aging. No "saccharine" poetry. Submit up to 6 poems at a time. Pays 50¢ to $1 per line.

MIDSTREAM—633 Third Ave., 21st Fl., New York, NY 10017. Attn: Poetry Ed. Poetry of Jewish/Zionist interest. "Brevity highly recommended." Pays $25, on publication. Allow 3 months for response.

THE MIRACULOUS MEDAL—475 E. Chelten Ave., Philadelphia, PA 19144-5785. William J. O'Brien, C.M., Ed. Catholic. Religious verse, to 20 lines. Pays 50¢ a line, on acceptance.

THE NATION—33 Irving Place, 8th Fl., New York, NY 10003. Grace

Schulman, Poetry Ed. Poetry of high quality. Pays after publication. SASE requried.

NATIONAL ENQUIRER—Lantana, FL 33464-0002. Kathy Martin, Fillers Ed. Short poems, to 8 lines, with traditional rhyming verse, of an amusing, philosophical, or inspirational nature. No experimental poetry. Original epigrams, humorous anecdotes, and "daffynitions." Submit seasonal/holiday material at least 2 months in advance. Pays $25, after publication. Material will not be returned; do not send SASE.

THE NEW REPUBLIC—1220 19th St. N.W., Washington, DC 20036. Attn: Mark Strand, Ed. Pays $100, after publication.

THE NEW YORKER—20 W. 43rd St., New York, NY 10036. Attn: Poetry Ed. First-rate poetry. Pays top rates, on acceptance. Include SASE.

PURPOSE—616 Walnut Ave., Scottdale, PA 15683-1999. James E. Horsch, Poetry Ed. Poetry, to 8 lines, with challenging Christian discipleship angle. Pays 85¢ to $2.50 a line, on acceptance.

ST. JOSEPH'S MESSENGER—P.O. Box 288, Jersey City, NJ 07303-0288. Sister Mary Kuiken, Ed. Light verse and traditional poetry, 4 to 40 lines. Pays $10 to $25, on publication.

THE SATURDAY EVENING POST—P.O. Box 567, Indianapolis, IN 46206. Steven Pettinga, Post Scripts Ed. Short narratives, jokes, and humorous, clean limericks. No conventional poetry. SASE required. Pays $15, on publication.

WARRIOR POETS—P.O. Box 7616, Wantagh, NY 11793. R.J. Erbacher, Ed.-in-Chief. Published 3 times per year. "The Magazine of Medieval Poetry." Poetry, any length; stories, 2,000 words, dealing with swords and chivalry, knights and maidens, love and bravery, sorcery and dragons, warriors, and poets. "Ancient stuff that rings with clashing swords, dragon roars, damsel's screams, and wizard's incantations." Payment is in copies, on publication. Guidelines.

WESTERN PEOPLE—P.O. Box 2500, Saskatoon, Sask., Canada S7K 2C4. Michael Gillgannon, Man. Ed. Short poetry with Western Canadian themes. Pays on acceptance. Send international reply coupons.

WRITER'S GUIDELINES & NEWS—(formerly *Yesterday's Magazette*) P.O. Box 18566, Sarasota, FL 34276. Ned Burke, Ed. Traditional poetry, to 24 lines. Pays in copies for poetry and short pieces.

YANKEE—Yankee Publishing Co., P.O. Box 520, Dublin, NH 03444. Jean Burden, Poetry Ed. Serious poetry of high quality, to 30 lines. Pays $50 per poem for all rights, $35 for first rights, on publication. SASE required.

YESTERDAY'S MAGAZETTE—See *Writer's Guidelines & News.*

COLLEGE, LITERARY, & LITTLE MAGAZINES

The thousands of literary journals, little magazines, and college quarterlies published today welcome work from novices and pros alike; editors are always interested in seeing traditional and experimental fiction, poetry, essays, reviews, short articles, criticism, and satire, and as long as the material is well-written, the fact that a writer is a beginner doesn't adversely affect his or her chances for acceptance.

Most of these smaller publications have small budgets and staffs, so they may be slow in their reporting time; several months is not unusual. In addition, they usually pay only in copies of the issue in which published work appears and some (particularly college magazines) do not read manuscripts during the summer.

Publication in the literary journals can, however, lead to recognition by editors of large-circulation magazines, who read the little magazines in their search for new talent. There is also the possibility of having one's work chosen for reprinting in one of the prestigious annual collections of work from the little magazines.

Because the requirements of these journals differ widely, it is always important to study recent issues before submitting work to one of them. Large libraries may carry a variety of journals, or a writer may send a postcard to the editor and ask the price of a sample copy.

For a complete list of literary and college publications and little magazines, writers may consult such reference works as *The International Directory of Little Magazines and Small Presses,* published annually by Dustbooks (P.O. Box 100, Paradise, CA 95967).

ABOUT SUCH THINGS—1701 Delancey St., Philadelphia, PA 19103. Laurel Garver, Man. Ed. Semiannual. Essays and reviews of arts and cultural topics. Free verse poetry. Fiction, to 3,000 words. "We seek contemporary voices that explore how Christian faith affects life in a broken world." Pays in 2 copies.

AFRICAN AMERICAN REVIEW—Dept. of English, Indiana State Univ., Terre Haute, IN 47809. Joe Weixlmann, Ed. Essays on African American literature, theater, film, art, and culture; interviews; poems; fiction; and book reviews. Submit up to 6 poems. Pays an honorarium and copies. Query for book review assignments; send 3 copies of all other submissions. Responds in 3 months.

AFRICAN VOICES—270 W. 96th St., New York, NY 10025. Carolyn A. Butts, Exec. Ed. Quarterly. Humorous, erotic, and dramatic fiction, 500 to 2,500 words, by ethnic writers. Nonfiction, 500 to 1,500 words, including investigative articles, artist profiles, essays, and first-person narratives. Pays in copies. SASE.

AGNI—Boston Univ., Creative Writing Program, 236 Bay State Rd., Boston, MA 02215. Askold Melnyczuk, Ed. Short stories and poetry. Manuscripts read October through January. Sample issue available for $9.

ALABAMA LITERARY REVIEW—Troy State Univ., 150 Smith Hall, Troy, AL 36082. William E. Hicks, Chief Ed. Annual. Contemporary, literary fiction and nonfiction, 3,500 words; short drama, to 25 pages; and poetry, to 2 pages. Thought-provoking B&W photos. Pays in copies (honorarium when available). Responds within 3 months.

ALASKA QUARTERLY REVIEW—Univ. of Alaska Anchorage, 3211 Providence Dr., Anchorage, AK 99508. Attn: Eds. Short stories, novel excerpts, short plays, and poetry (traditional and unconventional forms). Submit manuscripts between August 15 and May 15. Pays in subscription (and honorarium when funding is available).

ALBATROSS—P.O. Box 7787, North Port, FL 34287-0787. Richard Smyth, Richard Brobst, Eds. High-quality poetry; especially interested in ecological and nature poetry written in narrative form. Interviews with well-known poets. Submit 3 to 5 poems with brief bio. Pays in copies.

AMELIA—329 E St., Bakersfield, CA 93304. Frederick A. Raborg, Jr., Ed. Poetry, to 100 lines; critical essays, to 2,000 words; reviews, to 500 words; belles lettres, to 1,000 words; fiction, to 4,500 words; fine pen-and-ink sketches; photos. Pays $35 for fiction; $25 for criticism; $10 to $25 for other nonfiction and artwork; $2 to $25 for poetry. Annual contest.

THE AMERICAN BOOK REVIEW—Unit for Contemporary Literature, Illinois State Univ., Campus Box 4241, Normal, IL 61790-4241. Rebecca Kaiser, Man. Ed. Literary book reviews, 700 to 1,200 words. Pays $50 or 2-year subscription and copies. Query with clips of published reviews.

AMERICAN LITERARY REVIEW—Univ. of North Texas, English Dept., Denton, TX 76203-1307. Lee Martin, Ed. Short fiction and creative nonfiction, to 30 double-spaced pages, and poetry (submit 3 to 5 poems). Pays in copies.

THE AMERICAN POETRY REVIEW—1721 Walnut St., Philadelphia, PA 19103. Attn: Eds. Highest quality contemporary poetry. Responds in 10 weeks.

AMERICAN QUARTERLY—Dept. of English, Georgetown Univ., Washington, DC 20057. Lucy Maddox, Ed. Scholarly essays, 5,000 to 10,000 words, on any aspect of U.S. culture. Pays in copies.

THE AMERICAN SCHOLAR—1785 Massachusetts Ave. N.W., 4th Fl., Washington, DC 20036. Anne Fadiman, Ed. Articles, 3,500 to 4,000 words, on science, politics, literature, the arts, etc. Book reviews. Pays up to $500 for articles, $100 for reviews, on publication.

AMERICAN SHORT FICTION—Parlin Hall 108, Univ. of Texas, Austin, TX 78712-1164. Joseph E. Kruppa, Ed. Literary fiction only, any length. Pays $400 per story, on acceptance. Manuscripts read September 1 through May 31.

AMERICAN WRITING—4343 Manayunk Ave., Philadelphia, PA 19128. Alexandra Grilikhes, Ed. Semiannual. "We encourage experimentation, new writing that takes risks with form, point of view, and language. We're interested in the voice of the loner, states of being, and initiation. We strongly suggest reading a copy of the magazine before submitting your work." Fiction and nonfiction, to 3,500 words, and poetry. Pays in copies.

ANOTHER CHICAGO MAGAZINE—3709 N. Kenmore, Chicago, IL 60613. Attn: Ed. Semiannual. Fiction, essays on literature, and poetry. "We want writing that's urgent, new, and lives in the world." Pays in copies on acceptance, and small honorarium when possible.

ANTHOLOGY—P.O. Box 4411, Mesa, AZ 85211-4411. Sharon Skinner, Exec. Ed. Bimonthly. Stories, 1,000 to 5,000 words, any genre. Poetry, any style, to 100 lines. "We also accept stories based in the fictional city of Haven, where people make their own heroes." Payment is one copy. Send SASE for guidelines.

ANTIETAM REVIEW—41 S. Potomac St., Hagerstown, MD 21740. Susanne Kass and Ann Knox, Eds.-in-Chief. Fiction and nonfiction (interviews, essays), to 5,000 words; poetry and photography. Submissions from natives or residents of MD, PA, WV, VA, DE, or DC only. Pays from $20 to $100. Guidelines. Manuscripts read September through January.

THE ANTIGONISH REVIEW—St. Francis Xavier Univ., P.O. Box 5000, Antigonish, NS, Canada B2G 2W5. George Sanderson, Ed. Poetry; short stories, essays, book reviews, 1,800 to 2,500 words. Pays in copies.

ANTIOCH REVIEW—P.O. Box 148, Yellow Springs, OH 45387-0148. Robert S. Fogarty, Ed. Timely articles, 2,000 to 8,000 words, on social sciences, literature, and humanities. Quality fiction. Poetry. No inspirational poetry. Pays $10 per printed page, on publication. Poetry considered from September to May; other material considered year-round.

APPALACHIA—5 Joy St., Boston, MA 02108. Parkman Howe, Poetry Ed. Semiannual publication of the Appalachian Mountain Club. Oldest mountaineering journal in the country covers nature, conservation, climbing, hiking, canoeing, and ecology. Poems, to 30 lines. Pays in copies.

ARACHNE—2363 Page Rd., Kennedy, NY 14747-9717. Susan L. Leach, Ed. Semiannual. Fiction, to 1,500 words. Poems (submit up to 7). "We are looking for rural material." Pays in copies. Manuscripts read in January and July.

ARIZONA QUARTERLY—Univ. of Arizona, Main Library B-541, Tucson, AZ 85721. Edgar A. Dryden, Ed. Criticism of American literature and culture from a theoretical perspective. No poetry or fiction. Pays in copies.

ART TIMES—P.O. Box 730, Mt. Marion, NY 12456. Raymond J. Steiner, Ed. Fiction, to 1,500 words, and poetry, to 20 lines, for literate, art conscious readers (generally over 40 years old). Feature essays on the arts are staff-written. Pays $25 for fiction, in copies for poetry, on publication. Responds within six months.

ARTFUL DODGE—College of Wooster, Wooster, OH 44691. Daniel Bourne, Ed. Annual. Fiction, to 20 pages. Literary essays, especially those involving personal narrative, to 15 pages. Poetry, including translations of contemporary poets; submit 3 to 6 poems at a time; long poems encouraged. Pays $5 per page, on publication, plus 2 copies. Manuscripts read year-round.

THE ASIAN PACIFIC AMERICAN JOURNAL—The Asian American Writers' Workshop, 37 St. Marks Pl., New York, NY 10003-7801. Hanya Yanagihara, Eileen Tabios, Eds. Short stories, excerpts from longer fiction works by emerging or established Asian American writers. 4 copies of each submission required. Poetry (submit 10 poems). Pays in copies. Query required for reviews and interviews; queries preferred for other articles.

AURA LITERARY/ARTS REVIEW—P.O. Box 76, Univ. Center, UAB, Birmingham, AL 35294. Daniel Williams, Ed.-in-Chief. Fiction and essays on literature, to 5,000 words; poetry; B&W photos. Pays in copies. Guidelines.

BAMBOO RIDGE, THE HAWAII WRITERS' QUARTERLY— Bamboo Ridge Press, P.O. Box 61781, Honolulu, HI 96839-1781. Chock and Lum, Eds. Poetry, to 10 pages, and short stories, 25 pages, by writers in U.S. and abroad. Submit with SASE. Reports in 6 to 12 months. Pays 2 copies. Manuscripts read year-round.

BEACON STREET REVIEW—WLP Div., Emerson College, 100 Beacon St., Boston, MA 02116. Attn: Ed. Semiannual. Fiction, poetry, memoir, essays, to 20 pages. "Produced and edited by graduate students. We publish primarily writing by students in MFA programs." Send 3 copies of submission, short bio, and SASE. No payment.

THE BEAR DELUXE—(P.O. Box 10342, Portland, OR 97296. Thomas L. Webb, Ed. Quarterly. Unique environmental articles, 750 to 3,500 words; essays, 250 to 2,500 words; artist profiles, 750 to 1,500 words; and reviews, 100 to 1,000 words. Fiction, 750 to 4,500 words (2,500 is ideal). Poetry. Pays 5¢ a word, after publication, and subscription. Query for nonfiction.

BELLES LETTRES—1243 Maple View Dr., Charlottesville, MD 22902-8779. Janet Mullaney, Ed. Published 3 times a year; devoted to literature by or about women. Articles, 250 to 2,000 words: reviews, interviews, rediscoveries, and retrospectives; columns on publishing news, reprints, and nonfiction titles. Annual contest. Query required. Payment varies.

THE BELLINGHAM REVIEW—The Signpost Press, MS 9053, Western Washington Univ., Bellingham, WA 98225. Robin Hemley, Ed. Semiannual. Fiction and nonfiction, to 10,000 words, and poetry, any length. Pays in copies and subscription. Manuscripts read October to April. Contests. Guidelines.

BELLOWING ARK—P.O. Box 55564, Shoreline, WA 98155. Robert R. Ward, Ed. Bimonthly. Short fiction, poetry, and essays of varying lengths, that portray life as a positive, meaningful process. Interested in work from new writers. B&W photos; line drawings. Pays in copies. Manuscripts read year-round.

THE BELOIT FICTION JOURNAL—Box 11, Beloit College, Beloit, WI 53511. Clint McCown, Ed. Short fiction, one to 35 pages, on all themes. No pornography, political propaganda, religious dogma. Pays in copies. Manuscripts read Aug. 1 to Dec. 1.

BELOIT POETRY JOURNAL—24 Berry Cove Rd, Lamoine, ME 04605. Strong contemporary poetry, of any length or in any mode. Pays in copies. Guidelines. No simultaneous submissions.

BIBLIOPHILOS—Bibliophile Publishing, 200 Security Bldg., Fairmont, WV 26554. Dr. Gerald J. Bobango, Ed. Quarterly. Fiction and nonfiction, 1,500 to 3,000 words; poetry, to five printed pages (in batches of five). Reviews of history, literature, and literary criticism especially needed. Pays $25 to $50, on publication.

THE BITTER OLEANDER—4983 Tall Oaks Dr., Fayetteville, NY 13066-9776. Paul B. Roth, Ed./Pub. Short stories, 2,000 to 3,000 words. Poems, one to 100 lines. "Only highly imaginative poems and stories will suffice." Pays in copies. SASE.

BLACK BEAR REVIEW—Black Bear Publications, 1916 Lincoln St., Croydon, PA 19021-8026. Ave Jeanne, Ed. Semiannual. Contemporary poetry and art work. "We publish poems with social awareness, originality, and strength." Pays in one copy. Web site: http:members.aol.com/bbreview/index.htm

BLACK MOON: POETRY OF IMAGINATION—233 Northway Rd., Reistertown, MD 21136. Alan Britt, Ed. Imaginative poetry, long or short. Payment is one copy. Query. Guidelines.

THE BLACK WARRIOR REVIEW—The Univ. of Alabama, P.O. Box 862936, Tuscaloosa, AL 35486-0027. Christopher Chambers, Ed. Fiction; poetry; translations; reviews and essays. Pays about $100 for fiction; about $40 per poem, on publication. Annual awards. Manuscripts read year-round.

THE BLOOMSBURY REVIEW—P.O. Box 8928, Denver, CO 80201. Tom Auer, Ed. Marilyn Auer, Assoc. Ed. Book reviews, publishing features, interviews, essays, poetry. Pays $5 to $25, on publication.

BLUE UNICORN—22 Avon Rd., Kensington, CA 94707. Attn: Ed. Published in October, February, and June. "We are looking for originality of image, thought, and music; we rarely use poems over a page long." Submit up to 5 poems. Artwork used occasionally. Pays in one copy. Guidelines. Contest. SASE.

BLUELINE—English Dept., SUNY, Potsdam, NY 13676. Rick Henry, Ed. Essays and fiction, to 3,500 words, on Adirondack region or similar areas. Poems, to 75 lines; submit up to 5. Pays in copies. Manuscripts read September through November.

BORDERLANDS: TEXAS POETRY REVIEW—c/o Austin Writers' League, 1501 W. 5th St., Suite E-2, Austin, TX 78703-5155. Attn: Eds. Biannual. Outwardly directed poetry that exhibits social, political, spiritual, geographical, or historical awareness coupled with intelligence, creativity, and artistry. Bilingual poems and poems in two languages are acceptable when the poet has written both versions. Submit up to 5 poems with SASE. Also publishes interviews, essays (no more than 3,000 words), and reviews on contemporary poets and poets from the Southwest. Query for guidelines and contests. Pays one copy. Website: http://www.borderlands.org.

BOSTON REVIEW—E53-407, MIT, Cambridge, MA 02139. Matthew Howard, Man. Ed. Politics, literature, art, music, film, photography. Original fiction, to 5,000 words. Poetry. Pays $40 to $100. Manuscripts read year-round. Website: http://bostonreview.mit.edu.

BOTTOMFISH—De Anza College, 21250 Stevens Creek Blvd., Cupertino, CA 95014. David Denny, Ed. Annual. Short stories, short-shorts, poetry, creative nonfiction, interviews with writers and artists, photography, drawings, comics, and other visual art forms. Pays in copies. Submission period September to December only. Web site: http://laws.atc.fhda.edu/documents/bottomfish/bottomfish.html.

BOULEVARD—4579 Laclede Ave., #332, St. Louis, MO 63108-2103. Richard Burgin, Ed. Published 3 times a year. High-quality fiction and articles, to 30 pages; poetry. Pays to $300, on publication.

BRIAR CLIFF REVIEW—Briar Cliff College, 3303 Rebecca St., Sioux City, IA 51104. Tricia Currans-Sheehan, Man. Ed. Jeanne Emmons, Poetry Ed. Phil Hey, Fiction Ed. Prose, to 5,000 words: fiction, humor/satire, Siouxland history, thoughtful nonfiction. Also poetry, book reviews, and art. "We're an eclectic literary and cultural magazine focusing on, but not limited to, Siouxland writers and subjects." Pays in copies. Manuscripts read August through October.

THE BRIDGE—14050 Vernon St., Oak Park, MI 48237. Jack Zucker, Ed. Helen Zucker, Fiction Ed. Mitzi Alvin, Poetry Ed. Semiannual. Fiction, to 20 pages, and poetry to 200 lines. "Serious, realistic work with style." Pays in copies.

BUCKNELL REVIEW—Bucknell Univ., Lewisburg, PA 17837. Attn: Ed. Interdisciplinary journal in book form. Scholarly articles on arts, science, and letters. Pays in copies.

CALLALOO—Univ. of Virginia, Dept. of English, 322 Bryan Hall, Charlottesville, VA 22903. Charles H. Rowell, Ed. Fiction, poetry, drama, and popular essays by, and critical studies and bibliographies on Afro-American, Caribbean, and African artists and writers. Payment varies, on publication.

CALYX, A JOURNAL OF ART & LITERATURE BY WOMEN—P.O. Box B, Corvallis, OR 97339. M. Reaman, Man. Ed. Fiction, 5,000 words; book reviews, 1,000 words (please query about reviews); poetry, to 6 poems. Include short bio. Pays in copies and subscription. Guidelines. SASE. Submissions accepted October 1 to December 15.

THE CAPE ROCK—Dept. of English, Southeast Missouri State Univ., Cape Girardeau, MO 63701. Harvey E. Hecht, Ed. Semiannual. Poetry, to 70 lines, and B&W photography. (One photographer per issue; pays $100.) Pays in copies and $200 for best poem in each issue. Manuscripts read August to April.

THE CAPILANO REVIEW—Capilano College, 2055 Purcell Way, N. Vancouver, B.C., Canada V7J 3H5. Robert Sherrin, Ed. Experimental and literary fiction, 4,000 words; drama; poetry; photos and drawings. Pays $50 to $200, on publication.

THE CARIBBEAN WRITER—Univ. of the Virgin Islands, RR 02, Box 10,000, Kingshill, St. Croix, USVI 00850. Erika J. Waters, Ed. Annual. Fiction, to 15 pages (submit no more than 2 stories at a time), poems (no more than 5), personal essays (no more than 2), and one-act plays; the Caribbean should be central to the work. Blind submissions policy: place title only on manuscript; name, address, and title on separate sheet. Pays in copies. Annual deadline is September 30. E-mail submissions acceptable: qmars@uvi.edu

THE CAROLINA QUARTERLY—Greenlaw Hall CB#3520, Univ. of North Carolina, Chapel Hill, NC 27599-3520. Brian Carpenter, Ed. Fiction, to 5,000 words, by new or established writers. Poetry, to 300 lines; some nonfiction, artwork. Manuscripts read year-round.

THE CENTENNIAL REVIEW—312 Linton Hall, Michigan State Univ., East Lansing, MI 48824-1044. R.K. Meiners, Ed. Articles, 3,000 to 5,000 words, on sciences, humanities, and interdisciplinary topics. Pays in copies.

THE CHARITON REVIEW—Truman State Univ., Kirksville, MO 63501. Jim Barnes, Ed. Highest quality fiction, to 6,000 words. No "relatives" stories, essays, or poems. (Accepts 8 to 12 manuscripts each year.) Pays $5 per printed page.

CHATTAHOOCHEE REVIEW—Georgia Perimeter College, 2101 Womack Rd., Dunwoody, GA 30338-4497. Lawrence Hetrick, Ed. Quarterly. Fiction, essays, interviews, art, book reviews, and poetry. Pays on publication. Send SASE for guidelines and pay schedule.

CHELSEA—Box 773, Cooper Sta., New York, NY 10276. Richard Foerster, Ed. Alfredo de Palchi, Sr. Assoc. Ed. Andrea Lockett, Assoc. Ed. Fresh, original fiction and nonfiction, to 25 manuscript pages. Poems (submit 4 to 6). Translations welcome. "We are an eclectic literary magazine serving a sophisticated international audience. No racist, sexist, pornographic, or romance material." Query for book reviews. Pays $20 per page, on publication. Contests. Guidelines. Not accepting unsolicited manuscripts until June 1999.

CHICAGO REVIEW—5801 S. Kenwood Ave., Chicago, IL 60637. Andrew Rathmann, Ed. Essays, interviews, reviews, fiction, translations, poetry. Pays in copies plus one year's subscription. Manuscripts read year-round; replies in 2 to 3 months.

CHIRON REVIEW—702 No. Prairie, St. John, KS 67576-1516. Michael Hathaway, Ed. Contemporary fiction, to 4,000 words; articles, 500 to 1,000 words; and poetry, to 30 lines. Photos. Pays in copies. Poetry and chapbook contests. Website: http://members.xoom.com/chironreview.

CICADA—329 E St., Bakersfield, CA 93304. Frederick A. Raborg, Jr., Ed. Quarterly. Single haiku, sequences, or garlands; essays about the forms; haibun, tanka, renga, and fiction (one story per issue) related to haiku or Japan. Pays $10 plus one copy for fiction; $10 for "best of issue" poetry.

CIMARRON REVIEW—205 Morrill Hall, Oklahoma State Univ., Stillwater, OK 74078-0135. E. P. Walkiewicz, Ed. Poetry, fiction, essays. Seeks an individual, innovative style that focuses on contemporary themes. Pays $50 for stories and essays; $15 for poems, plus one-year subscription. Manuscripts read year-round.

CLOCKWATCH REVIEW—Dept. of English, Illinois Wesleyan Univ., Bloomington, IL 61702-2900. James Plath, Zarina Mullan Plath, Eds. Semiannual. Fiction, to 4,000 words, and poetry, to 36 lines. "Our preference is for fresh language, a believable voice, a mature style, and a sense of the unusual in the subject matter." Pays $25 for fiction, $5 for poetry, on acceptance, plus copies. Manuscripts read year-round.

THE COA—The Citizens of America, 30 Ford St., Glen Cove, NY 11542. John J. Maddox, Ed. Monthly. Fiction and nonfiction, 250 to 2,500 words; poetry, to 100 words; fillers. B&W photos and drawings also. Pays $40 to $100, on acceptance; $10 for photos. Web site: www.coamagazine.com.

COLLAGES & BRICOLAGES—P.O. Box 360, Shippenville, PA 16254. Marie-José Fortis, Michael Kressley, Eds. Annual. Fiction and nonfiction, plays, interviews, book reviews, and poetry. Surrealistic, feminist, and expressionistic drawings in ink. "I seek innovation and honesty. The magazine often focuses on one subject; query for themes." B&W photos; photo-collages. Pays in copies. Manuscripts read August through November.

COLORADO REVIEW—English Dept., Colorado State Univ., Fort Collins, CO 80523. David Milofsky, Ed. Short fiction and poetry on contemporary themes. Pays $5 per printed page for fiction and poetry. Manuscripts read September 1 to April 30.

COLUMBIA: A JOURNAL OF LITERATURE & ART—415 Dodge, Columbia Univ., New York, NY 10027. Attn: Ed. Biannual. Fiction and nonfiction; poetry; essays; interviews; visual art. Pays in copies. SASE for guidelines and contest rules. Manuscripts read September to May.

THE COMICS JOURNAL—Fantagraphics, Inc., 7563 Lake City Way, Seattle, WA 98115. Attn: Man. Ed. "Looking for freelancers with working knowledge of the diversity and history of the comics medium." Reviews, 2,500 to 5,000 words; domestic and international news, 500 to 7,000 words; commentaries, 500 to 1,500 words; interviews; and features, 2,500 to 5,000 words. Query for news and interviews. Pays 2¢ a word, on publication. Guidelines.

CONCHO RIVER REVIEW—Angelo State Univ., English Dept., San Angelo, TX 76909. James A. Moore, Ed. Semiannual. Fiction, essays, and book reviews, 1,500 to 5,000 words. Poetry, 500 to 1,500 words. "We tend to publish traditional stories with a strong sense of conflict, finely drawn characters, and crisp dialogue. Critical papers, articles, and personal essays with a Texas or Southwestern literary slant preferred. Query for book reviews." Payment is one copy.

CONFLUENCE—P.O. Box 336, Belpre, OH 45714-0336. David B. Prather, Poetry Ed. Daniel Born, Fiction Ed. Published annually by Marietta College and the Ohio Valley Literary Group. Poetry and short fiction. Pays in copies. Manuscripts read September through March.

CONFRONTATION—Dept. of English, C.W. Post of L.I.U., Brookville, NY 11548. Martin Tucker, Ed. Serious fiction, 750 to 6,000 words. Crafted poetry, 10 to 200 lines. Pays $10 to $150, on publication.

THE CONNECTICUT POETRY REVIEW—P.O. Box 818, Stonington, CT 06378. J. Claire White and Harley More, Eds. Poetry, 5 to 20 lines, and reviews, 700 words. Pays $5 per poem, $10 per review, on acceptance. Manuscripts read September to January and April to June.

CONNECTICUT RIVER REVIEW—P.O. Box 185, Ansonia, CT 06401-0185. Kevin Carey, Ed. Semiannual. Poetry. Submit up to 3 poems. Pays in one copy. Guidelines.

CRAZY QUILT—P.O. Box 632729, San Diego, CA 92163-2729. Attn: Eds. Fiction, to 4,000 words, poetry, one-act plays, literary criticism, and author interviews. Also B&W art, photographs. Pays in copies. Fiction read January through March. Other submissions read year-round.

CRAZYHORSE—English Dept., Univ. of Arkansas, Little Rock, AR 72204. Address Poetry Ed. or Criticism Ed. Mainstream poetry, nonfiction prose, and criticism.

THE CREAM CITY REVIEW—English Dept., Box 413, Univ. of Wisconsin, Milwaukee, WI 53201. Peter Whalen, Kyoko Yoshida, Co-Eds. Semiannual. "We serve a national audience interested in a diversity of writing (in terms of style, subject, genre) and writers (gender, race, class, publishing history, etc.). Both well-known and newly published writers of fiction, poetry, and essays are featured, along with B&W artwork." Pays in copies. Manuscripts read September 1 to April 30.

CREATIVE NONFICTION—5501 Walnut, Suite 202, Pittsburgh, PA 15232. Lee Gutkind, Ed. "No length requirements; seeking well-written prose, attentive to language, rich with detail and distinctive voice on any subject." Pays from $5 per published page. Send SASE for upcoming themes.

THE CRESCENT REVIEW—P.O. Box 15069, Chevy Chase, MD 20825. J.T. Holland, Ed. Short stories only. Pays in copies. Manuscripts read July through October and January through April.

CRITICAL INQUIRY—Univ. of Chicago Press, 202 Wieboldt Hall, 1050 E. 59th St., Chicago, IL 60637. W. J. T. Mitchell, Ed. Critical essays that offer a theoretical perspective on literature, music, visual arts, and popular culture. No fiction, poetry, or autobiography. Pays in copies. Manuscripts read year-round.

CUMBERLAND POETRY REVIEW—P.O. Box 120128, Acklen Sta.,

Nashville, TN 37212. Attn: Eds. High-quality poetry and criticism; translations. Send up to 6 poems with brief bio. No restrictions on form, style, or subject matter. Pays in copies.

CUTBANK—English Dept., Univ. of Montana, Missoula, MT 59812. Attn: Eds. Semiannual. Fiction, to 40 pages (submit one story at a time), and poems (submit up to 5 poems). All manuscripts are considered for the Richard Hugo Memorial Poetry Award and the A.B. Guthrie, Jr. Short Fiction Award. Pays in copies. Guidelines. Manuscripts read August 15 to March 15.

DENVER QUARTERLY—Univ. of Denver, Denver, CO 80208. Bin Ramke, Ed. Literary, cultural essays and articles; poetry; book reviews; fiction. Pays $5 per printed page, after publication. Manuscripts read September 15 to May 15.

DESCANT—T.C.U. Box 297270, Fort Worth, TX 76129. Neil Easterbrook, Ed. Fiction, to 6,000 words. Poetry, to 60 lines. No restriction on form or subject. Pays in copies. Frank O'Connor Award ($500) is given each year for best short story published in the volume. Betsy Colquitt Award ($500) is given each year for best poetry published in the volume. Submit material September through May only.

THE DEVIL'S MILLHOPPER—The Devil's Millhopper Press, USC/ Aiken, 471 University Pkwy., Aiken, SC 29801-6309. Stephen Gardner, Ed. Poetry. Send SASE for guidelines and contest information. Pays in copies.

THE DISTILLERY—Motlow State Community College, P.O. Box 88100, Tullahoma, TN 37388. Niles Reddick, Ed. Semiannual. Fiction, 3,000 words; poetry, submit 4 to 6 poems; critical essays; photos and art. Responds in 2 to 3 months. Pays in copies.

DOUBLE DEALER REDUX—632 Pirate's Alley, New Orleans, LA 70116. Rosemary Jams, Ed. Quarterly. Fiction, essays, and poetry. "We showcase the work of promising writers." No payment. Query. Contest.

DREAMS & VISIONS—Skysong Press, 35 Peter St. S., Orillia, Ontario, Canada L3V 5A8. Steve Stanton, Ed. Eclectic fiction, 2,000 to 6,000 words, that is "in some way unique and relevant to Christian readers today." Pays 1/2 ¢ per word.

EARTH'S DAUGHTERS—P.O. Box 41, Central Park Sta., Buffalo, NY 14215. Attn: Ed. Published 3 times a year. Fiction, to 1,000 words, poetry, to 40 lines, and B&W photos or drawings. "Finely crafted work with a feminist theme." Pays in copies. SASE for guidelines and themes.

ECLECTIC RAINBOWS—1538 Tennessee Walker Dr., Roswell, GA 30075. Linda T. Dennison, Ed./Pub. Annual. Essays (no nostalgia), articles, celebrity interviews, 1,000 to 4,000 words. Poetry, to 30 lines. Limited fiction (no science fiction or horror). "New Age emphasis is on personal and planetary growth and transformation. Be positive in approach; humorous point-of-view always welcome." Pays to $25, on publication. Guidelines. Contests.

EDGE CITY REVIEW—10912 Harpers Sq. Ct., Reston, VA 20191. T.L. Ponick, Ed. Literary fiction, to 3,500 words; essays, to 2,500 words; formal, metrical poetry. Reviews of small press books. "Prefer metrical poetry to free verse and coherent short fiction to self-consciously styled work. Political slant is conservative." Pays in copies.

EIGHTEENTH-CENTURY STUDIES—Dept. of French and Italian,

Kresge Hall 152, Northwestern Univ., Evanston, IL 60208-2204. Bernadette Fort, Ed. Quarterly. Articles, to 7,500 words. Blind submission policy: Submit 2 copies of manuscript; author's name and address should appear only on separate title page. No payment.

EPOCH—251 Goldwin Smith Hall, Cornell Univ., Ithaca, NY 14853-3201. Michael Koch, Ed. Serious fiction and poetry. Pays $5 a page for fiction and poetry. No submissions between April 15 and September 21. Guidelines.

EUREKA LITERARY MAGAZINE—Eureka College, P.O. Box 280, Eureka, IL 61530. Loren Logsdon, Ed. Nancy Perkins, Fiction Ed. Semiannual. Fiction, 15 to 25 pages, and poetry, submit up to 4 poems at a time. "We promote no specific political agenda or literary theory." Pays in copies.

EVENT—Douglas College, Box 2503, New Westminster, BC, Canada V3L 5B2. Calvin Wharton, Ed. Short fiction. Pays $22 per printed page, on publication.

EXQUISITE CORPSE—P.O. Box 25051, Baton Rouge, LA 70894. Andrei Codrescu, Ed. Fiction, nonfiction, and poetry for "a journal of letters and life." B&W photos and drawings. Read the magazine before submitting. Payment is 10 copies and one-year subscription. Manuscripts read year-round.

FICTION—c/o English Dept., City College of New York, Convent Ave. at 138th St., New York, NY 10031. Mark Jay Mirsky, Ed. Semiannual. Short stories and novel excerpts, to 5,000 words. "Read the magazine before submitting." Payment varies, on acceptance. Manuscripts not read in the summer.

FICTION INTERNATIONAL—English Dept., San Diego State Univ., San Diego, CA 92182-8140. Harold Jaffe, Ed. Innovative and politically committed fiction and theory. Query for annual themes. Pays in copies. Manuscripts read from September 1 to December 15.

THE FIDDLEHEAD—Campus House, Univ. of New Brunswick, Fredericton, N.B., Canada E3B 5A3. Attn: Ed. Serious fiction, 2,500 words. Pays about $10 per printed page, on publication. SAE with international reply coupons required. Manuscripts read year-round.

FIELD—Rice Hall, Oberlin College, Oberlin, OH 44074. Pamela Alexander, Martha Collins, Alberta Turner, David Walker, David Young, Eds. Serious poetry, any length, by established and unknown poets. Translations by qualified translators. Payment varies, on publication. Manuscripts read year-round.

FINE MADNESS—P.O. Box 31138, Seattle, WA 98103-1138. Attn: Ed. Poetry, to 10 pages. Fiction by invitation only. Pays in copies. No simultaneous submissions. Guidelines.

FIVE FINGERS REVIEW—P.O. Box 12955, Berkeley, CA 94712-3955. Annual. "Writing with a sense of experimentation, an awareness of tradition, and a willingness to explore artistic boundaries." Pays in copies.

FIVE POINTS—Georgia State University, University Plaza, Atlanta, GA 30303-3083. Ed. Three times yearly. Fiction, to 7,500 words. No simultaneous submissions. Pays $15 to $50 per printed page and copies, on publication.

THE FLORIDA REVIEW—English Dept., Univ. of Central Florida, Orlando, FL 32816. Russell Kesler, Ed. Semiannual. Mainstream and experimental fiction and nonfiction, to 7,500 words. Poetry, any style. Pays in copies.

FLYWAY LITERARY REVIEW—(formerly *Flyway*) 206 Ross Hall, Iowa State Univ., Ames, IA 50011. Debra Marquart, Ed. Poetry, fiction, creative nonfiction, and reviews. Pays in copies. Manuscripts read September through May.

FOLIO—Dept. of Literature, American Univ., Washington, DC 20016. Attn: Ed. Semiannual. Fiction, poetry, translations, art, and essays. Pays in 2 copies. Submissions read September through March 15. Contest.

THE FORMALIST—320 Hunter Dr., Evansville, IN 47711. William Baer, Ed. Metrical poetry. "Well-crafted poetry in a contemporary idiom which uses meter and the full range of traditional poetic conventions in vigorous and interesting ways. Especially interested in sonnets, couplets, tercets, ballads, the French forms, etc." Howard Nemerov Sonnet Award ($1,000); SASE for details.

THE FRACTAL—George Mason Univ., 4400 University Dr., MS 2D6, Fairfax, VA 22030. Christopher Elliot, Jessica Darago, Sr. Eds. Fantastic fiction, poetry, art, and nonfiction. Guidelines. Pays $25 for fiction; $50 for nonfiction; $5 for poetry, on publication. Send complete manuscript.

FREE INQUIRY—P.O. Box 664, Buffalo, NY 14226. Paul Kurtz, Ed. Tim Madigan, Exec. Ed. Articles, 500 to 5,000 words, for "literate and lively readership. Focus is on criticisms of religious belief systems, and how to lead an ethical life without a supernatural basis." Pays in copies.

FROGPOND—P.O. Box 2461, Winchester, VA 22604-1661. Jim Kacian, Ed. Published 3 times a year plus yearly supplement. Haiku and related writing, plus articles on haiku. Query for articles.

FUGUE—Univ. of Idaho, English Dept., Brink Hall, Room 200, Moscow, ID 83844-1102. Address Exec. Ed. Fiction and nonfiction to 6,000 words. Poetry, any style, 100 lines. Open to new writers. Include SASE. Pays in copies and small honorarium.

GEORGETOWN REVIEW—P.O. Box 6309 SS, Hattiesburg, MS 39406. Steve Conti, Ed. Semiannual. Fiction and poetry; new exciting voices. Guidelines. Contest.

THE GEORGIA REVIEW—Univ. of Georgia, Athens, GA 30602-9009. Stanley W. Lindberg, Ed. Short fiction; literary, interdisciplinary, and personal essays; book reviews; poetry; artwork. Translations and novel excerpts strongly discouraged. No simultaneous submissions. No submissions in June, July, or August.

THE GETTYSBURG REVIEW—Gettysburg College, Gettysburg, PA 17325. Peter Stitt, Ed. Quarterly. Poetry, fiction, essays, and essay reviews, 1,000 to 20,000 words. Pays $2 a line for poetry; $25 per printed page for prose. Allow 6 months for response. No simultaneous submissions.

GLIMMER TRAIN PRESS—710 S.W. Madison St., #504, Portland, OR 97205. Susan Burmeister-Brown, Ed. Quarterly. Fiction, 1,200 to 7,500 words. Eight stories in each issue. Pays $500, on acceptance. Submit material in January, April, July, and October. Allow 3 months for response. Short story award for new writers; SASE for details.

GRAIN—Box 1154, Regina, Sask., Canada S4P 3B4. Elizabeth Philips, Ed. Short stories, to 30 typed pages; poems, send up to 8; visual art. Pays $30 to $100 for stories and poems, $100 for cover art, $30 for other art. SASE with international reply coupons required or provide e-mail address. Manuscripts read year-round. Web site: www.skwriter.com.

GRAND STREET—214 Sullivan St., 6C, New York, NY 10012. Jean Stein, Ed. Quarterly. Poetry, any length. Pays $3 a line, on publication. Will not read unsolicited fiction or essays.

GRASSLANDS REVIEW—P.O. Box 626, Berea, OH 44017. Laura Kennelly, Ed. Semiannual. Short stories, 1,000 to 3,500 words. Poetry, any length. "We seek imagination without sloppiness, ideas without lectures, and delight in language. Our purpose is to encourage new writers." Pays in copies. Accepts manuscripts postmarked March or October only. Send SASE for annual contest guidelines.

GREEN MOUNTAIN REVIEW—Johnson State College, Johnson, VT 05656. Neil Shepard, Poetry Ed. Tony Whedon, Fiction Ed. Fiction and creative nonfiction, including literary essays, book reviews, and interviews, to 25 pages. Poetry. Manuscripts read September through April. Payment varies (depending on funding), on publication.

GREEN'S MAGAZINE—P.O. Box 3236, Regina, Sask., Canada S4P 3H1. David Green, Ed. Fiction for family reading, 1,500 to 4,000 words. Poetry, to 40 lines. No simultaneous submissions. Pays in copies. International reply coupons must accompany U.S. manuscripts. Manuscripts read year-round.

THE GREENSBORO REVIEW—English Dept., 134 McIver Bldg., UNCG, P.O. Box 26170, Greensboro, NC 27402-6170. Jim Clark, Ed. Semiannual. Poetry and fiction. Submission deadlines: September 15 and February 15. Pays in copies. Guidelines.

GULF COAST—English Dept., Univ. of Houston, Houston, TX 77204. Attn: Ed. Semiannual. Fiction (no genre fiction), nonfiction, poetry (submit up to 5), and translations. No payment.

HABERSHAM REVIEW—Piedmont College, Demorest, GA 30535-0010. Frank Gannon, Ed. Bobbi Jo Miller, Asst. Ed. Stephen R. Whited, Poetry Ed. Short stories, essays, satire, reviews, poetry. "Approximately two-thirds of each issue will have a southern focus." Pays in copies.

HALF TONES TO JUBILEE—Pensacola Junior College, English Dept., 1000 College Blvd., Pensacola, FL 32504. Walter F. Spara, Ed. Fiction, to 1,500 words, and poetry, to 60 lines. Pays in copies. Manuscripts read August 15 to May 15. Contest.

HAPPY—240 E. 35th St., Suite 11A, New York, NY 10016. Bayard, Ed. Quarterly. Fiction, to 6,000 words. "No previously published work. No pornography. No racist/sexist pandering. No bourgeois boredom." Pays $5 per 1,000 words, on publication, plus one copy.

HAWAII REVIEW—Dept. of English, Univ. of Hawaii, 1733 Donaggho Rd., Honolulu, HI 96822. Attn: Ed. Quality fiction, poetry, interviews, and essays. Manuscripts read year-round.

HAYDEN'S FERRY REVIEW—Box 871502, Arizona State Univ., Tempe, AZ 85287-1502. Attn: Ed. Semiannual. Fiction, essays, and poetry (submit up to 6 poems). Include brief bio and SASE. Deadline for Spring/Summer issue is September 30; Fall/Winter issue, February 28. Pays in copies.

THE HEARTLANDS TODAY—Firelands Writing Ctr. of Firelands College, Huron, OH 44839. Larry Smith and Nancy Dunham, Eds. Fiction, 1,000 to 4,500 words, and nonfiction, 1,000 to 3,000 words, about the contemporary Midwest. Poetry (submit 3 to 5 poems). "Writing must be set in the Midwest, but can include a variety of themes." B&W photos. Pays $10 to $20 honorarium, plus copies. Query for current themes. Contest. Manuscripts read January 1 to June 15.

HEAVEN BONE—P.O. Box 486, Chester, NY 10918. Steve Hirsch, Ed. Annual. "The Bridge Between Muse & Mind." Fiction, to 5,000 words. Magazine and book reviews, 250 to 2,500 words. Poetry (submit no more than 10 pages at a time). "Alternative-cultural, post-beat, surrealist, and yogic/anti-paranoiac." Allow 6 months for response. Pays in copies.

HEROES FROM HACKLAND—1225 Evans, Arkadelphia, AR 71923. Mike Grogan, Ed. Quarterly. Nostalgic articles, 750 to 1,500 words, on B-movies (especially westerns and serials), comic books, grade school readers, juvenile series books, cartoons, vintage autos, country music and pop music before 1956, and vintage radio and television. "We believe in heroes, especially those popular culture icons that serious critics label 'ephemera.' " Pays in copies.

HIGH PLAINS LITERARY REVIEW—180 Adams St., Suite 250, Denver, CO 80206. Robert O. Greer, Ed. Fiction, 3,000 to 6,500 words, as well as poetry, essays, reviews, interviews. "Designed to bridge the gap between the academic quarterlies and commercial reviews." Pays $10 a page for poetry; $5 a page for fiction, on publication.

THE HIGHLANDER—560 Green Bay Rd., Suite 204, Winnetka, IL 60093. Sharon Kennedy Ray, Man. Ed. Bimonthly. Articles, 1,300 to 1,900 words, related to Scottish history. "We do not want articles on modern Scotland." Pays $100 to $150, on acceptance.

THE HOLLINS CRITIC—P.O. Box 9538, Hollins University, Roanoke, VA 24020. R.H.W. Dillard, Ed. Published 5 times a year. Features an essay on a contemporary fiction writer, poet or dramatist, cover sketch, brief biography, and book list. Also, book reviews and poetry. Pays $25 for poetry, on publication.

HOME PLANET NEWS—P.O. Box 415, Stuyvesant Sta., New York, NY 10009. Enid Dame and Donald Lev, Eds. Quarterly art tabloid. Fiction, to 8 typed pages; reviews, 3 to 5 pages; and poetry, any length. Query for nonfiction. Pays in copies and subscription. Manuscripts read February through May.

THE HUDSON REVIEW—684 Park Ave., New York, NY 10021. Paula Deitz, Ed. Quarterly. Fiction, to 10,000 words. Essays, to 8,000 words. Poetry, submit up to 10. Payment varies, on publication. Guidelines. Reading periods: Nonfiction read January through April. Poetry read April through July. Fiction read June through November.

HURRICANE ALICE: A FEMINIST QUARTERLY—Dept. of English, Rhode Island College, Providence, RI 02908. Maureen Reddy, Ed. Articles, fiction, essays, interviews, and reviews, 500 to 3,000 words, with feminist perspective. Pays in copies.

ILLYA'S HONEY—432 Greenridge, Coppell, TX 75019. Stephen W. Brodie, Ed. Quarterly. Short fiction, any subject, any style, to 1,000 words; poetry, to 60 lines. "No forced rhyme or overly religious verse." Manuscripts read year-round.

INDIANA REVIEW—Ballantine 465, Indiana Univ., 1020 E. Kirkwood Ave., Bloomington, IN 47405-7103. Brian Leung, Ed. Simeon Berry, Assoc. Ed. We look for daring stories, poetry, and nonfiction that integrate theme, language, character, and form. We like polished writing, humor, and fiction which has consequence beyond the world of its narrator. Please read the magazine before submitting. Pays $5 per page.

INDIGENOUS FICTION—P.O. Box 2078, Redmond, WA 98073-2078. Sherry Decker, Man. Ed. Biannual. Mainstream fiction, occult fiction, mystery, fantasy, and science fiction, 2,500 to 4,500 words. Pays $10 to $20 plus copy, on publication.

INTERIM—Dept. of English, Univ. of Nevada, Las Vegas, NV 89154-5034. James Hazen, Ed. Semiannual. Poetry, any form or length; fiction, to 7,500 words (uses up to 2 stories per issue). Pays in copies and 2-year subscription. Responds in 2 months.

INTERNATIONAL POETRY REVIEW—Dept. of Romance Languages, Univ. of North Carolina, P.O. Box 26170, Greensboro, NC 27402-6170. Attn: Ed. Semiannual. Book reviews, interviews, and short essays, to 1,500 words. Original English poems and contemporary translations of poems. "We prefer material with cross-cultural or international dimension." Pays in copies.

INTERNATIONAL QUARTERLY—P.O. Box 10521, Tallahassee, FL 32302. Van K. Brock, Ed. Fiction and nonfiction, to 5,000 words; poetry. Pays in copies and subscription.

THE IOWA REVIEW—EPB 308, Univ. of Iowa, Iowa City, IA 52242. David Hamilton, Mary Hussmann, Eds. Essays, poems, stories, reviews. Pays $10 a page for prose; $1 a line for poetry, on publication. Manuscripts read September through January.

IRIS: A JOURNAL ABOUT WOMEN—The Women's Ctr., Box 323, HSC Univ. of Virginia, Charlottesville, VA 22908. Eileen Boris, Ed. Semiannual. Fiction, 2,500 to 8,000 words; personal essays, to 2,500 words; poetry. "Our readers are women; diverse in age and interests." Pays in subscription. Upcoming calls: Women on Peace; Gender, Race, and Money; and Southern Women.

THE JAMES WHITE REVIEW—P.O. Box 3356, Butler Quarter Sta., Minneapolis, MN 55403. Phil Willkie, Pub. "A Gay Men's Literary Quarterly." Short stories, to 9,000 words, and poetry, to 250 lines. Book reviews. Responds in 3 months.

JAPANOPHILE—P.O. Box 7977, Ann Arbor, MI 48107. Susan Lapp, Ed. Fiction, to 4,000 words, with a Japanese setting and at least one Japanese and at least one non-Japanese character. Articles, 2,000 words, that celebrate Japanese culture. "We seek to promote Japanese-American understanding. We are not about Japan-bashing or fatuous praise." Also seeks poetry that explores the images, people or experience of Japan, in addition to poetry that utilizes Japanese form, such as haiku. Pays to $25, on publication. Annual short story contest; deadline December 31.

JOURNAL OF NEW JERSEY POETS—County College of Morris, 214 Center Grove Rd., Randolph, NJ 07869-2086. Sander Zulauf, Ed. Semiannual. Serious contemporary poetry by current and former New Jersey residents. "Although our emphasis is on poets associated with New Jersey, we seek work that is universal in scope." Pays in copies.

KALEIDOSCOPE—United Disability Services, 701 S. Main St., Akron, OH 44311-1019. Darshan Perusek, Ph.D., Ed.-in-Chief. Semiannual. Fiction, essays, interviews, articles, and poetry relating to disability and the arts, to

5,000 words. Photos a plus. "We present balanced, realistic images of people with disabilities and publish pieces that challenge stereotypes." Submissions accepted from writers with or without disabilities. Pays $10 to $125. Guidelines recommended. Manuscripts read year-round; response may take up to 6 months.

KALLIOPE: A JOURNAL OF WOMEN'S LITERATURE & ART—Florida Community College at Jacksonville, 3939 Roosevelt Blvd., Jacksonville, FL 32205. Attn: Ed. Fiction, to 2,500 words; poetry; interviews of women writers, to 2,000 words; and B&W photos of fine art. Query for interviews only. Pays $10 or in copies.

KARAMU—Dept. of English, Eastern Illinois Univ., Charleston, IL 61920. Olga Abella, Lauren Smith, Eds. Annual. Contemporary or experimental fiction. Creative nonfiction prose, personal essays, and memoir pieces. Poetry. Pays in copies. Manuscripts read from September 1 to May 1.

KELSEY REVIEW—Mercer County Community College, P.O. Box B, Trenton, NJ 08690. Robin Schore, Ed. Fiction and nonfiction, to 2,000 words, and poetry by writers living or working in Mercer County, NJ. Pays in copies.

THE KENYON REVIEW—Kenyon College, Gambier, OH 43022. David H. Lynn, Ed. Published 3 times a year. Fiction, poetry, essays, literary criticism, and reviews. Pays $10 a printed page for prose, $15 a printed page for poetry, on publication. Manuscripts read September through March.

KIOSK—c/o English Dept., 306 Clemens Hall, SUNY Buffalo, Buffalo, NY 14260. Kevin Grauke (Fiction), Loren Goodman (Poetry), Eds. Fiction, to 20 pages, with a "strong sense of voice, narrative direction, and craftsmanship." Poetry "that explores boundaries, including the formally experimental." Address appropriate editor. Pays in copies. Manuscripts read September 1 to March 1.

LAMBDA BOOK REPORT—1773 T St., N.W., Suite One, Washington, DC 20009. Kanani Kauka, Sr. Ed. Reviews and features, 250 to 1,500 words, of gay and lesbian books. Pays $10 to $75, 60 days after publication. Queries preferred.

LATINO STUFF REVIEW—P.O. Box 440195, Miami, FL 33144. Nilda Cepero-Llevada, Ed./Pub. Short stories, 3,000 words; poetry, to one page; criticism and essays on literature, the arts, social issues. Bilingual publication focusing on Latino topics. Pays in copies.

THE LAUREL REVIEW—Northwest Missouri State Univ., Dept. of English, Maryville, MO 64468. William Trowbridge, David Slater, Beth Richards, Eds. Semiannual. Fiction, nonfiction, and poetry. Pays in copies and subscription.

THE LEADING EDGE—3163 JKHB, Provo, UT 84602. Loralee Leavitt, Ed. Semiannual. Science fiction and fantasy, to 12,000 words; poetry, to 600 lines; and articles, to 8,000 words, on science, scientific speculation, and literary criticism. No excessive profanity, overt violence, or excessive sexual situations. No simultaneous submissions. Pays 1¢ per word, on publication. Guidelines.

THE LEDGE—78-44 80th St., Glendale, NY 11385. Timothy Monaghan, Ed. Poetry; submit 3 to 5 poems at a time. "We publish provocative, well-crafted poems by well-known and lesser-known poets. Excellence is our main criterion." Pays in copies.

LIGHT—Box 7500, Chicago, IL 60680. John Mella, Ed. Quarterly. Light verse. Also fiction, reviews, and essays, to 2,000 words. Fillers, humor, jokes, quips. "If it has wit, point, edge, or barb, it will find a home here." Cartoons and line drawings. Pays in copies. Query for nonfiction.

LILITH, THE INDEPENDENT JEWISH WOMEN'S MAGAZINE— 250 W. 57th St., New York, NY 10107. Susan Weidman Schneider, Ed. Fiction, 1,500 to 2,000 words, on issues of interest to Jewish women.

LITERAL LATTE—61 E. 8th St., Suite 240, New York, NY 10003. Jenine Gordon Bockman, Ed./Pub. Bimonthly distributed to cafés and bookstores. Fiction and personal essays, to 6,000 words; poetry, to 2,000 words; art. Pays in subscription, honorarium, and copies. Contests and awards. Website: www.literal-latte.com.

LITERARY MAGAZINE REVIEW—Dept. of English Language and Lit., Univ. of Northern Iowa, 117 Baker Hall, Cedar Falls, IA 50614-0502. Grant Tracey, Ed. Reviews and articles concerning literary magazines, 1,000 to 1,500 words, for writers and readers of contemporary literature. Pays in copies. Query.

THE LITERARY REVIEW—Fairleigh Dickinson Univ., 285 Madison Ave., Madison, NJ 07940. Walter Cummins, Ed.-in-Chief. Astrid Dadourian, Man. Ed. Martin Green, Harry Keyishian, William Zander, Eds. Serious fiction; poetry; translations; essays and reviews on contemporary literature. Pays in copies.

LOLLIPOP—P.O. Box 441493, Boston, MA 02144. Scott Hefflon, Ed. Quarterly. Fiction, essays, and "edgy" commentary on music and youth culture, to 2,000 words; reviews and interviews related to underground culture; fillers; photos and drawings. Queries preferred. Pays $25 (for anything over 1,000 words), and $25 per illustration.

LONG SHOT—P.O. Box 6238, Hoboken, NJ 07030. Danny Shot, Nancy Mercado, Lynne Breitfeller, Andy Clausen, Eds. Fiction, poetry, and nonfiction, to 10 pages. B&W photos and drawings. Pays in copies.

THE LONG STORY—18 Eaton St., Lawrence, MA 01843. Attn: Ed. Stories, 8,000 to 20,000 words; prefer stories about common folks and a thematic focus. Pays in copies.

LYNX EYE—c/o Scribblefest Literary Group, 1880 Hill Dr., Los Angeles, CA 90041. Pam McCully, Kathryn Morrison, Eds. Quarterly. Short stories, vignettes, novel excerpts, one-act plays, essays, belle lettres, satires, 500 to 5,000 words; poetry, to 30 lines. Pays $10, on acceptance.

THE MACGUFFIN—Schoolcraft College, Dept. of English, 18600 Haggerty Rd., Livonia, MI 48152. Arthur J. Lindenberg, Ed. General, mainstream, and experimental fiction and nonfiction, 400 to 5,000 words. Poetry. "No religious, inspirational, confessional, romance, horror, or pornography." Pays in copies.

THE MALAHAT REVIEW—Univ. of Victoria, P.O. Box 1700, Stn CSC, Victoria, BC, Canada V8W 2Y2. Marlene Cookshaw, Ed. Fiction and poetry, including translations. Pays from $30 per published page, on acceptance.

MANOA—English Dept., Univ. of Hawaii, Honolulu, HI 96822. Frank Stewart, Ed. Ian MacMillan, Fiction Ed. Lisa Ottiger, Book Reviews Ed. Fiction, to 30 pages; essays, to 25 pages; book reviews, 4 to 5 pages; and poetry (submit 4 to 6 poems). "Writers are encouraged to read the journal carefully before submitting." Pays $25 for poetry and book reviews; $20 to $25 per page for fiction, on publication.

MANY MOUNTAINS MOVING—420 22nd St., Boulder, CO 80302. Naomi Horii, Ed. Semiannual. Fiction, nonfiction, and poetry by writers of all cultures. Pays in copies.

MASSACHUSETTS REVIEW—South College, Univ. of Massachusetts, Amherst, MA 01003. Attn: Ed. Poetry, fiction (15 to 20 pages), essays, translations, interviews, photographs, and art. Pays $50 prose, 35¢ a line poetry ($10 min.) Manuscripts read Oct. 1 to June 1. SASE with all manuscripts and inquiries. Guidelines.

THE MAVERICK PRESS—Rt. 2, Box 4915, Eagle Pass, TX 78852-9605. Carol Cullar, Ed. Short stories, to 1,500 words, and unrhymed poetry. Pays in copies. Query with SASE for themes. Website: www.hilconet. com/~mavpress

MEDIPHORS—P.O. Box 327, Bloomsburg, PA 17815. Eugene D. Radice, MD, Ed. "A literary journal of the health professions." Short stories, essays, and commentary, 4,500 words. "Topics should have some relation to medicine and health, but may be quite broad." Poems, to 30 lines. Humor. Pays in copies. Guidelines. Web site: www.mediphors.org.

MESSAGES FROM THE HEART—P.O. Box 64840, Tucson, AZ 85728. Lauren B. Smith, Ed. Quarterly. Heartfelt letters, diary excerpts, poems, or essays, to 800 words, that contain an element of hope. Drawings and B&W photos. Manuscripts read year-round. Pays in copies. Send SASE and $4 for sample copy.

MICHIGAN HISTORICAL REVIEW—Clarke Historical Library, Central Michigan Univ., Mt. Pleasant, MI 48859. Attn: Ed. Semiannual. Scholarly articles related to Michigan's political, social, economic, and cultural history; articles on American, Canadian, and Midwestern history that directly or indirectly explore themes related to Michigan's past. Manuscripts read year-round.

MID-AMERICAN REVIEW—Dept. of English, Bowling Green State Univ., Bowling Green, OH 43403. George Looney, Ed.-in-Chief. Michael Czyzniejewski, Fiction Ed. High-quality fiction, 10 to 20 pages, that is both character and language oriented. No simultaneous submissions. Pays to $50, on publication (pending funding). Manuscripts read September through May.

MIDWEST QUARTERLY—Pittsburg State Univ., Pittsburg, KS 66762. James B. M. Schick, Ed. Scholarly articles, 2,500 to 5,000 words, on contemporary academic and public issues; poetry. Pays in copies. Manuscripts read year-round.

THE MINNESOTA REVIEW—Dept. of English, Univ. of Missouri, Columbia, MO 65211. Attn: Ed. Politically committed fiction, 1,000 to 6,000 words; nonfiction, 5,000 to 7,500 words; and poetry, to 3 pages, for readers committed to social issues, including feminism, neomarxism, etc. Pays in copies. Responds in 2 to 4 months.

MISSISSIPPI MUD—7119 Santa Fe Ave., Dallas, TX 75223. Joel Weinstein, Ed. Short stories, to 50 pages, and novel excerpts, 50 to 100 pages; poetry, any length. Pays $25 for poems; $50 to $100 for fiction, on publication.

MISSISSIPPI REVIEW—Ctr. for Writers, Univ. of Southern Mississippi, Southern Sta., Box 5144, Hattiesburg, MS 39406-5144. Frederick Barthelme, Ed. Annual fiction/poetry competition. Deadline, May 31. Pays in copies.

THE MISSOURI REVIEW—1507 Hillcrest Hall, Univ. of Missouri-Columbia, Columbia, MO 65211. Greg Michalson, Man. Ed. Speer Morgan, Ed. Evelyn Somers, Nonfiction Ed. Poems, any length. "We do poetry features: 6 to 10 pages of poetry by 3 to 5 poets in each issue." Fiction and essays. Book reviews. Pays $20 per page (to $750) for essays; $125 to $300 for poetry and fiction, on acceptance. Manuscripts read year-round.

MODERN HAIKU—P.O. Box 1752, Madison, WI 53701-1752. Robert Spiess, Ed. Haiku and articles about haiku. Pays $1 per haiku, $5 a page for articles. Manuscripts read year-round.

MONTHLY REVIEW—122 W. 27th St., New York, NY 10001. Paul M. Sweezy, Harry Magdoff, Ellen Meiksins Wood, Eds. Analytical articles, 5,000 words, on politics and economics, from independent socialist viewpoint. Pays $25 for reviews, $50 for articles, on publication.

MUDDY RIVER POETRY REVIEW—28 Wessex Rd., Newton Centre, MA 02159. Zvi A. Sesling, Michael D. Sesling, Eds. Annual. Poems. "While free verse is preferred, nothing will be rejected if it is quality." No previously published poems. Payment is one copy.

MYSTERY TIME—P.O. Box 2907, Decatur, IL 62524. Linda Hutton, Ed. Semiannual. Suspense, 1,500 words, and poems about mysteries, up to 16 lines. "We prefer female protagonists. No gore or violence." Pays $5, on acceptance.

THE NAPLES REVIEW—626 Third St. N., Naples, FL 34102-5537. Mr. Leslie Waller, Ed. Quarterly. Articles, essays, short stories, novel excerpts, and plays, to 10 pages. Poetry, to 2 pages. Preference given to residents of Southwest Florida or subject matter related to the area. Pays in copies.

NEBO: A LITERARY JOURNAL—Dept. of English, Arkansas Tech. Univ., Russellville, AR 72801-2222. Attn: Ed. Poems (submit up to 5); mainstream fiction, to 3,000 words; critical essays, to 10 pages. Pays in one copy. Guidelines. Offices closed May through August. "Best time to submit is September through February."

NEBRASKA REVIEW—Writer's Workshop, FAB 212, Univ. of Nebraska at Omaha, Omaha, NE 68182-0324. James Reed, Ed. Susan Aizenberg, Poetry Ed. Short stories and personal essays, to 7,500 words. Poetry. Pays in copies and subscription.

NEW AUTHOR'S JOURNAL—1542 Tibbits Ave., Troy, NY 12180. Mario V. Farina, Ed. Fiction, to 2,000 words, and poetry. Topical nonfiction, to 1,000 words. Pays in copies. Manuscripts read year-round.

NEW DELTA REVIEW—c/o Dept. of English, Louisiana State Univ., Baton Rouge, LA 70803-5001. Attn: Eds. Semiannual. Fiction and nonfiction, to 5,000 words. Submit up to 4 poems, any length. Also essays, interviews, and reviews. "We want to see your best work." Pays in copies. Also awards prize for best poem and short story for each issue. Manuscripts read September through May.

NEW ENGLAND REVIEW—Middlebury College, Middlebury, VT

05753. Stephen Donadio, Ed. Jodee Stanley Rubins, Man. Ed. Fiction, nonfiction, and poetry of varying lengths. Also, speculative and interpretive essays, critical reassessments, statements by artists working in various media, interviews, testimonials, letters from abroad. "We are committed to exploration of all forms of contemporary cultural expresssion." Pays $10 per page ($20 minimum), on publication. Manuscripts read September through May.

NEW ENGLAND WRITERS' NETWORK—P.O. Box 483, Hudson, MA 01749-0483. Glenda Baker, Ed.-in-Chief. Short stories and novel excerpts, to 2,000 words. All genres except pornography and excessive violence. Personal and humorous essays, to 1,000 words. Upbeat, positive poetry, to 32 lines. Pays $10 for stories; $5 for essays; $3 for poems, plus one copy. Guidelines. Submit fiction, poetry, and essays June 1 to August 31 only.

NEW LAUREL REVIEW—828 Lesseps St., New Orleans, LA 70117. Lee Meitzen Grue, Ed. Annual. Fiction, 10 to 20 pages; nonfiction, to 10 pages; poetry, any length; translation. Library market. No inspirational verse. International readership. Read journal before submitting. Pays in one copy.

NEW LETTERS—Univ. House, Univ. of Missouri-Kansas City, 5101 Rockhill Rd., Kansas City, MO 64110-2499. James McKinley, Ed.-in-Chief. Fiction, 3,500 to 5,000 words. Poetry, submit 3 to 6 poems at a time. SASE for literary awards guidelines. Manuscripts read October 15 to May 15.

NEW ORLEANS REVIEW—Loyola Univ., New Orleans, LA 70118. Ralph Adamo, Ed. Serious fiction and poetry, personal essays, interviews, and B&W art.

THE NEW YORK QUARTERLY—P.O. Box 693, Old Chelsea Sta., New York, NY 10113. William Packard, Ed. Published 3 times a year. Poems of any style and persuasion, well-written and well-intentioned. Pays in copies. Manuscripts read year-round.

NEXUS—Wright State Univ., W016A Student Union, Dayton, OH 45435. Andre Hoilette, Adam Cline, Eds. Poetry, short, sudden, or flash fiction, essays, interviews, photography, and art. Specializes in works that highlight the human experience. Pays in 2 copies.

NIGHTSUN—School of Arts & Humanities, Frostburg State Univ., Frostburg, MD 21532-1099. Brad Barkley, Barbara Hurd, Karen Zealand, Eds. Annual. Short stories, about 12 pages, and poems, to 40 lines. Payment is 2 copies. Manuscripts read September through April.

NIMROD INTERNATIONAL JOURNAL—Univ. of Tulsa, 600 S. College Ave., Tulsa, OK 74104-3189. Dr. Francine Ringold, Ed.-in-Chief. Publishes 2 issues annually, one awards and one thematic. Quality poetry and fiction, experimental and traditional. Pays in copies. Annual awards for poetry and fiction. Guidelines. SASE.

96 INC.—P.O. Box 15559, Boston, MA 02215. Attn: Ed. Annual. Fiction, 1,000 to 7,500 words; interviews; and poetry of varying length. Pays in subscription, 4 copies, and modest payment, if funding is available.

THE NORTH AMERICAN REVIEW—Univ. of Northern Iowa, Cedar Falls, IA 50614-0516. Peter Cooley, Poetry Ed. Poetry of high quality. Pays from $20 per poem, on publication. Manuscripts read year-round.

NORTH ATLANTIC REVIEW—15 Arbutus Ln., Stony Brook, NY 11790-1408. John Gill, Ed. Annual. Fiction and nonfiction, to 5,000 words;

fillers, humor, photographs and illustrations. A special section on social or literary issues is a part of each issue. No poetry. Pays in copies. Responds in 6 months.

THE NORTH DAKOTA QUARTERLY—Univ. of North Dakota, Grand Forks, ND 58202-7209. Attn: Ed. Essays in the humanities and social sciences; fiction; reviews; and poetry. Limited market. Pays in copies.

NORTHEASTARTS—P.O. Box 94, Kittery, ME 03904. Mr. Leigh Donaldson, Ed. Fiction and nonfiction, to 750 words; poetry, to 30 lines; and short essays and reviews. "Both published and new writers are considered. No obscene or offensive material." Payment is 2 copies.

NORTHEAST CORRIDOR—Beaver College, 450 S. Easton Rd., Glenside, PA 19038. Susan Balée, Ed. Semiannual. Literary fiction, personal essays, and interviews, 10 to 20 pages. Poetry, to 40 lines (submit 3 to 5). "We seek the work of writers and artists living in or writing about the Northeast Corridor of America." Pays $25 for stories or essays, $10 for poems, on publication.

NORTHWEST REVIEW—369 PLC, Univ. of Oregon, Eugene, OR 97403. Janice MacRae, Fiction Ed. Fiction, commentary, essays, and poetry. Reviews. Pays in copies. Guidelines.

NORTHWOODS JOURNAL—P.O. Box 298, Thomaston, ME 04861. Robert W. Olmsted, Ed. Articles of interest to writers; fiction, 2,500 words. Poetry, any length. "Read guidelines first." Pays $4 per page, on acceptance.

NOTRE DAME REVIEW—Creative Writing Program, English Dept., Univ. of Notre Dame, Notre Dame, IN 46556. Attn: Man. Ed. Semiannual. Fiction, 50 to 60 pages. Essays, reviews, and poetry, 70 to 80 pages. Manuscripts read September through April. Payment varies, on publication.

OASIS—P.O. Box 626, Largo, FL 33779-0626. Neal Storrs, Ed. Short fiction and essays, any length, poetry, and translations from any language. "Literary language only. Style is paramount." Pays $15 to $25 for prose, $5 per poem, on publication. Guidelines. Responds same day.

OF UNICORNS AND SPACE STATIONS—P.O. Box 97, Bountiful, UT 84011-0097. Gene Davis, Ed. Science fiction and fantasy, to 5,000 words. Poetry related to science fiction, science, or fantasy. "Do not staple or fold long manuscripts." Pays 1¢ per word for fiction; $5 for poems, on publication. Website: www.genedavis.com/magazine/index.html.

OFFERINGS—P.O. Box 1667, Lebanon, MO 65536. Velvet Fackeldey, Ed. Quarterly. Poetry, to 30 lines, traditional and free verse. Students and unpublished writers encouraged. No payment.

THE OHIO REVIEW—344 Scott Quad., Ohio Univ., Athens, OH 45701-2979. Wayne Dodd, Ed. Short stories, poetry, essays, reviews. Pays $5 per page for prose, $1 a line for poetry, $20 minimum, plus copies, on publication. Submissions read September through May.

OLD CROW—FKB Press, P.O. Box 403, Easthampton, MA 01027. John Gibney, Ed. Semiannual. Fiction and nonfiction, 200 to 6,000 words. Poetry, to 500 lines. "International readership. Our purpose is to publish new and established writers who have something true to say which might raise the hairs on the backs of our readers' necks." Pays in copies. Rotating reading period.

THE OLD RED KIMONO—Humanities Div., Floyd College, Box 1864,

Rome, GA 30162. Jeff Mack, Kelly Deogg, Eds. Annual. Fiction, to 1,200 words. Poetry, submit 3 to 5 poems. "Poems and stories should be concise and imagistic. Nothing sentimental or didactic." Pays in copies.

100 WORDS—473 EPB, Univ. of Iowa, Iowa City, IA 52242. Cris Mattison, Ed. Bimonthly. Prose and poetry, to 100 words, on theme topics. Translations with original text. Send SASE for guidelines and themes.

OSIRIS—Box 297, Deerfield, MA 01342. Andrea Moorhead, Ed. Multilingual poetry journal founded in 1972, publishing poetry in English, French, German, with other languages in a bilingual format. Translations must have letter of permission from the poet or publisher. Pays in copies.

OTHER VOICES—Univ. of Illinois at Chicago, Dept. of English (M/C 162), 601 S. Morgan St., Chicago, IL 60607-7120. Lois Hauselman, Gina Frangello, Lisa Stolley, Eds. Semiannual. Fresh, innovative, accessible short stories, one-act plays, and novel excerpts. Pays in copies and modest honorarium. Manuscripts read October to April.

OUTERBRIDGE—College of Staten Island, English Dept. 2S-218, 2800 Victory Blvd., Staten Island, NY 10314. Charlotte Alexander, Ed. Annual. Well-crafted stories, about 20 pages, and poetry, to 4 pages, "directed to a wide audience of literate adult readers." Pays in 2 copies. Manuscripts read September to June.

PAINTBRUSH: A JOURNAL OF POETRY AND TRANSLATION—Language & Literature Div., Truman State Univ., Kirksville, MO 63501. Ben Bennani, Ed. Annual. Poetry, translations, interviews, and book reviews. Periodically publishes special monograph issues highlighting the work of individual writers. Query.

PAINTED BRIDE QUARTERLY—230 Vine St., Philadelphia, PA 19106. Kathleen Volk-Miller, Marion Wrenn, Eds. Fiction and poetry of varying lengths. Pays $5, plus subscription.

PALO ALTO REVIEW—Palo Alto College, 1400 W. Villaret, San Antonio, TX 78224-2499. Ellen Shull, Ed. Semiannual. Fiction and articles, 5,000 words. "We look for wide-ranging investigations of historical, geographical, scientific, mathematical, artistic, political, and social topics, anything that has to do with living and learning." Interviews; 200-word think pieces for "Food for Thought"; poetry, to 50 lines (send 3 to 5 poems at a time); reviews, to 500 words, of books, films, videos, or software. "Fiction shouldn't be too experimental or excessively avant-garde." Pays in copies. Send SASE for themes and guidelines.

PANGOLIN PAPERS—P.O. Box 241, Nordland, WA 98358. Pat Britt, Ed. Literary fiction, 100 to 7,000 words. No poetry or genre fiction. Pays in copies

PANHANDLER—English Dept., Univ. of W. Florida, Pensacola, FL 32514-5751. Laurie O'Brien, Ed. Semiannual. Fiction, 1,500 to 3,000 words; poetry, any length. Pays in copies. Responds within 6 months.

PARABOLA: THE MAGAZINE OF MYTH AND TRADITION—656 Broadway, New York, NY 10012. Attn: Eds. Quarterly. Articles, to 4,000 words, and fiction, 500 words, retelling traditional stories, folk and fairy tales. No poetry. "All submissions must relate to an upcoming theme. We are looking for a balance between scholarly and accessible writing devoted to the ideas of myth and tradition." Send SASE for guidelines and themes. Payment varies, on publication.

THE PARIS REVIEW— 541 E. 72nd St., New York, NY 10021. Attn: Fiction and Poetry Eds. Fiction and poetry of high literary quality. Pays on publication.

PARNASSUS— 205 W. 89th St., Apt. 8F, New York, NY 10024-1835. Herbert Leibowitz, Ed. Critical essays and reviews on contemporary poetry. International in scope. Pays in cash and copies. Manuscripts read year-round.

PARTING GIFTS— 3413 Wilshire, Greensboro, NC 27408. Robert Bixby, Ed. Fiction, to 1,000 words, and poetry, to 100 lines. Pays in copies. Manuscripts read January to June. Website: http://users.aol.com/marchst.

PARTISAN REVIEW— Boston Univ., 236 Bay State Rd., Boston, MA 02215. William Phillips, Ed.-in-Chief. Edith Kurzweil, Ed. Serious fiction, poetry, and essays. Payment varies. No simultaneous submissions. Manuscripts read September through to May.

PASSAGER: A JOURNAL OF REMEMBRANCE AND DISCOV-ERY—c/o Univ. of Baltimore, 1420 N. Charles St., Baltimore, MD 21201-5779. Mary Azrael, Kendra Kopelke, Eds. Fiction and essays, 3,000 words, of "remembrance and discovery." Poetry, to 40 lines. "We publish writers of all ages, but with an emphasis on new older writers." Pays in copies.

PASSAGES NORTH— Northern Michigan Univ., Dept. of English, 1401 Presque Isle Ave., Marquette, MI 49855. Kate Myers Hanson, Ed. Semiannual. Poetry, fiction, interviews, and literary nonfiction. Pays in copies. Manuscripts read September to May.

THE PATERSON LITERARY REVIEW—Passaic County Comm. College, College Blvd., Paterson, NJ 07505-1179. Maria Mazziotti Gillan, Ed. High-quality fiction and poetry, to 10 pages. Pays in copies. Manuscripts read January through May.

PEARL— 3030 E. Second St., Long Beach, CA 90803. Marilyn Johnson, Ed. Fiction, 500 to 1,200 words, and poetry, to 40 lines. "We are interested in accessible, humanistic poetry and fiction that communicates and is related to real life. Along with the ironic, serious, and intense, humor and wit are welcome." Pays in copies.

PEQUOD—New York Univ., English Dept., 19 University Pl., 2nd Fl., New York, NY 10003. Mark Rudman, Ed. Semiannual. Short stories, essays, and literary criticism, to 10 pages; poetry and translations, to 3 pages. Pays honorarium, on publication.

PEREGRINE: THE JOURNAL OF AMHERST WRITERS AND ARTISTS PRESS—P.O. Box 1076, Amherst, MA 01004. Nancy Rose, Man. Ed. Annual. Fiction, poetry, book reviews. "We seek unpretentious and memorable writing by new as well as established authors. We welcome work reflecting diversity of voice." Guidelines available with #10 SASE. Website: www.javanet.com/~awapress. Contest.

PERMAFROST—English Dept., Univ. of Alaska Fairbanks, P.O. Box 755720, Fairbanks, AK 99775. Ryan M. Johnson, Ed. Poetry, up to 5 poems; fiction and nonfiction, to 30 pages. Contests. Reading period: September through March 15.

PIEDMONT LITERARY REVIEW— 1017 Spanish Moss Lane, Breaux

Bridge, LA 70517. Poems, any length and style, rhymed and metered formal verse, or free verse, will be considered on basis of merit alone. Length limit of 40 lines preferred. Original previously unpublished work only. Submit up to 5 poems to Gail White, Poetry Ed. at above address. Submit Asian verse to Dorothy McLaughlin, 10 Atlantic Rd., Somerset, NJ 08873. Submit prose, to 2,400 words, to Dr. Olga Kronmeyer, Ed., 25 W. Dale Dr., Lynchburg, VA 24501. No pornography. Acquires first North American serial rights. Pays one copy. SASE.

PIG IRON PRESS—P.O. Box 237, Youngstown, OH 44501-0237. Jim Villani, Ed. Fiction and nonfiction, to 8,000 words. Poetry, to 100 lines. Write for upcoming themes; theme for 1999: The 20th Century. Pays $5 per page or poem, on publication. Manuscripts read year-round. Responds in 4 months.

THE PIKEVILLE REVIEW—Humanities Div., Pikeville College, 214 Sycamore St., Pikeville, KY 41501. Elgin M. Ward, Ed. Annual. Contemporary fiction, poetry, creative essays, and book reviews. Payment varies on publication.

PLEIADES—Dept. of English and Phil., Central Missouri State Univ., Warrensburg, MO 64093. R. M. Kinder, Kevin Prufer, Eds. Traditional and experimental poetry, fiction, criticism, translations, and reviews. Cross-genre especially welcome. Pays $10 for prose; $3 for poetry, on publication.

PLOUGHSHARES—Emerson College, 100 Beacon St., Boston, MA 02116-1596. Attn: Ed. Serious fiction, to 6,000 words. Poetry (submit up to 3 poems at a time). Pays $25 per page ($50 to $250), on publication, plus 2 copies and subscription. Manuscripts read August through March. Guidelines.

POEM—c/o English Dept., U.A.H., Huntsville, AL 35899. Nancy Frey Dillard, Ed. Serious lyric poetry. Pays in copies. Manuscripts read year-round; best to submit December to March or June to September.

POETRY—60 W. Walton St., Chicago, IL 60610. Joseph Parisi, Ed. Poetry of highest quality. Submit 3 to 4 poems. Allow 10 to 12 weeks for response. Pays $2 a line, on publication.

THE POET'S PAGE—P.O. Box 372, Wyanet, IL 61379. Ione K. Pence, Ed./Pub. Quarterly. Poetry, any length, style, and topic. Articles and essays on poetry and poetic forms, poets, styles, etc. Pays in copies.

POETS'PAPER—Anderie Poetry Press, P.O. Box 85, Easton, PA 18044-0085. Carole J. Heffley, Harriett Hunt, Eds. Semiannual. "Contemporary poetry that conveys an immediate, clear sense of recognition and thought." Rhymed metered verse as well as free verse. Submit up to 3 poems, any length. $500 annual prize in poetry. Responds in 4 to 6 weeks. SASE.

POTOMAC REVIEW—P.O. Box 354, Port Tobacco, MD 20677. Eli Flam, Ed. Regionally rooted quarterly with a conscience: to inform, entertain, and seek deeper values. Fiction and wide-ranging essays; occasional pieces, to 3,000 words. Poetry, submit 3 poems (to 5 pages total). Pays in copies or modest stipend for assigned nonfiction stories.

POTPOURRI—P.O. Box 8278, Prairie Village, KS 66208. Polly W. Swafford, Ed. Quarterly. Short stories, to 3,500 words. Literary essays, travel pieces, and humor, to 2,500 words. Poetry and haiku, to 75 lines. "We like clever themes that avoid reminiscence, depressing plots, and violence." Original B&W illustrations. Pays in one copy. Extra copies available at professional discount.

PRAIRIE SCHOONER—201 Andrews Hall, Univ. of Nebraska, Lincoln, NE 68588-0334. Hilda Raz, Ed. Short stories, poetry, essays, book reviews, and translations. Pays in copies. Manuscripts read September through May; responds in 3 months. Annual contests.

PRESS QUARTERLY—125 W. 72nd St., Suite 3-M, New York, NY 10023. Daniel Roberts, Ed. Short stories and poems that "deliver an invigorating dose of clear, humanized storytelling." Payment varies, on publication.

PRIMAVERA—Box 37-7547, Chicago, IL 60637. Attn: Editorial Board. Annual. Fiction and poetry that focus on the experiences of women; author need not be female. B&W photos and drawings. No simultaneous submissions; SASE. Pays in 2 copies. Responds within 3 months.

PRISM INTERNATIONAL—E462-1866 Main Mall, Creative Writing Program, Univ. of British Columbia, Vancouver, B.C., Canada V6T 1Z1. Attn: Ed. High-quality fiction, poetry, drama, creative nonfiction, and literature in translation, varying lengths. Include international reply coupons. Pays $20 per published page of prose, $40 per published page of poetry. Annual short fiction contest with $3,000 in prizes. Annual poetry prize of $500.

THE PROSE POEM—English Dept., Providence College, Providence, RI 02198. Peter Johnson, Ed. Prose poems. Book reviews, 4 to 6 pages. Pays in copies. Query for book reviews. Manuscripts read December through March.

PUCKERBRUSH REVIEW—76 Main St., Orono, ME 04473-1430. Constance Hunting, Ed. Semiannual. Literary fiction, criticism, and poetry of various lengths, "to bring literary Maine news to readers." Pays in 2 copies. Manuscripts read year-round.

PUDDING MAGAZINE: THE INTERNATIONAL JOURNAL OF APPLIED POETRY—c/o Pudding House Writers Resource Ctr., Bed & Breakfast for Writers, Johnstown, OH 43031. Jennifer Bosveld, Ed. Poems on popular culture, social concerns, personal struggle; articles/essays on poetry in the schools and in human services. Manuscripts read year-round; responds promptly. Check Web site for additional projects: puddinghouse.com.

PUERTO DEL SOL—New Mexico State Univ., Dept. of English, MSC 3E, P.O. Box 30001, Las Cruces, NM 88003-8001. K. West, Kevin McIlvoy, Antonya Nelson, and Gail Lavendar, Eds. Short stories and personal essays, to 30 pages; novel excerpts, to 65 pages; articles, to 45 pages, and reviews, to 15 pages. Poetry, photos. Pays in copies. Manuscripts read September through February.

PULP ETERNITY—Box 930068, Norcross, GA 30003. Steve Algieri, Ed. Quarterly. Fiction, to 10,000 words, and some nonfiction. Pays 3¢ per word, on publication. Query for nonfiction; send complete manuscript for fiction.

QUARTER AFTER EIGHT—Ellis Hall, Ohio Univ., Athens, OH 45701. Attn: Eds. Annual. Short fiction, novel excerpts, essays, criticism, investigations, and interviews, to 10,000 words. Submit no more than 2 pieces. Prose poetry (submit up to 5 poems); no traditional poetry. Pays in copies. Manuscripts read September through March. Guidelines. Annual prose contest.

QUARTERLY WEST—200 S. Central Campus Dr., Rm. 317, Univ. of UT, Salt Lake City, UT 84112. Margot Schilpp, Ed. Fiction, short-shorts, poetry, essays, translations, and reviews. Pays $25 to $100 for stories, $25 to $50 for poems. Manuscripts read year-round. Biennial novella competition in even-numbered years.

RAG MAG—P.O. Box 12, Goodhue, MN 55027-0012. Beverly Voldseth, Ed. Semiannual. Eclectic fiction and nonfiction, art, photos. Poetry, any length. No religious writing. Pays in copies. SASE for guidelines and themes. Not accepting submissions until LATE 1999.

RAMBUNCTIOUS REVIEW—1221 W. Pratt Blvd., Chicago, IL 60626. Richard Goldman, Nancy Lennon, Beth Hausler, Eds. Fiction, to 12 pages; poems, submit up to 5 at a time. Pays in copies. Manuscripts read September through May. Contests. Guidelines.

READER'S BREAK—Pine Grove Press, P.O. Box 85, Jamesville, NY 13078. Gertrude S. Eiler, Ed. Semiannual. Fiction, to 3,500 words, about relationships, tales of action, adventure, science fiction and fantasy, suspense, and mystery. Themes and plots may be historical, contemporary, or futuristic. Emphasis is on fiction but will consider nonfiction in story form. Poems, to 75 lines. Pays in one copy.

RE:AL, THE JOURNAL OF LIBERAL ARTS—Stephen F. Austin State Univ., P.O. Box 13007, SFA Sta., Nacogdoches, TX 75962. Attn: Eds. Experimental, genre, and historical fiction; reviews and scholarly nonfiction, 250 to 5,000 words. Poetry, to 10 pages. Pays in copies.

RED CEDAR REVIEW—Dept. of English, 17-C Morrill Hall, Michigan State Univ., E. Lansing, MI 48824-1036. Carrie Preston, Poetry Ed. Ari Kohen, Fiction Ed. Fiction, to 5,000 words; and poems, submit up to 5. Pays in copies. Manuscripts read year-round.

RED ROCK REVIEW—Dept. of English, Community College of Southern Nevada, 3200 E. Cheyenne Ave., N. Las Vegas, NV 89030. Dr. Richard Logsdon, Ed. Semiannual. Short fiction, to 5,000 words; book reviews, to 1,000 words; poetry, to 2 pages. "We're geared toward publishing the work of already established writers. No taboos." Payment varies, on acceptance.

REED MAGAZINE—Dept. of English, San Jose State Univ., One Washington Sq., San Jose, CA 95192-0090. Annual. Address Man. Ed. for fiction and nonfiction, to 10,000 words/submission. Address Poetry Ed. for poetry, to 40 lines/poem, with up to 10 poems per submission. Payment for all genres by copies. Book reviews by staff, and artwork is solicited. Manuscripts read to January 15.

RESPONSE: A CONTEMPORARY JEWISH REVIEW—Columbia University Post Office, P.O. Box 250892, New York, NY 10025. Chanita Baumhaft, Ed. Emily Katz, Asst. Ed. Independent journal of Jewish studies, culture, and literature. Publishes articles, essays, and fiction to 3500 words; poetry; book reviews; art; illustrated stories/comics. For nonfiction, query with one to two line abstract/proposal only. Pays in copies. E-mail: Response@Panix.com

REVIEW: LATIN AMERICAN LITERATURE AND ARTS—Americas Society, 680 Park Ave., New York, NY 10021. Alfred J. MacAdam, Ed. Semiannual. Work in English translation, 1,000 to 1,500 words, by and about young and established Latin American writers; essays and book reviews. Payment varies, on acceptance. Query.

RIVER CITY—Dept. of English, Univ. of Memphis, Memphis, TN 38152. Thomas Russell, Ed. Poems, short stories, essays, and interviews. No novel excerpts. Pay varies according to grants. Manuscripts read September through April. Guidelines. Contests.

RIVER OAK REVIEW—P.O. Box 3127, Oak Park, IL 60303. Semiannual. Address Fiction, Poetry, or Nonfiction Ed. No criticism, reviews, or translations. Limit prose to 20 pages; poetry to batches of no more than 4. Pays in copies, and small honorarium, as funding permits.

RIVER STYX—634 N. Grand Blvd., 12th Fl., St. Louis, MO 63103. Attn: Ed. Published 3 times a year. Poetry, fiction, personal essays, literary interviews, B&W photos, and color cover artwork. Payment is $8 per printed page plus subscription. Manuscripts read May through November; reports in 2 to 3 months.

ROCKFORD REVIEW—P.O. Box 858, Rockford, IL 61105. David Ross, Ed.-in-Chief. Published 3 times a year. Fiction, essays, and satire, 250 to 1,300 words. Experimental and traditional poetry, to 50 lines (shorter works preferred). One-act plays and other dramatic forms, to 10 pages. "We prefer genuine or satirical human dilemmas with coping or non-coping outcomes that ring the reader's bell." Submit up to 3 works at a time. Pays in copies; two $25 Editor's Choice Prizes awarded each issue.

ROSEBUD—P.O. Box 459, Cambridge, WI 53523. Rod Clark, Ed. Quarterly. Fiction, articles, profiles, 1,200 to 1,800 words, and poems; love, alienation, travel, humor, nostalgia, and unexpected revelation. Guidelines. Pays $45 plus copies, on publication.

ROSWELL LITERARY REVIEW—JoPop Publications, P.O. Box 8118, Roswell, NM 88202-8118. S. Joan Popek, Ed. Quarterly. Fiction, to 5,000 words, any genre, and poetry. No prose poetry. Pays from $5 to $15 for fiction, $1 to $10 for flash fiction. Poetry earns free copy. All payments made on acceptance.

SALAMANDER—48 Ackers Ave., Brookline, MA 02146. Jennifer Barber, Ed. Semiannual. "A magazine for poetry, fiction, and memoir." Short stories, including translations and novels in progress; creative nonfiction and memoirs. Poetry. "No criticism or essays (unless autobiographical). No science fiction." Pays an honorarium, on publication.

SANSKRIT LITERARY/ART PUBLICATION—Cone Ctr., Univ. of North Carolina/Charlotte, Charlotte, NC 28223-0001. Attn: Ed. Annual. Poetry, short fiction, photos, and fine art. Pays in copies. Manuscripts read in fall only; deadline October 30.

SANTA BARBARA REVIEW—P.O. Box 808, Summerland, CA 93067-0808. P.S. Leddy, Ed. Short stories; occasionally plays. Biographies and essays, to 6,500 words. Poems. Translations. B&W art and photos. Pays in copies.

SCANDINAVIAN REVIEW—15 E. 65th St., New York, NY 10021-6501. Attn: Ed. Published 3 times a year. Essays on contemporary Scandinavia: arts, sciences, business, politics, and culture of Scandinavia. Fiction and poetry, translated from Nordic languages. Photos. Pays from $100, on publication. Web site: www.amscan.org.

SCRIVENER—McGill Univ., 853 Sherbrooke St. W., Montreal, Quebec, Canada H3A 2T6. Attn: Eds. Poems, submit 5 to 15; prose, to 20 pages; reviews, to 5 pages. Photography and graphics. Pays in copies.

THE SEATTLE REVIEW—Padelford Hall, Box 354330, Univ. of Washington, Seattle, WA 98195. Colleen J. McElroy, Ed. Stories, to 20 pages; poetry; essays on the craft of writing; and interviews with northwest writers. Payment varies. Manuscripts read October through May.

SENECA REVIEW—Hobart & William Smith Colleges, Geneva, NY 14456. Deborah Tall, Ed. Poetry, translations, and essays on contemporary poetry. Pays in copies and 2-year subscription. Manuscripts read September through April.

SHENANDOAH—Washington and Lee Univ., Troubadour Theatre, 2nd Fl., Lexington, VA 24450-0303. R.T. Smith, Ed. Quarterly. Highest quality fiction, poetry, criticism, essays and interviews. "Read the magazine before submitting." Pays $25 per page for prose; $2.50 per line for poetry, on publication.

SING HEAVENLY MUSE! WOMEN'S POETRY & PROSE—P.O. Box 13320, Minneapolis, MN 55414. Attn: Ed. Short stories and essays, to 5,000 words. Poetry. Query for themes and reading periods. Pays in copies.

SKYLARK—2200 169th St., Hammond, IN 46323-2094. Pamela Hunter, Ed. "The Fine Arts Annual of Purdue Calumet." Fiction and articles, to 4,000 words. Poetry, to 21 lines. B&W prints and drawings. Pays in one copy. Manuscripts read November through April for fall publication.

SLIPSTREAM—Box 2071, Niagara Falls, NY 14301. Attn: Ed. Contemporary poetry, any length. Pays in copies. Reading for general issues in 1999. Fiction overstocked. Guidelines.

THE SMALL POND MAGAZINE—P.O. Box 664, Stratford, CT 06615. Napoleon St. Cyr, Ed. Published 3 times a year. Fiction, to 2,500 words; poetry, to 100 lines. Pays in copies. Query for nonfiction. Include short bio. Manuscripts read year-round. SASE required.

SMALL PRESS REVIEW—Box 100, Paradise, CA 95967. Len Fulton, Ed. Reviews, 200 words, of small literary books and magazines; tracks the publishing of small publishers and small-circulation magazines. Query.

SNAKE NATION REVIEW—Snake Nation Press, 110 #2 W. Force, Valdosta, GA 31601. Roberta George, Ed. Quarterly. Short stories, novel chapters, and informal essays, 5,000 words, and poetry, to 60 lines. Pays in copies and prizes.

SNOWY EGRET—P.O. Box 9, Bowling Green, IN 47833. Philip Repp, Ed. Poetry, fiction, and nonfiction, to 10,000 words. Natural history from artistic, literary, philosophical, and historical perspectives. Pays $2 per page for prose; $2 to $4 for poetry, on publication. Manuscripts read year-round.

SONORA REVIEW—Dept. of English, Univ. of Arizona, Tucson, AZ 85721. Attn: Fiction, Poetry, or Nonfiction Ed. (Address appropriate genre editor.) Annual contests; send for guidelines. Simultaneous submissions accepted (except for contest entries). Manuscripts read year-round.

THE SOUTH CAROLINA REVIEW—Dept. of English, Clemson Univ., Clemson, SC 29634-1503. Wayne Chapman, Ed. Semiannual. Fiction, essays, reviews, and interviews, to 4,000 words. Poems. Send complete manuscript. Pays in copies. Response time is 2 to 3 months. Manuscripts read September through May (but not in December). No multiple submissions.

SOUTH DAKOTA REVIEW—Box 111, Univ. Exchange, Vermillion, SD 57069-2390. Brian Bedard, Ed. Exceptional fiction, 3,000 to 5,000 words, and poetry, 10 to 25 lines. Critical articles, especially on American literature, Western American literature, theory and esthetics, creative nonfiction, 3,000 to 5,000 words. Pays in copies. Manuscripts read year-round; slower response time in the summer.

THE SOUTHERN CALIFORNIA ANTHOLOGY—c/o Master of Professional Writing Program, WPH 404, Univ. of Southern California, Los Angeles, CA 90089-4034. James Ragan, Ed.-in-Chief. Fiction, to 20 pages. Pays in copies. Manuscripts read September to January.

SOUTHERN EXPOSURE—P.O. Box 531, Durham, NC 27702. Chris Kromm, Ed. Quarterly forum on "Southern movements for social change." Short stories, to 3,600 words, essays, investigative journalism, and oral histories, 500 to 3,600 words. Pays $25 to $250, on publication. Query.

SOUTHERN HUMANITIES REVIEW—9088 Haley Ctr., Auburn Univ., AL 36849. Dan R. Latimer, Virginia M. Kouidis, Eds. Short stories, essays, and criticism, 3,500 to 15,000 words; poetry, to 2 pages. Responds within 3 months. No simultaneous submissions.

SOUTHERN POETRY REVIEW—Advancement Studies, Central Piedmont Community College, Charlotte, NC 28235. Ken McLaurin, Ed. Poems. No restrictions on style, length, or content. Manuscripts read September through May.

THE SOUTHERN REVIEW—43 Allen Hall, Louisiana State Univ., Baton Rouge, LA 70803-5005. James Olney and Dave Smith, Eds. Emphasis on contemporary literature with special interest in southern culture and history. Fiction and essays, 4,000 to 8,000 words. Serious poetry of highest quality. Pays $12 a page for prose, $20 a page for poetry, on publication. No manuscripts read in the summer.

SOUTHWEST REVIEW—307 Fondren Library W., Box 750374, Southern Methodist Univ., Dallas, TX 75275-0374. Elizabeth Mills, Sr. Fiction Ed. "A quarterly that serves the interests of the region but is not bound by them." Fiction, essays, poetry, and interviews with well-known writers, 3,000 to 7,500 words. Pays varying rates. Manuscripts read September 1 through May 31.

SOU'WESTER—Southern Illinois Univ. at Edwardsville, Edwardsville, IL 62026-1438. Fred W. Robbins, Ed. Nancy Avdoian, Assoc. Ed.; Susan Garrison, Fiction Ed., Leigh Ramsey, Poetry Ed., Allison Funk, Consulting Ed. Fiction, to 8,000 words. Poetry, any length. Pays in copies. Manuscripts not read in August.

THE SOW'S EAR POETRY REVIEW—19535 Pleasant View Dr., Abingdon, VA 24211-6827. Attn: Ed. Quarterly. Eclectic poetry and art. Submit one to 5 poems, any length, plus a brief biographical note. Interviews, essays, and articles, any length, about poets and poetry are also considered. B&W photos and drawings. Payment is one copy. Poetry and chapbook contests. Send SASE for guidelines.

SPARROW: THE YEARBOOK OF THE SONNET—(formerly *Sparrow Magazine*.) Sparrow Press, 103 Waldron St., W. Lafayette, IN 47906. Felix and Selma Stefanile, Eds./Pubs. Contemporary (14-line) sonnets, and occasionally formal poems in other structures. Submit up to 5 poems. Pays $3 per poem, on publication. A $25 sonnet prize is awarded to a contributor in each issue.

SPECTACLE—Pachanga Press, 101 Middlesex Turnpike, Suite 6, Box 155, Burlington, MA 01803. Richard Aguilar, Ed. Semiannual exploring American life, art, and passion. Personal essays on a theme. Send SASE for themes. Pays $30, in publication.

SPECTRUM—Univ. of California/ Santa Barbara, Box 14800, Santa

Barbara, CA 93107. Attn: Ed. Annual. Novel excerpts, short stories, various narrative, poetry, nonfiction essays, slides of art. Annual deadline is February 1.

SPOON RIVER POETRY REVIEW—Dept. of English, Stevenson Hall, Illinois State Univ., Normal, IL 61790-4240. Lucia Cordell Getsi, Ed. Poetry, any length. Pays in copies.

SPRING FANTASY—Women in the Arts, P.O. Box 2907, Decatur, IL 62524-2907. Linda Hutton, Ed. Fiction for adults and children; personal essays, to 1,500 words. Poetry, to 32 lines. Payment is one copy.

SPSM&H—329 E St., Bakersfield, CA 93304. Frederick A. Raborg, Jr., Ed. Romantic or Gothic short fiction, to 2,500 words, preferably in which the sonnet plays a part. Annual contest for romantic fiction. Pays $10, plus copy.

STAND MAGAZINE—Dept. of English, Hibbs Bldg., VCU, Richmond, VA 23284-2005. David Latané, U.S. Ed. School of English, Univ. of Leeds, Leeds, LS2 9JT, UK. John Kinsella and Michael Hulse, Eds. British quarterly. Fiction, 2,000 to 5,000 words, and poetry to 100 lines (submit up to 6 poems). No formulaic verse or genre fiction.

STATE STREET REVIEW—FCCJ North Campus, 4501 Capper Rd., Jacksonville, FL 32218-4499. John Hunt, Exec. Ed. Sohrab Fracis, Michele Boyette, Howard Denson, Eds. Semiannual. Fiction, to 6,000 words. Nonfiction, 2,000 words, on writers, poets, or on writing itself. Poetry. Pays in copies.

STORY QUARTERLY—P.O. Box 1416, Northbrook, IL 60065. Anne Brashler, Marie Hayes, Eds. Short stories and interviews. Pays in copies. Manuscripts read year-round.

THE STYLUS—9412 Huron Ave., Richmond, VA 23294. Roger Reus, Ed. Annual. Non-academic writings on authors, books, and occasionally the writing process itself. Original fiction and author interviews. Pays in copies.

THE SUN—The Sun Publishing Co., 107 N. Roberson St., Chapel Hill, NC 27516. Sy Safransky, Ed. Essays, interviews, and fiction, to 7,000 words; poetry; photos. "We're interested in all writing that makes sense and enriches our common space." Pays $300 to $500 for fiction; $300 to $1,000 for nonfiction; $50 to $200 for poetry, on publication.

SYCAMORE REVIEW—Purdue Univ., Dept. of English, West Lafayette, IN 47907. Sarah Griffiths, Ed.-in-Chief. Semiannual. Poetry, short fiction (no genre fiction), personal essays, drama, and translations. Pays in copies. Manuscripts read September to April.

TALKING RIVER REVIEW—Lewis-Clark State College, 500 8th Ave., Lewiston, ID 83501. Attn: Eds. Semiannual. Short stories, novel excerpts, and essays, to 7,500 words. Poetry, any length or style; submit up to 5 poems. "We publish emerging writing alongside established writers." Pays in copies and subscription. Manuscripts read September through February. Send poetry and prose under separate cover.

TALUS AND SCREE—P.O. Box 832, Newport, OR 97365. Carla Perry, Ed. Annual. Poetry, to five pages; short fiction, to 3,000 words; memoir vignettes; interviews; line drawings; and photos. Looking for humor, controversy, risk, and writing that goes over the edge. No pornography, self-indulgent word games, rhymed couplets, religious dogma, or misery, anger, lovelorn angst, etc. No pastoral poems. Prefer e-mail submissions: ocrisc@pioneer.net. Pays in copies and discount for more. Deadline August 15 every year. Guidelines and contest info available.

TAR RIVER POETRY—Dept. of English, East Carolina Univ., Greenville, NC 27858-4353. Peter Makuck, Ed. Poetry and reviews. "We prefer poems with strong imagery and figurative language. No trite, worn-out phrases, vague abstractions, or cliché situations." Pays in copies. Submit September through April.

THE TEXAS REVIEW—P.O. Box 2146, English Dept., Sam Houston State Univ., Huntsville, TX 77341. Paul Ruffin, Ed. Fiction, poetry, articles, to 20 typed pages. Reviews. Pays in copies and subscription. Annual book competitions in fiction and poetry. Write for guidelines.

THEMA—Box 8747, Metairie, LA 70011-8747. Virginia Howard, Ed. Theme-related fiction, to 20 pages, and poetry, to 2 pages. Pays $25 per story; $10 per short-short; $10 per poem; $10 for B&W art/photo, on acceptance. Send SASE for themes and guidelines.

32 PAGES—Rain Crow Publishing, 2127 W. Pierce Ave., Apt. 2B, Chicago, IL 60622-1824. Michael S. Manley, Pub. 4 to 6 times a year. Poetry, short fiction, creative nonfiction, and drama, to 8,000 words. Pays $5 per published page, on publication. Guidelines.

360 DEGREES: ART & LITERARY REVIEW—401 Georgia St., Vallejo, CA 94590. Karen Kinnison, Ed. Biannual art and literary review, featuring fiction and poetry (any length), and artwork. Send photocopies and photographs only. Payment is one copy.

THE THREEPENNY REVIEW—P.O. Box 9131, Berkeley, CA 94709. Wendy Lesser, Ed. Fiction, to 5,000 words. Pays to $200, on acceptance. Limited market. Send SASE for guidelines. Manuscripts read September through May.

TIGHTROPE—323 Pelham Rd., Amherst, MA 01002. Ed Rayher, Ed. Limited-edition, letterpress semiannual. Poetry, any length. Pays in copies. Manuscripts read year-round.

TIMBER CREEK REVIEW—3283 UNCG Station, Greensboro, NC 27413. J. M. Freiermuth, Ed. Quarterly. Fiction, 3,000 to 5,000 words; creative nonfiction, 2,000 to 4,000 words; and poetry, to 30 lines. "Not for children, or those easily offended." Pays $5 to $50 plus subscription for prose, author's copy for poetry, on publication.

TOMORROW: SPECULATIVE FICTION—See *www.tomorrowsf. com*

TRIQUARTERLY—Northwestern Univ., 2020 Ridge Ave., Evanston, IL 60208-4302. Susan Hahn, Ed. Serious, aesthetically informed and inventive poetry and prose, for an international and literate audience. Payment varies. Manuscripts read October through March. Allow 10 to 12 weeks for reply.

TWO RIVERS REVIEW—Anderie Poetry Press, 215 McCartney St., Easton, PA 18042. Philip Memmer, Ed. Semiannual. Excellent contemporary poetry, any style, from established poets and astonishing newcomers. Submit up to 3 poems, with SASE, any length. Responds in one month. Website: http://members.tripod.com/tworiversreview/index.html.

THE URBANITE: SURREAL & LIVELY & BIZARRE—Box 4737, Davenport, IA 52808. Mark McLaughlin, Ed. Published 3 times a year. Dark fantasy, horror (no gore), surrealism, reviews, and social commentary, to 3,000 words. Free verse poems, to 2 pages. Pays 2¢ to 3¢ a word; $10 for poetry, on acceptance. Query for themes.

URBANUS MAGAZINE—P.O. Box 192921, San Francisco, CA 94119. Peter Drizhal, Ed. Published 3 times a year. Fiction and nonfiction, 1,000 to 6,000 words, and poetry, to 40 lines, that reflect contemporary and urban influences for a "readership generally impatient with the mainstream approach." B&W photos and drawings. Pays $25 to $150 for articles, $15 to $20 for poems, on acceptance.

VERMONT INK—P.O. Box 3297, Burlington, VT 05401-3297. Donna Leach, Ed. Quarterly. Short stories, 2,000 words, that are well-written, entertaining, and "basically G-rated": adventure, historical, humor, mainstream, mystery and suspense, regional interest, romance, science fiction, and westerns. Poetry, to 25 lines, should be upbeat or humorous. Pays to $25 for stories; to $10 for poetry, on acceptance. Send complete manuscript with short bio and SASE.

THE VILLAGER—135 Midland Ave., Bronxville, NY 10708. Mary Hazzah, Fiction/Articles Ed. Eileen Mahoney, Poetry Ed. Fiction, 900 to 1,500 words, "in good taste": mystery, adventure, humor, romance. Short, preferably seasonal poetry. Pays in copies.

THE VINCENT BROTHERS REVIEW—4566 Northern Cir., Riverside, OH 45424-5733. Kimberly Willardson, Ed. Published 3 times a year. Fiction, nonfiction, poetry, fillers, and B&W art. "Read sample copies/back issues before submitting." Pays from $15 for fiction and nonfiction; $5 for poems; $10 for poetry used in "Page Left" feature. Guidelines.

VIRGINIA QUARTERLY REVIEW—One W. Range, Charlottesville, VA 22903. Attn: Ed. Quality fiction and poetry. Serious essays and articles, 3,000 to 6,000 words, on literature, science, politics, economics, etc. Pays $10 per page for prose, $1 per line for poetry, on publication.

VISIONS INTERNATIONAL—Black Buzzard Press, 1007 Ficklen Rd., Fredericksburg, VA 22405. Bradley R. Strahan, Ed. Published 3 times a year. Poetry, to 50 lines, and B&W drawings. (Query for art.) Read magazine before submitting. Pays in copies (or honorarium when funds available). Manuscripts read year-round.

WASCANA REVIEW OF CONTEMPORARY AND SHORT FICTION—c/o Dept. of English, Univ. of Regina, Regina, Sask., Canada S4S 0A2. Kathleen Wall, Ed. Short stories, 2,000 to 6,000 words; critical articles on short fiction and poetry; poetry. Pays $3 per page for prose, $10 for poetry, after publication.

WASHINGTON REVIEW—P.O. Box 50132, Washington, DC 20091-0132. Clarissa Wittenberg, Ed. Poetry; articles on literary, performing and fine arts in the Washington, D.C., area. Fiction, 1,000 to 2,500 words. Area writers preferred. Pays in copies. Responds in 3 months.

WEST BRANCH—Bucknell Hall, Bucknell Univ., Lewisburg, PA

17837. Karl Patten, Robert Taylor, Eds. Poetry and fiction. Pays in copies and subscriptions.

WESTERN HUMANITIES REVIEW—Univ. of Utah, Salt Lake City, UT 84112. Jenny Mueller, Man. Ed. Quarterly. Fiction and essays, to 30 pages, and poetry. Pays $35 for poetry, $50 to $100 for short stories and essays, on publication. Manuscripts read October through May; responds in 2 to 4 months.

WHETSTONE—P.O. Box 1266, Barrington, IL 60011. Attn: Eds. Fiction, poetry, and creative nonfiction, to 20 pages. Poems, submit up to 7. Payment varies, on publication.

WHISKEY ISLAND—Dept. of English, Cleveland State Univ., Cleveland, OH 44115. Attn: Ed. Fiction and nonfiction, under 6,500 words; Poetry up to 10 single-sided pages. We want a well-rounded magazine. Abstract and experimental works welcomed; social and ecological topics as well. Pays in copies.

THE WILLIAM AND MARY REVIEW—P.O. Box 8795, College of William and Mary, Williamsburg, VA 23187-8795. Brian Hatleberg, Ed. Annual. Fiction, 2,500 to 7,500 words; poetry, all genres (submit 4 to 6 poems); and art, all media. Pays in copies. Manuscripts read September through March. Responds in 3 months.

WIND MAGAZINE—P.O. Box 24548, Lexington, KY 40524. Charlie Hughes and Leatha Kendrick, Eds. Semiannual. Short stories, poems, and essays. Reviews of books from small presses and news of interest to the literary community. Pays in copies. Contests. Manuscripts read year-round. Web site: http://www.lit-arts.com/wind.

WINDSOR REVIEW—Dept. of English, Univ. of Windsor, Windsor, Ont., Canada N9B 3P4. Attn: Ed. Short stories, poetry, and original art. Pays $15 for poetry; $50 for fiction, on publication. Responds in one to 3 months.

WITNESS—Oakland Community College, 27055 Orchard Lake Rd., Farmington Hills, MI 48334. Peter Stine, Ed. Thematic journal. Fiction and essays, 5 to 20 pages, and poems (submit up to 3). Pays $6 per page for prose, $10 per page for poetry, on publication.

THE WORCESTER REVIEW—6 Chatham St., Worcester, MA 01609. Rodger Martin, Ed. Poetry (submit up to 5 poems at a time), fiction, and critical articles about poetry with a New England connection. Pays in copies. Responds within 9 months.

WRITERS FORUM—Univ. of Colorado, 1420 Austin Bluffs Pkwy., Colorado Springs, CO 80933-7150. C. Kenneth Pellow, Ed. Annual. Mainstream and experimental fiction, 1,000 to 8,000 words. Emphasis on Western themes and writers. Up to five poems by one author considered. Manuscripts read year-round. Pays in copies.

WRITERS' INTERNATIONAL FORUM and WRITERS' INTERNATIONAL FORUM FOR YOUNG AUTHORS—P.O. Box 516, Tracyton, WA 98393-0516. Sandra Haven, Ed. Online journal. Fiction and essays, also Christian manuscripts, to 2,500 words; all genres except horror; no graphic violence or sex, no derogatory language. Competitions with $250 first prize, merchandise prizes and awards, including a Special Young Authors Award.

Guidelines and entry information with SASE or at web site: http://www.bristolservicesintl.com

WRITERS ON THE RIVER—P.O. Box 40828, Memphis, TN 38174-0828. Mick Denington, Ed. Florence Bruce, Asst. Ed.; Russell Strauss, Prose Ed.; Wanda Rider, Poetry Ed. Family oriented. Publishes poetry, one page; fiction and nonfiction: adventure, fantasy, historical and regional, mainstream, humor, mystery/suspense, to 2, 500 words. Accepts submissions only from states bordering the Mississippi River, and Alabama. Pays in copies.

WWW.TOMORROWSF.COM—(formerly *Tomorrow: Speculative Fiction*) P.O. Box 6038, Evanston, IL 60204. Algis Budrys, Ed. Bimonthly electronic magazine. Nonfiction, any length, on science. Also, some cartoons and poetry. Pays 4¢ to 7¢ per word for nonfiction; $25 for cartoons; and 50¢ per line for poetry.

YALE REVIEW—Yale Univ., P.O. Box 208243, New Haven, CT 06520-8243. J.D. McClatchy, Ed. Susan Bianconi, Man. Ed. Serious poetry, to 200 lines, and fiction, 3,000 to 5,000 words. Pays average of $400.

YARROW—English Dept., Lytle Hall, Kutztown State Univ., Kutztown, PA 19530. Harry Humes, Ed. Semiannual. Poetry. "Just good, solid, clear writing. We don't have room for long poems." Pays in copies. Manuscripts read year-round.

ZOETROPE: ALL STORY—260 Fifth Ave., Suite 1200, New York, NY 10001. Adrienne Brodeur, Ed.-in-Chief. Stories and one-act plays under 7,000 words. Pays good rates, on acceptance. No submissions from June 1 through August 31. Please include SASE and allow five months for a response.

ZYZZYVA—41 Sutter, Suite 1400, San Francisco, CA 94104. Howard Junker, Ed. Publishes work of West Coast writers only: fiction, essays, and poetry. Pays $50, on acceptance. Manuscripts read year-round.

GREETING CARDS & NOVELTY ITEMS

Companies selling greeting cards and novelty items (T-shirts, coffee mugs, buttons, etc.) often have their own specific requirements for the submission of ideas, verse, and artwork. In general, however, each verse or message should be typed double-space on a 3x5 or 4x6 card. Use only one side of the card, and be sure to put your name and address in the upper left-hand corner. Keep a copy of every verse or idea you send. (It's also advisable to keep a record of what you've submitted to each publisher.) Always enclose an SASE, and do not send out more than ten verses or ideas in a group to any one publisher. Never send original artwork unless a publisher indicates a definite interest in using your work.

AMBERLEY GREETING CARD COMPANY—11510 Goldcoast Dr., Cincinnati, OH 45249-1695. Dave McPeek, Ed. Humorous ideas for cards: birthday, illness, friendship, anniversary, congratulations, "miss you," etc. Send SASE for market letter before submitting ideas. Pays $150. Buys all rights.

AMERICAN GREETINGS—One American Rd., Cleveland, OH 44144. Kathleen McKay, Ed. Recruitment. Send #10 SASE to receive Humorous Writing guidelines. Current need is for humor only.

BLUE MOUNTAIN ARTS, INC.—P.O. Box 1007, Boulder, CO 80306. Attn: Ed. Dept. TW. Poetry and prose about love, friendship, family, philosophies, etc. Also material for special occasions and holidays: birthdays, get well, Christmas, Valentine's Day, Easter, etc. Submit seasonal material 5 months in advance of holiday. No artwork. Include SASE. Pays $200 per poem.

BRILLIANT ENTERPRISES—117 W. Valerio St., Santa Barbara, CA 93101-2927. Ashleigh Brilliant, Ed. Illustrated epigrams. Send SASE and $2 for a catalogue and samples. Pays $50, on acceptance.

COMSTOCK CARDS—600 S. Rock, Suite 15, Reno, NV 89502-4115. David Delacroix, Ed. Adult humor, outrageous or sexual, for greeting cards, invitations, and notepads. SASE for guidelines. Payment varies, on publication.

DAYSPRING GREETING CARDS—P.O. Box 1010, Siloam Springs, AR 72761. Attn: Freelance Ed. Inspirational material for everyday occasions and most holidays. Currently only accepting free-lance copy submissions from published greeting card authors. Qualified writers should send samples of their published greeting cards (no more than 5 cards or copies). Also, the words "Previously Published" must be written on the lower left corner of the mailing envelopes containing copy submissions. Payment is $50 on acceptance. Send SASE for guidelines, or email to: info@dayspring.com, and type in the word "write" for guidelines.

DESIGN DESIGN, INC.—P.O. Box 2266, Grand Rapids, MI 49501-2266. Tom Vituj, Creative Dir. Short verses for both humorous and sentimental concepts for greeting cards. Everyday (birthday, get well, just for fun, etc.) and seasonal (Christmas, Valentine's Day, Easter, Mother's Day, Father's Day, Graduation, Halloween, Thanksgiving) material. Flat fee payment on publication. Please include SASE for return.

DUCK & COVER—P.O. Box 21640, Oakland, CA 94620. Jim Buser, Ed. Outrageous, off the wall, original one-liners for buttons and magnets. SASE for guidelines. Pays $25, on publication.

EPHEMERA, INC.—P.O. Box 490, Phoenix, OR 97535. Attn: Ed. Provocative, irreverent, and outrageously funny slogans for novelty buttons, magnets, and stickers. Submit typed list of slogans with SASE. Pays $40 per slogan, on acceptance. SASE for guidelines; also available from web site: www.ephemera-inc.com.

HALLMARK CARDS, INC.—Box 419580, Mail Drop 288, Kansas City, MO 64141. No unsolicited submissions.

KATE HARPER DESIGNS—P.O. Box 2112, Berkeley, CA 94702. Attn: Guidelines TW. Quotes, to 20 words, about work, life, technology, political themes, current social issues, etc., from everyday people for hand-assembled "quotation" cards that take a lighthearted look at life in the 90s. Submit original quotes on index card, one quote per card. No drawings, artwork, or visuals.

Send SASE for guidelines before submitting. Payment varies, on acceptance. Also accepting submissions from children under 13. Send SASE for guidelines format. No cover letter necessary. E-mail: kateharp@aol.com.

LAFFS BY MARCEL—Schurman Design, 101 New Montgomery, 6th Fl., San Francisco, CA 94105. Attn: Deanne Quinones. Sophisticated, humorous birthday, everyday, and seasonal ideas.

OATMEAL STUDIOS—Box 138 TW, Rochester, VT 05767. Attn: Ed. Humorous, clever, and new ideas needed for all occasions. Send legal-size SASE for guidelines.

PANDA INK—P.O. Box 5129, West Hills, CA 91308-5129. Ruth Ann Epstein, Ed. Judaica, metaphysical, cute, whimsical, or beautiful sentiment for greeting cards, bookmarks, clocks, and pins. Currently overstocked; accepting no submissions. Payment varies, on acceptance.

PARAMOUNT CARDS—P.O. Box 6546, Providence, RI 02940-6546. Attn: Editorial Freelance. Humorous, traditional, and inspirational card ideas for birthday, relative's birthday, friendship, romance, get well, Christmas, Valentine's Day, Easter, Mother's Day, Father's Day, and Graduation. Submit each idea (5 to 10 per submission) on 3x5 card with name and address on each, along with SASE. Payment varies, on acceptance.

PLUM GRAPHICS—P.O. Box 136, Prince Station, New York, NY 10012. Yvette Cohen, Ed. Editorial needs change frequently; write for guidelines (new guidelines 3 times per year). Queries required. Pays $40 per card, on publication.

RED FARM STUDIO—1135 Roosevelt Ave., P.O. Box 347, Pawtucket, RI 02862. Attn: Production Coord. Traditional cards for birthday, get well, wedding, anniversary, friendship, new baby, sympathy, congrats, and Christmas; also light humor. Pays $4 a line. Send SASE.

VAGABOND CREATIONS, INC.—2560 Lance Dr., Dayton, OH 45409. George F. Stanley, Jr., Ed. Greeting cards with graphics only on cover (no copy) and short punch line inside: birthday, everyday, Valentine's Day, Christmas, and graduation. Mildly risqué humor with double entendre acceptable. Ideas for illustrated theme stationery. Pays $15, on acceptance.

WEST GRAPHICS PUBLISHING—1117 California Dr., Burlingame, CA 94010. Attn: Production Dept. Outrageous humor concepts, all occasions (especially birthday) and holidays, for photo and illustrated card lines. Submit on 3x5 cards: concept on one side; name, address, and phone number on other. Pays $100, 30 days after publication.

HUMOR, FILLERS, & SHORT ITEMS

Magazines noted for their filler departments, plus a cross-section of publications using humor, short items, jokes, quizzes, and cartoons, follow. However, almost all magazines use some type of filler material from time to time, and writers can find dozens of markets by studying copies of magazines at a library or newsstand.

THE AMERICAN FIELD—542 S. Dearborn, Chicago, IL 60605. B.J. Matthys, Man. Ed. Short fact items and anecdotes on hunting dogs and field trials for bird dogs. Pays varying rates, on acceptance.

AMERICAN SPEAKER—Attn: Current Comedy, 1101 30th St. N.W., Washington, DC 20007. Aram Bakshian, Ed.-in-Chief. Original, funny, performable jokes on news, fads, topical subjects, business, etc., for "Current Comedy" section of *American Speaker* Magazine. Jokes for roasts, retirement dinners, and for speaking engagements. Humorous material specifically geared for public speaking situations such as microphone feedback, introductions, long events, etc. Also interested in longer original jokes and anecdotes that can be used by public speakers. No poems, puns, ethnic jokes, or sexist material. Pays $12, on publication. Guidelines.

THE ANNALS OF IMPROBABLE RESEARCH—AIR, P.O. Box 380853, Cambridge, MA 02238. Marc Abrahams, Ed. Science humor, science reports and analysis, one to 4 pages. B&W photos. "This journal is the place to find the mischievous, funny, iconoclastic side of science. An insider's journal that lets anyone sneak into the company of wonderfully mad scientists." Guidelines. No payment. Web site: www.improbable.com.

ARMY MAGAZINE—2425 Wilson Blvd., Arlington, VA 22210-0860. Mary B. French, Ed.-in-Chief. True anecdotes on military subjects. Pays $25 to $50, on publication.

ASIAN PAGES—P.O. Box 11932, St. Paul, MN 55111-0932. Cheryl Weiberg, Ed.-in-Chief. Profiles and news events, 500 words; short stories, 500 to 750 words; poetry, 100 words; and Asian-related fillers, 50 words. "All material must have a strong, non-offensive Asian slant." Pays $40 for articles, $25 for photos/cartoons, on publication.

THE ATLANTIC MONTHLY—77 N. Washington St., Boston, MA 02114. Attn: Ed. Sophisticated humorous or satirical pieces, 1,000 to 3,000 words. Some light poetry. No unsolicited material. Pays from $500 for prose, on acceptance.

ATLANTIC SALMON JOURNAL—P.O. Box 429, St. Andrews, N.B., Canada E0G 2X0. Jim Gourlay, Ed. Fillers, 50 to 100 words, on salmon politics, conservation, and nature. Pays $25 for fillers, on publication.

BICYCLING—135 N. 6th St., Emmaus, PA 18098. Attn: Eds. Anecdotes, helpful cycling tips, and other items for "Bike Shorts" section, 150 to 250 words. Pays $25 to $50, on acceptance.

BYLINE—Box 130596, Edmond, OK 73013. Marcia Preston, Ed.-in-Chief. Humor, 50 to 400 words, about writing. Pays $15 to $25 for humor, on acceptance.

CAPPER'S—1503 S.W. 42nd St., Topeka, KS 66609-1265. Ann Crahan, Ed. Letters, to 300 words, sharing heartwarming experiences, nostalgic accounts, household hints, poems, and recipes, for "Heart of the Home." Poetry to 16 lines. Pays on acceptance. Freelance articles on historical, informational, unusual items to 700 words. Pays on publication. Query only for serial fiction. Jokes, submit up to 6 at a time. Pays varying rates (and in gift certificates), on publication.

CATHOLIC DIGEST—2115 Summit Ave., St. Paul, MN 55105-1081. Attn: Filler Ed. Articles, 200 to 500 words, on instances of kindness, for "Hearts Are Trumps." Stories about conversions, for "Open Door." Accounts of good deeds, for "People Are Like That." Humorous pieces, 50 to 300 words, on parish life, for "In Our Parish." Amusing signs, for "Signs of the Times." Jokes; fillers. No fiction. Pays $2 per line, on publication.

CHICKADEE—179 John St., Suite 500, Toronto, Ont., Canada M5T 3G5. Kat Mototsune, Ed. Juvenile poetry, 10 to 15 lines. Fiction, 800 words. Pays on acceptance. Enclose $2.00 money order and IRC for reply.

CHILDREN'S PLAYMATE—1100 Waterway Blvd., P.O. Box 567, Indianapolis, IN 46206. Terry Harshman, Ed. Articles and fiction, puzzles, games, mazes, poetry, crafts, and recipes for 6- to 8-year-olds, emphasizing health, fitness, sports, safety, and nutrition. Pays to 17¢ a word (varies for puzzles and poems), on publication.

THE CHURCH MUSICIAN—127 Ninth Ave. N., Nashville, TN 37234-0160. Jere V. Adams, Ed. Humorous fillers with a music slant for church music leaders, pastors, organists, pianists, and members of the music council or other planning groups. (No clippings.) Pays 5½¢ a word, on publication.

COLUMBIA JOURNALISM REVIEW—Columbia Univ., 700 Journalism Bldg., New York, NY 10027. Gloria Cooper, Man. Ed. Amusing mistakes in news stories, headlines, photos, etc. (original clippings required), for "Lower Case." Pays $25, on publication.

COUNTRY WOMAN—P. O. Box 989, Greendale, WI 53129. Kathy Pohl, Exec. Ed. Short rhymed verse, 4 to 20 lines, seasonal and country-related. All material must be positive and upbeat. Pays $10 to $15, on acceptance.

CRACKED—Globe Communications, Inc., 3 E. 54th St., 15th Fl., New York, NY 10022-3108. Lou Silverstone, Andy Simmons, Eds. Cartoon humor, one to 5 pages, for 10- to 15-year-old readers. No text pieces accepted. "Queries are not necessary, but read the magazine before submitting material!" Pays from $100 per page, on acceptance.

CYCLE WORLD—1499 Monrovia Ave., Newport Beach, CA 92663. David Edwards, Ed.-in-Chief. News items on motorcycle industry, legislation, trends. Pays on publication.

ELYSIAN FIELDS QUARTERLY—2034 Marshall Ave., St. Paul, MN 55104. Tom Goldstein, Ed. Essays, interviews, humor, and opinion pieces, varying lengths, all related to baseball. Payment is in copies. SASE for guidelines.

FACES—Cobblestone Publishing, 30 Grove St., Suite C, Peterborough, NH 03458-1454. Elizabeth Crooker, Ed. Puzzles, mazes, crosswords, and picture puzzles for children. Send SASE for list of monthly themes before submitting.

FAMILY CIRCLE—375 Lexington Ave., New York, NY 10017. Uses some short humor, 750 words. No fiction. Payment varies, on acceptance.

THE FAMILY DIGEST—P.O. Box 40137, Fort Wayne, IN 46804. Corine B. Erlandson, Ed. Family- or Catholic parish-oriented anecdotes, 10 to 125 words, of funny or unusual real-life parish and family experiences. Pays $20, 4 to 8 weeks after acceptance.

FARM AND RANCH LIVING—5400 S. 60th St., Greendale, WI

53129. Nick Pabst, Ed. Fillers on rural people and living, including farming-related jokes, 200 words. Pays from $25, on acceptance and publication.

FATE—P.O. Box 64383, St. Paul, MN 55164-0383. Attn: Ed. Factual fillers, to 300 words, on strange, psychic, or paranormal happenings. True stories, to 500 words, on personal mystic experiences. Pays 10¢ a word for fillers (minimum $10), $25 for personal accounts. SASE for guidelines. E-mail: fate@llewellyn.com.

FIELD & STREAM—2 Park Ave., New York, NY 10016. Slaton White, Ed. Fillers on hunting, fishing, camping, etc., to 500 words. Cartoons. Pays $75 to $250, sometimes more, for fillers; $100 for cartoons, on acceptance.

FINESCALE MODELER—P.O. Box 1612, Waukesha, WI 53187. Terry Thompson, Ed. One-page hints and tips on building nonoperating, scale models. Payment varies, on acceptance.

GAMES—P.O. Box 184, Ft. Washington, PA 19034. R. Wayne Schmittberger, Ed.-in-Chief. Pencil puzzles, visual brainteasers, and pop culture tests. Humor and playfulness a plus; quality a must. Pays top rates, on publication.

GERMAN LIFE—Zeitgeist Publishing, 1068 National Hwy., La Vale, MD 21502. Heidi Whitesell, Ed. Fillers, 50 to 200 words, on German culture, its past and present, and how America has been influenced by its German element: history, travel, people, the arts, and social and political issues; also humor and cartoons. Articles, 500 to 2,000 words. Pays to $80 for fillers; $300 to $500 for articles, on publication. Queries preferred for articles.

GLAMOUR—350 Madison Ave., New York, NY 10017. Attn: Viewpoint Ed. Articles, 1,000 words, for "Viewpoint" section: opinion pieces for women. Pays $500, on acceptance.

GUIDEPOSTS—16 E. 34th St., New York, NY 10016. Catherine Scott, Asst. Ed. Inspirational anecdotes, to 250 words. Pays $10 to $75, on acceptance.

IRISH EDITION—903 E. Willow Grove Ave., Wyndmoor, PA 19038-7909. Jane M. Duffin, Ed. Fillers, humor, and puzzles, all geared toward Irish-American and Irish-born audience. Payment is negotiable, and is made on acceptance. Query.

MAD MAGAZINE—1700 Broadway, 5th Fl., New York, NY 10019. Attn: Eds. Humorous pieces on a wide variety of topics. Two- to 8-panel cartoons (not necessary to include sketches with submission). Pays top rates, on acceptance. Guidelines strongly recommended; must include SASE for response. Web site: www.madmag.com.

MATURE LIVING—127 Ninth Ave. N., MSN 140, Nashville, TN 37234. Attn: Ed. Brief, humorous, original items. "Grandparents Brag Board" items; Christian inspirational pieces for senior adults, 125 words. Pays $15 to $25.

MATURE YEARS—201 Eighth Ave. S., P.O. Box 801, Nashville, TN 37202. Marvin W. Cropsey, Ed. Poems, cartoons, puzzles, jokes, anecdotes, to 300 words, for older adults. Allow 2 months for manuscript evaluation. "A Christian magazine that seeks to build faith. We always show older adults in a favorable light." Include name, address, social security number with all submissions.

MID-WEST OUTDOORS—111 Shore Dr., Hinsdale, IL 60521-5885.

Gene Laulunen, Man. Ed. Where to and how to fish and hunt in the Midwest, 700 to 1,500 words, with 2 photos. Pays $15 to $30, on publication.

NATIONAL ENQUIRER—Lantana, FL 33464. Kathy Martin, Fillers Ed. Short, humorous or philosophical fillers, witticisms, anecdotes, jokes, tart comments. Original items only. Short poetry, 8 lines or less, with traditional rhyming verse, amusing, philosophical, or inspirational in nature. No obscure or artsy poetry. Submit seasonal/holiday material at least 3 months in advance. Pays $25, after publication.

NEW HUMOR MAGAZINE—P.O. Box 216, Lafayette Hill, PA 19444. Edward Savaria, Jr., Ed. Currently overstocked; not accepting submissions.

THE NEW YORKER—20 W. 43rd St., New York, NY 10036. Attn: Newsbreaks Dept. Amusing mistakes in newspapers, books, magazines, etc. Pays $10, on acceptance.

OUTDOOR LIFE—2 Park Ave., New York, NY 10016. Todd W. Smith, Ed. Short instructive items, 900 to 1,100 words, on hunting, fishing, boating, and outdoor equipment; regional pieces on lakes, rivers, specific geographic areas of special interest to hunters and fishermen. Not soliciting materals at present.

PLAYBOY—9242 Beverly Blvd., Beverly Hills, CA 90210. Attn: Party Jokes Ed. or After Hours Ed. Jokes; short original material on new trends, lifestyles, personalities; humorous news items. Pays $100 for jokes; $50 to $350 for "After Hours" items, on publication.

PLAYGIRL—801 Second Ave., New York, NY 10017. Sandra Mardenfeld, Man. Ed. Humorous pieces, 800 to 1,500 words, on romance and relationships with a sexual twist, from male or female perspective, 800 to 1,000 words. Pays varying rates, after acceptance. Query.

READER'S DIGEST—Readers Digest Road, Pleasantville, NY 10570-7000. Consult "Wanted: Your Laugh Lines" page for guidelines. No submissions acknowledged or returned.

REAL PEOPLE—450 7th Ave., Suite 1701, New York, NY 10123-0073. Brad Hamilton, Ed. True stories, to 500 words, about interesting people for "Real Shorts" section: strange occurrences, everyday weirdness, occupations, etc.; may be funny, sad, or hair-raising. Also humorous items, to 75 words, taken from small-circulation newspapers, etc. Pays $25 to $50, on publication.

RHODE ISLAND MONTHLY—70 Elm St., Providence, RI 02903. Paula M. Bodah, Ed. Short pieces, to 500 words, on Rhode Island and southeastern Massachusetts: places, customs, people and events. Pays $50 to $150. Query.

ROAD KING—Hammock Publishing, 3322 W. End Ave., Suite 700, Nashville, TN 37203. Attn: Fillers Ed. Trucking-related cartoons and fillers. Payment is negotiable, on publication.

THE ROTARIAN—1560 Sherman Ave., Evanston, IL 60201-3698. Charles W. Pratt, Ed. Occasional humor articles. Payment varies, on acceptance. No payment for fillers, anecdotes, or jokes.

SACRAMENTO MAGAZINE—4471 D St., Sacramento, CA 95819. Krista Minard, Ed. "City Lights," interesting and unusual people, places, and behind-the-scenes news items, to 400 words. All material must have Sacramento tie-in. Payment varies, on publication.

THE SATURDAY EVENING POST—P.O. Box 567, Indianapolis, IN

46206. Steven Pettinga, Post Scripts Ed. Humor and satire, to 100 words, that is upbeat and positive. No lurid references. Light verse, cartoons, jokes, for verse. Original material only. SASE required. Pays $15 for verse; $125 for cartoons, on publication.

SKI MAGAZINE—929 Pearl St., Suite 200, Boulder, CO 80302. Andrew Bigford, Ed.-in-Chief. Short, 100- to 300-word items on news, events, and people in skiing for "Ski Life" department. Pays on acceptance.

SPORTS AFIELD—250 W. 55th St., New York, NY 10019. Attn: Almanac Ed. Unusual, useful tips and information, 100 to 300 words, for "Almanac" section: on kayaking, hiking, skiing, mountain biking, rock climbing, fishing, and natural history. Pays on publication.

STAR—660 White Plains Rd., Tarrytown, NY 10591. Attn: Ed. Topical articles, 50 to 800 words, on show business and celebrities, health, fitness, parenting, and diet and food. Pays varying rates.

TECH DIRECTIONS—3970 Varsity Dr., Box 8623, Ann Arbor, MI 48107-8623. Tom Bowden, Man. Ed. Cartoons, puzzles, brainteasers, and humorous anecdotes of interest to technology and industrial education teachers and administrators. Pays $20 for cartoons; $25 for puzzles, brainteasers, and other short classroom activities; $5 for humorous anecdotes, on publication.

THOUGHTS FOR ALL SEASONS: THE MAGAZINE OF EPI-GRAMS—478 N.E. 56th St., Miami, FL 33137. Michel P. Richard, Ed. Epigrams and puns, one to 4 lines, and poetry, to one page. "Writers are advised not to submit material until they have examined a copy of the magazine." Payment is one copy.

TOUCH—Box 7259, Grand Rapids, MI 49510. Carol Smith, Man. Ed. Puzzles based on the NIV Bible, for Christian girls ages 8 to 14. Pays $10 to $15 per puzzle, on publication. Send SASE for theme update.

TRAVEL SMART—40 Beechdale Rd., Dobbs Ferry, NY 10522-3098. Attn: Ed. Interesting and useful travel-related tips. Practical, specific, information for vacation or business travel. Fresh, original material. Pays $5 to $150. Query for over 250 words.

TRUE CONFESSIONS—233 Park Ave. S., New York, NY 10003. Pat Byrdsong, Ed. Warm, inspirational first-person fillers, to 300 words, about love, marriage, family life, prayer for "Woman to Woman," "My Moment with God," "My Man," and "Incredible But True." Also, short stories, 1,000 to 2,000 words. Pays after publication. Buys all rights.

WISCONSIN TRAILS—P.O. Box 5650, Madison, WI 53705. Attn: Ed. Short articles/fillers, 300 to 800 words, about Wisconsin: places to go, things to do, nature, experiences, etc. Query. No clippings or phone calls. E-mail: editor@wistrails.com.

JUVENILE & YOUNG ADULT MAGAZINES

JUVENILE MAGAZINES

AMERICAN GIRL—8400 Fairway Pl., P.O. Box 998, Middleton, WI 53562-0998. Attn: Asst. to the Magazine Dept. Bimonthly. Articles, to 800 words, and contemporary or historical fiction, to 3,000 words, for girls ages 8 to 12. "We do not want 'teenage' material, i.e. articles on romance, make-up, dating, etc." Payment varies, on acceptance. Query for articles; include photo leads with historical queries.

APPLESEEDS—Cobblestone Publishing Co., 99 Perkins Point Rd., Newcastle, ME 04553. Barbara Burt, Co-Ed. Nine times yearly. Multidisciplinary social studies magazine for children 7 to 10. Feature articles, 400 to 600 words; fillers, including short fiction, profiles, and activities, to 300 words. All material must be theme-related. Queries required; send SASE for guidelines and theme list. Pays $50 per page. Web site: www.cobblestonepub.com.

BABYBUG—Carus Publishing Co., P.O. Box 300, Peru, IL 61354. Marianne Carus, Ed.-in-Chief. Paula Morrow, Ed. Stories, to 4 sentences; poems, and action rhymes, to 8 lines, for infants and toddlers, 6 months to 2 years. Pays from $25, on publication. Guidelines.

BOYS' QUEST—P.O. Box 227, Bluffton, OH 45817-4610. Attn: Ed. Bimonthly. Fiction and nonfiction, 500 words, for boys ages 6 to 12. "We are looking for articles, stories, and poetry that deal with timeless topics such as pets, nature, hobbies, science, games, sports, careers, simple cooking, etc." B&W photos a plus. Pays 5¢ a word, on publication. Send SASE for guidelines.

CALIFORNIA CHRONICLES—Cobblestone Publishing Co., 555 De Haro St., Suite 334, San Francisco, CA 94107. Submissions Five times yearly. California history, geography, and culture for children 9 to 14. Feature articles, 500 to 1,000 words. Fillers, including puzzles, recipes, and activities related to California history, 150 to 300 words. All submissions must be theme-related. Query; send SASE for guidelines and theme list first. Pays 20¢ to 25¢ per word. Web site: www.cobblestonepub.com.

CALLIOPE: WORLD HISTORY FOR YOUNG PEOPLE— Cobblestone Publishing, Inc., 30 Grove St., Peterborough, NH 03458. Rosalie Baker and Charles Baker, Eds. Theme-based magazine, published 9 times yearly. Articles, 750 to 1,000 words, with lively, original approach to world history (East/West) through the Renaissance. Shorts, 200 to 750 words, on little-known information related to issue's theme. Fiction, to 1,200 words: historical, biographical, adventure, or retold legends. Activities for children, to 800 words. Puzzles and games. Pays 20¢ to 25¢ a word, on publication. Guidelines and themes.

CHICKADEE MAGAZINE—179 John St., Suite 500, Toronto, Ont., Canada M5T 3G5. Hilary Bain, Ed. Adventure, folktale, and humorous stories and poems for 6- to 9-year-olds. Also puzzles, activities, and observation games. No religious material. Pays varying rates, on acceptance. Submit complete manuscript with $2.00 check or money order for return postage. Send $4.28 (Canadian dollars) for guidelines.

CHILD LIFE—1100 Waterway Blvd., P.O. Box 567, Indianapolis, IN 46206. Lise Hoffman, Ed. Nostalgia and some health-related material, the latter generated in-house or assigned, for 9- to 11-year-olds. Currently not accepting manuscripts for publication.

CHILDREN'S DIGEST—1100 Waterway Blvd., P.O. Box 567, Indianapolis, IN 46206. David Lee, Ed. Not considering new material at this time.

CHILDREN'S PLAYMATE—1100 Waterway Blvd., P.O. Box 567, Indianapolis, IN 46206. Terry Harshman, Ed. General-interest and health-related short stories (health, fitness, nutrition, safety, and exercise), 500 to 600 words, for 6- to 8-year-olds. Easy recipes and how-to crafts pieces with simple instructions. Poems, puzzles, dot-to-dots, mazes, hidden pictures. Pays to 17¢ a word, from $30 for poetry, on publication. Buys all rights.

CLICK—332 S. Michigan Ave., Suite 1100, Chicago, IL 60604. Attn: Ed. Ten times a year. Articles, to 850 words for readers 3 to 7, about natural, physical, or social sciences, the arts, technology, math, and history. Fiction, if the goal of the story is to address a question about the world. Pays 25¢ a word, on publication.

CLUBHOUSE—Box 15, Berrien Springs, MI 49103. Krista Phillips Hainey, Ed. Currently overstocked; not considering new material at this time. Action-oriented Christian stories, 800 to 1,200 words. Children in stories should be wise, brave, funny, kind, etc. Pays $25 to $35 for stories.

CLUBHOUSE JR. —8605 Explorer Dr., Colorado Springs, CO 80920. Jesse Florea, Ed. Articles on Christian values aimed at children ages 4 to 8. Nonfiction, to 500 words, on real people, science, and nature; fiction, 250 to 1,000 words; Bible stories, 250 to 800 words; rebus stories, to 200 words; poetry, to 250 words; and one-page puzzles. Pays $75 to $200 for all material except poetry, rebus stories, and puzzles. SASE for guidelines.

COBBLESTONE: DISCOVER AMERICAN HISTORY —30 Grove St., Suite C, Peterborough, NH 03458-1454. Meg Chorlian, Ed. Theme-related articles, biographies, plays, and short accounts of historical events, 700 to 800 words, for 8- to 15-year-olds; also supplemental nonfiction, 300 to 600 words. Fiction, 700 to 800 words. Activities (crafts, recipes, etc.) that can be done either by children alone or with adult supervision. Poetry, to 100 lines. Crossword and other word puzzles using the vocabulary of the issue's theme. Pays 20¢ to 25¢ a word, on publication. (Payment varies for activities and poetry.) Send SASE for guidelines and themes.

CONTACT KIDS—(formerly *3-2-1 Contact*) 1 Lincoln Plaza, Children's Television Workshop, New York, NY 10023. Curtis Slepian, Ed. No unsolicited manuscripts or queries.

CRAYOLA KIDS—Meredith Custom Publishing, 1912 Grand Ave., Des Moines, IA 50309-3379. Barbara Hall Palar, Ed. Bimonthly for families with children 3 to 8 years old. Hands-on crafts and seasonal activities, one to 4 pages. Puzzle ideas related to issue themes. Pays $50 to $250, on acceptance. Send SASE for themes. Query with resumé and work samples.

CRICKET—P.O. Box 300, Peru, IL 61354-0300. Marianne Carus, Ed.-in-Chief. Articles and fiction, 200 to 2,000 words, for 9- to 14-year-olds. (Include bibliography with nonfiction.) Poetry, to 30 lines. Pays to 25¢ a word, to $3 a line for poetry, on publication. Guidelines.

DISCOVERY TRAILS—(formerly *Junior Trails*) 1445 Boonville Ave., Springfield, MO 65802-1894. Sinda Zinn, Ed. Fiction, 800 to 1,000 words, with a Christian focus, believable characters, and moral emphasis. Articles, 200 to 400 words, on science, nature, biography. Pays 7¢ to 10¢ a word, on acceptance.

FACES—Cobblestone Publishing, 30 Grove St., Suite C, Peterborough, NH 03458-1454. Elizabeth Crooker, Ed. In-depth feature articles, 800 words, with an anthropology theme. Shorts, 300 to 600 words, related to themes. Fiction, to 800 words, on legends, folktales, stories from around the world, etc., related to theme. Activities, to 700 words, including recipes, crafts, games, etc., for children. Published monthly, September through May. Pays 20¢ to 25¢ a word. Write for guidelines and themes.

FOOTSTEPS—150 Page St., New Bedford, MA 02740. Charles Baker III, Ed. Fiction and nonfiction on African American history and culture, for children 8 to 14. Features, 600 to 750 words; fiction, to 700 words; articles, activities, and fillers, to 600 words. Cultural sensitivity and historical accuracy a must. Query; send SASE for guidelines and theme lists. Pays 20¢ to 25¢ per word, on publication.

THE FRIEND—50 E. North Temple, 23rd Fl., Salt Lake City, UT 84150-3226. Vivian Paulsen, Man. Ed. Stories and articles, 1,000 to 1,200 words. Stories, to 250 words, for younger readers and preschool children. Pays from 9¢ a word, from $25 per poem, on acceptance. Prefers completed manuscripts. Guidelines available with SASE.

GIRLS' LIFE—Monarch Avalon, Inc., 4517 Harford Rd., Baltimore, MD 21214. Kelly White, Sr. Ed. Features of various lengths and one-page departments that entertain and educate girls ages 7 to 14. Payment varies, on publication. Query with resumé and clips. Send SASE for guidelines.

THE GOLDFINCH—State Historical Society of Iowa, 402 Iowa Ave., Iowa City, IA 52240-1806. Quarterly. Articles, 200 to 800 words, and short fiction on Iowa history for young people. "All articles must correspond to an upcoming theme." Pays $25 per article, on acceptance. Query for themes.

GUIDEPOSTS FOR KIDS—P.O. Box 638, Chesterton, IN 46304. Mary Lou Carney, Ed. Issue-oriented, thought-provoking articles, 1,000 to 1,500 words. Secondary features: playful and entertaining nonfiction, to 700 words. Fiction, mysteries, contemporary, and holiday stories, 700 to 1,300 words. "Not preachy. Child protagonist. Dialogue-filled and value-driven." Pays competitive rates, on acceptance. Query for articles.

HIGHLIGHTS FOR CHILDREN—803 Church St., Honesdale, PA 18431-1824. Beth Troop, Manuscript Coord. Easy-to-read stories, to 800 words for 6- to 8-year-olds; and fiction, to 800 words, for 8-year-olds and up. Humor, adventure, mysteries, sports, history, especially holidays, patriotic tales, first-person accounts, back-to-school issues, biographies, black history, world history and cultures. "We'd also like to see stories that don't fit in any of those categories, but are good, meaningful stories for children." Pays from 14¢ a word, on acceptance. SASE for guidelines.

HOPSCOTCH, THE MAGAZINE FOR GIRLS—P.O. Box 164, Bluffton, OH 45817-0164. Marilyn Edwards, Ed. Bimonthly. Articles and fiction, 600 to 1,000 words, and short poetry for girls ages 6 to 12. Special interest in articles, with photos, about girls involved in worthwhile activities. "We believe young girls deserve the right to enjoy a season of childhood before they become young adults; we are not interested in such topics as sex, romance, cosmetics, hairstyles, etc." Pays 5¢ a word, on publication. Send SASE for guidelines.

HUMPTY DUMPTY'S MAGAZINE—1100 Waterway Blvd., P.O. Box 567, Indianapolis, IN 46206. Nancy Axelrad, Ed. General-interest publication with an emphasis on health and fitness for 4- to 6-year-olds. Easy-to-read fiction, to 300 words, with health and nutrition, safety, exercise, or hygiene as theme; humor and light approach preferred. Creative nonfiction. No-cook recipes using healthful ingredients. Short verse, narrative poems. Pays to 22¢ a word, from $25 for poems, on publication. Buys all rights.

JACK AND JILL—1100 Waterway Blvd., P.O. Box 567, Indianapolis, IN 46206. Daniel Lee, Ed. Articles, 500 to 800 words, for 7- to 10-year-olds, on sports, fitness, health, nutrition, safety, exercise. Features, 500 to 700 words, on history, biography, life in other countries, etc. Fiction, to 700 words. Short poems, games, puzzles, projects, recipes. Photos. Pays 10¢ to 20¢ a word, extra for photos, on publication.

JUNIOR SCHOLASTIC—Scholastic, Inc., 555 Broadway, New York, NY 10012. Lee Baier, Ed. On-the-spot reports from countries in the news. Payment varies, on acceptance. Query.

JUNIOR TRAILS—See *Discovery Trails.*

KID CITY—Children's Television Workshop, 1 Lincoln Plaza, New York, NY 10023. We do not accept any free-lance work.

KIDS TRIBUTE—71 Barber Greene Rd., Don Mills, Ont., Canada M3C 2A2. Doug Wallace, Ed. Quarterly. Movie- or entertainment-related articles, 500 words, for 8- to 13-year-olds. Pays $150 to $200 (Canadian), on acceptance. Query required.

KIDS' WALL STREET NEWS: THE NEWS AND FINANCIAL PUBLICATION FOR THE YOUTH OF OUR WORLD—P.O. Box 1207, Rancho Santa Fe, CA 92067. Attn: Ed. Bimonthly. Departments include "Adventure, Sports Arena," "Think about This," "Money & Banking," among others. Articles to 500 words. Submit material on a Mac format disk, with hard copy. Photos, graphs, and artwork. Payment is made on publication.

KIDZ CHAT—(formerly *R-A-D-A-R*) Standard Publishing, 8121 Hamilton Ave., Cincinnati, OH 45231. Gary Thacker, Ed. Weekly Sunday school take-home paper. Articles, 225 words, on animals and the environment. Fiction, 475 words, dealing with Sunday school lesson themes with 8- to 10-year-old as main character. Pays 5¢ to 7¢ a word, on acceptance. SASE for guidelines and themes.

LADYBUG—P.O. Box 300, Peru, IL 61354-0300. Marianne Carus, Ed.-in-Chief. Paula Morrow, Ed. Picture stories and read-aloud stories, 300 to 750 words, for 2- to 6-year-olds; poetry, to 20 lines; songs and action rhymes; crafts, activities, and games. Pays 25¢ a word for stories; $3 a line for poetry, on publication. Guidelines.

LAX MAG FOR KIDS—U.S. Lacrosse, 113 West University Parkway, Baltimore, MD 21210. Victoria Morehead, Ed. Aimed at 6- to 15-year olds. Articles, 2 to 3 pages; short stories; poetry; fillers of varying lengths; photographs; and drawings. All material must pertain to lacrosse. Pays varying rates, on publication. Query.

MUSE—The Cricket Magazine Group, 332 S. Michigan Ave., Suite 1100, Chicago, IL 60604. Submissions Ed. Ten times a year. Articles, 1,000 to 2,500 words, on problems connected with a discipline or area of practical knowledge, for children ages 8 to 14. Guidelines. Query with resumé, writing samples, list of possible topics, and SASE. Pays 50¢ a word, within 60 days of acceptance.

MY FRIEND—Pauline Books & Media, Daughters of St. Paul, 50 St. Pauls Ave., Boston, MA 02130. Sister Kathryn James Hermes, Ed. "The Catholic Magazine for Kids." Fun stories, 150 to 900 words, with Christian values for 6- to 12-years-olds. Buys first rights. Pays $35 to $100 for stories, $5 for fillers. Query for artwork. Guidelines.

NATIONAL GEOGRAPHIC WORLD—1145 17th St. N.W., Washington, DC 20036-4688. Susan Tejada, Ed. Picture magazine for young readers, ages 8 and older. Natural history, adventure, archaeology, geography, science, the environment, and human interest. Proposals for picture stories only. No unsolicited manuscripts.

NATURE FRIEND—2727 TR 421, Sugarcreek, OH 44681. Stanley K. Brubaker, Ed. Monthly. Articles for children that "increase their awareness of God; teach them to be kind to animals, plants, and nature; and illustrate spiritual lessons." Also publishes some poetry, fillers, and games. Pays 5¢ per word for articles; $15 for games and fillers. SASE for guidelines.

NEW MOON, THE MAGAZINE FOR GIRLS AND THEIR DREAMS—P.O. Box 3620, Duluth, MN 55803-3620. Deb Mylin, Bridget Grosser, Man. Eds. "Our goal is to celebrate girls and support their efforts to hang on to their voices, strengths, and dreams as they move from being girls to becoming women." Profiles of girls and women, 300 to 1,000 words. Science and math experiments, 300 to 600 words. Submissions from both girls and women. Queries preferred. Pays 6¢ to 12¢ a word, on publication. Also publishes companion newsletter, *New Moon Network: For Adults Who Care About Girls.*

ODYSSEY: ADVENTURES IN SCIENCE—(formerly *Odyssey: Science That's Out of This World*) Cobblestone Publishing, 30 Grove St., Suite C, Peterborough, NH 03458. Elizabeth Lindstrom, Ed. Features, 750 to 1,000 words, on science and technology, for 10 to 16-year-olds. Science-related fiction, myths, legends, and science fiction stories. Activities. Pays 20¢ to 25¢ a word, on publication. Guidelines and themes.

ON THE LINE—616 Walnut, Scottdale, PA 15683-1999. Mary Clemens Meyer, Ed. Monthly magazine for 9- to 14-year-olds. Nature, general nonfiction, and how-to articles, 350 to 500 words; fiction, 1,000 to 1,800 words; poetry, puzzles, cartoons. Pays to 5¢ a word, on acceptance.

OWL MAGAZINE—The Owl Group, Bayard Press, 179 John St., Suite 500, Toronto, Ont., Canada M5T 3G5. Elizabeth Siegel, Ed. Articles, 500 to 1,000 words, for 9- to 12-year-olds, about animals, science, people, technology, new discoveries, activities. Pays varying rates, on acceptance. Enclose $2.00 money order and SAE for reply. Guidelines.

PLAYS, THE DRAMA MAGAZINE FOR YOUNG PEOPLE—120 Boylston St., Boston, MA 02116-4615. Elizabeth Preston, Man. Ed. Wholesome one-act comedies, dramas, skits, satires, farces, and creative dramatic material suitable for school productions at junior high, middle, and lower grade levels. Plays with modern settings preferred. Also uses dramatized classics, folktales and fairy tales, puppet plays. No religious plays or musicals. Pays good rates, on acceptance. Buys all rights. Query for classics, folk and fairy tales. Guidelines.

POCKETS—1908 Grand Ave., Box 189, Nashville, TN 37202-0189. Janet Knight, Ed. Ecumenical magazine for 6- to 12-year-olds. Fiction and scripture stories, 600 to 1,500 words; short poems; games and family communication activities; role model stories; and stories about children involved in justice and environmental projects. Pays from 14¢ a word, $2 per line for poetry, on acceptance. Guidelines and themes. Annual fiction contest; send SASE for details. Website: www.upperroom.org/pockets

POWER AND LIGHT—6401 The Paseo, Kansas City, MO 64131. Beula J. Postlewait, Preteen Ed. Fiction, 500 to 800 words, for grades 5 and 6, with Christian emphasis. Pays 5¢ a word for multi-use rights, 1³/₄¢ a word for reprints. Pays $15 for cartoons and puzzles.

R-A-D-A-R—See *Kidz Chat.*

RANGER RICK—National Wildlife Federation, 8925 Leesburg Pike, Vienna, VA 22184. Gerald Bishop, Ed. Photographers and artists wishing to send unsolicited portfolios should first write for photo and art guidelines. No unsolicited article queries or manuscripts.

SCIENCEWORLD—Scholastic, Inc., 555 Broadway, New York, NY 10012-3999. Mark Bregman, Ed. Science articles, 750 words, and news articles, 200 words, on life science, earth science, physical science, technology, environmental science and/or health for readers in grades 7 to 10 (ages 12 to 15). "Articles should include current, exciting science news. Writing should be lively and show an understanding of teens' perspectives and interests." Pays $100 to $125 for news items; $200 to $650 for features. Query with a well-researched proposal, suggested sources, 2 to 3 clips of your work, and an SASE.

SHOFAR—43 Northcote Dr., Melville, NY 11747. Gerald H. Grayson, Ed. Short stories, 500 to 1,000 words; articles, 500 to 1,000 words; poetry, to 50 lines; short fillers, games, puzzles, and cartoons for Jewish children, 9 to 13. All material must have a Jewish theme. Pays 10¢ a word, on publication. Submit holiday pieces at least 6 months in advance.

SKIPPING STONES—P.O. Box 3939, Eugene, OR 97403. Arun N. Toké, Exec. Ed. "A Multicultural Children's Magazine." Articles, approximately 500 to 750 words, relating to relationships (support groups, networking and community), cross cultural communications and living abroad, humor unlimited, religions, nature, traditions, and cultural celebrations in other countries, for 8- to 16-year-olds. "Especially invited to submit are youth from diverse backgrounds. We print art, poetry, songs, games, stories, and photographs from around the world and include many different languages (with English translation)." Payment is one copy, on publication. Annual Youth Honor Awards; send SASE for guidelines. Query for upcoming themes.

SOCCER JR.—27 Unquowa Rd., Fairfield, CT 06430. Joe Provey, Ed. Fiction and fillers about soccer for readers ages 8 and up. Pays $450 for a feature or story; $250 for department pieces, on acceptance. Query.

SPIDER—Carus Publishing Co. P.O. Box 300, Peru, IL 61354. Attn: Submissions Ed. Fiction, 300 to 1,000 words, for 6- to 9-year-olds: realistic, easy-to-read stories, fantasy, folk and fairy tales, science fiction, fables, myths. Articles, 300 to 800 words, on nature, animals, science, technology, environment, foreign culture, history (include short bibliography with articles). Serious, humorous, or nonsense poetry, to 20 lines. Puzzles, activities, and games, to 4 pages. Pays 25¢ a word, $3 per line for poetry, on publication.

SPORTS ILLUSTRATED FOR KIDS—Time & Life Bldg., 1271 Ave. of the Americas, New York, NY 10020. Stephen Malley, Deputy Man. Ed. Articles, 1,000 words, (submit to Bob Der) and short features, 500 to 600 words, (submit to Nick Friedman) for 8- to 13-year-olds. "Most articles are staff-written. Department pieces are the best bet for free lancers." Read magazine and guidelines to learn about specific departments. Puzzles and games (submit to Nick Friedman). No fiction or poetry. Pays $500 for departments, $1,000 to $1,250 for articles, on acceptance. Query required.

STONE SOUP, THE MAGAZINE BY YOUNG WRITERS AND ARTISTS—Box 83, Santa Cruz, CA 95063-0083. Gerry Mandel, Ed. Stories, free-verse poems, plays, book reviews by children under 14. "Preference given to writing based on real-life experiences." Pays $25. Web site: www.stonesoup. com.

STORY FRIENDS—Mennonite Publishing House, Scottdale, PA 15683. Rose Stutzman, Ed. Stories, 350 to 800 words, for 4- to 9-year-olds, on Christian faith and values in everyday experiences. Poetry. Pays to 5¢ a word, to $10 per poem, on acceptance.

SUPERSCIENCE—Scholastic, Inc., 555 Broadway, New York, NY 10012. Attn: Ed. Science news and hands-on experiments for grades 4 through 6. Article topics are staff-generated and assigned to writers; send resumé and children's and science writing clips. Include large SASE for editorial calendar and sample issue. Pays $50 to $650, on acceptance.

SURPRISES—1200 N. 7th St., Minneapolis, MN 55411. Tim Drake, Ed. Bimonthly. Articles, 50 to 250 words, for readers 5 to 11. Puzzles, games, artwork. Pays $25 to $100, on publication.

TOUCH—Box 7259, Grand Rapids, MI 49510. Carol Smith, Man. Ed. Upbeat fiction and features, 500 to 1,000 words, for Christian girls ages 8 to 14; personal life, nature, crafts. Puzzles. Pays 2½¢ a word, extra for photos, on publication. Query with SASE for theme update.

TURTLE MAGAZINE FOR PRESCHOOL KIDS—1100 Waterway Blvd., Box 567, Indianapolis, IN 46206. Terry Harshman, Ed. Heavily illustrated articles with an emphasis on health and nutrition for 2- to 5-year-olds. Humorous, entertaining fiction. Also, crafts, recipes, activities, and simple science experiments. Simple poems. Action rhymes and read-aloud stories, to 300 words. Pays to 22¢ a word for stories; from $25 for poems; payment varies for activities. Pays on publication. Buys all rights. Send SASE for guidelines.

U.S. KIDS, A WEEKLY READER MAGAZINE—P.O. Box 567, Indianapolis, IN 46206. Nancy S. Axelrad, Ed. Articles, 500 words, for readers 6 to 9, on real children involved in health, fitness, sports, nutrition activities. Also interested in kids' community efforts, fun hobbies, science, nature, etc. Fiction, 500 words (no fantasy); some poetry.

WILD OUTDOOR WORLD—Box 1329, Helena, MT 59624. Carolyn Cunningham, Ed. Dir. Articles, 600 to 800 words, on North American wildlife, for readers ages 8 to 12. Pays $100 to $300, on acceptance. Query.

YOUNG JUDEAN—50 W. 58th St., New York, NY 10019. Edie Schaffron, Ed. Quarterly. Articles, 500 to 1,000 words, with photos, for 9- to 12-year-olds, on Israel, Jewish holidays, Jewish-American life, Jewish history. Fiction, 500 to 1,000 words, on Jewish themes. Fillers, humor, reviews. No payment.

ZILLIONS—Consumers Union of the United States, 101 Truman Ave., Yonkers, NY 10703-9925. Karen McNulty, Man. Ed. Bimonthly. Articles, up to 1,000 words, on consumer education (money, product testing, health, etc.), for kids ages 8 to 12. "We are the *Consumer Reports* for kids." Pays $500 to $2,000, on publication. Guidelines.

YOUNG ADULT MAGAZINES

ALIVE NOW!—P.O. Box 189, Nashville, TN 37202. Attn: Ed. Short essays, 250 to 400 words, with Christian emphasis for adults and young adults. Poetry, one page. B&W photos. Pays $20 to $30, on publication. Query with SASE for themes.

ALL ABOUT YOU—6420 Wilshire Blvd., Los Angeles, CA 90048-5515. Roxanne Camron, Ed. Dir. Beth Mayall, Ed. Articles, 1,000 to 1,500 words, on issues of interest to middle school girls. Payment varies, on acceptance. Queries.

BOYS' LIFE—1325 W. Walnut Hill Ln., P.O. Box 152079, Irving, TX 75015-2079. Published monthly by the Boy Scouts of America. Articles and fiction, 500 to 1,500 words, for 8- to 18-year-old boys. Pays from $350 for major articles, $750 for fiction, on acceptance. Query for articles; send complete manuscript for fiction. SASE.

CAMPUS LIFE—465 Gundersen Dr., Carol Stream, IL 60188. Chris Lutes, Ed. Articles reflecting Christian values and world view, for high school and college students. Humor, general fiction, and true, first-person experiences. "If we have a choice of fiction, how-to, and a strong first-person story, we'll go with the true story every time." Photo-essays, cartoons. Pays 15¢ to 20¢ a word, on acceptance. Query.

CICADA—P.O. Box 300, Peru, IL 61354. Submissions Ed. Bimonthly literary magazine. Nonfiction personal experience with coming-of-age theme, 2,000 to 5,000 words; realistic, contemporary, historical fiction, science fiction, fantasy, and humor, 2,000 to 15,000 words; poetry, to 25 lines; and book reviews, to 700 words. Send complete manuscript with SASE. Guidelines available. Pays to 25¢ per word for prose and $3 per line for poetry, on publication.

COLLEGE BOUND—See *Go Girl.*

CRACKED—Globe Communications, Inc., 3 E. 54th St., 15 Fl., New York, NY 10022-3108. Lou Silverstone, Andy Simmons, Eds. Cartoon humor, one to 5 pages, for 10- to 15-year-old readers. Cartoons/comic book style work; no short stories or poetry. "Read magazine before submitting." Pays $100 per page, on acceptance.

GO GIRL—Ramholtz Publishing, Inc., 2071 Clove Rd., Suite 206, Staten Island, NY 10304. Gina La Guardia, Ed. Published as an annual supplement to *College Bound.* Articles, 100 to 400 words, addressing the social and academic needs of adolescent females, including academic, fitness, beauty, and fashion topics. Send SASE for guidelines. Queries preferred. Pays $15 to $100, 30 days after publication. Web site: www.go-girl.com.

GUIDEPOSTS FOR TEENS—P.O. Box 638, Chesterton, IN 46304. Tanya Dean, Man. Ed. Bimonthly. "Value-centered" fiction and articles. First-person true stories about teens in dangerous, miraculous, and inspiring situations, 700 to 1,500 words. How-to pieces, 750 to 1,000 words; quizzes and humor with a spiritual point, 250 to 750 words. Queries preferred; send SASE for guidelines. Pays $25 to $100 for fillers and $175 to $500 for stories and departments, on acceptance. E-mail: gp4t@guideposts.org

JUMP: FOR GIRLS WHO DARE TO BE REAL—Weider Publications, Inc., 21100 Erwin St., Woodland Hills, CA 91367. Submissions. Published ten times yearly. Feature articles, 1,500 to 2,500 words, and columns, 600 to 800 words, on topics of interest to teen girls: new products, food and nutrition, sports, health, outrageous trends, and personal experience. Web site: www.jumponline.com

KEYNOTER—3636 Woodview Trace, Indianapolis, IN 46268. Julie A. Carson, Exec. Ed. Articles, 1,300 to 1,500 words, for high school leaders: general-interest features; self-help; contemporary teenage problems. No fillers, poetry, first-person accounts, or fiction. Pays $150 to $350, on acceptance. Query preferred.

LAX MAG FOR KIDS—U.S. Lacrosse, 113 West University Parkway, Baltimore, MD 21210. Victoria Morehead, Ed. Aimed at 6- to 15-year olds. Articles, 2 to 3 pages; short stories; poetry; fillers of varying lengths; photographs; and drawings. All material must pertain to lacrosse. Pays varying rates, on publication. Query.

LISTEN MAGAZINE—55 W. Oak Ridge Dr., Hagerstown, MD 21740. Lincoln Steed, Ed. Articles, 1,200 to 1,500 words, providing teens with "a vigorous, positive, educational approach to the problems arising from the use of tobacco, alcohol, and other drugs." Pays $30 to $200, on acceptance.

THE LOOK—P.O. Box 272, Cranford, NJ 07016-0272. John R. Hawks, Pub. Articles, 1,500 to 3,000 words, on fashion, student life, employment, relationships, and profiles of interest to local (NJ) readers ages 16 to 26. Also, beach stories and articles about the New Jersey shore. Pays $30 to $200, on publication.

MERLYN'S PEN: FICTION, ESSAYS, AND POEMS BY AMERICA'S TEENS—P.O. Box 1058, Dept. WR, East Greenwich, RI 02818. R. James Stahl, Ed. Writing by students in grades 6 through 12. Short stories and essays, to 5,000 words; reviews; travel pieces; and poetry, to 200 lines. Responds in 10 weeks. Pays $20 to $200, plus copies. Guidelines.

NEW ERA—50 E. North Temple, Salt Lake City, UT 84150. Richard M. Romney, Ed. Articles, 150 to 1,500 words, and fiction, to 2,000 words, for young Mormons. Poetry. Photos. Pays 5¢ to 20¢ a word, 25¢ a line for poetry, on acceptance. Query.

REACT—Parade Publications, 711 Third Ave., New York, NY 10017. Attn: Man. Ed. Weekly. Articles, to 800 words, on national and international news, entertainment, sports, social issues related to teenagers, and profiles of notable young people for readers 12 to 17. Payment varies, on acceptance. Query with related clips.

SCHOLASTIC UPDATE—555 Broadway, New York, NY 10012-3999. Herbert Buchsbaum, Ed. Biweekly. News articles, 500 words or 1,000 to 1,500 words, for teenagers. Pays $150 to $1,000, on acceptance. Send SASE for guidelines before querying.

SCIENCE WORLD—Scholastic, Inc., 555 Broadway, New York, NY 10012-3999. Attn: Eds. Articles, 750 words, on life science, earth science, physical science, environmental science, or health science for 7th to 10th graders (ages 12 to 15). Science news pieces, 200 words. Submit well-researched proposal, including suggested sources, 2 to 3 clips of your work, and SASE. Pays $100 to $125 for news items; $200 to $650 for features.

SEVENTEEN—850 Third Ave., New York, NY 10022. Susan Brenna, Features Ed. Articles, to 2,500 words, on subjects of interest to teenagers. Sophisticated, well-written fiction, 1,000 to 4,000 words, for young adults. Personal essays, to 1,200 words, by writers 23 and younger for "Voice." Pays varying rates, on acceptance.

SISTERS IN STYLE—233 Park Ave. S., 5th Fl., New York, NY 10003. Cynthia Marie Horner, Ed. Dir. Bimonthly. "For Today's Young Black Woman." Beauty and fashion articles, quizzes, and advice for African-American teens. No fiction or poetry. Payment varies, on publication. Query.

STRAIGHT—8121 Hamilton Ave., Cincinnati, OH 45231. Heather E. Wallace, Ed. Articles on current situations and issues for Christian teens. Humor. Well-constructed fiction, 1,000 to 1,500 words, showing teens using Christian principles. Poetry by teenagers. Photos. Pays about 5¢ to 7¢ a word, on acceptance. Guidelines.

'TEEN—6420 Wilshire Blvd., Los Angeles, CA 90048-5515. Attn: Ed. Short stories, 2,500 to 4,000 words: mystery, teen situations, adventure, romance, humor for teens. Pays from $250 to $450, on acceptance. Buys all rights.

TEEN LIFE—1445 Boonville Ave., Springfield, MO 65802-1894. Tammy Bicket, Ed. Not currently accepting material. Articles, 500 to 1,000 words, and fiction, to 1,200 words, for 13- to 19-year-olds; strong evangelical emphasis. Interviews with Christian athletes and other well-known Christians; true stories; up-to-date factual articles. Send SASE for current topics. Pays on acceptance.

TEEN VOICES—P.O. Box 120-027, Boston, MA 02112-0027. Shannon Berning, Man. Ed. Quarterly. Fiction and nonfiction, 200 to 400 words; and poetry, any length. Submissions by teenage girls only. Photo of writer and short bio preferred. Pays in copies.

TIGER BEAT—Sterling/MacFadden Partnership, 233 Park Ave. S., New York, NY 10003. Louise Barile, Ed. Articles, to 4 pages, on young people in show business and the music industry. Pays varying rates, on acceptance. Query.

WHAT! A MAGAZINE—108-93 Lombard Ave., Winnipeg, Manitoba, Canada R3B 3B1. Stuart Slayen and Leslie Malkin, Eds. Published 5 times a year and distributed in high schools. Articles, 650 to 2,000 words, on contemporary issues for teenage readers. Pays $100 to $500 (Canadian), on publication. Queries preferred.

YM—685 Third Ave., New York, NY 10017. Maria Baugh, Man. Ed. Articles, to 2,500 words, on entertainment, lifestyle, fashion, beauty, relationships, health, for women ages 14 to 19. Payment varies, on acceptance. Query with clips.

YOU!—29963 Mulholland Hwy., Agoura Hills, CA 91301. Attn: Submissions Ed. Articles, 200 to 1,000 words, on topics related to teenagers, especially moral issues, faith, and contemporary pop culture viewed from the Catholic/Christian perspective. No payment.

YOUNG AND ALIVE—4444 S. 52nd St., Lincoln, NE 68506. Richard J. Kaiser, Man. Ed. Gaylena Gibson, Ed. Quarterly. Feature articles, 800 to 1,400 words, for blind and visually impaired young adults on adventure, biography, camping, careers, health, history, hobbies, holidays, marriage, nature, practical Christianity, sports, and travel. Photos. Pays 3¢ to 5¢ a word, $5 to $20 for photos, on acceptance. Guidelines.

YOUNG SALVATIONIST—The Salvation Army, 615 Slaters Ln., P.O. Box 269, Alexandria, VA 22313. Attn: Tim Clark, Man. Ed. Articles for teens, 600 to 1,200 words, with Christian perspective; fiction, 800 to 1,200 words; short fillers. Pays 10¢ to 15¢ a word, on acceptance.

YOUTH UPDATE—*St. Anthony Messenger Press,* 1615 Republic St., Cincinnati, OH 45210. Attn: Ed. Articles on timely topics for Catholic teens. Avoid cuteness, glib phrases and clichés, academic or erudite approaches, preachiness. Pays 15¢ a word, on acceptance. Query with outline and SASE.

THE DRAMA MARKET

Community, regional, and civic theaters and college dramatic groups offer the best opportunities today for playwrights to see their work produced, whether on the stage or in dramatic readings. Indeed, aspiring playwrights will be encouraged to hear that many well-known playwrights received their first recognition in the regional theaters. Payment is generally nominal, but regional and university theaters usually buy only the right to produce a play, and all further rights revert to the author. Since most directors like to work closely with authors on any revisions necessary, theaters will often pay the playwright's expenses while in residence during rehearsals. The thrill of seeing your play come to life on the stage is one of the pleasures of being on hand for rehearsals and performances. In addition to producing plays and giving dramatic readings, many theaters also sponsor competitions or new play festivals.

Aspiring playwrights should query college and community theaters in their region to find out which ones are interested in seeing original scripts. Dramatic associations of interest to playwrights include the Dramatists Guild (1501 Broadway, Suite 701, New York, NY 10036), and Theatre Communications Group, Inc. (355 Lexington Ave., New York, NY 10017), which publishes the annual *Dramatists Sourcebook. The Playwright's Companion,* published by Feedback Theatrebooks (305 Madison Ave., Suite 1146, New York, NY 10165), is an annual directory of theaters, play publishers, and prize contests seeking scripts. See the *Organizations for Writers* list for details on dramatists' associations.

Some of the theaters on this list require that playwrights submit all or some of the following with scripts—cast list, synopsis, resumé, recommendations, return postcard—and with scripts and queries, SASEs must always be enclosed.

While the almost unlimited television offerings on commercial, educational, and cable TV stations, in addition to the hundreds of films released yearly, may lead free-lance writers to believe that opportunities to sell movie and television scripts are infinite, unfortunately, this is not true. With few exceptions, TV and film producers and programmers will read scripts and queries submitted only through recognized agents. (For a list of agents, see page 876.) Writers who want to try their hand at writing directly for this very limited market should be prepared to learn the special techniques and acceptable format of scriptwriting, either by taking a workshop through a university or at a writers conference, or by reading one or more of the many books that have been written on this subject. Also, experience in playwriting and knowledge of dramatic structure gained through working in amateur, community, or professional theaters can be helpful.

REGIONAL & UNIVERSITY THEATERS

ACTORS THEATRE OF LOUISVILLE—316 W. Main St., Louisville, KY 40202. Michael Bigelow Dixon, Lit. Mgr. Ten-minute comedies and dramas, to 10 pages. Longer one-act and full-length plays accepted from literary agents, and from playwrights with letter of recommendation from another professional theatre. SASE. Annual contest. Guidelines.

ACTORS' PLAYHOUSE AT THE MIRACLE THEATRE—280 Miracle Mile, Coral Gables, FL 33134. One-act musicals, children's plays, adaptations, and bilingual material (Spanish/English). Maximum 8 actors to play any number of roles; suitable for touring. Enclose resumé, recommendations, cast list, synopsis, and score or lead sheet, with vocal tape. Allow 3 to 6 months for response. Pay is made following production and is negotiable. Submit to Earl Maulding.

A. D. PLAYERS—2710 W. Alabama, Houston, TX 77098. Attn: Lit. Mgr. Jeannette Clift George, Artistic Dir. Full-length or one-act comedies, dramas, musicals, children's plays, and adaptations with Christian world view. Submit scripts and cast list with SASE. Readings. Pays negotiable rates.

ALABAMA SHAKESPEARE FESTIVAL—The State Theatre, 1 Festival Dr., Montgomery, AL 36117-4605. Lit. Mgr. Full-length scripts with southern and/or African-American themes, issues, or history; and scripts with southern and/or African-American authors. One work per author; query.

ALLIANCE THEATRE COMPANY—1280 Peachtree St. N.E., Atlanta, GA 30309. Attn: Lit. Dept. Dramas, comedies, and musicals, especially those that speak to a culturally diverse community; plays with compelling stories and engaging characters, told in adventurous or stylish ways. No unsolicited manuscripts or telephone inquiries. Letter of inquiry with synopsis and no more than 10 pages of sample dialogue accepted only with SASE for reply.

AMERICAN LITERATURE THEATRE PROJECT—Fountain Theatre, 5060 Fountain Ave., Los Angeles, CA 90029. Simon Levy, Prod. Dramaturg. One-act and full-length stage adaptations of classic and contemporary American literature. Sets and cast size are unrestricted. Send synopsis and SAS postcard. Rate of payment is standard, as set by the Dramatists Guild.

AMERICAN LIVING HISTORY THEATER—P.O. Box 752, Greybull, WY 82426. Dorene Ludwig, Artistic Dir. One-act, (one or 2 characters preferred) historically accurate (primary source materials only) dramas dealing with marketable American historical and literary characters and events. Submit treatment and letter with SASE. Responds within 6 months. Pays varying rates.

AMERICAN PLACE THEATRE—111 W. 46th St., New York, NY 10036. Martin Blank, Artistic Assoc. "No unsolicited manuscripts accepted.

Agent submission only. We seek challenging, innovative works and do not favor obviously commercial material."

AMERICAN THEATRE OF ACTORS—314 W. 54th St., New York, NY 10019. James Jennings, Artistic Dir. Full-length dramas for a cast of 2 to 6. Submit complete play and SASE. Reports in one to 2 months.

ARENA STAGE—1101 Sixth St. S.W., Washington, DC 20024. Cathy Madison, Lit. Mgr. No unsolicited manuscripts; send synopsis, 10 pages of dialogue, bio, and reviews if available. Currently looking for American settings and themes.

ARKANSAS REPERTORY THEATRE COMPANY—601 S. Main, P.O. Box 110, Little Rock, AR 72203-0110. Brad Mooy, Lit. Mgr. Full-length comedies, dramas, and musicals; prefer up to 8 characters. Send synopsis, cast list, resumé, and return postage; do not send complete manuscript. Reports in 3 months.

BARTER THEATER—P.O. Box 867, Abingdon, VA 24212-0867. Richard Rose, Artistic Dir. Full-length dramas, comedies, adaptations, and children's plays. Submit synopsis, dialogue sample, and SASE. Allow 6 to 8 months for report. Royalty policies consistent with industry standard.

BERKSHIRE THEATRE FESTIVAL—Box 797, Stockbridge, MA 01262. Kate Maguire, Producing Dir. Full-length comedies, musicals, and dramas; cast to 8. Submit through agent only.

BOARSHEAD THEATER—425 S. Grand Ave., Lansing, MI 48933. John Peakes, Artistic Dir. Full-length comedies and dramas with simple sets and cast of up to 10. Send precis, 5 to 10 pages of dialogue, cast list with descriptions, and SAS postcard for reply; do not send complete manuscript.

BRISTOL RIVERSIDE THEATRE—Box 1250, Bristol, PA 19007. Susan D. Atkinson, Producing/Artistic Dir. Full-length plays with up to 15 actors and a simple set.

CALIFORNIA UNIVERSITY THEATRE—California, PA 15419. Dr. Richard J. Helldobler, Chairman. Unusual, avant-garde, and experimental one-act and full-length comedies and dramas, children's plays, and adaptations. Cast size varies. Submit synopsis with short, sample scene(s). Payment available.

CENTER STAGE—700 N. Calvert St., Baltimore, MD 21202. James Magruder, Resident Dramaturg. Full-length comedies, dramas, translations, adaptations. No unsolicited manuscripts. Send synopsis, a few sample pages, resumé, cast list, and production history. Allow 8 to 10 weeks for reply.

CHILDSPLAY, INC.—Box 517, Tempe, AZ 85280. David Saar, Artistic Dir. Multigenerational plays running 45 to 120 minutes: dramas, musicals, and adaptations for family audiences. Productions may need to travel. Submissions accepted July through December. Send synopsis and 10-page dialogue sample. Reports in 2 to 6 months.

CIRCLE IN THE SQUARE/UPTOWN—1633 Broadway, New York, NY 10019-6795. Michael Breault, Artistic Assoc. Accepts agented material only. SASE.

CITY THEATRE COMPANY—57 S. 13th St., Pittsburgh, PA 15203. Literary Dept. Full-length cutting-edge comedies and dramas; especially interested in women and minorities. Cast to 10; simple sets. Query September to May. Royalty.

CLASSIC STAGE COMPANY—136 E. 13th St., New York, NY 10003. Barry Edelstein, Artistic Dir. Celise Kalke, Literary Assoc. Produces full-length translations and adaptations of classic literature. Submit synopsis with cast list and ten pages of sample dialogue. No unsolicited scripts.

THE CONSERVATORY THEATRE ENSEMBLE—c/o Tamalpais High School, 700 Miller Ave., Mill Valley, CA 94941. Susan Brashear, Artistic Dir. Comedies, dramas, children's plays, adaptations, and scripts addressing high school issues for largely female cast (about 3 women per man). "One-act plays of approximately 30 minutes are especially needed, as we produce 50 short plays each season using teenage actors." Send synopsis and resumé.

CROSSROADS THEATRE CO.—7 Livingston Ave., New Brunswick, NJ 08901. Ricardo Khan, Artistic Dir. Full-length and one-act dramas, comedies, musicals, and adaptations; issue-oriented experimental plays that offer honest, imaginative, and insightful examinations of the African-American experience. Also interested in African and Caribbean plays and plays exploring cross-cultural issues. No unsolicited scripts; queries only, with synopsis, cast list, resumé, and SASE.

DELAWARE THEATRE COMPANY—200 Water St., Wilmington, DE 19801-5030. Cleveland Morris, Artistic Dir. Full-length comedies, dramas, and musicals. Prefer cast of no more than 10. SASE required. Reports in 6 months. No longer accepting unsolicited manuscripts, except from local authors. Agent submissions in the form of synopses or letters of inquiries will be considered. The "Connections" competition has been suspended for the time being.

DENVER CENTER THEATRE COMPANY—1050 13th St., Denver, CO 80204. Bruce K. Sevy, Assoc. Artistic Dir./New Play Development. New play festival in June. Primus prize to female playwright. Send SASE; request guidelines and information. Note: deadlines changing.

DETROIT REPERTORY THEATRE—13103 Woodrow Wilson Ave., Detroit, MI 48238. Barbara Busby, Lit. Mgr. Full-length comedies and dramas. Scripts accepted October to April. Enclose SASE. Pays royalty.

STEVE DOBBINS PRODUCTIONS—650 Geary Blvd., San Francisco, CA 94102. Alan Ramos, Lit. Dir. Full-length comedies, dramas, and musicals. Cast of up to 12. Query with synopsis and resumé. No unsolicited manuscripts. Reports in 6 months. Offers workshops and readings. Pays 4% to 6% of gross.

DORSET THEATRE FESTIVAL—Box 519, Dorset, VT 05251. Jill Charles, Artistic Dir. Accepts queries or scripts from resident writers only. Residencies at Dorset Colony House for Writers available September to November, March to May; inquire. E-mail: theatre@sover.net. Web site: www.theatredirectories.com.

EAST WEST PLAYERS—244 S. San Pedro St., # 301, Los Angeles, CA 90012. Tim Dang, Artistic Dir. Ken Narasaki, Lit. Mgr. Produces 4 to 5 new plays annually. Original plays, translations, adaptations, musicals, and youth theater, "all of which must illuminate the Asian or Asian-American experience, or resonate in a significant fashion if cast with Asian-American actors." Readings. Prefer to see query letter with synopsis and 10 pages of dialogue; complete scripts also considered. Reports in 5 to 6 weeks for query; 6 months for complete script.

ENSEMBLE STUDIO THEATRE—549 W. 52nd St., New York, NY

10019. Attn: Lit. Mgr. Send full-length or one-act comedies and dramas with resumé and SASE, September to April. Specializing in developmental theatre.

FLORIDA STUDIO THEATRE—1241 N. Palm Ave., Sarasota, FL 33577. Chris Angermann, New Play Development. Innovative plays with universal themes. Query with synopsis and SASE. Also accepting musicals and musical revues.

WILL GEER THEATRICUM BOTANICUM—Box 1222, Topanga, CA 90290. Attn: Lit. Dir. All types of scripts for outdoor theater, with large playing area. Submit synopsis with SASE. Pays varying rates.

THE GOODMAN THEATRE—200 S. Columbus Dr., Chicago, IL 60603. Susan V. Booth, Lit. Mgr. Queries from recognized literary agents or producing organizations required for full-length comedies or dramas. No unsolicited scripts.

THE GUTHRIE THEATER—725 Vineland Pl., Minneapolis, MN 55403. Attn: Lit. Dept. Full-length dramas and adaptations of world literature, classic masterworks, oral traditions, and folktales. No unsolicited scripts; send query with synopsis, resumé, professional recommendation, and SASE. Reports in 3 to 4 months.

HIPPODROME STATE THEATRE—25 S.E. Second Pl., Gainesville, FL 32601. Tamerin Dygert, Dramaturg. Full-length plays with unit sets and casts of up to 8. Agent submissions and professional recommendations only; no unsolicited material. Submissions accepted May through August. Send synopsis only, with reviews and professional recommendation.

HOLLYWOOD THESPIAN COMPANY—12838 Kling St., Studio City, CA 91604-1127. Rai Tasco, Artistic Dir. Full-length comedies and dramas for integrated cast. Include cast list and SAS postcard with submission.

HORIZON THEATRE COMPANY—P. O. Box 5376, Station E, Atlanta, GA 31107. Jeff and Lisa Adler, Artistic Dirs. Full-length comedies, dramas, and satires. Encourages submissions by women writers. Cast of no more than 10. Submit synopsis with cast list, resumé, and recommendations. Pays percentage. Readings. Reports in 6 months.

HUNTINGTON THEATRE COMPANY—264 Huntington Ave., Boston, MA 02115-4606. Scott Edmiston, Lit. Assoc. Full-length comedies and dramas. Query with synopsis, cast list, and resumé.

ILLINOIS THEATRE CENTER—371 Artists' Walk, Park Forest, IL 60466. Attn: Producing Dir. Full-length comedies, dramas, musicals, and adaptations, for unit/fragmentary sets, and up to 8 cast members. Send summary and SAS postcard. No unsolicited manuscripts. Pays negotiable rates. Workshops and readings offered.

INVISIBLE THEATRE—1400 N. First Ave., Tucson, AZ 85719. Deborah Dickey, Lit. Mgr. Letter of introduction from theatre professional must accompany submissions for full-length comedies, dramas, musicals, and adaptations. Submit after October 2000. Cast of up to 10; simple set. Also one-act plays. Pays royalty.

JEWISH REPERTORY THEATRE—1395 Lexington Ave., New York, NY 10128. Ran Avni, Artistic Dir. Full-length comedies, dramas, musicals, and adaptations, with up to 10 cast members, relating to the Jewish experience. Pays varying rates. Enclose SASE.

KUMU KAHUA THEATRE, INC.—46 Merchant St., Honolulu, HI 96813. Harry Wong III, Artistic Dir. Full-length plays especially relevant to life in Hawaii. Prefer simple sets for arena and in-the-round productions. Submit resumé and synopsis January through April. Pays $50 per performance. Readings. Contests.

LIVE OAK THEATRE—See *State Theater Company.*

LOS ANGELES DESIGNERS' THEATRE—P.O. Box 1883, Studio City, CA 91614-0883. Richard Niederberg, Artistic Dir. Full-length comedies, dramas, musicals, fantasies, or adaptations. Religious, political, social, and controversial themes encouraged. Nudity, "adult" language, etc., O.K. "Please detail in the cover letter what the writer's proposed involvement with the production would be beyond the usual. Do not submit material that needs to be returned." Send proposals; not scripts. Payment varies. E-mail: LADESIGNERS@Juno.com.

THE MAGIC THEATRE—Fort Mason Ctr., Bldg. D, San Francisco, CA 94123. Kent Nicholson, Lit. Mgr. Comedies and dramas. "Special interest in political, non-linear, and multicultural work for mainstage productions." Query with synopsis, resumé, first 10 to 20 pages of script, and SASE; no unsolicited manuscripts. Pays varying rates.

MANHATTAN THEATRE CLUB—311 W. 43rd St., New York, NY 10036. Attn: Christian Parker Full-length and one-act comedies, dramas, and musicals. No unsolicited manuscripts or queries; agent submissions only.

METROSTAGE—P.O. Box 329, Alexandria, VA 22313. Carolyn Griffin, Prod. Art. Dir. Full-length comedies, dramas, and children's plays; casts of no more than 8. Send synopsis, 10 page dialogue sample, resumé, reading/production history, and return post card. Responds in 2 months.

MILL MOUNTAIN THEATRE—One Market Sq., Second Fl., Roanoke, VA 24011-1437. Literary Dept. One-act comedies and dramas, 25 to 35 minutes. For full-length plays, send letter, resumé, and synopsis. Send SASE for guidelines for new play competition. Payment varies.

MISSOURI REPERTORY THEATRE—4949 Cherry St., Kansas City, MO 64110. Felicia Londré, Dramaturg. Full-length comedies and dramas. Query with synopsis, cast list, resumé, and SAS postcard. Royalty. Allow 6 months for response. New scripts seldom produced.

MUSICAL THEATRE WORKS—440 Lafayette St., New York, NY 10003. Lonny Price, Art. Dir. Please call or write for submission guidelines.

NATIONAL BLACK THEATRE—2033 Fifth Ave., Harlem, NY 10035. Attn: Tunde Samuel. Drama, musicals, and children's plays. "Scripts should reflect African and African-American lifestyle. Historical, inspirational, and ritualistic forms appreciated." Workshops and readings.

NATIONAL PLAYWRIGHTS CONFERENCE, EUGENE O'NEILL THEATRE CENTER—234 W. 44th St., Suite 901, New York, NY 10036. Mary F. McCabe, Man. Dir. Annual competition to select new stage plays and teleplays/screenplays for development during the summer at organization's Waterford, CT, location. Submission deadline: December 1. Send #10-size SASE in the fall for guidelines. Pays stipend, plus travel/living expenses during conference.

NEW ENSEMBLE ACTORS THEATRE PROJECT OF SALT &

PEPPER MIME CO.—320 E. 90th St., #1B, New York, NY 10128. Ms. Scottie Davis, Dir. One-acts, all genres, conducive to "nontraditional" casting, surreal sets with mimetic concepts. One- or 4-person cast. Send resumé to 250 W. 65th St., New York, NY 10023. Scripts reviewed from May to December. Works also considered for readings, critiques, storyplayers, and experimental development. Logging fee/Application required.

NEW THEATRE, INC.—P.O. Box 173, Boston, MA 02117-0173. Attn: NEWorks Submissions Program. New full-length scripts for readings, workshop, and main stage productions. Include SASE.

NEW TUNERS/THE THEATRE BUILDING—1225 W. Belmont Ave., Chicago, IL 60657. John Sparks, Artistic Dir. Full-length musicals only, for cast to 15; no wing/fly space. Send query with brief synopsis, cassette tape of score, cast list, resumé, SASE, and SAS postcard. Pays on royalty basis.

NEW YORK STATE THEATRE INSTITUTE—155 River St., Troy, NY 12180. Attn: Patricia Di Benedetto Snyder, Producing Artistic Dir. Emphasis on new, full-length plays and musicals for family audiences. Query with synopsis and cast list. Payment varies.

ODYSSEY THEATRE ENSEMBLE—2055 S. Sepulveda Blvd., Los Angeles, CA 90025. Ron Sossi, Artistic Dir. Full-length comedies, dramas, musicals, and adaptations: provocative subject matter, or plays that stretch and explore the possibilities of theater. Query Sally Essex-Lopresti, Lit. Mgr., with synopsis, 8 to 10 pages of sample dialogue, and resumé. Pays variable rates. Allow 2 to 6 months for reply to script; 2 to 4 weeks for queries. Workshops and readings.

OLDCASTLE THEATRE COMPANY—Bennington Center for the Arts, P.O. Box 1555, Bennington, VT 05201. Eric Peterson, Dir. Full-length comedies, dramas, and musicals for a small cast (up to 10). Submit synopsis and cast list in the winter. Reports in 6 months. Offers workshops and readings. Pays expenses for playwright to attend rehearsals. Royalty.

PENGUIN REPERTORY COMPANY—Box 91, Stony Point, Rockland County, NY 10980. Joe Brancato, Artistic Dir. Full-length comedies and dramas with cast size to 5. Submit script, resumé, and SASE. Payment varies.

PEOPLE'S LIGHT AND THEATRE COMPANY—39 Conestoga Rd., Malvern, PA 19355. Alda Cortese, Lit. Mgr. Full-length comedies, dramas, adaptations. No unsolicited manuscripts; query with synopsis, and 10 pages of script. Reports in 6 months. Payment negotiable.

PIER ONE THEATRE—Box 894, Homer, AK 99603. Lance Petersen, Lit. Dir. Full-length and one-act comedies, dramas, musicals, children's plays, and adaptations. Submit complete script; include piano score with musicals. Pays 8% of ticket sales for mainstage musicals; other payment varies.

PLAYHOUSE ON THE SQUARE—51 S. Cooper in Overton Sq., Memphis, TN 38104. Jackie Nichols, Artistic Dir. Full-length comedies, dramas; cast of up to 15. Contest deadline is April for fall production. Pays $500.

PLAYWRIGHTS HORIZONS—416 W. 42nd St., New York, NY 10036. Address Literary Dept. Full-length, original comedies, dramas, and musicals by American authors. No one-acts or screenplays. Synopses discouraged; send script, resumé and SASE, include tape for musicals. Off Broadway contract.

PLAYWRIGHTS' PLATFORM—164 Brayton Rd., Boston, MA 02135. Attn: Lit. Dir. Script development workshops and public readings for New England playwrights only. Full-length and one-act plays of all kinds. No sexist or racist material. Residents of New England send scripts with short synopsis, resumé, SAS postcard, and SASE. Readings conducted at Massachusetts College of Art (Boston).

POPLAR PIKE PLAYHOUSE—7653 Old Poplar Pike, Germantown, TN 38138. Frank Bluestein, Artistic Dir. Full-length and one-act comedies, dramas, musicals, and children's plays. Submit synopsis with SAS postcard and resumé. Pays $300.

PRINCETON REPERTORY COMPANY—44 Nassau St., Suite 350, Princeton, NJ 08542. Victoria Liberatori, Artistic Dir. One-act plays on classical subject matter only, considered for reading and/or workshop. Submit synopsis (no more than two pages), cast list, resumé, and three pages of dialogue sample. Responds within two years.

THE PUERTO RICAN TRAVELING THEATRE—141 W. 94th St., New York, NY 10025. Miriam Colon Valle, Artistic Dir. Full-length and one-act comedies, dramas, and musicals; cast of up to 8; simple sets. "We prefer plays based on the contemporary Hispanic experience, material with social, cultural, or psychological content." Payment negotiable.

THE REPERTORY THEATRE OF ST. LOUIS—Box 191730, St. Louis, MO 63119. Attn: Lit. Dir. Query with brief synopsis, technical requirements, and cast size. Unsolicited manuscripts will be returned unread.

ROUND HOUSE THEATRE—12210 Bushey Dr., Silver Spring, MD 20902. Attn: Production Mgr. Full-length comedies, dramas, and adaptations; cast of up to 10; prefer simple set. Send one-page synopsis with 3 or 4 sample pages, cast list, and technical requirements. No unsolicited manuscripts.

SEATTLE REPERTORY THEATRE—155 Mercer St., Seattle, WA 98109. Sharon Ott, Artistic Dir. Full-length comedies, dramas, and adaptations. Submit synopsis, 10-page sample, SAS postcard, and resumé to Kurt Beattie, Associate Artistic Dir. New plays series with workshops throughout the year.

SOCIETY HILL PLAYHOUSE—507 S. 8th St., Philadelphia, PA 19147. Walter Vail, Dramaturg. Full-length dramas, comedies, and musicals with up to 6 cast members and simple set. Submit synopsis and SASE. Reports in 6 months. Nominal payment.

SOUTH COAST REPERTORY—P. O. Box 2197, Costa Mesa, CA 92628. John Glore, Lit. Mgr. Full-length comedies, dramas, musicals, juveniles. Query with synopsis and resumé. Payment varies.

SOUTHERN APPALACHIAN REPERTORY THEATRE—P.O. Box 1720, Mars Hill, NC 28754. James W. Thomas, Artistic Dir. Full-length comedies, dramas, musicals, and plays including (but not limited to) scripts with Appalachian theme. Submit resumé, recommendations, full script, and SASE. Send SASE for information on Southern Appalachian Playwright's Conference (held in April each year). Pays $500 royalty if play is selected for production during the summer season. Deadline for submissions is October 31 each year.

STAGES REPERTORY THEATRE—3201 Allen Pkwy., #101, Houston, TX 77019, Rob Bundy, Artistic Dir. Plays for Children's Theatre Playwright Festival, Texas Playwrights' Festival, Women's Repertory Project, and

Hispanic Playwrights' Festival. Submissions accepted October 1 through February 14 only. Send for guidelines on each theme.

STATE THEATER COMPANY—(formerly *Live Oak Theatre*) 719 Congress Ave., Austin, TX 78701. Full-length plays and adaptations. Please send SASE for guidelines.

MARK TAPER FORUM—135 N. Grand Ave., Los Angeles, CA 90012. Pier Carlo Talenti, Lit. Man. Full-length comedies, dramas, musicals, 50-minute juveniles, adaptations. Query.

THE TEN MINUTE MUSICALS PROJECT—Box 461194, W. Hollywood, CA 90046. Michael Koppy, Prod. One-act musicals. Include audio cassette, libretto, and lead sheets with submission. "We are looking for complete short musicals." Pays $250. Phone: 323-651-4899.

THEATER OF THE FIRST AMENDMENT—George Mason University, Institute of the Arts MSN 3E6, Fairfax, VA 22030. Rick Davis, Artistic Dir. Full-length and one-act comedies, drama, and adaptations. Send synopsis and resumé with return post card.

THEATRE AMERICANA—Box 245, Altadena, CA 91003-0245. Attn: Playreading Chair. Full-length comedies and dramas, preferably with American theme. No children's plays or musicals. Language and subject matter should be suitable for a community audience. Send bound manuscript with cast list, resumé, and SASE, by February 1. No payment. Allow 3 to 6 months for reply. Submit no more than 2 entries per season.

THEATRE/TEATRO—Bilingual Foundation of the Arts, 421 N. Ave., #19, Los Angeles, CA 90031. Agustin Coppola, Lit. Mgr. Margarita Galban, Artistic Dir. Full-length plays about the Hispanic experience; small casts. Submit manuscript with SASE. Pays negotiable rates.

THEATREWORKS—1100 Hamilton Ct., Menlo Park, CA 94025. Attn: Lit. Dept. Full-length comedies, dramas, and musicals. Submit complete script or synopsis with SAS postcard and SASE, cast list, theatre resumé, and production history. For musicals, include cassette of up to 6 songs and lyrics for all songs. Responds in 4 months for submissions made March to July; 5 months for submissions August to January. Payment is negotiable.

THEATREWORKS/USA—151 W. 26th St., 7th Fl., New York, NY 10001. Barbara Pasternack, Lit. Mgr. One-hour children's musicals and plays with music for 5-person cast. Playwrights must be within commutable distance to New York City. Submit outline or treatment, sample scenes, and music in spring, summer. Pays royalty and commission.

WALNUT STREET THEATRE COMPANY—825 Walnut St., Philadelphia, PA 19107. Beverly Elliott, Lit. Mgr. Mainstage: Full-length comedies, dramas, musicals, and popular, upbeat adaptations; also, one- to 4-character plays for studio stage. Submit 10 to 20 sample pages with SAS postcard, character breakdown, and synopsis. Musical submissions must include an audio cassette or CD. Responds only with SASE. Reports in 6 months. Payment varies.

THE WESTERN STAGE—156 Homestead Ave., Salinas, CA 93901. Michael Roddy, Dramaturg. Harvey Landa, Exec. Dir. Ongoing submissions; send query. Prefers adaptations of works of literary significance and/or large cast shows. Two or more shows chosen to workshop yearly.

GARY YOUNG MIME THEATRE—23724 Park Madrid, Calabasas, CA 91302. Gary Young, Artistic Dir. Comedy monologues and vignettes, for children and adults. Overstocked; not seeking new material.

PLAY PUBLISHERS

ALABAMA LITERARY REVIEW—Troy State Univ., 150 Smith Hall, Troy, AL 36082. Ed Hicks, Ed. Full-length and one-act comedies and dramas, to 50 pages. Query preferred. Responds to queries in 2 weeks; 2 to 3 months for complete manuscripts. Do not submit material in August. Payment is in copies; honorarium when available.

AMELIA—329 E St., Bakersfield, CA 93304. Frederick A. Raborg, Jr., Ed. One-act comedies and dramas; no longer than 45 minutes running time. Responds in 2 to 3 months. Payment is $35, on acceptance.

ANCHORAGE PRESS—Box 8067, New Orleans, LA 70182. Attn: Ed. Plays and musicals that have been proven in multiple production, for children ages 6 to 18. "We publish 8 to 10 new playbooks and one to 3 new hardcover books each year." Royalty.

ART CRAFT PUBLISHING COMPANY—See *Heuer Publishing Company.*

BAKER'S PLAYS—P.O. Box 69922, Quincy, MA 02269-9222. Ray Pape, Assoc. Ed. Full-length plays, one-act plays for young audiences, musicals, chancel dramas. Prefers produced plays; plays suitable for high school, community and regional theaters; "Plays from Young Authors" division features plays by high school playwrights. Send resumé; include press clippings if play has been produced. Responds within 2 to 6 months. E-mail: info@bakersplays.com. Web site: www.bakersplays.com.

CALLALOO—Dept. of English, Univ. of Virginia, Charlottesville, VA 22903. Charles H. Rowell, Ed. One-act dramas by and about African-American, Caribbean, and African writers. Scripts read September through May. Responds in 3 to 6 months. Payment varies, on publication.

I. E. CLARK PUBLICATIONS— P.O. Box 246, Schulenburg, TX 78956. Donna Cozzaglio, Ed. One-act and full-length plays and musicals, for children, young adults, and adults. Serious drama, comedies, classics, fairytales, melodramas, and holiday plays. "We seldom publish a play that has not been produced." Responds in 2 to 6 months. Royalty.

COLLAGES & BRICOLAGES—P.O. Box 360, Shippenville, PA 16254. Marie-José Fortis, Ed. Michael Kressley, Art Ed. One-act avant-garde comedies and dramas, maximum 25 pages. Manuscripts read August through November; responds in one to 3 months. Payment is in copies.

CONFRONTATION—Dept. of English, C.W. Post of L.I.U., Greenvale, NY 11548. Martin Tucker, Ed. One-act comedies, dramas, and adaptations. Manuscripts read September through May. Responds in 6 to 8 weeks. Pays $25 to $100, on publication.

CONTEMPORARY DRAMA SERVICE—Meriwether Publishing Co., Box 7710, 885 Elkton Dr., Colorado Springs, CO 80903. Arthur Zapel, Ed. Easy-to-stage comedies, skits, one-acts, large-cast musicals, and full-length comedy plays for schools and churches. (Junior high through college level; no elementary level material.) Adaptations of classics and improvised material for classroom use. Character education plays and comedy monologues and duets. Chancel drama for Christmas and Easter church use. Enclose synopsis. Books on theater arts subjects, scene books, and anthologies. Textbooks for speech and drama. Pays by fee arrangement or royalty.

DRAMATIC PUBLISHING COMPANY — 311 Washington St., Woodstock, IL 60098. Linda Habjan, Ed. Full-length and one-act plays and musicals for the professional, stock, amateur, and children's theater market. Send SASE. Royalty. Responds within 4 to 6 months. E-mail: plays@dramaticpublishing.com. Web site: www.dramaticpublishing.com.

DRAMATICS—Educational Theatre Assoc., 2343 Auburn Ave., Cincinnati, OH 45219. Don Corathers, Ed. One-act and full-length plays for high school production. Pays $100 to $400 for one-time, non-exclusive publication rights, on acceptance.

ELDRIDGE PUBLISHING COMPANY—P. O. Box 1595, Venice, FL 34284. Nancy Vorhis, Ed. Dept. One-act and full-length plays and musicals suitable for performance by schools, churches, and community theatre groups. Comedies, tragedies, dramas, skits, spoofs, and religious plays (all holidays). Submit complete manuscript with cover letter, biography, and SASE. Responds in 2 months. Flat fee for religious plays, royalties for full-length plays and one-acts; paid on publication. E-mail: info@histage.com. Web site: http.//www.histage.com.

SAMUEL FRENCH, INC.— 45 W. 25th St., New York, NY 10010. Lawrence Harbison, Ed. Full-length plays and musicals for dinner, community, stock, college, and high school theaters. One-act plays, 20 to 45 minutes. Children's plays, 45 to 60 minutes. Royalty.

HEUER PUBLISHING COMPANY—Art Craft Publishing Company, P.O. Box 248, Cedar Rapids, IA 52406. C. Emmett McMullen, Ed. One-act comedies and dramas for contest work; two- and three-act comedies, mysteries, farces, and musicals, with one interior setting, for middle school and high school production. Pays royalty or flat fee. E-mail: editor@hitplays.com. Web site: www.hitplays.com.

LYNX EYE—c/o Scribblefest Literary Group, 1880 Hill Dr., Los Angeles, CA 90041. Pam McCully, Kathryn Morrison, Co-Eds. One-act plays, 500 to 5,000 words, for thoughtful adults who enjoy interesting reading and writing. Also, short stories, vignettes, novel excerpts, essays, satires; poetry, to 30 lines. Pays $10, on acceptance.

NATIONAL DRAMA SERVICE—MSN 166, 127 Ninth Ave. N., Nashville, TN 37234. Attn: Ed. Scripts, 2 to 7 minutes long: drama in worship, puppets, clowns, Christian comedy, mime, movement, readers theater, creative worship services, and monologues. "We publish dramatic material that communicates the message of Christ. We want scripts that will give even the smallest church the opportunity to enhance their ministry with drama." Payment varies, on acceptance. Guidelines.

PIONEER DRAMA SERVICE—P. O. Box 4267, Englewood, CO 80155. Attn: Ed. Full-length and one-act plays as well as musicals, melodramas, and children's theatre. No unproduced plays or plays with largely male casts or multiple sets. Query preferred. Royalty. E-mail: piodrama@aol.com. Web site: www.pioneerdrama.com.

PLAYERS PRESS, INC.—P.O. Box 1132, Studio City, CA 91614-0132. Robert W. Gordon, Ed. One-act and full-length comedies, dramas, and musicals. "No manuscript will be considered unless it has been produced." Query with manuscript-size SASE and 2 #10 SASEs for correspondence. Include resumé and/or biography. Responds in 3 to 12 months. Royalty.

PLAYS, THE DRAMA MAGAZINE FOR YOUNG PEOPLE—120 Boylston St., Boston, MA 02116-4615. Elizabeth Preston, Man. Ed. One-act plays, with simple contemporary sets, for production by young people, 7 to 17: comedies, dramas, farces, skits, holiday plays. Also adaptations of classics, biography plays, puppet plays, and creative dramatics. No musicals or plays with religious themes. Maximum lengths: lower grades and skits, 10 double-spaced pages; middle grades, 15 pages; junior and senior high, 20 pages. Guidelines. Pays good rates, on acceptance. Query for adaptations of folk tales and classics. Buys all rights.

PRISM INTERNATIONAL—Dept. of Creative Writing, Univ. of British Columbia, Buch E462, 1866 Main Mall, Vancouver, BC, Canada V6T 1Z1. Jennica Harper, Drama Ed. One-act plays and translations of contemporary work. Responds in 4 to 6 months. Pays $20 per page, on publication, $10 per page web rights. Send request with SASE for rules to register for new drama contest. E-mail: prism@interchange.ubc.ca. Web site: http://www.arts.ubc.ca/prism.

RAG MAG—P.O. Box 12, Goodhue, MN 55027. Beverly Voldseth, Ed. Semiannual. Full-length and one-act comedies and dramas. SASE for guidelines. Send complete play. No plays read May through August. Pays in copy.

ROCKFORD REVIEW—P.O. Box 858, Rockford, IL 61105. David Ross, Ed. One-act comedies, dramas, and satires, to 1,300 words. "We prefer genuine or satirical human dilemmas with coping or non-coping outcomes that illuminate the human condition." Publishes one to 2 plays per issue. Pays in copies (plus invitation to attend reading-reception in the summer). Two $25 Editor's Choice Prizes awarded each issue.

SINISTER WISDOM—P.O. Box 3252, Berkeley, CA 94703. Margo Mercedes Rivera, Ed. Quarterly. One-act (no longer than 15 pages) lesbian drama. "We are particularly interested in work that reflects the diversity of our experiences: as lesbians of color, ethnic lesbians, Jewish, old, young, working class, poor, disabled, fat. Only material by born-woman lesbians is considered." Responds in 3 to 9 months; write for upcoming themes. Payment is in 2 copies, on publication. SASE.

SMITH AND KRAUS, INC.—P.O. Box 127, Main St., Lyme, NH 03768. Marisa Smith, Pres. Publishes monologue and scene anthologies, biographies of playwrights, translations, books on career developement (in theater) and the art of theater, and teaching texts for young actors (K-12). Does not accept full-length and one-act plays unless the play in question has been produced within the year and is therefore eligible for the "Best Scene and Monologue Series for the Year." Does not return manuscripts. Response time is 3 months. Pays on publication.

BOOK PUBLISHERS

The following list includes the major book publishers for adult and juvenile fiction and nonfiction and a representative number of small publishers from across the country, as well as a number of university presses.

Before submitting a complete manuscript to an editor, it is advisable to send a brief query letter describing the proposed book, and an SASE. The letter should also include information about the author's special qualifications for dealing with a particular topic and any previous publication credits. An outline of the book (or a synopsis for fiction) and a sample chapter may also be included.

While it is common practice to submit a book manuscript to only one publisher at a time, it is becoming more and more acceptable to submit the same query or proposal to more than one editor simultaneously. When sending multiple queries, *always* make note of it in each submission.

Book manuscripts may be packaged in typing paper boxes (available from a stationery store) and sent by first-class mail, or, more common and less expensive, by "Special Fourth Class Rate—Manuscript." For rates, details of insurance, and so forth, inquire at your local post office. With any submission to a publisher, be sure to enclose sufficient postage for the manuscript's return.

Royalty rates for hardcover books usually start at 10% of the retail price of the book and increase after a certain number of copies have been sold. Paperbacks generally have a somewhat lower rate, about 5% to 8%. It is customary for the publishing company to pay the author a cash advance against royalties when the book contract is signed or when the finished manuscript is received. Some publishers pay on a flat-fee basis.

While most of the publishers on this list consider either unsolicited manuscripts or queries, an increasing number now read only agented submissions. Since finding an agent is not an easy task, especially for newcomers, writers are advised to try to sell their manuscripts directly to the publisher first.

Writers seeking publication of their book-length poetry manuscripts are encouraged to enter contests that offer publication as the prize (see *Literary Prize Offers,* page 824); many presses that once considered unsolicited poetry manuscripts by emerging or unpublished writers now limit their reading of such manuscripts to those entered in their contests for new writers.

ABBEVILLE PRESS—22 Cortlandt St., New York, NY 10007. Attn: Submissions Ed. Illustrated adult nonfiction books on art, architecture, gardening, fashion, interior design, decorative arts, cooking, and travel, as well as illustrated children's books. Submit outline, sample illustrations, and sample chapters to Susan Costello. For juveniles, submit complete manuscript. Do not send original art or transparencies. Royalty.

ACADEMIC PRESS—Harcourt, Brace & Co., 525 B St., Suite 1900, San Diego, CA 92101. Attn: Ed. Dept. Scientific and technical books and journals for research-level scientists, students, and professionals; upper-level undergraduate and graduate science texts.

ACE BOOKS—325 Hudson St., New York, NY 10014. Susan Allison, V.P., Ed.-in-Chief. Science fiction and fantasy. Query with first 3 chapters and outline to Anne Sowards, Ed. Royalty.

ADAMS-BLAKE PUBLISHING—8041 Sierra St., Fair Oaks, CA 95628. Monica Blane, Ed. Books on business, careers, and technology. Query or send complete manuscript. Multiple submissions accepted. Royalty. See www.adams-blake.com for guidelines.

ADAMS-HALL PUBLISHING—P.O. Box 491002, Los Angeles, CA 90049. Sue Ann Bacon, Marketing Dir. Business and personal finance books with wide market appeal. Query with proposed book idea, a listing of current competitive books, author qualifications, the reason that the book is unique, and SASE. Royalty.

ADAMS MEDIA CORPORATION—260 Center St., Holbrook, MA 02343. Edward Walters, Ed.-in-Chief. Nonfiction trade books on business and careers, financial planning, self-improvement, family and parenting, relationships, pets, humor, inspiration, and historical biography. Query with outline, at least 2 sample chapters, and SASE. Unsolicted material without SASE will not be returned. Royalty.

ADRENALINE BOOKS—See *Thunder's Mouth Press.*

AFRICAN AMERICAN IMAGES—1909 W. 95 St., Chicago, IL 60643. Attn: Ed. Publishes books from an Africentric frame of reference that promote self-esteem, collective values, liberation, and skill development. Solutions for African Americans. Juvenile fiction and nonfiction as well. Responds within ten weeks. Multiple queries are accepted, and payment is made on a royalty basis. Send complete manuscript.

ALABASTER—See *Multnomah Publishers.*

ALASKA NORTHWEST BOOKS—2208 N.W. Market St., Suite 406, Seattle, WA 98107. Ellen Harkins Wheat, Sr. Ed. Nonfiction, 50,000 to 100,000 words, with an emphasis on natural world and history of Alaska and the Pacific Northwest: travel books; cookbooks; field guides; children's books; outdoor recreation; natural history; native culture; lifestyle. Send query or sample chapters with outline. Guidelines.

ALGONQUIN BOOKS OF CHAPEL HILL—Box 2225, Chapel Hill, NC 27515. Shannon Ravenel, Ed. Dir. Trade books, literary fiction and nonfiction, for adults.

ALLWORTH COMMUNICATIONS, INC.—10 E. 23rd St., Suite 400, New York, NY 10010. Nicole Potter, Ed. Helpful books for professional artists, designers, writers, and photographers. Query with outline and sample chapters. Royalty.

ALPINE PUBLICATIONS—225 S. Madison Ave., Loveland, CO 80537. B.J. McKinney, Pub. Nonfiction books, 35,000 to 60,000 words, on dogs and horses. Submit outline and sample chapters or complete manuscript. Royalty.

ALYSON PUBLICATIONS—P.O. Box 4371, Los Angeles, CA 90078. Attn: Ed. Gay and lesbian adult fiction and nonfiction books, from 65,000 words. *Alyson Wonderland* imprint: Children's picture books with gay and lesbian themes; young adult titles, from 65,000 words. Query with outline only. Royalty. See www.alyson.com for guidelines.

AMERICAN EDUCATION PUBLISHING—c/o Landoll, Inc., 425 Orange St., Ashland, OH 44805. Attn: Ed. Dir. Children's books, 10 to 64 pages. Submit writing samples for consideration as a free-lance, flat fee writer.

AMERICAN PARADISE PUBLISHING—P.O. Box 37, St. John, USVI 00831. Gary M. Goodlander, Ed. "We are interested in 'hopelessly local' books, between 80 and 300 pages. We need useful, practical books that help our Virgin Island readers lead better and more enjoyable lives." Guidebooks, cookbooks, how-to books, books on sailing, yacht cruising, hiking, snorkeling, sportfishing, local history, and West Indian culture, specifically aimed at Caribbean readers/tourists. Query with outline and sample chapters. Royalty.

ANCHOR BOOKS—Imprint of Bantam, Doubleday, Dell, 1540 Broadway, New York, NY 10036. Gerald Howard, Ed.-in-Chief. Adult trade paperbacks and hardcovers. Original fiction, nonfiction, multicultural, sociology, psychology, philosophy, women's interest, etc. No unsolicited manuscripts.

ANCHORAGE PRESS—Box 8067, New Orleans, LA 70182. Attn: Acquisitions Ed. Dramatic publishers. Plays for children ages 4 to 18. "We publish 8 to 10 new playbooks and one to 3 new hardcover books each year." Royalty.

ANHINGA PRESS—P.O. Box 10595, Tallahassee, FL 32302-0595. Rick Campbell, Ed. Poetry books. (Publishes 3 books a year.) Query or send complete manuscripts. Flat fee. Annual poetry prize of $2,000 plus publication; send #10 SASE for details.

ANTIQUE TRADER BOOKS—See *Landmark Specialty Books.*

APPALACHIAN MOUNTAIN CLUB BOOKS—5 Joy St., Boston, MA 02108. Attn: Ed. Dept. Regional (New England) and national nonfiction titles, 250 to 400 pages, for adult audience; juvenile and young adult nonfiction. Topics include guidebooks on non-motorized backcountry recreation, nature, outdoor recreation skills (how-to books), mountain history/biography, search and rescue, conservation, and environmental management. Query with outline and sample chapters. Multiple queries considered. Royalty.

ARABESQUE—See *Kensington Publishing Corp.*

ARCADE PUBLISHING—141 Fifth Ave., New York, NY 10010. Richard Seaver, Pub./Ed., Jeannette Seaver, Assoc. Pub., Cal Barksdale, Coates Bateman, Eds. Fiction and nonfiction. No unsolicited manuscripts. Query.

ARCHON BOOKS—See *Shoe String Press.*

ARCHWAY/MINSTREL BOOKS—Pocket Books, 1230 Ave. of the Americas, New York, NY 10020. Patricia MacDonald, V.P./ Ed. Dir. Young adult contemporary fiction (suspense thrillers, romances) and nonfiction (popular current topics), for ages 12 to 16. *Minstrel Books*: young reader fiction including thrillers, adventure, fantasy, humor, animal stories, for ages 6 to 11. Send query, outline, sample chapters to Attn: Manuscript Proposals.

ARTHUR A. LEVINE BOOKS—Imprint of Scholastic, Inc., 555 Broadway, New York, NY 10012. Arthur A. Levine, Ed. Dir. Primarily picture books and fiction for children of all ages.

AVALON BOOKS—401 Lafayette St., New York, NY 10003. Wilhelm H. Mickelsen, Pres. Veronica Mixon, Exec. Ed. Hardcover books, 40,000 to 50,000 words: romances, mysteries, and westerns. No explicit sex. Query with first 3 chapters and outline; nonreturnable. SASE for guidelines.

AVERY PUBLISHING GROUP—120 Old Broadway, Garden City Park, NY 11040. Attn: Man. Ed. Nonfiction, from 40,000 words, on health, childbirth, child care, healthful cooking. Query. Royalty.

AVISSON PRESS, INC.—3007 Taliaferro Rd., Greensboro, NC 27408. Martin L. Hester, Exec. Ed. Helpful nonfiction books on health, lifestyle, finance, etc., for older Americans; books on teenage issues, teen problems, and parenting; young adult biography (for readers 10 to 18). Query with outline or sample chapter, bio and SASE. Royalty.

AVON BOOKS—1350 Ave. of the Americas, Room 231, New York, NY 10019. Attn: Avon Editorial. Genre fiction, general fiction and nonfiction. Send one- to two-page query letter describing book and up to 35 sample pages with SASE. *Avon Hardcover*: adult commercial fiction and nonfiction. *Avon Eos*: science fiction, fantasy, 75,000 to 100,000 words. *Avon Romance*: historical or contemporary romance, 100,000 words. *Camelot*: fiction and nonfiction for 7- to 10-year-olds. No picture books. *Flare*: fiction and nonfiction for ages 12 and up.

BAEN BOOKS—Baen Publishing Enterprises, P.O. Box 1403, Riverdale, NY 10471-1403. Jim Baen, Pres./Ed.-in-Chief. Strongly plotted science fiction; innovative fantasy. Query with synopsis and manuscript. Advance and royalty. Guidelines available for letter-sized SASE.

BAKER BOOK HOUSE—P. O. Box 6287, Grand Rapids, MI 49516-6287. Rebecca Cooper, Asst. Ed. Religious nonfiction: books for trade, clergy, seminarians, collegians. Literary fiction. Royalty.

BALBOA—See *Tiare Publications.*

BALLANTINE BOOKS—201 E. 50th St., New York, NY 10022. Attn: Editorial Dept. General fiction and nonfiction. Accepts material only through agents.

BALSAM PRESS—36 E. 22nd St., 9th Fl., New York, NY 10010. Barbara Krohn, Exec. Ed. General and illustrated adult nonfiction. Query. Royalty.

BANCROFT PRESS—P.O. Box 65360, Baltimore, MD 21209-9945. Bruce Bortz, Sarah Azizi, Eds. Trade fiction and nonfiction, literary and commercial, including topics such as finance, sports, parenting, humor, history, and biography; also, some young adult fiction. No poetry or children's. For fiction, send complete manuscript, cover letter, and resumé to Sarah Azizi. For nonfiction, send complete manuscript or at least 5 chapters, cover letter, and resumé to Bruce Bortz. Responds in 2 to 3 months. Include SASE. Royalty.

BANTAM SPECTRA BOOKS—1540 Broadway, New York, NY 10036. Anne Lesley Groell, Ed. Patrick LoBrutto, Sr. Ed. Science fiction and fantasy, with emphasis on storytelling and characterization. First three chapters and synopsis with SASE; no unsolicited manuscripts. Royalty.

BANTAM, DOUBLEDAY, DELL—Div. of Random House, 1540 Broadway, New York, NY 10036. Irwyn Applebaum, Pres./Pub. Adult fiction and nonfiction. Mass-market titles, submit queries to the following imprints: *Crime Line*, crime and mystery fiction; *Domain*, frontier fiction, historical sagas, traditional westerns; *Spectra*, science fiction and fantasy; *Bantam Nonfiction*, wide variety of commercial nonfiction, including true crime, health and nutrition, sports, reference. Agented queries and manuscripts only.

BARRON'S EDUCATIONAL SERIES, INC.—250 Wireless Blvd., Hauppauge, NY 11788. Grace Freedson, Acquisitions Dir. Juvenile nonfiction (science, nature, history, hobbies, and how-to) and picture books for ages 3 to 6. Adult nonfiction (business, pet care, childcare, sports, test preparation, cookbooks, foreign language instruction). Query with SASE. Guidelines.

BATSFORD BRASSEY, INC.—(formerly Brassey's, Inc.) 4380 MacArthur Blvd., 2nd Fl., Washington, DC 20007. Don McKeon, Ed. Dir. Nonfiction books, 75,000 to 130,000 words. National and international affairs, history, foreign policy, defense, military biography, sports. No fiction. Query with synopsis, author bio, outline, sample chapters, and SASE. Royalty. E-mail: dmckeon@batsfordbrassey.com.

BAUHAN, PUBLISHER, WILLIAM L.—Box 443, Dublin, NH 03444. William L. Bauhan, Ed. Biographies, fine arts, gardening, architecture, and history books with an emphasis on New England. Submit query with outline and sample chapter.

BAYLOR UNIVERSITY PRESS—P.O. Box 97363, Baylor Univ., Waco, TX 76798-7363. Janet L. Burton, Academic Publications Coordinator. Scholarly nonfiction, especially oral history and church-state issues. Query with outline. Royalty.

BEACON PRESS—25 Beacon St., Boston, MA 02108. Attn: Kathy Daneman. General nonfiction: world affairs, women's studies, anthropology, history, philosophy, religion, gay and lesbian studies, nature writing, African-American studies, Latino studies, Asian-American studies, Native-American studies. Series: "Concord Library" (nature writing); "Barnard New Women Poets". Query. Agented manuscripts only.

BEAR & COMPANY, INC.—P.O. Drawer 2860, Santa Fe, NM 87504. John Nelson, Ed. Nonfiction "that will help transform our culture philosophically, environmentally, and spiritually." Query with outline, sample chapters, and SASE. Royalty.

BEHRMAN HOUSE—235 Watchung Ave., W. Orange, NJ 07052. Adult and juvenile nonfiction, varying lengths, in English and in Hebrew, on Jewish subjects. Query with outline and sample chapters. Flat fee or royalty.

BELLWETHER-CROSS PUBLISHING—18319 Highway 20 W., E. Dubuque, IL 61025. Jill Crow, Ed. Educational materials in most disciplines from high school through college. Also, trade nonfiction in a variety of topics. For educational materials, query with proposed book idea, list of current competitive books, and bio. For trade nonfiction, query with outline and sample chapters. SASE. Royalty.

BENCHMARK BOOKS—99 White Plains Rd., Tarrytown, NY 10591-9001. Judith Whipple, Ed. Dir. Books, 3,000 to 30,000 words, for young readers (grades 3 up) on science, sports, the arts, wildlife, math, and health. Series include: "Cultures of the World," "Cultures of the Past," "Biomes of the World," "Life Issues," "Discovering Math," and others. Query with outline. Royalty or flat fee. No single title submissions.

BERKLEY PUBLISHING GROUP —375 Hudson St., New York, NY 10014. General-interest fiction and nonfiction; science fiction, suspense, and mystery novels; romance. Submit through agent only. Publishes both reprints and originals. Paperback books, except for some hardcover mysteries and science fiction. Query required.

THE BESS PRESS—3565 Harding Ave., Honolulu, HI 96816. Revé Shapard, Ed. Nonfiction books about Hawaii and the Pacific for adults, children, and young adults. Query. Royalty.

BETHANY HOUSE PUBLISHERS—11400 Hampshire Ave. S., Minneapolis, MN 55438. Attn: Ed. Dept. Religious fiction and nonfiction. Query with sample chapters. Royalty.

BETTER HOMES AND GARDENS BOOKS—See *Meredith Corp. Book Publishing.*

BEYOND WORDS PUBLISHING—20827 N.W. Cornell Rd., Suite 500, Hillsboro, OR 97124. Attn: Adult Acquisitions Ed. or Children's Acquisitions Ed. Books on personal growth, women, and spiritual issues. Adult nonfiction books, 150 to 250 pages. Children's picture books, 32, 48, 60, or 80 pages. Submit outline and sample chapters for adult titles; complete manuscript for juvenile titles. Royalty.

BICK PUBLISHING HOUSE—307 Neck Rd., Madison, CT 06443. Dale Carlson, Ed. Books, 64 to 250 pages, on wildlife rehabilitation, special needs/disabilities, psychology. Submit outline and sample chapters. Royalty.

BINFORD & MORT PUBLISHING—5245 N.E. Elam Young Pkwy., Suite C, Hillsboro, OR 97124. P.L. Gardenier, Ed. Nonfiction on subjects related to the Pacific Coast and the Northwest. Lengths vary. Query. Royalty.

BIRCH LANE PRESS—See *Carol Publishing Group.*

BLACK BELT PRESS—Black Belt Publishing, P.O. Box 551, Montgomery, AL 36101. Attn: Submission Ed. Regional titles of national interest: history, especially African American or civil rights, biography, folklore, contemporary Southern fiction. Query with cover letter, synopsis or outline, author bio, and SASE for reply. Royalty varies. Web site: www.black-belt.com.

BLACK BUTTERFLY CHILDREN'S BOOKS—Writers and Readers Publishing, P.O. Box 461, Village Station, New York, NY 10014. Deborah Dyson, Ed. Titles featuring black children and other children of color, ages 9 to 13, for Young Beginners series. Picture books for children up to 11; board books for toddlers. Query. Royalty.

BLACK BUZZARD PRESS—Vias, Visions-International, 1007 Ficklen Rd., Fredericksburg, VA 22405. Bradley R. Strahan, Ed. Poetry manuscripts, to 30 pages. Query with SASE. Royalty.

BLACKBIRCH PRESS, INC.—260 Amity Rd., P.O. Box 3573, Woodbridge, CT 06525. Attn: Ed. Publishes books in a series, for 6- to 16-year olds. Series include "The Library of Famous Women" and "Building America." E-mail queries acceptable: staff@blackbirch.com. Web site: www.blackbirch. com.

BLAIR, PUBLISHER, JOHN F.—1406 Plaza Dr., Winston-Salem, NC 27103. Carolyn Sakowski, Pres. Books, 70,000 to 100,000 words: biography, history, folklore, and guidebooks, with southeastern tie-in. Query. Royalty.

BLOOMBERG PRESS—P.O. Box 888, Princeton, NJ 08542-0888. Jared Kieling, Ed. Nonfiction, varying lengths, on topics such as business, finance, and small business. Query with outline and sample chapter or send complete manuscript. SASE. Pays varying rates. Royalty.

BLUE DOLPHIN PUBLISHING, INC.—P.O. Box 8, Nevada City, CA 95959. Paul M. Clemens, Ed. Books, 200 to 300 pages, on comparative spiritual traditions, lay and transpersonal psychology, self-help, health, healing, and "whatever helps people grow in their social awareness and conscious evolution." Query with outline, sample chapters, and SASE. Royalty.

BLUE HERON PUBLISHING—1234 S.W. Stark St., Portland, OR 97205. Dennis Stovall, Ed. Adult and young adult books on writing and teaching writing, Northwestern and Western fiction for adults, universities and high schools (especially multicultural themes). SASE for guidelines or e-mail bhp@ teleport.com. Query. Web site: www.teleport.com/~bhp.

BLUE MOON BOOKS—See *Thunder's Mouth Press.*

BOA EDITIONS, LTD.—260 East Ave., Rochester, NY 14604. Steven Huff, Thomas Ward, Eds. Books of poetry, approximately 70 pages. Query. Royalty.

BOB JONES UNIVERSITY PRESS—See *Journey Books*.

BONUS BOOKS—160 E. Illinois St., Chicago, IL 60611. Benjamin Strong, Man. Ed. Nonfiction; topics vary widely. Query with sample chapters and SASE. Royalty.

BOTTOM DOG PRESS, INC.—c/o Firelands College, Huron, OH 44839. Larry Smith, Dir. Collections of personal essays, fiction, 50 to 200 pages, and poetry for combined chapbook publication (30 to 50 poems). Subjects should be midwestern or working class in focus. Must treat the Midwest as working class culture. "Interested writers should query first." Do not send manuscripts. Royalty.

BOYDS MILLS PRESS—815 Church St., Honesdale, PA 18431. Beth Troop, Manuscript Coord. Hardcover trade books for children. Fiction: picture books; middle-grade fiction with fresh ideas and involving story; young adult novels of literary merit. Nonfiction should be "fun, entertaining, and informative." Send outline and sample chapters for young adult novels and nonfiction, complete manuscripts for all other categories. Royalty.

BRANDEN PUBLISHING COMPANY—17 Station St., Box 843, Brookline Village, MA 02147. Attn: Ed. Dept. Novels, biographies, and autobiographies. Especially books by or about women, 250 to 350 pages. Also considers queries on history, computers, business, performance arts, and translations. Query only with SASE. Royalty. Web site: www.branden.com

BRASSEY'S, INC.—See *Batsford Brassey, Inc.*

BRAZILLER PUBLISHERS, GEORGE—171 Madison Ave., Suite 1103, New York, NY 10016. Attn: Ed. Dept. Fiction and nonfiction. Art history, collections of essays and short stories, anthologies. Send art history manuscripts to Art Ed.; others to Fiction Editor. Send outline with sample chapters.

BREAKAWAY BOOKS—Box 24, Halcottsville, NY 12438. Garth Battista, Pub. Literary sports novels or collections of essays or stories. "Our goal is to bring to light literary writing on the athletic experience." Royalty.

BRIDGE WORKS—Box 1798, Bridgehampton, NY 11932. Barbara Phillips, Pres./Ed. Dir. Mainstream adult literary fiction and nonfiction, 50,000 to 75,000 words. Royalty.

BRISTOL PUBLISHING ENTERPRISES—P.O. Box 1737, San Leandro, CA 94577. Lisa Tooker, Ed. Cookbooks. Query with outline, sample chapters, resumé, and SASE. Royalty.

BROADMAN AND HOLMAN PUBLISHERS—127 Ninth Ave. N., Nashville, TN 37234-0115. Richard P. Rosenbaum, Jr., V. P. Trade, academic, religious and inspirational nonfiction. Query with SASE. Royalty. Guidelines.

BROADWAY BOOKS—A Div. of Bantam, Doubleday, Dell, 1540 Broadway, New York, NY 10036. John Sterling, Ed.-in-Chief. Adult nonfiction; small and very selective fiction list. No unsolicited submissions.

BROWNDEER PRESS—Imprint of Harcourt Children's Books, 9 Monroe Pkwy., Suite 240, Lake Oswego, OR 97035-1487. Linda Zuckerman, Ed. Dir. Picture books, humorous fiction for middle-grade readers. Also, easy readers and chapter books. Considers submissions from agents, published authors, or members of SCBWI only. Query; send complete manuscript for picture books. SASE required for all correspondence.

BUCKNELL UNIVERSITY PRESS—Bucknell Univ., Lewisburg, PA 17837. Scholarly nonfiction. Query. Royalty.

BULFINCH PRESS—3 Center Plaza, Boston, MA 02108. Attn: Ed. Dept. Illustrated fine art and photography books. Query with outline or proposal, sample artwork, vita, and SASE.

BURFORD BOOKS—32 Morris Ave., Springfield, NJ 07081. Peter Burford, Pub. Books, 100 to 300 pages, related to sports, the outdoors, and military history. Query with outline. Royalty.

C&T PUBLISHING—P.O. Box 1456, Lafayette, CA 94549. Barbara Kuhn, Ed.-in-Chief. Quilting books, 64 to 200 finished pages. "Our focus is how-to, although we will consider picture, inspirational, or history books on quilting." Send query, outline, or sample chapters. Multiple queries considered. Royalty.

CALENDAR ISLANDS PUBLISHERS—477 Congress St., Suite 404-406, Portland, ME 04101. Peter Stillman, Ed. Nonfiction, on teaching English from junior high level through college. Query with outline and sample chapter; multiple queries considered. Pays in royalties.

CALYX BOOKS—P.O. Box B, Corvallis, OR 97339. Margarita Donnelly, Micki Reaman, Eds. Feminist publisher. Novels, short stories, poetry, nonfiction, translations, and anthologies by women. Accepts submissions for books from August 1 to September 15, 1999 and from January 1 to March 15, 2000. Send SASE or e-mail calyx@proaxis.com for guidelines before submitting.

CAMELOT BOOKS—See *Avon Books.*

CANDLEWICK PRESS—2067 Massachusetts Ave., Cambridge, MA 02140. Elizabeth Bicknell, Ed.-in-Chief. No unsolicited material.

CAPSTONE PRESS, INC.—6117 Blue Circle Dr., Suite 150, Minnetonka, MN 55343. Attn: Ed. Dept. High interest/low-reading level and early reader nonfiction for children, specifically, reluctant and new readers. Send SASE for catalogue of series themes. Query with references and resumé; no manuscripts will be accepted. Flat fee. Web site: www.capstone-press.com.

CAROL PUBLISHING GROUP—120 Enterprise Ave., Secaucus, NJ 07094. Hillek Black and Carrie Cantor, Eds. General nonfiction. *Citadel Press*: biography (celebrity preferred), autobiography, film, history, and self-help, 70,000 words. *Birch Lane Press*: adult nonfiction, 75,000 words. *Lyle Stuart*: adult nonfiction, 75,000 words, of a controversial nature, gaming, etc.; address Hillek Black, Ed. Also *University Books*. Query with SASE required. Royalty.

CAROLRHODA BOOKS—241 First Ave. N., Minneapolis, MN 55401. Rebecca Poole, Ed. Complete manuscripts for ages 4 to 12: biography, science, nature, history, photo-essays; historical fiction. Guidelines. Hardcover. Accepts submissions from March 1 to 31 and from October 1 to 31.

CAROUSEL PRESS—P.O. Box 6038, Berkeley, CA 94706-0038. Carole T. Meyers, Ed. Travel guides, especially round-ups. Send letter, table of contents, and sample chapter. "We publish one or 2 new books each year and will consider out-of-print books that the author wants to update." Modest advance and royalty.

CARROLL AND GRAF PUBLISHERS, INC.—19 W. 21st St., Suite

601, New York, NY 10001. Kent E. Carroll, Exec. Ed. General fiction and nonfiction. No unagented submissions.

CASABLANCA PRESS—Imprint of *Sourcebooks, Inc.* 121 N. Washington St., Naperville, IL 60540. Todd Stocke, Ed. Nonfiction, specializing in self-help, relationship, and gift. Query with outline and sample chapters. Pays in royalties.

CASSANDRA PRESS—P.O. Box 150868, San Rafael, CA 94915. Attn: Ed. Dept. New age, holistic health, metaphysical, and psychological books. Query with outline and sample chapters, or complete manuscript. Include SASE. Royalty (no advance).

CATBIRD PRESS—16 Windsor Rd., North Haven, CT 06473. Hrissi Haldezos, Ed. Adult fiction and nonfiction with "a fresh, sophisticated approach." Translations, especially Czech, German, and French. Query with outline and sample chapters. Accepts multiple queries and pays on a royalty basis.

THE CATHOLIC UNIVERSITY OF AMERICA PRESS—620 Michigan Ave. N.E., Washington, DC 20064. David J. McGonagle, Dir. Scholarly nonfiction: American and European history (both ecclesiastical and secular); Irish studies; American and European literature; philosophy; political theory; theology. Query with prospectus, annotated table of contents, or introduction and resumé. Royalty.

CELESTIAL ARTS—See *Ten Speed Press.*

CHAPTERS BOOKS—See *Houghton Mifflin Company.*

CHARLESBRIDGE PUBLISHING—85 Main St., Watertown, MA 02172. Attn: Submissions Ed. Children's picture books, primarily nonfiction. Send complete manuscript. Exclusive submissions only: must indicate on envelope and cover letter. Pays royalty or flat fee. Web site: www.charlesbridge.com.

CHATHAM PRESS—P. O. Box A, Old Greenwich, CT 06870. Roger H. Lourie, Man. Dir. Books on the Northeast coast, gardening, New England maritime subjects, and the ocean. Large photography volumes. Query with outline, sample chapters, illustrations, and SASE. Royalty.

CHELSEA GREEN PUBLISHING CO.—P.O. Box 428, White River Junction, VT 05001. Jim Schley, Ed.-in-Chief. Nonfiction: natural history, environmental issues, solar energy and shelter, organic agriculture, and ecological lifestyle books with strong backlist potential. Query with outline and SASE. Royalty. Web site: www.chelseagreen.com.

CHELSEA HOUSE PUBLISHERS—1974 Sproul Rd., Broomall, PA 19008. Attn: Acquisitions Ed. Juvenile books (for ages 8 up) for publication in a series format. Series include: "Women of Achievement" and "Overcoming Adversity" among others. No unsolicited manuscripts. Query with writing sample for consideration of assignments and SASE. Flat fee.

CHICAGO REVIEW PRESS—814 N. Franklin St., Chicago, IL 60610. Cynthia Sherry, Ed. Nonfiction: activity books for children, general nonfiction, architecture, parenting, how-to, and regional gardening and other regional topics. Query with outline and sample chapters.

CHILD AND FAMILY PRESS—Child Welfare League of America, 440 First St. N.W., Third Fl., Washington, DC 20001. Submissions Juvenile picture books, fiction, and nonfiction, 24 to 32 pages. (The CWLA also publishes adult nonfiction on parenting and family topics.) Please send complete manuscript. Multiple queries are considered. Pays in royalties. Web: www.cwla.org.

CHILDREN'S BOOK PRESS—246 First St., Suite 101, San Francisco, CA 94105. Submissions Ed. Bilingual and multicultural picture books, 750 to 1,500 words, for children in grades K through 6. "We publish folktales and contemporary stories reflecting the traditions and culture of the emerging majority in the U.S. and worldwide. Ultimately, we want to help encourage a more international, multicultural perspective on the part of all young people." Query. Pays advance on royalties.

CHILDREN'S PRESS—Grolier Publishing Co., Sherman Turnpike, Danbury, CT 06816. Attn: Submissions Ed. Science, social studies, and biography, 10,000 to 25,000 words, for supplementary use in libraries and classrooms. Royalty or outright purchase. Currently overstocked; not accepting unsolicited manuscripts. No phone inquiries.

CHINA BOOKS—2929 24th St., San Francisco, CA 94110. Greg Jones, Sr. Ed. Books relating to China or Chinese culture. Adult nonfiction, varying lengths. Juvenile picture books, fiction, nonfiction, and young adult books. Query. Royalty. Manuscript guidelines available at www.chinabooks.com.

CHRONICLE BOOKS—85 Second St., San Francisco, CA 94105. Attn: Ed. Dept. Fiction, art, photography, architecture, design, nature, food, giftbooks, regional topics. Children's books. Send proposal or complete manuscript for fiction with SASE.

CHRONIMED PUBLISHING—See *John Wiley & Sons, Inc.*

CITADEL PRESS—See *Carol Publishing Group.*

CLARION BOOKS—215 Park Ave. S., New York, NY 10003. Dinah Stevenson, Ed. Dir. Currently overstocked.

CLARK CITY PRESS—P.O. Box 1358, Livingston, MT 59047. Attn: Ed. Dept. Collections of poems, short stories, and essays; novels, biographies. Royalty. Currently overstocked; not accepting any new submissions.

CLARKSON N. POTTER, PUBLISHERS—201 E. 50th St., New York, NY 10022. Lauren Shakely, Ed. Dir. Illustrated trade books about such topics as cooking, gardening, and decorating. Submissions accepted through agents only.

CLEIS PRESS—P.O. Box 14684, San Francisco, CA 94114. Frédérique Delacoste, Ed. Fiction and nonfiction, 200 pages, by women. No poetry. Send SASE with 2 first-class stamps for catalogue before querying. Royalty.

CLOVER PARK PRESS—P.O. Box 5067-T, Santa Monica, CA 90409-5067. Martha Grant, Acquisitions Ed. Nonfiction adult books on California (history, natural history, travel, culture, or the arts), biography of extraordinary women, nature, travel, exploration, scientific/medical discovery, travel, adventure. Query with outline, sample chapter, author bio, and SASE.

COLLIER BOOKS—See *Macmillan Reference USA.*

CONARI PRESS—2550 Ninth St., Suite 101, Berkeley, CA 94710. Claudia Schaab, Managing Ed. Adult nonfiction: women's issues, personal growth, parenting, and spirituality. Submit outline, sample chapters, and $6\frac{1}{2}''$ × $9\frac{1}{2}''$ SASE. Royalty.

CONCORDIA PUBLISHING HOUSE—3558 S. Jefferson Ave., St. Louis, MO 63118. Attn: Book Development. Practical family books and devotionals. Must have explicit Christian content. No poetry. Query. Royalty.

CONFLUENCE PRESS—Lewis-Clark State College, 500 8th Ave.,

Lewiston, ID 83501-2698. James R. Hepworth, Dir. Literary fiction, essay collections, literary criticism, regional history, natural history, biography, and poetry. SASE for guidelines. Royalty.

COPPER CANYON PRESS—P.O. Box 271, Port Townsend, WA 98368. Sam Hamill, Ed. Poetry books only. No unsolicited manuscripts. Send SASE for guidelines. Royalty.

CORNELL UNIVERSITY PRESS—Sage House, 512 E. State St., Ithaca, NY 14851. Frances Benson, Ed.-in-Chief. Scholarly nonfiction, 60,000 to 120,000 words. Query with outline. Royalty.

COTLER BOOKS, JOANNA—See *HarperCollins Children's Books.*

COUNTERPOINT—1627 I St. N.W., Suite 850, Washington, DC 20006. Jack Shoemaker, Ed.-in-Chief. Adult literary nonfiction, including art, religion, history, biography, science, and current affairs; literary fiction. All submissions through agent only. Royalty.

CRAFTSMAN BOOK COMPANY—6058 Corte del Cedro, P.O. Box 6500, Carlsbad, CA 92018. Laurence D. Jacobs, Ed. How-to construction and estimating manuals and software for professional builders, 450 pages. Query. Royalty. Paperback. Web site: www.craftsman-book.com

CRIME LINE—See *Bantam, Doubleday, Dell.*

THE CROSSING PRESS—P.O. Box 1048, Freedom, CA 95019. Elaine Goldman Gill, Pub. Caryle Hirshberg, Acq. Ed. Natural and alternative health, spirituality, personal growth, self-help, empowerment, and cookbooks. Royalty.

CUMBERLAND HOUSE PUBLISHING—431 Harding Industrial Dr., Nashville, TN 37211. Mary Sanford, Ed. Adult nonfiction, to 100,000 words and mysteries. Query with outline and sample chapters. Royalty.

CURBSTONE PRESS—321 Jackson St., Willimantic, CT 06226. Alexander Taylor, Pub./Ed. Fiction, nonfiction, poetry books, and picture books that reflect a commitment to social change, with an emphasis on contemporary writing from Latin America and Latino communities in the U.S. Agented material only. Royalty.

DALKEY ARCHIVE PRESS—Illinois State Univ., Campus Box 4241, Normal, IL 61790-4241. John O'Brien, Sr. Ed. Avant-garde, experimental fiction, publishes only reprints "of the highest literary quality." No unsolicited manuscripts.

DANIEL AND COMPANY, JOHN—P.O. Box 21922, Santa Barbara, CA 93121. John Daniel, Pub. Books, to 200 pages, in the field of belles lettres and literary memoirs; stylish and elegant writing; essays and short fiction dealing with social issues; one poetry title per year. Send synopsis or outline with no more than 50 sample pages and SASE. Allow 6 to 8 weeks for response. Royalty.

DAVIES-BLACK PUBLISHING—3803 E. Bayshore Rd., Palo Alto, CA 94303. Melinda Adams Merino, Acquisitions Ed. Books, 250 to 400 manuscript pages. Professional and trade titles in business and careers. Web site: www. cpp-db.com.

DAVIS PUBLICATIONS, INC.—50 Portland St., Worcester, MA 01608. Books, 100 to 300 manuscript pages, for the art education market; mainly for teachers of art, grades K through 12. Must have an educational component.

Grades K through 8, address Claire M. Golding; grades 9 through 12, address Helen Ronan. Query with outline and sample chapters. Royalty.

DAW BOOKS, INC.—375 Hudson St., 3rd Fl., New York, NY 10014-3658. Elizabeth R. Wollheim, Pres. & Pub. Sheila E. Gilbert, Exec. V.P. & Pub. Peter Stampfel, Submissions Ed. Science fiction and fantasy, 85,000 words and up. No short stories, collections, or anthologies. Royalty.

DAWN PUBLICATIONS—P.O. Box 2010, Nevada City, CA 95959. Glenn J. Hovemann, Ed. Dept. Nature awareness books for children. Children's picture books with a positive, uplifting message to awaken a sense of appreciation and kinship with nature. For children's works, submit complete manuscript and specify intended age. SASE for guidelines. Royalty.

DEARBORN FINANCIAL PUBLISHING, INC.—155 N. Wacker Dr., Chicago, IL 60606-1719. Carol Luitjens, V.P. Cynthia Zigmund, Ed. Dir. Professional and Consumer books and courses on financial services, real estate, banking, small business, investing, etc. Query with outline and sample chapters. Royalty and flat fee.

DEE PUBLISHER, INC., IVAN R.—1332 N. Halsted St., Chicago, IL 60622-2637. Ivan R. Dee, Pres. Nonfiction books on history, politics, biography, literature, and theater. Query with outline and sample chapters. Royalty.

DEL REY BOOKS—201 E. 50th St., New York, NY 10022. Shelly Shapiro, Ed. Dir. Veronica Chapman, Jenni Smith, and Steve Saffel, Eds. Science fiction and fantasy, 60,000 to 120,000 words; first novelists welcome. Fantasy with magic basic to plotline. Query with SASE; no unsolicited manuscripts. Royalty.

DELACORTE PRESS—1540 Broadway, New York, NY 10036. Leslie Schnur, Jackie Cantor, Tom Spain, Eds. General adult fiction and nonfiction. Accepts material from agents only.

THE DELACORTE PRESS BOOKS FOR YOUNG READERS—1540 Broadway, New York, NY 10036. Attn: Ed. Dept. Unsolicited young adult manuscripts are accepted only for the Delacorte Press Prize for a first young adult novel. This must be a work of fiction written for ages 12 to 18, by a previously unpublished author. Send SASE for rules and guidelines.

DELL BOOKS—1540 Broadway, New York, NY 10036. Commercial fiction (including romance, mystery, and westerns) and nonfiction (including health, war, and spirituality). Agented submissions only.

DELTA BOOKS—1540 Broadway, New York, NY 10036. Attn: Ed. Dept., Book Proposal. General-interest nonfiction, submit detailed chapter outline with sample chapters and fiction, submit full manuscript with narrative synopsis (no more than 10 pages). Poetry not considered. Allow 3 months for reply. SASE.

DI CAPUA BOOKS, MICHAEL—See *HarperCollins Children's Books.*

DIAL PRESS—1540 Broadway, New York, NY 10036. Susan Kamil, VP & Ed. Dir. Quality fiction and nonfiction. No unsolicited material.

DIMI PRESS—3820 Oak Hollow Ln. S.E., Salem, OR 97302-4774. Dick Lutz, Pres. Books on unusual things in nature, e.g., unique animals, different cultures, astonishing natural events or disasters. Also, books on travel (no travel guides). Query. Royalty.

DK INK—Imprint of Dorling Kindersley, 95 Madison Ave., New York, NY 10016. Neal Porter, VP & Pub. Picture books and fiction for middle-grade and older readers. Not currently accepting unsolicited manuscripts. Royalty.

DOMAIN—See *Bantam, Doubleday, Dell.*

DOUBLEDAY AND CO.—Division of *Bantam Doubleday Dell,* 1540 Broadway, New York, NY 10036. Stephen Rubin, Pub./Pres. Proposals from literary agents only. No unsolicited material.

DUNNE BOOKS, THOMAS—175 Fifth Ave., New York, NY 10010. Thomas L. Dunne, Ed. Adult fiction (mysteries, trade, etc.) and nonfiction (history, biographies, science, politics, humor, etc.). Query with outline, sample chapters, and SASE. Royalty.

DUQUESNE UNIVERSITY PRESS—600 Forbes Ave., Pittsburgh, PA 15282. Attn: Ed. Dept. Scholarly publications in the humanities and social sciences; creative nonfiction (book-length only) by emerging writers. Guidelines.

DUTTON CHILDREN'S BOOKS—375 Hudson St., New York, NY 10014. Lucia Monfried, Assoc. Pub. & Ed.-in-Chief. Picture books, easy-to-read books; fiction and nonfiction for preschoolers to young adults. Submit outline and first 3 chapters with query for fiction and nonfiction, complete manuscripts for picture books and easy-to-read books. Manuscripts should be well written with fresh ideas and child appeal. Include SASE.

EAKIN PRESS—P.O. Drawer 90159, Austin, TX 78709-0159. Melissa Roberts, Sr. Ed. Adult nonfiction, 60,000 to 80,000 words: Texana, regional cookbooks, Mexico and the Southwest, WWII, military. Children's books: history, culture, geography, etc., of Texas and the Southwest. Juvenile picture books, 5,000 to 10,000 words; fiction, 20,000 to 30,000 words; young adult fiction, 25,000 to 40,000 words. Query; responds in 90 days. Royalty.

EASTERN WASHINGTON UNIVERSITY PRESS—Mail Stop 14, Eastern Washington Univ., 526 5th St., Cheney, WA 99004-2431. Attn: Eds. Literary essays, history, social commentary, and other academic subjects. Limited fiction and well-researched historical novels (one title every 2 years or so). One or 2 books of poetry, 60 to 150 pages, each year. "We are a small regional university press, publishing titles that reflect our regional service, our international contacts, our strong creative writing program, and research and interests of our exceptional faculty." Send complete manuscript, query with outline, or Mac-compatible diskette. Royalty.

EERDMANS PUBLISHING COMPANY, INC., WM. B.—255 Jefferson Ave. S.E., Grand Rapids, MI 49503. Jon Pott, Ed.-in-Chief. Protestant, Roman Catholic, and Orthodox theological nonfiction; religious history and biography; ethics; philosophy; literary studies; spiritual growth. For children's religious books, query Judy Zylstra, Ed., Eerdmans Books for Young Readers. Royalty.

ELEMENT BOOKS—160 North Washington St., 4th Floor, Boston, MA 02114. Roberta Scimone, Acquisitions Ed. Books on world religions, ancient wisdom, astrology, meditation, women's studies, and alternative health and healing. Study recent catalogue. Query with outline and sample chapters. Royalty. No phone calls, please.

ENCANTO—See *Kensington Publishing Corp.*

ENSLOW PUBLISHERS, INC.—P.O. Box 398, 40 Industrial Way, Berkeley Heights, NJ 07922. Brian D. Enslow, Ed./Pub. No fiction; nonfiction books for young people only. Areas of emphasis are children's and young adult books for ages 10 to 18 in the fields of social studies, science, and biography. Also reference books for all ages and easy reading books for teenagers.

ENTREPRENEUR BOOKS—2392 Morse Ave., Irvine, CA 92614. Marla Markman, Man. Ed. Publishes trade paperbacks, around 80,000 words, and business start-up guides, 30,000 to 60,000 words. Books have sidebars, information boxes, and graphics. Topics include raising money, sales and marketing, staffing, etc. Looking for material for a general audience as well as a business one. Payment varies from $6,000 to $15,000, (depending on type of book) with half as an advance and half upon completion of the book.

EPICENTER PRESS—P.O. Box 82368, Kenmore, WA 98028. Kent Sturgis, Pub. Quality nonfiction trade books, contemporary western art and photography titles, and destination travel guides emphasizing Alaska and the West Coast. "We are a regional press whose interests include but are not limited to the arts, history, environment, and diverse cultures and lifestyles of the North Pacific and high latitudes."

ERIKSSON, PUBLISHER, PAUL S.—P.O. Box 125, Forest Dale, VT 05745. Attn: Ed. Dept. General nonfiction (send outline and cover letter); some fiction (send 3 chapters with query). Royalty.

EVANS & CO., INC., M.—216 E. 49th St., New York, NY 10017. Attn: Ed. Dept. Books on health, self-help, popular psychology, and cookbooks. Limited list of commercial fiction. Query with outline, sample chapter, and SASE. Royalty.

EVENT HORIZON PRESS—P.O. Box 2006, Palm Springs, CA 92263. Joseph Cowles, Pub. Adult fiction and nonfiction. Currently overstocked; no unsolicited manuscripts.

EXCALIBUR PUBLICATIONS—P.O. Box 35369, Tucson, AZ 85740-5369. Alan M. Petrillo, Ed. Books on military history, firearms history, antique arms and accessories, military personalities, tactics and strategy, history of battles. Query with outline and 3 sample chapters. SASE. Royalty or flat fee.

FACTS ON FILE, INC.—11 Penn Plaza, New York, NY 10001. Reference and trade books on science, health, literature, language, history, the performing arts, ethnic studies, popular culture, sports, etc. (No fiction, poetry, computer books, technical books or cookbooks.) Query with outline, sample chapter, and SASE. Royalty. Hardcover.

FAIRVIEW PRESS—2450 Riverside Ave. S., Minneapolis, MN 55454. Lane Stiles, Managing Ed. Stephanie Billecke, Ed. Adult books, 80,000 words, on aging, grief & bereavement, family issues, health, medicine, and patient education. Query with outline and sample chapters. Royalty.

FANFARE—1540 Broadway, New York, NY 10036. Beth de Guzman, Wendy McCurdy, Sr. Eds. Stephanie Kip, Ed. Historical and contemporary women's fiction, about 90,000 to 150,000 words. Study field before submitting. Query. Paperback and hardcover.

FARRAR, STRAUS & GIROUX—19 Union Sq. W., New York, NY 10003. Adult and juvenile literary fiction and nonfiction.

THE FEMINIST PRESS AT THE CITY UNIVERSITY OF NEW YORK—City College; Wingate Hall Convent Ave. at 138th St., New York, NY 10031. Florence Howe, Pub. Reprints of significant "lost" fiction, original memoirs, autobiographies, biographies; multicultural anthologies; handbooks;

bibliographies. "We are especially interested in international literature, women and peace, women and music, and women of color." Royalty.

FIREBRAND BOOKS—141 The Commons, Ithaca, NY 14850. Nancy K. Bereano, Ed. Feminist and lesbian fiction and nonfiction. Royalty. Paperback and library edition cloth.

FIRESIDE BOOKS—1230 Ave. of the Americas, New York, NY 10020. No unsolicited manuscripts.

FIRST STORY PRESS—1800 Business Park Dr., Suite 205, Clarksville, TN 37040. Judith Pierson, Ed. Children's picture books of varying lengths. No stories about death, illness, family problems, or grandparents. Send one complete manuscript per envelope. SASE. Royalties.

FLARE BOOKS—See *Avon Books*.

FODOR'S TRAVEL GUIDES—201 E. 50th St., New York, NY 10022. Karen Cure, Ed. Dir. Travel guides for both foreign and US destinations. "For our Gold Guides, our flagship series, we generally hire writers who live in the area they will write about or who have a very intimate knowledge of the area they will cover; we're open to new ideas beyond our Gold Guides as well." Gold Guides follow established format. Send writing sample, and, for proposals for new books, a sample chapter, outline, and statement about your guide's intended audience.

FONT & CENTER PRESS—P.O. Box 95, Weston, MA 02493. Ilene Horowitz, Ed./Pub. Cookbooks. How-to books. Alternative history for adults and young adults. Send proposal, outline, and sample chapter(s). Responds in 3 months. SASE required. Royalty.

FORGE—Tom Doherty Associates, 175 Fifth Ave., 14th Fl., New York, NY 10010. Melissa Ann Singer, Sr. Ed. General fiction; limited nonfiction, from 80,000 words. Also interested in literary fiction, particularly women's. Query with complete synopsis and first 3 chapters to Ginger Clark, Ed. Asst. Advance and royalty.

FORTRESS PRESS—Box 1209, Minneapolis, MN 55440. Dr. Henry French, Ed. Dir. Books in the areas of biblical studies, theology, ethics, professional ministry, and church history for academic and professional markets, including libraries. Query.

THE FREE PRESS—See *Macmillan Reference USA*.

FREE SPIRIT PUBLISHING—400 First Ave. N., Suite 616, Minneapolis, MN 55401-1724. Tim Woessner, Ed. Asst. Nonfiction self-help for kids and teens, with an emphasis on school success, self-awareness, self-esteem, creativity, social action, lifeskills, and special needs. Creative classroom activities for teachers; adult books on raising, counseling, or educating children. Queries only. Request free catalog and guidelines. Advance and royalty.

FRONT STREET BOOKS, INC.—20 Battery Park Ave., #403, Asheville, NC 28801. Stephen Roxburgh, Pres./Pub. Fiction, poetry, and picture books for children. Query with sample chapters. Royalty.

FRONT STREET/CRICKET BOOKS—332 S. Michigan Ave., Suite 1100, Chicago, IL 60604. Fiction, for 7- to 12-year-olds. Send complete manuscripts to Submissions Ed. Royalty.

FULCRUM PUBLISHING—350 Indiana St., Suite 350, Golden, CO 80401. Attn: Submissions Dept. Adult trade nonfiction: gardening, travel, nature, history, education, and Native American culture; focus on western regional topics. No fiction. Send cover letter, sample chapters, table of contents, author credentials, and market analysis. Royalty.

GIBBS SMITH PUBLISHER—P.O. Box 667, Layton, UT 84041. Madge Baird, Ed. Dir. Adult nonfiction. Query. Royalty.

GIBBS SMITH, JUNIOR—P.O. Box 667, Layton, UT 84041. Suzanne Taylor, Ed. Juvenile books: western/cowboy; activity; how-to; nature/environment; and humor. Fiction picture books, to 1,000 words; nonfiction books, to 10,000 words, for readers 4 to 12. Royalty.

GINIGER CO. INC., THE K.S.—250 W. 57th St., Suite 414, New York, NY 10107. Attn: Ed. Dept. General nonfiction. Query with SASE; no unsolicited manuscripts. Royalty.

GLENBRIDGE PUBLISHING LTD.—6010 W. Jewell Ave., Lakewood, CO 80232. James A. Keene, Ed. Nonfiction books on a variety of topics, including business, history, and psychology. Query with sample chapter and SASE. Royalty.

GLOBE PEQUOT PRESS, THE—6 Business Park Rd., Box 833, Old Saybrook, CT 06475. Elizabeth Taylor, Submissions Ed. Nonfiction with national and regional focus; travel; outdoor recreation; home-based business. Query with sample chapter, contents, and one-page synopsis. SASE required. Royalty or flat fee.

GODINE PUBLISHER, DAVID R.—9 Hamilton Place, Boston, MA 02108. No unsolicited manuscripts. Royalty.

GOLD 'N' HONEY—See *Multnomah Publishers.*

GOLDEN BOOKS FAMILY ENTERTAINMENT—888 Seventh Ave., New York, NY 10106-4100. Thea Feldman, VP/Pub., children's publishing group. Children's fiction and nonfiction: picture books, storybooks, concept books, novelty books. No unsolicited manuscripts. Royalty or flat fee.

GOLDEN WEST PUBLISHERS—4113 N. Longview, Phoenix, AZ 85014. Hal Mitchell, Ed. Cookbooks and nonfiction Western history and travel books. Currently seeking writers for state and regional cookbooks. Query. Royalty or flat fee.

GRAYWOLF PRESS—2402 University Ave., Suite 203, St. Paul, MN 55114. Attn: Ed. Dept. Literary fiction (short story collections and novels), poetry, and essays.

GREAT QUOTATIONS—1967 Quincy Ct., Glendale Heights, IL 60139. Diane Voreis, Ed. General adult titles, 80 to 365 pages, with strong, clever, descriptive titles and brief, upbeat text. "We publish small, quick-read gift books." Query with outline and sample chapters or send complete manuscript. Royalty.

GREENWILLOW BOOKS—1350 Ave. of the Americas, New York, NY 10019. Susan Hirschman, Ed.-in-Chief. Children's books for all ages. Picture books.

GROSSET AND DUNLAP, INC.—Div. of Putnam Publishing Group, 345 Hudson St., New York, NY 10014. Jane O'Connor, Pub. Mass-market children's books. Not currently accepting unsolicited manuscripts. Royalty.

GROVE/ATLANTIC MONTHLY PRESS—841 Broadway, 4th Fl., New York, NY 10003-4793. Morgan Entrekin, Pub. Distinguished fiction and nonfiction. Query; no unsolicited manuscripts. Royalty.

GRYPHON HOUSE, INC.—P.O. Box 207, Beltsville, MD 20705. Kathy Charner, Ed.-in-Chief. Resource books, 150 to 500 pages, for parents and teachers of young children from birth to 8 years old. Query with outline and sample chapters. Royalty.

GULLIVER BOOKS—See *Harcourt Brace & Co. Children's Book Div.*

GULLIVER GREEN—See *Harcourt Brace & Co. Children's Book Div.*

HACHAI PUBLISHING—156 Chester Ave., Brooklyn, NY 11218. Dina Rosenfeld, Ed. Full-color children's picture books, 32 pages, for readers ages 2 to 8; Judaica, Bible tales. Query or send complete manuscript. Flat fee. Web site: www.hachai.com.

HANCOCK HOUSE PUBLISHERS, LTD.—1431 Harrison Ave., Blaine, WA 98230. Attn: Ed. Dept. Adult nonfiction: guidebooks, biographies, natural history, popular science, conservation, animal husbandry, and falconry. Some juvenile nonfiction. Query with outline and sample chapters or send complete manuscript. Multiple queries considered. Royalty.

HARCOURT BRACE & CO.—525 B St., Suite 1900, San Diego, CA 92101. Attn: Ed. Dept. Adult trade nonfiction and fiction. No unsolicited manuscripts. Queries accepted with SASE.

HARCOURT CHILDREN'S BOOK DIV.—525 B St., Suite 1900, San Diego, CA 92101-4495. Attn: Manuscript Submissions. Juvenile fiction and nonfiction for beginning readers through young adults under the following imprints: *Browndeer Press, Gulliver Books, Red Wagon Books, Odyssey Classics, Silver Whistle, Magic Carpet Books, Libros Viajeros, Harcourt Brace Big Books, Gulliver Green, Harcourt Brace Young Classics, Harcourt Brace Paperbacks,* and *Voyager Books.* Query with SASE; manuscripts accepted from agents.

HARCOURT BRACE PAPERBACKS—See *Harcourt Brace & Co. Children's Book Div.*

HARCOURT BRACE PROFESSIONAL PUBLISHING—525 B St., Suite 1900, San Diego, CA 92101-4495. Attn: Sidney Bernstein, V.P. & Pub. Professional books for practitioners in accounting, auditing, tax and financial planning, law, business management. Query. Royalty and work-for-hire.

HARLEQUIN BOOKS/CANADA—225 Duncan Mill Rd., Don Mills, Ont., Canada M3B 3K9. Randall Toye, Ed. Dir. *Mira Books*: Dianne Moggy, Ed. Dir. Contemporary women's fiction, to 100,000 words. Query. *Harlequin Superromance*: Paula Eykelhof, Sr. Ed. Contemporary romance, to 85,000 words, with a mainstream edge. Query. *Harlequin Temptation*: Birgit Davis-Todd, Sr. Ed. Sensuous, humorous contemporary romances, to 60,000 words. *Duets*: Malle Vallik, Assoc. Sr. Ed. The lighter side of love, to 55,000 words. Query.

HARLEQUIN BOOKS/U.S.—300 E. 42nd St., 6th Fl., New York, NY 10017. Denise O'Sullivan, Assoc. Sr. Ed. Contemporary romances, 70,000 to 75,000 words. Send for tip sheets, SASE. *Harlequin American Romances*: bold, exciting romantic adventures, "where anything is possible and dreams come true." *Harlequin Intrigue*: set against a backdrop of mystery and suspense, worldwide locales. Melissa Jeglinski, Assoc. Sr. Ed. Query. Paperback.

HARPER SAN FRANCISCO—353 Sacramento St., Suite 500, San Francisco, CA 94111-3653. Attn: Acquisitions Ed. Books on spirituality and religion. No unsolicited manuscripts; query required.

HARPERCOLLINS CHILDREN'S BOOKS—10 E. 53rd St., New

York, NY 10022-5299. Picture books, chapter books, and fiction and nonfiction for middle-grade and young adult readers. "Our imprints (*HarperTrophy* paperbacks, *Joanna Cotler Books, and Michael di Capua Books*) are committed to producing imaginative and responsible children's books. All publish from preschool to young adult titles." Guidelines. Royalty.

HARPERCOLLINS PUBLISHERS—10 E. 53rd St., New York, NY 10022-5299. Adult Trade Department: Address Man. Ed. Fiction, nonfiction (biography, history, etc.), reference. Submissions from agents only. College texts: Address College Dept. No unsolicited manuscripts; query only.

HARPERPAPERBACKS—HarperCollins, 10 E. 53rd St., New York, NY 10022. Carolyn Marino, Ed. Dir., John Douglas, Exec. Ed., Science Fiction/Fantasy. Jessica Lichtenstein, Sr. Ed. Laura Cifelli, Caitlin Blasdell, Eds. Leslie Stern, Assoc. Ed.

HARPERPRISM—10 E. 53rd St., New York, NY 10022-5299. John Douglas, Exec. Ed. Caitlin Blasdell, Sr. Ed. Science fiction/fantasy. No unsolicited manuscripts; query.

HARPERTROPHY—See *HarperCollins Children's Books.*

HARVARD COMMON PRESS—535 Albany St., Boston, MA 02118. Bruce Shaw, Ed. Adult nonfiction: cookbooks, travel guides, books on childcare and parenting, health, small business, etc. Send outline, analysis of competing books, and sample chapters or complete manuscript. SASE. Royalty.

HARVARD UNIVERSITY PRESS—79 Garden St., Cambridge, MA 02138-1499. Mary Ann Lane, Managing Ed. No free-lance submissions: "We hire no writers."

HARVEST HOUSE PUBLISHERS—1075 Arrowsmith, Eugene, OR 97402. LaRae Weikert, Editorial Managing Dir. No longer accepts unsolicited material.

HAWORTH PRESS, INC.—10 Alice St., Binghamton, NY 13904-1580. Bill Palmer, Ed. Scholarly press interested in research-based adult nonfiction: psychology, social work, gay and lesbian studies, women's studies, family and marriage; some recreation and entertainment. Send outline with sample chapters or complete manuscript. Royalty.

HAY HOUSE—P.O. Box 5100, Carlsbad, CA 92018-5100. Attn: Ed. Dir. Self-help books on health, self-awareness, spiritual growth, astrology, psychology, philosophy, women's and men's issues, metaphysics, and the environment. Query with outline, a few sample chapters, and SASE. Royalties.

HAZELDEN EDUCATIONAL MATERIALS—Box 176, Center City, MN 55012. Betty Greydanus, Ed. Asst. Self-help books, curricula, videos, audios, and pamphlets relating to addiction, recovery, spirituality, mental health, chronic illness, family issues, and wholeness. Query with outline and sample chapters. Multiple queries considered. Royalty.

HEALTH COMMUNICATIONS, INC.—3201 S.W. 15th St., Deerfield Beach, FL 33442. Christine Belleris, Ed. Dir. Books, 250 pages, on self-help, recovery, inspiration, and personal growth for adults. Query with outline and 2 sample chapters and SASE. Royalty.

HEALTH PRESS—P.O. Box 1388, Santa Fe, NM 87504. K. Schwartz, Ed. Health-related adult and children's books, 100 to 300 pages. "We're seeking cutting-edge, original manuscripts that will excite, educate, and help readers." Author must have credentials, or preface/intro must be written by M.D., Ph.D., etc. Controversial topics are desired; must be well researched and documented. Submit outline, table of contents, and first chapter with SASE. Royalty.

HEARST BOOKS —See *William Morrow and Co., Inc.*

HEARTSONG PRESENTS—P.O. Box 719, Uhrichsville, OH 44683. Rebecca Germany, Man. Ed. Contemporary and historical romances, 50,000 to 55,000 words, that present a conservative, evangelical Christian world view. Pays flat fee.

HEBREW UNION COLLEGE PRESS—3101 Clifton Ave., Cincinnati, OH 45220. Barbara Selya, Ed. Scholarly books, 200 pages, on very specific topics in Judaic studies. "Our usual print run is 500 books, and our target audience is mainly rabbis and professors." Query with outline and sample chapters. No payment.

HEINEMANN—361 Hanover St., Portsmouth, NH 03801. Attn: Ed. Dept. Practical theatre, drama education, professional education, K-12, and literacy education. Query.

HEMINGWAY WESTERN STUDIES SERIES—Boise State University, 1910 University Dr., Boise, ID 83725. Tom Trusky, Ed. Artists' and eccentric format books (multiple editions) relating to Rocky Mountain environment, race, religion, gender and other public issues. Guidelines.

HIGGINSON BOOK COMPANY—148 Washington St., Salem, MA 01970. Attn: Ed. Dept. Nonfiction genealogy and local history only, 20 to 1,000 pages. Specializes in reprints. Query. Royalty. E-mail: higginsn@cove.com.

HIGHSMITH PRESS—P.O. Box 800, Fort Atkinson, WI 53538-0800. Donald Sager, Pub. Adult books, 80 to 360 pages, on professional library science, education, and reference. Teacher activity and curriculum resource books, 48 to 240 pages, for pre-K through 12. Query with outline and sample chapters. Royalty. Guidelines available at web site: www.hpress.highsmith.com.

HIPPOCRENE BOOKS—171 Madison Ave., New York, NY 10016. George Blagowidow, Ed. Dir. Language instruction books and foreign language dictionaries, international cookbooks, travel guides, military history, Polish interest books. Send outline and sample chapters with SASE for reply. Multiple queries considered. Royalty.

HOHM PRESS—P.O. Box 2501, Prescott, AZ 86302. Adult nonfiction including religion, women's, parenting, holistic health, poetry, and children's. Query. Royalty.

HOLIDAY HOUSE, INC.—425 Madison Ave., New York, NY 10017. Regina Griffin, V. P. Lisa Hopp, Assoc. Ed. General juvenile fiction and nonfiction. Query with SASE. Royalty. Hardcover only.

HOLT AND CO., HENRY—115 W. 18th St., New York, NY 10011. Distinguished works of biography, history, fiction, and natural history; humor; child activity books; parenting books; books for the entrepreneurial business person; and health books. "Virtually all submissions come from literary agents or from writers whom we publish."

HOME BUILDER PRESS—National Assoc. of Home Builders, 1201 15th St. N.W., Washington, DC 20005-2800. Doris M. Tennyson, Sr. Acquisitions Ed. How-to and business management books, 150 to 200 manuscript pages, for builders, remodelers, developers, other building industry professionals, and consumers. Writers should be experts in homebuilding, remodeling, land development, sales, marketing, or related aspects of the building industry. Query with outline and sample chapter. Royalty. For author's packet TW, call Thayer Long (800) 368-5242, ext. 395.

HOMESTEAD PUBLISHING—P.O. Box 193, Moose, WY 83012. Carl Schreier, Pub. Fiction, guidebooks, art, history, natural history, and biography. Royalty.

HORIZON BOOKS—Christian Publications, 3825 Hartzdale Dr., Camp Hill, PA 17011. George McPeek, Ed. Adult and young adult nonfiction, from 35,000 to 50,000 words, on a variety of topics from an evangelical Christian perspective. Query; multiple queries considered. Pays in royalties.

HOUGHTON MIFFLIN COMPANY—222 Berkeley St., Boston, MA 02116-3764. Attn: Ed. Dept. Fiction: literary, historical. Nonfiction: history, biography, psychology. No unsolicited submissions. Children's book division, address Children's Trade Books: picture books, fiction, and nonfiction for all ages. Query. Royalty.

HOWARD UNIVERSITY PRESS—2225 Georgia Ave. N.W., Washington, DC 20017. Ed Gordon, Dir. Nonfiction books, 300 to 500 manuscript pages, on African diaspora, history, political science, literary criticism, biography, women's studies. Query with outline and sample chapters. Royalty.

HOWELL PRESS—1713-2D Allied Ln., Charlottesville, VA 22903. Ed. Nonfiction, especially history, transportation, cooking, gardening, motor sports, aviation, regional topics, Civil War, and quilting. Query with outline and sample chapters; multiple queries are considered. Pays either royalty or flat fee, as negotiated. Web site: www.howellpress.com.

HP BOOKS—375 Hudson St., New York, NY 10014. Attn: Ed. Dept. How-tos on cooking, automotive topics. Query with SASE.

HUMANICS PUBLISHING GROUP—P.O. Box 7400, Atlanta, GA 30357. W. Arthur Bligh, Acquisitions Ed. Inspiring trade books, 100 to 300 pages: self-help, spiritual, instructional, philosophy, and health for body, mind, and soul. Also, children's educational books/teacher resource guides for grades K through 6. "We are interested in books that people go to for help, guidance, and inspiration." Query with outline and SASE required. Royalty.

HUNGRY MIND PRESS—1648 Grand Ave., St. Paul, MN 55105. Pearl Kilbride, Ed. Fiction; memoirs; contemporary affairs; cultural criticism; travel essays; nonfiction. No genre fiction, self-help, religious, or poetry. "Books that examine the human experience, encourage reflection, and enrich everyday life. We want to involve writers in the planning and marketing of their books and build a strong relationship with booksellers." Query with outline and sample chapters. Royalty.

HUNTER HOUSE PUBLISHERS—P.O. Box 2914, Alameda, CA 94501-0914. Nonfiction for health, family, and community. Topics include health, women's health, personal growth, lifestyle, sexuality and relationships, writing, memoirs, violence intervention and prevention, human rights, diversity, counseling resources, and teaching resources. Send for guidelines.

HUNTER PUBLISHING, INC.—130 Campus Dr., Edison, NJ 08818. Kim André, Acquisitions Dept. Travel guides to the U.S., South America, and the Caribbean.

HYPERION—114 Fifth Ave., New York, NY 10011. Material accepted from agents only. No unsolicited manuscripts or queries considered.

HYSTERIA PUBLICATIONS—P.O. Box 38581, Bridgeport, CT 06605. Deborah Werksman, Ed. Humorous books that are "progressive, provocative, liberating, funny, and insightful," 96 to 112 finished pages. A division of *Sourcebooks, Inc.*. Also acquires gift, self-help, parenting, business, and media for *Sourcebooks*. Query with sample chapters or complete manuscript. SASE for guidelines. Royalty.

IMPACT PUBLISHERS, INC.—P.O. Box 6016, Atascadero, CA 93423-6016. Attn: Acquisitions Ed. Popular and professional psychology books, from 200 pages. Personal growth, relationships, families, communities, and health for adults. Children's books for "Little Imp" series on issues of self-esteem. "Writers must have advanced degrees and professional experience in human-service fields." Query with outline and sample chapters. Royalty.

INDIANA UNIVERSITY PRESS—601 N. Morton St., Bloomington, IN 47404-3797. Attn: Ed. Dept. Scholarly nonfiction, especially cultural studies, literary criticism, music, history, women's studies, African-American studies, science, philosophy, African studies, Middle East studies, Russian studies, anthropology, regional, etc. Query with outline and sample chapters. Royalty.

INNER TRADITIONS INTERNATIONAL, INC.—One Park St., Rochester, VT 05767. Jon Graham, Acquisitions Ed. Books representing the spiritual, cultural, and mythic traditions of the world, focusing on inner wisdom and the perennial philosophies and alternative modalities of healing. Query. Royalty.

INNISFREE PRESS, INC.—136 Roumfort Rd., Philadelphia, PA 19119-1632. Marcia Broucek, Ed. Adult nonfiction, from 40,000 to 60,000 words, on spirituality, self-help, women's issues, and psychology. "No fiction, poetry, or disease 'survival' stories." Accepts multiple queries and pays on a royalty basis. Query with outline and sample chapters.

INTERLINK PUBLISHING GROUP, INC.—46 Crosby St., Northampton, MA 01060. Picture books, to 32 pages, for children age 3 to 8. Query with sample illustrations. No multiple queries. Royalty.

INSTRUCTOR BOOKS—See *Scholastic Professional Books*.

INTERNATIONAL MARINE—A Div. of McGraw-Hill, Box 220, Camden, ME 04843. Jonathan Eaton, Ed. Dir. Books on boating (sailing and power). Imprint: *Seven Seas Press*.

INTIMATE MOMENTS—See *Silhouette Books*.

IRONWEED PRESS—P.O. Box 754208, Parkside Station, Forest Hills, NY 11375. Attn: Ed. Literary, multicultural fiction, especially Asian fiction, to 50,000 words. Nonfiction biographies and scholarly works, same length. Accepts multiple queries and pays on a royalty basis. Query with outline, sample chapters, or complete manuscript.

ISLAND PRESS—1718 Connecticut Ave. N.W., Suite 300, Washington, DC 20009. Dan Sayre, Ed.-in-Chief. Nonfiction focusing on natural history, literary science, the environment, and natural resource management. "We want solution-oriented material to solve environmental problems. For our imprint, *Shearwater Books*, we want books that express new insights about nature and the environment." Query or send manuscript. SASE required.

ITHACA BOOKS, INC.— 3500 W. Olive Ave., Suite 980, Burbank, CA 91505. Christopher J. Husa, Man. Dir. Books, 10,000 to 12,000 words, for children ages 8 to 13, based on true stories of adventure, exploration, and discovery. "Accuracy is critical; research is essential." Royalty.

JAI PRESS, INC.— 100 Prospect St., P.O. Box 811, Stamford, CT 06904. Roger A. Dunn, Man. Ed. Research and technical reference books on such subjects as business, economics, management, sociology, political science, computer science, life sciences, and chemistry. Query or send complete manuscript. Royalty.

JALMAR PRESS— P.O. Box 1185, Torrance, CA 90505. Dr. Bradley L. Winch, Pub. Nonfiction books for parents, teachers, and caregivers. "Our emphasis is on helping children and adults live from the inside/out so that they become personally and socially responsible." Special interest in peaceful conflict resolution, whole brain learning, self-esteem, emotional intelligence, stress management, and character education. Multiple queries considered. Submit outline. Royalty.

JAMES BOOKS, ALICE— Univ. of Maine at Farmington, 98 Main St., Farmington, ME 04938. Peg Peoples, Program Dir. Cooperative publishes books of poetry (48 to 72 pages) by writers through two annual competitions. The New England/New York Competition publishes manuscripts by writers living in New England (deadline is September); authors become active cooperative members. The Beatrice Hawley Competition is open to poets nationwide (deadline is December); authors do not become members. Also offers Jane Kenyon Chapbook Award (deadline June). "We emphasize the publication of poetry by women, but also welcome all manuscripts of high literary quality." Authors paid with 100 copies of their books. Request guidelines with SASE. Web site: www.umf.maine.edu/~ajb.

THE JEWISH PUBLICATION SOCIETY— 1930 Chestnut St., Philadelphia, PA 19103. Dr. Ellen Frankel, Ed.-in-Chief. Adult nonfiction, juvenile fiction, and young adult titles, all related to judaism. Query with outline. Multiple queries considered. Royalty.

JIST WORKS— 720 N. Park Ave., Indianapolis, IN 46202. Michael Cunningham, Managing Ed. Career and "life decision" books for people all reading and academic levels. Also business, welfare-to-work titles, and trade topics for consumers. Query with outline and sample chapters. Payment made on a royalty or flat fee basis.

THE JOHNS HOPKINS UNIVERSITY PRESS— 2715 N. Charles St., Baltimore, MD 21218. No unsolicited poetry or fiction considered.

JONA BOOKS— P.O. Box 336, Bedford, IN 47421. Joe Glasgow, Ed. Nonfiction: biographies, Native American history, old west, and military history. Fiction: action adventure, alternative history, historical fiction, mysteries, and military science fiction. Contracts negotiated; no advances. SASE for guidelines. Web site: www.kiva.net/~jonabook.

JONATHAN DAVID PUBLISHERS, INC.— 68-22 Eliot Ave., Middle Village, NY 11379. Alfred J. Kolatch, Ed.-in-Chief. General nonfiction (how-to, sports, cooking and food, self-help, etc.) and books on Judaica. Query with outline, sample chapter, resumé, and SASE. Royalty or outright purchase.

JOURNEY BOOKS— Division of Bob Jones University Press, 1700 Wade Hampton Blvd., Greenville, SC 29614. Gloria Repp, Ed. Books for young readers, ages 6 to 12, that reflect "The highest Christian standards of thought, feeling, and action." Fiction, 8,000 to 40,000 words. Nonfiction, 10,000 to 30,000 words. Young adult books, 40,000 to 60,000 words. Read guidelines, then submit sample chapters. Pays on royalty or flat fee basis.

JOVE BOOKS—375 Hudson Street, New York, NY 10014. Fiction and nonfiction. No unsolicited manuscripts.

JUDSON PRESS—P.O. BOX 851, Valley Forge, PA 19482-0851. Acq. Ed. Adult, juvenile, and young adult nonfiction of varying lengths. Publishes practical Christian resources for pastor and laity, devotional materials, and African American church resources. Query with outline, sample chapters, and author qualifications. Send for guidelines. Pays royalties or flat fee.

JUST US BOOKS—356 Glenwood Ave., East Orange, NJ 07017. No unsolicited material.

KALMBACH BOOKS—21027 Crossroads Cir., Waukesha, WI 53187. Terry Spohn, Sr. Acquisitions Ed. Adult nonfiction, 18,000 to 50,000 words, on scale modeling, railroading, model railroading, and toy trains. Send outline with sample chapters. Accepts multiple queries. Royalty.

KAR-BEN COPIES—6800 Tildenwood Ln., Rockville, MD 20852. Judye Groner, Ed. Books on Jewish themes for preschool and elementary children (to age 9): picture books, fiction, and nonfiction. Complete manuscript preferred; SASE. Royalty. Web site: www.karben.com

KEATS PUBLISHING, INC.—2020 Ave. of the Stars, Suite 300, Los Angeles, CA 90067. Peter Hoffman, Sr. Ed. Health, nutrition, alternative and complimentary medicine, preventive health care, New Age, and spirituality. Royalty.

KENSINGTON PUBLISHING CORP.—(*Kensington Books, Pinnacle,* and *Zebra* imprints) 850 Third Ave., 16th Fl., New York, NY 10022. Paul Dinas, Ed.-in-Chief. Ann LaFarge, Exec. Ed. Popular fiction; historical and contemporary romance; *Splendor Romances* (110,000 words); *Arabesque* (African American) romances; regencies (80,000 words); *Encanto* (Hispanic romances in English or Spanish); westerns; thrillers; true crime; nonfiction. Agented material only. SASE for guidelines. Web: www.kensingtonbooks.com.

KENT STATE UNIVERSITY PRESS—Kent State Univ., Kent, OH 44242. John T. Hubbell, Dir. Julia Morton, Ed.-in-Chief. Interested in scholarly works in history and literary criticism of high quality, any titles of regional interest for Ohio, scholarly biographies, archaeological research, the arts, and general nonfiction.

KNOPF BOOKS FOR YOUNG READERS, ALFRED A.—201 E. 50th St., New York, NY 10022. Distinguished juvenile fiction and nonfiction. Query; no unsolicited manuscripts. Royalty. Guidelines.

KNOPF, INC., ALFRED A.—201 E. 50th St., New York, NY 10022. Attn: Sr. Ed. Distinguished adult fiction and general nonfiction. Query for nonfiction.

KODANSHA AMERICA, INC.—114 Fifth Ave., New York, NY 10011. Attn: Ed. Dept. Nonfiction books, 50,000 to 200,000 words, on cross-cultural, Asian and other international subjects. Query with outline, sample chapters, and SASE. Royalty.

KRAUSE PUBLICATIONS, INC.—700 E. State St., Iola, WI 54990-

0001. Paul Kennedy, Acq. Ed. Antiques and collectibles, sewing and crafts, automotive topics, numismatics, sports, philatelics, outdoors, guns and knives, toys, records and comics.

LANDMARK SPECIALTY BOOKS—150 W. Brambleton Ave., Norfolk, VA 23510. Allan W. Miller, Man. Ed. Collector guides and reference books, 200 pages, on antiques and collectibles. Query with outline and sample chapter. Royalty. Imprints *Antique Trader Books* and *Tuff Stuff Books*.

LARK BOOKS—50 College St., Asheville, NC 28801. Carol Taylor, Pub. Distinctive books for creative people in crafts, how-to, leisure activities, and "coffee table" categories. Query with outline. Royalty.

LEADERSHIP PUBLISHERS, INC.—P.O. Box 8358, Des Moines, IA 50301-8358. Dr. Lois F. Roets, Ed. Reference books for teachers of talented and gifted students, grades K to 12, and teacher reference books. No fiction or poetry. Send SASE for catalogue and writer's guidelines before submitting. "We're getting too many manuscripts that have nothing to do with our area of publication." Query or outline. Royalty for books; flat fee for booklets.

LEE & LOW BOOKS—95 Madison Ave., New York, NY 10016. Philip Lee, Pub. Louise May, Sr. Ed. Focus is on fiction and nonfiction picture books for children ages 2 to 10. "Our goal is to meet the growing need for books that address children of color and to provide books on subjects and stories they can identify with. Of special interest are stories set in contemporary America. Folklore and animal stories not considered." Include SASE. Advance/royalty.

LERNER PUBLISHING GROUP—241 First Ave. N, Minneapolis, MN 55401. Jennifer Martin, Submissions Ed. Divisions include *Carolrhoda Books* and *Runestone Press*. Nonfiction for children of all grade levels, including nature, geography, natural and physical science, current events, history, world art and cultures, sports, and biographies (especially series). Submissions accepted during March and October only. Multiple queries are considered. Please allow six months for response. Pays mostly flat fee, but negotiated per contract.

LIBROS VIAJEROS—See *Harcourt Brace & Co. Children's Book Div.*

LIMELIGHT BOOKS—See *Tiare Publications*.

LINCOLN-HERNDON PRESS, INC.—818 S. Dirksen Pkwy., Springfield, IL 62703. Jean Saul, Asst. Pub. American humor that reveals American history. Humor collections. Query.

LINNET BOOKS, LINNET PROFESSIONAL BOOKS—See *Shoe String Press*.

LITTLE, BROWN & CO.—1271 Avenue of the Americas, New York, NY 10020. No unsolicited manuscripts.

LITTLE, BROWN & CO. CHILDREN'S BOOK DEPT.—3 Center Plaza, Boston, MA 02108. Attn: Ed. Dept. Juvenile fiction and nonfiction and picture books. No unsolicited manuscripts. Accepts agented material only.

LLEWELLYN PUBLICATIONS—P.O. Box 64383, St. Paul, MN 55164-0383. Nancy J. Mostad, Acquisitions Mgr. Books, from 75,000 words, on subjects of self-help, how-to, alternative health, astrology, metaphysics, new age, and the occult. Metaphysical/occult fiction. "We're interested in any kind of story (mystery, historical, gothic, occult, metaphysical adventure), just as long as the theme is authentic occultism, and the work is both entertaining and educational." Query with sample chapters. Multiple queries considered. Royalty.

LONGSTREET PRESS— 2140 Newmarket Pkwy., Suite 122, Marietta, GA 30067. Editorial Dept. Nonfiction, varying lengths, appealing to a general audience. Query with outline and sample chapters. Accepts very little fiction, and only through an agent. SASE. Allow 5 months for response. Royalty.

LOTHROP, LEE & SHEPARD BOOKS— 1350 Ave. of the Americas, New York, NY 10019. Susan Pearson, Ed.-in-Chief. Juvenile fiction and nonfiction, picture books. Does not review unsolicited material. Royalty.

LOUISIANA STATE UNIVERSITY PRESS— P.O. Box 25053, Baton Rouge, LA 70894-5053. Attn: Ed. Dir. Scholarly adult nonfiction, dealing with the U.S. South, its history and its culture. Query with outline and sample chapters. Royalty.

LOVE AND LAUGHTER— See *Harlequin Books/Canada*.

LUCENT BOOKS— P.O. Box 289011, San Diego, CA 92198-9011. Lori Shein, Man. Ed. Books, 18,000 to 25,000 words, for junior high/middle school students. "Overview" series: current issues (political, social, historical, environmental topics). Other series include "World History," "The Way People Live" (exploring daily life and culture of communities worldwide, past and present), "Modern Nations." No unsolicited material; work is by assignment only. Flat fee. Query for guidelines and catalogue.

LYLE STUART— See *Carol Publishing Group*.

LYONS PRESS— 123 W. 18th St., New York, NY 10011. Bryan Oettel, Ed. Books, 100 to 300 pages, on cooking, gardening, sports, woodworking, natural history, and science. Query with outline. Royalty.

MCCLANAHAN BOOK CO.— 23 W. 26th St., New York, NY 10010. Kenn Goin, Ed. Dir. Mass-market books for children, preschool to third grade. "Most books published as part of a series." Majority of work is done on a "Work for Hire" basis. Flat fee. Query; no unsolicited manuscripts accepted.

MCELDERRY BOOKS, MARGARET K.— 1230 6th Ave., New York, NY 10020. Emma Dryden, Senior Ed. Children's and young adult books, including picture books; quality fiction; fantasy; beginning chapter books; humor; and realism. Request guidelines before querying.

MCFARLAND & COMPANY, INC., PUBLISHERS— Box 611, Jefferson, NC 28640. Robert Franklin, Pres./Ed.-in-Chief. Steve Wilson, Sr. Ed., Virginia Tobiassen, Ed. Scholarly and reference books, from 225 manuscript pages, in many fields, except mathematical sciences. Particularly interested in general reference, performing arts, sports, women's studies, and African American studies. No fiction, new age, inspirational, children's, poetry, or exposés. Submit complete manuscripts or query with outline and sample chapters. Royalty.

MCGREGOR PUBLISHING— 4532 W. Kennedy Blvd., Suite 233, Tampa, FL 33609. Lonnie Herman, Pub. Nonfiction, especially biography, sports, self-help. Query with outline and sample chapters. Royalty.

MACMILLAN REFERENCE USA— 1633 Broadway, New York, NY 10019. Attn: Ed. Dept. General Book Division: Religious, sports, science, travel, and reference books. No fiction. Paperbacks: *Collier Books,* history, psychology, contemporary issues, sports, popular information, childcare, health. *The Free Press,* college texts and professional books in social sciences, humanities. Query. Royalty.

MACMURRAY & BECK, INC.—Alta Court, 1490 Lafayette St., Suite 108, Denver, CO 80218. Frederick Ramey, Exec. Dir. Quality fiction and narrative nonfiction.

MADISON BOOKS—4720 Boston Way, Lanham, MD 20706. James E. Lyons, Pub. Full-length nonfiction: history, biography, contemporary affairs, trade reference. Query required. Royalty.

MADLIBS—See *Price Stern Sloan, Inc.*

MAGIC ATTIC PRESS—866 Spring St., Westbrook, ME 04092. Ed. Series fiction for young girls, ages 7 to 12. Submit writing samples only: a portion of a work in progress or a chapter from a finished book (to 10 pages); include resumé, and SASE.

MAGIC CARPET BOOKS—See *Harcourt Brace & Co. Children's Book Div.*

MAGINATION PRESS—750 First St., N.E., Washington, DC 20002. Darcie Conner Johnston, Ed. Children's picture books dealing with the psychotherapeutic treatment or resolution of serious childhood problems. Picture books for children 4 to 11; nonfiction for children 8 to 18. Most books are written by mental health professionals. Submit complete manuscript. Royalty.

MARKOWSKI INTERNATIONAL PUBLISHERS—See *Possibility Press.*

MARLOWE AND COMPANY—See *Thunder's Mouth Press.*

MEADOWBROOK PRESS—5451 Smetana Dr., Minnetonka, MN 55343. Joseph Gredler, Submissions Ed. Upbeat, useful books, 60,000 words, on pregnancy, childbirth, and parenting; shorter works of humor, party planning, and children's activities; fiction anthologies and humorous poetry for children; adult light verse. Send for guidelines; include SASE with all submissions. Royalty or flat fee.

MEGA-BOOKS, INC.—240 E. 60th St., New York, NY 10022. John Craddock, Pres. Book packager. Young adult books, 150 pages, children's books. Query for guidelines. Flat fee.

MENASHA RIDGE PRESS—700 S. 28th St., Suite 206, Birmingham, AL 35233. Bud Zehmer, Sr. Acquisitions Ed. Outdoor/action travel guidebooks (mountain biking, canoeing, backpacking, etc.), to 224 pages. Query with sample chapters and table of contents. Pays flat fee or royalty.

MEREDITH CORP. BOOK PUBLISHING—(*Better Homes and Gardens Books* and *Ortho Books*) 1716 Locust St., Des Moines, IA 50309-3023. James D. Blume, Ed.-in-Chief. Books on gardening, crafts, decorating, do-it-yourself, cooking, health; mostly staff-written. "Interested in free-lance writers with expertise in these areas." Limited market. Query with SASE.

THE MICHIGAN STATE UNIVERSITY PRESS—1405 S. Harrison Rd., Suite 25, E. Lansing, MI 48823-5202. Scholarly nonfiction, with concentrations in history, regional history, women's studies, African-American history, contemporary culture; also Native American Series, Rhetoric Series, and Lotus Poetry Series. Submit prospectus, table of contents, and sample chapters to Acquisitions Ed. Authors should refer to The Chicago Manual of Style, 14th Edition, for formats and styles.

MILKWEED EDITIONS—430 First Ave. N., Suite 400, Minneapolis, MN 55401-1743. Emilie Buchwald, Ed. "We publish excellent award-winning fiction, poetry, essays, and nonfiction about the natural world, the kind of writing that makes for good reading." Publishes about 17 books a year. Send SASE for guidelines before submitting manuscript. Royalty. Also publishes *Milkweeds for Young Readers*: high quality novels for middle grades.

THE MILLBROOK PRESS—2 Old New Milford Rd., Brookfield, CT 06804. Meghann French, Ed. Asst. Nonfiction for early elementary grades through grades 7 and up, appropriate for the school and public library or trade market, encompassing curriculum-related topics and extracurricular interests. Some picture books. Imprint: *Copper Beech Books*. Query with outline, sample chapter, and SASE. Allow 6 to 8 weeks for response. Royalty.

MIRA BOOKS—See *Harlequin Books/Canada*.

THE MIT PRESS—5 Cambridge Center, Cambridge, MA 02142. Larry Cohen, Ed.-in-Chief. Books on computer science/artificial intelligence; cognitive sciences; economics; finance; architecture; aesthetic and social theory; linguistics; technology studies; environmental studies; and neuroscience.

MONDO PUBLISHING—One Plaza Rd., Greenvale, NY 11548. Attn: Submissions Ed. Picture books, nonfiction, and early chapter books for readers ages 4 to 10. "We want to create beautiful books that children can read on their own and find so enjoyable that they'll want to come back to them time and time again." Query. Royalty.

MONTANA HISTORICAL SOCIETY—P.O. Box 201201, Helena, MT 59620. Martha Kohl, Ed. Books on Montana history. Query. Royalty.

MOON HANDBOOKS—Moon Publications, Inc., P.O. Box 3040, Chico, CA 95927-3040. Karen Bleske, Ed. Dir. Travel guides, 400 to 500 pages. Will consider multiple submissions. Query. Royalty.

MOREHOUSE PUBLISHING—4775 Linglestown Rd., Harrisburg, PA 17112. Debra Farrington, Ed. Dir. Theology, pastoral care, church administration, spirituality, Anglican studies, history of religion, books for children. Query with outline, contents, and sample chapter and SASE. Royalty.

MORGAN REYNOLDS, INC.—620 S. Elm St., Suite 384, Greensboro, NC 27406. John Riley, Pub. Young adult biography and history, 20,000 words. Queries preferred. Multiple queries considered. Pays royalty. Web site: www.morganreynolds.com.

MORROW AND CO., INC., WILLIAM—The Hearst Corp. 1350 Ave. of the Americas, New York, NY 10019. Attn: Eds. Adult fiction and nonfiction: no unsolicited manuscripts. Betty Kelly, VP & Ed.-in-Chief. *Mulberry Books* (children's paperbacks), Paulette Kaufmann, Ed. Dir.; *Hearst Books* (general nonfiction), Jacqueline Deval, VP & Pub., Elizabeth Rice, Ed. Dir.; *Rob Weisbach Books*, Rob Weisbach, Pub. & Pres., Colin Dickerman, Sr. Ed.

MOUNTAIN PRESS PUBLISHING—1301 S. 3rd W., P.O. Box 2399, Missoula, MT 59806. Attn: Kathleen Ort, Ed.-in-Chief. Nonfiction, 300 pages: natural history, field guides, geology, Western history, Americana, and outdoor guides. Query with outline and sample chapters; multiple queries discouraged. Royalty.

THE MOUNTAINEERS BOOKS—1001 S.W. Klickitat Way, Suite 201, Seattle, WA 98134. Margaret Foster, Ed.-in-Chief. Nonfiction books on non-competitive aspects of outdoor sports such as mountaineering, backpacking, walking, trekking, canoeing, kayaking, bicycling, skiing; independent adventure travel. Field guides, how-to and where-to guidebooks, biographies of outdoor people; accounts of expeditions. Natural history and conservation. Submit sample chapters, outline, and bio. Royalty.

MUIR PUBLICATIONS, JOHN—P.O. Box 613, Santa Fe, NM 87504-0613. Cassandra Conyers, Acquisitions Mgr. Travel guidebooks for adults. Natural health topics for adults and children. Send manuscript or query with sample chapters. No fiction. Advance and royalties.

MULBERRY BOOKS—See *William Morrow and Co., Inc.*

MULTNOMAH PUBLISHERS—204 W. Adams Ave., P.O. Box 1720, Sisters, OR 97759. Attn: Ed. Evangelical, Christian publishing house with 3 imprints: *Multnomah Books*, message-driven, clean, moral, uplifting fiction, and nonfiction; address Ed. Dept. *Alabaster*, contemporary women's fiction that upholds strong Christian values; address Karen Ball, Ed. *Gold 'n' Honey*, developmentally appropriate stories for children; address *Gold'n'Honey* Ed. Submit 2 or 3 sample chapters with outline, cover letter, and SASE. Royalty. Web: www.MultnomahBooks.com

MUSTANG PUBLISHING CO., INC.—Box 770426, Memphis, TN 38177. Rollin A. Riggs, Ed. Nonfiction for 18- to 40-year-olds, specializing in travel, humor, and how-to. Send queries for 100- to 300-page books, with outlines and sample chapters. No phone calls. Royalty. SASE required.

THE MYSTERIOUS PRESS—Time and Life Bldg., 1271 Ave. of the Americas, New York, NY 10020. William Malloy, Ed.-in-Chief. Mystery/suspense novels. Agented manuscripts only.

NAIAD PRESS, INC.—Box 10543, Tallahassee, FL 32302. Barbara Grier, Ed. Adult fiction, 48,000 to 50,000 words, with lesbian themes and characters: mysteries, romances, gothics, ghost stories, westerns, regencies, spy novels, etc. Query with letter and one-page précis only. Royalty.

NAL—(formerly *Topaz*) 375 Hudson St., New York, NY 10014. Audrey LeFehr, Ex. Ed. Query.

NATIONAL GEOGRAPHIC CHILDREN'S BOOKS—1145 17th St. N.W., Washington, DC 20036-4688. Nancy Laties Feresten, Pub. Dir. Mostly nonfiction, but also folklore, family reference, and nonfiction-based fictional picture books for children ages 2 to 12. Subjects of interest include adventure, exploration, history, science, nature, geography, and the multicultural society. Send complete manuscript for shorter books; outline and sample chapter for longer ones.

NATUREGRAPH PUBLISHERS—P.O. Box 1047, Happy Camp, CA 96039. Barbara Brown, Ed. Nonfiction: Native-American culture, natural history, outdoor living, land, Indian lore, and how-to. Query. Royalty.

THE NAVAL INSTITUTE PRESS—, Annapolis, MD 21402. Attn: Acquisitions Dept. Nonfiction, 60,000 to 100,000 words: military histories; biographies; ship guides. Occasional military fiction, 75,000 to 110,000 words. Query with outline and sample chapters. Royalty.

NEW HORIZON PRESS—P.O. Box 669, Far Hills, NJ 07931. Joan Dunphy, Ed.-in-Chief. True stories, 96,000 words, dealing with contemporary issues, especially true crime, that revolve around a hero or heroine. Royalty. Query.

NEW LEAF PRESS, INC.—P.O. Box 726, Green Forest, AR 72638. Jim Fletcher, Acquisitions Ed. Nonfiction, 100 to 400 pages, for Christian readers:

how to live the Christian life, devotionals, gift books. Query with outline and sample chapters. Royalty.

NEW READERS PRESS—(formerly *Signal Hill Publications*) 1320 Jamesville Ave., Box 131, Syracuse, NY 13210. Terrie Lipke, Ed. Fiction, 5,000 to 9,000 words, for adults who read at low levels for use in basic and ESL programs, volunteer literacy programs, and job training programs. Guidelines. Query; no unsolicited manuscripts. Royalty.

NEW RIVERS PRESS—420 N. 5th St., Suite 910, Minneapolis, MN 55401. Ed. Collections of short stories, essays, and poems from emerging writers in upper Midwest. Send SASE for guidelines to the Minnesota Voices Project or Headwaters Literary Competitions.

NEW WORLD LIBRARY—14 Pamaron Way, Novato, CA 94949. Attn: Submissions Ed. Inspirational and practical nonfiction books and audio cassettes on spirituality, personal growth, health and wellness, business and prosperity, religion, recovery, multicultural studies, and women's studies. "Dedicated to awakening individual and global potential." Query with outline, sample chapter, and SASE. Multiple queries accepted. Royalty.

NEW YORK UNIVERSITY PRESS—70 Washington Sq. S., New York, NY 10012. Scholarly nonfiction. Submit manuscript and/or proposal with sample chapters and curriculum vitae.

NEWCASTLE PUBLISHING—13419 Saticoy St., N. Hollywood, CA 91605. Daryl Jacoby, Pub. Nonfiction manuscripts, 200 to 250 pages, for older adults on personal health, health care issues, psychology, and relationships. "We are not looking for fads or trends. We want books with a long shelf life." Multiple queries considered. Royalty.

NORTH COUNTRY PRESS—RR 1, Box 1358, Unity, ME 04988. Patricia Newell, Mary Kenney, Eds. Nonfiction with a Maine and/or New England tie-in with emphasis on the outdoors; also limited fiction (Maine-based mysteries). "Our goal is to publish high-quality books for people who love New England." Query with SASE, outline, and sample chapters. No unsolicited manuscripts. Royalty.

NORTHEASTERN UNIVERSITY PRESS—360 Huntington Ave., 416 CP, Boston, MA 02115. John Weingartner, Terri Teleen, Eds. Nonfiction, 50,000 to 200,000 words: trade and scholarly titles in music, criminal justice, women's studies, ethnic studies, law, sociology, environmental studies, and American history. Submit query with outline and sample chapter or complete manuscript. Royalty.

NORTHERN ILLINOIS UNIVERSITY PRESS—DeKalb, IL 60115. Mary L. Lincoln, Dir. Books, 250 to 450 typescript pages, for scholars and informed general readers. Submit history, regional topics, literature and Russian studies topics to Mary Lincoln; philosophy, politics, anthropology, economics, and other social sciences to Martin Johnson. Query with outline. Royalty.

NORTHLAND PUBLISHING—P.O. Box 1389, Flagstaff, AZ 86002. Nonfiction books on Western arts; Native American culture, myth, art, and crafts; Western regional nonfiction; and cookbooks. Unique children's picture books, 350 to 1,500 words, with contemporary themes. Query with outline, sample chapters. For children's books, send complete manuscript. Written queries only. Include SASE with all submissions or queries. Royalty.

NORTHWORD PRESS—5900 Green Oak Dr., Minnetonka, MN 55343.

Acq. Ed. Nonfiction nature and wildlife books for children and adults. Send SASE with 7 first-class stamps for catalogue and SASE for guidelines. Royalty or flat fee.

NORTON AND CO., INC., W.W.—500 Fifth Ave., New York, NY 10110. Attn: Ed. High-quality literary fiction and nonfiction. No occult, paranormal, religious, genre fiction (formula romance, science fiction, westerns), arts and crafts, young adult, or children's books. No unsolicited manuscripts.

NTC/CONTEMPORARY PUBLISHING GROUP—4255 W. Touhy Ave., Lincolnwood, IL 60646. John T. Nolan, Ed. Dir. Trade nonfiction, 100 to 400 pages, on health, fitness, sports, cooking, business, popular culture, finance, women's issues, quilting, crafts, and general reference. Query with outline, sample chapter, and SASE. Royalty.

ODYSSEY CLASSICS—See *Harcourt Brace & Co. Children's Book Div.*

OHIO UNIVERSITY PRESS/SWALLOW PRESS—Scott Quadrangle, Athens, OH 45701. David Sanders, Dir. Scholarly nonfiction, 350 to 450 manuscript pages, especially literary criticism, regional studies, African studies. *Swallow Press*: general interest and frontier Americana. Query with outline and sample chapters. Royalty. Annual Hollis Summers Poetry Award Competition. Contest guidelines available at: www.ohiou.edu/oupress/.

THE OLIVER PRESS—Charlotte Square, 5707 W. 36th St., Minneapolis, MN 55416. Teresa Faden, Ed. Collective biographies for young adults. Submit proposals for books, 20,000 to 25,000 words, on people who have made an impact in such areas as history, politics, crime, science, and business. Contracts negotiated.

ONJINJINKTA PUBLISHING—P.O. Box 25490, Seattle, WA 98125. Peter Orullian, Ed. Inspirational, self-improvement. Adult and juvenile fiction and nonfiction. Young adult books. Accepts multiple queries and pays an advance and royalties. Query with outline and sample chapters.

OPEN COURT PUBLISHING CO.—332 S. Michigan Ave., Suite 1100, Chicago, IL 60604. Attn: Acquisitions Dept. Scholarly books on philosophy, eastern thought, and related areas. Trade books of a thoughtful nature on social issues, Jungian thought, psychology, public policy, education, social issues, and contemporary culture. Send sample chapters with outline and resumé. Royalty.

ORCHARD BOOKS—95 Madison Ave., New York, NY 10016. Sarah Caguiat, Ed. Ana Cerro, Ed. Juvenile fiction. Picture books and middle-grade fiction, 100 to 150 pages. Limited amount of nonfiction. No unsolicited manuscripts. Query only.

ORCHISES PRESS—P.O. Box 20602, Alexandria, VA 22320-1602. Roger Lathbury, Ed. Nonfiction books, 128 to 500 pages; and intellectually sophisticated, technically expert poetry books, 48 to 128 pages. No fiction. Query with sample chapters. Royalty.

OREGON STATE UNIVERSITY PRESS—101 Waldo Hall, Corvallis, OR 97331. Attn: Ed. Dept. Scholarly books in a limited range of disciplines and books of particular importance to the Pacific Northwest, especially dealing with the history, natural history, culture, and literature of the region or with natural resource issues. Query with summary of manuscript.

OSBORNE/MCGRAW HILL—2600 Tenth St., Berkeley, CA 94710.

Scott Rogers, Ed.-in-Chief. Computer books for general and technical audience. Query. Royalty.

OUR SUNDAY VISITOR PUBLISHING—200 Noll Plaza, Huntington, IN 46750. Jacquelyn M. Lindsey, Mike Dubruiel, Acquisitions Eds. Catholic-oriented books of various lengths. No fiction. Query with outline and sample chapters. Royalty.

THE OVERLOOK PRESS—386 W. Broadway, 4th Fl., New York, NY 10012. Tracy Carns, Pub. Dir. Literary fiction, some fantasy/science fiction, foreign literature in translation, general nonfiction, including art, architecture, design, film, history, biography, crafts/lifestyle, martial arts, Hudson Valley regional interest, and children's books. Query with outline, sample chapters and SASE. Royalty.

OWEN PUBLISHERS, INC., RICHARD C.—Children's Book Dept., P.O. Box 585, Katonah, NY 10536. Janice Boland, Ed. Fiction and nonfiction. Brief storybooks, approximately 45 to 100 words, suitable for 5- and 7-year-old beginning readers for the "Books for Young Learners" collection. Also articles and fiction, 100 to 700 words, that interest, inform, inspire, fascinate, and entertain, for 7- and 8-year olds for "Books for Fluent Readers" collection. Royalties for writers. Flat fee for illustrators. Writers must send SASE for guidelines before submitting.

OXFORD UNIVERSITY PRESS—198 Madison Ave., New York, NY 10016. Attn: Ed. Dept. Authoritative books on literature, history, philosophy, etc.; college textbooks, medical, scientific, technical and reference books. Query. Royalty.

PANTHEON BOOKS—Div. of *Random House,* 201 E. 50th St., New York, NY 10022. Attn: Ed. Dept. Quality fiction and nonfiction. Query required. Royalty.

PAPIER-MACHE PRESS—P.O. Box 2428, Watsonville, CA 95077. Sandra Martz, Ed. Theme anthologies. "We emphasize, but are not limited to, the publication of books for midlife and older women." Write for guidelines. Royalty.

PARA PUBLISHING—P.O. Box 8206-238, Santa Barbara, CA 93118-8206. Dan Poynter, Ed. Adult nonfiction books on parachutes and skydiving only. Author must present evidence of having made at least 1,000 jumps. Query. Royalty.

PAULIST PRESS—997 Macarthur Blvd., Mahwah, NJ 07430. Donald Brophy, Man. Ed. Adult nonfiction, 100 to 400 pages; and picture books, 8 to 10 pages, for readers 5 to 7 or 8 to 10. For adult books, query with outline and sample chapters. For juvenile books, submit complete manuscript to Karen Scialabba, Ed. Royalty.

PEACHTREE PUBLISHERS, LTD.—494 Armour Cir. N.E., Atlanta, GA 30324. Attn: Ed. Dept. Wide variety of juvenile, and young adult books, fiction and nonfiction. No religious material, science fiction/fantasy, romance, mystery/detective, and historical fiction; no business, scientific, or technical books. Send outline and sample chapters. SASE required. Royalty.

PELICAN PUBLISHING CO., INC.—P.O. Box 3110, Gretna, LA 70054. Nina Kooij, Ed.-in-Chief. General nonfiction: Americana, regional, architecture, travel, cookbooks. Royalty.

PENGUIN PUTNAM BOOKS—375 Hudson St., New York, NY 10014. Attn: Ed. Dept. Adult fiction and nonfiction paperbacks. Royalty.

THE PERMANENT PRESS—4170 Noyac Rd., Sag Harbor, NY 11963. Judith Shepard, Ed. Original and arresting novels. Query. Royalty.

PERSEUS BOOKS—One Jacob Way, Reading, MA 01867-3999. Adult nonfiction, varying lengths, on science, business, psychology, parenting, and health. Query with outline and sample chapters. Multiple queries considered. Royalty.

PERSPECTIVES PRESS—P.O. Box 90318, Indianapolis, IN 46290-0318. Pat Johnston, Pub. Nonfiction books on infertility, adoption, closely related reproductive health and child welfare issues (foster care, etc.). "Writers must read our guidelines before submitting." Query. Royalty. See web site for guidelines: www.perspectivespress.com.

PHILOMEL BOOKS—345 Hudson St., New York, NY 10014. Patricia Lee Gauch, VP & Pub. Michael Green, Sr. Ed. Juvenile picture books and young adult fiction, particularaly fantasy and historical. Fresh, original work with compelling characters and "a sense of the dramatic." Query required.

PINEAPPLE PRESS—P.O. Box 3899, Sarasota, FL 34230. June Cussen, Ed. Serious fiction and nonfiction, Florida-oriented, 60,000 to 125,000 words. Query with outline, sample chapters, and SASE. Royalty.

PINNACLE BOOKS—850 Third Ave., New York, NY 10022. Paul Dinas, Ed.-in-Chief Nonfiction books: true crime, celebrity biographies, and humor. Unsolicited material not accepted.

PIPPIN PRESS—229 E. 85th St., Gracie Sta., Box 1347, New York, NY 10028. Barbara Francis, Pub. Small chapter books for children ages 7 to 10, with historical fiction and fantasy themes, as well as ethnic stories and humorous mysteries; imaginative nonfiction for children of all ages. Query with SASE only; no unsolicited manuscripts. Royalty.

PLANET DEXTER—One Jacob Way, Reading, MA 01867-3999. Nonfiction books for children ages 8 to 12. All product developed internally. No unsolicited submissions.

PLAYERS PRESS, INC.—P.O. Box 1132, Studio City, CA 91614. Robert Gordon, Ed. Plays and musicals for children and adults; juvenile and adult nonfiction related to theatre, film, television, and the performing arts. Lengths vary. Query. Royalty.

PLEASANT COMPANY—8400 Fairway Pl., Middleton, WI 58562-0998. Jennifer Hirsch, Submissions Ed. Books, 10,000 to 40,000 words, for 8- to 12-year-old girls: historical mystery/suspense, contemporary fiction, and contemporary advice and activity. "We have a small 'concept-driven' list and do not use inexperienced writers." Query with outline and sample chapters or send complete manuscript. Pays on a flat fee or royalty basis.

PLENUM PUBLISHING CORP.—10 E. 53rd St., New York, NY 10022. Linda Greenspan Regan, Exec. Ed. Trade nonfiction, approximately 300 pages, on popular science, criminology, psychology, social science, anthropology, and health. Query required. Royalty. Hardcover.

PLUME BOOKS—200 Madison Ave., New York, NY 10016. Attn: Ed. Dept. Nonfiction: hobbies, business, health, cooking, child care, psychology, history, popular culture, biography, and politics. Fiction: serious literary and gay. Query.

POCKET BOOKS—1230 Ave. of the Americas, New York, NY 10020. Adult and young adult fiction and nonfiction. Mystery line: police procedurals, private eye, and amateur sleuth novels, 60,000 to 70,000 words. Royalty.

POISONED PEN PRESS—6962 E. 1st Ave., #103, Scottsdale, AZ 85251. Louis Silverstein, Ed. Adult mysteries only. Pays on a royalty basis. Query with outline, sample chapters, and SASE.

POPULAR PRESS—Bowling Green State Univ., Bowling Green, OH 43403. Ms. Pat Browne, Ed. Nonfiction, 250 to 400 pages, examining some aspect of popular culture. Query with outline. Flat fee or royalty.

POSSIBILITY PRESS—(formerly *Markowski Publishers, Success Publishers*) One Oakglade Cir., Hummelstown, PA 17036. Marjorie L. Markowski, Ed. Nonfiction, 35,000 to 55,000 words: personal development, self-help, sales and marketing, leadership training, network marketing, motivation, and success topics. "Our mission is to help the people of the world grow and become the best they can be." SASE for guidelines. Query with outline and 3 sample chapters. Royalty. E-mail: PossPress@aol.com.

POTTER, CLARKSON—See *Clarkson N. Potter, Publishers.*

PRAEGER PUBLISHERS—88 Post Rd. W., Westport, CT 06881-5007. Attn: Pub. General nonfiction; scholarly and textbooks in the social sciences. Query with outline. Royalty.

PRESIDIO PRESS—505B San Marin Dr., Suite 300, Novato, CA 94945-1340. Attn: Ed. Dept. Nonfiction: military history and military affairs, from 90,000 words. Fiction: selected military and action-adventure works from 100,000 words. Query. Royalty.

PRICE STERN SLOAN, INC.—345 Hudson St., New York, NY 10014. Ed. Witty or edgy middle grade fiction and nonfiction, calendars, and novelty juvenile titles. Imprints include *Troubador Press, Wee Sing, MadLibs.* Royalty. No longer accepting unsolicited manuscripts.

PRIMA PUBLISHING—3875 Atherton Rd., Rocklin, CA 95765. Ben Dominitz, Pub. Steven K. Martin, Ed. Dir. Susan Silva, Jamie Miller, Eds. Nonfiction on variety of subjects, including business, health, self-help, entertainment, computers, inspiration, and cookbooks. "We want books with originality, written by highly qualified individuals." Advance against royalty.

PRUETT PUBLISHING COMPANY—7464 Arapahoe Rd., Suite A-9, Boulder, CO 80303. Jim Pruett, Pub. Nonfiction: outdoors and recreation, western U.S. history, travel, natural history and the environment, fly fishing. Query. Royalty.

PUTNAM'S SONS, G.P.—345 Hudson St., New York, NY 10014. Attn: Children's Ed. Dept. General trade nonfiction and fiction for ages 2 to 18. Mostly picture books and middle-grade novels. No unsolicited manuscripts. Royalty.

QED PRESS—155 Cypress St., Fort Bragg, CA 95437. Cynthia Frank, Ed. Health & healing, self-help, and how to fold paper airplanes. Query with outline and sample chapters. Royalty.

QUEST BOOKS—Theosophical Publishing House, 306 W. Geneva Rd., P. O. Box 270, Wheaton, IL 60189-0270. Brenda Rosen, Exec. Ed. Nonfiction books on Eastern and Western religion and philosophy, holism, healing, transpersonal psychology, men's and women's spirituality, creativity, meditation, yoga, ancient wisdom. Query. Royalty.

QUILL TRADE PAPERBACKS—Imprint of William Morrow and Co., Inc., 1350 Ave. of the Americas, New York, NY 10019. Trade paperback adult fiction and nonfiction. Submit through agent only.

QUIXOTE PRESS—1854 345th Ave., Wever, IA 52658. Bruce Carlson, Pres. Adult fiction and nonfiction including humor, folklore, and regional cookbooks; some juvenile fiction. Query with sample chapters and outline. Royalty.

RAGGED MOUNTAIN PRESS—A Div. of McGraw-Hill, Box 220, Camden, ME 04843. Jonathan Eaton, Ed. Dir. Tom McCarthy, Acquisitions Ed. Books on outdoor recreation.

RAINBOW BOOKS, INC.—Box 430, Highland City, FL 33846. Betsy Lampe, Ed. Adult mysteries, to 75,000 words. Self-help and how-to nonfiction, of varying lengths. Send SASE for guidelines. Pays royalties.

RAINTREE STECK-VAUGHN PUBLISHERS—466 Southern Blvd., Chatham, NJ 07928. Walter Kossmann, Frank Sloan, Eds. Nonfiction books, 5,000 to 30,000 words, for school and library market: biographies for grades 3 and up; and science, social studies, and history books for primary grades through high school. Query with outline and sample chapters; SASE required. Flat fee or royalty.

RANDOM HOUSE JUVENILE DIV.—201 E. 50th St., New York, NY 10022. Kate Klimo, Pub. Dir. Fiction and nonfiction for beginning readers; paperback fiction line for 7- to 9-year-olds. No unsolicited manuscripts. Agented material only.

RED CRANE BOOKS—2008 Rosina St., Suite B, Santa Fe, NM 87505. Marianne O'Shaughnessy, Ed. Art and folk art, bilingual material with Spanish and English, cookbooks, essays, gardening, herbal guides, natural history, novels, social and political issues and social history. No children's books. Send a short synopsis, 2 sample chapters, resumé, and SASE.

RED SAGE PUBLISHING, INC.—P.O. Box 4844, Seminole, FL 33775. Alexandria Kendall, Acquisitions Ed. Novella submissions for anthologies. Sensual romantic fiction, 20,000 to 30,000 words. "Love scenes should be sophisticated, erotic, and emotional. Push the envelope beyond the normal romance novel." Query with first 10 pages and synopsis. Royalty.

THE RED SEA PRESS—11-D Princess Rd., Suites D, E, F, Lawrenceville, NJ 08648. Kassahun Checole, Pub. Adult nonfiction, 360 double-spaced manuscript pages. "We focus on nonfiction material with a specialty on the Horn of Africa." Query. Royalty.

RED WAGON BOOKS—Imprint of Harcourt Children's Books, 525 B St., Suite 1900, San Diego, CA 92101-4495. Attn: Acquisitions Ed. No unsolicited manuscripts. Query with SASE.

RENAISSANCE HOUSE—Primer Publishers, 5738 N. Central Ave., Phoenix, AZ 85012. Regional guidebooks. Guidebooks on CO, AZ, CA, and the Southwest. "We use only manuscripts written to our specifications for new or ongoing series. Not accepting unsolicited manuscripts at this time."

REPUBLIC OF TEXAS PRESS—See *Wordware Publishing.*

RISING MOON—Imprint of *Northland Publishing*, P.O. Box 1389, Flagstaff, AZ 86002. Aimee Jackson, Associate Ed. Picture books for ages 5 to 8. Send complete manuscript. Fiction and nonfiction, ages 8 to 12; no longer accepts unsolicited manuscripts. Interested in material on contemporary subjects. Considers multiple queries and pays on a royalty basis.

RISING TIDE PRESS—3831 N. Oracle Rd., Tucson, AZ 85705. Lee Boojamra, Ed. Books for, by, and about lesbians. Fiction, 60,000 to 80,000 words: romance, mystery, and science fiction/fantasy. Nonfiction, 40,000 to 60,000 words. Royalty. Reports in 3 months. SASE for guidelines or e-mail RTPress@aol.com.

RIZZOLI INTERNATIONAL PUBLICATIONS, INC.—300 Park Ave. S., New York, NY 10010. Manuela Soares, Children's Book Ed. Original manuscripts that introduce children to fine art, folk art, and architecture of all cultures for a small list. Nonfiction and fiction for all ages. Query with SASE or response card. Royalty.

ROC—375 Hudson St., New York, NY 10014. Laura Anne Gilman, Exec. Ed. Jennifer Heddle, Asst. Ed. Science fiction, fantasy. Send agented manuscripts to Laura Anne Gilman; unagented manuscripts to Jennifer Heddle.

ROCKBRIDGE PUBLISHING—Imprint of Howell Press, Inc., P.O. Box 351, Berryville, VA 22611. Katherine Tennery, Ed. Book-length nonfiction on the Civil War, Virginia history, and travel guides to Virginia. Query. Royalty.

RODALE—400 S. 10th St., Emmaus, PA 18098. Pat Corpora, Pres. Sally Reith, Asst. Acquisitions Ed. Books on health (men's, women's alternative, senior), gardening, cookbooks, spirituality, fitness, and pets. Query with resumé, table of contents/outline, and two sample chapters. Royalty and outright purchase. "We have a large in-house writing staff; the majority of our books are conceived and developed in-house. We're always looking for truly competent free-lancers to write chapters for books." Payment on a work-for-hire basis.

ROYAL FIREWORKS PRESS—Box 399, First Ave., Unionville, NY 10988. Charles Morgan, Ed. Adult science fiction and mysteries. Juvenile and young adult fiction, biography, and educational nonfiction. Submit complete manuscripts with a brief plot overview. No multiple queries. Allow a three-week response time. Royalty.

RUNESTONE PRESS—See *Lerner Publishing Group.*

RUNNING PRESS—125 S. 22nd St., Philadelphia, PA 19103. Attn: Asst. to Ed. Dir. Trade nonfiction: art, craft, how-to, self-help, science, lifestyles. Young adult books and interactive packages. Query with outline or table of contents and two- to three-page writing sample. Royalty for some projects; flat fee for others.

RUTGERS UNIVERSITY PRESS—100 Joyce Kilmer Ave., Piscataway, NJ 08854-8099. Paula Kantenwein, Editorial Asst. Nonfiction, 70,000 to 100,000 words. Query with outline and sample chapters. Royalty.

RUTLEDGE HILL PRESS—211 Seventh Ave. N., Nashville, TN 37219. Mike Towle, Ed. Market-specific nonfiction. Query with outline and sample chapters. Royalty.

ST. ANTHONY MESSENGER PRESS—1615 Republic St., Cincinnati, OH 45210-1298. Lisa Biedenbach, Man. Ed. Inspirational nonfiction for Catholics, supporting a Christian lifestyle in our culture; prayer aids, scripture, church history, education, practical spirituality, parish ministry, liturgy resources,

Franciscan resources, family-based religious education program, and children's books. Query with 500-word summary. Royalty.

ST. MARTIN'S PRESS—175 Fifth Ave., New York, NY 10010. Attn: Ed. Dept. General adult fiction and nonfiction. Query. Royalty.

SAINT MARY'S PRESS—702 Terrace Heights, Winona, MN 55987-1320. Stephan Nagel, Ed.-in-Chief. Progressive Catholic publisher. Fiction, to 40,000 words, for young adults ages 11 to 17, "that gives insight into the struggle of teens to become healthy, hopeful adults and also sheds light on Catholic experience, history, or cultures." Query with outline and sample chapter. Royalty.

SANDLAPPER PUBLISHING, INC.—P.O. Drawer 730, Orangeburg, SC 29116-0730. Amanda Gallman, Book Ed. Nonfiction books on South Carolina history, culture, cuisine. Query with outline, sample chapters, and SASE. No phone calls, please.

SASQUATCH BOOKS—615 2nd Ave., Suite 260, Seattle, WA 98104. Attn: Ed. Dept. Regional books on a wide range of nonfiction topics: travel, natural history, gardening, cooking, history, and public affairs. Books should have a Pacific Northwest and/or West Coast subject or theme. Query with SASE. Royalty.

SCARECROW PRESS—4720 Boston Way, Lanham, MD 20706. Shirley Lambert, Assoc. Pub. Reference works and bibliographies, from 150 pages, especially in the areas of library and information science, cinema, TV, radio, and theater, mainly for use by libraries. Query or send complete manuscript; multiple queries considered. Royalty. Web: www.scarecrowpress.com.

SCHOCKEN BOOKS—201 E. 50th St., New York, NY 10022. Attn: Ed. Dept. General nonfiction: Judaica, women's studies, education, history, religion, psychology, cultural studies. Query with book proposal/outline and 2 sample chapters. Royalty.

SCHOLASTIC, INC.—555 Broadway, New York, NY 10012. No unsolicited manuscripts.

SCHOLASTIC PROFESSIONAL BOOKS—555 Broadway, New York, NY 10012-3999. Attn: Adrienne Rozier. Books by and for teachers of kindergarten through eighth grade. *Instructor Books*: practical, activity/resource books on teaching reading and writing, science, math, etc. *Teaching Strategies Books*: 64 to 96 pages on new ideas, practices, and approaches to teaching. Query with outline, sample chapters or activities, contents page, and resumé. Flat fee or royalty. Multiple queries considered. 8½" × 11" SASE for guidelines.

SCHWARTZ BOOKS, ANNE—Atheneum Publishers, 1230 Ave. of the Americas, New York, NY 10020. Anne Schwartz, Ed. Dir. Picture books, juvenile fiction, and nonfiction as well as illustrated collections. Query; no unsolicited manuscripts.

SCOTT FORESMAN—1900 E. Lake Ave., Glenview, IL 60025. Paul McFall, Pres. Elementary and secondary textbooks. Royalty or flat fee.

SEAL PRESS—3131 Western Ave., Suite 410, Seattle, WA 98121-1041. Jennie Goode, Man Ed. Feminist/women's studies books: popular culture and lesbian studies; parenting; domestic violence; health and recovery; sports and outdoors. Query. Royalty.

SEASIDE PRESS—See *Wordware Publishing.*

SEVEN SEAS PRESS—See *International Marine.*

SEVEN STORIES PRESS—140 Watts St., New York, NY 10013. Dan Simon and Paul Abruzzo, Eds. Small press. Fiction and nonfiction. Query with SASE. Royalty.

SHAMBHALA PUBLICATIONS—300 Mass. Ave., Boston, MA 02115. Attn: Laura Stone. "Publishes books of quality, with special interest in philosophy, religion, cultural studies, psychology, health, and global concerns." Publishes very little contemporary fiction, poetry, or art. Pays royalties. Query with outline and sample chapters.

SHAW PUBLISHERS, HAROLD—388 Gunderson Dr., Box 567, Wheaton, IL 60189. Nonfiction, 120 to 320 pages, with an evangelical Christian perspective. Some fiction and literary books. Query. Flat fee or royalty.

SHEARWATER BOOKS—See *Island Press.*

SHOE STRING PRESS—P.O. Box 657, 2 Linsley St., North Haven, CT 06473-2517. Diantha C. Thorpe, Ed./Pub. Books for children and teenagers, including juvenile nonfiction for ages 10 and older. Resources for teachers and librarians that share high standards of scholarship and practical experience. Imprints include *Linnet Books, Archon Books,* and *Linnet Professional Publications.* Submit outline and sample chapters. Royalty.

SIERRA CLUB BOOKS—85 Second St., San Francisco, CA 94105. Attn: Ed. Dept. Nonfiction: environment, natural history, the sciences, outdoors and regional guidebooks, nature photography; children's fiction and nonfiction. Query with SASE. Royalty.

SIGNAL HILL PUBLICATIONS—See *New Readers Press.*

SILHOUETTE BOOKS—300 E. 42nd St., New York, NY 10017. Isabel Swift, V.P. Ed. Tara Gavin, Ed. Dir. *Silhouette Romance*: Mary Theresa Hussey, Sr. Ed. Contemporary romances, 53,000 to 58,000 words. *Special Edition*: Karen Taylor Richman, Sr. Ed. Sophisticated contemporary romances, 75,000 to 80,000 words. *Silhouette Desire*: Joan Marlow Golan, Ed. Sensuous contemporary romances, 53,000 to 60,000 words. *Intimate Moments*: Leslie Wainger, Exec. Sr. Ed. Sensuous, exciting contemporary romances, 80,000 words. Historical romance: 95,000 to 105,000 words, and more; query with synopsis and 3 sample chapters to Tracy Farrell, Sr. Ed. Query with synopsis and SASE to appropriate editor. Tipsheets available.

SILVER MOON PRESS—160 Fifth Ave., Suite 622, New York, NY 10010.

SILVER WHISTLE—See *Harcourt Brace & Co. Children's Book Div.*

SIMON & SCHUSTER—1230 Ave. of the Americas, New York, NY 10020. Adult books. No unsolicited material; manuscripts must be submitted by an agent.

SIMON & SCHUSTER BOOKS FOR YOUNG READERS—1230 Ave. of the Americas, New York, NY 10020. Stephanie Owens Lurie, Assoc. Pub./V.P./Ed. Dir. Books for ages preschool through high school: picture books to young adult; nonfiction for all age levels. Hardcover only. Request guidelines before querying. SASE required for reply.

SINGER MEDIA CORP.—Seaview Business Park, 1030 Calle Cordillera, #106, San Clemente, CA 92673. Helen J. Lee, Acquisitions Dir. International literary agency and syndicate specializing in licensing foreign rights to books in the fields of business, management, celebrity biographies, self-help, occult, and fiction in all genres. Previously published books only. No poetry. Query first with SASE.

SKYLARK BOOKS—See *Yearling Books.*

SMITH AND KRAUS, INC.—P.O. Box 127, Main St., Lyme, NH 03768. Marisa Smith, Pres. Material of interest to the theatre community, collections of major American playwrights, annuals; Monologues, scenes, and plays that have been published in the current theatrical year; Plays and material for grades K through 12. Nonfiction on stagecraft, design, costuming, and makeup. No manuscripts returned. Response time is 3 months. Pays on publication.

SOHO PRESS—853 Broadway, New York, NY 10003. Juris Jurjevics, Pub. Mysteries, thrillers, and contemporary fiction and nonfiction, from 60,000 words. Send SASE and complete manuscript. Royalty.

SOUNDPRINTS—353 Main Ave., Norwalk, CT 06851. Stephanie Smith, Ed. Asst. Factual children's books, 800 to 2,000 words, about oceanic and back-yard animals, habitats, and history for young readers in preschool through fifth grade. No anthropomorphism. "Read one of our current stories in the relevant series before submitting or send SASE for guidelines." Pays flat fee.

SOURCEBOOKS—P.O. Box 372, Naperville, IL 60566. Todd Stocke, Ed. How-to and reference titles, including business; parenting; self-help; new age; gift-oriented; humor; law; and health. Query with outline and sample chapters. Royalty.

SOUTH END PRESS—7 Brookline St., #1, Cambridge, MA 02139-4146. Acq. Ed. Nonfiction on leftist politics. Query with sample chapters; multiple queries are accepted. Pays royalties.

SOUTHERN ILLINOIS UNIVERSITY PRESS—P.O. Box 3697, Carbondale, IL 62902-3697. James Simmons, Ed. Dir. Nonfiction on the humanities, 200 to 300 pages. Query with outline and sample chapters. Royalty.

SOUTHERN METHODIST UNIVERSITY PRESS—Box 415, Dallas, TX 75275. Kathryn Lang, Sr. Ed. Literary fiction. Nonfiction: scholarly studies in religion; medical ethics (death and dying); film; theater; scholarly works on Texas or Southwest. No juvenile material, science fiction, or poetry. Query. Royalty.

SPECIAL EDITION—See *Silhouette Books.*

SPECTACLE LANE PRESS—Box 1237, Mt. Pleasant, SC 29465-1237. Attn: Ed. Dept. Humor books, 500 to 5,000 words, on subjects of strong, current interest, illustrated with cartoons. Buys text or text/cartoon packages. Occasional nonfiction, non-humor books on provocative subjects of popular appeal. Advance against royalties.

SPECTRA—See *Bantam Books.*

SPINSTERS INK—32 E. First St., #330, Duluth, MN 55802. Nancy Walker, Acquisitions Ed. Adult fiction and nonfiction books, 200-plus pages, that deal with significant issues in women's lives from a feminist perspective and encourage change and growth. Main characters and/or narrators must be women. Query with synopsis. Royalty.

SPLENDOR ROMANCES—See *Kensington Publishing Corp.*

STACKPOLE BOOKS—5067 Ritter Rd., Mechanicsburg, PA 17055. Judith Schnell, Ed. Dir. Books on the outdoors, nature, fishing, carving, wood-working, sports, sporting literature, cooking, gardening, history, and military reference. Query. Royalty; advance. Unsolicited materials will not be returned.

STA-KRIS, INC.—P.O. Box 1131, Marshalltown, IA 50158. Kathy Wag-oner, Pres. Nonfiction adult-level gift books that portray universal feelings, truths, and values; or have a special-occasion theme. Query with bio, list of credits, complete manuscript, and SASE.

STANDARD PUBLISHING—8121 Hamilton Ave., Cincinnati, OH 45231. Attn: Acquisitions Ed. Christian education resources and children's books. No unsolicited material except for Program books, which include mate-rial for special days such as Easter, Mother's Day, Father's Day, Thanksgiving, and Christmas. Guidelines.

STANFORD UNIVERSITY PRESS—Stanford University, Stanford, CA 94305-2235. Norris Pope, Dir. "For the most part, we publish academic scholarship." No original fiction or poetry. Query with outline and sample chapters. Royalty.

STARBURST PUBLISHERS—Box 4123, Lancaster, PA 17604. David A. Robie, Ed. Dir. Health, inspiration, Christian, and self-help books. Query with outline for nonfiction book, synopsis for fiction book, and 3 sample chap-ters. Royalty. SASE. Web site: www.starburstpublishers.com.

STARRHILL PRESS—Black Belt Publishing, LLC, P.O. Box 551, Montgomery, AL 36101. Attn: Submission Ed. Affordable, succinct titles on American arts and letters. Query with cover letter, outline, author bio, and SASE for reply. Royalty varies. Web site: www.black-belt.com.

STEERFORTH PRESS—105-106 Chelsea St., Box 70, S. Royalton, VT 05068. Michael Moore, Ed. Adult nonfiction and some literary fiction. Fifteen books a year: novels; serious works of history, biography, politics, current af-fairs. Query with SASE. Royalty.

STEMMER HOUSE PUBLISHERS, INC.—2627 Caves Rd., Owings Mills, MD 21117. Barbara Holdridge, Ed. Adult nonfiction and juvenile picture books. Specializes in art, design, cookbooks, horticultural, and children's titles. Query with SASE. Royalty.

STERLING PUBLISHING CO., INC.—387 Park Ave. S., New York, NY 10016. Sheila Anne Barry, Acquisitions Dir. How-to, hobby, woodworking, alternative health and healing, fiber arts, crafts, dolls and puppets, ghosts, wine, nature, oddities, new consciousness, puzzles, juvenile humor and activities, ju-venile nature and science, medieval history, Celtic topics, gardening, alternative lifestyle, business, pets, recreation, sports and games books, reference, and home decorating. Query with outline, sample chapter, and sample illustrations. Royalty.

STODDART PUBLISHING—34 Lesmill Rd., N. York, Ontario, M3B 2T6, Canada. Adult literary fiction, and nonfiction including business, sports, humor, and politics, all varying lengths. Query with outline and sample chap-ters. Multiple queries considered. Royalty.

STONE MOUNTAIN PUBLISHING—P.O. Box 1501, Lorton, VA 22199-1501. Ron Jackson, Ed, Adult fiction and nonfiction. True crime, West-ern, action/adventure and romance, from 40,000 words. Pays advance against royalties.

STONEYDALE PRESS—523 Main St., Box 188, Stevensville, MT 59870. Dale A. Burk, Ed. Adult nonfiction, primarily how-to, on outdoor recreation with emphasis on big game hunting; some regional history of Northern Rockies. "We're a very specialized market. Query with outline and sample chapters essential." Royalty.

STOREY COMMUNICATIONS—Schoolhouse Rd., Pownal, VT 05261. Pam Art, Pub. How-to books for country living. Adult books, 100 to 350 pages, on gardening, animals, crafts, building, beer, and how-to. Royalty or flat fee.

STORY LINE PRESS—Three Oaks Farm, P.O. Box 1240, Ashland, OR 97520. Robert McDowell, Ed. Fiction, nonfiction, and poetry of varying lengths. Query. Royalty.

STRAWBERRY HILL PRESS—3848 S.E. Division St., Portland, OR 97202-1641. Carolyn Soto, Ed. Nonfiction: biography, autobiography, history, cooking, health, how-to, philosophy, performance arts, and Third World. Query with sample chapters, outline, and SASE. Royalty.

SUCCESS PUBLISHERS—See *Possibility Press.*

SYRACUSE UNIVERSITY PRESS—621 Skytop Rd., Ste. 110, Syracuse, NY 13244-5290.

TAYLOR PUBLISHING CO.—1550 W. Mockingbird Ln., Dallas, TX 75235. Attn: Ed. Dept. Adult nonfiction: gardening, sports, health, popular culture, celebrity biographies, parenting, and history. Query with outline, sample chapter, author bio, and SASE. Royalty.

TEACHING STRATEGIES BOOKS—See *Scholastic Professional Books.*

TEMPLE UNIVERSITY PRESS—1601 N. Broad St., USB 306, Philadelphia, PA 19122-6099. Janet Francendese, Ed. Adult nonfiction. Query with outline and sample chapters. Royalty.

TEN SPEED PRESS—P.O. Box 7123, Berkeley, CA 94707. Attn: Ed. Dept. Self-help and how-to on careers, recreation, etc.; natural science, history, cookbooks. Imprints include: *Tricycle Press* and *Celestial Arts.* Query with outline, sample chapters, and SASE. Paperback. Royalty.

THIRD WORLD PRESS—P.O. Box 19730, Chicago, IL 60619. Attn: Ed. Board. "Progressive Black Publishing." Adult fiction, nonfiction, and poetry, as well juvenile fiction and young adult books. Query with outline. Royalty. Send SASE or e-mail twpress3@aol.com for guidelines.

THUNDER'S MOUTH PRESS—Avalon Publishing Group, 841 Broadway, 4th Fl., New York, NY 10012. Neil Ortenberg, Pub. Joyce Watkins, Ed. Nonfiction: popular culture, music, and biography, to 300 pages. Royalty. Under *Adrenaline Books* imprint, publishes extreme adventure sports stories. Also publishes *Marlowe and Company* line; adult trade nonfiction focusing on health, religion, sprirituality, and self-help. *Blue Moon Books* publishes erotic fiction, especially Victorian and SM/BD themes. Royalty. None currently accepting unsolicited manuscripts.

TIA CHUCHA PRESS—P.O. Box 476969, Chicago, IL 60647. Luis Rodriguez, Ed. Poetry, 60 to 100 pages. Annual deadline: June 30. Royalty.

TIARE PUBLICATIONS—P.O. Box 493, Lake Geneva, WI 53147. Gerry L. Dexter, Ed. General nonfiction, *Limelight* imprint; jazz discographies and commentaries, *Balboa* imprint. Query with outline and sample chapters. Royalties.

TILBURY HOUSE—2 Mechanic St., #3, Gardiner, ME 04345. Attn: Acquisitions Ed. Children's books that deal with cultural diversity or the environment, appeal to children and parents as well as the educational market, and offer possibilities for developing a separate teacher's guide. Adult books: nonfiction books about Maine or the Northeast. Query with outline and sample chapters.

TIMES BOOKS—201 E. 50th St., New York, NY 10022. Peter Bernstein, Pub. No unsolicited manuscripts or queries accepted.

TOPAZ—See *NAL.*

TRANS NATIONAL GROUP—133 Federal St., Boston, MA 02110. Debra Lance, Book Development Mgr. Books for members of the Golf Society of the United States and the Adventure Club of North America. Subjects include golfing, backpacking, bicycling, camping, canoeing, fishing, hiking, mountain biking, outdoor photography, and skiing. Submit proposal with brief description of audience, resumé, and published clips. Pays flat fee. Responds in 2 months.

TRICYCLE PRESS—Ten Speed Press, P.O. Box 7123, Berkeley, CA 94707. Nicole Geiger, Pub. Children's books: Picture books, submit complete manuscripts. Activity books, submit about 20 pages and complete outline. "Real life" books that help children cope with issues. SASE required. Do not send original artwork. Responds in 10-20 weeks. Royalty.

TROUBADOR PRESS—See *Price Stern Sloan, Inc.*

TUFF STUFF BOOKS—See *Landmark Specialty Books.*

TURTLE BOOKS— 866 United Nations Plaza, Suite 525, New York, NY 10017. John Whitman, Pub. Children's picture books only. Submit complete manuscript with SASE. Royalty.

TURTLE POINT PRESS—103 Hog Hill Rd., Chappaqua, NY 10514. Jonathan D. Rabinowitz, Pres. Forgotten literary fiction, historical and biographical; some contemporary fiction, 200 to 400 typed pages. Also publishes imprint *Books & Co.* Query with sample chapters. Multiple queries considered. Royalty.

TWENTY-FIRST CENTURY BOOKS—The Millbrook Press, 2 Old New Milford Rd., Brookfield, CT 06804. Attn: Submissions Ed. Juvenile nonfiction, 10,000 to 30,000 words, for use in school and public libraries. Science, history, health, and social studies books for grades 5 and up. No fiction, workbooks, or picture books. Also accepts single titles for middle-grade and young adult readers. "Books are published primarily in series of four or more; not all titles in a series are necessarily by the same author." Query with SASE. Royalty.

TYNDALE HOUSE—351 Executive Dr., Box 80, Wheaton, IL 60189. Ron Beers, V.P. Adult fiction and nonfiction on subjects of concern to Christians. Picture books with religious focus for preschool and early readers. No unsolicited manuscripts. Send 9 x 12 SASE with 9 first-class stamps for catalogue and guidelines.

UAHC PRESS— 633 Third Ave., New York, NY 10017. Rabbi Hara Person, Man. Ed. Religious educational titles on or related to Judaism. Adult nonfiction; textbooks for Jewish educaton; juvenile picture books and nonfiction; and young adult nonfiction titles. Query with outline. Royalty.

UNIVERSITY BOOKS—See *Carol Publishing Group.*

UNIVERSITY OF ALABAMA PRESS—P.O. Box 870380, Tuscaloosa, AL 35487-0380. Attn: Ed. Dept. Scholarly and general regional nonfiction. Submit to appropriate editor: Nicole Mitchell, Ed. (history, public administration, political science, women's studies); Curtis Clark, Ed. (English, rhetoric and communication, Judaic studies); Judith Knight, Ed. (archaeology, anthropology). Send complete manuscript or proposal. Royalty.

UNIVERSITY OF ARIZONA PRESS—1230 N. Park Ave., Suite 102, Tucson, AZ 85719-4140. Christine R. Szuter, Interim Dir. Patti Hartmann, Acquiring Ed. Scholarly and popular nonfiction: Arizona, American West, anthropology, archaeology, behavioral sciences, environmental science, geography, Latin America, Native Americans, natural history, space sciences, women's studies. Query with outline, sample chapters, and current curriculum vitae or resumé. Royalty.

UNIVERSITY OF ARKANSAS PRESS—Div. of The Univ. of Arkansas, McIlroy House, 201 Ozark Ave., Fayetteville, AR 72701. John Coghlan, Dir. Short stories, nonfiction, and poetry. Query. Royalty.

UNIVERSITY OF CALIFORNIA PRESS—2120 Berkeley Way, Berkeley, CA 94720. Attn: Acquisitions Dept. Scholarly nonfiction. Query with cover letter, outline, sample chapters, curriculum vitae, and SASE.

UNIVERSITY OF GEORGIA PRESS—330 Research Dr., Athens, GA 30602-4901. Karen Orchard, Dir. Short story collections and poetry, scholarly nonfiction and literary criticism, Southern and American history, regional studies, biography and autobiography. For nonfiction, query with outline and sample chapters. Poetry collections considered in Sept. and Jan. only; short fiction in April and May only. A $15 fee is required for all poetry and fiction submissions. Royalty. SASE for competition guidelines.

UNIVERSITY OF HAWAII PRESS—2840 Kolowalu St., Honolulu, HI 96822. Patricia Crosby, Pam Kelley, and Sharon Yamamoto, Eds. Scholarly books on Asian, Asian American, and Pacific studies from disciplines as diverse as the arts, history, language, literature, natural science, philosophy, religion, and the social sciences. Query with outline and sample chapters. Royalty.

UNIVERSITY OF ILLINOIS PRESS—1325 S. Oak St., Champaign, IL 61820. Willis G. Regier, Dir. Scholarly and regional nonfiction. Rarely considers multiple submissions. Query. Royalty.

UNIVERSITY OF MINNESOTA PRESS—111 Third Ave. S., Suite 290, Minneapolis, MN 55401-2520. Nonfiction: literary and cultural theory, social and political theory; communications/media; anthropology; geography; international relations; Native American studies; regional titles, 50,000 to 225,000 words. Query with detailed prospectus or introduction, table of contents, sample chapter, and resumé. Royalty.

UNIVERSITY OF MISSOURI PRESS—2910 LeMone Blvd., Columbia, MO 65201-8227. Beverly Jarrett, Dir./Ed.in-Chief. Mr. Clair Wilcox, Acquisitions Ed. Scholarly books on American and European history; American, British, and Latin American literary criticism; political philosophy; intellectual history; regional studies; and short fiction.

UNIVERSITY OF NEBRASKA PRESS—312 N. 14th St., Lincoln, NE 68588-0484. Attn: Ed.-in-Chief. Specializes in the history of the American West, Native-American studies, literary and cultural nonfiction, fiction in translation, music, Jewish studies, and sports history. Send proposals with summary, a sample chapter, and resumé. Write for guidelines for annual North American Indian Prose Award.

UNIVERSITY OF NEVADA PRESS—MS 166, Reno, NV 89557. Margaret Dalrymple, Ed.-in-Chief. Fiction, nonfiction, and poetry. Nonfiction areas include history, biography, political science, natural history, regional (Nevada), mining, gaming, and Basque studies. Query first, with outline or table of contents, a synopsis, the estimated length and completion date of the manuscript, and resumé. Payment is on a royalty basis.

UNIVERSITY OF NEW MEXICO PRESS—University of New Mexico, Albuquerque, NM 87131. Elizabeth C. Hadas, Ed. Dir. David V. Holtby, Larry Ball, Dana Asbury, and Barbara Guth, Eds. Scholarly nonfiction on social and cultural anthropology, archaeology, Western history, art, and photography. Query. Royalty.

UNIVERSITY OF NORTH TEXAS PRESS—P.O. Box 311336, Denton, TX 76203-1336. Frances B. Vick, Dir. Charlotte M. Wright, Assoc. Dir. Books on Western Americana, Texan culture, history (including regional), women's studies, multicultural studies, and folklore. Series include: "War and the Southwest" (perspectives, histories, and memories of war from authors living in the Southwest); "Western Life Series"; and "Texas Writers" (critical biographies of Texas writers). Send manuscript or query with sample chapters; no multiple queries. Royalty.

UNIVERSITY OF OKLAHOMA PRESS—1005 Asp Ave., Norman, OK 73019-0445. John Drayton, Dir. Books, to 300 pages, on the history of the American West, Indians of the Americas, congressional studies, classical studies, literary criticism, natural history, and women's studies. Query. Royalty.

UNIVERSITY OF PENNSYLVANIA PRESS—4200 Pine St., Philadelphia, PA 19104-4011. Eric Halper, Dir. Scholarly nonfiction. Query.

UNIVERSITY OF PITTSBURGH PRESS—3347 Forbes Ave., Pittsburgh, PA 15261. Attn: Editor Scholarly nonfiction (philosophy of science, Latin American studies, political science, urban environmental history, culture, composition, and literacy); poetry. Send SASE for rules and reading periods.

UNIVERSITY OF SOUTH CAROLINA PRESS—937 Assembly St., Carolina Plaza, 8th Fl., Columbia, SC 29208. Acquisitions Ed. Books on history, literature, rhetoric, religious studies, and international relations. No original fiction. Submit outline with sample chapters. Royalty.

UNIVERSITY OF TENNESSEE PRESS—293 Communications Bldg., Knoxville, TN 37996-0325. Attn: Joyce Harrison. Nonfiction, American topics only, and humanities disciplines only. Regional trade and regional fiction, 200 to 400 manuscript pages. No poetry, translations, children's books, plays, or textbooks. Query with outline and sample chapters. Royalty.

UNIVERSITY OF TEXAS PRESS—Div. of University of Texas, Box 7819, Austin, TX 78713-7819. Joanna Hitchcock, Dir. Nonfiction books, 75,000 to 100,000 words. "Our press is located in the heart of Texas, but our books know no regional or even national boundaries." Query with outline. Royalty.

UNIVERSITY OF WISCONSIN PRESS—2537 Daniels St., Madison, WI 53718-6772. Attn: Acquisitions Ed. Trade nonfiction, scholarly books and regional titles on the Midwest. Offers Brittingham Prize in Poetry and Pollak Prize in Poetry; query for details. Web site: www.wisc.edu/wisconsinpress/.

UNIVERSITY PRESS OF COLORADO—P.O. Box 849, Niwot, CO 80544. Attn: Ed. Dept. Scholarly books in the humanities, social sciences, and applied sciences. Fiction for new series.

UNIVERSITY PRESS OF MISSISSIPPI—3825 Ridgewood Rd., Jackson, MS 39211-6492. Seetha Srinivasan, Dir. & Ed.-in-Chief. Scholarly and trade titles in American literature, history, and culture; southern studies; African-American, women's and American studies; popular culture; folklife; art and architecture; natural sciences; health; and other liberal arts.

UNIVERSITY PRESS OF NEW ENGLAND—23 S. Main St., Hanover, NH 03755-2048. Attn: Ed. Dept. General and scholarly nonfiction. American history, literature, and cultural studies. Jewish studies, women's studies, studies of the New England region, environmental studies, and performance studies. *Hardscrabble Books* imprint: fiction of New England, Weslyan University Poetry Series.

VAN NOSTRAND REINHOLD—See *John Wiley & Sons.*

VANDAMERE PRESS—P.O. Box 5243, Arlington, VA 22205. Jerry Frank, Assoc. Acquisitions Ed. General trade, fiction and nonfiction, including history, military, parenting, healthcare/disability studies, and travel. Also books about the nation's capital for a national audience. Prefer to see outline with sample chapter for nonfiction; for fiction send 4 or 5 sample chapters. Multiple queries considered. Royalty. SASE required.

VIKING—375 Hudson St., New York, NY 10014. Barbara Grossman, Pub. Fiction and nonfiction. Nonfiction: psychology, sociology, child-rearing and development, cookbooks, sports, and popular culture. Query. Royalty.

VIKING CHILDREN'S BOOKS—345 Hudson St., New York, NY 10014. Attn: Ed. Dept. Fiction and nonfiction, including biography, history, and sports, for ages 7 to 14. Humor and picture books for ages 3 to 8. Query Children's Book Dept. with outline and sample chapter. For picture books, please send entire manuscript. SASE required. Advance and royalty.

VILLARD BOOKS—201 E. 50th St., New York, NY 10022. Attn: Assoc. Ed. How-to, biography, humor, etc. "We look for authors who are promotable and books we feel we can market well." Royalty.

VINTAGE BOOKS—201 E. 50th St., New York, NY 10022. Attn: Ed. Dept. Quality fiction and serious nonfiction. Query with sample chapters for fiction; query for nonfiction.

VOYAGER BOOKS—See *Harcourt Brace & Co. Children's Book Div.*

VOYAGEUR PRESS—123 N. Second St., Stillwater, MN 55082. Todd R. Berger, Acquisitions Ed. Books, 15,000 to 100,000 words, on wildlife, travel, Americana, collectibles, natural history, hunting and fishing, regional topics; and Native American fiction, any length. "Photography is very important for most of our books." Guidelines. Query with outline and sample chapters. Royalty.

WALKER AND COMPANY—435 Hudson St., New York, NY 10014. Attn: Ed. Dept. Adult fiction: mysteries. Adult nonfiction: biography, history, science, natural history, health, psychology, popular science, and music. Juvenile nonfiction, including biography, science, history, music, and nature. Juvenile fiction: Picture books, middle grade and young adult novels. Query with synopsis and SASE. Guidelines. Royalty.

WARNER BOOKS—1271 Ave. of the Americas, New York, NY 10020. No unsolicited manuscripts or proposals.

WASHINGTON STATE UNIVERSITY PRESS—Cooper Publications Bldg., P.O. Box 645910, Pullman, WA 99164-5910. Keith Petersen, Acquisitions Ed. Glen Lindeman, Ed. Books on northwest history, prehistory, natural history, and culture, 200 to 350 pages. Query. Royalty.

WASHINGTON WRITERS PUBLISHING HOUSE—P.O. Box 15271, Washington, DC 20003. Attn: Ed. Dept. Poetry books, 50 to 60 pages, by writers in the greater Washington, DC and Baltimore area only. Send SASE for guidelines.

WATTS, FRANKLIN—Sherman Turnpike, Danbury, CT 06813. Curriculum-oriented nonfiction for grades K to 12, including science, history, social studies, and biography. No unsolicited submissions.

WEE SING—See *Price Stern Sloan, Inc.*

WEISBACH BOOKS, ROB—See *William Morrow and Co., Inc.*

SAMUEL WEISER, INC.—Box 612, York Beach, ME 03910. Eliot Stearnes, Ed. Nonfiction, including psychology, Eastern philosophy, esoteric studies, and alternative health. Query with sample chapters or complete manuscipt. Multiple queries accepted. Pays royalty. E-mail: email@weiserbooks.com.

WEISS ASSOCIATES, DANIEL—33 W. 17th St., New York, NY 10011. Alfred Nerz, Ed. Asst. Book packager. Young adult books, 36,000 words; middle grade books, 29,000 words; elementary books, 10,000 to 12,000 words. Royalty and flat fee.

WESLEYAN UNIVERSITY PRESS—110 Mt. Vernon St., Middletown, CT 06459-0433. Tom Radko, Dir. Wesleyan Poetry series: 64 to 80 pages. Query. Royalty.

WESTMINSTER JOHN KNOX PRESS—100 Witherspoon St., Louisville, KY 40202. Richard Brown, Dir. Books that inform, interpret, challenge, and encourage religious faith and living. Royalty. Send SASE for guidelines.

WHISPERING COYOTE PRESS—7130 Alexander Dr., Dallas, TX 75214. Ms. Lou Alpert, Ed. Picture books, 32 pages, for readers ages 4 to 12. Submit complete manuscript with SASE. Royalty.

WHITECAP BOOKS—351 Lynn Ave., N. Vancouver, BC, Canada V7J 2C4. Robert McCullough, Dir. of Pub. Operations. Juvenile books, 32 to 84 pages, and adult books, varying lengths, on such topics as natural history, gardening, cookery, and regional subjects. Query with table of contents, synopsis, and one sample chapter. Royalty and flat fee.

WHITMAN, ALBERT—6340 Oakton, Morton Grove, IL 60053. Kathleen Tucker, Ed. Picture books for preschool children; novels, biographies, mysteries, and nonfiction for middle-grade readers. Send complete manuscript for picture books, 3 chapters and outline for longer fiction; query for nonfiction. Royalty.

WILDERNESS PRESS—2440 Bancroft Way, Berkeley, CA 94704. Caroline Winnett, Ed. Nonfiction: outdoor sports, recreation, and travel in the western U.S. Royalty.

WILEY & SONS, INC. JOHN—605 Third Ave., New York, NY 10158-0012. Attn: Ed. Dept. Nonfiction: science/technology; business/management; travel; cooking; biography; psychology; computers; language; history; current affairs; health; finance. Send proposals with outline, bio, market information, and sample chapter. Royalty.

WILEY CHILDREN'S BOOKS—605 Third Ave., New York, NY 10158-0012. Kate Bradford, Ed. Nonfiction books, 96 to 128 pages, for 8- to 12-year-old children. Query. Royalty.

WILLIAMSON PUBLISHING CO.—P.O. Box 185, Charlotte, VT 05445. Attn: Susan Williamson. Active learning books for children and teachers. No children's picture books or fiction. Writers must send annotated table of contents, 2 sample chapters, and SASE.

WILLOWISP PRESS—801 94th Ave. N., St. Petersburg, FL 33702. Attn: Acquisitions Ed. Beginning chapter books, 2,000 to 6,000 words. Juvenile books for children in grades pre-K through 8. Picture books, 300 to 800 words. Fiction, 14,000 to 18,000 words, for grades 3 through 5; 20,000 to 24,000 words for grades 5 through 8. Requirements for nonfiction vary. Query with outline, sample chapter, and SASE. Guidelines. Royalty or flat fee.

WILSHIRE BOOK COMPANY—12015 Sherman Rd., N. Hollywood, CA 91605-3781. Melvin Powers, Pub. Nonfiction: self-help, motivation/inspiration/spiritual, psychology, recovery, how-to, entrepreneurship, mail order, horsemanship, and Internet marketing; minimum, 60,000 words. Fiction: allegories that teach principles of psychological/spiritual growth. Send synopsis/detailed chapter outline, 3 chapters, and SASE. Royalty.

WINDSWEPT HOUSE PUBLISHERS—Rte. 3 198, Mt. Desert, ME 04660-0159. Ed. Children's picture books; young adult novels; adult fiction and nonfiction.

WOODBINE HOUSE—6510 Bells Mill Rd., Bethesda, MD 20817. Susan Stokes, Ed. Books for or about people with disabilities only. Current needs include parenting, reference, special ed., picture books, and novels or nonfiction chapter books for young readers. Query or submit complete manuscript with SASE. Guidelines. Royalty.

WORD PUBLISHING—545 Marriott Dr., Ste. 750, Box 141000, Nashville, TN 37214. Lee Gessner, Dep. Pub. Fiction and nonfiction, 65,000 to 95,000 words, dealing with the relationship and/or applications of biblical principles to everyday life. Query with outline and sample chapters. Royalty.

WORDWARE PUBLISHING—2320 Los Rio Blvd., Suite 200, Plano, TX 75074. James S. Hill, Pub. *Wordware Computer Books.* Ginnie Bivona, Ed., *Republic of Texas Press:* Texana, Southwest regional, historical nonfiction including tales and legends of the old west and "legendary" characters, military history, women of the west and country humor. Ginnie Bivona, Ed., *Seaside Press*: Cities uncovered history/guidebooks, pet care, humor. Query with sample chapters, manuscript completion date, and author experience. Royalty.

WORKMAN PUBLISHING CO., INC.—708 Broadway, New York, NY 10003. Attn: Ed. Dept. General nonfiction. Normal contractual terms based on agreement.

WORLDWIDE LIBRARY—225 Duncan Mill Rd., Don Mills, Ont., Canada M3B 3K9. Randall Toye, Ed. Dir. Feroze Mohammed, Sr. Ed. Action adventure series for *Gold Eagle* imprint; mystery fiction reprints only. No unsolicited manuscripts.

WRITE WAY PUBLISHING—P.O. Box 441278, Aurora, CO 80044. Adult fiction, including whodunits, mysteries, soft science fiction, and fantasy, 65,000 to 120,000 wrods. Query with first two chapters. Considers multiple queries. Royalty.

WYNDHAM HALL PRESS—52857 C.R. 21, Bristol, IN 46507. Milton L. Clayton, Pub. Academic nonfiction. Submit complete manuscript. Royalty. Web site: www.wyndhamhall.com.

WYRICK & COMPANY—1-A Pinckney St., Charleston, SC 29401. Charles L. Wyrick, Jr., Ed. Fiction, particularly fiction set in the South; and some nonfiction, including gardening, fine arts, antiques, food and cooking, history and memoirs, photography, travel and guidebooks, and maritime interests. No poetry, children's, romance, science fiction, fantasy, technical, or how-to books. Accepts queries, book proposals, and complete manuscripts, all with SASE. Multiple queries considered. Royalty.

YALE UNIVERSITY PRESS—Box 209040, New Haven, CT 06520-9040. Adult nonfiction, 400 manuscript pages. Query. Royalty.

YEARLING BOOKS—1540 Broadway, New York, NY 10036. Attn: Ed. Dept. Not accepting unsolicited material. Imprints include *Skylark Books.*

ZOLAND BOOKS—384 Huron Ave., Cambridge, MA 02138. Ronald Pease, Ed. Dir. Fiction, poetry, and nonfiction, including art and photography. Royalty. Query.

ZONDERVAN PUBLISHING HOUSE—5300 Patterson S.E., Grand Rapids, MI 49530. Attn: Manuscript Review. Christian titles. General fiction and nonfiction; academic and professional books. Query with outline, sample chapter, and SASE. Royalty. Guidelines.

SYNDICATES

Syndicates buy material from writers and artists to sell to newspapers all over the country and the world. Authors are paid either a percentage of the gross proceeds or an outright fee. Of course, features by people well known in their fields have the best chance of being syndicated. In general, syndicates want columns that have been popular in a local newspaper or magazine. Since most syndicated fiction has been published previously in magazines or books, beginning fiction writers should try to sell their stories to magazines before submitting them to syndicates.

Always query syndicates before sending manuscripts, since their needs change frequently, and be sure to enclose SASEs with queries and manuscripts.

ARKIN MAGAZINE SYNDICATE—500 Bayview Dr., Suite F, N. Miami Beach, FL 33160. Mitzi Roberg, Ed. Dir. Articles, 750 to 2,200 words, for trade and professional magazines. Must have small-business slant, be written in layman's language, and offer solutions to business problems. Articles should apply to many businesses, not just a specific industry. No columns. Pays 3¢ to 10¢ a word, on acceptance. SASE required; query not necessary.

CONTEMPORARY FEATURES SYNDICATE—P. O. Box 1258, Jackson, TN 38302-1258. Lloyd Russell, Ed. Articles, 1,000 to 10,000 words: how-to, money savers, business, etc. Self-help pieces for small business. Pays from $25, on acceptance. Query.

HARRIS & ASSOCIATES FEATURES—15915 Caminito Aire Puro, San Diego, CA 92128. Dick Harris, Ed. Sports- and family-oriented features, to 1,200 words; fillers and short humor, 500 to 800 words. Queries preferred. Pays varying rates.

HISPANIC LINK NEWS SERVICE—1420 N St. N.W., Washington, DC 20005. Charles A. Ericksen, Ed. Trend articles, opinion and personal experience pieces, and general features with Hispanic focus, 650 to 700 words; editorial cartoons. Pays $25 for op-ed columns and cartoons, on acceptance. Send SASE for guidelines.

THE HOLLYWOOD INSIDE SYNDICATE—Box 49957, Los Angeles, CA 90049-0957. John Austin, Dir. Feature articles, 750 to 2,500 words, on TV and film personalities with B&W photo(s). Article suggestions for 3-part series. Pieces on unusual medical and scientific breakthroughs. Pays on percentage basis for features, negotiated rates for ideas, on publication. E-mail: hollywood@ce32.net.

LOS ANGELES TIMES SYNDICATE—Times Mirror Sq., Los Angeles, CA 90053. Commentary, features, columns, editorial cartoons, comics, puzzles and games; news services and online products. Send SASE for submission guidelines.

NATIONAL NEWS BUREAU—P.O. Box 43039, Philadelphia, PA 19129. Harry Jay Katz, Ed. Articles, 500 to 1,500 words, interviews, consumer news, how-tos, travel pieces, reviews, entertainment pieces, features, etc. Pays on publication.

NEW YORK TIMES SYNDICATION SALES—122 E. 42nd St., New York, NY 10168. Gloria Brown Anderson, Pres. and Ed.-in-Chief. Carolee Morrison, International Ed. Articles on international, seasonal, health, lifestyle, and entertainment topics, to 1,500 words (Previously published or unpublished). Query with published article or tear sheet and SASE. No calls please. Pays 50% royalty on collected sales.

NEWSPAPER ENTERPRISE ASSOCIATION—200 Madison Ave., 4th Fl., New York, NY 10016. Robert Levy, Exec. Ed. Ideas for new concepts in syndicated columns. No single stories or stringers. Payment by contractual arrangement.

SINGER MEDIA CORP.—#106, 1030 Calle Cordillera, San Clemente, CA 92673. Helen J. Lee, V.P. International syndication, some domestic. Subjects must be of global interest. Features: celebrity interviews and profiles, women's, health, fitness, self-help, business, computer, etc., all lengths; psychological quizzes; puzzles (no word puzzles), single-panel cartoons (with no bubbles), and games for children or adults. Pays 50%.

TRIBUNE MEDIA SERVICES—435 N. Michigan Ave., #1400, Chicago, IL 60611. Mark Mathes, Ed. Continuing columns, comic strips, features, electronic databases, puzzles and word games. Query with clips. Web site: www.tms.tribune.com.

UNITED FEATURE SYNDICATE—200 Madison Ave., 4th Fl., New York, NY 10016-3903. Diana Loevy, V.P./Ed. Dir. No one-shots or series. Payment by contractual arrangement. Send samples with SASE.

LITERARY PRIZE OFFERS

Writers seeking the thrill of competition should review the extensive list of literary prize offers, many of them designed to promote the unpublished writer. All of the competitions listed here are for unpublished manuscripts and usually offer publication in addition to a cash prize. The prestige that comes with winning some of the more established awards can do much to further a writer's career, as editors, publishers, and agents are likely to consider the future work of the prize winner more closely.

There are hundreds of literary contests open to writers in all genres, and the following list covers a representative number of them. The summaries given below are intended merely as guides; since submission requirements are more detailed than space allows, writers should send an SASE for complete guidelines before entering any contest. Writers are also advised to check the monthly "Prize Offers" column of *The Writer* Magazine (120 Boylston St., Boston, MA 02116-4615) for additional contest listings and up-to-date contest requirements. Deadlines are annual unless otherwise noted.

ACADEMY OF AMERICAN POETS—Walt Whitman Award, 584 Broadway, Suite 1208, New York, NY 10012-3250. An award of $5,000 plus publication and a one-month residency at the Vermont Studio Center is offered for a book-length poetry manuscript by a poet who has not yet published a volume of poetry. Deadline: November 15. Entry fee.

ACADEMY OF MOTION PICTURE ARTS AND SCIENCES—The Nicholl Fellowships, 8949 Wilshire Blvd., Beverly Hills, CA 90211-1972. Up to five fellowships of $25,000 each are awarded for original screenplays that display exceptional craft and engaging storytelling. Deadline: May 1. Entry fee.

ACTORS THEATRE OF LOUISVILLE—Ten-Minute Play Contest, 316 W. Main St., Louisville, KY 40202-4218. A prize of $1,000 is offered for a previously unproduced ten-page script. Deadline: December 1.

AMERICAN ACADEMY OF ARTS AND LETTERS—Richard Rogers Awards, 633 W. 155th St., New York, NY 10032. Offers subsidized productions or staged readings in New York City by a nonprofit theater for a musical, play with music, thematic review, or any comparable work. Deadline: November 1.

AMERICAN ANTIQUARIAN SOCIETY—Fellowships for Historical Research, 185 Salisbury St., Worcester, MA 01609-1634. Attn: John B. Hench. At least three fellowships are awarded to creative and performing artists, writers, film makers, and journalists for research on pre-20th century American history. Residencies are four- to eight-weeks; travel expenses and stipends of $1,200 per month are offered. Deadline: October 5, 1999.

THE AMERICAN-SCANDINAVIAN FOUNDATION—Translation Prize, 725 Park Ave., New York, NY 10021. A prize of $2,000 is awarded for an outstanding English translation of poetry, fiction, drama, or literary prose originally written in Danish, Finnish, Icelandic, Norwegian, or Swedish. Second prize is $500. Deadline: June 1.

ANHINGA PRESS—Anhinga Prize for Poetry, P.O. Box 10595, Tallahassee, FL 32302-0595. A $2,000 prize will be awarded for an unpublished full-length collection of poetry, 48 to 72 pages, by a poet who has published no more than one full-length collection. Deadline: March 15. Entry fee.

ARMY MAGAZINE—Essay Contest, Box 1560, Arlington, VA 22210. Prizes of $1,000, $500, and $250 plus publication are awarded for essays on a given theme. Deadline: May 31.

THE ASSOCIATED WRITING PROGRAMS—Awards Series, Tallwood House, Mail Stop 1E3, George Mason Univ., Fairfax, VA 22030. In the categories of poetry, short fiction, the novel, and nonfiction, the prize is book publication and a $2,000 honorarium. Deadline: February 29. Entry fee.

ASSOCIATION OF JEWISH LIBRARIES—Sydney Taylor Manuscript Competition, 1327 Wyntercreek Ln., Dunwoody, GA 30338. Attn: Paula Sandfelder, Coordinator. Offers $1,000 for the best fiction manuscript, 64 to 200 pages, by an unpublished book author, writing for readers 8 to 11. Stories must have a positive Jewish focus. Deadline: January 15.

BAKER'S PLAYS—High School Playwriting Contest, P.O. Box 69922, Quincy, MA 02269. Plays about the high school experience, written by high school students, are eligible for awards of $500, $250, and $100. Deadline: January 31.

BANKS CHANNEL BOOKS—Carolina Novel Award, P.O. Box 4446, Wilmington, NC 28406. Awards publication plus a $1,000 advance for an original, unpublished novel by a North or South Carolina writer. Deadline: July 31 of even-numbered years. Entry fee.

BANTAM DOUBLEDAY DELL BOOKS FOR YOUNG READERS—Marguerite de Angeli Prize, Dept. BFYR, 1540 Broadway, New York, NY 10036. A prize of $1,500 and a $3,500 advance against royalties is awarded for a middle-grade fiction manuscript that explores the diversity of the American experience. Open to U.S. and Canadian writers who have not previously published a novel for middle-grade readers. Deadline: June 30.

BARNARD COLLEGE—New Women Poets Prize, Women Poets at Barnard, Columbia Univ., 3009 Broadway, New York, NY 10027-6598. Attn: Directors. A prize of $1,500 and publication by Beacon Press is offered for an unpublished poetry manuscript, 50 to 100 pages, by a female poet who has never published a book of poetry. Deadline: October 15.

THE BELLETRIST REVIEW—Fiction Contest, Marmarc Publications, P.O. Box 596, Plainville, CT 06062-0596. Prize of $200 plus publication is awarded for an unpublished short story, 2,500 to 5,000 words. Deadline: July 15. Entry fee.

THE BELLINGHAM REVIEW—Tobias Wolff Award in Fiction/49th

Parallel Poetry Award, MS-9053, Western Washington Univ., Bellingham, WA 98225. Tobias Wolff Award in Fiction: Offers prizes of $500 plus publication, $250, and $100 for a short story or novel excerpt. Deadline: March 1. Annie Dillard Award in Nonfiction: Offers prizes of $500 plus publication, $250, and $100 for previously unpublished essays. Deadline: March 1. 49th Parallel Poetry Award: Offers publication and prizes of $500, $250, and $100 for individual poems. Deadline: November 30. Entry fees.

BEVERLY HILLS THEATRE GUILD/JULIE HARRIS PLAY-WRIGHT AWARD— 2815 N. Beachwood Dr., Los Angeles, CA 90068-1923. Attn: Marcella Meharg. Offers prize of $5,000, $2,000, and $1,000 for an unpublished full-length play. Deadline: November 1.

THE BEVERLY HILLS THEATRE GUILD PLAY COMPETITION FOR CHILDREN'S THEATRE— 2815 N. Beachwood Dr., Los Angeles, CA 90068-1923. A prize of $750 is awarded to the winning playscript, 40 to 50 minutes playing time, suitable for children ages 7 to 14. Runner-up receives $250. Deadline: February 28. Entry fee.

BIRMINGHAM-SOUTHERN COLLEGE—Hackney Literary Awards, Box 549003, Birmingham, AL 35254. A prize of $5,000 is awarded for an unpublished novel, any length. Deadline: September 30. Also, a $5,000 prize is shared for the winning short story, to 5,000 words, and poem of up to 50 lines. Deadline: December 31. Entry fees.

BLUE MOUNTAIN CENTER—Richard J. Margolis Award, 294 Washington St., Suite 610, Boston, MA 02108. A prize of $1,000 is awarded annually to a promising journalist or essayist whose work combines warmth, humor, wisdom, and a concern with social issues. Applications should include up to 30 pages of published or unpublished work. Deadline: June 1.

BOISE STATE UNIVERSITY—The Rocky Mountain Artists' Book Competition, Hemingway Western Studies Center, Boise, ID 83725. Tom Trusky, Ed. A prize of $500 and publication is awarded for up to 3 books; manuscripts (text and/or visual content) and proposals are considered for the short-run printing of books on public issues, especially the Inter-Mountain West. Deadline: year-round.

BOSTON REVIEW—Poetry Contest, *Boston Review,* E53-407 MIT, Cambridge, MA 02139. Annual poetry contest for original, unpublished poems, up to ten pages. Winner receives $1,000 plus publication in *Boston Review.* Send up to five poems. Deadline: June 15. Entry fee.

BOX TURTLE PRESS, INC.—Mudfish Poetry Prize, 184 Franklin St., New York, NY 10013. Awards $500 plus publication in *Mudfish.* Deadline: April 30. Entry fee.

ARCH AND BRUCE BROWN FOUNDATION—P.O. Box 45231, Phoenix, AZ 85064. Offers $1,000 grants for gay and lesbian-positive fiction. Deadline: May 31.

BUCKNELL UNIVERSITY—The Philip Roth Residence in Creative Writing, Stadler Center for Poetry, Bucknell Univ., Lewisburg, PA 17837. Attn: Cynthia Hogue, Dir. The fall residency, which includes studio, lodging, meals, and a $1,000 stipend, may be used by a writer, over 21, not currently enrolled in a university, to work on a first or second book. The residency is awarded in odd-numbered years to a fiction writer, and in even-numbered years to a poet. Deadline: March 1.

CASE WESTERN RESERVE UNIVERSITY—Marc A. Klein Playwriting Award, Dept. of Theater Arts, 10900 Euclid Ave., Cleveland, OH 44106-7077. A prize of $1,000 plus production is offered for an original, previously unproduced full-length play by a student currently enrolled at an American college or university. Deadline: May 15.

CENTER FOR BOOK ARTS—Poetry Chapbook Prize, Center for Book Arts, 626 Broadway, 5th Floor, New York, NY 10012. Offers $1,000, publication and a public reading for poetry manuscript, to 500 lines. Deadline: December 31. Entry fee.

CHELSEA AWARD COMPETITION—P.O. Box 1040, York Beach, ME 03910. Attn: Ed. Prizes of $750 plus publication are awarded for the best unpublished short fiction and poetry. Deadlines: June 15 (fiction); December 15 (poetry). Entry fees.

THE CHICAGO TRIBUNE—Nelson Algren Awards, 435 N. Michigan Ave., Chicago, IL 60611. A first prize of $5,000 and three runner-up prizes of $1,000 are awarded for outstanding unpublished short stories, 2,500 to 10,000 words, by American writers. Deadline: February 1.

CLAREMONT GRADUATE SCHOOL—Kingsley Tufts Poetry Awards, 160 E. 10th St., Claremont, CA 91711. An award of $50,000 is given an American poet whose work is judged most worthy. An award of $5,000 is given to an emerging poet whose work displays extraordinary promise. Books of poetry published or manuscripts completed in the calendar year are considered. Deadline: September 15.

CLEVELAND STATE UNIVERSITY POETRY CENTER—Poetry Center Prize, Dept. of English, Rhodes Tower, Rm. 1815, 1983 E. 24th St., Cleveland, OH 44115-2440. Publication and $1,000 are awarded for a previously unpublished book-length volume of poetry. Deadline: March 1. Entry fee.

COALITION FOR THE ADVANCEMENT OF JEWISH EDUCATION—David Dornstein Memorial Creative Writing Contest, 261 W. 35th St., Floor 12A, New York, NY 10001. Publication and prizes of $700, $200, and $100 are awarded for the three best original, previously unpublished short stories, to 5,000 words, on a Jewish theme or topic, by writers age 18 to 35. Deadline: December 31.

COLONIAL PLAYERS, INC.—Promising Playwright Award, 98 Tower Dr., Stevensville, MD 21666. Attn: Fran Marchano. A prize of $750 plus possible production will be awarded for the best full-length play by a resident of MD, DC, VA, WV, DE, or PA. Deadline: December 31 (of even-numbered years).

COLORADO STATE UNIVERSITY—Colorado Prize for Poetry, *Colorado Review,* Dept. of English, Fort Collins, CO 80523. Offers $1,500 plus publication for a book-length collection of original poems. Deadline: January 10. Entry fee.

COMMUNITY CHILDREN'S THEATRE OF KANSAS CITY—8021 E. 129th Terrace, Grandview, MO 64030. Attn: Mrs. Blanche Sellens, Dir. A prize of $500, plus production, is awarded for the best play, up to one hour long, to be performed by adults for elementary school audiences. Deadline: January 31.

COMMUNITY WRITERS ASSOCIATION—CWA Writing Contest,

P.O. Box 12, Newport, RI 02840-0001. A prize of $500 is offered for short stories, to 2,000 words, and poetry, any length. Deadline: June 1. Entry fee.

EUGENE V. DEBS FOUNDATION—Bryant Spann Memorial Prize, Dept. of History, Indiana State Univ., Terre Haute, IN 47809. Offers a prize of $1,000 for a published or unpublished article or essay on themes relating to social protest or human equality. Deadline: April 30.

DEEP SOUTH WRITERS CONFERENCE—Contest Clerk, Drawer 44691, Univ. of Southwestern Louisianna, Lafayette, LA 70504-4691. Prizes ranging from $50 to $300 are offered for unpublished manuscripts in the following categories: Fiction (including science fiction); Novel; Nonfiction; Poetry; Drama; and French literature. Deadline: July 15. Miller Award: offers $500 for a play dealing with some aspect of the life of Edward de Vere (1550-1604), the 17th Earl of Oxford. Deadline: July 15 (of odd-numbered years). Entry fee.

DELACORTE PRESS—Prize for First Young Adult Novel, Random House, Inc., 1540 Broadway, New York, NY 10036. A writer who has not previously published a young adult novel may submit a book-length manuscript with a contemporary setting suitable for readers ages 12 to 18. The prize is $1,500, plus a $6,000 advance, and hardcover and paperback publication. Deadline: December 31.

DRURY COLLEGE—Playwriting Contest, 900 N. Benton Ave., Springfield, MO 65802. Attn: Sandy Asher, Writer-in-Residence. Prizes of $300 and two $150 honorable mentions, plus possible production, are awarded for original, previously unproduced one-act plays. Deadline: December 1 (of even-numbered years).

DUBUQUE FINE ARTS PLAYERS—One-Act Playwriting Contest, 330 Clarke Dr., Dubuque, IA 52001. Attn: Jennifer G. Stabenow, Coordinator. Prizes of $600, $300 and $200 plus possible production are awarded for unproduced, original one-act plays of up to 40 minutes. Deadline: January 31. Entry fee.

DUKE UNIVERSITY—Dorothea Lange-Paul Taylor Prize, Prize Committee, Center for Documentary Studies, Box 90802, Duke Univ., Durham, NC 27708-0802. A grant of up to $10,000 is awarded to a writer and photographer working together in the formative stages of a documentary project that will ultimately result in a publishable work. Deadline: January 31. Entry fee.

ELF: ECLECTIC LITERARY FORUM—Ruth Cable Memorial Prize, P.O. Box 392, Tonawanda, NY 14150. Awards of $500 and three $50 prizes are given for poems up to 50 lines. Short Fiction Prize awards $500 plus publication and two $50 prizes for stories, to 3,500 words. Deadline: March 31. Fiction deadline: August 31. Entry fee.

EMPORIA STATE UNIVERSITY—Bluestem Award, English Dept., Emporia State Univ., Emporia, KS 66801-5087. A prize of $1,000 plus publication is awarded for a previously unpublished book of poems by a U.S. author. Deadline: March 1. Entry fee.

THE FLORIDA REVIEW—The Editors' Awards (specify Fiction, Nonfiction, or Poetry), Dept. of English, Univ. of Central Florida, Orlando, FL 32816-0001. Attn: Russell Kesler, Ed. Prizes of $500 plus publication are offered for short stories, essays, and creative nonfiction to 7,500 words, as well as groups of 3 to 5 poems, to 25 lines. Deadline: March 15. Entry fee.

FLORIDA STUDIO THEATRE—Shorts Contest, 1241 N. Palm Ave., Sarasota, FL 34236. Attn: Christian Angermann. Short scripts, songs, and other performance pieces on a given theme are eligible for a prize of $500. Deadline: February 15.

THE FORMALIST—Howard Nemerov Sonnet Award, 320 Hunter Dr., Evansville, IN 47711. A prize of $1,000 plus publication is offered for a previously unpublished, original sonnet. Deadline: June 15. Entry fee.

FOUR WAY BOOKS—Intro Prize in Poetry, P.O. Box 535, Village Sta., New York, NY 10014. Attn: K. Clarke. Awards $3,500 ($2,000 honorarium plus $1,500 author tour money) and publication for a book-length collection of poems by a U.S. poet. Deadline: March 31. Entry fee.

GEORGE MASON UNIVERSITY—Greg Grummer Award in Poetry, 4400 Univ. Dr., Fairfax, VA 22030-4444. A prize of $500 plus publication is offered for an outstanding previously unpublished poem. Deadline: December 15. Entry fee.

GEORGE WASHINGTON UNIVERSITY—Jenny McKean Moore Writer-in-Washington, Dept. of English, Washington, DC 20052. Attn: Prof. Christopher Sten. A salaried teaching position for two semesters is offered to a creative writer (of various mediums in alternate years) having "significant publications and a demonstrated commitment to teaching. The writer need not have conventional academic credentials." The Deadline: November 15.

THE GEORGETOWN REVIEW FICTION AND POETRY CONTEST—P.O. Box 6309, Southern Station, Hattiesburg, MS 39406-6309. A prize of $1,000 for a short story of no more than 25 pages or 6,500 words and $500 for a single poem, any length, plus publication and subscription. Deadline: October 1. Entry fee.

GLIMMER TRAIN PRESS—Semiannual Short Story Award for New Writers, 710 S.W. Madison St., #504, Portland, OR 97205. Writers whose fiction has never appeared in a nationally distributed publication are eligible to enter their stories of 1,200 to 7,500 words. Prizes are $1,200 plus publication, $500, and $300. Deadlines: March 31; September 30. Entry fee.

GREENFIELD REVIEW LITERARY CENTER—North American Native Authors First Book Awards, P.O. Box 308, 2 Middle Grove Rd., Greenfield Center, NY 12833. Attn: Joseph Bruchac, Dir. Native Americans of American Indian, Aleut, Inuit, or Metis ancestry who have not yet published a book are eligible to enter poetry, 64 to 100 pages, and prose, 200 to 300 pages (fiction or nonfiction) for $500 prizes plus publication. Deadline: March 15.

GROLIER POETRY PRIZE—6 Plympton St., Cambridge, MA 02138. Two $150 honorariums are awarded for poetry manuscripts of up to 10 double-spaced pages, including no more than five previously unpublished poems, by writers who have not yet published a book of poems. Deadline: May 1. Entry fee.

HEEKIN GROUP FOUNDATION—Fiction Fellowships Competition, Box 1534, Sisters, OR 97759. Awards the following fellowships to beginning career writers: two $1,500 Tara Fellowships in Short Fiction; two $3,000 James Fellowships for a Novel in Progress; one $2,000 Mary Molloy Fellowship for a Juvenile Novel in Progress (address H.G.F., P.O. Box 209, Middlebury, VT 05753; and one $2,000 Cuchulain Fellowhip for Rhetoric (Essay). Writers who have never published a novel, a children's novel, more than five short stories in national publication, or an essay are eligible to enter. Deadline: December 1. Entry fee.

HELICON NINE EDITIONS—Literary Prizes, 3607 Pennsylvania, Kansas City, MO 64111. Marianne Moore Poetry Prize: offers $1,000 for an original unpublished poetry manuscript of at least 48 pages. Willa Cather Fiction Prize: offers $1,000 for an original novella or short story collection, from 150 to 300 pages. Deadline: May 1. Entry fee.

LORIAN HEMINGWAY SHORT STORY COMPETITION—P.O. Box 993, Key West, FL 33041. Awards a $1,000 prize to an original, unpublished work short story, to 3,000 words by a writer whose fiction has never appeared in a nationally distributed publication. Deadline: June 1. Entry fee.

HIGHLIGHTS FOR CHILDREN—Fiction Contest, 803 Church St., Honesdale, PA 18431. Three $1,000 prizes plus publication are offered for stories on a given subject, up to 900 words. Deadline: February 28.

RUTH HINDMAN FOUNDATION—H.E. Francis Award, Dept. of English, Univ. of Alabama, Huntsville, AL 35899. A prize of $1,000 is awarded for a short story of up to 5,000 words. Deadline: December 31. Entry fee.

L. RON HUBBARD'S WRITERS OF THE FUTURE CONTEST—P.O. Box 1630, Los Angeles, CA 90078. Unpublished fiction writers are eligible to enter science fiction or fantasy short stories under 10,000 words, or novellas under 17,000 words. Quarterly prizes: $1,000, $750, and $500. Annual prize: $4,000. Deadlines: March 31; June 30; September 30; December 31.

INSTITUTE OF HISPANIC CULTURE—José Martí Award, 3315 Sul Ross, Houston, TX 77098. Prizes of $1,000, $600, and $400 are awarded for essays, 15 to 20 pages, on a given theme. Deadline: August 31.

INTERNATIONAL QUARTERLY—Crossing Boundaries Awards, P.O. Box 10521, Tallahassee, FL 32303-0521. Offers four prizes of $500 each plus publication for poetry, fiction, nonfiction, and "Crossing Boundaries," a category that includes "atypical work and innovative or experimental writing." Manuscripts, to 5,000 words; up to 5 poems per poetry submission. Deadline: March 1. Entry fee.

IUPUI CHILDREN'S THEATRE—Playwriting Competition, Indiana University-Purdue University at Indianapolis, 425 University Blvd., Suite 309, Indianapolis, IN 46202. Offers four $1,000 prizes plus staged readings for plays for young people. Deadline: September 1 (of even-numbered years).

ALICE JAMES BOOKS—Beatrice Hawley Award, Univ. of Maine at Farmington, 98 Main St., Farmington, ME 04938. A prize of publication plus 100 free copies is offered for the best poetry manuscript, 60 to 70 pages. Deadline: December 1. Entry fee.

JOE JEFFERSON PLAYERS ORIGINAL PLAY COMPETITION—P.O. Box 66065, Mobile, AL 36660. A prize of $1,000 plus production is offered for an original, previously unproduced play. Deadline: March 1.

JEWISH COMMUNITY CENTER THEATRE—Dorothy Silver Playwriting Competition, 3505 Mayfield Rd., Cleveland Heights, OH 44118. Attn: Elaine Rembrandt, Dir. Offers $1,000 and a staged reading for an original, previously unproduced full-length play, on some aspect of the Jewish experience. Deadline: December 15.

CHESTER H. JONES FOUNDATION—National Poetry Competition,

P. O. Box 498, Chardon, OH 44024. Prizes of $1,000, $750, $500, $250, and $100, as well as several $50 and $10 prizes are awarded for original, unpublished poems of up to 32 lines. Deadline: March 31. Entry fee.

JAMES JONES SOCIETY—First Novel Fellowship, c/o Dept. of English, Wilkes Univ., Wilkes-Barre, PA 18766. An award of $2,500 is offered for a first novel-in-progress by an American. Deadline: March 1. Entry fee.

THE JOURNAL: THE LITERARY MAGAZINE OF O.S.U.—The Ohio State Univ. Press, 1070 Carmack Rd., Columbus, OH 43210-1002. Attn: David Citino, Poetry Ed. Awards $1,000 plus publication for at least 48 pages of original, unpublished poetry. Deadline: September 30. Entry fee.

KALLIOPE: A JOURNAL OF WOMEN'S ART—Sue Saniel Elkind Poetry Contest, Florida Community College at Jacksonville, 3939 Roosevelt Blvd., Jacksonville, FL 32205. Publication and $1,000 are awarded for the best poem, under 50 lines, written by a woman. Deadline: November 1. Entry fee.

KEATS/KERLAN MEMORIAL FELLOWSHIP—The Ezra Jack Keats Memorial Fellowship Committee, 109 Walter Library, 117 Pleasant St. S.E., Univ. of Minnesota, Minneapolis, MN 55455. A $1,500 fellowship is awarded to a talented writer and/or illustrator of children's books who wishes to use the Kerlan Collection for furtherance of his or her artistic development. Deadline: May 1.

KENT STATE UNIVERSITY PRESS—Stan and Tom Wick Poetry Prize, P.O. Box 5190, Kent, OH 44242-0001. Publication and $1,000 are offered for a book of poems, 48 to 68 pages, by a writer who has not previously published a collection of poetry. Deadline: May 1. Entry fee.

LOVE CREEK PRODUCTIONS—One-Act Play Festivals, 162 Nesbit St., Weehawken, NJ 07087-6817. One-act plays and theme-based plays are awarded production or staged readings. Deadlines vary.

AMY LOWELL POETRY TRAVELLING SCHOLARSHIP—Choate, Hall & Stewart, Exchange Pl., 53 State St., Boston, MA 02109-2891. Attn: F. Davis Dassori. A scholarship of approximately $29,000 is awarded for a poet to spend the year abroad to advance the art of poetry. Deadline: October 15.

THE MADISON REVIEW—Dept. of English, 600 N. Park St., Helen C. White Hall, Univ. of Wisconsin-Madison, Madison, WI 53706. Phyllis Smart Young Prize in Poetry: awards $500 plus publication for a group of three unpublished poems. Chris O'Malley Prize in Fiction: awards $500 plus publication for an unpublished short story. Deadline: September 30. Entry fees.

MIDDLEBURY COLLEGE—Katharine Bakeless Nason Prizes, c/o Bread Loaf Writers' Conference, Middlebury College, Middlebury, VT 05753. Attn: Carol Knauss. Publication and fellowships to the Bread Loaf Writers' Conference are offered for previously unpublished first books of poetry, fiction, and nonfiction. Deadline: March 1. Entry fee.

MID-LIST PRESS—First Series Awards, 4324 12th Ave. S., Minneapolis, MN 55407-3218. Publication and an advance against royalties are awarded for first books in the following categories: a novel in any genre, from 50,000 words; poetry, from 65 pages; short fiction, from 50,000 words; creative nonfiction, from 50,000 words. Deadline: February 1 (novel and poetry); July 1 (short fiction and creative nonfiction). Entry fees.

MIDWEST RADIO THEATRE WORKSHOP—MRTW Script Competition, 115 Dikeman St., Hempstead, NY 11550. Workshop Script Contest: offers $800 in prizes, to be divided among two to four winners, and free workshop participation for contemporary radio scripts, 25 to 30 minutes long. Deadline: November 15. Entry fee.

MILL MOUNTAIN THEATRE—New Play Competition, 2nd Fl., One Market Square, Roanoke, VA 24011-1437. Attn: Jo Weinstein. Offers a $1,000 prize and staged reading, with possible full production, for an unpublished, unproduced, full-length or one-act play or musical. Cast size to ten. Deadline: January 1.

MISSISSIPPI REVIEW—Prize for Short Fiction and Poetry, The Center for Writers, Univ. of Southern Mississippi, Box 5144, Hattiesburg, MS 39406-5144. Attn: R. Fortenberry. Publication and $1,000 are offered for the best short story; $500 plus publication for the best poem. Deadline: May 31. Entry fee.

THE MISSOURI REVIEW—Editors' Prize, 1507 Hillcrest Hall, UMC, Columbia, MO 65211. Publication plus $1,500 is awarded for a short fiction manuscript (25 pages); $1,000 for an essay (25 pages); and $1,500 for poetry (10 pages). Deadline: October 15. Entry fee.

THE MOUNTAINEERS BOOKS—The Barbara Savage/"Miles from Nowhere" Memorial Award, 1001 S. W. Klickitat Way, Suite 201, Seattle, WA 98134. Offers a $3,000 cash award, plus publication and a $12,000 guaranteed advance against royalties for an outstanding unpublished, book-length manuscript of a nonfiction, personal-adventure narrative. Deadline: May 1 (of even-numbered years).

NATIONAL ENDOWMENT FOR THE ARTS—Nancy Hanks Center, 1100 Pennsylvania Ave. N.W., Room 720, Washington, DC 20506. Attn: Dir., Literature Program. Offers fellowships to writers and translators of poetry, fiction, plays, and creative nonfiction. Deadline: varies.

NATIONAL FEDERATION OF STATE POETRY SOCIETIES—Poetry Manuscript Contest, 3520 State Rt. 56, Mechanicsburg, OH 43044. Attn: Amy Zook, Chairman. A prize of $1,000 is awarded for the best manuscript of poetry, 35 to 60 pages. Deadline: October 15. Entry fee.

NATIONAL POETRY SERIES—P.O. Box G, Hopewell, NJ 08525. Attn: Coordinator. Sponsors Annual Open Competition for unpublished book-length poetry manuscripts. Five manuscripts are selected for publication, and each winner receives a $1,000 award. Deadline: February 15. Entry fee.

NEW ENGLAND POETRY CLUB—Annual Contests, 11 Puritan Rd., Arlington, MA 02172. Attn: Virginia Thayer. Prizes range from $100 to $500 in various contests for members, nonmembers, and students. Deadline: April 15. Entry fee.

NEW ENGLAND THEATRE CONFERENCE—John Gassner Memorial Playwriting Award, c/o Dept. of Theatre, Northeastern Univ., 360 Huntington Ave., Boston, MA 02115. A $1,000 first prize and a $500 second prize are offered for unpublished, unproduced full-length plays written by New England residents or members of the NETC. Deadline: April 15. Entry fee.

NEW ISSUES PRESS/WESTERN MICHIGAN UNIVERSITY—New Issues Poetry Prize, Western Michigan Univ., Kalamazoo, MI 49008-5092. Attn: Herbert Scott, Ed. Awards $1,000 plus publication for a book-length collection of poetry by a poet who has never before published a full-length collection. Deadline: November 30. Entry fee. *The Green Rose Prize in Poetry*—Open to poets who have had one or more full-length collections of poetry published, the winner receives a prize of $1,000 plus publication. Deadline: September 30. Entry fee.

NEW LETTERS—University of Missouri-Kansas City, 5100 Rockhill Rd., Kansas City, MO 64110-2499. Offers $750 for the best short story, to 5,000 words; $750 for the best group of three to six poems; $500 for the best essay, to 5,000 words. The work of each winner and first runner-up will be published. Deadline: May 15. Entry fee.

NEW YORK UNIVERSITY PRESS—New York University Press Prizes, 70 Washington Sq. S., 2nd Fl., New York, NY 10012-1091. Awards $1,000 plus publication to a book-length poetry manuscript and a book-length fiction manuscript. Deadline: May 1.

NIMROD/HARDIMAN AWARDS—*Nimrod International Journal*, 600 S. College Ave., Tulsa, OK 74104-3189. Katherine Anne Porter Prize: offers prizes of $2,000 and $1,000 for fiction, to 7,500 words. Pablo Neruda Prize: offers prizes of $2,000 and $1,000 for one long poem or a selection of poems. Deadline: April 15. Entry fees.

NORTH CAROLINA WRITERS' NETWORK—International Literature Prizes, 3501 Hwy. 54 West, Studio C, Chapel Hill, NC 27516. Thomas Wolfe Fiction Prize: offers $500 for a previously unpublished short story or novel excerpt. Deadline: August 31. Paul Green Playwrights Prize: offers $500 for a previously unproduced, unpublished play. Deadline: September 30. Randall Jarrell Poetry Prize: offers $500 for a previously unpublished poem. Deadline: November 1. Entry fees.

NORTHEASTERN UNIVERSITY PRESS—Samuel French Morse Poetry Prize, English Dept., 406 Holmes Hall, Northeastern Univ., Boston, MA 02115. Attn: Prof. Guy Rotella, Chairman. Offers $1,000 plus publication for a full-length poetry manuscript by a U.S. poet who has published no more than one book of poems. Deadline: August 1 (for inquiries); September 15 (for entries). Entry fee.

NORTHERN KENTUCKY UNIVERSITY—Y.E.S. New Play Festival, Dept. of Theatre, FA 227, Nunn Dr., Highland Hts., KY 41099-1007. Attn: Sandra Forman, Project Dir. Awards three $400 prizes plus production for previously unproduced full-length plays and musicals. Deadline: October 31 (of even-numbered years).

NORTHERN MICHIGAN UNIVERSITY—Mildred & Albert Panowski Playwriting Competition, Forest Roberts Theatre, Northern Michigan Univ., 1401 Presque Isle Ave., Marquette, MI 49855-5364. Awards $2,000, plus production for an original, full-length, previously unproduced and unpublished play. Deadline: November 20.

O'NEILL THEATER CENTER—National Playwrights Conference, 234 W. 44th St., Suite 901, New York, NY 10036. Attn: Mary F. McCabe. Offers stipend, staged readings, and room and board at the conference, for new stage and television plays. Deadline: December 1. Entry fee.

OFF CENTER THEATER—Women Playwright's Festival, Tampa Bay

Performing Arts Center, P.O. Box 518, Tampa, FL 33601. A $1,000 prize, production, and travel are offered for the best play about women, written by a woman; runner up receives staged reading. Deadline: September 15. Entry fee.

OHIO UNIVERSITY PRESS—Hollis Summers Poetry Prize, Scott Quadrangle, Athens, OH 45701. A $500 prize plus publication is awarded for an original collection of poetry, 60 to 95 pages. Deadline: October 31. Entry fee.

OLD DOMINION UNIVERSITY—Vassar Miller Prize in Poetry, c/o English Dept., Old Dominion University, Norfolk, VA 23529. Attn: Scott Cairns, Series Ed. Awards $1,000 plus publication by the University of North Texas Press for an original, unpublished poetry manuscript, 50 to 80 pages. Deadline: November 30. Entry fee.

PASSAGES NORTH—Elinor Benedict Poetry Prize, Dept. of English, Northern Michigan Univ., 1401 Presque Isle Ave., Marquette, MI 49855. $500 prize for unpublished poem. Deadline: December 1. Entry fee.

PATHWAY PRODUCTIONS—National Playwriting Contest, 9561 E. Daines Dr., Temple City, CA 91780. (E-mail: PathWayPro@earthlink.net) Awards $200 plus a workshop production to plays for and about teenagers. Deadline April 1.

PEN WRITERS FUND—PEN American Center, 568 Broadway, New York, NY 10012. Attn: India Amos, Writers Fund Coordinator. Grants and interest-free loans of up to $500 are available to published writers or produced playwrights facing unanticipated financial emergencies. If the emergency is due to HIV- and AIDS-related illness, professional writers and editors qualify through the Fund for Writers and Editors with AIDS; all decisions are confidential. Deadline: year-round.

PEN WRITING AWARDS FOR PRISONERS—PEN American Center, 568 Broadway, New York, 10012. County, state, and federal prisoners are eligible to enter one unpublished manuscript, to 5,000 words, in each of these categories: fiction, drama, and nonfiction. Prisoners may submit up to 10 poems (any form) in the poetry category (to 20 pages total) in the poetry category. Prizes of $100, $50, and $25 are awarded in each category. Deadline: September 1.

PEREGRINE SMITH POETRY SERIES—Gibbs Smith, Publisher, P.O. Box 667, Layton, UT 84041. Offers a $500 prize plus publication for a previously unpublished 64-page poetry manuscript. Deadline: April 30. Entry fee.

PETERLOO POETS—Open Competition, 2 Kelly Gardens, Calstock, Cornwall PL18 9SA, U.K. Prizes totalling 5,100 British pounds, including a grand prize of £4,000 plus publication, are awarded for poems of up to 40 lines. Deadline: March 1. Entry fee.

PHILADELPHIA FESTIVAL OF WORLD CINEMA—"Set in Philadelphia" Screenwriting Competition, 3701 Chestnut St., Philadelphia, PA 19104-3195. A $5,000 prize is awarded for the best screenplay, 85 to 130 pages, set primarily in the greater Philadelphia area. Deadline: January 1. Entry fee.

PIG IRON PRESS—Kenneth Patchen Competition, P.O. Box 237, Youngstown, OH 44501. Awards paperback publication, $500, and 20 copies of the winning manuscript of fiction (in even-numbered years) and poetry (in odd-numbered years). Deadline: December 31. Entry fee.

PIONEER DRAMA SERVICE—Shubert Fendrich Memorial Playwriting Contest, P.O. Box 4267, Englewood, CO 80155-4267. A prize of publication plus a $1,000 advance is offered for a previously produced, though unpublished, full-length play suitable for community theater. Deadline: March 1.

PLAYBOY—College Fiction Contest, 680 N. Lake Shore Dr., Chicago, IL 60611. Prizes of $3,000 plus publication, and $500, are offered for a short story, up to 25 pages, by a college student. Deadline: January 1.

THE PLAYWRIGHTS' CENTER—Jerome Fellowships, 2301 Franklin Ave. E., Minneapolis, MN 55406. Five emerging playwrights are offered a $7,000 stipend and 12-month residency; housing and travel are not provided. Deadline: September 16.

POCKETS—Fiction Contest, c/o Lynn W. Gilliam, Assoc. Ed., P.O. Box 189, Nashville, TN 37202-0189. A $1,000 prize goes to the author of the winning 1,000- to 1,600-word story for children in grades 1 to 6. Deadline: August 15.

POETS AND PATRONS OF CHICAGO—Poets and Patrons of Chicago, 1206 Hutchings, Glenview, IL 60025. Attn: Agnes Wathall Tatera. Prizes are $75 and $25 for original, unpublished poems of up to 40 lines. Deadline: September 1.

POETS CLUB OF CHICAGO—130 Windsor Park Dr., C-323, Carol Stream, IL 60188. Attn: LaVone Holt. Shakespearean/Petrarchan Sonnet Contest, with prizes of $50, $35, and $15. Deadline: September 1.

PRISM INTERNATIONAL—Short Fiction Contest, Creative Writing Dept., Univ. of B.C., E462-1866 Main Mall, Vancouver, B.C., V6T 1Z1. Publication, a $2,000 first prize, and five $200 prizes are awarded for stories of up to 25 pages. Deadline: December 31. Entry fee.

RIVER CITY—Writing Awards in Fiction, Dept. of English, Univ. of Memphis, Memphis, TN 38152. Awards of $2,000 plus publication, $500, and $300 are offered for previously unpublished short stories, to 7,500 words. Deadline: December 1. Entry fee.

ROME ART & COMMUNITY CENTER—Milton Dorfman Poetry Prize, 308 W. Bloomfield St., Rome, NY 13440. Offers prizes of $500, $200, and $100 for the best original, unpublished poems. Deadline: November 1. Entry fee.

ST. MARTIN'S PRESS/MALICE DOMESTIC CONTEST—Thomas Dunne Books, 175 Fifth Ave., New York, NY 10010. Offers publication plus a $10,000 advance against royalties, for a best first traditional mystery novel. Deadline: October 15.

ST. MARTIN'S PRESS/PRIVATE EYE NOVEL CONTEST—PWA Contest, 175 Fifth Ave., New York, NY 10010. Co-sponsored by Private Eye Writers of America. The writer of the best first private eye novel, from 60,000 words, receives publication plus $10,000 against royalties. Deadline: August 1.

SARABANDE BOOKS—Poetry and Short Fiction Prizes, P.O. Box 4999, Louisville, KY 40204. Prizes are $2,000, publication, and a standard royalty contract in the competition for the Kathryn A. Morton Prize in Poetry (for a collection of poems, from 48 pages) and the Mary McCarthy Prize in Short Fiction (for a collection of short stories or novellas, 150 to 300 pages). Deadline: February 15. Entry fee.

SHENANARTS—Shenandoah International Playwrights Retreat, Rt. 5, Box 167-F, Staunton, VA 24401. Full fellowships are offered to playwrights to attend the four-week retreat held each August. Each year the retreat focuses on plays having to do with a specific region of the world. Deadline: February 1.

SIENA COLLEGE—International Playwrights' Competition, Siena College, 515 Loudon Rd., Loudonville, NY 12211-1462. Offers $2,000 plus campus residency expenses for the winning full-length script; no musicals. Deadline: June 30 (of even-numbered years).

SILVERFISH REVIEW PRESS—The Gerald Cable Book Award, P.O. Box 3541, Eugene, OR 97403. Attn: Rodger Moody, Series Ed. Awards $1,000 plus publication to a book-length manuscript of poetry by an author who has not yet published a full-length collection. Deadline: November 1. Entry fee.

SNAKE NATION PRESS—Fiction and Poetry Contests, 110 #2 W. Force St., Valdosta, GA 31601. Attn: Nancy Phillips. Violet Reed Haas Prize: Offers publication plus $500 for a previously unpublished book of poetry, 50 to 75 pages. Deadline: January 15. *Snake Nation Review* Contest Issues: Prizes are publication plus $300, $200, and $100 for short stories; $100, $75, and $50 for poems. Deadlines: April 1; September 1. Entry fee.

SONORA REVIEW—Contests, Univ. of Arizona, Dept. of English, Tucson, AZ 85721. Poetry, Nonfiction Contest: offers $250 plus publication for the best poem; $100 plus publication for the best nonfiction. Deadline: July 1 for poetry and nonfiction. Short Story Contest: offers $250 plus publication for the best short story. Deadline: December 1. Entry fees.

THE SOUTHERN ANTHOLOGY—The Southern Prize, 2851 Johnston St., #123, Lafayette, LA 70503. A prize of $600 and publication are awarded for the best original, previously unpublished short story or novel excerpt, up to 7,500 words, or poem. Deadline: May 30. Entry fee.

SOUTHERN POETRY REVIEW—Guy Owen Poetry Prize, Southern Poetry Review, Advancement Studies Dept., Central Piedmont Community College, Charlotte, NC 28235. Attn: Ken McLaurin, Ed. A prize of publication plus $500 is awarded for the best original, previously unpublished poem. Deadline: April 30. Entry fee.

THE SOW'S EAR PRESS—19535 Pleasant View Dr., Abingdon, VA 24211-6827. Chapbook Competition: offers a prize of $500 plus 50 published copies for the best poetry manuscript, as well as two $100 prizes. Deadline: April 30. Poetry Competition: offers prizes of $500, $100, and $50 for a previously unpublished poem of any length. Deadline: October 31. Entry fees.

SPOON RIVER POETRY REVIEW—Editors' Prize, 4240 Dept. of English, Illinois State Univ., Normal, IL 61790-4240. Publication and a $500 prize, as well as two $100 prizes, are awarded for single poems. Deadline: May 1. Entry fee.

STATE UNIVERSITY OF NEW YORK AT STONY BROOK—Short Fiction Prize, Dept. of English, Humanities Bldg., State Univ., Stony Brook, NY 11794-5350. Attn: Carolyn McGrath. A prize of $1,000 is offered for the best short story, up to 5,000 words, written by an undergraduate currently enrolled full-time in an American or Canadian college. Deadline: February 28.

STORY LINE PRESS—Nicholas Roerich Poetry Prize, Three Oaks Farm, P.O. Box 1240, Ashland, OR 97520-0055. A prize of $1,000 plus publication is awarded for an original book of poetry by a poet who has never before published a book of poetry. Deadline: October 31. Entry fee.

SUNY FARMINGDALE—Paumanok Poetry Award, English Dept., Knapp Hall, SUNY Farmingdale, Farmingdale, NY 11735. Prizes of $1,000 and two $500 prizes are offered for entries of three to five poems. Deadline: September 15. Entry fee.

SYRACUSE UNIVERSITY PRESS—John Ben Snow Prize, 1600 Jamesville Ave., Syracuse, NY 13244-5160. Attn: Dir. Awards a $1,500 advance, plus publication, for an unpublished book-length nonfiction manuscript about New York State, especially upstate or central New York. Deadline: December 31.

TEN MINUTE MUSICALS PROJECT—Box 461194, W. Hollywood, CA 90046. Attn: Michael Koppy, Prod. Musicals of 7 to 20 minutes are eligible for a $250 advance against royalties and musical anthology productions at theaters in the U.S. and Canada. Deadline: August 31.

DAVID THOMAS CHARITABLE TRUST—Open Competitions, P.O. Box 4, Nairn IV12 4HU, Scotland, UK. The trust sponsors a number of theme-based poetry and short story contests open to beginning writers, with prizes ranging from £25 to £1,200. Deadline: varies. Entry fee.

TRITON COLLEGE—Salute to the Arts Poetry Contest, 2000 Fifth Ave., River Grove, IL 60171. Winning original, unpublished poems, to 60 lines, on designated themes, are published by Triton College. Deadline: April 1.

UNICO NATIONAL—Ella T. Grasso Literary Award Contest, 72 Burroughs Pl., Bloomfield, NJ 07003. A prize of $1,000 is awarded for the best essay or short story, 1,500 to 2,000 words, on the Italian-American experience; two $250 prizes also awarded. Deadline: April 1.

U.S. NAVAL INSTITUTE—Arleigh Burke Essay Contest, *Proceedings Magazine*, 291 Wood Rd., Annapolis, MD 21402-5034. Awards prizes of $3,000, $2,000, and $1,000 plus publication, for essays on the advancement of professional, literary, or scientific knowledge in the naval or maritime services, and the advancement of the knowledge of sea power. Deadline: December 31. Also sponsors several smaller contests; deadlines vary.

UNIVERSITIES WEST PRESS—Emily Dickinson Award in Poetry, Universities West Press, P.O. Box 22310, Flagstaff, AZ 86002-2310. A prize of $1,000 plus publication is awarded for an unpublished poem. Deadline: August 31. Entry fee.

UNIVERSITY OF AKRON PRESS—The Akron Poetry Prize, 374B Bierce Library, Akron, OH 44325-1703. Publication and $500 are offered for a previously unpublished collection of poems. Deadline: June 30. Entry fee.

UNIVERSITY OF CALIFORNIA IRVINE—Chicano/Latino Literary Contest, Dept. of Spanish and Portuguese, UCI, Irvine, CA 92697-5275. Attn: Alejandro Morales, Dir. A first prize of $1,000 plus publication, and prizes of $500 and $250 are awarded in alternating years for poetry, drama, novels, and short stories. Deadline: April 30.

UNIVERSITY OF GEORGIA PRESS—Flannery O'Connor Award for Short Fiction, Univ. of Georgia Press, 330 Research Dr., Athens, GA 30602-4901. Two prizes of $1,000 plus publication are awarded for book-length collections of short fiction. Deadline: July 31. Entry fees.

UNIVERSITY OF GEORGIA PRESS CONTEMPORARY POETRY SERIES—Athens, GA 30602-4901. Offers publication of manuscripts from poets who have published at least one volume of poetry. Deadline: January 31. Publication of book-length poetry manuscripts is offered to poets who have never had a book of poems published. Deadline: September 30. Entry fee.

UNIVERSITY OF HAWAII AT MANOA—Kumu Kahua Playwriting Contest, Dept. of Drama and Theatre, 1770 East-West Rd., Honolulu, HI 96822. Awards $500 and $400 for full-length plays on the Hawaiian experience; $200 for plays on any topic. Also conducts contest for plays written by Hawaiian residents. Deadline: January 1.

UNIVERSITY OF IOWA—Iowa Publication Awards for Short Fiction, Iowa Writers' Workshop, 102 Dey House, Iowa City, IA 52242-1000. The John Simmons Short Fiction Award and the Iowa Short Fiction Award, both for unpublished full-length collections of short stories, offer publication under a standard contract. Deadline: September 30.

UNIVERSITY OF IOWA PRESS—The Iowa Poetry Prize, 100 Kuhl House, Iowa City, IA 52242-1000. Two $1,000 prizes, plus publication, are awarded for poetry manuscripts, 50 to 150 pages, by writers who have published at least one book of poetry. Deadline: May 31.

UNIVERSITY OF MASSACHUSETTS PRESS—Juniper Prize, Amherst, MA 01003. Offers a prize of $1,000 plus publication for a book-length manuscript of poetry; awarded in odd-numbered years to writers who have never published a book of poetry, and in even-numbered years to writers who have published a book or chapbook of poetry. Deadline: September 30. Entry fee.

UNIVERSITY OF NEBRASKA-OMAHA—Awards in Poetry and Fiction, *The Nebraska Review*, Univ. of Nebraska-Omaha, Omaha, NE 68182-0324. Offers $500 each plus publication to the winning short story (to 5,000 words) and the winning poem (or group of poems). Deadline: November 30. Entry fee.

UNIVERSITY OF NEBRASKA PRESS—North American Indian Prose Award, 312 N. 14th St., Lincoln, NE 68588-0484. Previously unpublished book-length manuscripts of biography, autobiography, history, literary criticism, and essays will be judged for originality, literary merit, and familiarity with North American Indian life. A $1,000 advance and publication are offered. Deadline: July 1.

UNIVERSITY OF PITTSBURGH PRESS—3347 Forbes Ave., Pittsburgh, PA 15261. Agnes Lynch Starrett Poetry Prize: offers $3,000 plus publication in the Pitt Poetry Series for a book-length collection of poems by a poet who has not yet published a volume of poetry. Deadline: April 30. Entry fee. Drue Heinz Literature Prize: offers $10,000 plus publication and royalty contract for an unpublished collection of short stories or novellas, 150 to 300 pages, by a writer who has previously published a book-length collection of fiction or at least three short stories or novellas in nationally distributed magazines. Deadline: June 30.

UNIVERSITY OF SOUTHERN CALIFORNIA—Ann Stanford Poetry Prize, Master of Professional Writing Program, WPH 404, Univ. of Southern California, Los Angeles, CA 90089-4034. Publication plus prizes of $750,

$250, and $100 are awarded; submit up to five poems. Deadline: April 15. Entry fee.

UTAH STATE UNIVERSITY PRESS—May Swenson Poetry Award, Utah State Univ. Press, Logan, UT 84322-7800. Awards $750, plus publication and royalties to a collection of poems, 50 to 100 pages. Deadline: September 30. Entry fee.

VETERANS OF FOREIGN WARS—Voice of Democracy Audio Essay Competition, VFW National Headquarters, 406 W. 34th St., Kansas City, MO 64111. Several national scholarships totalling over $120,000 are awarded to high school students for short, tape-recorded essays. Themes change annually. Deadline: November 1.

YALE UNIVERSITY PRESS—Yale Series of Younger Poets Prize, Box 209040, Yale Sta., New Haven, CT 06520-9040. Attn: Ed. Series publication is awarded for a book-length manuscript of poetry written by a poet under 40 who has not previously published a volume of poems. Deadline: February 29. Entry fee.

WRITERS COLONIES

Writers colonies offer solitude and freedom from everyday distractions so that writers can concentrate on their work. Though some colonies are quite small, with space for just three or four writers at a time, others can provide accommodations for as many as thirty or forty. The length of a residency may vary, too, from a couple of weeks to five or six months. These programs have strict admissions policies, and writers must submit a formal application or letter of intent, a resumé, writing samples, and letters of recommendation. As an alternative to the traditional writers colony, a few of the organizations listed offer writing rooms for writers who live nearby. Write for application information first, enclosing a stamped, self-addressed envelope. Residency fees are subject to change.

THE EDWARD F. ALBEE FOUNDATION, INC.
14 Harrison St.
New York, NY 10013
(212) 266-2020
David Briggs, *Foundation Secretary*
Located on Long Island, "The Barn," or the William Flanagan Memorial Creative Persons Center, is maintained by the Albee Foundation. "The standards for admission are, simply, talent and need." Twelve writers are accepted each season for one-month residencies, available from June 1 to October 1; applications, including writing samples, project description, and resumé, are accepted from January 1 to April 1. There is no fee, though residents are responsible for their own food and travel expenses.

ALTOS DE CHAVÓN
c/o Parsons School of Design
2 W. 13th St., Rm. 707
New York, NY 10011
(212) 229-5370
Stephen D. Kaplan, *Arts/Education Director*

Altos de Chavón is a nonprofit center for the arts in the Dominican Republic committed to education, design innovation, international creative exchange, and the promotion of Dominican culture. Residencies average 12 weeks and provide the emerging or established artist an opportunity to live and work in a setting of architectural and natural beauty. All artists are welcome to apply, though writers should note there are no typewriters, the library is oriented more toward the design profession, and the apartments housing writers also accommodate university students. Two to three writers are chosen each year for the program. The fee is $350 per month for an apartment with kitchenette; linen and cleaning services are available at an extra cost. Applications include a letter of interest, writing sample, and resumé; deadline for application is July 15.

MARY ANDERSON CENTER FOR THE ARTS
101 St. Francis Dr.
Mount St. Francis, IN 47146
(812) 923-8602
e-mail: maca@iglou.com
Debra Carmody, *Executive Director*

Founded in 1989, the artists' residency and retreat is situated on the grounds of a Franciscan friary. Space is available for seven residents at a time, including private rooms, working space, and a visual artists' studio; meals are provided. Two-week to three-month residencies are available and are granted based on project proposal and the artist's body of work; applications are accepted year-round. Fees are $30 per day, but can be reduced in some cases. There is a non-refundable $15 application fee.

ATLANTIC CENTER FOR THE ARTS
1414 Art Center Ave.
New Smyrna Beach, FL 32168
(904) 427-6975; (800) 393-6975
web site: www.atlantic-centerarts.org
Nicholas Conroy, *Program Director*

The center is located on the east coast of central Florida, with 67 acres of pristine hammockland on a tidal estuary. All buildings, connected by raised wooden walkways, are handicapped accessible and air conditioned. The center provides a unique environment for sharing ideas, learning, and collaborating on interdisciplinary projects. Master artists meet with talented artists for readings and critiques, with time out for individual work. Residencies are one to three weeks. Fees are $100 a week for tuition and $25 a day for housing; off-site, tuition-only plans are available; financial aid is limited. Application deadlines vary.

BERLINER KÜNSTLERPROGRAM
Artists-in-Berlin Program
Jägerstr. 23
D-10117 Berlin, Germany

030-2022080; fax: 030-2041267
e-mail: bkp.berlin@daad.de

One-year residencies are offered to well-known and emerging writers, filmmakers, and composers to promote cultural exchange. Up to 20 residencies are offered for periods beginning between January 1 and June 30. Room, board, travel, and living expenses are awarded. Application, project description, and copies of publications are due by January 1 of the year preceding the residency.

BLUE MOUNTAIN CENTER

Blue Mountain Lake, NY 12812-0109
(518) 352-7391
Harriet Barlow, *Director*

Hosts month-long residencies for artists and writers from mid-June to late October. Established fiction and nonfiction writers, poets, and playwrights whose work evinces social and ecological concern are eligible; 14 residents are accepted per session. Residents are not charged for their time at Blue Mountain, although all visitors are invited to contribute to the studio construction fund. There is no application form; apply by sending a brief biographical sketch, a plan for work at Blue Mountain, five to 10 slides or a writing sample of any length, an indication of preference for an early summer, late summer, or fall residence, and a $20 application fee, attention: *Admissions Committee*. Applications are due February 1.

BYRDCLIFFE ARTS COLONY

Artists' Residency Program
Woodstock Guild
34 Tinker St.
Woodstock, NY 12498
(914) 679-2079
e-mail: wguild@ulster.net
web site: www.woodstockguild.org
Attn: *Director*

The Villetta Inn, located on the 400-acre arts colony, offers private studios and separate bedrooms, a communal kitchen, and a peaceful environment for fiction writers, poets, playwrights, and visual artists. One-month residencies are offered from June to September. Fee is $500 per month. Submit application, resumé, writing sample, and two letters of recommendation; the deadline is April 1. Send SASE for application.

THE CAMARGO FOUNDATION

125 Park Square Ct.
400 Sibley St.
St. Paul, MN 55101-1982
Dr. William Reichard, *U.S. Secretariat*

The Camargo Foundation maintains a center of studies in France for the benefit of nine scholars and graduate students each semester who wish to pursue projects in the humanities and social sciences relative to France and Francophone culture. In addition, one artist, one composer, and one writer are accepted each semester. The foundation offers furnished apartments and a reference library in the city of Cassis. Research should be at an advanced stage and not require resources unavailable in the Marseilles-Aix-Cassis region. Fellows must be in residence at the foundation; the award is exclusively a residential grant. Application materials include: application form, curriculum vitae, three letters of recommendation, and project description. Writers, artists, and composers are required to send work samples. Applications are due February 1.

CENTRUM
P.O. Box 1158
Port Townsend, WA 98368
(360) 385-3102
Marlene Bennett, *Program Facilitator*

Writers are awarded one-month residencies between September and May. Applicants selected by a peer jury receive free housing and a $300 stipend. Previous residents may return on a space-available basis for a monthly fee. Applications are due September 8. The application fee is $10.

DJERASSI RESIDENT ARTISTS PROGRAM
2325 Bear Gulch Rd.
Woodside, CA 94062
(650) 747-1250; fax: (650) 747-0105
e-mail: drap@djerassi.org
web site: www.djerassi.org
Judy Freeland, *Residency Coordinator*

The Djerassi Program offers living and working spaces in a rural setting, for writers in the categories of prose (fiction), drama (playwrights, screenwriters), music (composers, librettists, lyricists), and poetry. Residencies are from four to five weeks. There are no fees other than the $25 application fee. The application deadline is February 15 for a residency in the year 2001. Send an SASE for application packet.

DORLAND MOUNTAIN ARTS COLONY
Box 6
Temecula, CA 92593
(909) 302-3837
e-mail: dorland@ez2.net
web site: www.ez2.net/dorland/
Attn: *Admissions Committee*

Dorland is a nature preserve and "retreat for creative people" located in the Palomar Mountains of Southern California. "Without electricity, residents find a new, natural rhythm for their work." Novelists, playwrights, poets, nonfiction writers, composers, and visual artists are encouraged to apply for residencies of one to two months. The fee of $300 a month includes cottage, fuel, and firewood. Send SASE for application; deadlines are March 1 and September 1.

DORSET COLONY HOUSE
Box 510
Dorset, VT 05251
(802) 867-2223
John Nassivera, *Director*

Writers and playwrights are offered low-cost rooms with kitchen facilities at the historic Colony House in Dorset, Vermont. Residencies are one week to one month, and are available in the fall and spring. Applications are accepted year-round, and up to eight writers stay at a time. The fee is $125 per week; financial aid is limited. For more information, send SASE.

FINE ARTS WORK CENTER IN PROVINCETOWN
24 Pearl St.
Provincetown, MA 02657
Hunter O'Hanian, *Executive Director*

Fellowships, including living and studio space and monthly stipends, are available at the Fine Arts Work Center on Cape Cod, for fiction writers and poets to work independently. Residencies are for seven months, October through April; apply before December 1 deadline. Five poets and five fiction writers are accepted. Send SASE for details; indicate that you are a writer in the request.

GLENESSENCE WRITERS COLONY
1447 West Ward Ave.
Ridgecrest, CA 93555
(760) 446-5894
Allison Swift, *Director*

Glenessence is a luxury villa located in the Upper Mojave Desert, offering private rooms with bath, pool, spa, courtyard, shared kitchen, fitness center, and library. Children, pets, and smoking are prohibited. Residencies are offered at $565 per month; meals are not provided. Reservations are made on a first-come basis. Seasonal: March through May; September through November.

THE TYRONE GUTHRIE CENTRE
Annaghmakerrig, Newbliss
County Monaghan
Ireland
(353) 47-54003; fax: (353) 47-54380
G. Millar, *Administrator*

Set on a 450-acre country estate, the center offers peace and seclusion to writers and other artists to enable them to get on with their work. All art forms are represented. One- to three-month residencies are offered throughout the year, at the rate of 2,000 pounds per month; financial assistance is available to Irish citizens only. A number of longer term self-catering houses in the old farmyard are also available at £300 per week. Writers chosen on the basis of c.v., samples of published work, and outline of intended project. Writers may apply for acceptance year-round.

THE HAMBIDGE CENTER
P.O. Box 339
Rabun Gap, GA 30568
(706) 746-5718; fax: (706) 746-9933
e-mail: Hambidge@rabun.net
web site: www.rabun.net/~Hambidge

The Hambidge Center for Creative Arts and Sciences is located on 600 pristine acres of quiet woods in the north Georgia mountains. Eight private cottages are available for fellows. All fellowships are partially underwritten, residents are asked to contribute $125 per week. Two-week to six-week residencies, year-round, are offered to serious artists from all disciplines. Send SASE for application form. Application deadlines: November 1 for May to October; May 1 for November to April.

HEADLANDS CENTER FOR THE ARTS
944 Fort Barry
Sausalito, CA 94965
(415) 331-2787

Programs at the Headlands Center, located on 13,000 acres of open coastal space, are available to residents of Ohio, North Carolina, and California. Application requirements vary by state. Applications are due in June and decisions are announced in October for residencies beginning in February. There are no residency or application fees. Send SASE for more information.

HEDGEBROOK
2197 E. Millman Rd.
Langley, WA 98260
(360) 321-4786

Hedgebrook provides women writers, published or not, of all ages and from all cultural backgrounds, with a natural place to work. Established in 1988, the retreat is located on 30 acres of farmland and woods on Whidbey Island in Washington State. Each writer has her own cottage, equipped with electricity and woodstove. A bathhouse serves all six cottages. Writers gather for dinner in the farmhouse every evening and frequently read in the living room/library afterwards. Limited travel scholarships are available. Residencies range from one week to two months. April 1 is the application deadline for residencies from mid-June to mid-December; October 1 for mid-January to late May. Applicants are chosen by a selection committee composed of writers. There is a $15 fee to apply; send SASE for application.

KALANI OCEANSIDE RETREAT, INSTITUTE FOR CULTURE AND WELLNESS
Artist-in-Residence Program
RR2, Box 4500
Pahoa-Beach Road, HI 96778
(808) 965-7828; (800) 800-6886; fax: (808) 965-0527
e-mail: kalani@kalani.com
web site: www.kalani.com
Richard Koob, *Program Coordinator*

Located in a rural coastal setting of 113 botanical acres, Kalani Oceanside Retreat hosts and sponsors educational programs "with the aloha experience that is its namesake: harmony of heaven and earth." Residencies range from two weeks to two months and are available throughout the year. Fees range from $33 to $55 per day, meals available at additional fee. Applications accepted year-round.

THE MACDOWELL COLONY
100 High St.
Peterborough, NH 03458
(603) 924-3886
web site: www.macdowellcolony.org
Pat Dodge, *Admissions Coordinator*

Studios, room, and board are available for writers to work without interruption in a woodland setting. Through 2001, writers are given a stipend of up to $1,000 depending on financial need. Selection is competitive. Apply by January 15 for stays May through August; April 15 for September through December; and September 15 for January through April. Residencies last up to eight weeks, and 80 to 90 writers are accepted each year. Send SASE for application.

THE MILLAY COLONY FOR THE ARTS
444 East Hill Rd.
P.O. Box 3
Austerlitz, NY 12017-0003
(518) 392-3103
Gail Giles, *Director of Admissions*

At Steepletop, the former home of Edna St. Vincent Millay, writers are provided studios, universally accessible living quarters, and meals at no cost. Residencies last one month. Application deadlines are February 1, May 1, and September 1. Send SASE for more information and application. Applications can also be accessed by e-mail (application@millaycolony.org).

MILLETT FARM: AN ART COLONY FOR WOMEN
295 Bowery
New York, NY 10003
Kate Millett, *Director*

Summer residencies are offered to women writers and visual artists at a picturesque tree farm in rural New York. In return for housing, all residents contribute four hours of work each weekday morning and contribute $80 a week toward meals. Preference is given to writers who can stay all summer or at least six weeks. Also, one week intensive class with Kate Millett. For more information send an SASE.

MOLASSES POND WRITERS' RETREAT AND WORKSHOP
RR 1, Box 85C
Milbridge, ME 04658
(207) 546-2506
Martha Barron Barrett and Sue Wheeler, *Coordinators*

Led by published authors who teach writing at the University of New Hampshire, this one-week workshop is held in June and includes time set aside for writing, as well as manuscript critique and writing classes. Up to 10 writers participate, staying in a colonial farmhouse with private bed/work rooms for each participant and common areas for meals and classes. The $400 fee covers lodging, meals, and tuition. Applicants must be serious about their work. No children's literature or poetry. Submit statement of purpose and 15 to 20 pages of fiction or nonfiction between February 15 and March 1.

MONTANA ARTISTS REFUGE
Box 8
Basin, MT 59631
(406) 225-3525

Writers are offered apartment and studio space in a relaxed and unpretentious atmosphere, where they can work with other artists or in solitude.

Residencies range from three months to one year, and rents range from $260 to $450 per month. Limited financial aid is available. Deadline for summer (May–Sept.) is May 1 each year. Applications for other dates are ongoing. Send SASE for information.

JENNY McKEAN MOORE WRITER-IN-WASHINGTON

Dept. of English
The George Washington University
Washington, DC 20052
Attn: Prof. Faye Moskowitz

The fellowship allows for a writer to teach two paid semesters (salary: $48,000) at The George Washington University. Teaching duties include a poetry workshop each semester for students from the metropolitan community who may have had little formal education; and one class each semester for university students. Fiction and poetry alternate years. Applications include letter, indicating publications and other projects, extent of teaching experience, and other qualifications.The application must also include a resumé and fifteen to twenty-five sample pages of your work. The application deadline is November 15.

NEW YORK MILLS ARTS RETREAT AND REGIONAL CULTURAL CENTER

24 N. Main Ave.
P.O. Box 246
New York Mills, MN 56567
(218) 385-3339
Kent Scheer, *Retreat Coordinator*

Five to seven emerging artists, writers, filmmakers, or musicians are accepted during the nine month season. Each artist receives financial assistance through a stipend, ranging from $750 for a two-week residency to $1,500 for four weeks, provided by the Jerome Foundation. Retreatants live in a small house in the heart of this community of 1,000 people. The Cultural Center, housed in a restored 1895 general store, is an innovative nonprofit organization offering gallery exhibits, musical performances, theater, literary events, educational programs, the Great American Think-Off philosophy competition, and the Continental Divide Film and Music Festival. There is a review process twice a year; the deadlines are April 1 and October 1.

THE NORTHWOOD UNIVERSITY

Alden B. Dow Creativity Center
3225 Cook Rd.
Midland, MI 48640-2398
(517) 837-4478; fax: (517) 837-4468
e-mail: creativity@northwood.edu

The Fellowship Program allows individuals time away from their ongoing daily routines to pursue their project ideas without interruption. A project idea should be innovative, creative, and have potential for impact in its field. Four ten-week residencies, lasting from early-June to mid-August, are awarded yearly. There is a $10 application fee. A $750 stipend plus room and board are provided. No spouses or families. Applications are due December 31.

OX-BOW
37 S. Wabash Ave.
Chicago, IL 60603
(312) 899-7455

One-week residencies are available mid-June to mid-August for writers who wish to reside and work in a secluded, natural environment. Recipients are required to pay $380 room and board, per week. Primarily a program for the visual arts, the mission of Ox-Bow is to nurture the creative process through instruction, example, and community. Resident writers are encouraged to present a reading of their work and to participate in the community life at Ox-Bow. For application form write or call. Application deadline is May 14.

RAGDALE FOUNDATION
1260 N. Green Bay Rd.
Lake Forest, IL 60045
(847) 234-1063
Suellen Rocca, *Admissions*

Uninterrupted time and peaceful space allow writers a chance to finish works in progress, to begin new works, to solve thorny creative problems, and to experiment in new genres. The foundation is located 30 miles north of Chicago, on 55 acres of prairie. Residencies of two weeks to two months are available for writers, artists, and composers. The fee is $15 a day; some full and partial fee waivers available, based solely on financial need. Send SASE for deadline information. Application fee: $20.

SASKATCHEWAN WRITERS GUILD
Writers/Artists Colonies and Individual Retreats
P.O. Box 3986
Regina, Saskatchewan S4P 3R9
Canada
(306) 757-6310
Attn: *Colony Coordinator*

The Saskatchewan Colonies are at two locations: St. Peter's Abbey, near Humboldt, provides a six-week summer colony (July–August) and a two-week winter colony in February, for up to eight writers and artists at a time; applicant stays vary. Individual retreats of up to two weeks are offered year-round at St. Peter's, for up to three residents at a time. Only Canadian residents are eligible for individual retreats. Emma Lake, near Prince Albert, is the site of a two-week colony in August. A fee of $125 (Saskatchewan Writers Guild members) or $175 (nonmembers) per week includes room and board. Submit resumé, short project description, two references, and a 10-page writing sample. Among applicants of equal ability, priority is given to Saskatchewan residents. December 1 deadline for winter colony; May 1 deadline for summer colonies. Apply at least four weeks in advance of preferred retreat dates.

THE JOHN STEINBECK ROOM
Long Island University
Southampton College Library
Southampton, NY 11968
(516) 287-8382
Robert Gerbereux, *Library Director*

The John Steinbeck Room at Long Island University provides a basic research facility to writers who have either a current contract with a book publisher or a confirmed assignment from a magazine editor. The room is available for a period of six months with one six-month renewal permissible. Send SASE for application.

THE THURBER HOUSE RESIDENCIES
c/o Thurber House
77 Jefferson Ave.
Columbus, OH 43215
(614) 464-1032; fax: (614) 228-7445
Michael J. Rosen, *Literary Director*
Residencies in the restored home of James Thurber are awarded to journalists, poets, and playwrights. Residents work on their own writing projects, and in addition to other duties, teach one class at the Ohio State University. A stipend of $5,000 per quarter is provided. A letter of interest and curriculum vitae must be received by December 15, at which time applications are reviewed for the upcoming academic year.

UCROSS FOUNDATION
Residency Program
30 Big Red Lane
Clearmont, WY 82835
(307) 737-2291; fax: (307) 737-2322
Sharon Dynak, *Executive Director*
Residencies, two to eight weeks, in the foothills of the Big Horn Mountains in Wyoming, allow writers, artists, and scholars to concentrate on their work without interruption. Two residency sessions are scheduled annually: February to June and August to December. There is no charge for room, board, or studio space. Application deadlines are March 1 for the fall session and October 1 for the spring session. Send SASE for more information.

VERMONT STUDIO CENTER
P.O. Box 613
Johnson, VT 05656
(802) 635-2727; fax: (802) 635-2730;
e-mail: vscvt@pwshift.com
web site: www.vermontstudiocenter.com
Attn: *Registrar*
The Vermont Studio Center offers two-week studio sessions for up to 12 writers from February through April, led by prominent writers and teachers focusing on fiction, creative nonfiction, and poetry. Independent writers' retreats from two to 12 weeks are available year-round for those seeking more solitude. Room, working studio, and meals are included in all programs. The fee is $3,000 for a month-long residency. Financial assistance is available based on both merit and need. Applications are accepted year-round. Application fee: $25.

VILLA MONTALVO ARTIST RESIDENCY PROGRAM
P.O. Box 158
Saratoga, CA 95071
(408) 961-5818

Kathryn Funk, *Artist Residency Program Director*
Villa Montalvo, in the foothills of the Santa Cruz Mountains south of San Francisco, offers one- to three-month residencies free of charge to writers, visual artists, and composers. Several merit-based fellowships are available. The application deadlines are September 1 and March 1; send self-addressed label and 55¢ postage to receive brochure and application form. Application fee is $20.

VIRGINIA CENTER FOR THE CREATIVE ARTS
Box VCCA
Sweet Briar, VA 24595
(804) 946-7236
e-mail: vcca@vcca.com
web site: www.vcca.com
Suny Monk, *Executive Director*
A working retreat for writers, composers, and visual artists in Virginia's Blue Ridge Mountains. Residencies from two weeks to two months are available year-round. Application deadlines are the 15th of January, May, and September; about 300 residents are accepted each year. A limited amount of financial assistance is available. Send SASE for more information.

THE WRITERS ROOM
10 Astor Pl., 6th Fl.
New York, NY 10003
(212) 254-6995; fax: (212) 533-6059
Donna Brodie, *Executive Director*
Located in the East Village, The Writers Room provides subsidized work space to all types of writers at all stages of their careers. "We offer urban writers a quiet place to escape from noisy neighbors, children, roommates, and other distractions of city life." The Room holds 30 desks separated by partitions, a typing room with five desks, a kitchen, and a library. Open 24 hours a day, 365 days a year. There is a one-time $50 application fee; fees for the three-month period include $175 for a "floater" desk. Part-time memberships at reduced rates are also available. Call, fax or write for application (no visits without appointment).

THE WRITERS STUDIO
The Mercantile Library Association
17 E. 47th St.
New York, NY 10017
(212) 755-6710
Harold Augenbraum, *Director*
The Writers Studio is a quiet place in which writers can rent space conducive to the production of good work. A carrel, locker, small reference collection, electrical outlets, and membership in the Mercantile Library of New York are available at the cost of $200 per three-month residency. Submit application, resumé, and writing samples; applications are considered year-round.

HELENE WURLITZER FOUNDATION OF NEW MEXICO
Box 545
Taos, NM 87571

(505) 758-2413; fax: (505) 758-2559

Rent-free and utility-free studios in Taos are offered to writers and creative artists in all media. "All artists are given the opportunity to be free of the shackles of a 9-to-5 routine." Residency is usually three months. The foundation is open from April 1 through September 30 and on a limited basis October through March. Residencies are assigned into the year 2001, but cancellations do occur. Write or fax for an application.

YADDO
Box 395
Saratoga Springs, NY 12866-0395
(518) 584-0746; fax: (518) 584-1312
e-mail: CHWAIT@yaddo.org
Candace Wait, *Program Coordinator*

Visual artists, writers, choreographers, film/video artists, performance artists, composers, and collaborators are invited for stays from two weeks to two months. Room, board, and studio space are provided. No stipends. Deadlines are January 15 and August 1. There is a $20 application fee; send SASE for form.

WRITERS CONFERENCES

Each year, hundreds of writers conferences are held across the country. The following list, arranged by state, represents a sampling of conferences; each listing includes the location of the conference, the month during which it is usually held, and the name and address of the person from whom specific information may be received. Writers are advised to write directly to conference directors for full details. Always enclose an SASE. Additional conferences are listed annually in the May issue of *The Writer* Magazine (120 Boylston St., Boston, MA 02116-4615).

ALABAMA

WRITING TODAY—Birmingham, AL. April. Martha Ross, Dir., Writing Today, Birmingham-Southern College, Box 549003, Birmingham, AL 35254.

SCBWI "WRITING & ILLUSTRATING FOR KIDS"—Birmingham, AL. October. Joan Broerman, Reg. Adv., Southern Breeze SCBWI, P.O. Box 26282, Birmingham, AL 35260.

ALASKA

SITKA SYMPOSIUM ON HUMAN VALUES & THE WRITTEN WORD—Sitka, AK. June. Carolyn Servid, Dir., The Island Institute, P.O. Box 2420, Sitka, AK 99835.

NATIONAL FEDERATION OF PRESS WOMEN ANNUAL CONFERENCE—Anchorage, AK. September. Carol S. Pierce, Dir., NFPW, Box 5556, Arlington, VA 22205.

ARIZONA

DESERT DREAMS 2000—Phoenix, AZ. March, April. Alison Kinnaird, P.O. Box 1771, Chandler, AZ 85244-1771.

ARKANSAS

ARKANSAS WRITER'S CONFERENCE—Little Rock, AR. June. Peggy Vining, 6817 Gingerbread Ln., Little Rock, AR 72204.

OZARK CREATIVE WRITERS, INC.—Eureka Springs, AR. October. Marcia Camp, 75 Robinwood Dr., Little Rock, AR 72227.

CALIFORNIA

SAN DIEGO STATE UNIVERSITY ANNUAL WRITERS' CONFERENCE—San Diego, CA. January. Diane Dunaway, Coord., 8465 Jane St., San Diego, CA 92129.

JACK LONDON'S WRITERS' CONFERENCE—S. San Francisco, CA. March. Mariann M. Jackson, Dir., 327 B St., Redwood City, CA 94063-1017.

IWWG EARLY SPRING IN CALIFORNIA CONFERENCE—Santa Cruz, CA. March. Hannelore Hahn, Dir., IWWG, P.O. Box 810, Gracie Station, New York, NY 10028.

WRITERS' FORUM—Pasadena, CA. March. Meredith Brucker, Dir., Pasadena City College, 1570 E. Colorado Blvd., Pasadena, CA 91106-2003.

MOUNT HERMON CHRISTIAN WRITERS' CONFERENCE—Mount Hermon, CA. March. David R. Talbott, Dir., P.O. Box 413, Mount Hermon, CA 95041.

SANTA BARBARA WRITERS' CONFERENCE—Santa Barbara, CA. June. Barnaby and Mary Conrad, Dirs., P.O. Box 304, Carpinteria, CA 93014.

FOOTHILL WRITERS' CONFERENCE—Los Altos Hills, CA. June. Kim Wolterbeek, Dir., Foothill Writers' Conference, 12345 El Monte Rd., Los Altos Hills, CA 94022.

WRITERS' AND ILLUSTRATORS' CONFERENCE IN CHILDREN'S LITERATURE—Los Angeles, CA. August. Lin Oliver, Dir., SCBWI, 8271 Beverly Blvd., Los Angeles, CA 90048.

CAT WRITERS' ASSOCIATION WRITERS' CONFERENCE—Anaheim, CA. November. Amy D. Shojai, Dir., Cat Writers' Assoc., P.O. Box 1904, Sherman, TX 75091.

WRITING AND EDITING SEMINARS—Various dates and locations, CA. Louise Purwin Zobel, 23350 Sereno, Villa 30, Cupertino, CA 95014.

COLORADO

COLORADO CHRISTIAN WRITERS' CONFERENCE—Estes Park, CO. May. Marlene Bagnull, Dir., 316 Blanchard Rd., Drexel Hill, PA 19026.

STEAMBOAT SPRINGS WRITERS' CONFERENCE—Steamboat Springs, CO. July. Harriet Freiberger, Dir., P.O. Box 774284, Steamboat Springs, CO 80477.

PUBLISHING INSTITUTE AT THE UNIVERSITY OF DENVER—Denver, CO. July-August. Elizabeth Geiser, Dir., Publishing Institute, 2075 S. Univ. Blvd., #D-114, Denver, CO 80210.

CONNECTICUT

WESLEYAN WRITERS' CONFERENCE—Middletown, CT. June. Anne Greene, Dir., Wesleyan Writers' Conference, Middletown, CT 06459.

DISTRICT OF COLUMBIA

WASHINGTON INDEPENDENT WRITERS SPRING WRITER'S CONFERENCE—Washington, DC. May. Isolde Chapin, Dir., 220 Woodward Bldg., 733 15th St. N.W., Washington, DC 20005.

ROMANCE WRITERS OF AMERICA CONFERENCE—Washington, DC. July. Allison Kelley, RWA Exec. Dir., 3707 FM 1960 W., Suite 555, Houston, TX 77068.

FLORIDA

KEY WEST LITERARY SEMINAR: THE AMERICAN NOVEL—Key West, FL. January. Admin. Miles Frieden, 4 Portside Ln., Searsport, ME 04974.

FLORIDA SUNCOAST WRITERS' CONFERENCE—St. Petersburg, FL. February. Betty Moss, Dir., Dept. of English, Univ. of South Florida, Tampa, FL 33620.

SOUTHWEST FLORIDA WRITERS' CONFERENCE—Ft. Myers, FL. March. Jeri Magg, 723 Sand Dollar Dr., Sanibel, FL 33957.

SOUTH FLORIDA WRITERS CONFERENCE—Coral Gables, FL. March. Judith Welsh, Dir., National Writers Association, P.O. Box 570415, Miami, FL 33257-0415.

SLEUTH FEST 2000—Ft. Lauderdale, FL. March, April. Dianne Ell, Dir., 1432 S.E. 8th St., Deerfield Beach, FL 33441.

MARJORIE KINNON RAWLINGS WRITERS WORKSHOP—Gainesville, FL. July, August. Director, P.O. Box 12246, Gainesville, FL 32604.

FLORIDA REGION SCBWI CONFERENCE—Palm Springs, FL. September. Barbara Casey, Reg. Adv., 2158 Portland Ave., Wellington, FL 33414.

GEORGIA

SPRING MINGLE 2000—Atlanta, GA. March. Joan Broerman, Reg. Adv., Southern Breeze SCBWI, P.O. Box 26282, Birmingham, AL 35260.

SANDHILLS WRITERS CONFERENCE—Augusta, GA. March. Anthony Kellman, Dir., Augusta State Univ., Dept. of Lang, Lit. & Comm., 2500 Walton Way, Augusta, GA 30904.

SOUTHEASTERN WRITER'S ASSOC. SUMMER WORKSHOP—St. Simons Island, GA. June. Cappy Hall-Rearick, Pres., 114 Gould St., St. Simons Island, GA 31522.

ILLINOIS

MISSISSIPPI VALLEY WRITERS' CONFERENCE—Rock Island, IL. June. David R. Collins, Dir., 3403 45th St., Moline, IL 61265.

WRITE-TO-PUBLISH CONFERENCE—near Chicago, IL. June. Lin Johnson, Dir., 9731 N. Fox Glen Dr., #6F, Niles, IL 60714-5861.

OF DARK AND STORMY NIGHTS—Rolling Meadows, IL. June. Wiley Spurgeon, Dir., P.O. Box 1944, Muncie, IN 47308-1944.

ANNUAL ROMANCE WRITERS OF AMERICA CONFERENCE— Chicago, IL. July, August. Director, 13700 Veterans Memorial, #315, Houston, TX 77014.

AUTUMN AUTHORS' AFFAIR—near Chicago, IL. Autumn. Nancy McCann, Dir., 1507 Burnham Ave., Calumet City, IN 60409.

INDIANA

BUTLER UNIVERSITY CHILDREN'S LITERATURE CONFERENCE—Indianapolis, IN. January. Valiska Gregory, Dir., Butler University, 4600 Sunset Dr., Indianapolis, IN 46208.

INDIANA UNIVERSITY WRITERS' CONFERENCE—Bloomington, IN. June. Maura Stanton, Dir., IU Writers' Conference, Ballantine 464, Bloomington, IN 47405.

MIDWEST WRITERS WORKSHOP—Muncie, IN. July. Earl Conn, Dir., Ball State Univ., Dept. of Journalism, Muncie, IN 47306.

KANSAS

WRITERS' WORKSHOP IN SCIENCE FICTION—Lawrence, KS. July. James Gunn, Dir., Univ. of Kansas, English Dept., Lawrence, KS 66045.

KENTUCKY

GREEN RIVER NOVELS-IN-PROGRESS WORKSHOP— Louisville, KY. March. Mary E. O'Dell, Dir., Green River Writers, Inc., 11906 Locust Rd., Middletown, KY 40243-1413.

WRITERS' RETREAT WORKSHOP—Erlanger, KY. May-June. Gail Provost Stockwell, Dir., 2507 S. Boston Pl., Tulsa, OK 74114.

ANNUAL APPALACHIAN WRITERS WORKSHOP—Hindman, KY. July. Mike Mullins, Dir., Hindman Settlement School, Box 844, Hindman, KY 41822.

GREEN RIVER WORKSHOP WEEKEND & WRITERS RETREAT—Louisville, KY. July. Mary E. O'Dell, Dir., Green River Writers, Inc., 11906 Locust Rd., Middletown, KY 40243-1413.

MAINE

DOWNEAST MAINE WRITER'S WORKSHOPS—Stockton Springs, ME. July, August. Janet J. Barron, Dir., P.O. Box 446, Stockton Springs, ME 04981.

IN CELEBRATION OF CHILDREN'S LITERATURE—Gorham, ME. July. Joyce Martin, Dir., Univ. of Southern Maine, 305 Bailey Hall, Gorham, ME 04038.

STONECOAST WRITERS CONFERENCE—Freeport, ME. July, August. Barbara Hope, Dir., Univ. of Southern Maine, 96 Falmouth St., Portland, MR 04104.

STATE OF MAINE WRITERS' CONFERENCE—Ocean Park, ME. August. June A. Knowles, Mary E. Pitts, Co-Chairs, 18 Hill Rd., Belmont, MA 02478.

MARYLAND

SANDY COVE CHRISTIAN WRITERS' CONFERENCE—North East, MD. October. Jim Watkins, Dir., Sandy Cove Ministries, 60 Sandy Cove Rd., North East, MD 21901-5436.

MASSACHUSETTS

BOOK ARTS WORKSHOPS—Kingston, MA. May, June, July. Lilas Cingolani, Dir., Box 52, Kingston, MA 02364.

CAPE COD WRITERS CONFERENCE—Craigville Beach, MA. August. Cape Cod Writers' Center, P.O. Box 186, Barnstable, MA 02630.

TRURO CENTER FOR THE ARTS AT CASTLE HILL WRITERS WORKSHOPS—Truro, MA. Various dates. Mary Stackhouse, Dir., P.O. Box 756, Truro, MA 02666.

MICHIGAN

39TH ANNUAL WRITERS' CONFERENCE, SPONSORED BY OAKLAND UNIVERSITY AND DETROIT WOMEN WRITERS—Rochester, MI. October. Gloria J. Boddy, Dir., Oakland Univ., 231 Varner Hall, Rochester, MI 48309-4401.

MINNESOTA

HOW TO WRITE A CHILDREN'S PICTURE BOOK—Coon Rapids, MN. June. Brenda Dickinson, Dir., Continuing Education Dept., 11200 Mississippi Blvd. N.W., Coon Rapids, MN 55433.

SPLIT ROCK ARTS PROGRAM—Duluth, MN. July, August. Andrea Gilats, Dir., Univ. of Minnesota, 335 Nolte Ctr., 315 Pillsbury Dr. S.E., Minneapolis, MN 55455.

WRITING TO SELL 16TH ANNUAL WORKSHOP—Minneapolis, MN. August. Joyce Banaszak, Dir., Minneapolis Writers Workshop, P.O. Box 24356, Minneapolis, MN 55424.

MISSISSIPPI

NATCHEZ LITERARY CELEBRATION—Natchez, MS. June. Carolyn Vance Smith, Dir., P.O. Box 894, Natchez, MS 39121.

Missouri

WRITING AND LITERATURE CAMP—Springfield, MO. June. Dr. John Bushman, Dir., The Writing Conference, P.O. Box 27288, Shawnee Mission, KS 66225-7288.

NEW LETTERS WEEKEND WRITERS' CONFERENCE—Kansas City, MO. June. James McKinley, Dir., UMKC, Arts & Sciences Cont. Ed., 4825 Troost, Room 215, Kansas City, MO 64110.

AMERICAN TRANSLATORS ASSOCIATION ANNUAL CONFERENCE—St. Louis, MO. November. Walter Bacak, Dir., 1800 Diagonal Rd., #220, Alexandria, VA 22314.

New Hampshire

MOLASSES POND WRITER'S RETREAT/WORKSHOP—Wakefield, NH. June. Martha Barron Barrett, Dir., 36 Manning St., Portsmouth, NH 03801.

ODYSSEY FANTASY WRITING WORKSHOP—Manchester, NH. June-July. Jeanne Cavelos, Dir., Odyssey, 20 Levesque Ln., Mont Vernon, NH 03057.

NEW ENGLAND WRITERS CONFERENCE—Hanover, NH. July. Dr. Frank & Susan Anthony, Dirs., Box 483, Windsor, VT 05089.

ANNUAL FESTIVAL OF POETRY—Franconia, NH. August. Donald Sheehan, Dir., P.O. Box 74, Franconia, NH 03580.

New Jersey

THE COLLEGE OF NEW JERSEY WRITERS' CONFERENCE—Ewing, NJ. April. Jean Hollander, Dir., The College of New Jersey, Dept. of English, P.O. Box 7718, Ewing, NJ 08628-0718.

New Mexico

WRITING WOMEN'S LIVES—Santa Fe, NM. May. Robin Jones, Dir., Recursos, 826 Camino del Monte Rey, Santa Fe, NM 87505.

TAOS SCHOOL OF WRITING—Taos Ski Valley, NM. July. Norman Zollinger, Dir., P.O. Box 20496, Albuquerque, NM 87154.

SANTA FE WRITER'S CONFERENCE—Santa Fe, NM. July. Robin Jones, Dir., Recursos, 826 Camino del Monte Rey, Santa Fe, NM 87505.

WRITING YOURSELF—Santa Fe, NM. October. Stephen Lewis, Dir., Recursos, 826 Camino del Monte Rey, Santa Fe, NM 87505.

GLORIETA CHRISTIAN WRITERS' CONFERENCE—Glorieta, NM. October. Mona Gansberg Hodgson, Dir., P.O. Box 999, Cottonwood, AZ 86326.

New York

Big Apple Writing WORKSHOPS—New York, NY. April, October. Hannelore Hahn, Dir., IWWG, P.O. Box 810, Gracie Station, New York, NY 10028.

THE WRITERS' CENTER AT CHAUTAUQUA—Chautauqua, NY. June, August. Mary Jean Irion, Dir., 149 Kready Ave., Millersville, PA 17551.

MARYMOUNT MANHATTAN COLLEGE WRITER'S CONFERENCE—New York, NY. June. Lewis Burke Frumkes, Dir., The Writing Center, Marymount Manhattan College, 221 E. 71st St., New York, NY 10021.

CHENANGO VALLEY WRITER'S CONFERENCE—Hamilton, NY. June. Matt Leone, Dir., Dept. of Summer Programs, Colgate Univ., Hamilton, NY 13346.

MANHATTANVILLE'S SUMMER WRITERS' WORKSHOPS—Purchase, NY. June. Ruth Dowd, Dir., Manhattanville College, 2900 Purchase St., Purchase, NY 10577.

FEMINIST WOMEN'S WRITING WORKSHOPS—Geneva, NY. July. Margo Gumosky, Dir., P.O. Box 6583, Ithaca, NY 14851.

NEW YORK STATE SUMMER WRITERS' INSTITUTE—Saratoga Springs, NY. July. Robert Boyers, Dir., Skidmore College, Saratoga Springs, NY 12866.

ROBERT QUACKENBUSH'S CHILDREN'S BOOK WRITING & ILLUSTRATING WORKSHOPS—New York, NY. July. Robert Quackenbush, Dir., Quackenbush Studios, 460 E. 79th St., New York, NY 10021.

"REMEMBER THE MAGIC" SUMMER CONFERENCE—Saratoga Springs, NY. August. Hannelore Hahn, Dir., IWWG, P.O. Box 810, Gracie Station, New York, NY 10028.

NORTH CAROLINA

NORTH CAROLINA WRITERS' NETWORK SPRING GALA—Chapel Hill, NC. June. Bobbie Collins-Perry, Dir., P.O. Box 954, Carrboro, NC 27510.

NORTH CAROLINA WRITERS' NETWORK'S ANNUAL FALL CONFERENCE—Fayetteville, NC. November. Bobbi Collins-Perry, Dir., P.O. Box 954. Carrboro, NC 27510.

OHIO

WESTERN RESERVE WRITERS' MINI CONFERENCE—Kirtland, OH. March. Lea Leever Oldham, Dir., 34200 Ridge Rd., #110, Willoughby, OH 44094.

HUDSON WRITERS' MINI CONFERENCE—Hudson, OH. May. Lea Leever Oldham, Dir., 34200 Ridge Rd., #110, Willoughby, OH 44094.

THE HEIGHTS WRITER'S CONFERENCE—Beachwood, OH. May. Lavern Hall, Dir.,Writer's World Press, 35 N. Chillicothe Rd., Suite D, Aurora, OH 44202.

KENYON REVIEW WRITERS WORKSHOP—Gambier, OH. June, July. David Lynn, Dir., Kenyon Review, Gambier, OH 43022.

VALLEY WRITERS' CONFERENCE—Youngstown, OH. August. Nancy Christie, Dir., P.O. Box 4610, Youngstown, OH 44515.

ANTIOCH WRITERS' WORKSHOP—Yellow Springs, OH. August. Director, P.O. Box 494, Yellow Springs, OH 45387.

SKYLINE WRITERS' CONFERENCE—N. Royalton, OH. August. Lilie Kilburn, Dir., Skyline Writers' Club, P.O. Box 33343, N. Royalton, OH 44133.

WESTERN RESERVE WRITERS & FREELANCE CONFERENCE—Kirtland, OH. September. Lea Leever Oldham, Dir., 34200 Ridge Rd., #110, Willoughby, OH 44094.

COLUMBUS WRITERS CONFERENCE—Columbus, OH. September. Angela Palazzolo, Dir., P.O. Box 20548, Columbus, OH 43220.

CLEVELAND HEIGHTS/UNIVERSITY HEIGHTS WRITERS MINI CONFERENCE—Cleveland Heights, OH. October. Lea Leever Oldham, Dir., 34200 Ridge Rd., #110, Willoughby, OH 44094.

OKLAHOMA

NORTHWEST OKLAHOMA WRITERS' WORKSHOP—Enid, OK. April. Bev Walton-Porter, Dir., Enid Writers Club, P.O. Box 5994, Enid, OK 73702.

SHORT COURSE ON PROFESSIONAL WRITING—Norman, OK. June. J. Madison Davis, Dir., Univ. of Oklahoma, 226 Copeland Hall, Norman, OK 73019.

OREGON

FISHTRAP GATHERING & WORSHOPS—Wallowa Lake, OR. February, July. Rich Wandschneider, Dir., Fishtrap, P.O. Box 38, Enterprise, OR 97828.

THE FLIGHT OF THE MIND WRITING WORKSHOPS FOR WOMEN—McKenzie Bridge, OR. June-July. Ruth Gundle, Dir., Flight of the Mind, 622 S.E. 29th Ave., Portland, OR 97214.

THE WRITER'S WAY—Portland, OR. August. Cherie Walter, Dir., Willamette Writers, 9045 S.W. Barbur Blvd., Suite 5A, Portland, OR 97219

COOS BAY WRITERS CONFERENCE—Coos Bay, OR. Summer. Mary Scheirman, Dir., 2463 Union, North Bend, OR 97459.

PENNSYLVANIA

GREATER PHILADELPHIA CHRISTIAN WRITERS CONFERENCE—Philadelphia, PA. Spring. Marlene Bagnull, Dir., 316 Blanchard Rd., Drexel Hill, PA 19026.

PENNWRITERS ANNUAL CONFERENCE—Harrisburg, PA. May. Elizabeth Darrach, Dir., 492 Letort Rd., Millersville, PA 17551-9660.

ST. DAVID'S CHRISTIAN WRITERS' CONFERENCE—Beaver Falls, PA. June. Audrey Stallsmith, Registrar, 87 Pines Rd. E., Hadley, PA 16130.

BUCKNELL SEMINAR FOR YOUNGER POETS—Lewisburg, PA. June. Cynthia Hogue, Dir., Bucknell Univ., Stadler Center for Poetry, Lewisburg, PA 17837.

LIGONIER VALLEY WRITERS CONFERENCE—Ligonier, PA. July. Ligonier Valley Writers, P.O. Box B, Ligonier, PA 15658.

MID-ATLANTIC MYSTERY—Philadelphia, PA. October. Deen Kogan, Dir., 507 S. 8th St., Philadelphia, PA 19147.

RHODE ISLAND

NEW ENGLAND SCREENWRITERS CONFERENCE—Providence, RI. August. Robert Hofmann, Dir., Community Writers Assoc., P.O. Box 312, Providence, RI 02901-0312.

SOUTH CAROLINA

SOUTH CAROLINA PLAYWRIGHTS' CONFERENCE—Beaufort, SC. June. Bill Rauch, Dir., 1001 Bay St., Beaufort, SC 29902.

SOUTH CAROLINA WRITERS WORKSHOP—Myrtle Beach, FL. October. South Carolina Writers Workshop, P.O. Box 7104, Columbia, SC 29202.

TENNESSEE

AMERICAN CHRISTIAN WRITERS CONFERENCES—Various locations and dates. Reg A. Forder, Dir., Box 110390, Nashville, TN 37222.

SEWANEE WRITERS CONFERENCE—Sewanee, TN. July, August. Wyatt Prunty, Dir., 310 St. Luke's Hall, 735 University Ave., Sewanee, TN 37383.

TEXAS

WRITER'S ROUNDTABLE CONFERENCE 2000—Dallas, TX. March, April. Deborah Morris, Dir., P.O. Box 461572, Garland, TX 75046-1572.

AGENTS! AGENTS! AGENTS! & EDITORS TOO!—Austin, TX. July. Jim Bob McMillan, Dir., Austin Writers League, 1501 W. 5th St., Suite E-2, Austin, TX 78758.

THE CRAFT OF WRITING—Austin, TX. October. Jim Bob McMillan, Dir., Austin Writers League, 1501 W. 5th St., Suite E-2, Austin, TX 78758.

UTAH

SAN JUAN WRITERS' WORKSHOP—Bluff, UT. March. Scott Russel Sanders, Canyonlands Field Institute, P.O. Box 68, Moab, UT 84532.

SOUTHERN UTAH WRITERS CONFERENCE—Cedar City, UT. July. David Lee, Dir., c/o Dean David Nyman, Southern Utah Univ., School of Cont. Ed., Cedar City, UT 84720.

DESERT WRITERS WORKSHOP—Moab, UT. November. Ann Haymond Zwinger (Nonfiction), Alison Hawthorne Deming (Poetry), or Roy Porvin (Fiction), Canyonlands Field Institute, P.O. Box 68, Moab, UT 84532.

VERMONT

WILDBRANCH WORKSHOP IN OUTDOOR, NATURAL HISTORY, & ENVIRONMENTAL WRITING—Craftsbury Common, VT. June. David W. Brown, Dir., Wildbranch, Sterling College, Craftsbury Common, VT 05827.

BREAD LOAF WRITERS' CONFERENCE—Middlebury, VT. August. Michael Collier, Dir., Bread Loaf Writers' Conference, Middlebury College, Middlebury, VT 05753.

VIRGINIA

HIGHLAND SUMMER CONFERENCE—Radford, VA. June. Grace Toney Edwards, Dir., c/o Jo Ann Asbury, Radford Univ., Appalachian Reg. Studies Center., P.O. Box 7014, Radford, VA 24142.

SHENANDOAH INTERNATIONAL PLAYWRIGHT'S RETREAT—Staunton, VA. July-September. Robert Graham Small, Dir., Pennyroyal Farm, Rt. 5, Box 167-F, Staunton, VA 24401.

WASHINGTON

WRITER'S WEEKEND AT THE BEACH—Ocean Park, WA. February. Birdie Etchison, Dir., P.O. Box 877, Ocean Park, WA 98640.

WASHINGTON STATE SCBWI CONFERENCE—Seattle, WA. April. Donna Bergman, Dir., 4037 56th Ave. S.W., Seattle, WA 98116-3501.

CLARION WEST SCIENCE FICTION & FANTASY WRITERS WORKSHOP—Seattle, WA. June-July. Leslie Howle, Dir., 340 15th Ave. E., Suite 350, Seattle, WA 98112.

PORT TOWNSEND WRITERS' CONFERENCE—Port Townsend, WA. July. Sam Hamill, Dir., Centrum, Box 1158, Port Townsend, WA 98368.

TOUCH OF SUCCESS SEMINARS—San Juan Islands, WA (aboard yacht). August. Bill Thomas, Dir., Box 201, Quilcene, WA 98376.

WISCONSIN

GREEN LAKE WRITERS CONFERENCE—Green Lake, WI. June, July. Blythe Ann Cooper, Dir., Green Lake Conference Center, 2511 State Hwy. 23, Green Lake, WI 54941.

SCBWI FALL WRITER'S WORKSHOP—Green Bay, WI. October. Patricia Curtis Pfitsch, Dir., Rt. 1, Box 137, Gays Mills, WI 54631.

WYOMING

JACKSON HOLE WRITERS CONFERENCE—Jackson Hole, WY. July. Barbara Barnes, Dir., P.O. Box 3972, Laramie, WY 82071.

STATE ARTS COUNCILS

State arts councils sponsor grants, fellowships, and other programs for writers. To be eligible for funding, a writer *must* be a resident of the state in which he is applying. Write or call for more information; 1-800 numbers are toll free for in-state calls only; numbers preceded by TDD indicate Telecommunications Device for the Deaf; TTY indicates Teletypewriter.

ALABAMA STATE COUNCIL ON THE ARTS
201 Monroe St., Suite 110
Montgomery, AL 36130
(334) 242-4076; fax: (334) 240-3269
Albert B. Head, *Executive Director*

ALASKA STATE COUNCIL ON THE ARTS
411 W. 4th Ave., Suite 1E
Anchorage, AK 99501-2343
(907) 269-6610; fax: (907) 269-6601
e-mail: info@aksca.org
Shannon Planchon, *Grants Officer*

ARIZONA COMMISSION ON THE ARTS
417 W. Roosevelt
Phoenix, AZ 85003
(602) 255-5882; fax: (602) 256-0282
Attn: Jill Bernstein, Public Information and Literature Dir.

ARKANSAS ARTS COUNCIL
1500 Tower Bldg.
323 Center St.
Little Rock, AR 72201
(501) 324-9766; fax: (501) 324-9154
e-mail: info@dah.state.ar.us
web site: http://heritage.state.ar.us
James E. Mitchell, *Executive Director*

CALIFORNIA ARTS COUNCIL
1300 I St., Suite 930
Sacramento, CA 95814
(916) 322-6555; fax: (916) 322-6575
e-mail: cac@cwo.com
web site: http://www.cac.ca.gov
Adam Gottlieb, *Communications Director*

COLORADO COUNCIL ON THE ARTS
750 Pennsylvania St.
Denver, CO 80203-3699
(303) 894-2617; fax: (303) 894-2615
Fran Holden, *Executive Director*

CONNECTICUT COMMISSION ON THE ARTS
1 Financial Plaza
Hartford, CT 06103
(860) 566-4770; fax: (860) 566-6462
John Ostrout, *Executive Director*

DELAWARE DIVISION OF THE ARTS
(For Delaware residents only)
Carvel State Bldg.
820 N. French St.
Wilmington, DE 19801
(302) 577-8278; fax: (302) 577-6561
Barbara King, *Artist Services Coordinator*

FLORIDA ARTS COUNCIL
Dept. of State
Div. of Cultural Affairs
The Capitol
Tallahassee, FL 32399-0250
(850) 487-2980; fax: (850) 922-5259
TTY: (850) 488-5779
web site: www.dos.state.fl.us
Attn: Ms. Peg Richardson

GEORGIA COUNCIL FOR THE ARTS
260 14th St. N.W., Suite 401
Atlanta, GA 30318
(404) 685-2787; fax: (404) 685-2788
Caroline Ballard Leake, *Executive Director*
Rick George, *Grants Manager, Literature*

HAWAII STATE FOUNDATION ON CULTURE AND THE ARTS
44 Merchant St.
Honolulu, HI 96813
(808) 586-0300; fax: (808) 586-0308
Holly Richards, *Executive Director*

IDAHO COMMISSION ON THE ARTS
Box 83720
Boise, ID 83720-0008
(208) 334-2119; fax (208) 334-2488
Attn: Cort Conley

ILLINOIS ARTS COUNCIL
James R. Thompson Center
100 W. Randolph, Suite 10-500
Chicago, IL 60601
(312) 814-6750; (800) 237-6994; fax: (312) 814-1471
Loretta Brockmezor, *Director of Lit. Programs*

INDIANA ARTS COMMISSION
402 W. Washington St., Rm. 072
Indianapolis, IN 46204-2741
(317) 232-1268; TDD: (317) 233-3001; fax: (317) 232-5595
Dorothy Ilgen, *Executive Director*

IOWA ARTS COUNCIL
600 E. Locust
Des Moines, IA 50319-0290
(515) 282-6500; fax: (515) 242-6498
Attn: Stephen Poole

KANSAS ARTS COMMISSION
700 S.W. Jackson, Suite 1004
Topeka, KS 66603-3761
(785) 296-3335; fax: (785) 296-4989; TTY: (800) 766-3777
Robert T. Burtch, *Editor*
David Wilson, *Executive Director*

KENTUCKY ARTS COUNCIL
31 Fountain Pl.
Frankfort, KY 40601
(502) 564-3757; fax: (502) 564-2839; TDD: (502) 564-3757
Attn: Gerri Combs, *Executive Director*

LOUISIANA STATE ARTS COUNCIL
Box 44247
Baton Rouge, LA 70804
(504) 342-8180; fax: (504) 342-8173
James Borders, *Executive Director*

MAINE ARTS COMMISSION
25 State House Station
Augusta, ME 04333-0025
(207) 287-2724; fax: (207) 287-2335; TDD: (207) 287-6740
web site: www.mainearts.com
Alden C. Wilson, *Director*

MARYLAND STATE ARTS COUNCIL
Arts-in-Education Program
601 N. Howard St.
Baltimore, MD 21201
(410) 767-6555; fax: (410) 333-1062
Pamela Dunne, *Artists-in-Education Program Coordinator*

MASSACHUSETTS CULTURAL COUNCIL
120 Boylston St., 2nd Floor
Boston, MA 02116-4802
(617) 727-3668; (800) 232-0960; TTY: (617) 338-9153
fax: (617) 727-0044
Attn: Michael Brady

MICHIGAN COUNCIL FOR ARTS AND CULTURAL AFFAIRS
525 W. Ottawa
P.O. Box 30705
Lansing, MI 48909-8205
(517) 241-4011; fax: (517) 241-3979
Betty Boone, *Executive Director*

MINNESOTA STATE ARTS BOARD
Park Square Court
400 Sibley St., Suite 200
St. Paul, MN 55101-1928
(651) 215-1600; (800) 8MN-ARTS; fax: (651) 215-1602
Lori Hindbjorgen, *Artist Assistance Program Associate*

COMPAS: WRITERS & ARTISTS IN THE SCHOOLS
304 Landmark Center
75 W. Fifth St.
St. Paul, MN 55102
(651) 292-3254; fax: (651) 292-3258
Daniel Gabriel, *Director*

MISSISSIPPI ARTS COMMISSION
239 N. Lamar St., Suite 207
Jackson, MS 39201
(601) 359-6030; fax: (601) 359-6008
Lynn Adams Wilkins, *Community Arts Director*

MISSOURI ARTS COUNCIL
Wainwright Office Complex
111 N. 7th St., Suite 105
St. Louis, MO 63101-2188
(314) 340-6845; fax: (314) 340-7215
Michael Hunt, *Program Administrator for Literature*

MONTANA ARTS COUNCIL
P.O. Box 202201
Helena, MT 59620-2201
(406) 444-6430; fax: (406) 444-6548
e-mail: mac@state.mt.us
web site: www.art.state.mt.us
Arlynn Fishbaugh, *Executive Director*

NEBRASKA ARTS COUNCIL
3838 Davenport St.
Omaha, NE 68131-2329
(402) 595-2122; fax: (402) 595-2334
Jennifer Severin, *Executive Director*

NEVADA ARTS COUNCIL
602 N. Curry St.
Carson City, NV 89703
(702) 687-6680; fax: (702) 687-6688
Susan Boskoff, *Executive Director*

NEW HAMPSHIRE STATE COUNCIL ON THE ARTS
Phenix Hall
40 N. Main St.
Concord, NH 03301-4974
(603) 271-2789; fax: (603) 271-3584; TDD: (800) 735-2964
Audrey Sylvester, *Artist Services Coordinator*

NEW JERSEY STATE COUNCIL ON THE ARTS
Artist Services
P.O. Box 306
Trenton, NJ 08625
(609) 292-6130; fax: (609) 989-1440
Beth Vogel, *Program Officer, Arts Education & Artists Services*

NEW MEXICO ARTS
P.O. Box 1450
Santa Fe, NM 87501
(505) 827-6490; fax: (505) 827-6043
Randy Forrester, *Local and Performing Arts Coordinator*

NEW YORK STATE COUNCIL ON THE ARTS
915 Broadway
New York, NY 10010
(212) 387-7022; fax: (212) 387-7164/7168
e-mail: KMASTERSON@NYSCA.org
Kathleen Masterson, *Director, Literature Program*

NORTH CAROLINA ARTS COUNCIL
Dept. of Cultural Resources
Raleigh, NC 27601-2807
(919) 733-2111 ext. 22; fax: (919) 733-4834
e-mail: dmcgill@ncacmail.dcr.state.nc.us
Deborah McGill, *Literature Director*

NORTH DAKOTA COUNCIL ON THE ARTS
418 E. Broadway, Suite 70
Bismarck, ND 58501-4086
(701) 328-3954; fax: (701) 328-3963

OHIO ARTS COUNCIL
727 E. Main St.
Columbus, OH 43205-1796
(614) 466-2613; fax: (614) 466-4494
Bob Fox, *Literature Program Coordinator*

OKLAHOMA ARTS COUNCIL
P.O. Box 52001-2001
Oklahoma City, OK 73152-2001
(405) 521-2931; fax: (405) 521-6418
Betty Price, *Executive Director*

OREGON ARTS COMMISSION
775 Summer St. N.E.
Salem, OR 97310
(503) 986-0088; fax: (503) 986-0260;
e-mail: oregon.artscomm@state.or.us
web site: http://art.econ.state.or.us
Attn: *Assistant Director*

PENNSYLVANIA COUNCIL ON THE ARTS
Room 216, Finance Bldg.
Harrisburg, PA 17120
(717) 787-6883; fax (717) 783-2538
James Woland, *Literature Program*

INSTITUTE OF PUERTO RICAN CULTURE
P.O. Box 4184
San Juan, PR 00902-4184
Luis E. Diaz Hernandez, *Executive Director*

RHODE ISLAND STATE COUNCIL ON THE ARTS
95 Cedar St., Suite 103
Providence, RI 02903
(401) 222-3880; fax: (401) 521-1351
e-mail: info@risca.state.ri.us
web site: www.risca.state.ri.us
Randall Rosenbaum, *Executive Director*

SOUTH CAROLINA ARTS COMMISSION
1800 Gervais St.
Columbia, SC 29201
(803) 734-8696; fax: (803) 734-8526
Sara June Goldstein, *Director, Literary Arts Program*

SOUTH DAKOTA ARTS COUNCIL
800 Governors Dr.
Pierre, SD 57501-2294
(605) 773-3131; fax: (605) 773-6962
e-mail: <sdac@stlib.state.sd.us>
Attn: Dennis Holub, *Executive Director*

TENNESSEE ARTS COMMISSION
401 Charlotte Ave.
Nashville, TN 37243-0780
(615) 741-1701; fax: (615) 741-8559
e-mail: aswanson@mail.state.tn.us
Attn: Alice Swanson

TEXAS COMMISSION ON THE ARTS
P.O. Box 13406
Austin, TX 78711-3406
(512) 463-5535; fax: (512) 475-2699
Attn: Gaye Greever McElwain

UTAH ARTS COUNCIL
617 E. South Temple
Salt Lake City, UT 84102-1177
(801) 236-7553; fax: (801) 236-7556
Guy Lebeda, *Literary Coordinator*

VERMONT ARTS COUNCIL
136 State St., Drawer 33
Montpelier, VT 05633-6001
(802) 828-3291; fax: (802) 828-3363
e-mail: info@arts.vca.state.vt.us
web site: www.state.vt.us/vermont-arts
Michele Bailey, Artist Grants Coordinator

VIRGINIA COMMISSION FOR THE ARTS
223 Governor St.
Richmond, VA 23219
(804) 225-3132; fax: (804) 225-4327
e-mail: pbaggett.arts@state.va.us
web site: www.artswire.org/vacomm
Peggy J. Baggett, *Executive Director*

WASHINGTON STATE ARTS COMMISSION
234 E. 8th Ave.
P.O. Box 42675
Olympia, WA 98504-2675
(360)586-2421; fax: (360) 586-5357
e-mail: bitsyb@wsac.wa.gov
web site: www.wa.gov/art
Bitsy Bidwell, *Community Arts Development Manager*

WEST VIRGINIA DIVISION OF CULTURE & HISTORY
WV Commission on the Arts
Culture and History Division
The Cultural Center, Capitol Complex
1900 Kanawha Blvd. E.
Charleston, WV 25305-0300
(304) 558-0220; fax: (304) 558-2779
Kate McComas, Program Coordinator

WISCONSIN ARTS BOARD
101 E. Wilson St., 1st Floor
Madison, WI 53702
(608) 266-0190; fax: (608) 267-0380
e-mail: ARTSBOARD@ARTS.STATE.WI.US
George Tzougros, *Executive Director*

WYOMING ARTS COUNCIL
2320 Capitol Ave.
Cheyenne, WY 82002
(307) 777-7742; fax: (307) 777-5499
e-mail: mshay@missc.state.wy.us
Michael Shay, *Literature Program Manager*

ORGANIZATIONS FOR WRITERS

ACADEMY OF AMERICAN POETS
584 Broadway, Suite 1208
New York, NY 10012
(212) 274-0343; fax: (212) 274-9427
web site: http://www.poets.org.
Jonathan Galassi, *President*
    The Academy was founded in 1934 to support American poets at all
stages of their careers and to foster the appreciation of contemporary
poetry. The largest organization in the country dedicated specifically to the
art of poetry, the Academy sponsors programs nationally. In addition to
the Walt Whitman Award, these include the Academy Fellowship for distinguished poetic achievement; the Tanning Prize for outstanding and proven
mastery in the art of poetry; the Lenore Marshall Poetry Prize; the James
Laughlin Award; the Raiziss/de Palchi Translation Award; the Harold Morton Landon Translation Award; poetry prizes at more than 160 colleges and
universities; a national series of poetry readings and poets' residencies;
and the American Poets Fund and the Atlas Fund, which provide financial
assistance to poets and non-commercial publishers of poetry, respectively.
Membership is open to all. Annual dues: $25 and up.

AMERICAN SOCIETY OF JOURNALISTS AND AUTHORS, INC.

1501 Broadway, Suite 302
New York, NY 10036
(212) 997-0947
e-mail: ASJA@compuserve.com
web site: http://www.asja.org
Alexandra Owens, *Executive Director*

A nationwide organization of independent writers of nonfiction dedicated to promoting high standards of nonfiction writing through monthly meetings, annual writers' conferences, etc. The ASJA produces a free electronic bulletin board for free-lance writers on contract issues in the new-media age, and the organization offers extensive benefits and services including referral services, numerous discount services, and the opportunity to explore professional issues and concerns with other writers. Members also receive a monthly newsletter with confidential market information. Membership is open to professional free-lance writers of nonfiction; qualifications are judged by the membership committee. Call or write for application details.

THE ASSOCIATED WRITING PROGRAMS

Tallwood House, Mail Stop 1E3
George Mason University
Fairfax, VA 22030
(703) 993-4301; fax: (703) 993-4302
web site: http://www.awpwriter.org
Attn: *Membership*

The AWP seeks to serve writers and teachers in need of community, support, information, inspiration, contacts, and ideas. *The Writer's Chronicle* provides publishing opportunities, job listings, and an active exchange of ideas on writing and teaching, including an annual conference. Members receive six issues of *The Writer's Chronicle* and seven issues of *AWP Job List*. Publications include *The AWP Official Guide to Creative Writing Programs*. Annual dues: $57, *individual*; $37, *student*.

THE AUTHORS GUILD, INC.

330 W. 42nd St., 29th Fl.
New York, NY 10036-6902
(212) 563-5904; fax: (212) 564-5363
e-mail: staff@authorsguild.org
web site: www.authorsguild.org
Attn: *Membership Committee*

As the largest organization of published writers in America, membership offers writers free reviews of publishing and agency contracts, access to group health insurance, and seminars on subjects of concern to authors. The Authors Guild also lobbies on behalf of all authors on issues such as copyright, taxation, and freedom of expression. A writer who has published a book in the last seven years with an established publisher, or has published three articles in periodicals of general circulation within the last eighteen months is eligible for active voting membership. An unpublished writer who has received a contract offer may be eligible for associate membership. All members of the Authors Guild automatically become members of its parent organization, the Authors League of America. First year annual dues: $90.

THE AUTHORS LEAGUE OF AMERICA, INC.
330 W. 42nd St.
New York, NY 10036-6902
(212) 564-8350; fax: (212) 564-5363
e-mail: Authors@pipeline.com
Attn: *Membership Committee*
A national organization representing over 14,000 authors and dramatists on matters of joint concern, such as copyright, taxes, and freedom of expression. Membership is restricted to authors and dramatists who are members of the Authors Guild and the Dramatists Guild.

THE DRAMATISTS GUILD OF AMERICA, INC.
1501 Broadway, Suite 701
New York, NY 10036-3909
(212) 398-9366
John Weidman, *President*; Christopher Wilson, *Executive Director*
The national professional association of playwrights, composers, and lyricists, the guild was established to protect dramatists' rights and to improve working conditions. Services include use of the guild's contracts; a toll-free number for members in need of business advice; access to discount tickets; access to third-party health insurance programs and a group term life insurance plan; and numerous seminars. The Frederick Loew room is available to members for readings and rehearsals at a nominal fee. Publications currently include *The Dramatists Guild Resource Directory*, and *The Dramatists Magazine*. All playwrights, produced or not, are eligible for membership. Annual dues: $125, *active*; $75, *associate*; $35, *student*.

INTERNATIONAL ASSOCIATION OF CRIME WRITERS (NORTH AMERICAN BRANCH)
P.O. Box 8674
New York, NY 10116-8674
(212) 243-8966
Jim Weikart, *Acting President*
This international association was founded in 1987 to promote communications among crime writers worldwide, encourage translation of crime writing into other languages, and defend authors against censorship and other forms of tyranny. The IACW sponsors a number of conferences, publishes a quarterly newsletter, *Border Patrol*, and annually awards the Hammett prize for literary excellence in crime writing to a work of fiction or nonfiction by a U.S. or Canadian author. Membership is open to published authors of crime fiction, nonfiction, and screenplays. Agents, editors, and booksellers in the mystery field are also eligible to apply. Annual dues: $50.

INTERNATIONAL ASSOCIATION OF THEATRE FOR CHILDREN AND YOUNG PEOPLE
724 Second Ave. S.
Nashville, TN 37210

(615) 254-5719; fax: (615) 254-3255
e-mail: USASSITEJ@aol.com

The development of professional theater for young audiences and international exchange are the organization's primary mandates. Provides a link between professional theaters, artists, directors, training institutions, and arts agencies; sponsors festivals and forums for interchange among theaters and theater artists. Annual dues: $65, *individual*; $35, *retiree*; $30, *student*.

THE INTERNATIONAL WOMEN'S WRITING GUILD
Box 810, Gracie Station
New York, NY 10028-0082
(212) 737-7536; fax: (212) 737-9469
e-mail: iwwg@iwwg-com
web site: http://www.iwwg.com
Hannelore Hahn, *Executive Director & Founder*

Founded in 1976, serving as a network for the personal and professional empowerment of women through writing. Services include six issues of a 32-page newsletter, a list of literary agents, independent small presses, and publishing services, access to health insurance plan at group rates, access to writing conferences and related events throughout the U.S., including the annual "Remember the Magic" summer conference at Skidmore College in Saratoga Springs, NY, regional writing clusters, and year-round supportive networking. Any woman may join regardless of portfolio. Annual dues: $35; $45 *international*.

MIDWEST RADIO THEATRE WORKSHOP
KOPN
915 E. Broadway
Columbia, MO 65201
(573) 874-5676; fax: (314) 499-1662
e-mail: mrtw@mrtw.org
Sue Zizza, *Director*

Founded in 1979, the MRTW is the only national resource for American radio dramatists, providing referrals, technical assistance, educational materials, and workshops. MRTW coordinates an annual national radio script contest, publishes an annual radio scriptbook, and distributes a script anthology with primer. Send SASE for more information.

MYSTERY WRITERS OF AMERICA, INC.
17 E. 47th St., 6th Fl.
New York, NY 10017
(212) 888-8171; fax: (212) 888-8107
Mary Beth Becker, *Executive Director*

The MWA exists for the purpose of raising the prestige of mystery and detective writing, and of defending the rights and increasing the income of all writers in the field of mystery, detection, and fact crime writing. Each year, the MWA presents the Edgar Allan Poe Awards for the best mystery writing in a variety of fields. The four classifications of membership are: *active*, open to any writer who has made a sale in the field of mystery, suspense, or crime writing; *associate*, for professionals in allied fields; *corresponding*, for writers living outside the U.S.; *affiliate*, for unpublished writers. Annual dues: $65; $32.50 *corresponding members*.

NATIONAL ASSOCIATION OF SCIENCE WRITERS, INC.
P.O. Box 294
Greenlawn, NY 11740
(516) 757-5664
e-mail: diane@nasw.ORG
Diane McGurgan, *Executive Director*
The NASW promotes the dissemination of accurate information regarding science through all media, and conducts a varied program to increase the flow of news from scientists, to improve the quality of its
presentation, and to communicate its meaning to the reading public. Anyone who has been actively engaged in the dissemination of science information is eligible to apply for membership. Members must be principally
involved in reporting on science through newspapers, magazines, TV, or
other media that reach the public directly. Also, members report on science
through limited-circulation publications and other media. Annual dues:
$60.

NATIONAL CONFERENCE OF EDITORIAL WRITERS
6223 Executive Blvd.
Rockville, MD 20852
(301) 984-3015; fax: (301) 231-0026
e-mail: ncewhqs@erols.com
web site: www.ncew.org
A nonprofit professional organization established in 1947, NCEW exists to improve the quality of editorial pages and broadcast editorials, and
to promote high standards among opinion writers and editors . The association offers members networking opportunities, regional meetings, page exchanges, foreign tours, educational opportunities and seminars, an annual
convention, and a subscription to the quarterly journal *The Masthead.*
Membership is open to opinion writers and editors for general-circulation
newspapers, radio or television stations, and syndicated columnists; teachers and students of journalism; and others who determine editorial policy.
Annual dues are based on circulation or broadcast audience and range from
$85 to $150 (journalism educators: $75; students: $50).

THE NATIONAL LEAGUE OF AMERICAN PEN WOMEN, INC.
The Pen Arts Building
1300 17th St. N.W.
Washington, DC 20036-1973
(202) 785-1997
Judith La Fourest, *National President*
Founded in 1897, the league promotes development of the creative
talents of professional women in the arts. Membership is through local
branches, available by invitation from current members in the categories of
Art, Letters, and Music.

THE NATIONAL WRITERS ASSOCIATION
3140 S. Peoria, #295
Aurora, CO 80014
(303) 841-0246; fax: (303) 751-8593
web site: www.nationalwriters.com
Sandy Whelchel, *Executive Director*
New and established writers, poets, and playwrights throughout the

U.S. and worldwide may become members of the NWA, a full-time, customer-service-oriented association founded in 1937. Members receive a bimonthly newsletter, *Authorship*, and may attend the annual June conference. Annual dues: $85, *professional*; $65, *regular*; add $25 outside the U.S., Canada, and Mexico.

NATIONAL WRITERS UNION
113 University Place, 6th Fl.
New York, NY 10003
(212) 254-0279
Jonathan Tasini, *President*

Dedicated to bringing about equitable payment and fair treatment of free-lance writers through collective action. Membership is over 4,500 and includes book authors, poets, cartoonists, journalists, and technical writers in 14 chapters nationwide. The union offers its members contract and agent information, group health insurance, press credentials, grievance handling, a quarterly magazine, and sample contracts and resource materials. It sponsors workshops and seminars across the country. Membership is open to writers who have published a book, play, three articles, five poems, one short story or an equivalent amount of newsletter, publicity, technical, commercial, government, or institutional copy, or have written an equivalent amount of unpublished material and are actively seeking publication. Annual dues: $90 to $195.

NEW DRAMATISTS
424 W. 44th St.
New York, NY 10036
(212) 757-6960
Todd London, *Artistic Director*

New Dramatists is dedicated to finding gifted playwrights and giving them the time, space, and tools to develop their craft. Services include readings and workshops; a director-in-residence program; national script distribution for members; artist work spaces; international playwright exchange programs; script copying facilities; and a free ticket program. Membership is open to residents of New York City and the surrounding tri-state area. National memberships are offered to those outside the area who can spend time in NYC in order to take advantage of programs. Apply between July 15 and September 15. No annual dues.

NORTHWEST PLAYWRIGHTS GUILD
318 S.W. Palatine Hill Rd.
Portland, OR 97219
(503) 452-4778
e-mail: bjscript@teleport.com
Bill Johnson, *Office Manager*

The guild supports and promotes playwrights living in the Northwest through play development, staged readings, and networking for play competitions and production opportunities. Members receive monthly and quarterly newsletters. Annual dues: $25.

OUTDOOR WRITERS ASSOCIATION OF AMERICA, INC.
RD 1, Box 177
Spring Mills, PA 16875

Eileen King, *Meeting Director*

A non-profit, international organization representing professional communicators who report and reflect upon America's diverse interests in the outdoors. Membership, by nomination only, includes a monthly publication, *Outdoors Unlimited*; annual conference; annual membership directory; contests. The association also provides scholarships to qualified students.

PEN AMERICAN CENTER
568 Broadway
New York, NY 10012
(212) 334-1660
Michael Roberts, *Executive Director*

PEN American Center is one of more than 130 centers worldwide that compose International PEN. The 2,600 members of the American Center are poets, playwrights, essayists, editors, and novelists, as well as literary translators and those agents who have made a substantial contribution to the literary community. PEN American headquarters is in New York City, and branches are located in Boston, Chicago, New Orleans, Portland, Oregon, and San Francisco. Among the activities, programs, and services sponsored are literary events and awards, outreach projects to encourage reading, assistance to writers in financial need, and international and domestic human rights campaigns on behalf of many writers, editors, and journalists censored or imprisoned because of their writing. Membership is open to writers who have published two books of literary merit, as well as editors, agents, playwrights, and translators who meet specific standards; apply to membership committee.

THE PLAYWRIGHTS' CENTER
2301 Franklin Ave. E.
Minneapolis, MN 55406
(612) 332-7481
Carlo Cuesta, *Executive Director*

The Playwrights' Center fuels the theater by providing services that support playwrights and playwriting. Members receive applications for all programs, a calendar of events, eligibility to participate in special activities, including classes, outreach programs, and PlayLabs. For membership information, contact Jennifer Kane, Development and Communications Director. Annual dues: $40.

POETRY SOCIETY OF AMERICA
15 Gramercy Park
New York, NY 10003
(212) 254-9628; fax: (212) 673-2352
1-(888) USA-POEM, for a free brochure
web site: www.poetrysociety.org
Elise Paschen, *Executive Director*

Founded in 1910, the PSA seeks to raise the awareness of poetry, to deepen the understanding of it, and to encourage more people to read, listen to, and write poetry. To this end, the PSA presents national series of readings including "Tributes in Libraries" and "Poetry in Public Places," mounts poetry posters on mass transit vehicles through "Poetry in Motion," and broadcasts an educational poetry series on cable television. The

PSA also offers annual contests for poetry, seminars, poetry festivals, and publishes a newsletter. Annual dues: from $40 ($25 for students).

POETS AND WRITERS, INC.
72 Spring St.
New York, NY 10012
(212) 226-3586; fax: (212) 226-3963
web site: http://www.pw.org
Elliot Figman, *Executive Director*
    Poets & Writers, Inc., was founded in 1970 to foster the development of poets and fiction writers and to promote communication throughout the literary community. A non-membership organization, it offers information for writers; *Poets & Writers Magazine* and other publications; as well as support for readings and workshops at a wide range of venues.

PUBLICATION RIGHTS CLEARINGHOUSE
National Writers Union
113 University Pl., 6th Fl.
New York, NY 10003
(212) 254-0279; fax: (212) 254-0673
e-mail: nwu@nwu.org
web site: www.nwu.org
Naomi Zauderer, *Director*
    Publication Rights Clearinghouse, the collective-licensing agency of the National Writers Union, was created in 1996 to help writers license and collect royalties for the reuse of their published works in electronic databases and other media. It is modeled after similar organizations that have long existed in the music industry. Writers license non-exclusive secondary rights to the PRC; the PRC licenses those rights to secondary users and distributes payment to the writers. Enrollment is open to both NWU members and non-members.

ROMANCE WRITERS OF AMERICA
3707 FM 1960 West, Suite 555
Houston, TX 77068
(713) 440-6885; fax: (713) 440-7510
Allison Kelley, *Executive Director*
    An international organization with over 150 local chapters across the U.S., Canada, Europe, and Australia; membership is open to any writer, published or unpublished, interested in the field of romantic fiction. Annual dues of $65, plus $10 application fee for new members; benefits include annual conference, contest, market information, and monthly professional journal, *Romance Writers' Report*.

SCIENCE-FICTION AND FANTASY WRITERS OF AMERICA, INC.
532 La Guardia Pl., #632
New York, NY 10012-1428
Robert J. Sawyer, Pres.
    An organization whose purpose it is to foster and further the professional interests of science fiction and fantasy writers. Presents the annual Nebula Award for excellence in the field and publishes the *Bulletin* and *SFWA Handbook* for its members (also available to non-members).

Any writer who has sold a work of science fiction or fantasy is eligible for membership. Annual dues: $50, *active* ; $35, *affiliate*; plus $10 installation fee; send for application and information.

SISTERS IN CRIME
P.O. Box 442124
Lawrence, KS 66044-8933
e-mail: sistersincrime@juno.com
Medora Sale, *President*
Sisters in Crime was founded in 1986 to combat discrimination against women in the mystery field, educate publishers and the general public as to inequalities in the treatment of female authors, and raise the level of awareness of their contribution to the field. Membership is open to all and includes writers, readers, editors, agents, booksellers, and librarians. Publications include a quarterly newsletter and Books in Print membership directory. Annual dues: $35, U.S.; $40, foreign. Members interested in mysteries for young readers may join Mysteries for Minors (Katherine Hall Page, Chair, P.O. Box 442124, Lawrence, KS 66044-8933) with no additional dues.

SOCIETY OF AMERICAN TRAVEL WRITERS
4101 Lake Boone Trail, Suite 201
Raleigh, NC 27607
(919) 787-5181; fax: (919) 787-4916
Executive Director
The Society of American Travel Writers represents writers and other professionals who strive to provide travelers with accurate reports on destinations, facilities, and services. Active membership is limited to travel writers and free lancers who have a steady volume of published or distributed work about travel. Application fees: $250, *active*; $500, *associate*. Annual dues: $130, *active*; $250, *associate*.

SOCIETY OF CHILDREN'S BOOK WRITERS & ILLUSTRATORS
8271 Beverly Blvd.
Los Angeles, CA 90048
web site: www.scbwi.org
Lin Oliver, *Executive Director*
A national organization of authors, editors, publishers, illustrators, librarians, and educators, the SCBWI offers a variety of services to people who write, illustrate, or share an interest in children's literature. Full memberships are open to those who have had at least one children's book or story published. Associate memberships are open to all those with an interest in children's literature. Annual dues: $50.

SOCIETY OF ENVIRONMENTAL JOURNALISTS
P.O. Box 27280
Philadelphia, PA 19118
(215) 836-9970; fax: (215) 836-9972
e-mail: SEJ@SEJ.ORG
web site: http://www.SEJ.org
Beth Parke, *Executive Director*
Dedicated to improving the quality, accuracy, and visibility of envi-

ronmental reporting, the society serves 1,200 members with a quarterly newsletter, the *SEJournal*, national and regional conferences, World Wide Web (www.SEJ.org), and membership directory. Annual dues: $40; $30, *student*.

SOCIETY OF PROFESSIONAL JOURNALISTS
16 S. Jackson St.
Greencastle, IN 46135-0077
(765) 653-3333; fax: (765) 653-4631
web site: http://spj.org
With 13,500 members and 300 chapters, the Society seeks to serve the interests of print, broadcast, and wire journalists. Services include legal counsel on journalism issues, jobs-for-journalists career search newsletter, professional development seminars, and awards that encourage journalism. Members receive *Quill*, a monthly magazine that explores current issues in the field. SPJ promotes ethics and freedom of information programs. Annual dues: $70, *professional*; $35, *student*.

THE SONGWRITERS GUILD FOUNDATION
1560 Broadway, Suite 1306
New York, NY 10036
(212) 768-7902; fax: (212) 768-9048
George Wurzbach, *National Projects Director*
Open to published and unpublished songwriters, the Guild provides members with songwriter-publisher contracts, reviews contracts, collects royalties from publishers, offers group health and life insurance plans, conducts workshops and critique sessions, and provides a newsletter. Annual dues: $55, *associate*; $70 and up, *full member*.

THEATRE COMMUNICATIONS GROUP
355 Lexington Ave.
New York, NY 10017
(212) 697-5230
Ben Cameron, *Executive Director*
TCG, a national organization for the American theater, provides services to facilitate the work of playwrights, literary managers, and other theater professionals. Publications include the annual *Dramatists Sourcebook* and a line of theater books including plays. Individual members receive *American Theatre* magazine. Annual dues: $35, *individual*.

WESTERN WRITERS OF AMERICA, INC.
1012 Fair St.
Franklin, TN 37064
(615) 791-1444
e-mail: TNcrutch@aol.com
James A. Crutchfield, *Secretary/Treasurer*
Membership is open to qualified professional writers of fiction and nonfiction related to the history and literature of the American West. Its chief purpose is to promote a more widespread distribution, readership, and appreciation of the West and its literature. Holds annual convention in the last week of June. Sponsors annual Spur Awards, Owen Wister Award, and Medicine Pipe Bearer's Award for published work and produced screenplays. Annual dues: $75.

WRITERS GUILD OF AMERICA, EAST, INC.
555 W. 57th St.
New York, NY 10019
(212) 767-7800; fax: (212) 582-1909
web site: http://www.wgaeast.org
Mona Mangan, *Executive Director*

WRITERS GUILD OF AMERICA, WEST, INC.
7000 W. 3rd St.
Los Angeles, CA 90048
(213) 951-4000; fax: (213) 782-4800
web site: www.wga.org
Brian Walton, *Executive Director*

The Writers Guild of America (East and West) represents writers in motion pictures, broadcast, cable and new media industries, including news and entertainment. In order to qualify for membership, a writer must fulfill current requirements for employment or sale of material in one of these fields.

The basic dues are $25 per quarter for both organizations. In addition, there are quarterly dues based on percentage of the member's earnings in any one of the fields over which the guild has jurisdiction. The initiation fee is $1,500 for WGAE, for writers living east of the Mississippi, and $2,500 for WGAW, for those living west of the Mississippi.

WRITERS INFORMATION NETWORK,
THE PROFESSIONAL ASSOCIATION FOR CHRISTIAN
WRITERS
P.O. Box 11337
Bainbridge Island, WA 98110
(206) 842-9103; fax: (206) 842-0536
e-mail: WritersInfoNetwork@juno.com
web site: http://www.bluejaypub.com/win/
Elaine Wright Colvin, *Director/Publisher*

W.I.N. was founded in 1983 to provide a link between Christian writers and the religious publishing industry. Offered are a bimonthly magazine, *The WIN-Informer Magazine,* and market news, editorial services, advocacy and grievance procedures, referral services, and conferences. Annual dues: $33; $37, *foreign.*

LITERARY AGENTS

As the number of book publishers that will consider only agented submissions grows, more writers are turning to agents to sell their manuscripts. The agents in the following list handle both literary and dramatic material. Included in each listing are such important details as type of material represented, submission procedure, and commission. Since agents derive their income from the sales of their clients' work, they must represent writers who are selling fairly regularly to good markets. Nonetheless, many of the agents listed here note they will consider unpublished writers. Always query an agent first, and enclose a self-addressed, stamped envelope; most agents will not respond without it. Do not send any manuscripts until the agent has asked you to do so; and be wary of agents who charge fees for reading manuscripts. All of the following agents have indicated they do *not* charge reading fees, however some charge for copyright fees, manuscript retyping, photocopies, copies of books for use in the sale of other rights, and long distance calls.

To learn more about agents and their role in publishing, the Association of Authors' Representatives, Inc., publishes a canon of ethics as well as an up-to-date list of AAR members, available for $7 (check or money order) and a 55¢ legal-size SASE. Write to: Association of Authors' Representatives, Inc., 10 Astor Pl., 3rd Fl., New York, NY 10003.

Another good source which lists agents and their policies is *Literary Market Place,* a directory found in most libraries.

BRET ADAMS LTD.—448 W. 44th St., New York, NY 10036. Attn: Bruce Ostler or Bret Adams. Screenplays, teleplays, stage plays, and musicals. Unproduced writers considered. Query with synopsis, bio, resumé, and SASE. Commission: 10%.

LEE ALLAN AGENCY—7464 N. 107th St., Milwaukee, WI 53224-3706. Attn: Mr. Lee A. Matthias. Adult genre fiction, nonfiction. Screenplays. Unpublished writers considered. Query with SASE. Commission: 15% books; 10% scripts. Fees: photocopying, overnight shipping, telephone. "Go to a bookstore and locate the exact place in the store where your book would be displayed. If it realistically fits a popular market niche, is not derivative or imitative, meets the size constraints, and you can't make it any better yourself, you are ready to find an agent."

JAMES ALLEN LITERARY AGENT—538 E. Harford St., P.O. Box 909, Milford, PA 18337. Attn: James Allen. All types of adult fiction except Westerns; considers very few new authors. Query with 2- to 3-page synopsis; no multiple queries. Commission: 10% domestic; 20% foreign, film/TV. Representatives in Hollywood and all principle foreign countries.

MICHAEL AMATO AGENCY—1650 Broadway, Rm. 307, New York, NY 10019. Attn: Michael Amato. Screenplays. Query. Commission: 10%.

MARCIA AMSTERDAM AGENCY—41 W. 82nd St., #9A, New York, NY 10024. Attn: Marcia Amsterdam. Adult and young adult fiction; mainstream nonfiction. Screenplays and teleplays: comedy, romance, psychological suspense. Query with resumé; multiple queries O.K.; two-week exclusive for requested submissions. Commission: 15% books; 10% scripts.

THE AXELROD AGENCY—54 Church St., Lenox, MA 01240. Attn: Steven Axelrod. Adult fiction and nonfiction. No science fiction, fantasy, or westerns. Unpublished writers considered. Query; multiple queries O.K. Commission: 10% domestic; 20% foreign.

MALAGA BALDI LITERARY AGENCY—2112 Broadway, Suite 403, New York, NY 10023. Attn: Malaga Baldi. Adult fiction and nonfiction. Unpublished writers considered. Query first; "if I am interested, I ask for proposal,

outline, and sample pages for nonfiction, complete manuscript for fiction."
Multiple queries O.K. Commission: 15%. Response time: 10 weeks minimum.

THE BALKIN AGENCY—P.O. Box 222, Amherst, MA 01004. Attn:
Rick Balkin. Adult nonfiction. Unpublished writers considered. Query with outline; no multiple queries. Commission: 15% domestic; 20% foreign. "Most
interested in serious nonfiction."

VIRGINIA BARBER AGENCY—101 Fifth Ave., New York, NY 10003.
Adult fiction and nonfiction. No unsolicited manuscripts. Query with outline,
sample pages, bio/resumé and SASE. No multiple queries. Commission: 15%
domestic; 20% foreign.

BARNWOOD PRESS & AGENCY—72 Hudson Point Lane, Ossining,
NY 10562. Attn: Diana Dehli Gould. Commercial and literary fiction and nonfiction. Special interest in ethnic/history and lesbian/gay subjects; also literature
for young adults. No science fiction, fantasy, horror, genre romance, or children's manuscripts. Query with SASE. Commission: 15% domestic; 20% foreign.

LORETTA BARRETT BOOKS—101 Fifth Ave., New York, NY 10003.
Attn: Loretta Barrett. Adult fiction and nonfiction. Unpublished writers consid-
ered. Query with outline and SASE; include sample pages for nonfiction only.
Commission: 15%. Response time: 4 weeks.

REID BOATES LITERARY AGENCY—Box 328, 69 Cooks Cross-
road, Pittstown, NJ 08867-0328. Attn: Reid Boates. Adult mainstream fiction
and nonfiction. Unpublished writers rarely considered. SASE. Query with outline and sample pages; no multiple queries. Commission: 15%.

BOOK DEALS, INC.—Civic Opera Bldg., 20 N. Wacker Dr., Suite 1928,
Chicago, IL 60606. Caroline Carney, President. General-interest adult fiction
and nonfiction. Query with outline, first 20 pages, and bio. Commission: 15%
domestic; 20% foreign.

GEORGES BORCHARDT, INC.—136 E. 57th St., New York, NY
10022. Adult fiction and nonfiction. Unpublished writers considered by recommendation only. No unsolicited queries or submissions. Commission: 15%.

BRANDT & BRANDT LITERARY AGENTS—1501 Broadway, New
York, NY 10036. Adult fiction and nonfiction. Unpublished writers considered
occasionally. Unsolicited query by letter only; no multiple queries. Commission: 15%.

THE HELEN BRANN AGENCY—94 Curtis Rd., Bridgewater, CT
06752. Attn: Carol White. Adult fiction and nonfiction. Unpublished writers
considered. Commission: 15%.

ANDREA BROWN LITERARY AGENCY, INC.—P.O. Box 371027,
Montara, CA 94037. Attn: Laura Rennert. Juvenile fiction and nonfiction only.
Unpublished writers considered. Query with outline, sample pages, bio and
resumé, and SASE; no faxes. Commission: 15% domestic; 20% foreign.

KNOX BURGER ASSOCIATES, LTD.—39 1/2 Washington Square S.,
New York, NY 10012. Adult fiction and nonfiction. No science fiction, fantasy,
or romance. Highly selective. Query with SASE; no multiple queries. Commission: 15%.

SHEREE BYKOFSKY ASSOCIATES, INC.— 16 W. 36th St., 13th Fl.,
New York, NY 10018. Mostly adult nonfiction; some adult fiction. Unpublished

writers considered. Query with outline, up to 3 sample pages or proposal, and SASE. Multiple queries O.K. if indicated as such. Commission: 15%.

MARTHA CASSELMAN—P.O. Box 342, Calistoga, CA 94515-0342. Martha Casselman, Agent. Nonfiction, especially interested in cookbooks. Unpublished writers considered. Query with outline, bio/resumé, and SASE for return. Multiple queries O.K. if noted as such. Commission: 15%.

CASTIGLIA LITERARY AGENCY—1155 Camino del Mar, Suite 510, Del Mar, CA 92014. Attn: Julie Castiglia, Winifred Golden. Fiction: commercial, ethnic and literary. Nonfiction: psychology, health, women's issues, science, biography, spirituality, Eastern religions, finance, business, and technology. Query with outline, sample pages, bio and resumé. No multiple queries. Commission: 15%. "Please do not query on the phone. Attend workshops and writers' conferences before approaching an agent."

HY COHEN LITERARY AGENCY, LTD.—P.O. Box 43770, Upper Montclair, NJ 07043. Attn: Hy Cohen. Adult fiction, nonfiction, and juvenile. Unpublished writers considered. Unsolicited queries and manuscripts O.K., "with SASE, please!" Multiple submissions recommended. Commission: 10% domestic; 20% foreign.

RUTH COHEN, INC.—P.O. Box 7626, Menlo Park, CA 94025. Attn: Ruth Cohen. Adult mysteries and women's fiction; quality juvenile fiction and nonfiction. Unpublished writers seriously considered. Query with first 10 pages, synopsis, bio and resumé, and SASE. Commission: 15%.

DON CONGDON ASSOCIATES, INC.—156 Fifth Ave., Suite 625, New York, NY 10010. Adult fiction and nonfiction. Query with outline; no multiple queries. Commission: 10% domestic.

THE DOE COOVER AGENCY—P.O. Box 668, Winchester, MA 01890. Attn: Doe Coover, Colleen Mohyde. Adult literary and commercial fiction and general nonfiction including social sciences, journalism, science, business, biography, memoir, and cookbooks. Unpublished writers considered. Query with outline and bio/resumé; no unsolicited manuscripts. Commission: 15%.

RICHARD CURTIS ASSOCIATES, INC.—171 E. 74th St., 2nd Fl., New York, NY 10021. Attn: Pam Valvera. Adult fiction and nonfiction. Unpublished writers considered. Query with outline, bio/resumé, two chapters, and SASE; no multiple queries. Commission: 15% domestic; 20% foreign.

CURTIS BROWN LTD.—10 Astor Pl., New York, NY 10003. General trade fiction and nonfiction; also juvenile. Unpublished writers considered. Query with SASE; no multiple queries. Commission: unspecified.

SANDRA DIJKSTRA LITERARY AGENCY—1155 Camino del Mar, Suite 515C, Del Mar, CA 92014. Attn: Sandra Zane. Adult and children's fiction and nonfiction. Query with outline and bio/resumé. For fiction, submit first 50 pages and synopsis; for nonfiction, submit proposal. Commission: 15% domestic, 20% foreign. SASE.

THE JONATHAN DOLGER AGENCY—49 E. 96th St., 9B, New York, NY 10128. Attn: Tom Wilson. Adult trade fiction and nonfiction. Considers unpublished writers. Query with outline and SASE. Commission: 15%. "No category mysteries, romance, or science fiction."

DWYER & O'GRADY, INC.—P.O. Box 239, Lempster, NH 03605.

Attn: Elizabeth O'Grady. Specialize in children's books for ages 6 to 12. Require strong story line, dialogue, and character development. Unpublished writers considered. Query with bio/resumé. Commission: 15% domestic, 20% foreign, film, and merchandise. "Our primary focus is the representation of illustrators who also write their own stories; however, we represent authors who write for the children's market."

JANE DYSTEL LITERARY MANAGEMENT—One Union Square W., Suite 904, New York, NY 10003. Web site: www.dystel.com. Attn: Jane Dystel, Miriam Goderich, Todd Keithley, Jessica D. Jones, Jo Fagan. Adult fiction and nonfiction; some picture books and children's books. Unpublished writers considered. Query with bio/resumé, sample pages, and outline; no multiple queries. Commission: 15%.

EDUCATIONAL DESIGN SERVICES—P.O. Box 253, Wantaugh, NY 11793. Attn: Bertram L. Linder. Educational texts only. Unpublished writers considered. Query with outline, sample pages or complete manuscript, bio/resumé, and SASE. No multiple queries. Commission: 15% domestic, 25% foreign.

ETHAN ELLENBERG LITERARY AGENCY—548 Broadway, Suite 5E, New York, NY 10012. Ethan Ellenberg, Agent. Commercial and literary fiction and nonfiction. Specialize in first novels, thrillers, children's books, romance, science fiction, and fantasy. Nonfiction: health, new age/spirituality, pop-science, biography. No poetry or short stories. Query with first 3 chapters, synopsis, and SASE. "We respond within 2 weeks if interested." Commission: 15% domestic; 20% foreign.

ANN ELMO AGENCY—60 E. 42nd St., New York, NY 10165. Adult fiction, nonfiction, and plays. Juvenile for middle grades and up. No picture books. Unpublished writers considered. Please query first with outline, sample pages, and bio/resumé. No multiple queries. Commission: 15% domestic, 10% foreign.

FELICIA ETH—555 Bryant St., Suite 350, Palo Alto, CA 94301. Attn: Felicia Eth. Mostly adult nonfiction; some fiction. Unpublished writers considered. Query with outline, sample pages, and bio/resumé. Multiple queries O.K. if noted. Commission: 15% domestic; 20% foreign. "I am a small, very selective agent. My preference is for provocative, original subjects presented in a strong creative voice."

FARBER LITERARY AGENCY—14 E. 75th St., New York, NY 10021. Attn: Ann Farber. Adult fiction, nonfiction, and stage plays; juvenile books. Considers unpublished writers. Query with outline, sample pages, and SASE. Commission: 15% "with services of attorney."

JOYCE FLAHERTY—816 Lynda Ct., St. Louis, MO 63122. Attn: Joyce Flaherty. Adult fiction and nonfiction. Query with outline or proposal, first chapter, and bio. SASE. Commission: 15% domestic; 30% foreign.

FLANNERY LITERARY—1140 Wickfield Ct., Naperville, IL 60563-3303. Attn: Jennifer Flannery. Juvenile fiction and nonfiction, from board books through young adult novels. Unpublished writers considered. Query with SASE (no phone or fax queries); multiple queries O.K. Commission: 15%.

FOGELMAN LITERARY AGENCY—7515 Greenville Ave., Suite 712, Dallas, TX 75231. Attn: Linda M. Kruger. Romance. Nonfiction. Query with SASE. Commission: 15% domestic; 10% foreign.

ROBERT A. FREEDMAN DRAMATIC AGENCY, INC.—1501 Broadway, Suite 2310, New York, NY 10036. Attn: Robert A. Freedman or Selma Luttinger. Screenplays, teleplays, and stage plays. Send query, outline, and bio/resumé; multiple queries O.K. Commission: 10%.

SAMUEL FRENCH, INC.—45 W. 25th St., New York, NY 10010. Stage plays. Unpublished writers considered. Query with complete manuscript; unsolicited and multiple queries O.K.

GELFMAN SCHNEIDER—250 W. 57th St., Suite 2515, New York, NY 10107. Attn: Jane Gelfman. Adult fiction and nonfiction. Unpublished writers only considered if recommended by other writers or teachers. Query with outline, sample pages, and bio; no multiple queries. Commission: 15% domestic; 20% foreign.

GOODMAN ASSOCIATES—500 West End Ave., New York, NY 10024. Attn: Elise Simon Goodman. Adult fiction and nonfiction. Unpublished writers considered. Query with outline, sample pages, and bio/resumé. Multiple queries O.K. Commission: 15% domestic; 20% foreign.

GRAYBILL & ENGLISH, L.L.C.—1920 N. St. N.W., Suite 620, Washington, DC 20036. Attn: Nina Graybill. Adult commercial and literary fiction and nonfiction. For nonfiction, query with outline; for fiction, query with synopsis and up to 3 sample chapters. Multiple queries O.K. Commission: 15% domestic, 20% foreign.

SANFORD J. GREENBURGER—55 Fifth Ave., 15th Fl., New York, NY 10003. Attn: Faith Hornby Hamlin. Nonfiction, including sports books, health, business, psychology, parenting, science, biography, gay; juvenile books. Unpublished writers with strong credentials considered. Query with outline, sample pages, bio, and SASE; multiple queries O.K. Commission: 15% domestic; 20% foreign.

THE CHARLOTTE GUSAY LITERARY AGENCY—10532 Blythe, Los Angeles, CA 90064. Adult mainstream and literary fiction, nonfiction, and some young adult novels for film. Screenplays/Books to Film. Query with one-page outline and SASE. Then if we request to see your project, for fiction send a one-page synopsis and the first three chapters. For nonfiction, send the proposal, which includes overview, contents, bio, audience/marketing, and first three chapters. Multiple queries are discourage, but if you do so, please advise. Commission:10% dramatic, 15% literary.

JOY HARRIS LITERARY AGENCY, INC.—156 Fifth Ave., Suite 617, New York, NY 10010. Adult fiction and nonfiction. Unpublished writers considered. Query with outline, sample pages, and bio/resumé. No multiple queries. Commission: 15%.

HEACOCK LITERARY AGENCY, INC.—1523 Sixth St., Suite 14, Santa Monica, CA 90401. Attn: Rosalie Grace Heacock, Pres. Adult nonfiction. Published and unpublished writers welcome to query with outline, bio/resumé, and SASE. Queries unaccompanied by SASE will not be answered. No multiple queries. Commission: 15%.

FREDERICK HILL ASSOCIATES—1842 Union St., San Francisco, CA 94123. Attn: Irene Moore. Branch office: 505 N. Robertson Blvd., Los Angeles, CA 90048. Adult fiction and nonfiction. Unpublished writers considered. Query with outline and bio/resumé; multiple queries O.K. Commission: 15% domestic, 20% foreign.

JOHN L. HOCHMANN BOOKS—320 E. 58th St., New York, NY 10022. Attn: John L. Hochmann. Mainly nonfiction: biography, social history, health and food, college textbooks. Represent published authors, but unpublished writers considered, "provided they demonstrate thorough knowledge of their subjects." Query with outline, sample pages, bio/resumé, and SASE. No multiple queries. Commission: 15% for domestic/Canadian; plus 15% foreign language and U.K. "Do not submit jacket copy. Submit detailed outlines and proposals that include evaluations of competing books."

BARBARA HOGENSON AGENCY—165 West End Ave., Suite 19-C, New York, NY 10023. Attn: Barbara Hogenson. Adult fiction, nonfiction. Screenplays and stage plays. Query with bio and synopsis, SASE; multiple queries O.K. Commission: 10% scripts; 15% books.

IMG LITERARY AGENCY—825 7th Ave., New York, NY 10019. Attn: Mark Reiter, Carolyn Krupp. Adult fiction and nonfiction. Unpublished writers considered. Query with outline, sample pages, and bio/resumé. No multiple queries. Commission: 15% domestic.

SHARON JARVIS & CO.—Toad Hall, Inc., RR2, Box 2090, Laceyville, PA 18623. Adult fiction and nonfiction. Unpublished writers considered. Query with bio or resumé, and outline or synopsis. No unsolicited manuscripts. Commission: 15%. "Pay attention to what's selling and what's commercial."

JCA LITERARY AGENCY, INC.—27 W. 20th St., Suite 1103, New York, NY 10011. Adult fiction and nonfiction. Unpublished writers considered. Query with sample pages; multiple queries O.K. Commission: 15% domestic, 20% foreign.

NATASHA KERN LITERARY AGENCY, INC.—P.O. Box 2908, Portland, OR 97208-2908. Attn: Natasha Kern. Adult nonfiction including investigative journalism, popular psychology and sociology, self-help, natural science, New Age/inspiration, health and alternative health, parenting, business, animals, controversial, gay, and women's issues, celebrity biographies, gardening, etc.; and fiction, including mainstream women's, medical and historical thrillers, mysteries, psychological suspense, magical realism, novels of the West, romance, and mainstream historical and contemporary novels. See web site www.natashakern.com for detailed submission instructions. For fiction, query with SASE; for nonfiction, send book proposal with SASE. Commission: 15% domestic; 20% foreign.

LOUISE B. KETZ AGENCY—1485 First Ave., Suite 4B, New York, NY 10021. Attn: Louise B. Ketz. Adult nonfiction on science, business, sports, history, and reference. Considers unpublished writers "with proper credentials." Query with outline, sample pages, and bio/resumé; multiple queries occasionally considered. Commission: 15%.

KIDDE, HOYT & PICARD—335 E. 51st St., New York, NY 10022. Attn: Katharine Kidde, Laura Langlie. Mainstream, literary, and romantic fiction; general nonfiction. Writers should have been published to be considered. Query; include past writing experience, credits. Multiple queries O.K. Commission: 15%.

KIRCHOFF/WOHLBERG, INC.—866 United Nations Plaza, Suite 525, New York, NY 10017. Attn: Liza Voges. Juvenile fiction and nonfiction only. Unpublished writers considered. Query; multiple submissions O.K. Commission: 15%.

HARVEY KLINGER, INC.—301 W. 53rd St., New York, NY 10019. Attn: Harvey Klinger, Laurie E. Liss, David Dunton. Commercial and literary fiction and nonfiction. Unpublished writers considered. Query with outline and bio/resumé. No multiple queries. Commission: 15% domestic, 25% foreign.

BARBARA S. KOUTS—P.O. Box 560, Bellport, NY 11713. Attn: Barbara S. Kouts. Adult fiction, nonfiction, and juvenile for all ages. Unpublished writers considered. Query with bio/resumé. Multiple queries O.K. Commission: 10%.

PETER LAMPACK AGENCY, INC.—551 Fifth Ave., Suite 1613, New York, NY 10176. Attn: Loren Soeiro, Agent. Adult fiction and nonfiction including mainstream, mystery, suspense, thrillers, and literature. No romance, science fiction, fantasy, horror, or Westerns. No theatrical plays, screenplays, or teleplays. Unpublished writers considered. Query with synopsis/outline, up to 10 sample pages, SASE, and bio/resumé. Commission: 15% domestic; 20% foreign.

MICHAEL LARSEN/ELIZABETH POMADA—1029 Jones St., San Francisco, CA 94109. Attn: M. Larsen, nonfiction; E. Pomada, fiction. Fiction: literary, commercial, and genre. Nonfiction: general, including biography, business, nature, health, history, arts, travel. Unpublished writers welcome. Query for fiction with first 10 pages, synopsis, SASE, and phone number; send #10 SASE for brochure. For nonfiction, query with SASE. Commission: 15%. For more information see web site: www.larsen-pomada.com.

THE MAUREEN LASHER AGENCY—P.O. Box 888, Pacific Palisades, CA 90272. Attn: Ann Cashman. Adult fiction and nonfiction. Unpublished writers considered. Query with outline, sample pages, and bio/resumé. No multiple queries. Commission: 15%.

ELLEN LEVINE LITERARY AGENCY, INC.—15 E. 26th St., Suite 1801, New York, NY 10010. Attn: Elizabeth Kaplan, Diana Finch, Louise Quayle. Adult fiction and nonfiction. Query with SASE. Commission: 15%.

LICHTMAN, TRISTER, SINGER & ROSS—See *Gail Ross Literary Agency.*

NANCY LOVE LITERARY AGENCY—250 E. 65th St., New York, NY 10021. Attn: Sherrie Sutton. Adult fiction: mysteries and thrillers; and nonfiction: health, parenting, inspirational, current affairs, biography, memoirs, psychology. Unpublished writers considered. For nonfiction, query with proposal; for fiction, query with first chapter. Commission: 15%.

MCINTOSH & OTIS, INC.—353 Lexington Ave., New York, NY 10016. Adult fiction, nonfiction, and screenplays; juvenile fiction and nonfiction. Unpublished writers considered. Query with sample pages; include SASE. Allow 4 to 6 weeks for response. Commission: 15%.

DONALD MAASS LITERARY AGENCY—157 W. 57th St., Suite 703, New York, NY 10019. Attn: Donald Maass, Pres. Jennifer Jackson, Associate. Adult fiction: science fiction, fantasy, mystery, suspense, horror, frontier, romance, mainstream, literary. Unpublished writers considered. Query with first 5 sample pages, synopsis, and SASE. Commission: 15% domestic; 20% foreign.

GINA MACCOBY LITERARY AGENCY—P.O. Box 60, Chappaqua, NY 10514. Adult fiction and nonfiction; juvenile for all ages. No computer books, horror, science fiction, diet books, or cookbooks. Unpublished writers considered. Query with SASE; multiple queries O.K. Commission: 15%. No unsolicited manuscripts.

CAROL MANN LITERARY AGENCY — 55 Fifth Ave., New York, NY 10003. Attn: Carol Mann. 30% fiction; 70% nonfiction, including health, fitness, inspiration, alternative medicine, and self-help. Query with outline, sample pages, bio and resumé, and SASE. Commission: 15%.

MANUS ASSOCIATES, INC. — 417 E. 57th St., Suite 5D, New York, NY 10022. Attn: Janet Wilkens Manus. West coast office: 375 Forest Ave., Palo Alto, CA 94301. Adult fiction and nonfiction. No science fiction/fantasy, category romance, westerns, childrens, or original screenplays. Unpublished writers considered. Query with synopsis, three sample chapters, and bio/resumé. Multiple queries O.K. "on occasion." Commission: 15%.

THE MARTON AGENCY, INC. — One Union Square W., Rm. 612, New York, NY 10003-3303. Attn: Tonda Marton. Plays only. Not considering new work at this time. Commission: 10%.

JED MATTES, INC. — 2095 Broadway, #302, New York, NY 10023-2895. Adult fiction and nonfiction. Unpublished writers considered. Query. Commission: 15% domestic; 20% foreign.

HELMUT MEYER LITERARY AGENCY — 330 E. 79th St., New York, NY 10021. Attn: Helmut Meyer, Literary Agent. Adult nonfiction. Telephone query or query by mail with outline, sample pages, and bio/resumé. No multiple queries. Commission: 15%.

HENRY MORRISON, INC. — Box 235, Bedford Hills, NY 10507. Adult fiction and nonfiction; book-length only. Unpublished writers considered. Query with outline; multiple queries O.K. Commission: 15% domestic; 25% foreign. Fees: photocopying, shipping. "We are concentrating on a relatively small list of clients, and work toward building them in the U.S. and international marketplaces. We tend to avoid autobiographical novels and extremely literary novels, but always seek good nonfiction on major political and historical subjects."

MULTIMEDIA PRODUCT DEVELOPMENT — 410 S. Michigan Ave., Suite 724, Chicago, IL 60605. Jane Jordan Browne, Pres. Adult fiction and nonfiction, as well as juvenile fiction and nonfiction. "We are interested in commercial, overnight sellers in the areas of mainstream fiction and nonfiction." No short stories, poems, screenplays, articles, or software. Query with bio and SASE. Commission: 15% domestic; 20% foreign.

JEAN V. NAGGAR LITERARY AGENCY — 216 E. 75th St., New York, NY 10021. Attn: Jean Naggar, Frances Kuffel, or Anne Engel (nonfiction). Adult mainstream fiction and nonfiction. Very few unpublished writers considered. Query with outline, SASE, bio, and resumé. Commission: 15% domestic, 20% foreign.

RUTH NATHAN AGENCY — 53 E. 34th St., Suite 207, New York, NY 10016. Decorative arts, show business, biography. Selected historical fiction, pre-1500. No unsolicited queries. Commission: 15%. "To writers seeking an agent: Please note what my specialties are. Do not send science fiction, fantasy, children's books, or business books. Unsolicited manuscripts are not accepted."

NEW ENGLAND PUBLISHING ASSOCIATES — P.O. Box 5, Chester, CT 06412. Adult nonfiction, especially women's studies, history, biography, literature, business, and reference. Unpublished writers considered. Query with outline, sample pages, and bio/resumé. See web site for submission guidelines: http://nepa.com/nepa. Commission: 15% domestic; 20% foreign.

THE RICHARD PARKS AGENCY—138 E. 16th St., 5B, New York, NY 10003. Attn: Richard Parks. Adult nonfiction; fiction by referral only. Unpublished writers considered. Query with bio and resumé. Commission: 15% domestic; 20% foreign. "No phone calls or faxed queries, please."

PERKINS, RUBIE, AND ASSOCIATES—240 W. 35th St., New York, NY 10001. Attn: Lori Perkins or Peter Rubie. Adult fiction and nonfiction; some middle grade and young adult. Unpublished writers considered. Query with outline, sample pages, bio, and resumé; multiple queries O.K. Commission: 15% U.S.; 20% foreign.

JAMES PETER ASSOCIATES, INC.—P.O. Box 772, Tenafly, NJ 07670. Attn: Bert Holtje. Adult nonfiction. Unpublished writers considered. Query with outline, sample pages, and bio/resumé. No multiple queries. Commission: 15% domestic, 20% foreign.

ALISON PICARD, LITERARY AGENT—P.O. Box 2000, Cotuit, MA 02635. Attn: Alison Picard. Adult fiction, nonfiction, and juvenile. Unpublished writers considered. Query; multiple queries O.K. Commission: 15%.

PINDER LANE & GARON-BROOKE ASSOCIATES, LTD.—159 W. 53rd St., #14-E, New York, NY 10019. Attn: Jean Free. Adult fiction and nonfiction including thrillers, romance, contemporary, biography, lifestyle, and haelth. Unpublished writers considered. Query with outline, bio/resumé, and SASE; no multiple queries. Commission: 15% domestic, 30% foreign.

SUSAN ANN PROTTER—110 W. 40th St., Suite 1408, New York, NY 10018. Adult fiction and nonfiction only, specializing in mysteries, crime, thrillers and science fiction; health, psychology, parenting, self-help, biographies, history, popular science, medicine, and alternative medicine. Query by mail only, with description, bio/resumé, synopsis, and SASE. Commission: 15%.

RAINES & RAINES—71 Park Ave., Suite 4A, New York, NY 10016. Attn: Keith Korman, Joan Raines, Theron Raines. Adult fiction, nonfiction, and juvenile for all ages. Query; no multiple queries. Commission: 15% domestic; 20% foreign. "Keep query to one page."

HELEN REES LITERARY AGENCY—123 N. Washington St., Boston, MA 02114. Literary and commercial fiction and nonfiction. No short stories, science fiction, children's, religious, sports, occult, or poetry. Unpublished writers considered. Query with outline and bio/resumé. No multiple queries. Commission: 15%.

JODY REIN BOOKS, INC.—7741 S. Ash Ct., Littleton, CO 80122. Attn: Jody Rein. Literary and commercial adult nonfiction. Query with SASE. Commission: 15%.

RENAISSANCE LITERARY/TALENT AGENCY, INC.—9220 Sunset Blvd., Suite 302, Los Angeles, CA 90069. Literary fiction and nonfiction. Unpublished, unproduced novelists considered. Query with bio and resumé. Commission: 10%.

GAIL ROSS LITERARY AGENCY—1666 Connecticut Ave. N.W., Suite 500, Washington, DC 20009. Attn: Robin Pinnel. Adult nonfiction. Unpublished writers considered. Query with outline, sample pages, resumé, and SASE. Multiple queries O.K. Commission: 15%.

JANE ROTROSEN AGENCY, LLC.— 318 E. 51st St., New York, NY 10022. Attn: Ruth Kagle. Adult fiction and nonfiction. Unpublished writers considered. Query with outline and bio; no unsolicited manuscripts. Commission: 15% U.S. and Canada; 20% foreign and film/TV.

PESHA RUBINSTEIN LITERARY AGENCY—1392 Rugby Rd., Teaneck, NJ 07666. Attn: Pesha Rubinstein. Commercial fiction: mysteries, women's fiction, and thrillers; nonfiction; humor; and juvenile. Unpublished writers considered. Query with first 10 pages, synopsis, and SASE. Commission: 15% domestic, 20% foreign.

RUSSELL & VOLKENING, INC.— 50 W. 29th St., New York, NY 10001. Adult and juvenile fiction and nonfiction; specializing in literary fiction and narrative nonfiction. Queries for juvenile books should be addressed to Jennie Dunham. No screenplays, horror, romance, science fiction, or poetry. Unpublished writers considered. Query with letter and SASE. Commission: 10%.

SANDUM & ASSOCIATES— 144 E. 84th St., New York, NY 10028. Attn: Howard E. Sandum. Primarily nonfiction. Query with sample pages and bio/resumé. Multiple queries O.K. Commission: 15% domestic; 10% when foreign or TV/film subagents are used. "We do not consider manuscripts in genres such as science fiction, romance, or horror unless surpassing literary qualities are present."

SEBASTIAN AGENCY—PMB 406, 1560 Van Ness Ave., San Francisco, CA 94109. Attn: Laurie Harper. Adult nonfiction only. Considers very few new writers. Query with outline, sample pages, and and bio/resumé. Commission: 15% domestic; 20% to 25% foreign.

BOBBE SIEGEL, RIGHTS LITERARY AGENT— 41 W. 83rd St., New York, NY 10024. Attn: Bobbe Siegel. Adult fiction and nonfiction. No children's books, poetry, short stories, romances, cookbooks, or humor. Unpublished writers considered. Query; multiple queries O.K. SASE required. Commission: 15%.

JACQUELINE SIMENAUER LITERARY AGENCY, INC.—7146 Estero Blvd., Suite 917 N., Fort Myers Beach, FL 33931. Attn: Jacqueline Simenauer, nonfiction. Fran Pardi, fiction. Nonfiction: medical, pop psychology, how-to/self-help, women's issues, health, alternative health, spirituality, New Age, fitness, diet, nutrition, current issues, true crime, business, Men's issues, celebrities, reference, cookbooks, social issues. Fiction: literary and mainstream commercial. Query with outline, synopsis, and SASE. Multiple queries O.K. Commission: 15% domestic; 20% foreign.

PHILIP G. SPITZER LITERARY AGENCY— 50 Talmage Farm Ln., East Hampton, NY 11937. Attn: Philip Spitzer. Adult fiction and nonfiction. Query. Commission: 15% domestic; 20% foreign.

GUNTHER STUHLMANN, AUTHOR'S REPRESENTATIVE—P.O. Box 276, Becket, MA 01223. Attn: Barbara Ward. Literary fiction and nonfiction, especially biography, letters, and history. No mysteries, romance, science fiction, or adventure. Unpublished writers sometimes considered. Query with SASE; no multiple queries. Commission: 10% North America; 15% Britain and Commonwealth; 20% foreign.

THE TANTLEFF OFFICE— 375 Greenwich St., Suite 700, New York, NY 10013. Attn: Charmaine Ferenczi, stage plays. John Santoianni, stage plays, film and television. Jack Tantleff, stage plays, film and television. Jill Bock, film and television. Stage plays, screenplays, teleplays. Unpublished writers considered. Query with synopsis, up to 10 sample pages, bio/resumé; multiple queries O.K. Commission: 10% scripts.

WALES LITERARY AGENCY, INC.—108 Hayes St., Seattle, WA 98109. E-mail: waleslit@aol.com. Attn: Elizabeth Wales, Adrienne Reed. Mainstream and literary fiction and nonfiction, including women's, nature writing, multicultural stories, and animal stories. Unpublished writers considered. Query with outline, sample pages, and SASE. Multiple queries O.K. Commission: 15%.

JOHN A. WARE LITERARY AGENCY—392 Central Park W., New York, NY 10025. Attn: John Ware. Adult fiction and nonfiction. "Literate, accessible, noncategory fiction, plus thrillers and mysteries." Nonfiction: biography, history, current affairs, investigative journalism, social criticism, Americana and folklore, science. Unpublished writers considered. Query letter only, with SASE; multiple queries O.K. Commission: 15% domestic, 20% foreign.

WATKINS/LOOMIS AGENCY—133 E. 35th St., Suite One, New York, NY 10016. Attn: Katherine Fausset. Adult fiction and nonfiction. Unpublished writers considered. Query with SASE; no multiple queries. Commission: 15%.

SANDRA WATT & ASSOCIATES—1750 N. Sierra Bonita, Los Angeles, CA 90046. Attn: Sandra Watt. Adult fiction (mystery, thrillers, women's novels, detective) and nonfiction (spiritual, new age, animals, humor, anthropology, art, true crime, and gardening. Some middle grade, young adult, and picture books. Unpublished writers considered. Query with outline; multiple submissions O.K. Commission: 15%. "We're probably a bit old-fashioned in loving a great story."

WIESER & WIESER, INC.—25 E. 21st St.,6th Fl., New York, NY 10010. Attn: Olga Wieser, Jake Elwell. Adult fiction and nonfiction. Unpublished writers considered. Query with outline, sample pages, bio/resumé, and SASE. Commission: 15%.

WRITERS HOUSE—21 W. 26th St., New York, NY 10010. Attn: Simon Lipskar, fiction. John Hodgeman, nonfiction; Alexa Lichtenstein, juvenile and young adult. Liza Landsman, multimedia. Adult fiction and nonfiction; juvenile for all ages; and young adult. Unpublished writers considered. "Query with one-page letter on why your project is excellent, what it's about, and why you're the wonderful author to write it." No multiple queries. Commission: 15% domestic; 20% foreign.

WRITERS' PRODUCTIONS—P.O. Box 630, Westport, CT 06881. Attn: David L. Meth. Adult fiction and nonfiction, both of literary quality. Children's books that fit into multimedia fantasies. Unpublished writers considered. Query with SASE. Commission: 15% domestic; 25% foreign, dramatic, multimedia, software sales, licensing, and merchandising.

ZACHARY SHUSTER LITERARY AGENCY—244 5th Ave., 11th Fl., New York, NY 10001-7604. Attn: Lane Zachary or Todd Shuster. Branch office: 45 Newbury St., Boston, MA 02116. Adult fiction and nonfiction. Juvenile fiction and nonfiction. Screenplays. Query with sample pages or submit complete manuscript. Commission: 15% domestic; 20% foreign.

SUSAN ZECKENDORF ASSOCIATES, INC.— 171 W. 57th St., New York, NY 10019. Attn: Susan Zeckendorf. Fiction: literary fiction; mysteries; thrillers; women's commercial fiction. Nonfiction: science; music; biography; social history. Unpublished writers considered. Query with outline and bio/resumé. Commission: 15% domestic; 20% foreign.

Glossary

Advance—The amount a publisher pays a writer before a book is published; it is deducted from the royalties earned from sales of the finished book.

Agented material—Submissions from literary or dramatic agents to a publisher. Some publishing companies accept agented material only.

All rights—Some magazines purchase all rights to the material they publish, which means that they can use it as they wish, as many times as they wish. They cannot purchase all rights unless the writer gives them written permission to do so.

Assignment—A contract, written or oral, between an editor and writer, confirming that the writer will complete a specific project by a certain date, and for a certain fee.

B&W—Abbreviation for black-and-white photographs.

Book outline—Chapter-by-chapter summary of a book, frequently in paragraph form, allowing an editor to evaluate the book's content, tone, and pacing, and determine whether he or she wants to see the entire manuscript for possible publication.

Book packager—Company that puts together all the elements of a book, from initial concept to writing, publishing, and marketing it. Also called **book producer** or **book developer.**

Byline—Author's name as it appears on a published piece.

Clips—Copies of a writer's published work, often used by editors to evaluate the writer's talent.

Column inch—One inch of a typeset column; often serves as a basis for payment.

Contributor's copies—Copies of a publication sent to a writer whose work is included in it.

Copy editing—Line-by-line editing to correct errors in spelling, grammar, and punctuation, and inconsistencies in style. Differs from **content editing**, which evaluates flow, logic, and overall message.

Copy—Manuscript pages before they are set into type.

Copyright—Legal protection of creative works from unauthorized use. Under the law, copyright is secured automatically when the work is set down for the first time in written or recorded form.

Cover letter—A brief letter that accompanies a manuscript or book proposal. A cover letter is *not* a query letter (see definition, page 892).

Deadline—The date on which a written work is due at the editor's office, agreed to by author and editor.

Draft—A complete version of an article, story, or book. **First drafts** are often called **rough drafts**.

Fair use—A provision of the copyright law allowing brief passages of copyrighted material to be quoted without infringing on the owner's rights.

Feature—An article that is generally longer than a news story and whose main focus is an issue, trend, or person.

Filler—Brief item used to fill out a newspaper or magazine column; could be a news item, joke, anecdote, or puzzle.

First serial rights—The right of a magazine or newspaper to publish a work for the first time in any periodical. After that, all rights revert to the writer.

Galleys—The first typeset proofs of a manuscript, before they are divided into pages.

Ghostwriter—Author of books, articles, and speeches that are credited to someone else.

Glossy—Black-and-white photo with a shiny, rather than a matte, finish.

Hard copy—The printed copy of material written on a computer.

Honorarium—A modest, token fee paid by a publication to an author in gratitude for a submission.

International reply coupon (IRC)—Included with any correspondence or submission to a foreign publication; allows the editor to reply by mail without incurring cost.

Kill fee—Fee paid for an article that was assigned but subsequently not published; usually a percentage of the amount that would have been paid if the work had been published.

Lead time—Time between the planning of a magazine or book and its publication date.

Libel—A false accusation or published statement that causes a person embarrassment, loss of income, or damage to reputation.

Little magazines—Publications with limited circulation whose content often deals with literature or politics.

Mass market—Books appealing to a very large segment of the reading public and often sold in such outlets as drugstores, supermarkets, etc.

Masthead—A listing of the names and titles of a publication's staff members.

Ms—Abbreviation for manuscript; mss is the plural abbreviation.

Multiple submissions—Also called **simultaneous submissions**. Complete manuscripts sent simultaneously to different publications. Once universally discouraged by editors, the practice is gaining more acceptance, though some still frown on it. **Multiple queries** are generally accepted, however, since reading them requires less of an invest-ment in time on the editor's part.

On speculation—Editor agrees to consider a work for publication "on speculation," without any guarantee that he or she will ultimately buy the work.

One-time rights—Editor buys manuscript from writer and agrees to publish it one time, after which the rights revert to the author for subse-quent sales.

Op-ed—A newspaper piece, usually printed opposite the editorial page, that expresses a personal viewpoint on a timely news item.

Over-the-transom—Describes the submission of unsolicited mate-rial by a free-lance writer; the term harks back to the time when mail was delivered through the open window above an office door.

Payment on acceptance—Payment to writer when manuscript is accepted.

Payment on publication—Payment to writer when manuscript is published.

Pen name—A name other than his or her legal name that an author uses on written work.

Public domain—Published material that is available for use without permission, either because it was never copyrighted or because its copy-right term is expired. Works published at least 75 years ago are consid-ered in the public domain.

Q-and-A format—One type of presentation for an interview article, in which questions are printed, followed by the interviewee's answers.

Query letter—A letter—usually no longer than one page—in which a writer proposes an article idea to an editor.

Rejection slip—A printed note in which a publication indicates that it is not interested in a submission.

Reporting time—The weeks or months it takes for an editor to evaluate a submission.

Reprint rights—The legal right of a magazine or newspaper to print an article, story, or poem after it has already appeared elsewhere.

Royalty—A percentage of the amount received from retail sales of a book, paid to the author by the publisher. For hardcovers, the royalty is generally 10% on the first 5,000 copies sold; 12½% on the next 5,000 sold; 15% thereafter. Paperback royalties range from 4% to 8%, depending on whether it's a trade or mass-market book.

SASE—Self-addressed, stamped envelope, required with all submissions that the author wishes returned—either for return of material or (if you don't need material returned) for editor's reply.

Slush pile—The stack of unsolicited manuscripts in an editor's office.

Tear sheet—The pages of a magazine or newspaper on which an author's work is published.

Unsolicited submission—A manuscript that an editor did not specifically ask to see.

Vanity publisher—Also called **subsidy publisher**. A publishing company that charges author all costs of printing a book. No reputable book publisher operates on this subsidy basis.

Work for hire—When a work is written on a "for hire" basis, all rights in it become the property of the publisher. Though the work-for-hire clause applies mostly to work done by regular employees of a company, some editors offer work-for-hire agreements to free lancers. Think carefully before signing such agreements, however, since by doing so you will essentially be signing away your rights and will not be able to try to resell your work on your own.

Writers guidelines—A formal statement of a publication's editorial needs, payment schedule, deadlines, and other essential information.

INDEX TO MARKETS